Today's Moral Issues, 7e

Bonevac

Macomb Community College

McGraw Hill create®
create.mheducation.com

Mc Graw Hill create®

ISBN-13: 9781307140293

ISBN-10: 1307140297

Contents

PREFACE

This book is a text for courses on contemporary moral issues. Such courses assume that philosophy has something important to contribute to contemporary moral problems. They try to bring philosophical theories to bear on practical questions. From one point of view, this seems difficult. Philosophy is in many ways the most abstract of all disciplines. The questions it addresses are very general: What is real? How do we know? What should we do? But philosophy is also the most practical of all disciplines. It aims at wisdom. Living wisely, displaying good judgment, understanding yourself and your surroundings—these offer immense benefits to all, no matter who they are, how they earn a living, or what kind of society they inhabit. Living wisely is a key to living well. For just that reason, Aristotle thought that philosophy was the highest human activity and that the contemplative life was the highest and happiest form of life possible for a human being.

Nevertheless, it is not always easy to bring theory and practice together in the classroom. Philosophical texts can be hard to read. Philosophers often write primarily for each other. And arguments about contemporary issues are rarely reflective; the underlying principles can be hard to discern.

Contemporary moral problems textbooks often amplify these difficulties. They contain mostly papers by professional philosophers written for a professional audience. They tend to omit underlying theoretical approaches altogether or segregate them in a separate section of the book. The first strategy leaves students with no moral compass. Students have trouble abstracting ethical principles and methods from treatments of particular issues; even the best students flounder when faced with issues that have not been treated explicitly in class. The result is that students emerge with only the vaguest idea of what ethical thinking is. The second strategy divides courses into two parts that are hard to unify. The theory usually strikes students as dry and irrelevant, while the practical part remains confusing or, at best, an exercise in applying theory.

This book tries to resolve the dilemma by tying theoretical and practical considerations together. *Today's Moral Issues* combines theoretical and practical readings on four general themes: first principles, liberty, rights and responsibilities, and justice and equality. The theoretical readings are closely related to the contemporary readings that follow. I have found that using philosophical texts helps students connect theory and practice, for writers such as Locke and Mill tend to be more concrete and practical in outlook than most secondary discussions of their thought. Their motivations are not difficult for most students to understand. And I have edited the theoretical texts closely to bring students into direct contact with their chief motivations and arguments.

The classic and contemporary theoretical approaches constitute a foundation for thinking about contemporary issues. Combining these texts with discussions of contemporary problems lets students see the dialectic between theory and practice in ethics. Faced with practical dilemmas and disagreements, it is easy to see why ethical thinkers have sought to construct theories. And contemporary issues provide opportunities not only to apply theories but also to test and evaluate them. Good students, I have found, attain not only a rich understanding of the theories, the issues, and how they are related, but also a real sense of what ethical thinking is all about.

Today's Moral Issues is unique in treating contemporary moral issues in the context of both political philosophy and ethics. Issues such as abortion, euthanasia, and the environment have political as well as personal dimensions. Others, such as freedom of speech, capital punishment, and economic, racial, sexual, and global equality, are almost entirely political. To treat them adequately, one must consider the proper ends of government and the bounds of state action.

New Features

This edition retains the virtues of earlier editions. It combines theoretical and practical treatments of ethical and political issues from a wide variety of perspectives and sources, including court cases, journalists, public figures, public policy researchers, and scientists as well as philosophers.

This edition also has some new virtues. It differs from earlier editions in some important ways:

1. Among the most contentious issues of current politics is gay marriage. I have expanded the book to include it.
2. More than 20 percent of the readings are new to this edition.
3. In the Theoretical Approaches sections, I have added readings from Confucius. In the sections dealing with issues, I have added pieces by R. G. Frey, the World Commission on Environment and Development, Thomas Nagel, Francis Beckwith, Rosalind Hursthouse, Stanley Kurtz, Andrew Koppelman, Maggie Gallagher, Toon Quaghebeur, Bernadete Dierckx de Casterlé, and Chris Gastmans, Carol Steiker, Amartya Sen, Elizabeth Anderson, Robert Rector and Rachel Sheffield, and Michael Huemer.
4. I have reworked and greatly expanded the Questions for Reflection, especially in the theoretical sections.
5. The Web page (*http://bonevac.info/tmi*) that accompanies the book has been expanded. It includes many features to help both students and instructors, including
   a. sample course syllabi
   b. extensive class notes for all sections of the book, with links to relevant parts of philosophical texts (where they are public domain and available online)
   c. a study guide summarizing key points
   d. a comprehensive glossary of terms
   e. practice exams
   f. suggested readings
   g. relevant court cases
   h. Web links to other sources of information on contemporary issues
   i. a guide to writing philosophical essays
   j. tips on multimedia presentations
   k. PowerPoint slides for each section of the text

Acknowledgments

This book and the ideas behind it have evolved considerably during the thirty years I have been teaching contemporary moral issues courses at the University of Pittsburgh and the University of Texas at Austin. I am grateful to the many instructors, teaching assistants, and students who have used earlier versions and helped me refine them. I am particularly grateful to the more than 10,000 students who have taken my contemporary moral problems course at the University of Texas at Austin. They have taught me much about what a course on moral issues ought to be.

I especially want to thank Nicholas Asher and Stephen Phillips, who have team-taught courses on contemporary moral problems with me. Their ideas have found expression here in more ways than I can distinguish. I am also grateful for the helpful criticism and advice I have received throughout the years from Randy Mayes, California State University, Sacramento; Bill Myers, Birmingham Southern College; David Bradshaw, University of Kentucky; and Jonathan Davis, University of Texas at Austin.

I would like to thank the reviewers whose comments have helped me clarify my own thinking and decide what issues and readings to include: for the first edition, L. E. Andrade, Illinois State University; Linda Bomstad, California State University, Sacramento; Karen Hanson, Indiana University; and Anita Silvers, San Francisco State University; for the second edition, Stephanie Beardman, Rutgers University; Ray Cebik, University of Tennessee, Knoxville; Deirdre Golash, American University; Patrick Lee, Franciscan University of Steubenville; Aaron Meskin, Rutgers University; Sharon Sytsma, Northern Illinois University; and Nathan Tierney, California Lutheran University; for the third edition, Naomi Azck, University of Albany, State University of New York; Stephen Carey, Virginia Commonwealth University; Scott Lehman, University of Connecticut; A. P. Roark, University of Washington; and Stewart Shapiro, Ohio State University at Newark; for the fourth edition, Abrol O. Fairweather, CSU, Hayward; A. R. Molina, University of Miami; Barbara Montero, NYU; Lawrence Pasternack, Oklahoma State University; Janice Staab, Southern Illinois University; Lawrence Stark, State University of New York at Albany; for the fifth edition, Jean Axelrod Cahan, University of Nebraska, Lincoln; Barbara Lowe, St. John Fisher College; Joseph Pappin III, University of South Carolina; and Wendy A. Ritch, Raritan Valley Community College; for the sixth edition, Hannah Phelps, Pacific Lutheran University; Diane Bowser, The Art Institute of Pittsburg; Lawrence Stratton, Villanova University; Jack Bayne, University of Massachusetts, Boston; Robert Pielke, El Camino College; and Peter Marton, Salem State College; and, for the seventh edition,

- Nicholas Power, University of West Florida
- Stephen Carey, Virginia Commonwealth University
- Tracie Mahaffey, Florida State University
- John Messerly, Shoreline Community College
- Sean Stidd, Wayne State University
- Corine Sutherland, Golden West College
- Dan Lioy, Marylhurst University

I am grateful to all of those at McGraw-Hill who have supported this book and worked to present my ideas. I want especially to thank my editors. Jim Bull was vital to the first two editions, and Ken King similarly vital to the next two. I am also deeply grateful to Jessica Cannavo, sponsoring editor; development editor, Craig Leonard; marketing coordinator: Angela R. FitzPatrick; copyeditor, Kay Mikel; project manager, Melissa M. Leick; design coordinator, Margarite Reynolds; and Louis Swaim, Buyer, for their support throughout my work on this project.

INTRODUCTION

MORAL ARGUMENTS

This is a book about moral issues. What are moral issues? To answer this question, we need to consider the definition of philosophy. If the word itself is any guide, philosophy is the love of wisdom. A simple definition of wisdom, in turn, is good judgment. Philosophy, then, is the love or pursuit of good judgment. Moral philosophy, or ethics, is the pursuit of good judgment about character and action—about what kind of person to be and about what to do. Ethics addresses questions about virtue and vice, good and bad, right and wrong.

Such questions, clearly, have varied answers; they are often the subject of controversy and debate. The moral issues considered in this book—abortion, euthanasia, pornography, capital punishment, affirmative action, and many others—are among the most controversial our society faces. Most of this book consists of moral arguments, in which a moral issue is considered and a particular position is supported or a particular conclusion is reached through reasoning.

How can we think through moral issues carefully and systematically? How do we develop arguments for ethical conclusions? These are questions that I attempt to answer in this introduction.

Arguments

Arguments are bits of reasoning in language. Frequently, we think of arguments as conflicts. In that sense, this book presents a series of arguments about issues such as abortion, euthanasia, and affirmative action. But philosophers and logicians primarily use "argument" in the sense that one argues for a conclusion. An argument starts with some assertions and tries to justify a thesis.

Components of Arguments

The initial assertions of an argument are its *premises*; the thesis that the argument tries to justify is its *conclusion*. Arguments consist of *statements*, sentences that can be true or false. Almost every sentence in this book falls into this category. Statements are declarative, in the indicative mood; they say something about the way the world is, correctly or incorrectly.

Here, for example, is a simple argument:

(1) Stealing is wrong.
∴ Stealing this book is wrong.

(This format lists the premises in the order in which they are given and then gives the conclusion. The symbol ∴ means "therefore.")

How can we recognize arguments? The premises of an argument are meant to support the conclusion. We can recognize arguments, then, by recognizing when some statements are offered in support of others. We can do this most easily, in turn, if we can distinguish premises from conclusions. But how can we pick out the conclusion of an argument? In English, various words and phrases can signal the premises or the conclusion of an argument.

- *Conclusion Indicators*: therefore, thus, hence, consequently, it follows that, in conclusion, as a result, then, must, accordingly, this implies that, this entails that, we may infer that
- *Premise Indicators*: because, as, for, since, given that, for the reason that

Beware: These words and phrases have other uses as well.

Extended or *complex* arguments contain other arguments. *Simple* arguments do not. Because extended arguments are good only if the simple arguments within them are good, it is best to break extended arguments down into their simple components and analyze them separately.

Validity and Soundness

To evaluate arguments, we need to ask, What distinguishes good from bad arguments? What makes a good argument good?

A good argument links its premises to its conclusion in the right way. In a (deductively) *valid* argument, the truth of the premises guarantees the truth of the conclusion. If the premises are all true, then the conclusion has to be true. Or, equivalently, if the conclusion of a valid argument is false, at least one premise must also be false. Consider, for example, the argument

(2) All promises ought to be kept.
Your promise to Joe is a promise.
∴ You ought to keep your promise to Joe.

In any circumstance in which the premises of this argument are true, the conclusion must be true as well. It is impossible to conceive of a state of affairs in which, while all promises ought to be kept, and your promise to Joe is a promise, you nevertheless should not keep your promise to Joe. If it is false that you should keep your promise to Joe, then either there are promises that shouldn't be kept, or your "promise" wasn't a real promise.

Valid arguments are only one species of good argument. Others are *inductively strong* (or *reliable*). The truth of the premises of such an argument does not guarantee the truth of its conclusion, but it does make the truth of the conclusion probable. Consider, for example, this argument:

(3) Every generous person I've ever known has also been kind.
∴ All generous people are kind.

It is possible for the premise to be true while the conclusion is false. There may be generous but nasty people I've never met. So the argument is invalid. Nevertheless, the premise lends some support to the conclusion. The argument is inductively strong; how strong depends on how many generous people I've known, among other things.

In general, good arguments not only are valid or inductively strong but also have true premises. A *sound* argument is a valid argument with true premises. In any valid argument, the truth of the premises guarantees the truth of the conclusion, so a sound argument also has a true conclusion. A *cogent* argument is an inductively strong argument with true premises. In a cogent argument, the truth of the conclusion is likely but not guaranteed.

Logic develops precise ways of determining whether arguments are valid (although the most powerful ways of evaluating arguments are intuitive). An argument is valid if the truth of the premises guarantees the truth of the conclusion. To show that an argument is invalid, therefore, one needs to show that the premises could all be true while the conclusion is false.

There are two ways of showing that an argument is invalid. The first, the *direct* method, is simply to describe such a situation; that is, we can show an argument to be invalid by depicting a possible circumstance in which the premises were all true but the conclusion was false.

The second way to show that an argument is invalid, devised by Aristotle, is based on the idea of *form* and is known as the method of *counterexamples*. To show that an argument is invalid using this method, we must produce another argument of the same form with true premises and a false conclusion. This introduction is too short to present a detailed discussion of form. But Aristotle's insight was that validity is *formal* in the sense that arguments can be classified into certain general patterns, or forms, of which individual arguments are instances. An argument form is valid if and only if every instance of it is valid. More to the point, an argument form is invalid if and only if some instance of it is invalid. To show that an argument form is invalid, then, find an instance with true premises and a false conclusion. To show that an *individual argument* is invalid, find an argument with true premises and a false conclusion that shares the *specific form* of the original argument: the most explicit form we can devise, displaying the most structure.

Making Moral Arguments

As we have seen, it is possible to attack an argument by showing that one of its premises is false. Even if the argument is valid or strong, such an attack shows that it is not sound or cogent and undercuts its conclusion.

Moral arguments typically have both moral and factual premises. Some statements are *factual* or *descriptive*. They say how the world is. Other statements are *evaluative, prescriptive*, or *normative*. They say how the world ought to be; more generally, they evaluate how the world is, characterizing it as right or wrong, acceptable or unacceptable, delightful or dismal. They include specifically evaluative terms. A *moral argument* is an argument with an evaluative conclusion. People who reach opposite conclusions may differ in moral principles, but they may also differ in factual assumptions. One of the chief purposes of a contemporary moral problems course is to teach people how to disentangle moral from factual issues. The distinction matters, because factual and moral conclusions require different kinds of support.

Consider a simple example:

(4) You promised to sublet the apartment.
You should keep your promises.
∴ You should sublet the apartment.

The first premise is factual. Whether you promised to sublet the apartment is a matter of fact. If it is disputed, we may ask about the facts: What exactly did you say? Is there any agreement in writing? Did you sign anything? Was it really this apartment? The second premise, in contrast, is evaluative. It speaks of how things ought to be, not how they are. Consequently, no amount of inquiry into the facts can help us determine its truth or falsehood. To justify it, we must appeal to more general moral principles.

The general pattern of moral arguments for particular conclusions is thus:

(5) Factual premise(s)
Moral premise(s)
∴ Moral conclusion

This is utterly familiar. You ought to return those books to the library. Why? You borrowed them (factual premise), they are due (factual premise), and you ought to return what you borrow when it is due (moral premise). Or, you may take vacation the last week of April. Why? It won't cause your coworkers any inconvenience (factual premise), and you may take vacation whenever it won't cause your coworkers any inconvenience (moral premise).

Arguing for a Moral Principle

(5) is a pattern for arguing to a particular moral conclusion. But how can one argue for general moral conclusions, such as the moral principles on which such arguments rely? How, in other words, does one support moral premises such as You ought to keep your promises, You ought to return what you borrow when it's due, or You may take vacation whenever it won't cause your coworkers any inconvenience?

In essence, there are two ways to argue for a moral generalization: from above and from below. To argue from above, appeal to a more general moral principle. John Stuart Mill, for example, would argue as follows for the generalization, You ought to keep your promises:

(6) You ought to follow the rules that will maximize human happiness.
Following the rule You ought to keep your promises will maximize human happiness.
∴ You ought to keep your promises.

Immanuel Kant would justify it differently:

(7) You ought to treat others as ends, not merely as means.
Keeping a promise to someone treats that person as an end, but breaking one treats him or her as a means to your ends.
∴ You ought to keep your promises.

Philosophers who prefer justifications from above tend, like Mill and Kant, to search for a single, very general moral principle that can justify other principles.

Moral principles may also be justified from below, by appeal to their instances. One could try to argue that it is wrong to break promises, for example, by generalizing from examples of particular situations:

(8) Say someone promises to marry you but doesn't show up at the altar; that would be wrong.

Say Frank borrows money from you, promising insincerely to repay it, and then absconds; that would be wrong.

Say the doctor makes an appointment to see you and then goes to play golf instead; that would be wrong.

Say Joan agrees to pay you $1,000 for landscaping her yard, you do the work, and she refuses to pay; that would be wrong.

∴ Breaking promises is wrong.

or more specific kinds of situations:

(9) Someone who agrees to marry someone on a particular day should show up for the wedding.

Someone who borrows money ought to repay it.

Someone who makes an appointment ought to keep it.

Someone who signs a contract ought to fulfill it.

∴ Breaking promises is wrong.

These arguments are not valid, but they are inductively strong if the examples are numerous and diverse enough.

The readings in this book contain many arguments for moral principles, some from above, some from below. Arguments from above are important, for they say something about *why* the moral principle holds. Kant's argument for promise keeping, for example, not only concludes that promises should be kept but also indicates that they should be kept because breaking them treats others as means to your own ends. Mill's argument, similarly, indicates that promise keeping is obligatory because it maximizes human happiness. Arguments from below are also important, for they link principles to particular cases about which we have strong moral intuitions. The more abstract and general a moral principle is, the fewer intuitions we have about whether it is correct. Moral theories therefore rely on both kinds of arguments.

Arguing against a Moral Principle

How does one argue *against* a moral principle? One tries to find a counterexample: an instance in which the principle seems to give the wrong result. Is it *always* right to keep promises, for instance? One can try to find examples of promises that should not be kept. Recall that, in a valid argument, the truth of the premises guarantees the truth of the conclusion, or, equivalently, the falsehood of the conclusion guarantees the falsehood of at least one premise. One can construct a valid argument from the principle to a false conclusion:

(10) One should always keep one's promises.

∴ If Herman promised to murder the entire city council, he should do it.

The absurdity of the conclusion shows that there is something wrong with the premise.

Many philosophers have objected to Kant's opinion that lying is always wrong by constructing a similar argument. Suppose that a distraught child runs to you begging for help. A homicidal maniac is chasing her. You hide her in a closet. The maniac bangs on your door and asks whether you know where she is. Surely you should not tell the truth.

Exceptions to Moral Principles

This example illustrates that most moral principles have exceptions. Most moral principles are true *other things being equal* (in Latin, *ceteris paribus*), but not universally. Plato recognized this about promise keeping and telling the truth:

> . . . are we to say that justice or right is simply to speak the truth and to pay back any debt one may have contracted? Or are these same actions sometimes right and sometimes wrong? I mean this sort of thing, for example: everyone would surely agree that if a friend has deposited weapons with you when he was sane, and he asks for them when he is out of his mind, you should not return them. The man who returns them is not doing right, nor is one who is willing to tell the whole truth to a man in such a state. (*Republic*, 331c)*

Although Keep your promises and Tell the truth are good moral rules in general, they can be overridden or defeated by other moral considerations. For that reason, they are called *defeasible*. Normally, you ought to keep your promises. Normally, you ought to tell the truth. But sometimes there are good reasons to break a promise or to lie, and then you have a moral conflict.

Philosophers often analyze such situations of moral conflict in terms of *prima facie* duties. W. D. Ross defined "prima facie duty" as a "characteristic (quite distinct from that of being a duty proper) which an

*Plato, *The Republic*, translated by Paul Shorey (Cambridge, Mass.: Loeb Classical Library, 1930).

act has, in virtue of being of a certain kind (e.g., the keeping of a promise), of being an act which would be a duty proper if it were not at the same time of another kind which is morally significant."* A prima facie obligation, that is, holds under normal circumstances; it holds all other things being equal, becoming *actual*—an obligation all things considered, or, in Ross's terms, "a duty proper"—unless some other moral consideration intervenes.

Prima facie obligations offer a way to explain the force of rules while allowing for exceptions. The idea, in essence, is that a prima facie rule applies unless some other rule conflicts with it. John Stuart Mill's secondary principles are paradigms of prima facie principles: They dictate obligations unless they come into conflict. In that case, Mill stipulates, the principle of utility, the sole rule in his system that has an absolute rather than prima facie character, resolves the conflict. This indicates a key difference between actual and prima facie obligation: Prima facie obligations can conflict, whereas actual obligations cannot. If a homicidal maniac asks whether you know where an innocent child is hiding, there is a moral conflict: You have a prima facie obligation to tell the truth and another to tell a lie. Only one can be actual—what you ought actually to do in that situation, all things considered. Saving a life is more important than never telling a lie, so your obligation to lie is actual, overriding your obligation to tell the truth.

Let's revisit Plato's puzzle about returning weapons to a friend who is out of his mind. Because unconditional statements of actual obligation *cannot* conflict, this pair is inconsistent:

(11) You have an actual obligation to return the weapons.
You have an actual obligation not to return the weapons.
You cannot be obliged, actually, all things considered, both to return the weapons and not to return them.
Because conditional prima facie obligations *can* conflict, this pair of statements is consistent:

(12) You have a prima facie obligation to return the weapons.
You have a prima facie obligation not to return the weapons.

In general, you have a prima facie obligation to do something whenever the circumstances trigger a defeasible moral rule. In Plato's case, there are defeasible rules that you ought to keep your promises and that you ought to prevent harm. Your promise gives rise to the prima facie obligation to return the weapons; your friend's madness gives rise to the prima facie obligation not to return them.

Moral conflicts such as those Plato describes have spurred philosophers to devise moral theories to help us compare different kinds of moral considerations and resolve conflicts generated by them.

Seeing that moral considerations can come into conflict helps to dissolve some of the motivation for relativism. In morality, it is often true that one person or culture sees things one way and another sees them quite differently. But even within the view of a single person and culture, there are many different perspectives, which it is the task of morality to relate, evaluate, and, in particular situations, reconcile. Reasonable people can differ on how to reconcile them. That is what makes a book like this both possible and important.

*W.D. Ross, *The Right and the Good* (Oxford: Oxford University Press, 1930), 19.

First Principles

PART I

FIRST PRINCIPLES

Most of our moral judgments concern particular things. We judge certain actions and certain people good or bad. There are many gradations: Acts or people may be heroic, splendid, admirable, acceptable, indifferent, unsatisfactory, despicable, or horrible, to mention just a few moral adjectives. There are also many dimensions of moral consideration: Acts or people may be honest, kind, loyal, trustworthy, noble, brave, generous, self-controlled, gentle, friendly, witty, pleasant, helpful, effective, efficient, or considerate, to mention just a few positive attributes. Usually, we apply these to particular actions or to particular people.

When people disagree about a moral judgment, they try to justify their views. They do this by constructing an argument that appeals to moral principles. Suppose, for example, that Jennifer killed Michael by breaking a baseball bat over his head. And say that you and I disagree about the morality of the act. I think it was wrong; you think it was justifiable. I might try to justify my judgment by constructing a simple argument:

1. Jennifer's killing Michael was murder. (Fact)
2. Murder is always wrong. (Moral principle)
3. Therefore, Jennifer's killing Michael was wrong. (Moral conclusion)

An argument for a particular moral conclusion generally contains both factual and moral premises, just as this one does. The first premise is factual; it purports to describe the way the world is. The second premise, in contrast, is moral. It does not describe the world as it is but evaluates a general category of action. Assertions like the first premise are often called *factual* or *descriptive*. Those like the second premise or the conclusion are often called *evaluative*, *prescriptive*, or *normative*.

The distinction between these kinds of assertions matters, for we resolve disagreements about them in very different ways. Suppose, for example, that you challenge my first premise. You deny, in other words, that Jennifer committed a murder. We might resolve our disagreement by clarifying our use of words and investigating the facts. If I defend my premise with further premises:

4. Murder is killing a human being with malice aforethought.
5. Jennifer killed Michael.
6. Michael was human.
7. Jennifer intended to do Michael harm.

you might challenge my definition of murder (4) or my description of the facts (5, 6, and 7). We might proceed to investigate whether Jennifer was really the killer and Michael really the victim; whether Jennifer intended to harm Michael or killed him accidentally; whether Michael was human or a robot; and whether my definition of murder is correct. All these issues concern definitions or matters of fact.

If you challenge my second premise, however, investigating matters of fact cannot resolve our disagreement. We differ not on how the world is but on how it ought to be. And, as David Hume stresses, there is no way to derive *ought* from *is;* no amount of factual information can determine how the world ought to be. To justify my premise, I must appeal to some broader moral principle—and ultimately, many philosophers have thought, to a first, most fundamental moral principle from which all others follow. The thinkers of the Enlightenment, especially, saw that if we could establish and agree upon a first principle of morality, all our disagreements would concern definitions and matters of fact and thus would be resolvable by investigation. Morality would lend itself to scientific inquiry as much as anything else.

The search for a first principle of morality has other sources. One stems from the great variety of things we call good. We say that certain actions, people, and even qualities (such as honesty) are good. What makes them all good? What do they have in common? Similarly, we call things as diverse as September 11, Hitler, deception, and cruelty wrong. What makes them all wrong? What do they have in common? To answer would be to give the first principle of morality. Why couldn't there be several such principles? Because we could raise the question, What makes *them* fundamental principles of morality? What do *they* all have in common?

To try to justify moral principles as well as particular moral judgments is to construct a moral theory. Moral theories are systematic attempts to provide and justify answers to questions such as What should I do? and What kind of person should I be? Confucius distinguishes these questions and develops two independent answers to them. The person who does the right thing follows the Way, observing the rules of propriety. The person of superior character is sincere, generous, kind, diligent, and serious, doing the right thing for the right reason. Most modern moral theories take the former question as basic. They focus on action and try to distinguish right from wrong in principled ways. But some theories focus instead on the latter question and try to distinguish good character traits from bad. Good traits are *virtues;* bad traits, *vices.*

Aristotle develops the classic theory of virtue. He distinguishes *intrinsic* goods, which are desired for their own sake, from *instrumental* goods, which are desired as means to other things. To justify any answers to the above questions, we must appeal to intrinsic goods. Suppose that someone asks why you are reading this book. "Because it's required for my ethics course," you answer. "But why do what's required?" "I want to get a good grade." "Why do you want a good grade?" "I want to have a good GPA." "Why?" "It will help me get a job." "Why do you want a job?" "I want money." "Why?" "I want things money can buy!" "Why do you want them?" To stop the chain of questions, you must appeal to something that is intrinsically good. Every time you appeal to an instrumental good, the questioner can ask in turn why you want *it.*

Aristotle contends that people desire only one thing for its own sake and never for the sake of something else: happiness. Any series of requests for justification leads eventually to the response, "Because I want to be happy!" If someone persists in asking why, there is nothing more to say: happiness is desirable for its own sake.

What is happiness? What is it to live well? Aristotle's answer relies on the idea that human beings have a function. Just as a good knife cuts well and a good teacher teaches well, a good person fulfills the function of a human being well. But what is the function of a person? It is what is most distinctive of human beings: to act rationally. A good person acts in accordance with virtue, and to act virtuously is to act rationally. A good person does the right thing at the right time, and in the right way, *for the right reason.* Virtue is thus a mean between extremes. The ability to find that mean Aristotle calls *practical wisdom.* To fear too much is cowardly, but to fear too little is rash. Courage is fearing what ought to be feared, when it ought to be feared, to the extent that it ought to be feared, and for the appropriate reason.

How does a person become virtuous? How, in other words, can someone become practically wise? Not by abstract thought, Aristotle says, but by doing virtuous things. Shakespeare's Polonius advised, "Assume a virtue if you have it not"; Aristotle agrees. If you do brave things, for example—initially, by forcing yourself to do them, by pretending to be brave—you gradually develop the habit of doing brave things. When the habit is ingrained and automatic, to the point of being "second nature," you *are* brave. In general, people become good by doing good things. There is no rule for becoming good or for distinguishing good from bad, right from wrong; a person of practical wisdom has a highly refined ability to draw the right distinctions and tell right from wrong.

St. Thomas Aquinas bases his views on ethics and political philosophy on those of Aristotle. But he adds many innovations, blending Aristotelian insights into a Christian worldview. He develops a comprehensive theory of natural law that remains influential today. Aquinas begins with Aristotle's idea that human good depends on human nature. To live well—to excel or flourish—is to fulfill one's function well. Just as an excellent knife cuts well and an excellent eye sees well, an excellent human being displays excellence in rational activity. As these examples suggest, different things have different functions. In general, the function of a thing depends on its nature. So, what something ought to do and be depends on its function, which in turn depends on its nature.

Aquinas adds God to this Aristotelian picture. God establishes the order of nature, determining the natures of things and their functions and their excellences. God thus indirectly establishes not only the physical laws that constitute the order of nature but also the *natural laws* that free beings ought to obey. Since human nature is distinctively rational, law itself is essentially a matter of reason.

Aquinas distinguishes several different kinds of law. *Eternal law* is the law of nature, established by God, that governs the entire universe. Everything in the universe obeys eternal law and does so necessarily. Science investigates eternal law and tries to describe it. *Natural law* is normative; it prescribes what things should do and be. Since a thing's nature determines its function and thus its virtue—what it ought to do and be—eternal law determines natural law. Natural law is the manifestation of eternal law in creatures capable of rational choice and activity. Natural law manifests the eternal law by way of "the light of natural reason." God imprints on us the natural ability to tell right from wrong.

Aquinas also distinguishes natural law from human law. Natural law is fully general and universal, but human law must apply to particular circumstances in specific ways. Natural law relates to human law as principles relate to conclusions drawn from them. One can think of natural law, then, as comprising the axioms of the moral law in general. Because natural law serves as an axiom of the moral law, it must be self-evident; it cannot be a conclusion from some other premise. Precepts of natural law must be both general and obvious. That might make it seem that natural law has little content. Pursue good; avoid evil. Everyone can agree to that. But what is good? What is evil?

Here, Aquinas appeals to human nature. As Aristotle argued, human excellence depends on our characteristic function, which depends in turn on our nature. This is true in two senses. What we are determines what we ought to do and be. And what we are tells us what we ought to do and be. The universe is ordered so that we naturally tend to pursue good and avoid evil. Our own dispositions thus provide a test. We are naturally disposed to pursue good and avoid evil. We have a natural tendency not only to have certain inclinations (toward food, drink, and sex, for example), but also to control them through the exercise of reason. If lust is natural, so are rationality, shame, and self-restraint.

Aquinas classifies the precepts of natural law into three groups: (1) laws of self-preservation, (2) laws of biological welfare, and (3) laws of reason.

Aquinas does not develop his theory of natural law into a comprehensive political philosophy. Nevertheless, several important theses follow from it.

First, human law aims at the common good. Second, the purpose of human law is to help people follow natural law—that is, to make them virtuous. Law is essentially paternalistic, restricting people's freedom for their own good. The law accomplishes this by training people to recognize right and wrong. Third, human law must be flexible. As Aristotle said, virtue is a mean; there is no strict rule for finding it. Human laws cannot take into account the full complexity of the world; they inevitably oversimplify. We must create law to regulate our behavior but also must allow for exceptions in those cases in which the law does not make sense. One might think that we may solve this problem by making law more specific. We might, for example, require people to return goods held in trust unless such return poses a risk to national security. But this only makes the problem worse. We are better off with general laws flexibly applied. Fourth, a law that is unjust or fails to promote the common good, in general or in a particular case, has no authority as law. It should not be obeyed.

Finally, just as people have a natural inclination to virtue, they have a natural inclination to live in certain social structures: in families, in communities, and in states. These social institutions are natural, not conventional; they thus have moral force. People are inherently social, as Aristotle observed. More specifically, they are naturally family members, members of communities, and citizens. Law, therefore, should serve to strengthen these natural institutions.

The Enlightenment produced a great challenge to morality in the thought of David Hume. Aristotle and Aquinas hold that ethics rests on right reason. The function of a human being is to act rationally; human excellence consists in doing so well. Acting ethically requires using practical wisdom, reasoning on the basis of the natural law. Hume argues that reason can lead us only to conclusions; it cannot lead us to action. There is a gap between *is* and *ought;* there is likewise a gap between *ought* and *does*. Acting rationally has a source in something other than reason.

That source, Hume maintains, is passion. We have a moral sense that leads us to act by generating within us feelings of approval or disapproval, satisfaction or uneasiness, pleasure or pain. If we witness one person harming another, for example, we not only reach the conclusion that the act is wrong but also feel revulsion toward the act and the person committing it. That revulsion is what leads us to act. In fact, it may also underlie our conclusion: "Reason is, and ought to be, the slave of the passions."

The Enlightenment produced two great and competing accounts of the foundations of morality. Immanuel Kant maintains that all of ethics reduces to a single principle, the categorical imperative. He articulates five versions of the principle, but he takes all to be equivalent. The two most important versions are

I. Act so that the maxim of your action might be willed as universal law.

II. Treat everyone as a end, not merely as a means.

The first means that you must act on the basis of principle; you cannot make an exception for yourself. You must act, in other words, in such a way that everyone could act on your principles. The second means that every human being deserves to be treated with respect, as an independent moral agent; you must not use people as means to your own ends.

Kant derives the categorical imperative from general considerations about morality. A first principle, he warns, must be necessarily true; it must hold no matter what the world is like, for as a moral assertion, it does not describe the world. It must be something we can know *a priori,* independently of experience. It must therefore be universal, applying to all rational agents capable of thinking and acting morally. And it must be categorical, of the form "Everyone always ought to . . . ," rather than hypothetical (of the form "If you want . . . , you ought to . . . "), for it must not depend on the goals we adopt for ourselves, even general goals such as happiness. What all hypothetical imperatives have in common is simply the form of law, that is, the idea of acting on principle as a moral agent. That leads to Kant's formulations of the categorical imperative. You must act on principle; you must respect yourself and others as moral agents.

The second great Enlightenment account of the foundations of morality rejects Kant's picture completely. Utilitarianism, a moral theory mentioned in Plato's dialogues, first advocated by Francis Hutcheson, and brought to full development by Jeremy Bentham and John Stuart Mill, can be summarized in two words: *Maximize good.* Utilitarians hold that all of ethics and political philosophy reduces to that one maxim, the principle of utility.

The principle seems simple but has a number of far-reaching consequences. First, utilitarians evaluate actions by the extent to which they maximize good. They evaluate actions, therefore, solely by examining their consequences. In determining whether an action or kind of action is right or wrong, we need to ask, Is it for the best? What effect does it have on the amount of good in the universe? Utilitarianism is thus a version of *consequentialism,* the view that the moral value of an action depends completely on its consequences.

Other moral philosophers contend that other features of actions are relevant to their moral value. Killing, for example, is generally a bad thing. But our judgment of a killer depends on other factors. Was the killing purely accidental, or did it result from negligence? Did it stem from a fit of rage, or was it premeditated? The prior actions, motives, intentions, and general state of mind of the agent, we think, make a moral difference. Utilitarians are committed to saying that all these things are irrelevant to evaluating the killing itself—but, they would say, they are highly relevant to evaluating the killer. Utilitarians need not banish motives, intentions, states of mind, and circumstances from ethics. But they must define their moral values ultimately in terms of the moral value of actions. We might say, for example, that an intention is good to the extent that it results in good actions, that a motive is good to the extent that it results in good intentions, that a character trait is good to the extent that it results in good motives, and so on.

Second, utilitarianism is a *universalist* theory: We must judge whether an action or kind of action maximizes the total amount of good in the universe. Thus, we must consider the consequences of the action for everyone it affects. We cannot consider ourselves alone, or just people in our community, or our fellow citizens; we must consider *everyone*. Most actions affect only a few people in any significant, identifiable way. Political decisions, however, often affect millions. In either case, we must be prepared to consider the effects on everyone affected.

Third, utilitarianism requires an independent theory of the good. The principle of utility tells us to maximize good, but it does not tell us what the good is. What, exactly, must we maximize? Bentham and Mill are *hedonists*: They believe that pleasure and pain are the only sources of value. The good, for both, is pleasure and the absence of pain. In the view of these philosophers, then, the principle of utility directs us to maximize the balance of pleasure over pain. Other utilitarians hold other theories of the good. Some, for example, identify the good with the satisfaction of desire. Some maintain that the good is indefinable and cannot be identified with anything else.

Whatever theory of the good a utilitarian holds, however, that theory must treat the good as a quantity to be maximized. The principle requires us to maximize good; good, therefore, must be the kind of thing that can be maximized. Certainly this means that we must be able to judge whether one circumstance contains more good than another. It probably also means that we must be able to quantify the amount of good in any given circumstance; that is, that we must be able to say how much good that circumstance contains—ideally, by assigning it a number.

Utilitarians tend to fall into two main categories. Some, called *act-utilitarians,* take the evaluation of individual actions as primary. They judge an action by the effects it has on the amount of good. Others, *rule-utilitarians,* take the evaluation of kinds of actions as primary. They judge rules by the effects of following them and then judge individual actions by appealing to the recommended rules. Bentham is an act-utilitarian; Mill often sounds like a rule-utilitarian, although it is possible to interpret him as an act-utilitarian or even a *character-utilitarian,* one who takes the evaluation of character traits as primary and holds that one should develop the virtues that tend to maximize everyone's happiness.

In most cases, act- and rule-utilitarians agree in their moral evaluations of individual actions. They disagree, however, (a) when an action maximizes good while violating rules that usually—but not in a particular case—maximize good, and (b) when an action does not maximize good in a particular case but does follow those rules. Both situations involve a conflict between the principle of utility and a rule designed to maximize good in general. Act-utilitarians consider it bizarre to say that we should follow the rule instead of the principle of utility; according to rule-utilitarianism itself, the rule derives its force solely from the principle in the first place. But rule-utilitarians believe that rules are indispensable to moral thinking. We cannot calculate what to do in every individual case; we must think about kinds of actions, formulate rules that, if followed, maximize good, and then follow those rules.

Rule-utilitarians encounter a special difficulty: the rules justified by the principle of utility may come into conflict with each other. Among the good-maximizing rules, for example, are some commanding us to avoid murder and to save innocent lives. But there may be cases in which we can save lives only by committing a murder. Which rule takes precedence? Mill suggests that, in such cases, we appeal to the principle of utility itself. In his theory, then, the principle has two roles. It determines which rules we should adopt and resolves conflicts between them.

Nel Noddings argues for an ethics of caring. Kant begins his ethical reflections by affirming that only one thing is good unconditionally, without qualification—a good will. But what is it to have a good will? Kant gives two answers: to act on the basis of principle, and to respect others as ends in themselves. He doesn't explore a more obvious, common-sense answer: to care about others. A good-hearted person cares about other people, values them, and tries to help them. That, Noddings argues, is the basis for ethics. We have natural feelings of caring; a mother, for example, naturally cares about her child.

As we grow, morally speaking, we learn to extend these feelings to others even when they don't arise naturally.

Caring, Noddings contends, makes the difference between "Something must be done" and "I must do something." It takes us from moral evaluation to action. Caring, in short, solves Hume's problem. Reason doesn't impel us to do anything. Caring pushes us beyond the conclusions of reason to acting morally.

CONFUCIUS

from *The Analects*

Kong Fuzi (K'ung Fu-Tzu)—Grand Master Kong, or, as he became known in the West, Confucius (551–479 B.C.E.*)—was a contemporary of Lao Tzu and the Buddha. Born into a poor family in Lu (now Shandong Province in northeastern China), he was completely self-educated. His father died when he was three. At nineteen, he married, and had a son and two daughters. He got a government job, first managing a state granary and then managing herds of cattle and sheep. But at twenty-two he quit his job and opened up a school. He rose from poverty and obscurity to become the most influential and revered person in the history of China.*

*Confucius begins with the question "What kind of person should I try to become?", and centers his answer on the concept of virtue (*ren*). He contrasts selfishness, a desire for personal gain, with righteousness (*yi *or* i*), a desire to do what is right just because it is right. The superior person does the right thing for the right reason—because it is the right thing to do—not in order to get something else.*

Confucius holds that different virtues pertain to different relationships. There are virtues to be displayed toward other people in general, virtues to be displayed to friends and family, and virtues to exhibit to oneself. All are important, but all rest on the virtues of the self, which are central to virtue in general.

The basic virtues toward others are faithfulness and the five key components of ren*: seriousness, generosity, sincerity, diligence, and kindness. The chief principle for dealing with other people is* zhong*, reciprocity (sometimes translated "altruism" or "likening to oneself"): "What you do not want done to yourself, do not do to others" (5:11, 12:2, 15:23). This so-called Silver Rule is a logically weaker cousin of the Golden Rule: "What you would have others do unto you, do so unto them." There are also virtues special to relationships with family and friends: filial piety—obedience, reverence, and service to one's parents and elders—and fraternal submission, service and trustworthiness to one's equals. These virtues are roots of* ren*. We learn how to treat others by learning how to interact with those closest to us. Most fundamental of all are the virtues of the self. Knowledge leads to virtuous thought, which leads to virtuous feelings, which leads in turn to virtuous action.*

Confucius, like Aristotle, thinks of virtue as a mean between extremes; the properly generous person, for example, gives appropriately, neither too much nor too little, to the right person in the right circumstances. The best way to find the mean is to follow the rules of propriety, the traditional social rules intended to regulate action and craft character. (Source: *From Confucius,* The Analects. *Translated by James Legge. The translation has been revised for readability and similarity of style to the Chinese.)*

1:1. The Master said, "Isn't it pleasant to learn and to apply what you've learned? Isn't it delightful to have friends coming from far away? Isn't he a person of complete virtue who doesn't get angry that others don't appreciate him?"

1:2. Yu said, "Few filial and fraternal people like to offend their superiors, and nobody who doesn't like to offend superiors likes to stir up rebellion. The superior person attends to the root of things. From the root grows the Way [*dao*]. Filial piety and fraternal submission are the root of virtue [*ren*]."

1:4. Zeng said, "Every day I examine myself on three points: whether, with others, I may have been unfaithful; whether, with friends, I may have been untrustworthy; whether I may have failed to master and practice the instructions of my teacher."

1:6. The Master said, "A youth at home should be filial; abroad, respectful to elders. He should be earnest and truthful. He should overflow with love to all and cultivate the friendship of the good. When he has time and opportunity after doing these things, he should study."

1:7. Zi Xia said, "If someone turns from the love of beauty to a sincere love of virtue; if he can serve his parents with all his strength; if he can serve his prince with his life; if his words to his friends are sincere; although people say he has not learned, I will certainly say that he has."

1:8. The Master said, "A scholar who is not serious will not be venerated, and his learning will not be solid. Hold faithfulness and sincerity as first principles. Have no friends not equal to yourself. When you have faults, do not be afraid to abandon them."

1:12. Yu said, "In practicing propriety, a natural ease is best. This is the excellence of the ancient kings, and in things small and great we follow them. Yet it is not to be observed in all cases. Anyone who knows and manifests such ease must regulate it by propriety."

1:14. The Master said, "A superior person doesn't seek gratification or comfort. He's earnest in what he does; he's careful in speech. He associates with people of principle to set himself right. Such a person truly loves to learn."

2:3. The Master said, "If the people are led by laws and restrained by punishments, they will try to avoid them without any sense of shame. If they are led by virtue and restrained by propriety, they will have a sense of shame and become good."

2:4. At fifteen, I had my mind bent on learning. At thirty, I stood firm. At forty, I had no doubts. At fifty, I knew the decrees of Heaven. At sixty, my ear obeyed truth. At seventy, I could follow what my heart desired without transgressing what was right."

2:10. The Master said, "See what a person does. Mark his motives. Examine his habits. How can anyone conceal his character? How can anyone conceal his character?"

2:14. The Master said, "The superior person is open-minded and not partisan. The mean person is partisan and not open-minded."

2:17. The Master said, "Yu, shall I teach you what knowledge is? When you know something, to maintain that you know it; when you don't know something, to admit that you don't know it—this is knowledge."

2:24. The Master said, ". . . To see what is right and not do it is cowardice."

4:2. The Master said, "Those without virtue can't abide long in a condition of poverty and hardship—or in a condition of enjoyment. The virtuous are at ease with virtue [*ren*]; the wise desire virtue."

4:3. The Master said, "Only the truly virtuous [*ren*] know what to love or hate in others."

4:10. The Master said, "The superior person in the world is not for anything or against anything; he follows what is right."

4:11. The Master said, "The superior person thinks of virtue; the small person thinks of comfort. The superior person thinks of the law; the small person thinks of favors."

4:15. The Master said, "Shen, my doctrine is one thread." Zeng replied, "Yes." The Master went out, and the other disciples asked, "What do his words mean?" Zeng said, "Our Master's doctrine is to be true to the principles of our nature and to exercise them benevolently toward others—this and nothing more."

4:16. The Master said, "The superior person's mind is conversant with righteousness [*yi*]; the inferior person's mind is conversant with gain."

4:17. The Master said, "When we see people of worth, we should think of equaling them; when we see people of a contrary character, we should turn inward and examine ourselves."

5:11. Zi Kong said, "What I don't want others to do to me, I also want not to do to others."

6:18. The Master said, "Those who know the Way aren't equal to those who love it, and those who love it aren't equal to those who delight in it."

6:24. Zai Wu asked, "A benevolent person, told 'Someone is in the well,' will go in after him, I suppose." Confucius said, "Why should he? A superior person may be made to go to the well, but not to go down into it. One may impose upon him, but not make a fool of him."

6:25. The Master said, "The superior person studies all learning extensively and restrains himself by propriety. So, he doesn't swerve from the Way."

6:27. The Master said, "Perfect is the virtue that accords with the Constant Mean! For a long time, its practice has been rare among the people."

6:28. Zi Kong said, "What would you say about someone who benefits people extensively and helps everyone? May he be called perfectly virtuous [*ren*]?" The Master said, "Why only virtuous? Must he not have the qualities of a sage? Even Yao and Shun [legendary rulers who lived as much as two millennia earlier] weren't like this. Someone of perfect virtue [*ren*], wishing to establish himself, establishes others; wishing to enlarge himself, enlarges others. To be able to judge others by what is right in ourselves is the art of virtue [*ren*]."

7:27. The Master said, "Maybe some act without knowing why. I don't. Hearing much, selecting what is good, and following it, seeing much and remembering it, are the second style of knowledge."

8:2. The Master said, "Respectfulness without propriety becomes laborious bustle. Caution without propriety becomes timidity. Boldness without propriety becomes insubordination; straightforwardness without propriety becomes rudeness."

12:1. Yan Yuan asked about perfect virtue [*ren*]. The Master said, "To subdue oneself and return to propriety is virtue. If a man can subdue himself and return to propriety for one day, all under heaven will ascribe virtue to him. Is the practice of virtue from oneself alone, or does it depend on others?" Yan Yuan said, "I want to ask about these steps." The Master replied, "Don't look at what is contrary to propriety; don't listen to what is contrary to propriety; don't speak what is contrary to propriety; don't make a move that is contrary to propriety."

12:2. Zhong Kong asked about perfect virtue [*ren*]. The Master said, "When you travel, act as if you were receiving a great guest. Employ the people as if you were assisting at a great sacrifice. Don't do to others what you wouldn't want done to yourself. Then no one in the country or in your family will complain about you."

12:9. Duke Ai asked Yu Zo, "Suppose the year is one of scarcity and the government faces a deficit. What is to be done?" Yu Zo replied, "Why not demand from the people a tenth of their income?" "With two tenths there isn't enough," said the Duke. "How could I get by on one tenth?" Yu Zo answered, "If the people have plenty, their ruler will not be needy alone. If the people are needy, their ruler can't enjoy plenty alone."

12:17. Qi Kang asked Confucius about government. He replied, "To govern [*cheng*] is to rectify [*cheng*]. If you lead correctly, who will dare to be incorrect?"

13:3. Zi Lu said, "The ruler of Wei is waiting for you to help him govern. What should be done first?" The Master replied, "Rectify names." "Really?" said Zi Lu. "You're wide of the mark. Why rectify names?" The Master said, "How uncultivated you are, Yu! A superior man shows a cautious reserve about what he doesn't know."

13:6. The Master said, "If a ruler acts correctly, he can govern without issuing orders. If he acts incorrectly, his orders won't be followed."

13:13. The Master said, "If a minister makes his own conduct correct, what difficulty will he have in governing? If he can't rectify himself, how can he rectify others?"

13:18. The Duke of She told Confucius, "Some of us are upright. If our father had stolen a sheep, we'd bear witness to it." Confucius said, "In my country the upright are different. The father conceals the misconduct of the son, and the son conceals the misconduct of the father. Uprightness is to be found in this."

14:30. The Master said, "The way of the superior person is threefold, but I am not equal to it. Virtuous [*ren*], he is free from anxieties; wise, he is free from perplexities; bold, he is free from fear." Zi Kong said, "Master, that's you."

14:36. Someone said, "What do you say about the principle of repaying injury with kindness?" The Master said, "How then will you repay kindness?

Repay kindness with kindness and injury with justice."

15:17. The Master said, "The superior person takes righteousness [*yi*] to be essential. He practices it according to propriety. He brings it forth in humility. He completes it with sincerity. This is indeed a superior person."

15:20. The Master said, "What the superior person seeks is in himself. What the inferior person seeks is in others."

15:23. Zi Kong asked, "Is there one word to serve as a rule for practice throughout life?" Confucius said, "It is reciprocity. What you don't want done to yourself, don't do to others."

16:10. Confucius said, "The superior person thoughtfully considers nine things: With his eyes, he wants to see clearly. With his ears, he wants to hear distinctly. In countenance, he wants to be warm. In demeanor, he wants to be respectful. In speech, he wants to be sincere. In business, he wants to be careful. When in doubt, he wants to ask others. When angry, he thinks of difficulties that might result. When he sees opportunity for gain, he thinks of righteousness."

17:6. Zi Qang asked Confucius about perfect virtue [*ren*]. Confucius said: "To be able to practice five things everywhere under Heaven constitutes perfect virtue." He begged to know what they were, and was told, "Seriousness, generosity, sincerity, diligence, and kindness. If you're serious, you won't be treated with disrespect. If you're generous, you'll win all hearts. If you're sincere, you'll be trusted. If you're diligent, you'll accomplish much. If you're kind, you'll enjoy the service of others."

17:8. The Master said, "Yu, have you heard the six things followed by the six confusions?" Yu replied, "I haven't." "Sit down and I'll tell you. The love of benevolence without the love of learning leads to an ignorant simplicity. The love of knowledge without the love of learning leads to dissipation of mind. The love of sincerity without the love of learning leads to recklessness. The love of straightforwardness without the love of learning leads to rudeness. The love of boldness without the love of learning leads to insubordination. The love of strength of character without the love of learning leads to extravagance."

20:3. The Master said, "Without recognizing the ordinances of heaven, it's impossible to be a superior person. Without acquaintance with propriety, it's impossible to establish one's character. Without knowing the force of words, it's impossible to know people."

QUESTIONS FOR REFLECTION

1. Which virtues are central, according to Confucius, and why?
2. What does Confucius mean by saying that filial piety and fraternal submission are the roots of virtue?
3. Confucius holds that loyalty to family and friends is more important than general social obligations. Consider his example. Do you agree with him? Are there other examples that would lead you to a different conclusion? If so, what does that imply about how these obligations should be balanced?
4. Is Confucius's doctrine "one thread"? If so, why does Zeng's explanation mention *two* things?
5. Contrast the roles of knowledge and propriety in helping the superior person find the mean and thus act virtuously.
6. Confucius is sometimes criticized for encouraging so much respect for tradition that change becomes impossible. Is that criticism fair, in your view?
7. What might Confucius mean by the rectification of names, and how does it relate to his key ethical concepts?

ARISTOTLE

from *Nicomachean Ethics*

Aristotle (384–322 B.C.E.), born in Stagira, was the son of Nicomachus, the court physician to Amyntas II, the king of Macedonia. Nicomachus died when Aristotle was a boy. After training in medicine, Aristotle entered Plato's Academy in Athens at the age of seventeen. He stayed twenty years, until Plato's death. In 342, he became the tutor of Alexander the Great, Amyntas's grandson, who was thirteen; Aristotle stayed at the Macedonian court as Alexander's teacher for three years, until Alexander was appointed regent. In 335, Aristotle returned to Athens to establish his own school, the Lyceum. When Alexander died in 323, Athenians became suspicious of Aristotle's links to Macedonia. Fearing that he might be executed, as Socrates had been, he fled Athens, "lest the Athenians sin twice against philosophy." He died a year later in Chalcis of chronic indigestion brought about by overwork.

Aristotle's influence on intellectual history has been immense. He wrote treatises on physics, biology, astronomy, psychology, logic, metaphysics, poetry, rhetoric, ethics, and politics. Through the Middle Ages, in Europe and the Islamic world, Aristotle was known simply as "the philosopher." His philosophy is still important; most Western and Islamic thought is to some degree Aristotelian. His scientific work, though now chiefly of historical interest, was remarkably sophisticated. It was not superseded for more than 1,500 years.

The Nicomachean Ethics *addresses the basic questions of moral philosophy: What is the good? What is virtue? What is happiness? Aristotle believes that the good, for human beings—what humans properly desire for its own sake—is happiness, which he thinks has its highest form in contemplative activity. Aristotle holds that people can attain virtue and happiness, however, only in the context of a good state governed in the proper way. Aristotle thus believes that ethics and politics are intertwined. (Source: Reprinted by permission of the publishers from* Aristotle's Nicomachean Ethics, *translated by W. D. Ross. Oxford University Press, 1925. Most notes have been omitted.)*

Happiness

BOOK I

4

Let us resume our inquiry and state, in view of the fact that all knowledge and every pursuit aims at some good, what it is that we say political science aims at and what is the highest of all goods achievable by action. Verbally there is very general agreement; for both the general run of men and people of superior refinement say that it is happiness, and identify living well and doing well with being happy; but with regard to what happiness is they differ, and the many do not give the same account as the wise. . . .

7

Let us again return to the good we are seeking, and ask what it can be. It seems different in different actions and arts; it is different in medicine, in strategy, and in the other arts likewise. What then is the good of each? Surely that for whose sake everything else is done. In medicine this is health, in strategy victory, in architecture a house, in any other sphere something else, and in every action and pursuit the end; for it is for the sake of this that all men do whatever else they do. Therefore, if there is an end for all that we do, this will be the good achievable by action, and if there are more than one, these will be the goods achievable by action.

So the argument has by a different course reached the same point; but we must try to state this even more clearly. Since there are evidently more than one end, and we choose some of these (e.g. wealth, flutes, and in general instruments) for the sake of something else, clearly not all ends are final ends; but the chief good is evidently something final. Therefore, if there is only one final end, this will be what we are seeking, and if there are more than one, the most final of these will be what we are seeking. Now we call that which is in itself worthy of pursuit more final than that which is worthy of pursuit for the sake of something else, and that which is never desirable for the sake of something else more final than the things that are desirable both in themselves and for the sake of that other thing, and therefore we call final without qualification that which is always desirable in itself and never for the sake of something else.

Now such a thing happiness, above all else, is held to be; for this we choose always for itself and never for the sake of something else, but honour, pleasure, reason, and every virtue we choose indeed for themselves (for if nothing resulted from them we should still choose each of them), but we choose them also for the sake of happiness, judging that by means of them we shall be happy. Happiness, on the other hand, no one chooses for the sake of these, nor, in general, for anything other than itself. . . .

. . . Happiness, then, is something final and self-sufficient, and is the end of action.

The Function of Man

Presumably, however, to say that happiness is the chief good seems a platitude, and a clearer account of what it is is still desired. This might perhaps be given, if we could first ascertain the function of man. For just as for a flute-player, a sculptor, or any artist, and, in general, for all things that have a function or activity, the good and the "well" is thought to reside in the function, so would it seem to be for man, if he has a function. Have the carpenter, then, and the tanner certain functions or activities, and has man none? Is he born without a function? Or as eye, hand, foot, and in general each of the parts evidently has a function, may one lay it down that man similarly has a function apart from all these? What then can this be? Life seems to be common even to plants, but we are seeking what is peculiar to man. Let us exclude, therefore, the life of nutrition and growth. Next there would be a life of perception, but *it* also seems to be common even to the horse, the ox, and every animal. There remains, then, an active life of the element that has a rational principle; of this, one part has such a principle in the sense of being obedient to one, the other in the sense of possessing one and exercising thought. And, as "life of the rational element" also has two meanings, we must state that life in the sense of activity is what we mean; for this seems to be the more proper sense of the term. Now if the function of man is an activity of soul which follows or implies a rational principle, and if we say "a so-and-so" and "a good so-and-so" have a function which is the same in kind, e.g. a lyre-player and a good lyre-player, and so without qualification in all cases, eminence in respect of goodness being added to the name of the function (for the function of a lyre-player is to play the lyre, and that of a good lyre-player is to do so well): if this is the case, [and we state the function of man to be a certain kind of life, and this to be an activity or actions of the soul implying a rational principle, and the function of a good man to be the good and noble performance of these, and if any action is well performed when it is performed in accordance with the appropriate excellence: if this is the case,] human good turns out to be activity of soul in accordance with virtue, and if there are more than one virtue, in accordance with the best and most complete.

But we must add "in a complete life." For one swallow does not make a summer, nor does one day; and so too one day, or a short time, does not make a man blessed and happy. . . .

Virtue

BOOK II

1

Virtue, then, being of two kinds, intellectual and moral, intellectual virtue in the main owes both its birth and its growth to teaching (for which reason it requires experience and time), while moral virtue comes about as a result of habit, whence also its name (*ethike*) is one that is formed by a slight variation from the word *ethos* (habit). From this it is also plain that none of the moral virtues arises in us by nature; for nothing that exists by nature can form a habit contrary to its nature. For instance the stone which by nature moves downwards cannot be habituated to move upwards, not even if one tries to train it by throwing it up ten thousand times; nor can fire be habituated to move downwards, nor can anything else that by nature behaves in one way be trained to behave in another. Neither by nature, then, nor contrary to nature do the virtues arise in us; rather we are adapted by nature to receive them, and are made perfect by habit.

Again, of all the things that come to us by nature we first acquire the potentiality and later exhibit the activity (this is plain in the case of the senses; for it was not by often seeing or often hearing that we got these senses, but on the contrary we had them before we used them, and did not come to have them by using them); but the virtues we get by first exercising them, as also happens in the case of the arts as well. For the things we have to learn before we can do them, we learn by doing them, e.g. men become builders by building and lyre-players by playing the lyre; so too we become just by doing just acts, temperate by doing temperate acts, brave by doing brave acts.

This is confirmed by what happens in states; for legislators make the citizens good by forming habits in them, and this is the wish of every legislator, and those who do not effect it miss their mark, and it is in this that a good constitution differs from a bad one.

Again, it is from the same causes and by the same means that every virtue is both produced and destroyed, and similarly every art; for it is from playing the lyre that both good and bad lyre-players are produced. And the corresponding statement is true of builders and of all the rest; men will be good or bad builders as a result of building well or badly. For if this were not so, there would have been no need of a teacher, but all men would have been born good or bad at their craft. This, then, is the case with the virtues also; by doing the acts that we do in our transactions with other men we become just or unjust, and by doing the acts that we do in the presence of danger, and being habituated to feel fear or confidence, we become brave or cowardly. The same is true of appetites and feelings of anger; some men become temperate and good-tempered, others self-indulgent and irascible, by behaving in one way or the other in the appropriate circumstances. Thus, in one word, states of character arise out of like activities. This is why the activities we exhibit must be of a certain kind; it is because the states of character correspond to the differences between these. It makes no small difference, then, whether we form habits of one kind or of another from our very youth; it makes a very great difference, or rather *all* the difference.

Virtue as a Mean

2

Since, then, the present inquiry does not aim at theoretical knowledge like the others (for we are inquiring not in order to know what virtue is, but in order to become good, since otherwise our inquiry would have been of no use), we must examine the nature of actions, namely how we ought to do them; for these determine also the nature of the states of character that are produced, as we have said. Now, that we must act according to the right rule is a common principle and must be assumed—it will be discussed later, i.e. both what the right rule is, and how it is related to the other virtues. But this must be agreed upon beforehand, that the whole account of matters of conduct must be given in outline and not precisely, as we said at the very beginning that the accounts we demand must be in accordance with the subject-matter; matters concerned with conduct and questions of what is good for us have no fixity, any more than matters of health. The general account being of this nature, the account of particular cases is yet more lacking in exactness; for they do not fall under any art or precept but the agents themselves must in each case consider what is appropriate to the occasion, as happens also in the art of medicine or of navigation.

But though our present account is of this nature we must give what help we can. First, then, let us consider this, that it is the nature of such things to be destroyed by defect and excess, as we see in the case of strength and of health (for to gain light on things imperceptible we must use the evidence of sensible things); both excessive and defective exercise destroys the strength, and similarly drink or food which is above or below a certain amount destroys the health, while that which is proportionate both produces and increases and preserves it. So too is it, then, in the case of temperance and courage and the other virtues. For the man who flies from and fears everything and does not stand his ground against anything becomes a coward, and the man who fears nothing at all but goes to meet every danger becomes rash; and similarly the man who indulges in every pleasure and abstains from none becomes self-indulgent, while the man who shuns every pleasure, as boors do, becomes in a way insensible; temperance and courage, then, are destroyed by excess and defect, and preserved by the mean.

But not only are the sources and causes of their origination and growth the same as those of their destruction, but also the sphere of their actualization will be the same; for this is also true of the things which are more evident to sense, e.g. of strength; it is produced by taking much food and undergoing much exertion, and it is the strong man that will be most able to do these things. So too is it with the virtues; by abstaining from pleasures we become temperate, and it is when we have become so that we are most able to abstain from them; and similarly too in the case of courage; for by being habituated to despise things that are terrible and to stand our ground against them we become brave, and it is when we have become so that we shall be most able to stand our ground against them. . . .

4

. . . Actions, then, are called just and temperate when they are such as the just or the temperate man would do; but it is not the man who does these that is just and temperate, but the man who also does them *as* just and temperate men do them. It is well said, then, that it is by doing just acts that the just man is produced, and by doing temperate acts the temperate man; without doing these no one would have even a prospect of becoming good. . . .

Practical Wisdom

6

We must, however, not only describe virtue as a state of character, but also say what sort of state it is. We may remark, then, that every virtue or excellence both brings into good condition the thing of which it is the excellence and makes the work of that thing be done well; e.g. the excellence of the eye makes both the eye and its work good; for it is by the excellence of the eye that we see well. Similarly the excellence of the horse makes a horse both good in itself and good at running and at carrying its rider and at awaiting the attack of the enemy. Therefore, if this is true in every case, the virtue of man also will be the state of character which makes a man good and which makes him do his own work well.

How this is to happen we have stated already, but it will be made plain also by the following consideration of the specific nature of virtue. In everything that is continuous and divisible it is possible to take more, less, or an equal amount, and that either in terms of the thing itself or relatively to us; and the equal is an intermediate between excess and defect. By the intermediate in the object I mean that which is equidistant from each of the extremes, which is one and the same for all men; by the intermediate relatively to us that which is neither too much nor too little—and this is not one, nor the same for all. For instance, if ten is many and two is few, six is the intermediate, taken in terms of the object; for it exceeds and is exceeded by an equal amount; this is intermediate according to arithmetical proportion. But the intermediate relatively to us is not to be taken so; if ten pounds are too much for a particular person to eat and two too little, it does not follow that the trainer will order six pounds; for this also is perhaps too much for the person who is to take it, or too little—too little for Milo,* too much for the beginner in athletic exercises. The same is true of running and wrestling. Thus a master of any art avoids excess and defect, but seeks the intermediate and chooses this—the intermediate not in the object but relatively to us.

If it is thus, then, that every art does its work well—by looking to the intermediate and judging its works by this standard (so that we often say of good works of art that it is not possible either to take away or to add anything, implying that excess and defect destroy the goodness of works of art, while the mean preserves it; and good artists, as we say, look to this in their work), and if, further, virtue is more exact and better than any art, as nature also is, then virtue must have the quality of aiming at the intermediate. I mean moral virtue; for it is this that is concerned with passions and actions, and in these there is excess, defect, and the intermediate. For instance, both fear and confidence and appetite and anger and pity and in general pleasure and pain may be felt both too much and too little, and in both cases not well; but to feel them at the right times, with reference to the right objects, towards the right people, with the right motive, and in the right way, is what is both intermediate and best, and this is characteristic of virtue. Similarly with regard to actions also there is excess, defect, and the intermediate. Now virtue is concerned with passions and actions, in which excess is a form of failure, and so is defect, while the intermediate is praised and is a form of success; and being praised and being successful are both characteristics of virtue. Therefore virtue is a kind of mean, since, as we have seen, it aims at what is intermediate.

Again, it is possible to fail in many ways (for evil belongs to the class of the unlimited, as the Pythagoreans conjectured, and good to that of the limited), while to succeed is possible only in one way (for which reason also one is easy and the other difficult—to miss the mark easy, to hit it difficult); for these reasons also, then, excess and defect are characteristic of vice, and the mean of virtue;

> For men are good in but one way, but bad in many.

Virtue, then, is a state of character concerned with choice, lying in a mean, i.e. the mean relative to us, this being determined by a rational principle, and by that principle by which the man of practical wisdom would determine it. Now it is a mean between two vices, that which depends on excess and that which depends on defect; and again it is a mean because the vices respectively fall short of or exceed what is right in both passions and actions, while virtue both finds and chooses that which is intermediate. Hence in respect of its substance and the definition which states its essence virtue is a mean, with regard to what is best and right an extreme.

But not every action nor every passion admits of a mean; for some have names that already imply badness, e.g. spite, shamelessness, envy, and in the case of actions adultery, theft, murder; for all of these and suchlike things imply by their names that they are themselves bad, and not the excesses or deficiencies of them. It is not possible, then, ever to be right with regard to them; one must always be wrong. Nor does goodness or badness with regard to such things depend on committing adultery with the right woman, at the right time, and in the right way, but simply to do any of them is to go wrong. It would be equally absurd, then, to expect that in unjust, cowardly, and voluptuous action there should be a mean, an excess, and a deficiency; for at that rate there would be a mean of excess and of deficiency, and excess of excess, and a deficiency of deficiency. But as there is no excess and deficiency of temperance and courage because what is intermediate is in a sense an extreme, so too of the actions we have mentioned there is no mean nor any excess and deficiency, but however they are done they are wrong; for in general there is neither a mean of excess and deficiency, nor excess and deficiency of a mean. . . .

*A famous wrestler.

QUESTIONS FOR REFLECTION

1. How does Aristotle argue that happiness is the highest human good?
2. What is virtue, according to Aristotle?
3. How may a person become virtuous?
4. It is sometimes said that Aristotle's theory says nothing helpful about what I ought to do. It tells me to act as a virtuous person would, but that is just like telling me to do the right thing; I need to know what that is. How might Aristotle reply?
5. In what sense is virtue a mean between extremes?
6. What is it to be a good person, according to Aristotle? What does this mean for legislation?
7. Some charge that Aristotle offers no help when we face a moral dilemma. Is that true? How would Aristotle respond to Plato's dilemma about the borrowed weapons?

ST. THOMAS AQUINAS

from *Summa Theologica* (1265–1273)

St. Thomas Aquinas (1224–1274), perhaps the greatest of all Catholic theologians and philosophers, was born in Roccasecca, Italy, and studied at Naples, Paris, and Cologne. At age thirty-two he was awarded a doctorate in theology at Paris; he joined the faculty there the next year. Starting in 1259 he spent a decade teaching at various Dominican monasteries near Rome, returning to Paris to teach in 1268. In 1272, at forty-eight, he joined the faculty in Naples and died just two years later.

Aquinas sought to reconcile Christian faith and reason in two massive works, Summa Theologica *and* Summa Contra Gentiles, *as well as in a number of shorter works, including several commentaries on Aristotle. He had immense influence. His "perennial philosophy" dominated European thought for four hundred years and remains influential today. (Source: Translated by the author from* Summa Theologica *by Thomas Aquinas [Rome: Ex typographica Senatus, 1886–1887. For English translations, see New York, Benziger Bros., 1947–1948; Westminster: Christian Classics, 1948] I, II.)*

Natural Law

The law commands and forbids. But it belongs to reason to command. Therefore, law is something pertaining to reason.

Law is a certain rule and measure of acts that induces people to act or refrain from acting, for *lex* [law] comes from *ligare* [to bind], because it binds one to act. Now the rule and measure of human acts is reason, the first principle of human acts . . . since it belongs to reason to direct to the end, which is the first principle in all matters of action. . . .* Law, properly speaking, concerns first and foremost an ordering of the common good. . . .

*Francisco Suárez disputes Aquinas's etymology, citing Cicero and Augustine, who contend that *lex* derives from *lectio* or *legendo*, whose root is *legere* [to read]. Modern scholarship supports Suárez, Cicero, and Augustine on this point.

Law, being a rule and measure, can be in someone in two ways: (a) as in him that rules and measures; (b) as in what is ruled and measured; a thing is ruled and measured to the extent that it partakes of a rule or measure. So, since all things subject to divine providence are ruled and measured by the eternal law, all things partake to some extent of the eternal law—to the extent, namely, that it is imprinted on them, they derive their inclinations to their proper acts and ends. Now the rational creature is subject to divine providence in a more excellent way than anything else, for it partakes of a share of providence, by being provident both for itself and for others. So, it has a share of the eternal reason, whereby it has a natural inclination to its proper act and end. This participation in the eternal law in the rational creature is called the *natural law*. Hence the Psalmist, after saying "offer up the sacrifice of justice," as though someone asked what the works of justice are, adds: "Many say, 'Who shows us good things?'" In answer, he says: "The light of your countenance, O Lord, is signed upon us." This implies that the light of natural reason, by which we discern what is good and what is evil, which pertains to the natural law, is nothing else than an imprint on us of the divine light. It is therefore evident that the natural law is nothing other than the rational creature's participation in the eternal law.

Human Law

A law is a certain dictate of practical reason. Now evidently the same procedure takes place in practical and in speculative reason, for each goes from principles to conclusions. In speculative reason, we draw the conclusions of the various sciences from naturally known, indemonstrable principles. The knowledge of them is not imparted to us by nature but acquired by the efforts of reason. So too it is from the precepts of the natural law, as from general and indemonstrable principles, that human reason needs to proceed to certain particular determinations of the laws. These particular determinations, devised by human reason, are called human laws. . . .

The proper effect of law is to lead its subjects to their proper virtue. Since virtue is "what makes its subjects good," it follows that the proper effect of law is to make its subjects good, either simply or in some particular respect. A tyrannical law, through not being according to reason, is not a law, absolutely speaking, but rather a perversion of law. . . .

First Principles

The precepts of the natural law are to practical reason what the first principles of demonstrations are to speculative reason, because both are self-evident principles. Consequently, the first principle in practical reason is one founded on the notion of good: namely, that good is what all things seek. Hence this is the first precept of law: Good is to be done and pursued, and evil is to be avoided. All other precepts of natural law are based on this. So, whatever practical reason naturally apprehends as man's good [or evil] belongs to the precepts of natural law as something to be done or avoided.

Inclinations

Good has the nature of an end, and evil the nature of a contrary. Hence, all those things to which people have a natural inclination are naturally apprehended by reason as being good and, consequently, as objects of pursuit. Their contraries are naturally apprehended as evil and objects of avoidance. So, the order of the precepts of natural law follows the order of natural inclinations.

First, people have an inclination to good in accordance with the nature they have in common with all substances. Every substance seeks the preservation of its own being according to its nature. By reason of this inclination, whatever preserves human life and wards off its obstacles belongs to the natural law. Second, people have an inclination to things that pertain to them more specially according to that nature which they have in common with other animals. In virtue of this inclination, those things are said to belong to the natural law "which nature has taught to all animals," such as sexual intercourse, the education of offspring, and so on. Third, people have an inclination to good according to the nature of their reason, which is proper to them. Thus, people have a natural inclination to know the truth about God and to live in society. In this respect, whatever pertains to this inclination belongs to natural law: for instance, to shun ignorance, to avoid offending those among whom one has to live, and other such things.

Virtue

[St. John] Damascene says that "virtues are natural."* Therefore, virtuous acts are also a subject of natural law. . . . We may speak of virtuous acts in two ways: first, as being virtuous; second, as being such and such acts. If, then, we speak of acts of virtue considered as virtuous, all virtuous acts belong to natural law. For to natural law belongs everything to which people are naturally inclined. Now each thing inclines naturally to what is suitable to it according to its form. Thus, fire is inclined to give heat.

*St. John Damascene (700?–754?), *De fide orthodoxa* I, 5; in J. P. Migne (ed.), *Patrologia Latina* (Paris: Garnier fratres et J.-P. Migne successores, 1879) 32, 1228.

So, since the rational soul is the proper form of a human being, people have a natural inclination to act according to reason. This is to act according to virtue. Consequently, considered in this way, all acts of virtue are prescribed by natural law, since each one's reason naturally dictates to him to act virtuously. But if we speak of virtuous acts considered in themselves, that is, in their proper species, not all virtuous acts are prescribed by natural law; many things are done virtuously to which nature does not incline us at first, but which, through the inquiry of reason, we have found conducive to living well.

Exceptions

Practical reason concerns contingent matters, as do human actions. Consequently, though the general principles are necessary, the more we descend to matters of detail, the more frequently we encounter deviations. . . .

Thus, it is right and true for all to act according to reason. From this principle, it follows that goods entrusted to someone else should be restored to their owner. Now this is true for the majority of cases, but it may happen in a particular case that it would be harmful, and therefore unreasonable, to restore goods held in trust: for instance, if they are claimed for the purpose of fighting against one's country.

This principle will be found to fail more often as we descend further into detail: for example, if one were to say that goods held in trust should be restored with such and such a guarantee or in such and such a way. The greater the number of conditions added, the greater the number of ways in which the principle may fail, so that it is not right to restore or not to restore. . . .

Becoming Virtuous

People have a natural aptitude for virtue, but the perfection of virtue must be acquired by a kind of training. . . . Now, it is hard to see how a man could train himself, since the perfection of virtue consists chiefly in withdrawing him from undue pleasures, to which, above all, he is inclined. This is especially true of the young, who are more capable of being trained. Consequently, a man needs to receive this training from another to arrive at the perfection of virtue. Some young people are inclined to acts of virtue by their good natural disposition or by custom, or rather by the gift of God. For them, paternal training suffices, which is by warnings. But some are depraved, prone to vice, and not easily amenable to words. It is necessary for them to be restrained from evil by force and fear in order that they might at least desist from evil-doing and leave others in peace. They themselves, by being habituated in this way, might be brought to do willingly what they earlier did from fear and thus become virtuous. Now this kind of training, which compels through fear of punishment, is the discipline of laws.

The Common Good

Whatever is for an end should be proportioned to it. Now the end of law is the common good, because, as Isidore says, "Law should be framed not for any private benefit but for the common good of all the citizens."* Hence human laws should be proportioned to the common good. . . .

Every law is directed to the common welfare of people and derives the force and nature of law accordingly. But it has no power to oblige morally if it is not so directed. Hence the Jurist says: "By no reason of law or favor of equity may we interpret harshly and render burdensome those useful measures enacted for the welfare of man."† Now, often the observance of some point of law conduces to the common welfare in the majority of instances and yet in some cases is very harmful. Since, then, lawgivers cannot have in view every single case, they shape the law according to what happens most frequently, by directing their attention to the common good. So, if a case arises where the observance of that law would be harmful to the general welfare, it should not be observed. For instance, suppose that, in a city under siege, there is a law that the gates of the city must be kept closed. This is good for public welfare as a gen-

*St. Isidore of Seville (560?–636), *Etymologiarum Libri* V, 21; in J. P. Migne (ed.), *Patrologia Latina* (Paris: Garnier fratres et J.-P. Migne successores, 1879) 82, 203.

†Domitian Ulpian (170?–228), *Digest* I, 3, 25; in P. Kruger (ed.), *Corpus Juris Civilis* (Berlin: Weidmannos, 1899, 1928), 34b.

eral rule. But if the enemy were in pursuit of certain citizens defending the city, it would be a great loss to the city if the gates were not opened to them. So, in that case, the gates ought to be opened, contrary to the letter of the law, in order to maintain the common welfare, which the lawgivers had in view.

QUESTIONS FOR REFLECTION

1. What is natural law? How does it relate to eternal law?
2. What role does natural law play in practical reason?
3. What is "the first precept of law"?
4. Explain the significance of natural inclinations for natural law.
5. What is virtue? How does it relate to inclination?
6. What is the goal of law? What is the status of laws that do not serve that goal?
7. Why, according to Aquinas, do many laws have exceptions?
8. How do we know when to make an exception to a law?
9. Some philosophers reject the idea of natural law, holding that the concept is nothing more than a way of declaring a prejudice to have universal validity. How might Aquinas try to convince them of the objectivity of natural law?

DAVID HUME

from *A Treatise of Human Nature* (1739)

David Hume (1711–1776), Scottish philosopher and historian, was a contemporary of Voltaire, Rousseau, Handel, Bach, and fellow Scot Adam Smith. A prodigy, Hume entered the University of Edinburgh at age twelve. His family urged him to study law. He disliked it and opted for a business career but found that unsatisfying as well.

At age twenty-three, Hume gave up business and went to France, where he wrote A Treatise of Human Nature, *his greatest philosophical work. Hume argued for a skeptical empiricism, maintaining that all knowledge comes from sense experience and that therefore we can have no objective knowledge of anything beyond experience. The* Treatise *has been and continues to be immensely influential, but at the time it was ignored. Disappointed by the lack of response—"It fell stillborn from the press," he would later write—he turned to more popular works, such as* Essays Moral and Political *(1742). At thirty-one, he was rejected for a professorship at the University of Edinburgh because of his skeptical religious views. He returned to philosophy, writing* An Inquiry Concerning Human Understanding *(1748) and* An Inquiry Concerning the Principles of Morals *(1751) to set out his empiricism in more accessible form.*

At forty-one, Hume became librarian of the Advocates' Library in Edinburgh and began his six-volume History of England *(1754–1761), which earned him a substantial reputation as a man of letters in England and France as well as in Scotland. One of Hume's most important works,* Dialogues Concerning Natural Religion, *was published three years after his death at age sixty-five to avoid the controversy that he knew its criticisms of religious arguments would bring.*

In his writings on ethics, Hume stresses the importance of feeling as opposed to reason. There is a gulf, he argued, between is *and* ought; *factual premises can never yield a moral conclusion on their own. Moreover, purely rational principles can never provide a motive for action. In morality, as in other areas where we seek to go beyond the data of sense experience, "reason is, and ought to be, the slave of the passions." (Source: From David Hume,* A Treatise of Human Nature, *edited by Selby-Bigge [Oxford: Clarendon Press, 1888]. Footnotes have been omitted.)*

BOOK III / OF MORALS

Part I. Of Virtue and Vice in General.

Section I. Moral Distinctions Not Deriv'd from Reason.

. . . Those who affirm that virtue is nothing but a conformity to reason; that there are eternal fitnesses and unfitnesses of things, which are the same to every rational being that considers them; that the immutable measures of right and wrong impose an obligation, not only on human creatures, but also on the Deity himself: All these systems concur in the opinion, that morality, like truth, is discern'd merely by ideas, and by their juxtaposition and comparison. In order, therefore, to judge of these systems, we need only consider, whether it be possible, from reason alone, to distinguish betwixt moral good and evil, or whether there must concur some other principles to enable us to make that distinction.

If morality had naturally no influence on human passions and actions, 'twere in vain to take such pains to inculcate it; and nothing wou'd be more fruitless than that multitude of rules and precepts, with which all moralists abound. Philosophy is commonly divided into *speculative* and *practical*; and as morality is always comprehended under the latter division, 'tis supposed to influence our passions and actions, and to go beyond the calm and indolent judgments of the understanding. And this is confirm'd by common experience, which informs us, that men are often govern'd by their duties, and are deter'd from some actions by the opinion of injustice, and impell'd to others by that of obligation.

Since morals, therefore, have an influence on the actions and affections, it follows, that they cannot be deriv'd from reason; and that because reason alone, as we have already prov'd, can never have any such influence. Morals excite passions, and produce or prevent actions. Reason of itself is utterly impotent in this particular. The rules of morality, therefore, are not conclusions of our reason. . . .

Nor does this reasoning only prove, that morality consists not in any relations, that are the objects of science; but if examin'd, will prove with equal certainty, that it consists not in any *matter of fact*, which can be discover'd by the understanding. This is the *second* part of our argument; and if it can be made evident, we may conclude, that morality is not an object of reason. But can there be any difficulty in proving, that vice and virtue are not matters of fact, whose existence we can infer by reason? Take any action allow'd to be vicious: Wilful murder, for instance. Examine it in all lights, and see if you can find that matter of fact, or real existence, which you call *vice*. In whichever way you take it, you find only certain passions, motives, volitions and thoughts. There is no other matter of fact in the case. The vice entirely escapes you, as long as you consider the object. You never can find it, till you turn your reflexion into your own breast, and find a sentiment of disapprobation, which arises in you, towards this action. Here is a matter of fact; but 'tis the object of feeling, not of reason. It lies in yourself, not in the object. So that when you pronounce any action or character to be vicious, you mean nothing, but that from the constitution of your nature you have a feeling or sentiment of blame from the contemplation of it. Vice and virtue, therefore, may be compar'd to sounds, colours, heat and cold, which, according to modern philosophy, are not qualities in objects, but perceptions in the mind: And this discovery in morals, like that other in physics, is to be regarded as a considerable advancement of the speculative sciences; tho', like that too, it has little or no influence on practice. Nothing can be more real, or concern us more, than our own sentiments of pleasure and uneasiness; and if these be favourable to virtue, and unfavourable to vice, no more can be requisite to the regulation of our conduct and behaviour.

I cannot forbear adding to these reasonings an observation, which may, perhaps, be found of some importance. In every system of morality, which I have hitherto met with, I have always remark'd, that the author proceeds for some time in the ordinary way of reasoning, and establishes the being of a God, or makes observations concerning human affairs; when of a sudden I am surpriz'd to find, that instead of the usual copulations of propositions, *is*, and *is not*, I meet with no proposition that is not connected with an *ought*, or an *ought not*. This change is imperceptible; but is, however, of the last consequence. For as this *ought*, or *ought not*, expresses some new relation or affirmation, 'tis necessary that it shou'd be observ'd and explain'd; and at the same time that a reason should be given, for what seems altogether inconceivable, how this new relation can be a deduction from others, which are entirely different from it. But as authors do not commonly use this precaution, I shall presume to recommend it to the readers; and am persuaded, that this small attention wou'd subvert all the vulgar systems of morality, and let us see, that the distinction of vice and virtue is not founded merely on the relations of objects, nor is perceiv'd by reason.

Section II. Moral Distinctions Deriv'd from a Moral Sense.

Thus the course of the argument leads us to conclude, that since vice and virtue are not discoverable merely by reason, or the comparison of ideas, it must be by means of some impression or sentiment they occasion, that we are able to mark the difference betwixt them. Our decisions concerning moral rectitude and depravity are evidently perceptions; and as all perceptions are either impressions or ideas, the exclusion of the one is a convincing argument for the other. Morality, therefore, is more properly felt than judg'd of; tho' this feeling or sentiment is commonly so soft and gentle, that we are apt to confound it with an idea, according to our common custom of taking all things for the same, which have any near resemblance to each other.

The next question is, Of what nature are these impressions, and after what manner do they operate upon us? Here we cannot remain long in suspense, but must pronounce the impression arising from virtue, to be agreeable, and that proceeding from vice to be uneasy. Every moment's experience must convince us of this. There is no spectacle so fair and beautiful as a noble and generous action; nor any which gives us more abhorrence than one that is cruel and treacherous. No enjoyment equals the satisfaction we receive from the company of those we love and esteem; as the greatest of all punishments is to be oblig'd to pass our lives with those we hate or contemn. A very play or romance may afford us instances of this pleasure, which virtue conveys to us; and pain, which arises from vice.

Now since the distinguishing impressions, by which moral good or evil is known, are nothing but *particular* pains or pleasures; it follows, that in all enquiries concerning these moral distinctions, it will be sufficient to shew the principles, which make us feel a satisfaction or uneasiness from the survey of any character, in order to satisfy us why the character is laudable or blameable. An action, or sentiment, or character is virtuous or vicious; why? because its view causes a pleasure or uneasiness of a particular kind. In giving a reason, therefore, for the pleasure or uneasiness, we sufficiently explain the vice or virtue. To have the sense of virtue, is nothing but to *feel* a satisfaction of a particular kind from the contemplation of a character. The very *feeling* constitutes our praise or admiration. We go no farther; nor do we enquire into the cause of the satisfaction. We do not infer a character to be virtuous, because it pleases: But in feeling that it pleases after such a particular manner, we in effect feel that it is virtuous. The case is the same as in our judgments concerning all kinds of beauty, and tastes, and sensations. Our approbation is imply'd in the immediate pleasure they convey to us. . . .

Thus we are still brought back to our first position, that virtue is distinguished by the pleasure, and vice by the pain, that any action, sentiment or character gives us by the mere view and contemplation. This decision is very commodious; because it reduces us to this simple question, *Why any action or sentiment upon the general view or survey, gives a certain satisfaction or uneasiness*, in order to shew the origin of its moral rectitude or depravity, without looking for any incomprehensible relations and qualities, which never did exist in nature, nor even in our imagination, by any clear and distinct conception. I flatter myself I have executed a great part of my present design by a state of the question, which appears to me so free from ambiguity and obscurity.

QUESTIONS FOR REFLECTION

1. Summarize Hume's arguments that "the rules of morality are not conclusions of our reason."
2. Why, according to Hume, are rational principles unable to motivate the will?
3. Where, according to Hume, do most moral arguments fail?
4. How, if at all, can one get from *is* to *ought*? How, that is, is it possible to justify a moral conclusion?
5. In what sense is Hume's position a critique of Aristotle?
6. Plato held that virtue is knowledge—and thus that vice results from ignorance or error. How does Hume argue against that position?
7. How do we distinguish vice from virtue, according to Hume?
8. "You borrowed money from me. So, you ought to pay it back." How do I get from a descriptive statement to a normative one, from an *is* to an *ought*? Not by way of feeling, but by way of a general principle: "People ought to pay their debts." How might Hume respond to this criticism?

IMMANUEL KANT

from *Fundamental Principles of the Metaphysics of Morals* (1785)

Immanuel Kant (1724–1804), a contemporary of Blake, Goethe, and Mozart, was born in Königsberg, in East Prussia (now Kaliningrad, part of the Russian republic). The son of a saddlemaker and grandson of a Scottish immigrant, Kant attended the University of Königsberg, from which he graduated at twenty-two. A year later he published his first philosophical work, a book on living forces. He was a private tutor for several years while continuing his studies. At twenty-nine, he received a master's degree and began teaching at Königsberg as a Privatdozent—roughly, an unpaid lecturer who collected fees from his students. He continued in that capacity for fifteen years. Finally, in 1770, he was appointed to a chair of logic and metaphysics at the University of Königsberg.

At the age of fifty-seven, Kant published the Critique of Pure Reason, *a work that earned him fame and that contemporary philosophers regard as one of the greatest works of the Western philosophical tradition. The decade that followed was extremely productive for Kant.* Prolegomena to Any Future Metaphysics *appeared in 1783;* Fundamental Principles of the Metaphysics of Morals *in 1785; the second edition of the* Critique of Pure Reason *in 1787; the* Critique of Practical Reason *in 1788; and the* Critique of Judgment *in 1790. Kant continued writing well into his seventies.*

Though known for his wit and conversational skill as well as for his intellect, Kant never married and never traveled more than a few miles from the place of his birth. His habits were so regular that, according to legend, neighbors would set their clocks by his afternoon walks.

Kant's Fundamental Principles of the Metaphysics of Morals *argues that only one thing is good without qualification (that is, in itself): a good will. He argues that rational beings will recognize that they are subject to the moral law, which he formulates in several versions of what he takes to be single moral principle: the categorical imperative. From it stem human rights, human dignity, and everything else essential to morality. (Source: Reprinted by permission from* Fundamental Principles of the Metaphysics of Morals, *translated by Thomas Kingsmill Abbott. New York: Longmans, Green, 1926.)*

A Good Will

Nothing can possibly be conceived in the world, or even out of it, which can be called good, without qualification, except a good will. Intelligence, wit, judgment, and the other talents of the mind, however they may be named, or courage, resolution, perseverance, as qualities of temperament, are undoubtedly good and desirable in many respects; but these gifts of nature may also become extremely bad and mischievous if the will which is to make use of them, and which, therefore, constitutes what is called character, is not good. It is the same with the gifts of fortune. Power, riches, honour, even health, and the general well-being and contentment with one's condition which is called happiness, inspire pride, and often presumption, if there is not a good will to correct the influence of these on the mind, and with this also to rectify the whole principle of acting and adapt it to its end. The sight of a being who is not adorned with a single feature of a pure and good will, enjoying unbroken prosperity, can never give pleasure to an impartial rational spectator. Thus a good will appears to constitute the indispensable condition even of being worthy of happiness.

There are even some qualities which are of service to this good will itself and may facilitate its action, yet which have no intrinsic unconditional value, but always presuppose a good will, and this qualifies the esteem that we justly have for them and does not permit us to regard them as absolutely good. Moderation in the affections and passions, self-control, and calm deliberation are not only good in many respects, but even seem to constitute part of the intrinsic worth of the person; but they are far from deserving to be called good without qualification, although they have been so unconditionally praised by the ancients. For without the principles of a good will, they may become extremely bad, and the coolness of a villain not only makes him far more dangerous, but also directly makes him more abominable in our eyes than he would have been without it.

A good will is good not because of what it performs or effects, not by its aptness for the attainment of some proposed end, but simply by virtue of the volition; that is, it is good in itself, and considered by itself is to be esteemed much higher than all that can be brought about by it in favour of any inclination, nay even of the sum total of all inclinations. Even if it should happen that, owing to special disfavour of fortune, or the niggardly provision of a step-motherly nature, this will should wholly lack power to accomplish its purpose, if with its greatest efforts it should yet achieve nothing, and there should remain only the good will (not, to be sure, a mere wish, but the summoning of all means in our power), then, [a good will,] like a jewel, . . . would still shine by its own light, as a thing which has its whole value in itself. Its usefulness or fruitfulness can neither add nor take away anything from this value. It would be, as it were, only the setting to enable us to handle it the more conveniently in common commerce, or to attract to it the attention of those who are not yet connoisseurs, but not to recommend it to true connoisseurs, or to determine its value.

We have then to develop the notion of a will which deserves to be highly esteemed for itself and is good without a view to anything further, a notion which exists already in the sound natural understanding, requiring rather to be cleared up than to be taught, and which in estimating the value of our actions always takes the first place and constitutes the condition of all the rest. In order to do this, we will take the notion of duty, which includes that of a good will, although implying certain subjective restrictions and hindrances. These, however, far from concealing it, or rendering it unrecognizable, rather bring it out by contrast and make it shine forth so much the brighter.

Duty and Inclination

I omit here all actions which are already recognized as inconsistent with duty, although they may be useful for this or that purpose, for with these the question whether they are done from duty cannot arise at all, since they even conflict with it. I also set aside those actions which really conform to duty, but to which men have no direct inclination, performing them because they are impelled thereto by some other inclination. For in this case we can readily distinguish whether the action which agrees with duty is done from duty, or from a selfish view. It is much harder to make this distinction when the action accords with duty and the subject has besides a direct inclination to it. For example, it is always a matter of duty that a dealer should not overcharge an inexperienced purchaser; and wherever there is much commerce the prudent tradesman does not overcharge, but keeps a fixed price for everyone, so that a child buys of him as well as any other. Men are thus honestly served; but this is not enough to make us believe that the tradesman has so acted from duty and from principles of honesty: his own advantage required it; it is out of the question in this case to suppose that he might besides have a direct inclination in favour of the buyers, so that, as it were, from love he should give no advantage to one over another. Accordingly the action was done neither from duty nor from direct inclination, but merely with a selfish view.

On the other hand, it is a duty to maintain one's life; and, in addition, everyone has also a direct inclination to do so. But on this account the anxious care which most men take for it has no intrinsic worth, and their maxim has no moral import. They preserve their life as duty requires, no doubt, but not because duty requires. On the other band, if adversity and hopeless sorrow have completely taken away the relish for life; if the unfortunate one, strong in mind, indignant at his fate rather than desponding or dejected, wishes for death, and yet preserves his life without loving it—not from inclination or fear, but from duty—then his maxim has a moral worth.

Moral Worth

To be beneficent when we can is a duty; and besides this, there are many minds so sympathetically constituted that, without any other motive of vanity or self-interest, they find a pleasure in spreading joy around them and can take delight in the satisfaction of others so far as it is their own work. But I maintain that in such a case an action of this kind, however proper, however amiable it may be, has nevertheless no true moral worth, but is on a level with other inclinations, e.g., the inclination to honour, which, if it is happily directed to that which is in fact of public utility and accordant with duty and consequently honourable, deserves praise and encouragement, but not esteem. For the maxim lacks the moral import, namely, that such actions be done from duty, not from inclination. Put the case that the mind of that philanthropist were clouded by sorrow of his own, extinguishing all sympathy with the lot of others, and that, while he still has the power to benefit others in distress, he is not touched by their trouble because he is absorbed with his own; and now suppose that he tears himself out of this dead insensibility, and performs the action without any inclination to it, but simply from duty, then first has his action its genuine moral worth. Further still; if nature has put little sympathy in the heart of this or that man; if he, supposed to be an upright man, is by temperament cold and indifferent to the sufferings of others, perhaps because in respect of his own he is provided with the special gift of patience and fortitude and supposes, or even requires, that others should have the same—and such a man would certainly not be the meanest product of nature—but if nature had not specially framed him for a philanthropist, would he not still find in himself a source from whence to give himself a far higher worth than that of a good-natured temperament could be? Unquestionably. It is just in this that the moral worth of the character is brought out which is incomparably the highest of all, namely, that he is beneficent, not from inclination, but from duty.

The second proposition is: That an action done from duty derives its moral worth, not from the purpose which is to be attained by it, but from the maxim by which it is determined, and therefore does not depend on the realization of the object of the action, but merely on the principle of volition by which the action has taken place, without regard to any object of desire. It is clear from what precedes that the purposes which we may have in view in our actions, or their effects regarded as ends and springs of the will, cannot give to actions any unconditional or moral worth. In what, then, can their worth lie, if it is not to consist in the will and in reference to its expected effect? It cannot lie anywhere but in the principle of the will without regard to the ends which can be attained by the action. For the will stands between its a priori principle, which is formal, and its a posteriori spring, which is material, as between two roads, and as it must be determined by something, it must be determined by the formal principle of volition when an action is done from duty, in which case every material principle has been withdrawn from it.

The third proposition, which is a consequence of the two preceding, I would express thus: Duty is the necessity of acting from respect for the law. I may have inclination for an object as the effect of my proposed action, but I cannot have respect for it, just for this reason, that it is an effect and not an energy of will. Similarly I cannot have respect for inclination, whether my own or another's; I can at most, if my own, approve it; if another's, sometimes even love it; i.e., look on it as favourable to my own interest. It is only what is connected with my will as a principle, by no means as an effect—what does not subserve my inclination, but overpowers it, or at least in case of choice excludes it from its calculation—in other words, simply the law of itself, which can be an object of respect, and hence a command. Now an action done from duty must wholly exclude the influence of inclination and with it every object of the will, so that nothing remains which can determine the will except objectively the law, and subjectively pure respect for this practical law, and consequently the maxim* that I should follow this law even to the thwarting of all my inclinations.

Thus the moral worth of an action does not lie in the effect expected from it, nor in any principle of action which requires to borrow its motive from this expected effect. For all these effects—agreeableness of one's condition and even the promotion of the happiness of others—could have been also brought about by other causes, so that for this there would have been no need of the will of a rational being; whereas it is in this alone that the supreme and unconditional good can be found. The pre-eminent good which we call moral can therefore consist in nothing else than the conception of law in itself, which certainly is only possible in a rational being, in so far as this conception, and not the expected effect, determines the will. This is a good which is already present in the person who acts accordingly, and we have not to wait for it to appear first in the result.

Conformity to Law

But what sort of law can that be, the conception of which must determine the will, even without paying any regard to the effect expected from it, in order that this will may be called good absolutely and without qualification? As I have deprived the will of every impulse which could arise to it from obedience to any law, there remains nothing but the universal conformity of its actions to law in general, which alone is to serve the will as a principle, i.e., I am never to act otherwise than so that I could also will that my maxim should become a universal law.

*A maxim is the subjective principle of volition. The objective principle (i.e., that which would also serve subjectively as a practical principle to all rational beings if reason had full power over the faculty of desire) is the practical law.

Here, now, it is the simple conformity to law in general, without assuming any particular law applicable to certain actions, that serves the will as its principle and must so serve it, if duty is not to be a vain delusion and a chimerical notion. The common reason of men in its practical judgements perfectly coincides with this and always has in view the principle here suggested. Let the question be, for example: May I when in distress make a promise with the intention not to keep it? I readily distinguish here between the two significations which the question may have:

Whether it is prudent, or whether it is right, to make a false promise? The former may undoubtedly be the case. I see clearly indeed that it is not enough to extricate myself from a present difficulty by means of this subterfuge, but it must be well considered whether there may not hereafter spring from this lie much greater inconvenience than that from which I now free myself, and as, with all my supposed cunning, the consequences cannot be so easily foreseen but that credit once lost may be much more injurious to me than any mischief which I seek to avoid at present, it should be considered whether it would not be more prudent to act herein according to a universal maxim and to make it a habit to promise nothing except with the intention of keeping it. But it is soon clear to me that such a maxim will still only be based on the fear of consequences. Now it is a wholly different thing to be truthful from duty and to be so from apprehension of injurious consequences. In the first case, the very notion of the action already implies a law for me; in the second case, I must first look about elsewhere to see what results may be combined with it which would affect myself. For to deviate from the principle of duty is beyond all doubt wicked; but to be unfaithful to my maxim of prudence may often be very advantageous to me, although to abide by it is certainly safer. The shortest way, however, and an unerring one, to discover the answer to this question whether a lying promise is consistent with duty, is to ask myself, "Should I be content that my maxim (to extricate myself from difficulty by a false promise) should hold good as a universal law, for myself as well as for others? and should I be able to say to myself, "Every one may make a deceitful promise when he finds himself in a difficulty from which he cannot otherwise extricate himself?" Then I presently become aware that while I can will the lie, I can by no means will that lying should be a universal law. For with such a law there would be no promises at all, since it would be in vain to allege my intention in regard to my future actions to those who would not believe this allegation, or if they overhastily did so would pay me back in my own coin. Hence my maxim, as soon as it should be made a universal law, would necessarily destroy itself.

I do not, therefore, need any far-reaching penetration to discern what I have to do in order that my will may be morally good. Inexperienced in the course of the world, incapable of being prepared for all its contingencies, I only ask myself: Canst thou also will that thy maxim should be a universal law? If not, then it must be rejected, and that not because of a disadvantage accruing from it to myself or even to others, but because it cannot enter as a principle into a possible universal legislation, and reason extorts from me immediate respect for such legislation. I do not indeed as yet discern on what this respect is based (this the philosopher may inquire), but at least I understand this, that it is an estimation of the worth which far outweighs all worth of what is recommended by inclination, and that the necessity of acting from pure respect for the practical law is what constitutes duty, to which every other motive must give place, because it is the condition of a will being good in itself, and the worth of such a will is above everything.

Thus, then, without quitting the moral knowledge of common human reason, we have arrived at its principle. And although, no doubt, common men do not conceive it in such an abstract and universal form, yet they always have it really before their eyes and use it as the standard of their decision. Here it would be easy to show how, with this compass in hand, men are well able to distinguish, in every case that occurs, what is good, what bad, conformably to duty or inconsistent with it, if, without in the least teaching them anything new, we only, like Socrates, direct their attention to the principle they themselves employ; and that, therefore, we do not need science and philosophy to know what we should do to be honest and good, yea, even wise and virtuous. Indeed we might well have conjectured beforehand that the knowledge of what every man is bound to do, and therefore also to know, would be within the reach of every man, even the commonest. Here we cannot forbear admiration when we see how great an advantage the practical judgement has over the theoretical in the common understanding of men. In the latter, if common reason ventures to depart from the laws of experience and from the perceptions of the senses, it falls into mere inconceivabilities and self-contradictions, at least into a chaos of uncertainty, obscurity, and instability. But in the practical sphere it is just when the common understanding excludes all sensible springs from practical laws that its power of judgement begins to show itself to advantage. It then becomes even subtle, whether it be that it chicanes with its own conscience or with other claims respecting what is to be called right, or whether it desires for its own instruction to determine honestly the worth of actions; and, in the latter case, it may even have as good a hope of hitting the mark as any philosopher whatever can promise himself. Nay, it is almost more sure of doing so, because the philosopher cannot have any other principle, while he may easily perplex his judgement by a multitude of considerations foreign to the matter, and so turn aside from the right way. Would it not therefore be wiser in moral concerns to acquiesce in the judgement of common reason, or at most only to call in philosophy for the purpose of rendering the system of morals more complete and intelligible, and its rules more convenient for use (especially for disputation), but not so as to draw off the common understanding from its happy simplicity, or to bring it by means of philosophy into a new path of inquiry and instruction?

Imperatives

The conception of an objective principle, in so far as it is obligatory for a will, is called a *command* (of reason), and the formula of the command is called an *imperative*.

All imperatives are expressed by the word *ought* [or *should*], and thereby indicate the relation of an objective law of reason to a will, which from its subjective constitution is not necessarily determined by it (an obligation). They say that something would be good to do or to forbear, but they say it to a will which does not always do a thing because it is conceived to be good to do it. That is practically good, however, which determines the will by means of the conceptions of reason, and consequently not from subjective causes, but objectively, that is, on principles which are valid for every rational being as such. It is distinguished from the pleasant, as that which influences the will only by means of sensation from merely subjective causes, valid only for the sense of this or that one, and not as a principle of reason, which holds for every one. . . .

Now all imperatives command either hypothetically or categorically. The former represent the practical necessity of a possible action as means to something else that is willed (or at least which one might possibly will). The categorical imperative would be that which represented an action as necessary of itself without reference to another end, i.e., as objectively necessary.

. . . If now the action is good only as a means to something else, then the imperative is hypothetical; if it is conceived as good in itself and consequently as being necessarily the principle of a will which of itself conforms to reason, then it is categorical. . . .

Accordingly the hypothetical imperative only says that the action is good for some purpose, possible or actual. . . . The categorical imperative . . . declares an action to be objectively necessary in itself without reference to any purpose, i.e., without any other end. . . .

Since every practical law represents a possible action as good and, on this account, for a subject who is practically determinable by reason, necessary, all imperatives are formulae determining an action which is necessary according to the principle of a will good in some respects. If now the action is good only as a means to something else, then the imperative is hypothetical; if it is conceived as good in itself and consequently as being necessarily the principle of a will which of itself conforms to reason, then it is categorical.

Thus the imperative declares what action possible by me would be good and presents the practical rule in relation to a will which does not forthwith perform an action simply because it is good, whether because the subject does not always know that it is good, or because, even if it knows this, yet its maxims might be opposed to the objective principles of practical reason.

Accordingly the hypothetical imperative only says that the action is good for some purpose, possible or actual. In the first case it is a problematical, in the second an assertorial practical principle. The categorical imperative which declares an action to be objectively necessary in itself without reference to any purpose, i.e., without any other end, is valid as an apodeictic (practical) principle.

Whatever is possible only by the power of some rational being may also be conceived as a possible purpose of some will; and therefore the principles of action as regards the means necessary to attain some possible purpose are in fact infinitely numerous. All sciences have a practical part, consisting of problems expressing that some end is possible for us and of imperatives directing how it may be attained. These may, therefore, be called in general imperatives of skill. Here there is no question whether the end is rational and good, but only what one must do in order to attain it. The precepts for the physician to make his patient thoroughly healthy, and for a poisoner to ensure certain death, are of equal value in this respect, that each serves to effect its purpose perfectly. Since in early youth it cannot be known what ends are likely to occur to us in the course of life, parents seek to have their children taught a great many things, and provide for their skill in the use of means for all sorts of arbitrary ends, of none of which can they determine whether it may not perhaps hereafter be an object to their pupil, but which it is at all events possible that he might aim at; and this anxiety is so great that they commonly neglect to form and correct their judgement on the value of the things which may be chosen as ends.

Prudence and Morality

There is one end, however, which may be assumed to be actually such to all rational beings (so far as imperatives apply to them, viz., as dependent beings), and, therefore, one purpose which they not merely may have, but which we may with certainty assume that they all actually have by a natural necessity, and this is happiness. The hypothetical imperative which expresses the practical necessity of an action as means to the advancement of happiness is assertorial. We are not to present it as necessary for an uncertain and merely possible purpose, but for a purpose which we may presuppose with certainty and a priori in every man, because it belongs to his being. Now skill in the choice of means to his own greatest well-being may be called prudence, in the narrowest sense. And thus the imperative which refers to the choice of means to one's own happiness, i.e., the precept of prudence, is still always hypothetical; the action is not commanded absolutely, but only as means to another purpose.

[Morality] concerns not the matter of the action, or its intended result, but its form and the principle of which it is itself a result; and what is essentially good in it consists in the mental disposition, let the consequence be what it may.

When I conceive a hypothetical imperative, in general I do not know beforehand what it will contain until I am given the condition. But when I conceive a categorical imperative, I know at once what it contains. For as the imperative contains besides the law only the necessity that the maxims shall conform to this law, while the law contains no conditions restricting it, there remains nothing but the general statement that the maxim of the action should conform to a universal law, and it is this conformity alone that the imperative properly represents as necessary.

The Categorical Imperative

There is therefore but one categorical imperative, namely, this: Act only on that maxim whereby thou canst at the same time will that it should become a universal law.

. . . Since the universality of the law according to which effects are produced constitutes what is properly called nature in the most general sense (as to form), that is, the existence of things so far as it is determined by general laws, the imperative of duty may be expressed thus: Act as if the maxim of thy action were to become by thy will a universal law of nature.

Illustrations

We will now enumerate a few duties, adopting the usual division of them into duties to ourselves and ourselves and to others, and into perfect and imperfect duties.

1. A man reduced to despair by a series of misfortunes feels wearied of life, but is still so far in possession of his reason that he can ask himself whether it would not be contrary to his duty to himself to take his own life. Now he inquires whether the maxim of his action could become a universal law of nature. His maxim is: "From self-love I adopt it as a principle to shorten my life when its longer duration is likely to bring more evil than satisfaction." It is asked then simply whether this principle founded on self-love can become a universal law of nature. Now we see at once that a system of nature of which it should be a law to destroy life by means of the very feeling whose special nature it is to impel to the improvement of life would contradict itself and, therefore, could not exist as a system of nature; hence that maxim cannot possibly exist as a universal law of nature and, consequently, would be wholly inconsistent with the supreme principle of all duty.

2. Another finds himself forced by necessity to borrow money. He knows that he will not be able to repay it, but sees also that nothing will be lent to him unless he promises stoutly to repay it in a definite time. He desires to make this promise, but he has still so much conscience as to ask himself: "Is it not unlawful and inconsistent with duty to get out of a difficulty in this way?" Suppose however that he resolves to do so: then the maxim of his action would be expressed thus: "When I think myself in want of money, I will borrow money and promise to repay it, although I know that I never can do so." Now this principle of self-love or of one's own advantage may perhaps be consistent with my whole future welfare; but the question now is, "Is it right?" I change then the suggestion of self-love into a universal law, and state the question thus: "How would it be if my maxim were a universal law?" Then I see at once that it could never hold as a universal law of nature, but would necessarily contradict itself. For supposing it to be a universal law that everyone when he thinks himself in a difficulty should be able to promise whatever he pleases, with the purpose of not keeping his promise, the promise itself would become impossible, as well as the end that one might have in view in it, since no one would consider that anything was promised to him, but would ridicule all such statements as vain pretenses.

3. A third finds in himself a talent which with the help of some culture might make him a useful man in many respects. But he finds himself in comfortable circumstances and prefers to indulge in pleasure rather than to take pains in enlarging and improving his happy natural capacities. He asks, however, whether his maxim of neglect of his natural gifts, besides agreeing with his inclination to indulgence, agrees also with what is called duty. He sees then that a system of nature could indeed subsist with such a universal law although men

(like the South Sea islanders) should let their talents rest and resolve to devote their lives merely to idleness, amusement, and propagation of their species—in a word, to enjoyment; but he cannot possibly will that this should be a universal law of nature, or be implanted in us as such by a natural instinct. For, as a rational being, he necessarily wills that his faculties be developed, since they serve him and have been given him, for all sorts of possible purposes.

4. A fourth, who is in prosperity, while he sees that others have to contend with great wretchedness and that he could help them, thinks: "What concern is it of mine? Let everyone be as happy as Heaven pleases, or as he can make himself; I will take nothing from him nor even envy him, only I do not wish to contribute anything to his welfare or to his assistance in distress!" Now no doubt if such a mode of thinking were a universal law, the human race might very well subsist and doubtless even better than in a state in which everyone talks of sympathy and good-will, or even takes care occasionally to put it into practice, but, on the other side, also cheats when he can, betrays the rights of men, or otherwise violates them. But although it is possible that a universal law of nature might exist in accordance with that maxim, it is impossible to will that such a principle should have the universal validity of a law of nature. For a will which resolved this would contradict itself, inasmuch as many cases might occur in which one would have need of the love and sympathy of others, and in which, by such a law of nature, sprung from his own will, he would deprive himself of all hope of the aid he desires. . . .

Exceptions?

If now we attend to ourselves on occasion of any transgression of duty, we shall find that we in fact do not will that our maxim should be a universal law, for that is impossible for us; on the contrary, we will that the opposite should remain a universal law, only we assume the liberty of making an exception in our own favor or (just for this time only) in favor of our inclination. Consequently if we considered all cases from one and the same point of view, namely, that of reason, we should find a contradiction in our own will, namely, that a certain principle should be objectively necessary as a universal law, and yet subjectively should not be universal, but admit of exceptions. . . .

Rational Nature

Supposing, however, that there were something whose existence has in itself an absolute worth, something which, being an end in itself, could be a source of definite laws; then in this and this alone would lie the source of a possible categorical imperative, i.e., a practical law.

Now I say: man and generally any rational being exists as an end in himself, not merely as a means to be arbitrarily used by this or that will, but in all his actions, whether they concern himself or other rational beings, must be always regarded at the same time as an end. All objects of the inclinations have only a conditional worth, for if the inclinations and the wants founded on them did not exist, then their object would be without value. . . . Beings whose existence depends not on our will but on nature's, have nevertheless, if they are irrational beings, only a relative value as means, and are therefore called things; rational beings, on the contrary, are called persons, because their very nature points them out as ends in themselves, that is, as something which must not be used merely as means, and so far therefore restricts freedom of action (and is an object of respect). These, therefore, are not merely subjective ends whose existence has a worth for us as an effect of our action, but objective ends, that is, things whose existence is an end in itself; an end moreover for which no other can be substituted, which they should subserve merely as means, for otherwise nothing whatever would possess absolute worth; but if all worth were conditioned and therefore contingent, then there would be no supreme practical principle of reason whatever.

. . . The foundation of this principle [the categorical imperative] is: rational nature exists as an end in itself. Man necessarily conceives his own existence as being so; so far, then, this is a subjective principle of human actions. But every other rational being regards its existence similarly, just on the same rational principle that holds for me: so that it is at the same time an objective principle, from which as a supreme practical law all laws of the will must be capable of being deduced. Accordingly the practical imperative will be as follows: So act as to treat humanity, whether in thine own person or in that of any other, in every case as an end withal, never as means only. . . .

Illustrations

We will now inquire whether this can be practically carried out. To abide by the previous examples:

Firstly, under the head of necessary duty to oneself: He who contemplates suicide should ask himself whether his action can be consistent with the idea of humanity as an end in itself. If he destroys himself in order to escape from painful circumstances, he uses a person merely as a means to maintain a tolerable condition up to the end of life. But a man is not a thing, that is to say, something which can be used merely as means, but must in all his actions be always considered as an end in himself. I cannot, therefore, dispose in any way of a man in my own person so as to mutilate him, to damage or kill him. (It belongs to ethics proper to define this principle more precisely, so as to avoid all misunderstanding, e.g., as to the amputation of the limbs in order to preserve myself, as to exposing my life to danger with a view to preserve it, etc. This question is therefore omitted here.)

Secondly, as regards necessary duties, or those of strict obligation, towards others: He who is thinking of making a lying promise to others will see at once that he would be using another man merely as a means, without the latter containing at the same time the end in himself. For he whom I propose by such a promise to use for my own purposes cannot possibly assent to my mode of acting towards him and, therefore, cannot himself contain the end of this action. This violation of the principle of humanity in other men is more obvious if we take in examples of attacks on the freedom and property of others. For then it is clear that he who transgresses the rights of men intends to use the person of others merely as a means, without considering that as rational beings they ought always to be esteemed also as ends, that is, as beings who must be capable of containing in themselves the end of the very same action.

Thirdly, as regards contingent (meritorious) duties to oneself: It is not enough that the action does not violate humanity in our own person as an end in itself, it must also harmonize with it. Now there are in humanity capacities of greater perfection, which belong to the end that nature has in view in regard to humanity in ourselves as the subject: to neglect these might perhaps be consistent with the maintenance of humanity as an end in itself, but not with the advancement of this end.

Fourthly, as regards meritorious duties towards others: The natural end which all men have is their own happiness. Now humanity might indeed subsist, although no one should contribute anything to the happiness of others, provided he did not intentionally withdraw anything from it; but after all this would only harmonize negatively not positively with humanity as an end in itself, if every one does not also endeavour, as far as in him lies, to forward the ends of others. For the ends of any subject which is an end in himself ought as far as possible to be my ends also, if that conception is to have its full effect with me. . . .

Ends in Themselves

This principle, that humanity and generally every rational nature is an end in itself (which is the supreme limiting condition of every man's freedom of action), is not borrowed from experience, firstly, because it is universal, applying as it does to all rational beings whatever, and experience is not capable of determining anything about them; secondly, because it does not present humanity as an end to men (subjectively), that is as an object which men do of themselves actually adopt as an end; but as an objective end, which must as a law constitute the supreme limiting condition of all our subjective ends, let them be what we will; it must therefore spring from pure reason. In fact the objective principle of all practical legislation lies (according to the first principle) in the rule and its form of universality which makes it capable of being a law (say, e.g., a law of nature); but the subjective principle is in the end; now by the second principle the subject of all ends is each rational being, in as much as it is an end in itself. Hence follows the third practical principle of the will, which is the ultimate condition of its harmony with universal practical reason, viz.: the idea of the will of every rational being as a universally legislative will.

On this principle all maxims are rejected which are inconsistent with the will being itself universal legislator. Thus the will is not subject simply to the law, but so subject that it must be regarded as itself giving the law and, on this ground only, subject to the law (of which it can regard itself as the author).

In the previous imperatives, namely, that based on the conception of the conformity of actions to general laws, as in a physical system of nature, and that based on the universal prerogative of rational beings as ends in themselves—these imperatives, just because they were conceived as categorical, excluded from any share in their authority all admixture of any interest as a spring of action; they were, however, only assumed to be categorical, because such an assumption was necessary to explain the conception of duty. But we could not prove independently that there are practical propositions which command categorically, nor can it be proved in this section; one thing, however, could be done, namely, to indicate in the imperative itself, by some determinate expression, that in the case of volition from duty all interest is renounced, which is the specific criterion of categorical as distinguished from hypothetical imperatives. This is done in the present (third) formula of the principle, namely, in the idea of the will of every rational being as a universally legislating will.

For although a will which is subject to laws may be attached to this law by means of an interest, yet a will which is itself a supreme lawgiver so far as it is such cannot possibly depend on any interest, since a will so dependent would itself still need another law restricting the interest of its self-love by the condition that it should be valid as universal law.

Thus the principle that every human will is a will which in all its maxims gives universal laws, provided it be otherwise justified, would be very well adapted to be the categorical imperative, in this respect, namely, that just because of the idea of universal legislation it is not based on interest, and therefore it alone among all possible imperatives can be unconditional. Or still better, converting the proposition, if there is a categorical imperative (i.e., a law for the will of every rational being), it can only command that everything be done from maxims of one's will regarded as a will which could at the same time will that it should itself give universal laws, for in that case only the practical principle and the imperative which it obeys are unconditional, since they cannot be based on any interest.

Autonomy

Looking back now on all previous attempts to discover the principle of morality, we need not wonder why they all failed. It was seen that man was bound to laws by duty, but it was not observed that the laws to which he is subject are only those of his own giving, though at the same time they are universal, and that he is only bound to act in conformity with his own will; a will, however, which is designed by nature to give universal laws. For when one has conceived man only as subject to a law (no matter what), then this law required some interest, either by way of attraction or constraint, since it did not originate as a law from his own will, but this will was according to a law obliged by something else to act in a certain manner. Now by this necessary consequence all the labour spent in finding a supreme principle of duty was irrevocably lost. For men never elicited duty, but only a necessity of acting from a certain interest. Whether this interest was private or otherwise, in any case the imperative must be conditional and could not by any means be capable of being a moral command. I will therefore call this the principle of autonomy of the will, in contrast with every other which I accordingly reckon as heteronomy. . . .

The conception of the will of every rational being as one which must consider itself as giving in all the maxims of its will universal laws, so as to judge itself and its actions from this point of view—this conception leads to another which depends on it and is very fruitful, namely that of a kingdom of ends.

By a kingdom I understand the union of different rational beings in a system by common laws. Now since it is by laws that ends are determined as regards their universal validity, hence, if we abstract from the personal differences of rational beings and likewise from all the content of their private ends, we shall be able to conceive all ends combined in a systematic whole (including both rational beings as ends in themselves, and also the special ends which each may propose to himself), that is to say, we can conceive a kingdom of ends, which on the preceding principles is possible.

For all rational beings come under the law that each of them must treat itself and all others never merely as means, but in every case at the same time as ends in themselves. Hence results a systematic union of rational beings by common objective laws, i.e., a kingdom which may be called a kingdom of ends, since what these laws have in view is just the relation of these beings to one another as ends and means. It is certainly only an ideal.

A rational being belongs as a member to the kingdom of ends when, although giving universal laws in it, he is also himself subject to these laws. He belongs to it as sovereign when, while giving laws, he is not subject to the will of any other.

A rational being must always regard himself as giving laws either as member or as sovereign in a kingdom of ends which is rendered possible by the freedom of will. He cannot, however, maintain the latter position merely by the maxims of his will, but only in case he is a completely independent being without wants and with unrestricted power adequate to his will.

Morality consists then in the reference of all action to the legislation which alone can render a kingdom of ends possible. This legislation must be capable of existing in every rational being and of emanating from his will, so that the principle of this will is never to act on any maxim which could not without contradiction be also a universal law and, accordingly, always so to act that the will could at the same time regard itself as giving in its maxims universal laws. If now the maxims of rational beings are not by their own nature coincident with this objective principle, then the necessity of acting on it is called practical necessitation, i.e., duty. Duty does not apply to the sovereign in the kingdom of ends, but it does to every member of it and to all in the same degree.

The practical necessity of acting on this principle, i.e., duty, does not rest at all on feelings, impulses, or inclinations, but solely on the relation of rational beings to one another, a relation in which the will of a rational being must always be regarded as legislative, since otherwise it could not be conceived as an end in itself. Reason then refers every maxim of the will, regarding it as legislating universally, to every other will and also to every action towards oneself; and this not on account of any other practical motive or any future advantage, but from the idea of the dignity of a rational being, obeying no law but that which he himself also gives.

The Kingdom of Ends

In the kingdom of ends everything has either value or dignity. Whatever has a value can be replaced by something else which is equivalent; whatever, on the other hand, is above all value, and therefore admits of no equivalent, has a dignity.

Whatever has reference to the general inclinations and wants of mankind has a market value; whatever, without presupposing a want, corresponds to a certain taste, that is to a satisfaction in the mere purposeless play of our faculties, has a fancy value; but that which constitutes the condition under which alone anything can be an end in itself, this has not merely a relative worth, i.e., value, but an intrinsic worth, that is, dignity.

Now morality is the condition under which alone a rational being can be an end in himself, since by this alone is it possible that he should be a legislating member in the kingdom of ends. Thus morality, and humanity as capable of it, is that which alone has dignity.

What then is it which justifies virtue or the morally good disposition, in making such lofty claims? It is nothing less than the privilege it secures to the rational being of participating in the giving of universal laws, by which it qualifies him to be a member of a possible kingdom of ends, a privilege to which he was already destined by his own nature as being an end in himself and, on that account, legislating in the kingdom of ends; free as regards all laws of physical nature, and obeying those only which he himself gives, and by which his maxims can belong to a system of universal law, to which at the same time he submits himself. For nothing has any worth except what the law assigns it. Now the legislation itself which assigns the worth of everything must for that very reason possess dignity, that is an unconditional incomparable worth; and the word respect alone supplies a becoming expression for the esteem which a rational being must have for it.

Autonomy then is the basis of the dignity of human and of every rational nature. . . . Although the conception of duty implies subjection to the law, we yet ascribe a certain dignity and sublimity to the person who fulfills all his duties. There is not, indeed, any sublimity in him, so far as he is subject to the moral law; but inasmuch as in regard to that very law he is likewise a legislator, and on that account alone subject to it, he has sublimity. We have also shown above that neither fear nor inclination, but simply respect for the law, is the spring which can give actions a moral worth. Our own will, so far as we suppose it to act only under the condition that its maxims are potentially universal laws, this ideal will which is possible to us is the proper object of respect; and the dignity of humanity consists just in this capacity of being universally legislative, though with the condition that it is itself subject to this same legislation.

QUESTIONS FOR REFLECTION

1. What is an imperative? What is the difference between hypothetical and categorical imperatives?
2. Why must a categorical imperative be established a priori—that is, independently of experience?
3. Kant gives several different formulations of the categorical imperative. What are they? Why does he take them to be equivalent?
4. G.W.F. Hegel claims that Kant's formula of universal law is empty, saying only that we must act according to principle, but doing nothing at all to distinguish good from bad principles. Can you give an example of a principle that would fail Kant's universalization test?
5. What is autonomy? How does it relate to dignity?
6. John Rawls claims that every maxim fails Kant's test, for it is always true that a maxim applied universally might get in the way of a rational agent's pursuit of his or her ends. It might frustrate my ends if no one helps anyone, for example, but it might also frustrate my ends to have to help someone. How might Kant respond?
7. John Stuart Mill alleges that Kant relies on consequences in applying the categorical imperative. What if everyone were to break promises? Then there would be no such thing as promising. Nothing follows, Mill says, unless we add, "and that would be bad." Is that a fair criticism? How might Kant reply?
8. Apply Kant's formula of universal law to murder by way of the maxim, "Kill anyone who infuriates you." It seems as if this could be a universal law, though a rational agent could not consistently will it. If so, it would seem to follow that the obligation not to murder is merely imperfect, and that murder, although wrong, is not unjust. How might Kant respond?
9. W. D. Ross points out how crucial the formulation of maxims is to Kant's application of the categorical imperative. A rational agent could will as a universal law a highly specific maxim, such as "Shoot Homer J. Simpson between 10 and 11 P.M. on August 31, 2013, for refusing to pay his $3,000 debt," but not "Shoot debtors." So, the outcome depends entirely on how specific the maxim is. Can Kant provide any principled way of determining how specific the maxim being tested ought to be?
10. Benjamin Constant complains about the universality of Kant's conclusions, worrying that Kant forbids lying even to a murderer who asks where his intended victim is. Does Kant's theory forbid lying even to save a life?
11. What is the kingdom of ends? How might Kant answer the charge that acting as a legislator in the kingdom of ends leads to unrealistically utopian conclusions because people in the world as it is often treat one another merely as means?

JEREMY BENTHAM

from *An Introduction to the Principles of Morals and Legislation* (1789)

Jeremy Bentham (1748–1832), an English utilitarian, was born in Houndsditch, London. He was a prodigious student, entering Queen's College, Oxford, at twelve and graduating at fifteen. He studied law at Lincoln's Inn and was admitted to the bar at nineteen. Bentham was so appalled by English law, however, that he never practiced it, even for a day. Instead, he devoted his life to legal reform.

Bentham wrote many thousands of pages of pamphlets, papers, and books, relatively few of which were published during his lifetime. He founded a group of powerful and ultimately very influential thinkers, the philosophical radicals, which included James Mill, economist David Ricardo, and legal theorist John Austin. Bentham also founded the Westminster Review, *a political journal, and University College, London, where his embalmed body still rests, seated, in a glass case in the library.*

Principles of Morals and Legislation, *the only major theoretical work of his own that Bentham saw in print, appeared in 1789, the year of the French Revolution. Bentham objects strongly to views of morality and politics that stress individual conscience or religious conviction; both, in his view, are little more than prejudice in disguise. Bentham also rejects doctrines of natural rights, such as those invoked by the French revolutionaries, calling them "nonsense on stilts." Instead, he proposes to base ethics and politics on a single principle, the principle of utility. Roughly, Bentham's version of this principle states that a good action increases the balance of pleasure over pain in the community of people affected by it; a bad action decreases the balance. From this principle, taken together with the facts about the effects of actions, Bentham maintains, all our correct moral and political judgments follow. (Source: Reprinted from Jeremy Bentham,* An Introduction to the Principles of Morals and Legislation. *London: Printed for T. Payne, 1789.)*

CHAPTER I / OF THE PRINCIPLE OF UTILITY

1. Nature has placed mankind under the governance of two sovereign masters, *pain* and *pleasure*. It is for them alone to point out what we ought to do, as well as to determine what we shall do. On the one hand the standard of right and wrong, on the other the chain of causes and effects, are fastened to their throne. They govern us in all we do, in all we say, in all we think: every effort we can make to throw off our subjection, will serve but to demonstrate and confirm, it. In words a man may pretend to abjure their empire: but in reality he will remain subject to it all the while. The *principle of utility* recognises this subjection, and assumes it for the foundation of that system, the object of which is to rear the fabric of felicity by the hands of reason and of law. Systems which attempt to question it, deal in sounds instead of senses, in caprice instead of reason, in darkness instead of light.

But enough of metaphor and declamation: it is not by such means that moral science is to be improved.

2. The principle of utility is the foundation of the present work: it will be proper therefore at the outset to give an explicit and determinate account of what is meant by it. By the principle of utility is meant that principle which approves or disapproves of every action whatsoever, according to the tendency which it appears to have to augment or diminish the happiness of the party whose interest is in question: or, what is the same thing in other words, to promote or to oppose that happiness. I say of every action whatsoever, and therefore not only of every action of a private individual, but of every measure of government.

3. By utility is meant that property in any object, whereby it tends to produce benefit, advantage, pleasure, good, or happiness, (all this in the present case comes to the same thing) or (what comes again to the same thing) to prevent the happening of mischief, pain, evil, or unhappiness to the party whose interest is considered: if that party be the community in general, then the happiness of the community: if a particular individual, then the happiness of that individual.

4. The interest of the community is one of the most general expressions that can occur in the phraseology of morals: no wonder that the meaning of it is often lost. When it has a meaning, it is this. The community is a fictitious *body*, composed of the individual persons who are considered as constituting as it were its *members*. The interest of the community then is, what?—the sum of the interests of the several members who compose it.

5. It is in vain to talk of the interest of the community, without understanding what is the interest of the individual. A thing is said to promote the interest, or to be *for* the interest, of an individual, when it tends to add to the sum total of his pleasures: or, what comes to the same thing, to diminish the sum total of his pains.

6. An action then may be said to be comformable to the principle of utility, or, for shortness sake, to utility, (meaning with respect to the community at large) when the tendency it has to augment the happiness of the community is greater than any it has to diminish it.

7. A measure of government (which is but a particular kind of action, performed by a particular person or persons) may be said to be conformable to or dictated by the principle of utility, when in like manner the tendency which it has to augment the happiness of the community is greater than any which it has to diminish it.

8. When an action, or in particular a measure of government, is supposed by a man to be conformable to the principle of utility, it may be convenient, for the purposes of discourse, to imagine a kind of law or dictate, called a law or dictate of utility; and to speak of the action in question, as being conformable to such law or dictate.

9. A man may be said to be a partisan of the principle of utility, when the approbation or disapprobation he annexes to any action, or to any measure, is determined by and proportioned to the tendency which he conceives it to have to augment or to diminish the happiness of the community: or in other words, to its conformity or uncomformity to the laws or dictates of utility.

10. Of an action that is conformable to the principle of utility one may always say either that it is one that ought to be done, or at least that it is not one that ought not to be done. One may say also, that it is right it should be done; at least that it is not wrong it should be done: that it is a right action; at least that it is not a wrong action. When thus interpreted, the words *ought*, and *right* and *wrong*, and others of that stamp, have a meaning: when otherwise, they have none.

11. Has the rectitude of this principle been ever formally contested? It should seem that it had, by those who have not known what they have been meaning. Is it susceptible of any direct proof? it should seem not: for that which is used to prove every thing else, cannot itself be proved: a chain of proofs must have their commencement somewhere. To give such proof is as impossible as it is needless.

12. Not that there is or ever has been that human creature breathing, however stupid or perverse, who has not on many, perhaps on most occasions of his life, deferred to it. By the natural constitution of the human frame, on most occasions of their lives men in general embrace this principle, without thinking of it: if not for the ordering of their own actions, yet for the

trying of their own actions, as well as of those of other men. There have been, at the same time, not many, perhaps, even of the most intelligent, who have been disposed to embrace it purely and without reserve. There are even few who have not taken some occasion or other to quarrel with it, either on account of their not understanding always how to apply it, or on account of some prejudice or other which they were afraid to examine into, or could not bear to part with. For such is the stuff that man is made of: in principle and in practice, in a right track and in a wrong one, the rarest of all human qualities is consistency.

13. When a man attempts to combat the principle of utility, it is with reasons drawn, without his being aware of it, from that very principle itself. His arguments, if they prove any thing, prove not that the principle is *wrong*, but that, according to the application he supposes to be made of it, it is *misapplied*. Is it possible for a man to move the earth? Yes; but he must first find out another earth to stand upon.

14. To disprove the propriety of it by arguments is impossible; but, from the causes that have been mentioned, or from some confused or partial view of it, a man may happen to be disposed not to relish it. Where this is the case, if he thinks the settling of his opinions on such a subject worth the trouble, let him take the following steps and at length, perhaps, he may come to reconcile himself to it.

1. Let him settle with himself, whether he would wish to discard this principle altogether; if so, let him consider what it is that. all his reasonings (in matters of politics especially) can amount to?

2. If he would, let him settle with himself, whether he would judge and act without any principle, or whether there is any other he would judge and act by?

3. If there be, let him examine and satisfy himself whether the principle he thinks he has found is really any separate intelligible principle; or whether it be not a mere principle in words, a kind of phrase, which at bottom expresses neither more nor less than the mere averment of his own unfounded sentiments; that is, what in another person he might be apt to call caprice?

4. If he is inclined to think that his own approbation or disapprobation, annexed to the idea of an act, without any regard to its consequences, is a sufficient foundation for him to judge and act upon, let him ask himself whether his sentiment is to be a standard of right and wrong, with respect to every other man, or whether every other man's sentiment has the same privilege of being a standard to itself?

5. In the first case, let him ask himself whether his principle is not despotical, and hostile to all the rest of human race?

6. In the second case, whether it is not anarchical, and whether at this rate there are not as many different standards of right and wrong as there are men? and whether even to the same man, the same thing, which is right to-day, may not (without the least change in its nature) be wrong to-morrow? and whether the same thing is not right and wrong in the same place at the same time? and in either case, whether all argument is not at an end? and whether, when two men have said, "I like this," and "I don't like it," they can (upon such a principle) have any thing more to say?

7. If he should have said to himself, No: for that the sentiment which he proposes as a standard must be grounded on reflection, let him say on what particulars the reflection is to turn? if on particulars having relation to the utility of the act, then let him say whether this is not deserting his own principle, and borrowing assistance from that very one in opposition to which he sets it up: or if not on those particulars, on what other particulars?

8. If he should be for compounding the matter, and adopting his own principle in part, and the principle of utility in part, let him say how far he will adopt it?

9. When he has settled with himself where he will stop, then let him ask himself how he justifies to himself the adopting it so far? and why he will not adopt it any farther?

10. Admitting any other principle than the principle of utility to be a right principle, a principle that it is right for a man to pursue; admitting (what is not true) that the word *right* can have a meaning without reference to utility, let him say whether there is any such thing as a *motive* that a man can have to pursue the dictates of it: if there is, let him say what that motive is, and how it is to be distinguished from those which enforce the dictates of utility: if not,

then lastly let him say what it is this other principle can be good for? . . .

CHAPTER II / OF PRINCIPLES ADVERSE TO THAT OF UTILITY

. . . 11. Among principles adverse to that of utility, that which at this day seems to have most influence the matters of government, is what may be called the principle of sympathy and antipathy. By the principle of sympathy and antipathy, I mean that principle which approves or disapproves of certain actions, not on account of their tending to augment the happiness, nor yet on account of their tending to diminish the happiness of the party whose interest is in question, hut merely because a man finds himself disposed to approve or disapprove of them: holding up that approbation or disapprobation as a sufficient reason for itself, and disclaiming the necessity of looking out for any extrinsic ground. Thus far in the general department of morals: and in the particular department of politics, measuring out the quantum (as well as determining the ground) of punishment, by the degree of the disapprobation.

12. It is manifest, that this is rather a principle in name than in reality: it is not a positive principle of itself, so much as a term employed to signify the negation of all principle. What one expects to find in a principle is something that points out some external consideration, as a means of warranting and guiding the internal sentiments of approbation and disapprobation: this expectation is but ill fulfilled by a proposition, which does neither more nor less than hold up each of those sentiments as a ground and standard for itself.

13. In looking over the catalogue of human actions (says a partisan of this principle) in order to determine which of them are to be marked with the seal of disapprobation, you need but to take counsel of your own feelings: whatever you find in yourself a propensity to condemn, is wrong for that very reason. For the same reason it is also meet for punishment: in what proportion it is adverse to utility, or whether it be adverse to utility at all, is a matter that makes no difference. In that same *proportion* also is it meet for punishment: if you hate much, punish much: if you hate little, punish little: punish as you hate. If you hate not at all, punish not at all: the fine feelings of the soul are not to be overborne and tyrannised by the harsh and rugged dictates of political utility.

14. The various systems that have been formed concerning the standard of right and wrong, may all be reduced to the principle of sympathy and antipathy. One account may serve for all of them. They consist all of them in so many contrivances for avoiding the obligation of appealing to any external standard, and for prevailing upon the reader to accept of the author's sentiment or opinion as a reason for itself. The phrase is different, but the principle the same.

15. It is manifest, that the dictates of this principle will frequently coincide with those of utility, though perhaps without intending any such thing. Probably more frequently than not: and hence it is that the business of penal justice is carried on upon that tolerable sort of footing upon which we see it carried on in common at this day. For what more natural or more general ground of hatred to a practice can there be, than the mischievousness of such practice? What all men are exposed to suffer by, all men will be disposed to hate. It is far yet, however, from being a constant ground: for when a man suffers, it is not always that he knows what it is he suffers by. A man may suffer grievously, for instance, by a new tax, without being able to trace up the cause of his sufferings to the injustice of some neighbour, who has eluded the payment of an old one.

16. The principle of sympathy and antipathy is most apt to err on the side of severity. It is for applying punishment in many cases which deserve none: in many cases which deserve some, it is for applying more than they deserve. There is no incident imaginable, be it ever so trivial, and so remote from mischief, from which this principle may not extract aground of punishment. Any difference in taste: any difference in opinion: upon one subject as well as upon another. No disagreement so trifling which perseverance and altercation will not render serious. Each becomes in the other's eyes an enemy, and if laws permit, a criminal. This is one of the circumstances by which the human race is distinguished (not much indeed to its advantage) from the brute creation.

17. It is not, however, by any means unexampled for this principle to err on the side of lenity. A near and perceptible mischief moves antipathy. A remote and imperceptible mischief, though not less real, has no

effect. Instances in proof of this will occur in numbers in the course of the work. It would be breaking in upon the order of it to give them here. . . .

19. There are two things which are very apt to be confounded, but which it imports us carefully to distinguish:—the motive or cause, which, by operating on the mind of an individual, is productive of any act: and the ground or reason which warrants a legislator, or other by-stander, in regarding that act with an eye of approbation. When the act happens, in the particular instance in question, to be productive of effects which we approve of, much more if we happen to observe that the same motive may frequently be productive, in other instances, of the like effects, we are apt to transfer our approbation to the motive itself, and to assume, as the just ground for the approbation we bestow on the act, the circumstance of its originating from that motive. It is in this way that the sentiment of antipathy has often been considered as a just ground of action. Antipathy, for instance, in such or such a case, is the cause of an action which is attended with good effects: but this does not make it a right ground of action in that case, any more than in any other. Still farther. Not only the effects are good, but the agent sees beforehand that they will be so. This may make the action indeed a perfectly right action: but it does not make antipathy a right ground of action. For the same sentiment of antipathy, if implicitly deferred to, may be, and very frequently is, productive of the very worst effects. Antipathy, therefore, can never be a right ground of action. No more, therefore, can resentment, which, as will be seen more particularly hereafter, is but a modification of antipathy. The only right ground of action, that can possibly subsist, is, after all, the consideration of utility, which if it is a right principle of action, and of approbation, in any one case, is so in every other. Other principles in abundance, that is, other motives, may be the reasons why such and such an act has been done: that is, the reasons or causes of its being done: but it is this alone that can be the reason why it might or ought to have been done. Antipathy or resentment requires always to be regulated, to prevent its doing mischief: to be regulated by what? always by the principle of utility. The principle of utility neither requires nor admits of any other regulator than itself.

[CHAPTER III . . .]

CHAPTER IV / VALUE OF A LOT OF PLEASURE OR PAIN, HOW TO BE MEASURED

1. Pleasures then, and the avoidance of pains, are the *ends* which the legislator has in view: it behooves him therefore to understand their *value*. Pleasures and pains are the *instruments* he has to work with: it behooves him therefore to understand their force, which is again, in other words, their value.
2. To a person considered by *himself*, the value of a pleasure or pain considered by *itself*, will be greater or less, according to the four following circumstances:

    1. Its *intensity*.
    2. Its *duration*.
    3. Its *certainty* or *uncertainty*.
    4. Its *propinquity* or *remoteness*.

3. These are the circumstances which are to be considered in estimating a pleasure or a pain considered each of them by itself. But when the value of any pleasure or pain is considered for the purpose of estimating the tendency of any *act* by which it is produced, there are two other circumstances to be taken into account; these are,

    5. Its *fecundity*, or the chance it has of being followed by sensations of the *same* kind: that is, pleasures, if it be a pleasure: pain, if it be a pain.
    6. Its *purity*, or the chance it has of *not* being followed by sensations of the *opposite* kind: that is, pains, if it be a pleasure: pleasures, if it be a pain.

These two last, however, are in strictness scarcely to be deemed properties of the pleasure or the pain itself; they are not, therefore, in strictness to be taken into the account of the value of that pleasure or that pain. They are in strictness to be deemed properties only of the act, or other event, by which such pleasure or pain has been produced; and accordingly are only to be taken into the account of the tendency of such act or such event.

4. To a *number* of persons, with reference to each of whom the value of a pleasure or a pain is considered, it will be greater or less, according to seven circumstances: to wit, the six preceding ones; *viz.*

1. Its *intensity*.
2. Its *duration*.
3. Its *certainty* or *uncertainty*.
4. Its *propinquity* or *remoteness*.
5. Its *fecundity*.
6. Its *purity*.

And one other; to wit:

7. Its *extent*; that is, the number of persons to whom it *extends;* or (in other words) who are affected by it.

5. To take an exact account then of the general tendency of any act, by which the interests of a community are affected, proceed as follows. Begin with any one person of those whose interests seem most immediately to be affected by it: and take an account,
   1. Of the value of each distinguishable *pleasure* which appears to be produced by it in the *first* instance.
   2. Of the value of each *pain* which appears to be produced by it in the *first* instance.
   3. Of the value of each pleasure which appears to be produced by it *after* the first. This constitutes the *fecundity* of the first *pleasure* and the *impurity* of the first *pain*.
   4. Of the value of each *pain* which appears to be produced by it after the first. This constitutes the *fecundity* of the first *pain*, and the *impurity* of the first pleasure.
   5. Sum up all the values of all the *pleasures* on the one side, and those of all the pains on the other. The balance, if it be on the side of pleasure, will give the *good* tendency of the act upon the whole, with respect to the interests of that *individual* person; if on the side of pain, the bad tendency of it upon the whole.
   6. Take an account of the *number* of persons whose interests appear to be concerned; and repeat the above process with respect to each. *Sum up* the numbers expressive of the degrees of *good* tendency, which the act has, with respect to each individual, in regard to whom the tendency of it is *good* upon the whole: do this again with respect to each individual, in regard to whom the tendency of it is *bad* upon the whole. Take the *balance;* which, if on the side of *pleasure,* will give the general *good tendency* of the act, with respect to the total number or community, of individuals concerned; if on the side of pain, the general *evil tendency*, with respect to the same community.

6. It is not to be expected that this process should be strictly pursued previously to every moral judgment, or to every legislative or judicial operation. It may, however, be always kept in view: and as near as the process actually pursued on these occasions approaches to it, so near will such process approach to the character of an exact one.

7. The same process is alike applicable to pleasure and pain, in whatever shape they appear: and by whatever denomination they are distinguished: to pleasure, whether it be called *good* (which is properly the cause or instrument of pleasure) or *profit* (which is distant pleasure, or the cause or instrument of distant pleasure,) or *convenience*, or *advantage, benefit emolument, happiness,* and so forth: to pain, whether it be called *evil,* (which corresponds to *good*) or *mischief,* or *inconvenience*, or *disadvantage*, or *loss*, or *unhappiness*, and so forth.

8. Nor is this a novel and unwarranted, any more than it is a useless theory. In all this there is nothing but what the practice of mankind, wheresoever they have a clear view of their own interest, is perfectly conformable to. An article of property, an estate inland, for instance, is valuable, on what account? On account of the pleasures of all kinds which it enables a man to produce, and what comes to the same thing the pains of all kinds which it enables him to avert. But the value of such an article of property is universally understood to rise or fall according to the length or shortness of the time which a man has in it: the certainty or uncertainty of its coming into possession: and the nearness or remoteness of the time at which, if at all, it is to come into possession. As to the *intensity* of the pleasures which a man may derive from it, this is never thought of, because it depends upon the use which each particular person may come to make of it; which cannot be estimated till the particular pleasures he may come to derive from it, or the particular pains he may come to exclude by means of it, are brought to view. For the same reason, neither does he think of the *fecundity* or *purity* of those pleasures. . . .

QUESTIONS FOR REFLECTION

1. What is Bentham's principle of utility? What is utility?
2. What does Bentham's principle imply about what ought to be done when (*a*) only one available option, on balance, augments the happiness of the community; (*b*) only one available option, on balance, diminishes the happiness of the community; (*c*) all available options augment, on balance, the happiness of the community; (*d*) all available options diminish, on balance, the happiness of the community? What, intuitively, ought to be done in such cases, from a utilitarian point of view? What does this indicate about Bentham's principle?
3. Actions that, on balance, augment the happiness of the community "ought to be done" or at least are not ones that "ought not to be done." Explain the difference. Why does Bentham waffle? (Consider the cases mentioned in the previous question.)
4. How does Bentham argue for the principle of utility?
5. What is the principle of sympathy and antipathy? Why does Bentham disapprove of it?
6. In Chapter IV, Bentham details the *moral calculus*, his method for computing the utility of actions. How does it work? What aspects of pleasure and pain does Bentham consider?
7. Suppose that the numerous Roman spectators enjoyed gladiatorial combat so much that their pleasure was greater than the gladiators' suffering. Must Bentham conclude that such combat was morally acceptable?
8. Would Bentham's moral calculus approve punishing an innocent person if that were the only way to prevent highly destructive riots?
9. Thomas Carlyle called utilitarianism a philosophy fit for swine because it identifies the good with feeling good and makes no place for rationality or human dignity. How might Bentham respond?
10. Bernard Williams imagines wandering into a village square, where twenty innocent people are about to be shot by firing squad. The squad's captain spots you and makes you an offer: If you execute one of them, he will let the other nineteen go free. What should you do? What does Bentham's theory tell you to do?
11. Judith Jarvis Thomson imagines a healthy young man who enters a hospital for routine medical tests. A doctor has patients who are dying, in need of heart, liver, lung, and kidney transplants. The doctor realizes that killing the young man and using his organs could save five people. Does the principle of utility direct the doctor to kill one to save five?

JOHN STUART MILL

from *Utilitarianism* (1861)

John Stuart Mill (1806–1873) was a contemporary of Darwin, Dickens, Marx, and Tolstoy. Born in London, he was the most influential philosopher of the English-speaking world during the nineteenth century. His father, James Mill (1773–1836), was the son of a Scottish shoemaker who had become a prominent supporter of philosophical radicalism, a school of thought that advocated representative democracy, universal suffrage, and a scientific approach to philosophy. The elder Mill had a highly unusual and ambitious plan for educating his son at home. Consequently, John Stuart Mill never attended any school or college. He learned to read Greek at three and Latin just a few years later; he was well read in classical literature and history by eight and studied philosophy, mathematics, and economics before reaching his teens. At seventeen, he became a clerk in the East India Company, which governed India under charter from the British government. He eventually became chief of his department and worked at the company until 1858. In that year, Harriet Taylor, Mill's wife of six years—whom in the dedication of On Liberty *he calls "the inspirer, and in part the author, of all that is best in my writings"—died while they were traveling together in France. Mill decided to devote his time fully to writing the works they had discussed together. The next few years saw the publication of Mill's most influential ethical works:* On Liberty *(1859),* Utilitarianism *(1861), and* On the Subjection of Women *(1869). In 1865, Mill won election to Parliament, despite his refusal to campaign or defend his views. (Source: Reprinted from John Stuart Mill,* Utilitarianism. *London: Longman's, 1907.)*

CHAPTER II / WHAT UTILITARIANISM IS

The Principle of Utility

. . . The creed which accepts as the foundation of morals "utility" or the "greatest happiness principle" holds that actions are right in proportion as they tend to promote happiness; wrong as they tend to produce the reverse of happiness. By happiness is intended pleasure and the absence of pain; by unhappiness, pain and the privation of pleasure. To give a clear view of the moral standard set up by the theory, much more requires to be said; in particular, what things it includes in the ideas of pain and pleasure, and to what extent this is left an open question. But these supplementary explanations do not affect the theory of life on which this theory of morality is grounded—namely, that pleasure and freedom from pain are the only things desirable as ends; and that all desirable things (which are as numerous in the utilitarian as in any other scheme) are desirable either for pleasure inherent in themselves or as means to the promotion of pleasure and the prevention of pain.

A Philosophy Fit for Swine?

Now such a theory of life excites in many minds, and among them some of the most estimable in feeling and purpose, inveterate dislike. To suppose that life has (as they express it) no higher end than pleasure—no better and nobler object of desire and pursuit—they designate as utterly mean and groveling, as a doctrine worthy only of swine, to whom the followers of Epicurus were, at a very early period, contemptuously likened; and modern holders of the doctrine are occasionally made the subject of equally polite comparison by its German, French, and English assailants.

When thus attacked, the Epicureans have always answered that it is not they, but their accusers, who represent human nature in a degrading light, since the accusation supposes human beings to be capable of no pleasures except those of which swine are capable. If this supposition were true, the charge could not be gainsaid, but would then be no longer an imputation; for if the sources of pleasure were precisely the same to human beings and to swine, the rule of life which is good enough for the one would be good enough for the other. The comparison of the Epicurean life to that of beasts is felt as degrading, precisely because a beast's pleasures do not satisfy a human being's conceptions of happiness. Human beings have faculties more elevated than the animal appetites and, when once made conscious of them, do not regard anything as happiness which does not include their gratification. I do not indeed, consider the Epicureans to have been by any means faultless in drawing out their scheme of consequences from the utilitarian principle. To do this in any sufficient manner, many Stoic, as well as Christian, elements require to be included. But there is no known Epicurean theory of life which does not assign to the pleasures of the intellect, of the feelings and imagination, and of the moral sentiments a much higher value as pleasures than to those of mere sensation. It must be admitted, however, that utilitarian writers in general have placed the superiority of mental over bodily pleasures chiefly in the greater permanency, safety, uncostliness, etc., of the former—that is, in their circumstantial advantages rather than in their intrinsic nature. And on all these points utilitarians have fully proved their case; but they might have taken the other and, as it may be called, higher ground with entire consistency. It is quite compatible with the principle of utility to recognize the fact that some kinds of pleasure are more desirable and more valuable than others. It would be absurd that, while in estimating all other things quality is considered as well as quantity, the estimation of pleasure should be supposed to depend on quantity alone.

Qualities of Pleasures

If I am asked what I mean by difference of quality in pleasures, or what makes one pleasure more valuable than another, merely as a pleasure, except its being greater in amount, there is but one possible answer. Of two pleasures, if there be one to which all or almost all who have experience of both give a decided preference, irrespective of any feeling of moral obligation to prefer it, that is the more desirable pleasure. If one of the two is, by those who are competently acquainted with both, placed so far above the other that they prefer it, even though knowing it to be attended with a greater amount of discontent, and would not resign it for any quantity of the other pleasure which their nature is capable of, we are justified in ascribing to the preferred enjoyment a superiority in quality so far outweighing quantity as to render it, in comparison, of small account.

Now it is an unquestionable fact that those who are equally acquainted with and equally capable of appreciating and enjoying both do give a most marked preference to the manner of existence which employs their higher faculties. Few human creatures would consent to be changed into any of the lower animals for a promise of the fullest allowance of a beast's pleasures; no intelligent human being would consent to be a fool, no instructed person would be an ignoramus, no person of feeling and conscience would be selfish and base, even though they should be persuaded that the fool, the dunce, or the rascal is better satisfied with his lot than they are with theirs. They would not resign what they possess more than he for the most complete satisfaction of all the desires which they have in common with him. If they ever fancy they would, it is only in cases of unhappiness so extreme that to escape from it they would exchange their lot for almost any other, however undesirable in their own eyes. A being of higher faculties requires more to make him happy, is capable probably of more acute suffering, and certainly accessible to it at more points, than one of an inferior type; but in spite of these liabilities, he can never really wish to sink into what he feels to be a lower grade of existence.

We may give what explanation we please of this unwillingness; we may attribute it to pride, a name which is given indiscriminately to some of the most and to some of the least estimable feelings of which mankind are capable; we may refer it to the love of liberty and personal independence, an appeal to which was with the Stoics one of the most effective means for the inculcation of it; to the love of power or to the love of excitement, both of which do really enter into and contribute to it; but its most appropriate appellation is a sense of dignity, which all human beings possess in one form or other, and in some, though by no means in exact, proportion to their higher faculties, and which is so essential a part of the happiness of those in whom it is strong that nothing which conflicts with it could be otherwise than momentarily an object of desire to them. Whoever supposes that this preference takes place at a sacrifice of happiness—that the superior being, in anything like equal circumstances, is not happier than the inferior—confounds the two very different ideas of happiness and content. It is indisputable that the being whose capacities of enjoyment are low has the greatest chance of having them fully satisfied; and a highly endowed being will always feel that any happiness which he can look for, as the world is constituted, is imperfect. But he can learn to bear its imperfections, if they are at all bearable; and they will not make him envy the being who is indeed unconscious of the imperfections, but only because he feels not at all the good which those imperfections qualify. It is better to be a human being dissatisfied than a pig satisfied; better to be Socrates dissatisfied than a fool satisfied. And if the fool, or the pig, are of a different opinion, it is because they only know their own side of the question. The other party to the comparison knows both sides.

Temptation

It may be objected that many who are capable of the higher pleasures occasionally, under the influence of temptation, postpone them to the lower. But this is quite compatible with a full appreciation of the intrinsic superiority of the higher. Men often, from infirmity of character, make their election for the nearer good, though they know it to be the less valuable; and this no less when the choice is between two bodily pleasures than when it is between bodily and mental. They pursue sensual indulgence to the injury of health, though perfectly aware that health is the greater good. It may be further objected that many who begin with youthful enthusiasm for everything noble, as they advance in years, sink into indolence and selfishness. But I do not believe that those who undergo this very common change voluntarily choose the lower description of pleasures in preference to the higher. I believe that, before they devote themselves exclusively to the one, they have already become incapable of the other. Capacity for the nobler feelings is in most natures a very tender plant, easily killed, not only by hostile influences, but by mere want of sustenance; and in the majority of young persons it speedily dies away if the occupations to which their position in life has devoted them, and the society into which it has thrown them, are not favorable to keeping that higher capacity in exercise. Men lose their high aspirations as they lose their intellectual tastes, because they have not time or opportunity for indulging them; and they addict themselves to inferior pleasures, not because they deliberately prefer them, but because they are either the only ones to which they have access or the only ones which they are any longer capable of enjoying. It may be questioned whether anyone who has remained equally susceptible to both classes of pleasures ever knowingly and calmly preferred the lower, though many, in all ages, have broken down in an ineffectual attempt to combine both.

Judging Quality

From this verdict of the only competent judges, I apprehend there can be no appeal. On a question which is the best worth having of two pleasures, or which of two modes of existence is the most grateful to the feelings, apart from its moral attributes, and from its consequences, the judgment of these who are qualified by knowledge of both, or, if they differ, that of the majority among them, must be admitted as final. And there needs be the less hesitation to accept this judgment respecting the quality of pleasures, since there is no other tribunal to be referred to even on the question of quantity. What means are there of determining which is the acutest of two pains, or the intensest of two pleasurable sensations, except the general suffrage of those who are familiar with both? Neither pains nor pleasures are homogeneous, and pain is always heterogeneous with pleasure. What is there to decide whether a particular pleasure is worth purchasing at the cost of a particular pain, except the feelings and judgment of the experienced? When, therefore, those feelings and judgment declare the pleasures derived from the higher faculties to be preferable *in kind*, apart from the question of intensity, to those of which the animal nature, disjoined from the higher faculties, is susceptible, they are entitled on this subject to the same regard.

Virtue

I have dwelt on this point as being part of a perfectly just conception of utility or happiness considered as the directive rule of human conduct. But it is by no means an indispensable condition to the acceptance of the utilitarian standard; for that standard is not the agent's own greatest happiness, but the greatest amount of happiness altogether; and if it may possibly be doubted whether a noble character is always the happier for its nobleness, there can be no doubt that it makes other people happier, and that the world in general is immensely a gainer by it. Utilitarianism, therefore, could only attain its end by the general cultivation of nobleness of character, even if each individual were only benefited by the nobleness of others, and his own, so far as happiness is concerned, were a sheer deduction from the benefit. But the bare enunciation of such an absurdity as this last renders refutation superfluous.

Universality

According to the greatest happiness principle, as above explained, the ultimate end, with reference to and for the sake of which all other things are desirable—whether we are considering our own good or that of other people—is an existence exempt as far as possible from pain, and as rich as possible in enjoyments, both in point of quantity and quality; the test of quality and the rule for measuring it against quantity being the preference felt by those who, in their opportunities of experience, to which must be added their habits of self-consciousness and self-observation, are best furnished with the means of comparison. This, being according to the utilitarian opinion the end of human action, is necessarily also the standard of morality, which may accordingly be defined "the rules and precepts for human conduct," by the observance of which an existence such as has been described might be, to the greatest extent possible, secured to all mankind; and not to them only, but, so far as the nature of things admits, to the whole sentient creation. . . .

Secondary Principles

It is a strange notion that the acknowledgment of a first principle is inconsistent with the admission of secondary ones. To inform a traveler respecting the place of his ultimate destination is not to forbid the use of landmarks and direction-posts on the way. The proposition that happiness is the end and aim of morality does not mean that no road ought to be laid down to that goal, or that persons going thither should not be advised to take one direction rather than another. Men really ought to leave off talking a kind of nonsense on this subject, which they would neither talk nor listen to on other matters of practical concernment. Nobody argues that the art of navigation is not founded on astronomy because sailors cannot wait to calculate the Nautical Almanac. Being rational creatures, they go to sea with it ready calculated; and all rational creatures go out upon the sea of life with their minds made up on the common questions of right and wrong, as well as on many of the far more difficult questions of wise and foolish. And this, as long as foresight is a human quality, it is to be presumed they will continue to do. Whatever we adopt as the fundamental principle of morality, we require subordinate principles to apply it by; the impossibility of doing without them, being common to all systems, can afford no argument against any one in particular; but gravely to argue as if no such secondary principles could be had, and as if mankind had remained till now, and always must remain, without drawing any general conclusions from the experience of human life is as high a pitch, I think, as absurdity has ever reached in philosophical controversy.

Exceptions?

The remainder of the stock arguments against utilitarianism mostly consist in laying to its charge the common infirmities of human nature, and the general difficulties which embarrass conscientious persons in shaping their course through life. We are told that a utilitarian will be apt to make his own particular case an exception to moral rules, and, when under temptation, will see a utility in the breach of a rule, greater than he will see in its observance. But is utility the only creed which is able to furnish us with excuses for evildoing and means of cheating our own conscience? They are afforded in abundance by all doctrines which recognize as a fact in morals the existence of conflicting considerations, which all doctrines do that have been believed by sane persons. It is not the fault of any creed, but of the complicated nature of human affairs, that rules of conduct cannot be so framed as to require no exceptions, and that hardly any kind of action can safely be laid down as either always obligatory or always condemnable. There is no ethical creed which does not temper the rigidity of its laws by giving a certain latitude, under the moral responsibility of the agent, for accommodation to peculiarities of circumstances; and under every creed, at the opening thus made, self-deception and dishonest casuistry get in. There exists no moral system under which there do not arise unequivocal cases of conflicting obligation. These are the real difficulties, the knotty points both in the theory of ethics and in the conscientious guidance of personal conduct. They are overcome practically, with greater or with less success, according to the intellect and virtue of the individual; but it can hardly be pretended that anyone will be the less qualified for dealing with them, from possessing an ultimate standard to which conflicting rights and duties can be referred. If utility is the ultimate source of moral obligations, utility may be invoked to decide between them when their demands are incompatible. Though the application of the standard may be difficult, it is better than none at all; while in other systems, the moral laws all claiming independent authority, there is no common umpire entitled to interfere between them; their claims to precedence one over another rest on little better than sophistry, and, unless determined, as they generally are, by the unacknowledged influence of consideration of utility, afford a free scope for the action of personal desires and partialities. We must remember that only in these cases of conflict between secondary principles is it requisite that first principles should be appealed to. There is no case of moral obligation in which some secondary principle is not involved; and if only one, there can seldom be any real doubt which one it is, in the mind of any person by whom the principle itself is recognized.

QUESTIONS FOR REFLECTION

1. What is Mill's principle of utility? What does he mean by "utility"?
2. Mill distinguishes qualities, as well as quantities, of pleasures. Why? How does Mill rank pleasures in terms of quality?
3. People sometimes choose pleasures of lower quality over those of higher quality. How does Mill explain this?
4. Henry Sidgwick holds that Mill's distinction between qualities of pleasures confronts him with a dilemma. Either differences in quality can be measured in terms of differences in quantity, in which case the distinction does not seem very important, or they cannot be, in which case the idea of maximizing the general happiness seems to make little sense. How do you think Mill might respond to this dilemma?
5. What objections against utilitarianism does Mill consider? How does he respond to them?
6. What are the roles of tradition and conscience in Mill's theory?
7. What are secondary principles? What role do they play in Mill's theory? How do we decide which secondary principles to adopt? What happens when these principles conflict?

NEL NODDINGS

from *Caring: A Feminine Approach to Ethics and Moral Education* (1984)

Nel Noddings (1929–   ), a highly regarded feminist philosopher and educational theorist, was educated at Montclair State College, Rutgers University, and Stanford University. She taught elementary and high school mathematics for seventeen years and had ten children of her own. At age forty-eight, she became professor of education at Stanford. She later taught at Colgate University, Columbia University, and Eastern Michigan University. Her ethics of caring is relational, basing moral value on human relationships and the emotions that arise from them. (Source: Caring: A Feminine Approach to Ethics and Moral Education. *Copyright ©1984, 2003 by the Regents of the University of California. Reprinted by permission.)*

AN ETHIC OF CARING

From Natural to Ethical Caring

David Hume long ago contended that morality is founded upon and rooted in feeling—that the "final sentence" on matters of morality, "that which renders morality an active virtue"—". . . this final sentence depends on some internal sense or feeling, which nature has made universal in the whole species. For what else can have an influence of this nature?"

What is the nature of this feeling that is "universal in the whole species"? I want to suggest that morality as an "active virtue" requires two feelings and not just one. The first is the sentiment of natural caring. There can be no ethical sentiment without the initial, enabling sentiment. In situations where we act on behalf of the other because we want to do so, we are acting in accord with natural caring. A mother's caretaking efforts in behalf of her child are not usually considered ethical but natural. Even maternal animals take care of their offspring, and we do not credit them with ethical behavior.

The second sentiment occurs in response to a remembrance of the first. Nietzsche speaks of love and memory in the context of Christian love and Eros, but what he says may safely be taken out of context to illustrate the point I wish to make here:

> There is something so ambiguous and suggestive about the word love, something that speaks to memory and to hope, that even the lowest intelligence and the coldest heart still feel something of the glimmer of this word. The cleverest woman and the most vulgar man recall the relatively least selfish moments of their whole life, even if Eros has taken only a low flight with them.

This memory of our own best moments of caring and being cared for sweeps over us as a feeling—as an "I must"—in response to the plight of the other and our conflicting desire to serve our own interests. There is a transfer of feeling analogous to transfer of learning. In the intellectual domain, when I read a certain kind of mathematical puzzle, I may react by thinking, "That is like the sailors, monkey, and coconuts problem," and then, "Diophantine equations" or "modulo arithmetic" or "congruences." Similarly, when I encounter an other and feel the natural pang conflicted with my own desires—"I must—I do not want to"—I recognize the feeling and remember what has followed it in my own best moments. I have a picture of those moments in which I was cared for and in which I cared, and I may reach toward this memory and guide my conduct by it if I wish to do so.

Recognizing that ethical caring requires an effort that is not needed in natural caring does not commit us to a position that elevates ethical caring over natural caring. Kant has identified the ethical with that which is done out of duty and not out of love, and that distinction in itself seems right. But an ethic built on caring strives to maintain the caring attitude and is thus dependent upon, and not superior to, natural caring. The source of ethical behavior is, then, in twin sentiments—one that feels directly for the other and one that feels for and with that best self, who may accept and sustain the initial feeling rather than reject it.

We shall discuss the ethical ideal, that vision of best self, in some depth. When we commit ourselves to obey the "I must" even at its weakest and most fleeting, we are under the guidance of this ideal. It is not just any picture. Rather, it is our best picture of ourselves caring and being cared for. It may even be colored by acquaintance with one superior to us in caring, but, as I shall describe it, it is both constrained and attainable. It is limited by what we have already done and by what we are capable of, and it does not idealize the impossible so that we may escape into ideal abstraction.

Now, clearly, in pointing to Hume's "active virtue" and to an ethical ideal as the source of ethical behavior, I seem to be advocating an ethic of virtue. This is certainly true in part. Many philosophers recognize the need for a discussion of virtue as the energizing factor in moral behavior, even when they have given their best intellectual effort to a careful explication of their positions on obligation and justification. when we discuss the ethical ideal, we shall be talking about "virtue," but we shall not let "virtue" dissipate into "the virtues" described in abstract categories. The holy man living abstemiously on top of the mountain, praying thrice daily, and denying himself human intercourse may display "virtues," but they are not the virtues of one-caring. The virtue described by the ethical ideal of one-caring is built up in relation. It reaches out to the other and grows in response to the other.

Since our discussion of virtue will be embedded in an exploration of moral activity we might do well to start by asking whether or under what circumstances we are obliged to respond to the initial "I must." Does it make sense to say that I am obliged to heed that which comes to me as obligation?

Obligation

There are moments for all of us when we care quite naturally. We just do care; no ethical effort is required. "Want" and "ought" are indistinguishable in such cases. I want to do what I or others might judge I ought to do. But can there be a "demand" to care? There can be, surely, no demand for the initial impulse that arises as a feeling, an inner voice saying "I must do something," in response to the need of the cared-for. This impulse arises naturally, at least occasionally, in the absence of pathology. We cannot demand that one have this impulse, but we shrink from one who never has it. One who never feels the pain of another, who never confesses the internal "I must" that is so familiar to most of us, is beyond our normal pattern of understanding. Her case is pathological, and we avoid her.

But even if I feel the initial "I must," I may reject it. I may reject it instantaneously by shifting from "I must do something" to "Something must be done," and removing myself from the set of possible agents through whom the action should be accomplished. I may reject it because I feel that there is nothing I can do. If I do either of these things without reflection upon what I might do in behalf of the cared-for, then I do not care: Caring requires me to respond to the initial impulse with an act of commitment: I commit myself either to overt action on behalf of the cared-for (I pick up my crying infant) or I commit myself to thinking about what I might do. In the latter case, as we have seen, I may or may not act overtly in behalf of the cared-for. I may abstain from action if I believe that anything I might do would tend to work against the best interests of the cared-for. But the test of my caring is not wholly in how things turn out; the primary test lies in an examination of what I considered, how fully I received the other, and whether the free pursuit of his projects is partly a result of the completion of my caring in him.

But am I obliged to embrace the "I must"? In this form, the question is a bit odd, for the "I must" carries obligation with it. It comes to us as obligation. But accepting and affirming the "I must" are different from feeling it, and these responses are what I am pointing to when I ask whether I am obliged to embrace the "I must." The question nags at us; it is a question that has been asked, in a variety of forms, over and over by moralists and moral theorists. Usually, the question arises as part of the broader question of justification. We ask something of the sort: Why must I (or should I) do what suggests itself to reason as "right" or as needing to be done for the sake of some other? We might prefer to supplement "reason" with "and/or feeling." This question is, of course, not the only thorny question in moral theory, but it is one that has plagued theorists who see clearly that there is no way to derive an "I ought" statement from a chain of facts. I may agree readily that "things would be better"—that is, that a certain state of affairs commonly agreed to be desirable might be attained—if a certain chain of events were to take place. But there is still nothing in this intellectual chain that can produce the "I ought." I may choose to remain an observer on the scene.

Now I am suggesting that the "I must" arises directly and prior to consideration of what it is that I might do. The initial feeling is the "I must." When it comes to me indistinguishable from the "I want," I proceed easily as one-caring. But often it comes to me conflicted. It may be barely perceptible, and it may be followed almost simultaneously by resistance. When someone asks me to get something for him or merely asks for my attention, the "I must" may be lost in a clamor of resistance. Now a second sentiment is required if I am to behave as one-caring. I care about myself as one-caring and, although I do not care naturally for the person who has asked something of me—at least not at this moment—I feel the genuine moral sentiment, the "I ought," that sensibility to which I have committed myself.

Let me try to make plausible my contention that the moral imperative arises directly. And, of course, I must try to explain how caring and what I am calling the "moral imperative" are related. When my infant cries in the night, I not only feel that I must do something but I want to do something. Because I love this child, because I am bonded to him, I want to remove his pain as I would want to remove my own. The "I must" is not a dutiful imperative but one that accompanies the "I want." If I were tied to a chair, for example, and wanted desperately to get free, I might say as I struggled, "I must do something; I must get out of these bonds." But this "must" is not yet the moral or ethical "ought." It is a "must" born of desire.

The most intimate situations of caring are, thus, natural. I do not feel that taking care of my own child is "moral" but, rather, natural. A woman who allows her own child to die of neglect is often considered sick rather than immoral; that is, we feel that either she or the situation into which she has been thrust must be pathological. Otherwise, the impulse to respond, to nurture the living infant, is overwhelming. We share the impulse with other creatures in the animal kingdom. Whether we want to consider this response as "instinctive" is problematic, because certain patterns of response may be implied by the term and because suspension of reflective consciousness seems also to be implied (and I am not suggesting that we have no choice), but I have no difficulty in considering it as innate. Indeed, I am claiming that the impulse to act in behalf of the present other is itself innate. It lies latent in each of us, awaiting gradual development in a succession of caring relations. I am suggesting that our inclination toward and interest in morality derives from caring. In caring, we accept the natural impulse to act on behalf of the present other. We are engrossed in the other. We have received him and feel his pain or happiness, but we are not compelled by this impulse. We have a choice; we may accept what we feel, or we may reject it. If we have a strong desire to be moral, we will not reject it, and this strong desire to be moral is derived, reflectively, from the more fundamental and natural desire to be and to remain related. To reject the feeling when it arises is either to be in an internal state of imbalance or to contribute willfully to the diminution of the ethical ideal.

But suppose in a particular case that the "I must" does not arise, or that it whispers faintly and disappears, leaving distrust, repugnance, or hate. Why, then, should I behave morally toward the object of my dislike? Why should I not accept feelings other than those characteristic of caring and, thus, achieve an internal state of balance through hate, anger, or malice?

The answer to this is, I think, that the genuine moral sentiment (our second sentiment) arises from an evaluation of the caring relation as good, as better than, superior to, other forms of relatedness. I feel the moral "I must" when I recognize that my response will either enhance or diminish my ethical ideal. It will serve either to increase or decrease the likelihood of genuine caring. My response affects me as one-caring. In a given situation with someone I am not fond of, I may be able to find all sorts of reasons why I should not respond to his need. I may be too busy. He may be undiscerning. The matter may be, on objective analysis, unimportant. But, before I decide, I must turn away from this analytic chain of thought and back to the concrete situation. Here is this person with this perceived need to which is attached this importance. I must put justification aside temporarily. Shall I respond? How do I feel as a duality about the "I" who will not respond?

I am obliged, then, to accept the initial "I must" when it occurs and even to fetch it out of recalcitrant slumber when it fails to awake spontaneously. The source of my obligation is the value I place on the relatedness of caring. This value itself arises as a product of actual caring and being cared-for and my reflection on the goodness of these concrete caring situations.

Now, what sort of "goodness" is it that attaches to the caring relation? It cannot be a fully moral goodness, for we have already described forms of caring that are natural and require no moral effort. But it cannot be a fully nonmoral goodness either, for it would then join a class of goods many of which are widely separated from the moral good. It is, perhaps, properly described as a "premoral good," one that lies in a region with the moral good and shades over into it. We cannot always decide with certainty whether our caring response is natural or ethical. Indeed, the decision to respond ethically, as one-caring may cause the lowering of barriers that previously prevented reception of the other, and natural caring may follow.

I have identified the source of our obligation and have said that we are obligated to accept, and even to call forth, the feeling "I must." But what exactly must I do? Can my obligation be set forth in a list or hierarchy of principles? So far, it seems that I am obligated to maintain an attitude and, thus, to meet the other as one-caring and, at the same time, to increase my own virtue as one-caring. If I am advocating an ethic of virtue, do not all the usual dangers lie in wait: hypocrisy, self-righteousness, withdrawal from the public domain? We shall discuss these dangers as the idea of an ethical ideal is developed more fully.

Let me say here, however, why it seems preferable to place an ethical ideal above principle as a guide to moral action. It has been traditional in moral philosophy to insist that moral principles must be, by their very nature as moral principles, universifiable. If I am obligated to do *X* under certain conditions, then under sufficiently similar conditions you also are obligated to do *X*. But the principle of universifiability seems to depend, as Nietzsche pointed out, on a concept of "sameness." In order to accept the principle, we should have to establish that human predicaments exhibit sufficient sameness, and this we cannot do without abstracting away from concrete situations those qualities that seem to reveal the sameness. In doing this, we often lose the very qualities or factors that gave rise to the moral question in the situation. That condition which makes the situation different and thereby induces genuine moral puzzlement cannot be satisfied by the application of principles developed in situations of sameness.

This does not mean that we cannot receive any guidance from an attempt to discover principles that seem to be universifiable. We can, under this sort of plan, arrive at the doctrine of "prima facie duty" described by W. D. Ross. Ross himself, however, admits that this doctrine yields no real guidance for moral conduct in concrete situations. It guides us in abstract moral thinking; it tells us, theoretically, what to do, "all other things being equal." But other things are rarely if ever equal. A and B, struggling with a moral decision, are two different persons with different factual histories, different projects and aspirations, and different ideals. It may indeed be right, morally right, for A to do *X* and B to do not-*X*. We may, that is, connect "right" and "wrong" to faithfulness to the ethical ideal. This does not cast us into relativism, because the ideal contains at its heart a component that is universal: Maintenance of the caring relation.

QUESTIONS FOR REFLECTION

1. What is natural caring?
2. What is ethical caring? How does it relate to natural caring?
3. How does Noddings connect caring to obligation?
4. Is Noddings a Humean? Why or why not? How does she go from "I care" to "I have an obligation to care"?
5. How does caring offer a basis for prima facie obligation?
6. Discuss and evaluate Noddings's criticisms of Ross.
7. Critics have charged that Noddings's ethics of care is incompatible with impartiality and justice. Surely a judge, for example, should not adopt a principle of deciding in favor of the party he or she cares most about. How might Noddings reply?
8. Aristotle might consider caring a virtue, which is a mean between extremes. It seems possible to care too much. Can Noddings account for that?
9. We tend, by nature, to care most for people closest to us and most like us. Does Noddings's view accordingly approve of (a) preferring our own children to the children of others? (b) tribalism? (c) patriotism or nationalism? (d) ethnocentrism or even racism? How can she draw distinctions between these forms of preference?
10. It seems impossible to care about people if you don't even know they exist. Does it follow from Noddings's view that you have no obligations to such people? Why or why not?

SEXUAL BEHAVIOR

Teenagers and young adults often think of "morals" and "sexual morals" as equivalent expressions. Throughout life, our sexual identities and relationships remain central to our happiness and our conceptions of ourselves. The social roles implicit in being a husband, wife, lover, father, or mother remain among the most important we adopt. Our actions in the context of sexual relationships can thus affect other people more profoundly than almost anything else we do. We can make someone happy or break someone's heart. We can even create someone. Sexual morality, for all these reasons, has special importance.

Bertrand Russell, one of the twentieth century's most renowned philosophers, argues for a liberalization of sexual morality. His language is quaint, but his attitude proved influential, helping to lead to the sexual revolution. Russell finds traditional restrictions on sexual behavior to be part superstition and part response to social and biological conditions that no longer hold. He adopts the perspective of a rule-utilitarian—unsurprisingly, perhaps, since his godfather was John Stuart Mill!—asking "what moral rules are most likely to promote human happiness." He advocates the acceptance of premarital and even extramarital sexual relationships, stressing that the pursuit of pleasure is good, though it must of course be constrained by other moral concerns. He also objects to traditional marriage, holding that a relationship in which only one partner works is no better than prostitution.

Thomas Mappes sees Kant's categorical imperative as providing the key, if not to all of morality, at least to sexual morality. Kant urged that we treat others as "ends in themselves," not as "means only." In other words, the categorical imperative insists that we not use people but, instead, treat them with the respect that we ourselves deserve as moral agents. Mappes contends, accordingly, that the cardinal principle of sexual behavior is "Don't use people." He discusses applications of the principle, pointing out that, while his theory is more permissive than traditional morality, it prohibits a variety of behaviors, from deception and harassment to rape.

Roger Scruton offers a justification of traditional sexual morality. He critiques utilitarian and Kantian points of view, arguing that only an Aristotelian approach to an ethics of character can provide an adequate account of human flourishing. The chief sexual virtue, Scruton believes, is chastity, which involves not abstaining from sexual behavior but restricting it to relationships of erotic love. The capacity to love is a virtue crucial to human flourishing, Scruton maintains, and must be cultivated carefully. Chastity is one aspect of that cultivation, for it is necessary for sexual integrity—that is, the union of one's sexuality with the rest of one's personality.

BERTRAND RUSSELL

Our Sexual Ethics

Bertrand Russell (1872–1970), winner of the Nobel Prize for literature in 1950, is arguably the greatest philosopher of the twentieth century. A Fellow of the Royal Society, Honorary Fellow of the British Academy, and winner of the Order of Merit, he taught at Trinity College, Cambridge; the University of Chicago; and the University of California at Los Angeles. (Source: The American Mercury *38 [May 1936].)*

I

Sex, more than any other element in human life, is still viewed by many, perhaps by most, in an irrational way. Homicide, pestilence, insanity, gold and precious stones—all the things, in fact, that are the objects of passionate hopes or fears—have been seen, in the past, through a mist of magic or mythology; but the sun of reason has now dispelled the mist, except here and there. The densest cloud that remains is in the territory of sex, as is perhaps natural since sex is concerned in the most passionate part of most people's lives.

It is becoming apparent, however, that conditions in the modern world are working to effect a change in the public attitude toward sex. As to what change, or changes, this will bring about, no one can speak with any certainty; but it is possible to note some of the forces now at work, and to discuss what their results are likely to be upon the structure of society.

Insofar as human nature is concerned, it cannot be said to be *impossible* to produce a society in which there is very little sexual intercourse outside of marriage. The conditions necessary for this result, however, are such as are made almost unattainable by modern life. Let us, then, consider what they are.

The greatest influence toward effecting monogamy is immobility in a region containing few inhabitants. If a man hardly ever has occasion to leave home and seldom sees any woman but his wife, it is easy for him to be faithful; but if he travels without her or lives in a crowded urban community, the problem is proportionately more difficult. The next greatest assistance to monogamy is superstition: those who genuinely believe that "sin" leads to eternal punishment might be expected to avoid it, and to some extent they do so, although not to so great an extent as might be expected. The third support of virtue is public opinion. Where, as in agricultural societies, all that a man does is known to his neighbors, he has powerful motives for avoiding whatever convention condemns. But all these causes of correct behavior are much less potent than they used to be. Fewer people live in isolation; the belief in hell-fire is dying out; and in large towns no one knows what his neighbor does. It is, therefore, not surprising that both men and women are less monogamous than they were before the rise of modern industrialism.

Of course, it may be said that, while an increasing number of people fail to observe the moral law, that is no reason for altering our standards. Those who sin, we are sometimes told, should know and recognize that they sin, and an ethical code is none the worse for being difficult to live up to. But I should reply that the question whether a code is good or bad is the same as the question whether or not it promotes human happiness. Many adults, in their hearts, still believe all that they were taught in childhood and feel wicked when their lives do not conform to the maxims of the Sunday school. The harm done is not merely to introduce a division between the conscious reasonable personality and the unconscious infantile personality; the harm lies also in the fact that the valid parts of conventional morality become discredited along with the invalid parts, and it comes to be thought that, if adultery is excusable, so are laziness, dishonesty, and unkindness. This danger is inseparable from a system which teaches the young, *en bloc*, a number of beliefs that they are almost sure to discard when they become mature. In the process of social and economic revolt, they are likely to throw over the good along with the bad.

The difficulty of arriving at a workable sexual ethic arises from the conflict between the impulse to jealousy and the impulse to polygamy. There is no doubt that jealousy, while in part instinctive, is to a very large degree conventional. In societies in which a man is considered a fit object for ridicule if his wife is unfaithful, he will be jealous where she is concerned, even if he no longer has any affection for her. Thus jealousy is intimately connected with the sense of property and is much less where this sense is absent. If faithfulness is no part of what is conventionally expected, jealousy is much diminished. But although there is more possibility of lessening jealousy than many people suppose, there are very definite limits so long as fathers have rights and duties. So long as this is the case, it is inevitable that men should desire some assurance that they are the fathers of their wives' children. If women are to have sexual freedom, fathers must fade out, and wives must no longer expect to be supported by their husbands. This may come about in time, but it will be a profound social change, and its effects, for good or ill, are incalculable.

In the meantime, if marriage and paternity are to survive as social institutions, some compromise is necessary between complete promiscuity and life-long monogamy. To decide on the best compromise at any given moment is not easy; and the decision should vary from time to time, according to the habits of the population and the reliability of birth-control methods. Some things, however, can be said with some definiteness.

In the first place, it is undesirable, both physiologically and educationally, that women should have children before the age of twenty. Our ethics should, therefore be such as to make this a rare occurrence.

In the second place, it is unlikely that a person without previous sexual experience, whether man or woman, will be able to distinguish between mere physical attraction and the sort of congeniality that is necessary in order to make marriage a success. Moreover, economic causes compel men, as a rule, to postpone marriage, and it is neither likely that they will remain chaste in the years from twenty to thirty nor desirable psychologically that they should do so; but it is much better that, if they have temporary relations, they should not be with professionals but with girls of their own class, whose motive is affection rather than money. For both these reasons, young unmarried people should have considerable freedom, as long as children are avoided.

In the third place, divorce should be possible without blame to either party and should not be regarded as in any way disgraceful. A childless marriage should be terminable at the wish of one of the partners, and any marriage should be terminable by mutual consent—a year's notice being necessary in either case. Divorce should, of course, be possible on a number of other grounds—insanity, desertion, cruelty, and so on; but mutual consent should be the most usual ground.

In the fourth place, everything possible should be done to free sexual relations from the economic taint. At present, wives, just as much as prostitutes, live by the sale of their sexual charms; and even in temporary free relations the man is usually expected to bear all the joint expenses. The result is that there is a sordid entanglement of money with sex, and that women's motives not infrequently have a mercenary element. Sex, even when blessed by the church, ought not to be a profession. It is right that a woman should be paid for housekeeping or cooking or the care of children, but not merely for having sexual relations with a man. Nor should a woman who has once loved and been loved by a man be able to live ever after on alimony when his love and hers have ceased. A woman, like a man, should work for her living, and an idle wife is no more intrinsically worthy of respect than a gigolo.

II

Two very primitive impulses have contributed, though in very different degrees, to the rise of the currently accepted code of sexual behavior. One of these is modesty and the other, as mentioned above, is jealousy. Modesty, in some form and to some degree, is almost universal in the human race and constitutes a taboo which must only be broken in accordance with certain forms and ceremonies, or, at the least, in conformity with some recognized etiquette. Not everything may be seen, and not all facts may be mentioned. This is not, as some moderns suppose, an invention of the Victorian age; on the contrary, anthropologists have found the most elaborate forms of prudery among primitive savages. The conception of the obscene has its roots deep in human nature. We may go against it from a love of rebellion, or from loyalty to the scientific spirit, or from a wish to feel wicked, such as existed in Byron; but we do not thereby eradicate it from among our natural impulses. No doubt convention determines, in a given community, exactly what is to be considered indecent, but the universal existence of *some* convention of the kind is conclusive evidence of a source which is not merely conventional. In almost every human society, pornography and exhibitionism are reckoned as offenses, except when, as not infrequently occurs, they form part of religious ceremonies.

Asceticism—which may or may not have a psychological connection with modesty—is an impulse which seems to arise only where a certain level of civilization has been reached, but may then become powerful. It is not to be found in the earlier books of the Old Testament, but it appears in the later books, in the Apocrypha and in the New Testament. Similarly, among the Greeks there is little of it in early times, but more and more as time goes on. In India, it arose at a very early date and acquired great intensity. I will not attempt to give a psychological analysis of its origin, but I cannot doubt that it is a spontaneous sentiment, existing, to some slight extent, in almost all civilized human beings. Its faintest form is reluctance to imagine a revered individual—especially a person possessed of religious sanctity—engaged in lovemaking, which is felt to be scarcely compatible with the highest degree of dignity. The wish to free the spirit from bondage to the flesh has inspired many of the great religions of the world and is still powerful even among modern intellectuals.

But jealousy, I believe, has been the most potent single factor in the genesis of sexual morality. Jealousy instinctively rouses anger; and anger, rationalized, becomes moral disapproval. The purely instinctive motive must have been reinforced, at an early stage in the development of civilization, by the desire of males to be certain of paternity. Without security in this respect the patriarchal family would have been impossible, and fatherhood, with all its economic implications, could not have become the basis of social institutions. It was, accordingly, wicked to have relations with another man's wife but not even mildly reprehensible to have relations with an unmarried woman. There were excellent practical reasons for condemning the adulterer, since he caused confusion and very likely bloodshed. The siege of Troy was an extreme example of the upheavals due to disrespect for the rights of husbands, but something of the sort, though on a smaller scale, was to be expected even when the parties concerned were less exalted. There were, of course, in those days, no corresponding rights of wives; a husband had no duty to his wife, though he had the duty of respecting the property of other husbands. The old system of the patriarchal family, with an ethic based on the feelings that we have been considering, was, in a sense, successful: men, who dominated, had considerable liberty, and women, who suffered, were in such complete subjection that their unhappiness seemed not important. It is the claim of women to equality with men that has done most to make a new system necessary in the world today. Equality can be secured in two ways: either by exacting from men the same strict monogamy as was, in the past, exacted from women; or by allowing women, equally with men, a certain relaxation of the traditional code. The first of these ways was preferred by most of the pioneers of women's rights and is still preferred by the churches; but the second has many more adherents in practice, although most of them are in doubt as to the theoretical justifiability of their own behavior. And those who recognize that *some* new ethic is required find it difficult to know just what its precepts should be.

There is another source of novelty, and that is the effect of the scientific outlook in weakening the taboo on sexual knowledge. It has come to be understood that various evils—for example, venereal disease—cannot be effectively combated unless they are spoken of much more openly than was formerly thought permissible; and it has also been found that reticence and ignorance are apt to have injurious effects upon the psychology of the individual. Both sociology and psychoanalysis have led serious students to deprecate the policy of silence in regard to sexual matters, and many practical educators, from experience with children, have adopted the same position. Those who have a scientific outlook on human behavior, moreover, find it impossible to label any action as "sin"; they realize that what we do has its origin in our heredity, our education, and our environment, and that is by control of these causes, rather than by denunciation, that conduct injurious to society is to be prevented.

In seeking a new ethic of sexual behavior, therefore, we must not ourselves be dominated by the ancient irrational passions which gave rise to the old ethic, though we should recognize that they may, by accident, have led to some sound maxims, and that, since they still exist, though perhaps in a weakened form, they are still among the data of our problem. What we have to do positively is to ask ourselves what moral rules are most likely to promote human happiness, remembering always that whatever the rules may be, they are not likely to be universally observed. That is to say, we have to consider the effect which the rules will in fact have, not that which they would have if they were completely effective.

III

Let us look at the next question of knowledge on sexual subjects, which arises at the earliest age and is the least difficult and doubtful of the various problems with which we are concerned. There is no sound reason, of any sort or kind, for concealing facts when talking to children. Their questions should be answered and their curiosity satisfied in exactly the same way in regard to sex as in regard to the habits of fishes, or any other subject that interests them. There should be no sentiment, because children cannot feel as adults do and see no occasion for high-flown talk. It is a mistake to begin with the loves of the bees and the flowers; there is no point in leading up to the facts of life by devious routes. The child who is told what he wants to know and allowed to see his parents naked will have no pruriency and no obsession of a sexual kind. Boys who are brought up in official ignorance think and talk much more about sex than boys who have always heard this topic treated on a level with any other. Official ignorance and actual knowledge teach them to be deceitful and hypocritical with their elders. On the other hand, real ignorance, when it is achieved, is likely to be a source of shock and anxiety, and to make adaptation to real life difficult. All ignorance is regrettable, but ignorance on so important a matter as sex is a serious danger.

When I say that children should be told about sex, I do not mean that they should be told only the bare physiological facts; they should be told whatever they wish to know. There should be no attempt to represent adults as more virtuous than they are, or sex as occurring only in marriage. There is no excuse for deceiving children. And when, as must happen in conventional families, they find that their parents have lied, they lose confidence in them and feel justified in lying to them. There are facts which I should not obtrude upon a child, but I would tell him anything sooner than say what is not true. Virtue which is based upon a false view of the facts is not real virtue. Speaking not only from theory but from practical experience, I am convinced that complete openness on sexual subjects is the best way to prevent children from thinking about them excessively, nastily, or unwholesomely, and also the almost indispensable preliminary to an enlightened sexual morality.

Where adult sexual behavior is concerned, it is by no means easy to arrive at a rational compromise between the antagonistic considerations that have each their own validity. The fundamental difficulty is, of course, the conflict between the impulse to jealousy and the impulse to sexual variety. Neither impulse, it is true, is universal: there are those (though they are few) who are never jealous, and there are those (among men as well as among women) whose affections never wander from the chosen partner.

If either of these types could be made universal, it would be easy to devise a satisfactory code. It must be admitted, however, that either type can be made more common by conventions designed to that end.

Much ground remains to be covered by a complete sexual ethic, but I do not think we can say anything very positive until we have more experience, both of the effects of various systems and of the changes resulting from a rational education in matters of sex. It is clear that marriage, as an institution, should only interest the state because of children and should be viewed as a purely private matter so long as it is childless. It is clear, also, that, even where there are children, the state is only interested through the duties of fathers, which are chiefly financial. Where divorce is easy, as in Scandinavia, the children usually go with the mother, so that the patriarchal family tends to disappear. If, as is increasingly happening where wage earners are concerned, the state takes over the duties that have hitherto fallen upon fathers, marriage will cease to have any *raison d'être* and will probably be no longer customary except among the rich and the religious.

In the meantime, it would be well if men and women could remember, in sexual relations, in marriage, and in divorce, to practice the ordinary virtues of tolerance, kindness, truthfulness, and justice. Those who, by conventional standards, are sexually virtuous too often consider themselves thereby absolved from behaving like decent human beings. Most moralists have been so obsessed by sex that they have laid much too little emphasis on other more socially useful kinds of ethically commendable conduct.

QUESTIONS FOR REFLECTION

1. Why, according to Russell, is premarital sex almost inevitable in modern societies? Why is the same true for adultery, in his view?
2. What does Russell mean by saying, "an idle wife is no more intrinsically worthy of respect than a gigolo"? Do you agree?
3. Why does Russell think jealousy is bound to decline? What effect will this have on sexual morality? Is the effect beneficial, according to Russell?
4. Upholders of traditional morality often attacked Russell as an immoralist preaching free love. Is he?
5. In what ways is Russell's argument based on utilitarianism?
6. How might a utilitarian object to Russell's views?
7. How might a Kantian object?
8. Are there, for Russell, any distinctively sexual virtues? If so, what are they?
9. Is there, for Russell, any connection between sex and love?

THOMAS A. MAPPES

Sexual Morality and the Concept of Using Another Person

Thomas A. Mappes is professor of philosophy at Frostburg State University, Maryland. (Source: From Thomas A. Mappes and Jane S. Zembaty [eds.], Social Ethics: Morality and Social Policy *[New York: McGraw-Hill, 1992]. Notes have been omitted. Reprinted by permission of the author.)*

The central tenet of *conventional* sexual morality is that nonmarital sex is immoral. A somewhat less restrictive sexual ethic holds that *sex without love* is immoral. If neither of these positions is philosophically defensible, and I would contend that neither is, it does not follow that there are no substantive moral restrictions on human sexual interaction. *Any* human interaction, including sexual interaction, may be judged morally objectionable to the extent that it transgresses a justified moral rule or principle. The way to construct a detailed account of sexual morality, it would seem, is simply to work out the implications of relevant moral rules or principles in the area of human sexual interaction.

As one important step in the direction of such an account, I will attempt to work out the implications of an especially relevant moral principle, the principle that it is wrong for one person to use another person. However ambiguous the expression "using another person" may seem to be, there is a determinate and clearly specificable sense according to which using another person is morally objectionable. Once this morally significant sense of "using another person" is identified and explicated, the concept of using another person can play an important role in the articulation of a defensible account of sexual morality.

I. The Morally Significant Sense of "Using Another Person"

Historically, the concept of using another person is associated with the ethical system of Immanuel Kant. According to a fundamental Kantian principle, it is morally wrong for A to use B *merely as a means* (to achieve A's ends). Kant's principle does not rule out A using B as a means, only A using B *merely* as a means, that is, in a way incompatible with respect for B as a person. In the ordinary course of life, it is surely unavoidable (and morally unproblematic) that each of us in numerous ways uses others as a means to achieve our various ends. A college teacher uses students as a means to achieve his or her livelihood. A college student uses instructors as a means of gaining knowledge and skills. Such human interactions, presumably based on the voluntary participation of the respective parties, are quite compatible with the idea of respect for persons. But respect for persons entails that each of us recognize the rightful authority of other persons (as rational beings) to conduct their individual lives as they see fit. We may legitimately recruit others to participate in the satisfaction of our personal ends, but they are used merely as a means whenever we undermine the voluntary or informed character of their consent to interact with us in some desired way. A coerces B at knifepoint to hand over $200. A uses B merely as a means. If A had requested of B a gift of $200, leaving B free to determine whether or not to make the gift, A would have proceeded in a manner compatible with respect for B as a person. C deceptively rolls back the odometer of a car and thereby manipulates D's decision to buy the car. C uses D merely as a means.

On the basis of these considerations, I would suggest that the morally significant sense of "using another person" is best understood by reference to the notion of *voluntary informed consent*. More specifically, A immorally uses B if and only if A intentionally acts in a way that violates the requirement that B's involvement with A's ends be based on B's voluntary informed consent. If this account is correct, using another person (in the morally significant sense) can arise in at least two important ways: via *coercion*, which is antithetical to voluntary consent, and via *deception*, which undermines the informed character of voluntary consent. . . .

II. Deception and Sexual Morality

. . . If we presume a state of affairs in which A desires some form of sexual interaction with B, we can say that this desired form of sexual interaction with B is A's end. Thus A sexually *uses* B if and only if A intentionally acts in a way that violates the requirement that B's sexual interaction with A be based on B's voluntary informed consent. It seems clear then that A may sexually use B in at least two distinctive ways, (1) via coercion and (2) via deception. However, before proceeding to discuss deception and then the more problematic case of coercion, one important point must be made. In emphasizing the centrality of coercion and deception as mechanisms for the sexual using of another person, I have in mind sexual interaction with a fully competent adult partner. We should also want to say, I think, that sexual interaction with a child inescapably involves the sexual using of another person. Even if a child "consents" to sexual interaction, he or she is, strictly speaking, incapable of *informed* consent. It's a matter of being *incompetent* to give consent. Similarly, to the extent that a mentally retarded person is rightly considered incompetent, sexual interaction with such a person amounts to the sexual using of that person, unless someone empowered to give "proxy consent" has done so. (In certain circumstances, sexual involvement might be in the best interests of a mentally retarded person.) We can also visualize the case of an otherwise fully competent adult temporarily disordered by drugs or alcohol. To the extent that such a person is rightly regarded as temporarily incompetent, winning his or her "consent" to sexual interaction could culminate in the sexual using of that person.

There are a host of clear cases in which one person sexually uses another precisely because the former employs deception in a way that undermines the informed character of the latter's consent to sexual interaction. Consider this example. One person, A, has decided, as a matter of personal prudence based on past experience, not to become sexually involved outside the confines of a loving relationship. Another person, B, strongly desires a sexual relationship with A but does not love A. B, aware of A's unwillingness to engage in sex without love, professes love for A, thereby hoping to win A's consent to a sexual relationship. B's ploy is successful; A consents. When the smoke clears and A becomes aware of B's deception, it would be both appropriate and natural for A to complain, "I've been used."

In the same vein, here are some other examples. (1) Mr. A is aware that Ms. B will consent to sexual involvement only on the understanding that in time the two will be married. Mr. A has no intention of marrying Ms. B but says that he will. (2) Ms. C has herpes and is well aware that Mr. D will never consent to sex if he knows of her condition. When asked by Mr. D, Ms. C denies that she has herpes. (3) Mr. E knows that Ms. F will not consent to sexual intercourse in the absence of responsible birth control measures. Mr. E tells Ms. F that he has had a vasectomy, which is not the case. (4) Ms. G knows that Mr. H. would not consent to sexual involvement with a married woman. Ms. G is married but tells Mr. H that she is single. (5) Ms. I is well aware that Ms. J is interested in a stable lesbian relationship and will not consent to become sexually involved with someone who is bisexual. Ms. I tells Ms. J that she is exclusively homosexual, whereas the truth is that she is bisexual.

If one person's consent to sex is predicated on false beliefs that have been intentionally and deceptively inculcated by one's sexual partner in an effort to win the former's consent, the resulting sexual interaction involves one person sexually using another. In each of the above cases, one person explicitly *lies* to another. False information is intentionally conveyed to win consent to sexual interaction, and the end result is the sexual using of another person.

As noted earlier, however, lying is not the only form of deception. Under certain circumstances, the simple withholding of information can be considered a form of deception. Accordingly, it is possible to sexually use another person not only by (deceptively) lying about relevant facts but also by (deceptively) not disclosing relevant facts. If A has good reason to believe that B would refuse to consent to sexual interaction should B become aware of certain factual information, and if A withholds disclosure of this information in order to enhance the possibility of gaining B's consent, then, if B does consent, A sexually uses B via deception. One example will suffice. Suppose that Mr. A meets Ms. B in a singles bar. Mr. A realizes immediately that Ms. B is the sister of Ms. C, a woman that Mr. A has been sexually involved with for a long time. Mr. A, knowing that it is very unlikely that Ms. B will consent to sexual interaction if she becomes aware of Mr. A's involvement with her sister, decides not to disclose this information. If Ms. B eventually consents to sexual interaction, since her consent is the product of Mr. A's deception, it is rightly thought that she has been sexually used by him.

III. Coercion and Sexual Morality

We have considered the case of deception. The present task is to consider the more difficult case of coercion. Whereas deception functions to undermine the *informed* character of voluntary consent (to sexual interaction), coercion either obliterates consent entirely (the case of occurrent coercion) or undermines the voluntariness of consent (the case of dispositional coercion).

Forcible rape is the most conspicuous, and most brutal, way of sexually using another person via coercion. Forcible rape may involve either occurrent coercion or dispositional coercion. A man who rapes a woman by the employment of sheer physical force, by simply overpowering her, employs occurrent coercion. There is literally no sexual *interaction* in such a case; only the rapist performs an action. In no sense does the woman consent to or participate in sexual activity. She has no choice in what takes place, or rather, physical force results in her choice being simply beside the point. The employment of occurrent coercion for the purpose of rape "objectifies" the victim in the strongest sense of that term. She is treated like a physical object. One does not interact with physical objects; one acts upon them. In a perfectly ordinary (not the morally significant) sense of the term, we "use" physical objects. But when the victim of rape is treated as if she were a physical object, there we have one of the most vivid examples of the immoral using of another person.

Frequently, forcible rape involves not occurrent coercion (or not *only* occurrent coercion) but dispositional coercion. In dispositional coercion, the relevant factor is not physical force but the threat of harm. The rapist threatens his victim with immediate and serious bodily harm. For example, a man threatens to kill or beat a woman if she resists his sexual demands. She "consents," that is, she submits to his demands. He may demand only passive participation (simply not struggling against him) or he may demand some measure of active participation. Rape that employs dispositional coercion is surely just as wrong as rape that employs occurrent coercion, but there is a notable difference in the mechanism by which the rapist uses his victim in the two cases. With occurrent coercion, the victim's consent is entirely bypassed. With dispositional coercion, the victim's consent is not bypassed. It is coerced. Dispositional coercion undermines the *voluntariness* of consent. The rapist, by employing the threat of immediate and serious bodily harm, may succeed in bending the victim's will. He may gain the victim's "consent." But he uses another person precisely because consent is coerced.

The relevance of occurrent coercion is limited to the case of forcible rape. Dispositional coercion, a notion that also plays an indispensable role in an overall account of forcible rape, now becomes our central concern. Although the threat of immediate and serious bodily harm stands out as the most brutal way of coercing consent to sexual interaction, we must not neglect the employment of other kinds of threats to this same end. There are numerous ways in which one person can effectively harm, and thus effectively threaten, another. Accordingly, for example, consent to sexual interaction might be coerced by threatening to damage someone's reputation. If a person consents to sexual interaction to avoid a threatened harm, then that person has been sexually used (via dispositional coercion). In the face of a threat, of course, it remains possible that a person will refuse to comply with another's sexual demands. It is probably best to describe this sort of situation as a case not of coercion, which entails the *successful* use of threats to gain compliance, but of *attempted* coercion. Of course, the moral fault of an individual emerges with the *attempt* to coerce. A person who attempts murder is morally blameworthy even if the attempt fails. The same is true for someone who fails in an effort to coerce consent to sexual interaction.

Consider now each of the following cases:

Case 1. Mr. Supervisor makes a series of increasingly less subtle sexual overtures to Ms. Employee. These advances are consistently and firmly rejected by Ms. Employee. Eventually, Mr. Supervisor makes it clear that the granting of "sexual favors" is a condition of her continued employment.

Case 2. Ms. Debtor borrowed a substantial sum of money from Mr. Creditor, on the understanding that she would pay it back within one year. In the meantime, Ms. Debtor has become sexually attracted to Mr. Creditor, but he does not share her interest. At the end of the one-year period, Mr. Creditor asks Ms. Debtor to return the money. She says she will be happy to return the money so long as he consents to sexual interaction with her.

Case 3. Mr. Theatregoer has two tickets to the most talked-about play of the season. He is introduced to a woman whom he finds sexually attractive and who shares his interest in the theater. In the course of their conversation, she expresses disappointment that the play everyone is talking about is sold out; she would love to see it. At this point, Mr. Theatregoer suggests that she be his guest at the theater. "Oh, by the way," he says, "I always expect sex from my dates."

Case 4. Ms. Jetsetter is planning a trip to Europe. She has been trying for some time to develop a sexual relationship with a man who has shown little interest in her. She knows, however, that he has always wanted to go to Europe and that it is only lack of money that has deterred him. Ms. Jetsetter proposes that he come along as her traveling companion, all expenses paid, on the express understanding that sex is part of the arrangement.

Cases 1 and 2 involve attempts to sexually use another person whereas cases 3 and 4 do not. To see why this is so, it is essential to introduce a distinction between two kinds of proposals, viz., the distinction between *threats* and *offers*. The logical form of a threat differs from the logical form of an offer in the following way. Threat: "If you *do not* do what I am proposing you do, I will bring about an *undesirable consequence* for you." Offer: "If you *do* what I am proposing you do, I will bring about a *desirable consequence* for you." The person who makes a threat attempts to gain compliance by attaching an undesirable consequence to the alternative of noncompliance. This person attempts to *coerce* consent. The person who makes an offer attempts to gain compliance by attaching a desirable consequence to the alternative of compliance. This person attempts not to coerce but to *induce* consent.

Since threats are morally problematic in a way that offers are not, it is not uncommon for threats to be advanced in the language of offers. Threats are represented as if they were offers. An armed assailant might say, "I'm going to make you an *offer*. If you give me your money, I will allow you to go on living." Though this proposal on the surface has the logical form of an offer, it is in reality a threat. The underlying sense of the proposal is this: "If you do not give me your money, I will kill you." If, in a given case, it is initially unclear whether a certain proposal is to count as a threat or an offer, ask the following question. Does the proposal in question have the effect of making a person *worse off upon noncompliance*? The recipient of an offer, upon noncompliance, *is not worse off* than he or she was before the offer. In contrast, the recipient of a threat, upon noncompliance, *is worse off* than he or she was before the threat. Since the "offer" of our armed assailant has the effect, upon noncompliance, of rendering its recipient worse off (relative to the preproposal situation of the recipient), the recipient is faced with a threat, not an offer.

The most obvious way for a coercer to attach an undesirable consequence to the path of noncompliance is by threatening to render the victim of coercion materially worse off than he or she has heretofore been. Thus a person is threatened with loss of life, bodily injury, damage to property, damage to reputation, etc. It is important to realize, however, that a person can also be effectively coerced by being threatened with the withholding of something (in some cases, what we would call a "benefit") to which the person is entitled. Suppose that A is mired in quicksand and is slowly but surely approaching death. When B happens along, A cries out to B for assistance. All B need do is throw A a rope. B is quite willing to accommodate A, "provided you pay me $100,000 over the next ten years." Is B making A an offer? Hardly! B, we must presume, stands under a moral obligation to come to the aid of a person in serious distress, at least when such assistance entails no significant risk, sacrifice of time, etc. A is entitled to B's assistance. Thus, in reality, B attaches an undesirable consequence to A's noncompliance with the proposal that A pay B $100,000. A is undoubtedly better off that B has happened along, but A is not rendered better off *by B's proposal*. Before B's proposal, A legitimately expected assistance from B, "no strings attached." In attaching a very unwelcome string, B's proposal effectively renders A worse off. What B proposes, then, is not an offer of assistance. Rather, B threatens A with the withholding of something (assistance) that A is entitled to have from B.

Since threats have the effect of rendering a person worse off upon noncompliance, it is ordinarily the case that a person does not welcome (indeed, despises) them. Offers, on the other hand, are ordinarily welcome to a person. Since an offer provides no penalty for noncompliance with a proposal but only an inducement for compliance, there is *in principle* only potential advantage in being confronted with an offer. In real life, of course, there are numerous reasons why a person may be less than enthusiastic about being presented with an offer. Enduring the presentation of trivial offers does not warrant the necessary time and energy expenditures. Offers can be both annoying and offensive; certainly this is true of some sexual offers. A person might also be unsettled by an offer that confronts him or her with a difficult decision. All this, however, is compatible with the fact that an offer is fundamentally welcome to a rational person in the sense that the *content* of an offer necessarily widens the field of opportunity and thus provides, in principle, only potential advantage.

With the distinction between threats and offers clearly in view, it now becomes clear why cases 1 and 2 do indeed involve attempts to sexually use another person whereas cases 3 and 4 do not. Cases 1 and 2 embody threats, whereas cases 3 and 4 embody offers. In case 1, Mr. Supervisor proposes sexual interaction with Ms. Employee and, in an effort to gain compliance, threatens her with the loss of her job. Mr. Supervisor thereby attaches an undesirable consequence to one of Ms. Employee's alternatives, the path of noncompliance. Typical of the threat situation, Mr. Supervisor's proposal has the effect of rendering Ms. Employee worse off upon noncompliance. Mr. Supervisor is attempting via (dispositional) coercion to sexually use Ms. Employee. The situation in case 2 is similar. Ms. Debtor, as *she* might be inclined to say, "offers" to pay Mr. Creditor the money she owes him *if* he consents to sexual interaction with her. In reality, Ms. Debtor is threatening Mr. Creditor, attempting to coerce his consent to sexual interaction, attempting to sexually use him. Though Mr. Creditor is not now in possession of the money Ms. Debtor owes him, he is *entitled* to receive it from her at this time. She threatens to deprive him of something to which he is entitled. Clearly, her proposal has the effect of rendering him worse off upon noncompliance. Before her proposal, he had the legitimate expectation, "no strings attached," of receiving the money in question.

Cases 3 and 4 embody offers; neither involves an attempt to sexually use another person. Mr. Theatregoer simply provides an inducement for the woman he has just met to accept his proposal of sexual interaction. He offers her the opportunity to see the play that everyone is talking about. In attaching a desirable consequence to the alternative of compliance, Mr. Theatregoer in no way threatens or attempts to coerce his potential companion. Typical of the offer situation, his proposal does not have the effect of rendering her worse off upon noncompliance. She now has a new opportunity; if she chooses to forgo this opportunity, she is no worse off. The situation in case 4 is similar. Ms. Jetsetter provides an inducement for a man that she is interested in to accept her proposal of sexual involvement. She offers him the opportunity to see Europe, without expense, as her traveling companion. Before Ms. Jetsetter's proposal, he had no prospect of a European trip. If he chooses to reject her proposal, he is no worse off than he has heretofore been. Ms. Jetsetter's proposal embodies an offer, not a threat. She cannot be accused of attempting to sexually use her potential traveling companion.

Consider now two further cases, 5 and 6, each of which develops in the following way. Professor Highstatus, a man of high academic accomplishment, is sexually attracted to a student in one of his classes. He is very anxious to secure her consent to sexual interaction. Ms. Student, confused and unsettled by his sexual advances, has begun to practice "avoidance behavior." To the extent that it is possible, she goes out of her way to avoid him.

Case 5. Professor Highstatus tells Ms. Student that, though her work is such as to entitle her to a grade of B in the class, she will be assigned a D unless she consents to sexual interaction.

Case 6. Professor Highstatus tells Ms. Student that, though her work is such as to entitle her to a grade of B, she will be assigned an A if she consents to sexual interaction.

It is clear that case 5 involves an attempt to sexually use another person. Case 6, however, at least at face value, does not. In case 5, Professor Highstatus *threatens* to deprive Ms. Student of the grade she deserves. In case 6, he *offers* to assign her a grade that is higher than she deserves. In case 5, Ms. Student would be worse off upon noncompliance with Professor Highstatus's proposal. In case 6, she would not be worse off upon noncompliance with his proposal. In saying that case 6 does not involve an attempt to sexually use another person, it is not being asserted that Professor Highstatus is acting in a morally legitimate fashion. In offering a student a higher grade than she deserves, he is guilty of abusing his institutional authority. He is under an obligation to assign the grades that students earn, as defined by the relevant course standards. In case 6, Professor Highstatus is undoubtedly acting in a morally reprehensible way, but in contrast to case 5, where it is fair to say that he both abuses his institutional authority *and* attempts to sexually use another person, we can plausibly say that in case 6 his moral failure is limited to abuse of his institutional authority.

There remains, however, a suspicion that case 6 might after all embody an attempt to sexually use another person. There is no question that the literal content of what Professor Highstatus conveys to Ms. Student has the logical form of an offer and not a threat. Still, is it not the case that Ms. Student may very well feel threatened? Professor Highstatus, in an effort to secure consent to sexual interaction, has announced that he will assign Ms. Student a higher grade than she deserves. Can she really turn him down without substantial risk? Is he not likely to retaliate? If she spurns him, will he not lower her grade or otherwise make it harder for her to succeed in her academic program? He does, after all, have power over her. Will he use it to her detriment? Surely he is not above abusing his institutional authority to achieve his ends; this much is abundantly clear from his willingness to assign a grade higher than a student deserves.

Is Professor Highstatus naive to the threat that Ms. Student may find implicit in the situation? Perhaps. In such a case, if Ms. Student reluctantly consents to sexual interaction, we may be inclined to say that he has *unwittingly* used her. More likely, Professor High-status is well aware of the way in which Ms. Student will perceive his proposal. He knows that threats need not be verbally expressed. Indeed, it may even be the case that he consciously exploits his underground reputation. "Everyone knows what happens to the women who reject Professor Highstatus's little offers." To the extent, then, that Professor Highstatus intends to convey a threat in case 6, he is attempting via coercion to sexually use another person.

Many researchers "have pointed out the fact that the possibility of sanctions for noncooperation is implicit in all sexual advances across authority lines, as between teacher and student." I do not think that this consideration should lead us to the conclusion that a person with an academic appointment is obliged in all circumstances to refrain from attempting to initiate sexual involvement with one of his or her students. Still, since even "good faith" sexual advances may be ambiguous in the eyes of a student, it is an interesting question what precautions an instructor must take to avoid unwittingly coercing a student to consent to sexual interaction.

Much of what has been said about the professor/student relationship in an academic setting can be applied as well to the supervisor/subordinate relationship in an employment setting. A manager who functions within an organizational structure is required to evaluate fairly his or her subordinates according to relevant corporate or institutional standards. An unscrupulous manager, willing to abuse his or her institutional authority in an effort to win the consent of a subordinate to sexual interaction, can advance threats and/or offers related to the managerial task of employee evaluation. An employee whose job performance is entirely satisfactory can be threatened with an unsatisfactory performance rating, perhaps leading to termination. An employee whose job performance is excellent can be threatened with an unfair evaluation, designed to bar the employee from recognition, merit pay, consideration for promotion, etc. Such threats, when made in an effort to coerce employee consent to sexual interaction, clearly embody the attempt to sexually use another person. On the other hand, the manager who (abusing his or her institutional authority) offers to provide an employee with an inflated evaluation as an inducement for consent to sexual interaction does not, at face value, attempt to sexually use another person. Of course, all of the qualifications introduced in the discussion of case 6 above are applicable here as well.

QUESTIONS FOR REFLECTION

1. How does Mappes interpret Kant's prohibition on using another person as a means only?
2. Can you think of cases where someone gives voluntary informed consent but is nevertheless in some sense used?
3. Conversely, can you think of cases in which someone is treated as an end without voluntary informed consent?
4. How does Mappes distinguish threats from offers? What, in his view, is the moral significance of the distinction? Do you agree?
5. What implications does Mappes's view have for sexual harassment?
6. How might a utilitarian criticize Mappes's argument?
7. Apply Mappes's view to prostitution. Do you agree with the result?
8. Kant would surely take prostitution as a paradigm case of using another person merely as a means. Where does Mappes's understanding of Kant diverge from Kant's understanding of Kant?
9. Are there any distinctively sexual virtues, according to Mappes?
10. Apply Kant's formula of universal law directly to a case of casual sex, using the maxim "I will, when not already in a sexual relationship, have sex with willing partners with whom there is a strong mutual attraction." Could a rational being will that maxim as a universal law?
11. What would Mappes say about "open" relationships, in which people allow each other to have sex with other people? Do you agree?
12. Apply Mappes's reasoning to polygamy.
13. Is there, for Mappes, any connection between sex and love?
14. How might a Kantian argue for the view that sex is morally acceptable only in the context of a loving relationship?

ROGER SCRUTON

from *Sexual Desire*

Roger Scruton, British writer and philosopher, is the author of The Aesthetics of Architecture, Kant, The Meaning of Conservatism, Art and Imagination, The Politics of Culture, Untimely Tracts, The Aesthetics of Music, *and many other books on philosophy, politics, and art. (Source: Roger Scruton,* Sexual Desire *[London: Weidenfeld and Nicolson, 1986]. Notes have been omitted.*

Sexual Morality

We must now attempt to apply the Aristotelian strategy [here] and ask whether there is such a thing as sexual virtue, and, if so, what is it, and how is it acquired? Clearly, sexual desire, which is an interpersonal attitude with the most far-reaching consequences for those who are joined by it, cannot be morally neutral. On the contrary, it is in the experience of sexual desire that we are most vividly conscious of the distinction between virtuous and vicious impulses, and most vividly aware that, in the choice between them, our happiness is at stake.

The Aristotelian strategy enjoins us to ignore the actual conditions of any particular person's life, and to look only at the permanent features of human nature. We know that people feel sexual desire; that they feel erotic love, which may grow from desire; that they may avoid both these feelings, by dissipation or self-restraint. Is there anything to be said about desire, other than that it falls within the general scope of the virtue of temperance, which enjoins us to desire only what reason approves?

The first, and most important, observation to be made is that the capacity for love in general, and for erotic love in particular, is a virtue. . . . [E]rotic love involves an element of mutual self-enhancement; it generates a sense of the irreplaceable value, both of the other and of the self, and of the activities which bind them. To receive and to give this love is to achieve something of incomparable value in the process of self fulfilment. It is to gain the most powerful of all interpersonal *guarantees*; in erotic love the subject becomes conscious of the full reality of his personal existence, not only in his own eyes, but in the eyes of another. Everything that he is and values gains sustenance from his love, and every project receives a meaning beyond the moment. All that exists for us as mere hope and hypothesis—the attachment to life and to the body—achieves under the rule of *erōs* the aspect of a radiant certainty. Unlike the cold glances of approval, admiration and pride, the glance of love sees value precisely in that which is the source of anxiety and doubt: in the merely contingent, merely "empirical," existence of the flesh, the existence which we did not choose, but to which we are condemned. It is the answer to man's fallen condition—to his *Geworfenheit.**

To receive erotic love, however, a person must be able to give it: or if he cannot, the love of others will be a torment to him, seeking from him that which he

*Literally, "thrownness." German philosopher Martin Heidegger used this term for the human condition of being thrown into the midst of possibilities not of our own making.—Ed.

cannot provide, and directing against him the fury of a disappointed right. It is therefore unquestionable that we have reason to acquire the capacity for erotic love, and, if this means bending our sexual impulses in a certain direction, that will be the direction of sexual virtue. Indeed, . . . the development of the sexual impulse towards love may be impeded: there are sexual habits which are vicious, precisely in neutralising the capacity for love. The first thing that can be said, therefore, is that we all have reason to avoid those habits and to educate our children not to possess them.

Here it may be objected that not every love is happy, that there are many—Anna Karenina, for example, or Phaedra—whose capacity for love was the cause of their downfall. But we must remind ourselves of the Aristotelian strategy. In establishing that courage or wisdom is a virtue, the Aristotelian does not argue that the possession of these virtues is in every particular circumstance bound to be advantageous. . . .

. . . We wish to know, in advance of any particular experience, which dispositions a person must have if he is successfully to express himself in sexual desire and to be fulfilled in his sexual endeavours. Love is the fulfilment of desire, and therefore love is its *telos*. A life of celibacy may also be fulfilled; but, assuming the general truth that most of us have a powerful, and perhaps overwhelming, urge to make love, it is in our interests to ensure that love—and not some other thing—is made.

Love, I have argued, is prone to jealousy, and the object of jealousy is defined by the thought of the beloved's desire. Because jealousy is one of the greatest of psychical catastrophes, involving the possible ruin of both partners, a morality based in the need for erotic love must forestall and eliminate jealousy. It is in the deepest human interest, therefore, that we form the habit of fidelity. This habit is natural and normal; but it is also easily broken, and the temptation to break it is contained in desire itself—in the element of generality which tempts us always to experiment, to verify, to detach ourselves from that which is too familiar in the interest of excitement and risk. Virtuous desire is faithful; but virtuous desire is also an artefact, made possible by a process of moral education which we do not, in truth, understand in its complexity.

If that observation is correct, a whole section of traditional sexual morality must be upheld. The fulfillment of sexual desire defines the nature of desire: *to telos phuseis estin*. And the nature of desire gives us our standard of normality. There are enormous varieties of human sexual conduct, and of "commonsense" morality: some societies permit or encourage polygamy, others look with indifference upon premarital intercourse, or regard marriage itself as no more than an episode in a relation that pre-exists and perhaps survives it. But no society, and no "commonsense" morality—not even, it seems, the morality of Samoa—looks with favour upon promiscuity or infidelity, unless influenced by a doctrine of "emancipation" or "liberation" which is dependent for its sense upon the very conventions which it defies. Whatever the institutional forms of human sexual union, and whatever the range of permitted partners, sexual desire is itself inherently "nuptial"; it involves concentration upon the embodied existence of the other, leading through tenderness to the "vow" of erotic love. It is a telling observation that the civilisation which has most tolerated the institution of polygamy—the Islamic—has also, in its erotic literature, produced what are perhaps the intensest and most poignant celebrations of monogamous love, precisely through the attempt to capture, not the institution of marriage, but the human datum of desire.

The nuptiality of desire suggests, in its turn, a natural history of desire: a principle of development which defines the "normal course" of sexual education. "Sexual maturity" involves incorporating the sexual impulse into the personality, and so making sexual desire into an expression of the subject himself, even though it is, in the heat of action, a force which also overcomes him. If the Aristotelian approach to these things is as plausible as I think it is, the virtuous habit will also have the character of a "mean": it will involve the disposition to desire what is desirable, despite the competing impulses of animal lust (in which the intentionality of desire may be demolished) and timorous frigidity (in which the sexual impulse is impeded altogether). Education is directed towards the special kind of temperance which shows itself, sometimes as chastity, sometimes as fidelity, sometimes as passionate desire, according to the "right judgment" of the subject. In wanting what is judged to be desirable, the virtuous person wants what may also be loved, and what may therefore be obtained without hurt or humiliation.

Virtue is a matter of degree, rarely attained in its completion, but always admired. Because traditional sexual education has pursued sexual virtue, it is worthwhile summarising its most important features, in order to see the power of the idea that underlies and justifies it.

The most important feature of traditional sexual education is summarised in anthropological language as the "ethic of pollution and taboo." The child was taught to regard his body as sacred, and as subject to pollution by misperception or misuse. The sense of pollution is by no means a trivial side-effect of the "bad sexual encounter": it may involve a penetrating disgust, at oneself, one's body and one's situation, such as is experienced by the victim of rape. Those sentiments—which arise from our "fear of the obscene"—express the tension contained within the experience of embodiment. At any moment we can become "mere body," the self driven from its incarnation, and its habitation ransacked. The most important root idea of personal morality is that I am *in* my body, not (to borrow Descartes' image) as a pilot in a ship, but as an incarnate self. My body is identical with me, and sexual purity is the precious guarantee of this.

Sexual purity does not forbid desire: it simply ensures the status of desire as an interpersonal feeling. The child who learns "dirty habits" detaches his sex from himself, sets it outside himself as something curious and alien. His fascinated enslavement to the body is also a withering of desire, a scattering of erotic energy and a loss of union with the other. Sexual purity sustains the *subject* of desire, making him present as a self in the very act which overcomes him. . . .

The child was traditionally brought up to achieve sexual fulfilment only *through* chastity, which is the condition which surrounds him on his first entering the adult world—the world of commitments and obligations. At the same time, he was encouraged to ponder certain "ideal objects" of desire. These, presented to him under the aspect of an idealised physical beauty, were never *merely* beautiful, but also endowed with the moral attributes that fitted them for love. This dual inculcation of "pure" habits and "ideal" love might seem, on the face of it, to be unworthy of the name of education. Is it not, rather, like the mere *training* of a horse or a dog, which arbitrarily forbids some things and fosters others, without offering the first hint of a reason why? And is it not the distinguishing mark of education that it engages with the rational nature of its recipient, and does not merely mould him indifferently to his own understanding of the process? Why, in short, is this moral education, rather than a transference into the sexual sphere—as Freud would have it—of those same processes of interdiction that train us to defecate, not in our nappies, but in a porcelain pot?

The answer is clear. The cult of innocence is an attempt to *generate* rational conduct, by incorporating the sexual impulse into the self-activity of the subject. It is an attempt to impede the impulse, until such a time as it may attach itself to the interpersonal project that leads to its fulfilment: the project of union with another person, who is wanted not merely for his body, but for the person who *is* this body. Innocence is the disposition to avoid sexual encounter, except with the person whom one may fully desire. Children who have lost their innocence have acquired the habit of gratification through the body alone, in a state of partial or truncated desire. Their gratification is detached from the conditions of personal fulfilment and wanders from object to object with no settled tendency to attach itself to any, pursued all the while by a sense of the body's obscene dominion. "Debauching of the innocent" was traditionally regarded as a most serious offence, and one that offered genuine *harm* to the victim. The harm in question was not physical, but moral: the undermining of the process which prepares the child to enter the world of *erōs*. (Thus Nabokov's Lolita, who passes with such rapidity from childish provocativeness to a knowing interest in the sexual act, finds, in the end, a marriage devoid of passion, and dies without knowledge of desire.)

The personal and the sexual can become divorced in many ways. The task of sexual morality is to unite them, to sustain thereby the intentionality of desire, and to prepare the individual for erotic love. Sexual morality is the morality of embodiment: the posture which strives to unite us with our bodies, precisely in those situations when our bodies are foremost in our thoughts. Without such a morality the human world is subject to a dangerous divide, a gulf between self and body, at the verge of which all our attempts at personal union falter and withdraw. Hence the prime focus of sexual morality is not the attitude to others, but the attitude to one's own body and its uses. Its aim is to safeguard the integrity of our embodiment. Only on that condition, it is thought, can we inculcate either innocence in the young or fidelity in the adult. . . .

Traditional sexual education was, despite its exaggerations and imbecilities, truer to human nature than the libertarian culture which has succeeded it. Through considering its wisdom and its shortcomings, we may understand how to resuscitate an idea of sexual virtue, in accordance with the broad requirements of the Aristotelian argument that I have, in this chapter, been presenting. The ideal of virtue remains one of "sexual integrity": of a sexuality that is entirely integrated into the life of personal affection, and in which the self and its responsibility are centrally involved and indissolubly linked to the pleasures and passions of the body. . . .

QUESTIONS FOR REFLECTION

1. What, according to Scruton, are the advantages of an Aristotelian approach to sexual ethics?
2. What is chastity, and why is it an important virtue, according to Scruton?
3. What is sexual integrity? How does it justify traditional sexual morality?
4. How might Scruton respond to a charge of cultural relativity, based on the thesis that what behavior promotes or retards the capacity for love depends on social norms governing the meaning of that behavior?
5. Imagine a debate between Russell and Scruton. What is the most important criticism that each might make against the other?
6. Imagine a debate between Mappes and Scruton. What is the most important criticism that each might make against the other?
7. The virtuous person, Aristotle says, will do the right thing, in the right circumstances, with the right person, and for the right reason. But this provides little guidance toward determining what things, circumstances, reasons, and so on are right. Is Scruton's view similarly unhelpful? Why or why not?
8. Ethical theories, ideally, not only help agents make decisions but help them justify those decisions. Does Scruton offer agents justification for engaging in or declining to engage in sexual behavior?

SEXUAL ORIENTATION AND GAY MARRIAGE

Attitudes about homosexuality have changed dramatically over the past several decades. What was once whispered about as "the love that dares not speak its name" is now celebrated in Gay Pride parades. Debates about laws against sodomy have given way to debates about gay marriage.

In part, these issues concern equality. Is it ever legitimate for the law to favor heterosexuals over homosexuals, or vice versa? Kant's categorical imperative tells us that we must treat similar cases similarly, acting only on the basis of rules we are willing to apply universally. So, the law can treat people with different sexual orientations differently only if that difference is morally relevant to the consideration in question. Advocates of equality maintain that sexual orientation is rarely, if ever, morally relevant to governmental decisions and rules.

These are also questions of liberty. Sexual relationships between consenting, competent adults, from the perspective of Mill's harm principle, are none of the government's business. They fall into the class of self-regarding actions that constitutes the realm of liberty surrounding each of us as individuals. So, government may not interfere with a person's freedom in regard to sexual orientation or behavior except to prevent harm to others. That implies that government should not restrict or discourage any particular sexual orientation or living arrangement between consenting, competent adults.

Those who question the harm principle, in contrast, worry that sexual roles and especially the institution of marriage constitute a crucial and only partially understood part of society's foundation. Changing them may have sweeping, unintended, and unforeseen effects. Marriage is, for example, society's unit for raising children as well as for allowing couples to seek satisfaction, happiness, and love. Strong bonds between spouses are important to individuals and to society at large. Anything that affects the institution of marriage and threatens the strength of those bonds may have dramatic effects on others, even though such effects might not become clear for generations.

In *Bowers* v. *Hardwick*, the Supreme Court upheld the constitutionality of laws against sodomy. There is no general right to liberty, the Court held; any such right would lead to anarchy. It would make law itself impossible. The liberties the law should protect are those implicit in the concept of ordered liberty, or, as that has been elaborated, deeply rooted in our history and traditions. Since our history and traditions are unaccepting of homosexuality, the Court decided, it does not fall within the realm of liberty that ought to be protected by the law.

Just seventeen years later, in *Lawrence* v. *Texas*, the Court reversed itself, striking down laws against sodomy as unconstitutional. The Court drew the boundaries of liberty more broadly than it had earlier, maintaining that people should be free to make fundamental choices concerning their conduct in the privacy of their own homes as long as no one is injured and no institutions are abused.

In *Goodridge* v. *Department of Public Health*, the Massachusetts Supreme Court extended this reasoning to the question of gay marriage. The majority decided that respect for the dignity and equality of all requires the state to sanction gay as well as heterosexual marriage. Restricting marriage to heterosexuals not only discriminates against others but also is an affront to their dignity, given the centrality of marriage to a person's self-definition. Indeed, the majority finds no rational basis for such a restriction. The dissent argues that restricting marriage to heterosexuals violates no rights and that there is a conceivable rational basis for it.

Stanley Kurtz tackles what he describes as the libertarian argument in favor of gay marriage, resting on something like Mill's harm principle. Why should the state regulate or restrict any form of self-regarding behavior? Kurtz rejects the libertarian position, arguing that shared moral codes are vital to society. Drawing an analogy to incest, Kurtz points out that there are connections, even if indirect, between supposedly self-regarding behavior and the lives of others. The prohibition of incest helps to reinforce a taboo that might be violated more often without it. The taboo, moreover, is important in keeping young people from being violated by those with great power over them. Kurtz speculates that restricting marriage to heterosexuals reinforces a similar taboo—in this case, against adultery—which recognition of gay marriage would undermine.

Finally, Andrew Koppelman and Maggie Gallagher debate the ethics of same-sex marriage, focusing on empirical issues about the effects of changing our society's concept of marriage.

JUSTICE BYRON WHITE

Majority Opinion in Bowers *v.* Hardwick *(1986)*

(*Source:* Bowers, Attorney General of Georgia *v.* Hardwick et al, *478 U.S. 186. Most legal references have been omitted.*)

Justice White delivered the opinion of the Court.

In August 1982, respondent Hardwick (hereafter respondent) was charged with violating the Georgia statute criminalizing sodomy by committing that act with another adult male in the bedroom of respondent's home. After a preliminary hearing, the District Attorney decided not to present the matter to the grand jury unless further evidence developed.

Respondent then brought suit in the Federal District Court, challenging the constitutionality of the statute insofar as it criminalized consensual sodomy. He asserted that he was a practicing homosexual, that the Georgia sodomy statute, as administered by the defendants, placed him in imminent danger of arrest, and that the statute for several reasons violates the Federal Constitution. . . .

This case does not require a judgment on whether laws against sodomy between consenting adults in general, or between homosexuals in particular, are wise or desirable. It raises no question about the right or propriety of state legislative decisions to repeal their laws that criminalize homosexual sodomy, or of state-court decisions invalidating those laws on state constitutional grounds. The issue presented is whether the Federal Constitution confers a fundamental right upon homosexuals to engage in sodomy and hence invalidates the laws of the many States that still make such conduct illegal and have done so for a very long time. The case also calls for some judgment about the limits of the Court's role in carrying out its constitutional mandate.

We first register our disagreement with the Court of Appeals and with respondent that the Court's prior cases have construed the Constitution to confer a right of privacy that extends to homosexual sodomy and for all intents and purposes have decided this case. . . . We think it evident that none of the rights announced in those cases bears any resemblance to the claimed constitutional right of homosexuals to engage in acts of sodomy that is asserted in this case. No connection between family, marriage, or procreation on the one hand and homosexual activity on the other has been demonstrated, either by the Court of Appeals or by respondent. Moreover, any claim that these cases nevertheless stand for the proposition that any kind of private sexual conduct between consenting adults is constitutionally insulated from state proscription is unsupportable. Indeed, the Court's opinion in *Carey* twice asserted that the privacy right, which the *Griswold* line of cases found to be one of the protections provided by the Due Process Clause, did not reach so far.

Precedent aside, however, respondent would have us announce, as the Court of Appeals did, a fundamental right to engage in homosexual sodomy. This we are quite unwilling to do. It is true that despite the language of the Due Process Clauses of the Fifth and Fourteenth Amendments, which appears to focus only on the processes by which life, liberty, or property is taken, the cases are legion in which those Clauses have been interpreted to have substantive content, subsuming rights that to a great extent are immune from federal or state regulation or proscription. Among such cases are those recognizing rights that have little or no textual support in the constitutional language. . . .

Striving to assure itself and the public that announcing rights not readily identifiable in the Constitution's text involves much more than the imposition of the Justices' own choice of values on the States and the Federal Government, the Court has sought to identify the nature of the rights qualifying for heightened judicial protection. In *Palko* v. *Connecticut* (1937), it was said that this category includes those fundamental liberties that are "implicit in the concept of ordered liberty," such that "neither liberty nor justice would exist if [they] were sacrificed." A different description of fundamental liberties appeared in *Moore* v. *East Cleveland* (1977) (opinion of Powell, J.), where they are characterized as those liberties that are "deeply rooted in this Nation's history and tradition."

It is obvious to us that neither of these formulations would extend a fundamental right to homosexuals to engage in acts of consensual sodomy. Proscriptions against that conduct have ancient roots. Sodomy was a criminal offense at common law and was forbidden by the laws of the original 13 States when they ratified the Bill of Rights. In 1868, when the Fourteenth Amendment was ratified, all but 5 of the 37 States in the Union had criminal sodomy laws. In fact, until 1961, all 50 States outlawed sodomy, and today, 24 States and the District of Columbia continue to provide criminal penalties for sodomy performed in private and between consenting adults. Against this background, to claim that a right to engage in such conduct is "deeply rooted in this Nation's history and tradition" or "implicit in the concept of ordered liberty" is, at best, facetious.

Nor are we inclined to take a more expansive view of our authority to discover new fundamental rights imbedded in the Due Process Clause. The Court is most vulnerable and comes nearest to illegitimacy when it deals with judge-made constitutional law having little or no cognizable roots in the language or design of the Constitution. That this is so was painfully demonstrated by the face-off between the Executive and the Court in the 1930's, which resulted in the repudiation of much of the substantive gloss that the Court had placed on the Due Process Clauses of the Fifth and Fourteenth Amendments. There should be, therefore, great resistance to expand the substantive reach of those Clauses, particularly if it requires redefining the category of rights deemed to be fundamental. Otherwise, the Judiciary necessarily takes to itself further authority to govern the country without express constitutional authority. The claimed right pressed on us today falls [far] short of overcoming this resistance.

Respondent, however, asserts that the result should be different where the homosexual conduct occurs in the privacy of the home. He relies on *Stanley* v. *Georgia* (1969), where the Court held that the First Amendment prevents conviction for possessing and reading obscene material in the privacy of one's home: "If the First Amendment means anything, it means that a State has no business telling a man, sitting alone in his house, what books he may read or what films he may watch."

Stanley did protect conduct that would not have been protected outside the home, and it partially prevented the enforcement of state obscenity laws; but the decision was firmly grounded in the First Amendment. The right pressed upon us here has no similar support in the text of the Constitution, and it does not qualify for recognition under the prevailing principles for construing the Fourteenth Amendment. Its limits are also difficult to discern. Plainly enough, otherwise illegal conduct is not always immunized whenever it occurs in the home. Victimless crimes, such as the possession and use of illegal drugs, do not escape the law where they are committed at home. *Stanley* itself recognized that its holding offered no protection for the possession in the home of drugs, firearms, or stolen goods. And if respondent's submission is limited to the voluntary sexual conduct between consenting adults, it would be difficult, except by fiat, to limit the claimed right to homosexual conduct while leaving exposed to prosecution adultery, incest, and other sexual crimes even though they are committed in the home. We are unwilling to start down that road.

Even if the conduct at issue here is not a fundamental right, respondent asserts that there must be a rational basis for the law and that there is none in this case other than the presumed belief of a majority of the electorate in Georgia that homosexual sodomy is immoral and unacceptable. This is said to be an inadequate rationale to support the law. The law, however, is constantly based on notions of morality, and if all laws representing essentially moral choices are to be invalidated under the Due Process Clause, the courts will be very busy indeed. Even respondent makes no such claim, but insists that majority sentiments about the morality of homosexuality should be declared inadequate. We do not agree, and are unpersuaded that the sodomy laws of some 25 States should be invalidated on this basis.

Accordingly, the judgment of the Court of Appeals is Reversed.

QUESTIONS FOR REFLECTION

1. Explain the sphere of liberty defined by *Palko* v. *Connecticut.*
2. Explain the sphere of liberty defined by *Moore* v. *East Cleveland.*
3. Why would neither support a right to homosexual sodomy, according to Justice White?
4. May laws be based on morality, in Justice White's view? Why, or why not?
5. Is Justice White's view closer to that of Aristotle, Burke, or Mill? Explain.

JUSTICE ANTHONY KENNEDY

Majority Opinion in Lawrence et al. *v.* Texas (2003)

(*Source:* John Geddes Lawrence and Tyron Garner, Petitioners *v.* Texas, *No. 02-102. Most legal references have been omitted.*)

Justice Kennedy delivered the opinion of the Court.

Liberty protects the person from unwarranted government intrusions into a dwelling or other private places. In our tradition the State is not omnipresent in the home. And there are other spheres of our lives and existence, outside the home, where the State should not be a dominant presence. Freedom extends beyond spatial bounds. Liberty presumes an autonomy of self that includes freedom of thought, belief, expression, and certain intimate conduct. The instant case involves liberty of the person both in its spatial and more transcendent dimensions.

I

The question before the Court is the validity of a Texas statute making it a crime for two persons of the same sex to engage in certain intimate sexual conduct.

In Houston, Texas, officers of the Harris County Police Department were dispatched to a private residence in response to a reported weapons disturbance. They entered an apartment where one of the petitioners, John Geddes Lawrence, resided. The right of the police to enter does not seem to have been questioned. The officers observed Lawrence and another man, Tyron Garner, engaging in a sexual act. The two petitioners were arrested, held in custody over night, and charged and convicted before a Justice of the Peace.

The petitioners were adults at the time of the alleged offense. Their conduct was in private and consensual.

II

We conclude the case should be resolved by determining whether the petitioners were free as adults to engage in the private conduct in the exercise of their liberty under the Due Process Clause of the Fourteenth Amendment to the Constitution. For this inquiry we deem it necessary to reconsider the Court's holding in *Bowers*. . . .

The facts in *Bowers* had some similarities to the instant case. A police officer, whose right to enter seems not to have been in question, observed Hardwick, in his own bedroom, engaging in intimate sexual conduct with another adult male. The conduct was in violation of a Georgia statute making it a criminal offense to engage in sodomy One difference between the two cases is that the Georgia statute prohibited the conduct whether or not the participants were of the same sex, while the Texas statute, as we have seen, applies only to participants of the same sex. Hardwick was not prosecuted, but he brought an action in federal court to declare the state statute invalid. He alleged he was a practicing homosexual and that the criminal prohibition violated rights guaranteed to him by the Constitution. The Court, in an opinion by Justice White, sustained the Georgia law. Chief Justice Burger and Justice Powell joined the opinion of the Court and filed separate, concurring opinions. Four Justices dissented.

The Court began its substantive discussion in *Bowers* as follows; "The issue presented is whether the Federal Constitution confers a fundamental right upon homosexuals to engage in sodomy and hence invalidates the laws of the many States that still make such conduct illegal and have done so for a very long time." That statement, we now conclude, discloses the Court's own failure to appreciate the extent of the liberty at stake. To say that the issue in *Bowers* was simply the right to engage in certain sexual conduct demeans the claim the individual put forward, just as it would demean a married couple were it to be said marriage is simply about the right to have sexual intercourse. The laws involved in *Bowers* and here are, to be sure, statutes that purport to do no more than prohibit a particular sexual act. Their penalties and purposes, though, have more far-reaching consequences, touching upon the most private human conduct, sexual behavior, and in the most private of places, the home. The statutes do seek to control a personal relationship that, whether or not entitled to formal recognition in the law, is within the liberty of persons to choose without being punished as criminals.

This, as a general rule, should counsel against attempts by the State, or a court, to define the meaning of the relationship or to set its boundaries absent injury to a person or abuse of an institution the law protects. It suffices for us to acknowledge that adults may choose to enter upon this relationship in the confines of their homes and their own private lives and still retain their dignity as free persons. When sexuality finds overt expression in intimate conduct with another person, the conduct can be but one element in a personal bond that is more enduring. The liberty protected by the Constitution allows homosexual persons the right to make this choice.

Having misapprehended the claim of liberty there presented to it, and thus stating the claim to be whether there is a fundamental right to engage in consensual sodomy, the *Bowers* Court said: "Proscriptions against that conduct have ancient roots." In academic writings, and in many of the scholarly *amicus* briefs filed to assist the Court in this case, there are fundamental criticisms of the historical premises relied upon by the majority and concurring opinions in *Bowers*. We need not enter this debate in the attempt to reach a definitive historical judgment, but the following considerations counsel against adopting the definitive conclusions upon which *Bowers* placed such reliance.

At the outset it should be noted that there is no longstanding history in this country of laws directed at homosexual conduct as a distinct matter. Beginning in colonial times there were prohibitions of sodomy derived from the English criminal laws passed in the first instance by the Reformation Parliament of 1533. The English prohibition was understood to include relations between men and women as well as relations between men and men. Nineteenth-century commentators similarly read American sodomy, buggery, and crime-against-nature statutes as criminalizing certain relations between men and women and between men and men. The absence of legal prohibitions focusing on homosexual conduct may be explained in part by noting that according to some scholars the concept of the homosexual as a distinct category of person did not emerge until the late 19th century. Thus early American sodomy laws were not directed at homosexuals as such but instead sought to prohibit nonprocreative sexual activity more generally. This does not suggest approval of homosexual conduct. It does tend to show that this particular form of conduct was not thought of as a separate category from like conduct between heterosexual persons.

Laws prohibiting sodomy do not seem to have been enforced against consenting adults acting in private. A substantial number of sodomy prosecutions and convictions for which there are surviving records were for predator acts against those who could not or did not consent, as in the case of a minor or the victim of an assault. As to these, one purpose for the prohibitions was to ensure there would be no lack of coverage if a predator committed a sexual assault that did not constitute rape as defined by the criminal law. Thus the model sodomy indictments presented in a 19th-century treatise addressed the predatory acts of an adult man against a minor girl or minor boy. Instead of targeting relations between consenting adults in private, 19th-century sodomy prosecutions typically involved relations between men and minor girls or minor boys, relations between adults involving force, relations between adults implicating disparity in status, or relations between men and animals.

To the extent that there were any prosecutions for the acts in question, 19th-century evidence rules imposed a burden that would make a conviction more difficult to obtain even taking into account the problems always inherent in prosecuting consensual acts committed in private. Under then-prevailing standards, a man could not be convicted of sodomy based upon testimony of a consenting partner, because the partner was considered an accomplice. A partner's testimony, however, was admissible if he or she had not consented to the act or was a minor, and therefore incapable of consent. The rule may explain in part the infrequency of these prosecutions. In all events that infrequency makes it difficult to say that society approved of a rigorous and systematic punishment of the consensual acts committed in private and by adults. The longstanding criminal prohibition of homosexual sodomy upon which the *Bowers* decision placed such reliance is as consistent with a general condemnation of nonprocreative sex as it is with an established tradition of prosecuting acts because of their homosexual character.

The policy of punishing consenting adults for private acts was not much discussed in the early legal literature. We can infer that one reason for this was the very private nature of the conduct. Despite the absence of prosecutions, there may have been periods in which there was public criticism of homosexuals as such and an insistence that the criminal laws be enforced to discourage their practices. But far from possessing "ancient roots," American laws targeting same-sex couples did not develop until the last third of the 20th century. The reported decisions concerning the prosecution of consensual, homosexual sodomy between adults for the years 1880–1995 are not always clear in the details, but a significant number involved conduct in a public place.

It was not until the 1970's that any State singled out same-sex relations for criminal prosecution, and only nine States have done so. Post-*Bowers* even some of these States did not adhere to the policy of suppressing homosexual conduct. Over the course of the last decades, States with same-sex prohibitions have moved toward abolishing them.

In summary, the historical grounds relied upon in *Bowers* are more complex than the majority opinion and the concurring opinion by Chief Justice Burger indicate. Their historical premises are not without doubt and, at the very least, are overstated.

It must be acknowledged, of course, that the Court in *Bowers* was making the broader point that for centuries there have been powerful voices to condemn homosexual conduct as immoral. The condemnation has been shaped by religious beliefs, conceptions of right and acceptable behavior, and respect for the traditional family. For many persons these are not trivial concerns but profound and deep convictions accepted as ethical and moral principles to which they aspire and which thus determine the course of their lives. These considerations do not answer the question before us, however. The issue is whether the majority may use the power of the State to enforce these views on the whole society through operation of the criminal law. "Our obligation is to define the liberty of all, not to mandate our own moral code." *Planned Parenthood of Southeastern Pa.* v. *Casey* (1992).

Chief Justice Burger joined the opinion for the Court in *Bowers* and further explained his views as follows: "Decisions of individuals relating to homosexual conduct have been subject to state intervention throughout the history of Western civilization. Condemnation of those practices is firmly rooted in Judeao-Christian moral and ethical standards." As with Justice White's assumptions about history, scholarship casts some doubt on the sweeping nature of the statement by Chief Justice Burger as it pertains to private homosexual conduct between consenting adults. In all events we think that our laws and traditions in the past half century are of most relevance here. These references show an emerging awareness that liberty gives substantial protection to adult persons in deciding how to conduct their private lives in matters pertaining to sex. "[H]istory and tradition are the starting point but not in all cases the ending point of the substantive due process inquiry." *County of Sacramento* v. *Lewis* (1998) (Kennedy, J., concurring).

This emerging recognition should have been apparent when *Bowers* was decided. In 1955 the American Law Institute promulgated the Model Penal Code and made clear that it did not recommend or provide for "criminal penalties for consensual sexual relations conducted in private." It justified its decision on three grounds: (1) The prohibitions undermined respect for the law by penalizing conduct many people engaged in;

(2) the statutes regulated private conduct not harmful to others; and (3) the laws were arbitrarily enforced and thus invited the danger of blackmail. In 1961 Illinois changed its laws to conform to the Model Penal Code. Other States soon followed.

In *Bowers* the Court referred to the fact that before 1961 all 50 States had outlawed sodomy, and that at the time of the Court's decision 24 States and the District of Columbia had sodomy laws. Justice Powell pointed out that these prohibitions often were being ignored, however. Georgia, for instance, had not sought to enforce its law for decades. ("The history of nonenforcement suggests the moribund character today of laws criminalizing this type of private, consensual conduct"). . . .

In our own constitutional system the deficiencies in *Bowers* became even more apparent in the years following its announcement. The 25 States with laws prohibiting the relevant conduct referenced in the *Bowers* decision are reduced now to 13, of which 4 enforce their laws only against homosexual conduct. In those States where sodomy is still proscribed, whether for same-sex or heterosexual conduct, there is a pattern of nonenforcement with respect to consenting adults acting in private. The State of Texas admitted in 1994 that as of that date it had not prosecuted anyone under those circumstances.

Two principal cases decided after *Bowers* cast its holding into even more doubt. In *Planned Parenthood of Southeastern Pa.* v. *Casey* (1992), the Court reaffirmed the substantive force of the liberty protected by the Due Process Clause. The *Casey* decision again confirmed that our laws and tradition afford constitutional protection to personal decisions relating to marriage, procreation, contraception, family relationships, child rearing, and education. In explaining the respect the Constitution demands for the autonomy of the person in making these choices, we stated as follows:

> *"These matters, involving the most intimate and personal choices a person may make in a lifetime, choices central to personal dignity and autonomy, are central to the liberty protected by the Fourteenth Amendment. At the heart of liberty is the right to define one's own concept of existence, of meaning, of the universe, and of the mystery of human life. Beliefs about these matters could not define the attributes of personhood were they formed under compulsion of the State."*

Persons in a homosexual relationship may seek autonomy for these purposes, just as heterosexual persons do. The decision in *Bowers* would deny them this right.

The second post-*Bowers* case of principal relevance is *Romer* v. *Evans* (1996). There the Court struck down class-based legislation directed at homosexuals as a violation of the Equal Protection Clause. *Romer* invalidated an amendment to Colorado's constitution which named as a solitary class persons who were homosexuals, lesbians, or bisexual either by "orientation, conduct, practices or relationships," and deprived them of protection under state antidiscrimination laws. We concluded that the provision was "born of animosity toward the class of persons affected" and further that it had no rational relation to a legitimate governmental purpose.

As an alternative argument in this case, counsel for the petitioners and some *amid* contend that *Romer* provides the basis for declaring the Texas statute invalid under the Equal Protection Clause. That is a tenable argument, but we conclude the instant case requires us to address whether *Bowers* itself has continuing validity. Were we to hold the statute invalid under the Equal Protection Clause some might question whether a prohibition would be valid if drawn differently, say, to prohibit the conduct both between same-sex and different-sex participants.

Equality of treatment and the due process right to demand respect for conduct protected by the substantive guarantee of liberty are linked in important respects, and a decision on the latter point advances both interests. If protected conduct is made criminal and the law which does so remains unexamined for its substantive validity, its stigma might remain even if it were not enforceable as drawn for equal protection reasons. When homosexual conduct is made criminal by the law of the State, that declaration in and of itself is an invitation to subject homosexual persons to discrimination both in the public and in the private spheres. The central holding of *Bowers* has been brought in question by this case, and it should be addressed. Its continuance as precedent demeans the lives of homosexual persons. . . .

The doctrine of *stare decisis* is essential to the respect accorded to the judgments of the Court and to the stability of the law. It is not, however, an inexorable command. In *Casey* we noted that when a

Court is asked to overrule a precedent recognizing a constitutional liberty interest, individual or societal reliance on the existence of that liberty cautions with particular strength against reversing course. The holding in *Bowers*, however, has not induced detrimental reliance comparable to some instances where recognized individual rights are involved. Indeed, there has been no individual or societal reliance on *Bowers* of the sort that could counsel against overturning its holding once there are compelling reasons to do so. *Bowers* itself causes uncertainty, for the precedents before and after its issuance contradict its central holding.

The rationale of *Bowers* does not withstand careful analysis. In this dissenting opinion in *Bowers* Justice Stevens came to these conclusions:

> *"Our prior cases make two propositions abundantly clear. First, the fact that the governing majority in a State has traditionally viewed a particular practice as immoral is not a sufficient reason for upholding a law prohibiting the practice; neither history nor tradition could save a law prohibiting miscegenation from constitutional attack. Second, individual decisions by married persons, concerning the intimacies of their physical relationship, even when not intended to produce offspring, are a form of 'liberty' protected by the Due Process Clause of the Fourteenth Amendment. Moreover, this protection extends to intimate choices by unmarried as well as married persons."*

Justice Stevens' analysis, in our view, should have been controlling in *Bowers* and should control here.

Bowers was not correct when it was decided, and it is not correct today. It ought not to remain binding precedent. *Bowers* v. *Hardwick* should be and now is overruled.

The present case does not involve minors. It does not involve persons who might be injured or coerced or who are situated in relationships where consent might not easily be refused. It does not involve public conduct or prostitution. It does not involve whether the government must give formal recognition to any relationship that homosexual persons seek to enter. The case does involve two adults who, with full and mutual consent from each other, engaged in sexual practices common to a homosexual lifestyle. The petitioners are entitled to respect for their private lives. The State cannot demean their existence or control their destiny by making their private sexual conduct a crime. Their right to liberty under the Due Process Clause gives them the full right to engage in their conduct without intervention of the government. "It is a promise of the Constitution that there is a realm of personal liberty which the government may not enter." *Casey*. The Texas statute furthers no legitimate state interest which can justify its intrusion into the personal and private life of the individual.

Had those who drew and ratified the Due Process Clauses of the Fifth Amendment or the Fourteenth Amendment known the components of liberty in its manifold possibilities, they might have been more specific. They did not presume to have this insight. They knew times can blind us to certain truths and later generations can see that laws once thought necessary and proper in fact serve only to oppress. As the Constitution endures, persons in every generation can invoke its principles in their own search for greater freedom.

The judgment of the Court of Appeals for the Texas Fourteenth District is reversed, and the case is remanded for further proceedings not inconsistent with this opinion.

It is so ordered.

QUESTIONS FOR REFLECTION

1. Why, according to Justice Kennedy, did *Bowers* v. *Hardwick* fail to define the issue in these cases correctly?
2. Are there any morally relevant differences between the facts of this case and those of *Bowers*?
3. Compare Justice Kennedy's rejection of attempts "to define the meaning of the relationship or to set its boundaries absent injury to a person or abuse of an institution the law protects" to Mill's harm principle.
4. How does Justice Kennedy's reading of the history of sodomy prohibitions differ from that of Justice White?
5. Justice Kennedy cites Justice Stevens's dissent in *Bowers*. On what conception of liberty does he rely?

MASSACHUSETTS CHIEF JUSTICE MARGARET H. MARSHALL AND JUSTICE ROBERT J. CORDY

Majority and Dissenting Opinions in Goodridge *v.* Department of Public Health (2003)

(*Source:* Hillary Goodridge & others *v.* Department of Public Health & another. *Massachusetts Supreme Judicial Court, SJC-08860.*)

Margaret H. Marshall, Chief Justice

Marriage is a vital social institution. The exclusive commitment of two individuals to each other nurtures love and mutual support; it brings stability to our society. For those who choose to marry, and for their children, marriage provides an abundance of legal, financial, and social benefits. In return it imposes weighty legal, financial, and social obligations. The question before us is whether, consistent with the Massachusetts Constitution, the Commonwealth may deny the protections, benefits, and obligations conferred by civil marriage to two individuals of the same sex who wish to marry. We conclude that it may not. The Massachusetts Constitution affirms the dignity and equality of all individuals. It forbids the creation of second-class citizens. In reaching our conclusion we have given full deference to the arguments made by the Commonwealth. But it has failed to identify any constitutionally adequate reason for denying civil marriage to same-sex couples.

We are mindful that our decision marks a change in the history of our marriage law. Many people hold deep-seated religious, moral, and ethical convictions that marriage should be limited to the union of one man and one woman, and that homosexual conduct is immoral. Many hold equally strong religious, moral, and ethical convictions that same-sex couples are entitled to be married, and that homosexual persons should be treated no differently than their heterosexual neighbors. Neither view answers the question before us. Our concern is with the Massachusetts Constitution as a charter of governance for every person properly within its reach. "Our obligation is to define the liberty of all, not to mandate our own moral code." *Lawrence* v. *Texas* (2003), quoting *Planned Parenthood of Southeastern Pa.* v. *Casey* (1992).

Whether the Commonwealth may use its formidable regulatory authority to bar same-sex couples from civil marriage is a question not previously addressed by a Massachusetts appellate court. It is a question the United States Supreme Court left open as a matter of Federal law in *Lawrence*, where it was not an issue. There, the Court affirmed that the core concept of common human dignity protected by the Fourteenth Amendment to the United States Constitution precludes government intrusion into the deeply personal realms of consensual adult expressions of intimacy and one's choice of an intimate partner. The Court also reaffirmed the central role that decisions whether to marry or have children bear in shaping one's identity. The Massachusetts Constitution is, if anything, more protective of individual liberty and equality than the Federal Constitution; it may demand broader protection for fundamental rights; and it is less tolerant of government intrusion into the protected spheres of private life.

Barred access to the protections, benefits, and obligations of civil marriage, a person who enters into an intimate, exclusive union with another of the same sex is arbitrarily deprived of membership in one of our community's most rewarding and cherished institutions. That exclusion is incompatible with the constitutional principles of respect for individual autonomy and equality under law.

. . .

III

A

. . . The plaintiffs' claim that the marriage restriction violates the Massachusetts Constitution can be analyzed in two ways. Does it offend the Constitution's guarantees of equality before the law? Or do the liberty and due process provisions of the Massachusetts Constitution secure the plaintiffs' right to marry their chosen partner? In matters implicating marriage, family life, and the upbringing of children, the two constitutional concepts frequently overlap, as they do here. Much of what we say concerning one standard applies to the other.

We begin by considering the nature of civil marriage itself. Simply put, the government creates civil marriage. In Massachusetts, civil marriage is, and since pre-Colonial days has been, precisely what its name implies: a wholly secular institution. No religious ceremony has ever been required to validate a Massachusetts marriage.

In a real sense, there are three partners to every civil marriage: two willing spouses and an approving State. While only the parties can mutually assent to marriage, the terms of the marriage—who may marry and what obligations, benefits, and liabilities attach to civil marriage—are set by the Commonwealth. Conversely, while only the parties can agree to end the marriage (absent the death of one of them or a marriage void *ab initio*), the Commonwealth defines the exit terms.

Civil marriage is created and regulated through exercise of the police power. "Police power" (now more commonly termed the State's regulatory authority) is an old-fashioned term for the Commonwealth's lawmaking authority, as bounded by the liberty and equality guarantees of the Massachusetts Constitution and its express delegation of power from the people to their government. In broad terms, it is the Legislature's power to enact rules to regulate conduct, to the extent that such laws are "necessary to secure the health, safety, good order, comfort, or general welfare of the community."

Without question, civil marriage enhances the "welfare of the community." It is a "social institution of the highest importance." Civil marriage anchors an ordered society by encouraging stable relationships over transient ones. It is central to the way the Commonwealth identifies individuals, provides for the orderly distribution of property, ensures that children and adults are cared for and supported whenever possible from private rather than public funds, and tracks important epidemiological and demographic data.

Marriage also bestows enormous private and social advantages on those who choose to marry. Civil marriage is at once a deeply personal commitment to another human being and a highly public celebration of the ideals of mutuality, companionship, intimacy, fidelity, and family. "It is an association that promotes a way of life, not causes; a harmony in living, not political faiths; a bilateral loyalty, not commercial or social projects." *Griswold* v. *Connecticut* (1965). Because it fulfils yearnings for security, safe haven, and connection that express our common humanity, civil marriage is an esteemed institution, and the decision whether and whom to marry is among life's momentous acts of self-definition. . . .

The benefits accessible only by way of a marriage license are enormous, touching nearly every aspect of life and death. The department states that "hundreds of statutes" are related to marriage and to marital benefits. With no attempt to be comprehensive, we note that some of the statutory benefits conferred by the Legislature on those who enter into civil marriage include, as to property: joint Massachusetts income tax filing; tenancy by the entirety (a form of ownership that provides certain protections against creditors and allows for the automatic descent of property to the surviving spouse without probate); extension of the benefit of the homestead protection (securing up to $300,000 in equity from creditors) to one's spouse and children; automatic rights to inherit the property of a deceased spouse who does not leave a will; the rights of elective share and of dower (which allow surviving spouses certain property rights where the decedent spouse has not made adequate provision for the survivor in a will); entitlement to wages owed to a deceased employee; eligibility to continue certain businesses of a deceased spouse; the right to share the medical policy of one's spouse; thirty-nine week continuation of health coverage for the spouse of a person who is laid off or dies; preferential options under the Commonwealth's pension system; preferential benefits in the Commonwealth's medical program; access to veterans' spousal benefits and preferences; financial protections for spouses of certain Commonwealth employees (fire fighters, police officers, prosecutors, among others) killed in the performance of duty; the equitable division of marital property on divorce; temporary and permanent alimony rights; the right to separate support on separation of the parties that does not result in divorce; and the right to bring claims for wrongful death and loss of consortium, and for funeral and burial expenses and punitive damages resulting from tort actions.

Exclusive marital benefits that are not directly tied to property rights include the presumptions of legitimacy and parentage of children born to a married couple; and evidentiary rights, such as the prohibition against spouses testifying against one another about their private conversations, applicable in both civil and criminal cases. Other statutory benefits of a personal nature available only to married individuals include qualification for bereavement or medical leave to care for individuals related by blood or marriage; an automatic "family member" preference to make medical decisions for an incompetent or disabled spouse who does not have a contrary health care proxy; the application of predictable rules of child custody, visitation, support, and removal out-of-State when married parents divorce; priority rights to administer the estate of a deceased spouse who dies without a will, and requirement that surviving spouse must consent to the appointment of any other person as administrator; and the right to interment in the lot or tomb owned by one's deceased spouse.

Where a married couple has children, their children are also directly or indirectly, but no less auspiciously, the recipients of the special legal and economic protections obtained by civil marriage. Notwithstanding the Commonwealth's strong public policy to abolish legal distinctions between marital and nonmarital children in providing for the support and care of minors, the fact remains that marital children reap a measure of family stability and economic security based on their parents' legally privileged status that is largely inaccessible, or not as readily accessible, to nonmarital children. Some of these benefits are social, such as the enhanced approval that still attends the status of being a marital child. Others are material, such as the greater ease of access to family-based State and Federal benefits that attend the presumptions of one's parentage.

It is undoubtedly for these concrete reasons, as well as for its intimately personal significance, that civil marriage has long been termed a "civil right." The United States Supreme Court has described the right to marry as "of fundamental importance for all individuals" and as "part of the fundamental 'right of privacy' implicit in the Fourteenth Amendment's Due Process Clause."

Without the right to marry—or more properly, the right to choose to marry—one is excluded from the full range of human experience and denied full protection of the laws for one's "avowed commitment to an intimate and lasting human relationship." *Baker* v. *State*. Because civil marriage is central to the lives of individuals and the welfare of the community, our laws assiduously protect the individual's right to marry against undue government incursion. Laws may not "interfere directly and substantially with the right to marry." *Zablocki* v. *Redhail*.

Unquestionably, the regulatory power of the Commonwealth over civil marriage is broad, as is the Commonwealth's discretion to award public benefits. Individuals who have the choice to marry each other and nevertheless choose not to may properly be denied the legal benefits of marriage. But that same logic cannot hold for a qualified individual who would marry if she or he only could.

B

For decades, indeed centuries, in much of this country (including Massachusetts) no lawful marriage was possible between white and black Americans. That long history availed not when the Supreme Court of California held in 1948 that a legislative prohibition against interracial marriage violated the due process and equality guarantees of the Fourteenth Amendment, or when, nineteen years later, the United States Supreme Court also held that a statutory bar to interracial marriage violated the Fourteenth Amendment. As both *Perez* and *Loving* make clear, the right to marry means little if it does not include the right to marry the person of one's choice, subject to appropriate government restrictions in the interests of public health, safety, and welfare. In this case, as in *Perez* and *Loving*, a statute deprives individuals of access to an institution of fundamental legal, personal, and social significance—the institution of marriage—because of a single trait: skin color in *Perez* and *Loving*, sexual orientation here. As it did in *Perez* and *Loving*, history must yield to a more fully developed understanding of the invidious quality of the discrimination.

The Massachusetts Constitution protects matters of personal liberty against government incursion as zealously, and often more so, than does the Federal Constitution, even where both Constitutions employ essentially the same language. . . . The individual liberty and equality safeguards of the Massachusetts Constitution protect both "freedom from" unwarranted government intrusion into protected spheres of life and "freedom to" partake in benefits created by the State for the common good. Both freedoms are involved here. Whether and whom to marry, how to express sexual intimacy, and whether and how to establish a family—these are among the most basic of every individual's liberty and due process rights. And central to personal freedom and security is the assurance that the laws will apply equally to persons in similar situations. "Absolute equality before the law is a fundamental principle of our own Constitution." *Opinion of the Justices* (1912). The liberty interest in choosing whether and whom to marry would be hollow if the Commonwealth could, without sufficient justification, foreclose an individual from freely choosing the person with whom to share an exclusive commitment in the unique institution of civil marriage.

The Massachusetts Constitution requires, at a minimum, that the exercise of the State's regulatory authority not be "arbitrary or capricious." . . . Any law failing to satisfy the basic standards of rationality is void.

The department posits three legislative rationales for prohibiting same-sex couples from marrying: (1) providing a "favorable setting for procreation"; (2) ensuring the optimal setting for child rearing, which the department defines as "a two-parent family with one parent of each sex"; and (3) preserving scarce State and private financial resources. We consider each in turn.

The judge in the Superior Court endorsed the first rationale, holding that "the state's interest in regulating marriage is based on the traditional concept that marriage's primary purpose is procreation." This is incorrect. Our laws of civil marriage do not privilege procreative heterosexual intercourse between married people above every other form of adult intimacy and every other means of creating a family. General Laws c. 207 contains no requirement that the applicants for a marriage license attest to their ability or intention to conceive children by coitus. Fertility is not a condition of marriage, nor is it grounds for divorce. People who have never consummated their marriage, and never plan to, may be and stay married. People who cannot stir from their deathbed may marry. While it is certainly true that many, perhaps most, married couples have children together (assisted or unassisted), it is the exclusive and permanent commitment of the marriage partners to one another, not the begetting of children, that is the sine qua non of civil marriage.

Moreover, the Commonwealth affirmatively facilitates bringing children into a family regardless of whether the intended parent is married or unmarried, whether the child is adopted or born into a family, whether assistive technology was used to conceive the child, and whether the parent or her partner is heterosexual, homosexual, or bisexual. If procreation were a necessary component of civil marriage, our statutes would draw a tighter circle around the permissible bounds of nonmarital child bearing and the creation of families by noncoital means. The attempt to isolate procreation as "the source of a fundamental right to marry" overlooks the integrated way in which courts have examined the complex and overlapping realms of personal autonomy, marriage, family life, and child rearing. Our jurisprudence recognizes that, in these nuanced and fundamentally private areas of life, such a narrow focus is inappropriate.

The "marriage is procreation" argument singles out the one unbridgeable difference between same-sex and opposite-sex couples, and transforms that difference into the essence of legal marriage. Like "Amendment 2" to the Constitution of Colorado, which effectively denied homosexual persons equality under the law and full access to the political process, the marriage restriction impermissibly "identifies persons by a single trait and then denies them protection across the board." *Romer* v. *Evans* (1996). In so doing, the State's action confers an official stamp of approval on the destructive stereotype that same-sex relationships are inherently unstable and inferior to opposite-sex relationships and are not worthy of respect.

The department's first stated rationale, equating marriage with unassisted heterosexual procreation, shades imperceptibly into its second: that confining marriage to opposite-sex couples ensures that children are raised in the "optimal" setting. Protecting the welfare of children is a paramount State policy. Restricting marriage to opposite-sex couples, however, cannot plausibly further this policy "The demographic changes of the past century make it difficult to speak of an average American family. The composition of families varies greatly from household to household." *Troxel* v. *Granville* (2000). Massachusetts has responded supportively to "the changing realities of the American family," and has moved vigorously to strengthen the modern family in its many variations. Moreover, we have repudiated the common-law power of the State to provide varying levels of protection to children based on the circumstances of birth. The "best interests of the child" standard does not turn on a parent's sexual orientation or marital status.

The department has offered no evidence that forbidding marriage to people of the same sex will increase the number of couples choosing to enter into opposite-sex marriages in order to have and raise children. There is thus no rational relationship between the marriage statute and the Commonwealth's proffered goal of protecting the "optimal" child rearing unit. Moreover, the department readily concedes that people in same-sex couples may be "excellent" parents. These couples (including four of the plaintiff couples) have children for the reasons others do—to love them, to care for them, to nurture them. But the task of child rearing for same-sex couples is made infinitely harder by their status as outliers to the marriage laws. While establishing the parentage of children as soon as possible is crucial to the safety and welfare of children, same-sex couples must undergo the sometimes lengthy and intrusive process of second-parent adoption to establish their joint parentage. While the enhanced income provided by marital benefits is an important source of security and stability for married couples and their children, those benefits are denied to families headed by same-sex couples. While the laws of divorce provide clear and reasonably predictable guidelines for child support, child custody, and property division on dissolution of a marriage, same-sex couples who dissolve their relationships find themselves and their children in the highly unpredictable terrain of equity jurisdiction. Given the wide range of public benefits reserved only for married couples, we do not credit the department's contention that the absence of access to civil marriage amounts to little more than an inconvenience to same-sex couples and their children. Excluding same-sex couples from civil marriage will not make children of opposite-sex marriages more secure, but it does prevent children of same-sex couples from enjoying the immeasurable advantages that flow from the assurance of "a stable family structure in which children will be reared, educated, and socialized."

No one disputes that the plaintiff couples are families, that many are parents, and that the children they are raising, like all children, need and should have the fullest opportunity to grow up in a secure, protected family unit. Similarly, no one disputes that, under the rubric of marriage, the State provides a cornucopia of substantial benefits to married parents and their children. The preferential treatment of civil marriage reflects the Legislature's conclusion that marriage "is the foremost setting for the education and socialization of children" precisely because it "encourages parents to remain committed to each other and to their children as they grow."

In this case, we are confronted with an entire, sizeable class of parents raising children who have absolutely no access to civil marriage and its protections because they are forbidden from procuring a marriage license. It cannot be rational under our laws, and indeed it is not permitted, to penalize children by depriving them of State benefits because the State disapproves of their parents' sexual orientation.

The third rationale advanced by the department is that limiting marriage to opposite-sex couples furthers the Legislature's interest in conserving scarce State and private financial resources. The marriage restriction is rational, it argues, because the General Court logically could assume that same-sex couples are more financially independent than married couples and thus less needy of public marital benefits, such as tax advantages, or private marital benefits, such as employer-financed health plans that include spouses in their coverage.

An absolute statutory ban on same-sex marriage bears no rational relationship to the goal of economy. First, the department's conclusory generalization—that same-sex couples are less financially dependent on each other than opposite-sex couples—ignores that many same-sex couples, such as many of the plaintiffs in this case, have children and other dependents (here, aged parents) in their care. The department does not contend, nor could it, that these dependents are less needy or deserving than the dependents of married couples. Second, Massachusetts marriage laws do not condition receipt of public and private financial benefits to married individuals on a demonstration of financial dependence on each other; the benefits are available to married couples regardless of whether they mingle their finances or actually depend on each other for support.

The department suggests additional rationales for prohibiting same-sex couples from marrying, which are developed by some amici. It argues that broadening civil marriage to include same-sex couples will trivialize or destroy the institution of marriage as it has historically been fashioned. Certainly our decision today marks a significant change in the definition of marriage as it has been inherited from the common law, arid understood by many societies for centuries. But it does not disturb the fundamental value of marriage in our society.

Here, the plaintiffs seek only to be married, not to undermine the institution of civil marriage. They do not want marriage abolished. They do not attack the binary nature of marriage, the consanguinity provisions, or any of the other gate-keeping provisions of the marriage licensing law. Recognizing the right of an individual to marry a person of the same sex will not diminish the validity or dignity of opposite-sex marriage, any more than recognizing the right of an individual to marry a person of a different race devalues the marriage of a person who marries someone of her own race. If anything, extending civil marriage to same-sex couples reinforces the importance of marriage to individuals and communities. That same-sex couples are willing to embrace marriage's solemn obligations of exclusivity, mutual support, and commitment to one another is a testament to the enduring place of marriage in our laws and in the human spirit.

It has been argued that, due to the State's strong interest in the institution of marriage as a stabilizing social structure, only the Legislature can control and define its boundaries. Accordingly, our elected representatives legitimately may choose to exclude same-sex couples from civil marriage in order to assure all citizens of the Commonwealth that (1) the benefits of our marriage laws are available explicitly to create and support a family setting that is, in the Legislature's view, optimal for child rearing, and (2) the State does not endorse gay and lesbian parenthood as the equivalent of being raised by one's married biological parents. These arguments miss the point. The Massachusetts Constitution requires that legislation meet certain criteria and not extend beyond certain limits. It is the function of courts to determine whether these criteria are met and whether these limits are exceeded. In most instances, these limits are defined by whether a rational basis exists to conclude that legislation will bring about a rational result. The Legislature in the first instance, and the courts in the last instance, must ascertain whether such a rational basis exists. To label the court's role as usurping that of the Legislature is to misunderstand the nature and purpose of judicial review. We owe great deference to the Legislature to decide social and policy issues, but it is the traditional and settled role of courts to decide constitutional issues.

The history of constitutional law "is the story of the extension of constitutional rights and protections to people once ignored or excluded." *United States* v. *Virginia* (1996) (construing equal protection clause of the Fourteenth Amendment to prohibit categorical exclusion of women from public military institutes).

This statement is as true in the area of civil marriage as in any other area of civil rights. As a public institution and a right of fundamental importance, civil marriage is an evolving paradigm. . . . Marriage has survived all of these transformations, and we have no doubt that marriage will continue to be a vibrant and revered institution.

We also reject the argument suggested by the department, and elaborated by some amici, that expanding the institution of civil marriage in Massachusetts to include same-sex couples will lead to interstate conflict. We would not presume to dictate how another State should respond to today's decision. But neither should considerations of comity prevent us from according Massachusetts residents the full measure of protection available under the Massachusetts Constitution. The genius of our Federal system is that each State's Constitution has vitality specific to its own traditions, and that, subject to the minimum requirements of the Fourteenth Amendment, each State is free to address difficult issues of individual liberty in the manner its own Constitution demands.

Several amici suggest that prohibiting marriage by same-sex couples reflects community consensus that homosexual conduct is immoral. Yet Massachusetts has a strong affirmative policy of preventing discrimination on the basis of sexual orientation.

The department has had more than ample opportunity to articulate a constitutionally adequate justification for limiting civil marriage to opposite-sex unions. It has failed to do so. The department has offered purported justifications for the civil marriage restriction that are starkly at odds with the comprehensive network of vigorous, gender-neutral laws promoting stable families and the best interests of children. It has failed to identify any relevant characteristic that would justify shutting the door to civil marriage to a person who wishes to marry someone of the same sex.

The marriage ban works a deep and scarring hardship on a very real segment of the community for no rational reason. The absence of any reasonable relationship between, on the one hand, an absolute disqualification of same-sex couples who wish to enter into civil marriage and, on the other, protection of public health, safety, or general welfare, suggests that the marriage restriction is rooted in persistent prejudices against persons who are (or who are believed to be) homosexual. "The Constitution cannot control such prejudices but neither can it tolerate them. Private biases may be outside the reach of the law, but the law cannot, directly or indirectly, give them effect." *Palmore* v. *Sidoti* (1984) (construing Fourteenth Amendment). Limiting the protections, benefits, and obligations of civil marriage to opposite-sex couples violates the basic premises of individual liberty and equality under law protected by the Massachusetts Constitution.

. . .

So ordered.

QUESTIONS FOR REFLECTION

1. Explain the Court's argument from equality.
2. What are the chief benefits associated with marriage, as sanctioned by the State? What role do they play in the argument?
3. What rights does restricting marriage to heterosexuals violate?
4. What are "fundamental" rights? How do we decide on the boundaries of this class?
5. The Court suggests that there is no rational basis for restricting marriage to heterosexuals. Why? Do you agree?

Robert J. Cordy Justice (dissenting, with whom Francis X. Spina and Martha B. Sosman, Justices, join).

The court's opinion concludes that the Department of Public Health has failed to identify any "constitutionally adequate reason" for limiting civil marriage to opposite-sex unions, and that there is no "reasonable relationship" between a disqualification of same-sex couples who wish to enter into a civil marriage and the protection of public health, safety, or general welfare. Consequently, it holds that the marriage statute cannot withstand scrutiny under the

Massachusetts Constitution. Because I find these conclusions to be unsupportable in light of the nature of the rights and regulations at issue, the presumption of constitutional validity and significant deference afforded to legislative enactments, and the "undesirability of the judiciary substituting its notions of correct policy for that of a popularly elected Legislature" responsible for making such policy, *Zayre Corp. v. Attorney Gen.* (1977), I respectfully dissent. Although it may be desirable for many reasons to extend to same-sex couples the benefits and burdens of civil marriage (and the plaintiffs have made a powerfully reasoned case for that extension), that decision must be made by the Legislature, not the court.

If a statute either impairs the exercise of a fundamental right protected by the due process or liberty provisions of our State Constitution, or discriminates based on a constitutionally suspect classification such as sex, it will be subject to strict scrutiny when its validity is challenged. If it does neither, a statute "will be upheld if it is 'rationally related to a legitimate State purpose.'" This test, referred to in State and Federal constitutional jurisprudence as the "rational basis test," is virtually identical in substance and effect to the test applied to a law promulgated under the State's broad police powers (pursuant to which the marriage statutes and most other licensing and regulatory laws are enacted): that is, the law is valid if it is reasonably related to the protection of public health, safety, or general welfare.

The Massachusetts marriage statute does not impair the exercise of a recognized fundamental right, or discriminate on the basis of sex in violation of the equal rights amendment to the Massachusetts Constitution. Consequently, it is subject to review only to determine whether it satisfies the rational basis test. Because a conceivable rational basis exists upon which the Legislature could conclude that the marriage statute furthers the legitimate State purpose of ensuring, promoting, and supporting an optimal social structure for the bearing and raising of children, it is a valid exercise of the State's police power.

A. *Limiting marriage to the union of one man and one woman does not impair the exercise of a fundamental right.* Civil marriage is an institution created by the State. In Massachusetts, the marriage statutes are derived from English common law, and were first enacted in colonial times. They were enacted to secure public interests and not for religious purposes or to promote personal interests or aspirations. As the court notes in its opinion, the institution of marriage is "the legal union of a man and woman as husband and wife," and it has always been so under Massachusetts law, colonial or otherwise.

The plaintiffs contend that because the right to choose to marry is a "fundamental" right, the right to marry the person of one's choice, including a member of the same sex, must also be a "fundamental" right. While the court stops short of deciding that the right to marry someone of the same sex is "fundamental" such that strict scrutiny must be applied to any statute that impairs it, it nevertheless agrees with the plaintiffs that the right to choose to marry is of fundamental importance ("among the most basic" of every person's "liberty and due process rights") and would be "hollow" if an individual was foreclosed from "freely choosing the person with whom to share . . . the . . . institution of civil marriage." Hence, it concludes that a marriage license cannot be denied to an individual who wishes to marry someone of the same sex. In reaching this result the court has transmuted the "right" to marry into a right to change the institution of marriage itself. This feat of reasoning succeeds only if one accepts the proposition that the definition of the institution of marriage as a union between a man and a woman is merely "conclusory" rather than the basis on which the "right" to partake in it has been deemed to be of fundamental importance. In other words, only by assuming that "marriage" includes the union of two persons of the same sex does the court conclude that restricting marriage to opposite-sex couples infringes on the "right" of same-sex couples [to] "marry."

The plaintiffs ground their contention that they have a fundamental right to marry a person of the same sex in a long line of Supreme Court decisions that discuss the importance of marriage. In context, all of these decisions and their discussions are about the "fundamental" nature of the institution of marriage as it has existed and been understood in this country, not as the court has redefined it today. Even in that context, its "fundamental" nature is derivative of the nature of the interests that underlie or are associated with it. An examination of those interests reveals that they are either not shared by same-sex couples or not implicated by the marriage statutes.

Supreme Court cases that have described marriage or the right to marry as "fundamental" have focused primarily on the underlying interest of every individual in procreation, which, historically, could only legally occur within the construct of marriage because sexual intercourse outside of marriage was a criminal act. In *Skinner* v. *Oklahoma,* the first case to characterize marriage as a "fundamental" right, the Supreme Court stated, as its rationale for striking down a sterilization statute, that "[m]arriage and procreation are fundamental to the veiy existence of the race." In concluding that a sterilized individual "is forever deprived of a basic liberty," the Court was obviously referring to procreation rather than marriage. . . . Similarly, in *Loving* v. *Virginia,* in which the United States Supreme Court struck down Virginia's antimiscegenation statute, the Court implicitly linked marriage with procreation in describing marriage as "fundamental to our very existence." In *Zablocki* v. *Redhail,* the Court expressly linked the right to marry with the right to procreate, concluding that "if [the plaintiff's] right to procreate means anything at all, it must imply some right to enter the only relationship in which the State . . . allows sexual relations legally to take place." Once again, in *Turner* v. *Safley,* striking a State regulation that curtailed the right of an inmate to marry, the Court included among the important attributes of such marriages the "expectation that [the marriage] ultimately will be fully consummated." Because same-sex couples are unable to procreate on their own, any right to marriage they may possess cannot be based on their interest in procreation, which has been essential to the Supreme Courts denomination of the right to marry as fundamental.

Supreme Court cases recognizing a right to privacy in intimate decision-making, e.g., *Griswold* v. *Connecticut* (striking down statute prohibiting use of contraceptives); *Roe* v. *Wade* (striking down statute criminalizing abortion), have also focused primarily on sexual relations and the decision whether or not to procreate, and have refused to recognize an "unlimited right" to privacy Massachusetts courts have been no more willing than the Federal courts to adopt a "universal[ ]" "privacy doctrine," *Marcoux* v. *Attorney Gen.* (1978), or to derive "controversial 'new' rights from the Constitution." *Aime* v. *Commonwealth* (1993).

What the *Griswold* Court found "repulsive to the notions of privacy surrounding the marriage relationship" was the prospect of "allow[ing] the police to search the sacred precincts of marital bedrooms for telltale signs of the use of contraceptives." When Justice Goldberg spoke of "marital relations" in the context of finding it "difficult to imagine what is more private or more intimate than a husband and wife's marital relations[hip]," *Griswold* v. *Connecticut,* he was obviously referring to sexual relations. Similarly, in *Lawrence* v. *Texas,* it was the criminalization of private sexual behavior that the Court found violative of the petitioners' liberty interest.

In Massachusetts jurisprudence, protected decisions generally have been limited to those concerning "whether or not to beget or bear a child"; how to raise a child; or whether or not to accept medical treatment, none of which is at issue here.

The marriage statute, which regulates only the act of obtaining a marriage license, does not implicate privacy in the sense that it has found constitutional protection under Massachusetts and Federal law. It does not intrude on any right that the plaintiffs have to privacy in their choices regarding procreation, an intimate partner or sexual relations. The plaintiffs' right to privacy in such matters does not require that the State officially endorse their choices in order for the right to be constitutionally vindicated.

Although some of the privacy cases also speak in terms of personal autonomy, no court has ever recognized such an open-ended right. "That many of the rights and liberties protected by the Due Process Clause sound in personal autonomy does not warrant the sweeping conclusion that any and all important, intimate, and personal decisions are so protected. . . ." *Washington* v. *Glucksberg* (1997). Such decisions are protected not because they are important, intimate, and personal, but because the right or liberty at stake is "so deeply rooted in our history and traditions, or so fundamental to our concept of constitutionally ordered liberty" that it is protected by due process. Accordingly, the Supreme Court has concluded that while the decision to refuse unwanted medical treatment is fundamental, *Cruzan* v. *Director, Mo. Dep't of Health* (1990), because it is deeply rooted in our nation's history and tradition, the equally personal and profound decision to commit suicide is not because of the absence of such roots.

While the institution of marriage is deeply rooted in the history and traditions of our country and our State, the right to marry someone of the same sex is not. No matter how personal or intimate a decision to marry someone of the same sex might be, the right to make it is not guaranteed by the right of personal autonomy.

The protected right to freedom of association, in the sense of freedom of choice "to enter into and maintain certain intimate human relationships," *Roberts* v. *United States Jaycees* (1984) (as an element of liberty or due process rather than free speech), is similarly limited and unimpaired by the marriage statute. As recognized by the Supreme Court, that right affords protection only to "certain kinds of highly personal relationships," such as those between husband and wife, parent and child, and among close relatives, that "have played a critical role in the culture and traditions of the Nation," and are "deeply rooted in this Nation's history and tradition." *Moore* v. *East Cleveland* (1977) (distinguishing on this basis between family and nonfamily relationships). Unlike opposite-sex marriages, which have deep historic roots, or the parent-child relationship, which reflects a "strong tradition" founded on "the history and culture of Western civilization" and "is now established beyond debate as an enduring American tradition," *Wisconsin* v. *Yoder* (1972); or extended family relationships, which have been "honored throughout our history," *Moore* v. *East Cleveland,* same-sex relationships, although becoming more accepted, are certainly not so "deeply rooted in this Nation's history and tradition" as to warrant such enhanced constitutional protection.

Although "expressions of emotional support and public commitment" have been recognized as among the attributes of marriage, which, "*[t]aken together* . . . form a constitutionally protected marital relationship" (emphasis added), *Turner* v. *Safley* (1987), those interests, standing alone, are not the source of a fundamental right to marry. While damage to one's "status in the community" may be sufficient harm to confer standing to sue, such status has never been recognized as a fundamental right.

Finally, the constitutionally protected interest in child rearing is not implicated or infringed by the marriage statute here. The fact that the plaintiffs cannot marry has no bearing on their independently protected constitutional rights as parents which, as with opposite-sex parents, are limited only by their continued fitness and the best interests of their children.

Because the rights and interests discussed above do not afford the plaintiffs any fundamental right that would be impaired by a statute limiting marriage to members of the opposite sex, they have no fundamental right to be declared "married" by the State.

Insofar as the right to marry someone of the same sex is neither found in the unique historical context of our Constitution nor compelled by the meaning ascribed by this court to the liberty and due process protections contained within it, should the court nevertheless recognize it as a fundamental right? The consequences of deeming a right to be "fundamental" are profound, and this court, as well as the Supreme Court, has been very cautious in recognizing them. Such caution is required by separation of powers principles. If a right is found to be "fundamental," it is, to a great extent, removed from "the arena of public debate and legislative action"; utmost care must be taken when breaking new ground in this field "lest the liberty protected by the Due Process Clause be subtly transformed into the policy preferences of [judges]." *Washington* v. *Glucksberg* (1997).

"[T]o rein in" the otherwise potentially unlimited scope of substantive due process rights, both Federal and Massachusetts courts have recognized as "fundamental" only those "rights and liberties which are, objectively, 'deeply rooted in this Nation's history and tradition,' . . . and 'implicit in the concept of ordered liberty.'" In the area of family-related rights in particular, the Supreme Court has emphasized that the "Constitution protects the sanctity of the family precisely because the institution of the family is deeply rooted." *Moore* v. *East Cleveland.*

Applying this limiting principle, the Supreme Court, as noted above, declined to recognize a fundamental right to physician-assisted suicide, which would have required "revers[ing] centuries of legal doctrine and practice, and strik[ing] down the considered policy choice of almost every State." *Washington* v. *Glucksberg.* While recognizing that public attitudes toward assisted suicide are currently the subject of "earnest and profound debate," the Court nevertheless left the continuation and resolution of that debate to the political arena, "as it should be in a democratic society"

Similarly, Massachusetts courts have declined to recognize rights that are not so deeply rooted. As this court noted in considering whether to recognize a right of terminally ill patients to refuse life-prolonging treatment, "the law always lags behind the most advanced thinking in every area," and must await "some common ground, some consensus." *Superintendent of Belchertown State Sch.* v. *Saihewicz* (1977), quoting Burger, The Law and Medical Advances (1967).

This is not to say that a statute that has no rational basis must nevertheless be upheld as long as it is of ancient origin. However, "[t]he long history of a certain practice . . . and its acceptance as an uncontroversial part of our national and State tradition do suggest that [the court] should reflect carefully before striking it down." *Colo* v. *Treasurer & Receiver Gen.* (1979). As this court has recognized, the "fact that a challenged practice 'is followed by a large number of states . . . is plainly worth considering in determining whether the practice "offends some principle of justice so rooted in the traditions and conscience of our people as to be ranked as fundamental."'" *Commonwealth* v. *Kostka* (1976), quoting *Leland* v. *Oregon* (1952).

Although public attitudes toward marriage in general and same-sex marriage in particular have changed and are still evolving, "the asserted contemporary concept of marriage and societal interests for which [plaintiffs] contend" are "manifestly [less] deeply founded" than the "historic institution" of marriage. Indeed, it is not readily apparent to what extent contemporary values have embraced the concept of same-sex marriage. Perhaps the "clearest and most reliable objective evidence of contemporary values is the legislation enacted by the country's legislatures," *Atkins* v. *Virginia* (2002), quoting *Pemy* v. *Lynaugh* (1989). No State Legislature has enacted laws permitting same-sex marriages; and a large majority of States, as well as the United States Congress, have affirmatively prohibited the recognition of such marriages for any purpose.

Given this history and the current state of public opinion, as reflected in the actions of the people's elected representatives, it cannot be said that "a right to same-sex marriage is so rooted in the traditions and collective conscience of our people that failure to recognize it would violate the fundamental principles of liberty and justice that lie at the base of all our civil and political institutions. Neither . . . [is] a right to same-sex marriage . . . implicit in the concept of ordered liberty, such that neither liberty nor justice would exist if it were sacrificed." *Baehr* v. *Lewin* (1993). The one exception was the Alaska Superior Court, which relied on that State's Constitution's express and broadly construed right to privacy. In such circumstances, the law with respect to same-sex marriages must be left to develop through legislative processes, subject to the constraints of rationality, lest the court be viewed as using the liberty and due process clauses as vehicles merely to enforce its own views regarding better social policies, a role that the strongly worded separation of powers principles in art. 30 of the Declaration of Rights of our Constitution forbids, and for which the court is particularly ill suited.

. . .

C. *The marriage statute satisfies the rational basis standard.*

. . . In analyzing whether a statute satisfies the rational basis standard, we look to the nature of the classification embodied in the enactment, then to whether the statute serves a legitimate State purpose, and finally to whether the classification is reasonably related to the furtherance of that purpose. With this framework, we turn to the challenged statute, which authorizes local town officials to issue licenses to couples of the opposite sex authorizing them to enter the institution of civil marriage.

1. *Classification.* The nature of the classification at issue is readily apparent. Opposite-sex couples can obtain a license and same-sex couples cannot. The granting of this license, and the completion of the required solemnization of the marriage, opens the door to many statutory benefits and imposes numerous responsibilities. The fact that the statute does not permit such licenses to be issued to couples of the same sex thus bars them from civil marriage. The classification is not drawn between men and women or between heterosexuals and homosexuals, any of whom can obtain a license to marry a member of the opposite sex; rather, it is drawn between same-sex couples and opposite-sex couples.

2. *State purpose.* The court's opinion concedes that the civil marriage statute serves legitimate State purposes, but further investigation and elaboration of those purposes is both helpful and necessary.

Civil marriage is the institutional mechanism by which societies have sanctioned and recognized particular family structures, and the institution of marriage has existed as one of the fundamental organizing principles of human society. Marriage has not been merely a contractual arrangement for legally defining the private relationship between two individuals (although that is certainly part of any marriage). Rather, on an institutional level, marriage is the "very basis of the whole fabric of civilized society," J. P Bishop,

Commentaries on the Law of Marriage and Divorce, and Evidence in Matrimonial Suits (1852), and it serves many important political, economic, social, educational, procreational, and personal functions.

Paramount among its many important functions, the institution of marriage has systematically provided for the regulation of heterosexual behavior, brought order to the resulting procreation, and ensured a stable family structure in which children will be reared, educated, and socialized. Admittedly, heterosexual intercourse, procreation, and child care are not necessarily conjoined (particularly in the modern age of widespread effective contraception and supportive social welfare programs), but an orderly society requires some mechanism for coping with the fact that sexual intercourse commonly results in pregnancy and childbirth. The institution of marriage is that mechanism.

The institution of marriage provides the important legal and normative link between heterosexual intercourse and procreation on the one hand and family responsibilities on the other. The partners in a marriage are expected to engage in exclusive sexual relations, with children the probable result and paternity presumed. Whereas the relationship between mother and child is demonstratively and predictably created and recognizable through the biological process of pregnancy and childbirth, there is no corresponding process for creating a relationship between father and child. Similarly, aside from an act of heterosexual intercourse nine months prior to childbirth, there is no process for creating a relationship between a man and a woman as the parents of a particular child. The institution of marriage fills this void by formally binding the husband-father to his wife and child, and imposing on him the responsibilities of fatherhood. The alternative, a society without the institution of marriage, in which heterosexual intercourse, procreation, and child care are largely disconnected processes, would be chaotic.

The marital family is also the foremost setting for the education and socialization of children. Children learn about the world and their place in it primarily from those who raise them, and those children eventually grow up to exert some influence, great or small, positive or negative, on society. The institution of marriage encourages parents to remain committed to each other and to their children as they grow, thereby encouraging a stable venue for the education and socialization of children. More macroscopically, construction of a family through marriage also formalizes the bonds between people in an ordered and institutional manner, thereby facilitating a foundation of interconnectedness and interdependency on which more intricate stabilizing social structures might be built.

This court, among others, has consistently acknowledged both the institutional importance of marriage as an organizing principle of society, and the State's interest in regulating it.

It is undeniably true that dramatic historical shifts in our cultural, political, and economic landscape have altered some of our traditional notions about marriage, including the interpersonal dynamics within it, the range of responsibilities required of it as an institution, and the legal environment in which it exists. Nevertheless, the institution of marriage remains the principal weave of our social fabric. A family defined by heterosexual marriage continues to be the most prevalent social structure into which the vast majority of children are born, nurtured, and prepared for productive participation in civil society, see Children's Living Arrangements and Characteristics: March, 2002, United States Census Bureau Current Population Reports at 3 (June, 2003) (in 2002, 69% of children lived with two married parents, 23% lived with their mother, 5% lived with their father, and 4% lived in households with neither parent present).

It is difficult to imagine a State purpose more important and legitimate than ensuring, promoting, and supporting an optimal social structure within which to bear and raise children. At the very least, the marriage statute continues to serve this important State purpose.

3. *Rational relationship.* The question we must turn to next is whether the statute, construed as limiting marriage to couples of the opposite sex, remains a rational way to further that purpose. Stated differently, we ask whether a conceivable rational basis exists on which the Legislature could conclude that continuing to limit the institution of civil marriage to members of the opposite sex furthers the legitimate purpose of ensuring, promoting, and supporting an optimal social structure for the bearing and raising of children.

In considering whether such a rational basis exists, we defer to the decision-making process of the

Legislature, and must make deferential assumptions about the information that it might consider and on which it may rely.

We must assume that the Legislature (1) might conclude that the institution of civil marriage has successfully and continually provided this structure over several centuries; (2) might consider and credit studies that document negative consequences that too often follow children either born outside of marriage or raised in households lacking either a father or a mother figure, and scholarly commentary contending that children and families develop best when mothers and fathers are partners in their parenting; and (3) would be familiar with many recent studies that variously: support the proposition that children raised in intact families headed by same-sex couples fare as well on many measures as children raised in similar families headed by opposite-sex couples; support the proposition that children of same-sex couples fare worse on some measures; or reveal notable differences between the two groups of children that warrant further study.

We must also assume that the Legislature would be aware of the critiques of the methodologies used in virtually all of the comparative studies of children raised in these different environments, cautioning that the sampling populations are not representative, that the observation periods are too limited in time, that the empirical data are unreliable, and that the hypotheses are too infused with political or agenda driven bias.

Taking all of this available information into account, the Legislature could rationally conclude that a family environment with married opposite-sex parents remains the optimal social structure in which to bear children, and that the raising of children by same-sex couples, who by definition cannot be the two sole biological parents of a child and cannot provide children with a parental authority figure of each gender, presents an alternative structure for child rearing that has not yet proved itself beyond reasonable scientific dispute to be as optimal as the biologically based marriage norm. Working from the assumption that a recognition of same-sex marriages will increase the number of children experiencing this alternative, the Legislature could conceivably conclude that declining to recognize same-sex marriages remains prudent until empirical questions about its impact on the upbringing of children are resolved.

The fact that the Commonwealth currently allows same-sex couples to adopt does not affect the rationality of this conclusion. The eligibility of a child for adoption presupposes that at least one of the child's biological parents is unable or unwilling, for some reason, to participate in raising the child. In that sense, society has "lost" the optimal setting in which to raise that child—it is simply not available. In these circumstances, the principal and overriding consideration is the "best interests of the child," considering his or her unique circumstances and the options that are available for that child. The objective is an individualized determination of the best environment for a particular child, where the normative social structure—a home with both the child's biological father and mother—is not an option. That such a focused determination may lead to the approval of a same-sex couple's adoption of a child does not mean that it would be irrational for a legislator, in fashioning statutory laws that cannot make such individualized determinations, to conclude generally that being raised by a same-sex couple has not yet been shown to be the absolute equivalent of being raised by one's married biological parents.

That the State does not preclude different types of families from raising children does not mean that it must view them all as equally optimal and equally deserving of State endorsement and support. For example, single persons are allowed to adopt children, but the fact that the Legislature permits single-parent adoption does not mean that it has endorsed single parenthood as an optimal setting in which to raise children or views it as the equivalent of being raised by both of one's biological parents. The same holds true with respect to same-sex couples—the fact that they may adopt children means only that the Legislature has concluded that they may provide an acceptable setting in which to raise children who cannot be raised by both of their biological parents. The Legislature may rationally permit adoption by same-sex couples yet harbor reservations as to whether parenthood by same-sex couples should be affirmatively encouraged to the same extent as parenthood by the heterosexual couple whose union produced the child.

In addition, the Legislature could conclude that redefining the institution of marriage to permit same-sex couples to marry would impair the State's interest in promoting and supporting heterosexual marriage as the social institution that it has determined best normalizes, stabilizes, and links the acts of procreation and child rearing. While the plaintiffs argue that they only want to take part in the same stabilizing institution, the Legislature conceivably could conclude that permitting their participation would have the unintended effect of undermining to some degree marriage's ability to serve its social purpose.

As long as marriage is limited to opposite-sex couples who can at least theoretically procreate, society is able to communicate a consistent message to its citizens that marriage is a (normatively) necessary part of their procreative endeavor; that if they are to procreate, then society has endorsed the institution of marriage as the environment for it and for the subsequent rearing of their children; and that benefits are available explicitly to create a supportive and conducive atmosphere for those purposes. If society proceeds similarly to recognize marriages between same-sex couples who cannot procreate, it could be perceived as an abandonment of this claim, and might result in the mistaken view that civil marriage has little to do with procreation: just as the potential of procreation would not be necessary for a marriage to be valid, marriage would not be necessary for optimal procreation and child rearing to occur. In essence, the Legislature could conclude that the consequence of such a policy shift would be a diminution in society's ability to steer the acts of procreation and child rearing into their most optimal setting.

The court recognizes this concern, but brushes it aside with the assumption that permitting same-sex couples to marry "will not diminish the validity or dignity of opposite-sex marriage," and that "we have no doubt that marriage will continue to be a vibrant and revered institution." Whether the court is correct in its assumption is irrelevant. What is relevant is that such predicting is not the business of the courts. A rational Legislature, given the evidence, could conceivably come to a different conclusion, or could at least harbor rational concerns about possible unintended consequences of a dramatic redefinition of marriage.

There is no question that many same-sex couples are capable of being good parents, and should be (and are) permitted to be so. The policy question that a legislator must resolve is a different one, and turns on an assessment of whether the marriage structure proposed by the plaintiffs will, over time, if endorsed and supported by the State, prove to be as stable and successful a model as the one that has formed a cornerstone of our society since colonial times, or prove to be less than optimal, and result in consequences, perhaps now unforeseen, adverse to the State's legitimate interest in promoting and supporting the best possible social structure in which children should be born and raised. Given the critical importance of civil marriage as an organizing and stabilizing institution of society, it is eminently rational for the Legislature to postpone making fundamental changes to it until such time as there is unanimous scientific evidence, or popular consensus, or both, that such changes can safely be made.

There is no reason to believe that legislative processes are inadequate to effectuate legal changes in response to evolving evidence, social values, and views of fairness on the subject of same-sex relationships. Deliberate consideration of, and incremental responses to rapidly evolving scientific and social understanding is the norm of the political process—that it may seem painfully slow to those who are already persuaded by the arguments in favor of change is not a sufficient basis to conclude that the processes are constitutionally infirm. The advancement of the rights, privileges, and protections afforded to homosexual members of our community in the last three decades has been significant, and there is no reason to believe that that evolution will not continue. Changes of attitude in the civic, social, and professional communities have been even more profound. Thirty years ago, The Diagnostic and Statistical Manual, the seminal handbook of the American Psychiatric Association, still listed homosexuality as a mental disorder. Today, the Massachusetts Psychiatric Society, the American Psychoanalytic Association, and many other psychiatric, psychological, and social science organizations have joined in an amicus brief on behalf of the plaintiffs' cause. A body of experience and evidence has provided the basis for change, and that body continues to mount. The Legislature is the appropriate branch, both constitutionally and practically, to consider and respond to it. It is not enough that we as Justices might be personally of the view that we have learned enough to decide what is best. So long as the question is at all debatable, it must be the Legislature that decides. The marriage statute thus meets the requirements of the rational basis test.

D. *Conclusion.* While "the Massachusetts Constitution protects matters of personal liberty against government intrusion at least as zealously, and often more so than does the Federal Constitution," this case is not about government intrusions into matters of personal liberty. It is not about the rights of same-sex couples to choose to live together, or to be intimate with each other, or to adopt and raise children together. It is about whether the State must endorse and support their choices by changing the institution of civil marriage to make its benefits, obligations, and responsibilities applicable to them. While the courageous efforts of many have resulted in increased dignity, rights, and respect for gay and lesbian members of our community, the issue presented here is a profound one, deeply rooted in social policy, that must, for now, be the subject of legislative not judicial action.

QUESTIONS FOR REFLECTION

1. Explain the rational basis test.
2. Why, according to Justice Cordy, is restricting marriage to heterosexuals compatible with individual rights?
3. Why does Justice Cordy reject arguments based on personal autonomy?
4. What significance do history and tradition have, in Justice Cordy's view?
5. How does Justice Cordy argue that there is a rational basis for restricting marriage to heterosexuals?

STANLEY KURTZ

The Libertarian Question

Stanley Kurtz is a research fellow at the Hoover Institution at Stanford University

There is a mystery at the heart of the gay-marriage debate. I call it the "libertarian question." The libertarian question (really a series of questions) goes like this: *Why should any form of adult consensual sex be illegal? What rational or compelling interest does the state have in regulating consensual adult sex? More specifically, how does the marriage of two gay men undermine my marriage? Will the fact that two married gay men live next door make me leave my wife? Hardly. So how, then, does gay marriage undermine heterosexual marriage? Why not get the state out of such matters altogether?*

The libertarian question is mysterious because, in modern society, we find it difficult to understand the continuing necessity of shared moral standards—and of collective taboos against actions that violate those standards. Traditional societies depend on shared moral sentiments and collective taboos. Modern democracies, for the most part, have rejected these forms of collective morality in favor of an emphasis on personal freedom. Yet the truth is, although their workings are mysterious to us, shared moral codes (and a structure of taboos that guards those codes) can never be entirely dispensed with.

Incest

Let's approach the libertarian question about gay marriage from a new angle. The flap over Senator Rick Santorum's remarks has raised the question of incest. If homosexual sex is declared private, why won't consensual adult incest fall under the same sort of protection? (In raising this question, Sen. Santorum was simply echoing Justice Byron White's decision in *Bowers* v. *Hardwick.)*

In his very useful exploration of the consensual incest problem, . . . William Saletan points to a case of incest in which a woman was drawn into a sexual relationship with her uncle while she was still a minor, but continued that relationship as an adult. The woman was found guilty of incest and sentenced to supervised probation. After violating probation (presumably to return to her uncle) she was sentenced to five years in jail. Why should this woman have been jailed?

The prevalence of consensual adult incest is difficult to judge. It may be relatively rare. The deeper problem, of course, is the sexual abuse of children by older family members. The impossibility of real consent, as well as the potential psychological damage in cases of incestuous child abuse, are matters of very serious concern. But incestuous child abuse can obviously be made illegal. What is wrong with consensual adult incest?

Let's return to the libertarian question. *If a man happens to walk around town arm and arm with his adult niece, is that going to make me abuse my teenaged niece?* In most cases, probably not. Clearly, however, there is a connection. Our collective horror at incest—even adult incest—acts as a protective barrier against the temptation to incest with minors. The very real dangers of child abuse within families shows us that a significant number of people are potentially susceptible to sexual interest in the children under their control. Our collective taboo on incest, as expressed in our laws, helps to offset that potential temptation.

The mechanism here is embodied in the law, but goes well beyond the mere mechanical workings of the law. The real mechanism is collective and psychological. The law on incest expresses a shared moral value. It is a collective statement. As such, it reinforces a sense of disgust that helps to ward off temptation.

To see the mechanism of our incest taboo at work, imagine a world in which consensual adult incest was legal. Once we see or hear of couples—even a relatively small number—who engage in legal, consensual, adult incestuous relationships, the whole idea of incest with minors becomes thinkable. Preventing incest with minors from becoming thinkable is the purpose of the taboo.

The reason we need an incest taboo is because there is no effective way for the state to protect children from sexual abuse by family members. Children are essentially at the mercy of the adults who care for them. So only by building into adults a psychological mechanism of disgust and horror at incest can society protect children from the psychological harm of abuse by close relatives. The taboo runs deeper than the law itself. Yet the law embodies and reinforces the taboo. Were the law to be eliminated—even for consenting adults only—the taboo on incest with minors would be weakened, or break down—maybe not in all families, or even most, but for far too many.

Homosexuality

The taboo against homosexuality works in a similar fashion. But what, exactly, does the taboo on homosexuality protect? There is more than one way to approach that question, but the short answer is: The taboo on homosexuality protects marriage. Or, to look at the same problem from a slightly different angle, the institution of Western marriage, in its most traditional form, has been protected by a many-sided taboo against all sexuality outside of its confines—and against non-procreative sexuality within it. Just as the taboo on incest reduces the temptation to child abuse, the taboo on non-marital and non-reproductive sexuality helps to cement marital unions, and helps prevent acts of adultery that would tear those unions apart.

As an ultimate symbol of sexuality for the sake of pleasure (rather than reproduction) homosexuality has traditionally been taboo. That taboo was embodied and expressed in sodomy laws. Rigorous enforcement of these laws was secondary—and in any case, next to impossible. The important thing was the statement of collective values made by the laws against sodomy. By making homosexuality taboo, the law reinforced the idea that the highest and proper purpose of sexuality itself was to bind and energize families.

Of course, over the last 30 years, the taboo on homosexuality, like the broader taboo on a purely pleasure-seeking sexuality inside and outside the confines of marriage, has substantially broken down. And it's not surprising that, as a consequence of our changed understanding of sexuality, the rates of divorce and out of wedlock birth have dramatically risen. Of course, at the same time as the divorce rate has risen, the weakening of the old taboos has substantially increased our personal freedom. And our new sexual freedom has benefited no one more than homosexuals, who no longer serve, in nearly the degree they once did, as ultimate symbols of forbidden sexuality.

On balance, I think we as a society have gained much from the weakening of the old sexual taboos, although it is important to keep in mind that we are in fact dealing with a trade-off here. Traditional sexual taboos protect marriage, and their weakening cannot help but weaken marriage—even as they increase personal freedom. But again, on balance, I believe that at least some of the weakening in the old sexual system has been worth the trade-off.

Adultery

What we need to understand—but do not—is that gay marriage will undermine the structure of taboos that continue to protect heterosexual marriage—and will do so far more profoundly than either the elimination of sodomy laws, or the general sexual loosening of the past thirty years. Above all, marriage is protected by the ethos of monogamy—and by the associated taboo against adultery. The real danger of gay marriage is that it will undermine the taboo on adultery, thereby destroying the final bastion protecting marriage: the ethos of monogamy.

Gay marriage threatens monogamy in two ways. First, gay marriage threatens monogamy because homosexual couples—particularly male homosexual couples—tend to see monogamy as nonessential, even to the most loyal and committed relationships. Of course, advocates argue that legal gay marriage will change all that—that marriage will make gays more monogamous. But it is just as likely (indeed, far more likely) that the effect will go in the other direction—openly non-monogamous married gay couples will break the connection between marriage and monogamy. . . .

Even more powerfully, gay marriage threatens monogamy through its tendency to lead, on a slippery slope, to the legalization of polygamy and polyamory. . . .

It's important to understand what the danger of openly non-monogamous gay marriages, and of legalized polygamy and polyamory, really is. The key problem here is not, say, that polygamous marriages are unfair or exploitative to women. (That is a legitimate concern, of course, but it is not the greatest social danger posed by legalized polygamy.) The real problem is the effect of openly non-monogamous gay unions, and of legalized polygamy and polyamory, on the ethos of monogamy.

Even in the wake of the sexual-cultural changes of the Sixties, there is still a strong consensus in our society that marriage means monogamy. That consensus is expressed in the taboo on adultery. Legal recognition for group marriage, and for openly non-monogamous gay unions, would effectively destroy the taboo on adultery. That doesn't meant that everyone would instantly go out and commit adultery—any more than everyone exposed to legal incestuous unions between consenting adults would engage in child abuse. But there would be a significant social effect—and it would be over and above the weakening of marriage that has already occurred in the wake of the changes since the Sixties.

The libertarian asks, *Just because two married gay men live next door, is that going to make me leave my wife?* In a way, the answer is "Yes." For one thing, as a new generation grows up exposed to gay couples who openly define their marriages in non-monogamous terms, the concept of marriage itself will gradually change. No doubt, movies and television in a post-gaymarriage world will be filled with stories of the "cutting edge" understandings of open marriage being pioneered by the new gay couples, even if the actual number of such married gay couples is relatively small.

A large segment of the gay community looks forward to gay marriage for precisely this reason. Many thoughtful gay activists see same-sex marriage as a chance to redefine marriage itself—stripping marriage of what they see as its outdated and constricting connection to monogamy. And of course, even more powerfully than openly non-monogamous gay marriages, legalized group marriage would destroy the taboo against adultery. (Lots of potential for movies and TV there.)

Still, the libertarian asks, *Would the group marriage next door really make me leave my wife?* Maybe not. Of course, the married commune next door might invite the two of you over for some fun, with potentially problematic results for your marriage. But even that is not the real problem. The deeper difficulty is simply the breaking of the taboo on adultery. Sodomy laws were barely enforced, yet they made a collective statement about social attitudes toward non-marital and non-reproductive sexuality. Similarly, incest laws are rarely invoked. Yet their existence reinforces the horror of incest, and helps prevent the sort of violations that make incestuous temptation thinkable.

So the mere social statement that marriage does not mean monogamy is where the real danger of legalized gay marriage and polyamory lie. And the collapse of consensus about shared social institutions really does [affect] us as individuals. Once we as a society no longer take it for granted that marriage means monogamy, you may not decide to leave your wife. But you may be more likely to give in to the temptation of an affair. And that could mean the end of your marriage, whether that's what you wanted going into the affair or not. . . .

As with the taboos on incest and sodomy, society can't enforce the taboo on adultery with laws. Laws on matters of sexual conduct do make a difference, but less as enforcement mechanisms than as embodiments of common values. Precisely because the state cannot monitor and prosecute adultery, society writes a taboo against the practice into our hearts. The laws of marriage as currently constituted embody and express that taboo. Transform those laws, and the taboo will disappear.

The ongoing need for shared social understandings on matters pertaining to the family and sexuality does not fit neatly into the libertarian playbook. Social and sexual taboos are the stuff of traditional societies. But the truth is, so long as we live, not merely as isolated individuals, but in families together, we shall be in need of social and sexual taboos.

If the controversy over Senator Rick Santorum's remarks has made it possible to openly discuss the real basis of our shared social and sexual understandings, then it will have done some good. Unlike Sen. Santorum, I would rather accept some disruption in family stability than go back to the days when homosexuality itself was deeply tabooed. The increase in freedom and fairness is worth it. Yet there has been a terrible social cost for the changes of the Sixties. We need to mitigate those costs. And we certainly do not need to risk the destruction of an already weakened family system by radically undermining the ethos of monogamy.

Gay marriage would set in motion a series of threats to the ethos of monogamy from which the institution of marriage may never recover. Yet up to now, our society has been unable to face the real costs and consequences of the proposed change. That is partly because of an understandable sympathy for the gay-rights movement. But it also reflects the sheer inability of modern folk to grasp the operation, necessity—or even the existence—of the system of moral consensus and prohibition upon which society itself depends.

QUESTIONS FOR REFLECTION

1. What is the importance of a shared moral code, according to Kurtz?
2. How is incest analogous to homosexuality, in his view?
3. Kurtz approves the weakening of the taboo against homosexuality. Why?
4. Why does he refuse to extend that reasoning to gay marriage?
5. How would approval of gay marriage harm heterosexual marriages, in Kurtz's opinion? Do you agree?

ANDREW KOPPELMAN

from *The Decline and Fall of the Case against Same-Sex Marriage*

Andrew Koppelman is Professor of Law and Political Science at Northwestern University. (Source: University of St. Thomas Law Journal: Fides et Iustitia. *Copyright © 2004, University of St. Thomas Law Journal. Notes have been omitted.)*

II. The Two Debates over Same-Sex Marriage

Now let's turn to the merits of the question whether same-sex marriage should be permitted. In recent years, for better or worse, discussions about gay rights have shifted away from AIDS prevention, HIV and health care, anti-gay violence, immigration, employment discrimination, sodomy laws, and the military's exclusion of gays. The Hawaii Supreme Court's 1993 decision that same-sex marriage is a constitutional right was eventually overruled by a state constitutional amendment, but it placed the issue onto the national agenda, where it remains prominent today.

The controversy over same-sex marriage involves a confusing congeries of issues. Questions about health insurance and hospital visitation intersect with deeper ones, about which family forms are valued and who is a full citizen. And at the center of it all is the word "marriage," which is emotionally fraught for reasons that have never been fully explained. I will begin by attempting an explanation.

One reason why the debate is so muddled is that we are really having two debates at once. The first is a normative debate about what relationships to value or even to sanctify. The second is a debate about administration—about which relationships ought to have legal consequences.

The normative debate concerns what relationships are intrinsically valuable. It is taking place within most religious denominations within the United States, creating divisions that sometimes approach schism. The key question is one about objective moral reality: Are same-sex relationships, as such, morally equal to heterosexual relationships, or do heterosexual relationships partake of a good that homosexual relationships cannot possibly share? The conservatives have some powerful resources: authoritative texts, longstanding traditions, the considered views of clergy, and a primitive revulsion that many feel toward homosexual sex. If their views have not carried the day, it is only because of the fundamental difficulty of having to maintain (as they must) that there is too much love in the world, and that we therefore must weed out love of the wrong kind.

The most powerful argument on the other side notices the strong resemblance between the most successful heterosexual couples and their gay counterparts, in terms of both care for spouses and the creation of a family environment in which children can thrive. Like things should be treated alike. Unless there is some salient moral difference between the two kinds of couple, they should be treated the same.

This argument has been powerful enough that the burden has been shifting to the opponents of same-sex marriage to explain just what the moral difference is.

The conservative view may or may not be linked to the view that homosexual relations are intrinsically wrong. Many Americans detach the two. The number of Americans who oppose same-sex marriage considerably exceeds the number who think that homosexual conduct is always wrong.

The administrative debate concerns what relationships between persons ought to be given legal recognition. Here the issue is nothing as exalted as intrinsic value. It is the more mundane questions of how resources should be allocated and unfair disruption of people's lives prevented. Like it or not, households, of whatever kind, and relationships of dependency exist. From those relationships, one can reasonably infer what the members of those households would want and need if some unprovided-for contingency arises, such as the illness or death of one of them. From this perspective, law ought to maximize welfare by reflecting people's preferences and providing the default options that they would probably have chosen had they been able to think about it. The task of constructing the law of marriage is analogous to the task of constructing the law of business corporations: How can the state maximize efficiency and satisfy people's preferences about their relationships by constructing sensible "one size fits all" default rules, while protecting the interests of third parties, notably children? Here it all turns on what we know about the effects of various practices and policies. And issues of sanctification are very far from our minds.

The American puzzle is that here the two debates have become conflated. In part this is because, during the Reformation, marriage stopped being a sacrament and was therefore handed over to the state, but never lost its quasi-mystical associations. Joseph Story in 1834 called civil marriage "a religious, as well as a natural and civil contract," and the Supreme Court in 1890 described "the holy state of matrimony" as "a sacred obligation." The state thus found itself in the peculiar business of administering a sacrament. Moreover, America has always thought of itself in religious terms, as "a city on a hill," and this idea survives in modern American civil religion. The First Amendment notwithstanding, religion of a peculiar kind has been an integral part of American identity.

This is why so many contemporary Americans are willing to split the difference by acquiescing in "civil unions," which have all the benefits of marriage without the name. Americans oppose same-sex marriage by overwhelming margins, typically two to one. But polls also show that the label of "marriage" is all that many really care about. So long as that line isn't crossed, they are quite willing to let the law recognize same-sex relationships. A poll in March 2000 found that health insurance for gay partners was supported by 58 percent of Americans, and 54 percent thought—contrary to the federal Defense of Marriage Act—that partners should get Social Security benefits. (Only 34 percent of those polled thought there should be legally sanctioned same-sex marriages.) When people are asked about giving gay couples all the same legal rights as married couples, the split is one-third in favor, one-third against, and one-third who don't care.

On the other hand, if the word "marriage" is used, not only do the numbers shift, but passions suddenly run very high. Richard Viguerie, the most experienced conservative direct-mail fundraiser in the country, told the *New York Times* after the Massachusetts decision legalizing same-sex marriage in that state that same-sex marriage will be a better fundraising issue than abortion. "I have never seen anything that has energized and provoked our grass roots like this issue, including *Roe* v. *Wade*," said Richard Land, president of the Ethics and Religious Liberty Commission of the Southern Baptist Convention, which has 16 million members. This presents a puzzle. According to what view of the world could same-sex marriage possibly be a more severe problem than abortion, when it is stipulated that abortion involves the killing of millions of babies?

If the legal issue of same-sex marriage is actually a religious one, then the puzzle can be solved. Abortion may be thought a great moral evil, but it is not one that the state participates in. The state merely tolerates it. If marriage is a state-administered sacrament, on the other hand, then state recognition of the wrong kind of marriage is a kind of sacrilege, a profaning of the temple. It's easy to see why that would raise the blood pressure of conservatives. Thus

President George W. Bush, announcing his support for a constitutional amendment prohibiting same-sex marriage: "Marriage cannot be severed from its cultural, religious and natural roots without weakening the good influence of society." Or Rep. Henry Hyde, during the debate over the federal Defense of Marriage Act:

> People don't think that the traditional marriage ought to be demeaned or trivialized by same-sex unions. If two men want to love each other, go right ahead. If you want to solemnize your love affair by some ceremony, create one. But don't take marriage, which for centuries has been a union between man and woman, and certainly is in this country, and try to say that what you're doing is American.

So why not just compromise and enact an equivalent without the label? In Vermont, Connecticut, and California, "civil unions" and "domestic partnerships" give same-sex couples nearly all the legal benefits of marriage. When California enacted its law, with no prodding from any court, the legislation was so uncontroversial that the national press hardly even picked up the story.

There are two reasons why gay rights advocates resist the "civil unions" compromise. First, they also buy into the sanctification narrative, and they want their relationships sanctified, too. Jonathan Rauch thus writes that "marriage is society's most fundamental institution. To bar any class of people from marrying as they choose is an extraordinary deprivation." Andrew Sullivan describes marriage as "the social institution that defines for many people the most meaningful part of their lives." More is at issue here than legal benefits.

When the normative debate shifts to this ground, asking what relationships the state ought to honor, the gay advocates are on stronger ground than they are in the religious sphere, because the dogmas and revelations that traditionalists rely on are not articulable in this context. It is a deeply entrenched American norm that government may not declare religious truth. The prohibitions of Leviticus may be a good reason for an orthodox rabbi to refuse to celebrate a same-sex marriage, but they don't offer a sensible conversational move for a legislator.

The second objection to civil unions is that gays don't want second-class status, and that's what civil unions amount to. They are unwilling to concede that their relationships are in any way different from heterosexual marriages: Couples of both types are equally able to form households, care for each other, and create environments in which children can thrive. The Massachusetts Supreme Judicial Court rejected such unions, because they "would have the effect of maintaining and fostering a stigma of exclusion that the Constitution prohibits." Here gays can draw on a second American redemption narrative, the long struggle for equality. This struggle, of course, also has a religious dimension, with themes of sacrifice and rebirth symbolized in the lives and deaths of Lincoln and King. The gay struggle for equality in many ways resembles the struggle against racism. Both narratives prominently feature vicious, irrational prejudice, gang violence met with official indifference, pervasive discrimination, and an unresponsive political system. Separate but equal has an unattractive history.

. . .

B. The Spectre of Family Decline

Opponents of same-sex marriage have lately abandoned the claim that homosexual conduct is intrinsically evil, and have shifted to a different kind of claim: that indisputably bad consequences will follow if same-sex marriage is recognized. Thus Maggie Gallagher argues that same-sex marriage "affirms that children do not need mothers and fathers, and that marriage has nothing to do with babies," and claims that if the state endorses this message, there will be an increase in "poverty and trauma caused by widespread fatherlessness." Stanley Kurtz claims that the recognition of same-sex relationships in the Scandinavian countries has led to a decline in heterosexual marriage. "Instead of encouraging a society-wide return to marriage, Scandinavian gay marriage has driven home the message that marriage itself is outdated, and that virtually any family form, including out-of-wedlock parenthood, is acceptable."

Their understanding of marriage is functionalist rather than essentialist. Marriage is not a timeless telos, . . . but rather is a human construct created to bring about certain desirable results. Same-sex marriage is bad, these writers claim, because it will make those desirable results occur less frequently.

The basic argument here is that same-sex marriage is a signifier for a kind of individualism that is corrosive of the kinds of commitments on which children depend. Same-sex marriage depends on the idea that "marriage is an essentially private, intimate, emotional relationship created by two people for their own personal reasons to enhance their own personal well-being." This idea, because it recognizes no moral constraints outside the preferences of the adult self, is dangerous to children, because it corrodes the idea that parents have obligations to children even if they did not choose to bring them into the world. "Far more than mothers, reliable fathers are cultural creations, products of specific ideals, norms, rituals, and mating and parenting practices."

Now, it is true that there is an individualistic philosophy abroad in our culture that is in tension with the idea of any moral constraint outside the choices of the self. That philosophy is indeed potentially corrosive of ties between parents and children. It is also internally incoherent, because authentic choice only makes sense against a background of values that are not themselves chosen. But what has this got to do with same-sex marriage?

Recall that a chronic difficulty for arguments against same-sex marriage is their vulnerability to empirical refutation. . . . The Gallagher-Kurtz position is likewise nicely immunized against this danger. There is no way to disprove its claim, in which the alleged causal chain runs through the unobservable consciousnesses of millions of people. The problem is that there's not much reason to believe it, either. It's hard to imagine how legal recognition of same-sex marriage would affect even one man's deliberations about whether to marry a woman or to stay with his children.

It is good for children to grow up in stable, loving households. But this tells us nothing about relationships between gay people, many of whom have stable loving households of their own and are raising children very competently. Gallagher argues that if same-sex marriage is recognized, "marriage will no longer be about producing and protecting the next generation, or about getting mothers and fathers for children. In the new regime, marriage will be about legally affirming the sexual and emotional lifestyles of adults in the governing class." But, as she acknowledges elsewhere, these two models of marriage "are not mutually exclusive." Marriage performs both functions: it is good for adults and good for children. Some marriages, notably childless ones, follow the second model. But same-sex couples with children are closer to the first.

It is just bad anthropology to claim that same-sex marriage is understood by Americans to stand for corrosive individualism. Kurtz makes a similar leap in his discussion of Scandinavia. He blames the declining rate of heterosexual marriage there on the recognition of same-sex marriage, but not a single country treated same-sex relationships as equal to marriage during the period he discusses. It is always dangerous to attribute a unitary cultural meaning to anything, particularly in a culture as pluralistic and fragmented as ours. But it's particularly dangerous with respect to same-sex marriage.

Some gay rights advocates, such as Michael Warner and Michel Foucault, are proponents of radical individualism. But it is noteworthy that none of them are advocates of same-sex marriage. They understand that marriage, as an institution, privileges some choices over others. That's why they have a problem with it.

When one reads the supporters of same-sex marriage, one gets a different set of predictions about the cultural consequences, because those writers attribute a different kind of significance to same-sex marriage. William Eskridge claims that same-sex marriage will move gay people "From Sexual Liberty to Civilized Commitment." Andrew Sullivan, Jonathan Rauch, and Gabriel Rotello all claim that same-sex marriage would change the behavior and self-understanding of gay people, toward monogamy and stable two-partner households. Michael Warner and Janet Halley agree, though they are deeply suspicious of this attempted normalization.

I don't think that there's enough evidence to support any of these claims. (Probably the strongest of them is Warner, who offers a detailed analysis of the political and cultural economy of the normalization process and a history of how it has in fact played out in recent New York City politics.) Each offers a plausible, but no more than plausible, scenario of the aftermath of marriage recognition. Which scenario prevails will depend on cultural variables that cannot now confidently be predicted. All one can say with confidence is that different people will attribute different meanings to the legal recognition of same-sex marriage. This is a pretty vague consideration to weigh against the concrete benefits of legal recognition.

Institutions simply don't have stable cultural meanings. For example, the YMCA began as a Christian organization that successfully crusaded in favor of censorship and managed to make it a crime to distribute truthful information about contraception. It is today associated with the best known popular song based on gay culture, which is sung by many Americans who grasp its homoerotic subtext dimly or not at all. Also, in arguments about marriage law, the spectre of polygamy gets tossed about, but the meaning of polygamy is similarly multifaceted. For the original Mormons, it stood for a certain type of institutionalization of patriarchy, with assumptions about gender that are not all that different from those held by contemporary opponents of same-sex marriage. For some modern Mormon polygamists, it stands for a certain kind of feminism, in which women have more freedom and power than they have in monogamous relationships. For other modern "polyamorists," it stands for a certain kind of liberation from traditional constraints, of just the kind that contemporary conservatives fear.

Some writers try to stabilize the Gallagher/Kurtz view by combining it with the NNL [New Natural Law] position. The advantage of NNL is that, if its premises are accepted, heterosexuality and homosexuality have a definite moral valence that is not hostage to the vagaries of popular culture. The result, though, is an unstable combination of consequentialism and nonconsequentialism. One might think, for example, that bad consequences follow if the culture becomes too far removed from the NNL view. The trouble with this move is that the NNL view is so obscure and unfamiliar that it is hard to maintain that its argument is a significant part of our culture's shared understandings.

As a causal claim, the Gallagher/Kurtz position is dubious. When one presses it to find out just what the mechanism is whereby recognition of same-sex marriage will induce heterosexual fathers to abandon their children, the answer appears to be that what keeps fathers around is the fathers' belief, correct or not, that marriage is mystically connected with biological inevitability. This delusion is understood by Kurtz, though perhaps not by Gallagher, to be embedded in other mystifications about gender, prominently males' delusions that they are the rulers of the women who in fact rule them. Call this the Grand Inquisitor view: people cannot behave well unless they are induced to do so by miracle, mystery, and authority. There's no way to conclusively refute the Grand Inquisitor view. People can sometimes be pretty stupid and self-destructive, and mystifications can sometimes induce them to behave better than they otherwise would. But in this context, the hypothesis is unduly pessimistic. I have three kids, and I don't think I stick around because I'm mystified or confused.

The claim that same-sex marriage symbolizes corrosive individualism can't be refuted, because anything can symbolize anything. There are dangers in this kind of symbolic politics. Symbolic dangers can't be contained, and can seem enormously threatening. There is no limit to what can be justified by invoking them.

The Gallagher/Kurtz claim is best understood, not as a causal one, but as a report of a mental association. Gay people appear to be in some way associated in many people's minds with social trends that they dislike. But an association is not an argument, and it is a terrible basis for social policy. Salem, Massachusetts in 1692, historians Paul Boyer and Stephen Nissenbaum observe, was in the throes of social and economic upheaval, as an older agrarian order was being replaced by a new commercial one. Those who were accused of witchcraft were, for the most part, much more involved in the commercial activities of the nearby port than their accusers were. Unable to understand the forces that were transforming their world, the Salem villagers "lashed out with accusations not only against those who seemed in one way or another to represent the new order, but also against those who reminded them how far they, themselves, had already been seduced from their traditional moorings." They hanged 19 people and had more than 100 other suspects in jail when the trials ended. It did no good. The commercial and secular world continued its inexorable advance. Opponents of same-sex marriage like to talk about morality, but their eagerness to scapegoat innocent people for social problems that those people have nothing to do with has moral implications of its own.

The Gallagher/Kurtz view rests on admirable motives. Both authors are clearly concerned about the well-being of children and eager to promote stable families in which children can thrive. But there is no reason to think that any heterosexual family will benefit from withholding marriage from same-sex couples. What is certain is that some children will be harmed when their families are denied recognition. Gallagher and Kurtz are fighting for a good cause, but they are firing on their own troops.

QUESTIONS FOR REFLECTION

1. What are the two debates Koppelman distinguishes?
2. Why does Koppelman reject civil unions as an adequate option for same-sex relationships?
3. How does Koppelman argue that same-sex marriage would be good for children?
4. What is the Grand Inquisitor view, and how does Koppelman see it operating in the same-sex marriage debate?
5. Is there any reason to think that gay marriage would threaten heterosexual couples? Why or why not?

MAGGIE GALLAGHER

from *(How) Will Gay Marriage Weaken Marriage as a Social Institution: A Reply to Andrew Koppelman*

(*Source:* University of St. Thomas Law Journal 5 *[2004]: 32–70. Notes are omitted.)*

II. Why Marriage?

The central question raised by the same-sex marriage debate is therefore the question that Koppelman cannot answer: why *this* sanctification narrative and not some other, or no sanctification narrative at all? What right does the government have, and what interests of the state are served by singling out this one kind of relationship for special legal attention? What business is it of the government to sustain or reinforce norms about people's private, intimate lives?

As we've seen, this is a very hard question for advocates of same-sex marriage to answer. Dependency, love, "like it or not people already live like this," none of these can reliably discriminate between the kinds of relationships that are legally defined as marriage and the kinds that, however intrinsically valued and socially important, are legally unregulated.

So what is the answer? Why does marriage exist as a legal institution? What justifies its continued existence?

A. The historical answer in the American legal tradition

Historically, the reason marriage exists as a legal institution is clear. A virtually uninterrupted series of both lower court decisions and Supreme Court decisions until quite recently affirmed the primary purpose of marriage as a *legal* institution is to manage the sexually-based phenomenon known as "procreation." This is not quite the same as saying "marriage is in order to produce children." Marriage is not a factory for childbearing. Marriage existed to encourage men and women to create the next generation in the right context and simultaneously to discourage the creation of children in other contexts—out of wedlock in fatherless homes.

The reason marriage was singled out for special legal attention is that it is the only human relationship that can both (a) produce the next generation of babies and (b) connect those babies to both their mother and father.

Note that throughout this period, some married couples have not had children and older couples were allowed to marry. Yet legislators, courts, and the public continued to understand marriage's prime purpose as regulating sexual relationships in the interests of managing procreation. They understood that because sexual relationships between men and women outside of marriage regularly give rise to children, "narrowly tailoring" marriage would defeat its core public purpose. When men and women engage in extended sexual careers outside of marriage, pregnancy is the almost invariable result. At any age getting men and women attracted to the opposite sex into stable marital unions was understood to protect the interests of children and society in a stable social order.

B. The cross-cultural answer: Marriage as a universal human institution

Nor was it only American society that understood marriage in these terms. Marriage is a virtually universal social institution. It by no means always looks like our own particular marriage system, which is deeply rooted in Judeo-Christian-Roman cultural assumptions. But everywhere marriage has something to do with bringing together a man and a woman into a public—not merely private—sexual union, in which the rights and responsibilities of the husband and wife towards each other and any children their sexual union produces are publicly—not privately—defined and enforced.

As twelve family scholars pointed out recently:

> Marriage exists in virtually every known human society. . . . [A]t least since the beginning of recorded history, in all the flourishing varieties of human cultures documented by anthropologists, marriage has been a universal human institution. As a virtually universal human idea, marriage is about regulating the reproduction of children, families, and society. . . . [M]arriage across societies is a publicly acknowledged and supported sexual union which creates kinship obligations and sharing of resources between men, women, and the children that their sexual union may produce.

Other scholars have written:

> Marriage is a universal social institution, albeit with myriad variations in social and cultural details. A review of the cross-cultural diversity in marital arrangements reveals certain common themes: some degree of mutual obligation between husband and wife, a right of sexual access (often but not necessarily exclusive), an expectation that the relationships will persist (although not necessarily for a lifetime), some cooperative investment in offspring, and some sort of recognition of the status of the couple's children. The marital alliance is fundamentally a reproductive alliance.

I am not arguing that simply because marriage has always been about this it cannot ever be changed. That would be un-American. The question is: Why do so many wildly different kinds of societies come up with some version of marriage? There are not that many universal human social institutions. What is it about human nature that leads culturally separate and distinct societies to independently come up with the same basic idea?

Here is what I think the answer is: Marriage as a universal social institution is grounded in certain universal features of human nature. When men and women have sex, they make babies. Reproduction may be optional for individuals, but it is not optional for societies. Societies that fail to have "enough" babies fail to survive. And babies are most likely to grow to functioning adulthood when they have the care and attention of both their mother and their father.

Marriage arises again and again in some form out of the basic human need for a social institution to manage these basic human sexual realities. Societies that fail to manage these realities fail to survive long enough to be recorded by anthropologists among the human alternatives.

C. Does this marriage idea still matter? Contemporary evidence from the social sciences

Sex makes babies. Society needs babies. Babies deserve mothers and fathers. Together these three ideas explain the public purposes of marriage, its shape and its form. Marriage intrinsically aims at an enduring, exclusive, sexual union between a man and a woman, because managing the procreative consequences of human sexual attraction is at the core of its reason for existence.

Notice that all three of the components of the marriage idea are now contested in the public square. So the question arises: Is each of these three core marriage propositions still true? Do we still need a legal and social institution whose purpose is to manage the procreative consequences of sexual attraction between men and women, or have we transcended this great, historic, cross-cultural universal human imperative through technology or other means?

1. Does sex make babies? Forty years after *Griswold* v. *Connecticut*, we now have considerable social experience testing these propositions. Does sex still make babies? Yes. Sex between men and women continues to make babies on a regular basis, with or without the conscious intention of the participants. The longer men and women engage in non-marital sexual careers, the greater the risk of a non-marital pregnancy. Despite legal contraception, numerous studies have shown that unintended pregnancy is the common, not rare, consequence of sexual relationships between men and women.

By their late thirties, 60 percent of American women had had at least one unintended pregnancy. Almost 4 in 10 women aged 40–44 had had at least one unplanned birth.

Similarly, a scholarly analysis of contraceptive failure rates in actual use concluded, "almost half of all pregnancies were unintended in 1994. Some 53 percent of these occurred among women who were using contraceptives."

Another analysis of the 1995 National Survey of Family Growth concluded:

> The risk of failure during typical use of reversible contraceptives in the United States is not low—overall, 9% of women become pregnant within one year of starting use. The typical woman who uses reversible methods of contraception continuously from her 15th to her 45th birthday will experience 1.8 contraceptive failures.

The typical woman who uses contraceptives continuously will experience almost two unintended pregnancies. Contraceptive technology lowers the odds of pregnancy, but never eliminates the risk, especially for people who engage in extended non-marital sexual careers. The existence of contraceptives does not eliminate the state's interest in preferring voluntary marital sexual unions between men and women to other kinds. *Virtually every child born to a married couple will have a mother and a father already committed to caring for him or her. Most children conceived in sexual unions outside of marriage will not.*

2. *Does society need babies?* The second historic purpose of marriage is to encourage men and women to make the next generation. Does society still need babies? The experience of most of the developed nations of the world makes clear that depopulation, not overpopulation, is the threat most to be feared in the contemporary context. America is one of the only developed nations that has birthrates even close to levels necessary to prevent steep depopulation.

Europe's total fertility rate (TFR) from 1995 to 2000 was 1.42 children per woman. (Demographers define "very low fertility" as a birthrate below 1.5 children.)

What are the consequences of these very low levels of procreation? At the April 2, 2004 meeting the Population Association of America, U.N. demographer Joseph Chamie warned,

> [a] growing number of countries view their low birth rates with the resulting population decline and ageing to be a serious crisis, jeopardizing the basic foundations of the nation and threatening its survival. Economic growth and vitality, defense, and pensions and health care for the elderly, for example, are all areas of major concern.

A paper presented at one recent United Nations conference indicates that fertility levels of 1.5 to 1.8 children per woman constitute a "[s]trong dearth calling for deep revision of population policy. . . . [H]igher risk of labour shortage and reduced capacity to integrate new immigrants; since the main engine of integration of foreigners is the school, this integration cannot happen if a minimal fertility is not realized among the resident population."

As fertility levels fall to 1.2 to 1.5 children per woman (the European average), the result is "[h]eavy and structural contraction, which digs a deep hole at the [base] of the age pyramid and consequently compromises the future of the society at large. . . . [T]he resident population is progressively replaced by a continuous and bulky inflow of immigrants."

As fertility falls to less than 1.2 children per woman, as in Spain and Italy, the situation becomes an

> [e]xtreme case that is less and less rare, namely in Southern Europe and in the former Eastern bloc. A severe amputation of the base of the age pyramid is taking place under our eyes. . . . Acute and rapid aging process; deep and longlasting migratory dependency that could be unbearable or unmanageable.

The familiar population explosion is replaced by a population implosion or "exponential decrease." Financial consequences include "[t]he growing transfer of resources for the elderly (pension and health costs) to the detriment of younger workers," which can create a "feedback effect, creating a disincentive to fertility."

Far from making marriage obsolete as a regulator of childbearing, widespread contraceptive and abortion rights may actually make more salient, not less, the traditional role of marriage in encouraging men and women to make the next generation that society needs.

High birth rates may not be better than lower birth rates; but societies that fail to reproduce do not survive. Every society needs an institution that encourages men and women to have children if they want them.

The more legal, cultural, and technological choice individuals have about whether or not to have children, the more need there is for a social institution that encourages men and women to have babies together, and that creates the conditions under which those children are likely to flourish.

3. ***Do moms and dads matter?*** By making marriage a permanent sexual union based on the fidelity of both spouses, the state seeks to increase the likelihood that children will be raised in "intact" families, cared for by their mother and father. State preferences for marriage over other kinds of unions transmit a clear message to the next generation: The man and the woman who make the baby are supposed to stick around, take care of each other and their baby too.

Many scholars have written extensively on the social science evidence of the importance of intact, married biological parents. A *Child Trends* research brief summed up the scholarly consensus on the family structures that have been well-studied to date:

> [R]esearch clearly demonstrates that family structure matters for children, and the family structure that helps children the most is a family headed by two biological parents in a low-conflict marriage. Children in single-parent families, children born to unmarried mothers, and children in stepfamilies or cohabiting relationships face higher risks of poor outcomes. . . . There is thus value for children in promoting strong, stable marriages between biological parents.

These benefits, it should be noted, are not the results of specific legal incentives to parents or partners. Children whose single mothers remarry, for example, do not do any better on average than children whose mothers remain single. The primary way that legal marriage protects child well-being, social science suggests, is by increasing the likelihood that the child's own mother and father will stay together in a harmonious household.

While scholars continue to disagree about the size of the marital advantage and the mechanisms by which it is conferred, the weight of social science evidence strongly supports the idea that family structure matters and that children do best when raised by their own mother and father in a decent, loving marriage.

III. How Does Marriage Law Matter?

Laws do more than incentivize or punish, as Mary Ann Glendon has pointed out. They educate directly and indirectly. They define the boundaries of organizations, institutions, and relationships in the public square. One of the most basic ways that the law of marriage helps regulate out-of-wedlock births, for example, is by defining a socially shared category of married births, without which the very idea of unmarried childbearing disappears.

If we cannot tell who is married, we cannot tell who is an unwed parent. We therefore cannot, in any shared public fashion, teach our children that it is best to wait until marriage before risking pregnancy. If we cannot tell who is married, we cannot tell who is committing adultery, either.

Thus one of the core ways the law of marriage protects marriage as a shared social institution is by defining its boundaries: Clearly marked entry and clearly marked exits mean that the category of marriage is sharply defined and contrasted with non-marriage.

By requiring a divorce, we clearly communicate that leaving a marriage is not just a private matter, a question of taste, like other love relationships. Marriage law helps sustain the core public (as opposed to private or sectarian) understandings of what marriage is and what purposes it serves.

The most important legal purpose of defining marriage is to communicate to the young the essential, broad characteristics of the normative (or ideal) sexual union. Marriage law actively reflects and communicates shared norms about marriage, and these allow marriage to function as a social institution, changing the behavior of men and women in ways that benefit not only them, but their children and the larger community.

To summarize the argument so far: Marriage law is important not because it distributes administrative benefits that help people live their private lives. The law of marriage serves the "sanctification narrative," sustaining the boundaries of marriage and the basic norms required of married people. The reason the state is justified in "imposing" such norms on people's intimate lives is that sex makes babies, societies need babies, and children deserve their own mothers and fathers. While marriage and children are optional for individuals, they are not for societies. Managing the sexually-based phenomenon known as "procreativity" is not optional, but essential if a civilization is to perpetuate itself over the long term. At least it has been in every known human society and (the evidence suggests) still is in our own.

IV. How Will Same-Sex Marriage Weaken Marriage as a Social Institution?: Some General Concerns

How will redefining marriage as a unisex institution affect marriage? Let me lay out some general concerns.

A. Change the public meaning of "marriage"

Social institutions, as Dan Cere has pointed out, are essentially "public markers of social meaning." They aren't simple, solid things. They consist largely of interlocking sets of ideas that regulate or affect the way people actually behave and the way they understand their relationships with others. "Meaning matters, and the institutions that bear it serve to structure our experiences and to steer them in a particular direction. They define our goals, focus attention on those goals, and direct us toward them." Similarly, Barbara Dafoe Whitehead pointed out the power of words as markers of shared meaning in a 1992 essay (on a different subject), "The Experts' Story of Marriage":

> [T]he marriage critics seek to devalorize marriage by stripping away its inherited mantle of meaning and by erasing the linguistic boundaries between marriage and non-marriage. This amounts to cultural hardball. For language—or more precisely, normative vocabulary—is one of the key cultural resources supporting and regulating any institution. Nothing is more essential to the integrity and strength of an institution than a common set of understandings, a shared body of opinion, about the meaning and purpose of the institution. And, conversely, nothing is more damaging to the integrity of an institution than an attack on this common set of understanding with the consequent fracturing of meaning.

Change the public meaning of a social institution, and you change the institution itself. As a matter of definition, if you widen the class of objects to which a category applies, you necessarily make the fit between the category and the object less tight.

How can we translate this general intellectual insight into specific terms that critics like Prof. Koppelman can perceive (if not necessarily agree with)?

Put it this way: Words, like social institutions, have no fixed meanings. There is no reason in the world why we—or the law—cannot redefine "cat" to mean "furry, domestic animal with four legs and a tail." Defining "cat" in this way has certain advantages. It reveals the deep underlying similarities for example between those two formerly opposite classifications: "dog" and "cat." Not to mention "gerbil," "rabbit," and "guinea pig."

What is lost in redefining "cat" in this way?

Well, there is one little thing: we now no longer have a word that means "cat." If we want to speak to each other about cats, we will either have to invent a new term, and hope it will still communicate the full valence of the old word (rich with historic associations and symbolic overtones), or we will have to do without a word for "cat" at all. One might reasonably foresee, without charting all the particular specific mechanisms, that it might become harder to communicate an idea for which we no longer have any word.

Instinct doesn't take human beings very far. Social institutions like marriage are created, sustained, and transmitted by words, and the images, symbols, and feelings, that surround words. Change the meaning of the word, and you change the thing itself.

One thing same-sex marriage indubitably does is displace certain formerly core public understandings about marriage: such as, that it has something to do with bringing together male and female, men with women, husbands and wives, mothers with fathers. Husband will no longer point to or imply wife. Mother no longer implies father.

Many thoughtful supporters of same-sex marriage recognize that some profound shift in our whole understanding of the world is wrapped up in this legal re-engineering of the meaning of marriage.

As Ladelle McWhorter acknowledged: "[Heterosexuals] are right, for example, that if same-sex couples get legally married, the institution of marriage will change, and since marriage is one of the institutions that support heterosexuality and heterosexual identities, heterosexuality and heterosexuals will change as well."

B. The legal "misfit": some specific concerns

What is true for the word itself is also true for the underlying legal apparatus. As the legal category of marriage is broadened to include both same- and opposite-sex couples, the fit between the legal forms of marriage and the thing being regulated will also become less good. This is a necessity of widening the definition of a legal class, widely understood in other contexts.

To see what I mean by this, take another look at the *San Francisco Chronicle* story. Patricia Robertson says registering as a marriage-like couple:

> may not be the most prudent decision for everyone. . . . Gay and lesbian relationships have not been as financially intertwined as marriage historically, which was traditionally structured on the basis that women were the property of men. . . . For a lot of LGBT (lesbian, gay, bisexual and transgender) people, being independent financially is an important part of who they are. . . . To be told by the law that their financial relationship is now expected to mimic that of a married couple is unknown territory.

The rules for marriage are continually revised and updated, but they are deeply grounded in assumptions that have arisen from experience in managing opposite-sex relationships.

Rules assuming financial obligations of spouses, for example, stem from the deep economic vulnerabilities imposed on women by pregnancy and childbearing. Even today, women with children cannot compete as effectively in the marketplace (on average) as childless women or men, and unwed mothers face the most serious economic risks of all.

Rules against adultery, for example (still on the books in 24 states) may not make sense for gay men, who at least some preliminary evidence suggests are more likely to stay together if they are NOT sexually exclusive and do not create nonmarital children when they have sex with other men. Either the rules/norms/values for sustaining permanent opposite-sex coupledom will be imposed on gay couples (who will chafe at the bad fit around the corners) or the rules will be expanded and redrawn at a more general level of unisex specificity that will make marriage as a legal form "fit" opposite-sex coupledom less well.

The latter is what the Ontario Court of Appeals explicitly demanded: that the legal and public meaning of marriage be revised to take into account the "needs, capacities and circumstances of same-sex couples, not . . . the needs, capacities and circumstances of opposite-sex couples." Many advocates for gay marriage, for example, now question the "rule of two" limiting marriage and its associated benefits to faithful couples, in part because of dramatic differences in how same-sex couples "generate" children. Right after *Goodridge,* two members of the board of the National Gay and Lesbian Law Association warned of the dangers of accepting the "primacy" of the "married, two-parent model":

> [S]ome same-sex couples may desire recognition of multiparty relationships. For example a same-sex couple who have a child with a known sperm donor [sic] or surrogate mother may wish to form a three-party relationship, with each party having recognized rights vis-a-vis the other parties and the child. Alternatively, a bisexual individual may wish to maintain a co-parenting relationship with a former partner even after each has formed a new primary relationship. Some LGBT individual may form polyamorous or ethically nonmonogamous relationships. . . . [I]t is therefore important to remain mindful of the diversity of real partnerships and households, and to engage critically the primacy of the married, two-parent model.

Or consider, to give another related suggestive example, the fit between the same-sex marriage and the "presumption of paternity," which is the legal presumption that the husband is the father of the wife's children. Traditionally, no one else has standing under the law to challenge the husband's claim to be the legal father of his wife's children if he asserts it—not even the wife. The law will automatically impose the legal obligation of paternity on the husband, unless he contests it on the grounds the children are not biologically his. The presumption of paternity is thus rooted in fused biological and social reality. In having sex with his wife, the husband assumes the risks of paternity. In promising sexual exclusivity to the husband, the wife accepts his right to claim her children as his own. The presumption of paternity accords not only with biological reality but with social reality as well: It is marriage to the mother that creates effective social fatherhood for most men. Outside of marriage to the mother of their child, only a minority of men remain effective fathers in their children's lives.

The *Goodridge* court listed the presumption of paternity as one of the prime benefits of marriage. Except that in order to make the presumption "fit" the new paradigm of unisex marriage, it transformed the traditional presumption of paternity into something entirely new, called a presumption of "parentage."

What will the presumption of parentage do? Well, no one knows exactly, as this is uncharted legal ground. But presumably the law will now grant a lesbian partner the status of co-parent of any children her spouse bears. Presumably it will apply as well to a gay man who has children with a surrogate mother, or when one man adopts a child. If one husband becomes a father, the other will be a father, too.

Immediately, however, one can see problems even with this adaptation of the presumption of paternity to a unisex right. First, there is the problem of "too many" parents. What happens to the parental rights of the other biological parent under the presumption of parentage? Then there is the problem of consent to parenthood (particularly acute in a system which elevates decisions about whether or not to have children into a constitutional right). Unlike heterosexual couples, who are presumed to consent to co-parenting by having marital sex, spouses in same-sex marriages will be able to impose parental obligations on their spouse without any expression of consent on their part at all. Either that, or the "presumption of parentage" in the law will now be contestable not because the spouse is not the biological parent, but because the spouse did not consent to the child. Can these new grounds for contesting parenthood be limited only to same-sex couples? Or will all men (thanks to the new presumption of parentage) have a new legal standing to reject the obligations of fatherhood on the grounds they only consented to sex and not to parenthood?

Either the legal incidents of marriage will be designed around opposite-sex sexual reality, or they will be designed around the allegedly more generic "gender neutral" same-sex sexual reality. In either case, one of the two groups is going to find the "fit" between the legal form and the relationship being regulated is not as good.

If the idea of marriage really does matter—if society really does need a social institution that manages opposite-sex attractions in the interests of children and society—then taking an already weakened social institution, subjecting it to radical new redefinitions, and hoping that there are no consequences is probably neither a wise nor a compassionate idea. Particularly since the class of people to be benefited is so small, and alternative mechanisms for meeting their social needs (ones perhaps even better designed for them than marriage) have hardly been seriously tried, much less exhausted.

QUESTIONS FOR REFLECTION

1. How has the American legal tradition generally viewed marriage?
2. Why, according to Gallagher, is marriage a nearly universal human institution?
3. How do falling birthrates in Europe fit into Gallagher's argument?
4. How do laws educate? What is the educational function of the current definition of marriage?
5. How would acceptance of gay marriage change the meaning of marriage?
6. What problems would a change in the meaning of marriage cause, according to Gallagher? How might Koppelman respond to her worries?

ANIMALS

Concern for the rights, interests, and welfare of animals is not new. In ancient India, Mahavira and the Buddha, founders of Jainism and Buddhism, respectively, taught that killing any sentient creature was wrong. The *Acaranga Sutra*, for example, proclaims, "All animals, living beings, organisms and sentient creatures should not be injured, governed, enslaved, tortured and killed." In the United States, Benjamin Franklin practiced vegetarianism for moral reasons. Eventually, he gave it up:

> I consider'd . . . the taking every fish as a kind of unprovoked murder, since none of them had, or ever could do us any injury that might justify the slaughter. All this seemed very reasonable. But I had formerly been a great lover of fish, and, when this came hot out of the fryingpan, it smelt admirably well. I balanc'd some time between principle and inclination, till I recollected that, when the fish were opened, I saw smaller fish taken out of their stomachs; then thought I, "If you eat one another, I don't see why we mayn't eat you." So I din'd upon cod very heartily, and continued to eat with other people, returning only now and then occasionally to a vegetable diet.*

Killing animals for meat or fur, using animals for research, factory farming, and other practices have become even more controversial in an affluent society in which such practices cannot be considered necessities of human survival.

Few people think that animals have no moral status. Someone who causes an animal gratuitous pain does something wrong. Yet to say that animals and humans are morally on a par also seems incorrect; for instance, someone who chooses to save a dog rather than a child from dying in a burning building surely makes a serious moral error. The difficulty is explaining what moral status animals do have, and why.

The International League of the Rights of Animals takes the extreme view that all animals have equal claims on life. That entails not only that killing animals for fur or meat, using animals in research, and so forth are wrong, but also that organizations promoting the humane treatment of animals are wrong to euthanize unwanted animals; that pet owners are wrong to spay, neuter, or confine their pets; and that zoos are immoral.

Peter Singer, a utilitarian, believes that all animals are equal in the sense that all suffering and all pleasure must be given moral weight, no matter who or what is suffering or feeling pleasure. From a utilitarian point of view, what matters is maximizing good. For a hedonistic utilitarian such as Bentham or Mill, the goal is maximizing the balance of pleasure over pain. Moral value depends solely on amounts of pleasure and pain; it makes no difference whether the pleasure or pain is felt by a human or an animal. This does not mean that it makes no moral difference whether one saves the life of a child or a dog, however, or that a hunter is the moral equivalent of a murderer. Just as Mill stresses that pleasures differ in quality—"It is better to be a human being dissatisfied than a pig satisfied"—Singer stresses that animals of different species have different capacities for pleasure and pain. Singer states that the same quantity of pain has the same moral value, no matter who feels it, but that humans are capable of greater suffering and greater happiness than animals are.

Tom Regan, a Kantian, also argues that animals deserve moral respect, but not solely because they have the capacity to suffer. Regan maintains that animals have rights just as humans do. Human life, we think, has inherent moral value; we would agree to that in the original position. Animal life, Regan says, also has inherent moral value, and any attempt to distinguish between degrees, levels, or kinds of inherent value to make human life more valuable faces serious difficulties. The distinction is bound to be arbitrary, Regan asserts, and also to imply that certain human lives are less valuable than others. We consider babies and people who are senile or comatose to have rights and to deserve full moral status.

**Autobiography*, in *The Works of Benjamin Franklin*, Volume I (Boston: Hilliard, Gray & Company, 1840), p. 46.

R. G. Frey steers away from talk of rights or even talk of moral status. He holds that animals do have moral standing—causing an animal gratuitous suffering is wrong—but nevertheless supports the use of animals in medical research under certain conditions. Animals matter from a moral point of view, but people matter more. Human lives are in general worth more than animal lives because they are of higher quality, containing a richer array of thoughts and experiences.

INTERNATIONAL LEAGUE OF THE RIGHTS OF ANIMALS

Universal Declaration of the Rights of Animals

(This declaration was adopted by the International League of the Rights of Animals and the affiliated national leagues in London, September 21–23, 1977. The declaration was solemnly proclaimed in Paris, October 15, 1978, at the House of the UNESCO. Detailed information on this declaration is available from Ligue Française des Droits de l'Animal.)

1. All animals are born with an equal claim on life and the same rights to existence.

2. All animals are entitled to respect. Man as an animal species shall not arrogate to himself the right to exterminate or inhumanely exploit other species. It is his duty to use his knowledge for the welfare of animals. All animals have the right to the attention, care, and protection of man.

3. No animals shall be ill-treated or be subject to cruel acts. If an animal has to be killed, this must be instantaneous and without distress.

4. All wild animals have the right to liberty in their natural environment, whether land, air, or water, and should be allowed to procreate. Deprivation of freedom, even for educational purposes, is an infringement of this right.

5. Animals of species living traditionally in a human environment have the right to live and grow at the rhythm and under the conditions of life and freedom peculiar to their species. Any interference by man with this rhythm or these conditions for purposes of gain is infringement of this right.

6. All companion animals have the right to complete their natural life span. Abandonment of an animal is a cruel and degrading act.

7. All working animals are entitled to a reasonable limitation of the duration and intensity of their work, to necessary nourishment, and to rest.

8. Animal experimentation involving physical or psychological suffering is incompatible with the rights of animals, whether it be for scientific, medical, commercial, or any other form of research. Replacement methods must be used and developed.

9. Where animals are used in the food industry they shall be reared, transported, lairaged, and killed without the infliction of suffering.

10. No animal shall be exploited for the amusement of man. Exhibitions and spectacles involving animals are incompatible with their dignity.

11. Any act involving the wanton killing of the animals is biocide, that is, a crime against life.

12. Any act involving the mass killing of wild animals is genocide, that is, a crime against the species.

Pollution or destruction of the natural environment leads to genocide.

13. Dead animals shall be treated with respect. Scenes of violence involving animals shall be banned from cinema and television, except for human education.

14. Representatives of movements that defend animal rights should have an effective voice at all levels of government. The rights of animals, like human rights, should enjoy the protection of law.

QUESTIONS FOR REFLECTION

1. For each proposition in the declaration, name a common social practice that it would prohibit.
2. Animal welfare organizations sometimes euthanize unwanted animals. Is this practice acceptable, according to the declaration?
3. Animal welfare organizations often encourage spaying or neutering animals and sometimes spay or neuter populations of wild dogs or cats, for example. Is this practice acceptable, according to the declaration?
4. Darwin described nature as "red in tooth and claw," governed by scarcity and natural selection, "the survival of the fittest." Is that portrait of nature consistent with the declaration? Why or why not?

PETER SINGER

from *Animal Liberation*

Peter Singer is professor of philosophy and director of the Center for Human Values at Princeton University. (Source: Reprinted from Animal Liberation *[New York Review of Books, 1975, 1990], by permission of the author. Copyright © 1975, 1990 by Peter Singer.)*

All Animals Are Equal . . .

"Animal Liberation" may sound more like a parody of other liberation movements than a serious objective. The idea of "The Rights of Animals" actually was once used to parody the case for women's rights. When Mary Wollstonecraft, a forerunner of today's feminists, published her *A Vindication of the Rights of Woman* in 1792, her views were widely regarded as absurd, and before long an anonymous publication appeared entitled *A Vindication of the Rights of Brutes*. The author of this satirical work (now known to have been Thomas Taylor, a distinguished Cambridge philosopher) tried to refute Mary Wollstonecraft's arguments by showing that they could be carried one stage further. If the argument for equality was sound when applied to women, why should it not be applied to dogs, cats, and horses? The reasoning seemed to hold for these "brutes" too; yet to hold that brutes had rights was manifestly absurd; therefore the reasoning by which this conclusion had been reached must be unsound, and if unsound when applied to brutes, it must also be unsound when applied to women, since the very same arguments had been used in each case.

In order to explain the basis of the case for the equality of animals, it will be helpful to start with an examination of the case for the equality of women. Let us assume that we wish to defend the case for women's rights against the attack by Thomas Taylor. How should we reply?

One way in which we might reply is by saying that the case for equality between men and women cannot validly be extended to nonhuman animals. Women have a right to vote, for instance, because they are just as capable of making rational decisions about the future as men are; dogs, on the other hand, are incapable of understanding the significance of voting, so they cannot have the right to vote. There are many other obvious ways in which men and women resemble each other closely, while humans and animals differ greatly. So, it might be said, men and women are similar beings and should have similar rights, while humans and nonhumans are different and should not have equal rights.

The reasoning behind this reply to Taylor's analogy is correct up to a point, but it does not go far enough. There *are* important differences between humans and other animals, and these differences must give rise to *some* differences in the rights that each have. Recognizing this obvious fact, however, is no barrier to the case for extending the basic principle of equality to nonhuman animals. The differences that exist between men and women are equally undeniable, and the supporters of Women's Liberation are aware that these differences may give rise to different rights. Many feminists hold that women have the right to an abortion on request. It does not follow that since these same feminists are campaigning for equality between men and women they must support the right of men to have abortions too. Since a man cannot have an abortion, it is meaningless to talk of his right to have one. Since a dog can't vote, it is meaningless to talk of its right to vote. There is no reason why either Women's Liberation or Animal Liberation should get involved in such nonsense. The extension of the basic principle of equality from one group to another does not imply that we must treat both groups in exactly the same way, or grant exactly the same rights to both groups. Whether we should do so will depend on the nature of the members of the two groups. The basic principle of equality does not require equal or identical *treatment*; it requires equal *consideration*. Equal consideration for different beings may lead to different treatment and different rights.

So there is a different way of replying to Taylor's attempt to parody the case for women's rights, a way that does not deny the obvious differences between humans and nonhumans but goes more deeply into the question of equality and concludes by finding nothing absurd in the idea that the basic principle of equality applies to so-called "brutes." At this point such a conclusion may appear odd; but if we examine more deeply the basis on which our opposition to discrimination on grounds of race or sex ultimately rests, we will see that we would be on shaky ground if we were to demand equality for blacks, women, and other groups of oppressed humans while denying equal consideration to nonhumans. To make this clear we need to see, first, exactly why racism and sexism are wrong.

When we say that all human beings, whatever their race, creed, or sex, are equal, what is it that we are asserting? Those who wish to defend hierarchical, inegalitarian societies have often pointed out that by whatever test we choose it simply is not true that all humans are created equal. Like it or not we must face the fact that humans come in different shapes and sizes; they come with different moral capacities, different intellectual abilities, different amounts of benevolent feeling and sensitivity to the needs of others, different abilities to communicate effectively, and different capacities to experience pleasure and pain. In short, if the demand for equality were based on the actual equality of all human beings, we would have to stop demanding equality.

Still, one might cling to the view that the demand for equality among human beings is based on the actual equality of the different races and sexes. Although, it may be said, humans differ as individuals there are no differences between the races and sexes *as such*. From the mere fact that a person is black or a woman we cannot infer anything about that person's intellectual or moral capacities. This, it may be said, is why racism and sexism are wrong. The white racist claims that whites are superior to blacks, but this is false—although there are differences among individuals, some blacks are superior to some whites in all of the capacities and abilities that could conceivably be relevant. The opponent of sexism would say the same: a person's sex is no guide to his or her abilities, and this is why it is unjustifiable to discriminate on the basis of sex.

The existence of individual variations that cut across the lines of race or sex, however, provides us with no defense at all against a more sophisticated opponent of equality, one who proposes that, say, the interests of all those with IQ scores below 100 be given less consideration than the interests of those with ratings over 100. Perhaps those scoring below the mark would, in this society, be made the slaves of those scoring higher. Would a hierarchical society of this sort really be so much better than one based on race or sex? I think not. But if we tie the moral principle of equality to the factual equality of the different races or sexes, taken as a whole, our opposition to racism and sexism does not provide us with any basis for objecting to this kind of inegalitarianism.

There is a second important reason why we ought not to base our opposition to racism and sexism on any kind of factual equality, even the limited kind that asserts that variations in capacities and abilities are spread evenly between the different races and sexes: we can have no absolute guarantee that these capacities and abilities really are distributed evenly, without regard to race or sex, among human beings. So far as actual abilities are concerned there do seem to be certain measurable differences between both races and sexes. These differences do not, of course, appear in each case, but only when averages are taken. More important still, we do not yet know how much of these differences is really due to the different genetic endowments of the different races and sexes, and how much is due to poor schools, poor housing, and other factors that are the result of past and continuing discrimination. Perhaps all of the important differences will eventually prove to be environmental rather than genetic. Anyone opposed to racism and sexism will certainly hope that this will be so, for it will make the task of ending discrimination a lot easier; nevertheless it would be dangerous to rest the case against racism and sexism on the belief that all significant differences are environmental in origin. The opponent of, say, racism who takes this line will be unable to avoid conceding that *if* differences in ability do after all prove to have some genetic connection with race, racism would in some way be defensible.

Fortunately there is no need to pin the case for equality to one particular outcome of a scientific investigation. The appropriate response to those who claim to have found evidence of genetically based differences in ability between the races or sexes is not to stick to the belief that the genetic explanation must be wrong, whatever evidence to the contrary may turn up: instead we should make it quite clear that the claim to equality does not depend on intelligence, moral capacity, physical strength, or similar matters of fact. Equality is a moral idea, not an assertion of fact. There is no logicially compelling reason for assuming that a factual difference in ability between two people justifies any difference in the amount of consideration we give to their needs and interests. *The principle of the equality of human beings is not a description of an alleged actual equality among humans: it is a prescription of how we should treat humans.*

Jeremy Bentham, the founder of the reforming utilitarian school of moral philosophy, incorporated the essential basis of moral equality into his system of ethics by means of the formula: "Each to count for one and none for more than one." In other words, the interests of every being affected by an action are to be taken into account and given the same weight as the like interests of any other being. A later utilitarian, Henry Sidgwick, put the point in this way: "The good of any one individual is of no more importance, from the point of view (if I may say so) of the Universe, than the good of any other." More recently the leading figures in contemporary moral philosophy have shown a great deal of agreement in specifying as a fundamental presupposition of their moral theories some similar requirement which operates so as to give everyone's interests equal consideration—although these writers generally cannot agree on how this requirement is best formulated.

It is an implication of this principle of equality that our concern for others and our readiness to consider their interests ought not to depend on what they are like or on what abilities they may possess. Precisely what this concern or consideration requires us to do may vary according to the characteristics of those affected by what we do: concern for the well-being of a child growing up in America would require that we teach him to read; concern for the well-being of a pig may require no more than that we leave him alone with other pigs in a place where there is adequate food and room to run freely. But the basic element—the taking into account of the interests of the being, whatever those interests may be—must, according to the principle of equality, be extended to all beings, black or white, masculine or feminine, human or nonhuman.

Thomas Jefferson, who was responsible for writing the principle of the equality of men into the American Declaration of Independence, saw this point. It led him to oppose slavery even though he was unable to free himself fully from his slaveholding background. He wrote in a letter to the author of a book that emphasized the notable intellectual achievements of Negroes in order to refute the then common view that they had limited intellectual capacities:

> Be assured that no person living wishes more sincerely than I do, to see a complete refutation of the doubts I have myself entertained and expressed on the grade of understanding allotted to them by nature, and to find that they are on a par with ourselves . . . but whatever be their degree of talent it is no measure of their rights. Because Sir Isaac Newton was superior to others in understanding, he was not therefore lord of the property or person of others.

Similarly when in the 1850s the call for women's rights was raised in the United States a remarkable black feminist named Sojourner Truth made the same point in more robust terms at a feminist convention:

> . . . they talk about this thing in the head; what do they call it? ["Intellect," whispered someone near by.] That's it. What's that got to do with women's rights or Negroes' rights? If my cup won't hold but a pint and yours holds a quart, wouldn't you be mean not to let me have my little half-measure full?

It is on this basis that the case against racism and the case against sexism must both ultimately rest; and it is in accordance with this principle that the attitude that we may call "speciesism," by analogy with racism, must also be condemned. Speciesism—the word is not an attractive one, but I can think of no better term—is a prejudice or attitude of bias toward the interests of members of one's own species and against those members of other species. It should be obvious that the fundamental objections to racism and sexism made by Thomas Jefferson and Sojourner Truth apply equally to speciesism. If possessing a higher degree of intelligence does not entitle one human to use another for his own ends, how can it entitle humans to exploit nonhumans for the same purpose?

Many philosophers and other writers have proposed the principle of equal consideration of interests, in some form or other, as a basic moral principle; but not many of them have recognized that this principle applies to members of other species as well as to our own. Jeremy Bentham was one of the few who did realize this. In a forward-looking passage written at a time when black slaves had been freed by the French but in the British dominions were still being treated in the way we now treat animals, Bentham wrote:

> The day *may* come when the rest of the animal creation may acquire those rights which never could have been withholden from them but by the hand of tyranny. The French have already discovered that the blackness of the skin is no reason why a human being should be abandoned without redress to the caprice of a tormentor. It may one day come to be recognized that the number of the legs, the villosity of the skin, or the termination of the *os sacrum* are reasons equally insufficient for abandoning a sensitive being to the same fate. What else is it that should trace the insuperable line? Is it the faculty of reason, or perhaps the faculty of discourse? But a full-grown horse or dog is beyond comparison a more rational, as well as a more conversable animal, than an infant of a day or a week or even a month, old. But suppose they were otherwise, what would it avail? The question is not, Can they *reason*? nor Can they *talk*? but, Can they *suffer*?

In this passage Bentham points to the capacity for suffering as the vital characteristic that gives a being the right to equal consideration. The capacity for suffering—or more strictly, for suffering and/or enjoyment or happiness—is not just another characteristic like the capacity for language or higher mathemetics. Bentham is not saying that those who try to mark "the insuperable line" that determines whether the interests of a being should be considered happen to have chosen the wrong characteristic. By saying that we must consider the interests of all beings with the capacity for suffering or enjoyment Bentham does not arbitrarily exclude from consideration any interests at all—as those who draw the line with reference to the possession of reason or language do. The capacity for suffering and enjoyment is *a prerequisite for having interests at all*, a condition that must be satisfied before we can speak of interests in a meaningful way. It would be nonsense to say that it was not in the interests of a stone to be kicked along the road by a schoolboy. A stone does not have interests because it cannot suffer. Nothing that we can do to it could possibly make any difference to its welfare. A mouse, on the other hand, does have an interest in not being kicked along the road, because it will suffer if it is.

If a being suffers there can be no moral justification for refusing to take that suffering into consideration. No matter what the nature of the being, the principle of equality requires that its suffering be counted equally with the like suffering—in so far as rough comparisons can be made—of any other being. If a being is not capable of suffering, or of experiencing enjoyment or happiness, there is nothing to be taken into account. So the limit of sentience (using the term as a convenient if not strictly accurate shorthand for the capacity to suffer and/or experience enjoyment) is the only defensible boundary of concern for the interests of others. To mark this boundary by some other characteristic like intelligence or rationality would be to mark it in an arbitrary manner. Why not choose some other characteristic, like skin color?

The racist violates the principle of equality by giving greater weight to the interests of members of his own race when there is a clash between their interests and the interests of those of another race. The sexist violates the principle of equality by favoring the interests of his own sex. Similarly the speciesist allows the interests of his own species to override the greater interests of members of other species. The pattern is identical in each case.

Most human beings are speciesists. . . . [o]rdinary human beings, not a few exceptionally cruel or heartless humans, but the overwhelming majority of humans—take an active part in, acquiesce in, and allow their taxes to pay for practices that require the sacrifice of the most important interests of members of other species in order to promote the most trivial interests of our own species. . . .

Animals can feel pain. As we saw earlier, there can be no moral justification for regarding the pain (or pleasure) that animals feel as less important than the same amount of pain (or pleasure) felt by humans. But what exactly does this mean, in practical terms? To prevent misunderstanding I shall spell out what I mean a little more fully.

If I give a horse a hard slap across its rump with my open hand, the horse may start, but it presumably feels little pain. Its skin is thick enough to protect it against a mere slap. If I slap a baby in the same way, however, the baby will cry and presumably does feel pain, for its skin is more sensitive. So it is worse to slap a baby than a horse, if both slaps are administered with equal force. But there must be some kind of blow—I don't know exactly what it would be, but perhaps a blow with a heavy stick—that would cause the horse as much pain as we cause a baby by slapping it with our hand. That is what I mean by "the same amount of pain" and if we consider it wrong to inflict that much pain on a baby for no good reason then we must, unless we are speciesists, consider it equally wrong to inflict the same amount of pain on a horse for no good reason.

There are other differences between humans and animals that cause other complications. Normal adult human beings have mental capacities which will, in certain circumstances, lead them to suffer more than animals would in the same circumstances. If, for instance, we decided to perform extremely painful or lethal scientific experiments on normal adult humans, kidnaped at random from public parks for this purpose, every adult who entered a park would become fearful that he would be kidnaped. The resultant terror would be a form of suffering additional to the pain of the experiment. The same experiments performed on nonhuman animals would cause less suffering since the animals would not have the anticipatory dread of being kidnaped and experimented upon. This does not mean, of course, that it would be *right* to perform the experiment on animals, but only that there is a reason, which is *not* speciesist, for preferring to use animals rather than normal adult humans, if the experiment is to be done at all. It should be noted, however, that this same argument gives us a reason for preferring to use human infants—orphans perhaps—or retarded humans for experiments, rather than adults, since infants and retarded humans would also have no idea of what was going to happen to them. So far as this argument is concerned nonhuman animals and infants and retarded humans are in the same category; and if we use this argument to justify experiments on nonhuman animals we have to ask ourselves whether we are also prepared to allow experiments on human infants and retarded adults; and if we make a distinction between animals and these humans, on what basis can we do it, other than a bare-faced—and morally indefensible—preference for members of our own species?

There are many areas in which the superior mental powers of normal adult humans make a difference: anticipation, more detailed memory, greater knowledge of what is happening, and so on. Yet these differences do not all point to greater suffering on the part of the normal human being. Sometimes an animal may suffer more because of his more limited understanding. If, for instance, we are taking prisoners in wartime we can explain to them that while they must submit to capture, search, and confinement they will not otherwise be harmed and will be set free at the conclusion of hostilities. If we capture a wild animal, however, we cannot explain that we are not threatening its life. A wild animal cannot distinguish an attempt to overpower and confine from an attempt to kill; the one causes as much terror as the other.

It may be objected that comparisons of the sufferings of different species are impossible to make, and that for this reason when the interests of animals and humans clash the principle of equality gives no guidance. It is probably true that comparisons of suffering between members of different species cannot be made precisely, but precision is not essential. Even if we were to prevent the infliction of suffering on animals only when it is quite certain that the interests of humans will not be affected to anything like the extent that animals are affected, we would be forced to make radical changes in our treatment of animals that would involve our diet, the farming methods we use, experimental procedures in many fields of science, our approach to wildlife and to hunting, trapping and the wearing of furs, and areas of entertainment like circuses, rodeos, and zoos. As a result, a vast amount of suffering would be avoided.

So far I have said a lot about the infliction of suffering on animals, but nothing about killing them. This omission has been deliberate. The application of the principle of equality to the infliction of suffering is, in theory at least, fairly straightforward. Pain and suffering are bad and should be prevented or minimized, irrespective of the race, sex, or species of the being that suffers. How bad a pain is depends on how intense it is and how long it lasts, but pains of the same intensity and duration are equally bad, whether felt by humans or animals. . . .

The belief that human life, and only human life, is sacrosanct is a form of speciesism. To see this, consider the following example.

Assume that, as sometimes happens, an infant has been born with massive and irreparable brain damage. The damage is so severe that the infant can never be any more than a "human vegetable," unable to talk, recognize other people, act independently of others, or develop a sense of self-awareness. The parents of the infant, realizing that they cannot hope for any improvement in their child's condition and being in any case unwilling to spend, or ask the state to spend, the thousands of dollars that would be needed annually for proper care of the infant, ask the doctor to kill the infant painlessly.

Should the doctor do what the parents ask? Legally, he should not, and in this respect the law reflects the sanctity of life view. The life of every human being is sacred. Yet people who would say this about the infant do not object to the killing of nonhuman animals. How can they justify their different judgments? Adult chimpanzees, dogs, pigs, and many other species far surpass the brain-damaged infant in their ability to relate to others, act independently, be self-aware, and any other capacity that could reasonably be said to give value to life. With the most intensive care possible, there are retarded infants who can never achieve the intelligence level of a dog. Nor can we appeal to the concern of the infant's parents, since they themselves, in this imaginary example (and in some actual cases) do not want the infant kept alive.

The only thing that distinguishes the infant from the animal, in the eyes of those who claim it has a "right to life," is that it is, biologically, a member of the species *Homo sapiens*, whereas chimpanzees, dogs, and pigs are not. But to use *this* difference as the basis for granting a right to life to the infant and not to the other animals is, of course, pure speciesism. It is exactly the kind of arbitrary difference that the most crude and overt kind of racist uses in attempting to justify racial discrimination.

This does not mean that to avoid speciesism we must hold that it is as wrong to kill a dog as it is to kill a normal human being. The only position that is irredeemably speciesist is the one that tries to make the boundary of the right to life run exactly parallel to the boundary of our own species. Those who hold the sanctity of life view do this, because while distinguishing sharply between humans and other animals they allow no distinctions to be made within our own species, objecting to the killing of the severely retarded and the hopelessly senile as strongly as they object to the killing of normal adults.

To avoid speciesism we must allow that beings which are similar in all relevant respects have a similar right to life—and mere membership in our own biological species cannot be a morally relevant criterion for this right. Within these limits we could still hold that, for instance, it is worse to kill a normal adult human, with a capacity for self-awareness, and the ability to plan for the future and have meaningful relations with others, than it is to kill a mouse, which presumably does not share all of these characteristics; or we might appeal to the close family and other personal ties which humans have but mice do not have to the same degree; or we might think that it is the consequences for other humans, who will be put in fear of their own lives, that makes the crucial difference; or we might think it is some combination of these factors, or other factors altogether.

Whatever criteria we choose, however, we will have to admit that they do not follow precisely the boundary of our own species. We may legitimately hold that there are some features of certain beings which make their lives more valuable than those of other beings; but there will surely be some nonhuman animals whose lives, by any standards, are more valuable than the lives of some humans. A chimpanzee, dog, or pig, for instance, will have a higher degree of self-awareness and a greater capacity for meaningful relations with others than a severely retarded infant or someone in a state of advanced senility. So if we base the right to life on these characteristics we must grant these animals a right to life as good as, or better than, such retarded or senile humans.

Now this argument cuts both ways. It could be taken as showing that chimpanzees, dogs, and pigs, along with some other species, have a right to life and we commit a grave moral offense whenever we kill them, even when they are old and suffering and our intention is to put them out of their misery. Alternatively, one could take the argument as showing that the severely retarded and hopelessly senile have no right to life and may be killed for quite trivial reasons, as we now kill animals.

Since the focus [here] is on ethical questions concerning animals and not on the morality of euthanasia I shall not attempt to settle this issue finally. I think it is reasonably clear, though, that while both of the positions just described avoid speciesism, neither is entirely satisfactory. What we need is some middle position which would avoid speciesism but would not make the lives of the retarded and senile as cheap as the lives of pigs and dogs now are, nor make the lives of pigs and dogs so sacrosanct that we think it wrong to put them out of hopeless misery. What we must do is bring nonhuman animals within our sphere of moral concern and cease to treat their lives as expendable for whatever trivial purposes we may have. At the same time, once we realize that the fact that a being is a member of our own species is not in itself enough to make it always wrong to kill that being, we may come to reconsider our policy of preserving human lives at all costs, even when there is no prospect of a meaningful life or of existence without terrible pain.

I conclude, then, that a rejection of speciesism does not imply that all lives are of equal worth. While self-awareness, intelligence, the capacity for meaningful relations with others, and so on are not relevant to the question of inflicting pain—since pain is pain, whatever other capacities, beyond the capacity to feel pain, the being may have—these capacities may be relevant to the question of taking life. It is not arbitrary to hold that the life of a self-aware being, capable of abstract thought, of planning for the future, of complex acts of communication, and so on, is more valuable than the life of a being without these capacities. To see the difference between the issues of inflicting pain and taking life, consider how we would choose within our own species. If we had to choose to save the life of a normal human or a mentally defective human, we would probably choose to save the life of the normal human; but if we had to choose between preventing pain in the normal human or the mental defective—imagine that both have received painful but superficial injuries, and we only have enough painkiller for one of them—it is not nearly so clear how we ought to choose. The same is true when we consider other species. The evil of pain is, in itself, unaffected by the other characteristics of the being that feels the pain; the value of life is affected by these other characteristics.

Normally this will mean that if we have to choose between the life of a human being and the life of another animal we would choose to save the life of the human; but there may be special cases in which the reverse holds true, because the human being in question does not have the capacities of a normal human being. So this view is not speciesist, although it may appear to be at first glance. The preference, in normal cases, for saving a human life over the life of an animal when a choice *has* to be made is a preference based on the characteristics that normal humans have, and not on the mere fact that they are members of our own species. This is why when we consider members of our own species who lack the characteristics of normal humans we can no longer say that their lives are always to be preferred to those of other animals. . . .

QUESTIONS FOR REFLECTION

1. Why, according to Singer, are racism and sexism wrong?
2. Singer contends that speciesism is analogous to racism and sexism, and wrong for the same reasons. What is speciesism? How is it similar to racism and sexism? Are there important differences?
3. Singer credits Bentham with seeing "the capacity for suffering as the vital characteristic that gives a being the right to equal consideration." What does this mean? Suppose that a person for some reason lacked the ability to suffer. Would he or she then deserve no moral consideration?
4. Is killing animals wrong in the same way and to the same degree that killing humans is wrong, according to Singer? If not, why not?
5. Does Singer's position support all fourteen propositions of the Universal Declaration of the Rights of Animals?

TOM REGAN

The Case for Animal Rights

Tom Regan is professor emeritus of philosophy at North Carolina State University. (Source: Reprinted from "The Case for Animal Rights," in In Defense of Animals, *ed. Peter Singer [New York: Perennial Library, 1986; originally published by Blackwell, 1985]. Reprinted by permission of Blackwell Publishers.)*

I regard myself as an advocate of animal rights—as a part of the animal rights movement. That movement, as I conceive it, is committed to a number of goals, including:

the total abolition of the use of animals in science,

the total dissolution of commercial animal agriculture;

the total elimination of commercial and sport hunting and trapping.

There are, I know, people who profess to believe in animal rights but do not avow these goals. Factory farming, they say, is wrong—it violates animals' rights—but traditional animal agriculture is all right. Toxicity tests of cosmetics on animals violates their rights, but important medical research—cancer research, for example— does not. The clubbing of baby seals is abhorrent, but not the harvesting of adult seals. I used to think I understood this reasoning. Not any more. You don't change unjust institutions by tidying them up.

What's wrong—fundamentally wrong—with the way animals are treated isn't the details that vary from case to case. It's the whole system. The forlornness of the veal calf is pathetic, heartwrenching; the pulsing pain of the chimp with electrodes planted deep in her brain is repulsive; the slow, tortuous death of the raccoon caught in the leg-hold trap is agonizing. But what is wrong isn't the pain, isn't the suffering, isn't the deprivation. These compound what's wrong. Sometimes—often—they make it much, much worse. But they are not the fundamental wrong.

The fundamental wrong is the system that allows us to view animals as *our resources*, here for *us*—to be eaten, or surgically manipulated, or exploited for sport or money. Once we accept this view of animals—as our resources—the rest is as predictable as it is regrettable. Why worry about their loneliness, their pain, their death? Since animals exist for us, to benefit us in one way or another, what harms them really doesn't matter—or matters only if it starts to bother us, makes us feel a trifle uneasy when we eat our veal escalope, for example. So, yes, let us get veal calves out of solitary confinement, give them more space, a little straw, a few companions. But let us keep our veal escalope.

But a little straw, more space and a few companions won't eliminate—won't even touch—the basic wrong that attaches to our viewing and treating these animals as our resources. A veal calf killed to be eaten after living in close confinement is viewed and treated in this way: but so, too, is another who is raised (as they say) "more humanely." To right the wrong of our treatment of farm animals requires more than making rearing methods "more humane"; it requires the total dissolution of commercial animal agriculture. . . .

What to do? Where to begin anew? The place to begin, I think, is with the utilitarian's view of the value of the individual—or, rather, lack of value. In its place, suppose we consider that you and I, for example, do have value as individuals—what we'll call *inherent value*. To say we have such value is to say that we are something more than, something different from, mere receptacles. Moreover, to ensure that we do not pave the way for such injustices as slavery or sexual discrimination, we must believe that all who have inherent value have it equally, regardless of their sex, race, religion, birthplace and so on. Similarly to be discarded as irrelevant are one's talents or skills, intelligence and wealth, personality or pathology, whether one is loved and admired or despised and loathed. The genius and the retarded child, the prince and the pauper, the brain surgeon and the fruit vendor, Mother Teresa and the most unscrupulous used-car salesman—all have inherent value, all possess it equally, and all have an equal right to be treated with respect, to be treated in ways that do not reduce them to the status of things, as if they existed as resources for others. My value as an individual is independent of my usefulness to you. Yours is not dependent on your usefulness to me. For either of us to treat the other in ways that fail to show respect for the other's independent value is to act immorally, to violate the individual's rights.

Some of the rational virtues of this view—what I call the rights view—should be evident. Unlike (crude) contractarianism, for example, the rights view *in principle* denies the moral tolerability of any and all forms of racial, sexual and social discrimination; and unlike utilitarianism, this view *in principle* denies that we can justify good results by using evil means that violate an individual's rights—denies, for example, that it could be moral to kill my Aunt Bea to harvest beneficial consequences for others. That would be to sanction the disrespectful treatment of the individual in the name of the social good, something the rights view will not—categorically will not—ever allow.

The rights view, I believe, is rationally the most satisfactory moral theory. It surpasses all other theories in the degree to which it illuminates and explains the foundation of our duties to one another—the domain of human morality. On this score it has the best reasons, the best arguments, on its side. Of course, if it were possible to show that only human beings are included within its scope, then a person like myself, who believes in animal rights, would be obliged to look elsewhere.

But attempts to limit its scope to humans only can be shown to be rationally defective. Animals, it is true, lack many of the abilities humans possess. They can't read, do higher mathematics, build a bookcase or make *baba ghanoush*. Neither can many human beings, however, and yet we don't (and shouldn't) say that they (these humans) therefore have less inherent value, less of a right to be treated with respect, than do others. It is the *similarities* between those human beings who most clearly, most noncontroversially have such value (the people reading this, for example), not our differences, that matter most. And the really crucial, the basic similarity is simply this: we are each of us the experiencing subject of a life, a conscious creature having an individual welfare that has importance to us whatever our usefulness to others. We want and prefer things, believe and feel things, recall and expect things. And all these dimensions of our life, including our pleasure and pain, our enjoyment and suffering, our satisfaction and frustration, our continued existence or our untimely death—all make a difference to the quality of our life as lived, as experienced, by us as individuals. As the same is true of those animals that concern us: (the ones that are eaten and trapped, for example), they too must be viewed as the experiencing subjects of a life, with inherent value of their own.

Some there are who resist the idea that animals have inherent value. "Only humans have such value," they profess. How might this narrow view be defended? Shall we say that only humans have the requisite intelligence, or autonomy, or reason? But there are many, many humans who fail to meet these standards and yet are reasonably viewed as having value above and beyond their usefulness to others. Shall we claim that only humans belong to the right species, the species *Homo sapiens*? But this is blatant speciesism. Will it be said, then, that all—and only—humans have immortal souls? Then our opponents have their work cut out for them. I am myself not ill-disposed to the proposition that there are immortal souls. Personally, I profoundly hope I have one. But I would not want to rest my position on a controversial ethical issue on the even more controversial question about who or what has an immortal soul. That is to dig one's hole deeper, not to climb out. Rationally, it is better to resolve moral issues without making more controversial assumptions than are needed. The question of who has inherent value is such a question, one that is resolved more rationally without the introduction of the idea of immortal souls than by its use.

Well, perhaps some will say that animals have some inherent value, only less than we have. Once again, however, attempts to defend this view can be shown to lack rational justification. What could be the basis of our having more inherent value than animals? Their lack of reason, or autonomy, or intellect? Only if we are willing to make the same judgment in the case of humans who are similarly deficient. But it is not true that such humans—the retarded child, for example, or the mentally deranged—have less inherent value than you or I. Neither, then, can we rationally sustain the view that animals like them in being the experiencing subjects of a life have less inherent value. *All* who have inherent value have it *equally*, whether they be human animals or not.

Inherent value, then, belongs equally to those who are the experiencing subjects of a life. Whether it belongs to others—to rocks and rivers, trees and glaciers, for example—we do not know and may never know. But neither do we need to know, if we are to make the case for animal rights. We do not need to know, for example, how many people are eligible to vote in the next presidential election before we can know whether I am. Similarly, we do not need to know how many individuals have inherent value before we can know that some do. When it comes to the case for animal rights, then, what we need to know is whether the animals that, in our culture, are routinely eaten, hunted and used in our laboratories, for example, are like us in being subjects of a life. And we do know this. We do know that many—literally, billions and billions—of these animals are the subjects of a life in the sense explained and so have inherent value if we do. And since, in order to arrive at the best theory of our duties to one another, we must recognize our equal inherent value as individuals, reason—not sentiment, not emotion—reason compels us to recognize the equal inherent value of these animals and, with this, their equal right to be treated with respect. . . .

. . . I can now say why [the rights view's] implications for farming and science, among other fields, are both clear and uncompromising. In the case of the use of animals in science, the rights view is categorically abolitionist. Lab animals are not our tasters; we are not their kings. Because these animals are treated routinely, systematically as if their value were reducible to their usefulness to others, they are routinely, systematically treated with a lack of respect, and thus are their rights routinely, systematically violated. This is just as true when they are used in trivial, duplicative, unnecessary or unwise research as it is when they are used in studies that hold out real promise of human benefits. We can't justify harming or killing a human being (my Aunt Bea, for example) just for these sorts of reasons. Neither can we do so even in the case of so lowly a creature as a laboratory rat. It is not just refinement or reduction that is called for, not just larger, cleaner cages, not just more generous use of anaesthetic or the elimination of multiple surgery, not just tidying up the system. It is complete replacement. The best we can do when it comes to using animals in science is—not to use them. That is where our duty lies, according to the rights view.

As for commercial animal agriculture, the rights view takes a similar abolitionist position. The fundamental moral wrong here is not that animals are kept in stressful close confinement or in isolation, or that their pain and suffering, their needs and preferences are ignored or discounted. All these *are* wrong, of course, but they are not the fundamental wrong. They are symptoms and effects of the deeper, systematic wrong that allows these animals to be viewed and treated as lacking independent value, as resources for us—as, indeed, a renewable resource. Giving farm animals more space, more natural environments, more companions does not right the fundamental wrong, any more than giving lab animals more anaesthesia or bigger, cleaner cages would right the fundamental wrong in their case. Nothing less than the total dissolution of commercial animal agriculture will do this, just as, for similar reasons I won't develop at length here, morality requires nothing less than the total elimination of hunting and trapping for commercial and sporting ends. The rights view's implications, then, as I have said, are clear and uncompromising. . . .

QUESTIONS FOR REFLECTION

1. Do you agree with Regan that a position rejecting, for example, factory farming and cosmetics research on animals, but not animal husbandry or medical experimentation, is incoherent? Why or why not?
2. What is an indirect-duty view? Why does Regan reject it?
3. Regan claims that Rawls cannot explain why it is wrong to harm young children or an older adult with mental retardation. Is this true?
4. Why does Regan reject utilitarianism? How might Mill respond?
5. What is inherent value? How does Regan decide who or what has inherent value? How does he defend his assertion that animals have it?
6. Does Regan's position support all fourteen propositions of the Universal Declaration of the Rights of Animals?

R. G. FREY

Moral Community and Animal Research in Medicine

R. G. Frey is Senior Research Fellow at the Social Philosophy and Policy Center at Bowling Green State University. *(Source: From* Ethics and Behavior *7 (1997): 123–136.* *References have been omitted.)*

My position on animal research in medicine is unlike the positions adopted by some of the other philosophers—Tom Beauchamp, Carl Cohen, and Tom Regan—in these pages.

I support the use of animals in medical research.* I reject, therefore, abolitionist accounts of the matter, such as Regan's, that recently have emerged from the "animal rights" lobby. Unlike Cohen, however, I do not reject these accounts on the ground that animals lack moral standing and so are not members of the moral community. Rather, as Beauchamp correctly divines, I reject them because I think moral standing is a matter of degree, and although animals possess it, normal adult humans possess it more. Mine, then, is a more complicated position on animal experimentation than those of the overly simplistic "stop all animal research now" and the overly convenient "permit all animal research now" schools. Not unnaturally, therefore, it attracts opposition from both camps.†

For purposes of exposition, I set out the essentials of my position on animal research around six points. Before doing so, however, I make two observations on matters to do with ethical theory: moral rights and utilitarianism.

Moral Rights

Nothing in my position on the morality of animal research turns on or involves talk of moral rights. There are a number of reasons for this, including some rather abstract ones having to do with the grounds or foundations of such putative rights. But I do not require any such abstract considerations to point to the fact, which all of us perfectly well realize, that the invocation of moral rights in moral/social debate today is a recipe for deadlock in our consideration of substantive issues.

Even among people who are enamored of moral rights today, massive disagreement exists about what rights we have. Do we have a right to die? Some rights theorists say yes, others say no. Do we have moral rights to welfare, wherein we have positive rights to goods that, if we ourselves cannot supply them, other people must supply them to us? Some rights theorists say yes, others say no. Do we have a

---

* I develop and defend my position on animal experimentation in a number of places (see Frey, 1987, 1988, 1993,1996).

† I do not mean to imply that, with regard to animals, only my views on experimentation attract opposition. Those who have followed the animal rights debates from the appearance of my books in the area (Frey, 1980, 1983) know otherwise.

moral right to a job and paid vacations? The United Nations Declaration of Human Rights says yes, many Americans, I suspect, say no. Does the fetus have a moral right to life? Have adults a moral right to whatever sexual orientation and practice they desire? Not even rights theorists agree about these matters, so it is difficult to see how anything substantive with regard to these important moral/social issues can be achieved, even among themselves, through an appeal to putative moral rights.

Of course, in the United States today, every group with a cause is eager to convert that cause into a moral right so as to enhance the cause's standing in our public debate, wherein the currency of public exchange has become claims to rights. It should come as no surprise, therefore, that we increasingly hear of homosexual rights, the rights of the disabled, the rights of children, and the rights of the homeless or disadvantaged, on the one hand, and, moving only slightly further afield, the rights of future generations not yet conceived, the rights of trees or the environment or ecosystems generally, and, of course, the rights of animals, on the other. Given that our public debate on moral/social issues unfortunately has taken this form, no one with a cause can afford not to claim a moral right for their group, else the group lose standing and respect in the shouting that so often passes as debate about rights.

In fact, this rush to moral rights has proved singularly unhelpful in the discussion of substantive issues because deadlock is reached almost immediately—one's opponents also recognize the currency of our public debate—when the opposing side either refuses to agree one has the right one claims or, worse yet, converts its own cause into a right. Thus, the right of a pregnant woman to control over her body runs up against the right to life of the fetus; the right of doctors to decide what is best for their patients, given the traditional understanding of the doctor's mission, runs up against patients' exercise of their right of autonomy in aid of intentionally terminating life; and the right of the homosexual to his or her sexual preference and lifestyle runs up against the right of individuals in their communities to determine what sexual/social practices will be permitted within those communities. The inevitable result is certainly a moral standoff, but it is usually a legal standoff as well.

Everybody who is party to these disputes knows full well that deadlock in moral rights claims immediately is reached when each side claims its right, and this in part explains why so many people with causes are eager to get into court. For if a judge decides in favor of one's cause, then, however deadlocked the parties may be morally, those who espouse one's cause might be favored with a legal right or at least a legal permission to practice whatever is at issue in one's cause. If so, then one might gain the upper hand over one's opponents because one can then legally demand, on pain of punishment, that one's opponents take account of this legal right or legal permission. And this, one hopes, gives one's cause much firmer support than does the mere appeal to moral rights. Alas, not even court decisions stem the controversy over rights. Thus, I do not have the faintest idea whether women have a moral right to an abortion during the first trimester of a pregnancy; but I know that one side of the abortion controversy has a U.S. Supreme Court decision in favor of its plea for a legal right and that the other side is working feverishly to get that same court to overturn the decision. A 1986 U.S. Supreme Court decision held that the U.S. Constitution does not fully protect homosexual activity, and homosexual groups are striving constantly—and may well have succeeded with a Supreme Court decision in a Colorado case in 1996—to get that decision overturned. All kinds of groups are trying to get court decisions in favor of rights-based, affirmative action policies overturned, as happened in the U.S. Supreme Court decision in 1996 on admissions to the University of Texas Law School. Does anybody really believe that, should the opponents of all these decisions prevail, those who currently have the upper hand will see the rightness of their cause in any way diminished and so will go away? What they will do, almost certainly, is to behave in exactly the way their opponents currently are behaving.

Until we are presented with a logic that enables us to argue about moral rights in a way that amounts to more than one side affirming and the other denying the right in question, I think we would do well to dispense with talk of moral rights in our attempts to come to grips with moral/social problems and to present and assess the considerations that we think relevant to reaching a view about what it would be right to do in the contexts of those problems. Rights claims simply divert us from this task, from the real issues, as we spend our time trying to figure out what a moral right is, who or what has one, and whose theory or story about the foundations of moral rights should be favored among the dozens offered. In this situation, if Beauchamp, Cohen, and Regan really believe that claims to rights are the way to discuss issues morally, I simply do not see how they can succeed.

Utilitarianism

Just as nothing in my position on animal experimentation turns on claims about moral rights, so nothing in it, contra Regan in these pages, turns on the fact that in normative ethical theory I am a utilitarian.* My position turns fundamentally on the notion of quality of life, and no one has ever thought that only utilitarians may make use of this notion. Moreover, what I submit makes up the quality of life—its content and richness—is open to people of any normative stance to adopt. Although Regan appears not to understand this (I am not concerned here with the rather simple objections he raises to utilitarianism or with the numerous devices with which those objections can be met), in fact, I suspect that he understands it full well but that he is in the age-old business, when one's own position is going to strike most people as rather incredible, of trying to paint the opposition in even worse colors.

The truth is that Regan is an abolitionist. He advocates shutting down all animal experimentation now (only occasionally in public debates with him have I heard him speak of a gradual shutdown), no matter how far advanced or promising or important the research is (e.g., in gene therapy) with respect to serious human illnesses. Do we continue with animal experiments until we find replacements for them? Regan is ambivalent on the matter, but I do not see why. If, as he maintains, it is immoral to experiment on animals at all, then what permits us to continue in our current immorality until replacements are found? No, the truth is that he wants animal experimentation stopped. Given the number of people who would be affected adversely by any such shutdown, given the numbers who have been saved already by the fruits of animal research, I fail to see why I am the person, if Regan is to be believed in these pages, who is playing fast and loose with human life. Until we can find replacements for animals (and it is important that Regan never, anywhere, submits that this is even likely over the entire range of medical experiments in which animals currently are used), humans pay the cost of Regan's abolitionism. Why are his opponents the ones who show lack of regard for other people?

In any event, nothing in my view about animal research involves anything that nonutilitarians may not accept.

Moral Community

For ease of exposition, I set out my position on animal experimentation in six planks. Each, of course, requires much more elaboration than I can give it here.

First, moral standing, or moral status, has nothing to do with the possession of moral rights (as indicated, I dispense with moral rights talk). Furthermore it does not require agency on the part of the subject. As people fall completely into the grip of Alzheimer's disease they may cease to be moral agents, neither making choices and weighing reasons for action nor directing their own lives, but few of us think as a result that they cease to be members of the moral community. The severely mentally enfeebled may never have become agents in the first place, but few of us hold that they, therefore, are not morally considerable and or that they are not part of the moral community.

In my view, moral standing, or considerability, turns on whether a creature is an experiential subject, with an unfolding series of experiences that, depending on their quality, can make the creature's life go well or badly. Such a creature has a welfare that can be affected positively or negatively depending on what we do to it. With a welfare that can be enhanced or diminished, a creature has a quality of life. So far as I am aware, no one denies that patients with Alzheimer's disease and the severely mentally enfeebled are such creatures and so are beings with a quality of life that can be affected positively or

* Many different types and versions of types of utilitarianism are on offer today. It would consume too many pages to go into this matter here.

negatively by what we do to them. Equally, however, very few informed people today deny that rodents, dogs, and chimps are such creatures.* They are experiential subjects with a welfare and quality of life that our actions can push up or down, and this is true whether or not they are held to have moral rights and whether or not they are held to be moral agents.

I do not think, therefore, that the moral community is shaped by who or what has moral rights or by who or what is a moral agent. It is shaped by who or what is an experiential subject and so is a creature with a welfare and a quality of life that can be affected by what we do to it. Such creatures have biographical lives that consist in the unfolding of experiences. Although there may well be cases where I am uncertain whether a creature is an experiential one (e.g., mere adaptation to environment does not suffice because plants can do this), I do not think rodents, dogs, chimps, and the usual experimental subjects are doubtful ones.

I reject Regan's abolitionism; the benefits animal research has conferred on us have proved substantial, and gene therapy alone holds out extraordinary prospects for us finally to come to grips with some of the most terrible human illnesses. But I also reject Cohen's view that animals are not members of the moral community. I think they have moral standing and so are part of that community, on exactly the same basis that we are, and I think that any account of our justification for using animals in experiments must take this fact into account. That is precisely what my middle position on animal research does.

Second, what is it about animals that is supposed not to count morally? The two most obvious candidates are their pains and sufferings and their lives. On my view, pain is pain, as much an evil for a dog as for a child, and the pains of both dog and child count morally. To give an example I use frequently, I can see no moral difference between pouring scalding water on a dog and pouring it on a child: If it is wrong to do this in the case of the child, and most people would agree it is wrong just because of the pain the child feels (and not because of the relationship the child may bear to one), I can see no reason why it is not wrong to do this to the dog. Where pain is concerned, species makes no difference; what matters is that both are experiential creatures and that pain typically represents an evil in the lives of all such creatures, if not intrinsically, then certainly instrumentally, with respect to the quality of life. Of course, it may be true that adult humans suffer in more and different ways than do animals, but that does not affect the point that animal pains are morally significant features of the world that we need to take into account in deciding how we are to act.

Moreover, animal researchers today often acknowledge this point. All kinds of hospital and institutional guidelines exist for conducting animal research, and research protocols routinely go into how the pain and suffering of a research animal is to be controlled, limited, mitigated where feasible, and justified in the course of the experiment. Often, the animal is euthanized before it recovers from anesthetic. The day when these sorts of concerns about animal suffering could be ignored, if it ever fully existed, has long since passed.

If, however, the pains and sufferings of animals count morally, it is hard to see why their lives do not. For one of the things that so concerns us about pain and suffering is how these things can seriously blight a life and diminish its quality, and this possibility exists in the cases of all those who can experience these things. Neither in ourselves nor in the "higher" animals do we take excruciating agony to be an indication, all other things being equal, of a high or desirable quality of life. Animals are not like test tubes, which are broken and discarded without a second thought; they are, as are we, living creatures with experiential lives and, thus, things with a welfare and a quality of life. For these very reasons, I think that their lives have *some* value. Furthermore, I think the deliberate, intentional destruction of things of (some) value must be justified.

Research scientists and others think, of course, that they can meet this demand of justification for the destruction of valuable animal lives. They, as do I, cite (actual and potential) human benefit as their defense.

Third, animal life has some value, but it does not have the same value as normal adult human life. I accept a quality-of-life view of the value of a life, in which it is not life, but quality of life, that determines

* Indeed, it is precisely because these animals are experiential subjects whose lives are affected positively or negatively by what we do to them that research protocols in our labs and medical schools demand that we justify what we do to them.

a life's value. Such views are a commonplace today, figuring as they do in virtually all the literature coming out of medical and social ethics having to do with the human condition. Experiential creatures generally, however, have a welfare and a quality of life, which can be increased or diminished by the quality of their experiences, including those that ensue as a result of our treatment of them. Their lives can go well or badly. It is not just humans of whom these things are true. So I think a quality-of-life view determines the value not only of human but also of animal life. I see no reason whatever to turn to a different account in the animal case.

I think that the value of a life is a function of its quality, its quality of its richness, and its richness of its capacities or scope for enrichment. Richness of content, in other words, determines a life's quality and value, and a creature's capacities or scope for enrichment determines richness of content. Elsewhere, I have had more to say about richness and scope for enrichment (Frey, 1987,1988,1993,1996). But much more work in the animal case remains to be done because a commitment to a quality-of-life view of the value of a life requires that we have access to the subjective experiences or inner lives of animals, that we be able, in terms appropriate to the species of animal in question, to determine to a reasonable degree how well or badly their lives are going. That we do this all the time, at least at some level, is clear; that is why we play fetch with our dogs, take them for walks and runs, and give them bones. But if quality-of-life judgments are sometimes difficult in the human case, even though a good deal of the time they seem unproblematic at least in broad measure, it stands to reason that they can be difficult in the animal case.

I accept that the dog has subjective experiences, that those experiences determine its quality of life, and that the quality of its life determines that life's value. We use behavior and behavioral studies to give us access to the inner lives of animals, of course; and what we use in a rough-and-ready way to begin with we can come to use with more assurance as empirical studies of animals make more information available to us. Perhaps I cannot know *exactly* what it would be like to be a dog, but I *can* come to know more and more in this regard as we learn more about them and their responses to their environments.

I do not think, obviously, that the lives of all experiential creatures have the same value. If the value of a life depends on its quality, and the quality of two animal lives can vary substantially, then those two lives will have a different value. This can be true even of animals of the same species, for example, two dogs.

But the really crucial point here is that most of us do not think animal life is as valuable as is human life, and I think we are right to think this. The richness of normal adult human life vastly exceeds that of animals, and our capacities for enrichment, in all their variety and extent, vastly exceed anything that we know or associate with them. Although it is true that the dog has a more acute sense of smell than we do, what we should need to think, in order to think the quality and value of its life approaches the quality and value of ours, is that the dog's sense of smell confers on its life a quality that approximates the quality that all our capacities for enrichment, along multidimensions that appear unavailable to the dog, confer on our lives. Some activities we share with the dog, but there are dimensions of enrichment in our lives—music, literature, science, reflection—that do not appear present in the lives of dogs. At the end of life, when we say of a man that he led a rich and full life, we mean something incomparably beyond what we mean were we to say this of a rodent, dog, or chimp.

It can, of course, be objected by "animal rightists" that animal lives are every bit as rich as the lives of normal adult humans, that, for example, the differences in capacities and, therefore, in the depth, extent, and variety of experiences between a normal adult human and a rodent, dog, or chimp do not convey varying degrees of richness on the respective lives. It is difficult to see the basis for this claim of equal richness. In the case of chimps, I am quite prepared to be convinced by more and more evidence that their similarities to us run deep and in ways reflected in their experiential lives. If this turns out to be true, and in creatures whose DNA is 99% the same as our own it may well, claims of equal richness will be appropriate, and my view would then say of chimps what it says of normal adult humans. But what about the cases of very common experimental animals, such as rodents or rabbits? In these cases, where as best we can tell there are wide discrepancies in capacities (and so in experiences) with normal adult humans, we need something to anchor the claim of equal richness. That anchor is not provided by the claim that the current life is the only life that a rodent or rabbit or normal adult human has, so that its life is as valuable to the rodent or rabbit as the human's current life is to the human. This only shows that a creature has to be alive in order to have a quality of life; it shows nothing about the quality of life a creature has.

I am, therefore, prepared to be persuaded that animal lives can be as rich as normal adult human lives. In the case of chimps, baboons, apes, and so forth, if this turns out to be true, the claims I make on behalf of normal adult humans I would make on their behalf.* In the case of some common experimental animals, however, I certainly need to be persuaded of the claim of equal richness.

There is nothing speciesist or discriminatory about my view. The reason normal adult human lives are more valuable than animal lives is not because of species but because of richness and scope for enrichment. I am not guilty, therefore, of discriminating in favor of humans because they are human. Indeed, my view plainly allows that the quality, and therefore value, of some human lives can fall well below that of some animal lives.

My position, therefore, is that animals are members of the moral community because they are experiential creatures with a welfare or well-being that can be affected by what we do to them. They have moral standing. But they do not have the same moral standing as do normal adult humans because the value of the lives of the latter far exceed the value of the lives of the former. The truth is that not all creatures who have moral standing have the same moral standing. It is this truth that now must be put to the human case.

Fourth, because not all human lives have the same quality, not all human lives have the same value. Indeed, there are some human lives of a quality so low that we would not wish them on anyone, and those who live these lives desperately seek release from them (and often today, in a public manner). Accordingly, it strikes me as foolish to pretend, as some moralists do, that these lives are as valuable as normal adult human lives. Those fully and finally in the grip of amyotrophic lateral sclerosis do not so pretend; why should we?

If, however, not all human life has the same value, then the possibility arises that the quality of life of a perfectly healthy baboon can exceed that of a human. So, *if* one is going to appeal to human benefit to justify animal research, and *if* the benefit in this case can be realized either through experimenting on the baboon or the human, then why use the baboon in preference to the human? A quality-of-life view of the value of a life gives a consistent answer over taking a life and saving a life: One saves the creature with the higher quality of life, and one sacrifices the creature with the lower quality of life. In this case, the human has the lower quality of life; so, if either the baboon or the human has to be used in order to realize the benefit, the human must, all other things being equal, be used. Clearly, my view on the value of life and so on this choice is not speciesist.

The only way I can see to avoid this implication of the possibility of human experiments is to come up with something that cedes a human life of any quality, however low, greater value than an animal life of any quality, however high. I can find no such thing. And it is well to remember that if one appeals to the side effects of any decision to proceed with such experiments in order to oppose it, these effects may possibly be overcome through education and careful argument that makes clear the moral basis of why one is proceeding.

Notice that my position here is *not* that we must experiment on humans, only that we must do so—or at least envisage such experiments—if certain conditions obtain, as I think they do. My position is that *if* we continue to employ an argument from benefit to justify animal experimentation in medicine, and *if* we continue to employ a discussion of the comparative value of human and animal life to justify using the animal in preference to the human, then, because not all human life has the same value as normal adult human life, we are faced with the prospect of human experiments, of, that is, using some humans as we currently use some animals. The antecedents here are accepted widely in the medical research community; with that the case, I see no way to avoid the conclusion. Many of us favor animal research in medicine, and it extracts from us, I suggest, a severe cost.

* In this eventuality, I should be prepared to support the Great Ape Project in its essence, which I take to be the conferral of moral standing on the great apes.

Fifth, a series of dodges by which to avoid this cost of the defense of animal experimentation all come to grief. I do not have space to go into all these, let alone at any depth; I simply list a couple of dodges and append a few remarks to each.

One might simply *insist* that any human life, however deficient, has a higher quality than does any animal life, however exemplary. Today, such insistence rings hollow, even at the level of appeal to intuitions. When we visit a hospital, a surgeon says to us, "Now you understand, this man has a very low quality of life. We are debating whether withholding treatment and writing a nonresuscitation order are appropriate here. We are debating whether to ask the family for permission to discontinue treatment." Neither the surgeon nor we fail to realize that what we are talking about here is the glaring discrepancy between this life and normal adult human life.

On a quality-of-life view of the value of a life, a life has a value only if it has a quality, and it has a quality, at bottom, only if it has experiences. Accordingly, the lives of anencephalic infants and those in a permanent vegetative state have no value.* What could possibly justify using perfectly healthy baboons in preference to these humans?

Of course, it may be said by some that these infants and patients have ceased to be human; but surely that is a point in favor of using them in preference to healthy animals? Anencephalic infants have had no quality of life and do not and will not have one. Why should they not, as a committee of the American Medical Association recommended in 1995, only to be overturned by a vote of the entire organization in 1996, be used as sources of organs for transplant? But the very emphasis today on xenograft, or cross-species transplantation, shows reluctance to use them in preference to healthy animals.

Why cannot we show a preference for our own kind? We can. The problem is how one defines *own kind*. If I define my own kind as White, heterosexual, and male, presumably many will protest against the bias they take to be implied in what I say. Why should the category *own kind* be any less biased defined around species? Besides, if asked which of two creatures is more my own kind, a healthy baboon or a human in a permanently vegetative state, I would choose the baboon, who remains an experiential creature. Only in our "outer shell," in our similarly looking bodies, do those in a permanently vegetative state form part of our own kind; and similarity in outer shell is hard to see as a morally relevant, let alone a morally decisive, characteristic.

Humans are agents in their own right, guiding their lives through autonomous choices and decisions about how they want to live; animals do not and cannot do these things. Neither, alas, do or can all humans, as I noted earlier. The severely mentally enfeebled have never done these things; anencephalic infants can never do them; and although patients fully in the grip of Alzheimer's disease once did them, they no longer do. There is no decisive break to appeal to here in order to advantage the human.

Why cannot we appeal to our tradition and claim that it is a part of that tradition that we accord more respect to humans than to animals and that we accord this respect to humans even in cases in which the only resemblance left is the resemblance of our outer shells? We can. But why should the fact that something is a part of my tradition vouch for its moral quality and correctness? In the tradition lived by many Whites in the American South, Blacks were accorded and endured an inferior status, but few today would cite this fact as a reason for accepting a continued inferior status for Blacks. There are vast numbers of things that, as one thinks through the moral rightness and wrongness of what one has imbibed as a part of the tradition or ethic within which one has been brought up, one rejects.

I could go on. All these dodges are ways of trying to assert a greater value for human life so as to be able *always* to forgo using a human instead of an animal life in medical research devoted to obtaining benefits for humans.

Sixth, it can be claimed that my position on animal research expresses doubts about the Judeo-Christian ethic, which has underpinned medical practice and research in Western Europe and the United States for a very long time. This is true. I, like Singer (1996) in his book *Rethinking Life and Death,* think that parts of this ethic need to be rethought, including the view discussed in this article, namely, that all human life has the same value. Under the Judeo-Christian ethic, all human life is equal in the eyes of God, however

* This does not deny, of course, that what we do to these humans may affect negatively the welfare of other humans, which, obviously on my view, must be taken into account.

deficient its quality. Increasingly, however, fewer and fewer are religious and accept this religious presupposition; and even among those who do accept it, parts of this traditional ethic are coming under intense scrutiny, as, for example, the abortion debate illustrates.

Let me give some other examples. In the case of seriously defective newborns, with respect to whether we should strive officiously to keep them alive, the equal-value view is coming under attack. In the case of euthanasia, it long has been under attack. In the case of suicide and physician-assisted suicide, it is under increasing attack. In all these cases, the mere invocation of the Judeo-Christian ethic and its pronouncements no longer settles matters among us morally. Argument and debate continue, including among those who take themselves to be religious. Thus, the modern rethinking of the value and importance of autonomy in individual lives, including its role in decisions to end those lives, remains firmly in opposition to any mere appeal to the traditional ethic to settle the matter. In the case of physician-assisted suicide, these individuals want release from a life they see as no longer worth living, and they almost never pretend that their lives now are as valuable as normal adult human life. (It is important to notice that this judgment about the value of one's life can defy treatment of the person for, say, depression. A person in the final stages of amyotrophic lateral sclerosis may well judge his or her quality of life adversely, even if treated for depression.) Indeed, it is precisely because they have concluded the opposite that they make their adverse judgment about continuing to live those lives.

We need to rethink the claim that all human lives are equally valuable. And we must be careful of those who want to foist off on us some substitute for, or alternative to, equal value, such as something that Regan (1982) calls "equal inherent worth." This is an abstraction for which I cannot see that Regan has any good argument, yet insistence on which is supposed to show that, even though human lives can be massively different in quality, they nevertheless are of equal worth. All Regan has done is to seek a secular analog for equality in the eyes of God so as to avoid the obvious truth that none of us, if we could choose between a normal adult human life and an adult human life stricken fully and finally with a progressive nervous disorder that eventually destroys all traces of human personality, would choose the latter, which, if Regan is correct, is of equal inherent worth with the former.

I think animal research in medicine is justified and that human benefit justifies it, and I think the comparative value of normal adult human life and animal life is what justifies using animals instead of humans. But not all human life has the same value as normal adult human life, and anencephalic infants and those in permanently vegetative states are cases in point. Unless we can cite something that always, completely, and without exception confers greater value on human than on animal life, whatever the quality of both, we can justify animal research only by conceding that some humans are candidates for research as well. If we reject the use of humans altogether, how can the argument we have considered license us to use animals? As I indicated, disadvantageous side effects to any decision to go forward with such experiments may disappear through education and through our carefully making the moral case for our actions. However, is this likely? Can we go forward? On the other hand, in the background all the time are the enormous benefits that medical research confers on us. Can we decide *not* to go forward?

As I said, a committee of the American Medical Association did at one point come out in favor of using anencephalic infants as organ donors, a source for transplant organs needed to save the lives of other infants. If anything, this represents the very kind of rethinking of the view that all human lives have equal value that I am suggesting we need to undertake.

Conclusion

I think this view of equal value and the Judeo-Christian ethic in which it is embedded explain the widespread appeal to slippery slope arguments so as to prevent any rethinking of the sort I suggest. The claim always can be made that, if we start with anencephalic infants and patients in a permanently vegetative state, we soon will be led inexorably down the slope of harvesting organs and killing until we begin to harvest from those with an enviable quality of life, a quality far removed from where we began. Slippery slope arguments are consequentialist in character, and although I do not deny that they can be powerful tools that cause us to pause in what we are about to do, we need to be clear on exactly what it is that is supposed to force us down the slope in the first place.

The fact is there are slippery slope arguments that no one accepts: Have orange juice for lunch today, and you will be led to have orange juice for lunch for the rest of your life. Absolutely no one believes this, and not because the example is a trivial one. What one wants to know, for example, is the causal mechanism that propels one down the slope.

In the case of Christianity, where killing is concerned, that mechanism has been supplied by a conception of human nature that is exceedingly pessimistic and negative. We are seen in the light of the Fall and Original Sin, seen, that is, as basically corrupt, evil creatures in need of redemption as we constantly make decisions for our own selfish convenience. In the light of this view of ourselves, slippery slope arguments are convincing: Given our corrupt nature, there is no way to stop the slide into evil as we permit cases of harvesting organs from anencephalic infants to carry us headlong into seizing children playing in the streets for their organs.

Apart from a dark religious perspective, however, why should we believe any such thing as this? Why, if one rethinks one's view about defective newborns, so that four operations in a row to eke out 2 more months of life are rejected in favor of withholding treatment, is one condemned to slide down the slope to the depths of evil and killing? Why, if one rethinks the case against physician-assisted suicide and comes out for limited, controlled decisions in favor of termination at the patient's request under safeguards, will the safeguards inevitably fail and the Nazi camps be ahead of us? Horrible consequences such as these, if they are to deter rethinking of basic parts of the ethic that traditionally has underlain medical practice and research in the United States, must be shown to be before us, not in some sense of being mere possibilities, but in a sense that indicates some likelihood of occurring. After all, I would never leave my house if the mere possibility of death in the streets is held to be sufficient to deter me. Nor will it do merely to point out that what was once unthinkable is today thinkable, even done. At the very least, leaving aside changes in moral opinions, likelihood of consequences coming to pass must reflect one's case for why all safeguards will fail, no matter what.

None of this is to say that slippery slope arguments cannot be powerful tools to force us to proceed carefully on rethinking any issue to do with taking life. Indeed, we should proceed carefully where something as important as taking life is concerned. But we should not be stopped in our tracks by an appeal to possible consequences that may ensue as the result of the operation of some view of human nature that a religion, a political ideology, or both asserts to be the case.

QUESTIONS FOR REFLECTION

1. What is morally distinctive about humans as opposed to animals, in Frey's view?
2. Do we have any obligations to animals, in Frey's opinion? If so, what is their source?
3. How does Frey defend the view that human lives are richer than animal lives? Richer in what sense?
4. What are Frey's utilitarian arguments in favor of animal experimentation? Is his view dependent on or independent of utilitarianism?
5. Which propositions in the Universal Declaration of the Rights of Animals does Frey's position contradict?
6. If some human lives are less rich than animal lives, would it be acceptable to use those humans in medical experiments, according to Frey? Do you find his conclusion objectionable?
7. Write a critique of Frey's article from a Kantian perspective.

THE ENVIRONMENT

Every living thing interacts with its environment. Humans have no choice, therefore, but to change the natural world. But two factors have turned such changes into a significant public policy issue. First, the world's population has grown rapidly during the past several centuries, greatly amplifying humanity's impact on the environment. Second, the technological advances of the Industrial Revolution not only have increased our ability to affect our surroundings but also have brought about new kinds of effects that, even today, we only partially understand.

Utilitarians often see environmental problems as arising not from misguided calculations but from what Garrett Hardin dubs *the tragedy of the commons*. Often, each party to a collective decision has reason to pursue his or her self-interest, given what the others are doing. If everyone pursues self-interest, however, everyone becomes worse off. Each possible polluter, for example, may believe that his or her additional pollution will make no significant difference to the environment but will yield substantial economic rewards. This may be true. Yet if each potential polluter reasons similarly and pollutes, the resulting environmental degradation may make everyone worse off than before.

This is a special case of what has become known as a *prisoners' dilemma*. Suppose that the police catch two criminals, Mug and Thug. They immediately separate them and interrogate them independently. Having caught them on a minor violation, but lacking the evidence to be confident of obtaining a conviction on a major charge, the police offer Mug a deal: "You can make it easy for us, and on yourself, or you can make it tough. If you confess, and your testimony against Thug lets us get him on the major charge, you walk out of here. We bargain on the small stuff; you get probation. If you don't confess, you do time. You know we have you on the small stuff. If you don't work with us, we don't cut any deals. You go to jail. And if we get you on the big one, you go to jail for a long time. What do you say?" They offer the same deal to Thug.

We can represent the situation in a simple table, where Mug and Thug must choose to confess or remain silent, and where the outcomes are pairs [effect on Mug, effect on Thug]:

		Thug	
		Confess	Remain Silent
Mug	Confess	[−2, −2]	[0, −5]
	Remain Silent	[−5, 0]	[−1, −1]

That is, if both remain silent, they each get a year in jail on minor charges. If both confess, the police cut a deal for cooperation, but both are convicted of the serious offense, so each gets two years. If one confesses and the other doesn't, the one who confesses goes free, but the one who remains silent is convicted of everything, without any deals, and gets five years.

Mug and Thug can't communicate, and they aren't sure, let's assume, what the other will do. Mug might reason as follows: "If Thug confesses, I'm better off confessing. I'll get only two years instead of five. If Thug doesn't confess, I'm still better off confessing; I walk instead of getting a year. So, no matter what Thug does, I'm better off confessing." Mug therefore confesses. Thug reasons similarly, of course, and also confesses. So each criminal spends two years in jail. Their reasoning appears impeccable. Yet, if they had both remained silent, they would have cut their sentences in half.

Here's how the prisoners' dilemma applies to environmental problems and leads to the tragedy of the commons. Imagine that, in place of Mug and Thug, we have two companies, Vanishing Inc. and Roco Co. Each faces a choice between polluting and installing pollution control equipment. Each reasons that its pollution will have minor effects on overall air and water quality, but that installing control equipment will have a big impact on its bottom line. So each pollutes. But the result may be a lower quality of life for everyone, and even economic harm to the companies themselves (through additional costs required to clean the water to be used in their industrial processes, for example, or to replace equipment more frequently, or to attract workers to such an unpleasant community, or to pay increased health care costs).

Again, we can represent the choice in a table where the pairs are [effect on Vanishing Inc., effect on Roco Co.]:

		Roco Co.	
		Pollute	Control
Vanishing Inc.	Pollute	[2, 2]	[4, 1]
	Control	[1, 4]	[3, 3]

Each company can reason that it is better off polluting, no matter what the other does. Suppose that you are the CEO of Vanishing Inc. If Roco Co. pollutes, you are better off polluting; you have to put up with the disadvantages of Roco's pollution anyway, and the control equipment is expensive. If Roco controls its pollution, you are still better off polluting, because you save the costs of the control equipment, and you gain the benefits of Roco's cleanup efforts. But Roco Co. faces the same situation and reasons similarly. So you both pollute. But this is the worst possible outcome: a tragedy of the commons. You would have been better off, jointly and singly, if you had both controlled your pollution. The two of you taken together would have been better off if even one of you had done so.

So far, prisoners' dilemmas make the point that people or companies acting independently and rationally to promote their own self-interest can produce substantial and avoidable harm to the community as a whole. But the point applies to act-utilitarians as well as to self-interested agents. Suppose that Mug and Thug are utilitarians and that no one else is affected by what happens to them, so that they are seeking to maximize their combined welfare. Summing their individual utilities to compute the effects on the two taken together, their choice becomes

		Thug	
		Confess	Remain Silent
Mug	Confess	–4	–5
	Remain Silent	5	2

Mug, the utilitarian, sees that he should do whatever Thug does. Thug, the utilitarian, recognizes this too. So Mug and Thug satisfy the demands of act-utilitarianism if they both remain silent *or if they both confess*. This shows that act-utilitarianism is *indeterminate*—it may be satisfied by different patterns of behavior with different utilities for the community as a whole.

If our companies act as utilitarians in the case outlined above, they solve their problem: each maximizes welfare overall by controlling pollution, achieving the best outcome. (Vanishing Inc. sees that the community is better off if it controls its pollution, no matter what Roco Co. does.) But small changes in the effects on the two companies change this:

		Roco Co.	
		Pollute	Control
Vanishing Inc.	Pollute	[2.1, 2.1]	[4, 0]
	Control	[0, 4]	[3, 3]

Now, the choice is just like Mug's and Thug's. Each company can reason, as an act-utilitarian, that it should do what the other company does. But that means that both can be good act-utilitarians even while polluting and achieving less than the best overall outcome.

This points to an important limitation of act-utilitarian (that is, cost-benefit or risk-benefit) analyses made by independent parties: Even when they accurately assess risks and benefits, different patterns of behavior with different implications for the community's welfare can pass all such tests. Only by cooperating can the criminals or the companies achieve the best combined outcome.

This might seem to be an argument for rule-utilitarianism. But it too can lead to suboptimal outcomes. Suppose that Pig Inc. and Poke Co. each pollute slightly less than some threshold harmful amount. Then, if both pollute, they together produce significant harms. But the pollution of just one produces no harm at all. They seem to face the following choice:

		Poke Co.	
		Pollute	Control
Pig Inc.	Pollute	[2, 2]	[4, 3]
	Control	[3, 4]	[3, 3]

Self-interest and act-utilitarianism imply that exactly one company should pollute. The polluting company does better economically without producing any environmental harm. Yet rule-utilitarianism tells each company to follow the rule that will produce the best outcome overall. If both follow the rule "Pollute," the overall utility is 4; if they follow the rule "Don't pollute," it is 6. So if the companies act as rule-utilitarians, they will both install controls, producing less than the best outcome for the community.

The World Commission on Environment and Development, in a report to the United Nations known as the Brundtland Report, seeks to overcome the issue of the proper role of government and rules by focusing on the concept of sustainability. Over the past few decades sustainability has emerged as the most important concept in environmental ethics. Sustainable development, the commission says, meets the needs of the present without compromising the ability of future generations to meet their needs. It addresses a difficult philosophical question—What do we owe future generations?—by saying that we owe them an undiminished capacity to meet their needs. This imposes constraints on us now, for environmentally destructive development and overuse of nonrenewable resources can leave future generations in a difficult position. Avoiding such a result requires cooperation, not only in the form of private efforts and government action, but also in the form of international agreements.

Daniel Bonevac examines the concept of sustainability, seeing its core as preservation of goods—of resources, capacities to meet needs, opportunities, welfare, or some other good. Lying at the root of environmentalists' use of the concept is the thesis that a policy is morally acceptable only if it preserves the relevant good. Kant asks, "What if everyone were to adopt this policy?" The Brundtland Report asks, "What if we were to keep following this policy over the long run?" Bonevac distinguishes two ways of interpreting the requirement of sustainability of relevant goods. One is plausible and implies the need for environmental concern and moderate steps to secure environmental goods. The other—upon which environmentalists rest—calls for fundamental transformations of economic relationships as well as humanity's relation to the environment and is implausible, having unwelcome implications for individual and group action across the board.

GARRETT HARDIN

from *The Tragedy of the Commons*

Garrett Hardin is professor emeritus of biology at the University of California at Santa Barbara. (Source: Excerpted with permission from Garrett Hardin, "The Tragedy of the Commons," Science *162 [1968]: 1243–1248.*

. . . In economic affairs, *The Wealth of Nations* (1776) popularized the "invisible hand," the idea that an individual who "intends only his own gain" is, as it were, "led by an invisible hand to promote the public interest." Adam Smith did not assert that this was invariably true, and perhaps neither did any of his followers. But he contributed to a dominant tendency of thought that has ever since interfered with positive action based on rational analysis, namely, the tendency to assume that decisions reached individually will, in fact, be the best decisions for an entire society. . . .

Tragedy of Freedom in a Commons

The rebuttal to the invisible hand in population control is to be found in a scenario first sketched in a little-known pamphlet in 1833 by a mathematical amateur named William Forster Lloyd (1794–1852). We may well call it "the tragedy of the commons," using the word "tragedy" as the philosopher Whitehead used it: "The essence of dramatic tragedy is not unhappiness. It resides in the solemnity of the remorseless working of things." He then goes on to say, "This inevitableness of destiny can only be illustrated in terms of human life by incidents which in fact involve unhappiness. For it is only by them that the futility of escape can be made evident in the drama."

The tragedy of the commons develops in this way. Picture a pasture open to all. It is to be expected that each herdsman will try to keep as many cattle as possible on the commons. Such an arrangement may work reasonably satisfactorily for centuries because tribal wars, poaching, and disease keep the numbers of both man and beast well below the carrying capacity of the land. Finally, however, comes the day of reckoning, that is, the day when the long-desired goal of social stability becomes a reality. At this point, the inherent logic of the commons remorselessly generates tragedy.

As a rational being, each herdsman seeks to maximize his gain. Explicitly or implicitly, more or less consciously, he asks, "What is the utility to me of adding one more animal to my herd?" This utility has one negative and one positive component.

1. The positive component is a function of the increment of one animal. Since the herdsman receives all the proceeds from the sale of the additional animal, the positive utility is nearly +1.

2. The negative component is a function of the additional overgrazing created by one more animal. Since, however, the effects of overgrazing are shared by all the herdsmen, the negative utility for any particular decisionmaking herdsman is only a fraction of −1.

Adding together the component partial utilities, the rational herdsman concludes that the only sensible course for him to pursue is to add another animal to his herd. And another . . . But this is the conclusion reached by each and every rational herdsman sharing a commons. Therein is the tragedy. Each man is locked into a system that compels him to increase his herd without limit—in a world that is limited. Ruin is the destination toward which all men rush, each pursuing his own best interest in a society that believes in the freedom of the commons. Freedom in a commons brings ruin to all.

Some would say that this is a platitude. Would that it were! In a sense, it was learned thousands of years ago, but natural selection favors the forces of psychological denial. The individual benefits as an individual from his ability to deny the truth even though society as a whole, of which he is a part, suffers. Education can counteract the natural tendency to do the wrong thing, but the inexorable succession of generations requires that the basis for this knowledge be constantly refreshed.

A simple incident that occurred a few years ago in Leominster, Massachusetts, shows how perishable the knowledge is. During the Christmas shopping season the parking meters downtown were covered with plastic bags that bore tags reading: "Do not open until after Christmas. Free parking courtesy of the mayor and city council." In other words, facing the prospect of an increased demand for already scarce space, the city fathers reinstituted the system of the commons. (Cynically, we suspect that they gained more votes than they lost by this retrogressive act.)

In an approximate way, the logic of the commons has been understood for a long time, perhaps since the discovery of agriculture or the invention of private property in real estate. But it is understood mostly only in special cases which are not sufficiently generalized. Even at this late date, cattlemen leasing national land on the Western ranges demonstrate no more than an ambivalent understanding, in constantly pressuring federal authorities to increase the head count to the point where overgrazing produces erosion and weed-dominance. Likewise, the oceans of the world continue to suffer from the survival of the philosophy of the commons. Maritime nations still respond automatically to the shibboleth of the "freedom of the seas." Professing to believe in the "inexhaustible resources of the oceans," they bring species after species of fish and whales closer to extinction.

The National Parks present another instance of the working out of the tragedy of the commons. At present, they are open to all, without limit. The parks themselves are limited in extent—there is only one Yosemite Valley—whereas population seems to grow without limit. The values that visitors seek in the parks are steadily eroded. Plainly, we must soon cease to treat the parks as commons or they will be of no value to anyone.

What shall we do? We have several options. We might sell them off as private property. We might keep them as public property, but allocate the right to enter them. The allocation might be on the basis of wealth, by the use of an auction system. It might be on the basis of merit, as defined by some agreed-upon standards. It might be by lottery. Or it might be on a first-come, first-served basis, administered to long queues. These, I think, are all objectionable. But we must choose—or acquiesce in the destruction of the commons that we call our National Parks.

Pollution

In a reverse way, the tragedy of the commons reappears in problems of pollution. Here it is not a question of taking something out of the commons, but of putting something in—sewage, or chemical, radioactive, and heat wastes into water; noxious and dangerous fumes into the air; and distracting and unpleasant advertising signs into the line of sight. The calculations of utility are much the same as before. The rational man finds that his share of the cost of the wastes he discharges into the commons is less than the cost of purifying his wastes before releasing them. Since this is true for everyone, we are locked into a system of "fouling our own nest," so long as we behave only as independent, rational, free enterprisers.

The tragedy of the commons as a food basket is averted by private property, or something formally like it. But the air and waters surrounding us cannot readily be fenced, and so the tragedy of the commons as a cesspool must be prevented by different means, by coercive laws or taxing devices that make it cheaper for the polluter to treat his pollutants than to discharge them untreated. We have not progressed as far with the solution of this problem as we have with the first. Indeed, our particular concept of private property, which deters us from exhausting the positive resources of the earth, favors pollution. The owner of a factory on the bank of a stream—whose property extends to the middle of the stream—often has difficulty seeing why it is not his natural right to muddy the waters flowing past his door. The law, always behind the times, requires elaborate stitching and fitting to adapt it to this newly perceived aspect of the commons. . . .

QUESTIONS FOR REFLECTION

1. How does the tragedy of the commons refute the idea behind the "invisible hand"?
2. Why would declaring free parking downtown during Christmas season decrease total happiness?
3. How does the tragedy of the commons apply to the national park system, in Hardin's view? Which of the options he outlines would you favor? Why?
4. Could we avoid the tragedy of the commons if everyone acted as a utilitarian? As a Kantian?
5. Imagine an apartment with several bedrooms, each rented to a separate student, around a common kitchen and living area. What would Hardin predict about the eventual condition of the kitchen and living area? How might the roommates try to prevent that outcome?
6. One way of dealing with a potential tragedy of the commons is for participants to agree on informal rules for sharing. Are there circumstances in which such informal rules might succeed? Are there circumstances in which they are likely to fail?
7. Governments sometimes seek to prevent tragedies of the commons by enforcing rules with which all participants must comply. What are the advantages and disadvantages of such an approach?
8. A famous New England prep school once built a new set of buildings. The first year, it built no sidewalks, letting students walk wherever they wished. At the end of the year, they noticed where students had worn paths, and installed sidewalks there. Could that strategy generalize to an approach to environmental tragedies of the commons?
9. Identify examples of potential tragedies of the commons in a typical family with children. How do people try to avoid them? Do their strategies support or undermine Hardin's position?
10. Analyze a particular environmental problem—deforestation, climate change, overuse of fossil fuels, or air pollution, for example—as a tragedy of the commons, and suggest a strategy for protecting the commons.

WORLD COMMISSION ON ENVIRONMENT AND DEVELOPMENT

from *Our Common Future: Report of the World Commission on Environment and Development*

Chapter 2: Towards Sustainable Development

1. Sustainable development is development that meets the needs of the present without compromising the ability of future generations to meet their own needs. It contains within it two key concepts:

- the concept of "needs," in particular the essential needs of the world's poor, to which overriding priority should be given; and
- the idea of limitations imposed by the state of technology and social organization on the environment's ability to meet present and future needs.

2. Thus the goals of economic and social development must be defined in terms of sustainability in all countries—developed or developing, market-oriented or centrally planned. Interpretations will vary, but must share certain general features and must flow from a consensus on the basic concept of sustainable development and on a broad strategic framework for achieving it.

3. Development involves a progressive transformation of economy and society. A development path that is sustainable in a physical sense could theoretically be pursued even in a rigid social and political setting. But physical sustainability cannot be secured unless development policies pay attention to such considerations as changes in access to resources and in the distribution of costs and benefits. Even the narrow notion of physical sustainability implies a concern for social equity between generations, a concern that must logically be extended to equity within each generation.

I. The Concept of Sustainable Development

4. The satisfaction of human needs and aspirations is the major objective of development. The essential needs of vast numbers of people in developing countries—for food, clothing, shelter, jobs—are not being met, and beyond their basic needs these people have legitimate aspirations for an improved quality of life. A world in which poverty and inequity are endemic will always be prone to ecological and other crises. Sustainable development requires meeting the basic needs of all and extending to all the opportunity to satisfy their aspirations for a better life.

5. Living standards that go beyond the basic minimum are sustainable only if consumption standards everywhere have regard for long-term sustainability. Yet many of us live beyond the world's ecological means, for instance in our patterns of energy use. Perceived needs are socially and culturally determined, and sustainable development requires the promotion of values that encourage consumption standards that are within the bounds of the ecological possible and to which all can reasonably aspire.

6. Meeting essential needs depends in part on achieving full growth potential, and sustainable development clearly requires economic growth in

places where such needs are not being met. Elsewhere, it can be consistent with economic growth, provided the content of growth reflects the broad principles of sustainability and non-exploitation of others. But growth by itself is not enough. High levels of productive activity and widespread poverty can coexist, and can endanger the environment. Hence sustainable development requires that societies meet human needs both by increasing productive potential and by ensuring equitable opportunities for all.

7. An expansion in numbers can increase the pressure on resources and slow the rise in living standards in areas where deprivation is widespread. Though the issue is not merely one of population size but of the distribution of resources, sustainable development can only be pursued if demographic developments are in harmony with the changing productive potential of the ecosystem.

8. A society may in many ways compromise its ability to meet the essential needs of its people in the future—by overexploiting resources, for example. The direction of technological developments may solve some immediate problems but lead to even greater ones. Large sections of the population may be marginalized by ill-considered development.

9. Settled agriculture, the diversion of watercourses, the extraction of minerals, the emission of heat and noxious gases into the atmosphere, commercial forests, and genetic manipulation are all examples or human intervention in natural systems during the course of development. Until recently, such interventions were small in scale and their impact limited. Today's interventions are more drastic in scale and impact, and more threatening to life-support systems both locally and globally. This need not happen. At a minimum, sustainable development must not endanger the natural systems that support life on Earth: the atmosphere, the waters, the soils, and the living beings.

10. Growth has no set limits in terms of population or resource use beyond which lies ecological disaster. Different limits hold for the use of energy, materials, water, and land. Many of these will manifest themselves in the form of rising costs and diminishing returns, rather than in the form of any sudden loss of a resource base. The accumulation of knowledge and the development of technology can enhance the carrying capacity of the resource base. But ultimate limits there are, and sustainability requires that long before these are reached, the world must ensure equitable access to the constrained resource and reorient technological efforts to relieve the pressure.

> *A communications gap has kept environmental, population, and development assistance groups apart for too long, preventing us from being aware of our common interest and realizing our combined power. Fortunately, the gap is closing. We now know that what unites us is vastly more important than what divides us.*
>
> *We recognize that poverty, environmental degradation, and population growth are inextricably related and that none of these fundamental problems can be successfully addressed in isolation. We will succeed or fail together.*
>
> *Arriving at a commonly accepted definition of "sustainable development" remains a challenge for all the actors in the development process.*
>
> —"Making Common Cause." U.S. Based Development, Environment, Population NGOs, WCED Public Hearing, Ottawa, May 26–27, 1986.

11. Economic growth and development obviously involve changes in the physical ecosystem. Every ecosystem everywhere cannot be preserved intact. A forest may be depleted in one part of a watershed and extended elsewhere, which is not a bad thing if the exploitation has been planned and the effects on soil erosion rates, water regimes, and genetic losses have been taken into account. In general, renewable resources like forests and fish stocks need not be depleted provided the rate of use is within the limits of regeneration and natural growth. But most renewable resources are part of a complex and interlinked ecosystem, and maximum sustainable yield must be defined after taking into account system-wide effects of exploitation.

12. As for non-renewable resources, like fossil fuels and minerals, their use reduces the stock available for future generations. But this does not mean that such resources should not be used. In general the rate of depletion should take into account the criticality of that resource, the availability of technologies tor minimizing depletion, and the likelihood of substitutes being available. Thus land should not be degraded beyond reasonable recovery. With minerals

and fossil fuels, the rate of depletion and the emphasis on recycling and economy of use should be calibrated to ensure that the resource does not run out before acceptable substitutes are available. Sustainable development requires that the rate of depletion of non-renewable resources should foreclose as few future options as possible.

13. Development tends to simplify ecosystems and to reduce their diversity of species. And species, once extinct, are not renewable. The loss of plant and animal species can greatly limit the options of future generations; so sustainable development requires the conservation of plant and animal species.

14. So-called free goods like air and water are also resources. The raw materials and energy of production processes are only partly converted to useful products. The rest comes out as wastes. Sustainable development requires that the adverse impacts on the quality of air, water, and other natural elements are minimized so as to sustain the ecosystem's overall integrity.

15. In essence, sustainable development is a process of change in which the exploitation of resources, the direction of investments, the orientation of technological development, and institutional change are all in harmony and enhance both current and future potential to meet human needs and aspirations.

II. Equity and the Common Interest

16. Sustainable development has been described here in general terms. How are individuals in the real world to be persuaded or made to act in the common interest? The answer lies partly in education, institutional development, and law enforcement. But many problems of resource depletion and environmental stress arise from disparities in economic and political power. An industry may get away with unacceptable levels or air and water pollution because the people who bear the brunt of it are poor and unable to complain effectively. A forest may be destroyed by excessive felling because the people living there have no alternatives or because timber contractors generally have more influence then forest dwellers.

17. Ecological interactions do not respect the boundaries of individual ownership and political jurisdiction. Thus:

- In a watershed, the ways in which a farmer up the slope uses land directly affect run-off on farms downstream.
- The irrigation practices, pesticides, and fertilizers used on one farm affect the productivity of neighbouring ones, especially among small farms.
- The efficiency of a factory boiler determines its rate of emission of soot and noxious chemicals and affects all who live and work around it.
- The hot water discharged by a thermal power plant into a river or a local sea affects the catch of all who fish locally.

18. Traditional social systems recognized some aspects of this interdependence and enforced community control over agricultural practices and traditional rights relating to water, forests, and land. This enforcement of the "common interest" did not necessarily impede growth and expansion though it may have limited the acceptance and diffusion of technical innovations.

19. Local interdependence has, if anything, increased because of the technology used in modern agriculture and manufacturing. Yet with this surge of technical progress, the growing "enclosure" of common lands, the erosion of common rights in forests and other resources, and the spread of commerce and production for the market, the responsibilities for decision making are being taken away from both groups and individuals. This shift is still under way in many developing countries.

> *If the desert is growing, forest disappearing, malnutrition increasing, and people in urban areas living in very bad conditions, it is not because we are lacking resources but the kind of policy implemented by our rulers, by the elite group. Denying people rights and peoples' interests is pushing us to a situation where it is only the poverty that has a very prosperous future in Africa. And it is our hope that your Commission, the World Commission, will not overlook these problems of human rights in Africa and will put emphasis on it. Because it is only free people, people who have rights, who are mature and responsible citizens, who then participate in the development and in the protection of the environment.*
>
> —Speaker from the floor, WCED Public Hearing, Nairobi, September 23, 1986.

20. It is not that there is one set of villains and another of victims. All would be better off if each person took into account the effect of his or her acts upon others. But each is unwilling to assume that others will behave in this socially desirable fashion, and hence all continue to pursue narrow self-interest. Communities or governments can compensate for this isolation through laws, education, taxes, subsidies, and other methods. Well-enforced laws and strict liability legislation can control harmful side effects. Most important, effective participation in decision-making processes by local communities can help them articulate and effectively enforce their common interest.

21. Interdependence is not simply a local phenomenon. Rapid growth in production has extended it to the international plane, with both physical and economic manifestations. There are growing global and regional pollution effects, such as in the more than 200 international river basins and the large number of shared seas.

22. The enforcement of common interest often suffers because areas of political jurisdiction and areas of impact do not coincide. Energy policies in one jurisdiction cause acid precipitation in another. The fishing policies of one state affect the fish catch of another. No supranational authority exists to resolve such issues, and the common interest can only be articulated through international cooperation.

23. In the same way, the ability of a government to control its national economy is reduced by growing international economic interactions. For example, foreign trade in commodities makes issues of carrying capacities and resource scarcities an international concern. If economic power and the benefits of trade were more equally distributed, common interests would be generally recognized. But the gains from trade are unequally distributed, and patterns of trade in, say, sugar affect not merely a local sugar-producing sector, but the economies and ecologies of the many developing countries that depend heavily on this product.

24. The search for common interest would be less difficult if all development and environment problems had solutions that would leave everyone better off. This is seldom the case, and there are usually winners and losers. Many problems arise from inequalities in access to resources. An inequitable land ownership structure can lead to overexploitation of resources in the smallest holdings, with harmful effects on both environment and development. Internationally, monopolistic control over resources can drive those who do not share in them to excessive exploitation of marginal resources. The differing capacities of exploiters to commandeer "free" goods—locally, nationally, and internationally—is another manifestation of unequal access to resources. "Losers" in environment/development conflicts include those who suffer more than their fair share of the health, property, and ecosystem damage costs of pollution.

25. As a system approaches ecological limits, inequalities sharpen. Thus when a watershed deteriorates, poor farmers suffer more because they cannot afford the same anti-erosion measures as richer farmers. When urban air quality deteriorates, the poor, in their more vulnerable areas, suffer more health damage than the rich, who usually live in more pristine neighbourhoods. When mineral resources become depleted, late-comers to the industrialization process lose the benefits of low-cost supplies. Globally, wealthier nations are better placed financially and technologically to cope with the effects of possible climatic change.

26. Hence, our inability to promote the common interest in sustainable development is often a product of the relative neglect of economic and social justice within and amongst nations.

QUESTIONS FOR REFLECTION

1. What are "needs"? How do they differ from "goods" or other desirable outcomes?
2. What does the commission mean by "compromising abilities to meet needs"? Is this equivalent to "failing to preserve abilities to meet needs"?

3. The commission holds that sustainability requires attention to present inequality: "A world in which poverty and inequity are endemic will always be prone to ecological and other crises." Why? Evaluate the argument.
4. What is the logical relationship between equity *between* generations and equity *within* generations?
5. "The report calls for increased economic growth to meet the needs of people who are poor now, but without increasing our use of non-renewable resources, which might disadvantage people in the future. That's impossible. You have to choose one or the other." Discuss.
6. The commission sees sustainable development as a solution to communications problems and to the tragedy of the commons that results. How?

DANIEL BONEVAC

Is Sustainability Sustainable?

Daniel Bonevac is Professor of Philosophy at the University of Texas at Austin.
(Source: Academic Questions 23 (2010): 84–101. Footnotes omitted. Reprinted by permission.)

The most important concept in current environmental thinking is *sustainability*. Environmental policies, economic policies, development, resource use—all of these things, according to the consensus, ought to be sustainable. But what is sustainability? What is its ethical foundation? There is little consensus about how these questions ought to be answered.

Many environmentalists are troubled by the plethora of understandings of sustainability in the literature. Andrew Dobson, for example, counts more than three hundred definitions! Others see this as a virtue, equating sustainability with other contested concepts such as happiness, justice, and rights. Either way, exploring the ethical significance of sustainability is a vital task.

Surprisingly, almost nothing has been done to justify sustainability as an ethical constraint. My aim is to investigate whether that can be done. I shall argue that the chief conceptions of sustainability in the environmental literature are not themselves sustainable. They often have innocuous interpretations that are plausible but do little to advance the environmentalists' or any other particular agenda. Their more radical interpretations, however, lack ethical foundations; they face obvious counterexamples when applied to individual lives and communities. There is no reason to take any of them as criteria that any environmental, economic, developmental, or resource management policy must meet, or even as goals toward which any such policy ought to strive.

. . .

Sustainability and Needs

Sustainability moved to center stage in environmental discussions in the report of the Brundtland Commission, formally the World Commission on Environment and Development, convened by the United Nations in 1983. Also known as *Our Common Future*, the Brundtland report was published by Oxford University Press in 1987: "Sustainable development is development that meets the needs of the present without compromising the ability of future generations to meet their own needs." Call a policy *Brundtland-sustainable* if it "meets the needs of the present without compromising the ability of future generations to meet their own needs." Is it true that a policy is ethically permissible only if it is Brundtland-sustainable?

In assessing sustainability under any of its definitions or interpretations, I shall use a three-pronged test.

1. Is it plausible at an individual level? Is sustainability an acceptable ethical constraint on individual action?

2. Is it plausible at a group, organizational, or communal level? Is sustainability an acceptable ethical constraint on collective action?
3. Is it satisfiable? Is it possible for any policy to meet the sustainability constraint being proposed?

If the answer to any of these questions is no, I shall judge that conception of sustainability to be itself unsustainable. Throughout, I shall consider sustainability solely as a *necessary* condition on permissible action. Whether it would be sufficient if adequately formulated is an interesting question that few environmentalists have addressed. I shall also assume that, for the foreseeable future, human beings must use some nonrenewable resources (e.g., oil, natural gas) to produce energy in order to live modern lives.

Let's ask, first, whether Brundtland-sustainability is a reasonable constraint on individual action. An individual's policy, rule for living, or "maxim," to use Kant's phrase, can fail to be Brundtland-sustainable in either of two ways. First, it may fail to meet the needs of the present. Jones's profligacy and fast living may get him into trouble now. Second, it may compromise the ability of future generations to meet their needs. Jones's running up large debts may impose a substantial burden on his children, for example. These two ways of failing to be Brundtland-sustainable stem from different sources. If Jones fails to meet his own needs, he is certainly imprudent; it is less clear that he is immoral. If Jones places such a great burden on his children that they cannot meet their own needs, then he does appear unequivocally to do something immoral.

The plausibility of Brundtland-sustainability as an ethical constraint, however, depends crucially on how we interpret "needs" and especially "compromise." If "compromise someone's ability to meet their needs" means "makes it *impossible* for someone to meet their own needs," then Brundtland-unsustainable policies are, on an individual level, *prima facie* impermissible. That is to say, on that interpretation, Brundtland-unsustainable policies are, all other things being equal, wrong. It is vital to include the "all other things being equal" phrase, for it might be impossible to act in such a way that everyone in a future generation is capable of meeting his needs. Or, it might be possible to do so only at a prohibitive moral cost.

Many environmentalists, however, are unhappy with this "expansionist" interpretation of the Brundtland definition. They recognize, correctly in my view, that most of our current economic, developmental, and environmental policies are already Brundtland-sustainable. So, a demand for Brundtland-sustainability in this sense does not support an agenda of sweeping policy change. It suggests that, at least in highly developed nations, policies are already largely environmentally acceptable. In developing nations, it suggests that policies toward deforestation, water usage, and the like need to be reformed. But the adjustments to the status quo this definition demands are relatively minor from a global point of view. The Brundtland report is pro-growth; Wilfred Beckerman describes its view in these terms: "the surest way to improve your environment is to get rich."

If we mean something weaker by "compromise," so that the implications of the constraint are more radical, the constraint loses much of its plausibility. Suppose, putting prudential issues aside, that the condition means that we must not do anything to decrease the probability that future generations will be able to meet their own needs. On an individual level, this prohibits Jones from doing anything that would make it less likely that his descendants will be able to meet their needs in the future. But anything he spends or uses now does that. Does this require Jones, then, to maximize the amount of money he leaves them? Does it require him to forego everything beyond meeting his own needs in order to promote the capacities of future generations? Does it prohibit him from using any nonrenewable resources beyond those he requires to meet his own needs? Any nonrenewable resources at all? Anything he uses, after all, will not be available to meet future needs. Since the principle seems to require Jones simultaneously to meet his own needs and to do nothing that compromises the ability to meet needs in the future, it is unsatisfiable if he must use any nonrenewable resources to meet his needs. Meeting his own needs, to the extent that he uses nonrenewable resources, necessarily compromises abilities to meet future needs.

On an individual level, then, Brundtland-sustainability is either plausible and easily satisfied or implausible and unsatisfiable. The situation is no better at an organizational level. Consider, for example, a sports team. Surely the team should not focus so exclusively on the short term that it cannot meet its needs in the future. But it seems much too strong to say that it can do nothing to meet needs now that lowers the probability of meeting its future needs. Should the team pursue an accomplished but aging star who can help the team this year, or young prospects who may do little for the team now but will increase its chances in the future? This is a real question, faced by many kinds of organizations. It is by no means clear that one should never pursue the person who can help the most now at some cost to one's future prospects. Again, Brundtland-sustainability is either easily satisfied or utterly implausible.

Preservation of Capital

Many environmentalists construe sustainability as preservation. We might cast the Brundtland definition in these terms: A policy is sustainable if it preserves abilities to meet needs. The most common definition of sustainability, however, understands it as preservation of capital. Robert M. Solow, followed by K. G. Maler, defined economic sustainability as maximizing the flow of income that could be generated from a given stock of assets (or capital) while at least maintaining them. David W. Pearce, Anil Markandya, and Edward B. Barbier treat sustainability as requiring that conditions necessary for equal access to the Earth's resource base be met for each generation. Richard C. Bishop writes: "To achieve sustainability policies should be considered that constrain the day to day operations of the economy in ways that enhance the natural resource endowments of future generations." Marco Keiner requires that each generation "leave a *lesser burden*" (italics in original) than they inherited, increasing the quantity and quality of ecological, human, and manmade resources.

Advocates of a capital-preservation view generally distinguish three kinds of capital:

- Economic (man-made capital)
- Social (human capital, social capital)
- Environmental (natural capital)

The simplest version of the view is that sustainability is preservation of environmental capital. It is also implausible, however, for modern human beings. Living a modern life entails using some nonrenewable natural resources. If we consider gross effects on the environment, therefore, we must consider this understanding of sustainability to be unsatisfiable. We might refine it to concern net effects; perhaps we can increase the stock of natural capital by adding renewable resources to compensate for our use of nonrenewable resources.

This raises the question of substitution. May we substitute renewable for nonrenewable resources? May we substitute economic or social capital for environmental capital? Should we be concerned with preserving economic and social capital as well as environmental capital? Or should we be concerned solely with the sum of all three, allowing substitutions of one kind for another? Answers to these questions lead to three different versions of the capital-preservation view.

Strong Sustainability

William E. Rees, Herman E. Daly, and Robert Costanza argue that we must preserve each kind of capital individually. This view, known as *strong sustainability*, does not allow substitution of one kind of capital for another. We may not justify diminishing natural capital by augmenting social or economic capital, even if the result is a net gain in utility as well as in the total amount of capital available for future generations.

On an individual level, strong sustainability is absurd. Anyone who pays tuition to obtain an education trades economic capital for human capital: impermissible, decrees the requirement of strong sustainability. This is also the case for anyone who uses natural resources to obtain economic or social capital—which includes, in a modern society, virtually everyone who works. Strong sustainability, at an individual level, is unsatisfiable in a modern setting.

Strong sustainability fares no better at a group level. It rules out pollution as well as employee training (the substitution of human for economic capital) and resource use of any sort. A firm would like to spend some money for a team-building exercise? Out of luck; that would substitute social for economic capital.

Strong sustainability actually rules out environmentalism. Fishing boats are not effective substitutes for fish, say its advocates. But it follows just as readily from their position that fish are not effective substitutes for fishing boats. We may not trade economic gains for environmental capital, but we also may not trade economic capital for environmental gains. So, strong sustainability appears to forbid environmental expenditures and programs.

To avoid this consequence, some advocates of strong sustainability prohibit substitutions only in one direction. Nothing can substitute for environmental capital, though other substitutions are permitted. This appears philosophically unmotivated. It also seems implausible. Suppose that allowing one obscure, highly localized species to go extinct would produce massive economic and social benefits for humanity, solving problems of poverty, hunger, impure drinking water, lack of medical care, etc. Is it really morally unacceptable to allow it to happen?

Weak Sustainability

John M. Hartwick, Robert M. Solow, and Vinod Thomas et al., argue for *weak sustainability*, which requires preservation of total capital, permitting substitution of one kind for another. It permits us to spend money on environmental improvements. It also permits the use of natural capital to accumulate economic capital. For that very reason, many environmentalists find it too weak to promote their goals. But it is not vacuous. We may substitute one sort of capital for another, but we must not decrease the total supply of capital. We must hand the Earth to future generations in at least as good shape as we found it, even if we alter the mix of economic, social, and environmental capital.

On an individual level, weak sustainability requires passing on to the future at least as much capital as we have at any point managed to acquire. We might do this is any number of ways: earning money and leaving it to heirs; constructing buildings, machines, or other goods; raising and educating children; training people in skills we have acquired; and improving the natural environment. Think of an individual's net impact on the world as a combination of all his effects on the natural, social, and economic aspects of the world. Weak sustainability requires that our net impact, individually and communally, be nonnegative. It requires that we contribute at least as much as we take. If you ask George Bailey's question, and wonder what the world would have been like if you had never been born, the answer should be that it would have been worse, or at least that it would have been no better.

"Leave the world no worse than you found it" has some appeal from an ethical point of view. But several points are worth noting:

- The slogan actually captures only a part of the weak sustainability thesis, which requires that capital *never* decrease. The unit of measurement is not a life but a moment; you may never do *anything* that would decrease net capital. You may never use a natural resource without a corresponding increase in human, social, or economic capital that is at least as great. This is an extraordinarily demanding standard. Solitary entertainments that use natural resources without compensating increases in human capital sufficient to balance that use (bowling alone? watching TV alone? reading a novel alone by anything other than natural light? going for a drive in the country?) are out.
- The principle is consequentialist, that is, concerned solely with results. As a necessary condition only, it does not commit one to consequentialism *tout court*. But it is incompatible with certain ethical views, for example, Kant's.
- The principle makes no allowance for the possibility that some people, through no fault of their own, may not be able to avoid net negative effects on capital. Perhaps it should be amended to read "Minimize your net harm to the world."
- The principle gives a huge role to moral luck. Accidents happen. Anomalies occur. Actions that might reasonably be expected to result in a net increase in capital sometimes do the opposite. Actions that might reasonably be expected to result in a net decrease in capital sometimes work out well. Jeremy Bentham, John Stuart Mill, and most other consequentialists judge actions according to their *tendencies* to have positive or negative effects, not according to the effects themselves. Adding an adjustment for that would yield "Minimize the net harm your actions might reasonably be expected to have."
- For reasons familiar from debates over consequentialism, the weak sustainability principle, even in this refined form, strikes many people as implausible without a *ceteris paribus* clause. Are there any circumstances that would justify a net decrease in capital that might have been avoided?

Consequentialism's critics have pointed to situations in which we might accept suboptimal consequences for the sake of human dignity, human rights, honoring contracts, keeping promises, or self-respect. In short, one might argue that weak sustainability neglects various kinds of moral capital that also deserve consideration and respect.

All of these arguments tell against strong sustainability as well, since preservation of each kind of capital entails preservation of total capital.

So far we have been considering weak sustainability as a constraint on individual action. All the arguments above apply if we think of it instead as a constraint on group action. Indeed, a collective perspective suggests additional arguments. Can a group ever permissibly use capital to achieve its ends now, at the expense of the future? Think again of a sports team that signs an aging star at considerable expense to help win the championship, or a business that issues debt to undertake an advertising campaign to improve sales this year. Environmentalists rightly complain that business tends to adopt a perspective that is too short-term, making these kinds of decisions that too often favor the present at the expense of the future. But it is quite another thing to say that such a decision is never justified.

Sensible Sustainability

The divide between advocates of strong and weak sustainability has led several writers to develop an intermediate position, *sensible sustainability*, which allows limited tradeoffs between economic, social, and environmental capital. Sensible sustainability is more plausible than strong sustainability, allowing substitution of one kind of capital for another in certain circumstances while promoting more stringent environmental controls than weak sustainability. Just how much more plausible or stringent, however, depends on how one specifies those circumstances.

Evaluating sensible sustainability is difficult without knowing under what conditions transfers from one kind of capital to another would be permitted. Since sensible sustainability is stronger than weak sustainability, however, all arguments against weak sustainability apply to sensible sustainability as well. In particular, sensible sustainability too is highly stringent. It never permits benefitting the present at the expense of the future. In fact, it never permits sacrificing capital at a later time for the sake of an earlier time, even if both times are in the future. To put this differently, the view prohibits sacrificing present capital for the sake of the future unless the future gains are permanent. If they are temporary, capital will decline at some future point, and that is impermissible. And, to be plausible at all as a moral constraint, it would need a *ceteris paribus* clause, making it a desideratum, at best, and not a necessary condition.

Preservation of Capacities or Opportunities

Mwangi-wa Githinji and Charles Perrings, and Bryan Norton construe sustainability as preservation of *opportunities*. Andrew Steer advocates a preservation-of-*capacities* view, but takes it to be equivalent to a capital-preservation view:

> If you conceive of sustainable development in terms of passing on to future generations the capacity to do what we have done, or the capacity to enjoy life to the full extent that we do, then what you are really passing on to those generations is a stock of capital—and I do not mean just machines and buildings.

He is surely wrong about the equivalence claim; we might become more or less efficient at using capital to generate capacities and opportunities, thus preserving opportunities without preserving capital or vice versa. This is not merely a theoretical possibility. Living standards have risen dramatically over the past two centuries due primarily to productivity increases.

Preservation of opportunities or capacities runs into the same objections as preservation of capital. It too is stringent, never permits present-future tradeoffs, and would at best hold *ceteris paribus*. But it also has its own special problems. On an individual level, it has no plausibility whatever. Every choice a person makes forecloses opportunities. To live is to choose, and to choose is to narrow one's range of future choices. The same holds at a group level.

When a group chooses one course of action, it forecloses others. There are capacities and opportunities we have that future generations will never have, because choices that we, they, and everyone in between makes will eliminate them. Those choices will of course create other possibilities. Whether they will be better or worse is a moral question for which there may or may not be any clear-cut answer. Whether they will exceed current opportunities in *quantity* seems both imponderable and irrelevant, *pace* Ralf Dahrendorf, since similarity of opportunities is a crucial variable (see Brian Barry) and since all the quantities are infinite. In any case, preservation of opportunities is simply impossible.

Even putting that aside, preserving opportunities would forbid contracts, since the point of a contract is to constrain future behavior. So, a person or organization obeying the opportunities-preservation requirement could not get married, get a job, sign a lease, take on a mortgage, sign a contract, sign a treaty, or enter into an international organization.

Much the same holds true for capacity-preservation. Choosing to develop some capacities leaves others undeveloped. Someone who had the capacity to become a first-rate lawyer may no longer have that capacity, having devoted his life to teaching philosophy or playing the gamba. It seems to follow that devoting one's life to developing some capacities at the expense of others is morally unacceptable. But that is just to say that one should not develop one's capacities. And that is absurd.

Preservation of Well-Being

John Hicks and Joseph E. Stiglitz are concerned with the sustainability of per capita *consumption*. John C.V. Pezzey speaks of non-declining per capita *utility*. Ian Goldin and L. Alan Winters construe a sustainable policy as one that does not compromise future *growth* for the sake of the present. John G. Riley, Gerhard Pfister and Ortwin Renn, and Partha Dasgupta and Karl-Göran Mäler speak of non-declining inter-temporal *welfare*. Herman E. Daly stresses non-declining *throughput*. John C.V. Pezzey and Michael A. Toman speak, perhaps most generally, of non-declining *well-being*. These are not equivalent to the capital-preservation, capacities-preservation, or opportunities-preservation views. Nor are they equivalent to one another. All these views, however, have a common structure, shared by the views we have already examined. All treat sustainability as preservation of something of value: capital, capacities, opportunities, growth, per capita consumption, per capita utility, welfare, or well-being (see Brian Barry). Their common thought is that we should not allow a designated thing of value to decline. The arguments I have directed against capital-preservation theories address that thought, and so apply to all preservation theories. But a variety of additional arguments pertain to preservation-of-well-being approaches, alongside the problems of intergenerational utility, welfare, or well-being comparisons noted by Bryan Norton.

One set of considerations concerns the justification for demanding non-declining well-being. Why should a non-declining profile be preferred to a declining profile or a profile that is not monotone in either direction, even if it offers less well-being overall (see Beckerman)? Imagine that you face a choice between two lives. In one, your level of well-being is low but steadily increasing. The other offers a much higher level of well-being at every point, but contains ups and downs. Must we really choose the former?

There are other problems. Imagine that we have a one-time opportunity for a sudden, significant, costless, but temporary increase in well-being. Should we seize it? Intuitively, the answer is yes; there is no cost to us or to the future, and there is a significant benefit. Why not? People often accept opportunities for temporary gains in well-being—trips to amusement parks, vacations, temporary but lucrative job assignments—without any sense that the inevitable decline in well-being at the end makes them impermissible. Yet a non-declining well-being requirement rules all these out. That remains true even if the memory of the temporary boon increases well-being for the rest of eternity over what it would have been otherwise.

Individual decision-making patterns suggest further objections. People often decide to accept declines in consumption, utility, etc., for a variety of reasons. People go to college, save for a mortgage, have children, pay for their children's educations, quit jobs, go on diets, and retire. All of these things may involve temporary or permanent declines in per capita consumption, utility, etc. Certainly they involve declines in income. But surely there is nothing immoral about them.

The same is true of groups. Organizations too choose to downsize, make charitable contributions, make investments, liquidate, and do other things that involve declines in consumption, growth, utility, etc. This is neither irrational nor immoral.

Indeed, environmentalism seems to demand it. Environmentalists often urge us individually and collectively to restrict our consumption, to settle for "enough" rather them maximizing our acquisition of goods, etc. Moreover, environmental policies are expensive; they demand declines in per capita consumption, utility, growth, etc. But the interpretations of sustainability discussed above would rule out these choices. It appears, then, that such interpretations are incompatible with environmentalism as generally understood.

One could argue that these arguments do not work against a preservation of well-being criterion. People get married, have children, go on diets, and the like to increase their well-being, not some more specific measure. Similarly, organizations downsize, make investments, etc., for the sake of their well-being. So, perhaps "don't act so as to decrease your well-being" is a good moral principle, even if more specific versions fail.

This principle, however, is either prudential rather than ethical or a version of ethical egoism. It rules out many instances of altruism. People and organizations who donate to charities, environmental groups, or the needy often decrease their own well-being (and utility, consumption, opportunities, etc.) for the sake of helping others. A well-being-preservation approach implies that acts of charity are acceptable only if they on balance benefit the giver. Worse, the principle rules out moral heroism—sacrificing oneself for the good of others. But we regard people and groups who do that as having gone above and beyond the call of duty, not as having failed to live up to it.

Finally, these conceptions of sustainability are unsatisfiable. The hard fact is that consumption, utility, welfare, well-being, abilities to meet needs, opportunities, and capacities sometimes decline. Herman E. Daly points out that we cannot bequeath utility to the future; we can only bequeath opportunities. It is up to future generations what they make of them. But utility, well-being, etc., decline for many reasons in addition to missed opportunities. Tornadoes strike. Earthquakes knock down buildings. Wars break out. Recessions happen. People get old. People make mistakes.

These are unfortunate events, but a principle that demands that we avoid them cannot be satisfied. One might as well direct people not to make mistakes, not to grow old, and not to die. All those things would be good, but we cannot, at present, anyway, achieve them.

Other Sustainability Concepts

I have discussed sustainability concepts that I take to be the most important and influential, arguing that they are either plausible but so weak that they fail to support the environmentalists' agenda or implausible and even unsatisfiable. I should, however, mention three families of definitions of sustainability that are widespread but, ultimately, less interesting.

The first is the conception of a sustainable policy as one that takes some account of environmental concerns. The United States Department of Energy, for example, offers this definition:

> Sustainable development is a strategy by which communities seek economic development approaches that also benefit the local environment and quality of life.

Margaret Thatcher, cited in David W. Pearce et al., similarly considers a policy sustainable "provided the environment is nurtured and safeguarded." These conditions are weak, plausible, even uncontroversial, but do little to support the environmentalist agenda.

The second is the conception of sustainability as remaining within the carrying capacity of the Earth. This too is uncontroversial, but very weak. No one favors destroying human life. It supports significant change in environmental policies, moreover, only in the presence of extremely strong empirical premises.

Finally, a growing body of writers is developing a conception of sustainability that includes equality and participatory democracy. These have nothing directly to do with environmental concerns. In fact, claims of such writers to the contrary, these values conflict frequently and directly with environmental goals. Sacrificing economic growth for environmental goals will harm the poor most of all by making it harder to move up the socioeconomic ladder. And "participatory democracy," if it means something more than assigning special privileges and powers to environmental groups and activists, will likely impede environmental goals as well, since the proportion of people willing to accept job losses, higher taxes, and lower standards of living in exchange for alleged long-term environmental benefits is likely to remain small for the foreseeable future. Defining sustainability in terms of equality and democracy seems to be an attempt to define away real conflicts between values, if not to shift the topic of discussion altogether.

QUESTIONS FOR REFLECTION

1. Explain Bonevac's three-pronged test. Is that a reasonable test for an ethical principle?
2. What is Brundtland-sustainability? Distinguish the expansive interpretation of it from a more restrictive interpretation.
3. Suppose a policy is analogous to a maxim. How does Brundtland-sustainability compare to Kant's categorical imperative?
4. How does strong sustainability differ from weak sustainability? Why does Bonevac conclude that strong sustainability rules out environmentalism itself? Do you agree?
5. "Leave the world no worse than you found it" sounds like a plausible ethical constraint. Think of a potential counterexample—one of Bonevac's or one of your own—and respond to it from the perspective of a defender of that constraint.
6. Why does Bonevac hold that preservation of capacities is impossible? How might a defender of that version of sustainability reply?

Liberty

PART II

LIBERTY

The central problem of political philosophy is the relation between people and their governments—between the rulers and the ruled. When rulers acquire power through force or inheritance, they have little need to take the interests of the people into account. In a democracy, however, the rulers acquire power through elections and therefore must consider the interests of the people to some degree. But even if the rulers follow the will of the majority perfectly, the possibility of conflict remains. Rule by the people, as John Stuart Mill points out, is really rule of each by all the rest. Nothing in the concept of democracy itself protects the minority from the majority's power. As a joke has it, sometimes democracy is like three wolves and a sheep voting on what to have for dinner. Edmund Burke therefore warned of the "oppression of the minority"; Alexis de Tocqueville similarly foresaw "the tyranny of the majority." Both generalize Aristotle's worry that "If justice is the will of the majority, . . . they will unjustly confiscate the property of the wealthy minority" (*Politics* VI, 3).

Two kinds of issues arise here. First, certain distinct and unpopular or disadvantaged groups may consistently lose elections to a more powerful majority. Democracy, unembellished, does little to protect their rights. Second, individuals have little protection from the majority's power. Voters out of step with the majority may find themselves without any rights at all.

The Bill of Rights—the first ten amendments to the United States Constitution—attempts to protect people from the unfettered power of undemocratic minorities and democratic majorities. By delineating people's rights, it carves out a sphere of individual liberty that government may not transgress. Philosophers such as John Stuart Mill seek to distinguish a sphere of personal liberty in a different way. A law is *paternalistic* if it restricts a person's liberty for his or her own good. Mill argues, with some important qualifications, that such laws are illegitimate. Mill's *harm principle* asserts that government may restrict a person's liberty only to prevent harm to others. To restrict liberty to prevent people from harming themselves or to promote their own good, Mill contends, goes beyond the proper bounds of government authority.

Many countries have a wide variety of paternalistic laws. They tend to fall into three categories:

1. *Laws promoting morality:* Laws regulating religious practices, diet, and various forms of sexual behavior—adultery, polygamy, polyandry, sodomy, prostitution, premarital sex, and pornography.
2. *Laws promoting health and safety:* Laws regulating alcohol, drugs (both medical and recreational), suicide, self-mutilation, voluntary euthanasia, working conditions, and the use of motorcycle helmets and seat belts.
3. *Laws promoting economic welfare:* Laws regulating wages, working hours, shopping hours (for example, "blue laws"), gambling, investments, and retirement (for example, Social Security).

Few people would accept all laws of this kind as legitimate, but just as few would find all objectionable. How can we distinguish legitimate from illegitimate paternalistic laws?

One way incorporates Mill's distinction between *self-regarding* and *other-regarding* actions. Roughly, a self-regarding action affects only the agent or agents of the action; an other-regarding action affects others. Mill's harm principle, in these terms, rules out government restriction of self-regarding actions.

There are several complications. Some self-regarding actions involve only a single agent—taking a drug or failing to wear a seat belt, for example. Others involve a group of agents; it takes at least two agents to indulge in prostitution, sodomy, gambling, or employment, for example. In either case, Mill says, we can consider the act self-regarding only if several conditions are satisfied. First, every agent must be acting freely; there must be no coercion. Everyone involved must consent to the action. We can treat ordinary, consensual sexual activity as self-regarding, but rape is clearly other-regarding. Second, every agent must be acting voluntarily. If any participant is in any way incapable of choosing—if he or she is a child, for example, or mentally incapacitated, drugged, or insane—then the action is other-regarding. Third, every agent must be reasonably well informed about the action. There must be no ignorance or deception about any important and relevant matters. Someone taking a dangerous drug while believing it to be aspirin is not exercising liberty in any meaningful sense. If any participant is ignorant or deceived about an important feature of the action, then that action counts as other-regarding. The harm principle protects from government intrusion only those actions that are undertaken freely and voluntarily by informed agents and that affect nobody but themselves.

Mill's harm principle has met with wide acceptance in certain realms, but it has also met serious objections. Aristotle, for example, holds a completely opposed view of liberty. He contends that the best government is that which produces the best citizens. The chief task of government, in his view, is to promote the good of its citizens by helping to educate and guide them. Edmund Burke and others take a more moderate view. They maintain that individual liberty is only one among many important and competing values. A society should value the individual liberty of its citizens, these philosophers charge, but it should also value harmony, order, justice, and equality, among others. These various values often come into conflict, both in our individual lives and in the political arena. The harm principle tries to resolve all such conflicts in favor of liberty. But, Burke holds, it is not obvious that any value wins out all of the time. Politics, in his view, is an art of balancing values, reconciling them when possible, seeking compromises between them when possible, and, if all else fails, resolving conflicts between them by appeal to analogy and the wisdom we have accumulated from the past.

The Supreme Court and various political philosophers of the twentieth century have responded to Mill's principle by distinguishing civil from economic liberties. Civil liberties—in the original sense of the term, liberties granted by society—have been interpreted as liberties relating in some way to a person's sense of identity or to the political process. It is not clear whether this distinction makes sense. In what category, for example, is the freedom to place an advertisement or produce a commercial in favor of a certain political position? Whatever the answer, Mill means his principle to apply to both civil and economic liberties. Some twentieth-century thinkers, however, have sought to apply it only to civil liberties, contending that liberty does take precedence over other values in such matters, whereas justice, equality, and other concerns often take precedence over liberty in economic matters.

ARISTOTLE

from *Nicomachean Ethics*

(Source: Reprinted from Aristotle's Nicomachean Ethics, *translated by W. D. Ross, 1925, by permission of Oxford University Press.)*

BOOK X

9

Developing Virtue

. . . Surely, as the saying goes, where there are things to be done the end is not to survey and recognize the various things, but rather to do them; with regard to virtue, then, it is not enough to know, but we must try to have and use it, or try any other way there may be of becoming good. Now if arguments were in themselves enough to make men good, they would justly, as Theognis says, have won very great rewards, and such rewards should have been provided; but as things are, while they seem to have power to encourage and stimulate the generous-minded among our youth, and to make a character which is gently born, and a true lover of what is noble, ready to be possessed by virtue, they are not able to encourage the many to nobility and goodness. For these do not by nature obey the sense of shame, but only fear, and do not abstain from bad acts because of their baseness but through fear of punishment; living by passion they pursue their own pleasures and the means to them, and avoid the opposite pains, and have not even a conception of what is noble and truly pleasant, since they have never tasted it. What argument would remould such people? It is hard, if not impossible, to remove by argument the traits that have long since been incorporated in the character; and perhaps we must be content if, when all the influences by which we are thought to become good are present, we get some tincture of virtue.

Now some think that we are made good by nature, others by habituation, others by teaching. Nature's part evidently does not depend on us, but as a result of some divine causes is present in those who are truly fortunate; while argument and teaching, we may suspect, are not powerful with all men, but the soul of the student must first have been cultivated by means of habits for noble joy and noble hatred, like earth which is to nourish the seed. For he who lives as passion directs will not hear argument that dissuades him, nor understand it if he does; and how can we persuade one in such a state to change his ways? And in general passion seems to yield not to argument but to force. The character, then, must somehow be there already with a kinship to virtue, loving what is noble and hating what is base.

Law

But it is difficult to get . . . a right training for virtue if one has not been brought up under right laws; for to live temperately and hardily is not pleasant to most people, especially when they are young. For this reason their nurture and occupations should be fixed by law; for they will not be painful when they have become customary. But it is surely not enough that when they are young they should get the right nurture and attention; since they must, even when they are grown up, practise and be habituated to them, we shall need laws for this as well, and generally speaking to cover the whole of life; for most people obey necessity rather than argument, and punishments rather than the sense of what is noble.

This is why some think that legislators ought to stimulate men to virtue and urge them forward by the motive of the noble, on the assumption that those who have been well advanced by the formation of habits will attend to such influences; and that punishments and penalties should be imposed on those who disobey and are of inferior nature, while the incurably bad should be completely banished. A good man (they think), since he lives with his mind fixed on what is noble, will submit to argument, while a bad man, whose desire is for pleasure, is corrected by pain like a beast of burden. This is, too, why they say the pains inflicted should be those that are most opposed to the pleasures such men love.

However that may be, if (as we have said) the man who is to be good must be well trained and habituated, and go on to spend his time in worthy occupations and neither willingly nor unwillingly do bad actions, and if this can be brought about if men live in accordance with a sort of reason and right order, provided this has force—if this be so, the paternal command indeed has not the required force or compulsive power (nor in general has the command of one man, unless he be a king or something similar), but the law *has* compulsive power, while it is at the same time a rule proceeding from a sort of practical wisdom and reason. And while people hate *men* who oppose their impulses, even if they oppose them rightly, the law in its ordaining of what is good is not burdensome.

Paternalism

In the Spartan state alone, or almost alone, the legislator seems to have paid attention to questions of nurture and occupations; in most states such matters have been neglected, and each man lives as he pleases, Cyclops-fashion, "to his own wife and children dealing law." Now it is best that there should be a public and proper care for such matters; but if they are neglected by the community it would seem right for each man to help his children and friends towards virtue, and that they should have the power, or at least the will, to do this.

It would seem from what has been said that he can do this better if he makes himself capable of legislating. For public control is plainly effected by laws, and good control by good laws; whether written or unwritten would seem to make no difference, nor whether they are laws providing for the education of individuals or of groups—any more than it does in the case of music or gymnastics and other such pursuits. For as in cities laws and prevailing types of character have force, so in households do the injunctions and the habits of the father, and these have even more because of the tie of blood and the benefits he confers; for the children start with a natural affection and disposition to obey. Further, private education has an advantage over public, as private medical treatment has; for while in general rest and abstinence from food are good for a man in a fever, for a particular man they may not be; and a boxer presumably does not prescribe the same style of fighting to all his pupils. It would seem, then, that the detail is worked out with more precision if the control is private; for each person is more likely to get what suits his case.

But the details can be best looked after, one by one, by a doctor or gymnastic instructor or any one else who has the general knowledge of what is good for every one or for people of a certain kind (for the sciences both are said to be, and are, concerned with what is universal); not but what some particular detail may perhaps be well looked after by an unscientific person, if he has studied accurately in the light of experience what happens in each case, just as some people seem to be their own best doctors, though they could give no help to any one else. Nonetheless, it will perhaps be agreed that if a man does wish to become master of an art or science he must go to the universal, and come to know it as well as possible; for, as we have said, it is with this that the sciences are concerned.

And surely he who wants to make men, whether many or few, better by his care must try to become capable of legislating, if it is through laws that we can become good. For to get any one whatever—any one who is put before us—into the right condition is not for the first chance comer; if any one can do it, it is the man who knows, just as in medicine and all other matters which give scope for care and prudence. . . .

QUESTIONS FOR REFLECTION

1. "Some think that we are made good by nature, others by habituation, others by teaching." How does Aristotle react to each of these suggestions?
2. What role does law play in making people good?
3. Are there limits on the power of law to guide character?
4. What does Aristotle's view imply about the acceptability of paternalistic laws?

JOHN STUART MILL

from *On Liberty* (1859)

On Liberty *is a classic statement of the importance of individual liberty. Its chapter "Of the Liberty of Thought and Discussion" is probably the most famous and influential defense of freedom of speech ever written. Mill was a staunch advocate of democracy but saw that majority rule, in itself, could allow the oppression of the minority. Mill wrote* On Liberty *to outline a realm of freedom that not even democratic majorities may transgress. (Source: London: Parker, 1859.)*

CHAPTER I / INTRODUCTORY

The Harm Principle

. . . The object of this essay is to assert one very simple principle, as entitled to govern absolutely the dealings of society with the individual in the way of compulsion and control, whether the means used be physical force in the form of legal penalties or the moral coercion of public opinion. That principle is that the sole end for which mankind are warranted, individually or collectively, in interfering with the liberty of action of any of their number is self-protection. That the only purpose for which power can be rightfully exercised over any member of a civilized community, against his will, is to prevent harm to others. His own good, either physical or moral, is not a sufficient warrant. He cannot rightfully be compelled to do or forbear because it will be better for him to do so, because it will make him happier, because, in the opinions of others, to do so would be wise or even right. These are good reasons for remonstrating with him, or reasoning with him, or persuading him, or entreating him, but not for compelling him or visiting him with any evil in case he do otherwise. To justify that, the conduct from which it is desired to deter him must be calculated to produce evil to someone else. The only part of the conduct of anyone for which he is amenable to society is that which concerns others. In the part which merely concerns himself, his independence is, of right, absolute. Over himself, over his own body and mind, the individual is sovereign.

It is, perhaps, hardly necessary to say that this doctrine is meant to apply only to human beings in the maturity of their faculties. We are not speaking of children or of young persons below the age which the law may fix as that of manhood or womanhood. Those who are still in a state to require being taken care of by others must be protected against their own actions as well as against external injury. . . . But as soon as mankind have attained the capacity of being guided to their own improvement by conviction or persuasion (a period long since reached in all nations with whom we need here concern ourselves), compulsion, either in the direct form or in that of pains and penalties for noncompliance, is no longer admissible as a means to their own good, and justifiable only for the security of others.

Utility

It is proper to state that I forgo any advantage which could be derived to my argument from the idea of abstract right as a thing independent of utility. I regard utility as the ultimate appeal on all ethical questions; but it must be utility in the largest sense, grounded on the permanent interests of man as a progressive being. Those interests, I contend, authorize the subjection of individual spontaneity to external control only in respect to those actions of each which concern the interest of other people. If anyone does an act hurtful to others, there is a *prima facie* case for punishing him by law or, where legal penalties are not safely applicable, by general disapprobation. There are also many positive acts for the benefit of others which he may rightfully be compelled to perform, such as to give evidence in a court of justice, to bear his fair share in the common defense or in any other joint work necessary to the interest of the society of which he enjoys the protection, and to perform certain acts of individual beneficence, such as saving a fellow creature's life or interposing to protect the defenseless against ill usage—things which whenever it is obviously a man's duty to do he may rightfully be made responsible to society for not doing. A person may cause evil to others not only by his actions but by his inaction, and in either case he is justly accountable to them for the injury. The latter case, it is true, requires a much more cautious exercise of compulsion than the former. To make anyone answerable for doing evil to others is the rule; to make him answerable for not preventing evil is, comparatively speaking, the exception. Yet there are many cases clear enough and grave enough to justify that exception. In all things which regard the external relations of the individual, he is *de jure* amenable to those whose interests are concerned, and, if need be, to society as their protector. There are often good reasons for not holding him to the responsibility; but these reasons must arise from the special expediencies of the case: either because it is a kind of case in which he is on the whole likely to act better when left to his own discretion than when controlled in any way in which society have it in their power to control him; or because the attempt to exercise control would produce other evils, greater than those which it would prevent. When such reasons as these preclude the enforcement of responsibility, the conscience of the agent himself should step into the vacant judgment seat and protect those interests of others which have no external protection; judging himself all the more rigidly, because the case does not admit of his being made accountable to the judgment of his fellow creatures.

The Sphere of Liberty

But there is a sphere of action in which society, as distinguished from the individual, has, if any, only an indirect interest: comprehending all that portion of a person's life and conduct which affects only himself or, if it also affects others, only with their free, voluntary, and undeceived consent and participation. When I say only himself, I mean directly and in the first instance; for whatever affects himself may affect others through himself: and the objection which may be grounded on this contingency will receive consideration in the sequel. This, then, is the appropriate region of human liberty. It comprises, first, the inward domain of consciousness, demanding liberty of conscience in the most comprehensive sense, liberty of thought and feeling, absolute freedom of opinion and sentiment on all subjects, practical or speculative, scientific, moral, or theological. The liberty of expressing and publishing opinions may seem to fall under a different principle, since it belongs to that part of the conduct of an individual which concerns other people, but, being almost of as much importance as the liberty of thought itself and resting in great part on the same reasons, is practically inseparable from it. Secondly, the principle requires liberty of tastes and pursuits, of framing the plan of our life to suit our own character, of doing as we like, subject to such consequences as may follow, without impediment from our fellow creatures, so long as what we do does not harm them, even though they should think our conduct foolish, perverse, or wrong. Thirdly, from this liberty of each individual follows the liberty, within the same limits, of combination among individuals; freedom to unite for any purpose not involving harm to others: the persons combining being supposed to be of full age and not forced or deceived.

No society in which these liberties are not, on the whole, respected is free, whatever may be its form of government; and none is completely free in which they do not exist absolute and unqualified. The only freedom which deserves the name is that of pursuing our own good in our own way, so long as we do not attempt to deprive others of theirs or impede their efforts to obtain it. Each is the proper guardian of his own health, whether bodily *or* mental and spiritual. Mankind are greater gainers by suffering each other to live as seems good to themselves than by compelling each to live as seems good to the rest. . . .

QUESTIONS FOR REFLECTION

1. What is the "one very simple principle"—usually called the *harm principle*—that Mill's essay aims to assert? What does it mean? What conditions and qualifications does Mill place on it? How does it counteract the "tyranny of the majority"?
2. Later philosophers have often stated Mill's harm principle in terms of a distinction between self-regarding and other-regarding actions. How might this distinction be drawn? How can Mill's principle be stated in terms of that distinction?

CHAPTER IV / OF THE LIMITS TO THE AUTHORITY OF SOCIETY OVER THE INDIVIDUAL

What, then, is the rightful limit to the sovereignty of the individual over himself? Where does the authority of society begin? How much of human life should be assigned to individuality, and how much to society?

Self-Regarding Actions

Each will receive its proper share if each has that which more particularly concerns it. To individuality should belong the part of life in which it is chiefly the individual that is interested; to society, the part which chiefly interests society.

Though society is not founded on a contract, and though no good purpose is answered by inventing a contract in order to deduce social obligations from it, everyone who receives the protection of society owes a return for the benefit, and the fact of living in society renders it indispensable that each should be bound to observe a certain line of conduct toward the rest. This conduct consists, first, in not injuring the interests of one another, or rather certain interests which, either by express legal provision or by tacit understanding, ought to be considered as rights; and secondly, in each person's bearing his share (to be fixed on some equitable principle) of the labors and sacrifices incurred for defending the society or its members from injury and molestation. These conditions society is justified in enforcing at all costs to those who endeavor to withhold fulfillment. Nor is this all that society may do. The acts of an individual may be hurtful to others or wanting in due consideration for their welfare, without going to the length of violating any of their constituted rights. The offender may then be justly punished by opinion, though not by law. As soon as any part of a person's conduct affects prejudicially the interests of others, society has jurisdiction over it, and the question whether the general welfare will or will not be promoted by interfering with it becomes open to discussion. But there is no room for entertaining any such question when a person's conduct affects the interests of no persons besides himself, or needs not affect them unless they like (all the persons concerned being of full age and the ordinary amount of understanding). In all such cases, there should be perfect freedom, legal and social, to do the action and stand the consequences. . . .

Objections

The distinction here pointed out between the part of a person's life which concerns only himself and that which concerns others, many persons will refuse to admit. How (it may be asked) can any part of the conduct of a member of society be a matter of indifference to the other members? No person is an entirely isolated being; it is impossible for a person to do anything seriously or permanently hurtful to himself without mischief reaching at least to his near connections, and often far beyond them. If he injures his property, he does harm to those who directly or indirectly derived support from it, and usually diminishes, by a greater or less amount, the general resources of the community. If he deteriorates his bodily or mental faculties, he not only brings evil upon all who depended upon him for any portion of their happiness, but disqualifies himself for rendering the services which he owes to his fellow creatures generally, perhaps becomes a burden on their affection or benevolence; and if such conduct were very frequent hardly any offense that is committed would detract more from the general sum of good. Finally, if by his vices or follies a person does no direct harm to others, he is nevertheless (it may be said) injurious by his example, and ought to be compelled to control himself for the sake of those whom the sight or knowledge of his conduct might corrupt or mislead.

And even (it will be added) if the consequences of misconduct could be confined to the vicious or thoughtless individual, ought society to abandon to their own guidance those who are manifestly unfit for it? If protection against themselves is confessedly due to children and persons under age, is not society equally bound to afford it to persons of mature years who are equally incapable of self-government? If gambling, or drunkenness, or incontinence, or idleness, or uncleanliness are as injurious to happiness, and as great a hindrance to improvement, as many or most of the acts prohibited by law, why (it may be asked) should not law, so far as is consistent with practicability and social convenience, endeavor to repress these also? And as a supplement to the unavoidable imperfections of law, ought not opinion at least to organize a powerful police against these vices and visit rigidly with social penalties those who are known to practice them? There is no question here (it may be said) about restricting individuality, or impeding the trial of new and original experiments in living. The only things it is sought to prevent are things which have been tried and condemned from the beginning of the world until now—things which experience has shown not to be useful or suitable to any person's individuality. There must be some length of time and amount of experience after which a moral or prudential truth may be regarded as established; and it is merely desired to prevent generation after generation from falling over the same precipice which has been fatal to their predecessors.

Rights and Duties

I fully admit that the mischief which a person does to himself may seriously affect, both through their sympathies and their interests, those nearly connected with him and, in a minor degree, society at large. When, by conduct of this sort, a person is led to violate a distinct and assignable obligation to any other person or persons, the case is taken out of the self-regarding class and becomes amenable to moral disapprobation in the proper sense of the term. If, for example, a man, through intemperance or extravagance, becomes unable to pay his debts, or, having undertaken the moral responsibility of a family, becomes from the same cause incapable of supporting or educating them, he is deservedly reprobated and might be justly punished; but it is for the breach of duty to his family or creditors, not for the extravagance. If the resources which ought to have been devoted to them had been diverted from them for the most prudent investment, the moral culpability would have been the same. George Barnwell murdered his uncle to get money for his mistress, but if he had done it to set himself up in business, he would equally have been hanged. Again, in the frequent case of a man who causes grief to his family by addiction to bad habits, he deserves reproach for his unkindness or ingratitude; but so he may for cultivating habits not in themselves vicious, if they are painful to those with whom he passes his life, or who from personal ties are dependent on him for their comfort. Whoever fails in the consideration generally due to the interests and feelings of others, not being compelled by some more imperative duty, or justified by allowable self-preference, is a subject of moral disapprobation for that failure, but not for the cause of it, nor for the errors, merely personal to himself, which may have remotely led to it. In like manner, when a person disables himself, by conduct purely self-regarding, from the performance of some definite duty incumbent on him to the public, he is guilty of a social offense. No person ought to be punished simply for being drunk; but a soldier or policeman should be punished for being drunk on duty. Whenever, in short, there is a definite damage, or a definite risk of damage, either to an individual or to the public, the case is taken out of the province of liberty and placed in that of morality or law.

But with regard to the merely contingent or, as it may be called, constructive injury which a person causes to society by conduct which neither violates any specific duty to the public, nor occasions perceptible hurt to any assignable individual except himself, the inconvenience is one which society can afford to bear, for the sake of the greater good of human freedom. . . .

Harms of Interference

But the strongest of all the arguments against the interference of the public with purely personal conduct is that, when it does interfere, the odds are that it interferes wrongly and in the wrong place. On questions of social morality, of duty to others, the opinion of the public, that is, of an overruling majority, though often wrong, is likely to be still oftener right, because on such questions they are only required to judge of their own interests, of the manner in which some mode of conduct, if allowed to be practiced, would affect themselves. But the opinion of a similar majority, imposed as a law on the minority, on questions of self-regarding conduct is quite as likely to be wrong as right, for in these cases public opinion means, at the best, some people's opinion of what is good or bad for other people, while very often it does not even mean that—the public, with the most perfect indifference, passing over the pleasure or convenience of those whose conduct they censure and considering only their own preference. There are many who consider as an injury to themselves any conduct which they have a distaste for, and resent it as an outrage to their feelings; as a religious bigot, when charged with disregarding the religious feelings of others, has been known to retort that they disregard his feelings by persisting in their abominable worship or creed. But there is no parity between the feeling of a person for his own opinion and the feeling of another who is offended at his holding it, no more than between the desire of a thief to take a purse and the desire of the right owner to keep it. And a person's taste is as much his own peculiar concern as his opinion or his purse. It is easy for anyone to imagine an ideal public which leaves the freedom and choice of individuals in all uncertain matters undisturbed and only requires them to abstain from modes of conduct which universal experience has condemned. But where has there been seen a public which set any such limit to its censorship? Or when does the public trouble itself about universal experience? In its interferences with personal conduct it is seldom thinking of anything but the enormity of acting or feeling differently from itself; and this standard of judgment, thinly disguised, is held up to mankind as the dictate of religion and philosophy by nine-tenths of all moralists and speculative writers. These teach that things are right because they are right; because we feel them to be so. They tell us to search in our own minds and hearts for laws of conduct binding on ourselves and on all others. What can the poor public do but apply these instructions and make their own personal feelings of good and evil, if they are tolerably unanimous in them, obligatory on all the world? . . .

QUESTIONS FOR REFLECTION

1. To what extent may people be punished by the opinions or behavior of others, independent of any legal coercion? Is Mill's view compatible with his analysis of the social stigma attending the expression of unpopular opinions?
2. Mill admits that distinguishing self-regarding from other-regarding actions is a matter of degree, for virtually every action affects someone other than the agent who performs it. What is Mill's criterion for determining whether an act affects others enough to count as other-regarding and, so, to be subject to government interference?
3. What arguments does Mill advance in this section in favor of the harm principle?

CHAPTER V / APPLICATIONS

Economic Freedom

Again, trade is a social act. Whoever undertakes to sell any description of goods to the public does what affects the interest of other persons, and of society in general; and thus his conduct, in principle, comes within the jurisdiction of society; accordingly, it was once held to be the duty of governments, in all cases which were considered of importance, to fix prices and regulate the process of manufacture. But it is now recognized, though not till after a long struggle, that both the cheapness and the good quality of commo-dities are most effectually provided for by leaving the producers and sellers perfectly free, under the sole check of equal freedom to the buyers for supplying themselves elsewhere. This is the so-called doctrine of "free trade," which rests on grounds different from, though equally solid with, the principle of individual liberty asserted in this essay. Restrictions on trade, or on production for purposes of trade, are indeed restraints; and all restraint, *qua* restraint, is an evil; but the restraints in question affect only that part of conduct which society is competent to restrain, and are wrong solely because they do not really produce the results which it is desired to produce by them. As the principle of individual liberty is not involved in the doctrine of free trade, so neither is it in most of the questions which arise respecting the limits of that doctrine, as, for example, what amount of public control is admissible for the prevention of fraud by adulteration; how far sanitary precautions, or arrangements to protect workpeople employed in dangerous occupations, should be enforced on employers. Such questions involve considerations of liberty only in so far as leaving people to themselves is better, *ceteris paribus,* than controlling them; but that they may be legitimately controlled for these ends is in principle undeniable. On the other hand, there are questions relating to interference with trade which are essentially questions of liberty, such as the Maine Law, already touched upon: the prohibition of the importation of opium into China; the restriction of the sale of poisons—all cases, in short, where the object of the interference is to make it impossible or difficult to obtain a particular commodity. These interferences are objectionable, not as infringements on the liberty of the producer or seller, but on that of the buyer.

Prevention of Harm

One of these examples, that of the sale of poisons, opens a new question: the proper limits of what may be called the functions of police; how far liberty may legitimately be invaded for the prevention of crime, or of accident. It is one of the undisputed functions of government to take precautions against crime before it has been committed, as well as to detect and punish it afterwards. The preventive function of government, however, is far more liable to be abused, to the prejudice of liberty, than the punitory function; for there is hardly any part of the legitimate freedom of action of a human being which would not admit of being represented, and fairly, too, as increasing the facilities for some form or other of delinquency. Nevertheless, if a public authority, or even a private person, sees anyone evidently preparing to commit a crime, they are not bound to look on inactive until the crime is committed, but may interfere to prevent it. If poisons were never bought or used for any purpose except the commission of murder, it would be right to prohibit their manufacture and sale. They may, however, be wanted not only for innocent but for useful purposes, and restrictions cannot be imposed in the one case without operating in the other. Again, it is a proper office of public authority to guard against accidents. If either a public officer or anyone else saw a person attempting to cross a bridge which had been ascertained to be unsafe, and there were no time to warn him of his danger, they might seize him and turn him back, without any real infringement of his liberty; for liberty consists in doing what one desires, and he does not desire to fall into the river. Nevertheless, when there is not a certainty, but only a danger of mischief, no one but the person himself can judge of the sufficiency of the motive which may prompt him to incur the risk; in this case, therefore (unless he is a child, or delirious, or in some state of excitement or absorption incompatible with the full use of the reflecting faculty), he ought, I conceive, to be only warned of the danger; not forcibly prevented from exposing himself to it. Similar considerations, applied to such a question as the sale of poisons, may enable us to decide which among the possible modes of regulation are or are not contrary to principle. Such a precaution, for example, as that of labeling the drug with some word expressive of its dangerous character may be enforced without violation of liberty: the buyer cannot wish not to know that the thing he possesses has poisonous qualities. . . .

Risks and Duties

The right inherent in society to ward off crimes against itself by antecedent precautions suggests the obvious limitations to the maxim that purely self-regarding misconduct cannot properly be meddled with in the way of prevention or punishment. Drunkenness, for example, in ordinary cases, is not a fit subject for legislative interference, but I should deem it perfectly legitimate that a person who had once been convicted of any act of violence to others under the influence of drink should be placed under a special legal restriction, personal to himself; that if he were afterwards found drunk, he should be liable to a penalty, and that if, when in that state, he committed another offense, the punishment to which he would be liable for that other offense should be increased in severity. The making himself drunk, in a person whom drunkenness excites to do harm to others, is a crime against others. So, again, idleness, except in a person receiving support from the public, or except when it constitutes a breach of contract, cannot without tyranny be made a subject of legal punishment; but if, either from idleness or from any other avoidable cause, a man fails to perform his legal duties to others, as for instance to support his children, it is no tyranny to force him to fulfill that obligation by compulsory labor if no other means are available.

Offense to Others

Again, there are many acts which, being directly injurious only to the agents themselves, ought not to be legally interdicted, but which, if done publicly, are a violation of good manners and, coming thus within the category of offenses against others, may rightly be prohibited. Of this kind are offenses against decency; on which it is unnecessary to dwell, the rather as they are only connected indirectly with our subject, the objection to publicity being equally strong in the case of many actions not in themselves condemnable, nor supposed to be so. . . .

Discouraging Vice

A further question is whether the State, while it permits, should nevertheless indirectly discourage conduct which it deems contrary to the best interests of the agent; whether, for example, it should take measures to render the means of drunkenness more costly, or add to the difficulty of procuring them by limiting the number of the places of sale. On this, as on most other practical questions, many distinctions require to be made. To tax stimulants for the sole purpose of making them more difficult to be obtained is a measure differing only in degree from their entire prohibition, and would be justifiable only if that were justifiable. Every increase of cost is a prohibition to those whose means do not come up to the augmented price; and to those who do, it is a penalty laid on them for gratifying a particular taste. Their choice of pleasures and their mode of expending their income, after satisfying their legal and moral obligations to the State and to individuals, are their own concern and must rest with their own judgment. These considerations may seem at first sight to condemn the selection of stimulants as special subjects of taxation for purposes of revenue. But it must be remembered that taxation for fiscal purposes is absolutely inevitable; that in most countries it is necessary that a considerable part of that taxation should be indirect; that the State, therefore, cannot help imposing penalties, which to some persons may be prohibitory, on the use of some articles of consumption. It is hence the duty of the State to consider, in the imposition of taxes, what commodities the consumers can best spare; and *a fortiori,* to select in preference those of which it deems the use, beyond a very moderate quantity, to be positively injurious. Taxation, therefore, of stimulants up to the point which produces the largest amount of revenue (supposing that the State needs all the revenue which it yields) is not only admissible, but to be approved of. . . .

Voluntary Slavery

It was pointed out in an early part of this essay that the liberty of the individual, in things wherein the individual is alone concerned, implies a corresponding liberty in any number of individuals to regulate by mutual agreement such things as regard them jointly, and regard no persons but themselves. This question presents no difficulty so long as the will of all the persons implicated remains unaltered; but since that will may change it is often necessary, even in things in which they alone are concerned, that they should enter into engagements with one another; and when they do, it is fit, as a general rule, that those engagements should be kept. Yet, in the laws, probably, of every country, this general rule has some exceptions. Not only are persons not held to engagements which violate the rights of third parties, but it is sometimes considered a sufficient reason for releasing them from an engagement that it is injurious to themselves. In this and most other civilized countries, for example, an engagement by which a person should sell himself, or allow himself to be sold, as a slave would be null and void, neither enforced by law nor by opinion. The ground for thus limiting his power of voluntarily disposing of his own lot in life is apparent, and is very clearly seen in this extreme case. The reason for not interfering, unless for the sake of others, with a person's voluntary acts is consideration for his liberty. His voluntary choice is evidence that what he so chooses is desirable, or at least endurable, to him, and his good is on the whole best provided for by allowing him to take his own means of pursuing it. But by selling himself for a slave, he abdicates his liberty; he forgoes any future use of it beyond that single act. He therefore defeats, in his own case, the very purpose which is the justification of allowing him to dispose of himself. He is no longer free, but is thenceforth in a position which has no longer the presumption in its favor that would be afforded by his voluntarily remaining in it. The principle of freedom cannot require that he should be free not to be free. It is not freedom to be allowed to alienate his freedom. These reasons, the force of which is so conspicuous in this peculiar case, are evidently of far wider application, yet a limit is everywhere set to them by the necessities of life, which continually require, not indeed that we should resign our freedom, but that we should consent to this and the other limitation of it.

Contracts

The principle, however, which demands uncontrolled freedom of action in all that concerns only the agents themselves requires that those who have become bound to one another, in things which concern no third party, should be able to release one another from the engagement; and even without such voluntary release there are perhaps no contracts or engagements, except those that relate to money or money's worth, of which one can venture to say that there ought to be no liberty whatever of retraction. Baron Wilhelm von Humboldt . . . states it as his conviction that engagements which involve personal relations or services should never be legally binding beyond a limited duration of time; and that the most important of these engagements, marriage, having the peculiarity that its objects are frustrated unless the feelings of both the parties are in harmony with it, should require nothing more than the declared will of either party to dissolve it. This subject is too important and too complicated to be discussed in a parenthesis, and I touch on it only so far as is necessary for purposes of illustration. If the conciseness and generality of Baron Humboldt's dissertation had not obliged him in this instance to content himself with enunciating his conclusion without discussing the premises, he would doubtless have recognized that the question cannot be decided on grounds so simple as those to which he confines himself. When a person, either by express promise or by conduct, has encouraged another to rely on his continuing to act in a certain way—to build expectations and calculations, and stake any part of his plan of life upon that supposition—a new series of moral obligations arises on his part toward that person, which may possibly be overruled, but cannot be ignored. And again, if the relation between two contracting parties has been followed by consequences to others; if it has placed third parties in any peculiar position, or, as in the case of marriage, has even called third parties into existence, obligations arise on the part of both the contracting parties toward those third persons, the fulfillment of which, or at all events the mode of fulfillment, must be greatly affected by the continuance or disruption of the relation between the original parties to the contract. It does not follow, nor can I admit, that these obligations extend to requiring the fulfillment of the contract at all costs to the happiness of the reluctant party; but they are a necessary element in the question; and, even if, as von Humboldt maintains, they ought to make no difference in the *legal* freedom of the parties to release themselves from the engagement (and I also hold that they ought not to make *much* difference), they necessarily make a great difference in the *moral* freedom. A person is bound to take all these circumstances into account before resolving on a step which may affect such important interests of others; and if he does not allow proper weight to those interests, he is morally responsible for the wrong. . . .

QUESTIONS FOR REFLECTION

1. Between 1905 and 1937, a period known as the *Lochner* era, the U.S. Supreme Court used a form of the harm principle to strike down laws regulating economic activity: laws setting a minimum wage, for example, or regulating working hours and conditions. Does the harm principle, in Mill's view, apply to economic transactions? How does the harm principle relate to what he calls the doctrine of "free trade"?
2. What is the point of Mill's example of someone about to cross an unsafe bridge? What does it indicate about the harm principle?
3. The United States, like many other countries, regulates advertising. Is such regulation compatible with Mill's position in *On Liberty?* What kinds of regulation, if any, might Mill be willing to accept?
4. Many governments impose "sin taxes" on items such as alcohol and cigarettes. What is Mill's criterion for determining whether such taxes are acceptable?
5. Mill insists that voluntary slavery ought to be prohibited, although it might appear to fall into the realm of individual liberty. Why? Is Mill's support for this prohibition consistent with the harm principle?

DRUG LEGALIZATION

Over the past several decades, drug use has grown from a fashion among a small collection of bohemian artists and musicians into a major social problem. The use of illegal and seriously harmful drugs can be found in almost any high school, college, or university in the United States; scores of cities routinely witness drug-related shootings and other forms of violence. Several times the government has declared a "war on drugs," but the result has seemed, at best, a stalemate. Frustration with this state of affairs has led some to call for the legalization of drugs.

Drug use may appear to be a self-regarding act that may harm the drug user but that has little effect on anyone else. Few contemporary advocates of legalization, however, have rested their case solely on Mill's harm principle. Many writers on both sides of the issue believe that nonusers suffer significant harms that must be taken into account; they have debated whether criminal penalties reduce or add to the harms to nonusers. Moreover, addictive drugs pose problems related to those Mill confronts in discussing voluntary slavery; people may initially choose, freely and voluntarily, to take an addictive drug, but their freedom does not last long. As Mill asks, do people have the freedom to surrender their freedom? Many contemporary writers share Mill's conviction that they do not and thus include harms to users of addictive drugs as morally relevant. This does not mean, however, that philosophical attitudes toward liberty are unrelated to discussions of the drug problem. Some writers clearly presuppose something akin to Mill's harm principle. Others assume the opposed principle of moral paternalism, holding that a government should promote the moral well-being of its citizens. Still others treat harms to users and harms to nonusers as morally equivalent, in effect denying the significance of the distinction between self-regarding and other-regarding actions.

Milton Friedman, a respected economist, argues that the war on drugs has been a costly failure. He urges decriminalization of drugs—that is, removing criminal penalties against their sale and use. He advocates treating drugs much as we now treat alcohol and cigarettes—as substances that should be regulated and whose users should be treated rather than jailed.

William Bennett, "drug czar" under Presidents Reagan and Bush, maintains that Friedman's proposal is flawed and even reckless. Bennett defends criminal penalties for drug use by arguing that they reduce harms both to drug users and to others. He contends that "government has a responsibility to craft and uphold laws that help educate citizens about right and wrong."

Ethan Nadelmann argues Friedman's case in greater detail. He holds that drug legalization would produce significant economic benefits, reduce crime, and revitalize the inner cities. James Q. Wilson further articulates Bennett's case, contending that the war on drugs is justifiable and moderately successful. He holds that enforcing criminal penalties has helped confine the drug problem to a relatively small portion of the population, while sheltering most people from harms associated with the drug trade. Legalization, he believes, would greatly increase drug use and the attendant harms to users and nonusers alike.

MILTON FRIEDMAN

An Open Letter to Bill Bennett

Milton Friedman was Senior Research Fellow at the Hoover Institution at Stanford University and professor emeritus of economics at the University of Chicago. He was awarded the Nobel Prize in economics in 1976.

Dear Bill:

In Oliver Cromwell's eloquent words, "I beseech you, in the bowels of Christ, think it possible you may be mistaken" about the course you and President Bush urge us to adopt to fight drugs. The path you propose of more police, more jails, use of the military in foreign countries, harsh penalties for drug users, and a whole panoply of repressive measures can only make a bad situation worse. The drug war cannot be won by those tactics without undermining the human liberty and individual freedom that you and I cherish.

You are not mistaken in believing that drugs are a scourge that is devastating our society. You are not mistaken in believing that drugs are tearing asunder our social fabric, ruining the lives of many young people, and imposing heavy costs on some of the most disadvantaged among us. You are not mistaken in believing that the majority of the public share your concerns. In short, you are not mistaken in the end you seek to achieve.

Your mistake is failing to recognize that the very measures you favor are a major source of the evils you deplore. Of course the problem is demand, but it is not only demand, it is demand that must operate through repressed and illegal channels. Illegality creates obscene profits that finance the murderous tactics of the drug lords; illegality leads to the corruption of law enforcement officials; illegality monopolizes the efforts of honest law forces so that they are starved for resources to fight the simpler crimes of robbery, theft and assault.

Drugs are a tragedy for addicts. But criminalizing their use converts that tragedy into a disaster for society, for users and non-users alike. Our experience with the prohibition of drugs is a replay of our experience with the prohibition of alcoholic beverages.

I append excerpts from a column that I wrote in 1972 on "Prohibition and Drugs." The major problem then was heroin from Marseilles; today, it is cocaine from Latin America. Today, also, the problem is far more serious than it was 17 years ago: more addicts, more innocent victims; more drug pushers, more law enforcement officials; more money spent to enforce prohibition, more money spent to circumvent prohibition.

Had drugs been decriminalized 17 years ago, "crack" would never have been invented (it was invented because the high cost of illegal drugs made it profitable to provide a cheaper version) and there would today be far fewer addicts. The lives of thousands, perhaps hundreds of thousands of innocent victims would have been saved, and not only in the U.S. The ghettos of our major cities would not be drug-and-crime-infested noman's lands. Fewer people would be in jails, and fewer jails would have been built.

Colombia, Bolivia and Peru would not be suffering from narco-terror, and we would not be distorting our foreign policy because of narco-terror. Hell would not, in the words with which Billy Sunday welcomed Prohibition, "be forever for rent," but it would be a lot emptier.

Decriminalizing drugs is even more urgent now than in 1972, but we must recognize that the harm done in the interim cannot be wiped out, certainly not immediately. Postponing decriminalization will only make matters worse, and make the problem appear even more intractable.

Alcohol and tobacco cause many more deaths in users than do drugs. Decriminalization would not prevent us from treating drugs as we now treat alcohol and tobacco: prohibiting sales of drugs to minors, outlawing the advertising of drugs and similar measures. Such measures could be enforced, while outright prohibition cannot be. Moreover, if even a small fraction of the money we now spend on trying to enforce drug prohibition were devoted to treatment and rehabilitation, in an atmosphere of compassion not punishment, the reduction in drug usage and in the harm done to the users could be dramatic.

This plea comes from the bottom of my heart. Every friend of freedom, and I know you are one, must be as revolted as I am by the prospect of turning the United States into an armed camp, by the vision of jails filled with casual drug users and of an army of enforcers empowered to invade the liberty of citizens on slight evidence. A country in which shooting down unidentified planes "on suspicion" can be seriously considered as a drug-war tactic is not the kind of United States that either you or I want to hand on to future generations.

Milton Friedman
Senior Research Fellow
Hoover Institution
Stanford University

Flashback

This is a truncated version of a column by Mr. Friedman in Newsweek *May 1, 1972, issue, as President Nixon was undertaking an earlier "drug war":*

"The reign of tears is over. The slums will soon be only a memory. We will turn our prisons into factories and our jails into storehouses and corncribs. Men will walk upright now, women will smile, and the children will laugh. Hell will be forever for rent."

That is how Billy Sunday, the noted evangelist and leading crusader against Demon Rum, greeted the onset of Prohibition in early 1920.

We know now how tragically his hopes were doomed.

Prohibition is an attempted cure that makes matters worse—for both the addict and the rest of us.

Consider first the addict. Legalizing drugs might increase the number of addicts, but it is not clear that it would. Forbidden fruit is attractive, particularly to the young. More important, many drug addicts are deliberately made by pushers, who give likely prospects that first few doses free. It pays the pusher to do so because, once hooked, the addict is a captive customer. If drugs were legally available, any possible profit from such inhumane activity would disappear, since the addict could buy from the cheapest source.

Whatever happens to the number of addicts, the individual addict would clearly be far better off if drugs were legal. Addicts are driven to associate with criminals to get the drugs, become criminals themselves to finance the habit, and risk constant danger of death and disease.

Consider next the rest of us. The harm to us from the addiction of others arises almost wholly from the fact that drugs are illegal. It is estimated that addicts commit one third to one half of all street crime in the U.S.

Legalize drugs, and street crime would drop dramatically.

Moreover, addicts and pushers are not the only ones corrupted. Immense sums are at stake. It is inevitable that some relatively low-paid police and other government officials—and some high-paid ones as well—will succumb to the temptation to pick up easy money.

Legalizing drugs would simultaneously reduce the amount of crime and raise the quality of law enforcement. Can you conceive of any other measure that would accomplish so much to promote law and order?

In drugs, as in other areas, persuasion and example are likely to be far more effective than the use of force to shape others in our image.

QUESTIONS FOR REFLECTION

1. Asserting that government prohibition of drug use is illegitimate in itself differs from asserting that it is a bad idea in practice. Certainly Friedman asserts the latter. How does he argue for this position? Does he also assert the former?

2. Friedman claims that the drug war undermines "human liberty and individual freedom." What is Friedman's conception of liberty? Is Friedman's argument compatible with Mill's harm principle?

WILLIAM J. BENNETT

A Response to Milton Friedman

William J. Bennett is a Washington Fellow of the Claremont Institute. He has served as director of the Office of National Drug Control Policy and as U.S. Secretary of Education. (Source: Reprinted by permission from The Wall Street Journal, *September 19, 1989, p. A30.*

DEAR MILTON:

There was little, if anything, new in your open letter to me calling for the legalization of drugs (*The Wall Street Journal,* Sept. 7). As the excerpt from your 1972 article made clear, the legalization argument is an old and familiar one, which has recently been revived by a small number of journalists and academics who insist that the only solution to the drug problem is no solution at all. What surprises me is that you would continue to advocate so unrealistic a proposal without pausing to consider seriously its consequences.

If the argument for drug legalization has one virtue it is its sheer simplicity. Eliminate laws against drugs, and street crime will disappear. Take the profit out of the black market through decriminalization and regulation, and poor neighborhoods will no longer be victimized by drug dealers. Cut back on drug enforcement, and use the money to wage a public health campaign against drugs, as we do with tobacco and alcohol.

Counting Costs

The basic premise of all these propositions is that using our nation's laws to fight drugs is too costly. To be sure, our attempts to reduce drug use do carry with them enormous costs. But the question that must be asked—and which is totally ignored by the legalization advocates—is what are the costs of *not* enforcing laws against drugs?

In my judgment, and in the judgment of virtually every serious scholar in this field, the potential costs of legalizing drugs would be so large as to make it a public policy disaster.

Of course, no one, including you, can say with certainty what would happen in the U.S. if drugs were suddenly to become a readily purchased product. We do know, however, that wherever drugs have been cheaper and more easily obtained, drug use—and addiction—has skyrocketed. In opium and cocaine-producing countries, addiction is rampant among the peasants involved in drug production.

Professor James Q. Wilson tells us that during the years in which heroin could be legally prescribed by doctors in Britain, the number of addicts increased forty-fold. And after the repeal of Prohibition—an analogy favored but misunderstood by legalization advocates—consumption of alcohol soared by 350%.

Could we afford such dramatic increases in drug use? I doubt it. Already the toll of drug use on American society—measured in lost productivity, in rising health insurance costs, in hospitals flooded with drug overdose emergencies, in drug-caused accidents, and in premature death—is surely more than we would like to bear.

You seem to believe that by spending just a little more money on treatment and rehabilitation, the costs of increased addiction can be avoided. That hope betrays a basic misunderstanding of the problems facing drug treatment. Most addicts don't suddenly decide to get help. They remain addicts either because treatment isn't available or because they don't seek it out. The National Drug Control Strategy announced by President Bush on Sept. 5 goes a long way in making sure that more treatment slots are available. But the simple fact remains that many drug users won't enter treatment until they are forced to—often by the very criminal justice system you think is the source of the problem.

As for the connection between drugs and crime, your unswerving commitment to a legalization solution prevents you from appreciating the complexity of the drug market. Contrary to your claim, most addicts do not turn to crime to support their habit. Research shows that many of them were involved in criminal activity before they turned to drugs. Many former addicts who have received treatment continue to commit crimes during their recovery. And even if drugs were legal, what evidence do you have that the habitual drug user wouldn't continue to rob and steal to get money for clothes, food or shelter? Drug addicts always want more drugs than they can afford, and no legalization scheme has yet come up with a way of satisfying that appetite.

The National Drug Control Strategy emphasizes the importance of reclaiming the streets and neighborhoods where drugs have wrought havoc because, I admit, the price of having drug laws is having criminals who will try to subvert them. Your proposal might conceivably reduce the amount of gang- and dealer-related crime, but it is fanciful to suggest that it would make crime vanish. Unless you are willing to distribute drugs freely and widely, there will always be a black market to undercut the regulated one. And as for the potential addicts, for the school children and for the pregnant mothers, all of whom would find drugs more accessible and legally condoned, your proposal would offer nothing at all.

So I advocate a larger criminal justice system to take drug users off the streets and deter new users from becoming more deeply involved in so hazardous an activity. You suggest that such policies would turn the country "into an armed camp." Try telling that to the public housing tenants who enthusiastically support plans to enhance security in their buildings, or to the residents who applaud police when a local crack house is razed. They recognize that drug use is a threat to the individual liberty and domestic tranquility guaranteed by the Constitution.

I remain an ardent defender of our nation's laws against illegal drug use and our attempts to enforce them because I believe drug use is wrong. A true friend of freedom understands that government has a responsibility to craft and uphold laws that help educate citizens about right and wrong. That, at any rate, was the Founders' view of our system of government.

Liberal Ridicule

Today this view is much ridiculed by liberal elites and entirely neglected by you. So while I cannot doubt the sincerity of your opinion on drug legalization, I find it difficult to respect. The moral cost of legalizing drugs is great, but it is a cost that apparently lies outside the narrow scope of libertarian policy prescriptions.

I do not have a simple solution to the drug problem. I doubt that one exists. But I am committed to fighting the problem on several fronts through imaginative policies and hard work over a long period of time. As in the past, some of these efforts will work and some won't. Your response, however, is to surrender and see what happens. To my mind that is irresponsible and reckless public policy. At a time when national intolerance for drug use is rapidly increasing, the legalization argument is a political anachronism. Its recent resurgence is, I trust, only a temporary distraction from the genuine debate on national drug policy.

William J. Bennett
Director
Office of National Drug Control Policy

QUESTIONS FOR REFLECTION

1. Bennett contends that legalizing drugs would increase harms to nonusers. How does he argue this position?
2. Part of Bennett's case rests on his view that enforcing criminal penalties against drug use decreases harms done by drugs to drug users themselves. What is his argument? Is Bennett's use of this argument compatible with Mill's harm principle?
3. Friedman claims that the drug war undermines "human liberty and individual freedom." How does Bennett respond to this allegation, if at all? What does this indicate about Bennett's conception of freedom and of the proper bounds of government authority?
4. In what sense is Bennett's position Aristotelian?
5. To what extent might Mill's views lend support to Bennett's position?

ETHAN A. NADELMANN

The Case for Legalization

Ethan A. Nadelmann is executive director of the Drug Policy Alliance. (Source: Public Interest *92 [Summer 1988]. Notes have been omitted.*

What can be done about the "drug problem"? Despite frequent proclamations of war and dramatic increases in government funding and resources in recent years, there are many indications that the problem is not going away and may even be growing worse. During the past year alone, more than thirty million Americans violated the drug laws on literally billions of occasions. Drug-treatment programs in many cities are turning people away for lack of space and funding. In Washington, D.C., drug-related killings, largely of one drug dealer by another, are held responsible for a doubling in the homicide rate over the past year. In New York and elsewhere, courts and prisons are clogged with a virtually limitless supply of drug-law violators. In large cities and small towns alike, corruption of policemen and other criminal-justice officials by drug traffickers is rampant. . . .

If there were a serious public debate on this issue, far more attention would be given to one policy option that has just begun to be seriously considered but that may well prove more successful than anything currently being implemented or proposed: legalization. . . .

There is, of course, no single legalization strategy. At one extreme is the libertarian vision of virtually no government restraints on the production and sale of drugs or any psychoactive substances, except perhaps around the fringes, such as prohibiting sales to children. At the other extreme is total government control over the production and sale of these goods. In between lies a strategy that may prove more successful than anything yet tried in stemming the problems of drug abuse and drug-related violence, corruption, sickness, and suffering. It is one in which government makes most of the substances that are now banned legally available to competent adults, exercises strong regulatory powers over all large-scale production and sale of drugs, makes drug-treatment programs available to all who need them, and offers honest drug-education programs to children. This strategy, it is worth noting, would also result in a net benefit to public treasuries of at least ten billion dollars a year, and perhaps much more.

There are three reasons why it is important to think about legalization scenarios, even though most Americans remain hostile to the idea. First, current drug-control policies have failed, are failing, and will continue to fail, in good part because they are fundamentally flawed. Second, many drug-control efforts are not only failing but also proving highly costly and counterproductive; indeed, many of the drug-related evils that Americans identify as part and parcel of the "drug problem" are in fact caused by our drug-prohibition policies. Third, there is good reason to believe that repealing many of the drug laws would not lead, as many people fear, to a dramatic rise in drug abuse. In this essay I expand on each of these reasons for considering the legalization option. Government efforts to deal with the drug problem will succeed only if the rhetoric and crusading mentality that now dominate drug policy are replaced by reasoned and logical analysis.

Why Current Drug Policies Fail

Most proposals for dealing with the drug problem today reflect a desire to point the finger at those most removed from one's home and area of expertise. New York Mayor Ed Koch, Florida Congressman Larry Smith, and Harlem Congressman Charles Rangel, who recognize government's inability to deal with the drug problem in the cities, are among the most vocal supporters of punishing foreign drug-producing countries and stepping up interdiction efforts. Foreign leaders and U.S. State Department and drug-enforcement officials stationed abroad, on the other hand, who understand all too well why it is impossible to crack down successfully on illicit drug production outside the United States, are the most vigorous advocates of domestic enforcement and demand-reduction efforts within the United States. In between, those agencies charged with drug interdiction, from the Coast Guard and U.S. Customs Service to the U.S. military, know that they will never succeed in capturing more than a small percentage of the illicit drugs being smuggled into the United States. Not surprisingly, they point their fingers in both directions. The solution, they promise, lies in greater source-control efforts abroad and greater demand-reduction efforts at home.

Trying to pass the buck is always understandable. But in each of these cases, the officials are half right and half wrong—half right in recognizing that they can do little to affect their end of the drug problem, given the suppositions and constraints of current drug-control strategies; half wrong (if we assume that their finger pointing is sincere) in expecting that the solution lies elsewhere. It would be wrong, however, to assume that the public posturing of many officials reflects their real views. Many of them privately acknowledge the futility of all current drug-control strategies and wonder whether radically different options, such as legalization, might not prove more successful in dealing with the drug problem. The political climate pervading this issue is such, however, that merely to ask that alternatives to current policies be considered is to incur a great political risk.

By most accounts, the dramatic increase in drug-enforcement efforts over the past few years has had little effect on the illicit drug market in the United States. The mere existence of drug-prohibition laws, combined with a minimal level of law-enforcement resources, is sufficient to maintain the price of illicit drugs at a level significantly higher than it would be if there were no such laws. Drug laws and enforcement also reduce the availability of illicit drugs, most notably in parts of the United States where demand is relatively limited to begin with. Theoretically, increases in drug-enforcement efforts should result in reduced availability, higher prices, and lower purity of illegal drugs. That is, in fact, what has happened to the domestic marijuana market (in at least the first two respects). But in general the illegal drug market has not responded as intended to the substantial increases in federal, state, and local drug-enforcement efforts.

Cocaine has sold for about a hundred dollars a gram at the retail level since the beginning of the 1980s. The average purity of that gram, however, has increased from 12 to 60 percent. Moreover, a growing number of users are turning to "crack," a potent derivative of cocaine that can be smoked; it is widely sold in ghetto neighborhoods now for five to ten dollars per vial. Needless to say, both crack and the 60 percent pure cocaine pose much greater threats to users than did the relatively benign powder available eight years ago. Similarly, the retail price of heroin has remained relatively constant even as the average purity has risen from 3.9 percent in 1983 to 6.1 percent in 1986. Throughout the southwestern part of the United States, a particularly potent form of heroin known as "black tar" has become increasingly prevalent. And in many cities, a powerful synthetic opiate, Dilaudid, is beginning to compete with heroin as the preferred opiate. The growing number of heroin-related hospital emergencies and deaths is directly related to these developments.

All of these trends suggest that drug-enforcement efforts are not succeeding and may even be backfiring. There are numerous indications, for instance, that a growing number of marijuana dealers in both the producer countries and the United States are switching to cocaine dealing, motivated both by the promise of greater profits and by government drug-enforcement efforts that place a premium on minimizing the bulk of the illicit product (in order to avoid detection). It is possible, of course, that some of these trends would be even more severe in the absence of drug laws and enforcement. At the same time, it is worth observing that the increases in the potency of illegal drugs have coincided with decreases in the potency of legal substances. Motivated in good part by health concerns, cigarette smokers are turning increasingly to lower-tar and lower-nicotine tobacco products, alcohol drinkers from hard liquor to wine and beer, and even coffee drinkers from regular to decaffeinated coffee. This trend may well have less to do with the nature of the substances than with their legal status. It is quite possible, for instance, that the subculture of illicit-drug use creates a bias or incentive in favor of riskier behavior and more powerful psychoactive effects. If this is the case, legalization might well succeed in reversing today's trend toward more potent drugs and more dangerous methods of consumption.

The most "successful" drug-enforcement operations are those that succeed in identifying and destroying an entire drug-trafficking organization. Such operations can send dozens of people to jail and earn the government millions of dollars in asset forfeitures. Yet these operations have virtually no effect on the availability or price of illegal drugs throughout much of the United States. During the past few years, some urban police departments have devoted significant manpower and financial resources to intensive crackdowns on street-level drug dealing in particular neighborhoods. Code-named Operation Pressure Point, Operation Clean Sweep, and so on, these massive police efforts have led to hundreds, even thousands, of arrests of low-level dealers and drug users and have helped improve the quality of life in the targeted neighborhoods. In most cases, however, drug dealers have adapted relatively easily by moving their operations to nearby neighborhoods. In the final analysis, the principal accomplishment of most domestic drug-enforcement efforts is not to reduce the supply or availability of illegal drugs, or even to raise their price; it is to punish the drug dealers who are apprehended, and cause minor disruptions in established drug markets.

The Failure of International Drug Control

Many drug-enforcement officials and urban leaders recognize the futility of domestic drug-enforcement efforts and place their hopes in international control efforts. Yet these too are doomed to fail—for numerous reasons. First, marijuana and opium can be grown almost anywhere, and the coca plant, from which cocaine is derived, is increasingly being cultivated successfully in areas that were once considered inhospitable environments. Wherever drug-eradication efforts succeed, other regions and countries are quick to fill the void; for example, Colombian marijuana growers rapidly expanded production following successful eradication efforts in Mexico during the mid-1970s. Today, Mexican growers are rapidly taking advantage of recent Colombian government successes in eradicating marijuana in the Guajira peninsula. Meanwhile, Jamaicans and Central Americans from Panama to Belize, as well as a growing assortment of Asians and Africans, do what they can to sell their own marijuana in American markets. And within the United States, domestic marijuana production is believed to be a multi-billion-dollar industry, supplying between 15 and 50 percent of the American market. . . .

Beyond the push-down/pop-up factor, international source-control efforts face a variety of other obstacles. In many countries, governments with limited resources lack the ability to crack down on drug production in the hinterlands and other poorly policed regions. In some countries, ranging from Colombia and Peru to Burma and Thailand, leftist insurgencies are involved in drug production for either financial or political profit and may play an important role in hampering government drug-control efforts. With respect to all three of the illicit crops, poor peasants with no comparable opportunities to earn as much money growing legitimate produce are prominently involved in the illicit business. In some cases, the illicit crop is part of a traditional, indigenous culture. Even where it is not, peasants typically perceive little or nothing immoral about taking advantage of the opportunity to grow the illicit crops. Indeed, from their perspective their moral obligation is not to protect the foolish American consumer of their produce but to provide for their families' welfare. And even among those who do perceive participation in the illicit drug market as somewhat unethical, the temptations held out by the drug traffickers often prove overwhelming.

No illicit drug is as difficult to keep out of the United States as heroin. The absence of geographical limitations on where it can be cultivated is just one minor obstacle.

American heroin users consume an estimated 6 tons of heroin each year. The 60 tons of opium required to produce that heroin represent just 2 or 3 percent of the estimated 2,000 to 3,000 tons of illicit opium produced during each of the past few years. Even if eradication efforts combined with what often proves to be the opium growers' principal nemesis—bad weather—were to eliminate three-fourths of that production in one year, the U.S. market would still require just 10 percent of the remaining crop. Since U.S. consumers are able and willing to pay more than any others, the chances are good that they would still obtain their heroin. In any event, the prospects for such a radical reduction in illicit opium production are scanty indeed.

As Peter Reuter argues, interdiction, like source control, is largely unable to keep illicit drugs out of the United States. Moreover, the past twenty years' experience has demonstrated that even dramatic increases in interdiction and source-control efforts have little or no effect on the price and purity of drugs. The few small successes, such as the destruction of the Turkish-opium "French Connection" in the early 1970s and the crackdown on Mexican marijuana and heroin in the late 1970s, were exceptions to the rule. The elusive goal of international drug control since then has been to replicate those unusual successes. It is a strategy that is destined to fail, however, as long as millions of Americans continue to demand the illicit substances that foreigners are willing and able to supply.

The Costs of Prohibition

The fact that drug-prohibition laws and policies cannot eradicate or even significantly reduce drug abuse is not necessarily a reason to repeal them. They do, after all, succeed in deterring many people from trying drugs, and they clearly reduce the availability and significantly increase the price of illegal drugs. These accomplishments alone might warrant retaining the drug laws, were it not for the fact that these same laws are also responsible for much of what Americans identify as the "drug problem." Here the analogies to alcohol and tobacco are worth noting. There is little question that we could reduce the health costs associated with use and abuse of alcohol and tobacco if we were to criminalize their production, sale, and possession. But no one believes that we could eliminate their use and abuse, that we could create an "alcohol-free" or "tobacco-free" country. Nor do most Americans believe that criminalizing the alcohol and tobacco markets would be a good idea. Their opposition stems largely from two beliefs: that adult Americans have the right to choose what substances they will consume and what risks they will take and that the costs of trying to coerce so many Americans to abstain from those substances would be enormous. It was the strength of these two beliefs that ultimately led to the repeal of Prohibition, and it is partly due to memories of that experience that criminalizing either alcohol or tobacco has little support today.

Consider the potential consequences of criminalizing the production, sale, and possession of all tobacco products. On the positive side, the number of people smoking tobacco would almost certainly decline, as would the health costs associated with tobacco consumption. Although the "forbidden fruit" syndrome would attract some people to cigarette smoking who would not otherwise have smoked, many more would likely be deterred by the criminal sanction, the moral standing of the law, the higher cost and unreliable quality of the illicit tobacco, and the difficulties involved in acquiring it. Non-smokers would rarely if ever be bothered by the irritating habits of their fellow citizens. The anti-tobacco laws would discourage some people from ever starting to smoke and would induce others to quit.

On the negative side, however, millions of Americans, including both tobacco addicts and recreational users, would no doubt defy the law, generating a massive underground market and billions in profits for organized criminals. Although some tobacco farmers would find other work, thousands more would become outlaws and continue to produce their crops covertly. Throughout Latin America, farmers and gangsters would rejoice at the opportunity to earn untold sums of gringo greenbacks, even as U.S. diplomats pressured foreign governments to cooperate with U.S. laws. Within the United States, government helicopters would spray herbicides on illicit tobacco fields; people would be rewarded by the government for informing on their neighbors who grow, sell, and smoke tobacco; urine tests would be employed to identify violators of the anti-tobacco laws; and a Tobacco Enforcement Administration (the T.E.A.) would employ undercover agents, informants, and wiretaps to uncover tobacco-law violators. Municipal, state, and federal judicial systems would be clogged with tobacco traffickers and "abusers." "Tobacco-related murders" would increase dramatically as criminal organizations competed with one another for turf and markets. Smoking would become an act of youthful rebellion, and no doubt some users would begin to experiment with more concentrated, potent, and dangerous forms of tobacco. Tobacco-related corruption would infect all levels of government, and respect for the law would decline noticeably. Government expenditures on tobacco-law enforcement would climb rapidly into the billions of dollars, even as budget balancers longingly recalled the almost ten billion dollars per year in tobacco taxes earned by the federal and state governments prior to prohibition. Finally, the state of North Carolina might even secede again from the Union.

This seemingly far-fetched tobacco-prohibition scenario is little more than an extrapolation based on the current situation with respect to marijuana, cocaine, and heroin. In many ways, our predicament resembles what actually happened during Prohibition. Prior to Prohibition, most Americans hoped that alcohol could be effectively banned by passing laws against its production and supply. During the early years of Prohibition, when drinking declined but millions of Americans nonetheless continued to drink, Prohibition's supporters placed their faith in tougher laws and more police and jails. After a few more years, however, increasing numbers of Americans began to realize that laws and policemen were unable to eliminate the smugglers, bootleggers, and illicit producers, as long as tens of millions of Americans continued to want to buy alcohol. At the same time, they saw that more laws and policemen seemed to generate more violence and corruption, more crowded courts and jails, wider disrespect for government and the law, and more power and profits for the gangsters. Repeal of Prohibition came to be seen not as a capitulation to Al Capone and his ilk but as a means of both putting the bootleggers out of business and eliminating most of the costs associated with the prohibition laws.

Today, Americans are faced with a dilemma similar to that confronted by our forebears sixty years ago. Demand for illicit drugs shows some signs of abating but no signs of declining significantly. Moreover, there are substantial reasons to doubt that tougher laws and policing have played an important role in reducing consumption. Supply, meanwhile, has not abated at all. Availability of illicit drugs, except for marijuana in some locales, remains high. Prices are dropping, even as potency increases. And the number of drug producers, smugglers, and dealers remains sizable, even as jails and prisons fill to overflowing. As was the case during Prohibition, the principal beneficiaries of current drug policies are the new and old organized-crime gangs. The principal victims, on the other hand, are not the drug dealers but the tens of millions of Americans who are worse off in one way or another as a consequence of the existence and failure of the drug-prohibition laws.

All public policies create beneficiaries and victims, both intended and unintended. When a public policy results in a disproportionate magnitude of unintended victims, there is good reason to reevaluate the assumptions and design of the policy. In the case of drug-prohibition policies, the intended beneficiaries are those individuals who would become drug abusers but for the existence and enforcement of the drug laws. The intended victims are those who traffic in illicit drugs and suffer the legal consequences. The unintended beneficiaries, conversely, are the drug producers and traffickers who profit handsomely from the illegality of the market, while avoiding arrest by the authorities and the violence perpetrated by other criminals. The unintended victims of drug-prohibition policies are rarely recognized as such, however. Viewed narrowly, they are the thirty million Americans who use illegal drugs, thereby risking loss of their jobs, imprisonment, and the damage done to health by ingesting illegally produced drugs; viewed broadly, they are all Americans, who pay the substantial costs of our present ill-considered policies, both as taxpayers and as the potential victims of crime. These unintended victims are generally thought to be victimized by the unintended beneficiaries (i.e., the drug dealers), when in fact it is the drug-prohibition policies themselves that are primarily responsible for their plight.

If law-enforcement efforts could succeed in significantly reducing either the supply of illicit drugs or the demand for them, we would probably have little need to seek alternative drug-control policies. But since those efforts have repeatedly failed to make much of a difference and show little indication of working better in the future, at this point we must focus greater attention on their costs. Unlike the demand and supply of illicit drugs, which have remained relatively indifferent to legislative initiatives, the costs of drug-enforcement measures can be affected—quite dramatically—by legislative measures. What tougher criminal sanctions and more police have failed to accomplish, in terms of reducing drug-related violence, corruption, death, and social decay, may well be better accomplished by legislative repeal of the drug laws and adoption of less punitive but more effective measures to prevent and treat substance abuse.

QUESTIONS FOR REFLECTION

1. Why, according to Nadelmann, have current drug policies failed?
2. In Nadelmann's view, what harms does drug prohibition produce?
3. How does Nadelmann relate drug use and drug prohibition to crime? Do you find his analysis persuasive? Why or why not?

JAMES Q. WILSON

Against the Legalization of Drugs

James Q. Wilson is Ronald Reagan Professor of Public Policy at Pepperdine University. (Source: Reprinted from Commentary *[February 1990], by permission; all rights reserved.)*

In 1972, the President appointed me chairman of the National Advisory Council for Drug Abuse Prevention. Created by Congress, the Council was charged with providing guidance on how best to coordinate the national war on drugs. (Yes, we called it a war then, too.) In those days, the drug we were chiefly concerned with was heroin. When I took office, heroin use had been increasing dramatically. Everybody was worried that this increase would continue. Such phrases as "heroin epidemic" were commonplace.

That same year, the eminent economist Milton Friedman published an essay in *Newsweek* in which he called for legalizing heroin. His argument was on two grounds: as a matter of ethics, the government has no right to tell people not to use heroin (or to drink or to commit suicide); as a matter of economics, the prohibition of drug use imposes costs on society that far exceed the benefits. Others, such as the psychoanalyst Thomas Szasz, made the same argument.

We did not take Friedman's advice. (Government commissions rarely do.) I do not recall that we even discussed legalizing heroin, though we did discuss (but did not take action on) legalizing a drug, cocaine, that many people then argued was benign. Our marching orders were to figure out how to win the war on heroin, not to run up the white flag of surrender.

That was 1972. Today, we have the same number of heroin addicts that we had then—half a million, give or take a few thousand. Having that many heroin addicts is no trivial matter; these people deserve our attention. But not having had an increase in that number for over fifteen years is also something that deserves our attention. What happened to the "heroin epidemic" that many people once thought would overwhelm us?

The facts are clear: a more or less stable pool of heroin addicts had been getting older, with relatively few new recruits. In 1976 the average age of heroin users who appeared in hospital emergency rooms was about twenty-seven; ten years later it was thirty-two. More than two-thirds of all heroin users appearing in emergency rooms are now over the age of thirty. Back in the early 1970's, when heroin got onto the national political agenda, the typical heroin addict was much younger, often a teenager. Household surveys show the same thing—the rate of opiate use (which includes heroin) has been flat for the better part of two decades. More fine-grained studies of inner-city neighborhoods confirm this. John Boyle and Ann Brunswick found that the percentage of young blacks in Harlem who used heroin fell from 8 percent in 1970–71 to about 3 percent in 1975–76.

Why did heroin lose its appeal for young people? When the young blacks in Harlem were asked why they stopped, more than half mentioned "trouble with the law" or "high cost" (and high cost is, of course, directly the result of law enforcement). Two-thirds said that heroin hurt their health; nearly all said they had had a bad experience with it. We need not rely, however, simply on what they said. In New York City in 1973–75, the street price of heroin rose dramatically and its purity sharply declined, probably as a result of the heroin shortage caused by the success of the Turkish government in reducing the supply of opium base and of the French government in closing down heroin-processing laboratories located in and around Marseilles. These were short-lived gains for, just as Friedman predicted, alternative sources of supply—mostly in Mexico—quickly emerged. But the three-year heroin shortage interrupted the easy recruitment of new users.

Health and related problems were no doubt part of the reason for the reduced flow of recruits. Over the preceding years, Harlem youth had watched as more and more heroin users died of overdoses, were poisoned by adulterated doses, or acquired hepatitis from dirty needles. The word got around: heroin can kill you. By 1974 new hepatitis cases and drug-overdose deaths had dropped to a fraction of what they had been in 1970.

Alas, treatment did not seem to explain much of the cessation in drug use. Treatment programs can and do help heroin addicts, but treatment did not explain the drop in the number of *new* users (who by definition had never been in treatment) nor even much of the reduction in the number of experienced users.

No one knows how much of the decline to attribute to personal observation as opposed to high prices or reduced supply. But other evidence suggests strongly that price and supply played a large role. In 1972 the National Advisory Council was especially worried by the prospect that U.S. servicemen returning to this country from Vietnam would bring their heroin habits with them. Fortunately, a brilliant study by Lee Robins of Washington University in St. Louis put that fear to rest. She measured drug use of Vietnam veterans shortly after they had returned home. Though many had used heroin regularly while in Southeast Asia, most gave up the habit when back in the United States. The reason: here, heroin was less available and sanctions on its use were more pronounced. Of course, if a veteran had been willing to pay enough—which might have meant traveling to another city and would certainly have meant making an illegal contact with a disreputable dealer in a threatening neighborhood in order to acquire a (possibly) dangerous dose—he could have sustained his drug habit. Most veterans were unwilling to pay this price, and so their drug use declined or disappeared.

Reliving the Past

Suppose we had taken Friedman's advice in 1972. What would have happened? We cannot be entirely certain, but at a minimum we would have placed the young heroin addicts (and, above all, the prospective addicts) in a very different position from the one in which they actually found themselves. Heroin would have been legal. Its price would have been reduced by 95 percent (minus whatever we chose to recover in taxes). Now that it could be sold by the same people who make aspirin, its quality would have been assured—no poisons, no adulterants. Sterile hypodermic needles would have been readily available at the neighborhood drugstore, probably at the same counter where the heroin was sold. No need to travel to big cities or unfamiliar neighborhoods—heroin could have been purchased anywhere, perhaps by mail order.

There would no longer have been any financial or medical reason to avoid heroin use. Anybody could have afforded it. We might have tried to prevent children from buying it, but as we have learned from our efforts to prevent minors from buying alcohol and tobacco, young people have a way of penetrating markets theoretically reserved for adults. Returning Vietnam veterans would have discovered that Omaha and Raleigh had been converted into the pharmaceutical equivalent of Saigon.

Under these circumstances, can we doubt for a moment that heroin use would have grown exponentially? Or that a vastly larger supply of new users would have been recruited? Professor Friedman is a Nobel Prize–winning economist whose understanding of market forces is profound. What did he think would happen to consumption under his legalized regime? Here are his words: "Legalizing drugs might increase the number of addicts, but it is not clear that it would. Forbidden fruit is attractive, particularly to the young."

Really? I suppose that we should expect no increase in Porsche sales if we cut the price by 95 percent, no increase in whiskey sales if we cut the price by a comparable amount—because young people only want fast cars and strong liquor when they are "forbidden." Perhaps Friedman's uncharacteristic lapse from the obvious implications of price theory can be explained by a misunderstanding of how drug users are recruited. In his 1972 essay he said that "drug addicts are deliberately made by pushers, who give likely prospects their first few doses free." If drugs were legal it would not pay anybody to produce addicts, because everybody would buy from the cheapest source. But as every drug expert knows, pushers do not produce addicts. Friends or acquaintances do. In fact, pushers are usually reluctant to deal with non-users because a non-user could be an undercover cop. Drug use spreads in the same way any fad or fashion spreads: somebody who is already a user urges his friends to try, or simply shows already-eager friends how to do it.

But we need not rely on speculation, however plausible, that lowered prices and more abundant supplies would have increased heroin usage. Great Britain once followed such a policy and with almost exactly those results. Until the mid-1960's, British physicians were allowed to prescribe heroin to certain classes of addicts. (Possessing these drugs without a doctor's prescription remained a criminal offense.) For many years this policy worked well enough because the addict patients were typically middle-class people who had become dependent on opiate painkillers while undergoing hospital treatment. There was no drug culture. The British system worked for many years, not because it prevented drug abuse, but because there was no problem of drug abuse that would test the system.

All that changed in the 1960's. A few unscrupulous doctors began passing out heroin in wholesale amounts. One doctor prescribed almost 600,000 heroin tablets—that is, over thirteen pounds—in just one year. A youthful drug culture emerged with a demand for drugs far different from that of the older addicts. As a result, the British government required doctors to refer users to government-run clinics to receive their heroin.

But the shift to clinics did not curtail the growth in heroin use. Throughout the 1960's the number of addicts increased—the late John Kaplan of Stanford estimated by fivefold—in part as a result of the diversion of heroin from clinic patients to new users on the streets. An addict would bargain with the clinic doctor over how big a dose he would receive. The patient wanted as much as he could get, the doctor wanted to give as little as was needed. The patient had an advantage in this conflict because the doctor could not be certain how much was really needed. Many patients would use some of their "maintenance" dose and sell the remaining part to friends, thereby recruiting new addicts. As the clinics learned of this, they began to shift their treatment away from heroin and toward methadone, an addictive drug that, when taken orally, does not produce a "high" but will block the withdrawal pains associated with heroin abstinence.

Whether what happened in England in the 1960's was a mini-epidemic or an epidemic depends on whether one looks at numbers or at rates of change. Compared to the United States, the numbers were small. In 1960 there were 68 heroin addicts known to the British government; by 1968 there were 2,000 in treatment and many more who refused treatment. (They would refuse in part because they did not want to get methadone at a clinic if they could get heroin on the street.) Richard Hartnoll estimates that the actual number of addicts in England is five times the number officially registered. At a minimum, the number of British addicts increased by thirtyfold in ten years; the actual increase may have been much larger.

In the early 1980's the numbers began to rise again, and this time nobody doubted that a real epidemic was at hand. The increase was estimated to be 40 percent a year. By 1982 there were thought to be 20,000 heroin users in London alone. Geoffrey Pearson reports that many cities—Glasgow, Liverpool, Manchester, and Sheffield among them—were now experiencing a drug problem that once had been largely confined to London. The problem, again, was supply. The country was being flooded with cheap, high-quality heroin, first from Iran and then from Southeast Asia.

The United States began the 1960's with a much larger number of heroin addicts and probably a bigger at-risk population than was the case in Great Britain. Even though it would be foolhardy to suppose that the British system, if installed here, would have worked the same way or with the same results, it would be equally foolhardy to suppose that a combination of heroin available from leaky clinics and from street dealers who faced only minimal law-enforcement risks would not have produced a much greater increase in heroin use than we actually experienced. My guess is that if we had allowed either doctors or clinics to prescribe heroin, we would have had far worse results than were produced in Britain, if for no other reason than the vastly larger number of addicts with which we began. We would have had to find some way to police thousands (not scores) of physicians and hundreds (not dozens) of clinics. If the British civil service found it difficult to keep heroin in the hands of addicts and out of the hands of recruits when it was dealing with a few hundred people, how well would the American civil service have accomplished the same tasks when dealing with tens of thousands of people?

Back to the Future

Now cocaine, especially in its potent form, crack, is the focus of attention. Now as in 1972 the government is trying to reduce its use. Now as then some people are advocating legalization. Is there any more reason to yield to those arguments today than there was almost two decades ago?

I think not. If we had yielded in 1972 we almost certainly would have had today a permanent population of several million, not several hundred thousand, heroin addicts. If we yield now we will have a far more serious problem with cocaine.

Crack is worse than heroin by almost any measure. Heroin produces a pleasant drowsiness and, if hygienically administered, has only the physical side effects of constipation and sexual impotence. Regular heroin use incapacitates many users, especially poor ones, for any productive work or social responsibility. They will sit nodding on a street corner, helpless, but at least harmless. By contrast, regular cocaine use leaves the user neither helpless nor harmless. When smoked (as with crack) or injected, cocaine produces instant, intense, and short-lived euphoria. The experience generates a powerful desire to repeat it. If the drug is readily available, repeat use will occur. Those people who progress to "bingeing" on cocaine become devoted to the drug and its effects to the exclusion of almost all other considerations—job, family, children, sleep, food, even sex. Dr. Frank Gawin at Yale and Dr. Everett Ellinwood at Duke report that a substantial percentage of all high-dose, binge users become uninhibited, impulsive, hypersexual, compulsive, irritable, and hyperactive. Their moods vacillate dramatically, leading at times to violence and homicide.

Women are much more likely to use crack than heroin, and if they are pregnant, the effects on their babies are tragic. Douglas Besharov, who has been following the effects of drugs on infants for twenty years, writes that nothing he learned about heroin prepared him for the devastation of cocaine. Cocaine harms the fetus and can lead to physical deformities or neurological damage. Some crack babies have for all practical purposes suffered a disabling stroke while still in the womb. The long-term consequences of this brain damage are lowered cognitive ability and the onset of mood disorders. Besharov estimates that about 30,000 to 50,000 such babies are born every year, about 7,000 in New York City alone. There may be ways to treat such infants, but from everything we now know the treatment will be long, difficult, and expensive. Worse, the mothers who are most likely to produce crack babies are precisely the ones who, because of poverty or temperament, are least able and willing to obtain such treatment. In fact, anecdotal evidence suggests that crack mothers are likely to abuse their infants.

The notion that abusing drugs such as cocaine is a "victimless crime" is not only absurd but dangerous. Even ignoring the fetal drug syndrome, crack-dependent people are, like heroin addicts, individuals who regularly victimize their children by neglect, their spouses by improvidence, their employers by lethargy, and their coworkers by carelessness. Society is not and could never be a collection of autonomous individuals. We all have a stake in ensuring that each of us displays a minimal level of dignity, responsibility, and empathy. We cannot, of course, coerce people into goodness, but we can and should insist that some standards must be met if society itself—on which the very existence of the human personality depends—is to persist. Drawing the line that defines those standards is difficult and contentious, but if crack and heroin use do not fall below it, what does?

The advocates of legalization will respond by suggesting that my picture is overdrawn. Ethan Nadelmann of Princeton argues that the risk of legalization is less than most people suppose. Over 20 million Americans between the ages of eighteen and twenty-five have tried cocaine (according to a government survey), but only a quarter million use it daily. From this Nadelmann concludes that at most 3 percent of all young people who try cocaine develop a problem with it. The implication is clear: make the drug legal and we only have to worry about 3 percent of our youth.

The implication rests on a logical fallacy and a factual error. The fallacy is this: the percentage of occasional cocaine users who become binge users *when the drug is illegal* (and thus expensive and hard to find) tells us nothing about the percentage who will become dependent when the drug is legal (and thus cheap and abundant). Drs. Gawin and Ellinwood report, in common with several other researchers, that controlled or occasional use of cocaine changes to compulsive and frequent use "when access to the drug increases" or when the user switches from snorting to smoking. More cocaine more potently administered alters, perhaps sharply, the proportion of "controlled" users who become heavy users.

The factual error is this: the federal survey Nadelmann quotes was done in 1985, *before* crack had become common. Thus the probability of becoming dependent on cocaine was derived from the responses of users who snorted the drug. The speed and potency of cocaine's action increases dramatically when it is smoked. We do not yet know how greatly the advent of crack increases the risk of dependency, but all the clinical evidence suggests that the increase is likely to be large.

It is possible that some people will not become heavy users even when the drug is readily available in its most potent form. So far there are no scientific grounds for predicting who will and who will not become dependent. Neither socioeconomic background nor personality traits differentiate between casual and intensive users. Thus, the only way to settle the question of who is correct about the effect of easy availability on drug use, Nadelmann or Gawin and Ellinwood, is to try it and see. But that social experiment is so risky as to be no experiment at all, for if cocaine is legalized and if the rate of its abusive use increases dramatically, there is no way to put the genie back in the bottle, and it is not a kindly genie.

Have We Lost?

Many people who agree that there are risks in legalizing cocaine or heroin still favor it because, they think, we have lost the war on drugs. "Nothing we have done has worked" and the current federal policy is just "more of the same." Whatever the costs of greater drug use, surely they would be less than the costs of our present, failed efforts.

That is exactly what I was told in 1972—and heroin is not quite as bad a drug as cocaine. We did not surrender and we did not lose. We did not win, either. What the nation accomplished then was what most efforts to save people from themselves accomplish: the problem was contained and the number of victims minimized, all at a considerable cost in law enforcement and increased crime. Was the cost worth it? I think so, but others may disagree. What are the lives of would-be addicts worth? I recall some people saying to me then, "Let them kill themselves." I was appalled. Happily, such views did not prevail.

Have we lost today? Not at all. High-rate cocaine use is not commonplace. The National Institute of Drug Abuse (NIDA) reports that less than 5 percent of high-school seniors used cocaine within the last thirty days. Of course this survey misses young people who have dropped out of school and miscounts those who lie on the questionnaire, but even if we inflate the NIDA estimate by some plausible percentage, it is still not much above 5 percent. Medical examiners reported in 1987 that about 1,500 died from cocaine use; hospital emergency rooms reported about 30,000 admissions related to cocaine abuse.

These are not small numbers, but neither are they evidence of a nationwide plague that threatens to engulf us all. Moreover, cities vary greatly in the proportion of people who are involved with cocaine. To get city-level data we need to turn to drug tests carried out on arrested persons, who obviously are more likely to be drug users than the average citizen. The National Institute of Justice, through its Drug Use Forecasting (DUF) project, collects urinalysis data on arrests in 22 cities. As we have already seen, opiate (chiefly heroin) use has been flat or declining in most of these cities over the last decade. Cocaine use has gone up sharply, but with great variation among cities. New York, Philadelphia, and Washington, D.C., all report that two-thirds or more of their arrestees tested positive for cocaine, but in Portland, San Antonio, and Indianapolis the percentage was one-third or less.

In some neighborhoods, of course, matters have reached crisis proportions. Gangs control the streets, shootings terrorize residents, and drug-dealing occurs in plain view. The police seem barely able to contain matters. But in these neighborhoods—unlike at Palo Alto cocktail parties—the people are not calling for legalization, they are calling for help. And often not much help has come. Many cities are willing to do almost anything about the drug problem except spend more money on it. The federal government cannot change that; only local voters and politicians can. It is not clear that they will.

It took about ten years to contain heroin. We have had experience with crack for only about three or four years. Each year we spend perhaps $11 billion on law enforcement (and some of that goes to deal with marijuana) and perhaps $2 billion on treatment. Large sums, but not sums that should lead anyone to say, "We just can't afford this any more."

The illegality of drugs increases crime, partly because some users turn to crime to pay for their habits, partly because some users are stimulated by certain drugs (such as crack or PCP) to act more violently or ruthlessly than they otherwise would, and partly because criminal organizations seeking to control drug supplies use force to manage their markets. These also are serious costs, but no one knows how much they would be reduced if drugs were legalized. Addicts would no longer steal to pay black-market prices for drugs, a real gain. But some, perhaps a great deal, of that gain would be offset by the great increase in the number of addicts. These people, nodding on heroin or living in the delusion-ridden high of cocaine, would hardly be ideal employees. Many would steal simply to support themselves, since snatch-and-grab, opportunistic crime can be managed even by people unable to hold a regular job or plan an elaborate crime. Those British addicts who get their supplies from government clinics are not models of law-abiding decency. Most are in crime, and though their per-capita rate of criminality may be lower thanks to the cheapness of their drugs, the total volume of crime they produce may be quite large. Of course, society could decide to support all unemployable addicts on welfare, but that would mean that gains from lowered rates of crime would have to be offset by large increases in welfare budgets.

Proponents of legalization claim that the costs of having more addicts around would be largely if not entirely offset by having more money available with which to treat and care for them. The money would come from taxes levied on the sale of heroin and cocaine.

To obtain this fiscal dividend, however, legalization's supporters must first solve an economic dilemma. If they want to raise a lot of money to pay for welfare and treatment, the tax rate on the drugs will have to be quite high. Even if they themselves do not want a high rate, the politicians' love of "sin taxes" would probably guarantee that it would be high anyway. But the higher the tax, the higher the price of the drug, and the higher the price the greater the likelihood that addicts will turn to crime to find the money for it and that criminal organizations will be formed to sell tax-free drugs at below-market rates. If we managed to keep taxes (and thus prices) low, we would get that much less money to pay for welfare and treatment and more people could afford to become addicts. There may be an optimal tax rate for drugs that maximizes revenue while minimizing crime, bootlegging, and the recruitment of new addicts, but our experience with alcohol does not suggest that we know how to find it.

. . .

If I Am Wrong . . .

No one can know what our society would be like if we changed the law to make access to cocaine, heroin, and PCP easier. I believe, for reasons given, that the result would be a sharp increase in use, a more widespread degradation of the human personality, and a greater rate of accidents and violence.

I may be wrong. If I am, then we will needlessly have incurred heavy costs in law enforcement and some forms of criminality. But if I am right, and the legalizers prevail anyway, then we will have consigned millions of people, hundreds of thousands of infants, and hundreds of neighborhoods to a life of oblivion and disease. To the lives and families destroyed by alcohol we will have added countless more destroyed by cocaine, heroin, PCP, and whatever else a basement scientist can invent.

Human character is formed by society; indeed, human character is inconceivable without society, and good character is less likely in a bad society. Will we, in the name of an abstract doctrine of radical individualism, and with the false comfort of suspect predictions, decide to take the chance that somehow individual decency can survive amid a more general level of deregulation?

I think not. The American people are too wise for that, whatever the academic essayists and cocktail-party pundits may say. But if Americans today are less wise than I suppose, then Americans at some future time will look back on us now and wonder, what kind of people were they that they could have done such a thing?

QUESTIONS FOR REFLECTION

1. Wilson contends that the war on drugs has been successful. What evidence does he adduce in support of this claim?
2. Wilson believes that legalizing drugs would increase drug use significantly, and he supports his view with an economic argument. What is that argument? Do you find it persuasive?
3. Wilson talks about heroin and cocaine, but not marijuana. Which of his arguments would apply to marijuana, in your view? Which would not?
4. Wilson rejects the view that cocaine use is a "victimless crime"—that is, a self-regarding act. Why?
5. Wilson does not accept Mill's harm principle; he advocates a rather different conception of individual liberty and societal responsibility. What is Wilson's conception? What role does it play in his argument? Compare Wilson's conception to that of Aristotle.
6. Many advocates of legalization recommend treatment over incarceration. Wilson, however, is skeptical of drug treatment, at least in the absence of laws outlawing drug use. Why? Do you find his arguments persuasive?

PORNOGRAPHY

Most philosophers defend freedom of thought, of speech, and of the press. Some, like Milton and Mill, are strongly committed to these freedoms; others, like Burke, acknowledge that they are goods but believe that they must be balanced against other goods. Nevertheless, virtually no one believes that these freedoms are completely unrestricted. Slander, libel, false advertising, harassment, inciting to riot, and public endangerment—shouting "Fire!" in a crowded theater, for example—have often been held up as exceptions. Thus the problem of determining the proper limits of these freedoms arises.

Pornography raises especially difficult questions about limits on freedom of thought, speech, and the press. The exceptions mentioned above are often thought to be exceptions because they risk or cause harm that outweighs their values as communications. Many people believe pornography to be harmful and base their opposition to it on that ground. But any harms caused by pornography are subtler and harder to detect than those of inciting to riot, for example. Consequently, the question of whether pornography is harmful has become an important focus of debate.

Also, the harm done by a speaker is usually weighed against the value of the communication. It is harder to slander a public official than a private citizen, for example, because the public's need for information about officials of government is much greater than its need for information about you or me; communication about the beliefs and behavior of public officials has greater value than communication about the rest of us. But what does pornography communicate? Often, it is hard to discern any message at all. Is pornography ever communication? These problems make weighing the value of a piece of pornography against its harmful effects very difficult.

Moreover, most of the arguments that Milton and Mill advance in favor of free speech rest on the supposition that speech communicates something that might be true or false. Mill argues that an opinion might be true; that, even if false, it might contain part of the truth; and that, even if totally false, its combat with the truth helps keep the truth alive. This argument makes sense for opinions, for propositions or bits of information that might be true or false. But does it make any sense applied to *Sex Orgies Illustrated?* Or *Deep Throat?* Or a *Playboy* centerfold? If not, on what does the case for freedom of pornographic speech rest?

The United States Supreme Court, in *Miller* v. *California,* decided that the government may regulate pornographic materials, banning those that are obscene. The Court moreover proposed criteria for determining whether something is obscene: (a) it must, judged by the average person applying contemporary community standards, appeal to a prurient (that is, arousing and unwholesome) interest in sex; (b) it must depict or describe sexual conduct in a patently offensive way; and (c) it must lack serious literary, artistic, political, or scientific value. The first two criteria pertain to harm; the third, to lack of any positive communicative value that might balance the harm.

Dissenters to the decisions have argued that sexual expression deserves protection against government interference. Some hold that such an expression may have positive value for individuals that outweighs any harm it causes; some claim that freedoms of thought, speech, and the press are all forms of freedom of expression, which is what properly defines the limits of government authority. Others believe that there is no fair and accurate way to distinguish obscene from nonobscene materials.

A recent and particularly crucial freedom of expression case is *Reno* v. *ACLU,* in which the Supreme Court struck down the Communications Decency Act as unconstitutional. The act regulated and provided criminal penalties for transmitting obscene or indecent "patently offensive" messages on the Internet. Justice John Paul Stevens, writing for the majority, found that the act abridged the freedom of speech guaranteed by the First Amendment. It made no mention of serious artistic or literary value, thus ignoring any positive value of a message that might balance its offensive or harmful aspects. More seriously, it went far beyond limiting offense by regulating the time, place, and manner of speech; it sought to regulate speech on the basis of its content.

Catharine MacKinnon asserts that pornography is a practice of sex discrimination and thus a violation of women's civil rights. She argues for the morality and constitutionality of ordinances that prohibit pornography. The Attorney General's Commission on Pornography argues at length that certain kinds of pornography, particularly those involving violence, are harmful and ought to be restricted. The commission argues that these forms of pornography harm not only the "users" (the viewers of the material) but also others with whom the users come into contact. The commission holds, however, that other forms of pornography see relatively harmless and should escape any government restrictions.

Wendy McElroy argues that feminism has exactly the opposite implications. Women who choose to produce or consume pornography are exercising freedom; MacKinnon's restrictions on pornography thus restrict the liberty of women. In general, censorship on grounds of sex discrimination treats woman as children whose interests must be protected by law because they are incapable of taking responsibility for their own actions.

CHIEF JUSTICE WARREN BURGER AND JUSTICE WILLIAM O. DOUGLAS

Majority and Dissenting Opinions in Miller *v.* California (1973)

(Source: Miller *v.* California *413 U.S. [1973]. Most legal references have been omitted.)*

. . . Mr. Chief Justice Burger delivered the opinion of the Court. . . .

I

This case involves the application of a State's criminal obscenity statute to a situation in which sexually explicit materials have been thrust by aggressive sales action upon unwilling recipients who had in no way indicated any desire to receive such materials. This Court has recognized that the States have a legitimate interest in prohibiting dissemination or exhibition of obscene material when the mode of dissemination carries with it a significant danger of offending the sensibilities of unwilling recipients or of exposure to juveniles. It is in this context that we are called on to define the standards which must be used to identify obscene material that a State may regulate without infringing on the First Amendment as applicable to the States through the Fourteenth Amendment. . . .

Apart from the initial formulation in the *Roth* case, no majority of the Court has at any given time been able to agree on a standard to determine what constitutes obscene, pornographic material subject to regulation under the States' police power. We have seen "a variety of views among the members of the Court unmatched in any other course of constitutional adjudication." This is not remarkable, for in the area of freedom of speech and press the courts must always remain sensitive to any infringement on genuinely serious literary, artistic, political, or scientific expression. This is an area in which there are few eternal verities. . . .

II

This much has been categorically settled by the Court, that obscene material is unprotected by the First Amendment. We acknowledge, however, the inherent dangers of undertaking to regulate any form of expression. State statutes designed to regulate obscene materials must be carefully limited. As a result, we now confine the permissible scope of such regulation to works which depict or describe sexual conduct. That conduct must be specifically defined by the applicable state law, as written or authoritatively construed. A state offense must also be limited to works which, taken as a whole, appeal to the prurient interest in sex, which portray sexual conduct in a patently offensive way, and which, taken as a whole, do not have serious literary, artistic, political, or scientific value.

The basic guidelines for the trier of fact must be: (a) whether "the average person, applying contemporary community standards" would find that the work, taken as a whole, appeals to the prurient interest; (b) whether the work depicts or describes, in a patently offensive way, sexual conduct specifically defined by the applicable state law; and (c) whether the work, taken as a whole, lacks serious literary, artistic, political, or scientific value. We do not adopt as a constitutional standard the "*utterly* without redeeming social value" test of *Memoirs* v. *Massachusetts;* that concept has never commanded the adherence of more than three Justices at one time.

We emphasize that it is not our function to propose regulatory schemes for the States. That must await their concrete legislative efforts. It is possible, however, to give a few. plain examples of what a state statute could define for regulation under part (b) of the standard announced in this opinion:

(a) Patently offensive representations or descriptions of ultimate sexual acts, normal or perverted, actual or simulated.
(b) Patently offensive representations or descriptions of masturbation, excretory functions, and lewd exhibition of the genitals.

Sex and nudity may not be exploited without limit by films or pictures exhibited or sold in places of public accommodation any more than live sex and nudity can be exhibited or sold without limit in such public places. At a minimum, prurient, patently offensive depiction or description of sexual conduct must have serious literary, artistic, political, or scientific value to merit First Amendment protection. For example, medical books for the education of physicians and related personnel necessarily use graphic illustrations and descriptions of human anatomy. In resolving the inevitably sensitive questions of fact and law, we must continue to rely on the jury system, accompanied by the safeguards that judges, rules of evidence, presumption of innocence, and other protective features provide, as we do with rape, murder, and a host of other offenses against sdciety and its individual members.

Mr. Justice Brennan, author of the opinions of the Court, or the plurality opinions, in *Roth* v. *United States; Jacobellis* v. *Ohio; Ginzburg* v. *United States* (1966); *Mishkin* v. *New York* (1966); and *Memoirs* v. *Massachusetts,* has abandoned his former position and now maintains that no formulation of this Court, the Congress, or the States can adequately distinguish obscene material unprotected by the First Amendment from protected expression. Paradoxically, Mr. Justice Brennan indicates that suppression of unprotected obscene material is permissible to avoid exposure to unconsenting adults, as in this case, and to juveniles, although he gives no indication of how the division between protected and unprotected materials may be drawn with greater precision for these purposes than for regulation of commercial exposure to consenting adults only. Nor does he indicate where in the Constitution he finds the authority to distinguish between a willing "adult" one month past the state law age of majority and a willing "juvenile" one month younger.

Under the holdings announced today, no one will be subject to prosecution for the sale or exposure of obscene materials unless these materials depict or describe patently offensive "hard core" sexual conduct specifically defined by the regulating state law, as written or construed. We are satisfied that these specific prerequisites will provide fair notice to a dealer in such materials that his public and commercial activities may bring prosecution. If the inability to define regulated materials with ultimate, god-like precision altogether removes the power of the States or the Congress to regulate, then "hard core" pornography may be exposed without limit to the juvenile, the passerby, and the consenting adult alike, as, indeed, Mr. Justice Douglas contends. In this belief, however, Mr. Justice Douglas now stands alone.

Mr. Justice Brennan also emphasizes "institutional stress" in justification of his change of view. Noting that "[t]he number of obscenity cases on our docket gives ample testimony to the burden that has been placed upon this Court," he quite rightly remarks that the examination of contested materials "is hardly a source of edification to the members of this Court." He also notes, and we agree, that "uncertainty of the standards creates a continuing source of tension between state and federal courts. . . ." "The problem is . . . that one cannot say with certainty that material is obscene until at least five members of this Court, applying inevitably obscure standards, have pronounced it so." . . .

It is certainly true that the absence, since *Roth,* of a single majority view of this Court as to proper standards for testing obscenity has placed a strain on both state and federal courts. But today, for the first time since *Roth* was decided in 1957, a majority of this Court has agreed on concrete guidelines to isolate "hard core" pornography from expression protected by the First Amendment. . . .

III

Under a National Constitution, fundamental First Amendment limitations on the powers of the States do not vary from community to community, but this does not mean that there are, or should or can be, fixed, uniform national standards of precisely what appeals to the "prurient interest" or is "patently offensive." These are essentially questions of fact, and our Nation is simply too big and too diverse for this Court to reasonably expect that such standards could be articulated for all 50 States in a single formulation, even assuming the prerequisite consensus exists. When triers of fact are asked to decide whether "the average person, applying contemporary community standards" would consider certain materials "prurient," it would be unrealistic to require that the answer be based on some abstract formulation. The adversary system, with lay jurors as the usual ultimate factfinders in criminal prosecutions, has historically permitted triers of fact to draw on the standards of their community, guided always by limiting instructions on the law. To require a State to structure obscenity proceedings around evidence of a *national* "community standard" would be an exercise in futility. . . .

It is neither realistic nor constitutionally sound to read the First Amendment as requiring that the people of Maine or Mississippi accept public depiction of conduct found tolerable in Las Vegas, or New York City. People in different States vary in their tastes and attitudes, and this diversity is not to be strangled by the absolutism of imposed uniformity. As the Court made clear in *Mishkin v. New York,* the primary concern with requiring a jury to apply the standard of "the average person, applying contemporary community standards" is to be certain that, so far as material is not aimed at a deviant group, it will be judged by its impact on an average person, rather than a particularly susceptible or sensitive person—or indeed a totally insensitive one. . . . We hold that the requirement that the jury evaluate the materials with reference to "contemporary standards of the State of California" serves this protective purpose and is constitutionally adequate.

IV

The dissenting Justices sound the alarm of repression. But, in our view, to equate the free and robust exchange of ideas and political debate with commercial exploitation of obscene material demeans the grand conception of the First Amendment and its high purposes in the historic struggle for freedom. It is a "misuse of the great guarantees of free speech and free press. . . ." The First Amendment protects works which, taken as a whole, have serious literary, artistic, political, or scientific value, regardless of whether the government or a majority of the people approve of the ideas these works represent. "The protection given speech and press was fashioned to assure unfettered interchange of ideas for the bringing about of political and social changes desired by the people" (emphasis added). But the public portrayal of hard-core sexual conduct for its own sake, and for the ensuing commercial gain, is a different matter.

There is no evidence, empirical or historical, that the stern 19th century American censorship of public distribution and display of material relating to sex in any way limited or affected expression of serious literary, artistic, political, or scientific ideas. On the contrary, it is beyond any question that the era following Thomas Jefferson to Theodore Roosevelt was an "extraordinarily vigorous period," not just in economics and politics, but in *belles lettres* and in "the outlying fields of social and political philosophies." We do not see the harsh hand of censorship of ideas—good or bad, sound or unsound—and "repression" of political liberty lurking in every state regulation of commercial exploitation of human interest in sex.

Mr. Justice Brennan finds "it is hard to see how state-ordered regimentation of our minds can ever be forestalled." These doleful anticipations assume that courts cannot distinguish commerce in ideas, protected by the First Amendment, from commercial exploitation of obscene material. Moreover, state regulation of hard-core pornography so as to make it unavailable to nonadults, a regulation which Mr. Justice Brennan finds constitutionally permissible, has all the elements of "censorship" for adults; indeed even more rigid enforcement techniques may be called for with such dichotomy of regulation. One can concede that the "sexual revolution" of recent years may have had useful byproducts in striking layers of prudery from a subject long irrationally kept from needed ventilation. But it does not follow that no regulation of patently offensive "hard core" materials is needed or permissible; civilized people do not allow unregulated access to heroin because it is a derivative of medicinal morphine.

In sum, we (a) reaffirm the *Roth* holding that obscene material is not protected by the First Amendment; (b) hold that such material can be regulated by the States, subject to the specific safeguards enunciated above, without a showing that the material is "*utterly* without redeeming social value"; and (c) hold that obscenity is to be determined by applying "contemporary community standards," not "national standards." The judgment of the Appellate Department of the Superior Court, Orange County, California, is vacated and the case remanded to that court for further proceedings not inconsistent with the First Amendment standards established by this opinion. . . .

Mr. Justice Douglas, dissenting.

I

Today we leave open the way for California to send a man to prison for distributing brochures that advertise books and a movie under freshly written standards defining obscenity which until today's decision were never the part of any law.

The Court has worked hard to define obscenity and concededly has failed. In *Roth v. United States*, it ruled that "[o]bscene material is material which deals with sex in a manner appealing to prurient interest." Obscenity, it was said, was rejected by the First Amendment because it is "utterly without redeeming social importance." The presence of a "prurient interest" was to be determined by "contemporary community standards." That test, it has been said, could not be determined by one standard here and another standard there, but "on the basis of a national standard." My Brother Stewart in *Jacobellis* commented that the difficulty of the Court in giving content to obscenity was that it was "faced with the task of trying to define what may be indefinable."

In *Memoirs v. Massachusetts* the *Roth* test was elaborated to read as follows: "[T]hree elements must coalesce: it must be established that (a) the dominant theme of the material taken as a whole appeals to a prurient interest in sex; (b) the material is patently offensive because it affronts contemporary community standards relating to the description or representation of sexual matters; and (c) the material is utterly without redeeming social value."

In *Ginzburg v. United States*, a publisher was sent to prison, not for the kind of books and periodicals he sold, but for the manner in which the publications were advertised. The "leer of the sensualist" was said to permeate the advertisements. The Court said, "Where the purveyor's sole emphasis is on the sexually provocative aspects of his publications, that fact may be decisive, in the determination of obscenity." As Mr. Justice Black said in dissent, ". . . Ginzburg . . . is now finally and authoritatively condemned to serve five years in prison for distributing printed matter about sex which neither Ginzburg nor anyone else could possibly have known to be criminal." That observation by Mr. Justice Black is underlined by the fact that the *Ginzburg* decision was five to four.

A further refinement was added by *Ginzburg v. New York*, where the Court held that "it was not irrational for the legislature to find that exposure to material condemned by the statute is harmful to minors."

But even those members of this Court who had created the new and changing standards of "obscenity" could not agree on their application. Some condemn it if its "dominant tendency might be to "deprave or corrupt' a reader." Others look not to the content of the book but to whether it is advertised "to appeal to the erotic interests of customers." Some condemn only "hard-core pornography"; but even then a true definition is lacking. It has indeed been said of that definition, "I could never succeed in [defining it] intelligibly," but "I know it when I see it."

Today we would add a new three-pronged test: "(a) whether 'the average person, applying contemporary community standards' would find that the work, taken as a whole, appeals to the prurient interest, . . . (b) whether the work depicts or describes, in a patently offensive way, sexual conduct specifically defined by the applicable state law, and (c) whether the work, taken as a whole, lacks serious literary, artistic, political, or scientific value."

Those are the standards we ourselves have written into the Constitution. Yet how under these vague tests can we sustain convictions for the sale of an article prior to the time when some court has declared it to be obscene?

Today the Court retreats from the earlier formulations of the constitutional test and undertakes to make new definitions. This effort, like the earlier ones, is earnest and well intentioned. The difficulty is that we do not deal with constitutional terms, since "obscenity" is not mentioned in the Constitution or Bill of Rights; And the First Amendment makes no such exception from "the press" which it undertakes to protect nor, as I have said on other occasions, in an exception necessarily implied, for there was no recognized exception to the free press at the time the Bill of Rights was adopted which treated "obscene" publications differently from other types of papers, magazines, and books. So there are no constitutional guidelines for deciding what is and what is not "obscene." The Court is at large because we deal with tastes and standards of literature. What shocks me may be sustenance for my neighbor. What causes one person to boil up in rage over one pamphlet or movie may reflect only his neurosis, not shared by others. We deal here with a regime of censorship which, if adopted, should be done by constitutional amendments after full debate by the people.

Obscenity cases usually generate tremendous emotional outbursts. They have no business being in the courts. If a constitutional amendment authorized censorship, the censor would probably be an administrative agency. Then criminal prosecutions could follow as, if, and when publishers defied the censor and sold their literature. Under that regime a publisher would know when he was on dangerous ground. Under the present regime—whether the old standards or the new ones are used—the criminal law becomes a trap. A brand new test would put a publisher behind bars under a new law improvised by the courts after the publication. That was done in *Ginzburg* and has all the evils of an *ex post facto* law.

My contention is that until a civil proceeding has placed a tract beyond the pale, no criminal prosecution should be sustained. For no more vivid illustration of vague and uncertain laws could be designed than those we have fashioned. As Mr. Justice Harlan has said:

"The upshot of all this divergence in viewpoint is that anyone who undertakes to examine the Court's decisions since *Roth* which have held particular material obscene or not obscene would find himself in utter bewilderment." *Interstate Circuit, Inc.* v. *Dallas.*

. . . In any case—certainly when constitutional rights are concerned—we should not allow men to go to prison or be fined when they had no "fair warning" that what they did was criminal conduct.

[II . . .]

III

While the right to know is the corollary of the right to speak or publish, no one can be forced by government to listen to disclosure that he finds offensive. That was the basis of my dissent in *Public Utilities Comm'n* v. *Pollak*, where I protested against making streetcar passengers a "captive" audience. There is no "captive audience" problem in these obscenity cases. No one is being compelled to look or to listen. Those who enter newsstands or bookstalls may be offended by what they see. But they are not compelled by the State to frequent those places; and it is only state or governmental action against which the First Amendment, applicable to the States by virtue of the Fourteenth, raises a ban.

The idea that the First Amendment permits government to ban publications that are "offensive" to some people puts an ominous gloss on freedom of the press. That test would make it possible to ban any paper or any journal or magazine in some benighted place. The First Amendment was designed "to invite dispute," to induce "a condition of unrest," to "create dissatisfaction with conditions as they are," and even to stir "people to anger." The idea that the First Amendment permits punishment for ideas that are "offensive" to the particular judge or jury sitting in judgment is astounding. No greater leveler of speech or literature has even been designed. To give the power to the censor, as we do today, is to make a sharp and radical break with the traditions of a free society. The First Amendment was not fashioned as a vehicle for dispensing tranquilizers to the people. Its prime function was to keep debate open to "offensive" as well as to "staid" people. The tendency throughout history has been to subdue the individual and to exalt the power of government. The use of the standard "offensive" gives authority to government that cuts the very vitals out of the First Amendment. As is intimated by the Court's opinion, the materials before us may be garbage. But so is much of what is said in political campaigns, in the daily press, on TV, or over the radio. By reason of the First Amendment—and solely because of it—speakers and publishers have not been threatened or subdued because their thoughts and ideas may be "offensive" to some.

The standard "offensive" is unconstitutional in yet another way. In *Coates* v. *City of Cincinnati,* we had before us a municipal ordinance that made it a crime for three or more persons to assemble on a street and conduct themselves "in a manner annoying to persons passing by." We struck it down, saying: "If three or more people meet together on a sidewalk or street corner, they must conduct themselves so as not to annoy any police officer or other person who should happen to pass by. In our opinion this ordinance is unconstitutionally vague because it subjects the exercise of the right of assembly to an unascertainable standard, and unconstitutionally broad because it authorizes the punishment of constitutionally protected conduct.

"Conduct that annoys some people does not annoy others. Thus, the ordinance is vague, not in the sense that it requires a person to conform his conduct to an imprecise but comprehensive normative standard, but rather in the sense that no standard of conduct is specified at all."

How we can deny Ohio the convenience of punishing people who "annoy" others and allow California power to punish people who publish materials "offensive" to some people is difficult to square with constitutional requirements.

If there are to be restraints on what is obscene, then a constitutional amendment should be the way of achieving the end. There are societies where religion and mathematics are the only free segments. It would be a dark day for America if that were our destiny. But the people can make it such if they choose to write obscenity into the Constitution and define it.

We deal with highly emotional, not rational, questions. To many the Song of Solomon is obscene. I do not think we, the judges, were ever given the constitutional power to make definitions of obscenity. If it is to be defined, let the people debate and decide by a constitutional amendment what they want to ban as obscene and what standards they want the legislatures and the courts to apply. Perhaps the people will decide that the path towards a mature, integrated society requires that all ideas competing for acceptance must have no censor. Perhaps they will decide otherwise. Whatever the choice, the courts will have some guidelines. Now we have none except our own predilections. . . .

QUESTIONS FOR REFLECTION

1. Explain the obscenity test proposed by the Court.
2. Many critics, including Justice Douglas, have attacked the Court's test for obscenity as vague. What sources of vagueness do you see in the Court's criteria? How might they be eliminated? Should they be eliminated?
3. Justice Brennan complains that it is impossible to distinguish obscene from nonobscene materials accurately. How does the majority defend its view against this complaint?
4. Why does the majority believe that obscenity is not protected by freedom of speech?
5. How does Justice Douglas argue for his contention that "obscenity cases . . . have no business being in the courts"? Do you agree?
6. Offensiveness forms part of the test of obscenity. Justice Douglas contends that offense does not justify government restriction. What are his arguments? How would Mill recommend treating offensive material? What is the difference between offense and harm?

CATHARINE MACKINNON

Pornography, Civil Rights, and Speech

Catharine MacKinnon is Elizabeth A. Long Professor of Law at the University of Michigan. (Source: Reprinted by permission of the Harvard Civil Rights/Civil Liberties Law Review. *Copyright © 1985 by the President and Fellows of Harvard College.)*

. . . There is a belief that this is a society in which women and men are basically equals. Room for marginal corrections is conceded, flaws are known to exist, attempts are made to correct what are conceived as occasional lapses from the basic condition of sex equality. Sex discrimination law has concentrated most of its focus on these occasional lapses. It is difficult to overestimate the extent to which this belief in equality is an article of faith for most people, including most women, who wish to live in self-respect in an internal universe, even (perhaps especially) if not in the world. It is also partly an expression of natural law thinking: if we are inalienably equal, we can't "really" be degraded.

This is a world in which it is worth trying. In this world of presumptive equality, people make money based on their training or abilities or diligence or qualifications. They are employed and advanced on the basis of merit. In this world of just deserts, if someone is abused, it is thought to violate the basic rules of the community. If it doesn't, victims are seen to have done something they could have chosen to do differently, by exercise of will or better judgment. Maybe such people have placed themselves in a situation of vulnerability to physical abuse. Maybe they have done something provocative. Or maybe they were just unusually unlucky. In such a world, if such a person has an experience, there are words for it. When they speak and say it, they are listened to. If they write about it, they will be published. If certain experiences are never spoken about, if certain people or issues are seldom heard from, it is supposed that silence has been chosen. The law, including much of the law of sex discrimination and the First Amendment, operates largely within the realm of these beliefs.

Feminism is the discovery that women do not live in this world, that the person occupying this realm is a man, so much more a man if he is white and wealthy. This world of potential credibility, authority, security, and just rewards, recognition of one's identity and capacity, is a world that some people do inhabit as a condition of birth, with variations among them. It is not a basic condition accorded humanity in this society, but a prerogative of status, a privilege, among other things, of gender.

I call this a discovery because it has not been an assumption. Feminism is the first theory, the first practice, the first movement, to take seriously the situation of all women from the point of view of all women, both on our situation and on social life as a whole. The discovery has therefore been made that the implicit social content of humanism, as well as the standpoint from which legal method has been designed and injuries have been defined, has not been women's standpoint. Defining feminism in a way that connects epistemology with power as the politics of women's point of view, this discovery can be summed up by saying that women live in another world: specifically, a world of *not* equality, a world of inequality. . . .

. . . In pornography, there it is, in one place, all of the abuses that women had to struggle so long even to begin to articulate, all the *unspeakable* abuse: the rape, the battery, the sexual harassment, the prostitution, and the sexual abuse of children. Only in the pornography it is called something else: sex, sex, sex, sex, and sex, respectively. Pornography sexualizes rape, battery, sexual harassment, prostitution, and child sexual abuse; it thereby celebrates, promotes, authorizes, and legitimizes them. More generally, it eroticizes the dominance and submission that is the dynamic common to them all. It makes hierarchy sexy and calls that "the truth about sex" or just a mirror of reality. Through this process pornography constructs what a woman is as what men want from sex. This is what the pornography means.

Pornography constructs what a woman is in terms of its view of what men want sexually, such that acts of rape, battery, sexual harassment, prostitution, and sexual abuse of children become acts of sexual equality. Pornography's world of equality is a harmonious and balanced place. Men and women are perfectly complementary and perfectly bipolar. . . .

. . . There, women substantively desire dispossession and cruelty. We desperately want to be bound, battered, tortured, humiliated, and killed. Or, to be fair to the soft core, merely taken and used. This is erotic to the male point of view. Subjection itself, with self-determination ecstatically relinquished, is the content of women's sexual desire and desirability. Women are there to be violated and possessed, men to violate and possess us, either on screen or by camera or pen on behalf of the consumer. On a simple descriptive level, the inequality of hierarchy, of which gender is the primary one, seems necessary for sexual arousal to work. Other added inequalities identify various pornographic genres or subthemes, although they are always added through gender: age, disability, homosexuality, animals, objects, race (including anti-Semitism), and so on. Gender is never irrelevant.

What pornography *does* goes beyond its content: it eroticizes hierarchy, it sexualizes inequality. It makes dominance and submission into sex. Inequality is its central dynamic; the illusion of freedom coming together with the reality of force is central to its working. Perhaps because this is a bourgeois culture, the victim must look free, appear to be freely acting. Choice is how she got there. Willing is what she is when she is being equal. It seems equally important that then and there she actually be forced and that forcing be communicated on some level, even if only through still photos of her in postures of receptivity and access, available for penetration. Pornography in this view is a form of forced sex, a practice of sexual politics, an institution of gender inequality.

From this perspective, pornography is neither harmless fantasy nor a corrupt and confused misrepresentation of an otherwise natural and healthy sexual situation. It institutionalizes the sexuality of male supremacy, fusing the erotization of dominance and submission with the social construction of male and female. To the extent that gender is sexual, pornography is part of constituting the meaning of that sexuality. Men treat women as who they see women as being. Pornography constructs who that is. Men's power over women means that the way men see women defines who women can be. Pornography is that way. Pornography is not imagery in some relation to a reality elsewhere constructed. It is not a distortion, reflection, projection, expression, fantasy, representation, or symbol either. It is a sexual reality.

. . . Pornography *participates* in its audience's eroticism through creating an accessible sexual object, the possession and consumption of which *is* male sexuality, as socially constructed; to be consumed and possessed as which, *is* female sexuality, as socially constructed; pornography is a process that constructs it that way.

The object world is constructed according to how it looks with respect to its possible uses. Pornography defines women by how we look according to how we can be sexually used. Pornography codes how to look at women, so you know what you can do with one when you see one. Gender is an assignment made visually, both originally and in everyday life. A sex object is defined on the basis of its looks, in terms of its usability for sexual pleasure, such that both the looking—the quality of the gaze, including its point of view—and the definition according to use become eroticized as part of the sex itself. This is what the feminist concept "sex object" means. In this sense, sex in life is no less mediated than it is in art. Men have sex with their image of a woman. It is not that life and art imitate each other; in this sexuality, they *are* each other.

To give a set of rough epistemological translations, to defend pornography as consistent with the equality of the sexes is to defend the subordination of women to men as sexual equality. What in the pornographic view is love and romance looks a great deal like hatred and torture to the feminist. Pleasure and eroticism become violation. Desire appears as lust for dominance and submission. The vulnerability of women's projected sexual availability, that acting we are allowed (that is, asking to be acted upon), is victimization. Play conforms to scripted roles. Fantasy expresses ideology, is not exempt from it. Admiration of natural physical beauty becomes objectification. Harmlessness becomes harm. Pornography is a harm of male supremacy made difficult to see because of its pervasiveness, potency, and, principally, because of its success in making the world a pornographic place. Specifically, its harm cannot be discerned, and will not be addressed, if viewed and approached neutrally, because it *is* so much of "what is." In other words, to the extent pornography succeeds in constructing social reality, it becomes invisible as harm. If we live in a world that pornography creates through the power of men in a male-dominated situation, the issue is not what the harm of pornography is, but how that harm is to become visible.

Obscenity law provides a very different analysis and conception of the problem of pornography. In 1973 the legal definition of obscenity became that which the average person, applying contemporary community standards, would find that, taken as a whole, appeals to the prurient interest; that which depicts or describes in a patently offensive way—you feel like you're a cop reading someone's *Miranda* rights—sexual conduct specifically defined by the applicable state law; and that which, taken as a whole, lacks serious literary, artistic, political or scientific value. Feminism doubts whether the average person gender-neutral exists; has more questions about the content and process of defining what community standards are than it does about deviations from them; wonders why prurience counts but powerlessness does not and why sensibilities are better protected from offense than women are from exploitation; defines sexuality, and thus its violation and expropriation, more broadly than does state law; and questions why a body of law that has not in practice been able to tell rape from intercourse should, without further guidance, be entrusted with telling pornography from anything less. Taking the work "as a whole" ignores that which the victims of pornography have long known: legitimate settings diminish the perception of injury done to those whose trivialization and objectification they contextualize. Besides, and this is a heavy one, if a woman is subjected, why should it matter that the work has other value? Maybe what redeems the work's value is what enhances its injury to women, not to mention that existing standards of literature, art, science, and politics, examined in a feminist light, are remarkably consonant with pornography's mode, meaning, and message. And finally—first and foremost, actually—although the subject of these materials is overwhelmingly women, their contents almost entirely made up of women's bodies, our invisibility has been such, our equation as a sex *with* sex has been such, that the law of obscenity has never even considered pornography a women's issue.

Obscenity, in this light, is a moral idea, an idea about judgments of good and bad. Pornography, by contrast, is a political practice, a practice of power and powerlessness. Obscenity is ideational and abstract; pornography is concrete and substantive. The two concepts represent two entirely different things. Nudity, excess of candor, arousal or excitement, prurient appeal, illegality of the acts depicted, and unnaturalness or perversion are all qualities that bother obscenity law when sex is depicted or portrayed. Sex forced on real women so that it can be sold at a profit and forced on other real women; women's bodies trussed and maimed and raped and made into things to be hurt and obtained and accessed, and this presented as the nature of women in a way that is acted on and acted out, over and over; the coercion that is visible and the coercion that has become invisible—this and more bothers feminists about pornography. Obscenity as such probably does little harm. Pornography is integral to attitudes and behaviors of violence and discrimination that define the treatment and status of half the population. . . .

QUESTIONS FOR REFLECTION

1. What is feminism, according to MacKinnon?
2. Why, in MacKinnon's view, is pornography discriminatory?
3. What are MacKinnon's arguments against the *Miller* decision? How might a defender of *Miller* respond?
4. How does MacKinnon distinguish obscenity from pornography?
5. To what extent is MacKinnon's position compatible with Mill's harm principle? With Kant's categorical imperative?

THE ATTORNEY GENERAL'S COMMISSION ON PORNOGRAPHY

The Question of Harm

(Source: From the United States Attorney General's Commission on Pornography, Attorney General's Commission on Pornography: Final Report *[Washington: U.S. Department of Justice, 1986].)*

5.1.2 What Counts as a Harm?

What is a harm? And why focus on harm at all? We do not wish in referring repeatedly to "harm" to burden ourselves with an unduly narrow conception of harm. To emphasize in different words what we said in the previous section, the scope of identifiable harms is broader than the scope of that with which government can or should deal. We refuse to truncate our consideration of the question of harm by defining harms in terms of possible government regulation. And we certainly reject the view that the only noticeable harm is one that causes physical or financial harm to identifiable individuals. An environment, physical, cultural, moral, or aesthetic, can be harmed, and so can a community, organization, or group be harmed independent of identifiable harms to members of that community.

Most importantly, although we have emphasized in our discussion of harms the kinds of harms that can most easily be observed and measured, the idea of harm is broader than that. To a number of us, the most important harms must be seen in moral terms, and the act of moral condemnation of that which is immoral is not merely important but essential. From this perspective there are acts that need be seen not only as causes of immorality but as manifestations of it. Issues of human dignity and human decency, no less real for their lack of scientific measurability, are for many of us central to thinking about the question of harm. And when we think about harm in this way, there are acts that must be condemned not because the evils of the world will thereby be eliminated, but because conscience demands it.

We believe it useful in thinking about harms to note the distinction between harm and offense. Although the line between the two is hardly clear, most people can nevertheless imagine things that offend them, or offend others, that still would be hard to describe as harms. . . .

In thinking about harms, it is useful to draw a rough distinction between primary and secondary harms. Primary harms are those in which the alleged harm is commonly taken to be intrinsically harmful, even though the precise way in which the harm is harmful might yet be further explored. Nevertheless, murder, rape, assault, and discrimination on the basis of race and gender are all examples of primary harms in this sense. We treat these acts as harms not because of where they will lead, but simply because of what they are.

In other instances, however, the alleged harm is secondary, not in the sense that it is in any way less important, but in the sense that the concern is not with what the act *is*, but where it will lead. Curfews are occasionally imposed not because there is anything wrong with people being out at night, but because in some circumstances it is thought that being out at night in large groups may cause people to commit other crimes. Possession of "burglar tools" is often prohibited because of what those tools may be used for. Thus, when it is urged that pornography is harmful because it causes some people to commit acts of sexual violence, because it causes promiscuity, because it encourages sexual relations outside of marriage, because it promotes so-called "unnatural" sexual practices, or because it leads men to treat women as existing solely for the sexual satisfaction of men, the alleged harms are secondary, again not in any sense suggesting that the harms are less important. The harms are secondary here because the allegation of harm presupposes a causal link between the act and the harm, a causal link that is superfluous if, as in the case of primary harms, the act quite simply *is* the harm.

Thus we think it important, with respect to every area of possible harm, to focus on whether the allegation relates to a harm that comes from the sexually explicit material itself, or whether it occurs *as a result* of something the material does. If it is the former, then the inquiry can focus directly on the nature of the alleged harm. But if it is the latter, then there must be a two-step inquiry. First it is necessary to determine if some hypothesized result is in fact harmful. In some cases, where the asserted consequent harm is unquestionably a harm, this step of the analysis is easy. With respect to claims that certain sexually explicit material increases the incidence of rape or other sexual violence, for example, no one could plausibly claim that such consequences were not harmful, and the inquiry can then turn to whether the causal link exists. In other cases, however, the harmfulness of the alleged harm is often debated. With respect to claims, for example, that some sexually explicit material causes promiscuity, encourages homosexuality, or legitimizes sexual practices other than vaginal intercourse, there is serious societal debate about whether the consequences themselves are harmful.

Thus, the analysis of the hypothesis that pornography causes harm must start with the identification of hypothesized harms, proceed to the determination of whether those hypothesized harms are indeed harmful, and then conclude with the examination of whether a causal link exists between the material and the harm. When the consequences of exposure to sexually explicit material are not harmful, or when there is no causal relationship between exposure to sexually explicit material and some harmful consequence, then we cannot say that the sexually explicit material is harmful. But if sexually explicit material of some variety is causally related to, or increases the incidence of, some behavior that *is* harmful, then it is safe to conclude that the material is harmful.

5.2.1 Sexually Violent Material

The category of material on which most of the evidence has focused is the category of material featuring actual or unmistakably simulated or unmistakably threatened violence presented in sexually explicit fashion with a predominant focus on the sexually explicit violence. Increasingly, the most prevalent forms of pornography, as well as an increasingly prevalent body of less sexually explicit material, fit this description. Some of this material involves sado-masochistic themes, with the standard accoutrements of the genre, including whips, chains, devices of torture, and so on. But another theme of some of this material is not sado-masochistic, but involves instead the recurrent theme of a man making some sort of sexual advance to a woman, being rebuffed, and then raping the woman or in some other way violently forcing himself on the woman. In almost all of this material, whether in magazine or motion picture form, the woman eventually becomes aroused and ecstatic about the initially forced sexual activity, and usually is portrayed as begging for more. There is also a large body of material, more "mainstream" in its availability, that portrays sexual activity or sexually suggestive nudity coupled with extreme violence, such as disfigurement or murder. The so-called "slasher" films fit this description, as does some material, both in films and in magazines, that is less or more sexually explicit than the prototypical "slasher" film. . . .

When clinical and experimental research has focused particularly on sexually violent material, the conclusions have been virtually unanimous. In both clinical and experimental settings, exposure to sexually violent materials has indicated an increase in the likelihood of aggression. More specifically, the research . . . shows a causal relationship between exposure to material of this type and aggressive behavior towards women.

Finding a link between aggressive behavior towards women and sexual violence, whether lawful or unlawful, requires assumptions not found exclusively in the experimental evidence. We see no reason, however, not to make these assumptions. The assumption that increased aggressive behavior towards women is causally related, for an aggregate population, to increased sexual violence is significantly supported by the clinical evidence, as well as by much of the less scientific evidence. They are also to all of us assumptions that are plainly justified by our own common sense. This is not to say that all people with heightened levels of aggression will commit acts of sexual violence. But it is to say that over a sufficiently large number of cases we are confident in asserting that an increase in aggressive behavior directed at women will cause an increase in the level of sexual violence directed at women.

Thus we reach our conclusions by combining the results of the research with highly justifiable assumptions about the generalizability of more limited research results. Since the clinical and experimental evidence supports the conclusion that there is a causal relationship between exposure to sexually violent materials and an increase in aggressive behavior directed towards women, and since we believe that an increase in aggressive behavior towards women will in a population increase the incidence of sexual violence in that population, we have reached the conclusion, unanimously and confidently, that the available evidence strongly supports the hypothesis that substantial exposure to sexually violent materials as described here bears a causal relationship to antisocial acts of sexual violence and, for some subgroups, possibly to unlawful acts of sexual violence.

Although we rely for this conclusion on significant scientific empirical evidence, we feel it worthwhile to note the underlying logic of the conclusion. The evidence says simply that the images that people are exposed to bears a causal relationship to their behavior. This is hardly surprising. What would be surprising would be to find otherwise, and we have not so found. We have not, of course, found that the images people are exposed to are a greater cause of sexual violence than all or even many other possible causes the investigation of which has been beyond our mandate. Nevertheless, it would be strange indeed if graphic representations of a form of behavior, especially in a form that almost exclusively portrays such behavior as desirable, did not have at least some effect on patterns of behavior.

Sexual violence is not the only negative effect reported in the research to result from substantial exposure to sexually violent materials. The evidence is also strongly supportive of significant attitudinal changes on the part of those with substantial exposure to violent pornography. These attitudinal changes are numerous. Victims of rape and other forms of sexual violence are likely to be perceived by people so exposed as more responsible for the assault, as having suffered less injury, and as having been less degraded as a result of the experience. Similarly, people with a substantial exposure to violent pornography are likely to see the rapist or other sexual offender as less responsible for the act and as deserving of less stringent punishment.

These attitudinal changes have been shown experimentally to include a larger range of attitudes than those just discussed. The evidence also strongly supports the conclusion that substantial exposure to violent sexually explicit material leads to a greater acceptance of the "rape myth" in its broader sense—that women enjoy being coerced into sexual activity, that they enjoy being physically hurt in sexual context, and that as a result a man who forces himself on a woman sexually is in fact merely acceding to the "real" wishes of the woman, regardless of the extent to which she seems to be resisting. The myth is that a woman who says "no" really means "yes," and that men are justified in acting on the assumption that the "no" answer is indeed the "yes" answer. We have little trouble concluding that this attitude is both pervasive and profoundly harmful, and that any stimulus reinforcing or increasing the incidence of this attitude is for that reason alone properly designated as harmful.

Two vitally important features of the evidence supporting the above conclusions must be mentioned here. The first is that all of the harms discussed here, including acceptance of the legitimacy of sexual violence against women but not limited to it, are more pronounced when the sexually violent materials depict the woman as experiencing arousal, orgasm, or other form of enjoyment as the ultimate result of the sexual assault. This theme, unfortunately very common in the materials we have examined, is likely to be the major, albeit not the only, component of what it is in the materials in this category that causes the consequences that have been identified.

The second important clarification of all of the above is that the evidence lends some support to the conclusion that the consequences we have identified here *do not vary with the extent of sexual explicitness so long as the violence is presented in an undeniably sexual context.* Once a threshold is passed at which sex and violence are plainly linked, increasing the sexual explicitness of the material, or the bizarreness of the sexual activity, seems to bear little relationship to the extent of the consequences discussed here. Although it is unclear whether sexually violent material makes a substantially greater causal contribution to sexual violence itself than does material containing violence alone, it appears that increasing the amount of violence after the threshold of connecting sex with violence is more related to increase in the incidence or severity of harmful consequences than is increasing the amount of sex. As a result, the so-called "slasher" films, which depict a great deal of violence connected with an undeniably sexual theme but less sexual explicitness than materials that are truly pornographic, are likely to produce the consequences discussed here to a greater extent than most of the materials available in "adults only" pornographic outlets.

Although we have based our findings about material in this category primarily on evidence presented by professionals in the behavioral sciences, we are confident that it is supported by the less scientific evidence we have consulted, and we are each personally confident on the basis of our own knowledge and experiences that the conclusions are justified. None of us has the least doubt that sexual violence is harmful, and that general acceptance of the view that "no" means "yes" is a consequence of the most serious proportions. We have found a causal relationship between sexually explicit materials featuring violence and these consequences, and thus conclude that the class of such materials, although not necessarily every individual member of that class, is on the whole harmful to society.

5.2.2 Non-Violent Materials Depicting Degradation, Domination, Subordination, or Humiliation

Current research has rather consistently separated out violent pornography, the class of materials we have just discussed, from other sexually explicit materials. With respect to further subdivision the process has been less consistent. A few researchers have made further distinctions, while most have merely classed everything else as "non-violent." We have concluded that more subdivision than that is necessary. Our examination of the variety of sexually explicit materials convinces us that once again the category of "non-violent" ignores significant distinctions within this category, and thus combines classes of material that are in fact substantially different.

The subdivision we adopt is one that has surfaced in some of the research. And it is also one that might explain a significant amount of what would otherwise seem to be conflicting research results. Some researchers have found negative effects from non-violent material, while others report no such negative effects. But when the stimulus material these researchers have used is considered, there is some suggestion that the presence or absence of negative effects from non-violent material might turn on the non-violent material being considered "degrading," a term we shall explain shortly. It appears that effects similar to although not as extensive as that involved with violent material can be identified with respect to such degrading material, but that these effects are likely absent when neither degradation nor violence is present.

An enormous amount of the most sexually explicit material available, as well as much of the material that is somewhat less sexually explicit, is material that we would characterize as "degrading," the term we use to encompass the undeniably linked characteristics of degradation, domination, subordination, and humiliation. The degradation we refer to is degradation of people, most often women, and here we are referring to material that, although not violent, depicts people, usually women, as existing solely for the sexual satisfaction of others, usually men, or that depicts people, usually women, in decidedly subordinate roles in their sexual relations with others, or that depicts people engaged in sexual practices that would to most people be considered humiliating. Indeed, forms of degradation represent the largely predominant proportion of commercially available pornography.

With respect to material of this variety, our conclusions are substantially similar to those with respect to violent material, although we make them with somewhat less confidence and our making of them requires more in the way of assumption than was the case with respect to violent material. The evidence, scientific and otherwise, is more tentative, but supports the conclusion that the material we describe as degrading bears some causal relationship to the attitudinal changes we have previously identified. That is, substantial exposure to material of this variety is likely to increase the extent to which those exposed will view rape or other forms of sexual violence as less serious than they otherwise would have, will view the victim of rape and other forms of sexual violence as significantly more responsible, and will view the offenders as significantly less responsible. We also conclude that the evidence supports the conclusion that substantial exposure to material of this type will increase acceptance of the proposition that women like to be forced into sexual practices, and, once again, that the woman who says "no" really means "yes."

With respect to material of this type, there is less evidence causally linking the material with sexual aggression, but this may be because this is a category that has been isolated in only a few studies, albeit an increasing number. The absence of evidence should by no means be taken to deny the existence of the causal link. But because the causal link is less the subject of experimental studies, we have been required to think more carefully here about the assumptions necessary to causally connect increased acceptance of rape myths and other attitudinal changes with increased sexual aggression and sexual violence. And on the basis of all the evidence we have considered, from all sources, and on the basis of our own insights and experiences, we believe we are justified in drawing the following conclusion: Over a large enough sample a population that believes that many women like to be raped, that believes that sexual violence or sexual coercion is often desired or appropriate, and that believes that sex offenders are less responsible for their acts, will commit more acts of sexual violence or sexual coercion than would a population holding these beliefs to a lesser extent.

We should make clear what we have concluded here. We are not saying that everyone exposed to material of this type had his attitude about sexual violence changed. We are saying only that the evidence supports the conclusion that substantial exposure to degrading material increases the likelihood for an individual and the incidence over a large population that these attitudinal changes will occur. And we are not saying that everyone with these attitudes will commit an act of sexual violence or sexual coercion. We are saying that such attitudes will increase the likelihood for an individual and the incidence for a population that acts of sexual violence, sexual coercion, or unwanted sexual aggression will occur. Thus, we conclude that substantial exposure to materials of this type bears some causal relationship to the level of sexual violence, sexual coercion, or unwanted sexual aggression in the population so exposed.

We need mention as well that our focus on these more violent or more coercive forms of actual subordination of women should not diminish what we take to be a necessarily incorporated conclusion: Substantial exposure to materials of this type bears some causal relationship to the incidence of various non-violent forms of discrimination against or subordination of women in our society. To the extent that these materials create or reinforce the view that women's function is disproportionately to satisfy the sexual needs of men, then the materials will have pervasive effects on the treatment of women in society far beyond the incidence of identifiable acts of rape or other sexual violence. We obviously cannot here explore fully all of the forms in which women are discriminated against in contemporary society. Nor can we explore all of the causes of that discrimination against women. But we feel confident in concluding that the view of women as available for sexual domination is one cause of that discrimination, and we feel confident as well in concluding that degrading material bears a causal relationship to the view that women ought to subordinate their own desires and beings to the sexual satisfaction of men.

Although the category of the degrading is one that has only recently been isolated in some research, in the literature generally, and in public discussion of the issue, it is not a small category. If anything, it constitutes somewhere between the predominant and the overwhelming portion of what is currently standard fare heterosexual pornography, and is a significant theme in a broader range of materials not commonly taken to be sexually explicit enough to be pornographic. But as with sexually violent materials, the extent of the effect of these degrading materials may not turn substantially on the amount of sexual explicitness once a threshold of undeniable sexual content is surpassed. The category therefore includes a great deal of what would now be considered to be pornographic, and includes a great deal of what would now be held to be legally obscene, but it includes much more than that. Since we are here identifying harms for a class, rather than identifying harms caused by every member of that class, and since we are here talking about the identification of harm rather than making recommendations for legal control, we are not reluctant to identify harms for a class of material considerably wider than what is or even should be regulated by law.

5.2.3 Non-Violent and Non-Degrading Materials

Our most controversial category has been the category of sexually explicit materials that are not violent and are not degrading as we have used that term. They are materials in which the participants appear to be fully willing participants occupying substantially equal roles in a setting devoid of actual or apparent violence or pain. This category is in fact quite small in terms of currently available materials. There is some, to be sure, and the amount may increase as the division between the degrading and the non-degrading becomes more accepted, but we are convinced that only a small amount of currently available highly sexually explicit material is neither violent nor degrading. We thus talk about a small category, but one that should not be ignored. . . .

. . . Although the social science evidence is far from conclusive, we are on the current state of the evidence persuaded that material of this type does not bear a causal relationship to rape and other acts of sexual violence. . . .

A larger issue is the very question of promiscuity. Even to the extent that the behavior depicted is not inherently condemned by some or any of us, the manner of presentation almost necessarily suggests that the activities are taking place outside of the context of marriage, love, commitment, or even affection. Again, it is far from implausible to hypothesize that materials depicting sexual activity without marriage, love, commitment, or affection bear some causal relationship to sexual activity without marriage, love, commitment, or affection. There are undoubtedly many causes for what used to be called the "sexual revolution," but it is absurd to suppose that depictions or descriptions of uncommitted sexuality were not among them. Thus, once again our disagreements reflect disagreements in society at large, although not to as great an extent. Although there are many members of this society who can and have made affirmative cases for uncommitted sexuality, none of us believes it to be a good thing. A number of us, however, believe that the level of commitment in sexuality is a matter of choice among those who voluntarily engage in the activity. Others of us believe that uncommitted sexual activity is wrong for the individuals involved and harmful to society to the extent of its prevalence. Our view of the ultimate harmfulness of much of this material, therefore, is reflective of our individual views about the extent to whether sexual commitment is purely a matter of individual choice.

Even insofar as sexually explicit material of the variety being discussed here is not perceived as harmful for the messages it carries or the symbols it represents, the very publicness of what is commonly taken to be private is cause for concern. Even if we hypothesize a sexually explicit motion picture of a loving married couple engaged in mutually pleasurable and procreative vaginal intercourse, the depiction of that act on a screen or in a magazine may constitute a harm in its own right (a "primary harm" in the terminology introduced earlier in this Chapter) solely by virtue of being shown. Here the concern is with the preservation of sex as an essentially private act, in conformity with the basic privateness of sex long recognized by this and all other societies. The alleged harm here, therefore, is that as soon as sex is put on a screen or put in a magazine it changes its character, regardless of what variety of sex is portrayed. And to the extent that the character of sex as public rather than private is the consequence here, then that to many would constitute a harm. . . .

A number of witnesses have testified about the effects on their own sexual relations, usually with their spouses, of the depiction on the screen and in magazines of sexual practices in which they had not previously engaged. A number of these witnesses, *all women,* have testified that men in their lives have used such material to strongly encourage, or coerce, them into engaging in sexual practices in which they do not choose to engage. To the extent that such implicit or explicit coercion takes place as a result of these materials, we all agree that it is a harm. There has been other evidence, however, about the extent to which such material might for some be a way of revitalizing their sex lives, or, more commonly, simply constituting a part of a mutually pleasurable sexual experience for both partners. On this we could not agree. For reasons relating largely to the question of publicness in the first sense discussed above, some saw this kind of use as primarily harmful. Others saw it as harmless and possibly beneficial in contexts such as this. Some professional testimony supported this latter view, but we have little doubt that professional opinion is also divided on the issue. . . .

QUESTIONS FOR REFLECTION

1. In answering the question "What is a harm?" the commission distinguishes primary from secondary harm. Explain this distinction. What, according to the commission, is its moral significance?
2. Why does the commission believe that sexually violent material is harmful?
3. The commission holds that nonviolent but degrading material is also harmful. What is "degrading" material? Why is it harmful?
4. What is the commission's opinion of nonviolent, nondegrading pornography? Is it harmful in any way? Should the government attempt to restrict access to such material, according to the commission? Do you agree?
5. Does the test for obscenity in *Miller* correspond to the distinction the commission makes between harmful and (largely) harmless pornography? If not, how might the test be revised to make it correspond?

WENDY McELROY

from *Sexual Correctness*

Wendy McElroy is the author of several libertarian critiques of feminism, including The Reasonable Woman *and* XXX: A Woman's Right to Pornography. *(Source: Reprinted from* Sexual Correctness: The Gender-Feminist Attack on Women *[Jefferson, NC: McFarland and Company, Inc., 1996]. Notes have been omitted.*

CHAPTER THREE / A FEMINIST DEFENSE OF PORNOGRAPHY

Pornography is haunting feminists, who make such bald and insupportable statements as "pornography is the theory: rape is the practice." Women who work in the porn industry, who consume pornography, or who simply disagree are all considered to be brainwashed victims of patriarchy. In other words, they are sick and need not be taken seriously. This chapter attacks the ideology and strategy behind the crusade to limit women's sexual choices. It denies that pornography degrades women.

Gender Feminists and Conservatives: An Unholy Alliance

Pornography has been a traditional battleground between conservatives, who advocate family values, and liberals, who champion freedom of expression. The political makeup of contemporary feminism is overwhelmingly liberal; the more extreme feminists—called radical or gender feminist—are socialist. Nevertheless since the mid-eighties there has been a startling sight. Feminists have been standing alongside conservatives to demand legislation against pornography. Antipornography feminists have even joined hands with fundamentalists in a common cause.

This alliance makes some feminists nervous. Lisa Duggan, Nan Hunter and Carole S. Vance, in their essay *False Promises,* summarized the amazement with which many liberal feminists view these recent events: "One is tempted to ask in astonishment, how can this be happening? . . . But in fact this new development is not as surprising as it at first seems. Pornography has come to be seen as a central cause of women's oppression by a significant number of feminists." They also expressed great concern about the future consequences of standing side by side with conservatives: "This analysis takes feminism very close—indeed far too close to measures that will ultimately support conservative, antisex, procensorship forces in American society for it is with these forces that women have formed alliances."

Gender feminists dismiss the dangers of this alliance. They discount the possibility that the legislation they seek could backlash against the feminist movement. Gender feminist Catharine MacKinnon obviated the question of whether or not to trust the law by observing: "We do not trust medicine, yet we insist it respond to women's needs. We do not trust theology, but we claim spirituality as more than a male preserve. We do not abdicate the control of technology because it was not invented by women." MacKinnon concludes by dismissing those who question using patriarchy to protect women: "If women are to restrict our demands for change to spheres we can trust, spheres we already control, there will not be any."

The unlikely alliance between feminists and conservatives, and the split within feminism itself, has led to strange spectacles. For example, when an antipornography ordinance was proposed in Indianapolis, the law was supported by the Moral Majority—even though it had been drafted by gender feminists. Within the local feminist community, however, the ordinance found no support. The issue of pornography is turning feminist against feminist.

The Drift within Feminism on Pornography

The current antipornography crusade within feminism is something new on the political scene. It is new in at least two important ways: (1) it signals a break in feminism from its liberal insistence on freedom of speech and (2) it offers a revolutionary definition of pornography. The battle over pornography has shifted to new ground.

Pornography is the *bête noire* of gender feminism. To them, pornography is gender violence and a violation of the civil rights of women. It victimizes not merely women who work in the industry or who are exposed to magazines and films; pornography damages *all* women because it contributes to the general degradation of women that is prevalent in our society. Indeed, some theorists go so far as to claim that pornography is *the* source of society's unhealthy attitude toward women. Pornography is considered to be so damaging that it is linked, in a cause and effect relationship, to violent crimes such as rape. Thus, eliminating this form of expression is viewed as self-defense, not censorship.

The legal theorist Catharine MacKinnon has been a key voice in the antipornography campaign. In her book *Feminism Unmodified,* MacKinnon defined the object of attack: "Pornography, in the feminist view, is a form of forced sex, a practice of sexual politics, an institution of gender inequality." MacKinnon claims that pornography is not just a form of expression; pornographic material is—in and of itself—an act of violence: "Pornography not only teaches the reality of male dominance. It is one way its reality is imposed as well as experienced. It is a way of seeing and treating women."

MacKinnon further erases the line between attitude and behavior, image and action:

> Male power makes authoritative a way of seeing and treating women, so that when a man looks at a pornographic picture—pornographic meaning that the woman is defined as to be acted upon, a sexual object, a sexual thing—the *viewing* is an *act,* an act of male supremacy. [Emphasis in the original.]

The wholesale condemnation of pornography is new in feminism. Since its revival in the early 1960s the movement has been dominated by socialists and liberals; both these traditions advocated freedom of speech. Moreover, pornography tended to be viewed as part of a larger trend toward sexual liberation—a liberation that feminists applauded because it ushered in such things as birth control and the unveiling of women's sexuality.

Lisa Duggan, Nan Hunter, and Carole S. Vance typified this attitude in acknowledging the possible benefits pornography offered to women. They note that pornography has "served to flout conventional sexual mores, to ridicule sexual hypocrisy and to underscore the importance of sexual needs." In short, pornography has liberated women from the status quo by transmitting many messages:

> It advocates sexual adventure, sex outside of marriage, sex for pleasure, casual sex, illegal sex, anonymous sex, public sex, voyeuristic sex. Some of these ideas appeal to women . . . who may interpret some images as legitimating their own sense of sexual urgency or desire to be sexually aggressive.

Pornography and feminism have much in common. Both deal with women as sexual beings and both attempt to bring this sexuality out into the open. Moreover, pornography and feminism share a history of being targeted by obscenity laws. In particular, the Comstock Laws of the 1870s were used not only against pornographic material but also against birth control information. Feminist material—especially lesbian material—has always suffered under laws regulating sexual expression.

Gender Feminists: The New Puritans

By the late 1970s sexual liberation was being viewed with suspicion by feminists. Pornography was being redefined as an enemy of women. In her book, *Our Blood,* gender feminist Andrea Dworkin spells this out: "In pornography, sadism is the means by which men establish their dominance. Sadism is the authentic exercise of power which confirms manhood; and the first characteristic of manhood is that its existence is based on the negation of the female." Dworkin explains that manhood requires the destruction of women's bodies and will. Why? Dworkin explains this as well:

> The sexual sadism actualizes male identity. . . . The common erotic project of destroying women makes it possible for men to unite into a brotherhood; this project is the only firm and trustworthy groundwork for cooperation among males and all male bonding is based on it.

Antiporn Strategy

The feminist attack on pornography is not merely another cry for censorship from those who hate sex. It is more sophisticated than that. Feminists are using a strategy that has proved successful with other issues, such as affirmative action. Pornography is being defined as a violation of women's civil rights. Thus, instead of advocating criminal proceedings against pornographers, feminists restrict themselves to civil suits. This approach avoids sticky constitutional questions; in particular, it avoids the First Amendment. It also turns the entire discussion of pornography on its head. Conventional arguments for and against pornography simply do not apply.

Traditional obscenity laws have focused on the connection between pornography and moral harm. One of the standard tests of obscenity came from Supreme Court Justice Brennan in his ruling on *Memoirs* v. *Massachusetts:*

> (a) The dominant theme of the material taken as a whole appeals to the prurient interest in sex; (b) the material is patently offensive because it affronts contemporary community standards relating to the description or representation of sexual matters; and (c) the material is utterly without redeeming social value.

Antipornography feminists dwell on the connection between pornography and political harm—namely, the oppression of women. Consider MacKinnon's presentation of how pornography differs from obscenity. She argues that obscenity is concerned with morality—white male morality. Pornography is concerned with politics—the politics of women's subjugation. She further distinguishes between the two: "Morality here means good and evil; politics means power and powerlessness. Obscenity is a moral idea; pornography is a political practice. Obscenity is abstract; pornography is concrete. The two concepts represent two entirely different things."

In the mid-eighties, gender feminists launched a campaign to pass antipornography ordinances on a city by city basis. By localizing the issue, they bypassed the problem of obtaining a national consensus, which had proven so difficult with the ERA. The first ordinance—drafted by MacKinnon and Dworkin—served as the model for future ones. This was the Minneapolis Ordinance of 1983. In addressing the Minneapolis City Council, MacKinnon declared the key theme of gender feminism's attack on pornography: namely, that pornography was a violation of civil rights—an act of discrimination against women:

> We are proposing . . . a statutory scheme that will situate pornography as a central practice in the subordination of women. . . . The understanding and the evidence which we will present to you today to support defining pornography as a practice of discrimination on the basis of sex is a new idea.

Further, pornography was now placed at the heart of how men oppress women: "Pornography conditions and determines the way in which men actually treat women . . . and we will show that it is central to the way in which women remain second-class citizens."

Under the ordinance's provisions, a woman who had worked in pornography—a *Playboy* centerfold, for example—could bring a civil lawsuit against her employers for having coerced her into a "pornographic performance." Laws and remedies already existed for fraud or for contracts signed under duress. The purpose of the ordinance was to make "coercion" into a civil matter.

The definition of coercion was all-important. The ordinance was clear. Coercion was deemed to be present even if the woman was of age, fully understood the nature of the performance, signed a contract and release, agreed to it before witnesses, was under no threat, and was fully paid. None of these factors provided evidence of consent.

In essence, consent was not possible. In principle, the woman could not be treated as a consenting adult. By definition, coercion was always present in a pornographic act.

MacKinnon later explained: "In the context of unequal power (between the sexes), one needs to think about the meaning of consent—whether it is a meaningful concept at all." Gloria Steinem, in her introduction to Linda Lovelace's exposé *Out of Bondage,* agreed: "The question is free will: Are the subjects of pornography there by choice, or by coercion, *economic* or physical." (Emphasis added.)

In other words, if the woman needed or wanted the money offered, this would constitute economic coercion. The politics of society made it impossible for women to fully consent to a pornographic act. Women who thought they had agreed were mistaken. Such women had been so damaged by a male dominated culture that they were not able to give true consent. Lisa Duggan, Nan Hunter, and Carole S. Vance observe: "Advocates of the ordinance effectively assume that women have been so conditioned by the pornographic world view that if their own experiences of the sexual acts . . . are not subordinating, then they must simply be victims of false consciousness."

My Background as a Defender of Pornography

Several years ago, antipornography feminists attempted to pass an ordinance in Los Angeles. I was among the feminists who went down to city hall to argue against the ordinance. The arguments I decided *not* to use are almost as revealing as the ones I settled on.

I decided not to argue that pornography is undefinable and, therefore, not appropriate for a legal system that requires a clear point of enforcement. The ordinance had defined what it meant by pornography in excruciating—if subjective—detail. To focus on definitions would be to divert the debate into the bogs of what constitutes "dehumanization" or "exploitation." I simply accepted the rule of thumb offered by Supreme Court Justice Potter Stewart in his ruling on *Jacobellis v. Ohio,* 1964: "I know it when I see it." I assumed that everyone was talking about the same thing.

I also abandoned appeals to the First Amendment. Antipornography feminists had a tangled web of counterarguments, which would require more time to answer than I would be allotted. MacKinnon's arguments are typical. She begins by attacking the Constitution as a "white male" document: "The First Amendment essentially presumes some level of social equality among people and hence essentially equal social access to the means of expression. In a context of inequality between the sexes, we cannot presume that that is accurate."

MacKinnon then adds the dual claims: freedom of speech is not necessary for human fulfillment and pornography is an act of violence, not a form of speech: "The First Amendment also presumes that for the mind to be free to fulfill itself, speech must be free and open. . . . Pornography amounts to terrorism and promotes not freedom but silence. Rather, it promotes freedom for men and enslavement and silence for women." If pornography was an act of violence, then the First Amendment was irrelevant.

I also avoided a discussion of privacy rights. Supreme Court Justice Thurgood Marshall (*Stanley v. Georgia,* 1969) had maintained: "If the First Amendment means anything, it means that a state has no business telling a man, sitting alone in his own house, what books he may read or what films he must watch." But, again, if pornography was violence, the issue of committing it in private was beside the point.

The only way to effectively challenge the new attack was to answer gender feminists in their own terms. The debate on pornography had been shifted to new ground. Thus, the key questions were: Are all women coerced into pornography? and How does pornography relate to violence against women? Everything seemed to return to the basic contention of feminists: pornography is an act of violence. It is an act committed upon and against unconsenting women. This is the level on which the assault on pornography must be addressed.

A Feminist Defense of Pornography

To begin with, I divided women into two categories: women who were directly involved with pornography—either in production or consumption and women who had no direct exposure. The first category is the litmus test. If women are degraded by pornography, surely the women closest to it would be the most deeply affected. At the heart of this question is the problem of pinning down subjective terms such as "degrading."

It was not possible to ask every woman who was involved in pornography whether or not she felt degraded by it. This left only one way to judge the matter. Namely, did women freely choose to work in the porn industry or to consume pornography?

The answer is clear: pornographic models and actresses sign contracts. Women who produce pornography, such as Ms. Hefner at *Playboy* or Candida Royalle at Femme Films, do so willingly. Women shopkeepers who stock pornography choose to fill in the order forms. Women who consume pornography—including me—pay money to do so.

However, gender feminists insist, no "healthy" woman would consent to the humiliation of pornography. Therefore, women who make this choice are so psychologically damaged by a male-dominated culture that they are incapable of true consent. In Indianapolis, the ordinance explicitly argued that women, like children, need special protection under the law.

Pause with me for a moment. Consider how insulting this is to women who have made an "unacceptable" choice with their bodies—that is, women who work in pornography. Antipornography feminists label these women as psychologically sick because they have made nonfeminist choices. These women are called victims of their culture.

But gender feminists were raised in the same culture. Presumably, these "enlightened" women wish us to believe that their choices are based on reason and knowledge; somehow, they have risen above the culture in which they were raised. They are unwilling, however, to grant such a courteous assumption to any woman who disagrees with them.

Gender feminists are adamant that women involved in the production of pornography cannot be held legally responsible for their actions because they are psychologically impaired by cultural influence. Their arguments need not be taken seriously, their contracts need not be respected. They are psychologically impaired. If a woman enjoys consuming pornography, it is not because she comes from another background, has a different emotional makeup, or has reasoned from different facts. No, it is because she is mentally incompetent. Like any three-year-old, she is unable to give informed consent regarding her own body.

The touchstone principle of feminism used to be, "a woman's body, a woman's right." Regarding date rape, feminists still declare, "No means no." The logical corollary of this is, "Yes means yes." Now, modern feminists are declaring that "yes" means nothing. It is difficult to believe that any form of pornography could be more degrading to women than this attitude.

As to whether cultural pressure has influenced women's decisions—of course it has. The culture we live in impacts on every choice we make. But to say that women who participate in pornography cannot make a choice because of cultural pressure, is to eliminate the possibility of choice in any realm. Because every choice of every person is made in the presence of cultural pressure—including the choice to become a feminist.

The Right to Pose Is the Right to Contract

The antipornography ordinances were intended to protect women from the consequences of their own actions. But what legal implications does this have for women's contracts—a right for which past generations fought hard? In the nineteenth century, women battled to become the legal equal of men, to have their consent taken seriously in the form of contracts, and to have control of their own bodies legally recognized. After the antipornography crusade, who will take a woman's consent seriously? When the Fifteenth Amendment was proposed in a form that enfranchised black men while ignoring women, the pioneering feminist Susan B. Anthony protested: "We have stood with the black man in the Constitution over a half a century. . . . Enfranchise him and we are left outside with lunatics, idiots and criminals."

To deprive women of the right to make their own contracts is to place them, once again, outside the constitution with lunatics, idiots, and criminals. Gender feminists are reducing a woman's consent to a legal triviality. Women are being granted the protection of no longer being taken seriously when they sign contracts. This is not a step toward dignity or freedom for women.

But what of the women who do not choose to be involved in pornography? What of the women who are offended by it? The simplistic answer is that they should not buy or consume it. Moreover, they should use any and all peaceful means to persuade others that pornography is not a proper form of expression.

The Bias of Researchers

The argument runs that whether or not women are directly exposed to pornography, they are still victimized. Pornography is the first step of a slippery slope that leads to explicit violence against women, such as rape. Thus, *every* woman is a victim, because every woman is in danger. This argument assumes: (1) that pornography impacts on men's behavior, (2) that the impact can be measured objectively, and (3) that it can be correlated with sexual violence.

Pornography probably does impact on people's behavior, but it is next to impossible to objectively measure that impact. Human psychology is extremely complex, especially in the area of sexual response. Moreover, the standard of measurement and the conclusions drawn from data usually depend on the bias of the researchers or of those who commission the research.

For example, in 1983 the Metropolitan Toronto Task Force on Violence against Women commissioned Thelma McCormack to study pornography's connection with sexual aggression. Her research did not support the assumption that there was one. Indeed, McCormack's study indicated that the effect of pornography might be cathartic. It might reduce the incidence of rape.

Her report, *Making Sense of Research on Pornography,* was discarded. The study was reassigned to David Scott, a nonfeminist committed to antipornography. Scott found a clear connection between pornography and sexual aggression. Students, journalists, and researchers who tried to obtain a copy of McCormack's paper were told that it was unavailable.

Statistics almost always contain assumptions and biases. Sometimes the bias is obvious and acknowledged. For example, a researcher who believes that sexual aggression is a learned behavior will naturally ask different questions than someone who believes aggression is an instinct. Other forms of bias are not so obvious.

However, for the sake of argument, let's assume that a correlation exists between pornography and rape. What would such a correlation prove? If a society with more pornography tended to have more rape, what would this say? A correlation is not a cause and effect relationship. It is a logical fallacy to assume that if A is correlated with B, then A causes B. Both might be caused by a totally separate factor, C. For example, there is a high correlation between the number of doctors in a city and the amount of alcohol consumed there. One does not cause the other. Both result from a third factor, the size of the city's population.

Similarly, a correlation between pornography and rape may indicate nothing more than a common cause for both, namely, that we live in a sexually repressed society. To further repress sex by restricting pornography might well increase the incidence of rape. Opening up the area of pornography might well diffuse sexual violence by making it more understandable.

Conclusion

There is great irony in the spectacle of gender feminists aligning themselves with their two greatest ideological enemies: conservatives and the patriarchal state. In using ordinances, antipornography feminists are legitimizing a system they themselves condemn as patriarchy. It is a strange leap of faith. After all, once a law is on the books, it is the state bureaucracy, not NOW, who will enforce it. In *Our Blood,* Andrea Dworkin excoriated patriarchal bureaucracy:

> Under patriarchy, no woman is safe to live her life, or to love, or to mother children. Under patriarchy, every woman is a victim, past, present, and future. Under patriarchy, every woman's daughter is a victim, past, present, and future. Under patriarchy, every woman's son is her potential betrayer and also the inevitable rapist or exploiter of another woman.

Now feminists are appealing to this same state as a protector.

The final irony is that it is the state—not free speech—that has been the oppressor of women. It was the state, not pornography, that burned women as witches. It was eighteenth-century law, not pornography, that defined women as chattel. Nineteenth-century laws allowed men to commit wayward women to insane asylums, to claim their wives' earnings, and to beat them with impunity. Twentieth-century laws refuse to recognize rape within marriage and sentence the sexes differently for the same crime. The state, not pornography, has raised barriers against women. And censorship, not freedom, will keep the walls intact.

One of the most important questions confronting feminism at the turn of this century is whether or not women's liberation can embrace sexual liberation. Can the freedom of women and freedom of speech become fellow travelers once more?

The feminist Myrna Kostash answered this question well: "To paraphrase Albert Camus, freedom to publish and read does not necessarily assure a society of justice and peace, but without these freedoms it has no assurance at all."

QUESTIONS FOR REFLECTION

1. How, according to McElroy, do restrictions on pornography harm women who neither produce nor consume pornography?
2. What is McElroy's chief argument against MacKinnon and the antipornography ordinances that she supports?
3. Apply Mill's harm principle to pornography. Does it generally agree or disagree with McElroy's position?
4. Apply Kant's categorical imperative to pornography. Does it generally agree or disagree with McElroy's position?

OFFENSIVE SPEECH AND BEHAVIOR

In response to racial incidents, colleges and universities across the country have been enacting speech codes to limit what can be said on campus. Some are narrow, proscribing only repeated harassment of individuals; others are broad, prohibiting "insensitive" speech and behavior. At least one restriction has been struck down by a court as unconstitutional. Off campus, legal scholars have proposed new rules for civil lawsuits related to racial insults, and complaints and lawsuits concerning sexual harassment have become commonplace. Many companies now have sexual harassment policies and complaint procedures. Many states have passed laws giving stiffer penalties to criminals motivated by prejudice.

Advocates of these changes point to equality, the protection of rights, and the benefits of a more inclusive social environment. Critics, however, see restrictions on speech that are hard to justify.

Freedoms of thought, speech, and the press have well-recognized exceptions. One may not slander a person, incite a mob to riot, or shout "Fire!" in a crowded theater that is not on fire. In Mill's words, "Acts, of whatever kind, which without justifiable cause do harm to others may be, and in the more important cases absolutely require to be, controlled by the unfavorable sentiments, and, when needful, by the active interference of mankind." In cases of the kinds just mentioned, the harm done to particular people outweighs any possible value the speech possesses.

Is that true of racial insults, sexual harassment, and other offensive speech? Undoubtedly, harassment of various kinds can cause harm. But often offensive speech is just that—offensive. If someone insults me, or makes lewd remarks to me, or makes an obscene gesture toward me, I am probably going to be offended. But it is not so clear that I will suffer harm. There seems to be a big difference between an obscene gesture and a punch in the nose. The childhood rhyme says "Sticks and stones will break my bones, but words will never hurt me." This seems wrong—words can hurt—but it nevertheless makes an important point: There are differences between offense and harm.

Plato presents the classic case for censorship. A society is only as good as its people. Good societies become good by encouraging virtue in their members. Some speech promotes virtue. Some speech has no effect on virtue. And some speech discourages virtue. That speech, Socrates argues, should be banned. Speech that contains lies, incites conflict, encourages cynicism or injustice, or discourages courage or self-control, harms society and ought to be prohibited.

John Stuart Mill presents the case for freedom of speech. What someone says might turn out to be true; to ban it on grounds of falsehood assumes infallibility. Even if it isn't true, it might contain part of the truth. Finally, even if what someone says is completely false, it strengthens the truth by forcing us to understand and defend the truth. Mill allows "time, place, and manner" restrictions on speech—to have the right to speak is not to have the right to speak anywhere, at any time, at any volume, and in any way. You have the right to say what you want to say, but you do not have the right to say it through a loudspeaker in my neighborhood in the middle of the night. Mill also allows us to restrict speech that threatens to result in imminent harm. You do not have the right to incite a crowd to riot, or, to take a famous example of Justice Oliver Wendell Holmes, Jr., in *Schenck* v. *United States* (1919), falsely [to] shout "Fire!" in a crowded theater:

> The most stringent protection of free speech would not protect a man falsely to shouting fire in a theater and causing a panic. . . . The question in every case is whether the words used are used in such circumstances and are of such a nature as to create a clear and present danger. . . .

Neither does Mill challenge the law of slander and libel. With these exceptions, however, Mill defends freedom of speech, insisting that speech may not be banned because it is offensive, insensitive, controversial, or false.

Stanley Fish argues that speech is never really free; all defenses of freedom of speech make exceptions. The exceptions, Fish contends, are based not on principle but on politics. Deciding what speech to allow is deciding what will be politically favored. Fish concludes by defending speech codes and other restrictions, maintaining that they produce social benefits.

Thomas Nagel advances a theory of rights based on the concept of inviolability, and argues that restrictions on speech violate rights, even when they appear, on balance, to have beneficial effects. He distinguishes between agent-neutral and agent-relative principles, and uses it to argue that freedom of speech is essential to autonomy.

In *Morse* v. *Frederick*, the Supreme Court addresses student freedom of speech. Joseph Frederick unfurled a 14-foot-long banner with the words "BONG HiTS 4 JESUS" to attract the attention of TV cameras filming the procession of the Olympic torch through Juneau, Alaska. He was among students on a school outing, just across the street from the school. When the principal ordered him to take the banner down, he refused. She confiscated the banner and suspended him for ten days. The Court's majority finds in favor of the principal, maintaining that student speech may be restricted for a variety of reasons, including the war on drugs. Justice Stevens, writing in dissent, argues that the speech deserves protection. It is either silly and meaningless, in which case it does not deserve punishment for advocating drug use, or it is protected political speech.

Much more serious are issues arising from clashes between Western societies and Islam. In less than five years, the following incidents occurred.

2004: A lecturer at the University of Copenhagen is assaulted for reading the Qur'an aloud in a lecture attended by non-Muslims.

2004: Theo van Gogh, a Dutch filmmaker, directs *Submission*, a film about the oppression of women in Islam. In retaliation, a Dutch Muslim of Moroccan descent murders him. Hirsi Ali, the film's writer, goes into hiding and lives under protection.

2005: The Danish newspaper *Jyllands-Posten* publishes cartoons of Mohammed, the most inflammatory of which shows him with a bomb in his turban. Riots occur throughout the Muslim world during the following year to protest the publication. More than 100 people are killed. Several of the cartoonists receive death threats and go into hiding.

2006: Canadian Ezra Levant, publisher of the *Western Standard*, reprints the Danish cartoons. Syed Soharwardy of the Islamic Supreme Council of Canada complains to the Alberta Human Rights and Citizenship Commission and to the Calgary police, who begin investigations.

2006: French philosopher Robert Redeker publishes comments critical of Mohammed; he receives death threats and goes into hiding.

2007: A British schoolteacher, Gillian Gibbons, is imprisoned and convicted in the Sudan for permitting her students to name a teddy bear Muhammad. Rioting crowds demand her execution. She is released after intervention by the British government.

2007: Lars Vilks, a Swedish artist, draws "Modogs," images of Mohammed's head on the body of a dog, for an exhibition on "The Dog in Art." The organizers refuse to show the drawings, as do several other galleries. Many Swedish newspapers publish them. Vilks receives death threats; Islamic countries lodge protests against the Swedish government.

2007: The Canadian Islamic Congress files complaints against *Maclean's* magazine for publishing "Islamophobic" articles, especially "The Future Belongs to Islam," by Mark Steyn.

2007: Geert Wilders, a Dutch politician, calls the Qur'an "a fascist book," compares it to *Mein Kampf*, and proposes that it be banned on the grounds that it incites hatred and violence. He receives death threats.

2008: Wilders produces *Fitna*, a film that juxtaposes verses of the Qur'an and photographs of terrorist acts. Jordan demands that he be prosecuted and puts out an international warrant for his arrest, charging him with blasphemy. Others offer rewards for his murder.

2008: Ezra Levant appears before the Alberta Human Rights and Citizenship Commission and films his appearances. His postings on his blog and on YouTube generate so much publicity that the commission eventually drops charges against him. He later testifies before the Human Rights Caucus of the U.S. Congress.

2008: A Dutch cartoonist writing under the name Gregorius Nekschot is arrested for publishing satirical cartoons about Muslims on his website.

2008: The Canadian Human Rights Commission drops charges against Mark Steyn and *Maclean's* magazine. The British Columbia Human Rights Commission, however, proceeds to hear the case.

2009: Geert Wilders is prosecuted for hate speech in the Netherlands. He is acquitted in 2011.

2010: Journalist and historian Lars Hedegaard is prosecuted in Denmark for insulting Islam. He is acquitted, but the prosecution appeals. In 2011, he is convicted.

2011: Elisabeth Sabaditsch-Wolff is prosecuted in Austria, charged with incitement to hatred and denigration of religious beliefs of a legally recognized religion. She is acquitted on the first charge but convicted on the second.

These incidents raise fundamental questions about freedom of speech. Some Muslims claim a right not to be offended. They insist that everyone observe restrictions expected of Muslims and demand that speech offensive to them be punished. In response, defenders of free speech argue that there is no right not to be offended. The ability to say offensive, even outrageous, things lies at the heart of liberty and the culture of free inquiry.

PLATO

from *The Republic*

Socrates (470–399 B.C.E.) was a contemporary of the great Greek playwrights Sophocles, Euripedes, and Aristophanes, as well as of the historians Thucydides and Herodotus. He is in many ways the central figure of Western philosophy. Socrates was the first person in the West to advance philosophical arguments. As his student Plato (427–347 B.C.E.) portrays him, Socrates put forward no particular theories of his own—indeed, he wrote nothing—but used arguments to clarify, investigate, and, usually, refute the views of others.

Socrates is the central character of many of Plato's works. Unlike most later philosophers, Plato wrote dialogues rather than essays or treatises. He never speaks in his own voice. In the early dialogues, Socrates asks what some virtue (for example, piety, self-control, courage, or friendship) is. Someone answers. Socrates analyzes the proposed definition and begins asking questions, leading the parties to the conversation to see that the definition cannot be right. Sometimes the definition is unclear; sometimes it includes too much; sometimes it does not include enough. Someone then proposes another definition, and the process continues. This constitutes the Socratic method *(also called* dialectic*). The early dialogues end with at least some of the participants leaving discouraged, embarrassed, or irritated at being unable to give a good definition. Socrates himself takes no position. In fact, he maintains that he knows only that he knows nothing.*

In Plato's Republic, *Socrates and other characters of the dialogue discuss the question "What is justice?" Socrates goes beyond criticizing the views of others and outlines the ideal state. He advocates a sweeping censorship. Those who are to be leaders—the guardians—must be brought up to be virtuous. This requires that they hear and read only what ennobles their characters. Anything that would debase them must be banned. (Source: Plato,* Republic, *translated by Benjamin Jowett, from* The Dialogues of Plato *[Oxford: Oxford University Press, 1892].)*

(Socrates, Adeimantus.)

Educating Leaders

Then we have found the desired natures; and now that we have found them, how are they [the guardians, that is, the leaders of the state] to be reared and educated? Is not this an inquiry which may be expected to throw light on greater inquiry which is our final end—How do justice and injustice grow up in States? for we do not want either to omit what is to the point or to draw out the argument to an inconvenient length.

Adeimantus thought that the inquiry would be of great service to us.

Then, I said, my dear friend, the task must not be given up, even if somewhat long.

Certainly not.

Come then, and let us pass a leisure hour in storytelling, and our story shall be the education of our heroes.

By all means.

And what shall be their education? . . .

You know also that the beginning is the most important part of any work, especially in the case of a young and tender thing; for that is the time at which the character is being formed and the desired impression is more readily taken.

Quite true.

Censorship

And shall we just carelessly allow children to hear any casual tales which may be devised by casual persons, and to receive into their minds ideas for the most part the very opposite of those which we should wish them to have when they are grown up?

We cannot.

Then the first thing will be to establish a censorship of the writers of fiction, and let the censors receive any tale of fiction which is good, and reject the bad; and we will desire mothers and nurses to tell their children the authorized ones only. Let them fashion the mind with such tales, even more fondly than they mould the body with their hands; but most of those which are now in use must be discarded.

Of what tales are you speaking? he said.

You may find a model of the lesser in the greater, I said; for they are necessarily of the same type, and there is the same spirit in both of them.

Very likely, he replied; but I do not as yet know what you would term the greater.

Those, I said, which are narrated by Homer and Hesiod, and the rest of the poets, who have ever been the great storytellers of mankind.

Lies

But which stories do you mean, he said; and what fault do you find with them?

A fault which is most serious, I said; the fault of telling a lie, and, what is more, a bad lie.

But when is this fault committed?

Whenever an erroneous representation is made of the nature of gods and heroes—as when a painter paints a portrait not having the shadow of a likeness to the original.

Yes, he said, that sort of thing is certainly very blamable; but what are the stories which you mean?

First of all, I said, there was that greatest of all lies in high places, which the poet told about Uranus, and which was a bad lie too—I mean what Hesiod says that Uranus did, and how Cronus retaliated on him. The doings of Cronus, and the sufferings which in turn his son inflicted upon him, even if they were true, ought certainly not to be lightly told to young and thoughtless persons; if possible, they had better be buried in silence. But if there is an absolute necessity for their mention, a chosen few might hear them in a mystery, and they should sacrifice not a common pig, but some huge and unprocurable victim; and then the number of the hearers will be very few indeed.

Why, yes, said he, those stories are extremely objectionable.

Yes, Adeimantus, they are stories not to be repeated in our State; the young man should not be told that in committing the worst of crimes he is far from doing anything outrageous; and that even if he chastises his father when he does wrong, in whatever manner, he will only be following the example of the first and greatest among the gods.

I entirely agree with you, he said; in my opinion those stories are quite unfit to be repeated.

Quarrels

Neither, if we mean our future guardians to regard the habit of quarreling among themselves as of all things the basest, should any word be said to them of the wars in heaven, and of the plots and fightings of the gods against one another, for they are not true. No, we shall never mention the battles of the giants, or let them be embroidered on garments; and we shall be silent about the innumerable other quarrels of gods and heroes with their friends and relatives. If they would only believe us we would tell them that quarreling is unholy, and that never up to this time has there been any quarrel between citizens; this is what old men and old women should begin by telling children; and when they grow up, the poets also should be told to compose them in a similar spirit. But the narrative of Hephaestus binding Hera his mother, or how on another occasion Zeus sent him flying for taking her part when she was being beaten, and all the battles of the gods in Homer—these tales must not be admitted into our State, whether they are supposed to have an allegorical meaning or not. For a young person cannot judge what is allegorical and what is literal; anything that he receives into his mind at that age is likely to become indelible and unalterable; and therefore it is most important that the tales which the young first hear should be models of virtuous thoughts.

The Problem of Evil

There you are right, he replied; but if anyone asks where are such models to be found and of what tales are you speaking—how shall we answer him?

I said to him, You and I, Adeimantus, at this moment are not poets, but founders of a State: now the founders of a State ought to know the general forms in which poets should cast their tales, and the limits which must be observed by them, but to make the tales is not their business.

Very true, he said; but what are these forms of theology which you mean?

Something of this kind, I replied: God is always to be represented as he truly is, whatever be the sort of poetry, epic, lyric, or tragic, in which the representation is given.

Right.

And is he not truly good? and must he not be represented as such?

Certainly.

And no good thing is hurtful?

No, indeed.

And that which is not hurtful hurts not?

Certainly not.

And that which hurts not does no evil?

No.

And can that which does no evil be a cause of evil?

Impossible.

And the good is advantageous?

Yes.

And therefore the cause of well-being?

Yes.

It follows, therefore, that the good is not the cause of all things, but of the good only?

Assuredly.

Then God, if he be good, is not the author of all things, as the many assert, but he is the cause of a few things only, and not of most things that occur to men. For few are the goods of human life, and many are the evils, and the good is to be attributed to God alone; of the evils the causes are to be sought elsewhere, and not in him.

That appears to me to be most true, he said.

Then we must not listen to Homer or to any other poet who is guilty of the folly of saying that two casks

> Lie at the threshold of Zeus, full of lots, one of good, the other of evil lots,

and that he to whom Zeus gives a mixture of the two

> Sometimes meets with evil fortune, at other times with good but that he to whom is given the cup of unmingled ill, Him wild hunger drives o'er the beauteous earth.

And again—

> Zeus, who is the dispenser of good and evil to us.

And if anyone asserts that the violation of oaths and treaties, which was really the work of Pandarus, was brought about by Athena and Zeus, or that the strife and contention of the gods were instigated by Themis and Zeus, he shall not have our approval; neither will we allow our young men to hear the words of AEschylus, that

> God plants guilt among men when he desires utterly to destroy a house.

And if a poet writes of the sufferings of Niobe—the subject of the tragedy in which these iambic verses occur—or of the house of Pelops, or of the Trojan War or on any similar theme, either we must not permit him to say that these are the works of God, or if they are of God, he must devise some explanation of them such as we are seeking: he must say that God did what was just and right, and they were the better for being punished; but that those who are punished are miserable, and that God is the author of their misery—the poet is not to be permitted to say; though he may say that the wicked are miserable because they require to be punished, and are benefited by receiving punishment from God; but that God being good is the author of evil to anyone is to be strenuously denied, and not to be said or sung or heard in verse or prose by anyone whether old or young in any well-ordered commonwealth. Such a fiction is suicidal, ruinous, impious.

I agree with you, he replied, and am ready to give my assent to the law.

Let this then be one of our rules and principles concerning the gods, to which our poets and reciters will be expected to conform—that God is not the author of all things, but of good only.

That will do, he said. . . .

BOOK III / THE ARTS IN EDUCATION

(*Socrates, Adeimantus.*)

Courage

Such, then, I said, are our principles of theology—some tales are to be told, and others are not to be told to our disciples from their youth upward, if we mean them to honor the gods and their parents, and to value friendship with one another.

Yes; and I think that our principles are right, he said.

But if they are to be courageous, must they not learn other lessons beside these, and lessons of such a kind as will take away the fear of death? Can any man be courageous who has the fear of death in him?

Certainly not, he said.

And can he be fearless of death, or will he choose death in battle rather than defeat and slavery, who believes the world below to be real and terrible?

Impossible.

Then we must assume a control over the narrators of this class of tales as well as over the others, and beg them not simply to revile, but rather to commend the world below, intimating to them that their descriptions are untrue, and will do harm to our future warriors.

That will be our duty, he said.

Then, I said, we shall have to obliterate many obnoxious passages, beginning with the verses

> I would rather be a serf on the land of a poor and portionless man than rule over all the dead who have come to naught. . . .

And we must beg Homer and the other poets not to be angry if we strike out these and similar passages, not because they are unpoetical, or unattractive to the popular ear, but because the greater the poetical charm of them, the less are they meet for the ears of boys and men who are meant to be free, and who should fear slavery more than death.

Undoubtedly.

Also we shall have to reject all the terrible and appalling names which describe the world below—Cocytus and Styx, ghosts under the earth, and sapless shades, and any similar words of which the very mention causes a shudder to pass through the inmost soul of him who hears them. I do not say that these horrible stories may not have a use of some kind; but there is a danger that the nerves of our guardians may be rendered too excitable and effeminate by them.

There is a real danger, he said.

Then we must have no more of them.

True.

Another and a nobler strain must be composed and sung by us.

Clearly.

And shall we proceed to get rid of the weepings and wailings of famous men?

They will go with the rest.

But shall we be right in getting rid of them? Reflect: our principle is that the good man will not consider death terrible to any other good man who is his comrade.

Yes; that is our principle.

And therefore he will not sorrow for his departed friend as though he had suffered anything terrible?

He will not.

Such an one, as we further maintain, is sufficient for himself and his own happiness, and therefore is least in need of other men.

True, he said.

And for this reason the loss of a son or brother, or the deprivation of fortune, is to him of all men least terrible.

Assuredly.

And therefore he will be least likely to lament, and will bear with the greatest equanimity any misfortune of this sort which may befall him.

Yes, he will feel such a misfortune far less than another. . . .

Self-Control

For if, my sweet Adeimantus, our youth seriously listen to such unworthy representations of the gods, instead of laughing at them as they ought, hardly will any of them deem that he himself, being but a man, can be dishonored by similar actions; neither will he rebuke any inclination which may arise in his mind to say and do the like. And instead of having any shame or self-control, he will be always whining and lamenting on slight occasions.

Yes, he said, that is most true.

Yes, 1 replied; but that surely is what ought not to be, as the argument has just proved to us; and by that proof we must abide until it is disproved by a better.

It ought not to be.

Neither ought our guardians to be given to laughter. For a fit of laughter which has been indulged to excess almost always produces a violent reaction.

So 1 believe.

Then persons of worth, even if only mortal men, must not be represented as overcome by laughter, and still less must such a representation of the gods be allowed.

Still less of the gods, as you say, he replied. . . .

The Right to Lie

Again, truth should be highly valued; if, as we were saying, a lie is useless to the gods, and useful only as a medicine to men, then the use of such medicines should be restricted to physicians; private individuals have no business with them.

Clearly not, he said.

Then if anyone at all is to have the privilege of lying, the rulers of the State should be the persons; and they, in their dealings either with enemies or with their own citizens, may be allowed to lie for the public good. But nobody else should meddle with anything of the kind; and although the rulers have this privilege, for a private man to lie to them in return is to be deemed a more heinous fault than for the patient or the pupil of a gymnasium not to speak the truth about his own bodily illnesses to the physician or to the trainer, or for a sailor not to tell the captain what is happening about the ship and the rest of the crew, and how things are going with himself or his fellow sailors.

Most true, he said.

If, then, the ruler catches anybody beside himself lying in the State,

> Any of the craftsmen, whether he be priest or physician or carpenter,

he will punish him for introducing a practice which is equally subversive and destructive of ship or State.

Most certainly, he said, if our idea of the State is ever carried out.

Temperance

In the next place our youth must be temperate?

Certainly.

Are not the chief elements of temperance, speaking generally, obedience to commanders and self-control in sensual pleasures?

True.

Then we shall approve such language as that of Diomede in Homer,

> Friend sit still and obey my word,

and the verses which follow,

> The Greeks marched breathing prowess, . . . in silent awe of their leaders.

and other sentiments of the same kind.

We shall.

What of this line,

> O heavy with wine, who hast the eyes of a dog and the heart of a stag,

and of the words which follow? Would you say that these, or any similar impertinences which private individuals are supposed to address to their rulers, whether in verse or prose, are well or ill spoken?

They are ill spoken.

They may very possibly afford some amusement, but they do not conduce to temperance. And therefore they are likely to do harm to our young men—you would agree with me there?

Yes. . . .

In the next place, we must not let them be receivers of gifts or lovers of money.

Certainly not.

Neither must we sing to them of

> Gifts persuading gods, and persuading reverend kings.

Neither is Phoenix, die tutor of Achilles, to be approved or deemed to have given his pupil good counsel when he told him that he should take the gifts of the Greeks and assist them; but that without a gift he should not lay aside his anger. Neither will we believe or acknowledge Achilles himself to have been such a lover of money that he look Agamemnon's gifts, or that when he had received payment he restored the dead body of Hector, but that without payment he was unwilling to do so.

Undoubtedly, he said, these are not sentiments which can be approved. . . .

Justice

And what shall we say about men? That is clearly the remaining portion of our subject.

Clearly so.

But we are not in a condition to answer this question at present, my friend.

Why not?

Because, if 1 am not mistaken, we shall have to say that about men; poets and storytellers are guilty of making the gravest misstatements when they tell us that wicked men are often happy, and the good miserable; and that injustice is profitable when undetected, but that justice is a man's own loss and another's gain—these things we shall forbid them to utter, and command them to sing and say the opposite.

To be sure we shall, he replied.

But if you admit that 1 am right in this, then 1 shall maintain that you have implied the principle for which we have been all along contending.

I grant the truth of your inference.

That such things are or are not to be said about men is a question which we cannot determine until we have discovered what justice is, and how naturally advantageous to the possessor, whether he seem to be just or not.

Most true, he said. . . .

QUESTIONS FOR REFLECTION

1. How would Socrates decide which religious stories and texts should be banned?
2. Which stories about heroes would Socrates censor? Why?
3. Why would Socrates punish liars? What kinds of lies do we punish by law today? Would it be good to extend punishment to all lies, in your view?
4. Think of some well-known fairy tales. Which would Socrates censor? Why?
5. Are there well-known (a) Shakespearean plays; (b) movies; or (c) Bible stories that Socrates would ban? Which, and why?
6. Socrates moves from the relatively uncontroversial thesis that young children should not hear or read certain kinds of stories to the controversial position that those stories should be banned. How might he argue for this move?
7. Who has the right to lie, and why?

JOHN STUART MILL

from On Liberty

(Source: London: Parker, 1859.)

CHAPTER II / OF THE LIBERTY OF THOUGHT AND DISCUSSION

. . . Let us suppose . . . that the government is entirely at one with the people, and never thinks of exerting any power of coercion unless in agreement with what it conceives to be their voice. But I deny the right of the people to exercise such coercion, either by themselves or by their government. The power itself is illegitimate. The best government has no more title to it than the worst. It is as noxious, or more noxious, when exerted in accordance with public opinion than when in opposition to it. If all mankind minus one were of one opinion, mankind would be no more justified in silencing that one person than he, if he had the power, would be justified in silencing mankind. Were an opinion a personal possession of no value except to the owner, if to be obstructed in the enjoyment of it were simply a private injury, it would make some difference whether the injury was inflicted only on a few persons or on many. But the peculiar evil of silencing the expression of an opinion is that it is robbing the human race, posterity as well as the existing generation—those who dissent from the opinion, still more than those who hold it. If the opinion is right, they are deprived of the opportunity of exchanging error for truth; if wrong, they lose, what is almost as great a benefit, the clearer perception and livelier impression of truth produced by its collision with error.

It is necessary to consider separately these two hypotheses, each of which has a distinct branch of the argument corresponding to it. We can never be sure that the opinion we are endeavoring to stifle is a false opinion; and if we were sure, stifling it would be an evil still.

Fallibility

First, the opinion which it is attempted to suppress by authority may possibly be true. Those who desire to suppress it, of course, deny its truth; but they are not infallible. They have no authority to decide the question for all mankind and exclude every other person from the means of judging. To refuse a hearing to an opinion because they are sure that it is false is to assume that *their* certainty is the same thing as *absolute* certainty. All silencing of discussion is an assumption of infallibility. . . .

The objection likely to be made to this argument would probably take some such form as the following. There is no greater assumption of infallibility in forbidding the propagation of error than in any other thing which is done by public authority on its own judgment and responsibility. Judgment is given to men that they may use it. Because it may be used erroneously, are men to be told that they ought not to use it at all? To prohibit what they think pernicious is not claiming exemption from error, but fulfilling the duty incumbent on them, although fallible, of acting on their conscientious conviction. If we were never to act on our opinions, because those opinions may be wrong, we should leave all our interests uncared for, and all our duties unperformed. An objection which applies to all conduct can be no valid objection to any conduct in particular. It is the duty of governments, and of individuals, to form the truest opinions they can; to form them carefully, and never impose them upon others unless they are quite sure of being right. But when they are sure (such reasoners may say), it is not conscientiousness but cowardice to shrink from acting on their opinions and allow doctrines which they honestly think dangerous to the welfare of mankind, either in this life or in another, to be scattered abroad without restraint, because other people, in less enlightened times, have persecuted opinions now believed to be true. Let us take care, it may be said, not to make the same mistake; but governments and nations have made mistakes in other things which are not denied to be fit subjects for the exercise of authority: they have laid on bad taxes, made unjust wars. Ought we therefore to lay on no taxes and, under whatever provocation, make no wars? Men and governments must act to the best of their ability. There is no such thing as absolute certainty, but there is assurance sufficient for the purposes of human life. We may, and must, assume our opinion to be true for the guidance of our own conduct; and it is assuming no more when we forbid bad men to pervert society by the propagation of opinions which we regard as false and pernicious.

I answer, that it is assuming very much more. There is the greatest difference between presuming an opinion to be true because, with every opportunity for contesting it, it has not been refuted, and assuming its truth for the purpose of not permitting its refutation. Complete liberty of contradicting and disproving our opinion is the very condition which justifies us in assuming its truth for purposes of action; and on no other terms can a being with human faculties have any rational assurance of being right.

Corrigibility

When we consider either the history of opinion or the ordinary conduct of human life, to what is it to be ascribed that the one and the other are no worse than they are? Not certainly to the inherent force of the human understanding, for on any matter not self-evident there are ninety-nine persons totally incapable of judging of it for one who is capable; and the capacity of the hundredth person is only comparative, for the majority of the eminent men of every past generation held many opinions now known to be erroneous, and did or approved numerous things which no one will now justify. Why is it, then, that there is on the whole a preponderance among mankind of rational opinions and rational conduct? If there really is this preponderance—which there must be unless human affairs are, and have always been, in an almost desperate state—it is owing to a quality of the human mind, the source of everything respectable in man either as an intellectual or as a moral being, namely, that his errors are corrigible. He is capable of rectifying his mistakes by discussion and experience. Not by experience alone. There must be discussion to show how experience is to be interpreted. Wrong opinions and practices gradually yield to fact and argument; but facts and arguments, to produce any effect on the mind, must be brought before it. Very few facts are able to tell their own story, without comments to bring out their meaning. The whole strength and value, then, of human judgment depending on the one property, that it can be set right when it is wrong, reliance can be placed on it only when the means of setting it right are kept constantly at hand. In the case of any person whose judgment is really deserving of confidence, how has it become so? Because he has kept his mind open to criticism of his opinions and conduct. Because it has been his practice to listen to all that could be said against him; to profit by as much of it as was just, and to expound to himself, and upon occasion to others, the fallacy of what was fallacious. Because he has felt that the only way in which a human being can make some approach to knowing the whole of a subject is by hearing what can be said about it by persons of every variety of opinion, and studying all modes in which it can be looked at by every character of mind. No wise man ever acquired his wisdom in any mode but this; nor is it in the nature of human intellect to become wise in any other manner. The steady habit of correcting and completing his own opinion by collating it with those of others, so far from causing doubt and hesitation in carrying it into practice, is the only stable foundation for a just reliance on it; for, being cognizant of all that can, at least obviously, be said against him and having taken up his position against all gain-sayers—knowing that he has sought for objections and difficulties instead of avoiding them, and has shut out no light which can be thrown upon the subject from any quarter—he has a right to think his judgment better than that of any person, or any multitude, who have not gone through a similar process. . . .

Justification

Let us now pass to the second division of the argument, and dismissing the supposition that any of the received opinions may be false, let us assume them to be true and examine into the worth of the manner in which they are likely to be held when their truth is not freely and openly canvassed. However unwillingly a person who has a strong opinion may admit the possibility that his opinion may be false, he ought to be moved by the consideration that, however true it may be, if it is not fully, frequently, and fearlessly discussed, it will be held as a dead dogma, not a living truth.

There is a class of persons (happily not quite so numerous as formerly) who think it enough if a person assents undoubtingly to what they think true, though he has no knowledge whatever of the grounds of the opinion and could not make a tenable defense of it against the most superficial objections. Such persons, if they can once get their creed taught from authority, naturally think that no good, and some harm, comes of its being allowed to be questioned. Where their influence prevails, they make it nearly impossible for the received opinion to be rejected wisely and considerately, though it may still be rejected rashly and ignorantly; for to shut out discussion entirely is seldom possible, and when it once gets in, beliefs not grounded on conviction are apt to give way before the slightest semblance of an argument. Waiving, however, this possibility—assuming that the true opinion abides in the mind, but abides as a prejudice, a belief independent of, and proof against, argument—this is not the way in which truth ought to be held by a rational being. This is not knowing the truth. Truth, thus held, is but one superstition the more, accidentally clinging to the words which enunciate a truth. . . .

Meaning

If, however, the mischievous operation of the absence of free discussion, when the received opinions are true, were confined to leaving men ignorant of the grounds of those opinions, it might be thought that this, if an intellectual, is no moral evil and does not affect the worth of the opinions, regarded in their influence on the character. The fact, however, is that not only the grounds of the opinion are forgotten in the absence of discussion, but too often the meaning of the opinion itself. The words which convey it cease to suggest ideas, or suggest only a small portion of those they were originally employed to communicate. Instead of a vivid conception and a living belief, there remain only a few phrases retained by rote; or, if any part, the shell and husk only of the meaning is retained, the finer essence being lost. The great chapter in human history which this fact occupies and fills cannot be too earnestly studied and meditated on.

It is illustrated in the experience of almost all ethical doctrines and religious creeds: They are all full of meaning and vitality to those who originate them, and to the direct disciples of the originators. Their meaning continues to be felt in undiminished strength, and is perhaps brought out into even fuller consciousness, so long as the struggle lasts to give the doctrine or creed an ascendancy over other creeds. At last it either prevails and becomes the general opinion, or its progress stops; it keeps possession of the ground it has gained, but ceases to spread further. When either of these results has become apparent, controversy on the subject flags, and gradually dies away. The doctrine has taken its place, if not as a received opinion, as one of the admitted sects or divisions of opinion; those who hold it have generally inherited, not adopted it; and conversion from one of these doctrines to another, being now an exceptional fact, occupies little place in the thoughts of their professors. Instead of being, as at first, constantly on the alert either to defend themselves against the world or to bring the world over to them, they have subsided into acquiescence and neither listen, when they can help it, to arguments against their creed, nor trouble dissentients (if there be such) with arguments in its favor. From this time may usually be dated the decline in the living power of the doctrine. . . .

. . . There are many reasons, doubtless, why doctrines which are the badge of a sect retain more of their vitality than those common to all recognized sects, and why more pains are taken by teachers to keep their meaning alive; but one reason certainly is that the peculiar doctrines are more questioned and have to be oftener defended against open gainsayers. Both teachers and learners go to sleep at their post as soon as there is no enemy in the field. . . .

Partial Truth

It still remains to speak of one of the principal causes which make diversity of opinion advantageous, and will continue to do so until mankind shall have entered a stage of intellectual advancement which at present seems at an incalculable distance. We have hitherto considered only two possibilities: that the received opinion may be false, and some other opinion, consequently, true; or that, the received opinion being true, a conflict with the opposite error is essential to a clear apprehension and deep feeling of its truth. But there is a commoner case than either of these: when the conflicting doctrines, instead of being one true and the other false, share the truth between them, and the nonconforming opinion is needed to supply the remainder of the truth of which the received doctrine embodies only a part. Popular opinions, on subjects not palpable to sense, are often true, but seldom or never the whole truth. They are a part of the truth, sometimes a greater, sometimes a smaller part, but exaggerated, distorted, and disjointed from the truths by which they ought to be accompanied and limited. Heretical opinions, on the other hand, are generally some of these suppressed and neglected truths, bursting the bonds which kept them down, and either seeking reconciliation with the truth contained in the common opinion, or fronting it as enemies, and setting themselves up, with similar exclusiveness, as the whole truth. The latter case is hitherto the most frequent, as, in the human mind, one-sidedness has always been the rule, and many-sidedness the exception. Hence, even in revolutions of opinion, one part of the truth usually sets while another rises. Even progress, which ought to super-add, for the most part only substitutes one partial and incomplete truth for another; improvement consisting chiefly in this, that the new fragment of truth is more wanted, more adapted to the needs of the time than that which it displaces. Such being the partial character of prevailing opinions, even when resting on a true foundation, every opinion which embodies somewhat of the portion of truth which the common opinion omits ought to be considered precious, with whatever amount of error and confusion that truth may be blended. No sober judge of human affairs will feel bound to be indignant because those who force on our notice truths which we should otherwise have overlooked, overlook some of those which we see. Rather, he will think that so long as popular truth is one-sided, it is more desirable than otherwise that unpopular truth should have one-sided assertors, too, such being usually the most energetic and the most likely to compel reluctant attention to the fragment of wisdom which they proclaim as if it were the whole. . . .

. . . only through diversity of opinion is there, in the existing state of human intellect, a chance of fair play to all sides of the truth. When there are persons to be found who form an exception to the apparent unanimity of the world on any subject, even if the world is in the right, it is always probable that dissentients have something worth hearing to say for themselves, and that truth would lose something by their silence. . . .

Summary

We have now recognized the necessity to the mental well-being of mankind (on which all their other well-being depends) of freedom of opinion, and freedom of the expression of opinion, on four distinct grounds, which we will now briefly recapitulate:

First, if any opinion is compelled to silence, that opinion may, for aught we can certainly know, be true. To deny this is to assume our own infallibility.

Secondly, though the silenced opinion be an error, it may, and very commonly does, contain a portion of truth; and since the general or prevailing opinion on any subject is rarely or never the whole truth, it is only by the collision of adverse opinions that the remainder of the truth has any chance of being supplied.

Thirdly, even if the received opinion be not only true, but the whole truth; unless it is suffered to be, and actually is, vigorously and earnestly contested, it will, by most of those who receive it, be held in the manner of a prejudice, with little comprehension or feeling of its rational grounds. And not only this, but, fourthly, the meaning of the doctrine itself will be in danger of being lost or enfeebled, and deprived of its vital effect on the character and conduct: the dogma becoming a mere formal profession, inefficacious for good, but cumbering the ground and preventing the growth of any real and heartfelt conviction from reason or personal experience. . . .

CHAPTER III / OF INDIVIDUALITY, AS ONE OF THE ELEMENTS OF WELL-BEING

. . . No one pretends that actions should be as free as opinions. On the contrary, even opinions lose their immunity when the circumstances in which they are expressed are such as to constitute their expression a positive instigation to some mischievous act. An opinion that corn dealers are starvers of the poor, or that private property is robbery, ought to be unmolested when simply circulated through the press, but may justly incur punishment when delivered orally to an excited mob assembled before the house of a corn dealer, or when handed about among the same mob in the form of a placard. Acts of whatever kind, which without justifiable cause do harm to others may be, and in the more important cases absolutely require to be, controlled by the unfavorable sentiments, and, when needful, by the active interference of mankind. The liberty of the individual must be thus far limited; he must not make himself a nuisance to other people. But if he refrains from molesting others in what concerns them, and merely acts according to his own inclination and judgment in things which concern himself, the same reasons which show that opinion should be free prove also that he should be allowed, without molestation, to carry his opinions into practice at his own cost. . . .

QUESTIONS FOR REFLECTION

1. How does Mill's defense of freedom of thought and discussion fit into the overall scheme of *On Liberty*? Is speech self-regarding or other-regarding? Is his defense an application of the harm principle or an extension of it?
2. "All silencing of discussion is an assumption of infallibility," Mill contends. How does he argue for this claim? Do you agree?
3. Why does Mill think that the expression even of obviously false opinions should be protected?
4. Some contemporary advocates of controlling certain forms of expression argue that although the government cannot ban the expression of certain views, it can ban certain ways of expressing them—ways involving pornography, say, or the use of racial epithets. What is Mill's view about such restrictions? What arguments does he advance in support of his position? Do you find his arguments persuasive?
5. Mill mentions one exception to freedom of speech: inciting a mob to violence. What general principle lies behind this exception? What other exceptions might Mill be willing to accept?

STANLEY FISH

from *There's No Such Thing as Free Speech, and It's a Good Thing, Too*

Stanley Fish is dean emeritus at the University of Illinois at Chicago. (Source: From Boston Review *vol. 17 no. 1 [February 1992]. Copyright © 1992 by the Boston Critic, Inc. Reprinted by permission.)*

Nowadays the First Amendment is the First Refuge of Scoundrels.

—*S. Johnson and S. Fish*

Lately, many on the liberal and progressive left have been disconcerted to find that words, phrases, and concepts thought to be their property and generative of their politics have been appropriated by the forces of neoconservatism. This is particularly true of the concept of free speech, for in recent years First Amendment rhetoric has been used to justify policies and actions the left finds problematical if not abhorrent: pornography, sexist language, campus hate speech. How has this happened? The answer I shall give in this essay is that abstract concepts like free speech do not have any "natural" content but are filled with whatever content and direction one can manage to put into them. "Free speech" is just the name we give to verbal behavior that serves the substantive agendas we wish to advance; and we give our preferred verbal behaviors *that* name when we can, when we have the power to do so, because in the rhetoric of American life, the label "free speech" is the one you want your favorites to wear. Free speech, in short, is not an independent value but a political prize, and if that prize has been captured by a politics opposed to yours, it can no longer be invoked in ways that further your purposes, for it is now an obstacle to those purposes. This is something that the liberal left has yet to understand, and what follows is an attempt to pry its members loose from a vocabulary that may now be a disservice to them.

Not far from the end of his *Areopagitica,* and after having celebrated the virtues of toleration and unregulated publication in passages that find their way into every discussion of free speech and the First Amendment, John Milton catches himself up short and says, of course I didn't mean Catholics, them we exterminate:

> I mean not tolerated popery, and open superstition, which as it extirpates all religious and civil supremacies, so itself should be extirpated . . . that also which is impious or evil absolutely against faith or manners no law can possibly permit that intends not to unlaw itself.

Notice that Milton is not simply stipulating a single exception to a rule generally in place; the kinds of utterance that might be regulated and even prohibited on pain of trial and punishment constitute an open set; popery is named only as a particularly perspicuous instance of the advocacy that cannot be tolerated. No doubt there are other forms of speech and action that might be categorized as "open superstitions" or as subversive of piety, faith, and manners, and presumably these too would be candidates for "extirpation." Nor would Milton think himself culpable for having failed to provide a list of unprotected utterances.

The list will fill itself out as utterances are put to the test implied by his formulation: Would this form of speech or advocacy, if permitted to flourish, tend to undermine the very purposes for which our society is constituted? One cannot answer this question with respect to a particular utterance in advance of its emergence on the world's stage; rather, one must wait and ask the question in the full context of its production and (possible) dissemination. It might appear that the result would be *ad hoc* and unprincipled, but for Milton the principle inheres in the core values in whose name individuals of like mind came together in the first place. Those values, which include the search for truth and the promotion of virtue, are capacious enough to accommodate a diversity of views. But at some point—again impossible of advance specification—capaciousness will threaten to become shapelessness, and at that point fidelity to the original values will demand acts of extirpation.

I want to say that all affirmations of freedom of expression are like Milton's, dependent for their force on an exception that literally carves out the space in which expression can then emerge. I do not mean that expression (saying something) is a realm whose integrity is sometimes compromised by certain restrictions but that restriction, in the form of an underlying articulation of the world that necessarily (if silently) negates alternatively possible articulations, is constitutive of expression. Without restriction, without an inbuilt sense of what it would be meaningless to say or wrong to say, there could be no assertion and no reason for asserting it. The exception to unregulated expression is not a negative restriction but a positive hollowing out of value—we are for *this,* which means we are against *that*—in relation to which meaningful assertion can then occur. It is in reference to that value—constituted as all values are by an act of exclusion—that some forms of speech will be heard as (quite literally) intolerable. Speech, in short, is never a value in and of itself but is always produced within the precincts of some assumed conception of the good to which it must yield in the event of conflict. When the pinch comes (and sooner or later it will always come) and the institution (be it church, state, or university) is confronted by behavior subversive of its core rationale, it will respond by declaring "of course we mean not tolerated———, that we extirpate," not because an exception to a general freedom has suddenly and contradictorily been announced, but because the freedom has never been general and has always been understood against the background of an originary exclusion that gives it meaning. . . .

Despite the apparent absoluteness of the First Amendment, there are any number of ways of getting around it, ways that are known to every student of the law. In general, the preferred strategy is to manipulate the distinction, essential to First Amendment jurisprudence, between speech and action. The distinction is essential because no one would think to frame a First Amendment that began "Congress shall make no law abridging freedom of action," for that would amount to saying "Congress shall make no law," which would amount to saying "There shall be no law," only actions uninhibited and unregulated. If the First Amendment is to make any sense, have any bite, speech must be declared not to be a species of action, or to be a special form of action lacking the aspects of action that cause it to be the object of regulation. The latter strategy is the favored one and usually involves the separation of speech from consequences. This is what Archibald Cox does when he assigns to the First Amendment the job of protecting "expressions separable from conduct harmful to other individuals and the community." The difficulty of managing this segregation is well known: speech always seems to be crossing the line into action, where it becomes, at least potentially, consequential. In the face of this categorical instability, First Amendment theorists and jurists fashion a distinction within the speech/action distinction: some forms of speech are not really speech because their purpose is to incite violence or because they are, as the court declares in *Chaplinsky* v. *New Hampshire* (1942), "fighting words," words "likely to provoke the average person to retaliation, and thereby cause a breach of the peace."

The trouble with this definition is that it distinguishes not between fighting words and words that remain safely and merely expressive but between words that are provocative to one group (the group that falls under the rubric "average person") and words that might be provocative to other groups, groups of persons not now considered average. And if you ask what words are likely to be provocative to those non-average groups, what are likely to be *their* fighting words, the answer is anything and everything, for as Justice Holmes said long ago (in *Gitlow* v. *New York*), every idea is an incitement to somebody, and since ideas come packaged in sentences, in words, every sentence is potentially, in some situation that might occur tomorrow, a fighting word and therefore a candidate for regulation.

This insight cuts two ways. One could conclude from it that the fighting words exception is a bad idea because there is no way to prevent clever and unscrupulous advocates from shoveling so many forms of speech into the excepted category that the zone of constitutionally protected speech shrinks to nothing and is finally without inhabitants. Or, alternatively, one could conclude that there was never anything in the zone in the first place and that the difficulty of limiting the fighting words exception is merely a particular instance of the general difficulty of separating speech from action. And if one opts for this second conclusion, as I do, then a further conclusion is inescapable: insofar as the point of the First Amendment is to identify speech separable from conduct and from the consequences that come in conduct's wake, there is no such speech and therefore nothing for the First Amendment to protect. Or, to make the point from the other direction, when a court invalidates legislation because it infringes on protected speech, it is not because the speech in question is without consequences but because the consequences have been discounted in relation to a good that is judged to outweigh them. Despite what they say, courts are never in the business of protecting speech per se, "mere" speech (a nonexistent animal); rather, they are in the business of classifying speech (as protected or regulatable) in relation to a value—the health of the republic, the vigor of the economy, the maintenance of the status quo, the undoing of the status quo—that is the true, if unacknowledged, object of their protection.

But if this is the case, a First Amendment purist might reply, why not drop the charade along with the malleable distinctions that make it possible, and declare up front that total freedom of speech is our primary value and trumps anything else, no matter what? The answer is that freedom of expression would only be a primary value if it didn't matter what was said, didn't matter in the sense that no one gave a damn but just liked to hear talk. There are contexts like that, a Hyde Park corner or a call-in talk show where people get to sound off for the sheer fun of it. These, however, are special contexts, artificially bounded spaces designed to assure that talking is not taken seriously. In ordinary contexts, talk is produced with the goal of trying to move the world in one direction rather than another. In these contexts—the contexts of everyday life—you go to the trouble of asserting that X is Y only because you suspect that some people are wrongly asserting that X is Z or that X doesn't exist. You assert, in short, because you give a damn, not about assertion—as if it were a value in and of itself—but about what your assertion is about. It may seem paradoxical, but free expression could only be a primary value if what you are valuing is the right to make noise; but if you are engaged in some purposive activity in the course of which speech happens to be produced, sooner or later you will come to a point when you decide that some forms of speech do not further but endanger that purpose.

Take the case of universities and colleges. Could it be the purpose of such places to encourage free expression? If the answer were "yes," it would be hard to say why there would be any need for classes, or examinations, or departments, or disciplines, or libraries, since freedom of expression requires nothing but a soapbox or an open telephone line. The very fact of the university's machinery—of the events, rituals, and procedures that fill its calendar—argues for some other, more substantive purpose. In relation to that purpose (which will be realized differently in different kinds of institutions), the flourishing of free expression will in almost all circumstances be an obvious good; but in some circumstances, freedom of expression may pose a threat to that purpose, and at that point it may be necessary to discipline or regulate speech, lest, to paraphrase Milton, the institution sacrifice itself to one of its *accidental* features.

Interestingly enough, the same conclusion is reached (inadvertently) by Congressman Henry Hyde, who is addressing these very issues in a recently offered amendment to Title VI of the Civil Rights Act. The first section of the amendment states its purpose, to protect "the free speech rights of college students" by prohibiting private as well as public educational institutions from "subjecting any student to disciplinary sanctions solely on the basis of conduct that is speech." The second section enumerates the remedies available to students whose speech rights may have been abridged; and the third, which is to my mind the nub of the matter, declares as an exception to the amendment's jurisdiction any "educational institution that is controlled by a religious organization," on the reasoning that the application of the amendment to such institutions "would not be consistent with the religious tenets of such organizations." In effect, what Congressman Hyde is saying is that at the heart of these colleges and universities is a set of beliefs, and it would be wrong to require them to tolerate behavior, including speech behavior, inimical to those beliefs. But insofar as this logic is persuasive, it applies across the board, for all educational institutions rest on some set of beliefs—no institution is "just there" independent of any purpose—and it is hard to see why the rights of an institution to protect and preserve its basic "tenets" should be restricted only to those that are religiously controlled. Read strongly, the third section of the amendment undoes sections one and two—the exception becomes, as it always was, the rule—and points us to a balancing test very much like that employed in Canadian law: given that any college or university is informed by a core rationale, an administrator faced with complaints about offensive speech should ask whether damage to the core would be greater if the speech were tolerated or regulated.

The objection to this line of reasoning is well known and has recently been reformulated by Benno Schmidt, former president of Yale University. According to Schmidt, speech codes on campuses constitute "well-intentioned but misguided efforts to give values of community and harmony a higher place than freedom" (*Wall Street Journal,* May 6, 1991). "When the goals of harmony collide with freedom of expression," he continues, "freedom must be the paramount obligation of an academic community." The flaw in this logic is on display in the phrase "academic community," for the phrase recognizes what Schmidt would deny, that expression only occurs in communities—if not in an academic community, then in a shopping mall community or a dinner party community or an airplane ride community or an office community. In these communities and in any others that could be imagined (with the possible exception of a community of major league baseball fans), limitations on speech in relation to a defining and deeply assumed purpose are inseparable from community membership.

Indeed, "limitations" is the wrong word because it suggests that expression, as an activity and a value, has a pure form that is always in danger of being compromised by the urgings of special interest communities; but independently of a community context informed by interest (that is, purpose), expression would be at once inconceivable and unintelligible. Rather than being a value that is threatened by limitations and constraints, expression, in any form worth worrying about, is a *product* of limitations and constraints, of the already-in-place presuppositions that give assertions their very particular point. Indeed, the very act of thinking of something to say (whether or not it is subsequently regulated) is already constrained—rendered impure, and because impure, communicable—by the background context within which the thought takes its shape. (The analysis holds too for "freedom," which in Schmidt's vision is an entirely empty concept referring to an urge without direction. But like expression, freedom is a coherent notion only in relation to a goal or good that limits and, by limiting, shapes its exercise.)

Arguments like Schmidt's only get their purchase by first imagining speech as occurring in no context whatsoever, and then stripping particular speech acts of the properties conferred on them by contexts. The trick is nicely illustrated when Schmidt urges protection for speech "no matter how obnoxious in content." "Obnoxious" at once acknowledges the reality of speech-related harms and trivializes them by suggesting that they are *surface* injuries that any large-minded ("liberated and humane") person should be able to bear. The possibility that speech-related injuries may be grievous and *deeply* wounding is carefully kept out of sight, and because it is kept out of sight, the fiction of a world of weightless verbal exchange can be maintained, at least within the confines of Schmidt's carefully denatured discourse.

To this Schmidt would no doubt reply, as he does in his essay, that harmful speech should be answered not by regulation but by more speech; but that would make sense only if the effects of speech could be canceled out by additional speech, only if the pain and humiliation caused by racial or religious epithets could be ameliorated by saying something like "So's your old man." What Schmidt fails to realize at every level of his argument is that expression is more than a matter of proffering and receiving propositions, that words do work in the world of a kind that cannot be confined to a purely cognitive realm of "mere" ideas.

It could be said, however, that I myself mistake the nature of the work done by freely tolerated speech because I am too focused on short-run outcomes and fail to understand that the good effects of speech will be realized, not in the present, but in a future whose emergence regulation could only inhibit. This line of reasoning would also weaken one of my key points, that speech in and of itself cannot be a value and is only worth worrying about if it is in the service of something with which it cannot be identical. My mistake, one could argue, is to equate the something in whose service speech is with some locally espoused value (e.g., the end of racism, the empowerment of disadvantaged minorities), whereas in fact we should think of that something as a now-inchoate shape that will be given firm lines only by time's pencil. That is why the shape now receives such indeterminate characterizations (e.g., true self-fulfillment, a more perfect polity, a more capable citizenry, a less partial truth); we cannot now know it, and therefore we must not prematurely fix it in ways that will bind successive generations to error.

This forward-looking view of what the First Amendment protects has a great appeal, in part because it continues in a secular form the Puritan celebration of millenarian hopes, but it imposes a requirement so severe that one would expect more justification for it than is usually provided. The requirement is that we endure whatever pain racist and hate speech inflicts for the sake of a future whose emergence we can only take on faith. In a specifically religious vision like Milton's, this makes perfect sense (it is indeed the whole of Christianity), but in the context of a politics that puts its trust in the world and not in the Holy Spirit, it raises more questions than it answers and could be seen as the second of two strategies designed to delegitimize the complaints of victimized groups. The first strategy, as I have noted, is to define speech in such a way as to render it inconsequential (on the model of "sticks and stones will break my bones, but . . ."); the second strategy is to acknowledge the (often grievous) consequences of speech but declare that we must suffer them in the name of something that cannot be named. The two strategies are denials from slightly different directions of the *present* effects of racist speech; one confines those effects to a closed and safe realm of pure mental activity; the other imagines the effects of speech spilling over into the world but only in an ever-receding future for whose sake we must forever defer taking action.

I find both strategies unpersuasive, but my own skepticism concerning them is less important than the fact that in general they seem to have worked; in the parlance of the marketplace (a parlance First Amendment commentators love), many in the society seemed to have bought them. Why? The answer, I think, is that people cling to First Amendment pieties because they do not wish to face what they correctly take to be the alternative. That alternative is *politics*, the realization (at which I have already hinted) that decisions about what is and is not protected in the realm of expression will rest not on principle or firm doctrine but on the ability of some persons to interpret—recharacterize or rewrite—principle and doctrine in ways that lead to the protection of speech they want heard and the regulation of speech they want silenced. (That is how George Bush can argue *for* flag-burning statutes and *against* campus hate-speech codes.) When the First Amendment is successfully invoked, the result is not a victory for free speech in the face of a challenge from politics but a *political victory* won by the party that has managed to wrap its agenda in the mantle of free speech.

It is from just such a conclusion—a conclusion that would put politics *inside* the First Amendment—that commentators recoil, saying things like "This could render the First Amendment a dead letter," or "This would leave us with no normative guidance in determining when and what speech to protect," or "This effaces the distinction between speech and action," or "This is incompatible with any viable notion of freedom of expression." To these statements (culled more or less at random from recent law review pieces) I would reply that the First Amendment has always been a dead letter if one understood its "liveness" to depend on the identification and protection of a realm of "mere" expression distinct from the realm of regulatable conduct; the distinction between speech and action has always been effaced in principle, although in practice it can take whatever form the prevailing political conditions mandate; we have never had any normative guidance for marking off protected from unprotected speech; rather, the guidance we have has been fashioned (and refashioned) in the very political struggles over which it then (for a time) presides. In short, the name of the game has always been politics, even when (indeed, especially when) it is played by stigmatizing politics as the area to be avoided.

In saying this, I would not be heard as arguing either for or against regulation and speech codes as a matter of general principle. Instead my argument turns away from general principle to the pragmatic (anti)principle of considering each situation as it emerges. The question of whether or not to regulate will always be a local one, and we cannot rely on abstractions that are either empty of content or filled with the content of some partisan agenda to generate a "principled" answer. Instead we must consider in every case what is at stake and what are the risks and gains of alternative courses of action. In the course of this consideration many things will be of help, but among them will not be phrases like "freedom of speech" or "the right of individual expression," because, as they are used now, these phrases tend to obscure rather than clarify our dilemmas. Once they are deprived of their talismanic force, once it is no longer strategically effective simply to invoke them in the act of walking away from a problem, the conversation could continue in directions that are now blocked by a First Amendment absolutism that has only been honored in the breach anyway. To the student reporter who complains that in the wake of the promulgation of a speech code at the University of Wisconsin there is now something in the back of his mind as he writes, one could reply, "There was always something in the back of your mind, and perhaps it might be better to have this code in the back of your mind than whatever was in there before." And when someone warns about the slippery slope and predicts mournfully that if you restrict one form of speech, you never know what will be restricted next, one could reply, "Some form of speech is always being restricted, else there could be no meaningful assertion; we have always and already slid down the slippery slope; someone is always going to be restricted next, and it is your job to make sure that the someone is not you." And when someone observes, as someone surely will, that antiharassment codes chill speech, one could reply that since speech only becomes intelligible against the background of what isn't being said, the background of what has already been silenced, the only question is the political one of which speech is going to be chilled, and, all things considered, it seems a good thing to chill speech like "nigger," "cunt," "kike," and "faggot." And if someone then says, "But what happened to free-speech principles?" one could say what I have now said a dozen times, free-speech principles don't exist except as a component in a bad argument in which such principles are invoked to mask motives that would not withstand close scrutiny. . . .

QUESTIONS FOR REFLECTION

1. Why, according to Fish, does freedom of speech always have exceptions?
2. Fish rejects the distinction between speech and action. Why? Do you agree?
3. How does Fish defend campus speech codes?
4. What does Fish mean when he says, "There's no such thing as free speech"? Why does he think "it's a good thing, too"?

THOMAS NAGEL

Personal Rights and Public Space

Thomas Nagel is University Professor of Philosophy and Law at New York University. (Source: from Philosophy and Public Affairs *24 (1995): 83-107. Reprinted by permission. Footnotes have been omitted.)*

. . . I begin with a familiar point from recent moral philosophy. The feature of rights that makes them morally and theoretically puzzling is a logical one. If they are taken as basic, it is impossible to interpret them in terms of a straightforward positive or negative evaluation of certain things' happening to people, or certain things' being done to them. The reason is that rights essentially set limits to what any individual may do to any other, even in the service of good ends—and those good ends include even the prevention of transgressions of those same limits by others. If there is a general right not to be murdered, for example, then it is impermissible to murder one person even to prevent the murders of two others. It is difficult to see how such a prohibition could be morally basic; in fact it seems paradoxical, if it cannot be justified by its utility in the long run.

We can describe this logical property of rights in terms of the distinction between *agent-neutral* and *agent-relative* principle* Agent-neutral values are the values of certain occurrences or states of affairs which give everyone a reason to promote or prevent them. If murder is bad in an agent-neutral sense, for example, it means that everyone has a reason to try to minimize the overall number of murders, independent of who commits them—and this might in some circumstances mean murdering a few to prevent the murder of a larger number. But if, on the other hand, murder is wrong in an *agent-relative* sense, this means that each agent is required not to commit murder *himself*, and nothing is directly implied about what he must do to prevent murders by others. The agent-relative prohibition against murder of course applies to those others—in this sense the agent-relative principle is just as *universal* as the agent-neutral one—but it governs each agent's conduct only with respect to the murders that *he* might commit. The same applies to torture, enslavement, and various other violations. If the prohibitions against them are agent-relative, then I may not torture someone even to prevent two others from being tortured by someone else, and so forth.

The logical peculiarity of noninstrumental rights can be described by saying that they cannot be given an interpretation in terms of agent-neutral values—not even in terms of the agent-neutral value of what they protect. Rights have a different logical character: They prohibit us from *doing* certain things to *anyone* but do not require that we count it equally a reason for action that it will prevent those same sorts of things *being done* to someone, but not by oneself.

If murder were merely an agent-neutrally bad type of *occurrence* and nothing more, then the badness of one murder would be outweighed by the badness of two or three others, and one could be justified in murdering one innocent person to prevent

* For fuller discussion of this distinction, and further references, see *The View from Nowhere* (New York: Oxford University Press, 1986), pp. 152–53,175–80.

three others from being murdered. But if there is a right not to be murdered, it does not give way when murdering one innocent person is the only means of preventing the murder of two or three others. A right is an agent-relative, not an agent-neutral, value: Rights tell us in the first instance what not to *do* to other people, rather than what to *prevent from happening to them*.

It is compatible with this conception of rights that they are not absolute, and that there may be some threshold, defined in consequential, agent-neutral terms, at which they give way. For example, even if there is a general right not to be tortured or murdered, perhaps there are evils great enough so that one would be justified in murdering or torturing an innocent person to prevent them. But this would not change the basic character of the right, since the threshold will be high enough so that the impermissibility of torture or murder to prevent evils below it cannot be explained in terms of the agent-neutral badness of torture or murder alone. Even if it is permissible to torture one person to save a thousand others from being tortured, this leaves unexplained why one may not torture one to save two.

It is this qualified independence of the best overall results, calculated in agent-neutral terms, that gives rights their distinctive character. Of course if rights are instrumental—derivative from the agent-neutral value or disvalue of certain sorts of outcomes—then there is no problem, because their agent-relative character is not something morally basic. But if they are not merely instrumental, then they can, as I have said, seem paradoxical; for how could it be wrong to harm one person to prevent greater harm to others? How are we to understand the value that rights assign to certain kinds of human inviolability, which makes this consequence morally intelligible?

III

This peculiar feature of rights has been the subject of extensive discussion, by Robert Nozick, Judith Jarvis Thomson, and Samuel Scheffler, among others. I am drawn to an answer to the question which has been proposed and developed by Frances Kamm, and which was also suggested by Warren Quinn. The answer focuses on the status conferred on all human beings by the *design* of a morality which includes agent-relative constraints of this kind. The status is that of a certain kind of *inviolability*, which we identify with the possession of rights, and the proposal is that we explain the agent-relative constraint against certain types of violations in terms of the universal but non-consequentialist value of inviolability itself.

Being inviolable is not a condition, like being happy, or free—just as being violable is not a condition, like being unhappy or oppressed. To be inviolable does not mean that one *will not be violated*. It is a moral *status:* It means that one *may not* be violated in certain ways—such treatment is inadmissible, and if it occurs, the person has been wronged. So someone's having or lacking this status is not equivalent to anything's happening or not happening to him. If he has it, he does not lose it when his rights are violated—rather, such treatment counts as a violation of his rights precisely because he has it.

This yields a kind of answer to the "paradox" of rights. It is true that a right may sometimes forbid us to do something that would minimize its violation—as when we are forbidden to kill one innocent person even to prevent two other innocents from being killed. But the alternative possibility differs from this one not only in the numbers of innocents killed. If there is no such right, and it is permissible to kill the one to save the two, that implies a profound difference in the status of everyone—not only of the one who is killed. For in the absence of such a right, no one is inviolable: Anyone may be killed if that would serve to minimize the number of killings. This difference of status holds true of everyone whether or not the situation will ever arise for him.

So even if we suppose, for the sake of argument, that in a moral world in which such rights exist and are moreover recognized and respected by most people, the chances of being killed would be higher than in a world in which there are no such rights (perhaps because the means available to control violators would be weaker than they would if utilitarian methods were employed)—still, this would not be the only difference between the two worlds. In the world with no rights and fewer killings, *no one* would be inviolable in a way in which, in the world with more rights and more killings, *everyone* would be—including the victims.

. . . Those who hold political power are usually inclined to use it to push people around. This can take more or less outrageous forms. Shooting demonstrators in Tienanmen Square is not in the same category as outlawing marijuana or making it illegal to deny that the holocaust took place. Still, these exercises of force by the state all destroy individual freedom under the authority of some misguided idea of legitimacy. We shouldn't be asked to trade in our autonomy completely in exchange for the benefits of political society: It is not, contrary to what Hobbes thought, necessary.

One of the things that prompts this discussion is a wish to account for the level of indignation provoked (at least in me) by exercises of state power that do not have terribly harmful effects. My objection to the censorship of pornography or holocaust denial is quite out of proportion to the actual harm done by such prohibitions. It is like the reaction when someone cheats you out of a sum which, in itself, you can easily afford to lose. A sense of wrong disproportionate to the resulting loss is a good sign that a sentiment of justice, fairness, or right has been aroused. I am aware that life without pornography is perfectly livable, and that the prosecution in Europe of negationists or sellers of Nazi memorabilia is overwhelmingly merely ridiculous. But that is just the point. It is not the consequences, but the idea that state power *may* be legitimately used in such ways that seems grossly wrong; instances of such use seem like serious injustices, however modest their actual costs, or even if there is a net gain. They simply have no right to control people in that way. In advancing this conception of inviolability, I shall concentrate on freedom of expression and sexual freedom.

V

The purely instrumental justification for basic rights of free expression is very strong. Freedom of the press and of public dissent protect everyone against abuses of power and official harm and neglect of all kinds. In instrumental value they are comparable in importance to democracy and the rule of law, and their personal value to writers and intellectuals, as Joseph Raz has observed, is dwarfed by comparison. However, since I believe that the justification of rights in terms of their beneficial effects is not the whole story, I want to concentrate on the value of the form of inviolability which it confers on everyone, not as an effect but in itself—in virtue of its normative essence, so to speak. This becomes important if we wish to extend the justification of free expression substantially beyond the domain of political advocacy, where its instrumental value is clearest.

That the expression of what one thinks and feels should be overwhelmingly one's own business, subject to restriction only when clearly necessary to prevent serious harms distinct from the expression itself, is a condition of being an independent thinking being. It is a form of moral recognition that you have a mind of your own: Even if you never *want* to say anything to which others would object, the idea that they *could* stop you if they did object is in itself a violation of your integrity.

As an aspect of status, freedom of expression is inseparable from freedom of thought. To stifle communication is to stifle an essential aspect of the process by which free thought operates, because we function, in thinking, as members of a collective enterprise. The sovereignty of each person's reason over his own beliefs and values requires that he be permitted to express them, expose them to the reactions of others, and defend them against objections. It also requires that he not be protected against exposure to views or arguments that might influence him in ways others deem pernicious, but that he have the responsibility to make up his own mind about whether to accept or reject them. Mental autonomy is restricted by shutting down both inputs and outputs—it is a status that can only be possessed collectively. (A dictator who controlled the speech of all his subjects would not himself be free.)

This is close to the argument Scanlon offers for his principle of free expression, except that his argument goes through the conditions of legitimacy in the exercise of state power, and its conclusion is a limit on legal restrictions of expression rather than a general moral right. "An autonomous person," says Scanlon, "cannot accept without independent consideration the judgment of others as to what he should believe or what he should do. He may rely on the judgment of others, but when he does so he must be prepared to advance independent reasons for thinking their judgment likely to be correct, and to weigh the evidential value of their opinion against contrary evidence.

Worst, of course, is the suppression of dissenting opinion because of the danger that it may persuade people, thus depriving the reigning orthodoxy of support. Apart from its epistemological stupidity, this is the ultimate insult not only to the dissenters but to the rest of us, their potential audience, who are not trusted to make up our own minds. But while this kind of thought control is an element in the repressive impulses to be found in modern liberal societies, it is not the main one. Most civilized threats to individual autonomy are motivated by the desire to prevent offense, insult, or social discomfort, or to insure a moral environment of one kind or another. The greater the ambitions of those who hold power to supply a certain kind of harmonious social environment, the greater will be the pressures on individuality and against variations in divisive individual expression. Prominent among the targets of such control are expressions of racial, religious, or sexual bigotry—so-called hate speech.

Because of the Bill of Rights, such regulations have been generally limited to the private, nonlegal sphere in the United States, but even this can be a substantial form of restriction. In Europe, Britain, and Canada, government is under no such inhibitions, and laws against the expression of racial or religious bigotry are common. Now it would be easy to criticize such laws on the ground that they lend themselves much too readily to abuse, catching the wrong people. For example, the eminent scholar Bernard Lewis was recently taken to court in France for having expressed doubt in an interview with *Le Monde* that the mass slaughter of Armenians during World War I qualified as an example of genocide—the doubt being about the motives of their Turkish killers.

But I do not want to make the case on those grounds, for I think it is already sufficiently inexcusable that anyone should be jailed or fined for denying that the holocaust took place, or selling books that deny it, or for conducting a mail-order business in Nazi medallions, small busts of Hitler, and so forth. Those restrictions are deeply offensive in themselves, and I believe they are damaging to the situation of Jews in societies that enforce them. They carry the message that the reality of the holocaust and the evil of Nazism are propositions which cannot stand up on their own—that they are so vulnerable to denial that they need to be given the status of dogma, protected against criticism and held as articles of faith rather than reason. To claim the need for such protection of one's beliefs invites only contempt. Willingness to permit the expression of bigotry and stupidity, and to denounce or ignore it without censoring it, is the only appropriate expression of the enlightened conviction that the proper ground of belief is reason and evidence rather than dogmatic acceptance.

I find it a personal affront to be protected from the expression of such claims by others—thinking as a person with a mind of my own. But it is also an affront that the state should have the power to silence anyone—and therefore to silence me, if I were to start spouting equally contemptible nonsense. The censorship of a fanatical bigot is an offense to us all.

The same can be said about the pressures to control racially offensive and sexist expression in the United States. And here again I am not just talking about the more ridiculous excesses of political correctness, but about the prohibition of hard-core, intentional expressions of hostility. The situation where those who hold such opinions or attitudes are prevented from expressing them publicly seems to me extremely unhealthy, with its suggestion that the opposite, right-thinking view is a dogma that cannot survive challenge, and cannot be justified on ordinary rational and evidential grounds. The status of blacks and women can only be damaged by this kind of protection.

Even if this were not the case, however—even if such restrictions did some social good, on balance—the offense would remain. That is because it is not just the burden imposed by actual restrictions that counts against them, but more importantly the assumption that such restrictions are subject to that kind of justification. The existence of a morally protected sphere of mental autonomy depends on the rejection of that assumption. The autonomy we value is defined not just by how we are treated, but by how we may be treated. To admit the right of the community to restrict the expressions of convictions or attitudes on the basis of their content alone is to rob everyone of authority over his own mental life. It makes us all, equally, less free.

I do not deny that direct personal insult, if it is offensive enough and not a part of public political commentary and debate, can legitimately be considered a form of assault liable to legal action. But that should be true whatever the content of the insult, and not only when it has to do with membership in a politically sensitive group. It is bad to be nasty and wounding, and while the law is not a very effective instrument for the imposition of civilized standards of discourse, perhaps it can be used in extreme cases—provided, again, this does not serve as an excuse to stifle political polemic or the criticism of public actors.

QUESTIONS FOR REFLECTION

1. What is the paradox of rights?
2. Explain the distinction between agent-neutral and agent-relative principles.
3. What is inviolability? Why is it important?
4. How does inviolability help to resolve the paradox of rights?
5. How does Nagel connect inviolability to autonomy?
6. Summarize Nagel's argument for freedom of speech.
7. Consider a case of highly objectionable speech. How would Nagel defend it? Do you find his defense persuasive?
8. Imagine a debate between Fish and Nagel. What would be the primary criticism each might make against the other?

CHIEF JUSTICE JOHN ROBERTS AND JUSTICE PAUL STEVENS

Majority and Dissenting Opinions in Morse *v.* Frederick (2007)

(Source: Morse v. Frederick *551 U.S. [2007]. Most legal references have been omitted.)*

[Mr.] Chief Justice Roberts delivered the opinion of the Court. . . .

At a school-sanctioned and school-supervised event, a high school principal saw some of her students unfurl a large banner conveying a message she reasonably regarded as promoting illegal drug use. Consistent with established school policy prohibiting such messages at school events, the principal directed the students to take down the banner. One student—among those who had brought the banner to the event—refused to do so. The principal confiscated the banner and later suspended the student. The Ninth Circuit held that the principal's actions violated the First Amendment, and that the student could sue the principal for damages.

Our cases make clear that students do not "shed their constitutional rights to freedom of speech or expression at the schoolhouse gate." *Tinker* v. *Des Moines Independent Community School Dist.* (1969). At the same time, we have held that "the constitutional rights of students in public school are not automatically coextensive with the rights of adults in other settings," *Bethel School Dist. No. 403* v. *Fraser* (1986), and that the rights of students "must be 'applied in light of the special characteristics of the school environment.'" *Hazelwood School Dist.* v. *Kuhlmeier* (1988) (quoting *Tinker*). Consistent with these principles, we hold that schools may take steps to safeguard those entrusted to their care from speech that can reasonably be regarded as encouraging illegal drug use. We conclude that the school officials in this case did not violate the First Amendment by confiscating the pro-drug banner and suspending the student responsible for it.

I

On January 24, 2002, the Olympic Torch Relay passed through Juneau, Alaska, on its way to the winter games in Salt Lake City, Utah. The torchbearers were to proceed along a street in front of Juneau-Douglas High School (JDHS) while school was in session. Petitioner Deborah Morse, the school principal, decided to permit staff and students to participate in the Torch Relay as an approved social event or class trip. Students were allowed to leave class to observe the relay from either side of the street. Teachers and administrative officials monitored the students' actions.

Respondent Joseph Frederick, a JDHS senior, was late to school that day. When he arrived, he joined his friends (all but one of whom were JDHS students) across the street from the school to watch the event. Not all the students waited patiently. Some became rambunctious, throwing plastic cola bottles and snowballs and scuffling with their classmates. As the torchbearers and camera crews passed by, Frederick and his friends unfurled a 14-foot banner bearing the phrase: "BONG HiTS 4 JESUS." The large banner was easily readable by the students on the other side of the street.

Principal Morse immediately crossed the street and demanded that the banner be taken down. Everyone but Frederick complied. Morse confiscated the banner and told Frederick to report to her office, where she suspended him for 10 days. Morse later explained that she told Frederick to take the banner down because she thought it encouraged illegal drug use, in violation of established school policy. Juneau School Board Policy No. 5520 states: "The Board specifically prohibits any assembly or public expression that . . . advocates the use of substances that are illegal to minors. . . ." In addition, Juneau School Board Policy No. 5850 subjects "[p]upils who participate in approved social events and class trips" to the same student conduct rules that apply during the regular school program.

Frederick administratively appealed his suspension, but the Juneau School District Superintendent upheld it, limiting it to time served (8 days). In a memorandum setting forth his reasons, the superintendent determined that Frederick had displayed his banner "in the midst of his fellow students, during school hours, at a school-sanctioned activity." He further explained that Frederick "was not disciplined because the principal of the school 'disagreed' with his message, but because his speech appeared to advocate the use of illegal drugs."

The superintendent continued:

> "The common-sense understanding of the phrase 'bong hits' is that it is a reference to a means of smoking marijuana. Given [Frederick's] inability or unwillingness to express any other credible meaning for the phrase, I can only agree with the principal and countless others who saw the banner as advocating the use of illegal drugs. [Frederick's] speech was not political. He was not advocating the legalization of marijuana or promoting a religious belief. He was displaying a fairly silly message promoting illegal drug usage in the midst of a school activity, for the benefit of television cameras covering the Torch Relay. [Frederick's] speech was potentially disruptive to the event and clearly disruptive of and inconsistent with the school's educational mission to educate students about the dangers of illegal drugs and to discourage their use."

Relying on our decision in *Fraser*, the superintendent concluded that the principal's actions were permissible because Frederick's banner was "speech or action that intrudes upon the work of the schools." The Juneau School District Board of Education upheld the suspension. . . .

II

At the outset, we reject Frederick's argument that this is not a school speech case—as has every other authority to address the question. The event occurred during normal school hours. It was sanctioned by Principal Morse "as an approved social event or class trip," and the school district's rules expressly provide that pupils in "approved social events and class trips are subject to district rules for student conduct." Teachers and administrators were interspersed among the students and charged with supervising them. The high school band and cheerleaders performed. Frederick, standing among other JDHS students across the street from the school, directed his banner toward the school, making it plainly visible to most students. Under these circumstances, we agree with the superintendent that Frederick cannot "stand in the midst of his fellow students, during school hours, at a school-sanctioned activity and claim he is not at school." There is some uncertainty at the outer boundaries as to when courts should apply school-speech precedents, but not on these facts.

III

The message on Frederick's banner is cryptic. It is no doubt offensive to some, perhaps amusing to others. To still others, it probably means nothing at all. Frederick himself claimed "that the words were just nonsense meant to attract television cameras." But Principal Morse thought the banner would be interpreted by those viewing it as promoting illegal drug use, and that interpretation is plainly a reasonable one.

As Morse later explained in a declaration, when she saw the sign, she thought that "the reference to a 'bong hit' would be widely understood by high school students and others as referring to smoking marijuana." She further believed that "display of the banner would be construed by students, District personnel, parents and others witnessing the display of the banner, as advocating or promoting illegal drug use"—in violation of school policy. ("I told Frederick and the other members of his group to put the banner down because I felt that it violated the [school] policy against displaying . . . material that advertises or promotes use of illegal drugs.")

We agree with Morse. At least two interpretations of the words on the banner demonstrate that the sign advocated the use of illegal drugs. First, the phrase could be interpreted as an imperative: "[Take] bong hits . . ."—a message equivalent, as Morse explained in her declaration, to "smoke marijuana" or "use an illegal drug." Alternatively, the phrase could be viewed as celebrating drug use—"bong hits [are a good thing]," or "[we take] bong hits"—and we discern no meaningful distinction between celebrating illegal drug use in the midst of fellow students and outright advocacy or promotion.

The pro-drug interpretation of the banner gains further plausibility given the paucity of alternative meanings the banner might bear. The best Frederick can come up with is that the banner is "meaningless and funny." The dissent similarly refers to the sign's message as "curious," "ambiguous," "nonsense," "ridiculous," "obscure," "silly," "quixotic," and "stupid." Gibberish is surely a possible interpretation of the words on the banner, but it is not the only one, and dismissing the banner as meaningless ignores its undeniable reference to illegal drugs.

The dissent mentions Frederick's "credible and uncontradicted explanation for the message—he just wanted to get on television." But that is a description of Frederick's motive for displaying the banner; it is not an interpretation of what the banner says. The way Frederick was going to fulfill his ambition of appearing on television was by unfurling a pro-drug banner at a school event, in the presence of teachers and fellow students.

Elsewhere in its opinion, the dissent emphasizes the importance of political speech and the need to foster "national debate about a serious issue," as if to suggest that the banner is political speech. But not even Frederick argues that the banner conveys any sort of political or religious message. Contrary to the dissent's suggestion, this is plainly not a case about political debate over the criminalization of drug use or possession.

IV

The question thus becomes whether a principal may, consistent with the First Amendment, restrict student speech at a school event, when that speech is reasonably viewed as promoting illegal drug use. We hold that she may.

In *Tinker*, this Court made clear that "First Amendment rights, applied in light of the special characteristics of the school environment, are available to teachers and students." *Tinker* involved a group of high school students who decided to wear black armbands to protest the Vietnam War. School officials learned of the plan and then adopted a policy prohibiting students from wearing armbands. When several students nonetheless wore armbands to school, they were suspended. The students sued, claiming that their First Amendment rights had been violated, and this Court agreed.

Tinker held that student expression may not be suppressed unless school officials reasonably conclude that it will "materially and substantially disrupt the work and discipline of the school." The essential facts of *Tinker* are quite stark, implicating concerns at the heart of the First Amendment. The students sought to engage in political speech, using the armbands to express their "disapproval of the Vietnam hostilities and their advocacy of a truce, to make their views known, and, by their example, to influence others to adopt them." Political speech, of course, is "at the core of what the First Amendment is designed to protect." *Virginia* v. *Black* (2003). The only interest the Court discerned underlying the school's actions was the "mere desire to avoid the discomfort and unpleasantness that always accompany an unpopular viewpoint," or "an urgent wish to avoid the controversy which might result from the expression." *Tinker*. That interest was not enough to justify banning "a silent, passive expression of opinion, unaccompanied by any disorder or disturbance."

This Court's next student speech case was *Fraser*. Matthew Fraser was suspended for delivering a speech before a high school assembly in which he employed what this Court called "an elaborate, graphic, and explicit sexual metaphor." Analyzing the case under *Tinker*, the District Court and Court of Appeals found no disruption, and therefore no basis for disciplining Fraser. This Court reversed, holding that the "School District acted entirely within its permissible authority in imposing sanctions upon Fraser in response to his offensively lewd and indecent speech."

The mode of analysis employed in *Fraser* is not entirely clear. The Court was plainly attuned to the content of Fraser's speech, citing the "marked distinction between the political 'message' of the armbands in *Tinker* and the sexual content of [Fraser's] speech." But the Court also reasoned that school boards have the authority to determine "what manner of speech in the classroom or in school assembly is inappropriate."

We need not resolve this debate to decide this case. For present purposes, it is enough to distill from *Fraser* two basic principles. First, *Fraser's* holding demonstrates that "the constitutional rights of students in public school are not automatically coextensive with the rights of adults in other settings." Had Fraser delivered the same speech in a public forum outside the school context, it would have been protected. In school, however, Fraser's First Amendment rights were circumscribed "in light of the special characteristics of the school environment." Second, *Fraser* established that the mode of analysis set forth in *Tinker* is not absolute. Whatever approach *Fraser* employed, it certainly did not conduct the "substantial disruption" analysis prescribed by *Tinker*.

Our most recent student speech case, *Kuhlmeier*, concerned "expressive activities that students, parents, and members of the public might reasonably perceive to bear the imprimatur of the school." Staff members of a high school newspaper sued their school when it chose not to publish two of their articles. The Court of Appeals analyzed the case under *Tinker*, ruling in favor of the students because it found no evidence of material disruption to classwork or school discipline. This Court reversed, holding that "educators do not offend the First Amendment by exercising editorial control over the style and content of student speech in school-sponsored expressive activities so long as their actions are reasonably related to legitimate pedagogical concerns." *Kuhlmeier* does not control this case because no one would reasonably believe that Frederick's banner bore the school's imprimatur. The case is nevertheless instructive because it confirms both principles cited above. *Kuhlmeier* acknowledged that schools may regulate some speech "even though the government could not censor similar speech outside the school." And, like *Fraser*, it confirms that the rule of *Tinker* is not the only basis for restricting student speech.

Drawing on the principles applied in our student speech cases, we have held in the Fourth Amendment context that "while children assuredly do not 'shed their constitutional rights . . . at the schoolhouse gate,' . . . the nature of those rights is what is appropriate for children in school." *Vernonia School Dist. 47J* v. *Acton* (1995) (quoting *Tinker*). In particular, "the school setting requires some easing of the restrictions to which searches by public authorities are ordinarily subject." *New Jersey* v. *T. L. O.* (1985).

Even more to the point, these cases also recognize that deterring drug use by schoolchildren is an "important—indeed, perhaps compelling" interest. Drug abuse can cause severe and permanent damage to the health and well-being of young people:

> "School years are the time when the physical, psychological, and addictive effects of drugs are most severe. Maturing nervous systems are more critically impaired by intoxicants than mature ones are; childhood losses in learning are lifelong and profound; children grow chemically dependent more quickly than adults, and their record of recovery is depressingly poor. And of course the effects of a drug-infested school are visited not just upon the users, but upon the entire student body and faculty, as the educational process is disrupted."

Just five years ago, we wrote: "The drug abuse problem among our Nation's youth has hardly abated since *Vernonia* was decided in 1995. In fact, evidence suggests that it has only grown worse."

The problem remains serious today. About half of American 12th graders have used an illicit drug, as have more than a third of 10th graders and about one-fifth of 8th graders. Nearly one in four 12th graders has used an illicit drug in the past month. Some 25% of high schoolers say that they have been offered, sold, or given an illegal drug on school property within the past year.

Congress has declared that part of a school's job is educating students about the dangers of illegal drug use. It has provided billions of dollars to support state and local drug-prevention programs, and required that schools receiving federal funds under the Safe and Drug-Free Schools and Communities Act of 1994 certify that their drug prevention programs "convey a clear and consistent message that . . . the illegal use of drugs [is] wrong and harmful."

Thousands of school boards throughout the country—including JDHS—have adopted policies aimed at effectuating this message. Those school boards know that peer pressure is perhaps "the single most important factor leading schoolchildren to take drugs," and that students are more likely to use drugs when the norms in school appear to tolerate such behavior. Student speech celebrating illegal drug use at a school event, in the presence of school administrators and teachers, thus poses a particular challenge for school officials working to protect those entrusted to their care from the dangers of drug abuse.

The "special characteristics of the school environment," and the governmental interest in stopping student drug abuse—reflected in the policies of Congress and myriad school boards, including JDHS—allow schools to restrict student expression that they reasonably regard as promoting illegal drug use. *Tinker* warned that schools may not prohibit student speech because of "undifferentiated fear or apprehension of disturbance" or "a mere desire to avoid the discomfort and unpleasantness that always accompany an unpopular viewpoint." The danger here is far more serious and palpable. The particular concern to prevent student drug abuse at issue here, embodied in established school policy, extends well beyond an abstract desire to avoid controversy.

Petitioners urge us to adopt the broader rule that Frederick's speech is proscribable because it is plainly "offensive" as that term is used in *Fraser*. We think this stretches *Fraser* too far; that case should not be read to encompass any speech that could fit under some definition of "offensive." After all, much political and religious speech might be perceived as offensive to some. The concern here is not that Frederick's speech was offensive, but that it was reasonably viewed as promoting illegal drug use.

Although accusing this decision of doing "serious violence to the First Amendment" by authorizing "viewpoint discrimination," the dissent concludes that "it might well be appropriate to tolerate some targeted viewpoint discrimination in this unique setting." Nor do we understand the dissent to take the position that schools are required to tolerate student advocacy of illegal drug use at school events, even if that advocacy falls short of inviting "imminent" lawless action. And even the dissent recognizes that the issues here are close enough that the principal should not be held liable in damages, but should instead enjoy qualified immunity for her actions. Stripped of rhetorical flourishes, then, the debate between the dissent and this opinion is less about constitutional first principles than about whether Frederick's banner constitutes promotion of illegal drug use. We have explained our view that it does. The dissent's contrary view on that relatively narrow question hardly justifies sounding the First Amendment bugle.

School principals have a difficult job, and a vitally important one. When Frederick suddenly and unexpectedly unfurled his banner, Morse had to decide to act—or not act—on the spot. It was reasonable for her to conclude that the banner promoted illegal drug use—in violation of established school policy—and that failing to act would send a powerful message to the students in her charge, including Frederick, about how serious the school was about the dangers of illegal drug use. The First Amendment does not require schools to tolerate at school events student expression that contributes to those dangers.

[Mr.] Justice Stevens, with whom Justice Souter and Justice Ginsburg join, dissenting.

A significant fact barely mentioned by the Court sheds a revelatory light on the motives of both the students and the principal of Juneau-Douglas High School (JDHS). On January 24, 2002, the Olympic Torch Relay gave those Alaska residents a rare chance to appear on national television. As Joseph Frederick repeatedly explained, he did not address the curious message—"BONG HiTS 4 JESUS"—to his fellow students. He just wanted to get the camera crews' attention. Moreover, concern about a nationwide evaluation of the conduct of the JDHS student body would have justified the principal's decision to remove an attention-grabbing 14-foot banner, even if it had merely proclaimed "Glaciers Melt!"

I agree with the Court that the principal should not be held liable for pulling down Frederick's banner. I would hold, however, that the school's interest in protecting its students from exposure to speech "reasonably regarded as promoting illegal drug use" cannot justify disciplining Frederick for his attempt to make an ambiguous statement to a television audience simply because it contained an oblique reference to drugs. The First Amendment demands more, indeed, much more. The Court holds otherwise only after laboring to establish two uncontroversial propositions: first, that the constitutional rights of students in school settings are not coextensive with the rights of adults, and second, that deterring drug use by schoolchildren is a valid and terribly important interest. As to the first, I take the Court's point that the message on Frederick's banner is not necessarily protected speech, even though it unquestionably would have been had the banner been unfurled elsewhere. As to the second, I am willing to assume that the Court is correct that the pressing need to deter drug use supports JDHS's rule prohibiting willful conduct that expressly "advocates the use of substances that are illegal to minors." But it is a gross non sequitur to draw from these two unremarkable propositions the remarkable conclusion that the school may suppress student speech that was never meant to persuade anyone to do anything.

In my judgment, the First Amendment protects student speech if the message itself neither violates a permissible rule nor expressly advocates conduct that is illegal and harmful to students. This nonsense banner does neither, and the Court does serious violence to the First Amendment in upholding—indeed, lauding—a school's decision to punish Frederick for expressing a view with which it disagreed.

I

In December 1965, we were engaged in a controversial war, a war that "divided this country as few other issues ever have." Having learned that some students planned to wear black armbands as a symbol of opposition to the country's involvement in Vietnam, officials of the Des Moines public school district adopted a policy calling for the suspension of any student who refused to remove the armband. As we explained when we considered the propriety of that policy, "[t]he school officials banned and sought to punish petitioners for a silent, passive expression of opinion, unaccompanied by any disorder or disturbance on the part of petitioners." The district justified its censorship on the ground that it feared that the expression of a controversial and unpopular opinion would generate disturbances. Because the school officials had insufficient reason to believe that those disturbances would "materially and substantially interfere with the requirements of discipline in the operation of the school," we found the justification for the rule to lack any foundation and therefore held that the censorship violated the First Amendment. Justice Harlan dissented, but not because he thought the school district could censor a message with which it disagreed. Rather, he would have upheld the district's rule only because the students never cast doubt on the district's anti-disruption justification by proving that the rule was motivated "by other than legitimate school concerns—for example, a desire to prohibit the expression of an unpopular point of view while permitting expression of the dominant opinion."

Two cardinal First Amendment principles animate both the Court's opinion in *Tinker* and Justice Harlan's dissent. First, censorship based on the content of speech, particularly censorship that depends on the viewpoint of the speaker, is subject to the most rigorous burden of justification:

> "Discrimination against speech because of its message is presumed to be unconstitutional. . . . When the government targets not subject matter, but particular views taken by speakers on a subject, the violation of the First Amendment is all the more blatant. Viewpoint discrimination is thus an egregious form of content discrimination. The government must abstain from regulating speech when the specific motivating ideology or the opinion or perspective of the speaker is the rationale for the restriction." *Rosenberger v. Rector and Visitors of Univ. of Va.* (1995).

Second, punishing someone for advocating illegal conduct is constitutional only when the advocacy is likely to provoke the harm that the government seeks to avoid.

However necessary it may be to modify those principles in the school setting, *Tinker* affirmed their continuing vitality. As other federal courts have long recognized, under *Tinker*, "regulation of student speech is generally permissible only when the speech would substantially disrupt or interfere with the work of the school or the rights of other students. . . . *Tinker* requires a specific and significant fear of disruption, not just some remote apprehension of disturbance."

Yet today the Court fashions a test that trivializes the two cardinal principles upon which *Tinker* rests. The Court's test invites stark viewpoint discrimination. In this case, for example, the principal has unabashedly acknowledged that she disciplined Frederick because she disagreed with the pro-drug viewpoint she ascribed to the message on the banner—a viewpoint, incidentally, that Frederick has disavowed. Unlike our recent decision in *Tennessee Secondary School Athletic Assn.* v. *Brentwood Academy* (2007), the Court's holding in this case strikes at "the heart of the First Amendment" because it upholds a punishment meted out on the basis of a listener's disagreement with her understanding (or, more likely, misunderstanding) of the speaker's viewpoint. "If there is a bedrock principle underlying the First Amendment, it is that the Government may not prohibit the expression of an idea simply because society finds the idea itself offensive or disagreeable." *Texas* v. *Johnson* (1989).

It is also perfectly clear that "promoting illegal drug use," comes nowhere close to proscribable "incitement to imminent lawless action." Encouraging drug use might well increase the likelihood that a listener will try an illegal drug, but that hardly justifies censorship:

> "Every denunciation of existing law tends in some measure to increase the probability that there will be violation of it. Condonation of a breach enhances the probability. Expressions of approval add to the probability. . . . Advocacy of law-breaking heightens it still further. But even advocacy of violation, however reprehensible morally, is not a justification for denying free speech where the advocacy falls short of incitement and there is nothing to indicate that the advocacy would be immediately acted upon." *Whitney* v. *California* (1927).

No one seriously maintains that drug advocacy (much less Frederick's ridiculous sign) comes within the vanishingly small category of speech that can be prohibited because of its feared consequences. Such advocacy, to borrow from Justice Holmes, "ha[s] no chance of starting a present conflagration." *Gitlow* v. *New York* (1925).

II

The Court rejects outright these twin foundations of *Tinker* because, in its view, the unusual importance of protecting children from the scourge of drugs supports a ban on all speech in the school environment that promotes drug use. Whether or not such a rule is sensible as a matter of policy, carving out pro-drug speech for uniquely harsh treatment finds no support in our case law and is inimical to the values protected by the First Amendment.

I will nevertheless assume for the sake of argument that the school's concededly powerful interest in protecting its students adequately supports its restriction on "any assembly or public expression that . . . advocates the use of substances that are illegal to minors. . . ." Given that the relationship between schools and students "is custodial and tutelary, permitting a degree of supervision and control that could not be exercised over free adults," it might well be appropriate to tolerate some targeted viewpoint discrimination in this unique setting. And while conventional speech may be restricted only when likely to "incit[e] imminent lawless action," it is possible that our rigid imminence requirement ought to be relaxed at schools.

But it is one thing to restrict speech that advocates drug use. It is another thing entirely to prohibit an obscure message with a drug theme that a third party subjectively—and not very reasonably—thinks is tantamount to express advocacy. Even the school recognizes the paramount need to hold the line between, on the one hand, non-disruptive speech that merely expresses a viewpoint that is unpopular or contrary to the school's preferred message, and on the other hand, advocacy of an illegal or unsafe course of conduct. The district's prohibition of drug advocacy is a gloss on a more general rule that is otherwise quite tolerant of non-disruptive student speech:

> "Students will not be disturbed in the exercise of their constitutionally guaranteed rights to assemble peaceably and to express ideas and opinions, privately or publicly, provided that their activities do not infringe on the rights of others and do not interfere with the operation of the educational program.
>
> "The Board will not permit the conduct on school premises of any willful activity . . . that interferes with

the orderly operation of the educational program or offends the rights of others. The Board specifically prohibits . . . any assembly or public expression that . . . advocates the use of substances that are illegal to minors. . . ."

There is absolutely no evidence that Frederick's banner's reference to drug paraphernalia "willful[ly]" infringed on anyone's rights or interfered with any of the school's educational programs. On its face, then, the rule gave Frederick wide berth "to express [his] ideas and opinions" so long as they did not amount to "advoca[cy]" of drug use. If the school's rule is, by hypothesis, a valid one, it is valid only insofar as it scrupulously preserves adequate space for constitutionally protected speech. When First Amendment rights are at stake, a rule that "sweep[s] in a great variety of conduct under a general and indefinite characterization" may not leave "too wide a discretion in its application." Therefore, just as we insisted in Tinker that the school establish some likely connection between the armbands and their feared consequences, so too JDHS must show that Frederick's supposed advocacy stands a meaningful chance of making otherwise-abstemious students try marijuana.

But instead of demanding that the school make such a showing, the Court punts. Figuring out just how it punts is tricky; "[t]he mode of analysis [it] employ[s] is not entirely clear." On occasion, the Court suggests it is deferring to the principal's "reasonable" judgment that Frederick's sign qualified as drug advocacy. At other times, the Court seems to say that it thinks the banner's message constitutes express advocacy. Either way, its approach is indefensible.

To the extent the Court defers to the principal's ostensibly reasonable judgment, it abdicates its constitutional responsibility. The beliefs of third parties, reasonable or otherwise, have never dictated which messages amount to proscribable advocacy. Indeed, it would be a strange constitutional doctrine that would allow the prohibition of only the narrowest category of speech advocating unlawful conduct, yet would permit a listener's perceptions to determine which speech deserved constitutional protection.

Such a peculiar doctrine is alien to our case law. In *Abrams* v. *United States* (1919), this Court affirmed the conviction of a group of Russian "rebels, revolutionists, [and] anarchists," on the ground that the leaflets they distributed were thought to "incite, provoke, and encourage resistance to the United States." Yet Justice Holmes' dissent—which has emphatically carried the day—never inquired into the reasonableness of the United States' judgment that the leaflets would likely undermine the war effort. The dissent instead ridiculed that judgment: "nobody can suppose that the surreptitious publishing of a silly leaflet by an unknown man, without more, would present any immediate danger that its opinions would hinder the success of the government arms or have any appreciable tendency to do so." In *Thomas* v. *Collins* (1945), we overturned the conviction of a union organizer who violated a restraining order forbidding him from exhorting workers. In so doing, we held that the distinction between advocacy and incitement could not depend on how one of those workers might have understood the organizer's speech. That would "pu[t] the speaker in these circumstances wholly at the mercy of the varied understanding of his hearers and consequently of whatever inference may be drawn as to his intent and meaning." In *Cox* v. *Louisiana* (1965), we vacated a civil rights leader's conviction for disturbing the peace, even though a Baton Rouge sheriff had "deem[ed]" the leader's "appeal to . . . students to sit in at the lunch counters to be 'inflammatory.'" We never asked if the sheriff's in-person, on-the-spot judgment was "reasonable." Even in *Fraser*, we made no inquiry into whether the school administrators reasonably thought the student's speech was obscene or profane; we rather satisfied ourselves that "[t]he pervasive sexual innuendo in Fraser's speech was plainly offensive to both teachers and students—indeed, to any mature person."

To the extent the Court independently finds that "BONG HiTS 4 JESUS" objectively amounts to the advocacy of illegal drug use—in other words, that it can most reasonably be interpreted as such—that conclusion practically refutes itself. This is a nonsense message, not advocacy. The Court's feeble effort to divine its hidden meaning is strong evidence of that. Frederick's credible and uncontradicted explanation for the message—he just wanted to get on television—is also relevant because a speaker who does not intend to persuade his audience can hardly be said to be advocating anything. But most importantly, it takes real imagination to read a "cryptic" message (the Court's characterization, not mine) with a slanting drug reference as an incitement to drug use. Admittedly, some high school students (including those who use drugs) are dumb. Most students, however, do not shed their brains at the schoolhouse gate, and most students know dumb advocacy when they see it. The notion that the message on this banner would actually persuade either the average student or even the dumbest one to change his or her behavior is most implausible. That the Court believes such a silly message can be proscribed as advocacy underscores the novelty of its position, and suggests that the principle it articulates has no stopping point.

Even if advocacy could somehow be wedged into Frederick's obtuse reference to marijuana, that advocacy was at best subtle and ambiguous. There is abundant precedent, including another opinion THE CHIEF JUSTICE announces today, for the proposition that when the "First Amendment is implicated, the tie goes to the speaker," *Federal Election Comm'n v. Wisconsin Right to Life, Inc.* (2007) and that "when it comes to defining what speech qualifies as the functional equivalent of express advocacy . . . we give the benefit of the doubt to speech, not censorship." If this were a close case, the tie would have to go to Frederick's speech, not to the principal's strained reading of his quixotic message.

Among other things, the Court's ham-handed, categorical approach is deaf to the constitutional imperative to permit unfettered debate, even among high school students, about the wisdom of the war on drugs or of legalizing marijuana for medicinal use. If Frederick's stupid reference to marijuana can in the Court's view justify censorship, then high school students everywhere could be forgiven for zipping their mouths about drugs at school lest some "reasonable" observer censor and then punish them for promoting drugs.

Consider, too, that the school district's rule draws no distinction between alcohol and marijuana, but applies evenhandedly to all "substances that are illegal to minors." Given the tragic consequences of teenage alcohol consumption—drinking causes far more fatal accidents than the misuse of marijuana—the school district's interest in deterring teenage alcohol use is at least comparable to its interest in preventing marijuana use. Under the Court's reasoning, must the First Amendment give way whenever a school seeks to punish a student for any speech mentioning beer, or indeed anything else that might be deemed risky to teenagers? While I find it hard to believe the Court would support punishing Frederick for flying a "WINE SiPS 4 JESUS" banner—which could quite reasonably be construed either as a protected religious message or as a pro-alcohol message—the breathtaking sweep of its opinion suggests it would.

III

Although this case began with a silly, nonsensical banner, it ends with the Court inventing out of whole cloth a special First Amendment rule permitting the censorship of any student speech that mentions drugs, at least so long as someone could perceive that speech to contain a latent pro-drug message. Our First Amendment jurisprudence has identified some categories of expression that are less deserving of protection than others—fighting words, obscenity, and commercial speech, to name a few. Rather than reviewing our opinions discussing such categories, I mention two personal recollections that have no doubt influenced my conclusion that it would be profoundly unwise to create special rules for speech about drug and alcohol use.

The Vietnam War is remembered today as an unpopular war. During its early stages, however, "the dominant opinion" that Justice Harlan mentioned in his *Tinker* dissent regarded opposition to the war as unpatriotic, if not treason. That dominant opinion strongly supported the prosecution of several of those who demonstrated in Grant Park during the 1968 Democratic Convention in Chicago and the vilification of vocal opponents of the war like Julian Bond. In 1965, when the Des Moines students wore their armbands, the school district's fear that they might "start an argument or cause a disturbance" was well founded. Given that context, there is special force to the Court's insistence that "our Constitution says we must take that risk; and our history says that it is this sort of hazardous freedom—this kind of openness—that is the basis of our national strength and of the independence and vigor of Americans who grow up and live in this relatively permissive, often disputatious, society." As we now know, the then-dominant opinion about the Vietnam War was not etched in stone.

Reaching back still further, the current dominant opinion supporting the war on drugs in general, and our anti-marijuana laws in particular, is reminiscent of the opinion that supported the nationwide ban on alcohol consumption when I was a student. While alcoholic beverages are now regarded as ordinary articles of commerce, their use was then condemned with the same moral fervor that now supports the war on drugs. The ensuing change in public opinion occurred much more slowly than the relatively rapid shift in Americans' views on the Vietnam War, and progressed on a state-by-state basis over a period of many years. But just as prohibition in the 1920's and early 1930's was secretly questioned by thousands of otherwise law-abiding patrons of bootleggers and speakeasies, today the actions of literally millions of otherwise law-abiding users of marijuana, and of the majority of voters in each of the several States that tolerate medicinal uses of the product, lead me to wonder whether the fear of disapproval by those in the majority is silencing opponents of the war on drugs. Surely our national experience with alcohol should make us wary of dampening speech suggesting—however inarticulately—that it would be better to tax and regulate marijuana than to persevere in a futile effort to ban its use entirely.

Even in high school, a rule that permits only one point of view to be expressed is less likely to produce correct answers than the open discussion of countervailing views. In the national debate about a serious issue, it is the expression of the minority's viewpoint that most demands the protection of the First Amendment. Whatever the better policy may be, a full and frank discussion of the costs and benefits of the attempt to prohibit the use of marijuana is far wiser than suppression of speech because it is unpopular.

I respectfully dissent.

QUESTIONS FOR REFLECTION

1. Imagine that you are presenting Joseph Frederick's case. How would you argue?
2. Imagine that you are presenting Principal Morse's case. How would you argue?
3. Explain and assess Chief Justice Roberts's argument that this is indeed a school speech case.
4. What (if anything) do you think Frederick's sign means?
5. What difference should the meaning of the sign make to the outcome of the case?
6. Explain the *Tinker* test. Do you find it justifiable? (Justice Thomas, in an opinion not reprinted here, would overrule it, maintaining that students, in school, have no freedom of speech.)
7. How would you apply the *Tinker* test to this case?
8. Explain Justice Stevens's reasons for dissenting.
9. How would you have decided this case? Write your own opinion, justifying your answer.

Rights and Responsibilities

PART III

RIGHTS AND RESPONSIBILITIES

We find it hard to talk for very long about ethics or politics without talking about rights. But talk of rights is young by philosophical standards. Rights first made their appearance in Western moral discourse about 350 years ago, in the writings of Thomas Hobbes. Hobbes and many later writers present rights in the context of a general theory of government. To understand their conceptions of rights, therefore, we must consider their overall political theories.

Hobbes revives an ancient idea: that a government is legitimate if people, given a choice, would voluntarily opt to be subject to its dominion. Facing this choice requires us to consider what life would be like without government, in what Hobbes calls the state of nature. Hobbes provides a brief but stunning glimpse of the state of nature where, in his view, life would be "solitary, poor, nasty, brutish, and short." Even the strongest and smartest would be vulnerable to the tricks and physical force of groups of others. No one would be safe; people would routinely fight each other to survive. To gain security, therefore, people would choose to form a government. They would be willing to sacrifice much of their freedom to gain relief from the brutality of the state of nature. The resulting compact among competing individuals underlies the legitimacy of government. Hobbes's account is thus a version of *social contract theory*.

Rights emerge at two levels of Hobbes's theory. First, people have some rights even in the state of nature. There are *natural* rights that do not depend on government. Second, people have rights bestowed by government, which they acquire through the social contract. These are *social,* or *civil,* rights. These kinds of rights rest on different foundations. Hobbes believes that natural rights must underlie civil rights, for civil rights are founded on a contract. That contract can bind the contracting parties only if they already recognize an obligation to keep promises and, correlatively, a right to have promises kept. This kind of right and obligation must be prior to civil rights, depending not on a social contract but on the nature of human beings.

In any version of social contract theory, we can ask two questions that determine much about the theory of government that results: (1) What do the parties hope to gain by entering into the social contract? (2) What are they willing to give up to achieve it? In Hobbes's theory, the parties hope to gain security, which, for them, is a matter of life and death. They are willing to give up much for the protection of government. As a result, in Hobbes's theory, there are few limitations on the government, which Hobbes calls by the name of a monster, *Leviathan.* People are willing to sacrifice even their natural rights in order to survive.

John Locke presents a very different social contract theory. He, too, considers government legitimate only if it would be chosen over the state of nature. But Locke's state of nature is far tamer than Hobbes's. Precisely because everyone is vulnerable to everyone else's revenge, few would commit crimes, and those few would meet severe punishment. In the state of nature, we would have natural rights of life, liberty, and property, which would give us the right to punish anyone who violated those rights. The chief danger Locke sees in this condition is that punishment, often at the hands of the people wronged or those closely associated with them, would tend to be harsh, indiscriminate, and unfair. Consequently, people would feel the need for an impartial judge who could enforce the law of nature. People would therefore contract to form a government to serve as impartial arbitrator of their disputes. What do they hope to gain? Impartiality. This is important, but not a matter of life and death, as in Hobbes, except in extreme cases. What, therefore, are people willing to give up? A limited amount, according to Locke. They would give up their right to enforce the laws of nature by themselves. But they would retain their natural rights to life, liberty, and property, as long as they did not violate the rights of others. And they would gain civil rights to impartial treatment as well. Stemming from Locke's conception of the social contract is a limited view of government, which has little role other than enforcement and arbitration.

Rights are fundamental to our modern conception of ethics and political philosophy. But they give rise to a serious problem. Rights frequently seem to come into conflict. Abortion, capital punishment, and many other public problems can be seen as involving conflicts of rights. How are such conflicts to be resolved? Social contract theory in itself provides little help.

Some philosophers have maintained that conflicts cannot arise, because rights stem from a single, underlying moral principle: the categorical imperative, the principle of utility, or the law of nature, for example. But Edmund Burke maintains that there is no such principle. There are fundamentally different kinds of moral considerations, Burke contends; there is no theory that can take all into account and tell us, in every particular case, which considerations ought to take precedence. What is right or wrong depends on the circumstances, Burke says, and those may be extremely complex, involving many different kinds of values. The best we can do is to seek the right balance between those values. For that purpose, moral sensitivity and practical experience matter more than moral theories or talk of rights.

John Stuart Mill explains a utilitarian theory of rights. Many obligations are general, allowing us to choose how and when to fulfill them. We ought to give to charity, for example, but we can choose how much to give to whom. No one else has a right to our charity. Other, *perfect* obligations permit us no such choice and do correspond to other people's rights. We ought to pay the rent, for example, but have no choice about how much to pay or to whom. The landlord has a right to the rent money. A right, then, is simply a perfect obligation that ought to be enforced by society to maximize happiness.

Finally, the General Assembly of the United Nations has issued a Universal Declaration of Human Rights that expresses a contemporary consensus, enumerating fundamental human rights inherent "in the dignity and worth of the human person."

THOMAS HOBBES

from *Leviathan* (1651)

Thomas Hobbes (1588–1679), a contemporary of Descartes, Milton, Galileo, and Rembrandt, was born prematurely in Malmesbury, Wiltshire, England, when his mother heard of the approach of the Spanish Armada. "Fear and I were born twins," he later quipped. He was raised by an uncle after his father, a vicar, was involved in a fistfight outside the door of his church. Hobbes attended Magdalen Hall, Oxford, at fourteen, completing his degree five years later. He became tutor to an earl's son, a position that provided him a good library and the means to travel. He became a member of an intellectual circle in France that included Mersenne, Gassendi, and Descartes. In 1636, he met Galileo. In 1640, when King Charles I dissolved Parliament, Hobbes fled England for Paris.

Over the next decade, while in his fifties, Hobbes wrote a series of notable works: Human Nature, De Corpore Politico (On the Body Politic), De Cive (On the State), *and several works on optics. In 1646–1647, he tutored the future King Charles II in Paris. In 1651, Hobbes published* Leviathan, *probably his greatest work, in which he argued for absolute and undivided sovereignty in the state. Hobbes there gave the first modern defense of social contract theory, which, despite our contemporary distaste for monarchy, continues to be influential.*

When Charles II was restored to the throne in 1660, Hobbes returned to England. He was seventy-two, but still an avid tennis player. The king, in gratitude for Hobbes's tutor and for his public defense of monarchy, granted him a government pension. In 1665, however, came the great plague; the great fire of London followed a year later. Parliament, taking these events as signs of divine displeasure, investigated anyone who was suspected of atheism. Hobbes's Leviathan *made him a target; he was forbidden to publish any further writings. Still vigorous, however, Hobbes continued to write, completing several major works while in his eighties. (Source: Reprinted from Thomas Hobbes,* Leviathan. *[Oxford: Clarendon Press, 1909]. Spelling and punctuation have been modernized for clarity.)*

PART I, CHAPTER XIII / OF THE NATURAL CONDITION OF MANKIND AS CONCERNING THEIR FELICITY AND MISERY

Equality

Nature has made men so equal in the faculties of body and mind, as that though there be found one man sometimes manifestly stronger in body, or of quicker mind than another; yet when all is reckoned together, the difference between man and man is not so considerable, as that one man can thereupon claim to himself any benefit to which another may not pretend as well as he. For as to the strength of body, the weakest has strength enough to kill the strongest, either by secret machination or by confederacy with others, that are in the same danger with himself.

And as to the faculties of the mind (setting aside the arts grounded upon words, and especially that skill of proceeding upon general and infallible rules, called science; which very few have, and but in few things; as being not a native faculty, born with us; nor attained, [as prudence] while we look after somewhat else), I find yet a greater equality amongst men than that of strength. For prudence is but experience; which equal time equally bestows on all men in those things they equally apply themselves unto. That which may perhaps make such equality incredible is but a vain conceit of one's own wisdom which almost all men think they have in a greater degree than the vulgar; that is, than all men but themselves and a few others, whom by fame, or for concurring with themselves, they approve. For such is the nature of men, that howsoever they may acknowledge many others to be more witty, or more eloquent, or more learned; yet they will hardly believe there be many so wise as themselves: For they see their own wit at hand, and other men's at a distance. But this proves rather that men are in that point equal, than unequal. For there is not ordinarily a greater sign of the equal distribution of anything, than that every man is contented with his share.

Conflict

From this equality of ability arises equality of hope in the attaining of our ends. And therefore if any two men desire the same thing, which nevertheless they cannot both enjoy, they become enemies; and in the way to their end (which is principally their own conservation, and sometimes their delectation only) endeavour to destroy or subdue one another. And from hence it comes to pass, that where an invader has no more to fear than another man's single power; if one plant, sow, build, or possess a convenient seat, others may probably be expected to come prepared with forces united to dispossess and deprive him not only of the fruit of his labour, but also of his life or liberty. And the invader again is in the like danger of another.

And from this diffidence of one another, there is no way for any man to secure himself, so reasonable, as anticipation; that is, by force or wiles to master the persons of all men he can, so long, till he see no other power great enough to endanger him: And this is no more than his own conservation requires and is generally allowed. Also because there be some, that taking pleasure in contemplating their own power in the acts of conquest, which they pursue farther than their security requires; if others, that otherwise would be glad to be at ease within modest bounds, should not by invasion increase their power, they would not be able, long time, by standing only on their defence, to subsist. And by consequence, such augmentation of dominion over men, being necessary to a man's conservation . . . ought to be allowed him.

Again, men have no pleasure (but on the contrary a great deal of grief) in keeping company where there is no power able to over-awe them all. For every man looks that his companion should value him at the same rate he sets upon himself: And upon all signs of contempt or undervaluing naturally endeavours, as far as he dares (which amongst them that have no common power to keep them in quite is far enough to make them destroy each other) to extort a greater value from his condemners, by damage; and from others, by the example.

The State of Nature

So that in the nature of man, we find three principal causes of quarrel. First, competition; secondly, diffidence; thirdly, glory.

The first makes men invade for gain; the second, for safety; and the third, for reputation. The first use violence to make themselves masters of other men's persons, wives, children, and cattle; the second, to defend them; the third, for trifles, as a word, a smile, a different opinion, and any other sign of undervalue, either direct in their persons, or by reflexion in their kindred, their friends, their nation, their profession, or their name.

Hereby it is manifest that during the time men live without a common power to keep them all in awe, they are in that condition which is called war; and such a war as is of every man against every man. For war consists not in battle only, or the act of fighting; but in a tract of time, wherein the will to contend by battle is sufficiently known: and therefore the notion of *time* is to be considered in the nature of war, as it is in the nature of weather. For as the nature of foul weather lies not in a shower or two of rain, but in an inclination thereto of many days together; So the nature of war consisteth not in actual fighting, but in the known disposition thereto during all the time there is no assurance to the contrary. All other time is peace.

Whatsoever therefore is consequent to a time of war, where every man is enemy to every man; the same is consequent to the time wherein men live without other security than what their own strength and their own invention shall furnish them withall. In such condition, there is no place for industry; because the fruit thereof is uncertain: and consequently no culture of the earth, no navigation, nor use of the commodities that may be imported by sea; no commodious building; no instruments of moving, and removing such things as require much force; no knowledge of the face of the earth; no account of time; no arts; no letters; no society; and which is worst of all, continual fear and danger of violent death; And the life of man, solitary, poor, nasty, brutish, and short.

It may seem strange to some man that has not well weighed these things that nature should thus dissociate and render man apt to invade and destroy one another: and he may therefore, not trusting to this inference made from the passions, desire perhaps to have the same confirmed by experience. Let him therefore consider with himself, when taking a journey, he arms himself and seeks to go well accompanied; when going to sleep, he locks his doors; when even in his house he locks his chests; and this when he knows there be laws and public officers armed to revenge all injuries shall be done him; what opinion he has of his fellow subjects, when he rides armed; of his fellow citizens, when he locks his doors; and of his children and servants when he locks his chests. Does he not there as much accuse mankind by his actions, as I do by my words? But neither of us accuse man's nature in it. The desires, and other passions of man, are in themselves no sin. No more are the actions, that proceed from those passions, till they know a law that forbids them: which till laws be made they cannot know: nor can any law be made, till they have agreed upon the person that shall make it.

It may peradventure be thought, there was never such a time, nor condition of war as this; and I believe it was never generally so, over all the world; but there are many places, where they live so now. For the savage people in many places of *America,* except the government of small families, that concord whereof depends on natural lust, have no government at all; and live at this day in that brutish manner, as I said before. Howsoever, it may be perceived what manner of life there would be where there were no common power to fear; by the manner of life, which men that have formerly lived under a peaceful government, use to degenerate into, in a civil war.

But though there had never been any time wherein particular men were in a condition of war one against another, yet in all times kings, and persons of sovereign authority, because of their independence, are in continual jealousies and in the state and posture of gladiators, having their weapons pointing and their eyes fixed on one another; that is, their forts, garrisons, and guns, upon the frontiers of their kingdoms and continual spies upon their neighbours; which is a posture of war. But because they uphold thereby the industry of their subjects, there does not follow it that misery which accompanies the liberty of particular men.

Justice

To this war of every man against every man, this also is consequent; that nothing can be unjust. The notions of right and wrong, justice and injustice have no place. Where there is no common power, there is no law: where no law, no injustice. Force and fraud are in war, and two cardinal virtues. Justice and injustice are none of the faculties neither of the body nor mind. If they were, they might be in a man that were alone in the world, as well as his senses and passions. They are qualities that relate to men in society, not in solitude. It is consequent also to the same condition, that there be no propriety, no dominion, no *mine* and *thine* distinct; but only that to be every man's, that he can get; and for so long as he can keep it. And thus much for the ill condition, which man by mere nature is actually placed in; though with a possibility to come out of it, consisting partly in the passions, partly in his reason.

The passions that incline men to peace are fear of death, desire of such things as are necessary to commodious living, and a hope by their industry to obtain them. And reason suggests convenient articles of peace, upon which men may be drawn to agreement. These articles are they, which otherwise are called the laws of nature, whereof I shall speak more particularly in the following chapters.

CHAPTER XIV / OF THE FIRST AND SECOND NATURAL LAWS AND OF CONTRACTS

Liberty

The right of nature, which writers commonly call *jus naturale,* is the liberty each man has to use his own power, as he wills himself, for the preservation of his own nature; that is to say, of his own life; and consequently, of doing anything which in his own judgment and reasons he shall conceive to be the aptest means thereunto.

By liberty is understood, according to the proper signification of the word, the absence of external impediments: which impediments may oft take away part of a man's power to do what he would but cannot hinder him from using the power left him, according as his judgment and reason shall dictate to him.

Laws of Nature

A law of nature (*lex naturalis*) is a precept, or general rule, found out by reason, by which a man is forbidden to do that which is destructive of his life or takes away the means of preserving the same and to omit that by which he thinks it may be best preserved. For though they that speak of this subject used to confound *jus,* and *lex, right* and *law;* yet they ought to be distinguished, because right, consists in liberty to do or to forbear, whereas law determines and binds to one of them: so that law and right differ as much as obligation and liberty, which in one and the same matter are inconsistent.

And because the condition of man (as has been declared in the precedent chapter) is a condition of war of everyone against everyone, in which case everyone is governed by his own reason; and there is nothing he can make use of that may not be a help unto him in preserving his life against his enemies; it follows that in such a condition, every man has a right to everything; even to one another's body. And therefore, as long as this natural right of every man to every thing endures, there can be no security to any man (how strong or wise soever he be) of living out the time which nature ordinarily allows men to live. And consequently it is a precept or general rule of reason, *That every man ought to endeavour peace, as far as he has hope of obtaining it; and when he cannot obtain it, that he may seek, and use, all helps and advantages of war.* The first branch of which rule contains the first and fundamental law of nature; which is *to seek peace and follow it.* The second, the sum of the right of nature, which is by *all means we can, to defend ourselves.*

From this fundamental law of nature, by which men are commanded to endeavour peace, is derived this second law: *That a man be willing, when others are so too, as far-forth, as for peace and defence of himself he shall think it necessary to lay down this right to all things and be contented with so much liberty against other men as he would allow other men against himself.* For as long as every man holds this right of doing any thing he likes, so long are all men in the condition of war. But if other men will not lay down their right, as well as he, then there is no reason for anyone to divest himself of his: For that were to expose himself to prey (which no man is bound to) rather than to dispose himself to peace. This is that law of the gospel: *Whatsoever you require that others should do to you, that do ye to them.* And that law of all men, *Quod tibi fieri non vis, alteri ne feceris.* *

*"What you do not want done to yourself, do not do to others." —Ed.

To *lay down* a man's *right* to any thing is to divest himself of the *liberty* of hindering another of the benefit of his own right to the same. For he that renounces or passes away his right gives not to any other man a right which he had not before; because there is nothing to which every man had not right by nature; but only stands out of his way, that he may enjoy his own original right without hindrance from him; not without hindrance from another. So that the effect which redounds to one man by another man's defect of right is but so much diminution of impediments to the use of his own right original. . . .

QUESTIONS FOR REFLECTION

1. What is Hobbes's conception of the state of nature? Why would a person's life in that state be "solitary, poor, nasty, brutish, and short"?
2. What, for Hobbes, is liberty? What is a law of nature? How does Hobbes distinguish law from right?
3. What are the first three laws of nature, according to Hobbes? How does he derive them from the state of nature?
4. What motivates us, in the state of nature, to contract to form associations and governments? What are we willing to give up? What do we hope to gain?
5. Why, according to Hobbes, are we obliged to fulfill contracts, even when doing so is not in our best interest?
6. "Whatsoever is done to a man conformable to his own will, signified to the doer, is no injury to him." This is Hobbes's statement of a traditional principle: "To the willing no injustice is done." How does Hobbes argue for this? How is this principle related to Mill's harm principle?
7. John Locke denies that the state of nature would be a state of war. What would the world be like if there were no governmental authority at all? How might Hobbes defend his view that it would be a war of all against all?
8. Francis Fukayama writes that Hobbes's state of nature contains "individuals whose main concern is to take care of themselves and whose primary social contacts are ones of conflict." Is that a fair ground for complaint against Hobbes?
9. Discuss Hobbes's principle that we would surrender liberty, keeping only as much as we are willing to allow others to exercise against us. How does it relate to Mill's harm principle?
10. Applying Hobbes's strategy to ethical theory in general, we might think of ethical principles as rules that reasonable people would choose to adopt for their own protection and benefit. How could such a strategy explain obligations to help others?

JOHN LOCKE

from *Second Treatise of Government* (1690)

John Locke (1632–1704), a contemporary of Boyle, Leibniz, and Newton, was born in Wrington, Somerset, England. The son of an attorney, he was raised in a liberal Puritan family. At the age of fourteen, he entered Westminster School, where he studied the classics, Hebrew, and Arabic. At twenty, he entered Christ's Church, Oxford, where he earned a B.A. in 1656. After receiving an M.A., he was appointed censor of moral philosophy at Oxford.

When his father died in 1661, Locke received a small inheritance. He began studying for a medical degree and, in 1667, became personal physician to the Earl of Shaftesbury. Locke received his medical degree in 1674; while completing his studies, he wrote the first two drafts of his Essay Concerning Human Understanding, *was appointed a fellow of the Royal Society, and was named secretary to the Council of Trade and Plantations.*

Locke spent several years in France, returning in 1679. Because of his ties to Shaftesbury, who had been implicated in a plot against the king, Locke was placed under surveillance; he fled to Holland in 1683. There he became an adviser to William of Orange, published a series of works, and wrote the third draft of the Essay. *The Glorious Revolution of 1688 enabled him to return to England in the company of the future queen, Mary. In 1689 and 1690, Locke published the philosophical work that made him internationally famous: the* Essay *and the* Two Treatises of Government. *He became commissioner of the Board of Trade and Plantations, where he served with great distinction until failing health forced him to retire.*

Locke's Second Treatise *presents a classically liberal theory of government. People in the state of nature would choose to sacrifice a portion of their liberty for the impartial judgment the government can provide. The people nevertheless retain most of their natural rights, which place limits on the power of government. In addition, they receive social rights from the government itself. The government's purpose is the protection of life, liberty, and property; it can act only with the consent of the governed. (Source: Reprinted from John Locke,* Two Treatises of Government. *[London: Printed for Awnsham Churchill, 1690]. Spelling and punctuation have been modernized for clarity.)*

CHAPTER II / OF THE STATE OF NATURE

Liberty and Equality

§. 4. To understand political power right and derive it from its original, we must consider what state all men are naturally in, and that is a state of perfect freedom to order their actions and dispose of their possessions and persons, as they think fit, within the bounds of the law of nature, without asking leave or depending upon the will of any other man.

A state also of equality, wherein all the power and jurisdiction is reciprocal, no one having more than another; there being nothing more evident than that creatures of the same species and rank, promiscuously born to all the same advantages of nature and the use of the same faculties should also be equal one amongst another without subordination or subjection, unless the lord and master of them all should, by any manifest declaration of his will, set one above another and confer on him, by an evident and clear appointment, an undoubted right to dominion and sovereignty.

§. 5. This equality of men by nature the judicious Hooker* looks upon as so evident in itself and beyond all question that he makes it the foundation of that obligation to mutual love amongst men, on which he builds the duties they owe one another and from whence he derives the great maxims of justice and charity. His words are,

> The like natural inducement has brought men to know that it is no less their duty to love others than themselves; for seeing those things which are equal must needs all have one measure; if I cannot but wish to receive good, even as much at every man's hands as any man can wish unto his own soul, how should I look to have any part of my desire herein satisfied, unless myself be careful to satisfy the like desire, which is undoubtedly in other men, being of one and the same nature? To have anything offered them repugnant to this desire must needs in all respects grieve them as much as me; so that if I do harm, I must look to suffer, there being no reason that others should show greater measure of love to me than they have by me shown unto them: my desire therefore to be loved of my equals in nature, as much as possible may be, imposes upon me a natural duty of bearing to them fully the like affection; from which relation of equality between ourselves and them that are as ourselves, what several rules and canons natural reason has drawn for direction of life no man is ignorant, *Eccl. Pol. Lib.* i.

The Law of Nature

§. 6. But though this be a state of liberty, yet it is not a state of license: though man in that state have an uncontrollable liberty to dispose of his person or possessions, yet he has not liberty to destroy himself or so much as any creature in his possession, but where some nobler use than its bare preservation calls for it. The state of nature has a law of nature to govern it, which obliges every one: and reason, which is that law, teaches all mankind who will but consult it that being all equal and independent, no one ought to harm another in his life, health, liberty, or possessions: for men being all the workmanship of one omnipotent and infinitely wise maker, all the servants of one sovereign master, sent into the world by his order and about his business; they are his property, whose workmanship they are, made to last during his, not one another's pleasure: and being furnished with like faculties, sharing all in one community of nature, there cannot be supposed any such subordination among us that may authorize us to destroy one another, as if we were made for one another's uses, as the inferior ranks of creatures are for ours. Every one, as he is bound to preserve himself and not to quit his station wilfully, so by the like reason, when his own preservation comes not in competition, ought he as much as he can to preserve the rest of mankind and may not, unless it be to do justice on an offender, take away or impair the life or what tends to the preservation of the life, the liberty, health, limb, or goods of another.

The Right to Punish

§. 7. And that all men may be restrained from invading others' rights and from doing hurt to one another, and the law of nature be observed which wills the peace and preservation of all mankind, the execution of the law of nature is, in that state, put into every

*Richard Hooker (1553–1600), English theologian and political philosopher, wrote *The Laws of Ecclesiastical Polity,* which focuses on reason and natural law as foundations of the state.—ED.

man's hands, whereby everyone has a right to punish the transgressors of that law to such a degree as may hinder its violation: for the law of nature would, as all other laws that concern men in this world, be in vain if there were no body that in the state of nature had a power to execute that law and thereby preserve the innocent and restrain offenders. And if any one in the state of nature may punish another for any evil he has done, every one may do so: for in that state of perfect equality, where naturally there is no superiority or jurisdiction of one over another, what any may do in prosecution of that law everyone must needs have a right to do.

§. 8. And thus, in the state of nature, one man comes by a power over another; but yet no absolute or arbitrary power to use a criminal, when he has got him in his hands, according to the passionate heats, or boundless extravagancy of his own will; but only to retribute to him, so far as calm reason and conscience dictate, what is proportionate to his transgression, which is so much as may serve for reparation and restraint: for these two are the only reasons why one man may lawfully do harm to another, which is that we call punishment. In transgressing the law of nature, the offender declares himself to live by another rule than that of reason and common equity, which is that measure God has set to the actions of men for their mutual security; and so he becomes dangerous to mankind, the tie which is to secure them from injury and violence being slighted and broken by him. Which being a trespass against the whole species and the peace and safety of it provided for by the law of nature, every man upon this score, by the right he has to preserve mankind in general, may restrain or, where it is necessary, destroy things noxious to them and so may bring such evil on anyone who has transgressed that law, as may make him repent the doing of it and thereby deter him, and by his example others, from doing the like mischief. And in the case, and upon this ground, every man has a right to punish the offender and be executioner of the law of nature.

§. 9. I doubt not but this will seem a very strange doctrine to some men: but before they condemn it, I desire them to resolve me, by what right any prince or state can put to death or punish an alien for any crime he commits in their country. It is certain their laws, by virtue of any sanction they receive from the promulgated will of the legislative, reach not a stranger: they speak not to him, nor, if they did, is he bound to hearken to them. The legislative authority, by which they are in force over the subjects of that commonwealth, has no power over him. Those who have the supreme power of making laws in England, France or Holland are to an Indian but like the rest of the world, men without authority: and therefore, if by the law of nature every man has not a power to punish offences against it as he soberly judges the case to require, I see not how the magistrates of any community can punish an alien of another country; since, in reference to him, they can have no more power than what every man naturally may have over another.

§. 10. Besides the crime which consists in violating the law and varying from the right rule of reason, whereby a man so far becomes degenerate and declares himself to quit the principles of human nature and to be a noxious creature, there is commonly injury done to some person or other, and some other man receives damage by his transgression: in which case he who has received any damage has, besides the right of punishment common to him with other men, a particular right to seek reparation from him that has done it: and any other person who finds it just may also join with him that is injured and assist him in recovering from the offender so much as may make satisfaction for the harm he has suffered.

§. 11. From these two distinct rights, the one of punishing the crime for restraint and preventing the like offence, which right of punishing is in everybody; the other of taking reparation, which belongs only to the injured party, comes it to pass that the magistrate, who by being magistrate has the common right of punishing put into his hands, can often, where the public good demands not the execution of the law, remit the punishment of criminal offenses by his own authority, but yet cannot remit the satisfaction due to any private man for the damage he has received. That he who has suffered the damage has a right to demand in his own name, and he alone can remit: the damnified person has this power of appropriating to himself the goods or service of the offender by right of self-preservation, as every man has a power to punish the crime to prevent its being committed again, by the right he has of preserving all mankind and doing all reasonable things he can in order to that end: and thus it is that every man in the state of nature has a power to kill a murderer, both to deter others from doing the like injury, which no reparation can compensate, by the example of the punishment that attends it from everybody, and also to secure men from the attempts of a criminal, who having renounced reason, the common rule and measure God has given to mankind, has by the unjust violence and slaughter he has committed upon one, declared war against all mankind and therefore may be destroyed as a lion or a tiger, one of those wild savage beasts with whom men can have no society nor security: and upon this is grounded that great law of nature, *Whoso sheddeth man's blood, by man shall his blood be shed.* And Cain was so fully convinced that every one had a right to destroy such a criminal that after the murder of his brother, he cries out, *Every one that findeth me, shall slay me;* so plain was it writ in the hearts of all mankind.

§. 12. By the same reason may a man in the state of nature punish the lesser breaches of that law. It will perhaps be demanded, with death? I answer, each transgression may be punished to that degree and with so much severity as will suffice to make it an ill bargain to the offender, give him cause to repent, and terrify others from doing the like. Every offence that can be committed in the state of nature may in the state of nature be also punished equally, and as far forth as it may, in a commonwealth: for though it would be besides my present purpose to enter here into the particulars of the law of nature or its measures of punishment, yet, it is certain there is such a law, and that too as intelligible and plain to a rational creature and a studier of that law as the positive laws of commonwealths; nay, possibly plainer, as much as reason is easier to be understood than the fancies and intricate contrivances of men following contrary and hidden interests put into words; for so truly are a great part of the municipal laws of countries, which are only so far right as they are founded on the law of nature, by which they are to be regulated and interpreted.

§. 13. To this strange doctrine, *viz.* That in the state of nature every one has the executive power of the law of nature, I doubt not but it will be objected that it is unreasonable for men to be judges in their own cases, that self-love will make men partial to themselves and their friends, and, on the other side, that ill nature, passion and revenge will carry them too far in punishing others; and hence nothing but confusion and disorder will follow and that therefore God has certainly appointed government to restrain the partiality and violence of men. I easily grant that civil government is the proper remedy for the inconveniences of the state of nature, which must certainly be great where men may be judges in their own case, since it is easy to be imagined that he who was so unjust as to do his brother an injury will scarce be so just as to condemn himself for it: but I shall desire those who make this objection to remember that absolute monarchs are but men; and if government is to be the remedy of those evils which necessarily follow from men's being judges in their own cases and the state of nature is therefore not to be endured, I desire to know what kind of government that is and how much better it is than the state of nature, where one man commanding a multitude has the liberty to be judge in his own case and may do to all his subjects whatever he pleases, without the least liberty to anyone to question or control those who execute his pleasure? and in whatsoever he does, whether led by reason, mistake or passion, must be submitted to? Much better it is in the state of nature, where men are not bound to submit to the unjust will of another, and if he that judges judges amiss in his own or any other case, he is answerable for it to the rest of mankind.

Hypothetical?

§. 14. It is often asked as a mighty objection, where are, or ever were there, any men in such a state of nature? To which it may suffice as an answer at present that since all princes and rulers of independent governments all through the world are in a state of nature, it is plain the world never was, nor ever will be, without numbers of men in that state. I have named all governors of independent communities, whether they are or are not in league with others: for it is not every compact that puts an end to the state of nature between men, but only this one of agreeing together mutually to enter into the community and make one body politic; other promises and compacts men may make one with another and yet still be in the state of nature. The promises and bargains for truck, &c. between the two men in the desert island, mentioned by Garcilasso de la Vega in his history of Peru, or between a Swiss and an Indian in the woods of America are binding to them, though they are perfectly in a state of nature in reference to one another: for truth and keeping of faith belongs to men as men and not as members of society.

§. 15. To those that say there were never any men in the state of nature, I will not only oppose the authority of the judicious Hooker, *Eccl. Pol. lib.* i. *sect.* 10. where he says, *The laws which have been hitherto mentioned,* i.e. the laws of nature, *do bind men absolutely, even as they are men, although they have never any settled fellowship, never any solemn agreement amongst themselves what to do, or not to do: but forasmuch as we are not by ourselves sufficient to furnish ourselves with competent store of things, needful for such a life as our nature doth desire, a life fit for the dignity of man; therefore to supply those defects and imperfections which are in us, as living single and solely by ourselves, we are naturally induced to seek communion and fellowship with others: this was the cause of men's uniting themselves at first in politic societies.* But I moreover affirm that all men are naturally in that state and remain so until by their own consents they make themselves members of some politic society; and I doubt not in the sequel of this discourse, to make it very clear.

CHAPTER III / OF THE STATE OF WAR

§. 16. The state of war is a state of enmity and destruction: and therefore declaring by word or action, not a passionate and hasty, but a sedate settled design upon another man's life, puts him in a state of war with him against whom he has declared such an intention, and so has exposed his life to the other's power to be taken away by him or any one that joins with him in his defence and espouses his quarrel; it being reasonable and just, I should have a right to destroy that which threatens me with destruction: for by the fundamental law of nature, man being to be preserved as much as possible, when all cannot be preserved, the safety of the innocent is to be preferred: and one may destroy a man who makes war upon him or has discovered an enmity to his being, for the same reason that he may kill a wolf or a lion; because such men are not under the ties of the common law of reason, have no other rule but that of force and violence, and so may be treated as beasts of prey those dangerous and noxious creatures that will be sure to destroy him whenever he falls into their power.

§. 17. And hence it is that he who attempts to get another man into his absolute power does thereby put himself into a state of war with him, it being to be understood as a declaration of a design upon his life: for I have reason to conclude that he who would get me into his power without my consent would use me as he pleased when he had got me there and destroy me too when he had a fancy to it; for nobody can desire to have me in his absolute power, unless it be to compel me by force to that which is against the right of my freedom, i.e. make me a slave. To be free from such force is the only security of my preservation, and reason bids me look on him, as an enemy to my preservation, who would take away that freedom which is the fence to it; so that he who makes an attempt to enslave me thereby puts himself into a state of war with me. He that in the state of nature would take away the freedom that belongs to anyone in that state must necessarily be supposed to have a design to take away every thing else, that freedom being the foundation of all the rest; as he that in the state of society would take away the freedom belonging to those of that society or commonwealth must be supposed to design to take away from them everything else and so be looked on as in a state of war.

§. 18. This makes it lawful for a man to kill a thief who has not in the least hurt him nor declared any design upon his life any farther than by the use of force so to get him in his power, as to take away his money, or what he pleases, from him; because using force where he has no right to get me into his power, let his pretence be what it will, I have no reason to suppose that he who would take away my liberty would not, when he had me in his power, take away everything else. And therefore it is lawful for me to treat him as one who has put himself into a state of war with me, i.e. kill him if I can; for to that hazard does he justly expose himself, whoever introduces a state of war and is aggressor in it.

The State of Nature

§. 19. And here we have the plain difference between the state of nature and the state of war, which however some men have confounded, are as far distant as a state of peace, good will, mutual assistance and preservation and a state of enmity, malice, violence and mutual destruction are one from another. Men living together according to reason, without a common superior on earth with authority to judge between them, is properly the state of nature. But force, or a declared design of force, upon the person of another, where there is no common superior on earth to appeal to for relief, is the state of war: and it is the want of such an appeal gives a man the right of war even against an aggressor, though he be in society and a fellow subject. Thus a thief, whom I cannot harm but by appeal to the law for having stolen all that I am worth, I may kill when he sets on me to rob me but of my horse or coat; because the law, which was made for my preservation where it cannot interpose to secure my life from present force, which, if lost, is capable of no reparation, permits me my own defence and the right of war, a liberty to kill the aggressor, because the aggressor allows not time to appeal to our common judge nor the decision of the law for remedy in a case where the mischief may be irreparable. Want of a common judge with authority puts all men in a state of nature: force without right upon a man's person makes a state of war, both where there is and is not a common judge.

Impartial Judgment

§. 20. But when the actual force is over, the state of war ceases between those that are in society and are equally on both sides subjected to the fair determination of the law; because then there lies open the remedy of appeal for the past injury and to prevent future harm: but where no such appeal is, as in the state of nature, for want of positive laws and judges with authority to appeal to, the state of war once begun continues, with a right to the innocent party to destroy the other whenever he can until the aggressor offers peace and desires reconciliation on such terms as may repair any wrongs he has already done and secure the innocent for the future; nay, where an appeal to the law and constituted judges lies open, but the remedy is denied by a manifest perverting of justice and a barefaced wresting of the laws to protect or indemnify the violence or injuries of some men or party of men, there it is hard to imagine anything but a state of war: for wherever violence is used and injury done, though by hands appointed to administer justice, it is still violence and injury, however coloured with the name, pretences, or forms of law, the end whereof being to protect and redress the innocent by an unbiased application of it to all who are under it; wherever that is not *bona fide* done, war is made upon the sufferers, who, having no appeal on earth to right them, they are left to the only remedy in such cases, an appeal to heaven.

§. 21. To avoid this state of war (wherein there is no appeal but to heaven, and wherein every the least difference is apt to end where there is no authority to decide between the contenders) is one great reason of men's putting themselves into society and quitting the state of nature: for where there is an authority, a power on earth from which relief can be had by appeal there the continuance of the state of war is excluded, and the controversy is decided by that power. Had there been any such court, any superior jurisdiction on earth, to determine the right between Jephtha and the Ammonities, they had never come to a state of war: but we see he was forced to appeal to heaven. *The Lord the Judge* (says he) *be judge this day between the children of* Israel *and the children of* Ammon, *Judg.* xi. 27. and then prosecuting and relying on his appeal, he leads out his army to battle: and therefore in such controversies, where the question is put, *who shall be judge?* It cannot be meant, who shall decide the controversy; everyone knows what Jephtha here tells us, that the Lord the Judge shall judge. Where there is no judge on earth, the appeal lies to God in heaven. That question then cannot mean, who shall judge whether another has put himself in a state of war with me and whether I may, as Jephtha did, appeal to heaven in it? of that I myself can only be judge in my own conscience, as I will answer it, at the great day, to the supreme judge of all men.

CHAPTER IV / OF SLAVERY

§. 22. The natural liberty of man is to be free from any superior power on earth and not to be under the will or legislative authority of man, but to have only the law of nature for his rule. The liberty of man in society is to be under no other legislative power but that established by consent in the commonwealth, nor under the dominion of any will or restraint of any law but what that legislative shall enact according to the trust put in it. Freedom then is not what Sir Robert Filmer tells us, *Observations*, A. 55. *a liberty for every one to do what he lists, to live as he pleases, and not to be tied by any laws:* but *freedom of men under government* is to have a standing rule to live by, common to every one of that society and made by the legislative power erected in it; a liberty to follow my own will in all things, where the rule prescribes not; and not to be subject to the inconstant, uncertain, unknown, arbitrary will of another man: as freedom of nature is to be under no other restraint but the law of nature.

§. 23. This freedom from absolute, arbitrary power is so necessary to and closely joined with a man's preservation that he cannot part with it, but by what forfeits his preservation and life together: for a man, not having the power of his own life, cannot by compact or his own consent enslave himself to anyone nor put himself under the absolute, arbitrary power of another to take away his life when he pleases. Nobody can give more power than he has himself; and he that cannot take away his own life cannot give another power over it. Indeed, having by his fault forfeited his own life by some act that deserves death, he to whom he has forfeited it may (when he has him in his power) delay to take it and make use of him to his own service, and he does him no injury by it: for whenever he finds the hardship of his slavery outweigh the value of his life, it is in his power, by resisting the will of his master, to draw on himself the death he desires. . . .

QUESTIONS FOR REFLECTION

1. In what sense is the state of nature a state of equality?
2. How does Locke distinguish liberty from license? Why is the state of nature characterized only by the former?
3. How does Locke argue for capital punishment?
4. What motivates us, in the state of nature, to contract to form a government? What are we willing to give up? What do we hope to gain?
5. Hobbes describes the state of nature as a "war of every man against every man." Locke, however, finds the state of nature different from a state of war. In what ways?
6. What, for Locke, is natural liberty? What is liberty in society? What is liberty under government?
7. How do we know that no one should harm another in his life, health, liberty, or possessions? From experience? Or in some other way?
8. How does the right to property relate to the right of self-preservation?
9. Locke relies on an idea of freedom as not being subject to the arbitrary will of another. What does that idea imply about the proper arrangement of political authority?
10. Thomas Pangle worries that "what were once held to be natural laws and natural rights, grounded in objectively verifiable knowledge, are now widely or generally held to be no more than the values or world-view created by or mysteriously historically dispensed to a particular historical culture." What implications would historical relativism have for Locke's argument?

EDMUND BURKE

from *Reflections on the Revolution in France* (1790)

Edmund Burke (1730–1797) was born in Ireland to a Protestant family of modest means and a mixed religious background. Educated at a Quaker school and at Trinity College, Dublin, he took a first-class honors degree in classics and proceeded to study law in London. He did not, however, practice law. Instead, he became a "man of letters": He edited the Annual Register *(a political journal) and belonged to Samuel Johnson's literary club. Burke's first two books appeared when he was twenty-seven; at thirty-seven, he became a member of the House of Commons. Eventually, he became paymaster-general and served as mastermind of the Rockingham Whigs. He was outspoken in his opposition to the Stamp Act, British military action against the American colonies, the oppression of Irish Catholics, and the East India Company's autocratic rule in much of India.*

Burke was almost sixty when the French Revolution began in 1789. King Louis XVI, an absolute monarch, had summoned the largely advisory States General, had lost control of it, and had seen it transform itself into the National Assembly. That body had abolished feudalism, seized the lands of the French church, and inspired the capture and imprisonment of the royal family. A young Frenchman, Charles-François Depont, wrote Burke to ask his opinion of the Revolution. His response was Reflections on the Revolution in France, *which has become a classic of European political thought. The book is sharply critical of the Revolution. Burke's worries about the extremism of the revolutionaries were soon justified. The Reign of Terror led to the execution of thousands, including the king, his family, and much of the French aristocracy.*

Burke is a thoroughly practical thinker. He rejects the Enlightenment view that a change in the social or political order can perfect human nature and society. More fundamentally, he rejects all attempts to analyze human problems in terms of a few basic principles. Profoundly skeptical of philosophical theorizing, Burke stresses the complexity of real ethical problems. Solving a moral or political problem, he believes, involves balancing various moral considerations—various kinds of goods and evils—in light of features of the particular situation giving rise to it. Liberty, in Burke's view, is one kind of good, but there are many others; liberty does not always take precedence. There is no theory, method, or set of rules for achieving a proper balance between liberty and other goods. Instead, Burke urges, we should reason by analogy, clinging to social mechanisms that have stood the test of time. Yet Burke was also a reformer, asserting that "the Law of Nature is change," but change to preserve in accord with natural law. (Source: Edmund Burke, Reflections on the Revolution in France *[London: J. Dodsley, 1790].)*

Liberty

. . . I flatter myself that I love a manly, moral, regulated liberty as well as any gentleman of that society, be he who he will; and perhaps I have given as good proofs of my attachment to that cause in the whole course of my public conduct. . . . But I cannot stand forward and give praise or blame to anything which relates to human actions, and human concerns, on a simple view of the object, as it stands stripped of every relation, in all the nakedness and solitude of metaphysical abstraction. Circumstances (which with some gentlemen pass for nothing) give in reality to every political principle its distinguishing color and discriminating effect. The circumstances are what render every civil and political scheme beneficial or noxious to mankind. Abstractedly speaking, government, as well as liberty, is good; yet could I, in common sense, ten years ago, have felicitated France on her enjoyment of a government (for she then had a government) without inquiry what the nature of that government was, or how it was administered? Can I now congratulate the same nation upon its freedom? Is it because liberty in the abstract may be classed amongst the blessings of mankind, that I am seriously to felicitate a madman, who has escaped from the protecting restraint and wholesome darkness of his cell, on his restoration to the enjoyment of light and liberty? Am I to congratulate a highwayman and murderer who has broke prison upon the recovery of his natural rights? This would be to act over again the scene of the criminals condemned to the galleys, and their heroic deliverer, the metaphysic Knight of the Sorrowful Countenance.*

Pluralism

When I see the spirit of liberty in action, I see a strong principle at work; and this, for a while, is all I can possibly know of it. The wild *gas*, the fixed air, is plainly broke loose; but we ought to suspend our judgment until the first effervescence is a little subsided, till the liquor is cleared, and until we see something deeper than the agitation of a troubled and frothy surface. I must be tolerably sure, before I venture publicly to congratulate men upon a blessing, that they have really received one. Flattery corrupts both the receiver and the giver, and adulation is not of more service to the people than to kings. I should, therefore, suspend my congratulations on the new liberty of France until I was informed how it had been combined with government, with public force, with the discipline and obedience of armies, with the collection of an effective and well-distributed revenue, with morality and religion, with the solidity of property, with peace and order, with civil and social manners. All these (in their way) are good things, too, and without them liberty is not a benefit whilst it lasts, and is not likely to continue long. The effect of liberty to individuals is that they may do what they please; we ought to see what it will please them to do, before we risk congratulations which may be soon turned into complaints. Prudence would dictate this in the case of separate, insulated, private men, but liberty, when men act in bodies, is *power.* Considerate people, before they declare themselves, will observe the use which is made of *power,* and particularly of so trying a thing as *new* power in *new* persons of whose principles, tempers, and dispositions they have little or no experience, and in situations where those who appear the most stirring in the scene may possibly not be the real movers. . . .

History

. . . The Revolution was made to preserve our *ancient,* indisputable laws and liberties and that *ancient* constitution of government which is our only security for law and liberty. If you are desirous of knowing the spirit of our constitution and the policy which predominated in that great period which has secured it to this hour, pray look for both in our histories, in our records, in our acts of parliament, and journals of parliament, and not in the sermons of the Old Jewry† and the after-dinner toasts of the Revolution Society. In the former you will find other ideas and another language. Such a claim is as ill-suited to our temper and wishes as it is unsupported by any appearance of authority.

*A reference to Don Quixote, who set criminals free only to be beaten by them.—Ed.

†The Courthouse, so called because it was built on the site of a former synagogue.—Ed.

The very idea of the fabrication of a new government is enough to fill us with disgust and horror. We wished at the period of the Revolution, and do now wish, to derive all we possess as *an inheritance from our forefathers*. Upon that body and stock of inheritance we have taken care not to inoculate any cyon* alien to the nature of the original plant. All the reformations we have hitherto made have proceeded upon the principle of reverence to antiquity; and I hope, nay, I am persuaded, that all those which possibly may be made hereafter will be carefully formed upon analogical precedent, authority, and example. . . .

You will observe that from Magna Carta to the Declaration of Right it has been the uniform policy of our constitution to claim and assert our liberties as an *entailed inheritance* derived to us from our forefathers, and to be transmitted to our posterity—as an estate specially belonging to the people of this kingdom, without any reference whatever to any other more general or prior right. By this means our constitution preserves a unity in so great a diversity of its parts. We have an inheritable crown, an inheritable peerage, and a House of Commons and a people inheriting privileges, franchises, and liberties from a long line of ancestors.

Evolution by Analogy

This policy appears to me to be the result of profound reflection, or rather the happy effect of following nature, which is wisdom without reflection, and above it. A spirit of innovation is generally the result of a selfish temper and confined views. People will not look forward to posterity, who never look backward to their ancestors. Besides, the people of England well know that the idea of inheritance furnishes a sure principle of conservation and a sure principle of transmission, without at all excluding a principle of improvement. It leaves acquisition free, but it secures what it acquires. Whatever advantages are obtained by a state proceeding on these maxims are locked fast as in a sort of family settlement, grasped as in a kind of mortmain† forever. By a constitutional policy, working after the pattern of nature, we receive, we hold, we transmit our government and our privileges in the same manner in which we enjoy and transmit our property and our lives. The institutions of policy, the goods of fortune, the gifts of providence are handed down to us, and from us, in the same course and order. Our political system is placed in a just correspondence and symmetry with the order of the world and with the mode of existence decreed to a permanent body composed of transitory parts, wherein, by the disposition of a stupendous wisdom, molding together the great mysterious incorporation of the human race, the whole, at one time, is never old or middle-aged or young, but, in a condition of unchangeable constancy, moves on through the varied tenor of perpetual decay, fall, renovation, and progression. Thus, by preserving the method of nature in the conduct of the state, in what we improve we are never wholly new; in what we retain we are never wholly obsolete. By adhering in this manner and on those principles to our forefathers, we are guided not by the superstition of antiquarians, but by the spirit of philosophic analogy. In this choice of inheritance we have given to our frame of polity the image of a relation in blood, binding up the constitution of our country with our dearest domestic ties, adopting our fundamental laws into the bosom of our family affections, keeping inseparable and cherishing with the warmth of all their combined and mutually reflected charities our state, our hearths, our sepulchres, and our altars.

Virtue

Through the same plan of a conformity to nature in our artificial institutions, and by calling in the aid of her unerring and powerful instincts to fortify the fallible and feeble contrivances of our reason, we have derived several other, and those no small, benefits from considering our liberties in the light of an inheritance. Always acting as if in the presence of canonized forefathers, the spirit of freedom, leading in itself to misrule and excess, is tempered with an awful gravity. This idea of a liberal descent inspires us with a sense of habitual native dignity which prevents that upstart insolence almost inevitably adhering to and disgracing those who are the first acquirers of any distinction. By this means

* A shoot, twig, or graft; old form of *scion*.—ED.

† Literally "dead hand," a legal device to make a corporation possess something in perpetuity; or, the condition of lands held in perpetuity.—ED.

our liberty becomes a noble freedom. It carries an imposing and majestic aspect. It has a pedigree and illustrating ancestors. It has its bearings and its ensigns armorial. It has its gallery of portraits, its monumental inscriptions, its records, evidences, and titles. We procure reverence to our civil institutions on the principle upon which nature teaches us to revere individual men: on account of their age and on account of those from whom they are descended. All your sophisters cannot produce anything better adapted to preserve a rational and manly freedom than the course that we have pursued, who have chosen our nature rather than our speculations, our breasts rather than our inventions, for the great conservatories and magazines of our rights and privileges. . . .

Compromise

. . . These opposed and conflicting interests which you considered as so great a blemish in your old and in our present constitution interpose a salutary check to all precipitate resolutions. They render deliberation a matter, not of choice, but of necessity; they make all change a subject of *compromise,* which naturally begets moderation; they produce *temperaments* preventing the sore evil of harsh, crude, unqualified reformations, and rendering all the headlong exertions of arbitrary power, in the few or in the many, for ever impracticable. Through that diversity of members and interests, general liberty had as many securities as there were separate views in the several orders. . . .

Oppression of the Minority

. . . I reprobate no form of government merely upon abstract principles. There may be situations in which the purely democratic form will become necessary. There may be some (very few, and very particularly circumstanced) where it would be clearly desirable. This I do not take to be the case of France or of any other great country. Until now, we have seen no examples of considerable democracies. The ancients were better acquainted with them. Not being wholly unread in the authors who had seen the most of those constitutions, and who best understood them, I cannot help concurring with their opinion that an absolute democracy, no more than absolute monarchy, is not to be reckoned among the legitimate forms of government. They think it rather the corruption and degeneracy than the sound constitution of a republic. If I recollect rightly, Aristotle observes that a democracy has many striking points of resemblance with a tyranny. Of this I am certain, that in a democracy the majority of the citizens is capable of exercising the most cruel oppressions upon the minority whenever strong divisions prevail in that kind of polity, as they often must; and that oppression of the minority will extend to far greater numbers and will be carried on with much greater fury than can almost ever be apprehended from the dominion of a single scepter. In such a popular persecution, individual sufferers are in a much more deplorable condition than in any other. Under a cruel prince they have the balmy compassion of mankind to assuage the smart of their wounds; they have the plaudits of the people to animate their generous constancy under their sufferings; but those who are subjected to wrong under multitudes are deprived of all external consolation. They seem deserted by mankind, overpowered by a conspiracy of their whole species. . . .

Liberty and Virtue

. . . A brave people will certainly prefer liberty accompanied with a virtuous poverty to a depraved and wealthy servitude. But before the price of comfort and opulence is paid, one ought to be pretty sure it is real liberty which is purchased, and that she is to be purchased at no other price. I shall always, however, consider that liberty as very equivocal in her appearance which has not wisdom and justice for her companions and does not lead prosperity and plenty in her train. . . .

The effects of the incapacity shown by the popular leaders in all the great members of the commonwealth are to be covered with the "all-atoning name" of liberty. In some people I see great liberty indeed; in many, if not in the most, an oppressive, degrading servitude. But what is liberty without wisdom and without virtue? It is the greatest of all possible evils; for it is folly, vice, and madness, without tuition or restraint. Those who know what virtuous liberty is cannot bear to see it disgraced by incapable heads on account of their having high-sounding words in their mouths. Grand, swelling sentiments of liberty I am sure I do not despise. They warm the heart; they enlarge and liberalize our minds; they animate our courage in time of conflict. Old as I am, I read the fine raptures of Lucan and Corneille with pleasure. Neither do I wholly condemn the little arts and devices of popularity. They facilitate the carrying of many points of moment; they keep the people together; they refresh the mind in its exertions; and they diffuse occasional gaiety over the severe brow of moral freedom. Every politician ought to sacrifice to the graces, and to join compliance with reason. But in such an undertaking as that in France, all these subsidiary sentiments and artifices are of little avail. To make a government requires no great prudence. Settle the seat of power, teach obedience, and the work is done. To give freedom is still more easy. It is not necessary to guide; it only requires to let go the rein. But to form a *free government,* that is, to temper together these opposite elements of liberty and restraint in one consistent work, requires much thought, deep reflection, a sagacious, powerful, and combining mind. This I do not find in those who take the lead in the National Assembly. Perhaps they are not so miserably deficient as they appear. I rather believe it. It would put them below the common level of human understanding. But when the leaders choose to make themselve bidders at an auction of popularity, their talents, in the construction of the state, will be of no service. They will become flatterers instead of legislators, the instruments, not the guides, of the people. If any of them should happen to propose a scheme of liberty, soberly limited and defined with proper qualifications, he will be immediately outbid by his competitors who will produce something more splendidly popular. Suspicions will be raised of his fidelity to his cause. Moderation will be stigmatized as the virtue of cowards, and compromise as the prudence of traitors, until, in hopes of preserving the credit which may enable him to temper and moderate, on some occasions, the popular leader is obliged to become active in propagating doctrines and establishing powers that will afterwards defeat any sober purpose at which he ultimately might have aimed. . . .

Change

. . . I wish my countrymen rather to recommend to our neighbors the example of the British constitution than to take models from them for the improvement of our own. In the former, they have got an invaluable treasure. They are not, I think, without some causes of apprehension and complaint, but these they do not owe to their constitution but to their own conduct. I think our happy situation owing to our constitution, but owing to the whole of it, and not to any part singly, owing in a great measure to what we have left standing in our several reviews and reformations as well as to what we have altered or superadded. Our people will find employment enough for a truly patriotic, free, and independent spirit in guarding what they possess from violation. I would not exclude alteration neither, but even when I changed, it should be to preserve. I should be led to my remedy by a great grievance. In what I did, I should follow the example of our ancestors. I would make the reparation as nearly as possible in the style of the building. A politic caution, a guarded circumspection, a moral rather than a complexional timidity were among the ruling principles of our forefathers in their most decided conduct. Not being illuminated with the light of which the gentlemen of France tell us they have got so abundant a share, they acted under a strong impression of the ignorance and fallibility of mankind. He that had made them thus fallible rewarded them for having in their conduct attended to their nature. Let us imitate their caution if we wish to deserve their fortune or to retain their bequests. Let us add, if we please, but let us preserve what they have left; and, standing on the firm ground of the British constitution, let us be satisfied to admire rather than attempt to follow in their desperate flights the aeronauts of France. . . .

Against Rights

. . . [I]t is vain to talk to them of the practice of their ancestors, the fundamental laws of their country, the fixed form of a constitution whose merits are confirmed by the solid test of long experience and an increasing public strength and national prosperity. They despise experience as the wisdom of unlettered men; and as for the rest, they have wrought underground a mine that will blow up, at one grand explosion, all examples of antiquity, all precedents, charters, and acts of parliament. They have "the rights of men." Against these there can be no prescription, against these no agreement is binding; these admit no temperament and no compromise; anything withheld from their full demand is so much of fraud and injustice. Against these their rights of men let no government look for security in the length of its continuance, or in the justice and lenity of its administration. The objections of these speculatists, if its forms do not quadrate with their theories, are as valid against such an old and beneficent government as against the most violent tyranny or the greenest usurpation. . . .

Real Rights

Far am I from denying in theory, full as far is my heart from withholding in practice (if I were of power to give or to withhold) the *real* rights of men. In denying their false claims of right, I do not mean to injure those which are real, and are such as their pretended rights would totally destroy. If civil society be made for the advantage of man, all the advantages for which it is made become his right. It is an institution of beneficence; and law itself is only beneficence acting by a rule. Men have a right to live by that rule; they have a right to do justice, as between their fellows, whether their fellows are in public function or in ordinary occupation. They have a right to the fruits of their industry and to the means of making their industry fruitful. They have a right to the acquisitions of their parents, to the nourishment and improvement of their offspring, to instruction in life, and to consolation in death. Whatever each man can separately do, without trespassing upon others, he has a right to do for himself; and he has a right to a fair portion of all which society, with all its combinations of skill and force, can do in his favor. In this partnership all men have equal rights, but not to equal things. He that has but five shillings in the partnership has as good a right to it as he that has five hundred pounds has to his larger proportion. But he has not a right to an equal dividend in the product of the joint stock; and as to the share of power, authority, and direction which each individual ought to have in the management of the state, that I must deny to be amongst the direct original rights of man in civil society; for I have in my contemplation the civil social man, and no other. It is a thing to be settled by convention.

Natural and Civil Rights

If civil society be the offspring of convention, that convention must be its law. That convention must limit and modify all the descriptions of constitution which are formed under it. Every sort of legislative, judicial, or executory power are its creatures. They can have no being in any other state of things; *and how can any man claim under the conventions of civil rights which do not so much as suppose its existence—rights which are absolutely repugnant to it?* One of the first motives to civil society, and which becomes one of its fundamental rules, is *that no man should be judge in his own cause.* By this each person has at once divested himself of the first fundamental right of uncovenanted man, that is, to judge for himself and to assert his own cause. He abdicates all right to be his own governor. He inclusively, in a great measure, abandons the right of self-defense, the first law of nature. Men cannot enjoy the rights of an uncivil and of a civil state together. That he may obtain justice, he gives up his right of determining what it is in points the most essential to him. That he may secure some liberty, he makes a surrender in trust of the whole of it.

Rights and Responsibilities

Government is not made in virtue of natural rights, which may and do exist in total independence of it, and exist in much greater clearness and in a much greater degree of abstract perfection; but their abstract perfection is their practical defect. By having a right to everything they want everything. Government is a contrivance of human wisdom to provide for human *wants.* Men have a right that these wants should be provided for by this wisdom. Among these wants is to be reckoned the want, out of civil society, of a sufficient restraint upon their passions. Society requires not only that the passions of individuals should be subjected, but that even in the mass and body, as well as in the individuals, the inclinations of men should frequently be thwarted, their will controlled, and their passions brought into subjection. This can only be done *by a power out of themselves,* and not, in the exercise of its function, subject to that will and to those passions which it is its office to bridle and subdue. In this sense the restraints on men, as well as their liberties, are to be reckoned among their rights. But as the liberties and the restrictions vary with times and circumstances and admit to infinite modifications, they cannot be settled upon any abstract rule; and nothing is so foolish as to discuss them upon that principle.

The moment you abate anything from the full rights of men, each to govern himself, and suffer any artificial, positive limitation upon those rights, from that moment the whole organization of government becomes a consideration of convenience. This it is which makes the constitution of a state and the due distribution of its powers a matter of the most delicate and complicated skill. It requires a deep knowledge of human nature and human necessities, and of the things which facilitate or obstruct the various ends which are to be pursued by the mechanism of civil institutions. The state is to have recruits to its strength, and remedies to its distempers. What is the use of discussing a man's abstract right to food or medicine? The question is upon the method of procuring and administering them. In that deliberation I shall always advise to call in the aid of the farmer and the physician rather than the professor of metaphysics.

Experience

The science of constructing a commonwealth, or renovating it, or reforming it, is, like every other experimental science, not to be taught *a priori.* Nor is it a short experience that can instruct us in that practical science, because the real effects of moral causes are not always immediate; but that which in the first instance is prejudicial may be excellent in its remoter operation, and its excellence may arise even from the ill effects it produces in the beginning. The reverse also happens: and very plausible schemes, with very pleasing commencements, have often shameful and lamentable conclusions. In states there are often some obscure and almost latent causes, things which appear at first view of little moment, on which a very great part of its prosperity or adversity may most essentially depend. The science of government being therefore so practical in itself and intended for such practical purposes—a matter which requires experience, and even more experience than any person can gain in his whole life, however sagacious and observing he may be—it is with infinite caution that any man ought to venture upon pulling down an edifice which has answered in any tolerable degree for ages the common purposes of society, or on building it up again without having models and patterns of approved utility before his eyes.

Complexity

These metaphysic rights entering into common life, like rays of light which pierce into a dense medium, are by the laws of nature refracted from their straight line. Indeed, in the gross and complicated mass of human passions and concerns the primitive rights of men undergo such a variety of refractions and reflections that it becomes absurd to talk of them as if they continued in the simplicity of their original direction. The nature of man is intricate; the objects of society are of the greatest possible complexity; and, therefore, no simple disposition or direction of power can be suitable either to man's nature or to the quality of his affairs. When I hear the simplicity of contrivance aimed at and boasted of in any new political constitutions, I am at no loss to decide that the artificers are grossly ignorant of their trade or totally negligent of their duty. The simple governments are fundamentally defective, to say no worse of them. If you were to contemplate society in but one point of view, all these simple modes of polity are infinitely captivating. In effect each would answer its single end much more perfectly than the more complex is able to attain all its complex purposes. But it is better that the whole should be imperfectly and anomalously answered than that, while some parts are provided for with great exactness, others might be totally neglected or perhaps materially injured by the over-care of a favorite member.

The pretended rights of these theorists are all extremes; and in proportion as they are metaphysically true, they are morally and politically false. The rights of men are in a sort of *middle,* incapable of definition, but not impossible to be discerned. The rights of men in governments are their advantages; and these are often in balances between differences of good, in compromises sometimes between good and evil, and sometimes between evil and evil. Political reason is a computing principle: adding, subtracting, multiplying, and dividing, morally and not metaphysically or mathematically, true moral denominations. . . .

Prejudice

You see, Sir, that in this enlightened age I am bold enough to confess that we are generally men of untaught feelings, that, instead of casting away all our old prejudices, we cherish them to a very considerable degree, and, to take more shame to ourselves, we cherish them because they are prejudices; and the longer they have lasted and the more generally they have prevailed, the more we cherish them. We are afraid to put men to live and trade each on his own private stock of reason, because we suspect that this stock in each man is small, and that the individuals would do better to avail themselves of the general bank and capital of nations and of ages. Many of our men of speculation, instead of exploding general prejudices, employ their sagacity to discover the latent wisdom which prevails in them. If they find what they seek, and they seldom fail, they think it more wise to continue the prejudice, with the reason involved, than to cast away the coat of prejudice and to leave nothing but the naked reason; because prejudice, with its reason, has a motive to give action to that reason, and an affection which will give it permanence. Prejudice is of ready application in the emergency; it previously engages the mind in a steady course of wisdom and virtue and does not leave the man hesitating in the moment of decision skeptical, puzzled, and unresolved. Prejudice renders a man's virtue his habit, and not a series of unconnected acts. Through just prejudice, his duty becomes a part of his nature. . . .

. . . Rage and frenzy will pull down more in half an hour than prudence, deliberation, and foresight can build up in a hundred years. The errors and defects of old establishments are visible and palpable. It calls for little ability to point them out; and where absolute power is given, it requires but a word wholly to abolish the vice and the establishment together. The same lazy but restless disposition which loves sloth and hates quiet directs the politicians when they come to work for supplying the place of what they have destroyed. To make everything the reverse of what they have seen is quite as easy as to destroy. No difficulties occur in what has never been tried. Criticism is almost baffled in discovering the defects of what has not existed; and eager enthusiasm and cheating hope have all the wide field of imagination in which they may expatiate with little or no opposition.

Change

At once to preserve and to reform is quite another thing. When the useful parts of an old establishment are kept, and what is superadded is to be fitted to what is retained, a vigorous mind, steady, persevering attention, various powers of comparison and combination, and the resources of an understanding fruitful in expedients are to be exercised; they are to be exercised in a continued conflict with the combined force of opposite vices, with the obstinacy that rejects all improvement and the levity that is fatigued and disgusted with everything of which it is in possession. But you may object—"A process of this kind is slow. It is not fit for an assembly which glories in performing in a few months the work of ages. Such a mode of reforming, possibly, might take up many years." Without question it might; and it ought. It is one of the excellences of a method in which time is amongst the assistants, that its operation is slow and in some cases almost imperceptible. If circumspection and caution are a part of wisdom when we work only upon inanimate matter, surely they become a part of duty, too, when the subject of our demolition and construction is not brick and timber but sentient beings, by the sudden alteration of whose state, condition, and habits multitudes may be rendered miserable. But it seems as if it were the prevalent opinion in Paris that an unfeeling heart and an undoubting confidence are the sole qualifications for a perfect legislator.

Far different are my ideas of that high office. The true lawgiver ought to have a heart full of sensibility. He ought to love and respect his kind, and to fear himself. It may be allowed to his temperament to catch his ultimate object with an intuitive glance, but his movements toward it ought to be deliberate. Political arrangement, as it is a work for social ends, is to be only wrought by social means. There mind must conspire with mind. Time is required to produce that union of minds which alone can produce all the good we aim at. Our patience will achieve more than our force. If I might venture to appeal to what is so much out of fashion in Paris, I mean to experience, I should tell you that in my course I have known and, according to my measure, have cooperated with great men; and I have never yet seen any plan which has not been mended by the observation of those who were much inferior in understanding to the person who took the lead in the business. By a slow but well-sustained progress the effect of each step is watched; the good or ill success of the first gives light to us in the second; and so, from light to light, we are conducted with safety through the whole series. We see that the parts of the system do not clash. The evils latent in the most promising contrivances are provided for as they arise. One advantage is as little as possible sacrificed to another. We compensate, we reconcile, we balance. We are enabled to unite into a consistent whole the various anomalies and contending principles that are found in the minds and affairs of men. From hence arises, not an excellence in simplicity, but one far superior, an excellence in composition. Where the great interests of mankind are concerned through a long succession of generations, that succession ought to be admitted into some share in the councils which are so deeply to affect them. If justice requires this, the work itself requires the aid of more minds than one age can furnish. It is from this view of things that the best legislators have been often satisfied with the establishment of some sure, solid, and ruling principle in government—a power like that which some of the philosophers have called a plastic nature; and having fixed the principle, they have left it afterwards to its own operation. . . .

QUESTIONS FOR REFLECTION

1. What does Burke mean by a "manly, moral, regulated liberty"?
2. Burke is a pluralist—he believes that there are fundamentally different kinds of moral value. What are some of these kinds? What kind of value is liberty? Is it unequivocally good?
3. Burke points out that "liberty, when men act in bodies, is *power*." What does he deduce from this? What, in your view, does Burke's observation imply about liberty?
4. Burke thinks that it is very important "to derive all we possess as *an inheritance from our forefathers*." Why does Burke place such an emphasis on tradition?
5. Burke worries that democracy allows the "oppression of the minority." Why? What can be done to guard against it?
6. What principles properly guide change?
7. How does Burke distinguish "real rights" from pretenders?
8. What real rights, in Burke's opinion, do people have? On what are these rights based?
9. What, according to Burke, is the purpose of government? Why does this lead Burke to claim that "the restraints on men, as well as their liberties, are to be reckoned among their rights"?
10. Why does reform require "infinite caution," in Burke's view? Why does Burke stress the importance of tradition?
11. What is the role of "natural feeling" and prejudice in Burke's theory?
12. How do we resolve conflicts between rights, according to Burke?

JOHN STUART MILL

from *Utilitarianism*

(Source: Reprinted from John Stuart Mill, Utilitarianism. *[London: Longman's, 1907].)*

Duty

. . . We do not call anything wrong unless we mean to imply that a person ought to be punished in some way or other for doing it—if not by law, by the opinion of his fellow creatures; if not by opinion, by the reproaches of his own conscience. This seems the real turning point of the distinction between morality and simple expediency. It is a part of the notion of duty in every one of its forms that a person may rightfully be compelled to fulfil it. Duty is a thing which may be *exacted* from a person, as one exacts a debt. Unless we think that it may be exacted from him, we do not call it his duty. Reasons of prudence, or the interest of other people, may militate against actually exacting it, but the person himself, it is clearly understood, would not be entitled to complain. There are other things, on the contrary, which we wish that people should do, which we like or admire them for doing, perhaps dislike or despise them for not doing, but yet admit that they are not bound to do; it is not a case of moral obligation; we do not blame them, that is, we do not think that they are proper objects of punishment. How we come by these ideas of deserving and not deserving punishment will appear, perhaps, in the sequel; but I think there is no doubt that this distinction lies at the bottom of the notions of right and wrong; that we call any conduct wrong, or employ, instead, some other term of dislike or disparagement, according as we think that the person ought, or ought not, to be punished for it; and we say it would be right to do so and so, or merely that it would be desirable or laudable, according as we would wish to see the person whom it concerns compelled, or only persuaded and exhorted, to act in that manner.

Perfect and Imperfect Obligation

This, therefore, being the characteristic difference which marks off, not justice, but morality in general from the remaining provinces of expediency and worthiness, the character is still to be sought which distinguishes justice from other branches of morality. Now it is known that ethical writers divide moral duties into two classes, denoted by the ill-chosen expressions, duties of perfect and of imperfect obligation; the latter being those in which, though the act is obligatory, the particular occasions of performing it are left to our choice, as in the case of charity or beneficence, which we are indeed bound to practice but not towards any definite person, nor at any prescribed time. In the more precise language of philosophic jurists, duties of perfect obligation are those duties in virtue of which a correlative *right* resides in some person or persons; duties of imperfect obligation are those moral obligations which do not give birth to any right. I think it will be found that this distinction exactly coincides with that which exists between justice and the other obligations of morality. In our survey of the various popular acceptations of justice, the term appeared generally to involve the idea of a personal right—a claim on the part of one or more individuals, like that which the law gives when it confers a proprietary or other legal right. Whether the injustice consists in depriving a person of a possession, or in breaking faith with him, or in treating him worse than he deserves, or worse than other people who have no greater claims—in each case the supposition implies two things: a wrong done, and some assignable person who is wronged. Injustice may also be done by treating a person better than others; but the wrong in this case is to his competitors, who are also assignable persons. It seems to me that this feature in the case—a right in some person, correlative to the moral obligation—constitutes the specific difference between justice and generosity of beneficence. Justice implies something which it is not only right to do, and wrong not to do, but which some individual person can claim from us as his moral right. No one has a moral right to our generosity or beneficence because we are not morally bound to practice those virtues towards any given individual. And it will be found with respect to this as to every correct definition that the instances which seem to conflict with it are those which most confirm it. For if a moralist attempts, as some have done, to make out that mankind generally, though not any given individual, have a right to all the good we can do them, he at once, by that thesis, includes generosity and beneficence within the category of justice. He is obliged to say that our utmost exertions are *due* to our fellow creatures, thus assimilating them to a debt; or that nothing less can be a sufficient *return* for what society does for us, thus classing the case as one of gratitude; both of which are acknowledged cases of justice, and not of the virtue of beneficence; and whoever does not place the distinction between justice and morality in general, where we have now placed it, will be found to make no distinction between them at all, but to merge all morality in justice. . . .

Criticism of Kant

. . . It is common enough, certainly, though the reverse of commendable, to feel resentment merely because we have suffered pain; but a person whose resentment is really a moral feeling, that is, who considers whether an act is blamable before he allows himself to resent it—such a person, though he may not say expressly to himself that he is standing up for the interest of society, certainly does feel that he is asserting a rule which is for the benefit of others as well as for his own. If he is not feeling this—if he is regarding the act solely as it affects him individually—he is not consciously just; he is not concerning himself about the justice of his actions. This is admitted even by anti-utilitarian moralists. When Kant (as before remarked) propounds as the fundamental principle of morals, "So act that thy rule of conduct might be adopted as a law by all rational beings," he virtually acknowledges that the interest of mankind collectively, or at least of mankind indiscriminately, must be in the mind of the agent when conscientiously deciding on the morality of the act. Otherwise he uses words without a meaning; for that a rule even of utter selfishness could not *possibly* be adopted by all rational beings—that there is any insuperable obstacle in the nature of things to its adoption—cannot be even plausibly maintained. To give any meaning to Kant's principle, the sense put upon it must be that we ought to shape our conduct by a rule which all rational beings might adopt *with benefit to their collective interest.*

Rights

To recapitulate: the idea of justice supposes two things—a rule of conduct and a sentiment which sanctions the rule. The first must be supposed common to all mankind and intended for their good. The other (the sentiment) is a desire that punishment may be suffered by those who infringe the rule. There is involved, in addition, the conception of some definite person who suffers by the infringement, whose rights (to use the expression appropriated to the case) are violated by it. And the sentiment of justice appears to me to be the animal desire to repel or retaliate a hurt or damage to oneself or to those with whom one sympathises, widened so as to include all persons, by the human capacity of enlarged sympathy and the human conception of intelligent self-interest.

From the latter elements the feeling derives its morality; from the former, its peculiar impressiveness and energy of self-assertion.

I have, throughout, treated the idea of a *right* residing in the injured person and violated by the injury, not as a separate element in the composition of the idea and sentiment, but as one of the forms in which the other two elements clothe themselves. These elements are a hurt to some assignable person or persons, on the one hand, and a demand for punishment, on the other. An examination of our own minds, I think, will show that these two things include all that we mean when we speak of violation of a right. When we call anything a person's right, we mean that he has a valid claim on society to protect him in the possession of it, either by the force of law or by that of education and opinion. If he has what we consider a sufficient claim, on whatever account, to have something guaranteed to him by society, we say that he has a right to it. If we desire to prove that anything does not belong to him by right, we think this done as soon as it is admitted that society ought not to take measures for securing it to him, but should leave him to chance or to his own exertions. Thus a person is said to have a right to what he can earn in fair professional competition, because society ought not to allow any other person to hinder him from endeavouring to earn in that manner as much as he can. But he has not a right to three hundred a year, though he may happen to be earning it; because society is not called on to provide that he shall earn that sum. On the contrary, if he owns ten thousand pounds three-per-cent stock, he *has* a right to three hundred a year because society has come under an obligation to provide him with an income of that amount.

To have a right, then, is, I conceive, to have something which society ought to defend me in the possession of. If the objector goes on to ask why it ought, I can give him no other reason than general utility. If that expression does not seem to convey a sufficient feeling of the strength of the obligation, nor to account for the peculiar energy of the feeling, it is because there goes to the composition of the sentiment, not a rational only but also an animal element—the thirst for retaliation; and this thirst derives its intensity, as well as its moral justification, from the extraordinarily important and impressive kind of utility which is concerned. The interest involved is that of security to everyone's feelings the most vital of all interests. All other earthly benefits are needed by one person, not needed by another; and many of them can, if necessary, be cheerfully foregone or replaced by something else; but security no human being can possibly do without; on it we depend for all our immunity from evil and for the whole value of all and every good, beyond the passing moment since nothing but the gratification of the instant could be of any worth to us if we could be deprived of everything the next instant by whoever was momentarily stronger than ourselves. Now this most indispensable of all necessaries, after physical nutriment, cannot be had unless the machinery for providing it is kept unintermittedly in active play. Our notion, therefore, of the claim we have on our fellow creatures to join in making safe for us the very groundwork of our existence gathers feelings around it so much more intense than those concerned in any of the more common cases of utility that the difference in degree (as is often the case in psychology) becomes a real difference in kind. The claim assumes that character of absoluteness, that apparent infinity and incommensurability with all other considerations which constitute the distinction between the feeling of right and wrong and that of ordinary expediency and inexpediency. The feelings concerned are so powerful, and we count so positively on finding a responsive feeling in others (all being alike interested), that *ought* and *should* grow into *must*, and recognized indispensability becomes a moral necessity, analogous to physical, and often not inferior to it in binding force.

QUESTIONS FOR REFLECTION

1. Distinguish perfect from imperfect duties. Which correspond to rights?
2. "To treat someone unjustly is to violate their rights." Does Mill agree? Do you?
3. What is a right, according to Mill? Explain, in these terms, what rights to life, liberty, and property are.
4. How does Mill's conception of rights differ from that of Locke?
5. Contrast Mill's conception of rights with that of Thomas Nagel (in Part II). Can Mill explain a connection between rights and inviolability?
6. Ronald Dworkin considers rights as trumps: They cannot be overridden by utilitarian considerations. If I have a right to life, for example, you cannot murder me, even to promote the greater good. Is Mill committed to denying that? Why or why not? Should he deny it? Are there cases in which rights should be overridden by the greater good?

UNITED NATIONS

Universal Declaration of Human Rights

(Source: United Nations General Assembly Resolution 217A [III] of 10 December 1948.)

Preamble

Whereas recognition of the inherent dignity and of the equal and inalienable rights of all members of the human family is the foundation of freedom, justice and peace in the world,

Whereas disregard and contempt for human rights have resulted in barbarous acts which have outraged the conscience of mankind, and the advent of a world in which human beings shall enjoy freedom of speech and belief and freedom from fear and want has been proclaimed as the highest aspiration of the common people,

Whereas it is essential, if man is not to be compelled to have recourse, as a last resort, to rebellion against tyranny and oppression, that human rights should be protected by the rule of law,

Whereas it is essential to promote the development of friendly relations between nations,

Whereas the peoples of the United Nations have in the Charter reaffirmed their faith in fundamental human rights, in the dignity and worth of the human person and in the equal rights of men and women and have determined to promote social progress and better standards of life in larger freedom,

Whereas Member States have pledged themselves to achieve, in co-operation with the United Nations, the promotion of universal respect for and observance of human rights and fundamental freedoms,

Whereas a common understanding of these rights and freedoms is of the greatest importance for the full realisation of this pledge,

Now, therefore,

The General Assembly,

Proclaims this Universal Declaration of Human Rights as a common standard of achievement for all peoples and all nations, to the end that every individual and every organ of society, keeping this Declaration constantly in mind, shall strive by teaching and education to promote respect for these rights and freedoms and by progressive measures, national and international, to secure their universal and effective recognition and observance, both among the peoples of Member States themselves and among the peoples of territories under their jurisdiction.

Article 1

All human beings are born free and equal in dignity and rights. They are endowed with reason and conscience and should act towards one another in a spirit of brotherhood.

Article 2

Everyone is entitled to all the rights and freedoms set forth in this Declaration, without distinction of any kind; such as race, colour, sex, language, religion, political or other opinion, national or social origin, property, birth or other status.

Furthermore, no distinction shall be made on the basis of the political, jurisdictional or international status of the country or territory to which a person belongs, whether it be independent, trust, non-self-governing or under any other limitation of sovereignty.

Article 3

Everyone has the right to life, liberty and security of person.

Article 4

No one shall be held in slavery or servitude; slavery and the slave trade shall be prohibited in all their forms.

Article 5

No one shall be subjected to torture or to cruel, inhuman or degrading treatment or punishment.

Article 6

Everyone has the right to recognition everywhere as a person before the law.

Article 7

All are equal before the law and are entitled without any discrimination to equal protection of the law. All are entitled to equal protection against any discrimination in violation of this Declaration and against any incitement to such discrimination.

Article 8

Everyone has the right to an effective remedy by the competent national tribunals for acts violating the fundamental rights granted him by the constitution or by law.

Article 9

No one shall be subjected to arbitrary arrest, detention or exile.

Article 10

Everyone is entitled in full equality to a fair and public hearing by an independent and impartial tribunal, in the determination of his rights and obligations and of any criminal charge against him.

Article 11

1. Everyone charged with a penal offence has the right to be presumed innocent until proved guilty according to law in a public trial at which he has had all the guarantees necessary for his defence.
2. No one shall be held guilty of any penal offence on account of any act or omission which did not constitute a penal offence, under national or international law, at the time when it was committed. Nor shall a heavier penalty be imposed than the one that was applicable at the time the penal offence was committed.

Article 12

No one shall be subjected to arbitrary interference with his privacy, family, home or correspondence, nor to attacks upon his honour and reputation. Everyone has the right to the protection of the law against such interference or attacks.

Article 13

1. Everyone has the right to freedom of movement and residence within the borders of each State.
2. Everyone has the right to leave any country, including his own, and to return to his country.

Article 14

1. Everyone has the right to seek and to enjoy in other countries asylum from persecution.
2. This right may not be invoked in the case of prosecutions genuinely arising from non-political crimes or from acts contrary to the purposes and principles of the United Nations.

Article 15

1. Everyone has the right to a nationality.

2. No one shall be arbitrarily deprived of his nationality nor denied the right to change his nationality.

Article 16

1. Men and women of full age, without any limitation due to race, nationality or religion, have the right to marry and to found a family. They are entitled to equal rights as to marriage, during marriage and at its dissolution.
2. Marriage shall be entered into only with the free and full consent of the intending spouses.
3. The family is the natural and fundamental group unit of society and is entitled to protection by society and the State.

Article 17

1. Everyone has the right to own property alone as well as in association with others.
2. No one shall be arbitrarily deprived of his property.

Article 18

Everyone has the right to freedom of thought, conscience and religion; this right includes freedom to change his religion or belief, and freedom, either alone or in community with others and in public or private to manifest his religion or belief in teaching, practice, worship and observance.

Article 19

Everyone has the right to freedom of opinion and expression; this right includes freedom to hold opinions without interference and to seek, receive and impart information and ideas through any media and regardless of frontiers.

Article 20

1. Everyone has the right to freedom of peaceful assembly and association.
2. No one may be compelled to belong to an association.

Article 21

1. Everyone has the right to take part in the government of his country, directly or through freely chosen representatives.
2. Everyone has the right equal access to public service in his country.
3. The will of the people shall be the basis of the authority of government; this will shall be expressed in periodic and genuine elections which shall be by universal and equal suffrage and shall be held by secret vote or by equivalent free voting procedures.

Article 22

Everyone, as a member of society, has the right to social security and is entitled to realisation, through national effort and international co-operation and in accordance with the organisation and resources of each State, of the economic, social and cultural rights indispensable for his dignity and the free development of his personality.

Article 23

1. Everyone has the right to work, to free choice of employment, to just and favourable conditions of work and protection against unemployment.
2. Everyone, without any discrimination, has the right to equal pay for equal work.
3. Everyone who works has the right to just and favourable remuneration ensuring for himself and his family an existence worthy of human dignity, and supplemented, if necessary, by other means of social protection.
4. Everyone has the right to form and to join trade unions for the protection of his interests.

Article 24

Everyone has the right to rest and leisure, including reasonable limitation of working hours and periodic holidays with pay.

Article 25

1. Everyone has the right to a standard of living adequate for the health and well-being of himself and of his family, Including food, clothing, housing and medical care and necessary social services, and the right to security in the event of unemployment, sickness, disability, widowhood, old

age or other lack of livelihood in circumstances beyond his control.

2. Motherhood and childhood are entitled to special care and assistance. All children, whether born in or out of wedlock, shall enjoy the same social protection.

Article 26

1. Everyone has the right to education. Education shall be free, at least in the elementary and fundamental stages. Elementary education shall be compulsory. Technical and professional education shall be made generally available and higher education shall be equally accessible to all on the basis of merit.
2. Education shall be directed to the full development of the human personality and to the strengthening of respect for human rights and fundamental freedoms. It shall promote understanding, tolerance and friendship among all nations, racial or religious groups, and shall further the activities of the United Nations for the maintenance of peace.
3. Parents have a prior right to choose the kind of education that shall be I given to their children.

Article 27

1. Everyone has the right freely to participate in the cultural life of the community, to enjoy the arts and to share in scientific advancement and its benefits.
2. Everyone has the right to the protection of the moral and material interests resulting from any scientific, literary or artistic production of which he is the author.

Article 28

Everyone is entitled to a social and international order in which the rights and freedoms set forth in this Declaration call be fully realised.

Article 29

1. Everyone has duties to the community in which alone the free and full development of his personality is possible.
2. In the exercise of his rights and freedoms, everyone shall be subject only to such limitations as are determined by law solely for the purpose of securing due recognition and respect for the rights and freedoms of others and of meeting the just requirements of morality, public order and the general welfare in a democratic society.
3. These rights and freedoms may in no case be exercised contrary to the purposes and principles of the United Nations.

Article 30

Nothing in this Declaration may be interpreted as implying for any State, group or person any right to engage in any activity or to perform any act aimed at the destruction of any of the rights and freedoms, set forth herein.

QUESTIONS FOR REFLECTION

1. Which of the Declaration's rights are recognized in the U.S. Constitution?
2. Which of the Declaration's rights are compatible with the theory of rights advanced by Locke? Kant?

ABORTION

Abortion raises notoriously difficult ethical problems. At root, these problems seem to revolve around rights. Opponents of abortion speak of the right to life of the fetus; pro-choice advocates speak of a woman's right to choose. Obviously, these two putative rights come into conflict over abortion. One cannot respect both the right to life of the fetus and the woman's right to choose if the woman chooses to abort. Consequently, the abortion issue seems to call for some neutral or well-grounded way of deciding when some rights take precedence over others.

Of course, not everyone grants the rights in question. Some argue that the fetus is not a person and, indeed, is sufficiently unlike a person that it has no rights. Others argue that the woman may have obligations toward a fetus inside her even if it is there through no choice of her own. They deny that, at least in some cases, a woman has a right to choose abortion. The abortion problem thus raises two other very difficult issues: (1) What kinds of beings have rights? Fetuses, severely ill or injured people, and animals all share many basic human characteristics but lack others common to typical, healthy adults. Which characteristics, if any, are essential to having rights? In general, how do we decide the boundaries of our moral categories? (2) What kinds of obligations do we have toward others? Under what circumstances do other people have rights against us—rights to have us do certain things to help them and to refrain from doing things to harm them? To what extent do such obligations depend on our willingness to assume them? These questions are crucial to the abortion issue and, moreover, reach far beyond it.

Abortion had been illegal in most areas of the United States until 1973, when the Supreme Court decided, in *Roe* v. *Wade*, that the Constitution guarantees a right to privacy, implying that the state may not restrict abortions in the first trimester (the first three months of pregnancy). The Court backed away from any decision about the ultimate moral status of the fetus; it treated fetuses as "potential people," having value if not rights. (Opponents of the decision contend that this failure to decide the status of the fetus is itself a decision, since the Court does not take the rights of fetuses into account.) Instead, the Court based its decision on the medical fact that first-trimester abortions are less risky than carrying a child to term, whereas later abortions are riskier. The government's interest in preserving the health and safety of the mother thus gives the government reason to restrict abortions, but only after the first trimester. The value of the fetus also gives the government reason to restrict abortions, but only after the fetus becomes "viable"—that is, able to survive outside the mother's body. Until then, the mother's right to privacy takes precedence. The Court's decision in *Roe* v. *Wade* raises profound constitutional questions and analogous moral questions: Is there a right to privacy? If so, what is it? How far does it extend? How does it relate to other rights? What obligations does it place on others? . . .

Judith Jarvis Thomson contends that the unacceptability of abortion does not follow automatically from the right to life of the fetus. She grants, for the sake of argument, that the fetus has such a right. She then maintains that under many circumstances, a woman nevertheless has no obligation to carry a child to term. She distinguishes some important conceptions of our obligations to others and argues that only on a very (and, she thinks, unacceptably) strong conception does the woman generally have an obligation not to abort.

Mary Anne Warren rejects Thomson's argument. If the fetus were a person with a right to life, Warren believes, abortion would generally be immoral. But Warren rejects the premise. A fetus, she contends, is at best a potential person, for it lacks basic defining features of personhood: consciousness, reasoning, self-motivated activity, communicative ability, and self-awareness. Since the rights of actual people take precedence over the rights (if there are any) of potential people, abortion is therefore permissible.

Don Marquis contends that abortion is immoral for the same reason that murdering an adult human is immoral—it deprives something that would have had a life like ours of its future. Marquis does not argue, as many anti-abortionists have, that the fetus has a right to life or that abortion is murder; he argues instead that it is *like* murder in that it deprives something that would have gone on to experience a life like ours of that very opportunity. Rosalind Hursthouse discusses the ethics of abortion from the perspective of virtue ethics. She finds standard arguments overly simplistic due to their reliance on rules and a conclusion about the moral status of the fetus. Whatever the exact circumstances and status of the fetus, she argues, abortion is a matter of serious moral concern. That does not mean that it is always or even usually wrong; pursuing an abortion in a given case might be selfish, callous, or irresponsible, but it might not be, depending on the circumstances. Expanding our moral vocabulary by thinking in terms of virtues and vices leads to no universal conclusions about abortion, but it does enable us to think about abortion with the sensitivity and seriousness that the issue deserves.

Francis Beckwith criticizes several pro-choice arguments, including the argument that a woman has a right to her own body and that childbirth is more dangerous than abortion. (Both arguments figure significantly in the Supreme Court's reasoning in *Roe v. Wade*.) He devotes most of his effort, however, to criticizing Thomson's argument. He finds her analogy with unplugging a famous violinist unpersuasive, and observes that our view of the case would be significantly different if the woman concerned were the violinist's mother, or if what was expected of her was a relatively minor inconvenience.

Finally, Alexander Pruss argues that abortion is wrong whenever it would be wrong to kill an adult. You were once a fetus. It would have been just as wrong to kill you earlier as it would be to kill you now. This argument does not depend on whether fetuses are persons, but only on whether persons were once fetuses.

JUSTICE HARRY BLACKMUN

Majority Opinion in Roe v. Wade (1973)

(Source: Roe v. Wade *410 U.S. 113 [1973]. Most legal references have been omitted.)*

Mr. Justice Blackmun delivered the opinion of the Court. . . .

I

The Texas statutes that concern us here are Arts. 1191–1194 and 1196 of the State's Penal Code. These make it a crime to "procure an abortion," as therein defined, or to attempt one, except with respect to "an abortion procured or attempted by medical advice for the purpose of saving the life of the mother." Similar statutes are in existence in a majority of the States. . . .

II

Jane Roe, a single woman who was residing in Dallas County, Texas, instituted this federal action in March 1970 against the District Attorney of the county. She sought a declaratory judgment that the Texas criminal abortion statutes were unconstitutional on their face and an injunction restraining the defendant from enforcing the statutes.

Roe alleged that she was unmarried and pregnant; that she wished to terminate her pregnancy by an abortion "performed by a competent, licensed physician, under safe, clinical conditions"; that she was unable to get a "legal" abortion in Texas because her life did not appear to be threatened by the continuation of her pregnancy; and that she could not afford to travel to another jurisdiction in order to secure a legal abortion under safe conditions. She claimed that the Texas statutes were unconstitutionally vague and that they abridged her right of personal privacy, protected by the First, Fourth, Fifth, Ninth, and Fourteenth Amendments. By an amendment to her complaint Roe purported to sue "on behalf of herself and all other women" similarly situated. . . .

VIII

The Constitution does not explicitly mention any right of privacy. In a line of decisions, however, going back perhaps as far as *Union Pacific R. Co.* v. *Botsford* (1891), the Court has recognized that a right of personal privacy, or a guarantee of certain areas or zones of privacy, does exist under the Constitution. . . . The decisions make it clear that only personal rights that can be deemed "fundamental" or "implicit in the concept of ordered liberty" are included in this guarantee of personal privacy. They also make it clear that the right has some extension to activities relating to marriage, procreation, contraception, family relationships, and child rearing and education.

This right of privacy, whether it be founded in the Fourteenth Amendment's concept of personal liberty and restrictions upon state action, as we feel it is, or, as the District Court determined, in the Ninth Amendment's reservation of rights to the people, is broad enough to encompass a woman's decision whether or not to terminate her pregnancy. The detriment that the State would impose upon the pregnant woman by denying this choice altogether is apparent. Specific and direct harm medically diagnosable even in early pregnancy may be involved. Maternity, or additional off-spring, may force upon the woman a distressful life and future. Psychological harm may be imminent. Mental and physical health may be taxed by child care. There is also the distress, for all concerned, associated with the unwanted child, and there is the problem of bringing a child into a family already unable, psychologically and otherwise, to care for it. In other cases, as in this one, the additional difficulties and continuing stigma of unwed motherhood may be involved. All these are factors the woman and her responsible physician necessarily will consider in consultation.

On the basis of elements such as these, appellant and some *amici* argue that the woman's right is absolute and that she is entitled to terminate her pregnancy at whatever time, in whatever way, and for whatever reason she alone chooses. With this we do not agree. Appellant's arguments that Texas either has no valid interest at all in regulating the abortion decision, or no interest strong enough to support any limitation upon the woman's sole determination, are unpersuasive. The Court's decisions recognizing a right of privacy also acknowledge that some state regulation in areas protected by that right is appropriate. As noted above, a State may properly assert important interests in safeguarding health, in maintaining medical standards, and in protecting potential life. At some point in pregnancy, these respective interests become sufficiently compelling to sustain regulation of the factors that govern the abortion decision. The privacy right involved, therefore, cannot be said to be absolute. In fact, it is not clear to us that the claim asserted by some *amici* that one has an unlimited right to do with one's body as one pleases bears a close relationship to the right of privacy previously articulated in the Court's decisions. The Court has refused to recognize an unlimited right of this kind in the past.

We, therefore, conclude that the right of personal privacy includes the abortion decision, but that this right is not unqualified and must be considered against important state interests in regulation. . . .

IX

The District Court held that the appellee failed to meet his burden of demonstrating that the Texas statute's infringement upon Roe's rights was necessary to support a compelling state interest, and that, although the appellee presented "several compelling justifications for state presence in the area of abortions," the statutes outstripped these justifications and swept "far beyond any areas of compelling state interest." Appellant and appellee both contest that holding. Appellant, as has been indicated, claims an absolute right that bars any state imposition of criminal penalties in the area. Appellee argues that the State's determination to recognize and protect prenatal life from and after conception constitutes a compelling state interest. As noted above, we do not agree fully with either formulation.

A. The appellee and certain *amici* argue that the fetus is a "person" within the language and meaning of the Fourteenth Amendment. In support of this, they outline at length and in detail the well-known facts of fetal development. If this suggestion of personhood is established, the appellant's case, of course, collapses, for the fetus' right to life would then be guaranteed specifically by the Amendment. The appellant conceded as much on reargument. On the other hand, the appellee conceded on reargument that no case could be cited that holds that a fetus is a person within the meaning of the Fourteenth Amendment.

The Constitution does not define "person" in so many words. Section 1 of the Fourteenth Amendment contains three references to "person." The first, in defining "citizens," speaks of "persons born or naturalized in the United States." The word also appears both in the Due Process Clause and in the Equal Protection Clause. "Person" is used in other places in the Constitution. . . . But in nearly all these instances, the use of the word is such that it has application only postnatally. None indicates, with any assurance, that it has any possible prenatal application.

All this, together with our observation that throughout the major portion of the 19th century prevailing legal abortion practices were far freer than they are today, persuades us that the word "person," as used in the Fourteenth Amendment, does not include the unborn. This is in accord with the results reached in those few cases where the issue has been squarely presented. Indeed, our decision in *United States* v. *Vuitch* (1971), inferentially is to the same effect, for we there would not have indulged in statutory interpretation favorable to abortion in specified circumstances if the necessary consequence was the termination of life entitled to Fourteenth Amendment protection.

This conclusion, however, does not of itself fully answer the contentions raised by Texas, and we pass on to other considerations.

B. The pregnant woman cannot be isolated in her privacy. She carries an embryo and, later, a fetus, if one accepts the medical definitions of the developing young in the human uterus. . . . The situation therefore is inherently different from marital intimacy, or bedroom possession of obscene material, or marriage, or procreation, or education, with which *Eisenstadt* and *Griswold, Stanley, Loving, Skinner,* and *Pierce* and *Meyer* were respectively concerned. As we have intimated above, it is reasonable and appropriate for a State to decide that at some point in time another interest, that of health of the mother or that of potential human life, becomes significantly involved. The woman's privacy is no longer sole and any right of privacy she possesses must be measured accordingly.

Texas urges that, apart from the Fourteenth Amendment, life begins at conception and is present throughout pregnancy, and that, therefore, the State has a compelling interest in protecting that life from and after conception. We need not resolve the difficult question of when life begins. When those trained in the respective disciplines of medicine, philosophy, and theology are unable to arrive at any consensus, the judiciary, at this point in the development of man's knowledge, is not in a position to speculate as to the answer.

It should be sufficient to note briefly the wide divergence of thinking on this most sensitive and difficult question. There has always been strong support for the view that life does not begin until live birth. This was the belief of the Stoics. It appears to be the predominant, though not the unanimous, attitude of the Jewish faith. It may be taken to represent also the position of a large segment of the Protestant community, insofar as that can be ascertained; organized groups that have taken a formal position on the abortion issue have generally regarded abortion as a matter for the conscience of the individual and her family. As we have noted, the common law found greater significance in quickening. Physicians and their scientific colleagues have regarded that event with less interest and have tended to focus either upon conception, upon live birth, or upon the interim point at which the fetus becomes "viable," that is, potentially able to live outside the mother's womb, albeit with artificial aid. Viability is usually placed at about seven months (28 weeks) but may occur earlier, even at 24 weeks. The Aristotelian theory of "mediate animation," that held sway throughout the Middle Ages and the Renaissance in Europe, continued to be official Roman Catholic dogma until the 19th century, despite opposition to this "ensoulment" theory from those in the Church who would recognize the existence of life from the moment of conception. The latter is now, of course, the official belief of the Catholic Church. As one brief *amicus* discloses, this is a view strongly held by many non-Catholics as well, and by many physicians. Substantial problems for precise definition of this view are posed, however, by new embryological data that purport to indicate that conception is a "process" over time, rather than an event, and by new medical techniques such as menstrual extraction, the "morning-after" pill, implantation of embryos, artificial insemination, and even artificial wombs.

In areas other than criminal abortion, the law has been reluctant to endorse any theory that life, as we recognize it, begins before live birth or to accord legal rights to the unborn except in narrowly defined situations and except when the rights are contingent upon live birth. For example, the traditional rule of tort law denied recovery for prenatal injuries even though the child was born alive. That rule has been changed in almost every jurisdiction. In most States, recovery is said to be permitted only if the fetus was viable, or at least quick, when the injuries were sustained, though few courts have squarely so held. In a recent development, generally opposed by the commentators, some

States permit the parents of a stillborn child to maintain an action for wrongful death because of prenatal injuries. Such an action, however, would appear to be one to vindicate the parents' interest and is thus consistent with the view that the fetus, at most, represents only the potentiality of life. Similarly, unborn children have been recognized as acquiring rights or interests by way of inheritance or other devolution of property, and have been represented by guardians *ad litem*. Perfection of the interests involved, again, has generally been contingent upon live birth. In short, the unborn have never been recognized in the law as persons in the whole sense.

X

In view of all this, we do not agree that, by adopting one theory of life, Texas may override the rights of the pregnant woman that are at stake. We repeat, however, that the State does have an important and legitimate interest in preserving and protecting the health of the pregnant woman, whether she be a resident of the State or a nonresident who seeks medical consultation and treatment there, and that it has still *another* important and legitimate interest in protecting the potentiality of human life. These interests are separate and distinct. Each grows in substantiality as the woman approaches term and, at a point during pregnancy, each becomes "compelling."

With respect to the State's important and legitimate interest in the health of the mother, the "compelling" point, in the light of present medical knowledge, is at approximately the end of the first trimester. This is so because of the now-established medical fact . . . that until the end of the first trimester mortality in abortion may be less than mortality in normal childbirth. It follows that, from and after this point, a State may regulate the abortion procedure to the extent that the regulation reasonably relates to the preservation and protection of maternal health. Examples of permissible state regulation in this area are requirements as to the qualifications of the person who is to perform the abortion; as to the licensure of that person; as to the facility in which the procedure is to be performed, that is, whether it must be a hospital or may be a clinic or some other place of less-than-hospital status; as to the licensing of the facility; and the like.

This means, on the other hand, that, for the period of pregnancy prior to this "compelling" point, the attending physician, in consultation with his patient, is free to determine, without regulation by the State, that, in his medical judgment, the patient's pregnancy should be terminated. If that decision is reached, the judgment may be effectuated by an abortion free of interference by the State.

With respect to the State's important and legitimate interest in potential life, the "compelling" point is at viability. This is so because the fetus then presumably has the capability of meaningful life outside the mother's womb. State regulation protective of fetal life after viability thus has both logical and biological justifications. If the State is interested in protecting fetal life after viability, it may go so far as to proscribe abortion during that period, except when it is necessary to preserve the life or health of the mother.

Measured against these standards, Art. 1196 of the Texas Penal Code, in restricting legal abortions to those "procured or attempted by medical advice for the purpose of saving the life of the mother," sweeps too broadly. The statute makes no distinction between abortions performed early in pregnancy and those performed later, and it limits to a single reason, "saving" the mother's life, the legal justification for the procedure. The statute, therefore, cannot survive the constitutional attack made upon it here. . . .

XI

To summarize and to repeat:

1. A state criminal abortion statute of the current Texas type, that excepts from criminality only a *life-saving* procedure on behalf of the mother, without regard to pregnancy stage and without recognition of the other interests involved, is violative of the Due Process Clause of the Fourteenth Amendment.

a. For the stage prior to approximately the end of the first trimester, the abortion decision and its effectuation must be left to the medical judgment of the pregnant woman's attending physician.

b. For the stage subsequent to approximately the end of the first trimester, the State, in promoting its interest in the health of the mother, may, if it chooses, regulate the abortion procedure in ways that are reasonably related to maternal health.

c. For the stage subsequent to viability, the State in promoting its interest in the potentiality of human life may, if it chooses, regulate, and even proscribe, abortion except where it is necessary, in appropriate medical judgment, for the preservation of the life or health of the mother.

2. The State may define the term "physician," as it has been employed in the preceding paragraphs of this Part XI of this opinion, to mean only a physician currently licensed by the State, and may proscribe any abortion by a person who is not a physician as so defined. . . .

QUESTIONS FOR REFLECTION

1. What, according to the majority, are the chief interests of the state in making a decision about abortion?
2. The majority bases its decision on the right of privacy. What is this right? How does the majority argue for it? What are its limitations?
3. The majority contends that the "compelling point" for balancing the rights and interests involved is viability. What is viability? Why does the majority settle on it as the compelling point? Do you find the argument convincing?
4. What role does the factual assumption that childbirth is more dangerous than abortion play in the argument? How much more dangerous is it? Are there circumstances in which we expect people to take comparable risks?
5. Suppose technology develops to the point where fetuses can be kept alive outside the mother's body even at early stages of pregnancy. What implications would that have for the morality of abortion? What implications would it have for the Court's reasoning?
6. In a companion case to this one (*Doe* v. *Bolton*), the Court decided that the state must consider psychological as well as physical risks to the mother, permitting even late-term abortions in such cases. Because psychological risk is difficult to assess, the result has been that late-term abortions are largely unrestricted. Some critics have charged that the Court, having decided these cases at the same time, knew that its trimester scheme would have little practical significance. What impact would a frank admission of that have had on the Court's argument?

JUDITH JARVIS THOMSON

A Defense of Abortion

Judith Jarvis Thomson is professor of philosophy at the Massachusetts Institute of Technology. *(Source: From* Philosophy and Public Affairs, *Vol. I, No. 1 [Fall 1971], pp. 47–66.*

Most opposition to abortion relies on the premise that the fetus is a human being, a person, from the moment of conception. The premise is argued for, but, as I think, not well. Take, for example, the most common argument. We are asked to notice that the development of a human being from conception through birth into childhood is continuous; then it is said that to draw a line, to choose a point in this development and say "before this point the thing is not a person, after this point it is a person" is to make an arbitrary choice, a choice for which in the nature of things no good reason can be given. It is concluded that the fetus is, or anyway that we had better say it is, a person from the moment of conception. But this conclusion does not follow. Similar things might be said about the development of an acorn into an oak tree, and it does not follow that acorns are oak trees, or that we had better say they are. Arguments of this form are sometimes called "slippery slope arguments"—the phrase is perhaps self-explanatory—and it is dismaying that opponents of abortion rely on them so heavily and uncritically.

I am inclined to agree, however, that the prospects for "drawing a line" in the development of the fetus look dim. I am inclined to think also that we shall probably have to agree that the fetus has already become a human person well before birth. Indeed, it comes as a surprise when one first learns how early in its life it begins to acquire human characteristics. By the tenth week, for example, it already has a face, arms and legs, fingers and toes; it has internal organs, and brain activity is detectable. On the other hand, I think that the premise is false, that the fetus is not a person from the moment of conception. A newly fertilized ovum, a newly implanted clump of cells, is no more a person than an acorn is an oak tree. But I shall not discuss any of this. For it seems to me to be of great interest to ask what happens if, for the sake of argument, we allow the premise. How, precisely, are we supposed to get from there to the conclusion that abortion is morally impermissible? Opponents of abortion commonly spend most of their time establishing that the fetus is a person, and hardly any time explaining the step from there to the impermissibility of abortion. Perhaps they think the step too simple and obvious to require much comment. Or perhaps instead they are simply being economical in argument. Many of those who defend abortion rely on the premise that the fetus is not a person, but only a bit of tissue that will become a person at birth; and why pay out more arguments than you have to? Whatever the explanation, I suggest that the step they take is neither easy nor obvious, that it calls for closer examination than it is commonly given, and that when we do give it this closer examination we shall feel inclined to reject it.

I propose, then, that we grant that the fetus is a person from the moment of conception. How does the argument go from here? Something like this, I take it. Every person has a right to life. So the fetus has a right to life. No doubt the mother has a right to decide what shall happen in and to her body; everyone would grant that. But surely a person's right to life is stronger and more stringent than the mother's right to decide what happens in and to her body, and so outweighs it. So the fetus may not be killed; an abortion may not be performed.

It sounds plausible. But now let me ask you to imagine this. You wake up in the morning and find yourself back to back in bed with an unconscious violinist. A famous unconscious violinist. He has been found to have a fatal kidney ailment, and the Society of Music Lovers has canvassed all the available medical records and found that you alone have the right blood type to help. They have therefore kidnapped you, and last night the violinist's circulatory system was plugged into yours, so that your kidneys can be used to extract poisons from his blood as well as your own. The director of the hospital now tells you, "Look, we're sorry the Society of Music Lovers did this to you—we would never have permitted it if we had known. But still, they did it, and the violinist now is plugged into you. To unplug you would be to kill him. But never mind, it's only for nine months. By then he will have recovered from his ailment, and can safely be unplugged from you." Is it morally incumbent on you to accede to this situation? No doubt it would be very nice of you if you did, a great kindness. But do you *have* to accede to it? What if it were not nine months, but nine years? Or longer still? What if the director of the hospital says, "Tough luck, I agree, but you've now got to stay in bed, with the violinist plugged into you, for the rest of your life. Because remember this. All persons have a right to life, and violinists are persons. Granted you have a right to decide what happens in and to your body, but a person's right to life outweighs your right to decide what happens in and to your body. So you cannot ever be unplugged from him." I imagine you would regard this as outrageous, which suggests that something really is wrong with that plausible-sounding argument I mentioned a moment ago.

In this case, of course, you were kidnapped; you didn't volunteer for the operation that plugged the violinist into your kidneys. Can those who oppose abortion on the ground I mentioned make an exception for a pregnancy due to rape? Certainly. They can say that persons have a right to life only if they didn't come into existence because of rape; or they can say that all persons have a right to life, but that some have less of a right to life than others, in particular, that those who came into existence because of rape have less. But these statements have a rather unpleasant sound. Surely the question of whether you have a right to life at all, or how much of it you have, shouldn't turn on the question of whether or not you are the product of a rape. And in fact the people who oppose abortion on the ground I mentioned do not make this distinction, and hence do not make an exception in case of rape.

Nor do they make an exception for a case in which the mother has to spend the nine months of her pregnancy in bed. They would agree that would be a great pity, and hard on the mother; but all the same, all persons have a right to life, the fetus is a person, and so on. I suspect, in fact, that they would not make an exception for a case in which, miraculously enough, the pregnancy went on for nine years, or even the rest of the mother's life.

Some won't even make an exception for a case in which continuation of the pregnancy is likely to shorten the mother's life; they regard abortion as impermissible even to save the mother's life. Such cases are nowadays very rare, and many opponents of abortion do not accept this extreme view. All the same, it is a good place to begin: a number of points of interest come out in respect to it.

1. Let us call the view that abortion is impermissible even to save the mother's life "the extreme view." I want to suggest first that it does not issue from the argument I mentioned earlier without the addition of some fairly powerful premises. Suppose a woman has become pregnant, and now learns that she has a cardiac condition such that she will die if she carries the baby to term. What may be done for her? The fetus, being a person, has a right to life, but as the mother is a person too, so has she a right to life. Presumably they have an equal right to life. How is it supposed to come out that an abortion may not be performed? If mother and child have an equal right to life, shouldn't we perhaps flip a coin? Or should we add to the mother's right to life her right to decide what happens in and to her body, which everybody seems to be ready to grant—the sum of her rights now outweighing the fetus' right to life?

The most familiar argument here is the following. We are told that performing the abortion would be directly killing the child, whereas doing nothing would not be killing the mother, but only letting her die. Moreover, in killing the child, one would be killing an innocent person, for the child has committed no crime, and is not aiming at his mother's death. And then there are a variety of ways in which this might be continued. (1) But as directly killing an innocent person is always and absolutely impermissible, an abortion may not be performed. Or, (2) as directly killing an innocent person is murder, and murder is always and absolutely impermissible, an abortion may not be performed. Or, (3) as one's duty to refrain from directly killing an innocent person is more stringent than one's duty to keep a person from dying, an abortion may not be performed. Or, (4) if one's only options are directly killing an innocent person or letting a person die, one must prefer letting the person die, and thus an abortion may not be performed.

Some people seem to have thought that these are not further premises which must be added if the conclusion is to be reached, but that they follow from the very fact that an innocent person has a right to life. But this seems to me to be a mistake, and perhaps the simplest way to show this is to bring out that while we must certainly grant that innocent persons have a right to life, the theses in (1) through (4) are all false. Take (2), for example. If directly killing an innocent person is murder, and thus is impermissible, then the mother's directly killing the innocent person inside her is murder, and thus is impermissible. But it cannot seriously be thought to be murder if the mother performs an abortion on herself to save her life. It cannot seriously be said that she *must* refrain, that she *must* sit passively by and wait for her death. Let us look again at the case of you and the violinist. There you are, in bed with the violinist, and the director of the hospital says to you, "It's all most distressing, and I deeply sympathize, but you see this is putting an additional strain on your kidneys, and you'll be dead within the month. But you *have* to stay where you are all the same. Because unplugging you would be directly killing an innocent violinist, and that's murder, and that's impermissible." If anything in the world is true, it is that you do not commit murder, you do not do what is impermissible, if you reach around to your back and unplug yourself from that violinist to save your life.

The main focus of attention in writings on abortion has been on what a third party may or may not do in answer to a request from a woman for an abortion. This is in a way understandable. Things being as they are, there isn't much a woman can safely do to abort herself. So the question asked is what a third party may do, and what the mother may do, if it is mentioned at all, is deduced, almost as an afterthought, from what it is concluded that third parties may do. But it seems to me that to treat the matter in this way is to refuse to grant to the mother that very status of person which is so firmly insisted on for the fetus. For we cannot simply read off what a person may do from what a third party may do. Suppose you find yourself trapped in a tiny house with a growing child. I mean a very tiny house, and a rapidly growing child—you are already up against the wall of the house and in a few minutes you'll be crushed to death. The child on the other hand won't be crushed to death; if nothing is done to stop him from growing he'll be hurt, but in the end he'll simply burst open the house and walk out a free man. Now I could well understand it if a bystander were to say, "There's nothing we can do for you. We cannot choose between your life and his, we cannot be the ones to decide who is to live, we cannot intervene." But it cannot be concluded that you too can do nothing, that you cannot attack it to save your life. However innocent the child may be, you do not have to wait passively while it crushes you to death. Perhaps a pregnant woman is vaguely felt to have the status of house, to which we don't allow the right of self-defense. But if the woman houses the child, it should be remembered that she is a person who houses it.

I should perhaps stop to say explicitly that I am not claiming that people have a right to do anything whatever to save their lives. I think, rather, that there are drastic limits to the right of self-defense. If someone threatens you with death unless you torture someone else to death, I think you have not the right, even to save your life, to do so. But the case under consideration here is very different. In our case there are only two people involved, one whose life is threatened, and one who threatens it. Both are innocent: the one who is threatened is not threatened because of any fault, the one who threatens does not threaten because of any fault. For this reason we may feel that we bystanders cannot intervene. But the person threatened can.

In sum, a woman surely can defend her life against the threat to it posed by the unborn child, even if doing so involves its death. And this shows not merely that the theses in (1) through (4) are false; it shows also that the extreme view of abortion is false, and so we need not canvass any other possible ways of arriving at it from the argument I mentioned at the outset.

2. The extreme view could of course be weakened to say that while abortion is permissible to save the mother's life, it may not be performed by the third party, but only by the mother herself. But this cannot be right either. For what we have to keep in mind is that the mother and the unborn child are not like two tenants in a small house which has, by an unfortunate mistake, been rented to both: the mother *owns* the house. The fact that she does adds to the offensiveness of deducing that the mother can do nothing from the supposition that third parties can do nothing. But it does more than this: it casts a bright light on the supposition that third parties can do nothing. Certainly it lets us see that a third party who says "I cannot choose between you" is fooling himself if he thinks this is impartiality. If Jones has found and fastened on a certain coat, which he needs to keep him from freezing, but which Smith also needs to keep him from freezing, then it is not impartiality that says "I cannot choose between you" when Smith owns the coat. Women have said again and again "This body is *my* body!" and they have reason to feel angry, reason to feel that it has been like shouting into the wind. Smith, after all, is hardly likely to bless us if we say to him, "Of course it's your coat, anybody would grant that it is. But no one may choose between you and Jones who is to have it."

We should really ask what it is that says "no one may choose" in the face of the fact that the body that houses the child is the mother's body. It may be simply a failure to appreciate this fact. But it may be something more interesting, namely the sense that one has a right to refuse to lay hands on people, even where it would be just and fair to do so, even where justice seems to require that somebody do so. Thus justice might call for somebody to get Smith's coat back from Jones, and yet you have a right to refuse to be the one to lay hands on Jones, a right to refuse to do physical violence to him. This, I think, must be granted. But then what should be said is not "no one may choose," but only "*I* cannot choose," and indeed not even this, but "*I* will not *act,*" leaving it open that somebody else can or should, and in particular that anyone in a position of authority, with the job of securing people's rights, both can and should. So this is no difficulty. I have not been arguing that any given third party must accede to the mother's request that he perform an abortion to save her life, but only that he may.

I suppose that in some views of human life the mother's body is only on loan to her, the loan not being one which gives her any prior claim to it. One who held this view might well think it impartiality to say "I cannot choose." But I shall simply ignore this possibility. My own view is that if a human being has any just, prior claim to anything at all, he has a just, prior claim to his own body. And perhaps this needn't be argued for here anyway, since, as I mentioned, the arguments against abortion we are looking at do grant that the woman has a right to decide what happens in and to her body.

But although they do grant it, I have tried to show that they do not take seriously what is done in granting it. I suggest the same thing will reappear even more clearly when we turn away from cases in which the mother's life is at stake, and attend, as I propose we now do, to the vastly more common cases in which a woman wants an abortion for some less weighty reason than preserving her own life.

3. Where the mother's life is not at stake, the argument I mentioned at the outset seems to have a much stronger pull. "Everyone has a right to life, so the unborn person has a right to life." And isn't the child's right to life weightier than anything other than the mother's own right to life, which she might put forward as ground for an abortion?

This argument treats the right to life as if it were unproblematic. It is not, and this seems to me to be precisely the source of the mistake.

For we should now, at long last, ask what it comes to, to have a right to life. In some views having a right to life includes having a right to be given at least the bare minimum one needs for continued life. But suppose that what in fact *is* the bare minimum a man needs for continued life is something he has no right at all to be given? If I am sick unto death, and the only thing that will save my life is the touch of Henry Fonda's cool hand on my fevered brow, then all the same, I have no right to be given the touch of Henry Fonda's cool hand on my fevered brow. It would be frightfully nice of him to fly in from the West Coast to provide it. It would be less nice, though no doubt well meant, if my friends flew out to the West Coast and carried Henry Fonda back with them. But I have no right at all against anybody that he should do this for me. Or again, to return to the story I told earlier, the fact that for continued life that violinist needs the continued use of your kidneys does not establish that he has a right to be given the continued use of your kidneys. He certainly has no right against you that *you* should give him continued use of your kidneys. For nobody has any right to use your kidneys unless you give him such a right; and nobody has the right against you that you shall give him this right—if you do allow him to go on using your kidneys, this is kindness on your part, and not something he can claim from you as his due. Nor has he any right against anybody else that *they* should give him continued use of your kidneys. Certainly he had no right against the Society of Music Lovers that they should plug him into you in the first place. And if you now start to unplug yourself, having learned that you will otherwise have to spend nine years in bed with him, there is nobody in the world who must try to prevent you, in order to see to it that he is given something he has a right to be given.

Some people are rather stricter about the right to life. In their view, it does not include the right to be given anything, but amounts to, and only to, the right not to be killed by anybody. But here a related difficulty arises. If everybody is to refrain from killing that violinist, then everybody must refrain from doing a great many different sorts of things. Everybody must refrain from slitting his throat, everybody must refrain from shooting him—and everybody must refrain from unplugging you from him. But does he have a right against everybody that they shall refrain from unplugging you from him? To refrain from doing this is to allow him to continue to use your kidneys. It could be argued that he has a right against us that *we* should allow him to continue to use your kidneys. That is, while he had no right against us that we should give him the use of your kidneys, it might be argued that he anyway has a right against us that we shall not now intervene and deprive him of the use of your kidneys. I shall come back to third-party interventions later. But certainly the violinist has no right against you that *you* shall allow him to continue to use your kidneys. As I said, if you do allow him to use them, it is a kindness on your part, and not something you owe him.

The difficulty I point to here is not peculiar to the right to life. It reappears in connection with all the other natural rights; and it is something which an adequate account of rights must deal with. For present purposes it is enough just to draw attention to it. But I would stress that I am not arguing that people do not have a right to life—quite to the contrary, it seems to me that the primary control we must place on the acceptability of an account of rights is that it should turn out in that account to be a truth that all persons have a right to life. I am arguing only that having a right to life does not guarantee having either a right to be given the use of or a right to be allowed continued use of another person's body—even if one needs it for life itself. So the right to life will not serve the opponents of abortion in the very simple and clear way in which they seem to have thought it would.

4. There is another way to bring out the difficulty. In the most ordinary sort of case, to deprive someone of what he has a right to is to treat him unjustly. Suppose a boy and his small brother are jointly given a box of chocolates for Christmas. If the older boy takes the box and refuses to give his brother any of the chocolates, he is unjust to him, for the brother has been given a right to half of them. But suppose that, having learned that otherwise it means nine years in bed with that violinist, you unplug yourself from him. You surely are not being unjust to him, for you gave him no right to use your kidneys, and no one else can have given him any such right. But we have to notice that in unplugging yourself, you are killing him; and violinists, like everybody else, have a right to life, and thus in the view we were considering just now, the right not to be killed. So here you do what he supposedly has a right you shall not do, but you do not act unjustly to him in doing it.

The emendation which may be made at this point is this: the right to life consists not in the right not to be killed, but rather in the right not to be killed unjustly. This runs a risk of circularity, but never mind: it would enable us to square the fact that the violinist has a right to life with the fact that you do not act unjustly toward him in unplugging yourself, thereby killing him. For if you do not kill him unjustly, you do not violate his right to life, and so it is no wonder you do him no injustice.

But if this emendation is accepted, the gap in the argument against abortion stares us plainly in the face: it is by no means enough to show that the fetus is a person, and to remind us that all persons have a right to life—we need to be shown also that killing the fetus violates its right to life, i.e., that abortion is unjust killing. And is it?

I suppose we may take it as a datum that in a case of pregnancy due to rape the mother has not given the unborn person a right to the use of her body for food and shelter. Indeed, in what pregnancy could it be supposed that the mother has given the unborn person such a right? It is not as if there were unborn persons drifting about the world, to whom a woman who wants a child says "I invite you in."

But it might be argued that there are other ways one can have acquired a right to the use of another person's body than by having been invited to use it by that person. Suppose a woman voluntarily indulges in intercourse, knowing of the chance it will issue in pregnancy, and then she does become pregnant; is she not in part responsible for the presence, in fact the very existence, of the unborn person inside her? No doubt she did not invite it in. But doesn't her partial responsibility for its being there itself give it a right to the use of her body? If so, then her aborting it would be more like the boy's taking away the chocolates, and less like your unplugging yourself from the violinist—doing so would be depriving it of what it does have a right to, and thus would be doing it an injustice.

And then, too, it might be asked whether or not she can kill it even to save her own life: If she voluntarily called it into existence, how can she now kill it, even in self-defense?

The first thing to be said about this is that it is something new. Opponents of abortion have been so concerned to make out the independence of the fetus, in order to establish that it has a right to life, just as its mother does, that they have tended to overlook the possible support they might gain from making out that the fetus is *dependent* on the mother, in order to establish that she has a special kind of responsibility for it, a responsibility that gives it rights against her which are not possessed by any independent person—such as an ailing violinist who is a stranger to her.

On the other hand, this argument would give the unborn person a right to its mother's body only if her pregnancy resulted from a voluntary act, undertaken in full knowledge of the chance a pregnancy might result from it. It would leave out entirely the unborn person whose existence is due to rape. Pending the availability of some further argument, then, we would be left with the conclusion that unborn persons whose existence is due to rape have no right to the use of their mothers' bodies, and thus that aborting them is not depriving them of anything they have a right to and hence is not unjust killing.

And we should also notice that it is not at all plain that this argument really does go even as far as it purports to. For there are cases and cases, and the details make a difference. If the room is stuffy, and I therefore open a window to air it, and a burglar climbs in, it would be absurd to say, "Ah, now he can stay, she's given him a right to the use of her house—for she is partially responsible for his presence there, having voluntarily done what enabled him to get in, in full knowledge that there are such things as burglars, and that burglars burgle." It would be still more absurd to say this if I had had bars installed outside my windows, precisely to prevent burglars from getting in, and a burglar got in only because of a defect in the bars. It remains equally absurd if we imagine it is not a burglar who climbs in, but an innocent person who blunders or falls in. Again, suppose it were like this: people-seeds drift about in the air like pollen, and if you open your windows, one may drift in and take root in your carpets or upholstery. You don't want children, so you fix up your windows with fine mesh screens, the very best you can buy. As can happen, however, and on very, very rare occasions does happen, one of the screens is defective; and a seed drifts in and takes root. Does the person-plant who now develops have a right to the use of your house? Surely not—despite the fact that you voluntarily opened your windows, you knowingly kept carpets and upholstered furniture, and you knew that screens were sometimes defective. Someone may argue that you are responsible for its rooting, that it does have a right to your house, because after all you *could* have lived out your life with bare floors and furniture, or with sealed windows and doors. But this won't do—for by the same token anyone can avoid a pregnancy due to rape by having a hysterectomy, or anyway by never leaving home without a (reliable!) army.

It seems to me that the argument we are looking at can establish at most that there are *some* cases in which the unborn person has a right to the use of its mother's body, and therefore *some* cases in which abortion is unjust killing. There is room for much discussion and argument as to precisely which, if any. But I think we should sidestep this issue and leave it open, for at any rate the argument certainly does not establish that all abortion is unjust killing.

5. There is room for yet another argument here, however. We surely must all grant that there may be cases in which it would be morally indecent to detach a person from your body at the cost of his life. Suppose you learn that what the violinist needs is not nine years of your life, but only one hour: all you need do to save his life is to spend one hour in that bed with him. Suppose also that letting him use your kidneys for that one hour would not affect your health in the slightest. Admittedly you were kidnapped. Admittedly you did not give anyone permission to plug him into you. Nevertheless it seems to me plain you *ought* to allow him to use your kidneys for that hour—it would be indecent to refuse.

Again, suppose pregnancy lasted only an hour, and constituted no threat to life or health. And suppose that a woman becomes pregnant as a result of rape. Admittedly she did not voluntarily do anything to bring about the existence of a child. Admittedly she did nothing at all which would give the unborn person a right to the use of her body. All the same it might well be said, as in the newly emended violinist story, that she *ought* to allow it to remain for that hour—that it would be indecent in her to refuse.

Now some people are inclined to use the term "right" in such a way that it follows from the fact that you ought to allow a person to use your body for the hour he needs, that he has a right to use your body for the hour he needs, even though he has not been given that right by any person or act. They may say that it follows also that if you refuse, you act unjustly toward him. This use of the term is perhaps so common that it cannot be called wrong; nevertheless it seems to me to be an unfortunate loosening of what we would do better to keep a tight rein on. Suppose that box of chocolates I mentioned earlier had not been given to both boys jointly, but was given only to the older boy. There he sits, stolidly eating his way through the box, his small brother watching enviously. Here we are likely to say "You ought not to be so mean. You ought to give your brother some of those chocolates." My own view is that it just does not follow from the truth of this that the brother has any right to any of the chocolates. If the boy refuses to give his brother any, he is greedy, stingy, callous—but not unjust. I suppose that the people I have in mind will say it does follow that the brother has a right to some of the chocolates, and thus that the boy does act unjustly if he refuses to give his brother any. But the effect of saying this is to obscure what we should keep distinct, namely the difference between the boy's refusal in this case and the boy's refusal in the earlier case, in which the box was given to both boys jointly, and in which the small brother thus had what was from any point of view clear title to half.

A further objection to so using the term "right" that from the fact that A ought to do a thing for B, it follows that B has a right against A that A do it for him, is that it is going to make the question of whether or not a man has a right to a thing turn on how easy it is to provide him with it; and this seems not merely unfortunate, but morally unacceptable. Take the case of Henry Fonda again. I said earlier that I had no right to the touch of his cool hand on my fevered brow, even though I needed it to save my life. I said it would be frightfully nice of him to fly in from the West Coast to provide me with it, but that I had no right against him that he should do so. But suppose he isn't on the West Coast. Suppose he has only to walk across the room, place a hand briefly on my brow—and lo, my life is saved. Then surely he ought to do it, it would be indecent to refuse. Is it to be said "Ah, well, it follows that in this case she has a right to the touch of his hand on her brow, and so it would be an injustice in him to refuse"? So that I have a right to it when it is easy for him to provide it, though no right when it's hard? It's rather a shocking idea that anyone's rights should fade away and disappear as it gets harder and harder to accord them to him.

So my own view is that even though you ought to let the violinist use your kidneys for the one hour he needs, we should not conclude that he has a right to do so—we would say that if you refuse, you are, like the boy who owns all the chocolates and will give none away, self-centered and callous, indecent in fact, but not unjust. And similarly, that even supposing a case in which a woman pregnant due to rape ought to allow the unborn person to use her body for the hour he needs, we should not conclude that he has a right to do so; we should conclude that she is self-centered, callous, indecent, but not unjust, if she refuses. The complaints are no less grave; they are just different. However, there is no need to insist on this point. If anyone does wish to deduce "he has a right" from "you ought," then all the same he must surely grant that there are cases in which it is not morally required of you that you allow that violinist to use your kidneys, and in which he does not have a right to use them, and in which you do not do him an injustice if you refuse. And so also for mother and unborn child. Except in such cases as the unborn person has a right to demand it—and we were leaving open the possibility that there may be such cases—nobody is morally *required* to make large sacrifices, of health, of all other interests and concerns, of all other duties and commitments, for nine years, or even for nine months, in order to keep another person alive.

6. We have in fact to distinguish between two kinds of Samaritan: the Good Samaritan and what we might call the Minimally Decent Samaritan. The story of the Good Samaritan, you will remember, goes like this:

> A certain man went down from Jerusalem to Jericho, and fell among thieves, which stripped him of his raiment, and wounded him, and departed, leaving him half dead.
>
> And by chance there came down a certain priest that way; and when he saw him, he passed by on the other side.
>
> And likewise a Levite, when he was at the place, came and looked on him, and passed by on the other side.
>
> But a certain Samaritan, as he journeyed, came where he was; and when he saw him he had compassion on him.
>
> And went to him, and bound up his wounds, pouring in oil and wine, and set him on his own beast, and brought him to an inn, and took care of him.
>
> And on the morrow, when he departed, he took out two pence, and gave them to the host, and said unto him, "Take care of him; and whatsoever thou spendest more, when I come again, I will repay thee."
>
> (Luke 10:30–35)

The Good Samaritan went out of his way, at some cost to himself, to help one in need of it. We are not told what the options were, that is, whether or not the priest and the Levite could have helped by doing less than the Good Samaritan did, but assuming they could have, then the fact they did nothing at all shows they were not even Minimally Decent Samaritans, not because they were not Samaritans, but because they were not even minimally decent.

These things are a matter of degree, of course, but there is a difference, and it comes out perhaps most clearly in the story of Kitty Genovese, who, as you will remember, was murdered while thirty-eight people watched or listened, and did nothing at all to help her. A Good Samaritan would have rushed out to give direct assistance against the murderer. Or perhaps we had better allow that it would have been a Splendid Samaritan who did this, on the ground that it would have involved a risk of death for himself. But the thirty-eight not only did not do this, they did not even trouble to pick up a phone to call the police. Minimally Decent Samaritanism would call for doing at least that, and their not having done it was monstrous.

After telling the story of the Good Samaritan, Jesus said "Go, and do thou likewise." Perhaps he meant that we are morally required to act as the Good Samaritan did. Perhaps he was urging people to do more than is morally required of them. At all events it seems plain that it was not morally required of any of the thirty-eight that he rush out to give direct assistance at the risk of his own life, and that it is not morally required of anyone that he give long stretches of his life—nine years or nine months—to sustaining the life of a person who has no special right (we were leaving open the possibility of this) to demand it.

Indeed, with one rather striking class of exceptions, no one in any country in the world is *legally* required to do anywhere near as much as this for anyone else. The class of exceptions is obvious. My main concern here is not the state of the law in respect to abortion, but it is worth drawing attention to the fact that in no state in this country is any man compelled by law to be even a Minimally Decent Samaritan to any person; there is no law under which charges could be brought against the thirty-eight who stood by while Kitty Genovese died. By contrast, in most states in this country women are compelled by law to be not merely Minimally Decent Samaritans, but Good Samaritans to unborn persons inside them. This doesn't by itself settle anything one way or the other, because it may well be argued that there should be laws in this country—as there are in many European countries—compelling at least Minimally Decent Samaritanism. But it does show that there is a gross injustice in the existing state of the law. And it shows also that the groups currently working against liberalization of abortion laws, in fact working toward having it declared unconstitutional for a state to permit abortion, had better start working for the adoption of Good Samaritan laws generally, or earn the charge that they are acting in bad faith.

I should think, myself, that Minimally Decent Samaritan laws would be one thing, Good Samaritan laws quite another, and in fact highly improper. But we are not here concerned with the law. What we should ask is not whether anybody should be compelled by law to be a Good Samaritan, but whether we must accede to a situation in which somebody is being compelled—by nature, perhaps—to be a Good Samaritan. We have, in other words, to look now at third-party interventions. I have been arguing that no person is morally required to make large sacrifices to sustain the life of another who has no right to demand them, and this even where the sacrifices do not include life itself; we are not morally required to be Good Samaritans or anyway Very Good Samaritans to one another. But what if a man cannot extricate himself from such a situation? What if he appeals to us to extricate him? It seems to me plain that there are cases in which we can, cases in which a Good Samaritan would extricate him. There you are, you were kidnapped, and nine years in bed with that violinist lie ahead of you. You have your own life to lead. You are sorry, but you simply cannot see giving up so much of your life to the sustaining of his. You cannot extricate yourself, and ask us to do so. I should have thought that—in light of his having no right to the use of your body—it was obvious that we do not have to accede to your being forced to give up so much. We can do what you ask. There is no injustice to the violinist in our doing so.

7. Following the lead of the opponents of abortion, I have throughout been speaking of the fetus merely as a person, and what I have been asking is whether or not the argument we began with, which proceeds only from the fetus' being a person, really does establish its conclusion. I have argued that it does not.

But of course there are arguments and arguments, and it may be said that I have simply fastened on the wrong one. It may be said that what is important is not merely the fact that the fetus is a person, but that it is a person for whom the woman has a special kind of responsibility issuing from the fact that she is its mother. And it might be argued that all my analogies are therefore irrelevant—for you do not have that special kind of responsibility for that violinist, Henry Fonda does not have that special kind of responsibility for me. And our attention might be drawn to the fact that men and women both *are* compelled by law to provide support for their children.

I have in effect dealt (briefly) with this argument in section 4 above; but a (still briefer) recapitulation now may be in order. Surely we do not have any such "special responsibility" for a person unless we have assumed it, explicitly or implicitly. If a set of parents do not try to prevent pregnancy, do not obtain an abortion, and then at the time of birth of the child do not put it out for adoption, but rather take it home with them, then they have assumed responsibility for it, they have given it rights, and they cannot *now* withdraw support from it at the cost of its life because they now find it difficult to go on providing for it. But if they have taken all reasonable precautions against having a child, they do not simply by virtue of their biological relationship to the child who comes into existence have a special responsibility for it. They may wish to assume responsibility for it, or they may not wish to. And I am suggesting that if assuming responsibility for it would require large sacrifices, then they may refuse. A Good Samaritan would not refuse—or anyway, a Splendid Samaritan, if the sacrifices that had to be made were enormous. But then so would a Good Samaritan assume responsibility for that violinist; so would Henry Fonda, if he is a Good Samaritan, fly in from the West Coast and assume responsibility for me.

8. My argument will be found unsatisfactory on two counts by many of those who want to regard abortion as morally permissible. First, while I do argue that abortion is not impermissible, I do not argue that it is always permissible. There may well be cases in which carrying the child to term requires only Minimally Decent Samaritanism of the mother, and this is a standard we must not fall below. I am inclined to think it a merit of my account precisely that it does *not* give a general yes or a general no. It allows for and supports our sense that, for example, a sick and desperately frightened fourteen-year-old schoolgirl, pregnant due to rape, may *of course* choose abortion, and that any law which rules this out is an insane law. And it also allows for and supports our sense that in other cases resort to abortion is even positively indecent. It would be indecent in the woman to request an abortion, and indecent in a doctor to perform it, if she is in her seventh month, and wants the abortion just to avoid the nuisance of postponing a trip abroad. The very fact that the arguments I have been drawing attention to treat all cases of abortion, or even all cases of abortion in which the mother's life is not at stake, as morally on a par ought to have made them suspect at the outset.

Secondly, while I am arguing for the permissibility of abortion in some cases, I am not arguing for the right to secure the death of the unborn child. It is easy to confuse these two things in that up to a certain point in the life of the fetus it is not able to survive outside the mother's body; hence removing it from her body guarantees its death. But they are importantly different. I have argued that you are not morally required to spend nine months in bed, sustaining the life of that violinist; but to say this is by no means to say that if, when you unplug yourself, there is a miracle and he survives, you then have a right to turn round and slit his throat. You may detach yourself even if this costs him his life; you have no right to be guaranteed his death, by some other means, if unplugging yourself does not kill him. There are some people who will feel dissatisfied by this feature of my argument. A woman may be utterly devastated by the thought of a child, a bit of herself, put out for adoption and never seen or heard of again. She may therefore want not merely that the child be detached from her, but more, that it die. Some opponents of abortion are inclined to regard this as beneath contempt—thereby showing insensitivity to what is surely a powerful source of despair. All the same, I agree that the desire for the child's death is not one which anybody may gratify, should it turn out to be possible to detach the child alive.

At this place, however, it should be remembered that we have only been pretending throughout that the fetus is a human being from the moment of conception. A very early abortion is surely not the killing of a person, and so is not dealt with by anything I have said here.

QUESTIONS FOR REFLECTION

1. What conclusions does Thomson draw from the violinist example? Do you agree with her interpretation of the example?
2. Do your feelings about the violinist case change if you add that the violinist is your own child?
3. How does Thomson argue against what she calls "the extreme view"?
4. What is a right to life, for Thomson? Why does she reject other accounts of this right?
5. What is Good Samaritanism? Minimally Decent Samaritanism? Which, according to Thomson, is required of us? What does this imply for the morality of abortion?
6. Some philosophers have found Thomson's view on the violinist example inconsistent with her view that you do not have the right to torture someone, even to save your own life. Are these consistent? Explain.

MARY ANNE WARREN

On the Moral and Legal Status of Abortion

Mary Anne Warren teaches at San Francisco State University. (Source: From "On the Moral and Legal Status of Abortion," The Monist, *vol. 57, no. 1 [January 1973], pp. 43–51. Notes have been omitted. Reprinted with permission from* The Monist *and Dr. Mary Anne Warren, San Francisco State University.)*

We will be concerned with both the moral status of abortion, which for our purposes we may define as the act which a woman performs in voluntarily terminating, or allowing another person to terminate, her pregnancy, and the legal status which is appropriate for this act. I will argue that, while it is not possible to produce a satisfactory defense of a woman's right to obtain an abortion without showing that a fetus is not a human being, in the morally relevant sense of that term, we ought not to conclude that the difficulties involved in determining whether or not a fetus is human make it impossible to produce any satisfactory solution to the problem of the moral status of abortion. For it is possible to show that, on the basis of intuitions which we may expect even the opponents of abortion to share, a fetus is not a person, and hence not the sort of entity to which it is proper to ascribe full moral rights.

Of course, while some philosophers would deny the possibility of any such proof, others will deny that there is any need for it, since the moral permissibility of abortion appears to them to be too obvious to require proof. But the inadequacy of this attitude should be evident from the fact that both the friends and the foes of abortion consider their position to be morally self-evident. Because proabortionists have never adequately come to grips with the conceptual issues surrounding abortion, most if not all, of the arguments which they advance in opposition to laws restricting access to abortion fail to refute or even weaken the traditional antiabortion argument, i.e., that a fetus is a human being, and therefore abortion is murder.

These arguments are typically one of two sorts. Either they point to the terrible side effects of the restrictive laws, e.g., the deaths due to illegal abortions, and the fact that it is poor women who suffer the most as a result of these laws, or else they state that to deny a woman access to abortion is to deprive her of her right to control her own body. Unfortunately, however, the fact that restricting access to abortion has tragic side effects does not, in itself, show that the restrictions are unjustified, since murder is wrong regardless of the consequences of prohibiting it; and the appeal to the right to control one's body, which is generally construed as a property right, is at best a rather feeble argument for the permissibility of abortion. Mere ownership does not give me the right to kill innocent people whom I find on my property, and indeed I am apt to be held responsible if such people injure themselves while on my property. It is equally unclear that I have any moral right to expel an innocent person from my property when I know that doing so will result in his death.

Furthermore, it is probably inappropriate to describe a woman's body as her property, since it seems natural to hold that a person is something distinct from her property, but not from her body.

Even those who would object to the identification of a person with his body, or with the conjunction of his body and his mind, must admit that it would be very odd to describe, say, breaking a leg, as damaging one's property, and much more appropriate to describe it as injuring oneself. Thus it is probably a mistake to argue that the right to obtain an abortion is in any way derived from the right to own and regulate property.

But however we wish to construe the right to abortion, we cannot hope to convince those who consider abortion a form of murder of the existence of any such right unless we are able to produce a clear and convincing refutation of the traditional antiabortion argument, and this has not, to my knowledge, been done. With respect to the two most vital issues which that argument involves, i.e., the humanity of the fetus and its implication for the moral status of abortion, confusion has prevailed on both sides of the dispute.

Thus, both proabortionists and antiabortionists have tended to abstract the question of whether abortion is wrong to that of whether it is wrong to destroy a fetus, just as though the rights of another person were not necessarily involved. This mistaken abstraction has led to the almost universal assumption that if a fetus is a human being, with a right to life, then it follows immediately that abortion is wrong (except perhaps when necessary to save the woman's life), and that it ought to be prohibited. It has also been generally assumed that unless the question about the status of the fetus is answered, the moral status of abortion cannot possibly be determined.

Two recent papers, one by B. A. Brody, and one by Judith Thomson, have attempted to settle the question of whether abortion ought to be prohibited apart from the question of whether or not the fetus is human. Brody examines the possibility that the following two statements are compatible: (1) that abortion is the taking of innocent human life, and therefore wrong; and (2) that nevertheless it ought not to be prohibited by law, at least under the present circumstances. Not surprisingly, Brody finds it impossible to reconcile these two statements, since, as he rightly argues, none of the unfortunate side effects of the prohibition of abortion is bad enough to justify legalizing the *wrongful* taking of human life. He is mistaken, however, in concluding that the incompatibility of (1) and (2), in itself, shows that "the legal problem about abortion cannot be resolved independently of the status of the fetus problem. . . ."

What Brody fails to realize is that (1) embodies the questionable assumption that if a fetus is a human being, then of course abortion is morally wrong, and that an attack on *this* assumption is more promising, as a way of reconciling the humanity of the fetus with the claim that laws prohibiting abortion are unjustified, than is an attack on the assumption that if abortion is the wrongful killing of innocent human beings then it ought to be prohibited. He thus overlooks the possibility that a fetus may have a right to life and abortion still be morally permissible, in that the right of a woman to terminate an unwanted pregnancy might override the right of the fetus to be kept alive. The immorality of abortion is no more demonstrated by the humanity of the fetus, in itself, than the immorality of killing in self-defense is demonstrated by the fact that the assailant is a human being. Neither is it demonstrated by the *innocence* of the fetus, since there may be situations in which the killing of innocent human beings is justified.

It is perhaps not surprising that Brody fails to spot this assumption, since it has been accepted with little or no argument by nearly everyone who has written on the morality of abortion. John Noonan is correct in saying that "the fundamental question in the long history of abortion is, How do you determine the humanity of a being?" He summarizes his own antiabortion argument, which is a version of the official position of the Catholic Church, as follows:

> . . . it is wrong to kill humans, however poor, weak, defenseless, and lacking in opportunity to develop their potential they may be. It is therefore morally wrong to kill Biafrans. Similarly, it is morally wrong to kill embryos.

Noonan bases his claim that fetuses are human upon what he calls the theologians' criterion of humanity: that whoever is conceived of human beings is human. But although he argues at length for the appropriateness of this criterion, he never questions the assumption that if a fetus is human then abortion is wrong for exactly the same reason that murder is wrong.

Judith Thomson is, in fact, the only writer I am aware of who has seriously questioned this assumption; she has argued that, even if we grant the antiabortionist his claim that a fetus is a human being, with the same right to life as any other human being, we can still demonstrate that, in at least some and perhaps most cases, a woman is under no moral obligation to complete an unwanted pregnancy. Her argument is worth examining, since if it holds up it may enable us to establish the moral permissibility of abortion without becoming involved in problems about what entitles an entity to be considered human, and accorded full moral rights. To be able to do this would be a great gain in the power and simplicity of the proabortion position, since, although I will argue that these problems can be solved at least as decisively as can any other moral problem, we should certainly be pleased to be able to avoid having to solve them as part of the justification of abortion.

On the other hand, even if Thomson's argument does not hold up, her insight, i.e., that it requires *argument* to show that if fetuses are human then abortion is properly classified as murder, is an extremely valuable one. The assumption she attacks is particularly invidious, for it amounts to the decision that it is appropriate, in deciding the moral status of abortion, to leave the rights of the pregnant woman out of consideration entirely, except possibly when her life is threatened. Obviously, this will not do; determining what moral rights, if any, a fetus possesses is only the first step in determining the moral status of abortion. Step two, which is at least equally essential, is finding a just solution to the conflict between whatever rights the fetus may have, and the rights of the woman who is unwillingly pregnant. While the historical error has been to pay far too little attention to the second step, Ms. Thomson's suggestion is that if we look at the second step first we may find that a woman has a right to obtain an abortion *regardless* of what rights the fetus has.

Our own inquiry will also have two stages. In Section I, we will consider whether or not it is possible to establish that abortion is morally permissible even on the assumption that a fetus is an entity with a full-fledged right to life. I will argue that in fact this cannot be established, at least not with the conclusiveness which is essential to our hopes of convincing those who are skeptical about the morality of abortion, and that we therefore cannot avoid dealing with the question of whether or not a fetus really does have the same right to life as a (more fully developed) human being.

In Section II, I will propose an answer to this question, namely, that a fetus cannot be considered a member of the moral community, the set of beings with full and equal moral rights, for the simple reason that it is not a person, and that it is personhood, and not genetic humanity, i.e., humanity as defined by Noonan, which is the basis for membership in this community. I will argue that a fetus, whatever its stage of development, satisfies none of the basic criteria of personhood, and is not even enough *like* a person to be accorded even some of the same rights on the basis of this resemblance. Nor, as we will see, is a fetus's *potential* personhood a threat to the morality of abortion, since, whatever the rights of potential people may be, they are invariably overridden in any conflict with the moral rights of actual people.

I

We turn now to Professor Thomson's case for the claim that even if a fetus has full moral rights, abortion is still morally permissible, at least sometimes, and for some reasons other than to save the woman's life. Her argument is based upon a clever, but I think faulty, analogy. She asks us to picture ourselves waking up one day, in bed with a famous violinist. Imagine that you have been kidnapped, and your bloodstream hooked up to that of the violinist, who happens to have an ailment which will certainly kill him unless he is permitted to share your kidneys for a period of nine months. No one else can save him, since you alone have the right type of blood. He will be unconscious all that time, and you will have to stay in bed with him, but after the nine months are over he may be unplugged, completely cured; that is, provided that you have cooperated.

Now then, she continues, what are your obligations in this situation? The antiabortionist, if he is consistent, will have to say that you are obligated to stay in bed with the violinist: for all people have a right to life, and violinists are people, and therefore it would be murder for you to disconnect yourself from him and let him die. . . . But this is outrageous, and so there must be something wrong with the same argument when it is applied to abortion. It would certainly be commendable of you to agree to save the violinist, but it is absurd to suggest that your refusal to do so would be murder. His right to life does not obligate you to do whatever is required to keep him alive; nor does it justify anyone else in forcing you to do so. A law which required you to stay in bed with the violinist would clearly be an unjust law, since it is no proper function of the law to force unwilling people to make huge sacrifices for the sake of other people toward whom they have no such prior obligation.

Thomson concludes that, if this analogy is an apt one, then we can grant the antiabortionist his claim that a fetus is a human being, and still hold that it is at least sometimes the case that a pregnant woman has the right to refuse to be a Good Samaritan towards the fetus, i.e., to obtain an abortion. For there is a great gap between the claim that *x* has a right to life, and the claim that *y* is obligated to do whatever is necessary to keep *x* alive, let alone that he ought to be forced to do so. It is *y*'s duty to keep *x* alive only if he has somehow contracted a *special* obligation to do so; and a woman who is unwillingly pregnant, e.g., who was raped, has done nothing which obligates her to make the enormous sacrifice which is necessary to preserve the conceptus.

This argument is initially quite plausible, and in the extreme case of pregnancy due to rape it is probably conclusive. Difficulties arise, however, when we try to specify more exactly the range of cases in which abortion is clearly justifiable even on the assumption that the fetus is human. Professor Thomson considers it a virtue of her argument that it does not enable us to conclude that abortion is *always* permissible. It would, she says, be "indecent" for a woman in her seventh month to obtain an abortion just to avoid having to postpone a trip to Europe. On the other hand, her argument enables us to see that "a sick and desperately frightened [. . .] schoolgirl pregnant due to rape may *of course* choose abortion, and that any law which rules this out is an insane law." . . . So far, so good; but what are we to say about the woman who becomes pregnant not through rape but as a result of her own carelessness, or because of contraceptive failure, or who gets pregnant intentionally and then changes her mind about wanting a child? With respect to such cases, the violinist analogy is of much less use to the defender of the woman's right to obtain an abortion.

Indeed, the choice of a pregnancy due to rape, as an example of a case in which abortion is permissible even if a fetus is considered a human being, is extremely significant; for it is only in the case of pregnancy due to rape that the woman's situation is adequately analogous to the violinist case for our intuitions about the latter to transfer convincingly. The crucial difference between a pregnancy due to rape and the *normal* case of an unwanted pregnancy is that in the normal case we cannot claim that the woman is in no way responsible for her predicament; she could have remained chaste, or taken her pills more faithfully, or abstained on dangerous days, and so on. If, on the other hand, you are kidnapped by strangers, and hooked up to a strange violinist, then you are free of any shred of responsibility for the situation, on the basis of which it could be argued that you are obligated to keep the violinist alive. Only when her pregnancy is due to rape is a woman clearly just as nonresponsible.

Consequently, there is room for the antiabortionist to argue that in the normal case of unwanted pregnancy a woman has, by her own actions, assumed responsibility for the fetus. For if *x* behaves in a way which he could have avoided, and which he knows involves, let us say, a 1 percent chance of bringing into existence a human being, with a right to life, and does so knowing that if this should happen then that human being will perish unless *x* does certain things to keep him alive, then it is by no means clear that when it does happen *x* is free of any obligation to what he knew in advance would be required to keep that human being alive.

The plausibility of such an argument is enough to show that the Thomson analogy can provide a clear and persuasive defense of a woman's right to obtain an abortion only with respect to those cases in which the woman is in no way responsible for her pregnancy, e.g., where it is due to rape. In all other cases, we would almost certainly conclude that it was necessary to look carefully at the particular circumstances in order to determine the extent of the woman's responsibility, and hence the extent of her obligation. This is an extremely unsatisfactory outcome, from the viewpoint of the opponents of restrictive abortion laws, most of whom are convinced that a woman has a right to obtain an abortion regardless of how and why she got pregnant.

Of course a supporter of the violinist analogy might point out that it is absurd to suggest that forgetting her pill one day might be sufficient to obligate a woman to complete an unwanted pregnancy. And indeed it is absurd to suggest this. As we will see, the moral right to obtain an abortion is not in the least dependent upon the extent to which the woman is responsible for her pregnancy. But unfortunately, once we allow the assumption that a fetus has full moral rights, we cannot avoid taking this absurd suggestion seriously. Perhaps we can make this point more clear by altering the violinist story just enough to make it more analogous to a normal unwanted pregnancy and less to a pregnancy due to rape, and then seeing whether it is still obvious that you are not obligated to stay in bed with the fellow.

Suppose, then, that violinists are peculiarily prone to the sort of illness the only cure for which is the use of someone else's bloodstream for nine months, and that because of this there has been formed a society of music lovers who agree that whenever a violinist is stricken they will draw lots and the loser will, by some means, be made the one and only person capable of saving him. Now then, would you be obligated to cooperate in curing the violinist if you had voluntarily joined this society, knowing the possible consequences, and then your name had been drawn and you had been kidnapped? Admittedly, you did not promise ahead of time that you would, but you did deliberately place yourself in a position in which it might happen that a human life would be lost if you did not. Surely this is at least a *prima facie* reason for supposing that you have an obligation to stay in bed with the violinist. Suppose that you had gotten your name drawn deliberately; surely *that* would be quite a strong reason for thinking that you had such an obligation.

It might be suggested that there is one important disanalogy between the modified violinist case and the case of an unwanted pregnancy, which makes the woman's responsibility significantly less, namely, the fact that the fetus *comes into existence* as the result of the woman's actions. This fact might give her a right to refuse to keep it alive, whereas she would not have had this right had it existed previously, independently, and then as a result of her actions become dependent upon her for its survival.

My own intuition, however, is that x has no more right to bring into existence, either deliberately or as a foreseeable result of actions he could have avoided, a being with full moral rights (y), and then refuse to do what he knew beforehand would be required to keep that being alive, than he has to enter into an agreement with an existing person, whereby he may be called upon to save that person's life, and then refuse to do so when so called upon. Thus, x's responsibility for y's existence does not seem to lessen his obligation to keep y alive, if he is also responsible for y's being in a situation in which only he can save him.

Whether or not this intuition is entirely correct, it brings us back once again to the conclusion that once we allow the assumption that a fetus has full moral rights, it becomes an extremely complex and difficult question whether and when abortion is justifiable. Thus the Thomson analogy cannot help us produce a clear and persuasive proof of the moral permissibility of abortion. Nor will the opponents of the restrictive laws thank us for anything less; for their conviction (for the most part) is that abortion is obviously *not* a morally serious and extremely unfortunate, even though sometimes justified act, comparable to killing in self-defense or to letting the violinist die, but rather is closer to being a morally neutral act, like cutting one's hair.

The basis of this conviction, I believe, is the realization that a fetus is not a person, and thus does not have a full-fledged right to life. Perhaps the reason why this claim has been so inadequately defended is that it seems self-evident to those who accept it. And so it is, insofar as it follows from what I take to be perfectly obvious claims about the nature of personhood, and about the proper grounds for ascribing moral rights, claims which ought, indeed, to be obvious to both the friends and foes of abortion. Nevertheless, it is worth examining these claims, and showing how they demonstrate the moral innocuousness of abortion, since this apparently has not been adequately done before.

II

The question which we must answer in order to produce a satisfactory solution to the problem of the moral status of abortion is this: How are we to define the moral community, the set of beings with full and equal moral rights, such that we can decide whether a human fetus is a member of this community or not? What sort of entity, exactly, has the inalienable rights to life, liberty, and the pursuit of happiness? Jefferson attributed these rights to all *men,* and it may or may not be fair to suggest that he intended to attribute them *only* to men. Perhaps he ought to have attributed them to all human beings. If so, then we arrive, first, at Noonan's problem of defining what makes a being human, and, second, at the equally vital question which Noonan does not consider, namely, What reason is there for identifying the moral community with the set of all human beings, in whatever way we have chosen to define that term?

On the Definition of "Human"

One reason why this vital second question is so frequently overlooked in the debate over the moral status of abortion is that the term "human" has two distinct, but not often distinguished, senses. This fact results in a slide of meaning, which serves to conceal the fallaciousness of the traditional argument that since (1) it is wrong to kill innocent human beings, and (2) fetuses are innocent human beings, then (3) it is wrong to kill fetuses. For if "human" is used in the same sense in both (1) and (2) then, which ever of the two senses is meant, one of these premises is question-begging. And if it is used in two different senses then of course the conclusion doesn't follow.

Thus, (1) is a self-evident moral truth, and avoids begging the question about abortion, only if "human being" is used to mean something like "a full-fledged member of the moral community." (It may or may not also be meant to refer exclusively to members of the species *Homo sapiens.*) We may call this the *moral sense* of "human." It is not to be confused with what we will call the *genetic* sense, i.e., the sense in which *any* member of the species is a human being, and no member of any other species could be. If (1) is acceptable only if the moral sense is intended, (2) is non-question-begging only if what is intended is the genetic sense.

In "Deciding Who Is Human," Noonan argues for the classification of fetuses with human beings by pointing to the presence of the full genetic code, and the potential capacity for rational thought. . . . It is clear that what he needs to show, for his version of the traditional argument to be valid, is that fetuses are human in the moral sense, the sense in which it is analytically true that all human beings have full moral rights. But, in the absence of any argument showing that whatever is genetically human is also morally human, and he gives none, nothing more than genetic humanity can be demonstrated by the presence of the human genetic code. And, as we will see, the *potential* capacity for rational thought can at most show that an entity has the potential for *becoming* human in the moral sense.

Defining the Moral Community

Can it be established that genetic humanity is sufficient for moral humanity? I think that there are very good reasons for not defining the moral community in this way. I would like to suggest an alternative way of defining the moral community, which I will argue for only to the extent of explaining why it is, or should be, self-evident. The suggestion is simply that the moral community consists of all and only *people,* rather than all and only human beings; and probably the best way of demonstrating its self-evidence is by considering the concept of personhood, to see what sorts of entity are and are not persons, and what the decision that a being is or is not a person implies about its moral rights.

What characteristics entitle an entity to be considered a person? This is obviously not the place to attempt a complete analysis of the concept of personhood, but we do not need such a full adequate analysis just to determine whether and why a fetus is or isn't a person. All we need is a rough and approximate list of the most basic criteria of personhood, and some idea of which, or how many, of these an entity must satisfy in order to properly be considered a person.

In searching for such criteria, it is useful to look beyond the set of people with whom we are acquainted, and ask how we would decide whether a totally alien being was a person or not. (For we have no right to assume that genetic humanity is necessary for personhood.) Imagine a space traveler who lands on an unknown planet and encounters a race of beings utterly unlike any he has ever seen or heard of. If he wants to be sure of behaving morally toward these beings, he has to somehow decide whether they are people, and hence have full moral rights, or whether they are the sort of thing which he need not feel guilty about treating as, for example, a source of food.

How should he go about making this decision? If he has some anthropological background, he might look for such things as religion, art, and the manufacturing of tools, weapons, or shelters, since these factors have been used to distinguish our human from our prehuman ancestors, in what seems to be closer to the moral than the genetic sense of "human." And no doubt he would be right to consider the presence of such factors as good evidence that the alien beings were people, and morally human. It would, however, be overly anthropocentric of him to take the absence of these things as adequate evidence that they were not, since we can imagine people who have progressed beyond, or evolved without ever developing, these cultural characteristics.

I suggest that the traits which are most central to the concept of personhood, or humanity in the moral sense, are, very roughly, the following:

1. consciousness (of objects and events external and/or internal to the being), and in particular the capacity to feel pain;
2. reasoning (the *developed* capacity to solve new and relatively complex problems);
3. self-motivated activity (activity which is relatively independent of either genetic or direct external control);
4. the capacity to communicate, by whatever means, messages of an indefinite variety of types, that is, not just with an indefinite number of possible contents, but on indefinitely many possible topics;
5. the presence of self-concepts, and self-awareness, either individual or racial, or both.

Admittedly, there are apt to be a great many problems involved in formulating precise definitions of these criteria, let alone in developing universally valid behavioral criteria for deciding when they apply. But I will assume that both we and our explorer know approximately what (1)–(5) mean, and that he is also able to determine whether or not they apply. How, then, should he use his findings to decide whether or not the alien beings are people? We needn't suppose that an entity must have *all* of these attributes to be properly considered a person; (1) and (2) alone may well be sufficient for personhood, and quite probably (1)–(3) are sufficient. Neither do we need to insist that any one of these criteria is *necessary* for personhood, although once again (1) and (2) look like fairly good candidates for necessary conditions, as does (3), if "activity" is construed so as to include the activity of reasoning.

All we need to claim, to demonstrate that a fetus is not a person, is that any being which satisfies *none* of (1)–(5) is certainly not a person. I consider this claim to be so obvious that I think anyone who denied it, and claimed that a being which satisfied none of (1)–(5) was a person all the same, would thereby demonstrate that he had no notion at all of what a person is—perhaps because he had confused the concept of a person with that of genetic humanity. If the opponents of abortion were to deny the appropriateness of these five criteria, I do not know what further arguments would convince them. We would probably have to admit that our conceptual schemes were indeed irreconcilably different, and that our dispute could not be settled objectively.

I do not expect this to happen, however, since I think that the concept of a person is one which is very nearly universal (to people), and that it is common to both proabortionists and antiabortionists, even though neither group has fully realized the relevance of this concept to the resolution of their dispute. Furthermore, I think that on reflection even the antiabortionists ought to agree not only that (1)–(5) are central to the concept of personhood, but also that it is a part of this concept that all and only people have full moral rights. The concept of a person is in part a moral concept; once we have admitted that *x* is a person we have recognized, even if we have not agreed to respect, *x*'s right to be treated as a member of the moral community. It is true that the claim that *x* is a *human being* is more commonly voiced as part of an appeal to treat *x* decently than is the claim that *x* is a person, but this is either because "human being" is here used in the sense which implies personhood, or because the genetic and moral senses of "human" have been confused.

Now if (1)–(5) are indeed the primary criteria of personhood, then it is clear that genetic humanity is neither necessary nor sufficient for establishing that an entity is a person. Some human beings are not people, and there may well be people who are not human beings. A man or woman whose consciousness has been permanently obliterated but who remains alive is a human being which is no longer a person; defective human beings, with no appreciable mental capacity, are not and presumably never will be people: and a fetus is a human being which is not yet a person, and which therefore cannot coherently be said to have full moral rights. Citizens of the next century should be prepared to recognize highly advanced, self-aware robots or computers, should such be developed, and intelligent inhabitants of other worlds, should such be found, as people in the fullest sense, and to respect their moral rights. But to ascribe full moral rights to an entity which is not a person is as absurd as to ascribe moral obligations and responsibilities to such an entity.

Fetal Development and the Right to Life

Two problems arise in the application of these suggestions for the definition of the moral community to the determination of the precise moral status of a human fetus. Given that the paradigm example of a person is a normal adult human being, then (1) How like this paradigm, in particular how far advanced since conception, does a human being need to be before it begins to have a right to life by virtue, not of being fully a person as of yet, but of being *like* a person? and (2) To what extent, if any, does the fact that a fetus has the *potential* for becoming a person endow it with some of the same rights? Each of these questions requires some comment.

In answering the first question, we need not attempt a detailed consideration of the moral rights of organisms which are not developed enough, aware enough, intelligent enough, etc., to be considered people, but which resemble people in some respects. It does seem reasonable to suggest that the more like a person, in the relevant respects, a being is, the stronger is the case for regarding it as having a right to life, and indeed the stronger its right to life is. Thus we ought to take seriously the suggestion that, insofar as "the human individual develops biologically in a continuous fashion . . . the rights of a human person might develop in the same way." But we must keep in mind that the attributes which are relevant in determining whether or not an entity is enough like a person to be regarded as having some of the same moral rights are no different from those which are relevant to determining whether or not it is full a person—i.e., are no different from (1)–(5)—and that being genetically human, or having recognizably human facial and other physical features, or detectable brain activity, or the capacity to survive outside the uterus, are simply not among these relevant attributes.

Thus it is clear that even though a seven- or eight-month fetus has features which make it apt to arouse in us almost the same powerful protective instinct as is commonly aroused by a small infant, nevertheless it is not significantly more personlike than is a very small embryo. It is *somewhat* more personlike; it can apparently feel and respond to pain, and it may even have a rudimentary form of consciousness, insofar as its brain is quite active. Nevertheless, it seems safe to say that it is not fully conscious, in the way that an infant of a few months is, and that it cannot reason, or communicate messages of indefinitely many sorts, does not engage in self-motivated activity, and has no self-awareness. Thus, in the *relevant* respects, a fetus, even a fully developed one, is considerably less personlike than is the average fish. And I think that a rational person must conclude that if the right to life of a fetus is to be based upon its resemblance to a person, then it cannot be said to have any more right to life than, let us say, a newborn guppy (which also seems to be capable of feeling pain), and that a right of that magnitude could never override a woman's right to obtain an abortion, at any stage of her pregnancy.

There may, of course, be other arguments in favor of placing legal limits upon the stage of pregnancy in which an abortion may be performed. Given the relative safety of the new techniques of artificially inducing labor during the third trimester, the danger to the woman's life or health is no longer such an argument. Neither is the fact that people tend to respond to the thought of abortion in the later stages of pregnancy with emotional repulsion, since mere emotional responses cannot take the place of moral reasoning in determining what ought to be permitted. Nor, finally, is the frequently heard argument that legalizing abortion, especially late in the pregnancy, may erode the level of respect for human life, leading, perhaps, to an increase in unjustified euthanasia and other crimes. For this threat, if it is a threat, can be better met by educating people to the kinds of moral distinctions which we are making here than by limiting access to abortion (which limitation may, in its disregard for the rights of women, be just as damaging to the level of respect for human rights).

Thus, since the fact that even a fully developed fetus is not personlike enough to have any significant right to life on the basis of its personlikeness shows that no legal restrictions upon the stage of pregnancy in which an abortion may be performed can be justified on the grounds that we should protect the rights of the older fetus; and since there is no other apparent justification for such restrictions, we may conclude that they are entirely unjustified. Whether or not it would be *indecent* (whatever that means) for a woman in her seventh month to obtain an abortion just to avoid having to postpone a trip to Europe, it would not, in itself, be *immoral,* and therefore it ought to be permitted.

Potential Personhood and the Right to Life

We have seen that a fetus does not resemble a person in any way which can support the claim that it has even some of the same rights. But what about its *potential*, the fact that if nurtured and allowed to develop naturally it will very probably become a person? Doesn't that alone give it at least some right to life? It is hard to deny that the fact that an entity is a potential person is a strong *prima facie* reason for not destroying it; but we need not conclude from this that a potential person has a right to life, by virtue of that potential. It may be that our feeling that it is better, other things being equal, not to destroy a potential person is better explained by the fact that potential people are still (felt to be) an invaluable resource, not to be lightly squandered. Surely, if every speck of dust were a potential person, we would be much less apt to conclude that every potential person has a right to become actual.

Still, we do not need to insist that a potential person has no right to life whatever. There may well be something immoral, and not just imprudent, about wantonly destroying potential people, when doing so isn't necessary to protect anyone's rights. But even if a potential person does have some *prima facie* right to life, such a right could not possibly outweigh the right of a woman to obtain an abortion, since the rights of any actual person invariably outweigh those of any potential person, whenever the two conflict. Since this may not be immediately obvious in the case of a human fetus, let us look at another case.

Suppose that our space explorer falls into the hands of an alien culture whose scientists decide to create a few hundred thousand or more human beings, by breaking his body into its component cells, and using these to create fully developed human beings, with, of course, his genetic code. We may imagine that each of these newly created men will have all of the original man's abilities, skills, knowledge, and so on, and also have an individual self-concept, in short that each of them will be a bona fide (though hardly unique) person. Imagine that the whole project will take only seconds, and that its chances of success are extremely high, and that our explorer knows all of this, and also knows that these people will be treated fairly. I maintain that in such a situation he would have every right to escape if he could, and thus to deprive all of these potential people of their potential lives; for his right to life outweighs all of theirs together, in spite of the fact that they are all genetically human, all innocent, and all have a very high probability of becoming people very soon, if only he refrains from acting.

Indeed, I think he would have a right to escape even if it were not his life which the alien scientists planned to take, but only a year of his freedom, or, indeed, only a day. Nor would he be obligated to stay if he had gotten captured (thus bringing all these people-potentials into existence) because of his own carelessness, or even if he had done so deliberately, knowing the consequences. Regardless of how he got captured he is not morally obligated to remain in captivity for *any* period of time for the sake of permitting any number of potential people to come into actuality, so great is the margin by which one actual person's right to liberty outweighs whatever right to life even a hundred thousand potential people have. And it seems reasonable to conclude that the rights of a woman will outweigh by a similar margin whatever right to life a fetus may have by virtue of its potential personhood.

Thus, neither a fetus's resemblance to a person, nor its potential for becoming a person provides any basis whatever for the claim that it has any significant right to life. Consequently, a woman's right to protect her health, happiness, freedom, and even her life, by terminating an unwanted pregnancy, will always override whatever right to life it may be appropriate to ascribe to a fetus, even a fully developed one. And thus, in the absence of any overwhelming social need for every possible child, the laws which restrict the right to obtain an abortion, or limit the period of pregnancy during which an abortion may be performed, are a wholly unjustified violation of a woman's most basic moral and constitutional rights.

Postscript on Infanticide

Since the publication of this article, many people have written to point out that my argument appears to justify not only abortion but infanticide as well. For a newborn infant is not significantly more personlike than an advanced fetus, and consequently it would seem that if the destruction of the latter is permissible, so too must be that of the former. Inasmuch as most people, regardless of how they feel about the morality of abortion, consider infanticide a form of murder, this might appear to represent a serious flaw in my argument.

Now, if I am right in holding that it is only people who have a full-fledged right to life, and who can be murdered, and if the criteria of personhood are as I have described them, then it obviously follows that killing a newborn infant isn't murder. It does *not* follow, however, that infanticide is permissible, for two reasons. In the first place, it would be wrong, at least in this country and in this period of history, and other things being equal, to kill a newborn infant, because even if its parents do not want it and would not suffer from its destruction, there are other people who would like to have it, and would, in all probability, be deprived of a great deal of pleasure by its destruction. Thus, infanticide is wrong for reasons analogous to those which make it wrong to wantonly destroy natural resources, or great works of art.

Secondly, most people, at least in this country, value infants, and would much prefer that they be preserved, even if foster parents are not immediately available. Most of us would rather be taxed to support orphanages than allow unwanted infants to be destroyed. So long as there are people who want an infant preserved, and who are willing and able to provide the means of caring for it, under reasonably humane conditions, it is, *ceteris paribus,* wrong to destroy it.

But, it might be replied, if this argument shows that infanticide is wrong, at least at this time and in this country, doesn't it also show that abortion is wrong? After all, many people value fetuses, are disturbed by their destruction, and would much prefer that they be preserved, even at some cost to themselves. Furthermore, as a potential source of pleasure to some foster family, a fetus is just as valuable as an infant. There is, however, a crucial difference between the two cases: so long as the fetus is unborn, its preservation, contrary to the wishes of the pregnant woman, violates her rights to freedom, happiness, and self-determination. Her rights override the rights of those who would like the fetus preserved, just as if someone's life or limb is threatened by a wild animal, his right to protect himself by destroying the animal overrides the rights of those who would prefer that the animal not be harmed.

The minute the infant is born, however, its preservation no longer violates any of its mother's rights, even if she wants it destroyed, because she is free to put it up for adoption. Consequently, while the moment of birth does not mark any sharp discontinuity in the degree to which an infant possesses the right to life, it does mark the end of its mother's right to determine its fate. Indeed, if abortion could be performed without killing the fetus, she would never possess the right to have the fetus destroyed, for the same reasons that she has no right to have an infant destroyed.

On the other hand, it follows from my argument that when an unwanted or defective infant is born into a society which cannot afford and/or is not willing to care for it, then its destruction is permissible. This conclusion will, no doubt, strike many people as heartless and immoral; but remember that the very existence of people who feel this way, and who are willing and able to provide care for unwanted infants, is reason enough to conclude that they should be preserved.

QUESTIONS FOR REFLECTION

1. Explain Warren's criticisms of Thomson.
2. Why does Warren reject the traditional pro-life and pro-choice arguments?
3. Distinguish the genetic and moral senses of "human." John Noonan argues for their equivalence. Why does Warren reject it?
4. What are the central features of personhood, according to Warren? To what extent does a fetus have them? When are they acquired?
5. How does Warren respond to the charge that her view implies that infanticide is permissible? Do you find her response convincing?
6. Warren says that the rights of a potential person can never outweigh those of an actual person. Do you agree? Why or why not?

DON MARQUIS

Why Abortion Is Immoral

Don Marquis is professor of philosophy at the University of Kansas. (Source: Reprinted from The Journal of Philosophy *LXXXVI, 4 [April 1989]: 183–202, with permission of the author and* The Journal of Philosophy.

The view that abortion is, with rare exceptions, seriously immoral has received little support in the recent philosophical literature. No doubt most philosophers affiliated with secular institutions of higher education believe that the anti-abortion position is either a symptom of irrational religious dogma or a conclusion generated by seriously confused philosophical argument. The purpose of this essay is to undermine this general belief. This essay sets out an argument that purports to show, as well as any argument in ethics can show, that abortion is, except possibly in rare cases, seriously immoral, that it is in the same moral category as killing an innocent adult human being.

The argument is based on a major assumption. Many of the most insightful and careful writers on the ethics of abortion—such as Joel Feinberg, Michael Tooley, Mary Anne Warren, H. Tristram Engelhardt, Jr., L. W. Sumner, John T. Noonan, Jr., and Philip Devine—believe that whether or not abortion is morally permissible stands or falls on whether or not a fetus is the sort of being whose life it is seriously wrong to end. The argument of this essay will assume, but not argue, that they are correct.

Also, this essay will neglect issues of great importance to a complete ethics of abortion. Some anti-abortionists will allow that certain abortions, such as abortion before implantation or abortion when the life of a woman is threatened by a pregnancy or abortion after rape, may be morally permissible. This essay will not explore the casuistry of these hard cases. The purpose of this essay is to develop a general argument for the claim that the overwhelming majority of deliberate abortions are seriously immoral.

I

A sketch of standard anti-abortion and pro-choice arguments exhibits how those arguments possess certain symmetries that explain why partisans of those positions are so convinced of the correctness of their own positions, why they are not successful in convincing their opponents, and why, to others, this issue seems to be unresolvable. An analysis of the nature of this standoff suggests a strategy for surmounting it.

Consider the way a typical anti-abortionist argues. She will argue or assert that life is present from the moment of conception or that fetuses look like babies or that fetuses possess a characteristic such as a genetic code that is both necessary and sufficient for being human. Anti-abortionists seem to believe that (1) the truth of all of these claims is quite obvious, and (2) establishing any of these claims is sufficient to show that abortion is morally akin to murder.

A standard pro-choice strategy exhibits similarities. The pro-choicer will argue or assert that fetuses are not persons or that fetuses are not rational agents or that fetuses are not social beings. Pro-choicers seem to believe that (1) the truth of any of these claims is quite obvious, and (2) establishing any of these claims is sufficient to show that an abortion is not a wrongful killing.

In fact, both the pro-choice and the anti-abortion claims do seem to be true, although the "it looks like a baby" claim is more difficult to establish the earlier the pregnancy. We seem to have a standoff. How can it be resolved?

As everyone who has taken a bit of logic knows, if any of these arguments concerning abortion is a good argument, it requires not only some claim characterizing fetuses, but also some general moral principle that ties a characteristic of fetuses to having or not having the right to life or to some other moral characteristic that will generate the obligation or the lack of obligation not to end the life of a fetus. Accordingly, the arguments of the anti-abortionist and the pro-choicer need a bit of filling in to be regarded as adequate.

Note what each partisan will say. The anti-abortionist will claim that her position is supported by such generally accepted moral principles as "It is always *prima facie* seriously wrong to take a human life" or "It is always *prima facie* seriously wrong to end the life of a baby." Since these are generally accepted moral principles, her position is certainly not obviously wrong. The pro-choicer will claim that her position is supported by such plausible moral principles as "Being a person is what gives an individual intrinsic moral worth" or "It is only seriously *prima facie* wrong to take the life of a member of the human community." Since these are generally accepted moral principles, the pro-choice position is certainly not obviously wrong. Unfortunately, we have again arrived at a standoff.

Now, how might one deal with this standoff? The standard approach is to try to show how the moral principles of one's opponent lose their plausibility under analysis. It is easy to see how this is possible. On the one hand, the anti-abortionist will defend a moral principle concerning the wrongness of killing which tends to be broad in scope in order that even fetuses at an early stage of pregnancy will fall under it. The problem with broad principles is that they often embrace too much. In this particular instance, the principle "It is always *prima facie* wrong to take a human life" seems to entail that it is wrong to end the existence of a living human cancer-cell culture, on the grounds that the culture is both living and human. Therefore, it seems that the anti-abortionist's favored principle is too broad.

On the other hand, the pro-choicer wants to find a moral principle concerning the wrongness of killing which tends to be narrow in scope in order that fetuses will *not* fall under it. The problem with narrow principles is that they often do not embrace enough. Hence, the needed principles such as "It is *prima facie* seriously wrong to kill only persons" or "It is *prima facie* wrong to kill only rational agents" do not explain why it is wrong to kill infants or young children or the severely retarded or even perhaps the severely mentally ill. Therefore, we seem again to have a standoff. The anti-abortionist charges, not unreasonably, that pro-choice principles concerning killing are too narrow to be acceptable; the pro-choicer charges, not unreasonably, that anti-abortionist principles concerning killing are too broad to be acceptable.

Attempts by both sides to patch up the difficulties in their positions run into further difficulties. The anti-abortionist will try to remove the problem in her position by reformulating her principle concerning killing in terms of human beings. Now we end up with: "It is always *prima facie* seriously wrong to end the life of a human being." This principle has the advantage of avoiding the problem of the human cancer-cell culture counterexample. But this advantage is purchased at a high price. For although it is clear that a fetus is both human and alive, it is not at all clear that a fetus is a human *being*. There is at least something to be said for the view that something becomes a human being only after a process of development, and that therefore first-trimester fetuses and perhaps all fetuses are not yet human beings. Hence, the anti-abortionist, by this move, has merely exchanged one problem for another.

The pro-choicer fares no better. She may attempt to find reasons why killing infants, young children, and the severely retarded is wrong which are independent of her major principle that is supposed to explain the wrongness of taking human life, but which will not also make abortion immoral. This is no easy task. Appeals to social utility will seem satisfactory only to those who resolve not to think of the enormous difficulties with a utilitarian account of the wrongness of killing and the significant social costs of preserving the lives of the unproductive. A pro-choice strategy that extends the definition of "person" to infants or even to young children seems just as arbitrary as an anti-abortion strategy that extends the definition of "human being" to fetuses. Again, we find symmetries in the two positions and we arrive at a standoff.

There are even further problems that reflect symmetries in the two positions. In addition to counter-example problems, or the arbitrary application problems that can be exchanged for them, the standard anti-abortionist principle "It is *prima facie* seriously wrong to kill a human being," or one of its variants, can be objected to on the grounds of ambiguity. If "human being" is taken to be a *biological* category, then the anti-abortionist is left with the problem of explaining why a merely biological category should make a moral difference. Why, it is asked, is it any more reasonable to base a moral conclusion on the number of chromosomes in one's cells than on the color of one's skin? If "human being," on the other hand, is taken to be a *moral* category, then the claim that a fetus is a human being cannot be taken to be a premise in the anti-abortion argument, for it is precisely what needs to be established. Hence, either the anti-abortionist's main category is a morally irrelevant, merely biological category, or it is of no use to the anti-abortionist in establishing (non-circularly, of course) that abortion is wrong.

Although this problem with the anti-abortionist position is often noticed, it is less often noticed that the pro-choice position suffers from an analogous problem. The principle "Only persons have the right to life" also suffers from an ambiguity. The term "person" is typically defined in terms of psychological characteristics, although there will certainly be disagreement concerning which characteristics are most important. Supposing that this matter can be settled, the pro-choicer is left with the problem of explaining why *psychological* characteristics should make a *moral* difference. If the pro-choicer should attempt to deal with this problem by claiming that an explanation is not necessary, that in fact we do treat such a cluster of psychological properties as having moral significance, the sharp-witted anti-abortionist should have a ready response. We do treat being both living and human as having moral significance. If it is legitimate for the pro-choicer to demand that the anti-abortionist provide an explanation of the connection between the biological character of being a human being and the wrongness of being killed (even though people accept this connection), then it is legitimate for the anti-abortionist to demand that the pro-choicer provide an explanation of the connection between psychological criteria for being a person and the wrongness of being killed (even though that connection is accepted).

Feinberg has attempted to meet this objection (he calls psychological personhood "commonsense personhood"):

> The characteristics that confer commonsense personhood are not arbitrary bases for rights and duties, such as race, sex or species membership; rather they are traits that make sense out of rights and duties and without which those moral attributes would have no point or function. It is because people are conscious; have a sense of their personal identities; have plans, goals, and projects; experience emotions; are liable to pains, anxieties, and frustrations; can reason and bargain, and so on—it is because of these attributes that people have values and interests, desires and expectations of their own, including a stake in their own futures, and a personal well-being of a sort we cannot ascribe to unconscious or nonrational beings. Because of their developed capacities they can assume duties and responsibilities and can have and make claims on one another. Only because of their sense of self, their life plans, their value hierarchies, and their stakes in their own futures can they be ascribed fundamental rights. There is nothing arbitrary about these linkages.

The plausible aspects of this attempt should not be taken to obscure its implausible features. There is a great deal to be said for the view that being a psychological person under some description is a necessary condition for having duties. One cannot have a duty unless one is capable of behaving morally, and a being's capability of behaving morally will require having a certain psychology. It is far from obvious, however, that having rights entails consciousness or rationality, as Feinberg suggests. We speak of the rights of the severely retarded or the severely mentally ill, yet some of these persons are not rational. We speak of the rights of the temporarily unconscious. The New Jersey Supreme Court based their decision in the Quinlan case on Karen Ann Quinlan's right to privacy, and she was known to be permanently unconscious at that time. Hence, Feinberg's claim that having rights entails being conscious is, on its face, obviously false.

Of course, it might not make sense to attribute rights to a being that would never in its natural history have certain psychological traits. This modest connection between psychological personhood and moral personhood will create a place for Karen Ann Quinlan and the temporarily unconscious. But then it makes a place for fetuses also. Hence, it does not serve Feinberg's pro-choice purposes. Accordingly, it seems that the pro-choicer will have as much difficulty bridging the gap between psychological personhood and personhood in the moral sense as the anti-abortionist has bridging the gap between being a biological human being and being a human being in the moral sense.

Furthermore, the pro-choicer cannot any more escape her problem by making person a purely moral category than the anti-abortionist could escape by the analogous move. For if person is a moral category, then the pro-choicer is left without the resources for establishing (noncircularly, of course) the claim that a fetus is not a person, which is an essential premise in her argument. Again, we have both a symmetry and a standoff between pro-choice and anti-abortion views.

Passions in the abortion debate run high. There are both plausibilities and difficulties with the standard positions. Accordingly, it is hardly surprising that partisans of either side embrace with fervor the moral generalizations that support the conclusions they pre-analytically favor, and reject with disdain the moral generalizations of their opponents as being subject to inescapable difficulties. It is easy to believe that the counterexamples to one's own moral principles are merely temporary difficulties that will dissolve in the wake of further philosophical research, and that the counterexamples to the principles of one's opponents are as straightforward as the contradiction between *A* and *O* propositions in traditional logic. This might suggest to an impartial observer (if there are any) that the abortion issue is unresolvable.

There is a way out of this apparent dialectical quandary. The moral generalizations of both sides are not quite correct. The generalizations hold for the most part, for the usual cases. This suggests that they are all *accidental* generalizations, that the moral claims made by those on both sides of the dispute do not touch on the *essence* of the matter.

This use of the distinction between essence and accident is not meant to invoke obscure metaphysical categories. Rather, it is intended to reflect the rather atheoretical nature of the abortion discussion. If the generalization a partisan in the abortion dispute adopts were derived from the reason why ending the life of a human being is wrong, then there could not be exceptions to that generalization unless some special case obtains in which there are even more powerful countervailing reasons. Such generalizations would not be merely accidental generalizations; they would point to, or be based upon, the essence of the wrongness of killing, what it is that makes killing wrong. All this suggests that a necessary condition of resolving the abortion controversy is a more theoretical account of the wrongness of killing. After all, if we merely believe, but do not understand, why killing adult human beings such as ourselves is wrong, how could we conceivably show that abortion is either immoral or permissible?

II

In order to develop such an account, we can start from the following unproblematic assumption concerning our own case: it is wrong to kill us. Why is it wrong? Some answers can be easily eliminated. It might be said that what makes killing us wrong is that a killing brutalizes the one who kills. But the brutalization consists of being inured to the performance of an act that is hideously immoral; hence, the brutalization does not explain the immorality. It might be said that what makes killing us wrong is the great loss others would experience due to our absence. Although such hubris is understandable, such an explanation does not account for the wrongness of killing hermits, or those whose lives are relatively independent and whose friends find it easy to make new friends.

A more obvious answer is better. What primarily makes killing wrong is neither its effect on the murderer nor its effect on the victim's friends and relatives, but its effect on the victim. The loss of one's life is one of the greatest losses one can suffer. The loss of one's life deprives one of all the experiences, activities, projects, and enjoyments that would otherwise have constituted one's future. Therefore, killing someone is wrong, primarily because the killing inflicts (one of) the greatest possible losses on the victim. To describe this as the loss of life can be misleading, however. The change in my biological state does not by itself make killing me wrong. The effect of the loss of my biological life is the loss to me of all those activities, projects, experiences, and enjoyments which would otherwise have constituted my future personal life. These activities, projects, experiences, and enjoyments are either valuable for their own sakes or are means to something else that is valuable for its own sake. Some parts of my future are not valued by me now, but will come to be valued by me as I grow older and as my values and capacities change. When I am killed, I am deprived both of what I now value which would have been part of my future personal life, but also what I would come to value. Therefore, when I die, I am deprived of all of the value of my future. Inflicting this loss on me is ultimately what makes killing me wrong. This being the case, it would seem that what makes killing *any* adult human being *prima facie* seriously wrong is the loss of his or her future.

How should this rudimentary theory of the wrongness of killing be evaluated? It cannot be faulted for deriving an "ought" from an "is," for it does not. The analysis assumes that killing me (or you, reader) is *prima facie* seriously wrong. The point of the analysis is to establish which natural property ultimately explains the wrongness of the killing, given that it is wrong. A natural property will ultimately explain the wrongness of killing, only if (1) the explanation fits with our intuitions about the matter and (2) there is no other natural property that provides the basis for a better explanation of the wrongness of killing. This analysis rests on the intuition that what makes killing a particular human or animal wrong is what it does to that particular human or animal. What makes killing wrong is some natural effect or other of the killing. Some would deny this. For instance, a divine-command theorist in ethics would deny it. Surely this denial is, however, one of those features of divine-command theory which renders it so implausible.

The claim that what makes killing wrong is the loss of the victim's future is directly supported by two considerations. In the first place, this theory explains why we regard killing as one of the worst of crimes. Killing is especially wrong, because it deprives the victim of more than perhaps any other crime. In the second place, people with AIDS or cancer who know they are dying believe, of course, that dying is a very bad thing for them. They believe that the loss of a future to them that they would otherwise have experienced is what makes their premature death a very bad thing for them. A better theory of the wrongness of killing would require a different natural property associated with killing which better fits with the attitudes of the dying. What could it be?

The view that what makes killing wrong is the loss to the victim of the value of the victim's future gains additional support when some of its implications are examined. In the first place, it is incompatible with the view that it is wrong to kill only beings who are biologically human. It is possible that there exists a different species from another planet whose members have a future like ours. Since having a future like that is what makes killing someone wrong, this theory entails that it would be wrong to kill members of such a species. Hence, this theory is opposed to the claim that only life that is biologically human has great moral worth, a claim which many anti-abortionists have seemed to adopt. This opposition, which this theory has in common with personhood theories, seems to be a merit of the theory.

In the second place, the claim that the loss of one's future is the wrong-making feature of one's being killed entails the possibility that the futures of some actual nonhuman mammals on our own planet are sufficiently like ours that it is seriously wrong to kill them also. Whether some animals do have the same right to life as human beings depends on adding to the account of the wrongness of killing some additional account of just what it is about my future or the futures of other adult human beings which makes it wrong to kill us. No such additional account will be offered in this essay. Undoubtedly, the provision of such an account would be a very difficult matter.

Undoubtedly, any such account would be quite controversial. Hence, it surely should not reflect badly on this sketch of an elementary theory of the wrongness of killing that it is indeterminate with respect to some very difficult issues regarding animal rights.

In the third place, the claim that the loss of one's future is the wrong-making feature of one's being killed does not entail, as sanctity of human life theories do, that active euthanasia is wrong. Persons who are severely and incurably ill, who face a future of pain and despair, and who wish to die will not have suffered a loss if they are killed. It is, strictly speaking, the value of a human's future which makes killing wrong in this theory. This being so, killing does not necessarily wrong some persons who are sick and dying. Of course, there may be other reasons for a prohibition of active euthanasia, but that is another matter. Sanctity-of-human-life theories seem to hold that active euthanasia is seriously wrong even in an individual case where there seems to be good reason for it independently of public policy considerations. This consequence is most implausible, and it is a plus for the claim that the loss of a future of value is what makes killing wrong that it does not share this consequence.

In the fourth place, the account of the wrongness of killing defended in this essay does straightforwardly entail that it is *prima facie* seriously wrong to kill children and infants, for we do presume that they have futures of value. Since we do believe that it is wrong to kill defenseless little babies, it is important that a theory of the wrongness of killing easily account for this. Personhood theories of the wrongness of killing, on the other hand, cannot straightforwardly account for the wrongness of killing infants and young children. Hence, such theories must add special ad hoc accounts of the wrongness of killing the young. The plausibility of such ad hoc theories seems to be a function of how desperately one wants such theories to work. The claim that the primary wrong-making feature of a killing is the loss to the victim of the value of its future accounts for the wrongness of killing young children and infants directly; it makes the wrongness of such acts as obvious as we actually think it is. This is a further merit of this theory. Accordingly, it seems that this value of a future-like-ours theory of the wrongness of killing shares strengths of both sanctity-of-life and personhood accounts while avoiding weaknesses of both. In addition, it meshes with a central intuition concerning what makes killing wrong.

The claim that the primary wrong-making feature of a killing is the loss to the victim of the value of its future has obvious consequences for the ethics of abortion. The future of a standard fetus includes a set of experiences, projects, activities, and such which are identical with the futures of adult human beings and are identical with the futures of young children. Since the reason that is sufficient to explain why it is wrong to kill human beings after the time of birth is a reason that also applies to fetuses, it follows that abortion is *prima facie* seriously morally wrong.

This argument does not rely on the invalid inference that, since it is wrong to kill persons, it is wrong to kill potential persons also. The category that is morally central to this analysis is the category of having a valuable future like ours; it is not the category of personhood. The argument to the conclusion that abortion is *prima facie* seriously morally wrong proceeded independently of the notion of person or potential person or any equivalent. Someone may wish to start with this analysis in terms of the value of a human future, conclude that abortion is, except perhaps in rare circumstances, seriously morally wrong, infer that fetuses have the right to life, and then call fetuses "persons" as a result of their having the right to life. Clearly, in this case, the category of person is being used to state the *conclusion* of the analysis rather than to generate the *argument* of the analysis.

The structure of this anti-abortion argument can be both illuminated and defended by comparing it to what appears to be the best argument for the wrongness of the wanton infliction of pain on animals. This latter argument is based on the assumption that it is *prima facie* wrong to inflict pain on me (or you, reader). What is the natural property associated with the infliction of pain which makes such infliction wrong? The obvious answer seems to be that the infliction of pain causes suffering and that suffering is a misfortune. The suffering caused by the infliction of pain is what makes the wanton infliction of pain on me wrong. The wanton infliction of pain on other adult humans causes suffering. The wanton infliction of pain on animals causes suffering. Since causing suffering is what makes the wanton infliction of pain wrong and since the wanton infliction of pain on animals causes suffering, it follows that the wanton infliction of pain on animals is wrong.

This argument for the wrongness of the wanton infliction of pain on animals shares a number of structural features with the argument for the serious *prima facie* wrongness of abortion. Both arguments start with an obvious assumption concerning what it is wrong to do to me (or you, reader). Both then look for the characteristic or the consequence of the wrong action which makes the action wrong. Both recognize that the wrong-making feature of these immoral actions is a property of actions sometimes directed at individuals other than postnatal human beings. If the structure of the argument for the wrongness of the wanton infliction of pain on animals is sound, then the structure of the argument for the *prima facie* serious wrongness of abortion is also sound, for the structure of the two arguments is the same. The structure common to both is the key to the explanation of how the wrongness of abortion can be demonstrated without recourse to the category of person. In neither argument is that category crucial.

This defense of an argument for the wrongness of abortion in terms of a structurally similar argument for the wrongess of the wanton infliction of pain on animals succeeds only if the account regarding animals is the correct account. Is it? In the first place, it seems plausible. In the second place, its major competition is Kant's account. Kant believed that we do not have direct duties to animals at all, because they are not persons. Hence, Kant had to explain and justify the wrongness of inflicting pain on animals on the grounds that "he who is hard in his dealings with animals becomes hard also in his dealing with men." The problem with Kant's account is that there seems to be no reason for accepting this latter claim unless Kant's account is rejected. If the alternative to Kant's account is accepted, then it is easy to understand why someone who is indifferent to inflicting pain on animals is also indifferent to inflicting pain on humans, for one is indifferent to what makes inflicting pain wrong in both cases. But, if Kant's account is accepted, there is no intelligible reason why one who is hard in his dealings with animals (or crabgrass or stones) should also be hard in his dealings with men. After all, men are persons: animals are no more persons than crabgrass or stones. Persons are Kant's crucial moral category. Why, in short, should a Kantian accept the basic claim in Kant's argument?

Hence, Kant's argument for the wrongness of inflicting pain on animals rests on a claim that, in a world of Kantian moral agents, is demonstrably false. Therefore, the alternative analysis, being more plausible anyway, should be accepted. Since this alternative analysis has the same structure as the anti-abortion argument being defended here, we have further support for the argument for the immorality of abortion being defended in this essay.

Of course, this value of a future-like-ours argument, if sound, shows only that abortion is *prima facie* wrong, not that it is wrong in any and all circumstances. Since the loss of the future to a standard fetus, if killed, is, however, at least as great a loss as the loss of the future to a standard adult human being who is killed, abortion, like ordinary killing, could be justified only by the most compelling reasons. The loss of one's life is almost the greatest misfortune that can happen to one. Presumably abortion could be justified in some circumstances, only if the loss consequent on failing to abort would be at least as great. Accordingly, morally permissible abortions will be rare indeed unless, perhaps, they occur so early in pregnancy that a fetus is not yet definitely an individual. Hence, this argument should be taken as showing that abortion is presumptively very seriously wrong, where the presumption is very strong—as strong as the presumption that killing another adult human being is wrong.

. . .

V

In this essay, it has been argued that the correct ethic of the wrongness of killing can be extended to fetal life and used to show that there is a strong presumption that any abortion is morally impermissible. If the ethic of killing adopted here entails, however, that contraception is also seriously immoral, then there would appear to be a difficulty with the analysis of this essay.

But this analysis does not entail that contraception is wrong. Of course, contraception prevents the actualization of a possible future of value. Hence, it follows from the claim that futures of value should be maximized that contraception is *prima facie* immoral. This obligation to maximize does not exist, however; furthermore, nothing in the ethics of killing in this paper entails that it does. The ethics of killing in this essay would entail that contraception is wrong only if something were denied a human future of value by contraception. Nothing at all is denied such a future by contraception, however.

Candidates for a subject of harm by contraception fall into four categories: (1) some sperm or other, (2) some ovum or other, (3) a sperm and an ovum separately, and (4) a sperm and an ovum together. Assigning the harm to some sperm is utterly arbitrary, for no reason can be given for making a sperm the subject of harm rather than an ovum. Assigning the harm to some ovum is utterly arbitrary, for no reason can be given for making an ovum the subject of harm rather than a sperm. One might attempt to avoid these problems by insisting that contraception deprives both the sperm and the ovum separately of a valuable future like ours. On this alternative, too many futures are lost. Contraception was supposed to be wrong, because it deprived us of one future of value, not two. One might attempt to avoid this problem by holding that contraception deprives the combination of sperm and ovum of a valuable future like ours. But here the definite article misleads. At the time of contraception, there are hundreds of millions of sperm, one (released) ovum and millions of possible combinations of all of these. There is no actual combination at all. Is the subject of the loss to be a merely possible combination? Which one? This alternative does not yield an actual subject of harm either. Accordingly, the immorality of contraception is not entailed by the loss of a future-like-ours argument simply because there is no nonarbitrarily identifiable subject of the loss in the case of contraception.

VI

The purpose of this essay has been to set out an argument for the serious presumptive wrongness of abortion subject to the assumption that the moral permissibility of abortion stands or falls on the moral status of the fetus. Since a fetus possesses a property, the possession of which in adult human beings is sufficient to make killing an adult human being wrong, abortion is wrong. This way of dealing with the problem of abortion seems superior to other approaches to the ethics of abortion, because it rests on an ethics of killing which is close to self-evident, because the crucial morally relevant property clearly applies to fetuses, and because the argument avoids the usual equivocations on "human life," "human being," or "person." The argument rests neither on religious claims nor on Papal dogma. It is not subject to the objection of "speciesism." Its soundness is compatible with the moral permissibility of euthanasia and contraception. It deals with our intuitions concerning young children.

Finally, this analysis can be viewed as resolving a standard problem—indeed, *the* standard problem—concerning the ethics of abortion. Clearly, it is wrong to kill adult human beings. Clearly, it is not wrong to end the life of some arbitrarily chosen single human cell. Fetuses seem to be like arbitrarily chosen human cells in some respects and like adult humans in other respects. The problem of the ethics of abortion is the problem of determining the fetal property that settles this moral controversy. The thesis of this essay is that the problem of the ethics of abortion, so understood, is solvable.

QUESTIONS FOR REFLECTION

1. Marquis argues that usual anti-abortion and pro-choice arguments have symmetric problems and so are at a standoff. Review his reasoning. Do you agree?
2. Why, according to Marquis, is it wrong to kill an adult human being?
3. Marquis argues that it is wrong to kill a fetus for just the same reason that it is wrong to kill an adult. How does his argument go? Do you find it convincing?
4. Marquis compares his argument to one for the wrongness of the wanton infliction of pain on animals. Do you find the arguments analogous?
5. Many have objected that on Marquis's grounds, it would be wrong to kill a sperm cell or an egg, for they too have a human future. How might Marquis respond?
6. Are there genetic abnormalities or other factors that might lead us to conclude that a fetus does not have a "life like ours" in its future? If so, would it be wrong to abort such a fetus on Marquis's grounds?

ROSALIND HURSTHOUSE

Virtue Theory and Abortion

Rosalind Hursthouse is Professor of Philosophy at the University of Auckland, New Zealand. *(Source: from* Philosophy and Public Affairs *20 [1991], 223–246. Reprinted by permission of the publishers.)*

As everyone knows, the morality of abortion is commonly discussed in relation to just two considerations: first, and predominantly, the status of the fetus and whether or not it is the sort of thing that may or may not be innocuously or justifiably killed; and second, and less predominantly (when, that is, the discussion concerns the *morality* of abortion rather than the question of permissible legislation in a just society), women's rights. If one thinks within this familiar framework, one may well be puzzled about what virtue theory, as such, could contribute. Some people assume the discussion will be conducted solely in terms of what the virtuous agent would or would not do. Others assume that only justice, or at most justice and charity, will be applied to the issue, generating a discussion very similar to Judith Jarvis Thomson's.

Now if this is the way the virtue theorist's discussion of abortion is imagined to be, no wonder people think little of it. It seems obvious in advance that in any such discussion there must be either a great deal of extremely tendentious application of the virtue terms *just, charitable,* and so on or a lot of rhetorical appeal to "this is what only the virtuous agent knows." But these are caricatures; they fail to appreciate the way in which virtue theory quite transforms the discussion of abortion by dismissing the two familiar dominating considerations as, in a way, fundamentally irrelevant. In what way or ways, I hope to make both clear and plausible.

Let us first consider women's rights. Let me emphasize again that we are discussing the *morality* of abortion, not the rights and wrongs of laws prohibiting or permitting it. If we suppose that women do have a moral right to do as they choose with their own bodies, or, more particularly, to terminate their pregnancies, then it may well follow that a *law* forbidding abortion would be unjust. Indeed, even if they have no such right, such a law might be, as things stand at the moment, unjust, or impractical, or inhumane: on this issue I have nothing to say in this article. But, putting all questions about the justice or injustice of laws to one side, and supposing only that women have such a moral right, *nothing* follows from this supposition about the morality of abortion, according to virtue theory, once it is noted (quite generally, not with particular reference to abortion) that in exercising a moral right I can do something cruel, or callous, or selfish, light-minded, self-righteous, stupid, inconsiderate, disloyal, dishonest—that is, act viciously. Love and friendship do not survive their parties' constantly insisting on their rights, nor do people live well when they think that getting what they have a right to is of preeminent importance; they harm others, and they harm themselves. So whether women have a moral right to terminate their pregnancies is irrelevant within virtue theory, for it is irrelevant to the question "In having an abortion in these circumstances, would the agent be acting virtuously or viciously or neither?"

What about the consideration of the status of the fetus—what can virtue theory say about that? One might say that this issue is not in the province of any moral theory; it is a metaphysical question, and an extremely difficult one at that. Must virtue theory then wait upon metaphysics to come up with the answer?

At first sight it might seem so. For virtue is said to involve knowledge, and part of this knowledge consists in having the *right* attitude to things. "Right" here does not just mean "morally right" or "proper" or "nice" in the modern sense; it means "accurate, true." One cannot have the right or correct attitude to something if the attitude is based on or involves false beliefs. And this suggests that if the status of the fetus is relevant to the rightness or wrongness of abortion, its status must be known, as a truth, to the fully wise and virtuous person.

But the sort of wisdom that the fully virtuous person has is not supposed to be recondite; it does not call for fancy philosophical sophistication, and it does not depend upon, let alone wait upon, the discoveries of academic philosophers. And this entails the following, rather startling, conclusion: that the status of the fetus—that issue over which so much ink has been spilt—is, according to virtue theory, simply not relevant to the rightness or wrongness of abortion (within, that is, a secular morality).

Or rather, since that is clearly too radical a conclusion, it is in a sense relevant, but only in the sense that the familiar biological facts are relevant. By "the familiar biological facts" I mean the facts that most human societies are and have been familiar with—that, standardly (but not invariably), pregnancy occurs as the result of sexual intercourse, that it lasts about nine months, during which time the fetus grows and develops, that standardly it terminates in the birth of a living baby, and that this is how we all come to be.

It might be thought that this distinction—between the familiar biological facts and the status of the fetus—is a distinction without a difference. But this is not so. To attach relevance to the status of the fetus, in the sense in which virtue theory claims it is not relevant, is to be gripped by the conviction that we must go beyond the familiar biological facts, deriving some sort of conclusion from them, such as that the fetus has rights, or is not a person, or something similar. It is also to believe that this exhausts the relevance of the familiar biological facts, that all they are relevant to is the status of the fetus and whether or not it is the sort of thing that may or may not be killed.

These convictions, I suspect, are rooted in the desire to solve the problem of abortion by getting it to fall under some general rule such as "You ought not to kill anything with the right to life but may kill anything else." But they have resulted in what should surely strike any nonphilosopher as a most bizarre aspect of nearly all the current philosophical literature on abortion, namely, that, far from treating abortion as a unique moral problem, markedly unlike any other, nearly everything written on the status of the fetus and its bearing on the abortion issue would be consistent with the human reproductive facts' (to say nothing of family life) being totally different from what they are. Imagine that you are an alien extraterrestrial anthropologist who does not know that the human race is roughly 50 percent female and 50 percent male, or that our only (natural) form of reproduction involves heterosexual intercourse, viviparous birth, and the female's (and only the female's) being pregnant for nine months, or that females are capable of childbearing from late childhood to late middle age, or that childbearing is painful, dangerous, and emotionally charged—do you think you would pick up these facts from the hundreds of articles written on the status of the fetus? I am quite sure you would not. And that, I think, shows that the current philosophical literature on abortion has got badly out of touch with reality.

Now if we are using virtue theory, our first question is not "What do the familiar biological facts show—what can be derived from them about the status of the fetus?" but "How do these facts figure in the practical reasoning, actions and passions, thoughts and reactions, of the virtuous and the nonvirtuous? What is the mark of having the right attitude to these facts and what manifests having the wrong attitude to them?" This immediately makes essentially relevant not only all the facts about human reproduction I mentioned above, but a whole range of facts about our emotions in relation to them as well. I mean such facts as that human parents, both male and female, tend to care passionately about their offspring, and that family relationships are among the deepest and strongest in our lives—and, significantly, among the longest-lasting.

These facts make it obvious that pregnancy is not just one among many other physical conditions; and hence that anyone who genuinely believes that an abortion is comparable to a haircut or an appendectomy is mistaken. The fact that the premature termination of a pregnancy is, in some sense, the cutting off of a new human life, and thereby, like the procreation of a new human life, connects with all our thoughts about human life and death, parenthood, and family relationships, must make it a serious matter. To disregard this fact about it, to think of abortion as nothing but the killing of something that does not matter, or as nothing but the exercise of some right or rights one has, or as the incidental means to some desirable state of affairs, is to do something callous and light-minded, the sort of thing that no virtuous and wise person would do. It is to have the wrong attitude not only to fetuses, but more generally to human life and death, parenthood, and family relationships.

Although I say that the facts make this obvious, I know that this is one of my tendentious points. In partial support of it I note that even the most dedicated proponents of the view that deliberate abortion is just like an appendectomy or haircut rarely hold the same view of spontaneous abortion, that is, miscarriage. It is not so tendentious of me to claim that to react to people's grief over miscarriage by saying, or even thinking, "What a fuss about nothing!" would be callous and light-minded, whereas to try to laugh someone out of grief over an appendectomy scar or a botched haircut would not be. It is hard to give this point due prominence within act-centered theories, for the inconsistency is an inconsistency in attitude about the seriousness of loss of life, not in beliefs about which acts are right or wrong. Moreover, an act-centered theorist may say, "Well, there is nothing wrong with *thinking* 'What a fuss about nothing!' as long as you do not say it and hurt the person who is grieving. And besides, we cannot be held responsible for our thoughts, only for the intentional actions they give rise to." But the character traits that virtue theory emphasizes are not simply dispositions to intentional actions, but a seamless disposition to certain actions and passions, thoughts and reactions.

To say that the cutting off of a human life is always a matter of some seriousness, at any stage, is not to deny the relevance of gradual fetal development. Notwithstanding the well-worn point that clear boundary lines cannot be drawn, our emotions and attitudes regarding the fetus do change as it develops, and again when it is born, and indeed further as the baby grows. Abortion for shallow reasons in the later stages is much more shocking than abortion for the same reasons in the early stages in a way that matches the fact that deep grief over miscarriage in the later stages is more appropriate than it is over miscarriage in the earlier stages (when, that is, the grief is solely about the loss of *this* child, not about, as might be the case, the loss of one's only hope of having a child or of having one's husband's child). Imagine (or recall) a woman who already has children; she had not intended to have more, but finds herself unexpectedly pregnant. Though contrary to her plans, the pregnancy, once established as a fact, is welcomed—and then she loses the embryo almost immediately. If this were bemoaned as a tragedy, it would, I think, be a misapplication of the concept of what is tragic. But it may still properly be mourned as a loss. The grief is expressed in such terms as "I shall always wonder how she or he would have turned out" or "When I look at the others, I shall think, 'How different their lives would have been if this other one had been part of them.'" It would, I take it, be callous and light-minded to say, or think, "Well, she has already *got* four children; what's the problem?"; it would be neither, nor arrogantly intrusive in the case of a close friend, to try to correct prolonged mourning by saying, "I know it's sad, but it's not a tragedy; rejoice in the ones you have." The application of *tragic* becomes more appropriate as the fetus grows, for the mere fact that one has lived with it for longer, conscious of its existence, makes a difference. To shrug off an early abortion is understandable just because it is very hard to be fully conscious of the fetus's existence in the early stages and hence hard to appreciate that an early abortion is the destruction of life. It is particularly hard for the young and inexperienced to appreciate this, because appreciation of it usually comes only with experience.

I do not mean "with the experience of having an abortion" (though that may be part of it) but, quite generally, "with the experience of life." Many women who have borne children contrast their later pregnancies with their first successful one, saying that in the later ones they were conscious of a new life growing in them from very early on. And, more generally, as one reaches the age at which the next generation is coming up close behind one, the counterfactuals "If I, or she, had had an abortion, Alice, or Bob, would not have been born" acquire a significant application, which casts a new light on the conditionals "If I or Alice have an abortion then some Caroline or Bill will not be born."

The fact that pregnancy is not just one among many physical conditions does not mean that one can never regard it in that light without manifesting a vice. When women are in very poor physical health, or worn out from childbearing, or forced to do very physically demanding jobs, then they cannot be described as self-indulgent, callous, irresponsible, or light-minded if they seek abortions mainly with a view to avoiding pregnancy as the physical condition that it is. To go through with a pregnancy when one is utterly exhausted, or when one's job consists of crawling along tunnels hauling coal, as many women in the nineteenth century were obliged to do, is perhaps heroic, but people who do not achieve heroism are not necessarily vicious. That they can view the pregnancy only as eight months of misery, followed by hours if not days of agony and exhaustion, and abortion only as the blessed escape from this prospect, is entirely understandable and does not manifest any lack of serious respect for human life or a shallow attitude to motherhood. What it does show is that something is terribly amiss in the conditions of their lives, which make it so hard to recognize pregnancy and childbearing as the good that they can be.

In relation to this last point I should draw attention to the way in which virtue theory has a sort of built-in indexicality. Philosophers arguing against anything remotely resembling a belief in the sanctity of life (which the above claims clearly embody) frequently appeal to the existence of other communities in which abortion and infanticide are practiced. We should not automatically assume that it is impossible that some other communities could be morally inferior to our own; maybe some are, or have been, precisely insofar as their members are, typically, callous or light-minded or unjust. But in communities in which life is a great deal tougher for everyone than it is in ours, having the right attitude to human life and death, parenthood, and family relationships might well manifest itself in ways that are unlike ours. When it is essential to survival that most members of the community fend for themselves at a very young age or work during most of their waking hours, selective abortion or infanticide might be practiced either as a form of genuine euthanasia or for the sake of the community and not, I think, be thought callous or light-minded. But this does not make everything all right; as before, it shows that there is something amiss with the conditions of their lives, which are making it impossible for them to live really well.

The foregoing discussion, insofar as it emphasizes the right attitude to human life and death, parallels to a certain extent those standard discussions of abortion that concentrate on it solely as an issue of killing. But it does not, as those discussions do, gloss over the fact, emphasized by those who discuss the morality of abortion in terms of women's rights, that abortion, wildly unlike any other form of killing, is the termination of a pregnancy, which is a condition of a woman's body and results in *her* having a child if it is not aborted. This fact is given due recognition not by appeal to women's rights but by emphasizing the relevance of the familiar biological and psychological facts and their connection with having the right attitude to parenthood and family relationships. But it may well be thought that failing to bring in women's rights still leaves some important aspects of the problem of abortion untouched.

Speaking in terms of women's rights, people sometimes say things like, "Well, it's her life you're talking about too, you know; she's got a right to her own life, her own happiness." And the discussion stops there. But in the context of virtue theory, given that we are particularly concerned with what constitutes a good human life, with what true happiness or *eudaimonia* is, this is no place to stop. We go on to ask, "And is this life of hers a good one? Is she living well?"

If we are to go on to talk about good human lives, in the context of abortion, we have to bring in our thoughts about the value of love and family life, and our proper emotional development through a natural life cycle. The familiar facts support the view that parenthood in general, and motherhood and childbearing in particular, are intrinsically worthwhile, are among the things that can be correctly thought to be partially constitutive of a flourishing human life. If this is right, then a woman who opts for not being a mother (at all, or again, or now) by opting for abortion may thereby be manifesting a flawed grasp of what her life should be, and be about—a grasp that is childish, or grossly materialistic, or shortsighted, or shallow.

I said "*may* thereby": this *need* not be so. Consider, for instance, a woman who has already had several children and fears that to have another will seriously affect her capacity to be a good mother to the ones she has—she does not show a lack of appreciation of the intrinsic value of being a parent by opting for abortion. Nor does a woman who has been a good mother and is approaching the age at which she may be looking forward to being a good grandmother. Nor does a woman who discovers that her pregnancy may well kill her, and opts for abortion and adoption. Nor, necessarily, does a woman who has decided to lead a life centered around some other worthwhile activity or activities with which motherhood would compete.

People who are childless by choice are sometimes described as "irresponsible," or "selfish," or "refusing to grow up," or "not knowing what life is about." But one can hold that having children is intrinsically worthwhile without endorsing this, for we are, after all, in the happy position of there being more worthwhile things to do than can be fitted into one lifetime. Parenthood, and motherhood in particular, even if granted to be intrinsically worthwhile, undoubtedly take up a lot of one's adult life, leaving no room for some other worthwhile pursuits. But some women who choose abortion rather than have their first child, and some men who encourage their partners to choose abortion, are not avoiding parenthood for the sake of other worthwhile pursuits, but for the worthless one of "having a good time," or for the pursuit of some false vision of the ideals of freedom or self-realization. And some others who say "I am not ready for parenthood yet" are making some sort of mistake about the extent to which one can manipulate the circumstances of one's life so as to make it fulfill some dream that one has. Perhaps one's dream is to have two perfect children, a girl and a boy, within a perfect marriage, in financially secure circumstances, with an interesting job of one's own. But to care too much about that dream, to demand of life that it give it to one and act accordingly, may be both greedy and foolish, and is to run the risk of missing out on happiness entirely. Not only may fate make the dream impossible, or destroy it, but one's own attachment to it may make it impossible. Good marriages, and the most promising children, can be destroyed by just one adult's excessive demand for perfection.

Once again, this is not to deny that girls may quite properly say "I am not ready for motherhood yet," especially in our society, and, far from manifesting irresponsibility or light-mindedness, show an appropriate modesty or humility, or a fearfulness that does not amount to cowardice. However, even when the decision to have an abortion is the right decision—one that does not itself fall under a vice-related term and thereby one that the perfectly virtuous could recommend—it does not follow that there is no sense in which having the abortion is wrong, or guilt inappropriate. For, by virtue of the fact that a human life has been cut short, some evil has probably been brought about, and that circumstances make the decision to bring about some evil the right decision will be a ground for guilt if getting into those circumstances in the first place itself manifested a flaw in character.

What "gets one into those circumstances" in the case of abortion is, except in the case of rape, one's sexual activity and one's choices, or the lack of them, about one's sexual partner and about contraception. The virtuous woman (which here of course does not mean simply "chaste woman" but "woman with the virtues") has such character traits as strength, independence, resoluteness, decisiveness, self-confidence, responsibility, serious-mindedness, and self-determination—and no one, I think, could deny that many women become pregnant in circumstances in which they cannot welcome or cannot face the thought of having *this* child precisely because they lack one or some of these character traits. So even in the cases where the decision to have an abortion is the right one, it can still be the reflection of a moral failing—not because the decision itself is weak or cowardly or irresolute or irresponsible or light-minded, but because lack of the requisite opposite of these failings landed one in the circumstances in the first place. Hence the common universalized claim that guilt and remorse are never appropriate emotions about an abortion is denied. They may be appropriate, and appropriately inculcated, even when the decision was the right one.

Another motivation for bringing women's rights into the discussion may be to attempt to correct the implication, carried by the killing-centered approach, that insofar as abortion is wrong, it is a wrong that only women do, or at least (given the preponderance of male doctors) that only women instigate. I do not myself believe that we can thus escape the fact that nature bears harder on women than it does on men, but virtue theory can certainly correct many of the injustices that the emphasis on women's rights is rightly concerned about. With very little amendment, everything that has been said above applies to boys and men too. Although the abortion decision is, in a natural sense, the woman's decision, proper to her, boys and men are often party to it, for well or ill, and even when they are not, they are bound to have been party to the circumstances that brought it up. No less than girls and women, boys and men can, in their actions, manifest self-centeredness, callousness, and light-mindedness about life and parenthood in relation to abortion. They can be self-centered or courageous about the possibility of disability in their offspring; they need to reflect on their sexual activity and their choices, or the lack of them, about their sexual partner and contraception; they need to grow up and take responsibility for their own actions and life in relation to fatherhood. If it is true, as I maintain, that insofar as motherhood is intrinsically worthwhile, being a mother is an important purpose in women's lives, being a father (rather than a mere generator) is an important purpose in men's lives as well, and it is adolescent of men to turn a blind eye to this and pretend that they have many more important things to do.

QUESTIONS FOR REFLECTION

1. Why does Hursthouse believe that appeals to women's rights cannot resolve the moral issue of abortion?
2. Hursthouse rejects arguments that depend on the moral standing of the fetus that go beyond familiar biological facts. Why?
3. Why is abortion a matter of profound moral significance, according to Hursthouse?
4. Hursthouse worries that an alien reading the philosophical literature on abortion would have no idea what the basic biological facts of human reproduction are. What, in her view, does that show about the literature?
5. Hursthouse shifts the question from "What do the biological facts show?" to "How do the biological facts figure in practical reasoning?" Explain the difference. Why is it important?
6. What do reactions to miscarriages tell us about the moral character of abortion, in Hursthouse's view? Do you agree?
7. List some vice terms that might be applied to abortions. What are some paradigm cases of abortions that exemplify these vices?
8. Are there virtuous abortions? If so, what are they like? What are some virtue terms that might apply to them? If not, why not?

FRANCIS J. BECKWITH

Personal Bodily Rights, Abortion, and Unplugging the Violinist

Francis J. Beckwith is professor of Philosophy & Church-State Studies at Baylor University. (Source: from International Philosophical Quarterly 32 *[1992]: 105–118. Reprinted by permission of the publishers.)*

Those who argue against abortion-rights (or *prolife* advocates) often try to show that the unborn entity during some period of its development is fully human (or "a person"), and hence, elective abortion, which entails the death of this unborn entity, is a serious moral wrong. Some defenders of abortion-rights (or *prochoice* advocates), however, do not see the status of the unborn as the decisive factor in whether or not abortion is morally justified. They argue that the unborn's presence in the pregnant woman's body entails a conflict of rights. Therefore, the unborn, regardless of whether or not it is fully human and has a full right to life, cannot use the body of another against her will. Hence, a pregnant woman's removal of an unborn entity from her body, even though it will probably result in its death, is no more immoral than an ordinary person's refusal to donate his kidney to another in need of one, even though this refusal will probably result in the death of the prospective recipient.

The most famous and influential argument from rights is the one presented by Judith Jarvis Thomson. Prior to analyzing that argument, however, I want to respond to two popular arguments which are much less sophisticated than Professor Thomson's, although they carry much rhetorical weight in the popular debate. These arguments, unlike Thomson's, do not assume for the sake of argument that the unborn is fully human, but merely ignore altogether the question of the unborn's full humanness.

I. Argument for a Woman's Right Over Her Own Body

This argument asserts that because a woman has a right to control her own body, she therefore has a right to undergo an abortion for any reason she deems fit. Although it is not obvious that either the law or sound ethical reasoning supports such a strong view of personal autonomy (e.g., laws against prostitution and suicide), this abortion-rights argument still logically fails even if we assume that such a strong view of personal autonomy is correct.

First, the unborn entity within the pregnant woman's body is not *part* of her body. The conceptus is a genetically distinct entity with its own individual gender, blood type, bone-structure and genetic code. Although the unborn entity is *attached* to her mother, it is not part of her mother. To say that the unborn entity is part of her mother is to claim that the mother possesses four legs, two heads, two noses, and with the case of a male conceptus, a penis and two testicles. Furthermore, since scientists have been able to achieve conception in a petri dish in the case of the "test-tube" baby, and this conceptus if it has white parents can be transferred to the body of a black woman and be born white, we know conclusively that the unborn is not part of the pregnant woman's body. Certainly a woman has a right to control her own body, but the unborn entity is not *part* of her body. Hence, abortion is not justified since no one's right to personal autonomy is so strong that it permits the arbitrary execution of others.

Second, this abortion-rights argument is guilty of special pleading. The concept of a personal right over one's own body presupposes the existence of a human person who possesses such a right. Such a right also presupposes that this right to personal autonomy should not interfere with another person's identical right. This is why smoking is being prohibited in more and more public places. Many studies have shown conclusively that a smoker's habit not only affects his own lungs, but also the lungs of others who choose not to smoke. The smoker's "secondary smoke" can cause the non-smoker to be ill and quite possibly acquire lung cancer if he is exposed to such smoke over a long period of time. Since the non-smoker has a personal right over his own body, and he chooses not to fill it with nicotine, the smoker's personal right to smoke and fill his own body with nicotine is limited by the non-smoker's personal right to remain healthy. This is because in the process of smoking the smoker passes on harmful secondary smoke to the unwilling non-smoker.

Suppose a smoker, in arguing against a prohibition of smoking in public places, continually appeals to his "personal right" to control his own body. And suppose he dismisses out of hand any counter-argument which appeals to the possible existence of other persons (non-smokers) whose rights his actions may obstruct. This sort of argumentation would be a case of *special pleading,* a fallacy which occurs when someone selects pieces of evidence which confirm his position (in this case, the smoker's legitimate right to personal autonomy) and ignores counter-examples which conflict with it (in this case, the non-smoker's legitimate right to personal autonomy). Therefore, in terms of the abortion issue, when the abortion-rights advocate appeals to a woman's right to control her own body while ignoring the possibility that this control may entail the death of another, he is guilty of selecting principles that support his position (i.e., every person has a right to personal autonomy) while ignoring principles which conflict with it (i.e., every person has an obligation not to kill another). Thus the abortion-rights advocate is guilty of special pleading.

Of course, if the unborn entity is not fully human, I believe that this abortion-rights argument has compelling force. But this means that one begs the question when one uses this argument without first demonstrating that the unborn entity is not fully human. Professor Baruch Brody adds to this observation that although "it is surely true that one way in which women have been oppressed is by their being denied authority over their own bodies . . . , it seems to be that, as the struggle is carried on for meaningful amelioration of such oppression, it ought not to be carried so far that it violates the steady responsibilities all people have to one another." To cite a number of examples, "parents may not desert their children, one class may not oppress another, one race or nation may not exploit another. For parents, powerful groups in society, races or nations in ascendancy, there are penalties [i.e., hardships] for refraining from these wrong actions, but those penalties can in no way be taken as the justification for such wrong actions. Similarly, if the fetus is a human being, the penalty of carrying it cannot, I believe, be used as justification for destroying it."

II. Argument from Abortion Being Safer Than Childbirth

This argument attempts to show that the pregnant woman has no moral obligation to carry her unborn offspring to term, regardless of whether or not it is fully human. The abortion-rights advocate argues that childbirth is an act which is not morally obligatory on the part of the pregnant woman, since an abortion is statistically less dangerous than childbirth. The statistic often quoted to support this argument is one found in the most recent edition of the *American Medical Association Encyclopedia of Medicine:* "Mortality is less than one per 100,000 when abortion is performed before the 13th week, rising to three per 100,000 after the 13th week. (For comparison, maternal mortality for full-term pregnancy is nine per 100,000.)"

This argument can be outlined in the following way.

1. Among moral acts one is not morally obligated to perform are those which can endanger one's life (e.g., the man who dove into the Potomac in the middle of winter to save the survivors of a plane crash).
2. Childbirth is more life-threatening than having an abortion.
3. Therefore, childbirth is an act one is not morally obligated to perform.
4. Therefore, abortion is justified.

The problem with this argument lies in the inference from (2) to (3). First, assuming that childbirth is on the average more life-threatening than abortion, it does not follow that abortion is justified in every case. The fact that one act, A, is more life-threatening on the average than another act, B, does not mean that one is not justified or obligated to perform A in *specific* situations where there is no prima facie reason to believe that A would result in death or severe physical impairment unless one resorts to B. To use an uncontroversial example, it is probably on the average less life-threatening to stay at home than to leave home and buy groceries (e.g., one can be killed in a car crash, purchase and take tainted Tylenol, or be murdered by a mugger), yet it seems foolish, not to mention counter-intuitive, always to act in every instance on the basis of that average. This is a form of the informal fallacy of division, which occurs when someone erroneously argues that what is true of a whole (the average) must also be true of its parts (every individual situation). One would commit this fallacy if one argued that because Beverly Hills is a wealthier city than Barstow every individual person who lives in Beverly Hills is wealthier than every individual person who lives in Barstow.

Second, one can also imagine a situation in which one is obligated to perform a particular *moral* action although there is statistically more risk in performing it than abstaining from it. That is to say, one can challenge the inference from (2) to (3) by pointing out that just because an act, X, is "more dangerous" *relative* to another act, Y, does not mean that one is *not* morally obligated to perform X. For example, it would be statistically "more dangerous" for me (a swimmer) to dive into a swimming pool to save my wife (a non-swimmer) from drowning than it would be for me to abstain from acting. Yet this does not mean that I am not morally obligated to save my wife's life. Sometimes my moral obligation is such that it *outweighs* the *relative* danger I avoid by not acting. One could then argue that although childbirth may be "more dangerous" than abortion, the special moral obligation one has to one's offspring far outweighs the relative danger one avoids by not acting on that moral obligation.

Of course, if a *specific* act, X, is *significantly* dangerous (i.e., there is a good chance that one will die or be severely harmed if one acts)—such as the act performed by that one man who dove into the freezing Potomac River in the dead of winter to save the survivors of an airplane crash—then it would seem that an individual would not be obligated to perform X. But if one had chosen to perform X, one would be performing an act of exceptional morality (what ethicists call "a supererogatory act"), although if one had refrained from X one would not be considered a bad or evil person. In light of the above observations, the abortion-rights argument in question can be strengthened if changed in the following way:

1. Among moral acts one is not morally obligated to *perform* are those which can endanger one's life.
2. A particular instance of childbirth, X, is more life-threatening to the pregnant woman than having an abortion.
3. Therefore, X is an act one is not morally obligated to perform.
4. Therefore, not-X via abortion is justified.

Although avoiding the pitfalls of the first argument, this one *does not* support the abortion-rights position. For it is perfectly consistent with the prolife assertion that abortion is justified if it is employed in order to save the life of the mother. Therefore, whether or not abortion is statistically safer than childbirth is irrelevant to whether or not abortion is justified in particular cases where sound medical diagnosis indicates that childbirth will pose no threat to the mother's life.

One other observation can be made about the argument from abortion being safer than childbirth. The AMA statistics are misused and do not really establish the abortion-rights position. The above statistics claim that the mortality rate for a woman in childbirth is 9 per 100,000 while mortality is less than 1 per 100,000 when abortion is performed before the 13th week, increasing to 3 per 100,000 after the 13th week. This is why abortion-rights advocates often claim that a first trimester abortion is nine times safer than childbirth. Although technically true if one assumes that the statistics are accurate, it is statistically insignificant. This becomes apparent when one converts the above "odds" into percentages. If the mortality of childbirth is 9 per 100,000, then a woman has a 99.991% chance of surviving. If the mortality of a first trimester abortion is 1 per 100,000, then a woman has a 99.999% chance of surviving. But the statistical difference between 99.991% and 99.999% (00.008%) is moot, especially if one considers the complex nature of both childbirth and abortion, about which there are so many variables which may account for the small difference in the mortality rates.

Considering that the supposed "fact" that childbirth is riskier than abortion played a substantial role in the U.S. Supreme Court opinions which made abortion legal, *Roe* v. *Wade* (410 U.S. 113 [1973]) and *Doe* v. *Bolton* (410 U.S. 179 [1973]), the exposing of the logical flaws of this claim helps to undermine the foundation of the Court's opinions.

III. Argument from Unplugging the Violinist

In an article, which by 1986 was "the most widely reprinted essay in all of contemporary philosophy," Professor Judith Jarvis Thomson presents a philosophically sophisticated version of the argument from a woman's right to control her body. Thomson argues that even if the unborn entity has a right to life, this does not mean that a woman must be forced to use her bodily organs to sustain its life. Just as one does not have a right to use another's kidney if one's kidney has failed, the unborn entity, although having a basic right to life, does not have a right to life so strong that it outweighs the pregnant woman's right to personal bodily autonomy.

It should be noted that Thomson's argument was not used in any of the landmark Supreme Court decisions which have sided with the abortion-rights position, such as *Roe* v. *Wade* (1973) or *Doe* v. *Bolton* (1973). Recently, however, Harvard law professor Laurence Tribe, whose influence on the Court's liberal wing is well-known, has suggested that it should have used Thomson's argument. Tribe writes: ". . . [P]erhaps the Supreme Court's opinion in *Roe*, by gratuitously insisting that the fetus *cannot* be deemed a person, needlessly insulted and alienated those for whom the view that the fetus is a person represents a fundamental article of faith or a bedrock personal commitment. . . . The Court should have instead said: Even if the fetus *is* a person, our Constitution forbids compelling a woman to carry it for nine months and become a mother."

1. Presentation of the Argument

This argument is called "the argument from unplugging the violinist" because of a story Thomson uses in order to illustrate her position:

> You wake up in the morning and find yourself back to back in bed with an unconscious violinist. A famous unconscious violinist. He has been found to have a fatal kidney ailment, and the Society of Music Lovers has canvassed all the available medical records and found that you alone have the right blood type to help. They have therefore kidnapped you, and last night the violinist's circulatory system was plugged into yours, so that your kidneys can be used to extract poisons from his blood as well as your own. The director of the hospital now tells you, "Look we're sorry the Society of Music Lovers did this to you—we would never have permitted it if we had known. But still, they did it, and the violinist now is plugged into you. To unplug you would be to kill him. But never mind, it's only for nine months. By then he will have recovered from his ailment, and can safely be unplugged from you." Is it morally incumbent on you to accede to this situation? No doubt it would be very nice of you if you did, a great kindness. But do you *have* to accede to it? What if it were not nine months, but nine years? Or still longer? What if the director of the hospital says, "Tough luck, I agree, but you've now got to stay in bed, with the violinist plugged into you, for the rest of your life. Because remember this. All persons have a right to life, and violinists are persons. Granted you have a right to decide what happens in and to your body, but

a person's right to life outweighs your right to decide what happens in and to your body. So you cannot ever be unplugged from him." I imagine that you would regard this as outrageous. . . .

Thomson concludes that by use of the violinist illustration she is "only arguing that having a right to life does not guarantee having either a right to be given the use of or a right to be allowed continued use of another person's body—even if one needs it for life itself." Thomson anticipates several objections to her argument, and in the process of responding to them further clarifies it. It is not important, however, that we go over these clarifications now, for some are not germane to the prolife position I am defending in this article, and the remaining will be dealt with in the following critique.

Although I believe that it would be difficult to find an ethicist who would seriously defend the position that it is *not* prima facie wrong to kill innocent human beings, Thomson's argument poses a special difficulty because she believes that since pregnancy constitutes an infringement on the pregnant woman's personal rights by the unborn entity, the ordinary abortion, although it results in the death of an innocent human being, is not prima facie wrong. I believe, however, that there are many flaws in Thomson's use of the violinist analogy.

2. A Critique of Thomson's Argument

I believe that there at least six problems with Thomson's argument. These can be put into two categories: ethical and ideological. First, under the ethical category, there are at least four problems with Thomson's argument:

1. *Thomson assumes volunteerism.* By using the violinist story as a paradigm for all relationships, which implies that moral obligations must be voluntarily accepted in order to have moral force, Thomson mistakenly infers that all true moral obligations to one's offspring are voluntary. But consider the following story. Suppose a couple has a sexual encounter which is fully protected by several forms of birth-control (condom, the Pill, IUD, etc.), but nevertheless results in conception. Instead of getting an abortion, the mother of the conceptus decides to bring it to term although the father is unaware of this decision. After the birth of the child the mother pleads with the father for child support. Because he refuses, she seeks legal action and takes him to court. Although he took every precaution to avoid fatherhood, thus showing that he did not wish to accept such a status, according to nearly all child support laws in this United States he would still be obligated to pay support *precisely because* of his relationship to this child. As Michael Levin points out, "All child-support laws make the parental body an indirect resource for the child. If the father is a construction worker, the state will intervene unless some of his calories he expends lifting equipment go to providing food for his children."

But this obligatory relationship is not based strictly on *biology*, for this would make sperm-donors morally responsible for children conceived by their seed. Rather, the father's responsibility for his offspring stems from the fact that he engaged in an act, sexual intercourse, which he fully realized could result in the creation of another human being, although he took every precaution to avoid such a result. This is not an unusual way to frame moral obligations, for we hold drunk people whose driving results in manslaughter responsible for their actions, even if they did not *intend* to kill someone prior to becoming intoxicated. Such special obligations, although not *directly* undertaken *voluntarily*, are necessary in any civilized culture in order to preserve the rights of the vulnerable, the weak, and the young, who can offer very little in exchange for the rights bestowed upon them by the strong, the powerful, and the post-uterine in Thomson's moral universe of the social contract. Thus, Thomson is simply wrong, in addition to ignoring the *natural* relationship between sexual intercourse and human reproduction when she claims that if a couple has "taken all reasonable precautions against having a child, they do not by virtue of their biological relationship to the child who comes into existence have a special responsibility for it" since "surely we do not have any such 'special responsibility' for a person unless we have assumed it, explicitly or implicitly." Hence, instead of providing reasons for rejecting any special responsibilities for one's offspring, Thomson simply dismisses the concept altogether.

2. *Thomson's argument is fatal to family morality.* It follows from the first criticism that Thomson's volunteerism is fatal to family morality, which has as one of its central beliefs that an individual has special

personal obligations to his offspring and family which he does not have to other persons. Although Thomson may not consider such a fatality as being all that terrible, since she may buy into the feminist dogma that the traditional family is "oppressive" to women, a great number of ordinary men and women, who have found joy, happiness, and love in family life, find Thomson's volunteerism to be counter-intuitive. Philosopher Christina Sommers has come to a similar conclusion:

> For it [the volunteerist thesis] means that there is no such thing as filial [sic] duty per se, no such thing as the special duty of mother to child, and generally no such thing as morality of special family or kinship relations. All of which is contrary to what people think. For most people think that we do owe special debts to our parents even though we have not voluntarily assumed our obligations to them. Most people think that what we owe to our children does not have its origin in any voluntary undertaking, explicit or implicit, that we have made to them. And "preanalytically," many people believe that we owe special consideration to our siblings even at times when we may not *feel* very friendly to them. . . . The idea that to be committed to an individual is to have made a voluntarily implicit or explicit commitment to that individual is generally fatal to family morality. For it looks upon the network of felt obligation and expectation that binds family members as a sociological phenomenon that is without presumptive moral force. The social critics who hold this view of family obligation usually are aware that promoting it in public policy must further the disintegration of the traditional family as an institution. But whether they deplore the disintegration or welcome it, they are bound in principle to abet it.

3. *A case can be made that the unborn does have a prima facie right to her mother's body.* Assuming that there is such a thing as a special parental obligation, which does *not* have to be voluntarily accepted in order to have moral weight, it is not obvious that the unborn entity in ordinary circumstances (that is, with the exception of when the mother's life is in significant danger) *does not* have a natural prima facie claim to her mother's body. There are several reasons to suppose that the unborn entity does have such a natural claim:

a. Unlike Thomson's violinist who is artificially attached to another person in order to save his life and is therefore not naturally dependent on any particular human being, the unborn entity is a human being who is by her very nature *dependent* on her mother, for this is how human beings are at this stage of their development.

b. This period of a human being's *natural* development occurs in the womb. This is the journey which *we all* must take and is a necessary condition for *any* human being's post uterine existence. And this fact alone brings out the most glaring disanalogy between the violinist and the unborn: the womb is the unborn's natural environment whereas being artificially hooked-up to a stranger is not the natural environment for the violinist. It would seem, then, that the unborn has a prima facie natural claim upon its mother's body. This brings us to my third point.

c. This same entity, when it becomes a newborn, has a natural claim upon her parents to care for her, regardless of whether her parents "wanted" her (see the above story of the irresponsible father). This is why we prosecute child-abusers, people who throw their babies in trash cans, and parents who abandon their children. Although it should not be ignored that pregnancy and childbirth entail certain emotional, physical, and financial sacrifices on the part of the pregnant woman, these sacrifices are also endemic of *parenthood* in general (which ordinarily lasts much longer than nine months), and do not seem to justify the execution of troublesome infants and younger children whose existence entails a natural claim to certain financial and bodily goods which are under the ownership of their parents.

d. If the unborn entity is fully human, as Thomson is willing to grant, why should the unborn's natural prima facie claim to her parents' goods differ before birth? Of course, a court will not force a parent to donate a kidney to her dying offspring, but this sort of dependence on the parent's body is highly unusual and is not part of the ordinary obligations associated with the *natural* process of human development, just as in the case of the violinist's artificial dependency on the reluctant music lover.

As Professor Schwarz points out: "So, the very thing that makes it plausible to say that the person in bed with the violinist has no duty to sustain him; namely, that he is a stranger unnaturally hooked up to him, is precisely what is absent in the case of the mother and her child." That is to say, the mother "does have an obligation to take care of her child, to sustain her, to protect her, and especially, to let her live in the only place where she can now be protected, nourished, and allowed to grow, namely the womb."

Now if Thomson responds to this by saying that birth is the threshold at which parents become fully responsible, then she has begged the question, for her violinist argument was supposed to show us *why* there is no parental responsibility before birth. That is to say, Thomson can not appeal to birth as the decisive moment at which parents become responsible in order to prove that birth is the time at which parents become responsible.

It is evident that Thomson's violinist illustration undermines the deep *natural bond* between mother and child by making it seem no different than two strangers artificially hooked-up to each other so that one can "steal" the service of the other's kidneys. Never has something so human, so natural, so beautiful, and so wonderfully demanding of our human creativity and love been reduced to such a brutal caricature.

I am not saying that the unborn entity has an *absolute* natural claim to her mother's body, but simply that she has a *prima facie* natural claim. For one can easily imagine a situation in which this natural claim is outweighed by other important prima facie values, such as when a pregnancy significantly endangers the mother's life. Since the continuation of such a pregnancy would most likely entail the death of both mother and child, and since it is better that one human should live rather than two die, I believe that terminating such a pregnancy via abortion is morally justified.

Now someone may respond to the above four criticisms by agreeing that Thomson's violinist illustration may not apply in cases of ordinary sexual intercourse, but only in cases in which pregnancy results from rape or incest, although it should be noted that Thomson herself does not press the rape argument. She writes: "Surely the question of whether you have a right to life at all, or of how you have it, shouldn't turn on the question of whether or not you are the product of rape."

But those who do press the rape argument may choose to argue in the following way. Just as the sperm-donor is not responsible for how his sperm is used or what results from its use (e.g., it may be stolen, or an unmarried woman may purchase it, inseminate herself, and give birth to a child), the raped woman, who did not voluntarily engage in intercourse, cannot be held responsible for the unborn human who is living inside her.

But there is a problem with this analogy: The sperm-donor's relinquishing of responsibility *does not result in the death of a human life* while the raped woman's does. The following story should help to illustrate the differences and similarities between these two cases.

Suppose that the sperm donated by the sperm-donor was stolen by an unscrupulous physician and inseminated into a woman. Although he is not morally responsible for the child which results from such an insemination, he is nevertheless forced by an unjust court to pay a large monthly sum for child support, a sum so large that it may drive him into serious debt, maybe even bankruptcy. This would be similar to the woman who became pregnant as a result of rape. She was unjustly violated and is supporting a human being against her will at an emotional and financial cost. Is it morally right for the sperm-donor to kill the child he is supporting in order to allegedly right the wrong which has been committed against him? Not at all, because such an act would be murder. Now if we assume, as does Thomson, that the raped woman is carrying a being who is fully human, her killing of the unborn entity by abortion, except if the pregnancy has a strong possibility of endangering her life, would be as unjust as the sperm-donor killing the child he is unjustly forced to support. As the victimized man may rightly refuse to pay the child support, the raped woman may rightly refuse to bring up her child after the pregnancy has to come to term. She can choose to put the child up for adoption. But in both cases, the killing of the child is not morally justified. Although neither the sperm-donor nor the rape victim has the same special obligation to their biological offspring as does the couple who voluntarily engaged in intercourse with no direct intention to produce a child, it seems that the more general obligation not to kill directly another human being does apply, which is supported by my fourth ethical objection.

4. *Thomson ignores the fact that abortion is indeed killing and not merely the withholding of treatment.* Thomson makes an excellent point in her use of the violinist

story, namely, that there are times when withholding and/or withdrawing of medical treatment is morally justified. For instance, I am not morally obligated to donate my kidney to Fred, my next door neighbor, simply because he needs a kidney in order to live. In other words, I am not obligated to risk my life so that Fred may live a few years longer. Fred should not expect that of me. If, however, I donate one of my kidneys to Fred, I will have acted above and beyond the call of duty, since I will have performed a supererogatory moral act. But this case is not analogous to pregnancy and abortion.

Levin argues that there is an essential disanalogy between abortion and the unplugging of the violinist. In the case of the violinist (as well as my relationship to Fred's welfare), "the person who withdraws [or withholds] his assistance is not completely responsible for the dependency on him of the person who is about to die, while the mother *is* completely responsible for the dependency of her fetus on her. When one is completely responsible for dependence, refusal to continue to aid is indeed killing." For example, "if a woman brings a newborn home from the hospital, puts it in its crib and refuses to feed it until it has starved to death, it would be absurd to say that she simply refused to assist it and had done nothing for which she should be criminally liable." In other words, just as the withholding of food kills the child after birth, in the case of abortion, it is the *abortion* which kills the child. In neither case is there any ailment from which the child suffers and which highly invasive medical treatment, with the cooperation of another's bodily organs, is necessary in order to cure this ailment and save the child's life.

Or consider a case parallel to rape. Suppose a person returns home after work to find a baby at his doorstep (like in the film with Tom Selleck, Ted Danson, and Steve Guttenberg, *Three Men and a Baby*). Suppose that no one else is able to take care of the child, but this person only has to take care of the child for nine months (after that time a couple will adopt the child). Imagine that this person will have some bouts with morning sickness, water retention, and other minor ailments. If we assume with Thomson that the unborn child is as much a person as you or I, would "withholding treatment" from this child and its subsequent death be justified on the basis that the homeowner was only "withholding treatment" of a child he did not *ask* for in order to benefit himself? Is any person, born or unborn, obligated to sacrifice his life because his death would benefit another person? Consequently, there is no doubt that such "withholding" of treatment (and it seems totally false to call ordinary shelter and sustenance "treatment") is indeed murder.

But is it even accurate to refer to abortion as the "withholding of support or treatment"? Professors Schwarz and R. K. Tacelli make the important point that although "a woman who has an abortion is indeed 'withholding support' from her unborn child. . . . abortion is far more than that. It is the active killing of a human person—by burning him, by crushing him, by dismembering him." Euphemistically calling abortion the "withholding of support or treatment" makes about as much sense as calling suffocating someone with a pillow the withdrawing of oxygen.

In summary, then, of the four problems with Thomson's argument under the ethical category, I agree with Professor Brody when he concludes that "Thomson has not established the truth of her claim about abortion, primarily because she has not sufficiently attended to the distinction between our duty to save *X's* life and our duty not to take it." But "once one attends to that distinction, it would seem that the mother, in order to regain control over her body, has no right to abort the fetus from the point at which it becomes a human being."

Turning our attention now to the ideological category, we find that there are at least two problems in the use of Thomson's argument by others. Whether or not Thomson agrees with the following points is not relevant to the following critique, since many who use her argument do agree with these points.

1. *Inconsistent use of the burden of pregnancy.* Thomson has to paint pregnancy in the most horrific of terms in order to make her argument seem plausible. Dr. Bernard Nathanson, an obstetrician/gynecologist and former abortion-provider, objects "strenuously to Thomson's portrayal of pregnancy as a nine-month involuntary imprisonment in bed. This casts an unfair and wrongheaded prejudice against the consideration of the state of pregnancy and skews the argument." Nathanson points out that "pregnancy is not a 'sickness'. Few pregnant women are bedridden and many, emotionally and physically, have never felt better. For these it is a stimulating experience,

even for mothers who originally did not 'want' to be pregnant." Unlike the person who is plugged into Thomson's violinist, "alpha [the unborn entity] does not hurt the mother by being 'plugged in,' . . . except in the case of well-defined medical indications." And "in those few cases where pregnancy *is* a medical penalty, it is a penalty lasting nine months."

Compare and contrast Thomson's portrayal of pregnancy with the fact that researchers have recently discovered that many people believe that a pregnant woman cannot work as effectively as a non-pregnant woman who is employed to do the same job in the same workplace. This has upset a number of feminists, and rightfully so. They argue that a pregnant woman is not incapacitated or ill, but can work just as effectively as a non-pregnant woman.

But why, then, do feminists who use Thomson's argument argue, when it comes to abortion, that pregnancy is similar to being bedridden and hooked up to a violinist for nine months? When it comes to equality in the workplace (and here I agree with the feminists) there is "no problem." But in the case of morally justifying abortion-rights, pregnancy is painted in the most horrific of terms. Although not *logically* fatal to the abortion-rights position, this sort of double-minded grandstanding is not conducive to good moral reasoning.

2. *The libertarian principles underlying Thomson's case are inconsistent with the state-mandated agenda of radical feminism.* If Thomson's violinist illustration works at all, it works contrary to the statist principles of radical feminism (of course, a libertarian feminist need not be fazed by this objection). Levin points out that "while appeal to an absolute right to the disposition of one's body coheres well with other strongly libertarian positions (laissez faire in the marketplace, parental autonomy in education of their children, freedom of private association), this appeal is most commonly made by feminists who are antilibertarian on just about every other issue." For example, "feminists who advocate state-mandated quotas, state-mandated comparable worth pay scales, the censorship of 'sexist' textbooks in the public schools, laws against 'sexually harassing speech' and legal limitations on private association excluding homosexuals, will go on to advocate abortion on the basis of an absolute libertarianism at odds with every one of those policies."

Although this criticism is *ad hominem*, as was the previous one, it serves to underscore the important political fact that many abortion rights advocates are more than willing to hold and earnestly defend contrary principles for the sake of legally mandating their ideological agenda.

QUESTIONS FOR REFLECTION

1. State the argument from a woman's right over her own body. What premises does Beckwith challenge, and why?
2. How does Beckwith dispute the argument that a woman has no moral obligation to undertake the risk of continuing a pregnancy?
3. Are there cases in which people have a duty to accept risks at least as great as the risk (in a typical case) of carrying a child to term?
4. Does Thomson's argument assume that obligations must be accepted voluntarily to have moral force? If so, could her argument be reframed to eliminate that assumption?
5. Are there cases in which people have obligations they have not accepted voluntarily? If so, give examples.
6. How do your reactions to Thomson's case change if the woman is the violinist's mother? What obligations, in general, do mothers have to their children?
7. How does Beckwith argue that the fetus has a prima facie claim to use of the mother's body? Do you agree? Are there boundaries to that claim?
8. Are any abortions morally permissible, from Beckwith's perspective?

ALEXANDER R. PRUSS

I Was Once a Fetus: That Is Why Abortion Is Wrong

Alexander R. Pruss is associate professor of philosophy at Baylor University.

0. Introduction

I am going to give an argument showing that abortion is wrong in exactly the same circumstances in which it is wrong to kill an adult. To argue further that abortion is always wrong would require showing that it is always wrong to kill an adult or that the circumstances in which it is not wrong—say, capital punishment—never befall a fetus. Such an argument will be beyond the scope of this paper, but since it is uncontroversial that it is wrong to kill an adult human being for the sorts of reasons for which most abortions are performed, it follows that most abortions are wrong.

The argument has three parts, of decreasing difficulty. The most difficult will be the first part where I will argue that I was once a fetus and before that I was an embryo. This argument will rest on simple considerations of the metaphysics of identity. The next part of the argument will be to show that it would have been at least as wrong to have killed me before I was born as it would be to kill me now. I will argue for this in more than one way, but the guiding intuition is clear: if you kill me earlier, the victim is the same but the harm is greater since I am deprived of more the earlier I die. Finally, the easiest part of the argument will be that I am not relevantly different from anybody else and the fetus which I was was not relevantly different from any other human fetus, and so the argument applies equally well to all fetuses.

The advantage of this argument over others is that it avoids talking of personhood, except in one of the independent arguments in part 2.

1. I Was Once a Fetus

The first part seems innocuous. After all, is it not biologically evident that first I was an embryo, then I was a fetus, then a neonate, then a baby, then a toddler, then a child, then an adolescent, and then an adult? Does not my mother talk of the time when she was "pregnant with me," thereby implying that it was I who was in her womb when she was pregnant? Is not the sonogram of my daughter the sonogram of that daughter of mine who will be born? Evident as it might be that I was once a fetus, given how clear it will be that abortion is wrong if I was once a fetus, it is clear that the opponent will have to focus his attack on this part of the argument. So more needs to be said.

About thirty years ago, nine months before I was born, a conception occurred. A sperm from my father fertilized an ovum from my mother. Within twenty-four hours, or sooner, a new organism came into existence, an organism that was neither a part of my mother nor of my father. For one, this organism was genetically distinct from both. For another, this organism's functioning is directed towards its own benefit—selfishly, the organism colonizes the womb, releases hormones that trigger changes in the woman beneficial to the organism, and so on. It certainly does not behave like a body part of either my mother or my father. Moreover, it clearly is not a part of my father—it need no longer have any interaction with him. But it could not really be a part of my mother, since the genetic contribution from my father is equal to that from the mother, so it is either a part of both or of neither. Thus, indeed, it is not a part of either. Besides, we can see that in the earliest days of this organism, the organism floats free, independently seeking nutrition in my mother's womb. This organism certainly is not a part of my mother.

Hence, we have on the scene a new individual organism, one that did not exist before. Let's give this organism a name: call it Bob. If we had a camera and looked at what was happening in the womb in which Bob is living, we will see an embryo developing, cells differentiating, a fetus forming, growing, and finally a birth. If we keep watching, we see a neonate, then an infant, then a toddler, then a child, then an adolescent and then an adult. It's all a continuous history. But recall what I am out to prove. I am out to prove that I was once a fetus and indeed an embryo against an opponent that will not grant this. My opponent will thus have to deny that I and Bob are one and the same entity. He will have to say that "Bob" and "Alex" name two different entities, rather than being two names for one and the same entity at different stages of its life.

In any case, we have on the scene Bob the embryo. And then all this development happens. I now need a simple metaphysical principle. If an organism that once existed has never died, then this organism still exists. I am not going to argue for this principle. Someone who thinks something can exist at time A and not exist at a later time B, without having ceased to exist in between, is beyond the reach of argument. The crucial question now is: Has Bob the embryo ever died? This is a question that the biologists can tell us the answer to. Bob's cells have divided, differentiated, and Bob has developed. But nowhere in the continuous history I described before have we seen anything we could identify as "the death of Bob." In fact, the whole process is the very opposite of the process of death: we have a process of growth. That embryo that was conceived nine months before my birth never died. True, it ceased to be an embryo after a while, and at the end of the nine months it ceased to be a fetus. But this is no more a literal death than my passing from childhood to adolescence or from adolescence to adulthood was a death.

Indeed, if Bob died, we would be mystified as to when he died. All we have in his life history is a process of growth and development. Now, it is true that not all deaths are alike—not all deaths involve an evident destruction. For instance, some philosophers think that the right way to describe an amoeba's splitting is to say that the original amoeba dies and from its ashes there arise two new amoebae. Likewise, some philosophers think that when two entities merge into a single unified entity, the original entities perish and a new one is formed. That in fact may be how we should understand the process of conception: the egg and sperm perish, and a new thing results. But again, for as long as Bob has existed, he has always been a single unified organism. But nothing like that happened in Bob's life history—Bob never split in two and never merged with anything else so as to lose his own identity. If I were an identical twin, matters would be slightly different as an argument could then be made that the pre-twinning embryo has indeed perished when it split in two. But that's not what happened to Bob. It is clear that Bob has not died in the prosaic way of having his organic functioning disrupted, and hasn't even died in these two more outré ways that philosophers discuss.

Furthermore, the very continuity in Bob's development speaks against the hypothesis that he died. When did that momentous event happen? When did Bob cease to exist? Could there have been some moment in Bob's growth where one millisecond Bob was alive and a millisecond later Bob was no longer around? Surely not.

Therefore, it is sufficiently established that Bob, that embryo who came into existence nine months before my birth, has never died. But by my metaphysical principle, if he has never died, he is still alive. Where, then, is Bob? But surely there is no mystery there. Every part of Bob—other than the cells in the placenta and the umbilical cord that were shed*—developed continuously into a part of

*One might try to argue that Bob died at birth, because of the loss of his placental cells and umbilical cord. But this is implausible. The loss of an organ does not kill a human being unless it disrupts general functioning, and in this case no disruption of general functioning occurred.

me, and every part of me has developed ultimately out of a part of Bob. It is thus quite futile to look for Bob outside of me. If Bob is anywhere, he is right here, where I am. It may be true that most of the original cells in Bob are no longer around, but that does not stop the survival of an organism: organisms replace their cells regularly, and do not perish thereby.

Now, Bob can't be a mere part of my body, because all of my body has continuously come from Bob's body. Therefore, one can't set aside some special part of my body and say "that part of me is Bob." So, where is Bob? The answer is simple: here. I am Bob. That embryo has grown to be a fetus, then to be a neonate, then an infant, then a child, then an adolescent and finally an adult. Bob is I and I am Bob. This was what I was trying to establish.

But this is a little too quick. I just said, vaguely, that Bob is here, and concluded that Bob is I. We need the following. Here where I stand there is only one large animal—Alexander Pruss. Bob is presumably right here—there is nowhere else for him to be. Bob has been growing for much of his life, and so Bob is also a large animal. The only large animal here is Alexander Pruss, and hence Bob and Alexander Pruss are one and the same animal. I, thus, am Bob. If Bob is here, and if no part of me is a large animal, and if Bob is a large animal, Bob and I must be one and the same entity.

Besides, given how organic development works, it is easy to see that every organ of mine is an organ of Bob's, since Bob's organs have developed into being my organs, and yet without any transplant happening. Thus, I and Bob are organisms having all of our organs in common. But the only way that can be is if I and Bob are the same organism, i.e., I am Bob. "Bob" and "Alex" are just different names for one and the same being: Alexander Robert Pruss.

There is only one way of countering this argument, and this is to deny that I am an animal, that I am an organism. This response seems absurd on the face of it, and it is right that we should see it as absurd. I am a rational animal. But there are three seemingly plausible ways of making this objection work. They are not the only ones, but they will be representative.

The first form this objection can take is Cartesian dualism. Souls and bodies are separate substances. What I really am is a soul, a spiritual substance. The body is simply a tool my soul owns and uses, much as I might use a hammer. My body is an organism, indeed an animal, but I am not myself an organism or animal. Thus, what Bob is is my body: he is an animal I own. This dualistic view has various paradoxical consequences. My wife has never kissed me—she has only kissed Bob, my body. You cannot touch me—you can only touch Bob. Likewise, rape is a mere property crime, then. Making philosophical sense of the meaning of sexuality is a lost cause: two persons' having sexual intercourse is nothing but the intercourse between the animals owned by each of the persons. My body is simply my property, and so stealing one of my kidneys is a mere property crime—it is not stealing a part of me. These consequences are ethically unacceptable. After all, the government can morally take away some of my property for the greater good, and does so in taxes. If my body were mere property, then the government would in principle have a right, when necessary, to extract a kidney from me as a tax payment. Finally, observe that if this is right, then the traditional rallying cry of abortion supporters "It's my body" is no different in principle from the silly argument that I can do whatever I like in my house because my house is my property.

There is too much absurdity there, and so this Cartesian view fails. But even if it did not fail, it could only be used by the proponent of abortion if he had good reason to deny that the soul substance was united with the embryo from conception—otherwise, the safer thing is to refrain from killing what might be I. But since the soul substance is unobservable, no such grounds are possible, apart from revelation-based religious arguments, and those should not be brought in in a secular societal context.

The arguments against the Cartesian view are not arguments against the existence of a soul. The Cartesian view that the soul is a separate substance, distinct from the body, is not the only view of the soul. The Aristotelian or Thomistic view is that the soul is that which makes an organism be the organism it is and develop as it does. Thus, the soul is not something over and beyond the organism—it constitutes the organism as what it is and what we are is organisms, organisms constituted by our souls. Thus as soon as there is a unitary organism, there is a soul. (Admittedly Aristotle and Thomas believed that the conceptus did not have the same soul as I do—but they were theorizing in the absence of empirical evidence about the conceptus being an animal that continuously grows and develops into me, or else they were going against what they should have said by their own lights.)

The Cartesian view is rather unpopular these days in secular circles. But there is a secular version of it, that replaces body-soul duality with body-brain duality: I am not my body, I am not an animal—I am a brain. This kind of a view will not help the abortion supporter all that much, since the brain develops relatively early in pregnancy—around six weeks after conception. But in fact the most trenchant objections against the "I am a soul" view can be made against the "I am a brain" view. Only in the course of brain surgery can my wife kiss me if I am a brain. Rape, still, is but a property crime. My kidneys are not parts of me, but mere property, and hence can be expropriated by the government if necessary.

And there is a further objection. My brain developed out of earlier cells guided by the genetic information already present in the embryo: there was, first, a neural tube, and earlier there were precursors to that. Brain development was gradual, cells specializing more and more and arranging themselves. At which point did I come to exist? And why should the cells that were the precursors of the brain cells not be counted as having been the same organ as the brain, but in inchoate form? If so, then perhaps I was there from conception, even on this view.

The third response to my argument is that I am not my body or my brain, but what I am is my body's intellectual functioning. This response requires a metaphysical answer. On this view, I do not think. Rather, I am nothing else than thought itself, or more precisely, I am nothing else than a process of thinking. We would do well to reject this view just because it contradicts the commonsensical fact that we think. But we can also reject this view for a deeper reason. If I am a particular process of thought, then it follows that were that process of thought not to have occurred, I would not have existed. Thus, when asleep, I exist not. Moreover, were I not to have engaged in the processes of thought that I have engaged in over my lifetime, but instead were I to have engaged in different processes of thought, then I would not have existed—there would then have been a different process of thought, and hence someone else, if what I am is the process of thought that I am. It follows that we cannot think otherwise than we do, because our very identity is defined by the process of thought we engage in. This fatalism, this deprivation of free will, is unacceptable.

As I said, there are views of who I am that compete with the view that I am an animal and that are not the same as these three, but they tend to be variations of these three. For instance, some think that what I am is a whole made up of two parts, a Cartesian soul and a body-animal. This view is open to the simple objection that two interacting parts do not automatically make for a whole. Moreover, there is the objection that surely I think, and yet my soul thinks, and since I am not a part of me, it follows absurdly that there are two thinkers here: I and my soul.

We see thus that I am Bob. I was once an embryo and a fetus. The embryo or fetus that was there was just I—in an earlier stage of my life. This completes the first and hardest step of the argument.

An objection. In the first two weeks or so after conception, the blastocyst was not an individual, and hence in particular is not the same individual as I am, because it was capable of twinning—of splitting into two or more individuals—which it in fact does in about one in 260 cases. While what is normally called "abortion" is not likely to be done at this time since the woman at this time rarely knows herself to be pregnant, nonetheless there are abortifacients that act this early—for instance the IUD, Emergency Birth Control or the Pill in those cases where these act through an abortifacient effect—and hence the question is not merely of theoretical interest.

This argument rests on the false principle that if it is merely possible that an organism will split in the future, then we do not have a genuine individual on the scene. But this is plainly false: amoebae are certainly individuals, but they are capable of splitting. What happens to the individuality when they split is disputed by philosophers. One might hold that the old amoeba continues existing as one of the two new ones, but we simply do not know as which one. Or one might hold, more plausibly, that the old perishes and a new one comes to be in its place. In the latter case, if I had had an identical twin, then I would have come to exist about two weeks after conception, not at conception, and the human being who came to exist at conception would no longer be alive.

But if we have an amoeba in front of us for a period of time during which it does not split, then it is the same amoeba, the same organism, over all of this time. This judgment is unaffected even should we learn that the amoeba could have split during this period of time, just as our judgment that someone is alive is unaffected by learning that she could have died yesterday. As long as the amoeba in fact does not split, it is one and the same individual as we had on the scene earlier.

One might argue that if one could know in the first two weeks that twinning was going to occur, then one would thereby know that the conceived embryo would cease to exist at two weeks of age, and one could abort it earlier, since one would not be depriving it of a long and meaningful life. Whether this argument is correct or not—and I am inclined to think it is not, since I think how good the life that one is being deprived of should not affect whether it is wrong for someone to deprive one of it—it does not matter in practice. We just cannot tell at the moment. And as in 259 out of 260 cases twinning will not occur, one needs to act on the presumption that it will not in fact occur.

2. If I Was a Fetus, It Would Have Been Wrong to Kill That Fetus

There are several paths to the conclusion of the second part of the argument, that if I was once a fetus (or an embryo for that matter), then it would have been wrong to kill that fetus, under exactly the same circumstances under which it would be wrong to kill me now.

The most powerful argument is to look at what is wrong with killing me now. Killing me now is a paradigmatic crime-with-a-victim, the victim being me. What would make killing me now wrong is the harm it would do to to me: it would deprive me, who am juridically innocent, of life, indeed of the rest of my life. Now, consider the hypothetical killing of the fetus that I once was. This killing would have exactly the same victim as killing me now would. Moreover, the harm inflicted on the victim would have been strictly greater, in the sense that any harm inflicted on me by killing me now would likewise have been inflicted on me by killing me when I was a child. I am now 29 years old. Suppose that left to nature's resources, I would die at 65. Then, killing me now would deprive me of years 29 through 65 of my life. However, killing me when I was a fetus would also deprive me of years 29 through 65 of my life—as well as the years from the moment of the killing up to 29. Given that murder is a crime whose wrongness comes from the harm to the victim, it is clear that when the victim is the same, and the harm greater, killing is if anything more wrong.

Of course, there may be circumstances in which it is acceptable to kill me now. It might be that under some circumstances capital punishment is justified. If so, then it might be right to kill the fetus under the same circumstances. However, it is also clear that the circumstances involved in capital punishment do not apply in the case of the fetus. Whether there are any other circumstances in which it would be acceptable to kill me now is a question that is beyond the scope of this paper, though I believe the answer is basically negative. In any case, we see that the wrongfulness of killing me when I was a fetus is at least as great as the wrongfulness of killing me now in relevantly similar circumstances. Thus, my moral status when I was a fetus with respect to being killed is the same, or more favorable than, my status now.

The reason for the "more favorable than now" option is that we have an intuition that it is particularly wrong to kill people earlier. Although there may be no duty thus to sacrifice one's life, we see nothing irrational in an older person sacrificing his life for a younger on the grounds that the older has literally less to lose by death. When I was a fetus, I had more to lose by death than I do now. Thus, to have killed me then would, strictly speaking, have been a greater harm.

Observe that nothing is said here about whether I was a person when I was a fetus. This is irrelevant. Whether I was a person then or not, killing me would have the same victim and greater harm as killing me now. Observe that if I was not a person when I was a fetus, then the harm in killing me then would have been even greater than if I was a person then. For, killing me when I was not a person would thus have deprived me of all of my personhood as lived out on earth, and this radical deprivation would have been a greater crime than killing me now which would not deprive me of ever having had a personhood lived out on earth.

That said, an independent argument shows that in fact I was a person when I was a fetus. This gives a second argument for why killing a fetus is wrong, and it is the only argument I give that depends on issues of personhood. The argument turns on the metaphysical notion of an "essential property." The essential property of a being is a property which that being cannot lack as long as that being exists. For instance, many philosophers think that being a horse is an essential property of a horse. If you take a horse like Silver Blaze and modify it to such a degree that it is no longer a horse, Silver Blaze will cease to exist and something else will come to exist in his place. Being material is an essential property of a rock: it could not exist without being material.

Now, it is likewise plausible that being a person is an essential property of every person. If someone were a person, and personhood were removed from her, she would cease to exist. If this is correct, then the fetus that I was was a person, since I am a person. If the fetus that I was were not a person, then it would be the case that I could have existed without being a person—which would be impossible.

Even more plausibly, it is an essential property of me to have a property that I will call human dignity. Human dignity is a property of me which makes it wrong for another human being to set out to kill me when I am juridically innocent. As before, I leave capital punishment as an open question. Human dignity is an essential property: it is part of the essence of who I am—were I to lack this intrinsic dignity, I would not be myself, I would not exist. But if human dignity understood in this way is an essential property and I have it, then the fetus that I was also had it—otherwise it wouldn't be an essential property.

Finally, there is a very different argument for the wrongfulness of killing the fetus that I was, based on John Rawls' concept of justice. Even though I take this concept to be incorrect, the more bases on which our argument can rest, the better the argument. Rawls bids us to imagine that we do not know which role in society we fill—imagining this is called entering under the "veil of ignorance." What kind of a society with what kinds of rules would I rationally come up with, on selfish grounds, if I did not know which role in this society I am going to live in? Rawls says that that kind of society is the just society, and its rules are the rules of justice. In such a society, for instance, we would forbid racism, because under the veil of ignorance we would not know whether we would end up having the role of victim or inflicter of racism, and we would not want to take the risk of being on the victim. Likewise, we would prohibit the murder of adults.

Would we forbid the killing of fetuses? This question depends on just how much we are to be ignorant of under the veil of ignorance. If we know that we are not fetuses, then we might not forbid the killing of fetuses when it is convenient to non-fetuses, because we would have no selfish reason to prohibit it. So is the fact of us not being fetuses something that is under the veil of ignorance or not? Well, we must be careful not to take too much out from under the veil. For instance, if racism is to end up being deemed unjust, our race must lie under the veil. Moreover, even our being conscious must fall under the veil—thereby showing how much the veil is just a figure of speech, since we cannot really be ignorant of our consciousness. The reason our being conscious must fall under the veil is that otherwise we might well enact that it is right to kill the unconscious for the sake of the conscious—to use the man in a coma for medical experiments, say. But at the same time, we can't put too much under the veil. We had better have an awareness of ourselves as human, since otherwise our "just society" will end up prohibiting all killing of animals, and this would make even most vegetarian farming wrong because of the moles and voles and other animals killed in the process of farming, as someone has once argued.

So where do we draw the line? I would propose this simple criterion. Under the veil, we are aware of which social roles it would be logically possible for us to fill, but not aware which of those roles we do in fact fill. It would not be logically possible for me to fill the role of a mole in the ground—I would not be myself then. So I know, even under the veil, that I am not a mole. However, it plainly is logically possible for me to fill the role of a fetus—it is possible, because I did fill the role of a fetus once! Thus, whether I am a fetus or not is something that must fall under the veil of ignorance, and hence the killing of fetuses will end up being prohibited in exactly the same way as that of adults: we just wouldn't want to take the risk that we might end up being a fetus that is being killed. Hence, justice requires a prohibition on killing fetuses in exactly the way in which it requires a prohibition on killing adults.

Later, Rawls modified his criterion by talking of an unselfish caretaker for someone making the decision under a veil of ignorance about what role her charge would fill. This takes care of the problem that we can hardly be ignorant of whether we are conscious, while a caretaker can be ignorant of whether her charge is conscious. But it does not affect the rest of the argument. The caretaker needs to be ignorant of some properties of her charge, such as the charge's profession in life, but not of others, such as that her charge is not an insect. Again, I would suggest that a natural way to draw the line is apt to make the caretaker be ignorant of whether her charge is a fetus or not. For at the very least the caretaker should be ignorant as to which of the roles her charge could fill she in fact fills, and certainly her charge could fill the role of a fetus. And if that were so, the caretaker, truly loving whoever is entrusted into her care, would not want to take the risk of enacting a system whereby her charge could be killed.

3. If It Was Wrong to Kill Me When I Was a Fetus, It Was Wrong to Kill Anyone When He Is a Fetus

If you cut me, do I bleed any more than the next guy? No. I was not and am not special. If it was wrong to kill me when I was a fetus, it was likewise wrong to kill anyone else when he was a fetus.

It might be argued that there are some special differences between the fetus that I was, which we have seen it would have been wrong to kill, and some other fetuses. For instance, I was wanted. But that I was wanted did not anywhere enter into my arguments against killing me when I was a fetus. It is wrong to kill me now no matter whether I am wanted by others or not. Killing me earlier, I have argued, is not significantly different from killing me now, and so whether I was wanted or not is irrelevant.

A different objection would be that, as far as I know, I did not endanger my mother's life. However, my arguments would continue to apply even if I did: the fetus needs to be protected at least to the extent to which we would protect an adult under relevantly similar circumstances. The fetus endangers the mother's life unintentionally. Whether it is acceptable to kill the fetus under those circumstances depends on whether it would be acceptable to kill me now were I to endanger my mother's life unintentionally. But the unintentional endangering case is different. As I announced, the aim of this paper is limited: it is to argue that killing fetuses is wrong under the same circumstances under which it is wrong to kill adults, but it is not the purpose of the paper to discuss the circumstances, if any, under which it is permissible to kill adults. I think it would not be acceptable to kill me were I endangering my mother's life unintentionally: I will simply say in support of this that were I alone in a space capsule, three days from rescue, with my mother, with only enough air for 1.5 days each, it would not be acceptable for my mother or her agent to kill me, I take it.

A yet different objection is: I was a healthy fetus, but some others are not. The wrong in killing me when I was a fetus would have been depriving me of a meaningful and long future life. But what if the fetus cannot be expected to have such a life? Again, I respond that the purpose of this paper is limited: I am not going to settle issues of euthanasia here. It is acceptable to kill such a fetus only if it is acceptable to kill an adult who cannot be expected to have a meaningful and long future life. Again, I think it is not acceptable to kill an adult under such circumstances. Human life is intrinsically worthwhile. But this is not a paper about euthanasia. If I have shown that the fetus is worthy of at least the same respect as an adult in comparable circumstances, I have done my task.

QUESTIONS FOR REFLECTION

1. Explain the overall structure of Pruss's argument. Suppose, for the sake of the argument, that the premises are true. Does the conclusion follow?
2. How does Pruss argue that he was once a fetus, and, before that, an embryo?
3. Evaluate that argument. Were you once a fetus?
4. Does the possibility of splitting into identical twins undermine Pruss's premise?
5. What is wrong with killing an adult, according to Pruss?
6. How does Pruss argue that it would have been wrong to kill him when he was a fetus?
7. How does Pruss argue for his third premise?
8. Pruss contends that "the fetus needs to be protected at least to the extent to which we would protect an adult under relevantly similar circumstances." Consider Thomson's violinist case. Does she succeed in showing that we would *not* protect an adult under circumstances relevantly similar to abortion in the case of rape?

EUTHANASIA AND PHYSICIAN-ASSISTED SUICIDE

Euthanasia, or mercy killing, presents some very difficult and painful dilemmas for doctors, patients, family members, and moral philosophers. Sometimes a patient's condition is so poor and holds so little hope of future recovery that death seems better than life. Is it ever morally justifiable to allow such patients to die by withholding treatment that would otherwise be given? Is it ever justifiable to kill them?

Clearly, this topic concerns both rights and liberty. The patient has a right to life and perhaps a right to die. The patient may also have the liberty to make certain fundamental decisions about whether to continue treatment. Frequently, however, euthanasia becomes a serious issue only after the patient is comatose or otherwise incapable of making a competent decision. Moreover, many factors seem to be morally relevant to the decision between life and death. Is the patient conscious? Suffering? If so, how much? What are the prospects for improvement? Is the patient terminally ill? What kind of life can the patient hope to lead, and for how long? The course of action being contemplated may also matter: Cessation of "heroic" lifesaving efforts? Withdrawal of food and water? A lethal injection?

The Supreme Court of New Jersey, in a much-publicized case, decided in 1976 to allow the parents of Karen Ann Quinlan to remove her from a respirator. She was comatose and diagnosed as having no chance of regaining consciousness. The court decided that Quinlan's right of privacy gave her or her guardian the right to decide the course of her treatment, since a respirator, which might be deemed ordinary for a curable patient, should count as extraordinary for someone with her poor prognosis.

Eight years later, the Supreme Court of Missouri reached the opposite verdict in a related case. Nancy Cruzan, after an automobile accident, was "in a persistent vegetative state." She was nevertheless not terminally ill and not reliant on a respirator or other extraordinary machinery for support. However, she did require a feeding tube. Her guardians requested that fluids and nutrition be withdrawn. The court found no justification for granting that request, arguing that Cruzan's condition was significantly different from Quinlan's and that the relevant state interest is life, not the quality of life, as the *Quinlan* court seemed to suggest.

The United States Supreme Court upheld that decision, saying that although a competent person might make an informed and voluntary choice to have hydration and nutrition withdrawn, the state has an interest in preserving life and demanding clear and convincing evidence of the patient's wishes.

J. Gay-Williams argues that euthanasia is invariably wrong. It is, he contends, contrary to everyone's natural inclination to continue living. Moreover, it is extremely dangerous for several reasons. First, we can never know that death is really preferable to continued life. Second, people may choose death out of ignorance, a temporary feeling of hopelessness, or consideration for their families. Finally, euthanasia would lead to a lowered respect for life that could have serious consequences for medical care and society's treatment of the infirm.

Closely related to the question of euthanasia is that of physician-assisted suicide. Dr. Jack Kevorkian has become famous for traveling the country assisting in the suicides of desperate patients. In 1997 two cases before the Supreme Court, *Vacco* v. *Quill* and *Washington* v. *Glucksberg*, raised the issue of a right to physician-assisted suicide. Six of America's most respected philosophers—Ronald Dworkin, Thomas Nagel, Robert Nozick, John Rawls, Thomas Scanlon, and Judith Jarvis

Thomson—filed an *amici curiae* (friends of the court) brief in favor of a right to assisted suicide. They contended that the right to liberty entails the freedom to make fundamental decisions, such as the decision to die, without governmental interference. The Supreme Court unanimously rejected their reasoning in both cases, contending instead that tradition and a concern for human life give the state sufficient reason to restrict or prohibit physician-assisted suicide.

Finally, Toon Quaghebeur, Bernadette Dierckx de Casterlé, and Chris Gastmans review arguments for and against euthanasia from the perspective of nurses who are responsible for caring for patients at the end of life. They take no position themselves but identify four key ethical concepts—autonomy, non-maleficence, beneficence, and justice—and observe that each has been used on each side of the debate. They also pay careful attention to the ethics of care, which they see as especially relevant to euthanasia and to the obligations of medical professionals. The moral status of euthanasia, they contend, depends not only on how autonomy, non-maleficence, beneficence, and justice are ranked against one another but also on how each is interpreted.

SUPREME COURT OF NEW JERSEY

Matter of Quinlan (1976)

(Source: Matter of Quinlan *70 N.J. 10, 355 A. 2d. 647 [1976]. Most legal references have been omitted.)*

The Litigation

The central figure in this tragic case is Karen Ann Quinlan, a New Jersey resident. At the age of 22, she lies in a debilitated and allegedly moribund state at Saint Clare's Hospital in Denville, New Jersey. The litigation has to do, in final analysis, with her life—its continuance or cessation—and the responsibilities, rights and duties, with regard to any fateful decision concerning it, of her family, her guardian, her doctors, the hospital, the State through its law enforcement authorities, and finally the courts of justice.

Due to extensive physical damage fully described in the able opinion of the trial judge, Judge Muir, supporting that judgment, Karen allegedly was incompetent. Joseph Quinlan sought the adjudication of that incompetency. He wished to be appointed guardian of the person and property of his daughter. It was proposed by him that such letters of guardianship, if granted, should contain an express power to him as guardian to authorize the discontinuance of all extraordinary medical procedures now allegedly sustaining Karen's vital processes and hence her life, since these measures, he asserted, present no hope of her eventual recovery. A guardian *ad litem* was appointed by Judge Muir to represent the interest of the alleged incompetent.

The Factual Base

On the night of April 15, 1975, for reasons still unclear, Karen Quinlan ceased breathing for at least two 15-minute periods. She received some ineffectual mouth-to-mouth resuscitation from friends. She was taken by ambulance to Newton Memorial Hospital. There she had a temperature of 100 degrees, her pupils were unreactive, and she was unresponsive even to deep pain. The history at the time of her admission to that hospital was essentially incomplete and uninformative.

Three days later, Dr. Morse examined Karen at the request of the Newton admitting physician, Dr. McGee. He found her comatose with evidence of decortication, a condition relating to derangement of the cortex of the brain causing a physical posture in which the upper extremities are flexed and the lower extremities are extended. She required a respirator to assist her breathing. Dr. Morse was unable to obtain an adequate account of the circumstances and events leading up to Karen's admission to the Newton Hospital. Such initial history or etiology is crucial in neurological diagnosis. Relying as he did upon the Newton Memorial records and his own examination, he concluded that prolonged lack of oxygen in the bloodstream, anoxia, was identified with her condition as he saw it upon first observation. When she was later transferred to Saint Clare's Hospital she was still unconscious, still on a respirator, and a tracheotomy had been performed. On her arrival Dr. Morse conducted extensive and detailed examinations. An electroencephalogram (EEG) measuring electrical rhythm of the brain was performed, and Dr. Morse characterized the result as "abnormal but it showed some activity and was consistent with her clinical state." Other significant neurological tests, including a brain scan, an angiogram, and a lumbar puncture were normal in result. Dr. Morse testified that Karen has been in a state of coma, lack of consciousness, since he began treating her. He explained that there are basically two types of coma, sleep-like unresponsiveness and awake unresponsiveness. Karen was originally in a sleep-like unresponsive condition but soon developed "sleep-wake" cycles, apparently a normal improvement for comatose patients occurring within three to four weeks. In the awake cycle she blinks, cries out and does things of that sort but is still totally unaware of anyone or anything around her.

Dr. Morse and other expert physicians who examined her characterized Karen as being in a "chronic persistent vegetative state." Dr. Fred Plum, one of such expert witnesses, defined this as a "subject who remains with the capacity to maintain the vegetative parts of neurological function but who . . . no longer has any cognitive function." . . .

It seemed to be the consensus not only of the treating physicians but also of the several qualified experts who testified in the case, that removal from the respirator would not conform to medical practices, standards and traditions.

The further medical consensus was that Karen in addition to being comatose is in a chronic and persistent "vegetative" state, having no awareness of anything or anyone around her and existing at a primitive reflex level. Although she does have some brain stem function (ineffective for respiration) and has other reactions one normally associates with being alive, such as moving, reacting to light, sound and noxious stimuli, blinking her eyes, and the like, the quality of her feeling impulses is unknown. She grimaces, makes stereotyped cries and sounds and has chewing motions. Her blood pressure is normal.

Karen is described as emaciated, having suffered a weight loss of at least 40 pounds, and undergoing a continuing deteriorative process. Her posture is described as fetal-like and grotesque; there is extreme flexion-rigidity of the arms, legs and related muscles and her joints are severely rigid and deformed.

From all of this evidence, and including the whole testimonial record, several basic findings in the physical area are mandated. Severe brain and associated damage, albeit of uncertain etiology, has left Karen in a chronic and persistent vegetative state. No form of treatment which can cure or improve that condition is known or available. As nearly as may be determined, considering the guarded area of remote uncertainties characteristic of most medical science predictions, she can *never* be restored to cognitive or sapient life. Even with regard to the vegetative level and improvement therein (if such it may be called) the prognosis is extremely poor and the extent unknown if it should in fact occur.

She is debilitated and moribund and although fairly stable at the time of argument before us (no new information having been filed in the meanwhile in expansion of the record), no physician risked the opinion that she could live more than a year and indeed she may die much earlier. Excellent medical and nursing care so far has been able to ward off the constant threat of infection, to which she is peculiarly susceptible because of the respirator, the tracheal tube, and other incidents of care in her vulnerable condition. Her life accordingly is sustained by the respirator and tubal feeding, and removal from the respirator would cause her death soon, although the time cannot be stated with more precision.

It is from this factual base that the Court confronts and responds to three basic issues:

1. Was the trial court correct in denying the specific relief requested by plaintiff, i.e., authorization for termination of the life-supporting apparatus, on the case presented to him? Our determination on that question is in the affirmative.
2. Was the court correct in withholding letters of guardianship from the plaintiff and appointing in his stead a stranger? On that issue our determination is in the negative.
3. Should this Court, in the light of the foregoing conclusions, grant declaratory relief to the plaintiff? On that question our Court's determination is in the affirmative.

This brings us to a consideration of the constitutional and legal issues underlying the foregoing determinations.

Constitutional and Legal Issues

The Right of Privacy

It is the issue of the constitutional right of privacy that has given us most concern, in the exceptional circumstances of this case. Here a loving parent, *qua* parent and raising the rights of his incompetent and profoundly damaged daughter, probably irreversibly doomed to no more than a biologically vegetative remnant of life, is before the court. He seeks authorization to abandon specialized technological procedures which can only maintain for a time a body having no potential for resumption or continuance of other than a "vegetative" existence.

We have no doubt, in these unhappy circumstances, that if Karen were herself miraculously lucid for an interval (not altering the existing prognosis of the condition to which she would soon return) and perceptive of her irreversible condition, she could effectively decide upon discontinuance of the life-support apparatus, even if it meant the prospect of natural death. . . .

We have no hesitancy in deciding . . . that no external compelling interest of the State could compel Karen to endure the unendurable, only to vegetate a few measurable months with no realistic possibility of returning to any semblance of cognitive or sapient life. We perceive no thread of logic distinguishing between such a choice on Karen's part and a similar choice which, under the evidence in this case, could be made by a competent patient terminally ill, riddled by cancer and suffering great pain; such a patient would not be resuscitated or put on a respirator . . . and *a fortiori* would not be kept *against his will* on a respirator.

Although the Constitution does not explicitly mention a right of privacy, Supreme Court decisions have recognized that a right of personal privacy exists and that certain areas of privacy are guaranteed under the Constitution. . . .

The court in *Griswold* found the unwritten constitutional right of privacy to exist in the penumbra of specific guarantees of the Bill of Rights "formed by emanations from those guarantees that help give them life and substance." Presumably this right is broad enough to encompass a patient's decision to decline medical treatment under certain circumstances, in much the same way as it is broad enough to encompass a woman's decision to terminate pregnancy under certain conditions. . . .

The claimed interests of the State in this case are essentially the preservation and sanctity of human life and defense of the right of the physician to administer medical treatment according to his best judgment. In this case the doctors say that removing Karen from the respirator will conflict with their professional judgment. The plaintiff answers that Karen's present treatment serves only a maintenance function; that the respirator cannot cure or improve her condition but at best can only prolong her inevitable slow deterioration and death; and that the interests of the patient, as seen by her surrogate, the guardian, must be evaluated by the court as predominant, even in the face of an opinion *contra* by the present attending physicians. Plaintiff's distinction is significant. The nature of Karen's care and the realistic chances of her recovery are quite unlike those of the patients discussed in many of the cases where treatments were ordered. In many of those cases the medical procedure required (usually a transfusion) constituted a minimal bodily invasion and the chances of recovery and return to functioning life were very good. We think that the State's interest *contra* weakens and the individual's right to privacy grows as the degree of bodily invasion increases and the prognosis dims. Ultimately there comes a point at which the individual's rights overcome the State interest. It is for that reason that we believe Karen's choice, if she were competent to make it, would be vindicated by the law. Her prognosis is extremely poor—she will never resume cognitive life. And the bodily invasion is very great—she requires 24 hour intensive nursing care, antibiotics, the assistance of a respirator, a catheter and feeding tube.

Our affirmation of Karen's independent right of choice, however, would ordinarily be based upon her competency to assert it. The sad truth, however, is that she is grossly incompetent and we cannot discern her supposed choice based on the testimony of her previous conversations with friends, where such testimony is without sufficient probative weight. . . . Nevertheless we have concluded that Karen's right of privacy may be asserted on her behalf by her guardian under the peculiar circumstances here present.

If a putative decision by Karen to permit this non-cognitive, vegetative existence to terminate by natural forces is regarded as a valuable incident of her right of privacy, as we believe it to be, then it should not be discarded solely on the basis that her condition prevents her conscious exercise of the choice. The only practical way to prevent destruction of the right is to permit the guardian and family of Karen to render their best judgment, subject to the qualifications hereinafter stated, as to whether she would exercise it in these circumstances. If their conclusion is in the affirmative, this decision should be accepted by a society the overwhelming majority of whose members would, we think, in similar circumstances, exercise such a choice in the same way for themselves or for those closest to them. It is for this reason that we determine that Karen's right of privacy may be asserted in her behalf, in this respect, by her guardian and family under the particular circumstances presented by this record.

Regarding Mr. Quinlan's right of privacy, we agree with Judge Muir's conclusion that there is no parental constitutional right that would entitle him to a grant of relief *in propria persona*. . . . Insofar as a parental right of privacy has been recognized, it has been in the context of determining the rearing of infants and, as Judge Muir put it, involved "continuing life styles." . . . Karen Quinlan is a 22-year-old adult. Her right of privacy in respect of the matter before the court is to be vindicated by Mr. Quinlan as guardian, as hereinabove determined.

The Medical Factor

. . . We glean from the record here that physicians distinguish between curing the ill and comforting and easing the dying; that they refuse to treat the curable as if they were dying or ought to die, and that they have sometimes refused to treat the hopeless and dying as if they were curable. In this sense, as we were reminded by the testimony of Drs. Korein and Diamond, many of them have refused to inflict an undesired prolongation of the process of dying on a patient in irreversible condition when it is clear that such "therapy" offers neither human nor humane benefit. We think these attitudes represent a balanced implementation of a profoundly realistic perspective on the meaning of life and death and that they respect the whole Judeo-Christian tradition of regard for human life. No less would they seem consistent with the moral matrix of medicine, "to heal," very much in the sense of the endless mission of the law, "to do justice."

Yet this balance, we feel, is particularly difficult to perceive and apply in the context of the development by advanced technology of sophisticated and artificial life-sustaining devices. For those possibly curable, such devices are of great value, and, as ordinary medical procedures, are essential. Consequently, as pointed out by Dr. Diamond, they are necessary because of the ethic of medical practice. But in light of the situation in the present case (while the record here is somewhat hazy in distinguishing between "ordinary" and "extraordinary" measures), one would have to think that the use of the same respirator or life support could be considered "ordinary" in the context of the possibly curable patient but "extraordinary" in the context of the forced sustaining by cardiorespiratory processes of an irreversibly doomed patient. . . .

The evidence in this case convinces us that the focal point of decision should be the prognosis as to the reasonable possibility of return to cognitive and sapient life, as distinguished from the forced continuance of that biological vegetative existence to which Karen seems to be doomed.

In summary of the present Point of this opinion, we conclude that the state of the pertinent medical standards and practices which guided the attending physicians in this matter is not such as would justify this Court in deeming itself bound or controlled thereby in responding to the case for declaratory relief established by the parties on the record before us. . . .

Declaratory Relief

. . . [W]e herewith declare the following affirmative relief on behalf of the plaintiff. Upon the concurrence of the guardian and family of Karen, should the responsible attending physicians conclude that there is no reasonable possibility of Karen's ever emerging from her present comatose condition to a cognitive, sapient state and that the life-support apparatus now being administered to Karen should be discontinued, they shall consult with the hospital "Ethics Committee" or like body of the institution in which Karen is then hospitalized. If that consultative body agrees that there is no reasonable possibility of Karen's ever emerging from her present comatose condition to a cognitive, sapient state, the present life-support system may be withdrawn and said action shall be without any civil or criminal liability therefor on the part of any participant, whether guardian, physician, hospital or others. We herewith specifically so hold.

QUESTIONS FOR REFLECTION

1. Which features of Karen Ann Quinlan's condition did the court find relevant to reaching a decision? Do you agree that these are all the relevant factors?
2. How did the court justify its decision? Do you find the justification persuasive?
3. In fact, when Karen Ann Quinlan was disconnected from life-support machinery after this decision, she did not die. If the court had known she would survive without the equipment, would the justification the court offered be weakened?

J. GAY-WILLIAMS

The Wrongfulness of Euthanasia

(Source: Reprinted from Ronald Munson [ed.], Intervention and Reflection: Basic Issues in Medical Ethics. *Belmont, CA: Wadsworth Publishing Company. Copyright © 1992 by Ronald Munson. Reprinted with permission.)*

My impression is that euthanasia—the idea, if not the practice—is slowly gaining acceptance within our society. Cynics might attribute this to an increasing tendency to devalue human life, but I do not believe this is the major factor. The acceptance is much more likely to be the result of unthinking sympathy and benevolence. Well-publicized, tragic stories like that of Karen Quinlan elicit from us deep feelings of compassion. We think to ourselves, "She and her family would be better off if she were dead." It is an easy step from this very human response to the view that if someone (and others) would be better off dead, then it must be all right to kill that person. Although I respect the compassion that leads to this conclusion, I believe the conclusion is wrong. I want to show that euthanasia is wrong. It is inherently wrong, but it is also wrong judged from the standpoints of self-interest and of practical effects.

Before presenting my arguments to support this claim, it would be well to define "euthanasia." An essential aspect of euthanasia is that it involves taking a human life, either one's own or that of another. Also, the person whose life is taken must be someone who is believed to be suffering from some disease or injury from which recovery cannot reasonably be expected. Finally, the action must be deliberate and intentional. Thus, euthanasia is intentionally taking the life of a presumably hopeless person. Whether the life is one's own or that of another, the taking of it is still euthanasia.

It is important to be clear about the deliberate and intentional aspect of the killing. If a hopeless person is given an injection of the wrong drug by mistake and this causes his death, this is wrongful killing but not euthanasia. The killing cannot be the result of accident. Furthermore, if the person is given an injection of a drug that is believed to be necessary to treat his disease or better his condition and the person dies as a result, then this is neither wrongful killing nor euthanasia. The intention was to make the patient well, not kill him. Similarly, when a patient's condition is such that it is not reasonable to hope that any medical procedures or treatments will save his life, a failure to implement the procedures or treatments is not euthanasia. If the person dies, this will be as a result of his injuries or disease and not because of his failure to receive treatment.

The failure to continue treatment after it has been realized that the patient has little chance of benefitting from it has been characterized by some as "passive euthanasia." This phrase is misleading and mistaken. In such cases, the person involved is not killed (the first essential aspect of euthanasia), nor is the death of the person intended by the withholding of additional treatment (the third essential aspect of euthanasia). The aim may be to spare the person additional and unjustifiable pain, to save him from the indignities of hopeless manipulations, and to avoid increasing the financial and emotional burden on his family. When I buy a pencil it is so that I can use it to write, not to contribute to an increase in the gross national product. This may be the unintended consequence of my action, but it is not the aim of my action. So it is with failing to continue the treatment of a dying person. I intend his death no more than I intend to reduce the GNP by not using medical supplies. His is an unintended dying, and so-called "passive euthanasia" is not euthanasia at all.

1. The Argument from Nature

Every human being has a natural inclination to continue living. Our reflexes and responses fit us to fight attackers, flee wild animals, and dodge out of the way of trucks. In our daily lives we exercise the caution and care necessary to protect ourselves. Our bodies are similarly structured for survival right down to the molecular level. When we are cut, our capillaries seal shut, our blood clots, and fibrogen is produced to start the process of healing the wound. When we are invaded by bacteria, antibodies are produced to fight against the alien organisms, and their remains are swept out of the body by special cells designed for clean-up work.

Euthanasia does violence to this natural goal of survival. It is literally acting against nature because all the processes of nature are bent towards the end of bodily survival. Euthanasia defeats these subtle mechanisms in a way that, in a particular case, disease and injury might not.

It is possible, but not necessary, to make an appeal to revealed religion in this connection. Man as trustee of his body acts against God, its rightful possessor, when he takes his own life. He also violates the commandment to hold life sacred and never to take it without just and compelling cause. But since this appeal will persuade only those who are prepared to accept that religion has access to revealed truths, I shall not employ this line of argument.

It is enough, I believe, to recognize that the organization of the human body and our patterns of behavioral responses make the continuation of life a natural goal. By reason alone, then, we can recognize that euthanasia sets us against our own nature. Furthermore, in doing so, euthanasia does violence to our dignity. Our dignity comes from seeking our ends. When one of our goals is survival, and actions are taken that eliminate that goal, then our natural dignity suffers. Unlike animals, we are conscious through reason of our nature and our ends. Euthanasia involves acting as if this dual nature—inclination towards survival and awareness of this as an end—did not exist. Thus, euthanasia denies our basic human character and requires that we regard ourselves or others as something less than fully human.

2. The Argument from Self-Interest

The above arguments are, I believe, sufficient to show that euthanasia is inherently wrong. But there are reasons for considering it wrong when judged by standards other than reason. Because death is final and irreversible, euthanasia contains within it the possibility that we will work against our own interest if we practice it or allow it to be practiced on us.

Contemporary medicine has high standards of excellence and a proven record of accomplishment, but it does not possess perfect and complete knowledge. A mistaken diagnosis is possible, and so is a mistaken prognosis. Consequently, we may believe that we are dying of a disease when, as a matter of fact, we may not be. We may think that we have no hope of recovery when, as a matter of fact, our chances are quite good. In such circumstances, if euthanasia were permitted, we would die needlessly. Death is final and the chance of error too great to approve the practice of euthanasia.

Also, there is always the possibility that an experimental procedure or a hitherto untried technique will pull us through. We should at least keep this option open, but euthanasia closes it off. Furthermore, spontaneous remission does occur in many cases. For no apparent reason, a patient simply recovers when those all around him, including his physicians, expected him to die. Euthanasia would just guarantee their expectations and leave no room for the "miraculous" recoveries that frequently occur.

Finally, knowing that we can take our life at any time (or ask another to take it) might well incline us to give up too easily. The will to live is strong in all of us, but it can be weakened by pain and suffering and feelings of hopelessness. If during a bad time we allow ourselves to be killed, we never have a chance to reconsider. Recovery from a serious illness requires that we fight for it, and anything that weakens our determination by suggesting that there is an easy way out is ultimately against our own interest. Also, we may be inclined towards euthanasia because of our concern for others. If we see our sickness and suffering as an emotional and financial burden on our family, we may feel that to leave our life is to make their lives easier. The very presence of the possibility of euthanasia may keep us from surviving when we might.

3. The Argument from Practical Effects

Doctors and nurses are, for the most part, totally committed to saving lives. A life lost is, for them, almost a personal failure, an insult to their skills and knowledge. Euthanasia as a practice might well alter this. It could have a corrupting influence so that in any case that is severe doctors and nurses might not try hard enough to save the patient. They might decide that the patient would simply be "better off dead" and take the steps necessary to make that come about. This attitude could then carry over to their dealings with patients less seriously ill. The result would be an overall decline in the quality of medical care.

Finally, euthanasia as a policy is a slippery slope. A person apparently hopelessly ill may be allowed to take his own life. Then he may be permitted to deputize others to do it for him should he no longer be able to act. The judgment of others then becomes the ruling factor. Already at this point euthanasia is not personal and voluntary, for others are acting "on behalf of" the patient as they see fit. This may well incline them to act on behalf of other patients who have not authorized them to exercise their judgment. It is only a short step, then, from voluntary euthanasia (self-inflicted or authorized), to directed euthanasia administered to a patient who has given no authorization, to involuntary euthanasia conducted as part of a social policy. Recently many psychiatrists and sociologists have argued that we define as "mental illness" those forms of behavior that we disapprove of. This gives us license then to lock up those who display the behavior. The category of the "hopelessly ill" provides the possibility of even worse abuse. Embedded in a social policy, it would give society or its representatives the authority to eliminate all those who might be considered too "ill" to function normally any longer. The dangers of euthanasia are too great to all to run the risk of approving it in any form. The first slippery step may well lead to a serious and harmful fall.

I hope that I have succeeded in showing why the benevolence that inclines us to give approval of euthanasia is misplaced. Euthanasia is inherently wrong because it violates the nature and dignity of human beings. But even those who are not convinced by this must be persuaded that the potential personal and social dangers inherent in euthanasia are sufficient to forbid our approving it either as a personal practice or as a public policy.

Suffering is surely a terrible thing, and we have a clear duty to comfort those in need and to ease their suffering when we can. But suffering is also a natural part of life with values for the individual and for others that we should not overlook. We may legitimately seek for others and for ourselves an easeful death. Euthanasia, however, is not just an easeful death. It is a wrongful death. Euthanasia is not just dying. It is killing.

QUESTIONS FOR REFLECTION

1. Why does Gay-Williams object to the phrase "passive euthanasia"?
2. Gay-Williams argues that euthanasia is unnatural. In what way? How does this argument lead to the moral conclusion that euthanasia is wrong?
3. Can euthanasia ever be in a patient's self-interest, according to Gay-Williams? Do you agree?
4. What is Gay-Williams's "slippery slope" argument? How persuasive is it?

RONALD DWORKIN, THOMAS NAGEL, ROBERT NOZICK, JOHN RAWLS, THOMAS SCANLON, AND JUDITH JARVIS THOMSON

The Brief of the Amici Curiae

Ronald Dworkin and Thomas Nagel are professors of philosophy at New York University. Thomas Scanlon is professor of philosophy at Harvard University, as were Robert Nozick and John Rawls before their deaths in 2002. Judith Jarvis Thomson is professor of philosophy at the Massachusetts Institute of Technology. *(Source: Reprinted from an* amici curiae *["friends of the court"] brief submitted to the United States Supreme Court in the cases* Washington v. Glucksberg *and* Vacco v. Quill, *1997. Notes have been omitted.)*

Argument

I. The Liberty Interest Asserted Here Is Protected by the Due Process Clause

Certain decisions are momentous in their impact on the character of a person's life—decisions about religious faith, political and moral allegiance, marriage, procreation, and death, for example. Such deeply personal decisions pose controversial questions about how and why human life has value. In a free society, individuals must be allowed to make those decisions for themselves, out of their own faith, conscience, and convictions. This Court has insisted, in a variety of contexts and circumstances, that this great freedom is among those protected by the Due Process Clause as essential to a community of "ordered liberty." *Palko* v. *Connecticut* (1937). In its recent decision in *Planned Parenthood* v. *Casey* (1992), the Court offered a paradigmatic statement of that principle:

> matters involving the most intimate and personal choices a person may make in a lifetime, choices central to a person's dignity and autonomy, are central to the liberty protected by the Fourteenth Amendment.

That declaration reflects an idea underlying many of our basic constitutional protections. As the Court explained in *West Virginia State Board of Education* v. *Barnette* (1943):

> If there is any fixed star in our constitutional constellation, it is that no official . . . can prescribe what shall be orthodox in politics, nationalism, religion, or other matters of opinion or force citizens to confess by word or act their faith therein.

A person's interest in following his own convictions at the end of life is so central a part of the more general right to make "intimate and personal choices" for himself that a failure to protect that particular interest would undermine the general right altogether. Death is, for each of us, among the most significant events of life. As the Chief Justice said in *Cruzan* v. *Missouri* (1990), "[t]he choice between life and death is a deeply personal decision of obvious and overwhelming finality." Most of us see death—whatever we think will follow it—as the final act of life's drama, and we want that last act to reflect our own convictions, those we have tried to live by, not the convictions of others forced on us in our most vulnerable moment.

Different people, of different religious and ethical beliefs, embrace very different convictions about which way of dying confirms and which contradicts the value of their lives. Some fight against death with every weapon their doctors can devise. Others will do nothing to hasten death even if they pray it will come soon. Still others, including the patient-plaintiffs in these cases, want to end their lives when they think that living on, in the only way they can, would disfigure rather than enhance the lives they had created. Some people make the latter choice not just to escape pain. Even if it were possible to eliminate all pain for a dying patient—and frequently that is not possible—that would not end or even much alleviate the anguish some would feel at remaining alive, but intubated, helpless, and often sedated near oblivion.

None of these dramatically different attitudes about the meaning of death can be dismissed as irrational. None should be imposed, either by the pressure of doctors or relatives or by the fiat of government, on people who reject it. Just as it would be intolerable for government to dictate that doctors never be permitted to try to keep someone alive as long as possible, when that is what the patient wishes, so it is intolerable for government to dictate that doctors may never, under any circumstances, help someone to die who believes that further life means only degradation. The Constitution insists that people must be free to make these deeply personal decisions for themselves and must not be forced to end their lives in a way that appalls them, just because that is what some majority thinks proper. . . .

III. State Interests Do Not Justify a Categorical Prohibition on All Assisted Suicide

The Solicitor General concedes that "a competent, terminally ill adult has a constitutionally cognizable liberty interest in avoiding the kind of suffering experienced by the plaintiffs in this case." He agrees that this interest extends not only to avoiding pain, but to avoiding an existence the patient believes to be one of intolerable indignity or incapacity as well. The Solicitor General argues, however, that states nevertheless have the right to "override" this liberty interest altogether, because a state could reasonably conclude that allowing doctors to assist in suicide, even under the most stringent regulations and procedures that could be devised, would unreasonably endanger the lives of a number of patients who might ask for death in circumstances when it is plainly not in their interests to die or when their consent has been improperly obtained.

This argument is unpersuasive, however, for at least three reasons. *First*, in *Cruzan*, this Court noted that its various decisions supported the recognition of a general liberty interest in refusing medical treatment, even when such refusal could result in death. The various risks described by the Solicitor General apply equally to those situations. For instance, a patient kept alive only by an elaborate and disabling life support system might well become depressed, and doctors might be equally uncertain whether the depression is curable: such a patient might decide for death only because he has been advised that he will die soon anyway or that he will never live free of the burdensome apparatus, and either diagnosis might conceivably be mistaken. Relatives or doctors might subtly or crudely influence that decision, and state provision for the decision may (to the same degree in this case as if it allowed assisted suicide) be thought to encourage it.

Yet there has been no suggestion that states are incapable of addressing such dangers through regulation. In fact, quite the opposite is true. In *McKay* v. *Bergstedt* (1990), for example, the Nevada Supreme Court held that "competent adult patients desiring to refuse or discontinue medical treatment" must be examined by two non-attending physicians to determine whether the patient is mentally competent, understands his prognosis and treatment options, and appears free of coercion or pressure in making his decision. See also: *id.* (in the case of terminally ill patients with natural life expectancy of less than six months, [a] patient's right of self-determination shall be deemed to prevail over state interests, whereas [a] non-terminal patient's decision to terminate life-support systems must first be weighed against relevant state interests by trial judge); [and] *In re Farrell* (1987) ([which held that a] terminally-ill patient requesting termination of life-support must be determined to be competent and properly informed about [his] prognosis, available treatment options and risks, and to have made the decision voluntarily and without coercion). Those protocols served to guard against precisely the dangers that the Solicitor General raises. The case law contains no suggestion that such protocols are inevitably insufficient to prevent deaths that should have been prevented.

Indeed, the risks of mistake are overall greater in the case of terminating life support. *Cruzan* implied that a state must allow individuals to make such decisions through an advance directive stipulating either that life support be terminated (or not initiated) in described circumstances when the individual was no longer competent to make such a decision himself, or that a designated proxy be allowed to make that decision. All the risks just described are present when the decision is made through or pursuant to such an advance directive, and a grave further risk is added: that the directive, though still in force, no longer represents the wishes of the patient. The patient might have changed his mind before he became incompetent, though he did not change the directive, or his proxy may make a decision that the patient would not have made himself if still competent. In *Cruzan*, this Court held that a state may limit these risks through reasonable regulation. It did not hold—or even suggest—that a state may avoid them through a blanket prohibition that, in effect, denies the liberty interest altogether.

Second, nothing in the record supports the [Solicitor General's] conclusion that no system of rules and regulations could adequately reduce the risk of mistake. As discussed above, the experience of states in adjudicating requests to have life-sustaining treatment removed indicates the opposite. The Solicitor General has provided no persuasive reason why the same sort of procedures could not be applied effectively in the case of a competent individual's request for physician-assisted suicide.

Indeed, several very detailed schemes for regulating physician-assisted suicide have been submitted to the voters of some states and one has been enacted. In addition, concerned groups, including a group of distinguished professors of law and other professionals, have drafted and defended such schemes. Such draft statutes propose a variety of protections and review procedures designed to insure against mistakes, and neither Washington nor New York attempted to show that such schemes would be porous or ineffective. Nor does the Solicitor General's brief: it relies instead mainly on flat and conclusory statements. It cites a New York Task Force report, written before the proposals just described were drafted, whose findings have been widely disputed and were implicitly rejected in the opinion of the Second Circuit below. The weakness of the Solicitor General's argument is signaled by his strong reliance on the experience in the Netherlands which, in effect, allows assisted suicide pursuant to published guidelines. The Dutch guidelines are more permissive than the proposed and model American statutes, however. The Solicitor General deems the Dutch practice of ending the lives of people like neonates who cannot consent particularly noteworthy, for example, but that practice could easily and effectively be made illegal by any state regulatory scheme without violating the Constitution.

The Solicitor General's argument would perhaps have more force if the question before the Court were simply whether a state has any rational basis for an absolute prohibition; if that were the question, then it might be enough to call attention to risks a state might well deem not worth running. But as the Solicitor General concedes, the question here is a very different one: whether a state has interests sufficiently compelling to allow it to take the extraordinary step of altogether refusing the exercise of a liberty interest of constitutional dimension. In those circumstances, the burden is plainly on the state to demonstrate that the risk of mistakes is very high, and that no alternative to complete prohibition would adequately and effectively reduce those risks. Neither of the Petitioners has made such a showing.

Nor could they. The burden of proof on any state attempting to show this would be very high. Consider, for example, the burden a state would have to meet to show that it was entitled altogether to ban public speeches in favor of unpopular causes because it could not guarantee, either by regulations short of an outright ban or by increased police protection, that such speeches would not provoke a riot that would result in serious injury or death to an innocent party.

Or that it was entitled to deny those accused of crime the procedural rights that the Constitution guarantees, such as the right to a jury trial, because the security risk those rights would impose on the community would be too great. One can posit extreme circumstances in which some such argument would succeed. See, e.g., *Korematsu* v. *United States* (1944) (permitting United States to detain individuals of Japanese ancestry during wartime). But these circumstances would be extreme indeed, and the *Korematsu* ruling has been widely and severely criticized.

Third, it is doubtful whether the risks the Solicitor General cites are even of the right character to serve as justification for an absolute prohibition on the exercise of an important liberty interest. The risks fall into two groups. The first is the risk of medical mistake, including a misdiagnosis of competence or terminal illness. To be sure, no scheme of regulation, no matter how rigorous, can altogether guarantee that medical mistakes will not be made. But the Constitution does not allow a state to deny patients a great variety of important choices, for which informed consent is properly deemed necessary, just because the information on which the consent is given may, in spite of the most strenuous efforts to avoid mistake, be wrong. Again, these identical risks are present in decisions to terminate life support, yet they do not justify an absolute prohibition on the exercise of the right.

The second group consists of risks that a patient will be unduly influenced by considerations that the state might deem it not in his best interests to be swayed by, for example, the feelings and views of close family members. But what a patient regards as proper grounds for such a decision normally reflects exactly the judgments of personal ethics—of why his life is important and what affects its value—that patients have a crucial liberty interest in deciding for themselves. Even people who are dying have a right to hear and, if they wish, act on what others might wish to tell or suggest or even hint to them, and it would be dangerous to suppose that a state may prevent this on the ground that it knows better than its citizens when they should be moved by or yield to particular advice or suggestion in the exercise of their right to make fateful personal decisions for themselves. It is not a good reply that some people may not decide as they really wish—as they would decide, for example, if free from the "pressure" of others. That possibility could hardly justify the most serious pressure of all—the criminal law which tells them that they may not decide for death if they need the help of a doctor in dying, no matter how firmly they wish it.

There is a fundamental infirmity in the Solicitor General's argument. He asserts that a state may reasonably judge that the risk of "mistake" to some persons justifies a prohibition that not only risks but ensures and even aims at what would undoubtedly be a vastly greater number of "mistakes" of the opposite kind—preventing many thousands of competent people who think that it disfigures their lives to continue living, in the only way left to them, from escaping that—to them—terrible injury. A state grievously and irreversibly harms such people when it prohibits that escape. The Solicitor General's argument may seem plausible to those who do not agree that individuals are harmed by being forced to live on in pain and what they regard as indignity. But many other people plainly do think that such individuals are harmed, and a state may not take one side in that essentially ethical or religious controversy as its justification for denying a crucial liberty.

Of course, a state has important interests that justify regulating physician-assisted suicide. It may be legitimate for a state to deny an opportunity for assisted suicide when it acts in what it reasonably judges to be the best interests of the potential suicide, and when its judgment on that issue does not rest on contested judgments about "matters involving the most intimate and personal choices a person may make in a lifetime, choices central to personal dignity and autonomy." *Casey*. A state might assert, for example, that people who are not terminally ill, but who have formed a desire to die, are, as a group, very likely later to be grateful if they are prevented from taking their own lives. It might then claim that it is legitimate, out of concern for such people, to deny any of them a doctor's assistance [in taking their own lives].

This Court need not decide now the extent to which such paternalistic interests might override an individual's liberty interest. No one can plausibly claim, however—and it is noteworthy that neither Petitioners nor the Solicitor General does claim—that any such prohibition could serve the interests of any significant number of terminally ill patients. On the contrary, any paternalistic justification for an absolute prohibition of assistance to such patients would of necessity appeal to a widely contested religious or ethical conviction many of them, including the patient-plaintiffs, reject. Allowing *that* justification to prevail would vitiate the liberty interest.

Even in the case of terminally ill patients, a state has a right to take all reasonable measures to ensure that a patient requesting such assistance has made an informed, competent, stable and uncoerced decision. It is plainly legitimate for a state to establish procedures through which professional and administrative judgments can be made about these matters, and to forbid doctors to assist in suicide when its reasonable procedures have not been satisfied. States may be permitted considerable leeway in designing such procedures. They may be permitted, within reason, to err on what they take to be the side of caution. But they may not use the bare possibility of error as justification for refusing to establish any procedures at all and relying instead on a flat prohibition.

Conclusion

Each individual has a right to make the "most intimate and personal choices central to personal dignity and autonomy." That right encompasses the right to exercise some control over the time and manner of one's death.

The patient-plaintiffs in these cases were all mentally competent individuals in the final phase of terminal illness and died within months of filing their claims.

Jane Doe described how her advanced cancer made even the most basic bodily functions such as swallowing, coughing, and yawning extremely painful and that it was "not possible for [her] to reduce [her] pain to an acceptable level of comfort and to retain an alert state." Faced with such circumstances, she sought to be able to "discuss freely with [her] treating physician [her] intention of hastening [her] death through the consumption of drugs prescribed for that purpose." *Quill* v. *Vacco* (2d Cir. 1996).

George A. Kingsley, in advanced stages of AIDS which included, among other hardships, the attachment of a tube to an artery in his chest which made even routine functions burdensome and the development of lesions on his brain, sought advice from his doctors regarding prescriptions which could hasten his impending death.

Jane Roe, suffering from cancer since 1988, had been almost completely bedridden since 1993 and experienced constant pain which could not be alleviated by medication. After undergoing counseling for herself and her family, she desired to hasten her death by taking prescription drugs. *Compassion in Dying* v. *Washington* (1994).

John Doe, who had experienced numerous AIDS-related ailments since 1991, was "especially cognizant of the suffering imposed by a lingering terminal illness because he was the primary caregiver for his long-term companion who died of AIDS" and sought prescription drugs from his physician to hasten his own death after entering the terminal phase of AIDS.

James Poe suffered from emphysema which caused him "a constant sensation of suffocating" as well as a cardiac condition which caused severe leg pain. Connected to an oxygen tank at all times but unable to calm the panic reaction associated with his feeling of suffocation even with regular doses of morphine, Mr. Poe sought physician-assisted suicide.

A state may not deny the liberty claimed by the patient-plaintiffs in these cases without providing them an opportunity to demonstrate, in whatever way the state might reasonably think wise and necessary, that the conviction they expressed for an early death is competent, rational, informed, stable, and uncoerced.

Affirming the decisions by the Courts of Appeals would establish nothing more than that there is such a constitutionally protected right in principle. It would establish only that some individuals, whose decisions for suicide plainly cannot be dismissed as irrational or foolish or premature, must be accorded a reasonable opportunity to show that their decision for death is informed and free. It is not necessary to decide precisely which patients are entitled to that opportunity. If, on the other hand, this Court reverses the decisions below, its decision could only be justified by the momentous proposition—a proposition flatly in conflict with the spirit and letter of the Court's past decisions—that an American citizen does not, after all, have the right, even in principle, to live and die in the light of his own religious and ethical beliefs, his own convictions about why his life is valuable and where its value lies.

QUESTIONS FOR REFLECTION

1. How do the philosophers argue that denying a right to physician-assisted suicide would undermine the general right to make "intimate and personal choices"? Do you find their argument convincing?
2. Would Mill's view in *On Liberty* support or contradict the philosophers' view on physician-assisted suicide? Explain.
3. Why do the philosophers find the possibility of error incapable of supporting a ban on euthanasia?
4. Many have alleged that allowing physician-assisted suicide would endanger the lives of patients who do not want to die. How do the philosophers respond to this argument?
5. Would Kant agree with the philosophers that facing death on something other than your own terms is an indignity? How would he view physician-assisted suicide?

CHIEF JUSTICE WILLIAM REHNQUIST

Majority Opinion in Washington et al. *v.* Glucksberg et al. (1997)

(Source: 117 S.Ct. 2258 [1997]. Most legal references have been omitted.)

Chief Justice Rehnquist delivered the opinion of the Court.

The question presented in this case is whether Washington's prohibition against "caus[ing]" or "aid[ing]" a suicide offends the Fourteenth Amendment to the United States Constitution. We hold that it does not.

It has always been a crime to assist a suicide in the State of Washington. In 1854, Washington's first Territorial Legislature outlawed "assisting another in the commission of self-murder." Today, Washington law provides: "A person is guilty of promoting a suicide attempt when he knowingly causes or aids another person to attempt suicide." "Promoting a suicide attempt" is a felony, punishable by up to five years' imprisonment and up to a $10,000 fine. At the same time, Washington's Natural Death Act, enacted in 1979, states that the "withholding or withdrawal of life-sustaining treatment" at a patient's direction "shall not, for any purpose, constitute a suicide." . . .

I

We begin, as we do in all due-process cases, by examining our Nation's history, legal traditions, and practices. In almost every State—indeed, in almost every western democracy—it is a crime to assist a suicide. The States' assisted-suicide bans are not innovations. Rather, they are longstanding expressions of the States' commitment to the protection and preservation of all human life. *Cruzan* ("[T]he States—indeed, all civilized nations—demonstrate their commitment to life by treating homicide as a serious crime. Moreover, the majority of States in this country have laws imposing criminal penalties on one who assists another to commit suicide"); see *Stanford* v. *Kentucky* (1989) ("[T]he primary and most reliable indication of [a national] consensus is . . . the pattern of enacted laws"). Indeed, opposition to and condemnation of suicide—and, therefore, of assisting suicide—are consistent and enduring themes of our philosophical, legal, and cultural heritages.

More specifically, for over 700 years, the Anglo-American common-law tradition has punished or otherwise disapproved of both suicide and assisting suicide. *Cruzan* (Scalia, J., concurring). In the 13th century, Henry de Bracton, one of the first legal-treatise writers, observed that "[j]ust as a man may commit felony by slaying another so may he do so by slaying himself." The real and personal property of one who killed himself to avoid conviction and punishment for a crime were forfeit to the king; however, thought Bracton, "if a man slays himself in weariness of life or because he is unwilling to endure further bodily pain . . . [only] his movable goods [were] confiscated." Thus, "[t]he principle that suicide of a sane person, for whatever reason, was a punishable felony was . . . introduced into English common law." Centuries later, Sir William Blackstone, whose *Commentaries on the Laws of England* not only provided a definitive summary of the common law but was also a primary legal authority for 18th and 19th-century American lawyers, referred to suicide as "self-murder" and "the pretended heroism, but real cowardice, of the Stoic philosophers, who destroyed themselves to avoid those ills which they had not the fortitude to endure. . . ." Blackstone emphasized that "the law has . . . ranked [suicide] among the highest crimes," *ibid*, although, anticipating later developments, he conceded that the harsh and shameful punishments imposed for suicide "borde[r] a little upon severity."

For the most part, the early American colonies adopted the common-law approach. . . .

That suicide remained a grievous, though nonfelonious, wrong is confirmed by the fact that colonial and early state legislatures and courts did not retreat from prohibiting assisting suicide. . . .

The earliest American statute explicitly to outlaw assisting suicide was enacted in New York in 1828, and many of the new States and Territories followed New York's example. Between 1857 and 1865, a New York commission led by Dudley Field drafted a criminal code that prohibited "aiding" a suicide and, specifically, "furnish[ing] another person with any deadly weapon or poisonous drug, knowing that such person intends to use such weapon or drug in taking his own life." By the time the Fourteenth Amendment was ratified, it was a crime in most States to assist a suicide. . . .

Though deeply rooted, the States' assisted-suicide bans have in recent years been reexamined and, generally, reaffirmed. Because of advances in medicine and technology, Americans today are increasingly likely to die in institutions, from chronic illnesses. Public concern and democratic action are therefore sharply focused on how best to protect dignity and independence at the end of life, with the result that there have been many significant changes in state laws and in the attitudes these laws reflect. Many States, for example, now permit "living wills," surrogate health-care decisionmaking, and the withdrawal or refusal of life-sustaining medical treatment. At the same time, however, voters and legislators continue for the most part to reaffirm their States' prohibitions on assisting suicide.

The Washington statute at issue in this case was enacted in 1975 as part of a revision of that State's criminal code. Four years later, Washington passed its Natural Death Act, which specifically stated that the "withholding or withdrawal of life-sustaining treatment . . . shall not, for any purpose, constitute a suicide" and that "[n]othing in this chapter shall be construed to condone, authorize, or approve mercy killing. . . ." In 1991, Washington voters rejected a ballot initiative which, had it passed, would have permitted a form of physician-assisted suicide. Washington then added a provision to the Natural Death Act expressly excluding physician-assisted suicide.

California voters rejected an assisted-suicide initiative similar to Washington's in 1993. On the other hand, in 1994, voters in Oregon enacted, also through ballot initiative, that State's "Death with Dignity Act," which legalized physician-assisted suicide for competent, terminally ill adults. Since the Oregon vote, many proposals to legalize assisted suicide have been and continue to be introduced in the States' legislatures, but none has been enacted. And just last year, Iowa and Rhode Island joined the overwhelming majority of States explicitly prohibiting assisted suicide. Also, on April 30, 1997, President Clinton signed the Federal Assisted Suicide Funding Restriction Act of 1997, which prohibits the use of federal funds in support of physician-assisted suicide.

Thus, the States are currently engaged in serious, thoughtful examinations of physician-assisted suicide and other similar issues. For example, New York State's Task Force on Life and the Law—an ongoing, blueribbon commission composed of doctors, ethicists, lawyers, religious leaders, and interested laymen—was convened in 1984 and commissioned with "a broad mandate to recommend public policy on issues raised by medical advances." Over the past decade, the Task Force has recommended laws relating to end-of-life decisions, surrogate pregnancy, and organ donation. After studying physician-assisted suicide, however, the Task Force unanimously concluded that "[l]egalizing assisted suicide and euthanasia would pose profound risks to many individuals who are ill and vulnerable. . . . [T]he potential dangers of this dramatic change in public policy would outweigh any benefit that might be achieved."

Attitudes toward suicide itself have changed since Bracton, but our laws have consistently condemned, and continue to prohibit, assisting suicide. Despite changes in medical technology and notwithstanding an increased emphasis on the importance of end-of-life decisionmaking, we have not retreated from this prohibition. Against this backdrop of history, tradition, and practice, we now turn to respondents' constitutional claim.

II

The Due Process Clause guarantees more than fair process, and the "liberty" it protects includes more than the absence of physical restraint. The Clause also provides heightened protection against government interference with certain fundamental rights and liberty interests. In a long line of cases, we have held that, in addition to the specific freedoms protected by the Bill of Rights, the "liberty" specially protected by the Due Process Clause includes the rights to marry, to have children, to direct the education and upbringing of one's children, to marital privacy, to use contraception, to bodily integrity, and to abortion. We have also assumed, and strongly suggested, that the Due Process Clause protects the traditional right to refuse unwanted lifesaving medical treatment.

But we "ha[ve] always been reluctant to expand the concept of substantive due process because guideposts for responsible decisionmaking in this unchartered area are scarce and open-ended." By extending constitutional protection to an asserted right or liberty interest, we, to a great extent, place the matter outside the arena of public debate and legislative action. We must therefore "exercise the utmost care whenever we are asked to break new ground in this field," lest the liberty protected by the Due Process Clause be subtly transformed into the policy preferences of the members of this Court.

Our established method of substantive-due-process analysis has two primary features: First, we have regularly observed that the Due Process Clause specially protects those fundamental rights and liberties which are, objectively, "deeply rooted in this Nation's history and tradition," and "implicit in the concept of ordered liberty," such that "neither liberty nor justice would exist if they were sacrificed," *Palko v. Connecticut* (1937). Second, we have required in substantive-due-process cases a "careful description" of the asserted fundamental liberty interest. Our Nation's history, legal traditions, and practices thus provide the crucial "guideposts for responsible decisionmaking," that direct and restrain our exposition of the Due Process Clause. As we stated recently in *Flores*, the Fourteenth Amendment "forbids the government to infringe . . . 'fundamental' liberty interests at all, no matter what process is provided, unless the infringement is narrowly tailored to serve a compelling state interest."

Justice Souter, relying on Justice Harlan's dissenting opinion in *Poe v. Ullman*, would largely abandon this restrained methodology, and instead ask "whether [Washington's] statute sets up one of those 'arbitrary impositions' or 'purposeless restraints' at odds with the Due Process Clause of the Fourteenth Amendment." In our view, however, the development of this Court's substantive-due-process jurisprudence, described briefly above, has been a process whereby the outlines of the "liberty" specially protected by the Fourteenth Amendment—never fully clarified, to be sure, and perhaps not capable of being fully clarified—have at least been carefully refined by concrete examples involving fundamental rights found to be deeply rooted in our legal tradition. This approach tends to rein in the subjective elements that are necessarily present in due-process judicial review. In addition, by establishing a threshold requirement—that a challenged state action implicate a fundamental right—before requiring more than a reasonable relation to a legitimate state interest to justify the action, it avoids the need for complex balancing of competing interests in every case.

Turning to the claim at issue here, the Court of Appeals stated that "[p]roperly analyzed, the first issue to be resolved is whether there is a liberty interest in determining the time and manner of one's death," or, in other words, "[i]s there a right to die?" Similarly, respondents assert a "liberty to choose how to die" and a right to "control of one's final days," and describe the asserted liberty as "the right to choose a humane, dignified death," and "the liberty to shape death." As noted above, we have a tradition of carefully formulating the interest at stake in substantive-due-process cases. For example, although *Cruzan* is often described as a "right to die" case, we were, in fact, more precise: we assumed that the Constitution granted competent persons a "constitutionally protected right to refuse life-saving hydration and nutrition." *Cruzan* (O'Connor, J., concurring) ("[A] liberty interest in refusing unwanted medical treatment may be inferred from our prior decisions"). The Washington statute at issue in this case prohibits "aid[ing] another person to attempt suicide," and, thus, the question before us is whether the "liberty" specially protected by the Due Process Clause includes a right to commit suicide which itself includes a right to assistance in doing so.

We now inquire whether this asserted right has any place in our Nation's traditions. Here, as discussed above, we are confronted with a consistent and almost universal tradition that has long rejected the asserted right, and continues explicitly to reject it today, even for terminally ill, mentally competent adults. To hold for respondents, we would have to reverse centuries of legal doctrine and practice, and strike down the considered policy choice of almost every State. . . .

The history of the law's treatment of assisted suicide in this country has been and continues to be one of the rejection of nearly all efforts to permit it. That being the case, our decisions lead us to conclude that the asserted "right" to assistance in committing suicide is not a fundamental liberty interest protected by the Due Process Clause. The Constitution also requires, however, that Washington's assisted-suicide ban be rationally related to legitimate government interests. This requirement is unquestionably met here. As the court below recognized, Washington's assisted-suicide ban implicates a number of state interests.

First, Washington has an "unqualified interest in the preservation of human life." *Cruzan*. The State's prohibition on assisted suicide, like all homicide laws, both reflects and advances its commitment to this interest. This interest is symbolic and aspirational as well as practical:

> While suicide is no longer prohibited or penalized, the ban against assisted suicide and euthanasia shores up the notion of limits in human relationships. It reflects the gravity with which we view the decision to take one's own life or the life of another, and our reluctance to encourage or promote these decisions.—New York Task Force.

Respondents admit that "[t]he State has a real interest in preserving the lives of those who can still contribute to society and enjoy life." The Court of Appeals also recognized Washington's interest in protecting life, but held that the "weight" of this interest depends on the "medical condition and the wishes of the person whose life is at stake." Washington, however, has rejected this sliding-scale approach and, through its assisted-suicide ban, insists that all persons' lives, from beginning to end, regardless of physical or mental condition, are under the full protection of the law. As we have previously affirmed, the States "may properly decline to make judgments about the 'quality' of life that a particular individual may enjoy," *Cruzan*. This remains true, as *Cruzan* makes clear, even for those who are near death.

Relatedly, all admit that suicide is a serious public-health problem, especially among persons in otherwise vulnerable groups. The State has an interest in preventing suicide, and in studying, identifying, and treating its causes.

Those who attempt suicide—terminally ill or not—often suffer from depression or other mental disorders. Research indicates, however, that many people who request physician-assisted suicide withdraw that request if their depression and pain are treated. The New York Task Force, however, expressed its concern that, because depression is difficult to diagnose, physicians and medical professionals often fail to respond adequately to seriously ill patients' needs. Thus, legal physician-assisted suicide could make it more difficult for the State to protect depressed or mentally ill persons, or those who are suffering from untreated pain, from suicidal impulses.

The State also has an interest in protecting the integrity and ethics of the medical profession. In contrast to the Court of Appeals' conclusion that "the integrity of the medical profession would [not] be threatened in any way by [physician-assisted suicide]," the American Medical Association, like many other medical and physicians' groups, has concluded that "[p]hysician-assisted suicide is fundamentally incompatible with the physician's role as healer." And physician-assisted suicide could, it is argued, undermine the trust that is essential to the doctor-patient relationship by blurring the time-honored line between healing and harming.

Next, the State has an interest in protecting vulnerable groups—including the poor, the elderly, and disabled persons—from abuse, neglect, and mistakes.

The Court of Appeals dismissed the State's concern that disadvantaged persons might be pressured into physician-assisted suicide as "ludicrous on its face." We have recognized, however, the real risk of subtle coercion and undue influence in end-of-life situations. *Cruzan*. Similarly, the New York Task Force warned that "[l]egalizing physician-assisted suicide would pose profound risks to many individuals who are ill and vulnerable. . . . The risk of harm is greatest for the many individuals in our society whose autonomy and well-being are already compromised by poverty, lack of access to good medical care, advanced age, or membership in a stigmatized social group." If physician-assisted suicide were permitted, many might resort to it to spare their families the substantial financial burden of end-of-life health-care costs.

The State's interest here goes beyond protecting the vulnerable from coercion; it extends to protecting disabled and terminally ill people from prejudice, negative and inaccurate stereotypes, and "societal indifference." The State's assisted-suicide ban reflects and reinforces its policy that the lives of terminally ill, disabled, and elderly people must be no less valued than the lives of the young and healthy, and that a seriously disabled person's suicidal impulses should be interpreted and treated the same way as anyone else's.

Finally, the State may fear that permitting assisted suicide will start it down the path to voluntary and perhaps even involuntary euthanasia. The Court of Appeals struck down Washington's assisted-suicide ban only "as applied to competent, terminally ill adults who wish to hasten their deaths by obtaining medication prescribed by their doctors." Washington insists, however, that the impact of the court's decision will not and cannot be so limited. If suicide is protected as a matter of constitutional right, it is argued, "every man and woman in the United States must enjoy it." The Court of Appeals' decision, and its expansive reasoning, provide ample support for the State's concerns. The court noted, for example, that the "decision of a duly appointed surrogate decision maker is for all legal purposes the decision of the patient himself"; that "in some instances, the patient may be unable to self-administer the drugs and . . . administration by the physician . . . may be the only way the patient may be able to receive them"; and that not only physicians, but also family members and loved ones, will inevitably participate in assisting suicide. Thus, it turns out that what is couched as a limited right to "physician-assisted suicide" is likely, in effect, a much broader license, which could prove extremely difficult to police and contain. Washington's ban on assisting suicide prevents such erosion.

This concern is further supported by evidence about the practic of euthanasia in the Netherlands. The Dutch government's own study revealed that in 1990, there were 2,300 cases of voluntary euthanasia (defined as "the deliberate termination of another's life at his request"), 400 cases of assisted suicide, and more than 1,000 cases of euthanasia without an explicit request. In addition to these latter 1,000 cases, the study found an additional 4,941 cases where physicians administered lethal morphine overdoses without the patients' explicit consent. This study suggests that, despite the existence of various reporting procedures, euthanasia in the Netherlands has not been limited to competent, terminally ill adults who are enduring physical suffering, and that regulation of the practice may not have prevented abuses in cases involving vulnerable persons, including severely disabled neonates and elderly persons suffering from dementia. The New York Task Force, citing the Dutch experience, observed that "assisted suicide and euthanasia are closely linked," and concluded that the "risk of . . . abuse is neither speculative nor distant." Washington, like most other States, reasonably ensures against this risk by banning, rather than regulating, assisting suicide.

We need not weigh exactingly the relative strengths of these various interests. They are unquestionably important and legitimate, and Washington's ban on assisted suicide is at least reasonably related to their promotion and protection. We therefore hold that Wash. Rev. Code §9A.36.060(1) (1994) does not violate the Fourteenth Amendment, either on its face or "as applied to competent, terminally ill adults who wish to hasten their deaths by obtaining medication prescribed by their doctors."

Throughout the Nation, Americans are engaged in an earnest and profound debate about the morality, legality, and practicality of physician-assisted suicide. Our holding permits this debate to continue, as it should in a democratic society. The decision of the *en banc* Court of Appeals is reversed, and the case is remanded for further proceedings consistent with this opinion.

QUESTIONS FOR REFLECTION

1. How is the history of prohibition on suicide and assisted suicide relevant to the Court's decision?
2. What philosophical view of rights would most closely correspond to the attitude the Court adopts?
3. What rationales does the Court find for prohibiting physician-assisted suicide?
4. How does the Court's decision respond to the philosophers' argument that people have the right to make "intimate and personal choices"?
5. Does the Court's decision depend on the distinction between killing and letting die?

TOON QUAGHEBEUR, BERNADETTE DIERCKX DE CASTERLÉ, AND CHRIS GASTMANS

Nursing and Euthanasia: A Review of Argument-Based Ethics Literature

Toon Quaghebeur is professor and vice-head of the Department of Health and Technology at the Catholic University of Leuven and Leuven University College, Leuven, Belgium. Bernadette Dierckx de Casterlé is professor at the Faculty of Medicine, Centre for Health Services and Nursing Research, at the Catholic University of Leuven. Chris Gastmans is professor at the Faculty of Medicine, Centre for Biomedical Ethics and Law, at the Catholic University of Leuven. *(Source: from Nursing Ethics 26 [2009]: 467–487. Reprinted by permission of the publishers. Footnotes omitted.)*

Results

Ethical arguments about euthanasia related to principles

The four principles of medical ethics—respect for autonomy, non-maleficence, beneficence and justice—comprise, in large measure, the nursing ethics debate on euthanasia. However, it seems too simple to state, as Snelling did, that the justification for euthanasia is based on the principles of beneficence and respect for autonomy, while its opponents rely on the principle of non-maleficence. The nursing ethics literature reveals that these principles are put forward, manipulated and interpreted to support arguments both for and against euthanasia.

Respect for autonomy In the nursing ethics literature, euthanasia as an ethically good practice is often justified on the basis of respect for an individual's autonomy. A person organizes his or her own private life so that the government, doctors and nurses cannot counteract what a euthanasia requester considers as the individual realization of his or her autonomous choice. Farsides states that doctors and nurses must respect a request for euthanasia as an expression of the patient's autonomy, even if they do not consider themselves capable of or want to carry out this request. Similarly, Willard indicated that caring for a patient is best achieved by respecting the patient's autonomy, even if he or she requests euthanasia. According to Kuhse, a good death is an autonomous death. Thus, the autonomous choice to die must not be counteracted by the maternal attitude of an unprincipled, feminine nursing ethics of care.

However, the nursing ethics literature also offers four criticisms against the characterization of euthanasia as a morally good practice on the basis of respect for a patient's autonomy. Appeals to autonomy in order to justify euthanasia seem problematic. The first criticism is that euthanasia itself, at least in part, carries the connotation of having too little respect for the autonomy of others. Schaart and Boer stated that euthanasia not only deals with a patient's autonomy regarding life in general or his or her life in particular, but also, and above all, deals with a patient's autonomy over and against other people. Blondeau argued that respect for a patient's autonomy cannot simply erase the importance of the social community. Just as life is a social practice, dying is also a social practice: it does not happen outside of a social network. McCabe stated that a one-sided choice to support a patient's autonomy undermines the autonomy of the nurses involved in caring for that patient. They are not obliged to honour every preference that a patient may express. Nurses do not have to advocate anything and everything a patient may want. Beech therefore argues that, for full respect of autonomy to occur, nurses as well as patients must be allowed an equal opportunity to exercise their autonomy. Similarly, Goodman also has problems with the notion that nurses' autonomy is violated by the act of euthanasia on the basis of respect for a patient's autonomy.

The second criticism is based on the idea that euthanasia does not really administer justice to the autonomy of the patient. Low and Pang consider respect for a patient's autonomy as important, but not absolute. They found it strange that advocates of euthanasia support patient autonomy by making this same autonomy senseless, because after euthanasia is completed the patient no longer enjoys his or her autonomy. Low and Pang thus consider euthanasia to be an escape, in which pain is alleviated by eliminating the patient. Euthanasia therefore illustrates an inability to deal with death. Blondeau also questions the quality of autonomy for a patient who flees from uncertainty and anxiety by choosing to die. According to Rumbold, on the basis of a patient's autonomy, euthanasia only confirms a defeatist perspective, in which there is no room for a positive answer to personal suffering. According to McCabe, respect for a patient's individual autonomy as justification for the act of euthanasia considers only those who can make, or have made, their wishes clear. The "non-autonomous" patient, who can no longer communicate with his or her environment, is made to suffer. One who uses the principle of respect for autonomy as justification for euthanasia therefore runs the risk of denying a person dignity once he or she is incapable of expressing himself or herself as an autonomous individual.

The third criticism lies in the argument that, if one considers euthanasia at least as a socially justified possibility of choice, a patient's autonomy is in danger because of growing social pressure on some specific patient populations.This type of social climate hinders a patient from making a well-considered and free decision. The possible occurrence of discrimination against vulnerable groups makes euthanasia dangerous. Begley fears that, because of the growing focus on the "procedure of care," a patient may be afraid to withdraw his or her euthanasia request once the procedure has started. Pollard and Winton, as well as Low and Pang, point out that the so-called free request for euthanasia does not always happen freely.

The last criticism is based on the misuse of autonomy to justify euthanasia. Indeed, McCabe criticizes how the nursing ethics literature currently uses the concept of autonomy to justify a link between nursing care and euthanasia. This type of autonomy concerns an asocial, individualistic concept of autonomy based on desires rather than on reason or understanding. According to McCabe, the application of autonomy in this way leads to a one-sided preference—utilitarianism or forced ethic of consequences in which "morally good" corresponds with "autonomously chosen."

Non-maleficence In the nursing ethics literature, a rejection of euthanasia mostly occurs on the basis of the non-maleficence principle. Owing to irreversible damage to patients' lives, Mclnerney and Seibold ardently plead against euthanasia. According to this perspective, euthanasia is too drastic an intervention to be used in end-of-life care. It makes dealing correctly with death almost impossible; it is also irreversible.

The principle of non-maleficence is applied in two ways. First, the sanctity and inviolability of life and the human person do not allow euthanasia to be considered as good ethical nursing practice. According to nurses, human life deserves respect, especially now when society is confronted with the problems of a population that is growing older and health care costs that are increasing.

Second, using this argument the gift character of life is often translated into a religious stance. The religiously interpreted resistance to euthanasia starts from the presupposition that life lies in God's hands and that our life is not our own. Religion helps us to see ourselves and others as persons. Fitzpatrick emphasizes that the problem with such reasoning is that it works only for those who share the same religious presupposition.

The principle of non-maleficence also has its opponents. Schaart and Boer and Zimbelman suggest that the fundamental norm, "respect for life," is not absolute. Kuhse and Singer reject the sanctity-of-life principle, which states that each human life is of equal dignity and inviolable. According to these authors, one must have good reasons for preferring the condition of allowing one to die over the condition of helping one to die. Moody also sweeps aside the sanctity-of-life principle and views it as an illusion.

Beneficence Nurses are also portrayed as patient advocates who must do good. The principle of beneficence generates an obligation to promulgate the important and legitimate interests of others. In the ethical debate on euthanasia, the principle of beneficence functions also as a two-edged sword that can be used for support or opposition.

If nurses want to do good for patients, then, according to some authors, quality-of-life arguments have to be employed, whereby the quality of one's life and its dignity is worth more than the length of life. In line with respect for the beneficence principle as an argument for euthanasia, Simpson refers to the concept of "wrongful life," which implies that a particular life is bad, intrinsically wrong, and harmful in comparison to death. Death is then precisely considered as good and right. According to Zimbelman, the quality-of-life argument ensures that health care workers do not become subject to biological idolatry—the error of vitalism—or therapeutic obstinacy. In this respect, Davis *et al.* discuss "the overall good of an individual patient" and state that what is medically good for a patient is not always what the patient wants.

Nevertheless, there are sharp remarks in the nursing ethics literature with respect to this argument in favour of euthanasia. These remarks question the direct link between doing good for a patient and euthanasia. The concept of beneficence carries with it an indistinctness: how is one to consider the "patient's best interests," and which necessary actions does one have to fulfil to meet them? In interpreting the significance of doing good for a patient, the patient's desire to die may not simply be identified with a desire to be killed. Van der Arend states that patients' interests are never served by causing their death, even if they believe so and if they desire to die. Goodman calls compassion an insufficiently strong motive for justifying euthanasia.

The nursing ethics literature on euthanasia poses many more questions. Can one rationally judge the worthlessness of someone's life? Is there something like a life not worth being lived? Is it not a contradiction to eliminate a life on the basis of seeking quality of that life? McCabe warns about ethics of desire that outstrip ethics of reason. When the feelings and wishes of patients or of other persons involved attain the upper hand, there is a threat of moral relativism whereby the feelings of the majority promulgating the patient's interests determine what is good ethical nursing practice.

Justice In promoting or protecting patients' interests, Kuhse defends the notion that euthanasia can be necessary from the point of view of justice. Here the principle of justice appears as an expression of good care for the patient.

Allmark states that one does not have to resort to a utilitarian way of thinking wherein euthanasia is considered to be an ethically justified form of good dying; for example, in cases in which it would be unjust and cruel to refuse a request for euthanasia. Justice here means that everyone receives according to their need and gives according to their possibilities.

The literature offers two warnings about using the principle of justice in the argument for euthanasia. First, the danger of being self-righteous (or the danger of calling something "just" to fit in its own domain) is very real. Self-gratification and self-serving behaviour are the characteristics of a new social movement, of which euthanasia is but a part. Second, the right to die does not morally obligate nurses actually to carry out patients' requests for euthanasia.

Ethical arguments about euthanasia related to the profession

According to some authors, violation of the non-maleficence principle is not only detrimental to the gift character of life, but it can also seriously harm the integrity of the nursing profession. Several ethical arguments for and against euthanasia emerge from the literature, and they prompt the nursing profession to reflect deeply on its attitude towards this problem.

Nursing practice based on trust Simpson and Kowalski both plead in favour of the argument that patients should always be able to trust that a nurse will not kill them. Euthanasia as such can create a dimension of suspicion that changes the very character of a nurse's role as healer and advocate. In this context, Zimbelman also warns of the distrust that can arise in institutions that co-opt into their policy the possibility of euthanasia. Confidence in the relationship between patient and nurse suffers from this type of policy. McCabe states that nurses' involvement in the execution of euthanasia truly harms society's trust in the nursing profession.

The nurse as independent moral actor In the same profession-orientated perspective, Aroskar refers to the integrity of nurses, who should never be used merely as means to achieving patients' goals, here meaning patients' wish for death. According to McCabe, when euthanasia is justified through utilitarian use of the principle of respect for autonomy, this runs counter to nursing's moral practice. Nurses are more than simple executers of patients' wishes. When nurses become involved in carrying out euthanasia, many issues are at stake: the true nature of nursing, the professional dignity of nurses and, above all, the autonomous character of nursing with regard to doctors and patients.

Professional integrity in the function of euthanasia Nevertheless, the professional integrity argument is also used to support euthanasia to the extent that professional integrity can be thought of as responsibility for a fellow human being and as respect for a patient's autonomy. In this context, White clearly states that assisted suicide, which in her article is understood to be euthanasia, is compatible with the professional integrity of nursing. This integrity specifically underlies nurses' motivation for respecting patient autonomy, promoting patient well-being and providing compassionate care. Here, euthanasia is in line with the proper character of the nursing profession, which focuses on protecting human dignity, promoting patients' interests and caring for patients.

Ethical arguments about euthanasia related to the concept of care

Framing euthanasia as an ethical problem from a care-orientated perspective has a different starting point from that of a principle- and profession-orientated perspective. The main question from this viewpoint is how to define good care.

Euthanasia as the pinnacle of care In the nursing ethics literature, some authors plead for the case that euthanasia is an expression of care for patients in distress. Ellis is in favour of permitting euthanasia so that dignified care can be delivered during dying in the same way that nurses strive to deliver patient care in life. Farsides therefore stresses that requests for euthanasia should not be considered a sign of care failure. Willard advances the notion that euthanasia is certainly not incompatible with care and is a moral possibility, even though other treatment options, such as palliative care, now exist. Particularly during the terminal phase of life it is critical that nurses acknowledge that patients are fellow human beings who are worthy of dignity and respect. This is crucial for all caring. For Kuhse, who sees no clear line separating palliative care and euthanasia, euthanasia is best seen as a form of specialized care. However, this view challenges some long-accepted principles, rules and laws that are unjust and stand in the way of good patient care. For Begley, who considers euthanasia to be part of terminal care, euthanasia is not opposed to care. In line with Kuhse, she even calls euthanasia a challenge for health care workers: "The challenge of euthanasia . . . is clear: are those who claim to be the advocates of the dying person ready to accept this challenge?" According to Begley, comprehensive care has to imply the possibility of euthanasia. Woods defends the idea that euthanasia should be an integral part of palliative care. For him, euthanasia is consistent with palliative care ethics because he regards it as being on a continuum with the use of palliative sedation.

Care as a challenge for euthanasia? There are also those who challenge Begley's position. It is not euthanasia that poses a challenge but the development of care for the patient in need. According to several nursing ethicists, euthanasia is in direct opposition to care. For them it is unthinkable that euthanasia would comprise a part of nursing caring practice.

The idea that care for a dying person should be improved is an argument often heard in the literature against making a link between euthanasia and good care. Coyle states that conditional legalization of euthanasia does not advance the goal of improving care for dying people. She offers some tools for nursing management. The basic condition for good care is the empathic attitude a nurse shows towards a patient. Suffering is not denied, and patients and their families actually feel that they are not left alone or abandoned. Nurses do not let their patients down; feelings of abandonment or despair have to be heard. Consistent with the principle of beneficence against euthanasia but from the care perspective, Coyle states that wanting to die is not the same as wanting to be killed. There is a difference between "I wish I was dead" and "kill me." According to Beech it can be argued that euthanasia is not conducive to care for dying people; it even undermines this kind of care. In carrying out euthanasia, health care professionals may become weary of death in general, which could lead to a less compassionate attitude towards caring for dying patients.

Similarly, Pollard and Winton accuse many of unjustly considering euthanasia as a rational alternative, a possibility in the care of elderly, dying and severely disabled people. According to both authors, a better care alternative is possible. Remmers interprets the longing for death as a cry for more attention and support in the dying process. Goodman therefore sees that the most important role of nurses is to offer the fittest, most respectful, supportive, skilled and compassionate care. She refuses to consider euthanasia as care and to justify it as a way of pain control. In this context, Gauthier asks himself, "whose pain does euthanasia really aim to relieve: that of the patient or that of the healthcare worker and the relatives?" Volkenandt also does not consider the choice between supportive care and euthanasia to be an ethical dilemma. Euthanasia does not meet his vision of good care, which acknowledges pain without eliminating the patient.

Low and Pang reject the idea that euthanasia is an option or possibility of choice in palliative care. They state that euthanasia radically counteracts the fundamental principles of medicine and nursing in general, and of palliative care in particular. For them, unconditional care is the cornerstone of palliative care—defined as care that does not unnecessarily postpone or hasten the end of life—and is incompatible with the possibility of euthanasia. These nurse ethicists consider euthanasia to be the opposite of palliative care. Killing opposes the most fundamental principles of palliative care, such as "doing good" and "not harming." From their perspective, euthanasia cannot be considered to be a confirmation of life; it degrades life and deprives a patient of his or her final growth in humanity.

This plea among nurse ethicists for adequate care that does not point at termination of life is also supported by Karkheck. To her, the issue of euthanasia illustrates the shortcomings in our care of terminally ill patients. As such, ethically justified end-of-life decisions do not include assisting with euthanasia, which denies patients their final stage of life. Bandman and Bandman are more explicit and believe that, in general, not intervening in the dying process is ethically preferable to killing. They consider euthanasia to be an intervention that is too aggressive and prefer the hospice concept of Cicely Saunders. These views also inspired Oduncu, who rejects killing as due care. Euthanasia relieves pain by eliminating the patient. According to Oduncu, it is not possible for euthanasia to be part of the duty of care giving. He pleads for skilled and compassionate care in accompanying dying people and prefers optimal instead of "maximal" (euthanasia included) but incomplete care. Along these lines, Arndt pleads for the development of "*individualisierende Pflege*" (individualizing care), which makes euthanasia superfluous. McCabe also believes that the ultimate concern of nursing care, that is, healing of patients, excludes euthanasia. For her, euthanasia is antithetical to nursing activity and cannot be considered to be a "nursing-as-healing praxis."

Discussion

Before discussing the main results of our review, we would like to make the following remark. It can be taken for granted that the arguments described are influenced by religious and other attitudes of the authors. In some cases, this religious background is incorporated and made explicit in the arguments. However, in other cases, the religious or personal underlying attitudes are not made explicit by the authors. In these cases, in order to avoid misinterpretation, we have chosen to present the arguments as they are described by the authors, without any reference to personal or other underlying attitudes.

Another observation we made is that only two studies originate from the Netherlands, the first country in the world to have passed an Act on euthanasia. From Belgium, the second country with euthanasia legislation, no study is included in our review. Most of those included were published before euthanasia legislation came into force in the Netherlands and Belgium. Based on these observations, we should be very cautious in interpreting the described arguments in the context of current (Dutch or Belgian) euthanasia legislation.

Principle- and care-orientated approaches to nursing ethics

The nursing ethics debate on euthanasia seems mostly to be influenced by two important approaches in nursing ethics: the principle-orientated approach and the care-orientated approach. It is striking that the concepts used in nursing ethics literature on euthanasia are substantially allied to principlism, a perspective expressed in the 1970s by Beauchamp and Childress. In the majority of the studies included (35 of 41), principle-based arguments are apparent. This observation could be partially explained by the fact that the main body of literature in this study is Anglo-Saxon in origin. The principle of respect for autonomy is predominant in the included studies and generally leads to an argument for euthanasia.

Until now, this principle-based thinking invited much criticism from the care perspective or care philosophy, among others. A care-based approach to ethics is a challenge to the principle-based approach. Indeed, the conceptual relationship between nursing ethics arguments and care-based arguments is becoming increasingly clear. In approximately half of the studies included (20 of 41), care-based arguments are advanced. This care-orientated literature mostly considers euthanasia as being incompatible with care (13 of 20).

Different from the principle-based arguments, those referring to the concept of care do not have such a clear definition of the main concept used. This makes these arguments more difficult to interpret. It is clear that publications using the concept of care do not share the same meaning of this concept. Some studies refer to care in the meaning of "clinical care," "palliative care," "terminal care" or "nursing care," while others refer to a more normative concept of care, as used in "care ethics literature." This "care literature" is the most difficult (and confusing) but at the same time the most interesting (and innovative) writing to be studied in the context of nursing and euthanasia. Further research is thus needed to clarify and interpret the exact meaning of the ethical arguments on euthanasia related to the concept of care.

As such, we state that the nursing ethics debate on euthanasia is strongly influenced by the fundamental ethical discussion of a principle-orientated approach and the care approach in nursing ethics.

QUESTIONS FOR REFLECTION

1. What is autonomy? Contrast concepts in the nursing literature with Kant's concept of autonomy.
2. "A good death is an autonomous death." Discuss.
3. How might autonomy be used to argue for the acceptability of euthanasia?
4. How might autonomy be viewed as a challenge to the practice of euthanasia?
5. How might autonomy apply to patients who are comatose or otherwise incapable of making their wishes known?
6. How could non-maleficence be used to argue in favor of the acceptability of euthanasia?
7. Is beneficence best understood as doing what is in the patient's best interests or as doing what the patient wants? How might these come apart in end-of-life cases?
8. How can beneficence be used to argue against euthanasia?
9. How does euthanasia pose special ethical problems for nurses and their professional role?
10. How do principle-based approaches differ from approaches based on the ethics of care in their treatment of the issue of euthanasia?

CAPITAL PUNISHMENT

Ordinarily, we think that people have a right to life and that governments, if they have any obligations at all, are obliged to protect that right. But many people believe that the government is nevertheless justified in putting certain kinds of criminals to death. Generally, they believe that the government needs to deprive some people of the right to life in order to protect that right for others—indeed, for the vast majority of its citizens. From this belief arises the issue of capital punishment: Can the government be justified in putting someone to death?

The death penalty raises important questions about the origin, status, and extent of the right to life. Most people believe that they have the right to defend themselves against an assailant. They believe, in particular, that they have the right to kill an attacker if their own lives are in danger. Some philosophers have extended this reasoning to the state as a whole. The murderer, for example, can be seen as attacking society; society is justified in using lethal force to defend itself. Of course, once apprehended, the murderer no longer threatens society in quite the same way. But if murderers are likely to murder again, the self-protection argument may apply. This strategy argues that the right to life is limited so that those who threaten death to others lose their own right to life or, at least, deserve to have it overridden by the rights of others.

Other philosophers have argued in favor of a right to retribution. Society, having suffered a serious harm, has the right to take retribution by punishing the offender. Moreover, the punishment that seems appropriate for causing death is suffering death. They have thus maintained that justice sometimes requires the death penalty.

Still others have stressed deterrence as a justification for capital punishment. Putting a criminal to death, in this view, deters others from committing similar crimes. Enforcing the death penalty thus promotes the good of society; it may save more lives than it costs. Statistical studies of the effects of capital punishment tend to be inconclusive; it is not clear whether the death penalty actually has this effect. But some studies report that each execution saves several lives by deterring prospective murderers.

These arguments raise large issues beyond those involving the right to life itself. What rights does society have to defend itself against criminal activity? What is the moral justification for punishment? When can the interests of a larger group justify violating the rights of an individual? Under what circumstances does a person lose or surrender rights? In each case, arguments for and against capital punishment take or presuppose controversial stands.

Cesare Beccaria presents a classic and influential argument against the death penalty. Government and law are founded on a social contract; the laws have legitimacy and authority only to the extent that those subject to them would agree to be subject to them. But no one would consent to be put to death. Indeed, no one would agree to give up any more of their liberty than necessary to preserve society. So, capital punishment is unjust. Beccaria argues on utilitarian grounds as well. The death penalty is ineffective in deterring crime and undermines respect for law.

In *Furman* v. *Georgia*, in 1972, the Supreme Court held that a Georgia capital punishment law was unconstitutional. The Court found that the death penalty, under the circumstances of its application there, was incompatible with human dignity and violated the Eighth Amendment prohibiting "cruel and unusual" punishment. Some members of the Court argued that the death penalty was in itself objectionable. The majority, however, concluded simply that its application was too haphazard, unprincipled, and unjust to count as constitutional.

In *Gregg* v. *Georgia*, four years later, the Court upheld Georgia's revision of its capital punishment law. Under that revision, the jury receives detailed instructions about the appropriateness of the death penalty. Certain kinds of circumstances are aggravating, tending to justify the death penalty; others are mitigating, tending to justify an alternative sentence. The Court decided that the death penalty, administered in this way, is constitutionally acceptable.

Strictly speaking, these decisions rest on legal rather than moral grounds. They are not, however, morally irrelevant. Cruel and unusual punishments are ethically as well as legally objectionable. Consequently, the legal arguments of the justices in these cases parallel moral arguments about the permissibility of capital punishment.

Ernest van den Haag goes beyond typical defenses of capital punishment in at least two ways. First, he argues that deterrence provides an argument for the death penalty, even if we cannot determine whether it succeeds in deterring or not. If there is a chance that it does, he contends, then we place innocent lives at risk by failing to carry it out. Second, he argues that certain special cases justify capital punishment, even if it is unacceptable in most cases. Thus, we may be justified in executing war criminals and criminals who murder in prison while already serving life terms, even if we are not justified in executing most murderers.

Hugo Adam Bedau advances several different arguments against the death penalty. He affirms the *Furman* Court's arguments that capital punishment is cruel, arbitrary, discriminatory, incompatible with human dignity, and ineffective as a deterrent. The changes wrought by *Gregg* do not alter these points. In addition, he contends that the death penalty is wrong for just the same reason that murder itself is wrong: It demonstrates disrespect for human life. When the government shows such disrespect, the consequences for society are far worse than when an individual does so.

Cass Sunstein and Adrian Vermeule point to recent evidence that the death penalty does effectively deter murder, and they argue that if so, the government has an obligation to impose it.

Carol Steiker argues that there is a significant moral difference between acting and failing to act, even for government. She points out that capital punishment is not like regulation; in executing a criminal, the government directly intends and causes someone's death. She draws analogies with the trolley problem, among other thought experiments, to illustrate the moral importance of that fact, and links it to the divide between deontological and consequentialist moral theories. Steiker then argues that the death penalty violates standards of proportionality and equality as well as human dignity.

CESARE BECCARIA

from *On Crimes and Punishments*

Cesare Beccaria (1738–1794), who was a member of a group called "the academy of fists," dedicated to reforming Italy's system of criminal justice, wrote On Crimes and Punishments *in 1764, when he was just twenty-six, after a study of Italy's prison system. His work, including a classic statement of the case against capital punishments, became influential throughout Europe. He later became a government official in Milan and, briefly, professor of political economy at the University of Milan. (Source:* On Crimes and Punishments *[Philadelphia: Philip H. Nicklin, 1819].)*

In every human society, there is an effort continually tending to confer on one part the height of power and happiness, and to reduce the other to the extreme of weakness and misery. The intent of good laws is to oppose this effort, and to diffuse their influence universally and equally. But men generally abandoned the care of their most important concerns to the uncertain prudence and discretion of those whose interest it is to reject the best and wisest institutions; and it is not till they have been led into a thousand mistakes in matters the most essential to their lives and liberties, and are weary of suffering, that they can be induced to apply a remedy to the evils with which they are oppressed. It is then they begin to conceive and acknowledge the most palpable truths which, from their very simplicity, commonly escape vulgar minds, incapable of analysing objects, accustomed to receive impressions, without distinction, and to be determined rather by the opinions of others than by the result of their own examination.

If we look into history we shall find that laws, which are, or ought to be, conventions between men in a state of freedom, have been, for the most part the work of the passions of a few, or the consequences of a fortuitous or temporary necessity; not dictated by a cool examiner of human nature, who knew how to collect in one point the actions of a multitude, and had this only end in view, *the greatest happiness of the greatest number.* Happy are those few nations who have not waited till the slow succession of human vicissitudes should, from the extremity of evil, produce a transition to good; but by prudent laws have facilitated the progress from one to the other! And how great are the obligations due from mankind to that philosopher, who, from the obscurity of his closet, had the courage to scatter among the multitude the seeds of useful truths, so long unfruitful!

CHAPTER 2 / OF THE RIGHT TO PUNISH

Every punishment which does not arise from absolute necessity, says the great Montesquieu, is tyrannical. A proposition which may be made more general thus: every act of authority of one man over another, for which there is not an absolute necessity, is tyrannical. It is upon this then that the sovereign's right to punish crimes is founded; that is, upon the necessity of defending the public liberty, entrusted to his care, from the usurpation of individuals; and punishments are just in proportion, as the liberty, preserved by the sovereign, is sacred and valuable.

(¶ 2.2) Let us consult the human heart, and there we shall find the foundation of the sovereign's right to punish; for no advantage in moral policy can be lasting which is not founded on the indelible sentiments of the heart of man. Whatever law deviates from this principle will always meet with a resistance which will destroy it in the end; for the smallest force continually applied will overcome the most violent motion communicated to bodies.

(¶ 2.3) No man ever gave up his liberty merely for the good of the public. Such a chimera exists only in romances. Every individual wishes, if possible, to be exempt from the compacts that bind the rest of mankind.

(¶ 2.4) The multiplication of mankind, though slow, being too great, for the means which the earth, in its natural state, offered to satisfy necessities which every day became more numerous, obliged men to separate again, and form new societies. These naturally opposed the first, and a state of war was transferred from individuals to nations.

(¶ 2.5) Thus it was necessity that forced men to give up a part of their liberty. It is certain, then, that every individual would choose to put into the public stock the smallest portion possible, as much only as was sufficient to engage others to defend it. The aggregate of these, the smallest portions possible, forms the right of punishing; all that extends beyond this, is abuse, not justice.

(¶ 2.6) Observe that by justice I understand nothing more than that bond which is necessary to keep the interest of individuals united, without which men would return to their original state of barbarity. All punishments which exceed the necessity of preserving this bond are in their nature unjust. We should be cautious how we associate with the word justice an idea of any thing real, such as a physical power, or a being that actually exists. I do not, by any means, speak of the justice of God, which is of another kind, and refers immediately to rewards and punishments in a life to come.

CHAPTER 28 / OF THE PUNISHMENT OF DEATH

The useless profusion of punishments, which has never made men better induces me to inquire, whether the punishment of death be really just or useful in a well governed state? What right, I ask, have men to cut the throats of their fellow-creatures? Certainly not that on which the sovereignty and laws are founded. The laws, as I have said before, are only the sum of the smallest portions of the private liberty of each individual, and represent the general will, which is the aggregate of that of each individual. Did any one ever give to others the right of taking away his life? Is it possible that, in the smallest portions of the liberty of each, sacrificed to the good of the public, can be contained the greatest of all good, life? If it were so, how shall it be reconciled to the maxim which tells us, that a man has no right to kill himself, which he certainly must have, if he could give it away to another?

(¶ 28.2) But the punishment of death is not authorised by any right; for I have demonstrated that no such right exists. It is therefore a war of a whole nation against a citizen whose destruction they consider as necessary or useful to the general good. But if I can further demonstrate that it is neither necessary nor useful, I shall have gained the cause of humanity.

(¶ 28.3) The death of a citizen cannot be necessary but in one case: when, though deprived of his liberty, he has such power and connections as may endanger the security of the nation; when his existence may produce a dangerous revolution in the established form of government. But, even in this case, it can only be necessary when a nation is on the verge of recovering or losing its liberty, or in times of absolute anarchy, when the disorders themselves hold the place of laws: but in a reign of tranquility, in a form of government approved by the united wishes of the nation, in a state well fortified from enemies without and supported by strength within, and opinion, perhaps more efficacious, where all power is lodged in the hands of a true sovereign, where riches can purchase pleasures and not authority, there can be no necessity for taking away the life of a subject.

(¶ 28.4) If the experience of all ages be not sufficient to prove, that the punishment of death has never prevented determined men from injuring society, if the example of the Romans, if twenty years' reign of Elizabeth, empress of Russia, in which she gave the fathers of their country an example more illustrious than many conquests bought with blood; if, I say, all this be not sufficient to persuade mankind, who always suspect the voice of reason, and who choose rather to be led by authority, let us consult human nature in proof of my assertion.

(¶ 28.5) It is not the intenseness of the pain that has the greatest effect on the mind, but its continuance; for our sensibility is more easily and more powerfully affected by weak but repeated impressions, than by a violent but momentary impulse. The power of habit is universal over every sensible being. As it is by that we learn to speak, to walk, and to satisfy our necessities, so the ideas of morality are stamped on our minds by repeated impression. The death of a criminal is a terrible but momentary spectacle, and therefore a less efficacious method of deterring others than the continued example of a man deprived of his liberty, condemned, as a beast of burden, to repair, by his labour, the injury he has done to society. If I commit such a crime, says the spectator to himself, I shall be reduced to that miserable condition for the rest of my life. A much more powerful preventive than the fear of death which men always behold in distant obscurity.

(¶ 28.6) The terrors of death make so slight an impression, that it has not force enough to withstand the forgetfulness natural to mankind, even in the most essential things, especially when assisted by the passions. Violent impressions surprise us, but their effect is momentary; they are fit to produce those revolutions which instantly transform a common man into a Lacedaemonian or a Persian; but in a free and quiet government they ought to be rather frequent than strong.

(¶ 28.7) The execution of a criminal is to the multitude a spectacle which in some excites compassion mixed with indignation. These sentiments occupy the mind much more than that salutary terror which the laws endeavor to inspire; but, in the contemplation of continued suffering, terror is the only, or at least predominant sensation. The severity of a punishment should be just sufficient to excite compassion in the spectators, as it is intended more for them than for the criminal.

(¶ 28.8) A punishment, to be just, should have only that degree of severity which is sufficient to deter others. Now there is no man who upon the least reflection, would put in competition the total and perpetual loss of his liberty, with the greatest advantages he could possibly obtain in consequence of a crime. Perpetual slavery, then, has in it all that is necessary to deter the most hardened and determined, as much as the punishment of death. I say it has more. There are many who can look upon death with intrepidity and firmness, some through fanaticism, and others through vanity, which attends us even to the grave; others from a desperate resolution, either to get rid of their misery, or cease to live: but fanaticism and vanity forsake the criminal in slavery, in chains and fetters, in an iron cage, and despair seems rather the beginning than the end of their misery. The mind, by collecting itself and uniting all its force, can, for a moment, repel assailing grief; but its most vigorous efforts are insufficient to resist perpetual wretchedness.

(¶ 28.9) In all nations, where death is used as a punishment, every example supposes a new crime committed; whereas, in perpetual slavery, every criminal affords a frequent and lasting example; and if it be necessary that men should often be witnesses of the power of the laws, criminals should often be put to death: but this supposes a frequency of crimes; and from hence this punishment will cease to have its effect, so that it must be useful and useless at the same time.

(¶ 28.10) I shall be told that perpetual slavery is as painful a punishment as death, and therefore as cruel. I answer, that if all the miserable moments in the life of a slave were collected into one point, it would be a more cruel punishment than any other; but these are scattered through his whole life, whilst the pain of death exerts all its force in a moment. There is also another advantage in the punishment of slavery, which is, that it is more terrible to the spectator than to the sufferer himself; for the spectator considers the sum of all his wretched moments whilst the sufferer, by the misery of the present, is prevented from thinking of the future. All evils are increased by the imagination, and the sufferer finds resources and consolations of which the spectators are ignorant, who judge by their own sensibility of what passes in a mind by habit grown callous to misfortune.

(¶ 28.11) Let us, for a moment, attend to the reasoning of a robber or assassin, who is deterred from violating the laws by the gibbet or the wheel. I am sensible, that to develop the sentiments of one's own heart is an art which education only can teach; but although a villain may not be able to give a clear account of his principles, they nevertheless influence his conduct. He reasons thus: "What are these laws that I am bound to respect, which make so great a difference between me and the rich man? He refuses me the farthing I ask of him, and excuses himself by bidding me have recourse to labour, with which he is unacquainted."

(¶ 28.12) "Who made these laws? The rich and the great, who never deigned to visit the miserable hut of the poor, who have never seen him dividing a piece of mouldy bread, amidst the cries of his famished children and the tears of his wife. Let us break those ties, fatal to the greatest part of mankind, and only useful to a few indolent tyrants. Let us attack injustice at its source. I will return to my natural state of independence. I shall live free and happy on the fruits of my courage and industry. A day of pain and repentance may come, but it will be short; and for an hour of grief I shall enjoy years of pleasure and liberty. King of a small number as determined as myself, I will correct the mistakes of fortune, and I shall see those tyrants grow pale and tremble at the sight of him, whom, with insulting pride, they would not suffer to rank with their dogs and horses."

(¶ 28.13) Religion then presents itself to the mind of this lawless villain, and, promising him almost a certainty of eternal happiness upon the easy terms of repentance, contributes much to lessen the horror of the last scene of the tragedy.

(¶ 28.14) But he who foresees that he must pass a great number of years, even his whole life, in pain and slavery, a slave to those laws by which he was protected, in sight of his fellow-citizens, with whom he lives in freedom and society, makes an useful comparison between those evils, the uncertainty of his success, and the shortness of the time in which he shall enjoy the fruits of his transgression. The example of those wretches, continually before his eyes, makes a much greater impression on him than a punishment, which instead of correcting, makes him more obdurate.

(¶ 28.15) The punishment of death is pernicious to society, from the example of barbarity it affords. If the passions, or the necessity of war, have taught men to shed the blood of their fellow creatures, the laws, which are intended to moderate the ferocity of mankind, should not increase it by examples of barbarity, the more horrible as this punishment is usually attended with formal pageantry. Is it not absurd, that the laws, which detest and punish homicide, should, in order to prevent murder, publicly commit murder themselves? What are the true and most useful laws? Those compacts and conditions which all would propose and observe in those moments when private interest is silent, or combined with that of the public. What are the natural sentiments of every person concerning the punishment of death? We may read them in the contempt and indignation with which every one looks on the executioner, who is nevertheless an innocent executor of the public will, a good citizen, who contributes to the advantage of society, the instrument of the general security within, as good soldiers are without. What then is the origin of this contradiction? Why is this sentiment of mankind indelible to the scandal of reason? It is that, in a secret corner of the mind, in which the original impressions of nature are still preserved, men discover a sentiment which tells them, that their lives are not lawfully in the power of any one, but of that necessity only which with its iron sceptre rules the universe.

(¶ 28.16) What must men think, when they see wise magistrates and grave ministers of justice, with indifference and tranquillity, dragging a criminal to death, and whilst a wretch trembles with agony, expecting the fatal stroke, the judge, who has condemned him, with the coldest insensibility, and perhaps with no small gratification from the exertion of his authority, quits his tribunal, to enjoy the comforts and pleasures of life? They will say, "Ah! those cruel formalities of justice are a cloak to tyranny, they are a secret language, a solemn veil, intended to conceal the sword by which we are sacrificed to the insatiable idol of despotism. Murder, which they would represent to us an horrible crime, we see practised by them without repugnance or remorse. Let us follow their example. A violent death appeared terrible in their descriptions, but we see that it is the affair of a moment. It will be still less terrible to him who, not expecting it, escapes almost all the pain." Such is the fatal though absurd reasonings of men who are disposed to commit crimes, on whom the abuse of religion has more influence than religion itself.

(¶ 28.17) If it be objected, that almost all nations in all ages have punished certain crimes with death, I answer, that the force of these examples vanishes when opposed to truth, against which prescription is urged in vain. The history of mankind is an immense sea of errors, in which a few obscure truths may here and there be found.

QUESTIONS FOR REFLECTION

1. What, according to Beccaria, gives the state the right to punish anyone?
2. What constrains the state's right to punish?
3. Why is capital punishment incompatible with social contract theory, in Beccaria's view?
4. What are Beccaria's utilitarian arguments against the death penalty? Do you find them convincing?

JUSTICE WILLIAM BRENNAN

Concurring Opinion in Furman v. Georgia (1972)

William Brennan was Justice of the United States Supreme Court from 1956 to 1990. (Source: Furman v. Georgia *408 U.S. 238 [1972]. Most legal references have been omitted.)*

. . . Mr. Justice Brennan, concurring.

The question presented in these cases is whether death is today a punishment for crime that is "cruel and unusual" and consequently, by virtue of the Eighth and Fourteenth Amendments, beyond the power of the State to inflict. . . .

III

. . . The question, then, is whether the deliberate infliction of death is today consistent with the command of the Clause that the State may not inflict punishments that do not comport with human dignity. I will analyze the punishment of death in terms of the principles set out above and the cumulative test to which they lead: It is a denial of human dignity for the State arbitrarily to subject a person to an unusually severe punishment that society has indicated it does not regard as acceptable, and that cannot be shown to serve any penal purpose more effectively than a significantly less drastic punishment. Under these principles and this test, death is today a "cruel and unusual" punishment.

Death is a unique punishment in the United States. In a society that so strongly affirms the sanctity of life, not surprisingly the common view is that death is the ultimate sanction. This natural human feeling appears all about us. There has been no national debate about punishment, in general or by imprisonment, comparable to the debate about the punishment of death. No other punishment has been so continuously restricted, nor has any State yet abolished prisons, as some have abolished this punishment. And those States that still inflict death reserve it for the most heinous crimes. Juries, of course, have always treated death cases differently, as have governors exercising their commutation powers. Criminal defendants are of the same view. "As all practicing lawyers know, who have defended persons charged with capital offenses, often the only goal possible is to avoid the death penalty." Some legislatures have required particular procedures, such as two-stage trials and automatic appeals, applicable only in death cases. "It is the universal experience in the administration of criminal justice that those charged with capital offenses are granted special considerations." This Court, too, almost always treats death cases as a class apart. And the unfortunate effect of this punishment upon the functioning of the judicial process is well known; no other punishment has a similar effect.

The only explanation for the uniqueness of death is its extreme severity. Death is today an unusually severe punishment, unusual in its pain, in its finality, and in its enormity. No other existing punishment is comparable to death in terms of physical and mental suffering. Although our information is not conclusive, it appears that there is no method available that guarantees an immediate and painless death. Since the discontinuance of flogging as a constitutionally permissible punishment, death remains as the only punishment that may involve the conscious infliction of physical pain. In addition, we know that mental pain is an inseparable part of our practice of punishing criminals by death, for the prospect of pending execution exacts a frightful toll during the inevitable long wait between the imposition of sentence and the actual infliction of death. As the California Supreme Court pointed out, "the process of carrying out a verdict of death is often so degrading and brutalizing to the human spirit as to constitute psychological torture." Indeed, as Mr. Justice Frankfurter noted, "the onset of insanity while awaiting execution of a death sentence is not a rare phenomenon." The "fate of ever-increasing fear and distress" to which the expatriate is subjected can only exist to a greater degree for a person confined in prison awaiting death.

The unusual severity of death is manifested most clearly in its finality and enormity. Death, in these respects, is in a class by itself. Expatriation, for example, is a punishment that "destroys for the individual the political existence that was centuries in the development," that "strips the citizen of his status in the national and international political community," and that puts "[h]is very existence" in jeopardy. Expatriation thus inherently entails "the total destruction of the individual's status in organized society." "In short, the expatriate has lost the right to have rights." Yet, demonstrably, expatriation is not "a fate worse than death." Although death, like expatriation, destroys the individual's "political existence" and his "status in organized society," it does more, for, unlike expatriation, death also destroys "[h]is very existence." There is, too, at least the possibility that the expatriate will in the future regain "the right to have rights." Death forecloses even that possibility.

Death is truly an awesome punishment. The calculated killing of a human being by the State involves, by its very nature, a denial of the executed person's humanity. The contrast with the plight of a person punished by imprisonment is evident. An individual in prison does not lose "the right to have rights." A prisoner retains, for example, the constitutional rights to the free exercise of religion, to be free of cruel and unusual punishments, and to treatment as a "person" for purposes of due process of law and the equal protection of the laws. A prisoner remains a member of the human family. Moreover, he retains the right of access to the courts. His punishment is not irrevocable. Apart from the common charge, grounded upon the recognition of human fallibility, that the punishment of death must inevitably be inflicted upon innocent men, we know that death has been the lot of men whose convictions were unconstitutionally secured in view of later, retroactively applied, holdings of this Court. The punishment itself may have been unconstitutionally inflicted, yet the finality of death precludes relief. An executed person has indeed "lost the right to have rights." As one 19th century proponent of punishing criminals by death declared, "When a man is hung, there is an end of our relations with him. His execution is a way of saying, 'You are not fit for this world, take your chance elsewhere.'"

In comparison to all other punishments today, then, the deliberate extinguishment of human life by the State is uniquely degrading to human dignity. . . .

QUESTIONS FOR REFLECTION

1. Justice Brennan offers some principles for determining whether a punishment "comports with human dignity." Explain them.
2. Why, in Justice Brennan's view, is capital punishment incompatible with human dignity? Would Kant agree?
3. How is human dignity connected to the "right to have rights," in Justice Brennan's view?
4. What is the moral significance of the rare application and seeming arbitrariness of the death penalty?
5. How, according to Justice Brennan, does the death penalty differ from imprisonment? What is the moral significance of those differences?
6. Suppose someone were to argue, "Everything Justice Brennan says about death at the hands of the state is also true of death resulting from a terminal illness." But it is absurd to conclude that death from natural causes is unconstitutional or morally unacceptable. So his reasoning must be flawed. How would you respond?

JUSTICES STEWART, POWELL, AND STEVENS

Majority Opinion in Gregg v. Georgia (1976)

(Source: Gregg v. Georgia *428 U.S. 153 [1976]. Most legal references have been omitted.)*

Judgment of the Court, and opinion of Mr. Justice Stewart, Mr. Justice Powell, and Mr. Justice Stevens, announced by Mr. Justice Stewart. . . .

III

. . . The Court on a number of occasions has both assumed and asserted the constitutionality of capital punishment. In several cases that assumption provided a necessary foundation for the decision, as the Court was asked to decide whether a particular method of carrying out a capital sentence would be allowed to stand under the Eighth Amendment. But until *Furman* v. *Georgia*, the Court never confronted squarely the fundamental claim that the punishment of death always, regardless of the enormity of the offense or the procedure followed in imposing the sentence, is cruel and unusual punishment in violation of the Constitution. Although this issue was presented and addressed in *Furman*, it was not resolved by the Court. Four Justices would have held that capital punishment is not unconstitutional *per se;* two Justices would have reached the opposite conclusion; and three Justices, while agreeing that the statutes then before the Court were invalid as applied, left open the question whether such punishment may ever be imposed. We now hold that the punishment of death does not invariably violate the Constitution. . . .

C

. . . The imposition of the death penalty for the crime of murder has a long history of acceptance both in the United States and in England. The common-law rule imposed a mandatory death sentence on all convicted murderers. And the penalty continued to be used into the 20th century by most American States, although the breadth of the common-law rule was diminished, initially by narrowing the class of murders to be punished by death and subsequently by widespread adoption of laws expressly granting juries the discretion to recommend mercy.

It is apparent from the text of the Constitution itself that the existence of capital punishment was accepted by the Framers. At the time the Eighth Amendment was ratified, capital punishment was a common sanction in every State. Indeed, the First Congress of the United States enacted legislation providing death as the penalty for specified crimes. The Fifth Amendment, adopted at the same time as the Eighth, contemplated the continued existence of the capital sanction by imposing certain limits on the prosecution of capital cases:

> "No person shall be held to answer for a capital, or otherwise infamous crime, unless on a presentment or indictment of a Grand Jury . . . ; nor shall any person be subject for the same offense to be twice put in jeopardy of life or limb; . . . nor be deprived of life, liberty, or property, without due process of law. . . ."

And the Fourteenth Amendment, adopted over three-quarters of a century later, similarly contemplates the existence of the capital sanction in providing that no State shall deprive any person of "life, liberty, or property" without due process of law.

For nearly two centuries, this Court, repeatedly and often expressly, has recognized that capital punishment is not invalid *per se*. . . .

The death penalty is said to serve two principal social purposes: retribution and deterrence of capital crimes by prospective offenders.

In part, capital punishment is an expression of society's moral outrage at particularly offensive conduct. This function may be unappealing to many, but it is essential in an ordered society that asks its citizens to rely on legal processes rather than self-help to vindicate their wrongs.

> "The instinct for retribution is part of the nature of man, and channeling that instinct in the administration of criminal justice serves an important purpose in promoting the stability of a society governed by law. When people begin to believe that organized society is unwilling or unable to impose upon criminal offenders the punishment they 'deserve,' then there are sown the seeds of anarchy—of self-help, vigilante justice, and lynch law." *Furman* v. *Georgia* (Stewart, J., concurring).

"Retribution is no longer the dominant objective of the criminal law," but neither is it a forbidden objective nor one inconsistent with our respect for the dignity of men. Indeed, the decision that capital punishment may be the appropriate sanction in extreme cases is an expression of the community's belief that certain crimes are themselves so grievous an affront to humanity that the only adequate response may be the penalty of death.

Statistical attempts to evaluate the worth of the death penalty as a deterrent to crimes by potential offenders have occasioned a great deal of debate. The results simply have been inconclusive. As one opponent of capital punishment has said:

> "[A]fter all possible inquiry, including the probing of all possible methods of inquiry, we do not know, and for systematic and easily visible reasons cannot know, what the truth about this 'deterrent' effect may be. . . .
>
> "The inescapable flaw is . . . that social conditions in any state are not constant through time, and that social conditions are not the same in any two states. If an effect were observed (and the observed effects, one way or another, are not large) then one could not at all tell whether any of this effect is attributable to the presence or absence of capital punishment. A 'scientific'—that is to say, a soundly based—conclusion is simply impossible, and no methodological path out of this tangle suggests itself."

Although some of the studies suggest that the death penalty may not function as a significantly greater deterrent than lesser penalties, there is no convincing empirical evidence either supporting or refuting this view. We may nevertheless assume safely that there are murderers, such as those who act in passion, for whom the threat of death has little or no deterrent effect. But for many others, the death penalty undoubtedly is a significant deterrent. There are carefully contemplated murders, such as murder for hire, where the possible penalty of death may well enter into the cold calculus that precedes the decision to act. And there are some categories of murder, such as murder by a life prisoner, where other sanctions may not be adequate.

The value of capital punishment as a deterrent of crime is a complex factual issue the resolution of which properly rests with the legislatures, which can evaluate the results of statistical studies in terms of their own local conditions and with a flexibility of approach that is not available to the courts. Indeed, many of the post-*Furman* statutes reflect just such a responsible effort to define those crimes and those criminals for which capital punishment is most probably an effective deterrent.

In sum, we cannot say that the judgment of the Georgia Legislature that capital punishment may be necessary in some cases is clearly wrong. Considerations of federalism, as well as respect for the ability of a legislature to evaluate, in terms of its particular State, the moral consensus concerning the death penalty and its social utility as a sanction, require us to conclude, in the absence of more convincing evidence, that the infliction of death as a punishment for murder is not without justification and thus is not unconstitutionally severe.

Finally, we must consider whether the punishment of death is disproportionate in relation to the crime for which it is imposed. There is no question that death as a punishment is unique in its severity and irrevocability. When a defendant's life is at stake, the Court has been particularly sensitive to ensure that every safeguard is observed. But we are concerned here only with the imposition of capital punishment for the crime of murder, and when a life has been taken deliberately by the offender, we cannot say that the punishment is invariably disproportionate to the crime. It is an extreme sanction, suitable to the most extreme of crimes.

We hold that the death penalty is not a form of punishment that may never be imposed, regardless of the circumstances of the offense, regardless of the character of the offender, and regardless of the procedure followed in reaching the decision to impose it.

IV

. . .

B

We now turn to consideration of the constitutionality of Georgia's capital-sentencing procedures. In the wake of *Furman*, Georgia amended its capital punishment statute, but chose not to narrow the scope of its murder provisions. Thus, now as before *Furman*, in Georgia "[a] person commits murder when he unlawfully and with malice aforethought, either express or implied, causes the death of another human being." All persons convicted of murder "shall be punished by death or by imprisonment for life."

Georgia did act, however, to narrow the class of murderers subject to capital punishment by specifying 10 statutory aggravating circumstances, one of which must be found by the jury to exist beyond a reasonable doubt before a death sentence can ever be imposed. In addition, the jury is authorized to consider any other appropriate aggravating or mitigating circumstances. The jury is not required to find any mitigating circumstances in order to make a recommendation of mercy that is binding on the trial court, but it must find a *statutory* aggravating circumstance before recommending a sentence of death.

These procedures require the jury to consider the circumstances of the crime and the criminal before it recommends sentence. No longer can a Georgia jury do as Furman's jury did: reach a finding of the defendant's guilt and then, without guidance or direction, decide whether he should live or die. Instead, the jury's attention is directed to the specific circumstances of the crime: Was it committed in the course of another capital felony? Was it committed for money? Was it committed upon a peace officer or judicial officer? Was it committed in a particularly heinous way or in a manner that endangered the lives of many persons? In addition, the jury's attention is focused on the characteristics of the person who committed the crime: Does he have a record of prior convictions for capital offenses? Are there any special facts about this defendant that mitigate against imposing capital punishment (*e.g.*, his youth, the extent of his cooperation with the police, his emotional state at the time of the crime)? As a result, while some jury discretion still exists, "the discretion to be exercised is controlled by clear and objective standards so as to produce non-discriminatory application."

As an important additional safeguard against arbitrariness and caprice, the Georgia statutory scheme provides for automatic appeal of all death sentences to the State's Supreme Court. That court is required by statute to review each sentence of death and determine whether it was imposed under the influence of passion or prejudice, whether the evidence supports the jury's finding of a statutory aggravating circumstance, and whether the sentence is disproportionate compared to those sentences imposed in similar cases.

In short, Georgia's new sentencing procedures require as a prerequisite to the imposition of the death penalty, specific jury findings as to the circumstances of the crime or the character of the defendant. Moreover, to guard further against a situation comparable to that presented in *Furman*, the Supreme Court of Georgia compares each death sentence with the sentences imposed on similarly situated defendants to ensure that the sentence of death in a particular case is not disproportionate. On their face these procedures seem to satisfy the concerns of *Furman*. No longer should there be "no meaningful basis for distinguishing the few cases in which [the death penalty] is imposed from the many cases in which it is not." . . .

V

The basic concern of *Furman* centered on those defendants who were being condemned to death capriciously and arbitrarily. Under the procedures before the Court in that case, sentencing authorities were not directed to give attention to the nature or circumstances of the crime committed or to the character or record of the defendant. Left unguided, juries imposed the death sentence in a way that could only be called freakish. The new Georgia sentencing procedures, by contrast, focus the jury's attention on the particularized nature of the crime and the particularized characteristics of the individual defendant. While the jury is permitted to consider any aggravating or mitigating circumstances, it must find and identify at least one statutory aggravating factor before it may impose a penalty of death. In this way the jury's discretion is channeled. No longer can a jury wantonly and freakishly impose the death sentence; it is always circumscribed by the legislative guidelines. In addition, the review function of the Supreme Court of Georgia affords additional assurance that the concerns that prompted our decision in *Furman* are not present to any significant degree in the Georgia procedure applied here.

For the reasons expressed in this opinion, we hold that the statutory system under which Gregg was sentenced to death does not violate the Constitution. Accordingly, the judgment of the Georgia Supreme Court is affirmed. . . .

QUESTIONS FOR REFLECTION

1. The majority argues that the death penalty is sometimes justified. What are the majority's chief arguments?
2. In *Furman* v. *Georgia*, Justice Brennan outlined arguments that the death penalty is incompatible with human dignity. Does the majority in *Gregg* v. *Georgia* accept those arguments? Does it present arguments that the death penalty is compatible with, or even required by, human dignity?

ERNEST VAN DEN HAAG

from *The Death Penalty: A Debate*

Ernest van den Haag was professor of jurisprudence and public policy at Fordham University. He died in 2002. (Source: Excerpts from Ernest van den Haag and Joseph P. Conrad, The Death Penalty: A Debate *[Plenum Press, 1983]. Copyright © 1983 by Plenum Publishing Corporation.)*

CHAPTER 4 / MORE ON THE DETERRENT EFFECT OF THE DEATH PENALTY

. . . Does capital punishment deter more than life imprisonment?

Science, logic, or statistics often have been unable to prove what common sense ells us to be true. Thus, the Greek philosopher Zeno some 2000 years ago found that he could not show that motion is possible; indeed, his famous paradoxes appear to show that motion is impossible. Though nobody believed them to be true, nobody succeeded in showing the fallacy of these paradoxes until the rise of mathematical logic less than a hundred years ago. But meanwhile, the world did not stand still. Indeed, nobody argued that motion should stop because it had not been shown to be logically possible. There is no more reason to abolish the death penalty than there was to abolish motion simply because the death penalty has not been, and perhaps cannot be, shown statistically to be a deterrent over and above other penalties. Indeed, there are two quite satisfactory, if nonstatistical, indications of the marginal deterrent effect of the death penalty.

In the first place, our experience shows that the greater the threatened penalty, the more it deters. *Ceteris paribus,* the threat of 50 lashes deters more than the threat of 5; a $1000 fine deters more than a $10 fine; 10 years in prison deter more than 1 year in prison—just as, conversely, the promise of a $1000 reward is a greater incentive than the promise of a $10 reward, etc. There may be diminishing returns. Once a reward exceeds, say, $1 million, the additional attraction may diminish. Once a punishment exceeds, say, 10 years in prison (net of parole), there may be little additional deterrence in threatening additional years. We know hardly anything about diminishing returns of penalties. It would still seem likely, however, that the threat of life in prison deters more than any other term of imprisonment.

The threat of death may deter still more. For it is a mistake to regard the death penalty as though it were of the same kind as other penalties. If it is not, then diminishing returns are unlikely to apply. And death differs significantly, in kind, from any other penalty. Life in prison is still life, however unpleasant. In contrast, the death penalty does not just threaten to make life unpleasant—it threatens to take life altogether. This difference is perceived by those affected. We find that when they have the choice between life in prison and execution, 99% of all prisoners under sentence of death prefer life in prison. By means of appeals, pleas for commutation, indeed by all means at their disposal, they indicate that they prefer life in prison to execution.

From this unquestioned fact a reasonable conclusion can be drawn in favor of the superior deterrent effect of the death penalty. Those who have the choice in practice, those whose choice has actual and immediate effects on their life and death, fear death more than they fear life in prison or any other available penalty. If they do, it follows that the threat of the death penalty, all other things equal, is likely to deter more than the threat of life in prison. One is most deterred by what one fears most. From which it follows that whatever statistics fail, or do not fail, to show, the death penalty is likely to be more deterrent than any other.

Suppose now one is not fully convinced of the superior deterrent effect of the death penalty. I believe I can show that even if one is genuinely uncertain as to whether the death penalty adds to deterrence, one should still favor it, from a purely deterrent viewpoint. For if we are not sure, we must choose either to (1) trade the certain death, by execution, of a convicted murderer for the probable survival of an indefinite number of murder victims whose future murder is less likely (whose survival is more likely)—if the convicted murderer's execution deters prospective murderers, as it might, or to (2) trade the certain survival of the convicted murderer for the probable loss of the lives of future murder victims more likely to be murdered because the convicted murderer's nonexecution might not deter prospective murderers, who could have been deterred by executing the convicted murderer.

To restate the matter: If we were quite ignorant about the marginal deterrent effects of execution, we would have to choose—like it or not—between the certainty of the convicted murderer's death by execution and the likelihood of the survival of future victims of other murderers on the one hand, and on the other his certain survival and the likelihood of the death of new victims. I'd rather execute a man convicted of having murdered others than put the lives of innocents at risk. I find it hard to understand the opposite choice.

However, I doubt that those who insist that the death penalty has not been demonstrated to be more deterrent than other penalties really believe that it is not. Or that it matters. I am fairly certain that the deterrent effect of the death penalty, or its absence, is not actually important to them. Rather, I think, they use the lack of statistical demonstration of a marginal deterrent effect to rationalize an opposition to the death penalty that has nonrational sources yet to be examined. In fact, although they use the alleged inconclusiveness of statistical demonstrations of deterrence as an argument to dissuade others from the death penalty, it can be shown that most abolitionists are not quite serious about the relevance of their own argument from insufficient deterrence.

In numerous discussions I have asked those who oppose capital punishment because, in their opinion, it will not deter capital crimes enough, whether they would favor the death penalty if it could be shown to deter more than life imprisonment does. My question usually led to some embarrassment and to attempts to dodge it by saying that additional deterrence has not been shown. However, when I persisted, conceding as much but asking abolitionists to give a hypothetical answer to a hypothetical question, they would admit that they would continue to oppose the death penalty—even if it were shown to deter more than life imprisonment. Which is to say that the argument based on the alleged lack of superior deterrence is factitious.

At times I have pursued the question. I would ask: "Suppose it were shown that every time we execute a person convicted of murder, ten fewer homicides are committed annually than were otherwise expected—would you still favor abolition?" The answer has been "yes" in all cases I can recall. I would persist: "Suppose every time we execute a convicted murderer, 500 fewer persons are murdered than otherwise would be expected to be murdered; suppose that, by executing the convicted murderer, we so much more deter others, who are not deterred by the threat of life imprisonment, that 500 victims will be spared?" After some hesitation, such staunch abolitionists as Professor Hugo Adam Bedau (Tufts University); Ramsey Clark, attorney general of the United States under President Johnson; Professor Charles Black (Yale); and Mr. Henry Schwarzchild, capital punishment project director of the American Civil Liberties Union, admitted that if they had the choice, they would rather see 500 innocents murdered than execute one convict found guilty of murder. This leads me to doubt the sincerity of abolitionist arguments based on the alleged lack of significant additional deterrent effect of capital punishment.

I also wonder why anyone would hold more precious the life of a convicted murderer than that of 500 innocents, if by executing him he could save them. . . .

CHAPTER 10 / SPECIAL CASES

There are some special cases—special because the threat of the death penalty is the only threat that may deter the crime. We do not know that it will. We do know that in these cases no other threat can.

Unless threatened with the death penalty, prisoners serving life sentences without parole can murder fellow prisoners or guards with impunity. Without the death penalty we give effective immunity, we promise impunity, to just those persons who are most likely to need deterrent threats if they are to be restrained. From a moral viewpoint one may add that if a prisoner already convicted of a crime sufficient to send him to prison for life commits a murder, the death penalty seems likely to be well deserved. At any rate, without the death penalty his fellow prisoners and the correctional officers can and will be victimized with impunity should he decide to murder them. To avoid threatening the convict with the only punishment available to restrain him, their lives are put at risk. This seems hard to justify.

The matter is all too well illustrated by the following:

> Two hard-case inmates apparently wangled their way into the warden's offices and stabbed the warden and his deputy to death with sharpened mess-hall knives.
>
> . . . investigators said that the death mission had been specifically ordered the night before at a meeting of Muslim inmates because Fromhold had resisted their demands "once too often." Fromhold was stabbed thirteen times in the back and chest; Warden Patrick Curran, 47, who dashed into his deputy's first-floor office, was stabbed three times in the back.
>
> Neither inmate had much to lose. Burton was doing life in the cold-blooded execution of a Philadelphia police sergeant, and Bowen was awaiting trial in another cop-killing and the shooting of an elderly couple.*

I can think of no reason for giving permanent immunity to homicidal life prisoners, thereby victimizing guards and other prisoners.

Outside prison, too, the threat of the death penalty is the only threat that is likely to restrain some criminals. Without the death penalty an offender having committed a crime that leads to imprisonment for life has nothing to lose if he murders the arresting officer. By murdering the officer or, for that matter, witnesses to their crimes, such criminals increase their chances of escape, without increasing the severity of the punishment they will suffer if caught. This is the case for all criminals likely to be given life imprisonment if caught who commit an additional crime such as murdering the arresting officer. Only the death penalty could rationally restrain them.

In some states the death penalty is threatened to those who murder a police officer in the performance of his duties. Thus, special protection is extended to police officers, who, after all, are specially exposed. They deserve that extra protection. But it seems to me that everyone deserves the protection against murder that the death penalty can provide.

There are still other cases in which the death penalty alone is likely to be perceived as the threat that may deter from the crime. Thus, there is little point in imprisoning a spy in wartime: He expects his side to win, to be liberated by it, and to become a hero. On the other hand, if he had to fear immediate execution, the victory of his side would help the spy little. This may deter some people from becoming spies. It may not deter the man who does not mind becoming a patriotic martyr, but it may deter a man who does his spying for money.

A deserter, too, afraid of the risk of death on the battlefield, afraid enough to desert, is not going to be restrained by the threat of a prison sentence. But he may be afraid of certain death by firing squad. So may be anyone who deserts for any reason whatsoever.

Even the death penalty cannot restrain certain crimes. Once a man has committed a first murder for which, if convicted, he would be punished by execution, he can commit additional murders without fear of additional punishment. The range of punishments is limited. The range of crimes is not. The death penalty is the most severe punishment we can impose. It is reserved for the most serious crimes. But we can

Newsweek, 11 June 1973.

add nothing for still more serious crimes such as multiple murders or torture murders.

Unlike death, which we will all experience, torture is repulsive to us. Thus, we will not apply it even to those who richly deserve it. It is, moreover, most unlikely that anyone not deterred by death would be deterred by torture or that death with torture would be more deterrent than death without. Thus, there is little point in trying to extend the range of punishment upward, beyond death.

Unfortunately, criminals can and sometimes do torture victims. They also can and sometimes do murder more than one person. The law cannot threaten more than death. But at least it should not threaten less. Although the threat of the death penalty may not restrain the second murder, it may restrain the first. . . .

CHAPTER 16 / THE ADVOCATE ADVOCATES

There are two basic arguments for the death penalty; they are independent of, yet consistent with, one another.

The first argument is moral: The death penalty is just; it is deserved for certain crimes. One can explain why one feels that certain crimes deserve the death penalty. But as usual with moral arguments, one cannot show this conviction to be *factually* correct (or, for that matter, incorrect) since moral arguments rest not on facts but on our evaluation of them. My evaluation leads me to believe that, e.g., premeditated murder or treason (a fact) is so grave and horrible a crime (an evaluation) as to deserve nothing less than the death penalty, that only the death penalty (a fact) is proportionate to the gravity of the crime (an evaluation).

My widely shared view is opposed by abolitionists, who claim that the death penalty is unjust for any crime, and inconsistent with human dignity. . . . Since most abolitionists believe, as I do, that punishments should be proportionate to the perceived gravity of crimes, the abolitionist claim seems to me logically precarious. It implies either that murder is not so horrible after all—not horrible enough, at any rate, to deserve death—or that the death penalty is too harsh a punishment for it, and indeed for any conceivable crime. I find it hard to believe that one can hold either view seriously, let alone both. . . .

I must confess that I have never understood the assorted arguments claiming that the death penalty is inconsistent with human dignity or that, somehow, society has no right to impose it. One might as well claim that death generally, or at least death from illness, is inconsistent with human dignity, or that birth is, or any suffering or any undesirable social condition. Most of these are unavoidable. At least death by execution can be avoided by not killing someone else, by not committing murder. One can preserve one's dignity in this respect if one values it. Incidentally, execution may be physically less humiliating and painful than death in a hospital. It is, however, morally more humiliating and meant to be: It indicates the extreme blame we attach to the crime of murder by deliberately expelling the murderer from among the living.

As for the dignity of society, it seems to me that by executing murderers it tries to keep its promise to secure the lives of innocents, to vindicate the law, and to impose retribution on those who so horribly violate it. To do anything less would be inconsistent with the dignity of society. . . .

QUESTIONS FOR REFLECTION

1. Van den Haag argues that we should accept the deterrent value of the death penalty, despite the inconclusive results of most statistical studies. What are his arguments?
2. In what special circumstances, according to van den Haag, is capital punishment justified, even if it is unacceptable in most cases? Do you agree?
3. Why, in van den Haag's view, is the death penalty compatible with human dignity?

HUGO ADAM BEDAU

The Case against the Death Penalty

(Source: ACLU website http://www.aclu.org/. Copyright © 1988 American Civil Liberties Union. Notes have been omitted. Reprinted by permission of the ACLU.)

Introduction

. . .

Despite the Supreme Court's 1976 ruling in *Gregg v. Georgia,* the ACLU continues to oppose capital punishment on moral and practical, as well as on constitutional, grounds:

- Capital punishment is cruel and unusual. It is a relic of the earliest days of penology, when slavery, branding, and other corporal punishments were commonplace. Like those other barbaric practices, executions have no place in a civilized society.
- Opposition to the death penalty does not arise from misplaced sympathy for convicted murderers. On the contrary, murder demonstrates a lack of respect for human life. For this very reason, murder is abhorrent, and any policy of state-authorized killings is immoral.
- Capital punishment denies due process of law. Its imposition is arbitrary and irrevocable. It forever deprives an individual of benefits of new evidence or new law that might warrant the reversal of a conviction or the setting aside of a death sentence.
- The death penalty violates the constitutional guarantee of the equal protection of the laws. It is applied randomly at best and discriminatorily at worst. It is imposed disproportionately upon those whose victims are white, on offenders who are people of color, and on those who are themselves poor and uneducated.
- The defects in death-penalty laws, conceded by the Supreme Court in the early 1970s, have not been appreciably altered by the shift from unfettered discretion to "guided discretion." These changes in death sentencing have proved to be largely cosmetic. They merely mask the impermissible arbitrariness of a process that results in an execution.
- Executions give society the unmistakable message that human life no longer deserves respect when it is useful to take it and that homicide is legitimate when deemed justified by pragmatic concerns.
- Reliance on the death penalty obscures the true causes of crime and distracts attention from the social measures that effectively contribute to its control. Politicians who preach the desirability of executions as a weapon of crime control deceive the public and mask their own failure to support anti-crime measures that will really work.
- Capital punishment wastes resources. It squanders the time and energy of courts, prosecuting attorneys, defense counsel, juries, and courtroom and correctional personnel. It unduly burdens the system of criminal justice, and it is therefore counterproductive as an instrument for society's control of violent crime. It epitomizes the tragic inefficacy and brutality of the resort to violence rather than reason for the solution of difficult social problems.

- A decent and humane society does not deliberately kill human beings. An execution is a dramatic, public spectacle of official, violent homicide that teaches the permissibility of killing people to solve social problems—the worst possible example to set for society. In this century, governments have too often attempted to justify their lethal fury by the benefits such killing would bring to the rest of society. The bloodshed is real and deeply destructive of the common decency of the community; the benefits are illusory.

Two conclusions buttress our entire case: Capital punishment does not deter crime, and the death penalty is uncivilized in theory and unfair and inequitable in practice.

Deterrence

The argument most often cited in support of capital punishment is that the threat of executions deters capital crimes more effectively than imprisonment. This claim is plausible, but the facts do not support it. The death penalty fails as a deterrent for several reasons.

1. Any punishment can be an effective deterrent only if it is consistently and promptly employed. Capital punishment cannot be administered to meet these conditions.

   Only a small proportion of first-degree murderers is sentenced to death, and even fewer are executed. Although death sentences since 1980 have increased in number to about 250 per year, this is still only 1 percent of all homicides known to the police. Of all those convicted on a charge of criminal homicide, only 2 percent—about 1 in 50—are eventually sentenced to death.

   The possibility of increasing the number of convicted murderers sentenced to death and executed by enacting mandatory death penalty laws was ruled unconstitutional in 1976 (*Woodson* v. *North Carolina*).

   Considerable delay in carrying out the death sentence is unavoidable, given the procedural safeguards required by the courts in capital cases. Starting with empaneling the trial jury, murder trials take far longer when the death penalty is involved. Post-conviction appeals in death-penalty cases are far more frequent as well. All these factors increase the time and cost of administering criminal justice.

   The sobering lesson is that we can reduce such delay and costs only by abandoning the procedural safeguards and constitutional rights of suspects, defendants, and convicts, with the attendant high risk of convicting the wrong person and executing the innocent.

2. Persons who commit murder and other crimes of personal violence either premeditate them or they do not. If the crime is premeditated, the criminal ordinarily concentrates on escaping detection, arrest, and conviction. The threat of even the severest punishment will not deter those who expect to escape detection and arrest. If the crime is not premeditated, then it is impossible to imagine how the threat of any punishment could deter it. Most capital crimes are committed during moments of great emotional stress or under the influence of drugs or alcohol, when logical thinking has been suspended. Impulsive or expressive violence is inflicted by persons heedless of the consequences to themselves as well as to others.

   Gangland killings, air piracy, drive-by shootings, and kidnapping for ransom are among the graver felonies that continue to be committed because some individuals think they are too clever to get caught. Political terrorism is usually committed in the name of an ideology that honors its martyrs; trying to cope with it by threatening death for terrorists is futile. Such threats leave untouched the underlying causes and ignore the many political and diplomatic sanctions (such as treaties against asylum for international terrorists) that could appreciably lower the incidence of terrorism.

   The attempt to reduce murders in the illegal drug trade by the threat of severe punishment ignores this fact: Anyone trafficking in illegal drugs is already betting his life in violent competition with other dealers. It is irrational to think that the death penalty—a remote threat at best—will deter murders committed in drug turf wars or by street-level dealers.

3. If, however, severe punishment can deter crime, then long-term imprisonment is severe enough to cause any rational person not to commit violent crimes. The vast preponderance of the evidence shows that the death penalty is no more effective than imprisonment in deterring murder and that it may even be an incitement to criminal violence in certain cases.
   a. Death-penalty states as a group do not have lower rates of criminal homicide than non-death-penalty states. During the 1980s, death-penalty states averaged an annual rate of 7.5 criminal homicides per 100,000 population; abolitionist states averaged a rate of 7.4.
   b. Use of the death penalty in a given state may increase the subsequent rate of criminal homicide in that state. In New York, for example, between 1907 and 1964, 692 executions were carried out. On the average, over this 57-year period, one or more executions in a given month aided a net increase of two homicides to the total committed in the next month.
   c. In neighboring states—one with the death penalty and the others without it—the one with the death penalty does not show a consistently lower rate of criminal homicide. For example, between 1972 and 1990, the homicide rate in Michigan (which has no death penalty) was generally as low as or lower than the neighboring state of Indiana, which restored the death penalty in 1973 and since then has sentenced 70 persons to death and carried out 2 executions.
   d. Police officers on duty do not suffer a higher rate of criminal assault and homicide in states that have abolished the death penalty than they do in death-penalty states. Between 1973 and 1984, for example, lethal assaults against police were not significantly more or less frequent in abolition states than in death-penalty states. There is "no support for the view that the death penalty provides a more effective deterrent to police homicides than alternative sanctions. Not for a single year was evidence found that police are safer in jurisdictions that provide for capital punishment."
   e. Prisoners and prison personnel do not suffer a higher rate of criminal assault and homicide from life-term prisoners in abolition states than they do in death-penalty states. Between 1984 and 1989, seventeen prison staff were murdered by prisoners in ten states; of these murders, 88 percent (15 of 17) occurred in death-penalty jurisdictions—just as about 88 percent of all the prisoners in those ten states were in death-penalty jurisdictions. Evidently, the threat of the death penalty "does not even exert an incremental deterrent effect over the threat of a lesser punishment in the abolitionist state."

Actual experience establishes these conclusions beyond a reasonable doubt. No comparable body of evidence contradicts them.

Three investigations since *Furman*, using methods pioneered by economists, reported findings in the opposite direction. Subsequently, several qualified investigators have independently examined these claims, and all have rejected them. The National Academy of Sciences, in its thorough report on the effects of criminal sanctions on crime rates, concluded: "It seems unthinkable to us to base decisions on the use of the death penalty" on such "fragile" and "uncertain" results. "We see too many plausible explanations for [these] findings . . . other than the theory that capital punishment deters murder."

Furthermore, cases have been clinically documented where the death penalty actually incited the capital crimes it was supposed to deter. These include instances of the so-called suicide-by-execution syndrome—persons who wanted but feared to take their own life and committed murder so that society would kill them.

It must, of course, be conceded that inflicting the death penalty guarantees that the condemned person will commit no further crimes. This is an incapacitative, not a deterrent, effect of executions. Furthermore, it is too high a price to pay when studies show that very few convicted murderers ever commit another crime of violence. A recent study examined the prison and post-release records of 533 prisoners on death row in 1972 whose sentences were reduced to life by the Supreme Court's ruling in *Furman*. The research showed that 6 had committed another murder. But the same study showed that in 4 other cases, an innocent man had been sentenced to death.

Recidivism among murderers does occasionally happen. But it happens less frequently than most people believe; the media rarely distinguish between a paroled murderer who murders again and other murderers who have a previous criminal record but not for homicide.

There is no way to predict which convicted murderers will kill again. Repeat murders could be prevented only by executing all those convicted of criminal homicide. Such a policy is too inhumane and brutal to be taken seriously. Society would never tolerate dozens of executions daily, yet nothing less would suffice. Equally effective but far less inhumane is a policy of life imprisonment without the possibility of parole.

Unfairness

Constitutional due process as well as elementary justice require that the judicial functions of trial and sentencing be conducted with fundamental fairness, especially where the irreversible sanction of the death penalty is involved. In murder cases (since 1930, 99 percent of all executions have been for this crime), there has been substantial evidence to show that courts have been arbitrary, racially biased, and unfair in the way in which they have sentenced some persons to prison but others to death.

Racial discrimination was one of the grounds on which the Supreme Court relied in *Furman* in ruling the death penalty unconstitutional. Half a century ago, Gunnar Myrdal, in his classic *American Dilemma* (1944), reported that "the South makes the widest application of the death penalty, and Negro criminals come in for much more than their share of the executions." Statistics confirm this discrimination, only it is not confined to the South. Between 1930 and 1990, 4,016 persons were executed in the United States. Of these, 2,129 (or 53 percent) were black. For the crime of murder, 3,343 were executed; 1,693 (or 51 percent) were black. During these years African-Americans were about 12 percent of the nation's population.

The nation's death rows have always had a disproportionately large population of African-Americans, relative to their fraction of the total population. Over the past century, black offenders, as compared with white, were often executed for crimes less often receiving the death penalty, such as rape and burglary. (Between 1930 and 1976, 455 men were executed for rape, of whom 405 [or 90 percent] were black.) A higher percentage of the blacks who were executed were juveniles; and blacks were more often executed than were whites without having their conviction reviewed by any higher court.

In recent years, it has been widely believed that such flagrant discrimination is a thing of the past. Since the revival of the death penalty in the mid-1970s, about half of those on death row at any given time have been black—a disproportionately large fraction given the black/white ratio of the total population, but not so obviously unfair if judged by the fact that roughly 50 percent of all those arrested for murder were also black. Nevertheless, when those under death sentence are examined more closely, it turns out that race is a decisive factor after all.

An exhaustive statistical study of racial discrimination in capital cases in Georgia, for example, showed that "the average odds of receiving a death sentence among all indicted cases were 4.3 times higher in cases with white victims." In 1987 these data were placed before the Supreme Court in *McCleskey* v. *Kemp* and the Court did not dispute the statistical evidence. The Court did hold, however, that the evidence failed to show that there was "a constitutionally significant risk of racial bias. . . ."

In 1990, the U.S. General Accounting Office reported to the Congress the results of its review of empirical studies on racism and the death penalty. The GAO concluded: "Our synthesis of the 28 studies shows a pattern of evidence indicating racial disparities in the charging, sentencing, and imposition of the death penalty after the *Furman* decision" and that "race of victim influence was found at all stages of the criminal justice system process. . . ."

These results cannot be explained away by relevant non-racial factors (such as prior criminal record or type of crime), and they lead to a very unsavory conclusion: In the trial courts of this nation, even at the present time, the killing of a white is treated much more severely than the killing of a black. Of the 168 persons executed between January 1977 and April 1992, only 29 had been convicted of the killing of a non-white, and only one of these 29 was himself white. Where the death penalty is involved, our criminal justice system essentially reserves the death penalty for murderers (regardless of their race) who kill white victims.

Both sex and socioeconomic class are also factors that enter into determining who receives a death sentence and who is executed. During the 1980s and 1990s, only about 1 percent of all those on death row were women, even though women commit about 15 percent of all criminal homicides. A third or more of the women under death sentence were guilty of killing men who had victimized them with years of violent abuse. Since 1930, only 33 women (12 of them black) have been executed in the United States.

Discrimination against the poor (and in our society racial minorities are disproportionately poor) is also well established. "Approximately ninety percent of those on death row could not afford to hire a lawyer when they were tried." A defendant's poverty, lack of firm social roots in the community, inadequate legal representation at trial or on appeal—all these have been common factors among death-row populations. As Justice William O. Douglas noted in *Furman*, "One searches our chronicles in vain for the execution of any member of the affluent strata in this society."

The demonstrated inequities in the actual administration of capital punishment should tip the balance against it in the judgment of fair-minded and impartial observers. "Whatever else might be said for the use of death as a punishment, one lesson is clear from experience: this is a power that we cannot exercise fairly and without discrimination."

Justice John Marshall Harlan, writing for the Court, noted: ". . . the history of capital punishment for homicides . . . reveals continual efforts, uniformly unsuccessful, to identify before the fact those homicides for which the slayer should die. . . . Those who have come to grips with the hard task of actually attempting to draft means of channeling capital sentencing discretion have confirmed the lesson taught by history. . . . To identify before the fact those characteristics of criminal homicides and their perpetrators which call for the death penalty, and to express these characteristics in language which can be fairly understood and applied by the sentencing authority, appears to be tasks which are beyond present human ability." (*McGautha* v. *California* [1971])

Yet in the *Gregg* decision, the majority of the Supreme Court abandoned the wisdom of Justice Harlan and ruled as though the new guided-discretion statutes could accomplish the impossible. The truth is that death statutes approved by the Court "do not effectively restrict the discretion of juries by any real standards. They never will. No society is going to kill everybody who meets certain preset verbal requirements, put on the statute books without awareness of coverage of the infinity of special factors the real world can produce."

Even if these statutes were to succeed in guiding the jury's choice of sentence, a vast reservoir of unfettered discretion remains: the prosecutor's decision to prosecute for a capital or lesser crime, the court's willingness to accept or reject a guilty plea, the jury's decision to convict for second-degree murder or manslaughter rather than capital murder, the determination of the defendant's sanity, the final decision by the governor on clemency.

Discretion in the criminal-justice system is unavoidable. The history of capital punishment in American society clearly shows the desire to mitigate the harshness of this penalty by narrowing its scope. Discretion, whether authorized by statutes or by their silence, has been the main vehicle to this end. But when discretion is used, as it always has been, to mark for death the poor, the friendless, the uneducated, the members of racial minorities, and the despised, then discretion becomes injustice.

Thoughtful citizens, who in contemplating capital punishment in the abstract might support it, must condemn it in actual practice.

Inevitability of Error

Unlike all other criminal punishments, the death penalty is uniquely irrevocable. Speaking to the French Chamber of Deputies in 1830, years after the excesses of the French Revolution, which he had witnessed, the Marquis de Lafayette said, "I shall ask for the abolition of the punishment of death until I have the infallibility of human judgment demonstrated to me." Although some proponents of capital punishment would argue that its merits are worth the occasional execution of innocent people, most would also insist that there is little likelihood of the innocent being executed. Yet a large body of evidence shows that innocent people are often convicted of crimes, including capital crimes, and that some of them have been executed.

Since 1900, in this country, there have been on the average more than four cases per year in which an entirely innocent person was convicted of murder. Scores of these persons were sentenced to death. In many cases, a reprieve or commutation arrived just hours, or even minutes, before the scheduled execution. These erroneous convictions have occurred in virtually every jurisdiction from one end of the nation to the other. Nor have they declined in recent years, despite the new death-penalty statutes approved by the Supreme Court. Consider this handful of representative cases:

- In 1975, only a year before the Supreme Court affirmed the constitutionality of capital punishment, two African-American men in Florida, Freddie Pitts and Wilbert Lee, were released from prison after twelve years awaiting execution for the murder of two white men. Their convictions were the result of coerced confessions, erroneous testimony of an alleged eyewitness, and incompetent defense counsel. Though a white man eventually admitted his guilt, a nine-year legal battle was required before the governor would grant Pitts and Lee a pardon. Had their execution not been stayed while the constitutional status of the death penalty was argued in the courts, these two innocent men probably would not be alive today.
- Just months after Pitts and Lee were released, authorities in New Mexico were forced to admit they had sentenced to death four white men—motorcyclists from Los Angeles—who were innocent. The accused offered a documented alibi at their trial, but the prosecution dismissed it as an elaborate ruse. The jury's verdict was based mainly on what was later revealed to be perjured testimony (encouraged by the police) from an alleged eyewitness. Thanks to persistent investigation by newspaper reporters and the confession of the real killer, the error was exposed and the defendants were released after eighteen months on death row.
- In Georgia in 1975, Earl Charles was convicted of murder and sentenced to death. A surviving victim of the crime erroneously identified Charles as the gunman; her testimony was supported by a jail-house informant who claimed he had heard Charles confess. Incontrovertible alibi evidence, showing that Charles was in Florida at the very time of the crime, eventually established his innocence—but not until he had spent more than three years under death sentence. His release was owing largely to his mother's unflagging efforts.
- In 1989, Texas authorities decided not to retry Randall Dale Adams after the appellate court reversed his conviction for murder. Adams had spent more than three years on death row for the murder of a Dallas police officer. He was convicted on the perjured testimony of a 16-year-old youth who was the real killer. Adams's plight was vividly presented in the 1988 docudrama, *The Thin Blue Line*, which convincingly told the true story of the crime and exposed the errors that resulted in his conviction.
- Another case in Texas from the 1980s tells an even more sordid story. In 1980, a black high school janitor, Clarence Brandley, and his white co-worker found the body of a missing 15-year-old white schoolgirl. Interrogated by the police, they were told, "One of you two is going to hang for this." Looking at Brandley, the officer said, "Since you're the nigger, you're elected." In a classic case of rush to judgment, Brandley was tried, convicted, and sentenced to death. The circumstantial evidence against him was thin, other leads were ignored by the police, and the courtroom atmosphere reeked of racism. In 1986, Centurion Ministries—a volunteer group devoted to freeing wrongly convicted prisoners—came to Brandley's aid. Evidence had meanwhile emerged that another man had committed the murder for which Brandley was awaiting execution. Brandley was not released until 1990.

Each of these five stories told above has a reassuring ending: The innocent prisoner is saved from execution and is released. But when prisoners are executed, no legal forum exists in which unanswered questions about their guilt can be resolved. In May 1992, Roger Keith Coleman was executed in Virginia despite widely publicized doubts surrounding his guilt and evidence that pointed to another person as the murderer—evidence that was never submitted at his trial. Not until late in the appeal process did anyone take seriously the possibility that the state was about to kill an innocent man, and then efforts to delay or nullify his execution failed. Was Coleman really innocent? At the time of his execution, his case was marked with many of the features found in other cases where the defendant was eventually cleared. Were Coleman still in prison, his friends and attorneys would have a strong incentive to resolve these questions. But with Coleman dead, further inquiry into the facts of the crime for which he was convicted is unlikely.

Overzealous prosecution, mistaken or perjured testimony, faulty police work, coerced confessions, the defendant's previous criminal record, inept defense counsel, seemingly conclusive circumstantial evidence, community pressure for a conviction—such factors help explain why the judicial system cannot guarantee that justice will never miscarry. And when it does miscarry, volunteers outside the criminal justice system—newspaper reporters, for example—and not the police or prosecutors are the ones who rectify the errors. To retain the death penalty in the face of the demonstrable failures of the system is unacceptable, especially as there are no strong counterbalancing factors in favor of the death penalty. . . .

Financial Costs

It is sometimes suggested that abolishing capital punishment is unfair to the taxpayer, as though life imprisonment were obviously more expensive than executions. If one takes into account all the relevant costs, the reverse is true. "The death penalty is not now, nor has it ever been, a more economical alternative to life imprisonment."

A murder trial normally takes much longer when the death penalty is at issue than when it is not. Litigation costs—including the time of judges, prosecutors, public defenders, and court reporters, and the high costs of briefs—are all borne by the taxpayer.

A 1982 study showed that were the death penalty to be reintroduced in New York, the cost of the capital trial alone would be more than double the cost of a life term in prison.

In Maryland, a comparison of capital trial costs with and without the death penalty for the years 1979–1984 concluded that a death penalty case costs "approximately 42 percent more than a case resulting in a non-death sentence." In 1988 and 1989 the Kansas legislature voted against reinstating the death penalty after it was informed that reintroduction would involve a first-year cost of "more than $11 million." Florida, with one of the nation's largest death rows, has estimated that the true cost of each execution is approximately $3.2 million, or approximately six times the cost of a life-imprisonment sentence.

The only way to make the death penalty a "better buy" than imprisonment is to weaken due process and curtail appellate review, which are the defendant's (and society's) only protections against the grossest miscarriages of justice. The savings in dollars would be at the cost of justice: In nearly half of the death-penalty cases given review under federal habeas corpus, the conviction is overturned.

QUESTIONS FOR REFLECTION

1. How does Bedau argue against the deterrent effect of the death penalty? Do you find his arguments convincing?
2. Which of Bedau's arguments are based on utility? Which are based on a concept of rights?
3. How would Bedau answer Locke's charge that a murderer has given up his right to life?
4. Suppose that Bedau's arguments are correct. Could imposing the death penalty ever be justifiable?

CASS R. SUNSTEIN AND ADRIAN VERMEULE

Is Capital Punishment Morally Required? The Relevance of Life-Life Tradeoffs

Cass R. Sunstein is Karl N. Llewellyn Distinguished Service Professor of Jurisprudence at the University of Chicago Law School. Adrian Vermeule is Bernard D. Meltzer Professor of Law at the University of Chicago.

1. Introduction

Many people believe capital punishment is morally impermissible. In their view, executions are inherently cruel and barbaric. Often they add that capital punishment is not, and cannot be, imposed in a way that adheres to the rule of law. They contend that as administered, capital punishment ensures the execution of (some) innocent people, and also that it reflects arbitrariness, in the form of random or invidious infliction of the ultimate penalty.

Defenders of capital punishment come in two different camps. Some are retributivists. Following Kant, they claim that for the most heinous forms of wrongdoing, the penalty of death is morally justified or perhaps even required. Other defenders of capital punishment are consequentialists and often also welfarists. They contend that the deterrent effect of capital punishment is significant and that it justifies the infliction of the ultimate penalty. Consequentialist defenses of capital punishment, however, tend to assume that capital punishment is (merely) morally permissible, as opposed to being morally obligatory.

Our goal here is to suggest that the debate over capital punishment is rooted in an unquestioned assumption, and that the failure to question that assumption is a serious moral error. The assumption is that for governments, acts are morally different from omissions. We want to raise the possibility that an indefensible form of the act-omission distinction is crucial to the most prominent objections to capital punishment—and that defenders of capital punishment, apparently making the same distinction, have failed to notice that on the logic of their theory, capital punishment is morally obligatory, not just permissible. We want to suggest, in other words, that capital punishment may be morally required not for retributive reasons, but in order to prevent the taking of innocent lives.

The suggestion bears not only on moral and political debates, but also on constitutional questions. In invalidating the death penalty for juveniles, for example, the Supreme Court did not seriously engage the possibility that capital punishment for juveniles may help to prevent the death of innocents, including the deaths of juvenile innocents. And if our suggestion is correct, it is connected to many questions outside of the context of capital punishment. If omissions by the state are often indistinguishable, in principle, from actions by the state, then a wide range of apparent failures to act—in the context not only of criminal and civil law, but of regulatory law as well—should be taken to raise serious moral and legal problems. Those who accept our arguments in favor of the death penalty may or may not welcome the implications for government action in general. In many situations, ranging from environmental quality to highway safety to relief of poverty, our arguments suggest that in light of imaginable empirical findings, government is obliged to provide far more protection than it now does, and that it should not be permitted to hide behind unhelpful distinctions between acts and omissions.

The foundation for our argument is a large and growing body of evidence that capital punishment may well have a deterrent effect, possibly a quite powerful one. A leading study suggests that each execution prevents some eighteen murders, on average. The particular numbers do not much matter. If the current evidence is even roughly correct, then a refusal to impose capital punishment will effectively condemn numerous innocent people to death. States that choose life imprisonment, when they might choose capital punishment, are ensuring the deaths of a large number of innocent people. On moral grounds, a choice that effectively condemns large numbers of people to death seems objectionable to say the least. For those who are inclined to be skeptical of capital punishment for moral reasons—a group that includes one of the current authors—the task is to consider the possibility that the failure to impose capital punishment is, prima facie and all things considered, a serious moral wrong.

Judgments of this sort are often taken to require a controversial commitment to either a consequentialist or a deontological view about the foundations of moral evaluation. One of our principal points, however, is that the choice between consequentialist and deontological approaches to morality does not seem crucial here; we will suggest that on certain empirical assumptions, theorists of both stripes might converge on the idea that capital punishment is morally obligatory. On consequentialist grounds, the death penalty seems morally obligatory if it is the only or most effective means of preventing significant numbers of murders; and much of our discussion will emphasize this point. For deontologists, a killing is a wrong under most circumstances, and its wrongness does not depend on its consequences or its effects on overall welfare. Many deontologists (of course not all) believe that capital punishment counts as a moral wrong. But in the abstract, any deontological injunction against the wrongful infliction of death turns out to be indeterminate on the moral status of capital punishment *if* it is necessary to prevent significant numbers of killings.

An unstated assumption animating much opposition to capital punishment, especially among self-conscious or intuitive deontologists is that capital punishment counts as an "act," while the refusal to impose it counts as an "omission," and that the two are altogether different from the moral point of view. We shall investigate this claim in some detail. But we doubt that the act-omission distinction can bear the moral weight given to it by the critics of capital punishment. Whatever its value as a moral concept where individuals are concerned, the act-omission distinction misfires in the general setting of government regulation. If government policies fail to protect people against air pollution, occupational risks, or racial discrimination, it is inadequate to put great moral weight on the idea that the failure to act is a mere "omission." No one believes that government can avoid responsibility to protect people against serious dangers, as for example by refusing to enforce regulatory statutes, simply by contending that such refusals are unproblematic omissions. If state governments impose light penalties on offenders, or treat certain offenses (say, domestic violence) as unworthy of attention, they should not be able to escape public retribution by contending that they are simply refusing to act. Where government is concerned, failures of protection, through refusals to punish and deter private misconduct, cannot be justified by pointing to the distinction between acts and omissions.

It has even become common to speak of "risk-risk tradeoffs," understood to arise when regulation of one risk (say, the risks associated with use of DDT) gives rise to another risk (say, the spread of malaria, against which DDT has been effective). Or suppose that an air pollutant creates adverse health effects but also has health benefits, as appears to be the case for ground-level ozone. No one believes that for moral reasons, social planners should refuse to take account of such tradeoffs; there is general agreement that whether a particular substance ought to be regulated depends on the overall effect of regulation on human well-being.

As an empirical matter, criminal law is pervaded by its own risk-risk tradeoffs. If the deterrent signal works, a failure to impose stringent penalties on certain crimes will increase the number of those crimes. A refusal to impose such penalties is, for that reason, problematic from the moral point of view. The very idea of "equal protection of the laws," in its oldest and most literal sense, attests to the importance of enforcing the criminal and civil law so as to safeguard the potential victims of private violence. What we are suggesting is that the death penalty produces a risk-risk tradeoff of its own, indeed what we will call a *life-life tradeoff*, to the extent that a refusal to impose capital punishment yields a significant increase in the number of deaths of innocent people.

Of course this point does not resolve the capital punishment debate. By itself, the act of execution may be a wrong, in a way that cannot be said for an act of imposing civil or criminal penalties on (say) environmental degradation. But the existence of life-life tradeoffs raises the possibility that for those who oppose killing, a rejection of capital punishment is not necessarily mandated. On the contrary, it may well be morally compelled. At the very least, those who object to capital punishment, and do so in the name of protecting life, must come to terms with the fact that the failure to inflict capital punishment might fail to protect life—and must, in our view, justify their position in ways that do not rely on question-begging claims about the distinction between acts and omissions.

We begin, in Part I, with the facts. Contrary to widely held beliefs, based on partial information or older studies, a wave of recent evidence suggests the possibility that capital punishment saves lives. One study finds that as a national average, each execution deters some eighteen murders. Our question whether capital punishment is morally obligatory is motivated by these findings; our central concern is that forgoing any given execution may be equivalent to condemning some eighteen unidentified people to a premature and violent death. Of course social science can always be disputed in this contentious domain, and we mean to outline, rather than to defend, the relevant evidence here. But the current findings do provide evidence of deterrence, and we think that it is illuminating to take those findings as given for purposes of analysis of the moral issues. Those who would like to abolish capital punishment, and who reject the social science, might find it useful to ask whether they would maintain their commitment to abolition if they were persuaded that capital punishment does have a strong deterrent effect; that is the principal issue that we mean to raise here.

In Part II, the centerpiece of the paper, we offer a few remarks on moral foundations and examine some standard objections to capital punishment that might seem plausible even in light of the current findings. We focus in particular on the crucial view that capital punishment is objectionable because it requires affirmative and intentional state "action," not merely an "omission." That distinction, we suggest, systematically misfires when applied to government, which is a moral agent with distinctive features. The act-omission distinction may not even be intelligible in the context of government, which always faces a choice among policy regimes, and in that sense cannot help but "act."

Even if the distinction between acts and omissions can be rendered intelligible in regulatory settings, its moral relevance is obscure. Some acts are morally obligatory, while some omissions are morally culpable. If capital punishment has significant deterrent effects, we suggest that for government to omit to impose it is morally blameworthy, even on a deontological account of morality. Deontological accounts typically recognize a consequentialist override to baseline prohibitions; if each execution saves eighteen lives, on average, then it is plausible to think that the override is triggered, in turn triggering an obligation to adopt capital punishment.

Once the act-omission distinction is rejected where government is concerned, it becomes clear that the most familiar, and plausible, objections to capital punishment deal with only one side of the ledger: the objections fail to take account of the exceedingly arbitrary deaths that capital punishment apparently deters. We consider rule-of-law concerns about the irreversibility of capital punishment and its possibly random or invidious administration; a strict-scrutiny principle that capital punishment should not be permitted if other means for producing the same level of deterrence are available; and concerns about slippery slopes from capital punishment to other practices. We suggest that while some of these complaints have merit, they do not count as decisive objections to capital punishment, because they embody a flawed version of the act-omission distinction and generally overlook the fact that the moral objections to capital punishment apply even more strongly to the murders that capital punishment deters.

. . .

2. Evidence

For many years, the deterrent effect of capital punishment was sharply disputed. But a great deal of recent evidence strengthens the claim that capital punishment has large deterrent effects. The reason for the shift is that a wave of sophisticated econometric studies have exploited a newly available form of data, so-called "panel data" that uses all information from a set of units (states or counties) and follows that data over an extended period of time. A leading study used county-level panel data from 3,054 U.S. counties between 1977 and 1996. The authors find that the murder rate is significantly reduced by both death sentences and executions. The most striking finding is that *on average, each execution results in eighteen fewer murders*.

Other econometric studies also find a substantial deterrent effect. In two papers, Paul Zimmerman uses state-level panel data from 1978 onwards to measure the deterrent effect of execution rates and execution methods. He estimates that each execution deters an average of fourteen murders. Using state-level data from 1977 to 1997, Mocan and Gittings find that each execution deters five murders on average. They also find that increases in the murder rate come from removing people from death row and also from commutations in death sentences. Yet another study, based on state-level data from 1997 to 1999, finds that a death sentence deters 4.5 murders and an execution deters three murders. The same study investigates the question of whether executions deter crimes of passion and murders by intimates. The answer is clear: these categories of murder are deterred by capital punishment. The deterrent effect of the death penalty is also found to be a function of the length of waits on death row, with a murder deterred for every 2.75 years of reduction in the period before execution.

In the period between 1972 and 1976, the Supreme Court produced an effective moratorium on capital punishment, and an extensive study exploits that fact to estimate the deterrent effect. Using state-level data from 1960 to 2000, the authors make before-and-after comparisons, focusing on the murder rate in each state before and after the death penalty was suspended and reinstated. The authors find a substantial deterrent effect. After suspending the death penalty, 91% of states faced an increase in homicides—and in 67% of states, the rate was decreased after reinstatement of capital punishment.

A recent study offers more refined findings. Disaggregating the data on a state-by-state basis, Joanna Shepherd finds that the nationwide deterrent effect of capital punishment is entirely driven by only six states—and that no deterrent effect can be found in the twenty-one other states that have restored capital punishment. What distinguishes the six from the twenty-one? The answer lies in the fact that states showing a deterrent effect are executing more people than states that do not. In fact the data show a "threshold effect": deterrence is found in states that had at least nine executions between 1977 and 1996. In states below that threshold, no deterrence can be found. This finding is intuitively plausible. Unless executions reach a certain level, murderers may act as if the death is so improbable as not to be worthy of concern. [Shepherd's] main lesson is that once the level of executions reaches a certain level, the deterrent effect of capital punishment is substantial.

All in all, the recent evidence of a deterrent effect from capital punishment seems impressive. But in studies of this kind, it is hard to control for confounding variables, and a degree of doubt inevitably remains. It remains possible that these findings will be exposed as statistical artifacts or will be found to rest on flawed econometric methods. More broadly, skeptics are likely to question the mechanisms by which capital punishment has a deterrent effect. On the skeptical view, many murderers lack a clear sense of the likelihood and perhaps even the existence of executions in their state; further problems for the deterrence claim are introduced by the fact that capital punishment is imposed infrequently and after long delays. In any case many murders are committed in a passionate state that does not lend itself to an all-things-considered analysis on the part of perpetrators.

As mentioned above, and as we discuss in Part IV, these suppositions are in some tension with existing evidence. But let us suppose that these doubts are reasonable. If so, should current findings be deemed irrelevant for purposes of policy and law? That would be an odd conclusion. In regulation as a whole, it is common to embrace some version of the Precautionary Principle—the idea that steps should be taken to prevent significant harm even if cause-and-effect relationships remain unclear and even if the risk is not likely to come to fruition. Even if we reject strong versions of the Precautionary Principle, it hardly seems sensible that governments should ignore evidence demonstrating a significant possibility that a certain step will save large numbers of innocent lives.

For capital punishment, critics often seem to assume that evidence on deterrent effects should be ignored if reasonable questions can be raised about it. But as a general rule, this is implausible. In most contexts, the existence of reasonable questions is hardly an adequate reason to ignore evidence of severe harm. If it were, many environmental controls would be in serious jeopardy. We do not mean to suggest that government should commit what many people consider to be, prima facie, a serious moral wrong simply on the basis of speculation that this step will do some good. But a degree of reasonable doubt does not seem sufficient to doom capital punishment, if the evidence suggests that significant deterrence occurs.

In any event, we will proceed by stipulating to the validity of this evidence, in order to isolate the question of its moral significance. Our primary concern here is not to reach a final judgment about the evidence, but how to evaluate capital punishment given the assumption of a substantial deterrent effect. Those who doubt the evidence might ask themselves how they would assess the moral questions if they were ultimately convinced that life-life tradeoffs were actually involved—as, for example, in hostage situations in which officials are authorized to use deadly force to protect the lives of innocent people.

If capital punishment does have a strong deterrent effect, there is a crucial implication: it must be the case that capital punishment is *not* a wholly capricious system of punishment, pervaded by false positives. At the very least, some or many prospective murderers must believe that the system has a high degree of accuracy. The simple reason is that if capital punishment were thoroughly error-prone and seen as such, the deterrent signal of the punishment would be so diluted that it would be extremely unlikely to produce such strong and consistent empirical traces as those described above. At the limit, if capital punishment were entirely random, falling with utter arbitrariness upon innocent and guilty alike, there would be no reason for any prospective criminal to factor it into calculation about the costs and benefits of crime. In this sense, it turns out, Justice Potter Stewart's comparison of capital punishment to being struck by lighting does not hold for current systems (a point on which we will expand below). We do not mean to overstate this point. Of course it remains undeniable that capital punishment is sometimes imposed erroneously, and undeniable too that it is sometimes imposed arbitrarily or on invidious grounds *within* the set of guilty defendants. Nothing we say here is meant to suggest that states should be content with erroneous or arbitrary death sentences. But the evidence suggests that there is at least a high degree of accuracy, in the sense of avoiding false positives, in the infliction of capital punishment.

3. Capital Punishment: Moral Foundations and Four Objections

Assume, then, that capital punishment does save significant numbers of innocent lives. On what assumptions should that form of punishment be deemed morally unacceptable, rather than morally obligatory? Why should the deaths of those convicted of capital murder, a large fraction of whom are guilty in fact, be considered a more serious moral wrong than the deaths of a more numerous group who are certainly innocents?

We consider, and ultimately reject, several responses. Our first general contention is that opposition to capital punishment trades on a form of the distinction between acts and omissions. Whatever the general force of that distinction, its application to government systematically fails, because government is a distinctive kind of moral agent. Our second general contention is that, apart from direct state involvement, the features that make capital punishment morally objectionable to its critics are also features of the murders that capital punishment deters. The principal difference, on the empirical assumptions we are making, is that in a legal regime without capital punishment, far more people die, and those people are innocent of any wrongdoing. No one denies that arbitrariness in the system of capital punishment is a serious problem. But even if the existing system is viewed in its worst light, it involves far less arbitrariness than does the world of homicide. Let us begin, however, with foundational issues.

Morality and Death

On a standard view, it is impossible to come to terms with the moral questions about capital punishment without saying something about the foundations of moral judgments. We will suggest, however, that sectarian commitments at the foundational level are for the most part irrelevant to the issues here. If it is stipulated that the evidence discussed in Part I is correct, both consequentialist and deontological accounts of morality will or should converge upon the view that capital punishment is morally obligatory. Consequentialists will do so because capital punishment minimizes killings overall. Deontologists will do so because an opposition to killing is, by itself, indeterminate in the face of life-life tradeoffs; because a legal regime with capital punishment has a strong claim to be more respectful of life's value than does a legal regime lacking capital punishment; and because modern deontologists typically subscribe to a consequentialist override or escape hatch, one that makes otherwise impermissible actions obligatory if necessary to prevent many deaths—precisely what we are assuming is true of capital punishment. Only those few deontologists who both insist upon a strong distinction between state actions and state omissions, *and* reject a consequentialist override, will believe the deterrent effect of capital punishment irrelevant in principle.

Suppose that we accept consequentialism and believe that government actions should be evaluated in terms of their effects on aggregate welfare. If so, the evidence of deterrence strongly supports a moral argument in favor of the death penalty—which, by hypothesis, seems to produce a net gain in overall welfare. Of course there are many complications here; for example, the welfare of many people might increase as a result of knowing that capital punishment exists, and the welfare of many other people might decrease for the same reason. A full consequentialist calculus would require a more elaborate assessment than we aim to provide here. The only point is that if capital punishment produces significantly fewer deaths on balance, there should be a strong consequentialist presumption on its behalf. To be sure, it is also possible to imagine forms of consequentialism that reject welfarism as implausibly reductionist and that see violations of rights as part of the set of consequences that must be taken into account in deciding what to do. For some such consequentialists, killings are, under ordinary circumstances, a violation of rights, and this point is highly relevant to any judgment about killings. But even if the point is accepted, capital punishment may be required, not prohibited, on consequentialist grounds, simply because and to the extent that it minimizes rights violations.

But imagine that we are deontologists, believing that actions by government and others should not be evaluated in consequentialist terms. How can capital punishment be morally permissible, let alone obligatory? Suppose, for example, that under ordinary circumstances, killing a human being is a wrong, and its wrongness does not depend on an inquiry into whether it produces a net increase in welfare. For many critics of capital punishment, a deontological intuition is central; evidence of deterrence is irrelevant because moral wrongdoing by the state is not justified even if it can be defended on utilitarian grounds. Compare a situation in which a state seeks to kill an innocent person, knowing that the execution will prevent a number of private killings; deontologists believe that the unjustified execution cannot be supported even if the state is secure in its knowledge of its beneficial effects. Of course it is contentious to claim that capital punishment is a moral wrong. But if it is, then significant deterrence might be entirely beside the point.

Despite all this, our claims here do not depend on accepting consequentialism or on rejecting the deontological objection to evaluating unjustified killings in consequentialist terms. The argument is instead that by itself and in the abstract, this objection is indeterminate on the moral status of capital punishment. To the extent possible, we intend to bracket the most fundamental questions and to suggest that whatever one's view of the foundations of morality, the objection to the death penalty is difficult to sustain under the empirical assumptions that we have traced. Taken in its most sympathetic light, a deontological objection to capital punishment is unconvincing *if* states that refuse to impose the death penalty produce, by that very refusal, significant numbers of additional deaths. For deontologists who emphasize life's value and object to the death penalty, the problem is acute if the refusal to impose that penalty predictably leads to significant additional murders. In a hostage situation, police officers are permitted to kill (execute) those who have taken hostages if this step is reasonably deemed necessary to save those who have been taken. If the evidence of deterrence is convincing, why is capital punishment so different in principle?

Of course we could envision a form of deontology that refuses any exercise in aggregation—one that would refuse to authorize, or compel, a violation of rights even, if the violation is necessary to prevent a significantly larger number of rights violations. But most modern deontologists reject this position, instead admitting a consequentialist override to baseline deontological prohibitions. Although the threshold at which the consequentialist override is triggered varies with different accounts, we will suggest below that if each execution deters some eighteen murders, the override is plausibly triggered.

To distill these points: the only moral accounts that are inconsistent with our argument are those that both (1) embrace a distinction between state actions and state omissions and (2) reject a consequentialist override. To those who subscribe to this complex of views, and who consider capital punishment a violation of rights, our argument will not be convincing. In the end, however, we believe that it is difficult to sustain the set of moral assumptions that would bar capital punishment if it is the best means of preventing significant numbers of innocent deaths. Indeed, we believe that those who think that they hold those assumptions are motivated by other considerations—especially a failure to give full weight to statistical lives—on which we focus in Part III.

Acts and Omissions

A natural response to our basic concern would invoke the widespread intuition that capital punishment involves intentional state "action," while the failure to deter private murders is merely an "omission" by the state. In our view, this appealing and intuitive line of argument goes rather badly wrong. The critics of capital punishment have been led astray by uncritically applying the act-omission distinction to a regulatory setting. Their position condemns the "active" infliction of death by governments but does not condemn the "inactive" production of death that comes from the refusal to maintain a system of capital punishment. The basic problem is that even if this selective condemnation can be justified at the level of individual behavior, it is difficult to defend for governments. A great deal of work has to be done to explain why "inactive," but causal, government decisions should not be part of the moral calculus. Suppose that we endorse the deontological position that it is wrong to take human lives, even if overall welfare is promoted by taking them. Why does the system of capital punishment violate that position, if the failure to impose capital punishment also takes lives?

Perhaps our argument about unjustified selectivity is blind to morally relevant factors that condemn capital punishment and that buttress the act-omission distinction in this context. There are two possible points here, one involving intention and the other involving causation. First, a government (acting through agents) that engages in capital punishment intends to take lives; it seeks to kill. A government that does not engage in capital punishment, and therefore provides less deterrence, does not intend to kill. The deaths that result are the unintended and unsought by-product of an effort to respect life. Surely—it might be said—this is a morally relevant difference. Second, a government that inflicts capital punishment ensures a simple and direct causal chain between its own behavior and the taking of human lives. When a government rejects capital punishment, the causal chain is much more complex; the taking of human lives is an indirect consequence of the government's decision, one that is mediated by the actions of a murderer. The government authorizes its agents to inflict capital punishment but does not authorize private parties to murder; indeed it forbids murder. Surely that is a morally relevant difference too.

In our view, both the argument from causation and the argument from intention go wrong by overlooking the distinctive features of government as a moral agent. Whatever the general status of the act-omission distinction as a matter of moral philosophy, the distinction is least impressive when applied to government. The most fundamental point is that unlike individuals, governments always and necessarily face a choice between or among possible policies for regulating third parties. The distinction between acts and omissions may not be intelligible in this context, and even if it is, the distinction does not make a morally relevant difference. Most generally, government is in the business of creating permissions and prohibitions. When it explicitly or implicitly authorizes private action, it is not omitting to do anything, or refusing to act. Moreover, the distinction between authorized and unauthorized private action—for example, private killing—becomes obscure when the government formally forbids private action but chooses a set of policy instruments that do not adequately or fully discourage it.

A system of punishments that only weakly deters homicide, relative to other feasible punishments, does not quite authorize homicide; but it is not properly characterized as an omission, and little turns on whether it can be so characterized. Suppose, for example, that government fails to characterize certain actions—say, sexual harassment—as tortious or as violative of civil rights law, and that it therefore permits employers to harass employees as they choose, or to discharge employees for failing to submit to sexual harassment. It would be unhelpful to characterize the result as a product of governmental "inaction." If employers are permitted to discharge employees for failing to submit to sexual harassment, it is because the law is allocating certain entitlements to employers rather than employees. Or consider the context of ordinary torts. When Homeowner B sues Factory A, complaining of air pollution, a decision not to rule for B is not a form of inaction; it is the allocation to Factory A of property right to pollute.

Let us apply these points, beginning with the causal version of the argument in favor of an act-omission distinction. For concreteness, suppose that government officials face a choice between two (and only two) packages of policies for reducing the murder rate. Suppose that Package A contains a range of legal instruments, such as ordinary imprisonment, imprisonment without parole (perhaps for life), post-incarceration programs to prevent recidivism, and so on. Package B contains all the same instruments *plus* capital punishment.

Stipulating to the validity of the evidence discussed in Part I, the crux of the issue is this: whatever the nature of the causal chain, Package A will inevitably ensure a significant increase in the number of deaths. Why should the length of the causal chain matter? In this setting, it is hard to make sense of the claim that capital punishment involves causal government "action" in some morally distinctive way. For government to opt for Package A—even in the sense of simply leaving in place previously—enacted laws that adopted Package A—is no less an "action" than it is to opt for Package B. Some criminal justice policy or other will necessarily be in place. The only interesting or even meaningful question government ever faces is not whether to act, but what action should be taken—what mix of criminal-justice policies government ought to pursue. The policy mix that does not include capital punishment is not an "omission" or a "failure to act" in any meaningful sense. If a government chooses that mix, it is allocating a certain set of rights to both murderers and their victims; the latter are certainly given a right to be free from murder, but the right is limited by the terms of the anticipated punishment. In the extreme case, suppose that a state failed to punish certain classes of murders (say, those of African-Americans), or that it punished such murders only infrequently, or that it punished such murders with a slap on the wrist. If so, the distinction between authorizing murder, and failing to prevent it, would become thin.

The allied idea that capital punishment involves "intentional" action, whereas merely allowing (undeterred) private murders to proceed does not, misfires for parallel reasons. Consider a situation in which regulators refuse to adopt motor vehicle or drug safety regulations that would prevent significant numbers of statistical deaths. Is the refusal acceptable because it leads to deaths that are not strictly speaking intended? The very concept of "intentional" action, and the moral relevance of intention, are both obscure when government is the pertinent moral agent. The executioner who administers the injection acts intentionally, but so does the private murderer. Proponents of this view presumably do not mean to focus narrowly on the actual individual who carries out the final action on the state's behalf. (Does it matter so much that the executioner is on the government's payroll? What if the executioner is a volunteer?) The real point is that in a regime of capital punishment the executioner acts pursuant to an explicit government policy, whereas (the idea runs) there is never a government policy to murder the particular citizens whose deaths would be deterred by capital punishment.

It is true that there is no such policy, but the moral relevance of its absence is obscure. If the point appears intuitively important, it is only because of the abstract or statistical character of the eighteen persons whose murders are deterred by each execution (a theme to which we return in Part III). The legal regime whose package of crime-control instruments happens not to include capital punishment does indeed embody an explicit government policy: a policy that inevitably and predictably opts for more murders over fewer. That the victims of those murders cannot be personally identified in advance does not seem a morally impressive basis for favoring the regime that makes their murders inevitable. Putting aside the intentional actions of low-level officials, the relevant policies in either regime will be set by a complex process of democratic and regulatory interaction among voters, legislators, administrators, and judges. In this large-scale process of collective decisionmaking, the concept of intention becomes too attenuated to bear the moral weight often put upon it; and the regime with capital punishment does not seem importantly different, on the score of intentions, than the regime without it.

In this light, the idea that the government "authorizes" capital punishment but "forbids" private murder is too simple. Two points are important. First, of course it is true that the government does not authorize private killings in a retail sense, barring cases of self-defense or defense of others. At the wholesale level, however, to adopt a package of criminal-justice policies that does not include capital punishment is to ensure the murders of a large number of (as yet unidentified) victims. The government's inability to identify the victims before the fact must be morally irrelevant. Second, there is a sense in which the regime without capital punishment comes perilously close to licensing private killings, because in that regime policymakers know or should know that the prohibition on murder is supported by a weaker deterrent signal. The cash value of a prohibition lies in the scheme of punishments that enforce it; where the enforcement scheme is feeble, the prohibition is as well. On the empirical assumptions we are making, a government that eschews capital punishment rejects an effective mechanism for enforcing the baseline prohibition of murder. In the extreme case, ineffective enforcement mechanisms make the prohibition of murder begin to look like something of a sham.

So far we have argued that the act-omission distinction is conceptually obscure when applied to government, whatever its merits when applied to individuals. Even if that argument fails, however, capital punishment may still be morally obligatory for governments. The relevant acts may be morally required, or the relevant omissions morally blameworthy. We begin with the idea that declining to adopt capital punishment is a culpable omission and then turn to the idea that adopting capital punishment is a morally obligatory act.

Suppose that there is some clear sense in which a system of capital punishment counts as relevantly "action" and that this is not the case for a refusal to impose capital punishment, which therefore counts as a kind of omission or failure to act. What is the moral importance of this distinction? Individuals, let us suppose, are prima facie obligated not to harm others, but have no obligation to assist them. Of course this view raises many puzzles, not least in the definition of the relevant categories, but let us accept it for present purposes and ask how it applies where government is the moral agent. The government cannot easily claim that it is under no duty to assist people, at least when they are at risk of criminal violence. In administrative law, it is greatly contested whether agency inaction is subject to some special immunity from judicial review, and any such immunity turns largely on pragmatic considerations involving the limits of oversight by federal judges. Likewise, governmental failure to protect people against private violence generally does not give rise to constitutional liability, but this too is largely because judges have a limited capacity to enforce liability in such cases. Apart from law, there is no reason to think that omissions of this kind are properly insulated from moral criticism if significant numbers of deaths are a predictable consequence.

Alternatively, and equivalently, we can put the point within the usual language of the act-omission distinction. It is standard that an omission can count as an action where there is a "duty" to act, especially where the party subject to the duty has himself created the conditions that threaten harm. Where government is concerned, these requirements will often be fulfilled, far more often than for typical private parties. Where citizens are murdering each other, government is not a bystander, innocent or otherwise, because the decision whether to murder is made, at least in part, in light of the government's criminal-justice policies. The background rules against which citizens act to threaten the lives of others or to protect their own, including rules about and limitations on self-defense, are themselves products of government action, including the action of the special bureaucracies that lawyers call criminal courts.

The previous points suggest that even if inflicting capital punishment is an "act" while declining to inflict it is an "omission," the omission may nonetheless be morally culpable. Conversely, the act may be morally obligatory if large numbers are saved. Even strict deontological accounts of the impermissibility of killing typically build in a threshold exception: when the threshold is crossed, the moral agent is obliged to commit otherwise impermissible acts in order to save third-party lives. Moral theorists are typically vague as to where the threshold lies, but if each execution saves eighteen lives, then we are right in the neighborhood at which most theorists blanch at the collateral costs of deontological prohibitions. We offer more general remarks on deontology and its relation to the act-omission distinction below. The point here is that capital punishment may be morally obligatory even if capital punishment counts as an act while failing to impose capital punishment counts as an omission.

We have questioned both the coherence and the moral relevance of the act-omission distinction as applied to capital punishment. We want to be clear, however, that in this setting, as elsewhere, rejecting the act-omission distinction only begins the analysis. For government to opt for a large highway-building project, for example, inevitably and predictably results in the deaths of a statistical set of workers who are no less real for being unidentifiable in advance. The reason the highway project is acceptable (if it is) might be either that more deaths would occur on net absent the project, or more broadly that the social benefits are higher than the costs. Likewise, capital punishment might or might not be shown to save lives, on net; might or might not turn out to be welfare-enhancing, all things considered; and might or might not turn out to be just, depending on whether we hold a welfarist conception of justice. Our point here is limited: the crucial questions that determine whether capital punishment is life-saving, welfare-enhancing, or otherwise just are not questions about the difference between actions and omissions.

Consider, in this regard, the "reasonable doubt" standard of criminal law, under which it is better that some number of guilty defendants go free than that an innocent person be convicted. It is possible to imagine a defense of the reasonable doubt standard on act-omission grounds: perhaps the government "acts" when it convicts and "fails to act" when it does not convict; perhaps government errors through action are much worse than government errors through inaction. Yet this seems an unlikely description. To acquit, or to decline to convict, is government "action" whether performed by a judge or by a jury acting as the state's agents, under rules and procedures set by the state. Yet the reasonable doubt standard can still be straightforwardly defended on a claim that the overall social consequences of false convictions are much worse than the overall social consequences of false acquittals. If so defended, the standard is perfectly sensible and need not be justified by reference to an obscure distinction between acts and omissions. So too in our setting: apart from the distinction between acts and omissions, there is a reasonable question about whether capital punishment really does provide net social benefits. The relevant material for answering that question, however, is the empirical evidence discussed in Part I, rather than conceptual arguments that struggle to adapt the act-omission distinction to the state.

Error, Arbitrariness, and Discrimination

Of course there are important objections to capital punishment that do not trade on (some version of) the distinction between acts and omissions. Some of the most powerful of these objections invoke values associated with the rule of law. There are three concerns here.

1. Some innocent people are executed, and their deaths are irreversible. No legal system can ensure complete accuracy in criminal convictions. Even under the "no reasonable doubt" standard, errors are made. But errors are sometimes said to be intolerable when the state is depriving people of their lives, precisely because mistaken deprivations cannot be reversed.
2. The death penalty inevitably contains a degree of arbitrariness. Justice Stewart famously made the point when he wrote that receiving the death penalty is "cruel and unusual in the same way that being struck by lightning is cruel and unusual." As we have seen Justice Stewart's point is overstated for current capital punishment systems. But if any such system operates as a kind of death lottery, in which similarly situated people are not treated similarly, perhaps it is unacceptable for that reason alone.
3. Even within the set of guilty defendants, the death penalty may be administered in a way that reflects objectionable or invidious discrimination. In 2003, 42% of the death row population was African-American and 56% was white. In some times and places, African-American defendants have been more likely to receive capital punishment than whites. More recently, those who kill white people appear to be more likely to receive capital punishment than those who kill African-Americans. The system of capital punishment might reflect a form of institutional racism; even if not, the system might simply operate against the background of racial injustice, which ensures intolerable inequalities in the imposition of death. In any event, capital defendants who are poor, or otherwise unlikely to have good lawyers are far more likely to face the death penalty as a result.

Some people believe that even if capital punishment could be morally acceptable if it were fairly administered, the inevitability of unfair administration means that we must eliminate it. These arguments point to strong reasons for reforming the existing system to increase accuracy and decrease arbitrariness. But the arguments do not succeed as objections to capital punishment as such. Once the act-omission distinction is no longer central, it becomes clear that *the standard moral objections to capital punishment apply even more powerfully to the murders that capital punishment prevents*. Those murders also cause irreversible deaths: the deaths of the victims of murder. Private murders are also often highly arbitrary, involving selectivity on any number of morally irrelevant or objectionable grounds. African-Americans, for example, are far more likely than other groups to be the victims of murder. In 2003, 48% of murder victims were white and 48% were African-American—meaning that the racial disparity in the probability of becoming a murder victim is even greater than the racial disparity in the probability of ending up on death row. An important corollary is that the benefits of capital punishment, to the extent that it operates as a powerful deterrent of murder, are likely to flow disproportionately to African-Americans.

To be sure, this effect will be attenuated if death sentences are imposed less frequently on those who murder African-Americans. In the most pessimistic projection, capital punishment is likely to be disproportionately inflicted on African-Americans, and because that punishment is most likely to be imposed when whites have been killed, the resulting savings are likely to go largely to whites. On this view, the "life-life tradeoffs" may turn out, all too often, to be "African-American life/white life tradeoffs." Perhaps it is unclear how to make that tradeoff, even if it involves larger numbers, and innocence, on one side of the ledger. But even on the current numbers, this projection is unrealistic. Most murder is intraracial, not interracial. Because African-Americans are disproportionately the victims of homicide, and because their murderers are disproportionately African-American, they have a great deal to gain from capital punishment—very plausibly more, on balance, than white people do. In any event, the more natural response to existing racial disparities is to lower them, rather than to eliminate the penalty altogether.

For the rule-of-law questions, as for all other, the core problem of capital punishment is that it presents a risk-risk tradeoff, or a life-life tradeoff. To say the least, it is extremely desirable to prevent arbitrary or irreversible deaths, but this consideration is on both sides of the ledger. The relevant analogy is not, say, to a policy that uses racial classifications to increase security or national wealth. The closer analogy would be one that uses racial classifications in order to minimize the overall use of racial classifications, or to hasten the day when racial classifications are no longer useful. A still closer analogy would be a policy that increases certain risks but that in the process decreases other risks of greater magnitude. Whatever the merits of such tradeoffs across different settings, a one-sided complaint about a harm or loss that is on both sides of the ledger is not a sufficient objection to a policy of this sort.

On this view, the crucial point is that a legal regime with capital punishment predictably produces far *fewer* arbitrary and irreversible deaths than a regime without capital punishment. In a sensible regime of capital punishment, legal rules, enforced by administrative, judicial and citizen oversight, attempt to reduce arbitrariness and error up to the point where further reductions would inflict unacceptable harms. Where killing is carried out by private parties, however, there are no such institutions for keeping arbitrariness in check. Most striking is the sheer size of the opportunity cost of forgone capital punishment. Stipulate that for every forgone execution (conducted under procedural safeguards), the cost is, on average, some eighteen arbitrary and irreversible murders—as some of the evidence in Part I suggests. Suppose, for example, that five hundred additional death row inmates were executed in the next year. Unless the marginal deterrent benefit of each additional execution diminishes very rapidly, the result would be to save thousands of innocent people—in all probability, far more people than were killed in the terrorist attacks of September 11, 2001. The people whose lives are lost, and whose deaths could be averted, are killed arbitrarily and without fair process. In short, rule-of-law criticisms of capital punishment either smuggle in the distinction between acts and omissions, or else overlook the fact that the same objections apply even more powerfully to the utterly arbitrary killings that capital punishment prevents.

QUESTIONS FOR REFLECTION

1. Outline the overall structure of Sunstein and Vermeule's argument.
2. Sunstein and Vermeule maintain that their argument applies from both consequentialist and deontological points of view. Why? Is there any difference in the form the argument takes in these two cases?
3. Is there an important moral distinction between action and omission for individual moral agents? Is killing someone, for example, worse than letting someone die?
4. Why, according to Sunstein and Vermeule, does the distinction between action and omission fail to apply to government?
5. How do Sunstein and Vermeule respond to objections that capital punishment is irreversible, liable to mistakes, or random?
6. Some argue against the death penalty because its administration, in practice, is discriminatory. How do Sunstein and Vermeule respond?
7. All the deterrence effect found in studies on capital punishment comes from six states. In other states, there appears to be no deterrence effect. Does that weaken their argument? Why or why not?
8. Denying the significance of the act-omission distinction for government has consequences for issues other than capital punishment. Give an example, and explain it.

CAROL S. STEIKER

No, Capital Punishment Is Not Morally Required: Deterrence, Deontology, and the Death Penalty

Carol S. Steiker is Professor of Law at Harvard Law School. (Source: from Stanford Law Review 751 [2006]: 751–789. Footnotes omitted.)

I. Private Murders Are Not Equivalent to Executions as a Moral Matter: Nonpurposeful versus Purposeful Killings

The central insight on which Sunstein and Vermeule stake their argument is that the government is a distinctive moral actor that is equally responsible for things it *lets happen* as for things it *does*. Because governments, unlike individuals, "always and necessarily face a choice between or among possible policies for regulating third parties," it would not be proper to characterize a governmental choice not to regulate to reduce a harm as a mere "omission" that might be excused on an individual level. For example, the lives the government would sacrifice by requiring a particular childhood vaccination (knowing that a small number of those vaccinated will die from the vaccine) should be viewed no differently from the lives that the government would sacrifice by *not* requiring such a vaccination (knowing that a large number of those unvaccinated will die from the spread of disease), even though the first set of deaths would result from government "action" and the second from government "inaction." The government always has to choose among competing policies and make "life-life tradeoffs" of this kind. This collapse of the traditional act/omission distinction for the government as moral agent represents an insight on the collective level parallel to the doctrine in substantive criminal law that holds that culpable "omissions" count as "acts" for the purposes of individual criminal liability whenever an individual has a "duty" to act. Government, by its very nature, always has a duty to act on behalf of its citizens and thus cannot evade responsibility for omissions merely because they are omissions. This general point seems both interesting and right, as far as it goes.

But while the point may go very far in the regulatory context (where Sunstein and Vermeule recognize that it may have "broad implications"), it does not go nearly as far as they suggest in the capital punishment context. Sunstein and Vermeule treat the use of capital punishment as simply another routine decision "in the general setting of government regulation" and thus miss the salience of an important moral distinction about the nature of government action in the context of capital punishment (and criminal justice more generally). In the regulatory context, when the government makes life-life tradeoffs, its treatment of lives on either side of the tradeoff is identical; it is risking lives whether it acts or fails to act, but in neither case is its purpose to take life. In the capital punishment context, this moral equivalence in the treatment of lives does not obtain; the government knowingly or recklessly loses or "takes" lives by not executing (assuming that it knows or thinks there is a good chance that executions deter), but it purposefully takes lives by executing. Sunstein and Vermeule wish to say that knowing or risking that *others* will act purposefully is the moral equivalent of acting purposefully oneself, or that even if it is not equivalent for individuals, it somehow becomes equivalent for the government (hence, their dramatic assertion that private murders should be viewed as the moral equivalent of government "executions"). But we do not recognize this moral equivalence for individual actors, and there is no good reason to do so for the government as actor, either. The collapse of the purposeful/nonpurposeful distinction is not the same as and does not follow from the collapse of the act/omission distinction. Rather, the difference between purposeful and nonpurposeful harms remains crucial for *both* acts and omissions.

To see that this is so on the individual level, consider again the substantive criminal law doctrine of treating certain culpable omissions as "acts" for the purposes of criminal liability. When individuals have a duty to act, their failure to do so counts as the actus reus or "bad act" component of criminal liability, but the collapse of the act/omission distinction here says nothing about whether the mens rea or "intent" component of criminal liability is met. Suppose a mother fails to protect her child from abuse by the mother's boyfriend, who intentionally murders the child. (Let us stipulate that the mother's failure to act is causally linked to the death of the child.) Because the mother has an ongoing duty to protect her child (the way the government has a duty to protect its citizens), it is no defense for her to say that her failure to act was merely an omission for which she was not responsible. However, the degree of her moral culpability depends on her mens rea: if she did not know, but should have known, of the risk of death to her child, she would be guilty of negligent homicide; if she knew of and consciously disregarded a substantial risk of death to her child, she would be guilty of reckless homicide (manslaughter); if she knew to a practical certainty that her child would die, she would be guilty of second-degree murder; and if her purpose in failing to act was to bring about the death of her child, she would be guilty of first-degree murder. To acknowledge that the mother had a duty to act to prevent the intentional murder of her child by another is not and should not be the same as saying that her omission constituted intentional murder. Thus, for Sunstein and Vermeule's point to hold, they must insist that when the act/omission distinction collapses for the government as actor, the mens rea distinctions that we normally insist upon for individuals must collapse as well.

But there are no good reasons to think that degrees of mens rea are meaningless for the government as actor. Consider the raging debate in the wake of Hurricane Katrina about the government's failure to maintain the Lake Pontchartrain levees. Everyone acknowledges that the government cannot disclaim responsibility for the disaster in New Orleans on the ground that its failure to maintain the levees was merely an omission for which it was not responsible. Rather, the debate is about *how culpable* an omission the failure was: whether the government was aware of the risks; whether the likelihood of such a terrible disaster rose to the level of knowledge; even, in some bizarre conspiracy theories, whether the government intended the levees to fail. There is no reason to think that any of these attributions of culpability are meaningless when applied to the government. Indeed, such a claim would prevent us from considering clearly relevant factors in assessing government action or inaction. In criminal law and in moral theory, the relevance of purposeful action is clear: those who purposefully transgress are more blameworthy because they have affirmatively chosen their course of action and its results (in terms of retributive justice), and they are more likely than those who do not act purposefully to act similarly in the future (in consequentialist terms).

What reasons do Sunstein and Vermeule offer to refute the quotidian moral significance of the difference between purposeful and nonpurposeful action, at least in the case of the government as actor? It turns out that they offer surprisingly little in the way of argument. They acknowledge that in the context of capital punishment, the government has a policy to kill when it executes and that no such policy exists toward private murders (just the opposite), but they insist that it is mere "intuition" that suggests that this difference is important. They then nod toward "a large philosophical literature that considers whether the concept of culpability for intentional wrongdoing applies meaningfully to governments" and "also large literatures in jurisprudence and literary theory that consider whether the concept of intention can meaningfully be transposed from individual to collective decisionmakers." But nothing in the few works they cite supports the abandonment of the moral distinction between purposeful and nonpurposeful action either in general or for the government as actor. The single work that they cite as the "large literature" on whether it is meaningful to hold governments accountable for intentional wrongdoing—Christopher Kutz's interesting book on complicity—is simply inapposite, as its central concern is fixing degrees of *individual* accountability for collective acts. The other "large literature" cited by Sunstein and Vermeule on the difficulty of determining governmental (as opposed to individual) "intention" in no way purports to claim that there is never any meaningful distinction between purposeful and nonpurposeful government action; rather, that literature explores the now-familiar problem of interpreting ambiguous governmental texts by reference to the multiple and conflicting "intentions" of collective actors. This literature is simply inapposite here as well: there is nothing ambiguous or problematic about the "intent" of capital punishment statutes with regard to the death of those executed. There is no question that laws permitting the use of capital punishment "intend" to kill those who are sentenced under them in a way that is meaningfully different from laws that prohibit private murder but do not allow for the most extreme of penal sanctions.

What Sunstein and Vermeule really mean to claim is that, at least in the context of killing, the moral difference between acting purposefully and acting knowingly or recklessly should not matter because *it is right* to take lives purposefully in order to save more lives than one knows (or risks) will be lost otherwise. We can see this clearly in their discussion of Bernard Williams's famous "Jim and the Indians" problem, in which they suggest (contra Williams) that Jim should think of himself as responsible for the lives of the nineteen additional Indians whom he knows will be killed if he refuses to kill one. We can see it even more clearly in their approach to the "trolley problem," in which they suggest (contra most people's moral intuition and Judith Jarvis Thomson's deontological account) that there is merely an emotional rather than a moral difference between, on the one hand, pushing a pedestrian off a footbridge into the path of a brakeless trolley car in order to prevent the death of five others on the track, and on the other hand, switching the same trolley onto a different track on which there is only one endangered person.

In this latter problem (unlike "Jim and the Indians"), there is no act/omission distinction at all. In each of the two versions of the trolley problem, there is affirmative action (pushing the pedestrian off the footbridge or switching the trolley onto a different track). The differences lie entirely in the attitude the actor has toward the death of the one and in the means the actor uses to bring about that death. In switching the trolley, the switcher knows that the one person on the alternate track will be hit by the trolley, but this is in no way the purpose of the action (the switcher would be thrilled if the one somehow avoided being hit), whereas in pushing someone from the footbridge, the pusher must intend that the one person be hit (otherwise the trolley would not derail and save the five). Moreover, the switcher merely redirects the source of an external threat to life, while the pusher directly interferes with the physical inviolability of the pedestrian in order to redistribute the harm caused by the brakeless trolley from the five to the one. In essence, the pusher denies that the pedestrian has a right not to be violated for the greater good. Sunstein and Vermeule want to characterize the widely held reluctance to legitimize the pusher's purposeful and direct violation of the pedestrian's rights in order to save others as a kind of cognitive error resulting from improper reliance on a "moral heuristic." They urge us to be open to reconsidering and abandoning such moral heuristics, especially when doing so would save lives.

It is important to see that this argument is not the same as and does not follow from the argument for collapsing the act/omission distinction for the government as actor; rather, it represents a core dispute between consequentialist and deontological moral theories. Sunstein and Vermeule insist, as consequentialists, that there is nothing intrinsically wrong with individuals or governments "using" the lives of some to promote the greater good, while deontologists insist that when it comes to lives and bodies, individuals have rights against such use that trump the greater good. The "trolley problem" can be followed by the "organ transplant" problem to illuminate this dispute. If it is right to sacrifice one to save five in the trolley example, is it also right for a doctor to sacrifice one healthy patient in order to save the lives of five desperately ill patients, each of whom needs the immediate transplant of one of five different vital organs?

Consequentialists would see nothing intrinsically wrong with such a sacrifice; any arguments against such a decision must flow from the bad consequences that might ensue if doctors were generally empowered to do such things (if a medical "institution" of involuntary organ donation were established). Deontologists would object to such an institution even under hypothetical conditions that could ensure that the overall consequences to society would be beneficial (conditions that some involuntary organ donation plans plausibly might meet). Better to knowingly allow the five terminally ill patients to die (along with the five people on the trolley track and Jim's nineteen Indians), says the deontologist, than to deny the right to personal inviolability of the healthy patient (or the pedestrian on the footbridge or the one Indian). Sunstein and Vermeule's insistence on the moral equivalence of purposeful executions and knowing provision of suboptimal deterrence of private murders is, at bottom, a claim about the moral rightness of taking life to save life. Their contention that disagreement with this claim is merely improper reliance on a moral heuristic is, at bottom, a rejection of deontological moral reasoning.

This is a very big claim, indeed, and it is by no means required by (or even related to) the claim that the act/omission distinction is inapplicable to the government as actor. One can agree that the government is "acting" when (if) it fails to provide optimal deterrence for private murders and that, therefore, it bears some moral responsibility for those deaths and has a moral obligation to try to prevent them. But this acknowledgement does not entail that the government is required to take any action that would prevent such murders, no matter how morally problematic that action might be. Sunstein and Vermeule's insistence that the government is morally obligated to retain capital punishment depends on collapsing a further distinction—the distinction between purposeful and nonpurposeful killing—a collapse that they support for individual as well as for government actors, as evidenced by their approach to "Jim and the Indians." The evasion of this further distinction is necessary to equilibrate the government's accountability for deaths it commands and for murders it forbids but fails to adequately deter, and thus to permit the choice to retain or abolish capital punishment to be portrayed as a "life-life tradeoff." But the collapse of this further distinction is no small thing; it is no mere gloss on the acceptance of either the distinctive moral agency of government or the necessity for "life-life tradeoffs" in general. Rather, it is a separate moral claim that goes to the heart of the divide between consequentialism and deontology—a claim that Sunstein and Vermeule neither recognize as distinct nor adequately defend.

Of course, Sunstein and Vermeule could (and do, briefly) claim that the government's purposeful killings are independently morally justified because the lives that it takes by executions are (usually) those of guilty murderers, while the lives that it knowingly or recklessly cedes to private murder are by definition those of innocents. But when they switch to this kind of moral justification for the state's purposeful killing, Sunstein and Vermeule have switched to the language of deontological moral theory (retributivism) and thus acknowledge the nonequivalence of the state's actions in taking life through execution and through suboptimal deterrence of private murder: they are no longer on the terrain of life-life tradeoffs at all. Yes, of course there are deontological justifications for purposeful killing in some situations, and there are special deontological arguments for killing guilty murderers, but these are not the kind of arguments that Sunstein and Vermeule purport to be making.

II. Private Murders Are Not Equivalent to Executions as a Matter of Justice: Regulation versus Punishment

The fact that the government affirmatively intends the deaths of those whom it executes points to an even more central problem with Sunstein and Vermeule's attempt to portray capital punishment as a "life-life tradeoff." When the government executes, it is not merely "killing" (though of course it is doing that); it is engaging in a distinctive governmental practice that we call criminal punishment, which involves the deliberate infliction of unpleasant consequences in response to an offender's wrongdoing. This purposefulness is one of the defining features of criminal punishment as a practice, along with the public affixing of blame and the solicitation of certain emotions, such as shame (on the part of the punished) and condemnation (on the part of the public). These features of punishment explain why it is viewed not merely as regulation by other means but rather as a problematic practice that requires some special justification. Being an act done by the state in the name of the collective, it requires not only moral but also political justification: we would appropriately characterize improper executions as not only morally wrong but also unjust. Sunstein and Vermeule portray the central deontological objections to capital punishment as entirely confined to the "capital" aspect of it, and thus they are able to make their argument from moral equivalence: if government killing by execution is wrong, so is government "killing" through inadequate deterrence. But if government executions are wrong not only because they are killings but also because they constitute unjust "punishment," then there is no equivalence between what the government is doing through executions and what it is doing through inadequate deterrence.

This Part will sketch three accounts of why capital punishment might be thought to constitute unjust punishment. Through these accounts, I hope to demonstrate that Sunstein and Vermeule's depiction of deontological objections to capital punishment as "abstract injunctions against the taking of life" does not do justice to rich, subtle, and widely held scruples about the justice of the death penalty and thus constitutes an evasion of the central deontological objections to capital punishment qua punishment. Without confronting and rebutting these objections, Sunstein and Vermeule cannot fairly assert the equivalence of executions and private murders and thus cannot fairly characterize the choice of capital punishment as a "life-life tradeoff." Moreover, these objections do not depend on the moral distinction between purposeful and nonpurposeful killing outlined in Part I; rather, these objections represent a separate and independent argument for the non-equivalence of executions and private murders.

A. Capital Punishment as a Failure of Proportionality

It is stunning how almost completely absent from Sunstein and Vermeule's account of capital punishment is any discussion of whether or not such punishment is deserved by the offenders who receive it. A venerable deontological tradition with roots in Kantian retributivism holds that punishment is justified only as a response to wrongdoing by the offender and not by its consequential effects. In its strongest form, retributivism imposes a duty to punish offenders according to their desert. In its weakest and perhaps most widely accepted form—as a side constraint on the useful deterrent, incapacitative, or rehabilitative functions that punishment can serve in a society—retributivism requires, at a bare minimum, that the uses of punishment be limited to situations in which the punishment is deserved by the offender and is proportional to the offender's wrongdoing. Under this theory, if the suffering caused by punishment is not deserved and is not proportional to the wrongdoing of those upon whom it is inflicted, then the infliction of such suffering constitutes a wrong—the imposition of unjust punishment—distinct from and worse than merely the suffering itself.

At first glance, a retributive argument might seem an odd one to make against capital punishment, as it is retributivism that offers some of the strongest arguments *in favor* of the death penalty. (Reconsider the depiction of a generic death penalty debate with which I began, in which retributive arguments are deployed by the proponent of capital punishment.) Kant's famous injunction—that a desert-island society about to disperse would still have an obligation to kill its last murderer—stands for the strong form of retributivism. This form of retributivism holds that the duty to impose deserved punishment exists regardless of any beneficial consequences that might be thought to flow from it. Kant's use of the death penalty as the quintessential example of deserved punishment for the crime of murder seems, at first blush, natural and unobjectionable.

But there is good reason to think that capital punishment—at least as imposed in our contemporary society—routinely and inevitably runs afoul of retributivism's bedrock proportionality constraint. It is rarely the case that execution as a form of suffering can confidently be viewed as disproportionate to the harms inflicted on the victims of capital murders. Rather, the strongest argument for such disproportionality lies in the reduced culpability of most convicted capital offenders; this is an argument that remains powerful even today, *after* the Supreme Court has recently declared that mentally retarded and juvenile offenders may no longer be executed for their crimes. Though capital defendants have usually committed (or participated in) heinous murders, they very frequently are extremely intellectually limited, are suffering from some form of mental illness, are in the powerful grip of a drug or alcohol addiction, are survivors of childhood abuse, or are the victims of some sort of societal deprivation (be it poverty, racism, poor education, inadequate health care, or some noxious combination of the above). In such circumstances, it is difficult to say that these defendants deserve all of the blame for their terrible acts; if their families or societies share responsibility—even in some small measure—for the tragic results, then the extreme punishment of death should be considered undeserved. Indeed, this point follows directly from Sunstein and Vermeule's own logic. If the government is responsible for private murders that it fails to prevent by providing adequate deterrence, is it not also responsible for private murders that it fails to prevent by providing adequate poverty relief, support for families, education, health care, and initiatives to promote racial equality? This recognition of the conflict between collective responsibility for crimogenic conditions and the imposition of individual criminal responsibility for crime is best captured by a *New Yorker* cartoon in which a jury foreperson delivers the following verdict: "We find that all of us, as a society, are to blame, but only the defendant is guilty."

For this point to hold, it is not necessary to say that there are no capital defendants in our society who could be deemed sufficiently blameworthy so as to deserve the death penalty, or that all capital defendants not sufficiently blameworthy for capital punishment are blameless for their actions and deserve no punishment at all, or that criminal defendants in general are blameless and undeserving of any criminal punishment. Rather, the more modest point is simply the uncontroversial empirical fact that in our contemporary society, those most likely to commit the worst crimes (capital murders) are, as a group, also most likely to have had their volitional capacities affected or impaired by societal conditions for which we collectively bear some responsibility. Thus, it cannot fairly be said that this group is deserving of our worst punishment, or, more affirmatively, it must be acknowledged that there is a retributive gap between the culpability of such offenders and the punishment inflicted upon them.

Moreover, from the standpoint of retributive justice, the strong evidence of discrimination (on the basis of race) or mere arbitrariness (on the basis of geography, among other things) in the imposition of capital punishment takes on a new and different significance from the disparate impact of the private murders that the government might fail to deter. The fact that the race of the defendant and/or the race of the victim frequently have been found to have salience in predicting whether a defendant will be sentenced to death shows not only that there is some racial skewing in the distribution of capital sentences, but also that there is reason to question the underlying moral and legal judgment that any particular murder is one for which capital punishment is a proportional response. Similarly, the fact that defendants from otherwise similar counties in the same state face radically different prospects of receiving capital punishment calls into question not only the procedures by which those deserving of capital punishment are chosen but also the reliability of the underlying judgment that any particular defendant so chosen deserves the death penalty. Unless one takes the position that capital punishment is a deserved and proportional response to *every* intentional killing no matter what the circumstances (a position neither required by retributivism nor permitted by American law), one can take no recourse in the argument that discrimination and arbitrariness merely exclude some deserving defendants from execution. Rather, discrimination and arbitrariness undermine our confidence in the very attribution of desert to the defendants chosen for execution.

The strongest case for a retributive gap, of course, lies in the conviction and execution of the innocent—a moral wrong that we have new reason to believe is disturbingly prevalent in our capital punishment system. Although all victims of private murder are, by definition, innocent, there is a special moral wrong in executing an innocent person, as one adds the horror of blame for heinous wrongdoing to the taking of life. Sunstein and Vermeule have nothing to say about this problem, other than to claim that, under the hypothetical conditions of deterrence to which they stipulate, the execution of the innocent could not be much of a problem, as future murderers would not be deterred by the death penalty under circumstances in which innocent defendants were likely to be punished instead of guilty perpetrators.

This rather lame assumption is far too insouciant. It is perfectly possible for an error-prone capital justice system to deter, under circumstances in which potential murderers are not aware of the innocence of those executed (either because *nobody* is aware of that fact or because potential murderers are not well informed of such events), or under circumstances in which well-informed potential murderers are not sensitive to significant changes in the likelihood of their conviction or execution because of the special salience of execution as a punishment. (This last point is exactly the argument Sunstein and Vermeule make about why our current capital punishment system—which, even in Texas, executes only a tiny fraction of murderers—might plausibly deter.) In light of the recent spate of death row exonerations, there is good reason to fear that the system of capital punishment might produce enormous retributive gaps too often to be considered a just system of punishment.

B. Capital Punishment as a Failure of Equality

There is a second and distinct flaw in the equivalence that Sunstein and Vermeule seek to maintain between racial inequality in the administration of capital punishment and racial inequality in the distribution of private murders. The racial inequalities in the administration of capital punishment—both the failure to give equal weight to the deaths of black victims as compared to white victims in similar cases and the greater willingness to take the lives of black defendants as compared to white defendants in similar cases—give rise to an inference of racial animus on the part of state actors (prosecutors and jurors). That is, these disparities reveal the unwillingness or inability, whether conscious or unconscious, of governmental actors to treat black citizens with equal concern and respect. But the racial inequality in the distribution of private murders does not plausibly reflect such pervasive animus on the part either of the murderers or the government. Of course, some murders are motivated by racial (or gender or other) animus. But as Sunstein and Vermeule recognize, the primary reason that the crime of murder has a disparate racial impact is that most murders are intraracial and that there is a higher murder rate among blacks than among whites. There is no reason to think that black murderers choose their black victims because of a conscious or unconscious racial animus toward members of their own race; rather, in our segregated society, black murderers most plausibly choose their victims because of their proximity—intimate, social, and geographical.

Sunstein and Vermeule's declared equivalence of racial disparity in punishment to racial disparity in victimization might hold up in a situation in which the government failed to provide adequate deterrence for crimes that were primarily the product of the perpetrators' private racial animus. In such circumstances, it would seem fair to say that the government was failing to give equal concern and respect to the victims of such racially animated crime. But the equivalence evaporates when there is much more evidence of racial animus in the imposition of punishment than in the distribution of crime. The distributional failings of capital punishment in terms of violations of the norm of equal concern and respect are simply qualitatively different from the distributional failings of private murders.

Sunstein and Vermeule could still argue (and they do, sort of) that the savings of disproportionately black lives under the hypothetical regime of deterrence to which they stipulate might (should?) make the racial discrimination that infects the capital punishment system "worth it," even to blacks. This is a familiar all-things-considered application of the utilitarian calculus. But it is *not* a proper "life-life tradeoff argument because it fails to acknowledge the difference in the kinds of discrimination that lie on either side of the trade. Sunstein and Vermeule do not seem to notice when their argument veers off the track of their novel claim that capital punishment should be viewed as a "life-life tradeoff" and onto the well-worn path of utilitarian calculation of overall costs and benefits.

C. Capital Punishment as a Failure of Dignity

A third major wellspring of deontological objection to the justice of capital punishment is the claim that, unlike many ordinary punishments, it violates human dignity. This view has been given its most prominent exposition in Justice Brennan's concurring opinion on the unconstitutionality of the death penalty as "cruel and unusual punishment" under the Eighth Amendment in *Furman v. Georgia.* This claim has an abstract, slippery quality to it that makes it difficult to assess whether the violence done to human dignity through the imposition of death as punishment is different in any meaningful way from the violence done to human dignity through the crime of murder. In what follows, I consider two common constructions of the claim and conclude that neither one offers a new ground to assert that the damage to human dignity from execution is distinct from the damage to human dignity from murder, at least under a hypothetical regime of proven deterrence. However, I offer a third construction of the argument from human dignity that does offer good reason to think that executions endanger that value in a way that is meaningfully different from and worse than private murders.

1. Punishments violate human dignity when they are excessive in relationship to their purposes.

Absent good reason to think that the American death penalty deters better than life imprisonment—that is, in the "real world" outside of Sunstein and Vermeule's stipulation to the contrary—this was and remains one of the primary arguments against the death penalty. As Justice Brennan wrote in *Furman v. Georgia:*

> The infliction of a severe punishment by the State cannot comport with human dignity when it is nothing more than the pointless infliction of suffering. If there is a significantly less severe punishment adequate to achieve the purposes for which the punishment is inflicted, the punishment inflicted is unnecessary and therefore excessive.

This argument is one on which consequentialists and deontologists can agree, as the utilitarian principle of parsimony and the deontological principle of proportionality both converge upon it in their own ways. However, this common and powerful argument is taken off the table for consequentialists by Sunstein and Vermeule's stipulation of marginal deterrence, and it is covered for deontologists by the arguments from proportionality that I address above. Thus, this version of the dignitary objection to the justice of capital punishment adds nothing to the reasons already on the table for considering executions differently from private murders.

2. Extreme punishments violate human dignity because they destroy the distinctive human capacities of the punished.

This argument for why capital punishment is wrong—that it totally annihilates the very personhood of the punished—powerfully captures what is distinctive about death as a punishment. To quote Justice Brennan again, "The true significance of these [examples of extreme] punishments is that they treat members of the human race as nonhumans, as objects to be toyed with and discarded." But because this version of the human dignity argument focuses exclusively on the effects of extreme punishments on the punished, it does not help to rebut the aspect of the "life-life tradeoff" argument that is my target here—the nonequivalence of the harms of executions and those of private murders. Private murders, too, totally annihilate the personhood of their victims; they are as cruel and degrading, from the perspective of their effects on their victims, as any execution.

There is, however, one feature of executions that distinguishes them from private murders from the perspective of their effects on the person killed. The suffering and degradation that is inflicted upon those executed is not only dehumanizing, it is dehumanization that is presented and publicly accepted as deserved. This is an important difference between killing as punishment and killing as murder, but it cannot count as a nonequivalence that matters unless it is one that also renders executions unjust. The possibility (indeed, the likelihood) that the imposition of blame and the assertion of moral desert that accompany executions are unjust is addressed above in the discussion of proportionality. Thus, this second version of the dignity argument, like the first, is already encompassed in the argument about proportionality and brings nothing new to the table regarding the equivalence of executions and private murders.

3. Extreme punishments violate human dignity because they destroy the distinctive human capacities of the society in whose name they are publicly inflicted.

I offer here a third formulation of the human dignity argument against capital punishment that both asserts a difference between executions and private murders and does not depend for its force on the punishment being in any way disproportionate or undeserved. The imposition of extreme punishments such as execution (or rape or torture), even in cases involving the most deserving of murderers (or rapists or torturers), violates human dignity—not because of what it does to the punished, but rather because of what it does to all of us. Death, from either execution or murder, by definition destroys the human capacities of the person killed, but inflicting death (or rape or torture) as punishment can, in addition, damage or destroy the human capacities of those of us in whose name the punishment is publicly inflicted.

This threat to dignity stems from certain sociological facts about the way punishment works as a social practice. Punishment is a public act; it is generally presented by the government as deserved by the recipient, and that imputation of desert is generally accepted by the public; the imposition of punishment tends to elicit gratifying emotions of satisfaction because the public condemnation and suffering of an offender assuage to some degree the anger and hatred provoked by the offense. Nothing in this characterization is meant as a normative justification of punishment practices. I mean to take no position here on whether the "retributive hatred" that wrongdoing inspires is a moral good, or whether the public satisfaction of vengeful urges offers a satisfactory consequentialist defense of punishment. Rather, I mean simply to suggest that when the purposeful infliction of extreme suffering is yoked with emotions of righteousness and satisfaction, it will inevitably suppress our ordinary human capacities for compassion and empathy. To be sure, the desire to punish may itself spring, at least in part, from compassion and empathy for crime victims. And not every kind of punishment necessarily suppresses to any great extent our capacities for compassion and empathy. But the inherent moral satisfaction that attends the practice of punishment when it includes the infliction of death or other very extreme forms of suffering does seem to permit, or even require, the weakening of important psychological constraints against brutality. In this way, brutal *punishment* poses threats to our human capacities distinct from and more insidious than other forms of brutality that might be authorized or tolerated by the government because punishment has a distinctive connection to powerful human emotions.

I do not wish to make here the consequentialist form of this argument—that the suppression of compassion and the weakening of psychological constraints against brutality will lead to greater incidence of violence or other bad behavior (though I will embrace this point later). Rather, I mean to make a deontological point about human dignity. From any normative perspective, punishment takes its justification from the distinctive human capacity for agency. In retributive terms, punishment is justified as the product of human agency: the duty to punish derives from the will of the wrongdoer in choosing to offend. In consequentialist terms, punishment is justified in order to protect human agency from private threats. My version of the deontological argument from human dignity recognizes that, in extreme forms, punishment as a practice can impair some of the human capacities that are necessary for full agency and thus can affect the necessary precondition for any justification of punishment. True human agency requires not only reason and volition, but also distinctively human affective attributes, such as the ability to feel empathy, compassion, pity, or love. By damaging or destroying human capacities to enter imaginatively into the pain of others, extreme punishments impair us as social agents, free to will and choose our destinies in an interrelated social world.

It is true that the failure of the government to provide optimal deterrence for private murder also might inure us to human suffering, by making murders more common and by implicitly communicating that they are not that serious a problem. But this potential impact on human capacities pales in comparison to the moral and emotional salience of the celebratory aspects of publicly endorsed executions. Given that homicide is seriously punished and condemned in our society even in the absence of capital punishment, any failure to provide optimal deterrence would clearly have a far more muted impact on the kinds of human capacities that are my concern here.

Thus, this formulation of the argument from human dignity suggests, along with the arguments from proportionality and equality, that executions are morally objectionable in ways distinct from and worse than private murders. As noted at the outset, I have bracketed my objection in Part I throughout this entire Part and accepted for purposes of argument that the government bears the same moral responsibility for private murders as it does for executions. What the foregoing is meant to show is that even under this assumption, the government can be seen as committing distinctive moral wrongs through execution because executions, as punishments, have the capacity to be morally problematic in ways that go beyond their wrongness as "killing."

QUESTIONS FOR REFLECTION

1. How does the act/omission distinction function in Sunstein and Vermeule's argument, as Steiker sees it?
2. How does Steiker argue in favor of the act/omission distinction?
3. What is the moral significance of the distinction between acting knowingly and acting recklessly or negligently?
4. How does Steiker use the trolley problem to argue for her position?
5. How is the "Jim and the Indians" puzzle relevant to capital punishment?
6. Summarize Steiker's argument from proportionality. How might Sunstein and Vermeule respond?
7. Steiker uses three arguments from dignity. Contrast them with one another and with Kant's conception of dignity.
8. Would your willingness to push a fat man in front of a runaway trolley change if you knew he was guilty of murder? If so, does that provide an argument against Steiker?

WAR

"War is hell." General William Tecumseh Sherman's warning to a graduating class of cadets in 1880 helps explain why war presents some of the most momentous ethical and political problems we face. War is systematized violence. A wrong decision may devastate or end thousands, even millions, of lives.

Philosophers traditionally distinguish two kinds of ethical questions concerning war. First is the issue of *jus ad bellum*—justice (in going) to war—which concerns the circumstances under which it is permissible to go to war. When may a nation declare war on another nation? Is it ever permissible for a nation to initiate a war? If so, when? Most people think a nation may defend itself from military attack. Other circumstances are less clear. May a nation declare war on nations allied with an attacker, who may be giving it economic and military aid? May a nation ever engage in preventive war, attacking in order to keep from being attacked?

These questions are perennial but have been given new dimensions by terrorism, the systematic use of violence against noncombatants to intimidate or coerce someone for political ends. Terrorism is plainly a form of aggression. Most philosophers hold that nations have a right to fight aggression for the same reason that individuals have rights to self-defense. Therefore, nations have a right to fight terrorism. But terrorists generally have no official affiliation with any nation. A country attacked by terrorists therefore may have no one to declare war against. There is no nation or identifiable group with whom to engage in diplomacy or deterrence. Terrorism, moreover, makes questions about preemptive war more acute. Especially in an age of biological, chemical, and nuclear weapons, waiting until *after* a terrorist attack to take action may seem irresponsible.

Thomas Aquinas articulates classical just war theory to answer these questions. For a nation to wage a war justly, three conditions must be fulfilled. First, the party waging war must be a legitimate government. Second, there must be a just cause. Aquinas does not elaborate an account of what these might be, but he does give examples: A nation that seizes territory unjustly, or that refuses to make amends for wrongs inflicted by its citizens, deserves to be attacked. Whether the wrongs inflicted must be against citizens of the nation waging war, or whether they may be against citizens of another nation, even the nation to be attacked, Aquinas does not say. May a nation wage war to protect people from their own tyrannical governments? Third, the party waging war must be seeking to advance good and avoid evil. Cruelty, pride, greed, and the lust for power are not acceptable motives. Since "Seek good and avoid evil" is the fundamental precept of natural law, Aquinas's third condition requires that a person wage war to uphold natural law. To phrase it another way, one must wage war not because it is to one's advantage but because it is the right thing to do.

Later writers, most prominently Francisco de Vitoria, have added further conditions: that war be a last resort; that war have a reasonable likelihood of success; and that the goods to be gained outweigh the evils of warfare.

Hugo Grotius, often considered the father of international law, develops just war theory by way of what Michael Walzer calls the domestic analogy. The right of a nation to defend itself, Grotius argues, is analogous to (and in fact derived from) each individual's right to defend him- or herself. The wrongs that would justify war are similarly analogous to the harms that would justify legal action against an individual. The basic just cause for waging war is thus an injury. It may of course be an actual injury resulting from an act of aggression on the part of another state. But it may also be injury resulting from the acts of citizens of another state who are not properly held accountable by that state and for which no compensation is made. The injury need not even be actual; it is enough if there is a threat of injury to persons and property. I may defend myself against an attacker, even with lethal force, before I have been injured; I do not have to wait until I have been hurt. Similarly, nations may defend themselves preemptively against threats; they do not have to wait until they have been attacked. But such a preemptive war must meet several conditions. First, the danger must be immediate. Second, it must be real; fear is not in itself a justification for going to war. Third, there must be no less extreme way of avoiding the danger.

Carl von Clausewitz gives a simple and classic answer to the problem of *jus* in bello. War is "politics by other means," "an act of violence intended to compel our opponent to fulfill our will." War, always horrible, has become even more cruel and destructive as the technology of killing has become more powerful, and war inevitably tends to escalate. The advantage goes to the side with fewer scruples. War thus tends toward what Clausewitz calls "the utmost use of force." It also aims at disarming the enemy, for only then is the enemy no longer a threat. Fulfilling our will, then, requires subjugation of the enemy. The more quickly and securely that is brought about, the better. Winning does and should take precedence over all other moral considerations. There is one fundamental rule: Do what it takes to win. Everything else is detail.

Mahatma Gandhi argues for pacifism, maintaining that war is always impermissible. Even under direct attack, we are not morally justified in responding with violence. It is better to be killed than to kill, in Gandhi's view. Gandhi argues on both deontological and consequentialist grounds. Killing and injuring others for our own purposes are wrong in themselves. Killing could be justified only on the condition that the victim actually benefit from the killing. So, thus euthanasia is not necessarily wrong—though Gandhi thinks that, faced with a suffering human being, we are never in a position to know with confidence that it would be the right thing to do. In any case, that makes no difference to the moral acceptability of war, for no one thinks that enemy soldiers themselves are better off dead or wounded. But even apart from its intrinsic morality, Gandhi claims, violence is counterproductive. War causes immense destruction; there is always a better way. Nonviolent resistance takes great courage, but it accomplishes great things.

Richard Posner and Gary Becker argue, on consequentialist grounds, that preventive war is justified, not only in the face of an immediate threat, as Grotius insists, but even if the threat is not immediate. Terrorism makes the argument for preventive war stronger, they argue, for terrorists cannot be retaliated against, and hence deterred, in the way that state agents can.

ST. THOMAS AQUINAS

Whether It Is Always Sinful to Wage War?

(Source: The Summa Theologica of St. Thomas Aquinas, *second and revised edition, 1920, literally translated by Fathers of the English Dominican Province.)*

In order for a war to be just, three things are necessary. First, the authority of the sovereign by whose command the war is to be waged. For it is not the business of a private individual to declare war, because he can seek for redress of his rights from the tribunal of his superior. Moreover it is not the business of a private individual to summon together the people, which has to be done in wartime. And as the care of the common weal is committed to those who are in authority, it is their business to watch over the common weal of the city, kingdom or province subject to them. And just as it is lawful for them to have recourse to the sword in defending that common weal against internal disturbances, when they punish evil-doers, according to the words of the Apostle: "He beareth not the sword in vain: for he is God's minister, an avenger to execute wrath upon him that doth evil"; so too, it is their business to have recourse to the sword of war in defending the common weal against external enemies. Hence it is said to those who are in authority: "Rescue the poor: and deliver the needy out of the hand of the sinner"; and for this reason Augustine says: "The natural order conducive to peace among mortals demands that the power to declare and counsel war should be in the hands of those who hold the supreme authority."

Secondly, a just cause is required, namely that those who are attacked, should be attacked because they deserve it on account of some fault. Wherefore Augustine says: "A just war is wont to be described as one that avenges wrongs, when a nation or state has to be punished, for refusing to make amends for the wrongs inflicted by its subjects, or to restore what it has seized unjustly."

Thirdly, it is necessary that the belligerents should have a rightful intention, so that they intend the advancement of good, or the avoidance of evil. Hence Augustine says: "True religion looks upon as peaceful those wars that are waged not for motives of aggrandizement, or cruelty, but with the object of securing peace, of punishing evil-doers, and of uplifting the good." For it may happen that the war is declared by the legitimate authority, and for a just cause, and yet be rendered unlawful through a wicked intention. Hence Augustine says: "The passion for inflicting harm, the cruel thirst for vengeance, an unpacific and relentless spirit, the fever of revolt, the lust of power, and such like things, all these are rightly condemned in war."

Whether it is lawful to kill a man in self-defense?

It is written (Exodus 22:2): "If a thief be found breaking into a house or undermining it, and be wounded so as to die; he that slew him shall not be guilty of blood." Now it is much more lawful to defend one's life than one's house. Therefore neither is a man guilty of murder if he kill another in defense of his own life.

Nothing hinders one act from having two effects, only one of which is intended, while the other is beside the intention. Now moral acts take their species according to what is intended, and not according to what is beside the intention, since this is accidental. Accordingly the act of self-defense may have two effects: one is the saving of one's life, the other is the slaying of the aggressor. Therefore this act, since one's intention is to save one's own life, is not unlawful, seeing that it is natural to everything to keep itself in "being," as far as possible. And yet, though proceeding from a good intention, an act may be rendered unlawful, if it be out of proportion to the end. Wherefore if a man, in self-defense, uses more than necessary violence, it will be unlawful: whereas if he repel force with moderation his defense will be lawful, because according to the jurists, "it is lawful to repel force by force, provided one does not exceed the limits of a blameless defense." Nor is it necessary for salvation that a man omit the act of moderate self-defense in order to avoid killing the other man, since one is bound to take more care of one's own life than of another's. But as it is unlawful to take a man's life, except for the public authority acting for the common good, as stated above (Article 3), it is not lawful for a man to intend killing a man in self-defense, except for such as have public authority, who while intending to kill a man in self-defense, refer this to the public good, as in the case of a soldier fighting against the foe, and in the minister of the judge struggling with robbers, although even these sin if they be moved by private animosity.

Whether one is guilty of murder through killing someone by chance?

On the contrary, Augustine says to Publicola (*Ep.* xlvii): "When we do a thing for a good and lawful purpose, if thereby we unintentionally cause harm to anyone, it should by no means be imputed to us." Now it sometimes happens by chance that a person is killed as a result of something done for a good purpose. Therefore the person who did it is not accounted guilty.

I answer that, according to the Philosopher (*Phys.* ii, 6) "chance is a cause that acts beside one's intention." Hence chance happenings, strictly speaking, are neither intended nor voluntary. And since every sin is voluntary, according to Augustine (*De Vera Relig.* xiv) it follows that chance happenings, as such, are not sins.

Nevertheless it happens that what is not actually and directly voluntary and intended, is voluntary and intended accidentally, according as that which removes an obstacle is called an accidental cause. Wherefore he who does not remove something whence homicide results whereas he ought to remove it, is in a sense guilty of voluntary homicide. This happens in two ways: first when a man causes another's death through occupying himself with unlawful things which he ought to avoid: secondly, when he does not take sufficient care. Hence, according to jurists, if a man pursue a lawful occupation and take due care, the result being that a person loses his life, he is not guilty of that person's death: whereas if he be occupied with something unlawful, or even with something lawful, but without due care, he does not escape being guilty of murder, if his action results in someone's death

QUESTIONS FOR REFLECTION

1. Explain Aquinas's first condition for a just war.
2. What constitutes a "just cause"?
3. Are Aquinas's examples of just causes for war analogous to injuries suffered by individual people that might justify legal action? Why or why not?
4. What are acceptable motives for waging war, in Aquinas's view?
5. Think about applying Aristotle's schema for virtue to the issue of waging war: One must wage war at the right times, in the right circumstances, and for the right reason. (a) Is this virtue a mean between extremes? If so, describe them. (b) Compare the results to Aquinas's just war theory.
6. Aquinas's position on self-defense is known as the doctrine of Double Effect. Explain why.
7. What implications does Aquinas's view of killing in self-defense have for warfare?

FRANCISCO DE VITORIA

from *The Law of War on Indians*

Francisco de Vitoria (1492–1546), the father of international law, was a Spanish Renaissance philosopher who founded the School of Salamanca. Ethnically Jewish, he studied at the University of Paris and joined the faculty there at age twenty-two. At thirty, he returned to Spain, teaching first at Valladolid and then at Salamanca. Renowned as a scholar and teacher, he advised King Charles V and influenced many later thinkers, despite the fact that he published nothing during his lifetime. His lecture notes were published after his death. (Source: Francisco de Vitoria, De Indis De Jure Belli, Relectiones Theologicae *XII; Part 3—*The Law of War on Indians. *Introduction by Ernest Nys, and translation [by John Pawley Bate] of the Introduction by Ernest Nys. A translation of the text, by John Pawley Bate.)*

Proper Authority

3. Herein let my first proposition be: Any one, even a private person, can accept and wage a defensive war. This is shown by the fact that force may be repelled by force. Hence any one can make this kind of war, without authority from any one else, for the defense not only of his person, but also of his property and goods. . . .

5. Second proposition: Every State has authority to declare and to make war. In course of proof of this be it noted that the difference herein between a private person and a State is that a private person is entitled, as said above, to defend himself and what belongs to him, but has no right to avenge a wrong done to him, nay, not even to recapt property that has been seized from him if time has been allowed to go by since the seizure. But defense can only be resorted to at the very moment of the danger, or, as the jurists say, *in continenti*, and so when the necessity of defense has passed there is an end to the lawfulness of war. In my view, however, one who has been contumeliously assaulted can immediately strike back, even if the assaulter was not proposing to make a further attack, for in the avoidance of shame and disgrace one who (for example) has had his ears boxed might immediately use his sword, not for the purpose of vengeance, but, as has been said, in order to avoid infamy and disgrace. But a State is within its rights not only in defending itself, but also in avenging itself and its subjects and in redressing wrongs. This is proved by what Aristotle says in the third book of his *Politics*, namely, that a State ought to be sufficient unto itself. But it can not adequately protect the public weal and the position of the State if it can not avenge a wrong and take measures against its enemies, for wrongdoers would become readier and bolder for wrongdoing, if they could do wrong with

impunity. It is, therefore, imperative for the due ordering of human affairs that this authority be allowed to States. . . .

Just Cause

10. Third question: What may be a reason and cause of just war? . . .

13. Fourth proposition: There is a single and only just cause for commencing a war, namely, a wrong received. The proof of this rests in the first place on the authority of St. Augustine, and it is the conclusion arrived at by St. Thomas and the opinion of all the doctors. Also, an offensive war is for the purpose of avenging a wrong and of taking measures against an enemy, as said above. But there can be no vengeance where there is no preceding fault and wrong. Therefore [There should be no offensive war without a preceding fault or wrong.] Also, a prince has no greater authority over foreigners than over his own subjects. But he may not draw his sword against his own subjects, unless they have done some wrong. Therefore not against foreigners either. This is confirmed by the text already cited from St. Paul about a prince: "He beareth not the sword in vain: for he is the minister of God, a revenger to execute wrath upon him that doeth evil." Hence it is clear that we may not turn our sword against those who do us no harm, the killing of the innocent being forbidden by natural law. I omit here any injunctions inconsistent herewith which God has given in special cases, for He is the Lord of life and death and it is within His competence to vary His dispositions.

Proportional Force

14. Fifth proposition: Not every kind and degree of wrong can suffice for commencing a war. The proof of this is that not even upon one's own fellow-countrymen is it lawful for every offense to exact atrocious punishments, such as death or banishment or confiscation of property. As, then, the evils inflicted in war are all of a severe and atrocious character, such as slaughter and fire and devastation, it is not lawful for slight wrongs to pursue the authors of the wrongs with war, seeing that the degree of the punishment ought to correspond to the measure of the offense (Deuteronomy, ch. 25).

15. The fourth question is about the law of war, namely, what kind and degree of stress is lawful in a just war. Here let my first proposition be: In war everything is lawful which the defense of the common weal requires. This is notorious, for the end and aim of war is the defense and preservation of the State. Also, a private person may do this in self-defense, as has been proved. Therefore much more may a State and a prince. . . .

Last Resort

21. Second proposition: It is essential for a just war that an exceedingly careful examination be made of the justice and causes of the war and that the reasons of those who on grounds of equity oppose it be listened to. For (as the comic poet says) "A wise man must make trial of everything by words before resorting to force," and he ought to consult the good and wise and those who speak with freedom and without anger or bitterness or greed, seeing that (as Sallust says) "where these vices hold sway, truth is not easily distinguished." This is self-evident. For truth and justice in moral questions are hard of attainment and so any careless treatment of them easily leads to error, an error which will be inexcusable, especially in a concern of great moment, involving danger and calamity to many, and they our neighbors, too, whom we are bound to love as ourselves. . . .

Killing the Innocent

34. With regard to another question, namely, what degree of stress is lawful in a just war, there are also many doubts. The first is: Whether it is lawful in war to kill the innocent. It seems that it is. . . .

35. With regard to this doubt, let my first proposition be: The deliberate slaughter of the innocent is never lawful in itself. . . . the basis of a just war is a wrong done, as has been shown

above. But wrong is not done by an innocent person. Therefore war may not be employed against him. Thirdly, it is not lawful within a State to punish the innocent for the wrongdoing of the guilty. Therefore this is not lawful among enemies. Fourthly, were this not so, a war would be just on both sides, although there was no ignorance, a thing which, as has been shown, is impossible. And the consequence is manifest, because it is certain that innocent folk may defend themselves against any who try to kill them. . . .

37. Second proposition: Sometimes it is right, in virtue of collateral circumstances, to slay the innocent even knowingly, as when a fortress or city is stormed in a just war, although it is known that there are a number of innocent people in it and although cannon and other engines of war can not be discharged or fire applied to buildings without destroying innocent together with guilty. The proof is that war could not otherwise be waged against even the guilty, and the justice of belligerents would be balked. In the same way, conversely, if a town be wrongfully besieged and rightfully defended, it is lawful to fire cannon-shot and other missiles on the besiegers and into the hostile camp, even though we assume that there are some children and innocent people there.

The Condition of Proportionality

Great attention, however, must be paid to the point already taken, namely, the obligation to see that greater evils do not arise out of the war than the war would avert. For if little effect upon the ultimate issue of the war is to be expected from the storming of a fortress or fortified town wherein are many innocent folk, it would not be right, for the purpose of assailing a few guilty, to slay the many innocent by use of fire or engines of war or other means likely to overwhelm indifferently both innocent and guilty. In sum, it is never right to slay the guiltless, even as an indirect and unintended result, except when there is no other means of carrying on the operations of a just war. . . .

QUESTIONS FOR REFLECTION

1. Does Vitoria's account of just cause match that of Aquinas?
2. Does his account of proper authority match that of Aquinas?
3. Vitoria adds to Aguinas's just war theory a condition of proportionality. What is that condition? How does he justify it?
4. Vitoria also requires that war be a last resort. Explain.
5. Can one ever kill innocent people intentionally, according to Vitoria?
6. Consider and evaluate this objection to the proportionality condition: "The short-term effects of war are always strongly negative. The long-term effects are speculative and uncertain. Therefore, if we insist on confidence that the goods to be gained outweigh the evils of war, we will never fight."
7. Consider and evaluate this objection to the last resort condition: "If the good wait until they've tried everything else, they will fight only when evil is at its strongest. The last resort condition thus inevitably puts the good side at a disadvantage, and, by giving the advantage to the aggressor, actually makes war more likely."

HUGO GROTIUS

from *On the Law of War and Peace*

Hugo Grotius (1583–1645), a Dutch judge, philosopher, and theologian, is the founder of international law. (Source: On the Law of War and Peace, *translated by A. C. Campbell [London, 1814].)*

BOOK I, CHAPTER 2 / INQUIRY INTO THE LAWFULNESS OF WAR

It has been said above that an investigation of the laws of nature implies an inquiry, whether any particular action may be done without injustice: now by an act of injustice is understood that, which necessarily has in it any thing repugnant to the nature of a reasonable and social being. So far from any thing in the principles of nature being repugnant to war, every part of them indeed rather favours it. For the preservation of our lives and persons, which is the end of war, and the possession or acquirement of things necessary and useful to life is most suitable to those principles of nature, and to use force, if necessary, for those occasions, is no way dissonant to the principles of nature, since all animals are endowed with natural strength, sufficient to assist and defend themselves.

. . . Now right reason and the nature of society which claims the second, and indeed more important place in this inquiry, prohibit not all force, but only that which is repugnant to society, by depriving another of his right. For the end of society is to form a common and united aid to preserve to every one his own. Which may easily be understood to have obtained, before what is now called property was introduced. For the free use of life and limbs was so much the right of every one, that it could not be infringed or attacked without injustice. So the use of the common productions of nature was the right of the first occupier, and for any one to rob him of that was manifest injustice. This may be more easily understood, since law and custom have established property under its present form. . . . It is not therefore contrary to the nature of society to provide and consult for ourselves, if another's right is not injured; the force therefore, which inviolably abstains from touching the rights of others, is not unjust. For as the same Cicero observes some where in his Epistles, that as there are two modes of contending, the one by argument, and the other by force, and as the former is peculiar to man, and the latter common to him with the brute creation, we must have recourse to the latter, when it is impossible to use the former. And again, what can be opposed to force, but force? Ulpian observes that Cassius says, it is lawful to repel force by force, and it is a right apparently provided by nature to repel arms with arms, with whom Ovid agrees, observing that the laws permit us to take up arms against those that bear them. . . .

III

Proofs of what has been advanced, may be drawn also from the consent of all, especially, of the wisest nations. There is a celebrated passage in Cicero's speech for Milo, in which, justifying recourse to force in defence of life, he bears ample testimony to the feelings of nature, who has given us this law, which is not written, but innate, which we have not received by instruction, hearing or reading, but the elements of it have been engraven in our hearts and minds with her own hand: a law which is not the effect of habit and acquirement, but forms a part in the original complexion of our frame: so that if our lives are threatened with assassination or open violence from the hands of robbers or enemies, any means of defence would be allowed and laudable. He proceeds, reason has taught this to the learned, necessity to the barbarians, custom to nations, and nature herself to wild beasts, to use every possible means of repelling force offered to their bodies, their limbs and their lives. Caius and Lawyer say natural reason permits us to defend ourselves against dangers. And Florentinus, another legal authority, maintains, that whatever any one does in defence of his person ought to be esteemed right. Josephus observes, that the love of life is a law of nature strongly implanted in all creatures, and therefore we look upon those as enemies, who would openly deprive us of it.

This principle is founded on reasons of equity, so evident, that even in the brute creation, who have no idea of right, we make a distinction between attack and defence. For when Ulpian had said, that an animal without knowledge, that is without the use of reason, could not possibly do wrong, he immediately adds, that when two animals fight, if one kills the other, the distinction of Quintius Mutius must be admitted, that if the aggressor were killed no damages could be recovered; but if the other, which was attacked, an action might be maintained. There is a passage in Pliny, which will serve for an explanation of this, he says that the fiercest lions do not fight with each other, nor do serpents bite serpents. But if any violence is done to the tamest of them, they are roused, and upon receiving any hurt, will defend themselves with the greatest alacrity and vigour.

IV

From the law of nature then which may also be called the law of nations, it is evident that all kinds of war are not to be condemned. . . .

BOOK II, CHAPTER 1 / DEFENSE OF PERSON AND PROPERTY

I

The causes of war by which are meant the justifiable causes, are now to be considered. For in some cases motives of interest operate distinctly from motives of justice. . . . Injury, or the prevention of injury forms the only justifiable cause of war. "And, *in the language of the same Augustin,* all the evil consequences of war are to be laid at the door of the aggressor." Thus the Roman Herald in a declaration of war makes a solemn appeal against the aggressor, as having violated the laws of nations, and refused proper satisfaction.

II

The grounds of war are as numerous as those of judicial actions. For where the power of law ceases, there war begins. Now there are methods in law to prevent intended injuries, as well as actions for those actually committed. For CIVIL INJURIES various methods of redress, or prevention are appointed by the law; and by the same power securities are provided to prevent the commission of crimes and misdemeanors. In civil cases, the party aggrieved may recover damages for the injuries sustained; and in crimes, which are offences against the public, the aggressor must submit to actual punishment. . . .

Now reparation or indemnity relates to what either does or did belong to us; which gives rise to real and personal actions. These ascertain our right to the damages, which are our due, either from an agreement, or from an injury received. A right which is termed in law a right by contract, or injury. Crimes, which are offences against society, are prosecuted by indictment, that is by an accusation in the name of the sovereign.

The justifiable causes generally assigned for war are three, defence, indemnity, and punishment, all which are comprised in the declaration of Camillus against the Gauls, enumerating all things, which it is right to defend, to recover, and the encroachment on which it is right to punish.

There is an omission in this enumeration, unless the word recover be taken in its most extensive sense. For recovering by war what we have lost, includes indemnity for the past, as well as the prosecution of our claim to a debt. Plato has not omitted to notice this distinction, for he has said, "that wars are made to punish not only oppression or robbery, but also fraud and deception." With whom Seneca agrees; for to command payment of what you owe, he calls, "an equitable sentence, stamped with the authority of the law of nations." Indeed the form which was prescribed for the Roman heralds to use in declarations of war, bears exactly the same import. For therein the aggressor is charged with having neither given, paid, nor done what was due. Sallust in one of his fragments, has made a Tribune, in his harangue to the people, say, "As a final settlement of all discussion; I demand restitution according to the law of nations."

St. Augustin, in defining those to be just wars, which are made to avenge injuries has taken the word avenge in a general sense of removing and preventing, as well as punishing aggressions. This appears to be his meaning from the following sentence of the passage, in which he does not enumerate the particular acts, which amount to injury, but adds, by way of illustration, that "the state or nation, which has neglected to punish the aggressions of its own subjects, or to make reparation for the losses occasioned by those aggressions, is a proper object of hostility and attack." Prompted by this natural knowledge of right and wrong, the Indian King, as we are informed by Diodorus, accused Semiramis of having commenced war against him without having received any injury, Thus the Romans expostulated with the Senones, that they ought not to attack a people who had given them no provocation. Aristotle in the second book and second chapter of his Analytics, says, war generally is made upon those who have first done an injury. Quintus Curtius describes the Abian Scythians, as the best acquainted with the principles of justice of any of the Barbarians. For they declined having recourse to arm; unless provoked by aggression. A just cause then of war is an injury, which though not actually committed, threatens our persons or property with danger.

III

It has already been proved that when our lives are threatened with immediate danger, it is lawful to kill the aggressor, if the danger cannot otherwise be avoided: an instance, as it has been shewn, on which the justice of private war rests. We must observe that this kind of defence derives its origin from the principle of self-preservation, which nature has given to every living creature, and not from the injustice or misconduct of the aggressor. Wherefore though he may be clear of guilt, as for instance a soldier in actual service, mistaking my person for that of another, or a madman in his frenzy, or a man walking in his sleep, none of these cases deprive me of the right of self-defence against those persons. For I am not bound to submit to the danger or mischief intended, any more than to expose myself to the attacks of a wild beast.

IV

It admits of some doubt, whether those, who unintentionally obstruct our defence, or escape, which are necessary to our preservation, may be lawfully maimed or killed. There are some, even Theologians, who think they may. And, certainly if we look to the law of nature alone, according to its principles, our own preservation should have much more weight with us, than the welfare of society. But the law of charity, especially the evangelical law, which has put our neighbour upon a level with ourselves, does not permit it.

Thomas Aquinas, if taken in a right sense, has justly observed, that in actual self-defence no man can be said to be purposely killed. Indeed, it may some times happen that there is no other way for a person to save himself, than by designedly doing an act, by which the death of an aggressor must inevitably ensue. Yet here the death of any one was not the primary object intended, but employed as the only means of security, which the moment supplied. Still it is better for the party assaulted, if he can safely do it, to repel or disable the aggressor than to shed his blood.

V

The danger must be immediate, which is one necessary point. Though it must be confessed, that when an assailant seizes any weapon with an apparent intention to kill me I have a right to anticipate and prevent the danger. For in the moral as well as the natural system of things, there is no point without some breadth. But they are themselves much mistaken, and mislead others, who maintain that any degree of fear ought, to be a ground for killing another, to prevent his SUPPOSED intention. It is a very just observation made by Cicero in his first book of Offices, that many wrongs proceed from fear; as when the person, who intends to hurt another, apprehends some danger to himself unless he took, that method. Clearchus, in Xenophon, says, I have known some men, who partly through misrepresentation, and partly through suspicion, dreading one another, in order to prevent the supposed intentions of their adversaries, have committed the most enormous cruelties against those who neither designed, nor wished them any harm.

Cato in his speech for the Rhodians, says, "Are we to prevent them by doing first, what we say they intended to do to us?" On this subject there is a remarkable passage in Aulus Gellius, "When a Gladiator prepares to enter the lists for combat, such is his lot that he must either kill his adversary, or be killed himself. But the life of man is not circumscribed by the hard terms of such an over-ruling necessity, as to oblige him to do an injury to prevent him from receiving one." Quintilian has quoted a passage from Cicero, wherein the orator asks, "Whoever made such a decision, or to whom could such a point be yielded without the most imminent danger, that you have a right to kill the person, by whom you say, you fear that you shall afterwards be killed yourself?" To which this passage of Euripides, may be applied, "If your husband, as you say, intended to have killed you, you ought to have waited, till he actually did make the attempt." Conformably to which Thucydides, in the first book of his history, has expressed himself in the following terms, "The issue of war is uncertain, nor ought we to be so far transported by our fears, as to engage in immediate and open hostilities." The same writer too in his luminous description of the dangerous factions, that had arisen in the Grecian states, condemns the approbation bestowed on the person, that injured or destroyed another from whom he himself apprehended injury or destruction."

Livy says, "Men, to guard against their alarms, make themselves objects of terror; averting the danger from their own heads, by imposing upon others the necessity of either doing or suffering the evil which they themselves fear." Vibius asked a person, that appeared armed in the forum, "Who gave you permission to shew your fear in this manner?" A question not inapplicable to the present subject, and much commended by Quintilian. Livia also in Dion says, that great infamy redounds to those, who by anticipation perpetrate the criminal act, which they fear.

Now if any one intend no immediate violence, but is found to have formed a conspiracy to destroy me by assassination, or poison, or by false accusation, perjury, or suborned witnesses, I have no right to kill him. For my knowledge of the danger may prevent it. Or even if it were evident that I could not avoid the danger without killing him; this would not establish my right to do so. For there is every presumption that my knowing it will lead me to apply for the legal remedies of prevention.

BOOK III, CHAPTER 1 / WHAT IS LAWFUL IN WAR

I

Having, in the preceding books, considered by what persons, and for what causes, war may be justly declared and undertaken, the subject necessarily leads to an inquiry into the circumstances, under which war may be undertaken, into the extent, to which it may be carried, and into the manner, in which its rights may be enforced. Now all these matters may be viewed in the light of privileges resulting simply from the law of nature and of nations, or as the effects of some prior treaty or promise. But the actions, which are authorised by the law of nature, are those that are first entitled to attention.

II

In the first place, as it has occasionally been observed, the means employed in the pursuit of any object must, in a great degree, derive the complexion of their moral character from the nature of the end to which they lead. It is evident therefore that we may justly avail ourselves of those means, provided they be lawful, which are necessary to the attainment of any right. RIGHT in this place means what is strictly so called, signifying the moral power of action, which any one as a member of society possesses. On which account, a person, if he has no other means of saving his life, is justified in using any forcible means of repelling an attack, though he who makes it, as for instance, a soldier in battle, in doing so, is guilty of no crime. For this is a right resulting not properly from the crime of another, but from the privilege of self-defence, which nature grants to every one. Besides, if any one has SURE and UNDOUBTED grounds to apprehend imminent danger from any thing belonging to another, he may seize it without any regard to the guilt or innocence of that owner. Yet he does not by that seizure become the proprietor of it. For that is not necessary to the end he has in view. He may DETAIN it as a precautionary measure, till he can obtain satisfactory assurance of security.

Upon the same principle any one has a natural right to seize what belongs to him, and is unlawfully detained by another: or, if that is impracticable, he may seize something of equal value, which is nearly the same as recovering a debt. Recoveries of this kind establish a property in the things so reclaimed; which is the only method of restoring the equality and repairing the breaches of violated justice. So too when punishment is lawful and just, all the means absolutely necessary to enforce its execution are also lawful and just, and every act that forms a part of the punishment, such as destroying an enemy's property and country by fire or any other way, falls within the limits of justice proportionable to the offence.

III

In the second place, it is generally known that it is not the ORIGIN only of a just war which is to be viewed as the principal source of many of our rights, but there may be causes growing out of that war which may give birth to additional rights. As in proceedings at law, the sentence of the court may give to the successful litigant other rights besides those belonging to the original matter of dispute. So those who join our enemies, either as allies or subjects, give us a right of defending ourselves against THEM also. So too a nation engaging in an unjust war, the injustice of which she knows and ought to know, becomes liable to make good all the expences and losses incurred, because she has been guilty of occasioning them. In the same manner those powers, who become auxiliaries in wars undertaken without any reasonable grounds, contract a degree of guilt and render themselves liable to punishment in proportion to the injustice of their measures. Plato approves of war conducted so far, as to compel the aggressor to indemnify the injured and the innocent.

IV

In the third place, an individual or belligerent power may, in the prosecution of a lawful object, do many things, which were not in the contemplation of the original design, and which in THEMSELVES it would not be lawful to do. Thus in order to obtain what belongs to us, when it is impossible to recover the specific thing, we may take more than our due, under condition of repaying whatever is above the real value. For the same reason it is lawful to attack a ship manned by pirates, or a house occupied by robbers, although in that ship, or that house there may be many innocent persons, whose lives are endangered by such attack.

But we have had frequent occasion to remark, that what is conformable to right taken in its strictest sense is not always lawful in a moral point of view. For there are many instances, in which the law of charity will not allow us to insist upon our right with the utmost rigour. A reason for which it will be necessary to guard against things, which fall not within the original purpose of an action, and the happening of which might be foreseen: unless indeed the action has a tendency to produce advantages, that will far outweigh the consequences of any accidental calamity, and the apprehensions of evil are by no means to be put in competition with the sure hopes of a successful issue. But to determine in such cases requires no ordinary penetration and discretion. But wherever there is any doubt, it is. always the safer way to decide in favour of another's interest, than to follow the bent of our own inclination. . . .

QUESTIONS FOR REFLECTION

1. How does Grotius link the right to wage war to an individual's right of self-defense?
2. Under what circumstances is it acceptable to go to war, in Grotius's view?
3. How does Grotius justify preventive war?
4. What conditions does Grotius place on preventive war?
5. War may itself generate additional rights and obligations, according to Grotius. What are they, and why do they arise?

CARL VON CLAUSEWITZ

On the Nature of War

Carl von Clausewitz (1780–1831) fought for Prussia during the Napoleonic wars, attaining the rank of Major General, and remains Western civilzation's most prominent military theorist. (Source: From Book I of On War, translated by J. J. Graham [London: K. Paul, Trench, Trubner, 1908]. Originally published 1832.)

CHAPTER I / WHAT IS WAR?

. . . War is nothing but a duel on an extensive scale. If we would conceive as a unit the countless number of duels which make up a War, we shall do so best by supposing to ourselves two wrestlers. Each strives by physical force to compel the other to submit to his will: each endeavours to throw his adversary, and thus render him incapable of further resistance.

War therefore is an act of violence intended to compel our opponent to fulfil our will.

Violence arms itself with the inventions of Art and Science in order to contend against violence. Self-imposed restrictions, almost imperceptible and hardly worth mentioning, termed usages of International Law, accompany it without essentially impairing its power. Violence, that is to say, physical force (for there is no moral force without the conception of States and Law), is therefore the *means*; the compulsory submission of the enemy to our will is the ultimate object. In order to attain this object fully, the enemy must be disarmed, and disarmament becomes therefore the immediate *object* of hostilities in theory. It takes the place of the final object, and puts it aside as something we can eliminate from our calculations.

3. Utmost Use of Force

Now, philanthropists may easily imagine there is a skilful method of disarming and overcoming an enemy without great bloodshed, and that this is the proper tendency of the Art of War. However plausible this may appear, still it is an error which must be extirpated; for in such dangerous things as War, the errors which proceed from a spirit of benevolence are the worst. As the use of physical power to the utmost extent by no means excludes the co-operation of the intelligence, it follows that he who uses force unsparingly, without reference to the bloodshed involved, must obtain a superiority if his adversary uses less vigour in its application. The former then dictates the law to the latter, and both proceed to extremities to which the only limitations are those imposed by the amount of counter-acting force on each side.

This is the way in which the matter must be viewed and it is to no purpose, it is even against one's own interest, to turn away from the consideration of the real nature of the affair because the horror of its elements excites repugnance.

If the Wars of civilised people are less cruel and destructive than those of savages, the difference arises from the social condition both of States in themselves and in their relations to each other. Out of this social condition and its relations War arises, and by it War is subjected to conditions, is controlled and modified. But these things do not belong to War itself; they are only given conditions; and to introduce into the philosophy of War itself a principle of moderation would be an absurdity.

Two motives lead men to War: instinctive hostility and hostile intention. In our definition of War, we have chosen as its characteristic the latter of these elements, because it is the most general. It is impossible to conceive the passion of hatred of the wildest description, bordering on mere instinct, without combining with it the idea of a hostile intention. On the other hand, hostile intentions may often exist without being accompanied by any, or at all events by any extreme, hostility of feeling. Amongst savages views emanating from the feelings, amongst civilised nations those emanating from the understanding, have the predominance; but this difference arises from attendant circumstances, existing institutions, [etc.], and, therefore, is not to be found necessarily in all cases, although it prevails in the majority. In short, even the most civilised nations may burn with passionate hatred of each other.

We may see from this what a fallacy it would be to refer the War of a civilised nation entirely to an intelligent act on the part of the Government, and to imagine it as continually freeing itself more and more from all feeling of passion in such a way that at last the physical masses of combatants would no longer be required; in reality, their mere relations would suffice—a kind of algebraic action.

Theory was beginning to drift in this direction until the facts of the last War [against Napoleon] taught it better. If War is an *act* of force, it belongs necessarily also to the feelings. If it does not originate in the feelings, it *reacts,* more or less, upon them, and the extent of this reaction depends not on the degree of civilisation, but upon the importance and duration of the interests involved.

Therefore, if we find civilised nations do not put their prisoners to death, do not devastate towns and countries, this is because their intelligence exercises greater influence on their mode of carrying on War, and has taught them more effectual means of applying force than these rude acts of mere instinct. The invention of gunpowder, the constant progress of improvements in the construction of firearms, are sufficient proofs that the tendency to destroy the adversary which lies at the bottom of the conception of War is in no way changed or modified through the progress of civilisation.

We therefore repeat our proposition, that War is an act of violence pushed to its utmost bounds; as one side dictates the law to the other, there arises a sort of reciprocal action, which logically must lead to an extreme. This is the first reciprocal action, and the first extreme with which we meet (*first reciprocal action*).

4. The Aim Is to Disarm the Enemy

We have already said that the aim of all action in War is to disarm the enemy, and we shall now show that this, theoretically at least, is indispensable.

If our opponent is to be made to comply with our will, we must place him in a situation which is more oppressive to him than the sacrifice which we demand; but the disadvantages of this position must naturally not be of a transitory nature, at least in appearance, otherwise the enemy, instead of yielding, will hold out, in the prospect of a change for the better. Every change in this position which is produced by a continuation of the War should therefore be a change for the worse. The worst condition in which a belligerent can be placed is that of being completely disarmed. If, therefore, the enemy is to be reduced to submission by an act of War, he must either be positively disarmed or placed in such a position that he is threatened with it. From this it follows that the disarming or overthrow of the enemy, whichever we call it, must always be the aim of Warfare. Now War is always the shock of two hostile bodies in collision, not the action of a living power upon an inanimate mass, because an absolute state of endurance would not be making War; therefore, what we have just said as to the aim of action in War applies to both parties. Here, then, is another case of reciprocal action. As long as the enemy is not defeated, he may defeat me; then I shall be no longer my own master; he will dictate the law to me as I did to him. This is the second reciprocal action, and leads to a second extreme (*second reciprocal action*).

5. Utmost Exertion of Powers

If we desire to defeat the enemy, we must proportion our efforts to his powers of resistance. This is expressed by the product of two factors which cannot be separated, namely, the sum of available means and the strength of the Will. The sum of the available means may be estimated in a measure, as it depends (although not entirely) upon numbers; but the strength of volition is more difficult to determine, and can only be estimated to a certain extent by the strength of the motives. Granted we have obtained in this way an approximation to the strength of the power to be contended with, we can then take of our own means, and either increase them so as to obtain a preponderance, or, in case we have not the resources to effect this, then do our best by increasing our means as far as possible. But the adversary does the same; therefore, there is a new mutual enhancement, which, in pure conception, must create a fresh effort towards an extreme. This is the third case of reciprocal action, and a third extreme with which we meet (*third reciprocal action*).

11. The Political Object Now Reappears

Here the question which we had laid aside forces itself again into consideration (see No. 2), viz., the political object of the War. The law of the extreme, the view to disarm the adversary, to overthrow him, has hitherto to a certain extent usurped the place of this end or object. Just as this law loses its force, the political must again come forward. If the whole consideration is a calculation of probability based on definite persons and relations, then the political object, being the original motive, must be an essential factor in the product. The smaller the sacrifice we demand from our opponent, the smaller, it may be expected, will be the means of resistance which he will employ; but the smaller his preparation, the smaller will ours require to be. Further, the smaller our political object, the less value shall we set upon it, and the more easily shall we be induced to give it up altogether.

Thus, therefore, the political object, as the original motive of the War, will be the standard for determining both the aim of the military force and also the amount of effort to be made. This it cannot be in itself, but it is so in relation to both the belligerent States, because we are concerned with realities, not with mere abstractions. One and the same political object may produce totally different effects upon different people, or even upon the same people at different times; we can, therefore, only admit the political object as the measure, by considering it in its effects upon those masses which it is to move, and consequently the nature of those masses also comes into consideration. It is easy to see that thus the result may be very different according as these masses are animated with a spirit which will infuse vigour into the action or otherwise. It is quite possible for such a state of feeling to exist between two States that a very trifling political motive for War may produce an effect quite disproportionate—in fact, a perfect explosion.

This applies to the efforts which the political object will call forth in the two States, and to the aim which the military action shall prescribe for itself. At times it may itself be that aim, as, for example, the conquest of a province. At other times the political object itself is not suitable for the aim of military action; then such a one must be chosen as will be an equivalent for it, and stand in its place as regards the conclusion of peace. But also, in this, due attention to the peculiar character of the States concerned is always supposed. There are circumstances in which the equivalent must be much greater than the political object, in order to secure the latter. The political object will be so much the more the standard of aim and effort, and have more influence in itself, the more the masses are indifferent, the less that any mutual feeling of hostility prevails in the two States from other causes, and therefore there are cases where the political object almost alone will be decisive.

If the aim of the military action is an equivalent for the political object, that action will in general diminish as the political object diminishes, and in a greater degree the more the political object dominates. Thus it is explained how, without any contradiction in itself, there may be Wars of all degrees of importance and energy, from a War of extermination down to the mere use of an army of observation. . . .

23. War Is Always a Serious Means for a Serious Object. Its More Particular Definition

Such is War; such the Commander who conducts it; such the theory which rules it. But War is no pastime; no mere passion for venturing and winning; no work of a free enthusiasm: it is a serious means for a serious object. All that appearance which it wears from the varying hues of fortune, all that it assimilates into itself of the oscillations of passion, of courage, of imagination, of enthusiasm, are only particular properties of this means.

The War of a community—of whole Nations, and particularly of civilised Nations—always starts from a political condition, and is called forth by a political motive. It is, therefore, a political act. Now if it was a perfect, unrestrained, and absolute expression of force, as we had to deduct it from its mere conception, then the moment it is called forth by policy it would step into the place of policy, and as something quite independent of it would set it aside, and only follow its own laws, just as a mine at the moment of explosion cannot be guided into any other direction than that which has been given to it by preparatory arrangements. This is how the thing has really been viewed hitherto, whenever a want of harmony between policy and the conduct of a War has led to theoretical distinctions of the kind. But it is not so, and the idea is radically false. War in the real world, as we have already seen, is not an extreme thing which expends itself at one single discharge; it is the operation of powers which do not develop themselves completely in the same manner and in the same measure, but which at one time expand sufficiently to overcome the resistance opposed by inertia or friction, while at another they are too weak to produce an effect; it is therefore, in a certain measure, a pulsation of violent force more or less vehement, consequently making its discharges and exhausting its powers more or less quickly—in other words, conducting more or less quickly to the aim, but always lasting long enough to admit of influence being exerted on it in its course, so as to give it this or that direction, in short, to be subject to the will of a guiding intelligence. Now, if we reflect that War has its root in a political object, then naturally this original motive which called it into existence should also continue the first and highest consideration in its conduct. Still, the political object is no despotic lawgiver on that account; it must accommodate itself to the nature of the means, and though changes in these means may involve modification in the political objective, the latter always retains a prior right to consideration. Policy, therefore, is interwoven with the whole action of War, and must exercise a continuous influence upon it, as far as the nature of the forces liberated by it will permit.

24. War Is a Mere Continuation of Policy by Other Means

We see, therefore, that War is not merely a political act, but also a real political instrument, a continuation of political commerce, a carrying out of the same by other means. All beyond this which is strictly peculiar to War relates merely to the peculiar nature of the means which it uses. That the tendencies and views of policy shall not be incompatible with these means, the Art of War in general and the Commander in each particular case may demand, and this claim is truly not a trifling one. But however powerfully this may react on political views in particular cases, still it must always be regarded as only a modification of them; for the political view is the object, War is the means, and the means must always include the object in our conception.

QUESTIONS FOR REFLECTION

1. Explain von Clausewitz's definition of war.
2. Why does war inevitably tend toward "the utmost use of force"?
3. What does escalation imply about the possibility of rules of war?
4. If escalation is inevitable, how can there be limited wars?
5. What does von Clausewitz mean in saying that war is a continuation of policy by other means?

MAHATMA GANDHI

Non-Violence in Various Aspects

Mohandas Karamchand (Mahatma) Gandhi (1869–1948) led India to independence through a campaign of nonviolent civil disobedience.
(Source: A Gandhi Anthology, *Book I [Ahmedabad: Navajivan Press, 1952].*

Where there is only a choice between cowardice and violence, I would advise violence. . . . But . . . non-violence is infinitely superior to violence.

Non-violence is the greatest force at the disposal of mankind. It is mightier than the mightiest weapon of destruction devised by the ingenuity of man.

In a family, when a father slaps his delinquent child the latter does not think of retaliating. He obeys his father not because of the deterrent effect of the slap but because of the offended love which he senses behind it. That . . . is an epitome of the way in which society should be governed.

My ethics not only permit me to claim but require me to own kinship with not merely the ape but the horse and the sheep, the lion and the leopard, the snake and the scorpion.

I do not want to live at the cost of the life even of a snake. I should let him bite me to death rather than kill him. . . . Snakes, tigers etc. are God's answer to the poisonous, wicked, evil thoughts we harbour. . . . If I want to rid the earth of venomous beasts and reptiles, I must rid myself of all venomous thoughts.

Himsa [violence] is an inherent necessity for life in the body. That is why a votary of *ahimsa* always prays for ultimate deliverance from the bondage of flesh.

I would not kill a human being for protecting a cow, as I will not kill a cow for saving a human life, be it ever so precious.

I cannot for a moment bear to see a dog . . . helplessly suffering the torture of a slow death. I do not kill a human being thus circumstanced because I have more hopeful remedies. I should kill a dog similarly situated because in its case I am without a remedy. Should my child be attacked by rabies and there was no hopeful remedy to relieve his agony, I should consider it my duty to take his life.

The principle of *ahimsa* is hurt by every evil thought, by undue haste, by lying, by hatred, by wishing ill to anybody. It is also violated by one's holding on to what the world needs.

Without *ahimsa* it is not possible to seek and find truth.

Under this rule there is no room for organized assassinations, there is no room for murders even openly committed, and there is no room for any violence even for the sake of your country and even for guarding the honour of precious ones that may be in your charge. After all that would be a poor defence of the honour. *Ahimsa* tells us that we may guard the honour of those who are in our charge by delivering ourselves into the hands of the man who would commit the sacrilege. And that requires far greater physical and mental courage than the delivering of blows. You may have some degree of physical power,—I do not say courage,—and you may use that power. But after that is expended, what happens? The other man is filled with wrath, and you have made him more angry by matching your violence against his; and when he has done you to death, the rest of his violence is delivered against your charge. But if you do not retaliate but stand your ground between your charge and the opponent simply receiving the blows without retaliating, what happens? I give you my promise that the whole of the violence will be expended on you and your charge will be left unscathed.

I am not a visionary. I claim to be a practical idealist. The religion of non-violence is not meant merely for *rishis* [seers] and saints. It is meant for the common people as well. Non-violence is the law of our species as violence is the law of the brute.

Non-violence in its dynamic condition means conscious suffering. It does not mean meek submission to the will of the evil-doer but it means the pitting of one's whole soul against the will of the tyrant. Working under this law of our being, it is possible for a single individual to defy the whole might of an unjust empire to save his honour, his religion, his soul, and lay the foundation for that empire's fall or its regeneration.

Truth is my God. Non-violence is the means of realizing Him.

Anger is the enemy of *ahimsa*; and pride is a monster that swallows it up.

Ahimsa is not mere non-killing. A person who remains smugly satisfied with the non-killing of noxious life but has no love in his heart for all that lives will be counted as least in the Kingdom of Heaven. True love is boundless like the ocean, and rising and swelling within one spreads itself out, and crossing all boundaries and frontiers envelops the whole world.

To me it is one of the most active forces in the world. It is like the sun that rises upon us unfailingly from day to day. [Indeed] it is infinitely greater than a million suns put together. It radiates life and light and peace and happiness.

The hardest metal yields to sufficient heat. Even so must the hardest heart melt before sufficiency of the heat of non-violence. And there is no limit to the capacity of non-violence to generate heat.

Ahimsa must express itself through acts of selfless service of the masses. I cannot think of a better symbol of or medium for its expression than the spinning-wheel.

Himsa does not merely mean indulgence in physical violence; resort to trickery, falsehood, intrigue, chicanery and deceitfulness—in short, all unfair and foul means come under the category of *himsa*, and acceptance of *ahimsa* necessarily implies renunciation of all these things.

A votary of *ahimsa* has therefore to be incorruptible, fair and square in his dealings, truthful, straightforward and utterly selfless. He must have also true humility.

It is the law of love that rules mankind. Had violence, i.e. hate, ruled us, we should have become extinct long ago. And yet the tragedy of it is that the so-called civilized men and nations conduct themselves as if the basis of society was violence.

I have been practising with scientific precision non-violence and its possibilities for an unbroken period of over fifty years. I have applied it in every walk of life, domestic, institutional, economic and political. I know of no single case in which it has failed. Where it has seemed sometimes to have failed, I have ascribed it to my imperfections. I claim no perfection for myself, but I claim to be a passionate seeker after Truth which is but another name for God. In the course of that search the discovery of non-violence came to me. Its spread is my life-mission. I have no interest in living except for the prosecution of that mission.

We dare not exchange non-violence even for Swaraj [independence]. For Swaraj thus got will be no true Swaraj.

Ahimsa does not simply mean non-killing. *Himsa* means causing pain to or killing any life out of anger or from a selfish purpose, or with the intention of injuring it. Refraining from so doing is *ahimsa*.

All have to destroy some life,

(a) for sustaining their own bodies.

(b) for protecting those under their care, or

(c) sometimes for the sake of those whose life is taken.

(a) and (b) mean *himsa* to a greater or less extent.
(c) means no *himsa* and is therefore *ahimsa*. *Himsa* in (a) and (b) is unavoidable.

A progressive *ahimsa*-ist will therefore commit the *himsa* contained in (a) and (b) as little as possible, only when it is unavoidable, and after full and mature deliberation and having exhausted all remedies to avoid it.

Taking life may be a duty. We do destroy as much life as we think necessary for sustaining our body.

Thus for food we take life, vegetable and other, and for health we destroy mosquitoes and the like by the use of disinfectants and we do not think that we are guilty of irreligion in doing so. . . . For the benefit of the species we kill carnivorous beasts. . . . Even manslaughter may be necessary in certain cases. Suppose a man runs amuck and goes furiously about, sword in hand, and killing any one that comes in his way and no one dares to capture him alive. Any one who despatches this lunatic will earn the gratitude of the community and be regarded as a benevolent man.

To say or write a distasteful word is surely not violent especially when the speaker or writer believes it to be true. The essence of violence is that there must be a violent intention behind a thought, word or act, i.e. an intention to do harm to the opponent so called.

The hardest heart [must soften] and the grossest ignorance must disappear before the rising sun of suffering without anger and without malice.

Non-violence presupposes the ability to strike. It is a conscious, deliberate restraint put upon one's desire for vengeance. But vengeance is any day superior to passive, effeminate and helpless submission. Forgiveness is higher still. Vengeance too is weakness. The desire for vengeance comes out of fear of harm, imaginary or real. A man who fears no one on earth would consider it troublesome even to summon up anger against one who is vainly trying to injure him.

Non-violence to be a potent force must begin with the mind. Non-violence of the mere body without the co-operation of the mind is non-violence of the weak or the cowardly and has therefore no potency. If we bear malice and hatred in our bosoms and pretend not to retaliate, it must recoil upon us and lead to our destruction. For abstention from mere bodily violence not to be injurious, it is at least necessary not to entertain hatred if we cannot generate active love.

From violence done to the foreign ruler, violence to our own people whom we may consider to be obstructing the country's progress is an easy natural step.

The spiritual weapon of self-purification, intangible as it seems, is the most potent means of revolutionizing one's environment and loosening external shackles. It is the straightest way to liberation, the surest and quickest.

Suffering injury in one's own person is on the contrary of the essence of non-violence and is the chosen substitute for violence to others. It is not because I value life low that I can countenance with joy thousands voluntarily losing their lives for Satyagraha but because I know that it results in the long run in the least loss of life, and what is more, it ennobles those who lose their lives and morally enriches the world for their sacrifice.

The main thing   is for women to know how to be fearless. It is my firm conviction that a fearless woman who knows that her purity is her best shield can never be dishonoured. However beastly the man, he will bow in shame before the flame of her dazzling purity. . . . It [the art of becoming fearless] can best be learnt from a living faith in God. Though He is invisible, He is our unfailing protector. He who has this faith is the most fearless of all.

But such faith or courage cannot be acquired in a day. Meanwhile we must try to explore other means. When a woman is assaulted, she may not stop to think in terms of *himsa* or *ahimsa*. Her primary duty is self-protection. She is at liberty to employ every method or means that comes to her mind in order to defend her honour. God has given her nails and teeth. She must use them with all her strength and if need be, die in the effort. . . . Whether a man crawls on his belly or whether a woman yields to the lust of man, it is symbolic of that same love of life which makes us stoop to anything. Therefore only he who loses his life shall save it; . . . To enjoy life one should give up the lure of life. That should be part of our nature.

If I had been a citizen of Switzerland . . . what I would have done would be to refuse passage to the invading army by refusing all supplies. Secondly by re-enacting a Thermopylae in Switzerland, [I] would have presented a living wall of men and women and children, and invited the invaders to walk over our corpses. The army would be brutal enough to walk over them, you might say. I would then say you will still have done your duty by allowing yourself to be annihilated. An army that dares to pass over the corpses of innocent men and women would not be able to repeat that experiment. You may, if you wish, refuse to believe in such courage on the part of the masses of men and women, but, then, you would have to admit that non-violence is made of sterner stuff. It was never conceived as a weapon of the weak but of the stoutest hearts.

QUESTIONS FOR REFLECTION

1. What does Gandhi mean by *ahimsa?*
2. Are there any circumstances under which violence is permissible?
3. How does Gandhi argue that nonviolence is more effective than violence at achieving good?
4. Suppose one were to argue that in war, one does not intend the deaths of the enemy; one intends to achieve certain objectives, and those deaths are unfortunate side effects of doing so. Thus one might argue that a just war, at any rate, does not violate *ahimsa*. How might Gandhi respond?
5. George Orwell wrote that Gandhi's nonviolent methods worked to free India from British rule but could not be expected to work against totalitarian governments that do not honor freedom of speech, are willing to be brutal in suppressing dissent, and are ruled by madmen: "It is difficult to see how Gandhi's methods could be applied in a country where opponents of the regime disappear in the middle of the night and are never heard of again." How might Gandhi respond? Do you agree with Orwell's criticism?
6. Orwell wrote that during World War II, "one question that every pacifist had a clear obligation to answer was: 'What about the Jews? Are you prepared to see them exterminated? If not, how do you propose to save them without resorting to war?'" How might a pacifist respond?
7. Evaluate Gandhi's actual response to Orwell's question: The Jews should have committed collective suicide, for that "would have aroused the world and the people of Germany to Hitler's violence."

RICHARD A. POSNER AND GARY S. BECKER

Preventive War

Richard A. Posner (1939–), senior lecturer at the University of Chicago Law School and author of forty books, is judge on the U.S. Court of Appeals, Seventh Circuit, where he served as chief judge from 1993 to 2000. Gary S. Becker (1930–) is university professor of economics, sociology, and business at the University of Chicago. He won the Nobel Prize in economics in 1992. (Source: Reprinted from The Becker-Posner Blog *[December 5, 2004]. Reprinted by permission of Creative Commons, http://creativecommons.org.)*

Posner:

The U.S. invasion of Iraq, the U.S. decision not to invade Afghanistan before the 9/11 attacks, and concern with the apparent efforts of Iran and North Korea to obtain nuclear weapons raise acutely the question when if ever a preemptive or preventive war is justified. If "preemptive war" is defined narrowly enough, it merges into defensive war, which is uncontroversial; if you know with certainty that you are about to be attacked, you are justified in trying to get in the first blow. Indeed, the essence of self-defense is striking the first blow against your assailant.

But what if the danger of attack is remote rather than imminent? Should imminence be an absolute condition of going to war, and preventive war thus be deemed always and everywhere wrong? Analytically, the answer is no. A rational decision to go to war should be based on a comparison of the costs and benefits (in the largest sense of these terms) to the nation. The benefits are the costs that the enemy's attack, the attack that going to war now will thwart, will impose on the nation. The fact that the attack is not imminent is certainly relevant to those costs. It is relevant in two respects. First, future costs may not have the same weight in our decisions as present costs. This is obvious when the costs are purely financial; if given a choice between $100 today and $100 in ten years, any rational person will take $100 now, if only because the money can be invested and through interest compounding grow to a much larger amount in ten years. But the appropriateness of thus discounting future costs is less clear when the issue is averting future costs that are largely nonpecuniary and have national or global impact.

Second, and more important, and well illustrated by the failure to find weapons of mass destruction in Iraq, if the threat of attack lies in the future it is difficult to gauge either its actual likelihood or its probable magnitude. But this is not a compelling argument against preventive war. What is true is that a defensive war is by definition waged only when the probability of an attack has become one; the attack has occurred. The probability of attack is always less than one if the putative victim wages a preventive war, because the attacker might have changed his mind before attacking.

But while the probability of a future attack is always less than one, the expected cost of the future attack—the cost that the attack will impose multiplied by the probability of the attack—may be very high, perhaps because the adversary is growing stronger and so will be able to deliver a heavier blow in the future than he could do today. It may be possible to neutralize his greater strength, but that will require a greater investment in defense. Suppose there is a probability of .5 that the adversary will attack at some future time, when he has completed a military build up, that the attack will, if resisted with only the victim's current strength, inflict a cost on the victim of 100, so that the expected cost of the attack is 50 (100 × .5), but that the expected cost can be reduced to 20 if the victim incurs additional defense costs of 15. Suppose further that at an additional cost of only 5, the victim can by a preventive strike today eliminate all possibility of the future attack. Since 5 is less than 35 (the sum of injury and defensive costs if the future enemy attack is not prevented), the preventive war is cost-justified.

A historical example that illustrates this analysis is the Nazi reoccupation of the Rhineland area of Germany in 1936, an area that had been demilitarized by the Treaty of Versailles. Had France and Great Britain responded to this treaty violation by invading Germany, in all likelihood Hitler would have been overthrown and World War II averted. (It is unlikely that Japan would have attacked the United States and Great Britain in 1941 had it not thought that Germany would be victorious.) The benefits of preventive war would in that instance have greatly exceeded the costs.

Becker:

Combating crime mainly relies on deterrence through punishment of criminals who recognize that there is a chance of being apprehended and convicted—the chances are greater for more serious crimes. If convicted, they can expect imprisonment or other punishments—again, punishments are generally more severe for more serious crimes. Apprehension and punishment reduce the gain from crimes; in this way, it deters others from criminal activities.

Individuals can also be punished simply for planning or intending to commit crimes. The evidence required to punish intent has to be convincing, but the standard is weaker for violent crimes, like plotting murder, since punishment after the crime does not do anything for those murdered. In addition, individuals who cannot be deterred are sometimes punished simply because it is considered likely [they] will commit crimes in the future. This is a major justification for forced hospitalization and psychological treatment of potentially violent and mentally unstable persons.

These arguments about intent apply much more strongly to preventive actions against terrorist organizations and rogue nations. The conventional approach to war in democratic states favors retaliation after attacks. This was the rationale for the Mutually Assured Destruction (MAD) doctrine during the height of the Cold War: the United States was prepared to unleash devastating nuclear destruction against the Soviet Union if attacked with nuclear weapons, and [vice] versa for the Soviets. That worked, although there were several close calls, as during the Cuban crisis.

But this approach is no longer adequate to fight terrorist organizations, states that sponsor terrorism, and dictatorial states that want to destroy their enemies. For it is becoming increasingly possible for terrorist organizations and governments to unleash biological, chemical, or nuclear weapons that will cause massive destruction. Retaliation may be slow and difficult if terrorists are widely dispersed so that it is hard to generate sufficiently severe reprisals to discourage their attacks. Rogue governments also are more capable of using these weapons surreptitiously, so that it might be many obstacles to determining who was responsible if they chose not to admit their responsibility. It is already difficult to know which groups are responsible for terrorist acts except when they brag about them.

In addition, many state-sponsors of terrorism often prey on the zeal of individuals who are willing to kill themselves in promoting what they consider a higher cause. These suicide bombers clearly cannot be punished after they commit their acts (although their families could be) because they forfeit their lives while attempting to kill and injure others. One can try to raise the probability that they will fail—through barriers, walls, and other protective activities—but free societies are so vulnerable that these can never be strong enough deterrents.

The only really effective approach is to stop them before they engage in their attacks. This is accomplished by tracking them down and imprisoning or killing them based on evidence that they intend to engage in suicidal attacks. Those planning such acts can also be punished on the basis of intent.

The same argument applies to dictators who are willing to use weapons of mass destruction to attack their enemies when they do not care if many of their populations are killed and maimed by retaliation from other countries. Dictators, like Saddam Hussein, may also greatly underestimate the likelihood of massive responses because sycophants feed them bad information, or they believe that democratic victimized states will be reluctant to make swift and decisive responses.

Admittedly, the evidence is usually more imperfect when trying to prevent attacks than when responding to attacks. Mistakes will be made, and the evidence of intent must be analyzed carefully. But criminals are convicted too on less than 100% certain evidence. As Posner says in his commentary, it is necessary to consider probabilities, not certainties.

Moreover, the degree of certainty required before preventive actions are justified has been considerably reduced below what it was in the past because the destructive power of weaponry has enormously increased. Perhaps most worrisome, the power of weapons continues to grow, and to become more easily accessible. Critics of preventive wars and other preventive actions against rogue states and terrorist groups ignore these major changes in weaponry and their availability. Democratic governments have to recognize that they no longer have the luxury of waiting to respond until they are attacked.

QUESTIONS FOR REFLECTION

1. It is sometimes rational to engage in a preventive war, even if the threat is not imminent, argues Posner. Why?
2. Posner's argument concerns rationality rather than morality as utilitarians conceive it; Posner evaluates costs and benefits for one nation, not for everyone affected. Could his argument be adapted to one taking consequences for everyone into account? Would such a calculation yield a similar result?
3. Should a leader or a citizen think of the decision to go to war in terms of effects on the nation's interests, or in terms of the effects on everyone affected?
4. Explain the link between question 3 and the issue dividing act-utilitarians and rule-utilitarians.
5. How do Posner and Becker respond to the objection that we never know enough to make a reasonable assessment of a non-imminent threat?
6. What analogies does Becker exploit in arguing for preventive war? How strong are they?
7. How does terrorism affect the decision to conduct preventive war, according to Becker? Do you agree?

Justice and Equality

PART IV

JUSTICE AND EQUALITY

Aristotle distinguishes several different senses of justice. He identifies one sense of justice with virtue as a whole, but specifically in relation to other people. Another sense of justice pertains to rectification—setting right previous wrongs. This section concerns *distributive justice:* the problem of distributing goods and obligations among the members of a society.

Aristotle holds a simple but extremely powerful theory of distributive justice. He believes that both goods and obligations ought to be distributed according to merit. He considers a group of people who have somehow obtained a flute. Who in the group should get the flute? The best flute player, Aristotle answers. Similarly, goods ought to go to those who deserve them—that is, those who can make the best use of them. This answer has very strong intuitive appeal. How should a professor assign grades? The top grades should go to those with the most merit, those who have performed best. Who should receive a Grammy Award? Those who have produced the best music. Who should receive political power? Those who have the most political virtue, Aristotle answers—the people with the greatest ability to bring about good government.

Aristotle's theory is a patterned theory of justice. It says that people should receive goods of a certain kind to the extent that they have merit of that kind. Thus, it answers the question of distributive justice in terms of who has what other characteristics now or at some other definite time. Jean-Jacques Rousseau, Karl Marx, Friedrich Engels, and John Rawls all propose very different theories of justice, but all specify who should get what in terms of who has what now or at some other time.

Rousseau's analysis of distributive justice is somewhat vague. He makes clear that no one should have too much and no one too little. Within the bounds this principle establishes, however, the general will rules. Recall that according to Rousseau's conception of the social contract, we would agree to form a government because we hope to gain from the cooperation it makes possible. We are willing to commit everything we have in the interests of cooperation and expect to receive in return our share of everything that anyone else has. Distribution, then, is in the hands of the community as a whole. Rousseau treats the community as a body with its own interests. He characterizes limits on the community's behavior in terms of the general will. Roughly, the community can legitimately do only what accords with the general will—that is, with the community's own self-interest. This seems to imply that a just distribution is one that accords with the interests of the community as a whole. What this distribution is, of course, is an empirical matter. But Rousseau feels confident enough to say that the multitude should not lack necessities and that the fortunate should not be able to pursue luxuries.

Marx and Engels take Rousseau's position to a more definite conclusion. They analyze social structures in terms of class struggle. They see moral language as little more than a tool in class struggle; consequently, they are reluctant to offer a general theory of justice. But Marx does provide a slogan that embodies such a theory: "From each according to his abilities, to each according to his needs!" This, too, is a patterned theory. It determines who should receive what by considering who has what abilities and needs. Note that Marx's theory has something in common with Aristotle's; both agree that responsibilities are functions of ability. Aristotle, however, believes that rewards should also be proportionate to ability; Marx believes that they should go to those in need, regardless of merit or contribution.

John Rawls offers another development of Rousseau's approach. Imagine being in the state of nature, choosing whether or not to submit to a government. To determine principles of justice, Rawls says, we must imagine that we make the choice based not on any contingent features of our own characters, but on the basis of what we share with all other human beings. Rawls thus imagines us making the choice from behind the *veil of ignorance,* in which we know everything we need to know about economics, political science, sociology, and so on, but know nothing about our own position in the social structure. What principles, Rawls asks, would we choose from behind the veil of ignorance? What institutions would be rational choices? He concludes that we would choose to minimize risk and so opt for a system that would make the least well off in society as well off as possible; that is, we would choose to maximize the welfare of the least advantaged. We would not choose to maximize good overall, as a utilitarian would, for we would fear coming out a loser in the social order. We would not choose absolute equality, for we have no reason to object to inequality as long as it does not disadvantage us, no matter where we might end up in the resulting society. Rawls thus advocates two principles of justice. The first is a principle of liberty, that each person should have the most liberty compatible with an equal liberty for all. The second has two parts: (a) inequalities should be to everyone's advantage (that is, those who receive less would be even worse off if others weren't receiving more) and (b) the positions to which benefits attach should be open to everyone. Part (a) is often called the *difference principle;* part (b) is a principle of equal opportunity. The difference principle has stirred by far the most controversy concerning Rawls's theory.

Rawls's approach to distributive justice is an end-state theory. We determine whether a set of institutions is just by looking at the distribution they produce—not now, perhaps, but at some point in the future when the distribution stabilizes. John Locke and Robert Nozick offer a very different theory of justice. How do we determine whether people hold their possessions justly? Locke and Nozick deny that any sort of structural account can provide an answer. Do you, for example, possess this book justly? To answer that question, in their view, we need to ask not about your abilities or your needs or your total wealth or whether your possession of the book benefits everyone, but about how you obtained it. Did you steal it? Did you buy it from someone who had the right to sell it? Locke takes property as a fundamental natural and civil right. The purpose of government, Locke insists, is to preserve property. Consequently, government cannot consider every good in society its own and reflect abstractly on how to distribute it. People acquire goods justly from nature. They buy and sell them justly. When an injustice occurs, they try to compensate for it. To determine whether a distribution is just, according to Locke and Nozick, we must see how it came about. Were the initial acquisitions just? Were subsequent transfers just? Were any injustices sufficiently rectified? If we can answer yes to these questions, then, Locke and Nozick believe, the distribution is just. Their theories are thus *historical* theories: whether a distribution is just depends on how it came about.

ARISTOTLE

from *Nicomachean Ethics*

(Source: Aristotle's Nichomachean Ethics, *translated by W. D. Ross [1925], by permission of Oxford University Press. Notes have been omitted, and punctuation has been modernized for clarity.)*

BOOK V

2

Distributive Justice

. . . Of particular justice and that which is just in the corresponding sense, (A) one kind is that which is manifested in distributions of honour or money or the other things that fall to be divided among those who have a share in the constitution (for in these it is possible for one man to have a share either unequal or equal to that of another), and (B) one is that which plays a rectifying part in transactions between man and man. Of this there are two divisions; of transactions (1) some are voluntary and (2) others involuntary—voluntary such transactions as sale, purchase, loan for consumption, pledging, loan for use, depositing, letting (they are called voluntary because the origin of these transactions is voluntary), while of the involuntary (a) some are clandestine, such as theft, adultery, poisoning, procuring, enticement of slaves, assassination, false witness, and (b) others are violent, such as assault, imprisonment, murder, robbery with violence, mutilation, abuse, insult.

3

Merit

(A) We have shown that both the unjust man and the unjust act are unfair or unequal; now it is clear that there is also an intermediate between the two unequals involved in either case. And this is the equal; for in any kind of action in which there is a more and a less, there is also what is equal. If, then, the unjust is unequal, the just is equal, as all men suppose it to be, even apart from argument. And since the equal is intermediate, the just will be an intermediate. Now equality implies at least two things. The just, then, must be both intermediate and equal and relative (i.e., for certain persons). And *qua* intermediate it must be between certain things (which are respectively greater and less); *qua* equal, it involves *two* things; *qua* just, it is for certain people. The just, therefore, involves at least four terms; for the persons for whom it is in fact just are two, and the things in which it is manifested, the objects distributed, are two. And the same equality will exist between the persons and between the things concerned; for as the latter—the things concerned—are related, so are the former; if they are not equal, they will not have what is equal, but this is the origin of quarrels and complaints—when either equals have and are awarded unequal shares, or unequals equal shares. Further, this is plain from the fact that awards should be "according to merit"; for all men agree that what is just in distribution must be according to merit in some sense, though they do not all specify the same sort of merit, but democrats identify it with the status of freeman, supporters of oligarchy with wealth (or with noble birth), and supporters of aristocracy with excellence.

The just, then, is a species of the proportionate (proportion being not a property only of the kind of number which consists of abstract units, but of number in general). For proportion is equality of ratios, and involves four terms at least (that discrete proportion involves four terms is plain, but so does continuous proportion, for it uses one term as two and mentions it twice; e.g., "as the line A is to the line B, so is the line B to the line C"; the line B, then, has been mentioned twice, so that if the line B be assumed twice, the proportional terms will be four); and the just, too, involves at least four terms, and the ratio between one pair is the same as that between the other pair; for there is a similar distinction between the persons and between the things. As the term A, then, is to B, so will C be to D, and therefore, *alternando,* as A is to C, B will be to D. Therefore also the whole is in the same ratio to the whole; and this coupling the distribution effects, and, if the terms are so combined, effects justly. The conjunction, then, of the term A with C and of B with D is what is just in distribution, and this species of the just is intermediate, and the unjust is what violates the proportion; for the proportional is intermediate, and the just is proportional. (Mathematicians call this kind of proportion geometrical; for it is in geometrical proportion that it follows that the whole is to the whole as either part is to the corresponding part.) This proportion is not continuous; for we cannot get a single term standing for a person and a thing.

This, then, is what the just is—the proportional; the unjust is what violates the proportion. Hence one term becomes too great, the other too small, as indeed happens in practice; for the man who acts unjustly has too much, and the man who is unjustly treated too little, of what is good. In the case of evil the reverse is true; for the lesser evil is reckoned a good in comparison with the greater evil, since the lesser evil is rather to be chosen than the greater, and what is worthy of choice is good, and what is worthier of choice a greater good. . . .

QUESTIONS FOR REFLECTION

1. How does Aristotle argue for his assertion that justice is equality?
2. What is merit? Which interpretations of it does he discuss?
3. What particular kinds of justice does Aristotle discuss? Explain each.
4. According to Aristotle's theory of distributive justice, the just is the proportional. What does this mean? What should be proportional to what?
5. Suppose that the good in question is political power. To what sense of merit is that good relevant? What would be a reasonable account of that sort of merit—a kind Aristotle calls political virtue?
6. Apply Aristotle's theory to the assignment of grades in a college course. Who should get the best grades, and why?
7. Apply Aristotle's theory to university admissions. Who should be accepted, and why? To what extent to current admissions policies match Aristotle's theory? Where do they diverge?
8. Apply Aristotle's theory to hiring at a private company. What are some common ways in which hiring decisions could count as unjust by Aristotle's criterion?

ARISTOTLE

from *Politics*

(Source: The Works of Aristotle, *Vol. X [Oxford: Clarendon Press, 1921], translated by Benjamin Jowett. Notes have been omitted, and punctuation has been modernized for clarity.)*

BOOK III

Section 12

Justice and Equality

In all sciences and arts the end is a good, and the greatest good and in the highest degree a good in the most authoritative of all—this is the political science of which the good is justice, in other words, the common interest. All men think justice to be a sort of equality; and to a certain extent they agree in the philosophical distinctions which have been laid down by us about Ethics. For they admit that justice is a thing and has a relation to persons, and that equals ought to have equality. But there still remains a question: equality or inequality of what? Here is a difficulty which calls for political speculation. For very likely some persons will say that offices of state ought to be unequally distributed according to superior excellence, in whatever respect, of the citizen, although there is no other difference between him and the rest of the community; for that those who differ in any one respect have different rights and claims. But, surely, if this is true, the complexion or height of a man, or any other advantage, will be a reason for his obtaining a greater share of political rights.

Merit

The error here lies upon the surface, and may be illustrated from the other arts and sciences. When a number of flute-players are equal in their art, there is no reason why those of them who are better born should have better flutes given to them; for they will not play any better on the flute, and the superior instrument should be reserved for him who is the superior artist. If what I am saying is still obscure, it will be made clearer as we proceed. For if there were a superior flute-player who was far inferior in birth and beauty, although either of these may be a greater good than the art of flute-playing, and may excel flute-playing in a greater ratio than he excels the others in his art, still he ought to have the best flutes given to him, unless the advantages of wealth and birth contribute to excellence in flute-playing, which they do not.

Commensurability

Moreover, upon this principle any good may be compared with any other. For if a given height may be measured against wealth and against freedom, height in general may be so measured. Thus if A excels in height more than B in virtue, even if virtue in general excels height still more, all goods will be commensurable; for if a certain amount is better than some other, it is clear that some other will be equal. But since no such comparison can be made, it is evident that there is good reason why in politics men do not ground their claim to office on every sort of inequality any more than in the arts. For if some be slow, and others swift, that is no reason why the one should have little and the others much; it is in gymnastic contests that such excellence is rewarded. Whereas the rival claims of candidates for office can only be based on the possession of elements which enter into the composition of a state. And therefore the noble, or freeborn, or rich, may with good reason claim office; for holders of offices must be freemen and taxpayers: a state can be no more composed entirely of poor men than entirely of slaves. But if wealth and freedom are necessary elements, justice and valor are equally so; for without the former qualities a state cannot exist at all, without the latter not well. . . .

QUESTIONS FOR REFLECTION

1. What is merit, according to Aristotle?
2. Aristotle denies that "any good may be compared with any other." Why? What is the significance of his denial?

JOHN LOCKE

from *Second Treatise of Government* (1690)

(Source: Reprinted from John Locke, Two Treatises of Government. *London: Printed for Awnsham Churchill, 1690. Spelling and punctuation have been modernized for clarity.)*

CHAPTER V / OF PROPERTY

§. 25. Whether we consider natural reason, which tells us that men, being once born, have a right to their preservation and consequently to meat and drink and such other things as nature affords for their subsistence, or revelation, which gives us an account of those grants God made of the world to Adam and to Noah and his sons, it is very clear that God, as King David says, Psal. cxv. 16., has given the earth to the children of men: given it to mankind in common. But this being supposed, it seems to some a very great difficulty how anyone should ever come to have a property in any thing: I will not content myself to answer that if it be difficult to make out property upon a supposition that God gave the world to Adam and his posterity in common, it is impossible that any man, but one universal monarch, should have any property upon a supposition that God gave the world to Adam and his heirs in succession, exclusive of all the rest of his posterity. But I shall endeavour to show how men might come to have a property in several parts of that which God gave to mankind in common, and that without any express compact of all the commoners.

§. 26. God, who has given the world to men in common, has also given them reason to make use of it to the best advantage of life and convenience. The earth and all that is therein is given to men for the support and comfort of their being. And though all the fruits it naturally produces and beasts it feeds belong to mankind in common, as they are produced by the spontaneous hand of nature, and nobody has originally a private dominion exclusive of the rest of mankind, in any of them, as they are thus in their natural state; yet being given for the use of men, there must of necessity be a means to appropriate them some way or other before they can be of any use or at all beneficial to any particular man. The fruit or venison which nourishes the wild Indian, who knows no inclosure and is still a tenant in common, must be his, and so his, *i.e.*, a part of him, that another can no longer have any right to it before it can do him any good for the support of his life.

Labor

§. 27. Though the earth and all inferior creatures be common to all men, yet every man has a property in his own person: this no body has any right to but himself. The labor of his body and the work of his hands, we may say, are properly his. Whatsoever then he removes out of the state that nature has provided, and left in it, he has mixed his labor with and joined to it something that is his own and thereby makes it his property. It being by him removed from the common state nature has placed it in, it has by this labor something annexed to it that excludes the common right of other men: for this labor being the unquestionable property of the laborer, no man but he can have a right to what that is once joined to, at least where there is enough, and as good, left in common for others.

§. 28. He that is nourished by the acorns he picked up under an oak or the apples he gathered from the trees in the wood has certainly appropriated them to himself. Nobody can deny but the nourishment is his. I ask then, when did they begin to be his? When he digested? Or when he ate? Or when he boiled? Or when he brought them home? Or when he picked them up? And it is plain, if the first gathering made them not his, nothing else could. That labor put a distinction between them and common: that added something to them more than nature, the common mother of all, had done; and so they became his private right. And will anyone say he had no right to those acorns or apples he thus appropriated, because he had not the consent of all mankind to make them his? Was it a robbery thus to assume to himself what belonged to all in common? If such a consent as that was necessary, man had starved, notwithstanding the plenty God had given him. We see in commons, which remain so by compact, that it is the taking any part of what is common and removing it out of the state nature leaves it in, which begins the property, without which the common is of no use. And the taking of this or that part does not depend on the express consent of all the commoners. Thus the grass my horse has bit, the turfs my servant has cut, and the ore I have digged in any place where I have a right to them in common with others became my property, without the assignation or consent of any body. The labor that was mine, removing them out of that common state they were in, has fixed my property to them.

§. 29. By making an explicit consent of every commoner necessary to anyone's appropriating to himself any part of what is given in common, children or servants could not cut the meat which their father or master had provided for them in common without assigning to everyone his peculiar part. Though the water running in the fountain be everyone's, yet who can doubt but that in the pitcher is his only who drew it out? His labor has taken it out of the hands of nature, where it was common and belonged equally to all her children, and has thereby appropriated it to himself.

§. 30. Thus this law of reason makes the deer that Indian's who has killed it; it is allowed to be his goods, who has bestowed his labor upon it, though before it was the common right of everyone. And amongst those who are counted the civilized part of mankind, who have made and multiplied positive laws to determine property, this original law of nature, for the beginning of property, in what was before common, still takes place; and by virtue thereof, what fish anyone catches in the ocean, that great and still remaining common of mankind, or what ambergris anyone takes up here, is by the labor that removes it out of that common state nature left it in made his property, who takes that pains about it. And even amongst us, the hare that anyone is hunting is thought his who pursues her during the chase: for being a beast that is still looked upon as common and no man's private possession, whoever has employed so much labor about any of that kind as to find and pursue her has thereby removed her from the state of nature, wherein she was common, and has begun a property.

Provisos

§. 31. It will perhaps be objected to this, that if gathering the acorns, or other fruits of the earth, etc., makes a right to them, then any one may ingross as much as he will. To which I answer, Not so. The same law of nature that does by this means give us property does also bound that property too. *God has given us all things richly,* 1 Tim. vi. 12., is the voice of reason confirmed by inspiration. But how far has he given it us? To enjoy. As much as anyone can make use of to any advantage of life before it spoils, so much he may by his labor fix a property in: whatever is beyond this is more than his share and belongs to others. Nothing was made by God for man to spoil or destroy. And thus, considering the plenty of natural provisions there was a long time in the world and the few spenders and to how small a part of that provision the industry of one man could extend itself and ingross it to the prejudice of others, especially keeping within the bounds, set by reason, of what might serve for his use, there could be then little room for quarrels or contentions about property so established.

§. 32. But the chief matter of property being now not the fruits of the earth and the beasts that subsist on it, but the earth itself, as that which takes in and carries with it all the rest; I think it is plain that property in that too is acquired as the former. As much land as a man tills, plants, improves, cultivates, and can use the product of, so much is his property. He by his labor does, as it were, enclose it from the common. Nor will it invalidate his right to say everybody else has an equal title to it and therefore he cannot appropriate, he cannot enclose, without the consent of all his fellow-commoners, all mankind. God, when he gave the world in common to all mankind, commanded man also to labor, and the penury of his condition required it of him. God and his reason commanded him to subdue the earth, *i.e.*, improve it for the benefit of life, and therein lay out something upon it that was his own, his labor. He that in obedience to this command of God, subdued, tilled and sowed any part of it thereby annexed to it something that was his property, which another had no title to nor could without injury take from him.

§. 33. Nor was this appropriation of any parcel of land, by improving it, any prejudice to any other man, since there was still enough and as good left; and more than the yet unprovided could use. So that, in effect, there was never the less left for others because of his enclosure for himself: for he that leaves as much as another can make use of does as good as take nothing at all. Nobody could think himself injured by the drinking of another man, though he took a good draught, who had a whole river of the same water left him to quench his thirst; and the case of land and water, where there is enough of both, is perfectly the same. . . .

Benefits to Others

§. 37. This is certain, that in the beginning, before the desire of having more than man needed had altered the intrinsic value of things, which depends only on their usefulness to the life of man or had agreed that a little piece of yellow metal which would keep without wasting or decay should be worth a great piece of flesh or a whole heap of corn; though men had a right to appropriate by their labor each one of himself as much of the things of nature as he could use, yet this could not be much, nor to the prejudice of others, where the same plenty was still left to those who would use the same industry. To which let me add, that he who appropriates land to himself by his labor does not lessen, but increases the common stock of mankind; for the provisions serving to the support of human life produced by one acre of enclosed and cultivated land are (to speak much within compass) ten times more than those which are yielded by an acre of land of an equal richness lying waste in common. And therefore he that encloses land and has a greater plenty of the conveniencies of life from ten acres than he could have from a hundred left to nature may truly be said to give ninety acres to mankind: for his labor now supplies him with provisions out of ten acres which were but the product of a hundred lying in common. I have here rated the improved land very low in making its product but as ten to one, when it is much nearer a hundred to one; for I ask whether in the wild woods and uncultivated waste of America, left to nature, without any improvement, tillage or husbandry, a thousand acres yield the needy and wretched inhabitants as many conveniencies of life as ten acres of equally fertile land do in Devonshire, where they are well cultivated?

Before the appropriation of land, he who gathered as much of the wild fruit, killed, caught, or tamed as many of the beasts as he could; he that so employed his pains about any of the spontaneous products of nature as any way to alter them from the state which nature put them in, by placing any of his labor on them, did thereby acquire a propriety in them: but if they perished in his possession, without their due use; if the fruits rotted or the venison putrified before he could spend it, he offended against the common law of nature and was liable to be punished; he invaded his neighbour's share, for he had no right farther than his use called for any of them, and they might serve to afford him conveniencies of life. . . .

Money

§. 44. From all which it is evident that though the things of nature are given in common, yet man, by being master of himself, and proprietor of his own person and the actions or labor of it had still in himself the great foundation of property; and that which made up the great part of what he applied to the support or comfort of his being, when invention and arts had improved the conveniencies of life, was perfectly his own and did not belong in common to others. . . .

§. 46. The greatest part of things really useful to the life of man, and such as the necessity of subsisting made the first commoners of the world look after, as it does the Americans now, are generally things of short duration such as, if they are not consumed by use, will decay and perish of themselves; gold, silver and diamonds are things that fancy or agreement has put the value on, more than real use and the necessary support of life. Now of those good things which nature has provided in common, everyone had a right (as has been said) to as much as he could use, and property in all that he could effect with his labor; all that his industry could extend to, to alter from the state nature had put in it, was his. He that gathered a hundred bushels of acorns or apples had thereby a property in them; they were his goods as soon as gathered. He was only to look that he used them before they spoiled, else he took more than his share and robbed others. And indeed it was a foolish thing, as well as dishonest, to hoard up more than he could make use of. If he gave away a part to any body else, so that it perished not uselessly in his possession, these he also made use of. And if he also bartered away plums that would have rotted in a week for nuts that would last good for his eating a whole year, he did no injury; he wasted not the common stock, destroyed no part of the portion of goods that belonged to others, so long as nothing perished uselessly in his hands. Again, if he would give his nuts for a piece of metal, pleased with its colour; or exchange his sheep for shells, or wool for a sparkling pebble or a diamond, and keep those by him all his life, he invaded not the right of others; he might heap up as much of these durable things as he pleased, the exceeding of the bounds of his just property not lying in the largeness of his possession, but the perishing of any thing uselessly in it.

§. 47. And thus came in the use of money, some lasting thing that men might keep without spoiling and that by mutual consent men would take in exchange for the truly useful but perishable supports of life.

§. 48. And as different degrees of industry were apt to give men possessions in different proportions, so this invention of money gave them the opportunity to continue and enlarge them: for supposing an island, separate from all possible commerce with the rest of the world, wherein there were but a hundred families, but there were sheep, horses and cows, with other useful animals, wholesome fruits, and land enough for corn for a hundred thousand times as many, but nothing in the island, either because of its commonness or perishableness fit to supply the place of money; what reason could any one have there to enlarge his possessions beyond the use of his family and a plentiful supply to its consumption, either in what their own industry produced or they could barter for like perishable, useful commodities with others? Where there is not something both lasting and scarce and so valuable to be hoarded up, there men will not be apt to enlarge their possessions of land, were it never so rich, never so free for them to take: for I ask, what would a man value ten thousand or a hundred thousand acres of excellent land, ready cultivated and well stocked too with cattle, in the middle of the inland parts of America, where he had no hopes of commerce with other parts of the world, to draw money to him by the sale of the product? It would not be worth the enclosing, and we should see him give up again to the wild common of nature whatever was more than would supply the conveniencies of life to be had there for him and his family.

Inequality

§. 49. Thus in the beginning all the world was America, and more so than that is now; for no such thing as money was any where known. Find out something that has the use and value of money amongst his neighbors; you shall see the same man will begin presently to enlarge his possessions.

§. 50. But since gold and silver, being little useful to the life of man in proportion to food, raiment, and carriage, has its value only from the consent of men, whereof labor yet makes in great part the measure, it is plain that men have agreed to a disproportionate and unequal possession of the earth, they having by a tacit and voluntary consent found out a way how a man may fairly possess more land than he himself can use the product of, by receiving in exchange for the over-plus gold and silver which may be hoarded up without injury to anyone, these metals not spoiling or decaying in the hands of the possessor. This partage of things in an inequality of private possessions, men have made practicable out of the bounds of society, and without compact, only by putting a value on gold and silver and tacitly agreeing in the use of money; for in governments, the laws regulate the right of property, and the possession of land is determined by positive constitutions.

§. 51. And thus, I think, it is very easy to conceive, without any difficulty, how labor could at first begin a title of property in the common things of nature and how the spending it upon our uses bounded it. So that there could then be no reason of quarreling about title nor any doubt about the largeness of possession it gave. Right and convenience went together; for as a man had a right to all he could employ his labor upon, so he had no temptation to labor for more than he could make use of. This left no room for controversy about the title, nor for encroachment on the right of others; what portion a man carved to himself was easily seen; and it was useless, as well as dishonest, to carve himself too much or take more than he needed.

CHAPTER VIII / OF THE BEGINNING OF POLITICAL SOCIETIES

Consent

§. 95. Men being, as has been said, by nature all free, equal, and independent, no one can be put out of this estate and subjected to the political power of another without his own consent. The only way whereby any one divests himself of his natural liberty and puts on the bonds of civil society is by agreeing with other men to join and unite into a community for their comfortable, safe, and peaceable living one amongst another, in a secure enjoyment of their properties and a greater security against any that are not of it. This any number of men may do, because it injures not the freedom of the rest; they are left as they were in the liberty of the state of nature. When any number of men have so consented to make one community or government, they are thereby presently incorporated and make one body politic, wherein the majority have a right to act and conclude the rest.

Majority

§. 96. For when any number of men have, by the consent of every individual, made a community, they have thereby made that community one body, with a power to act as one body, which is only by the will and determination of the majority: for that which acts any community, being only the consent of the individuals of it, and it being necessary to that which is one body to move one way, it is necessary the body should move that way whither the greater force carries it, which is the consent of the majority; or else it is impossible it should act or continue one body, one community, which the consent of every individual that united into it agreed that it should; and so everyone is bound by that consent to be concluded by the majority. And therefore we see that in assemblies empowered to act by positive laws, where no number is set by that positive law which empowers them, the act of the majority passes for the act of the whole and of course determines as having, by the law of nature and reason, the power of the whole.

§. 97. And thus every man, by consenting with others to make one body politic under one government, puts himself under an obligation to everyone of that society to submit to the determination of the majority and to be concluded by it; or else this original compact, whereby he with others incorporated into one society, would signify nothing and be no compact if he be left free and under no other ties than he was in before in the state of nature. For what appearance would there be of any compact? what new engagement if he were no farther tied by any decrees of the society than he himself thought fit and did actually consent to? This would be still as great a liberty as he himself had before his compact, or anyone else in the state of nature has, who may submit himself and consent to any acts of it if he thinks fit.

§. 98. For if the consent of the majority shall not, in reason, be received as the act of the whole and conclude every individual, nothing but the consent of every individual can make anything to be the act of the whole: but such a consent is next to impossible ever to be had, if we consider the infirmities of health and avocations of business, which in a number, though much less than that of a commonwealth, will necessarily keep many away from the public assembly. To which if we add the variety of opinions and contrariety of interest which unavoidably happen in all collections of men, the coming into society upon such terms would be only like Cato's coming into the theatre only to go out again. Such a constitution as this would make the mighty Leviathan of a shorter duration than the feeblest creatures and not let it outlast the day it was born in, which cannot be supposed until we can think that rational creatures should desire and constitute societies only to be dissolved, for where the majority cannot conclude the rest, there they cannot act as one body and consequently will be immediately dissolved again.

§. 99. Whosoever therefore out of a state of nature unite into a community must be understood to give up all the power necessary to the ends for which they unite into society to the majority of the community, unless they expressly agreed in any number greater than the majority. And this is done by barely agreeing to unite into one political society, which is all the compact that is, or needs be, between the individuals that enter into or make up a commonwealth. And thus that which begins and actually constitutes any political society is nothing but the consent of any number of freemen capable of a majority to unite and incorporate into such a society. And this is that, and that only, which did or could give beginning to any lawful government in the world. . . .

CHAPTER IX / OF THE ENDS OF POLITICAL SOCIETY AND GOVERNMENT

§. 123. If man in the state of nature be so free, as has been said; if he be absolute lord of his own person and possessions, equal to the greatest and subject to nobody, why will he part with his freedom? why will he give up this empire and subject himself to the dominion and control of any other power? To which it is obvious to answer that though in the state of nature he hath such a right, yet the enjoyment of it is very uncertain and constantly exposed to the invasion of others; for all being kings as much as he, every man his equal, and the greater part no strict observers of equity and justice, the enjoyment of the property he has in this state is very unsafe, very unsecure. This makes him willing to quit a condition which, however free, is full of fears and continual dangers; and it is not without reason that he seeks out and is willing to join in society with others who are already united, or have a mind to unite, for the mutual preservation of their lives, liberties and estates, which I call by the general name *property*.

§. 124. The great and chief end, therefore, of men's uniting into commonwealths, and putting themselves under government is the preservation of their property. To which in the state of nature there are many things wanting.

First, there wants an established, settled, known law, received and allowed by common consent to be the standard of right and wrong, and the common measure to decide all controversies between them; for though the law of nature be plain and intelligible to all rational creatures, yet men being biased by their interest, as well as ignorant for want of study of it, are not apt to allow of it as a law binding to them in the application of it to their particular cases.

§. 125. *Secondly,* in the state of nature there wants a known and indifferent judge with authority to determine all differences according to the established law; for everyone in that state being both judge and executioner of the law of nature, men being partial to themselves, passion and revenge is very apt to carry them too far and with too much heat in their own cases, as well as negligence and unconcernedness to make them too remiss in other men's.

§. 126. *Thirdly,* in the state of nature there often wants power to back and support the sentence when right and to give it due execution. They who by any injustice offended will seldom fail where they are able by force to make good their injustice; such resistance many times makes the punishment dangerous and frequently destructive to those who attempt it.

§. 127. Thus mankind, notwithstanding all the privileges of the state of nature, being but in an ill condition while they remain in it, are quickly driven into society. Hence it comes to pass that we seldom find any number of men live any time together in this state. The inconveniences that they are therein exposed to by the irregular and uncertain exercise of the power every man has of punishing the transgressions of others make them take sanctuary under the established laws of government and therein seek the preservation of their property. It is this makes them so willingly give up every one his single power of punishing, to be exercised by such alone as shall be appointed to it amongst them and by such rules as the community, or those authorized by them to that purpose, shall agree on. And in this we have the original right and rise of both the legislative and executive power, as well as of the governments and societies themselves.

Natural Rights

§. 128. For in the state of nature, to omit the liberty he has of innocent delights, a man has two powers.

The first is to do whatsoever he thinks fit for the preservation of himself and others within the permission of the law of nature, by which law, common to them all, he and all the rest of mankind are one community, make up one society, distinct from all other creatures. And were it not for the corruption and viciousness of degenerate men, there would be no need of any other, no necessity that men should separate from this great and natural community and by positive agreements combine into smaller and divided associations.

The other power a man has in the state of nature is the power to punish the crimes committed against that law. Both these he gives up when he joins in a private, if I may so call it, or particular politic society and incorporates into any commonwealth separate from the rest of mankind.

§. 129. The first power, *viz.*, of doing whatsoever he thought for the preservation of himself and the rest of mankind, he gives up to be regulated by laws made by the society, so far forth as the preservation of himself and the rest of that society shall require; which laws of the society in many things confine the liberty he had by the law of nature.

§. 130. Secondly, the power of punishing he wholly gives up and engages his natural force (which he might before employ in the execution of the law of nature, by his own single authority, as he thought fit) to assist the executive power of the society, as the law thereof shall require; for being now in a new state, wherein he is to enjoy many conveniencies from the labor, assistance, and society of others in the same community, as well as protection from its whole strength, he is to part also with as much of his natural liberty in providing for himself as the good, prosperity, and safety of the society shall require; which is not only necessary, but just, since the other members of the society do the like.

Limits of Government

§. 131. But though men, when they enter into society, give up the equality, liberty, and executive power they had in the state of nature, into the hands of the society to be so far disposed of by the legislative as the good of the society shall require, yet, it being only with an intention in everyone the better to preserve himself, his liberty and property (for no rational creature can be supposed to change his condition with an intention to be worse), the power of the society, or legislative constituted by them, can never be supposed to extend farther than the common good but is obliged to secure everyone's property by providing against those three defects above mentioned that made the state of nature so unsafe and uneasy. And so whoever has the legislative or supreme power of any commonwealth is bound to govern by established standing laws promulgated and known to the people, and not by extemporary decrees; by indifferent and upright judges, who are to decide controversies by those laws and to employ the force of the community at home only in the execution of such laws or abroad to prevent or redress foreign injuries and secure the community from inroads and invasion. And all this to be directed to no other end but the peace, safety, and public good of the people.

CHAPTER XI / OF THE EXTENT OF THE LEGISLATIVE POWER

§. 134. The great end of men's entering into society, being the enjoyment of their properties in peace and safety, and the great instrument and means of that being the laws established in that society, the first and fundamental positive law of all commonwealths is the establishing of the legislative power; as the first and fundamental natural law, which is to govern even the legislative itself, is the preservation of the society and (as far as will consist with the public good) of every person in it. This legislative is not only the supreme power of the commonwealth, but sacred and unalterable in the hands where the community have once placed it; nor can any edict of anybody else, in what form soever conceived or by what power soever backed, have the force and obligation of a law which has not its sanction from that legislative which the public has chosen and appointed; for without this the law could not have that which is absolutely necessary to its being a law, the consent of the society, over whom no body can have a power to make laws but by their own consent and by authority received from them; and therefore all the obedience, which by the most solemn ties anyone can be obliged to pay, ultimately terminates in this supreme power and is directed by those laws which it enacts; nor can any oaths to any foreign power whatsoever or any domestic subordinate power discharge any member of the society from his obedience to the legislative acting pursuant to their trust, nor oblige him to any obedience contrary to the laws so enacted or farther than they do allow, it being ridiculous to imagine one can be tied ultimately to obey any power in the society which is not the supreme.

Arbitrary Power

§. 135. Though the legislative, whether placed in one or more, whether it be always in being or only by intervals, though it be the supreme power in every commonwealth; yet,

First, it is not nor can possibly be absolutely arbitrary over the lives and fortunes of the people; for it being but the joint power of every member of the society given up to that person, or assembly which is legislator, it can be no more than those persons had in a state of nature before they entered into society and gave up to the community; for nobody can transfer to another more power than he has in himself, and nobody has an absolute arbitrary power over himself or over any other to destroy his own life or take away the life or property of another. A man, as has been proved, cannot subject himself to the arbitrary power of another; and having in the state of nature no arbitrary power over the life, liberty, or possession of another, but only so much as the law of nature gave him for the preservation of himself and the rest of mankind, this is all he does, or can give up to the commonwealth, and by it to the legislative power, so that the legislative can have no more than this. Their power, in the utmost bounds of it, is limited to the public good of the society. It is a power that has no other end but preservation and therefore can never have a right to destroy, enslave, or designedly to impoverish the subjects. The obligations of the law of nature cease not in society, but only in many cases are drawn closer and have by human laws known penalties annexed to them to enforce their observation. Thus the law of nature stands as an eternal rule to all men, legislators as well as others. The rules that they make for other men's actions, must, as well as their own and other men's actions, be conformable to the law of nature, *i.e.,* to the will of God, of which that is a declaration, and the fundamental law of nature being the preservation of mankind, no human sanction can be good or valid against it.

The Rule of Law

§. 136. *Secondly,* the legislative, or supreme authority, cannot assume to itself a power to rule by extemporary arbitrary decrees, but is bound to dispense justice and decide the rights of the subject by promulgated standing laws and known authorized judges; for the law of nature being unwritten and so nowhere to be found but in the minds of men, they who through passion or interest shall miscite or misapply it cannot so easily be convinced of their mistake where there is no established judge; and so it serves not, as it ought, to determine the rights and fence the properties of those that live under it, especially where everyone is judge, interpreter, and executioner of it too, and that in his own case; and he that has right on his side, having ordinarily but his own single strength, has not force enough to defend himself from injuries or to punish delinquents. To avoid these inconveniences, which disorder men's properties in the state of nature, men unite into societies that they may have the united strength of the whole society to secure and defend their properties and may have standing rules to bound it, by which everyone may know what is his. To this end it is that men give up all their natural power to the society which they enter into, and the community put the legislative power into such hands as they think fit, with this trust, that they shall be governed by declared laws, or else their peace, quiet, and property will still be at the same uncertainty as it was in the state of nature.

§. 137. Absolute arbitrary power, or governing without settled standing laws, can neither of them consist with the ends of society and government, which men would not quit the freedom of the state of nature for, and tie themselves up under, were it not to preserve their lives, liberties and fortunes, and by stated rules of right and property to secure their peace and quiet. It cannot be supposed that they should intend, had they a power so to do, to give to anyone, or more, an absolute arbitrary power over their persons and estates and put a force into the magistrate's hand to execute his unlimited will arbitrarily upon them. This were to put themselves into a worse condition than the state of nature, wherein they had a liberty to defend their right against the injuries of others and were upon equal terms of force to maintain it, whether invaded by a single man or many in combination. Whereas by supposing they have given up themselves to the absolute arbitrary power and will of a legislator, they have disarmed themselves and armed him to make a prey of them when he pleases; he being in a much worse condition, who is exposed to the arbitrary power of one man who has the command of 100,000, than he that is exposed to the arbitrary power of 100,000 single men; nobody being secure, that his will, who has such a command, is better than that of other men, though his force be 100,000 times stronger. And therefore, whatever form the commonwealth is under, the ruling power ought to govern by declared and received laws, and not by extemporary dictates and undetermined resolutions: for then mankind will be in a far worse condition than in the state of nature, if they shall have armed one, or a few men with the joint power of a multitude, to force them to obey at pleasure the exorbitant and unlimited decrees of their sudden thoughts or unrestrained, and until that moment unknown wills, without having any measures set down which may guide and justify their actions; for all the power the government has, being only for the good of the society, as it ought not to be arbitrary and at pleasure, so it ought to be exercised by established and promulgated laws that both the people may know their duty and be safe and secure within the limits of the law and the rulers too kept within their bounds and not be tempted by the power they have in their hands to employ it to such purposes and by such measures as they would not have known and own not willingly.

Consent

§. 138. *Thirdly,* the supreme power cannot take from any man any part of his property without his own consent; for the preservation of property being the end of government and that for which men enter into society, it necessarily supposes and requires that the people should have property, without which they must be supposed to lose that, by entering into society, which was the end for which they entered into it; too gross an absurdity for any man to own. Men therefore in society having property, they have such a right to the goods which by the law of the community are theirs, that nobody has a right to take their substance or any part of it from them without their own consent: without this they have no property at all; for I have truly no property in that which another can by right take from me when he pleases against my consent. Hence it is a mistake to think that the supreme or legislative power of any commonwealth can do what it will and dispose of the estates of the subject arbitrarily or take any part of them at pleasure. This is not much to be feared in governments where the legislative consists, wholly or in part, in assemblies which are variable, whose members upon the dissolution of the assembly are subjects under the common laws of their country equally with the rest. But in governments, where the legislative is in one lasting assembly always in being, or in one man, as in absolute monarchies, there is danger still that they will think themselves to have a distinct interest from the rest of the community and so will be apt to increase their own riches and power by taking what they think fit from the people; for a man's property is not at all secure, though there be good and equitable laws to set the bounds of it between him and his fellow subjects, if he who commands those subjects have power to take from any private man what part he pleases of his property and use and dispose of it as he thinks good.

§. 139. But government, into whatsoever hands it is put, being, as I have before shown, entrusted with this condition and for this end, that men might have and secure their properties, the prince or senate, however it may have power to make laws for the regulating of property between the subjects one amongst another, yet can never have a power to take to themselves the whole or any part of the subjects' property without their own consent: for this would be in effect to leave them no property at all. And to let us see that even absolute power, where it is necessary, is not arbitrary by being absolute but is still limited by that reason and confined to those ends which required it in some cases to be absolute, we need look no farther than the common practice of martial discipline: for the preservation of the army, and in it of the whole commonwealth, requires an absolute obedience to the command of every superior officer, and it is justly death to disobey or dispute the most dangerous or unreasonable of them; but yet we see that neither the sergeant that could command a soldier to march up to the mouth of a cannon or stand in a breach where he is almost sure to perish can command that soldier to give him one penny of his money; nor the general that can condemn him to death for deserting his post or for not obeying the most desperate orders can yet, with all his absolute power of life and death, dispose of one farthing of that soldier's estate or seize one jot of his goods, whom yet he can command anything, and hang for the least disobedience; because such a blind obedience is necessary to that end for which the commander has his power, *viz.*, the preservation of the rest, but the disposing of his goods has nothing to do with it.

§. 140. It is true, governments cannot be supported without great charge, and it is fit everyone who enjoys his share of the protection should pay out of his estate his proportion for the maintenance of it. But still it must be with his own consent, *i.e.*, the consent of the majority, giving it either by themselves or their representatives chosen by them; for if any one shall claim a power to lay and levy taxes on the people by his own authority and without such consent of the people, he thereby invades the fundamental law of property and subverts the end of government: for what property have I in that which another may be right to take when he pleases to himself?

Delegation

§. 141. *Fourthly,* the legislative cannot transfer the power of making laws to any other hands, for it being but a delegated power from the people, they who have it cannot pass it over to others. The people alone can appoint the form of the commonwealth, which is by constituting the legislative and appointing in whose hands that shall be. And when the people have said, We will submit to rules and be governed by laws made by such men and in such forms, nobody else can say other men shall make laws for them; nor can the people be bound by any laws but such as are enacted by those whom they have chosen and authorized to make laws for them. The power of the legislative, being derived from the people by a positive voluntary grant and institution, can be no other than what that positive grant conveyed, which being only to make laws and not to make legislators, the legislative can have no power to transfer their authority to making laws and place it in other hands.

The Bounds of Government

§. 142. These are the bounds which the trust that is put in them by the society and the law of God and nature have set to the legislative power of every commonwealth, in all forms of government.

First, they are to govern by promulgated established laws, not to be varied in particular cases, but to have one rule for rich and poor, for the favourite at court, and the country man at plough.

Secondly, these laws also ought to be designed for no other end ultimately but the good of the people.

Thirdly, they must not raise taxes on the property of the people without the consent of the people, given by themselves or their deputies. And this properly concerns only such governments where the legislative is always in being, or at least where the people have not reserved any part of the legislative to deputies, to be from time to time chosen by themselves.

Fourthly, the legislative neither must nor can transfer the power of making laws to any body else or place it anywhere but where the people have.

QUESTIONS FOR REFLECTION

1. Locke takes the right to property as natural. Why? What allows me to appropriate things I find in nature? Are there limits to my right of appropriation?
2. What, for Locke, justifies allowing a person to appropriate more than he or she needs?
3. How does money affect principles of property, in Locke's view?
4. What, for Locke, is the chief end of government? How does this end limit government action?
5. Why, according to Locke, is the minority bound to follow the majority's decision?
6. Robert Nozick criticizes Locke's view that I make something mine by mixing my labor with it. If I pour my bottle of tomato juice into the sea, mixing my property with it, I do not thereby own the sea; I lose my tomato juice. So why should mixing my labor with something make it mine?
7. Nozick continues: Even if mixing my labor with something gives me some right to it, why should I own the whole object rather than just the value I have added to it? How might Locke respond?
8. In what sense have you consented to the laws of the nation in which you live?
9. Can hypothetical consent create obligations? Surely I don't owe the bank money because I would have taken out a mortgage on a house I might have bought but didn't. So, why do I owe anyone anything because I would have consented to the social contract?
10. Some Lockeans rely on the idea of tacit consent—I have tacitly consented to the laws by remaining where I am. Can that tacit consent be withdrawn? If so, how?

JEAN-JACQUES ROUSSEAU

from *Discourse on the Origin of Inequality*

(*Source:* The Social Contract and Discourses, *translated by G. D. H. Cole. London: J. M. Dent & Sons, Ltd., 1913.*)

THE SECOND PART

Property

The first man who, having enclosed a piece of ground, bethought himself of saying *This is mine,* and found people simple enough to believe him, was the real founder of civil society. From how many crimes, wars and murders, from how many horrors and misfortunes might not any one have saved mankind, by pulling up the stakes, or filling up the ditch, and crying to his fellows, "Beware of listening to this impostor; you are undone if you once forget that the fruits of the earth belong to us all, and the earth itself to nobody." But there is great probability that things had then already come to such a pitch, that they could no longer continue as they were; for the idea of property depends on many prior ideas, which could only be acquired successively, and cannot have been formed all at once in the human mind. Mankind must have made very considerable progress, and acquired considerable knowledge and industry which they must also have transmitted and increased from age to age, before they arrived at this last point of the state of nature. Let us then go farther back, and endeavour to unify under a single point of view that slow succession of events and discoveries in the most natural order.

The State of Nature

Man's first feeling was that of his own existence, and his first care that of self-preservation. The produce of the earth furnished him with all he needed, and instinct told him how to use it. Hunger and other appetites made him at various times experience various modes of existence; and among these was one which urged him to propagate his species—a blind propensity that, having nothing to do with the heart, produced a merely animal act. The want once gratified, the two sexes knew each other no more; and even the offspring was nothing to its mother, as soon as it could do without her. . . .

Other men, it is true, were not then to him what they now are to us, and he had no greater intercourse with them than with other animals; yet they were not neglected in his observations. The conformities, which he would in time discover between them, and between himself and his female, led him to judge of others which were not then perceptible; and finding that they all behaved as he himself would have done in like circumstances, he naturally inferred that their manner of thinking and acting was altogether in conformity with his own. This important truth, once deeply impressed on his mind, must have induced him, from an intuitive feeling more certain and much more rapid than any kind of reasoning, to pursue the rules of conduct, which he had best observe towards them, for his own security and advantage.

Taught by experience that the love of well-being is the sole motive of human actions, he found himself in a position to distinguish the few cases, in which mutual interest might justify him in relying upon the assistance of his fellows; and also the still fewer cases in which a conflict of interests might give cause to suspect them. In the former case, he joined in the same herd with them, or at most in some kind of loose association, that laid no restraint on its members, and lasted no longer than the transitory occasion that formed it. In the latter case, every one sought his own private advantage, either by open force, if he thought himself strong enough, or by address and cunning, if he felt himself the weaker. . . .

Society

As ideas and feelings succeeded one another, and heart and head were brought into play, men continued to lay aside their original wildness; their private connections became every day more intimate as their limits extended. They accustomed themselves to assemble before their huts round a large tree; singing and dancing, the true offspring of love and leisure, became the amusement, or rather the occupation, of men and women thus assembled together with nothing else to do. Each one began to consider the rest, and to wish to be considered in turn; and thus a value came to be attached to public esteem. Whoever sang or danced best, whoever was the handsomest, the strongest, the most dexterous, or the most eloquent, came to be of most consideration; and this was the first step towards inequality, and at the same time towards vice. From these first distinctions arose on the one side vanity and contempt and on the other shame and envy: and the fermentation caused by these new leavens ended by producing combinations fatal to innocence and happiness.

Injury

As soon as men began to value one another, and the idea of consideration had got a footing in the mind, every one put in his claim to it, and it became impossible to refuse it to any with impunity. Hence arose the first obligations of civility even among savages; and every intended injury became an affront; because, besides the hurt which might result from it, the party injured was certain to find in it a contempt for his person, which was often more insupportable than the hurt itself.

Thus, as every man punished the contempt shown him by others, in proportion to his opinion of himself, revenge became terrible, and men bloody and cruel. This is precisely the state reached by most of the savage nations known to us: and it is for want of having made a proper distinction in our ideas, and seen how very far they already are from the state of nature, that so many writers have hastily concluded that man is naturally cruel, and requires civil institutions to make him more mild; whereas nothing is more gentle than man in his primitive state, as he is placed by nature at an equal distance from the stupidity of brutes, and the fatal ingenuity of civilised man. Equally confined by instinct and reason to the sole care of guarding himself against the mischiefs which threaten him, he is restrained by natural compassion from doing any injury to others, and is not led to do such a thing even in return for injuries received. For, according to the axiom of the wise Locke, *There can be no injury, where there is no property.*

Morality

But it must be remarked that the society thus formed, and the relations thus established among men, required of them qualities different from those which they possessed from their primitive constitution. Morality began to appear in human actions, and every one, before the institution of law, was the only judge and avenger of the injuries done him, so that the goodness which was suitable in the pure state of nature was no longer proper in the newborn state of society. Punishments had to be made more severe, as opportunities of offending became more frequent, and the dread of vengeance had to take the place of the rigour of the law. Thus, though men had become less patient, and their natural compassion had already suffered some diminution, this period of expansion of the human faculties, keeping a just mean between the indolence of the primitive state and the petulant activity of our egoism, must have been the happiest and most stable of epochs.

The more we reflect on it, the more we shall find that this state was the least subject to revolutions, and altogether the very best man could experience; so that he can have departed from it only through some fatal accident, which, for the public good, should never have happened. The example of savages, most of whom have been found in this state, seems to prove that men were meant to remain in it, that it is the real youth of the world, and that all subsequent advances have been apparently so many steps towards the perfection of the individual, but in reality towards the decrepitude of the species.

So long as men remained content with their rustic huts, so long as they were satisfied with clothes made of the skins of animals and sewn together with thorns and fishbones, adorned themselves only with feathers and shells, and continued to paint their bodies different colours, to improve and beautify their bows and arrows and to make with sharp-edged stones fishing boats or clumsy musical instruments; in a word, so long as they undertook only what a single person could accomplish, and confined themselves to such arts as did not require the joint labor of several hands, they lived free, healthy, honest and happy lives, so long as their nature allowed, and as they continued to enjoy the pleasures of mutual and independent intercourse. But from the moment one man began to stand in need of the help of another; from the moment it appeared advantageous to any one man to have enough provisions for two, equality disappeared, property was introduced, work became indispensable, and vast forests became smiling fields, which man had to water with the sweat of his brow, and where slavery and misery were soon seen to germinate and grow up with the crops.

Civilization

Metallurgy and agriculture were the two arts which produced this great revolution. The poets tell us it was gold and silver, but, for the philosophers, it was iron and corn, which first civilised men, and ruined humanity. Thus both were unknown to the savages of America, who for that reason are still savage: the other nations also seem to have continued in a state of barbarism while they practised only one of these arts. One of the best reasons, perhaps, why Europe has been, if not longer, at least more constantly and highly civilised than the rest of the world, is that it is at once the most abundant in iron and the most fertile in corn. . . .

Justice

The cultivation of the earth necessarily brought about its distribution; and property, once recognised, gave rise to the first rules of justice; for, to secure each man his own, it had to be possible for each to have something. Besides, as men began to look forward to the future, and all had something to lose, every one had reason to apprehend that reprisals would follow any injury he might do to another. This origin is so much the more natural, as it is impossible to conceive how property can come from anything but manual labor: for what else can a man add to things which he does not originally create, so as to make them his own property? It is the husbandman's labor alone that, giving him a title to the produce of the ground he has tilled, gives him a claim also to the land itself, at least till harvest; and so, from year to year, a constant possession which is easily transformed into property. When the ancients, says Grotius, gave to Ceres* the title of Legislatrix, and to a festival celebrated in her honour the name of Thesmophoria, they meant by that that the distribution of lands had produced a new kind of right: that is to say, the right of property, which is different from the right deducible from the law of nature.

In this state of affairs, equality might have been sustained, had the talents of individuals been equal, and had, for example, the use of iron and the consumption of commodities always exactly balanced each other; but, as there was nothing to preserve this balance, it was soon disturbed; the strongest did most work; the most skilful turned his labor to best account; the most ingenious devised methods of diminishing his labor: the husbandman wanted more iron, or the smith more corn, and, while both labored equally, the one gained a great deal by his work, while the other could hardly support himself. Thus natural inequality unfolds itself insensibly with that of combination, and the difference between

*Ceres was the goddess of agriculture.—Ed.

men, developed by their different circumstances, becomes more sensible and permanent in its effects, and begins to have an influence, in the same proportion, over the lot of individuals.

Hypocrisy

Matters once at this pitch, it is easy to imagine the rest. I shall not detain the reader with a description of the successive invention of other arts, the development of language, the trial and utilisation of talents, the inequality of fortunes, the use and abuse of riches, and all the details connected with them which the reader can easily supply for himself. I shall confine myself to a glance at mankind in this new situation.

Behold then all human faculties developed, memory and imagination in full play, egoism interested, reason active, and the mind almost at the highest point of its perfection. Behold all the natural qualities in action, the rank and condition of every man assigned him; not merely his share of property and his power to serve or injure others, but also his wit, beauty, strength or skill, merit or talents: and these being the only qualities capable of commanding respect, it soon became necessary to possess or to affect them.

It now became the interest of men to appear what they really were not. To be and to seem became two totally different things; and from this distinction sprang insolent pomp and cheating trickery, with all the numerous vices that go in their train. On the other hand, free and independent as men were before, they were now, in consequence of a multiplicity of new wants, brought into subjection, as it were, to all nature, and particularly to one another; and each became in some degree a slave even in becoming the master of other men: if rich, they stood in need of the services of others; if poor, of their assistance; and even a middle condition did not enable them to do without one another. Man must now, therefore, have been perpetually employed in getting others to interest themselves in his lot, and in making them, apparently at least, if not really, find their advantage in promoting his own. Thus he must have been sly and artful in his behaviour to some, and imperious and cruel to others; being under a kind of necessity to ill use all the persons of whom he stood in need, when he could not frighten them into compliance, and did not judge it his interest to be useful to them. Insatiable ambition, the thirst of raising their respective fortunes, not so much from real want as from the desire to surpass others, inspired all men with a vile propensity to injure one another, and with a secret jealousy, which is the more dangerous, as it puts on the mask of benevolence, to carry its point with greater security. In a word, there arose rivalry and competition on the one hand, and conflicting interests on the other, together with a secret desire on both of profiting at the expense of others. All these evils were the first effects of property, and the inseparable attendants of growing inequality.

Rich and Poor

Before the invention of signs to represent riches, wealth could hardly consist in anything but lands and cattle, the only real possessions men can have. But, when inheritances so increased in number and extent as to occupy the whole of the land, and to border on one another, one man could aggrandise himself only at the expense of another; at the same time the supernumeraries, who had been too weak or too indolent to make such acquisitions, and had grown poor without sustaining any loss, because, while they saw everything change around them, they remained still the same, were obliged to receive their subsistence, or steal it, from the rich; and this soon bred, according to their different characters, dominion and slavery, or violence and rapine. The wealthy, on their part, had no sooner begun to taste the pleasure of command, than they disdained all others, and, using their old slaves to acquire new, thought of nothing but subduing and enslaving their neighbours; like ravenous wolves, which, having once tasted human flesh, despise every other food and thenceforth seek only men to devour.

Thus, as the most powerful or the most miserable considered their might or misery as a kind of right to the possessions of others, equivalent, in their opinion, to that of property, the destruction of equality was attended by the most terrible disorders. Usurpations by the rich, robbery by the poor, and the unbridled passions of both, suppressed the cries of natural compassion and the still feeble voice of justice, and filled men with avarice, ambition and vice. Between the title of the strongest and that of the first occupier, there arose perpetual conflicts, which never ended but in battles and bloodshed. The newborn state of society thus gave rise to a horrible state of war; men thus harassed and depraved were no longer capable of retracing their steps or renouncing the fatal acquisitions they had made, but, laboring by the abuse of the faculties which do them honor, merely to their own confusion, brought themselves to the brink of ruin.

*Attonitus novitate mali, divesque miserque, Effugere optat opes; et quæ modo voverat odit.**

Strong and Weak

It is impossible that men should not at length have reflected on so wretched a situation, and on the calamities that overwhelmed them. The rich, in particular, must have felt how much they suffered by a constant state of war, of which they bore all the expense, and in which, though all risked their lives, they alone risked their property. Besides, however speciously they might disguise their usurpations, they knew that they were founded on precarious and false titles; so that, if others took from them by force what they themselves had gained by force, they would have no reason to complain. Even those who had been enriched by their own industry, could hardly base their proprietorship on better claims. It was in vain to repeat, "I built this well; I gained this spot by my industry." Who gave you your standing, it might be answered, and what right have you to demand payment of us for doing what we never asked you to do? Do you not know that numbers of your fellow creatures are starving, for want of what you have too much of? You ought to have had the express and universal consent of mankind, before appropriating more of the common subsistence than you needed for your own maintenance. Destitute of valid reasons to justify and sufficient strength to defend himself, able to crush individuals with ease, but easily crushed himself by a troop of bandits, one against all, and incapable, on account of mutual jealousy, of joining with his equals against numerous enemies united by the common hope of plunder, the rich man, thus urged by necessity, conceived at length the profoundest plan that ever entered the mind of man: this was to employ in his favour the forces of those who attacked him, to make allies of his adversaries, to inspire them with different maxims, and to give them other institutions as favourable to himself as the law of nature was unfavourable.

With this view, after having represented to his neighbours the horror of a situation which armed every man against the rest, and made their possessions as burdensome to them as their wants, and in which no safety could be expected either in riches or in poverty, he readily devised plausible arguments to make them close with his design. "Let us join," said he, "to guard the weak from oppression, to restrain the ambitious, and secure to every man the possession of what belongs to him: let us institute rules of justice and peace, to which all without exception may be obliged to conform; rules that may in some measure make amends for the caprices of fortune, by subjecting equally the powerful and the weak to the observance of reciprocal obligations. Let us, in a word, instead of turning our forces against ourselves, collect them in a supreme power which may govern us by wise laws, protect and defend all the members of the association, repulse their common enemies, and maintain eternal harmony among us."

Far fewer words to this purpose would have been enough to impose on men so barbarous and easily seduced; especially as they had too many disputes among themselves to do without arbitrators, and too much ambition and avarice to go long without masters. All ran headlong to their chains, in hopes of securing their liberty; for they had just wit enough to perceive the advantages of political institutions, without experience enough to enable them to foresee the dangers. The most capable of foreseeing the dangers were the very persons who expected to benefit by them; and even the most prudent judged it not inexpedient to sacrifice one part of their freedom to ensure the rest; as a wounded man has his arm cut off to save the rest of his body.

*[Ovid, Metamorphoses xi, 127.

Both rich and poor, shocked at their new-found ills,
Would fly from wealth, and lose what they had sought.]

State of Nature among Nations

Such was, or may well have been, the origin of society and law, which bound new fetters on the poor, and gave new powers to the rich; which irretrievably destroyed natural liberty, eternally fixed the law of property and inequality, converted clever usurpation into unalterable right, and, for the advantage of a few ambitious individuals, subjected all mankind to perpetual labor, slavery and wretchedness. It is easy to see how the establishment of one community made that of all the rest necessary, and how, in order to make head against united forces, the rest of mankind had to unite in turn. Societies soon multiplied and spread over the face of the earth, till hardly a corner of the world was left in which a man could escape the yoke, and withdraw his head from beneath the sword which he saw perpetually hanging over him by a thread. Civil right having thus become the common rule among the members of each community, the law of nature maintained its place only between different communities, where, under the name of the right of nations, it was qualified by certain tacit conventions, in order to make commerce practicable, and serve as a substitute for natural compassion, which lost, when applied to societies, almost all the influence it had over individuals, and survived no longer except in some great cosmopolitan spirits, who, breaking down the imaginary barriers that separate different peoples, follow the example of our Sovereign Creator, and include the whole human race in their benevolence.

But bodies politic, remaining thus in a state of nature among themselves, presently experienced the inconveniences which had obliged individuals to forsake it; for this state became still more fatal to these great bodies than it had been to the individuals of whom they were composed. Hence arose national wars, battles, murders, and reprisals, which shock nature and outrage reason; together with all those horrible prejudices which class among the virtues the honor of shedding human blood. The most distinguished men hence learned to consider cutting each other's throats a duty; at length men massacred their fellow creatures by thousands without so much as knowing why, and committed more murders in a single day's fighting, and more violent outrages in the sack of a single town, than were committed in the state of nature during whole ages over the whole earth. Such were the first effects which we can see to have followed the division of mankind into different communities. . . .

Three Stages of Inequality

If we follow the progress of inequality in these various revolutions, we shall find that the establishment of laws and of the right of property was its first term, the institution of magistracy the second, and the conversion of legitimate into arbitrary power the third and last; so that the condition of rich and poor was authorized by the first period; that of powerful and weak by the second; and only by the third that of master and slave, which is the last degree of inequality, and the term at which all the rest remain, when they have got so far, till the government is either entirely dissolved by new revolutions, or brought back again to legitimacy.

To understand this progress as necessary we must consider not so much the motives for the establishment of the body politic, as the forms it assumes in actuality, and the faults that necessarily attend it: for the flaws which make social institutions necessary are the same as make the abuse of them unavoidable. . . .

Master and Slave

This is the last term of inequality, the extreme point that closes the circle, and meets that from which we set out. Here all private persons return to their first equality, because they are nothing; and, subjects having no law but the will of their master, and their master no restraint but his passions, all notions of good and all principles of equity again vanish. There is here a complete return to the law of the strongest, and so to a new state of nature, differing from that we set out from; for the one was a state of nature in its first purity, while this is the consequence of excessive corruption. There is so little difference between the two states in other respects, and the contract of government is so completely dissolved by despotism, that the despot is master only so long as he remains the strongest; as soon as he can be expelled, he has no right to complain of violence. The popular insurrection that ends in the death or deposition of a Sultan is as lawful an act as those by which he disposed, the day before, of the lives and fortunes of his subjects. As he was maintained by force alone, it is force alone that overthrows him. Thus everything takes place according to the natural order; and, whatever may be the result of such frequent and precipitate revolutions, no one man has reason to complain of the injustice of another, but only of his own ill fortune or indiscretion.

Human Nature

If the reader thus discovers and retraces the lost and forgotten road, by which man must have passed from the state of nature to the state of society; if he carefully restores, along with the intermediate situations which I have just described, those which want of time has compelled me to suppress, or my imagination has failed to suggest, he cannot fail to be struck by the vast distance which separates the two states. It is in tracing this slow succession that he will find the solution of a number of problems of politics and morals, which philosophers cannot settle. He will feel that, men being different in different ages, the reason why Diogenes could not find a man was that he sought among his contemporaries a man of an earlier period. He will see that Cato died with Rome and liberty, because he did not fit the age in which he lived; the greatest of men served only to astonish a world which he would certainly have ruled, had he lived five hundred years sooner. In a word, he will explain how the soul and the passions of men insensibly change their very nature; why our wants and pleasures in the end seek new objects; and why, the original man having vanished by degrees, society offers to us only an assembly of artificial men and factitious passions, which are the work of all these new relations, and without any real foundation in nature. We are taught nothing on this subject, by reflection, that is not entirely confirmed by observation. The savage and the civilized man differ so much in the bottom of their hearts and in their inclinations, that what constitutes the supreme happiness of one would reduce the other to despair. The former breathes only peace and liberty; he desires only to live and be free from labor; even the *ataraxia* of the Stoic falls far short of his profound indifference to every other object. Civilized man, on the other hand, is always moving, sweating, toiling and racking his brains to find still more laborious occupations: he goes on in drudgery to his last moment, and even seeks death to put himself in a position to live, or renounces life to acquire immortality. He pays his court to men in power, whom he hates, and to the wealthy, whom he despises; he stops at nothing to have the honour of serving them; he is not ashamed to value himself on his own meanness and their protection; and, proud of his slavery, he speaks with disdain of those, who have not the honor of sharing it. What a sight would the perplexing and envied labors of a European minister of State present to the eyes of a Carib[b]ean! How many cruel deaths would not this indolent savage prefer to the horrors of such a life, which is seldom even sweetened by the pleasure of doing good! But, for him to see into the motives of all this solicitude, the words *power* and *reputation,* would have to bear some meaning in his mind; he would have to know that there are men who set a value on the opinion of the rest of the world; who can be made happy and satisfied with themselves rather on the testimony of other people than on their own. In reality, the source of all these differences is, that the savage lives within himself, while social man lives constantly outside himself, and only knows how to live in the opinion of others, so that he seems to receive the consciousness of his own existence merely from the judgment of others concerning him. It is not to my present purpose to insist on the indifference to good and evil which arises from this disposition, in spite of our many fine works on morality, or to show how, everything being reduced to appearances, there is but art and mummery in even honor, friendship, virtue, and often vice itself, of which we at length learn the secret of boasting; to show, in short, how, always asking others what we are, and never daring to ask ourselves, in the midst of so much philosophy, humanity and civilisation, and of such sublime codes of morality, we have nothing to show for ourselves but a frivolous and deceitful appearance, honor without virtue, reason without wisdom, and pleasure without happiness. It is sufficient that I have proved that this is not by any means the original state of man, but that it is merely the spirit of society, and the inequality which society produces, that thus transform and alter all our natural inclinations.

Inequality

I have endeavoured to trace the origin and progress of inequality, and the institution and abuse of political societies, as far as these are capable of being deduced from the nature of man merely by the light of reason, and independently of those sacred dogmas which give the sanction of divine right to sovereign authority. It follows from this survey that, as there is hardly any inequality in the state of nature, all the inequality which now prevails owes its strength and growth to the development of our faculties and the advance of the human mind, and becomes at last permanent and legitimate by the establishment of property and laws. Secondly, it follows that moral inequality, authorised by positive right alone, clashes with natural right, whenever it is not proportionate to physical inequality; a distinction which sufficiently determines what we ought to think of that species of inequality which prevails in all civilised countries; since it is plainly contrary to the law of nature, however defined, that children should command old men, fools wise men, and that the privileged few should gorge themselves with superfluities, while the starving multitude are in want of the bare necessities of life.

QUESTIONS FOR REFLECTION

1. What is Rousseau's conception of the state of nature in the *Discourse on the Origin of Inequality?* Does it differ from that of *On the Social Contract?*
2. Why, in Rousseau's view, does property give rise to deception?
3. How does Rousseau criticize the right to property?
4. What stages of inequality does Rousseau discuss? What is the final stage?
5. A research question: Compare Rousseau's conception of the master-slave stage with Hegel's account of that relationship.
6. If the source of unjust inequality is private property, is the solution its abolition? Why, or why not?
7. All rights are civil rights, Rousseau contends, in the sense that they come from the state; there are no natural rights. How does he argue for that conclusion?
8. Locke insists that rights to life, health, liberty, and property are natural rights. Rousseau denies it. What practical difference does it make? What are three kinds of governmental action that Locke would prohibit but Rousseau would permit?

JEAN-JACQUES ROUSSEAU

from *On the Social Contract*

(*Source:* The Social Contract and Discourses, *translated by G. D. H. Cole. London: J. M. Dent & Sons, Ltd., 1913.*)

Book I

CHAPTER IX / REAL PROPERTY

Each member of the community gives himself to it, at the moment of its foundation, just as he is, with all the resources at his command, including the goods he possesses. This act does not make possession, in changing hands, change its nature, and become property in the hands of the Sovereign; but, as the forces of the city are incomparably greater than those of an individual, public possession is also, in fact, stronger and more irrevocable, without being any more legitimate, at any rate from the point of view of foreigners. For the State, in relation to its members, is master of all their goods by the social contract, which, within the State, is the basis of all rights; but, in relation to other powers, it is so only by the right of the first occupier, which it holds from its members.

The right of the first occupier, though more real than the right of the strongest, becomes a real right only when the right of property has already been established. Every man has naturally a right to everything he needs; but the positive act which makes him proprietor of one thing excludes him from everything else. Having his share, he ought to keep to it, and can have no further right against the community. This is why the right of the first occupier, which in the state of nature is so weak, claims the respect of every man in civil society. In this right we are respecting not so much what belongs to another as what does not belong to ourselves.

In general, to establish the right of the first occupier over a plot of ground, the following conditions are necessary: first, the land must not yet be inhabited; secondly, a man must occupy only the amount he needs for his subsistence; and, in the third place, possession must be taken, not by an empty ceremony, but by labour and cultivation, the only sign of proprietorship that should be respected by others, in default of a legal title. . . .

It may also happen that men begin to unite one with another before they possess anything, and that, subsequently occupying a tract of country which is enough for all, they enjoy it in common, or share it out among themselves, either equally or according to a scale fixed by the Sovereign. However the acquisition be made, the right which each individual has to his own estate is always subordinate to the right which the community has over all: without this, there would be neither stability in the social tie, nor real force in the exercise of Sovereignty.

I shall end this chapter and this book by remarking on a fact on which the whole social system should rest: *i.e.*, that, instead of destroying natural inequality, the fundamental compact substitutes, for such physical inequality as nature may have set up between men, an equality that is moral and legitimate, and that men, who may be unequal in strength or intelligence, become every one equal by convention and legal right.*

Book II

CHAPTER III / WHETHER THE GENERAL WILL IS FALLIBLE

It follows from what has gone before that the general will is always right and tends to the public advantage; but it does not follow that the deliberations of the people are always equally correct. Our will is always for our own good, but we do not always see what that is; the people is never corrupted, but it is often deceived, and on such occasions only does it seem to will what is bad.

There is often a great deal of difference between the will of all and the general will; the latter considers only the common interest, while the former takes private interest into account, and is no more than a sum of particular wills: but take away from these same wills the pluses and minuses that cancel one another, and the general will remains as the sum of the differences.

If, when the people, being furnished with adequate information, held its deliberations, the citizens had no communication one with another, the grand total of the small differences would always give the general will, and the decision would always be good. But when factions arise, and partial associations are formed at the expense of the great association, the will of each of these associations becomes general in relation to its members, while it remains particular in relation to the State: it may then be said that there are no longer as many votes as there are men, but only as many as there are associations. The differences become less numerous and give a less general result. Lastly, when one of these associations is so great as to prevail over all the rest, the result is no longer a sum of small differences, but a single difference; in this case there is no longer a general will, and the opinion which prevails is purely particular.

It is therefore essential, if the general will is to be able to express itself, that there should be no partial society within the State, and that each citizen should think only his own thoughts. . . . But if there are partial societies, it is best to have as many as possible and to prevent them from being unequal. . . . These precautions are the only ones that can guarantee that the general will shall be always enlightened, and that the people shall in no way deceive itself.

CHAPTER IV / THE LIMITS OF THE SOVEREIGN POWER

If the State is a moral person whose life is in the union of its members, and if the most important of its cares is the care for its own preservation, it must have a universal and compelling force, in order to move and dispose each part as may be most advantageous to the whole. As nature gives each man absolute power over all his members, the social compact gives the body politic absolute power over all its members also; and it is this power which, under the direction of the general will, bears, as I have said, the name of Sovereignty. . . .

Each man alienates, I admit, by the social compact, only such part of his powers, goods and liberty as it is important for the community to control; but it must also be granted that the Sovereign is sole judge of what is important.

Every service a citizen can render the State he ought to render as soon as the Sovereign demands it; but the Sovereign, for its part, cannot impose upon its subjects any fetters that are useless to the community, nor can it even wish to do so; for no more by the law of reason than by the law of nature can anything occur without a cause.

The undertakings which bind us to the social body are obligatory only because they are mutual; and their nature is such that in fulfilling them we cannot work for others without working for ourselves. Why is it that the general will is always in the right, and that all continually will the happiness of each one, unless it is because there is not a man who does not think of "each" as meaning him, and consider himself in voting for all? This proves that equality of rights and the idea of justice which such equality creates originate in the preference each man gives to himself, and accordingly in the very nature of man. . . .

*Under bad governments, this equality is only apparent and illusory: it serves only to keep the pauper in his poverty and the rich man in the position he has usurped. In fact, laws are always of use to those who possess and harmful to those who have nothing: from which it follows that the social state is advantageous to men only when all have something and none too much.

It should be seen from the foregoing that what makes the will general is less the number of voters than the common interest uniting them; for, under this system, each necessarily submits to the conditions he imposes on others: and this admirable agreement between interest and justice gives to the common deliberations an equitable character which at once vanishes when any particular question is discussed, in the absence of a common interest to unite and identify the ruling of the judge with that of the party.

From whatever side we approach our principle, we reach the same conclusion, that the social compact sets up among the citizens an equality of such a kind, that they all bind themselves to observe the same conditions and should therefore all enjoy the same rights. Thus, from the very nature of the compact, every act of Sovereignty, *i.e.*, every authentic act of the general will, binds or favors all the citizens equally; so that the Sovereign recognizes only the body of the nation, and draws no distinctions between those of whom it is made up. What, then, strictly speaking, is an act of Sovereignty? It is not a convention between a superior and an inferior, but a convention between the body and each of its members. It is legitimate, because based on the social contract, and equitable, because common to all; useful, because it can have no other object than the general good, and stable, because guaranteed by the public force and the supreme power. So long as the subjects have to submit only to conventions of this sort, they obey no one but their own will; and to ask how far the respective rights of the Sovereign and the citizens extend, is to ask up to what point the latter can enter into undertakings with themselves, each with all, and all with each.

We can see from this that the sovereign power, absolute, sacred and inviolable as it is, does not and cannot exceed the limits of general conventions, and that every man may dispose at will of such goods and liberty as these conventions leave him; so that the Sovereign never has a right to lay more charges on one subject than on another, because, in that case, the question becomes particular, and ceases to be within its competency.

When these distinctions have once been admitted, it is seen to be so untrue that there is, in the social contract, any real renunciation on the part of the individuals, that the position in which they find themselves as a result of the contract is really preferable to that in which they were before. Instead of a renunciation, they have made an advantageous exchange: instead of an uncertain and precarious way of living they have got one that is better and more secure; instead of natural independence they have got liberty, instead of the power to harm others security for themselves, and instead of their strength, which others might overcome, a right which social union makes invincible. Their very life, which they have devoted to the State, is by it constantly protected; and when they risk it in the State's defence, what more are they doing than giving back what they have received from it? What are they doing that they would not do more often and with greater danger in the state of nature, in which they would inevitably have to fight battles at the peril of their lives in defence of that which is the means of their preservation? All have indeed to fight when their country needs them; but then no one has ever to fight for himself. Do we not gain something by running, on behalf of what gives us our security, only some of the risks we should have to run for ourselves, as soon as we lost it? . . .

CHAPTER XI / THE VARIOUS SYSTEMS OF LEGISLATION

If we ask in what precisely consists the greatest good of all, which should be the end of every system of legislation, we shall find it reduce itself to two main objects, liberty and equality—liberty, because all particular dependence means so much force taken from the body of the State, and equality, because liberty cannot exist without it.

I have already defined civil liberty; by equality, we should understand, not that the degrees of power and riches are to be absolutely identical for everybody; but that power shall never be great enough for violence, and shall always be exercised by virtue of rank and law; and that, in respect of riches, no citizen shall ever be wealthy enough to buy another, and none poor enough to be forced to sell himself:* which implies, on the part of the great, moderation in goods and position, and, on the side of the common sort, moderation in avarice and covetousness.

*If the object is to give the State consistency, bring the two extremes as near to each other as possible; allow neither rich men nor beggars. These two estates, which are naturally inseparable, are equally fatal to the common good; from the one come the friends of tyranny, and from the other tyrants. It is always between them that public liberty is put up to auction: the one buys, and the other sells.

Such equality, we are told, is an unpractical ideal that cannot actually exist. But if its abuse is inevitable, does it follow that we should not at least make regulations concerning it? It is precisely because the force of circumstances tends continually to destroy equality that the force of legislation should always tend to its maintenance. . . .

QUESTIONS FOR REFLECTION

1. What is Rousseau's conception of the state of nature in *On the Social Contract?* Does it differ from that of *Discourse on the Origin of Inequality?*
2. What principles of distributive justice does Rousseau advocate? Are they compatible with one another?
3. According to Rousseau, are there any limits on government power? If so, what are they?
4. Explain Rousseau's concept of the sovereign. What constraints must the sovereign obey?
5. What incentive to those who "gorge themselves on luxuries" have to enter into the social contract?
6. How does Rousseau argue for his position that everyone must have something to gain from the social contract?
7. In order that everyone gain from the social contract, Rousseau says, everyone should have something, and no one should have too much. The reason that everyone should have something is obvious. But why should no one have too much?
8. Francis Fukayama worries that Rousseau's state of nature assumes isolated individuals, to an even greater degree than that of Hobbes or Locke, for "not even the family is necessary for human sustenance or happiness." Is that a fair complaint? What effect does it have on Rousseau's theory?

KARL MARX AND FRIEDRICH ENGELS

from *Manifesto of the Communist Party* (1848)

Karl Marx (1818–1883) was born in Treves, in the German Rhineland, to a Jewish family that had converted to Lutheranism. He earned his doctorate at Jena in 1841 and edited a newspaper in Cologne. Friedrich Engels (1820–1895), born in Barmen, also in the Rhineland, was the son of a textile manufacturer. He worked for his father in a cotton mill in Manchester, England, as a clerk, manager, and part owner. He met Marx in Cologne in 1842 and again in Paris in 1844. In 1848, a year that brought revolution to Paris as well as to Berlin, Vienna, Venice, Milan, and Parma, they collaborated to write The Communist Manifesto.

Although a vision of justice lies behind much of their work, Marx and Engels wrote little about it. The Communist Manifesto *contains some of their most explicit comments about distributive justice and details the theory of class struggle. (Source: Karl Marx and Friedrich Engels,* Manifesto of the Communist Party, *New York: International Publishers, 1932.)*

I. Bourgeois and Proletarians*

Class Struggle

The history of all hitherto existing society is the history of class struggles.

Freeman and slave, patrician and plebeian, lord and serf, guild-master and journeyman, in a word, oppressor and oppressed, stood in constant opposition to one another, carried on an uninterrupted, now hidden, now open fight, a fight that each time ended, either in a revolutionary reconstitution of society at large, or in the common ruin of the contending classes. . . .

. . . Society as a whole is more and more splitting up into two great hostile camps, into two great classes directly facing each other: Bourgeoisie and Proletariat. . . .

The Bourgeoisie

The bourgeoisie, historically, has played a most revolutionary part.

The bourgeoisie, wherever it has got the upper hand, has put an end to all feudal, patriarchal, idyllic relations. It has pitilessly torn asunder the motley feudal ties that bound man to his "natural superiors," and has left remaining no other nexus between man and man than naked self-interest, than callous "cash payment." It has drowned the most heavenly

*By bourgeoisie is meant the class of modern Capitalists, owners of the means of social production and employers of wage-labor. By proletariat, the class of modern wage-laborers who, having no means of production of their own, are reduced to selling their labor-power in order to live.

ecstasies of religious fervour, of chivalrous enthusiasm, of philistine sentimentalism, in the icy water of egotistical calculation. It has resolved personal worth into exchange value, and in place of the numberless indefeasible chartered freedoms, has set up that single, unconscionable freedom—Free Trade. In one word, for exploitation, veiled by religious and political illusions, it has substituted naked, shameless, direct, brutal exploitation.

The bourgeoisie has stripped of its halo every occupation hitherto honoured and looked up to with reverent awe. It has converted the physician, the lawyer, the priest, the poet, the man of science, into its paid wage-laborers.

The bourgeoisie has torn away from the family its sentimental veil, and has reduced the family relation to a mere money relation. . . .

The bourgeoisie cannot exist without constantly revolutionising the instruments of production, and thereby the relations of production, and with them the whole relations of society. Conservation of the old modes of production in unaltered form, was, on the contrary, the first condition of existence for all earlier industrial classes. Constant revolutionising of production, uninterrupted disturbance of all social conditions, everlasting uncertainty and agitation distinguish the bourgeois epoch from all earlier ones. All fixed, fast-frozen relations, with their train of ancient and venerable prejudices and opinions, are swept away, all new-formed ones become antiquated before they can ossify. All that is solid melts into air, all that is holy is profaned, and man is at last compelled to face with sober senses, his real conditions of life, and his relations with his kind.

Civilization

The need of a constantly expanding market for its products chases the bourgeoisie over the whole surface of the globe. It must nestle everywhere, settle everywhere, establish connections everywhere.

The bourgeoisie has through its exploitation of the world-market given a cosmopolitan character to production and consumption in every country. To the great chagrin of Reactionists, it has drawn from under the feet of industry the national ground on which it stood. All old-established national industries have been destroyed or are daily being destroyed. They are dislodged by new industries, whose introduction becomes a life and death question for all civilized nations, by industries that no longer work up indigenous raw material, but raw material drawn from the remotest zones; industries whose products are consumed, not only at home, but in every quarter of the globe. In place of the old wants, satisfied by the productions of the country, we find new wants, requiring for their satisfaction the products of distant lands and climes. In place of the old local and national seclusion and self-sufficiency, we have intercourse in every direction, universal interdependence of nations. And as in material, so also in intellectual production. The intellectual creations of individual nations become common property. National one-sidedness and narrow-mindedness become more and more impossible, and from the numerous national and local literatures, there arises a world literature.

The bourgeoisie, by the rapid improvement of all instruments of production, by the immensely facilitated means of communication, draws all, even the most barbarian, nations into civilisation. The cheap prices of its commodities are the heavy artillery with which it batters down all Chinese walls, with which it forces the barbarians' intensely obstinate hatred of foreigners to capitulate. It compels all nations, on pain of extinction, to adopt the bourgeois mode of production; it compels them to introduce what it calls civilisation into their midst, *i.e.*, to become bourgeois themselves. In one word, it creates a world after its own image.

The bourgeoisie has subjected the country to the rule of the towns. It has created enormous cities, has greatly increased the urban population as compared with the rural, and has thus rescued a considerable part of the population from the idiocy of rural life. Just as it has made the country dependent on the towns, so it has made barbarian and semi-barbarian countries dependent on the civilised ones, nations of peasants on nations of bourgeois, the East on the West.

The bourgeoisie keeps more and more doing away with the scattered state of the population, of the means of production, and of property. It has agglomerated population, centralized means of production, and has concentrated property in a few hands. The necessary consequence of this was political centralization. Independent, or but loosely connected provinces, with separate interests, laws, government and systems of taxation, became lumped together into one nation, with one government, one code of laws, one national class-interest, one frontier and one customs-tariff. . . .

Industrial Society

. . . Modern bourgeois society with its relations of production, of exchange and of property, a society that has conjured up such gigantic means of production and of exchange, is like the sorcerer, who is no longer able to control the powers of the nether world whom he has called up by his spells. For many a decade past the history of industry and commerce is but the history of the revolt of modern productive forces against modern conditions of production, against the property relations that are the conditions for the existence of the bourgeoisie and of its rule. It is enough to mention the commercial crises that by their periodical return put on its trial, each time more threateningly, the existence of the entire bourgeois society. In these crises a great part not only of the existing products, but also of the previously created productive forces, are periodically destroyed. In these crises there breaks out an epidemic that, in all earlier epochs, would have seemed an absurdity—the epidemic of overproduction. Society suddenly finds itself put back into a state of momentary barbarism; it appears as if a famine, a universal war of devastation had cut off the supply of every means of subsistence; industry and commerce seem to be destroyed; and why? Because there is too much civilisation, too much means of subsistence, too much industry, too much commerce. The productive forces at the disposal of society no longer tend to further the development of the conditions of bourgeois property; on the contrary, they have become too powerful for these conditions, by which they are fettered, and so soon as they overcome these fetters, they bring disorder into the whole of bourgeois society, endanger the existence of bourgeois property. The conditions of bourgeois society are too narrow to comprise the wealth created by them. And how does the bourgeoisie get over these crises? On the one hand by enforced destruction of a mass of productive forces; on the other, by the conquest of new markets, and by the more thorough exploitation of the old ones. That is to say, by paving the way for more extensive and more destructive crises, and by diminishing the means whereby crises are prevented.

The weapons with which the bourgeoisie felled fuedalism to the ground are now turned against the bourgeoisie itself.

The Proletariat

But not only has the bourgeoisie forged the weapons that bring death to itself; it has also called into existence the men who are to wield those weapons—the modern working class—the proletarians.

In proportion as the bourgeoisie, *i.e.*, capital, is developed, in the same proportion is the proletariat, the modern working class, developed—a class of laborers, who live only so long as they find work, and who find work only so long as their labor increases capital. These laborers, who must sell themselves piecemeal, are a commodity, like every other article of commerce, and are consequently exposed to all the vicissitudes of competition, to all the fluctuations of the market.

Owing to the extensive use of machinery and to division of labor, the work of the proletarians has lost all individual character, and consequently, all charm for the workman. He becomes an appendage of the machine, and it is only the most simple, most monotonous, and most easily acquired knack, that is required of him. Hence, the cost of production of a workman is restricted, almost entirely, to the means of subsistence that he requires for his maintenance, and for the propagation of his race. But the price of a commodity, and therefore also of labor, is equal to its cost of production. In proportion, therefore, as the repulsiveness of the work increases, the wage decreases. Nay more, in proportion as the use of machinery and division of labor increases, in the same proportion the burden of toil also increases, whether by prolongation of the working hours, by increase of the work exacted in a given time or by increased speed of the machinery, etc.

Modern industry has converted the little workshop of the patriarchal master into the great factory of the industrial capitalist. Masses of laborers, crowded into the factory, are organised like soldiers. As privates of the industrial army they are placed under the command of a perfect hierarchy of officers and sergeants. Not only are they slaves of the bourgeois class, and of the bourgeois State; they are daily and hourly enslaved by the machine, by the over-looker, and, above all, by the individual bourgeois manufacturer himself. The more openly this despotism proclaims gain to be its end and aim, the more petty, the more hateful and the more embittering it is.

The less the skill and exertion of strength implied in manual labor, in other words, the more modern industry becomes developed, the more is the labor of men superseded by that of women. Differences of age and sex have no longer any distinctive social validity for the working class. All are instruments of labor, more or less expensive to use, according to their age and sex. . . .

Oppression

Hitherto, every form of society has been based, as we have already seen, on the antagonism of oppressing and oppressed classes. But in order to oppress a class, certain conditions must be assured to it under which it can, at least, continue its slavish existence. The serf, in the period of serfdom, raised himself to membership in the commune, just as the petty bourgeois, under the yoke of feudal absolutism, managed to develop into a bourgeois. The modern laborer, on the contrary, instead of rising with the progress of industry, sinks deeper and deeper below the conditions of existence of his own class. He becomes a pauper, and pauperism develops more rapidly than population and wealth. And here it becomes evident, that the bourgeoisie is unfit any longer to be the ruling class in society, and to impose its conditions of existence upon society as an overriding law. It is unfit to rule because it is incompetent to assure an existence to its slave within his slavery, because it cannot help letting him sink into such a state, that it has to feed him, instead of being fed by him. Society can no longer live under this bourgeoisie, in other words, its existence is no longer compatible with society.

The essential condition for the existence, and for the sway of the bourgeois class, is the formation and augmentation of capital; the condition for capital is wage-labor. Wage-labor rests exclusively on competition between the laborers. The advance of industry, whose involuntary promoter is the bourgeoisie, replaces the isolation of the laborers, due to competition, by their revolutionary combination, due to association. The development of Modern Industry, therefore, cuts from under its feet the very foundation on which the bourgeoisie produces and appropriates products. What the bourgeoisie, therefore, produces, above all, is its own grave-diggers. Its fall and the victory of the proletariat are equally inevitable.

II Proletarians and Communists

Private Property

The distinguishing feature of Communism is not the abolition of property generally, but the abolition of bourgeois property. But modern bourgeois private property is the final and most complete expression of the system of producing and appropriating products, that is based on class antagonisms, on the exploitation of the many by the few.

In this sense, the theory of the Communists may be summed up in the single sentence: Abolition of private property. . . .

You are horrified at our intending to do away with private property. But in your existing society, private property is already done away with for nine-tenths of the population; its existence for the few is solely due to its non-existence in the hands of those nine-tenths. You reproach us, therefore, with intending to do away with a form of property, the necessary condition for whose existence is the nonexistence of any property for the immense majority of society.

In one word, you reproach us with intending to do away with your property. Precisely so; that is just what we intend.

Individuality

From the moment when labor can no longer be converted into capital, money, or rent, into a social power capable of being monopolised, *i.e.*, from the moment when individual property can no longer be transformed into bourgeois property, into capital, from that moment, you say, individuality vanishes.

You must, therefore, confess that by "individual" you mean no other person than the bourgeois, than the middle-class owner of property. This person must, indeed, be swept out of the way, and made impossible.

Communism deprives no man of the power to appropriate the products of society; all that it does is to deprive him of the power to subjugate the labor of others by means of such appropriation.

Incentives

It has been objected that upon the abolition of private property all work will cease, and universal laziness will overtake us.

According to this, bourgeois society ought long ago to have gone to the dogs through sheer idleness; for those of its members who work, acquire nothing, and those who acquire anything, do not work. The whole of this objection is but another expression of the tautology: that there can no longer be any wage-labor when there is no longer any capital.

Culture

All objections urged against the Communistic mode of producing and appropriating material products, have, in the same way, been urged against the Communistic modes of producing and appropriating intellectual products. Just as, to the bourgeois, the disappearance of class property is the disappearance of production itself, so the disappearance of class culture is to him identical with the dissappearance of all culture.

That culture, the loss of which he laments, is, for the enormous majority, a mere training to act as a machine.

But don't wrangle with us so long as you apply, to our intended abolition of bourgeois property, the standard of your bourgeois notions of freedom, culture, law, etc. Your very ideas are but the outgrowth of the conditions of your bourgeois production and bourgeois property, just as your jurisprudence is but the will of your class made into a law for all, a will, whose essential character and direction are determined by the economical conditions of existence of your class. . . .

Does it require deep intuition to comprehend that man's ideas, views and conceptions, in one word, man's consciousness, changes with every change in the conditions of his material existence, in his social relations and in his social life?

What else does the history of ideas prove, than that intellectual production changes its character in proportion as material production is changed? The ruling ideas of each age have ever been the ideas of its ruling class. . . .

The Revolution

We have seen above, that the first step in the revolution by the working class, is to raise the proletariat to the position of ruling class, to win the battle of democracy.

The proletariat will use its political supremacy to wrest, by degrees, all capital from the bourgeoisie, to centralise all instruments of production in the hands of the State, *i.e.*, of the proletariat organized as the ruling class; and to increase the total of productive forces as rapidly as possible.

Of course, in the beginning, this cannot be effected except by means of despotic inroads on the rights of property, and on the conditions of bourgeois production; by means of measures, therefore, which appear economically insufficient and untenable, but which, in the course of the movement, outstrip themselves, necessitate further inroads upon the old social order, and are unavoidable as a means of entirely revolutionising the mode of production.

These measures will of course be different in different countries.

Nevertheless in the most advanced countries, the following will be pretty generally applicable.

1. Abolition of property in land and application of all rents of land to public purposes.
2. A heavy progressive or graduated income tax.
3. Abolition of all right of inheritance.
4. Confiscation of the property of all emigrants and rebels.
5. Centralisation of credit in the hands of the State, by means of a national bank with State capital and an exclusive monopoly.
6. Centralisation of the means of communication and transport in the hands of the State.
7. Extention of factories and instruments of production owned by the State; the bringing into cultivation of wastelands, and the improvement of the soil generally in accordance with a common plan.
8. Equal liability of all to labor. Establishment of industrial armies, especially for agriculture.

9. Combination of agriculture with manufacturing industries; gradual abolition of the distinction between town and country, by a more equable distribution of the population over the country.
10. Free education for all children in public schools. Abolition of children's factory labor in its present form. Combination of education with industrial production, etc., etc.

When, in the course of development, class distinctions have disappeared, and all production has been concentrated in the hands of a vast association of the whole nation, the public power will lose its political character. Political power, properly so called, is merely the organised power of one class for oppressing another. If the proletariat during its contest with the bourgeoisie is compelled, by the force of circumstances, to organise itself as a class, if, by means of a revolution, it makes itself the ruling class, and, as such, sweeps away by force the old conditions of production, then it will, along with these conditions, have swept away the conditions for the existence of class antagonisms and of classes generally, and will thereby have abolished its own supremacy as a class.

In place of the old bourgeois society, with its classes and class antagonisms, we shall have an association, in which the free development of each is the condition for the free development of all.

IV. Position of the Communists in Relation to the Various Existing Opposition Parties

. . . In short, the Communists everywhere support every revolutionary movement against the existing social and political order of things.

In all these movements they bring to the front, as the leading question in each, the property question, no matter what its degree of development at the time.

Finally, they labor everywhere for the union and agreement of the democratic parties of all countries.

The Communists disdain to conceal their views and aims. They openly declare that their ends can be attained only by the forcible overthrow of all existing social conditions. Let the ruling classes tremble at a Communistic revolution. The proletarians have nothing to lose but their chains. They have a world to win.

WORKING MEN OF ALL COUNTRIES, UNITE!

QUESTIONS FOR REFLECTION

1. What is the bourgeoisie? What is the proletariat?
2. Why, according to Marx and Engels, are the bourgeoisie and the proletariat in conflict?
3. What arguments do Marx and Engels advance for the abolition of private property? What objections might be raised against that program?
4. What practical measures do Marx and Engels advocate? How are these measures related to the primary aim of communism?
5. Bernard Henri-Levy has argued that Marxism is incompatible with political freedom; the Gulag is just as essential to communism, he has said, as Auschwitz was to Nazism. Is the *Communist Manifesto* incompatible with freedom?
6. Bertrand Russell writes, "Marx's doctrine that all historical events have been motivated by class conflicts is a rash and untrue extension to world history of certain features prominent in England and France a hundred years ago"—the conditions of the early industrial revolution. To what extent do class conflicts motivate events in contemporary America?
7. Ludwig von Mises complains that although Marx's fundamental concept is class conflict, Marx never defined "class" or explained what gave a class unity and distinguished it from others. Can you devise a definition? Under it, how many classes are there in contemporary American society?

KARL MARX

from *Estranged Labour, Economic and Philosophical Manuscripts of 1844*

(Source: From Economic and Philosophic Manuscripts of 1844 *[Moscow: Progress Publishers, 1932].)*

We have started out from the premises of political economy. We have accepted its language and its laws. We presupposed private property; the separation of labour, capital, and land, and likewise of wages, profit, and capital; the division of labour; competition; the conception of exchange value, etc. From political economy itself, using its own words, we have shown that the worker sinks to the level of a commodity, and moreover the most wretched commodity of all; that the misery of the worker is in inverse proportion to the power and volume of his production; that the necessary consequence of competition is the accumulation of capital in a few hands and hence the restoration of monopoly in a more terrible form; and that, finally, the distinction between capitalist and landlord, between agricultural worker and industrial worker, disappears and the whole of society must split into the two classes of property owners and propertyless workers. . . .

We now have to grasp the essential connection between private property, greed, the separation of labour, capital and landed property, exchange and competition, value and the devaluation of man, monopoly, and competition, etc.—the connection between this entire system of estrangement and the money system.

We must avoid repeating the mistake of the political economist, who bases his explanations on some imaginary primordial condition. Such a primordial condition explains nothing. It simply pushes the question into the grey and nebulous distance. It assumes as facts and events what it is supposed to deduce—namely, the necessary relationships between two things, between, for example, the division of labour and exchange. Similarly, theology explains the origin of evil by the fall of Man—i.e., it assumes as a fact in the form of history what it should explain.

We shall start out from an actual economic fact.

The worker becomes poorer the more wealth he produces, the more his production increases in power and extent. The worker becomes an ever cheaper commodity the more commodities he produces. The devaluation of the human world grows in direct proportion to the increase in value of the world of things. Labour not only produces commodities; it also produces itself and the workers as a commodity and it does so in the same proportion in which it produces commodities in general.

This fact simply means that the object that labour produces, its product, stands opposed to it as something alien, as a power independent of the producer. The product of labour is labour embodied and made material in an object, it is the objectification of labour. The realization of labour is its objectification. In the sphere of political economy, this realization of labour appears as a loss of reality for the worker, objectification as loss of and bondage to the object, and appropriation as estrangement, as alienation.

So much does the realization of labour appear as loss of reality that the worker loses his reality to the point of dying of starvation. So much does objectification appear as loss of the object that the worker is robbed of the objects he needs most not only for life but also for work. Work itself becomes an object which he can only obtain through an enormous effort and with spasmodic interruptions. So much does the appropriation of the object appear as estrangement that the more objects the worker produces, the fewer can he possess and the more he falls under the domination of his product, of capital.

All these consequences are contained in this characteristic, that the worker is related to the product of labour as to an alien object. For it is clear that, according to this premise, the more the worker exerts himself in his work, the more powerful the alien, objective world becomes which he brings into being over against himself, the poorer he and his inner world become, and the less they belong to him. It is the same in religion. The more man puts into God, the less he retains within himself. The worker places his life in the object; but now it no longer belongs to him, but to the object. The greater his activity, therefore, the fewer objects the worker possesses. What the product of his labour is, he is not. Therefore, the greater this product, the less is he himself. The externalisation of the worker in his product means not only that his labour becomes an object, an external existence, but that it exists outside him, independently of him and alien to him, and begins to confront him as an autonomous power; that the life which he has bestowed on the object confronts him as hostile and alien.

Let us now take a closer look at objectification, at the production of the worker, and the estrangement, the loss of the object, of his product, that this entails.

The workers can create nothing without nature, without the sensuous external world. It is the material in which his labour realizes itself, in which it is active and from which, and by means of which, it produces.

But just as nature provides labour with the means of life, in the sense of labour cannot live without objects on which to exercise itself, so also it provides the means of life in the narrower sense, namely the means of physical subsistence of the worker.

The more the worker appropriates the external world, sensuous nature, through his labour, the more he deprives himself of the means of life in two respects: firstly, the sensuous external world becomes less and less an object belonging to his labour, a means of life of his labour; and, secondly, it becomes less and less a means of life in the immediate sense, a means for the physical subsistence of the worker.

In these two respects, then, the worker becomes a slave of his object; firstly, in that he receives an object of labour, i.e., he receives work, and, secondly, in that he receives means of subsistence. Firstly, then, so that he can exist as a worker, and secondly as a physical subject. The culmination of this slavery is that it is only as a worker that he can maintain himself as a physical subject and only as a physical subject that he is a worker.

(The estrangement of the worker in his object is expressed according to the laws of political economy in the following way:

1. the more the worker produces, the less he has to consume;
2. the more value he creates, the more worthless he becomes;
3. the more his product is shaped, the more misshapen the worker;
4. the more civilized his object, the more barbarous the worker;
5. the more powerful the work, the more powerless the worker;
6. the more intelligent the work, the duller the worker and the more he becomes a slave of nature.)

Political economy conceals the estrangement in the nature of labour by ignoring the direct relationship between the worker (labour) and production. It is true that labour produces marvels for the rich, but it produces privation for the worker. It produces palaces, but hovels for the worker. It produces beauty, but deformity for the worker. It replaces labour by machines, but it casts some of the workers back into barbarous forms of labour and turns others into machines. It produces intelligence, but it produces idiocy and cretinism for the worker.

The direct relationship of labour to its products is the relationship of the worker to the objects of his production. The relationship of the rich man to the objects of production and to production itself is only a consequence of this first relationship, and confirms it. Later, we shall consider this second aspect. Therefore, when we ask what is the essential relationship of labour, we are asking about the relationship of the worker to production.

Up to now, we have considered the estrangement, the alienation of the worker, only from one aspect—i.e., the worker's relationship to the products of his labour. But estrangement manifests itself not only in the result, but also in the act of production, within the activity of production itself. How could the product of the worker's activity confront him as something alien if it were not for the fact that in the act of production he was estranging himself from himself? After all, the product is simply the résumé of the activity, of the production. So if the product of labour is alienation, production itself must be active alienation, the alienation of activity, the activity of alienation. The estrangement of the object of labour merely summarizes the estrangement, the alienation in the activity of labour itself.

What constitutes the alienation of labour?

Firstly, the fact that labour is external to the worker—i.e., does not belong to his essential being; that he, therefore, does not confirm himself in his work, but denies himself, feels miserable and not happy, does not develop free mental and physical energy, but mortifies his flesh and ruins his mind. Hence, the worker feels himself only when he is not working; when he is working, he does not feel himself. He is at home when he is not working, and not at home when he is working. His labour is, therefore, not voluntary but forced, it is forced labour. It is, therefore, not the satisfaction of a need but a mere means to satisfy needs outside itself. Its alien character is clearly demonstrated by the fact that as soon as no physical or other compulsion exists, it is shunned like the plague. External labour, labour in which man alienates himself, is a labour of self-sacrifice, of mortification. Finally, the external character of labour for the worker is demonstrated by the fact that it belongs not to him but to another, and that in it he belongs not to himself but to another. Just as in religion the spontaneous activity of the human imagination, the human brain, and the human heart, detaches itself from the individual and reappears as the alien activity of a god or of a devil, so the activity of the worker is not his own spontaneous activity. It belongs to another; it is a loss of his self.

The result is that man (the worker) feels that he is acting freely only in his animal functions—eating, drinking, and procreating, or at most in his dwelling and adornment—while in his human functions, he is nothing more than animal.

It is true that eating, drinking, and procreating, etc., are also genuine human functions. However, when abstracted from other aspects of human activity and turned into final and exclusive ends, they are animal.

We have considered the act of estrangement of practical human activity, of labour, from two aspects:

(1) the relationship of the worker to the product of labour as an alien object that has power over him. The relationship is, at the same time, the relationship to the sensuous external world, to natural objects, as an alien world confronting him, in hostile opposition.

(2) The relationship of labour to the act of production within labour. This relationship is the relationship of the worker to his own activity as something which is alien and does not belong to him, activity as passivity, power as impotence, procreation as emasculation, the worker's own physical and mental energy, his personal life—for what is life but activity?—as an activity directed against himself, which is independent of him and does not belong to him. Self-estrangement, as compared with the estrangement of the object mentioned above. . . .

Estranged labour not only (1), estranges nature from man and (2) estranges man from himself, from his own function, from his vital activity; because of this, it also estranges man from his species. It turns his species-life into a means for his individual life. Firstly, it estranges species-life and individual life, and, secondly, it turns the latter, in its abstract form, into the purpose of the former, also in its abstract and estranged form.

For in the first place labour, life activity, productive life itself, appears to man only as a means for the satisfaction of a need, the need to preserve physical existence. But productive life is species-life. It is life-producing life. The whole character of a species, its species-character, resides in the nature of its life activity, and free conscious activity constitutes the species-character of man. Life appears only as a means of life.

The animal is immediately one with its life activity. It is not distinct from that activity; it is that activity. Man makes his life activity itself an object of his will and consciousness. He has conscious life activity. It is not a determination with which he directly merges. Conscious life activity directly distinguishes man from animal life activity. Only because of that is he a species-being. Or, rather, he is a conscious being—i.e., his own life is an object for him, only because he is a species-being. Only because of that is his activity free activity. Estranged labour reverses the relationship so that man, just because he is a conscious being, makes his life activity, his essential being, a mere means for his existence. . . .

It is, therefore, in his fashioning of the objective that man really proves himself to be a species-being. Such production is his active species-life. Through it, nature appears as his work and his reality. The object of labour is, therefore, the objectification of the species-life of man: for man produces himself not only intellectually, in his consciousness, but actively and actually, and he can therefore contemplate himself in a world he himself has created. In tearing away the object of his production from man, estranged labour therefore tears away from him his species-life, his true species-objectivity, and transforms his advantage over animals into the disadvantage that his inorganic body, nature, is taken from him.

In the same way as estranged labour reduces spontaneous and free activity to a means, it makes man's species-life a means of his physical existence.

Consciousness, which man has from his species, is transformed through estrangement so that species-life becomes a means for him.

(3) Estranged labour, therefore, turns man's species-being—both nature and his intellectual species-power—into a being alien to him and a means of his individual existence. It estranges man from his own body, from nature as it exists outside him, from his spiritual essence, his human existence.

(4) An immediate consequence of man's estrangement from the product of his labour, his life activity, his species-being, is the estrangement of man from man. When man confronts himself, he also confronts other men. What is true of man's relationship to his labour, to the product of his labour, and to himself, is also true of his relationship to other men, and to the labour and the object of the labour of other men.

In general, the proposition that man is estranged from his species-being means that each man is estranged from the others and that all are estranged from man's essence.

Man's estrangement, like all relationships of man to himself, is realized and expressed only in man's relationship to other men.

In the relationship of estranged labour, each man therefore regards the other in accordance with the standard and the situation in which he as a worker finds himself.

We started out from an economic fact, the estrangement of the worker and of his production. We gave this fact conceptual form: estranged, alienated labour. We have analyzed this concept, and in so doing merely analyzed an economic fact.

Let us now go on to see how the concept of estranged, alienated labour must express and present itself in reality.

If the product of labour is alien to me, and confronts me as an alien power, to whom does it then belong?

To a being other than me.

Who is this being?

The gods? It is true that in early times most production—e.g., temple building, etc., in Egypt, India, and Mexico—was in the service of the gods, just as the product belonged to the gods. But the gods alone were never the masters of labour. The same is true of nature. And what a paradox it would be if the more man subjugates nature through his labour and the more divine miracles are made superfluous by the miracles of industry, the more he is forced to forgo the joy of production and the enjoyment of the product out of deference to these powers.

The alien being to whom labour and the product of labour belong, in whose service labour is performed, and for whose enjoyment the product of labour is created, can be none other than man himself.

If the product of labour does not belong to the worker, and if it confronts him as an alien power, this is only possible because it belongs to a man other than the worker. If his activity is a torment for him, it must provide pleasure and enjoyment for someone else. Not the gods, not nature, but only man himself can be this alien power over men.

Consider the above proposition that the relationship of man to himself becomes objective and real for him only through his relationship to other men. If, therefore, he regards the product of his labour, his objectified labour, as an alien, hostile, and powerful object which is independent of him, then his relationship to that object is such that another man—alien, hostile, powerful, and independent of him—is its master. If he relates to his own activity as unfree activity, then he relates to it as activity in the service, under the rule, coercion, and yoke of another man.

Every self-estrangement of man from himself and nature is manifested in the relationship he sets up between other men and himself and nature. Thus, religious self-estrangement is necessarily manifested in the relationship between layman and priest, or, since we are dealing here with the spiritual world, between layman and mediator, etc. In the practical, real world, self-estrangement can manifest itself only in the practical, real relationship to other men. The medium through which estrangement progresses is itself a practical one. So through estranged labour man not only produces his relationship to the object and to the act of production as to alien and hostile powers; he also produces the relationship in which other men stand to his production and product, and the relationship in which he stands to these other men. Just as he creates his own production as a loss of reality, a punishment, and his own product as a loss, a product which does not belong to him, so he creates the domination of the non-producer over production and its product. Just as he estranges from himself his own activity, so he confers upon the stranger an activity which does not belong to him.

Up to now, we have considered the relationship only from the side of the worker. Later on, we shall consider it from the side of the non-worker.

Thus, through estranged, alienated labour, the worker creates the relationship of another man, who is alien to labour and stands outside it, to that labour. The relation of the worker to labour creates the relation of the capitalist—or whatever other word one chooses for the master of labour—to that labour. Private property is therefore the product, result, and necessary consequence of alienated labour, of the external relation of the worker to nature and to himself.

Private property thus derives from an analysis of the concept of alienated labour—i.e., alienated man, estranged labour, estranged life, estranged man.

It is true that we took the concept of alienated labour (alienated life) from political economy as a result of the movement of private property. But it is clear from an analysis of this concept that, although private property appears as the basis and cause of alienated labour, it is in fact its consequence, just as the gods were originally not the cause but the effect of the confusion in men's minds. Later, however, this relationship becomes reciprocal.

It is only when the development of private property reaches its ultimate point of culmination that this, its secret, re-emerges; namely, that it is

(a) the product of alienated labour, and

(b) the means through which labour is alienated, the realization of this alienation. . . .

Wages are an immediate consequence of estranged labour, and estranged labour is the immediate cause of private property. If the one falls, then the other must fall too.

(2) It further follows from the relation of estranged labour to private property that the emancipation of society from private property, etc., from servitude, is expressed in the political form of the emancipation of the workers. This is not because it is only a question of their emancipation, but because in their emancipation is contained universal human emancipation.

QUESTIONS FOR REFLECTION

1. Why are workers alienated from the products of their labor?
2. Why does labor alienate us from ourselves?
3. What role does private property play in the estrangement of labor?
4. We must work to live. Is there a kind of work that would not lead to estrangement? If so, what would it be like?
5. Kant said that everyone should be treated as an end-in-himself, not merely as a means. Assess the hypothesis that Marx's central complaint against capitalism is that it forces the worker to use *himself* merely as a means.
6. Marx's prediction that workers would become more and more impoverished has not been borne out; the living standards of workers have risen dramatically since his time. What impact does this have on his argument?

KARL MARX

from *Critique of the Gotha Program*

(Source: Karl Marx, Critique of the Gotha Program. *New York: International Publishers, 1933.)*

. . . What is "a fair distribution"?

Do not the bourgeois assert that the present-day distribution is "fair"? And is it not, in fact, the only "fair" distribution on the basis of the present-day mode of production? Are economic relations regulated by legal conceptions or do not, on the contrary, legal relations arise from economic ones? Have not also the socialist sectarians the most varied notions about "fair" distribution?

To understand what is implied in this connection by the phrase "fair distribution," we must take the first paragraph and this one together. The latter presupposes a society wherein "the instruments of labour are common property and the total labour is cooperatively regulated," and from the first paragraph we leam that "the proceeds of labour belong undiminished with equal right to all members of society."

"To all members of society"? To those who do not work as well? What remains then of the "undiminished proceeds of labour"? Only to those members of society who work? What remains then of the "equal right" of all members of society?

But "all members of society" and "equal right" are obviously mere phrases. The kernel consists in this, that in this communist society every worker must receive the "undiminished" Lassallean* "Proceeds of Labour."

*Ferdinand Lassalle (1825–1864), German socialist and correspondent of Marx, founded the first political party for German workers in 1863. It is the ancestor of today's German Social Democratic Party. —Ed.

Let us take first of all the words "proceeds of labour" in the sense of the product of labour; then the co-operative proceeds of labour are the *total social product.*

From this must now be deducted:

First, cover for replacement of the means of production used up.

Secondly, additional portion for expansion of production.

Thirdly, reserve or insurance funds to provide against accidents, dislocations caused by natural calamities, etc.

These deductions from the "undiminished proceeds of labour" are an economic necessity and their magnitude is to be determined according to available means and forces, and partly, by computation of probabilities, but they are in no way calculable by equity.

There remains the other part of the total product, intended to serve as means of consumption.

Before this is divided among the individuals, there has to be deducted again, from it:

First, the general costs oj administration not belonging to production.

This part will, from the outset, be very considerably restricted in comparison with present-day society and it diminishes in proportion as the new society develops.

Secondly, that which is intended for the common satisfaction of needs, such as schools, health services, etc.

From the outset this part grows considerably in comparison with present-day society and it grows in proportion as the new society develops.

Thirdly, funds for those unable to work, etc., in short, for what is included under so-called official poor relief today.

Only now do we come to the "distribution" which the programme, under Lassallean influence, alone has in view in its narrow fashion, namely, to that part of the means of consumption which is divided among the individual producers of the co-operative society.

The "undiminished proceeds of labour" have already unnoticeably become converted into the "diminished" proceeds, although what the producer is deprived of in his capacity as a private individual benefits him directly or indirectly in his capacity as a member of society.

Just as the phrase of the "undiminished proceeds of labour" has disappeared, so now does the phrase of the "proceeds of labour" disappear altogether.

Within the co-operative society based on common ownership of the means of production, the producers do not exchange their products; just as little does the labour employed on the products appear here *as the value* of these products, as a material quality possessed by them, since now, in contrast to capitalist society, individual labour no longer exists in an indirect fashion but directly as a component part of the total labour. The phrase "proceeds of labour," objectionable also today on account of its ambiguity, thus loses all meaning.

What we have to deal with here is a communist society, not as it has *developed* on its own foundations, but, on the contrary, just as it *emerges* from capitalist society; which is thus in every respect, economically, morally and intellectually, still stamped with the birth marks of the old society from whose womb it emerges. Accordingly, the individual producer receives back from society—after the deductions have been made—exactly what he gives to it. What he has given to it is his individual quantum of labour. For example, the social working day consists of the sum of the individual hours of work; the individual labour time of the individual producer is the part of the social working day contributed by him, his share in it. He receives a certificate from society that he has furnished such and such an amount of labour (after deducting his labour for the common funds), and with this certificate he draws from the social stock of means of consumption as much as costs the same amount of labour. The same amount of labour which he has given to society in one form he receives back in another.

Here obviously the same principle prevails as that which regulates the exchange of commodities, as far as this is exchange of equal values. Content and form are changed, because under the altered circumstances no one can give anything except his labour, and because, on the other hand, nothing can pass to the ownership of individuals except individual means of consumption. But, as far as the distribution of the latter among the individual producers is concerned, the same principle prevails as in the exchange of commodity equivalents: a given amount of labour in one form is exchanged for an equal amount of labour in another form.

Hence, *equal right* here is still in principle—*bourgeois right*, although principle and practice are no longer at loggerheads, while the exchange of equivalents in commodity exchange only exists *on the average* and not in the individual case.

In spite of this advance, this *equal right* is still constantly stigmatised by a bourgeois limitation. The right of the producers is *proportional* to the labour they supply; the equality consists in the fact that measurement is made with an *equal standard*, labour.

But one man is superior to another physically or mentally and so supplies more labour in the same time, or can labour for a longer time; and labour, to serve as a measure, must be defined by its duration or intensity, otherwise it ceases to be a standard of measurement. This *equal* right is an unequal right for unequal labour. It recognises no class differences, because everyone is only a worker like everyone else; but it tacitly recognises unequal individual endowment and thus productive capacity as natural privileges. It is, *therefore, a right of inequality, in its content, like every right*. Right by its very nature can consist only in the application of an equal standard; but unequal individuals (and they would not be different individuals if they were not unequal) are measurable only by an equal standard in so far as they are brought under an equal point of view, are taken from one *definite* side only, for instance, in the present case, are regarded *only as workers* and nothing more is seen in them, everything else being ignored. Further, one worker is married, another not; one has more children than another, and so on and so forth.

Thus, with an equal performance of labour, and hence an equal share in the social consumption fund, one will in fact receive more than another, one will be richer than another, and so on. To avoid all these defects, right instead of being equal would have to be unequal.

But these defects are inevitable in the first phase of communist society as it is when it has just emerged after prolonged birth pangs from capitalist society. Right can never be higher than the economic structure of society and its cultural development conditioned thereby.

In a higher phase of communist society, after the enslaving subordination of the individual to the division of labour, and therewith also the antithesis between mental and physical labour, has vanished; after labour has become not only, a means of life but life's prime want; after the productive forces have also increased with the all-round development of the individual, and all the springs of co-operative wealth flow more abundantly—only then can the narrow horizon of bourgeois right be crossed in its entirety and society inscribe on its banner: From each according to his ability, to each according to his needs!

I have dealt more at length with the "undiminished proceeds of labour," on the one hand, and with "equal right" and "fair distribution," on the other, in order to show what a crime it is to attempt, on the one hand, to force on our Party again, as dogmas, ideas which in a certain period had some meaning but have now become obsolete verbal rubbish, while again perverting, on the other, the realistic outlook, which it cost so much effort to instil into the Party but which has now taken root in it, by means of ideological nonsense about right and other trash so common among the democrats and French Socialists.

Quite apart from the analysis so far given, it was in general a mistake to make a fuss about so-called *distribution* and put the principal stress on it.

Any distribution whatever of the means of consumption is only a consequence of the distribution of the conditions of production themselves. The latter distribution, however, is a feature of the mode of production itself. The capitalist mode of production, for example, rests on the fact that the material conditions of production are in the hands of non-workers in the form of property in capital and land, while the masses are only owners of the personal condition of production, of labour power. If the elements of production are so distributed, then the present-day distribution of the means of consumption results automatically If the material conditions of production are the co-operative property of the workers themselves, then there likewise results a distribution of the means of consumption different from the present one. Vulgar socialism (and from it in turn a section of the democracy) has taken over from the bourgeois economists the consideration and treatment of distribution as independent of the mode of production and hence the presentation of socialism as turning principally on distribution. After the real relation has long been made clear, why retrogress again? . . .

QUESTIONS FOR REFLECTION

1. Why does Marx consider every right a right of inequality? What does this mean?
2. What is Marx's conception of distributive justice?
3. Distributing "to each according to his needs," John Stuart Mill argues, gives people no incentive to develop their talents or work hard. Instead, it gives them incentive to increase their needs. Is that a fair criticism of Marx's position?
4. Many contemporary Marxists replace Marx's criterion with a simpler one: Government should meet people's needs. Is that an improvement, in your view?
5. Who will decide people's abilities and needs? Mikhail Bakunin writes that Marxism means "the rule of the great masses of the people by a privileged minority." Is he correct?
6. Sigmund Freud argues that socialism requires a basic change in human nature, so that people work together without conflict for the common good. But he says "such an alteration in human nature is very improbable." Does human nature need to change for Marx's theory to work?

JOHN RAWLS

Justice as Fairness

John Rawls (1921–2002) was professor of philosophy at Harvard University, winner of the Schock Prize for logic and philosophy, and recipient of a National Humanities medal. (Source: The Journal of Philosophy LIV (1957). *Reprinted by permission.)*

The fundamental idea in the concept of justice is that of fairness. It is this aspect of justice for which utilitarianism, in its classical form, is unable to account, but which is represented, even if misleadingly so, in the idea of the social contract. To establish these propositions I shall develop, but of necessity only very briefly, a particular conception of justice by stating two principles which specify it and by considering how they may be thought to arise. The parts of this conception, are familiar; but perhaps it is possible by using the notion of fairness as a framework to assemble and to look at them in a new way.

Principles of Justice

1. Throughout I discuss justice as a virtue of institutions constituting restrictions as to how they may define offices and powers, and assign rights and duties; and not as a virtue of particular actions, or persons. Justice is but one of many virtues of institutions, for these may be inefficient, or degrading, or any of a number of things, without being unjust. Essentially justice is the elimination of arbitrary distinctions and the establishment, within the structure of a practice, of a proper balance between competing claims. I do not argue that the principles given below are *the* principles of justice. It is sufficient for my purposes that they be typical of the family of principles which might reasonably be called principles of justice as shown by the background against which they may be thought to arise.

The first principle is that each person participating in a practice, or affected by it, has an equal right to the most extensive liberty compatible with a like liberty for all; and the second is that inequalities are arbitrary unless it is reasonable to expect that they will work out for everyone's advantage and unless the offices to which they attach, or from which they may be gained, are open to all. These principles express justice as a complex of three ideas: liberty, equality, and reward for contributions to the common advantage.

The first principle holds, of course, only *ceteris paribus:* while there must always be a justification for departing from the initial position of equal liberty (which is defined by the pattern of rights and duties), and the burden of proof is placed upon him who would depart from it, nevertheless, there can be, and often there is, a justification for doing so. One can view this principle as containing the principle that similar cases be judged similarly, or if distinctions are made in the handling of cases, there must be some relevant difference between them (a principle which follows from the concept of a judgment of any kind). It could be argued that justice requires only an equal liberty; but if a greater liberty were possible for all without loss or conflict, then it would be irrational to settle on a lesser liberty. There is no reason for circumscribing rights until they mutually interfere with one another. Therefore no serious distortion of the concept of justice is likely to follow from including within it the concept of the greatest equal liberty instead of simply equal liberty.

The second principle specifies what sorts of inequalities are permissible, where by inequalities it seems best to understand not any difference between offices and positions, since structural differences are not usually an issue (people do not object to there being different offices as such, and so to there being the offices of president, senator, governor, judge, and so on), but differences in the benefits and burdens attached to them either directly or indirectly, such as prestige and wealth, or liability to taxation and compulsory service. An inequality is allowed only if there is reason to believe that the practice with the inequality will work to the advantage of *every* party. This is interpreted to require, first, that there must normally be evidence acceptable to common sense and based on a common fund of knowledge and belief which shows that this is in fact likely to be the case. The principle does not rule out, however, arguments of a theological or metaphysical kind to justify inequalities (e.g., a religious basis for a caste system) provided they belong to common belief and are freely acknowledged by people who may be presumed to know what they are doing.

Second, an inequality must work for the common advantage; and since the principle applies to practices, this implies that the representative man in *every* office or position of the practice, when he views it as a going institution, must find it reasonable to prefer his condition and prospects with the inequality to what they would be without it. And finally, the various offices to which special benefits and burdens attach are required to be open to all; and so if, for example, it is to the common advantage to attach benefits to offices (because by doing so not only is the requisite talent attracted to them, but encouraged to give its best efforts once there), they must be won in a fair competition in which contestants are judged on their merits. If some offices were not open, those excluded would normally be justified in feeling wronged, even if they benefited from the greater efforts of those who were allowed to compete for them. Assuming that offices are open, it is necessary only to consider the design of the practices themselves and how they jointly, as a system, work together. It is a mistake to fix attention on the varying relative positions of particular persons and to think that each such change, as a once-for-all transaction, must be in itself just. The system must be judged from a general point of view: unless one is prepared to criticize it from the standpoint of a representative man holding some particular office, one has no complaint against it.

The Original Position

2. Given these principles, one might try to derive them from *a priori* principles of reason, or offer them as known by intuition. These are familiar steps, and, at least in the case of the first principle, might be made with some success. I wish, however, to look at the principles in a different way.

Consider a society where certain practices are already established, and whose members are mutually self-interested: their allegiance to the established practices is founded on the prospect of self-advantage. It need not be supposed that they are incapable of acting from any other motive; if one thinks of the members of this society as families, the individuals thereof may be bound by ties of sentiment and affection. Nor must they be mutually self-interested under all circumstances, but only under those circumstances in which they ordinarily participate in their common practices. Imagine also that the persons in this society are rational: they know their own interests more or less accurately; they are capable of tracing out the likely consequences of adopting one practice rather than another and of adhering to a decision once made; they can resist present temptations and attractions of immediate gain; and the knowledge, or the perception, of the difference between their condition and that of others is not, in itself, a source of great dissatisfaction. Finally, they have roughly similar needs and interests and are sufficiently equal in power and ability to assure that in normal circumstances none is able to dominate the others.

Now suppose that on some particular occasion several members of this society come together to discuss whether any of them has a legitimate complaint against their established institutions. They try first to arrive at the principles by which complaints, and so practices themselves, are to be judged. Their procedure for this is the following: each is to propose the principles upon which he wishes his complaints to be tried with the understanding that, if acknowledged, the complaints of others will be similarly tried, and that no complaints will be heard at all until everyone is roughly of one mind as to how complaints are to be judged. They understand further that the principles proposed and acknowledged on this occasion are to be binding on future occasions. Thus each will be wary of proposing principles which give him a peculiar advantage, supposing them to be accepted, in his present circumstances, since he will be bound by it in future cases the circumstances of which are unknown and in which the principle might well be to his detriment. Everyone is, then, forced to make in advance a firm commitment, which others also may reasonably be expected to make, and no one is able to tailor the canons of a legitimate complaint to fit his own special condition, Therefore each person will propose principles of a general kind which will, to a large degree, gain their sense from the various applications to be made of them. These principles will express the conditions in accordance with which each is least unwilling to have his interests limited in the design of practices on the supposition that the interests of others will be limited likewise. The restrictions which would so arise might be thought of as those a person would keep in mind if he were designing a practice in which his enemy were to assign him his place.

In this account of a hypothetical society the character and respective situations of the parties reflect the circumstances in which questions of justice may be said to arise, and the procedure whereby principles are proposed and acknowledged represents constraints, analogous to those of having a morality, whereby rational and mutually self-interested parties are brought to act reasonably, Given all conditions as described, it would be natural to accept the two principles of justice. Since there is no way for anyone to win special advantage for himself, each might consider it reasonable to acknowledge equality as an initial principle. There is however, no reason why they should regard this position as final; for if there are inequalities which satisfy the second principle, the immediate gain which equality would allow can be considered as intelligently invested in view of its future return. If, as is quite likely, these inequalities work as incentives to draw out better efforts, the members of this society may look upon them as concessions to human nature: they, like us, may think that people ideally should want to serve one another. But as they are mutually self-interested, their acceptance of these inequalities is merely the acceptance of the relations in which they actually stand. They have no title to complain of one another. And so; provided the conditions of the principle are met, there is no reason why they should reject such inequalities in the design of their social practices. Indeed, it would be short-sighted of them to do so, and could result, it seems, only from their being dejected by the bare knowledge, or perception, that others are better situated. Each person will, however, insist on a common advantage, for none is willing to sacrifice anything for the others.

These remarks are not, of course, offered as a proof that persons so circumstanced would settle upon the two principles, but only to show that the principles of justice could have such a background; and so can be viewed as those principles which mutually self-interested and rational persons, when similarly situated and required to make in advance a firm commitment, could acknowledge as restrictions governing the assignment of rights and duties in their common practices, and thereby accept as limiting their rights against one another.

Fair Play

3. That the principles of justice can be regarded in this way is an important fact about them. It brings out the idea that fundamental to justice is the concept of fairness which relates to right dealing between persons who are cooperating with or competing against one another, as when one speaks of fair games, fair competition, and fair bargains. The question of fairness arises when free persons, who have no authority over one another, are engaging in a joint activity and amongst themselves settling or acknowledging the rules which define it and which determine the respective shares in its benefits and burdens. A practice will strike the parties as fair if none feels that, by participating in it, he, or any of the others, is taken advantage of, or forced to give in to claims which he does not regard as legitimate. This implies that each has a conception of legitimate claims which he thinks it reasonable that others as well as himself should acknowledge. If one thinks of the principles of justice

as arising in the way described, then they do define this sort of conception. A practice is just, then, when it satisfies the principles which those who participate in it could propose to one another for mutual acceptance under the aforementioned circumstances. Persons engaged in a just, or fair, practice can face one another honestly, and support their respective positions, should they appear questionable, by reference to principles which it is reasonable to expect each to accept. It is this notion of the possibility of mutual acknowledgment which makes the concept of fairness fundamental to justice. Only if such acknowledgment is possible, can there be true community between persons in their common practices; otherwise their relations will appear to them as founded to some extent on force and violence. If, in ordinary speech, fairness applies more particularly to practices in which there is a choice whether to engage or not, and justice to practices in which there is no choice and one must play, the element of necessity does not alter the basic conception of the possibility of mutual acceptance, although it may make it much more urgent to change unjust than unfair institutions.

Now if the participants in a practice accept its rules as fair, and so have no complaint to lodge against it, there arises a prima facie duty (and a corresponding prima facie right) of the parties to each other to act in accordance with the practice when it falls upon them to comply. When any number of persons engage in a practice, or conduct a joint undertaking, according to rules, and thus restrict their liberty, those who have submitted to these restrictions when required have a right to a similar acquiescence on the part of those who have benefited by their submission. These conditions will, of course, obtain if a practice is correctly acknowledged to be fair, for in this case, all who participate in it will benefit from it. The rights and duties so arising are special rights and duties in that they depend on previous voluntary actions—in this case, on the parties' having engaged in a common practice and accepted its benefits. It is not, however, an obligation which presupposes a deliberate performative act in the sense of a promise, or contract, and the like. It is sufficient that one has knowingly participated in a practice acknowledged to be fair and accepted the resulting benefits. This prima facie obligation may, of course, be overridden: it may happen, when it comes one's turn to follow a rule, that other considerations will justify not doing so. But one cannot, in general, be released from this obligation by denying the justice of the practice only when it falls on one to obey. If a person rejects a practice, he should, as far as possible, declare his intention in advance, and avoid participating in it or accepting its benefits.

This duty may be called that of fair play, which is, perhaps, to extend the ordinary notion; for acting unfairly is usually not so much the breaking of any particular rule, even if the infraction is difficult to detect (cheating), but taking advantage of loopholes or ambiguities in rules, availing oneself of unexpected or special circumstances which make it impossible to enforce them, insisting that rules be enforced when they should be suspended, and, more generally, acting contrary to the intention of a practice. (Thus one speaks of the sense of fair play: acting fairly is not simply following rules; what is fair must be felt or perceived.) Nevertheless, it is not an unnatural extension of the duty of fair play to have it include the obligation which participants in a common practice owe to each other to act in accordance with it when their performance falls due. Consider the tax dodger, or the free rider.

The duty of fair play stands beside those of fidelity and gratitude as a fundamental moral notion; and like them it implies a constraint on self-interest in particular cases. I make this point to avoid a misunderstanding: the conception of the mutual acknowledgment of principles under special circumstances is used to analyze the concept of justice. I do not wish to imply that the acceptance of justice in actual conduct depends solely on an existing equality of conditions. My own view, which is perhaps but one of several compatible with the preceding analysis, and which I can only suggest here, is that the acknowledgment of the duty of fair play, as shown in acting on it, and wishing to make amends and the like when one has been at fault, is one of the forms of conduct in which participants in a common practice show their recognition of one another as persons. In the same way that, failing a special explanation, the criterion for the recognition of suffering is helping him who suffers, acknowledging the duty of fair play is the criterion for recognizing another as a person with similar capacities, interests, and feelings as oneself. The acceptance by participants in a common practice of this duty is a reflection in each of the recognition of the aspirations of the others to be realized by their joint activity. Without this acceptance they would recognize one another as but complicated objects in a complicated routine. To recognize another as a person one must respond to him and act towards him as one; and these forms of action and response include, among other things, acknowledging the duty of fair play. These remarks are unhappily obscure; their purpose here is to forestall the misunderstanding mentioned above.

The conception at which we have arrived, then, is that the principles of justice may be thought of as arising once the constraints of having a morality are imposed upon rational and mutually self-interested parties who are related and situated in a special way. A practice is just if it is in accordance with the principles which all who participate in it might reasonably be expected to propose or to acknowledge before one another when they are similarly circumstanced and required to make a firm commitment in advance; and thus when it meets standards which the parties could accept as fair should occasion arise for them to debate its merits. Once persons knowingly engage in a practice which they acknowledge to be fair and accept the benefits of doing so, they are bound by the duty of fair play which implies a limitation on self-interest in particular cases. . . .

QUESTIONS FOR REFLECTION

1. What is the original position? What is the role of the veil of ignorance?
2. Why might rational agents in the original position reject the principle of utility?
3. People in the original position should be viewed as equal in what sense?
4. Explain Rawls's first principle. Give an example of something ruled out by the principle.
5. How does Rawls's first principle differ from Mill's harm principle? From Hobbes's law of nature?
6. Explain Rawls's second principle. Give an example of something ruled out by each part of the principle.
7. Rawls justifies his principles by saying that rational agents in the original position would agree to them. Do you concur?
8. Describe a situation in which Rawls's second principle would disagree with (a) the principle of utility, (b) the historical theory of Locke and Nozick, (c) Aristotle's meritocratic theory, (d) the maxim of Marx and Engels, and (e) Rousseau's conception of justice. In each case, do you find Rawls's theory more or less plausible than its competitor? Why?
9. Various writers have challenged Rawls's claim that the first principle of justice should always take precedence over the second. Are there cases in which basic liberties ought to be restricted to secure equal opportunity or a fairer distribution? Why, or why not?
10. Amartya Sen observes that people have very different desires and needs, and worries that Rawls, by taking the set of basic goods as the same for everyone, overlooks "widespread and real differences," producing a "partially blind morality." Is that a fair criticism of Rawls?

ROBERT NOZICK

from *Anarchy, State, and Utopia* (1974)

Robert Nozick was professor of philosophy at Harvard University. (Source: From Anarchy, State, and Utopia *by Robert Nozick. Copyright © 1974 by Basic Books, Inc.; reprinted by permission of Basic Books, a division of HarperCollins Publishers Inc.)*

CHAPTER 7 / DISTRIBUTIVE JUSTICE

The minimal state is the most extensive state that can be justified. Any state more extensive violates people's rights. Yet many persons have put forth reasons purporting to justify a more extensive state. . . . In this chapter we consider the claim that a more extensive state is justified, because necessary (or the best instrument) to achieve distributive justice.

The term "distributive justice" is not a neutral one. Hearing the term "distribution," most people presume that some thing or mechanism uses some principle or criterion to give out a supply of things. Into this process of distributing shares some error may have crept. So it is an open question, at least, whether *re*distribution should take place; whether we should do again what has already been done once, though poorly. However, we are not in the position of children who have been given portions of pie by someone who now makes last minute adjustments to rectify careless cutting. There is no *central* distribution, no person or group entitled to control all the resources, jointly deciding how they are to be doled out. What each person gets, he gets from others who give to him in exchange for something, or as a gift. In a free society, diverse persons control different resources, and new holdings arise out of the voluntary exchanges and actions of persons. There is no more a distributing or distribution of shares than there is a distributing of mates in a society in which persons choose whom they shall marry. The total result is the product of many individual decisions which the different individuals involved are entitled to make. Some uses of the term "distribution," it is true, do not imply a previous distributing appropriately judged by some criterion (for example, "probability distribution"); nevertheless, despite the title of this chapter, it would be best to use a terminology that clearly is neutral. We shall speak of people's holdings; a principle of justice in holdings describes (part of) what justice tells us (requires) about holdings. I shall state first what I take to be the correct view about justice in holdings, and then turn to the discussion of alternate views.

Section I

The Entitlement Theory

The subject of justice in holdings consists of three major topics. The first is the *original acquisition of holdings*, the appropriation of unheld things. This includes the issues of how unheld things may come to be held, the process, or processes, by which unheld things may come to be held, the things that may come to be held by these processes, the extent of what comes to be held by a particular process, and so on. We shall refer to the complicated truth about this topic, which we shall not formulate here, as the principle of justice in acquisition. The second topic concerns the *transfer of holdings* from one person to another. By what processes may a person transfer holdings to another? How may a person acquire a holding from another who holds it? Under this topic come general descriptions of voluntary exchange, and gift and (on the other hand) fraud, as well as reference to particular conventional details fixed upon in a given society. The complicated truth about this subject (with placeholders for conventional details) we shall call the principle of justice in transfer. (And we shall suppose it also includes principles governing how a person may divest himself of a holding, passing it into an unheld state.)

If the world were wholly just, the following inductive definition would exhaustively cover the subject of justice in holdings.

1. A person who acquires a holding in accordance with the principle of justice in acquisition is entitled to that holding.
2. A person who acquires a holding in accordance with the principle of justice in transfer, from someone else entitled to the holding, is entitled to the holding.
3. No one is entitled to a holding except by (repeated) applications of 1 and 2.

The complete principle of distributive justice would say simply that a distribution is just if everyone is entitled to the holdings they possess under the distribution.

Justice Preservation

A distribution is just if it arises from another just distribution by legitimate means. The legitimate means of moving from one distribution to another are specified by the principle of justice in transfer. The legitimate first "moves" are specified by the principle of justice in acquisition. Whatever arises from a just situation by just steps is itself just. The means of change specified by the principle of justice in transfer preserve justice. As correct rules of inference are truth-preserving, and any conclusion deduced via repeated application of such rules from only true premises is itself true, so the means of transition from one situation to another specified by the principle of justice in transfer are justice-preserving, and any situation actually arising from repeated transitions in accordance with the principle from a just situation is itself just. The parallel between justice-preserving transformations and truth-preserving transformations illuminates where it fails as well as where it holds. That a conclusion could have been deduced by truth-preserving means from premises that are true suffices to show its truth. That from a just situation a situation *could* have arisen via justice-preserving means does not suffice to show its justice. The fact that a thief's victims voluntarily *could* have presented him with gifts does not entitle the thief to his ill-gotten gains. Justice in holdings is historical; it depends upon what actually has happened. We shall return to this point later.

Injustice

Not all actual situations are generated in accordance with the two principles of justice in holdings: the principle of justice in acquisition and the principle of justice in transfer. Some people steal from others, or defraud them, or enslave them, seizing their product and preventing them from living as they choose, or forcibly exclude others from competing in exchanges. None of these are permissible modes of transition from one situation to another. And some persons acquire holdings by means not sanctioned by the principle of justice in acquisition. The existence of past injustice (previous violations of the first two principles of justice in holdings) raises the third major topic under justice in holdings: the rectification of injustice in holdings. If past injustice has shaped present holdings in various ways, some identifiable and some not, what now, if anything, ought to be done to rectify these injustices? What obligations do the performers of injustice have toward those whose position is worse than it would have been had the injustice not been done? Or, than it would have been had compensation been paid promptly? How, if at all, do things change if the beneficiaries and those made worse off are not the direct parties in the act of injustice, but, for example, their descendants? Is an injustice done to someone whose holding was itself based upon an unrectified injustice? How far back must one go in wiping clean the historical slate of injustices? What may victims of injustice permissibly do in order to rectify the injustices being done to them, including the many injustices done by persons acting through their government? I do not know of a thorough or theoretically sophisticated treatment of such issues. Idealizing greatly, let us suppose theoretical investigation will produce a principle of rectification. This principle uses historical information about previous situations and injustices done in them (as defined by the first two principles of justice and rights against interference), and information about the actual course of events that flowed from these injustices, until the present, and it yields a description (or descriptions) of holdings in the society. The principle of rectification presumably will make use of its best estimate of subjunctive information about what would have occurred (or a probability distribution over what might have occurred, using the expected value) if the injustice had not taken place. If the actual description of holdings turns out not to be one of the descriptions yielded by the principle, then one of the descriptions yielded must be realized.

The general outlines of the theory of justice in holdings are that the holdings of a person are just if he is entitled to them by the principles of justice in acquisition and transfer, or by the principle of rectification of injustice (as specified by the first two principles). If each person's holdings are just, then the total set (distribution) of holdings is just. To turn these general outlines into a specific theory we would have to specify the details of each of the three principles of justice in holdings: the principle of acquisition of holdings, the principle of transfer of holdings, and the principle of rectification of violations of the first two principles. I shall not attempt that task here. (Locke's principle of justice in acquisition is discussed below.)

Historical Principles and End-Result Principles

The general outlines of the entitlement theory illuminate the nature and defects of other conceptions of distributive justice. The entitlement theory of justice in distribution is *historical;* whether a distribution is just depends upon how it came about. In contrast, *current time-slice principles* of justice hold that the justice of a distribution is determined by how things are distributed (who has what) as judged by some *structural* principle(s) of just distribution. A utilitarian who judges between any two distributions by seeing which has the greater sum of utility and, if the sums tie, applies some fixed equality criterion to choose the more equal distribution, would hold a current time-slice principle of justice. As would someone who had a fixed schedule of trade-offs between the sum of happiness and equality. According to a current time-slice principle, all that needs to be looked at, in judging the justice of a distribution, is who ends up with what; in comparing any two distributions one need look only at the matrix presenting the distributions. No further information need be fed into a principle of justice. It is a consequence of such principles of justice that any two structurally identical distributions are equally just. (Two distributions are structurally identical if they present the same profile, but perhaps have different persons occupying the particular slots. My having ten and your having five, and my having five and your having ten are structurally identical distributions.) Welfare economics is the theory of current time-slice principles of justice. The subject is conceived as operating on matrices representing only current information about distribution. This, as well as some of the usual conditions (for example, the choice of distribution is invariant under relabeling of columns), guarantees that welfare economics will be a current time-slice theory, with all of its inadequacies.

Most persons do not accept current time-slice principles as constituting the whole story about distributive shares. They think it relevant in assessing the justice of a situation to consider not only the distribution it embodies, but also how that distribution came about. If some persons are in prisons for murder or war crimes, we do not say that to assess the justice of the distribution in the society we must look only at what this person has, and that person has, and that person has, . . . at the current time. We think it relevant to ask whether someone did something so that he *deserved* to be punished, deserved to have a lower share. Most will agree to the relevance of further information with regard to punishments and penalties. Consider also desired things. One traditional socialist view is that workers are entitled to the produce and full fruits of their labor; they have earned it; a distribution is unjust if it does not give the workers what they are entitled to. Such entitlements are based upon some past history. No socialist holding this view would find it comforting to be told that because the actual distribution *A* happens to coincide structurally with the one he desires *D, A* therefore is no less just than *D*; it differs only in that the "parasitic" owners of capital receive under *A* what the workers are entitled to under *D*, and the workers receive under *A* what the owners are entitled to under *D*, namely very little. This socialist rightly, in my view, holds onto the notions of earning, producing, entitlement, desert, and so forth, and he rejects current time-slice principles that look only to the structure of the resulting set of holdings. (The set of holdings resulting from what? Isn't it implausible that how holdings are produced and come to exist has no effect at all on who should hold what?) His mistake lies in his view of what entitlements arise out of what sorts of productive processes.

We construe the position we discuss too narrowly by speaking of *current* time-slice principles. Nothing is changed if structural principles operate upon a time sequence of current time-slice profiles and, for example, give someone more now to counterbalance the less he has had earlier. A utilitarian or an egalitarian or any mixture of the two over time will inherit the difficulties of his more myopic comrades. He is not helped by the fact that *some* of the information others consider relevant in assessing a distribution is reflected, unrecoverably, in past matrices. Henceforth, we shall refer to such unhistorical principles of distributive justice, including the current time-slice principles, as *end-result principles* or *end-state principles*.

In contrast to end-result principles of justice, *historical principles* of justice hold that past circumstances or actions of people can create differential entitlements or differential deserts to things. An injustice can be worked by moving from one distribution to another structurally identical one, for the second, in profile the same, may violate people's entitlements or deserts; it may not fit the actual history.

Patterning

The entitlement principles of justice in holdings that we have sketched are historical principles of justice. To better understand their precise character, we shall distinguish them from another subclass of the historical principles. Consider, as an example, the principle of distribution according to moral merit. This principle requires that total distributive shares vary directly with moral merit; no person should have a greater share than anyone whose moral merit is greater. (If moral merit could be not merely ordered but measured on an interval or ratio scale, stronger principles could be formulated.) Or consider the principle that results by substituting "usefulness to society" for "moral merit" in the previous principle. Or instead of "distribute according to moral merit," or "distribute according to usefulness to society," we might consider "distribute according to the weighted sum of moral merit, usefulness to society, and need," with the weights of the different dimensions equal. Let us call a principle of distribution *patterned* if it specifies that a distribution is to vary along with some natural dimension, weighted sum of natural dimensions, or lexicographic ordering of natural dimensions. And let us say a distribution is patterned if it accords with some patterned principle. (I speak of natural dimensions, admittedly without a general criterion for them, because for any set of holdings some artificial dimensions can be gimmicked up to vary along with the distribution of the set.) The principle of distribution in accordance with moral merit is a patterned historical principle, which specifies a patterned distribution. "Distribute according to I.Q." is a patterned principle that looks to information not contained in distributional matrices. It is not historical, however, in that it does not look to any past actions creating differential entitlements to evaluate a distribution; it requires only distributional matrices whose columns are labeled by I.Q. scores. The distribution in a society, however, may be composed of such simple patterned distributions, without itself being simply patterned. Different sectors may operate different patterns, or some combination of patterns may operate in different proportions across a society. A distribution composed in this manner, from a small number of patterned distributions, we also shall term "patterned." And we extend the use of "pattern" to include the overall designs put forth by combinations of end-state principles.

Almost every suggested principle of distributive justice is patterned: to each according to his moral merit, or needs, or marginal product, or how hard he tries, or the weighted sum of the foregoing, and so on. The principle of entitlement we have sketched is *not* patterned. There is no one natural dimension or weighted sum or combination of a small number of natural dimensions that yields the distributions generated in accordance with the principle of entitlement. The set of holdings that results when some persons receive their marginal products, others win at gambling, others receive a share of their mate's income, others receive gifts from foundations, others receive interest on loans, others receive gifts from admirers, others receive returns on investment, others make for themselves much of what they have, others find things, and so on, will not be patterned. Heavy strands of patterns will run through it; significant portions of the variance in holdings will be accounted for by pattern-variables. If most people most of the time choose to transfer some of their entitlements to others only in exchange for something from them, then a large part of what many people hold will vary with what they held that others wanted. More details are provided by the theory of marginal productivity. But gifts to relatives, charitable donations, bequests to children, and the like, are not best conceived, in the first instance, in this manner. Ignoring the strands of pattern, let us suppose for the moment that a distribution actually arrived at by the operation of the principle of entitlement is random with respect to any pattern. Though the resulting set of holdings will be unpatterned, it will not be incomprehensible, for it can be seen as arising from the operation of a small number of principles. These principles specify how an initial distribution may arise (the principle of acquisition of holdings) and how distributions may be transformed into others (the principle of transfer of holdings). The process whereby the set of holdings is generated will be intelligible, though the set of holdings itself that results from this process will be unpatterned.

The writings of F. A. Hayek focus less than is usually done upon what patterning distributive justice requires. Hayek argues that we cannot know enough about each person's situation to distribute to each according to his moral merit (but would justice demand we do so if we did have this knowledge?); and he goes on to say, "our objection is against all attempts to impress upon society a deliberately chosen pattern of distribution, whether it be an order of equality or of inequality." However, Hayek concludes that in a free society there will be distribution in accordance with value rather than moral merit; that is, in accordance with the perceived value of a person's actions and services to others. Despite his rejection of a patterned conception of distributive justice, Hayek himself suggests a pattern he thinks justifiable: distribution in accordance with the perceived benefits given to others, leaving room for the complaint that a free society does not realize exactly this pattern. Stating this patterned strand of a free capitalist society more precisely, we get "To each according to how much he benefits others who have the resources for benefiting those who benefit them." This will seem arbitrary unless some acceptable initial set of holdings is specified, or unless it is held that the operation of the system over time washes out any significant effects from the initial set of holdings. As an example of the latter, if almost anyone would have bought a car from Henry Ford, the supposition that it was an arbitrary matter who held the money then (and so bought) would not place Henry Ford's earnings under a cloud. In any event, *his* coming to hold it is not arbitrary. Distribution according to benefits to others *is* a major patterned strand in a free capitalist society, as Hayek correctly points out, but it is only a strand and does not constitute the whole pattern of a system of entitlements (namely, inheritance, gifts for arbitrary reasons, charity, and so on) or a standard that one should insist a society fit. Will people tolerate for long a system yielding distributions that they believe are unpatterned? No doubt people will not long accept a distribution they believe is *unjust*. People want their society to be and to look just. But must the look of justice reside in a resulting pattern rather than in the underlying generating principles? We are in no position to conclude that the inhabitants of a society embodying an entitlement conception of justice in holdings will find it unacceptable. Still, it must be granted that were people's reasons for transferring some of their holdings to others always irrational or arbitrary, we would find this disturbing. (Suppose people always determined what holdings they would transfer, and to whom, by using a random device.) We feel more comfortable upholding the justice of an entitlement system if most of the transfers under it are done for reasons. This does not mean necessarily that all deserve what holdings they receive. It means only that there is a purpose or point to someone's transferring a holding to one person rather than to another; that usually we can see what the transferrer thinks he's gaining, what cause he thinks he's serving, what goals he thinks he's helping to achieve, and so forth. Since in a capitalist society people often transfer holdings to others in accordance with how much they perceive these others benefiting them, the fabric constituted by the individual transactions and transfers is largely reasonable and intelligible. (Gifts to loved ones, bequests to children, charity to the needy also are nonarbitrary components of the fabric.) In stressing the large strand of distribution in accordance with benefit to others, Hayek shows the point of many transfers, and so shows that the system of transfer of entitlements is not just spinning its gears aimlessly. The system of entitlements is defensible when constituted by the individual aims of individual transactions. No over-arching aim is needed, no distributional pattern is required.

To think that the task of a theory of distributive justice is to fill in the blank in "to each according to his ____________" is to be predisposed to search for a pattern; and the separate treatment of "from each according to his ____________" treats production and distribution as two separate and independent issues. On an entitlement view these are *not* two separate questions. Whoever makes something, having bought or contracted for all other held resources used in the process (transferring some of his holdings for these cooperating factors), is entitled to it. The situation is *not* one of something's getting made, and there being an open question of who is to get it. Things come into the world already attached to people having entitlements over them. From the point of view of the historical entitlement conception of justice in holdings, those who start afresh to complete "to each according to his ____________" treat objects as if they appeared from nowhere, out of nothing. A complete theory of justice might cover this limit case as well; perhaps here is a use for the usual conceptions of distributive justice.

So entrenched are maxims of the usual form that perhaps we should present the entitlement conception as a competitor. Ignoring acquisition and rectification, we might say:

> From each according to what he chooses to do, to each according to what he makes for himself (perhaps with the contracted aid of others) and what others choose to do for him and choose to give him of what they've been given previously (under this maxim) and haven't yet expended or transferred.

This, the discerning reader will have noticed, has its defects as a slogan. So as a summary and great simplification (and not as a maxim with any independent meaning) we have:

> *From each as they choose, to each as they are chosen.*

How Liberty Upsets Patterns

It is not clear how those holding alternative conceptions of distributive justice can reject the entitlement conception of justice in holdings. For suppose a distribution favored by one of these nonentitlement conceptions is realized. Let us suppose it is your favorite one and let us call this distribution D_1; perhaps everyone has an equal share, perhaps shares vary in accordance with some dimension you treasure. Now suppose that Wilt Chamberlain is greatly in demand by basketball teams, being a great gate attraction. (Also suppose contracts run only for a year, with players being free agents.) He signs the following sort of contract with a team: In each home game, twenty-five cents from the price of each ticket of admission goes to him. (We ignore the question of whether he is "gouging" the owners, letting them look out for themselves.) The season starts, and people cheerfully attend his team's games; they buy their tickets, each time dropping a separate twenty-five cents of their admission price into a special box with Chamberlain's name on it. They are excited about seeing him play; it is worth the total admission price to them. Let us suppose that in one season one million persons attend his home games, and Wilt Chamberlain winds up with $250,000, a much larger sum than the average income and larger even than anyone else has. Is he entitled to this income? Is this new distribution D_2, unjust? If so, why? There is *no* question about whether each of the people was entitled to the control over the resources they held in D_1; because that was the distribution (your favorite) that (for the purposes of argument) we assumed was acceptable. Each of these persons *chose* to give twenty-five cents of their money to Chamberlain. They could have spent it on going to the movies, or on candy bars, or on copies of *Dissent* magazine, or of *Monthly Review*. But they all, at least one million of them, converged on giving it to Wilt Chamberlain in exchange for watching him play basketball. If D_1 was a just distribution, and people voluntarily moved from it to D_2, transferring parts of their shares they were given under D_1 (what was it for if not to do something with?), isn't D_2 also just? If the people were entitled to dispose of the resources to which they were entitled (under D_1), didn't this include their being entitled to give it to, or exchange it with, Wilt Chamberlain? Can anyone else complain on grounds of justice? Each other person already has his legitimate share under D_1. Under D_1, there is nothing that anyone has that anyone else has a claim of justice against. After someone transfers something to Wilt Chamberlain, third parties *still* have their legitimate shares; *their* shares are not changed. By what process could such a transfer among two persons give rise to a legitimate claim of distributive justice on a portion of what was transferred, by a third party who had no claim of justice on any holding of the others *before* the transfer? To cut off objections irrelevant here, we might imagine the exchanges occurring in a socialist society, after hours. After playing whatever basketball he does in his daily work, or doing whatever other daily work he does, Wilt Chamberlain decides to put in *overtime* to earn additional money. (First his work quota is set; he works time over that.) Or imagine it is a skilled juggler people like to see, who puts on shows after hours.

Why might someone work overtime in a society in which it is assumed their needs are satisfied? Perhaps because they care about things other than needs. I like to write in books that I read, and to have easy access to books for browsing at odd hours. It would be very pleasant and convenient to have the resources of Widener Library in my back yard. No society, I assume, will provide such resources close to each person who would like them as part of his regular allotment (under D_1). Thus, persons either must do without some extra things that they want, or be allowed to do something extra to get some of these things. On what basis could the inequalities that would eventuate be forbidden? Notice also that small factories would spring up in a socialist society, unless forbidden. I melt down some of my personal possessions (under D_1) and build a machine out of the material. I offer you, and others, a philosophy lecture once a week in exchange for your cranking the handle on my machine, whose products I exchange for yet other things, and so on. (The raw materials used by the machine are given to me by others who possess them under D_1, in exchange for hearing lectures.) Each person might participate to gain things over and above their allotment under D_1. Some persons even might want to leave their job in socialist industry and work full time in this private sector. . . . Here I wish merely to note how private property even in means of production would occur in a socialist society that did not forbid people to use as they wished some of the resources they are given under the socialist distribution D_1. The socialist society would have to forbid capitalist acts between consenting adults.

The general point illustrated by the Wilt Chamberlain example and the example of the entrepreneur in a socialist society is that no end-state principle or distributional patterned principle of justice can be continuously realized without continuous interference with people's lives. Any favored pattern would be transformed into one unfavored by the principle, by people choosing to act in various ways; for example, by people exchanging goods and services with other people, or giving things to other people, things the transferrers are entitled to under the favored distributional pattern. To maintain a pattern one must either continually interfere to stop people from transferring resources as they wish to, or continually (or periodically) interfere to take from some persons resources that others for some reason chose to transfer to them. (But if some time limit is to be set on how long people may keep resources others voluntarily transfer to them, why let them keep these resources for *any* period of time? Why not have immediate confiscation?) It might be objected that all persons voluntarily will choose to refrain from actions which would upset the pattern. This presupposes unrealistically (1) that all will most want to maintain the pattern (are those who don't, to be "reeducated" or forced to undergo "self-criticism"?), (2) that each can gather enough information about his own actions and the ongoing activities of others to discover which of his actions will upset the pattern, and (3) that diverse and far-flung persons can coordinate their actions to dovetail into the pattern. Compare the manner in which the market is neutral among persons' desires, as it reflects and transmits widely scattered information via prices, and coordinates persons' activities.

It puts things perhaps a bit too strongly to say that every patterned (or end-state) principle is liable to be thwarted by the voluntary actions of the individual parties transferring some of their shares they receive under the principle. For perhaps some *very* weak patterns are not so thwarted. Any distributional pattern with any egalitarian component is overturnable by the voluntary actions of individual persons over time; as is every patterned condition with sufficient content so as actually to have been proposed as presenting the central core of distributive justice. Still, given the possibility that some weak conditions or patterns may not be unstable in this way, it would be better to formulate an explicit description of the kind of interesting and contentful patterns under discussion, and to prove a theorem about their instability. Since the weaker the patterning, the more likely it is that the entitlement system itself satisfies it, a plausible conjecture is that any patterning either is unstable or is satisfied by the entitlement system. . . .

QUESTIONS FOR REFLECTION

1. Outline Nozick's entitlement theory. What principles would be required if the world were perfect? What principle is needed because it is not?
2. How do historical principles differ from end-result principles?
3. What is a patterned theory of justice? Is Nozick's theory patterned? Can a theory be both patterned and historical?
4. Why, according to Nozick, are patterned theories of justice incompatible with liberty?
5. Hal Varian charges that Nozick has no way to compensate for randomness: "If a process can be radically affected by turns of fortune that are arbitrary from a moral point of view, it seems unreasonable to attach great moral significance to the outcome of such a process." Does the randomness of good fortune make the distribution of it unjust?
6. Socialists worry that there is no more frontier; almost everything has been owned for hundreds of years. So, they say, there are few original acquisitions from nature these days, and most chains of transfers going back to an original acquisition include many uncorrected injustices. Nozick ought to conclude that the current distribution is massively unjust and in need of rectification. Does that argument against Nozick succeed, in your view?
7. Recall the tragedy of the commons: People acting rationally out of self-interest or even out of concern for the common good can nevertheless produce less than the best outcome, using too many resources, for example. James Dick sees no way for Nozick to avoid such tragedies. Is that right? Could Nozick justify interferences in people's lives to prevent tragedies of the commons?

ECONOMIC EQUALITY

The central problem of distributive justice is how goods should be allotted to members of a society. In many societies, the prevailing methods of allotment leave some people with very little. Some may not have enough to eat; some may have inadequate housing or no housing at all. Some may lack basic medical care. Some may receive no, or very poor, education. How should society respond to these problems?

Clearly, this question raises two major issues. One is philosophical: What are the proper principles of distribution? What, in other words, is the correct theory of distributive justice? The other is practical: Given a set of principles of distribution, how can we devise policies to bring about distributions in accord with them? Answering the first question defines our obligations to help others; answering the second defines a way of fulfilling them in practice. The first question is prior. Only if we know what we are trying to accomplish can we judge how well various policies accomplish it.

These questions go to the root of our conception of political and economic organization. A society that alters its laws about capital punishment, abortion, or pornography, for example, may bring about significant changes by doing so, but it does not fundamentally change the way it is organized. Changing one's conception of distribution, however, can change social organization. Socialism, capitalism, communism, and other forms of economic organization aim at satisfying different principles of distribution. Within each system arise important questions about policies for satisfying them.

John Stuart Mill argues in favor of welfare programs that redistribute wealth to those in need. Recognizing that people will be harmed if they become dependent on such help, however, he seeks to limit assistance to a level significantly below what people could gain by working.

Philosopher John Hospers argues in favor of libertarianism, the view that the government may act only to prevent harm to others. Taking Mill's harm principle and applying it broadly, Hospers finds little justification for any government action concerning distribution. The government may of course enforce laws against stealing, for example, because that involves direct harm to others. But nothing justifies government action to take from A and give to B simply because B has less than A. Hospers argues that all other conceptions of government and of distributive justice give people rights over the lives of others—rights that, in his view, they do not have.

Amartya Sen criticizes utilitarianism and Rawls for failing to take account of the wide variation in people's needs and desires. Maximizing utility will not promote equality, Sen argues, and trying to equalize welfare, if possible at all, would promote other kinds of injustices. Focusing on the same set of basic goods for everyone is bound to overlook important differences. Sen takes the idea of capabilities as fundamental, and argues that we should try to promote an equality of capabilities.

Social theorist Charles Murray addresses the practical problem of welfare. He assumes that government is justified in attempting to eliminate poverty, homelessness, and other social problems but asks how it can do so. Murray draws several laws about social programs, which imply that such programs inevitably do more harm than good. Murray concludes that a society without any welfare programs at all would be better off than one in which government expends a great deal of energy and money trying to redistribute income and other goods. If Murray is right, there is a sense in which the practical problem of welfare policy may be prior to the question of distributive justice: perhaps no policies can achieve anything worth achieving—on any plausible conception of justice—without doing even greater harm. If so, then what conception of justice is correct makes no difference for social policy, for no combination of welfare programs could bring about a just distribution.

Elizabeth Anderson defends equality in a different way. She decries attempts to pursue equality in ways vulnerable to conservative criticisms and rejects what she calls "luck egalitarianism," the idea that the government should seek to remove the effects of luck from our lives. She outlines a vision of democratic equality that, she argues, has a deeper philosophical foundation and avoids the disadvantages of a focus on luck.

Robert Rector and Rachel Sheffield report on the state of America's poor in 2005. Very few are homeless or hungry. A typical poor household has air conditioning, a car, two television sets, cable or satellite TV, a VCR, a DVD player, a microwave, a washer and dryer, and various other amenities. Its members are well nourished and live in a house or apartment larger than that of the average European. Focusing on transfers to the poor as the government currently defines the term directs large amounts of help to people who are not poor in any traditional sense and makes it harder to address problems of real deprivation.

JOHN STUART MILL

from *Principles of Political Economy*

(Source: John Stuart Mill, Principles of Political Economy *[London: Longmans, Green and Co., 1909].)*

. . .

[T]he argument against governmental interference grounded on the maxim that individuals are the best judges of their own interest, cannot apply to the very large class of cases, in which those acts of individuals with which the government claims to interfere, are not done by those individuals for their own interest, but for the interest of other people. This includes, among other things, the important and much agitated subject of public charity. Though individuals should, in general, be left to do for themselves whatever it can reasonably be expected that they should be capable of doing, yet when they are at any rate not to be left to themselves, but to be helped by other people, the question arises whether it is better that they should receive this help exclusively from individuals, and therefore uncertainly and casually, or by systematic arrangements, in which society acts through its organ, the state.

This brings us to the subject of Poor Laws; a subject which would be of very minor importance if the habits of all classes of the people were temperate and prudent, and the diffusion of property satisfactory but of the greatest moment in a state of things so much the reverse of this, in both points, as that which the British islands present.

Apart from any metaphysical considerations respecting the foundation of morals or of the social union, it will be admitted to be right that human beings should help one another; and the more so, in proportion to the urgency of the need: and none needs help so urgently as one who is starving. The claim to help, therefore, created by destitution, is one of the strongest which can exist; and there is prima facie the amplest reason for making the relief of so extreme an exigency as certain to those who require it, as by any arrangements of society it can be made.

On the other hand, in all cases of helping, there are two sets of consequences to be considered; the consequences of the assistance itself, and the consequences of relying on the assistance. The former are generally beneficial, but the latter, for the most part, injurious; so much so, in many cases, as greatly to outweigh the value of the benefit. And this is never more likely to happen than in the very cases where the need of help is the most intense. There are few things for which it is more mischievous that people should rely on the habitual aid of others, than for the means of subsistence and unhappily there is no lesson which they more easily learn. The problem to be solved is therefore one of peculiar nicety as well as importance; how to give the greatest amount of needful help, with the smallest encouragement to undue reliance on it.

Energy and self-dependence are, however, liable to be impaired by the absence of help, as well as by its excess. It is even more fatal to exertion to have no hope of succeeding by it, than to be assured of succeeding without it. When the condition of any one is so disastrous that his energies are paralyzed by discouragement, assistance is a tonic, not a sedative: it braces instead of deadening the active faculties: always provided that the assistance is not such as to dispense with self-help, by substituting itself for the person's own labour, skill, and prudence, but is limited to affording him a better hope of attaining success by those legitimate means. This accordingly is a test to which all plans of philanthropy and benevolence should be brought, whether intended for the benefit of individuals or of classes, and whether conducted on the voluntary or on the government principle.

In so far as the subject admits of any general doctrine or maxim, it would appear to be this—that if assistance is given in such a manner that the condition of the person helped is as desirable as that of the person who succeeds in doing the same thing without help, the assistance, if capable of being previously calculated on, is mischievous: but if, while available to everybody, it leaves to every one a strong motive to do without it if he can, it is then for the most part beneficial. This principle, applied to a system of public charity, is that of the Poor Law of 1834. If the condition of a person receiving relief is made as eligible as that of the labourer who supports himself by his own exertions, the system strikes at the root of all individual industry and self-government; and, if fully acted up to, would require as its supplement an organized system of compulsion, for governing and setting to work like cattle, those who had been removed from the influence of the motives that act on human beings. But if, consistently with guaranteeing all persons against absolute want, the condition of those who are supported by legal charity can be kept considerably less desirable than the condition of those who find support for themselves, none but beneficial consequences can arise from a law which renders it impossible for any person, except, by his own choice, to die from insufficiency of food. That in England at least this supposition can be realized, is proved by the experience of a long period preceding the close of the last century, as well as by that of many highly pauperized districts in more recent times, which have been dispauperized by adopting strict rules of poor-law administration, to the great and permanent benefit of the whole labouring class. There is probably no country in which, by varying the means suitably to the character of the people, a legal provision for the destitute might not be made compatible with the observance of the conditions necessary to its being innocuous.

Subject to these conditions, I conceive it to be highly desirable, that the certainty of subsistence should be held out by law to the destitute able-bodied, rather than that their relief should depend on voluntary charity. In the first place, charity almost always does too much or too little: it lavishes its bounty in one place, and leaves people to starve in another. Secondly, since the state must necessarily provide subsistence for the criminal poor while undergoing punishment, not to do the same for the poor who have not offended is to give a premium on crime. And lastly, if the poor are left to individual charity, a vast amount of mendicity is inevitable. What the state may and should abandon to private charity, is the task of distinguishing between one case of real necessity and another. Private charity can give more to the more deserving. The state must act by general rules. It cannot undertake to discriminate between the deserving and the undeserving indigent. It owes no more than subsistence to the first, and can give no less to the last. What is said about the injustice of a law which has no better treatment for the merely unfortunate poor than for the ill-conducted, is founded on a misconception of the province of law and public authority. The dispensers of public relief have no business to be inquisitors. Guardians and overseers are not fit to be trusted to give or withhold other people's money according to their verdict on the morality of the person soliciting it; and it would show much ignorance of the ways of mankind to suppose that such persons, even in the almost impossible case of their being qualified, will take the trouble of ascertaining and sifting the past conduct of a person in distress, so as to form a rational judgment on it. Private charity can make these distinctions; and in bestowing its own money, is entitled to do so according to its own judgment. It should understand that this is its peculiar and appropriate province, and that it is commendable or the contrary, as it exercises the function with more or less discernment. But the administrators of a public fund ought not to be required to do more for anybody, than that minimum which is due even to the worst. If they are, the indulgence very speedily becomes the rule, and refusal the more or less capricious or tyrannical exception.

QUESTIONS FOR REFLECTION

1. Why, according to Mill, is government assistance to the poor preferable to private charity?
2. What are the disadvantages of government assistance?
3. How, according to Mill, should one structure welfare programs to maximize their good effects and minimize their disadvantages?
4. The Poor Law of 1834 required those receiving assistance, if not disabled, to live and work in workhouses and to surrender, while receiving assistance, the right to vote. Those requirements remained in effect until 1948. Would Mill support them?
5. How does Mill distinguish the deserving poor from the undeserving poor? Can government programs distinguish them? Should they be distinguished?

JOHN HOSPERS

What Libertarianism Is

John Hospers is professor emeritus of philosophy at the University of Southern California. He ran for president on the Libertarian Party ticket in 1972. *(Source: Reprinted by permission from Tibor R. Machan [ed.],* The Libertarian Alternative: Essays in Social and Political Philosophy *[Chicago: Nelson-Hall, 1974]. Copyright © 1974 by Nelson-Hall, Inc.)*

The political philosophy that is called libertarianism (from the Latin *libertas*, liberty) is the doctrine that every person is the owner of his own life, and that no one is the owner of anyone else's life; and that consequently every human being has the right to act in accordance with his own choices, unless those actions infringe on the equal liberty of other human beings to act in accordance with *their* choices.

There are several other ways of stating the same libertarian thesis:

1. *No one is anyone else's master, and no one is anyone else's slave.* Since I am the one to decide how my life is to be conducted, just as you decide about yours, I have no right (even if I had the power) to make you my slave and be your master, nor have you the right to become the master by enslaving me. Slavery is *forced* servitude, and since no one owns the life of anyone else, no one has the right to enslave another. Political theories past and present have traditionally been concerned with who should be the master (usually the king, the dictator, or government bureaucracy) and who should be the slaves, and what the extent of the slavery should be. Libertarianism holds that no one has the right to use force to enslave the life of another, or any portion or aspect of that life.
2. *Other men's lives are not yours to dispose of.* I enjoy seeing operas; but operas are expensive to produce.Opera-lovers often say, "The state (or the city, etc.) should subsidize opera, so that we can all see it. Also it would be for people's betterment, cultural benefit, etc." But what they are advocating is nothing more or less than legalized plunder. They can't pay for the productions themselves, and yet they want to see opera, which involves a large number of people and their labor; so what they are saying in effect is, "Get the money through legalized force. Take a little bit more out of every worker's paycheck every week to pay for the operas we want to see." But I have no right to take by force from the workers' pockets to pay for what I want.

Perhaps it would be better if he *did* go to see opera—then I should try to convince him to go voluntarily. But to take the money from him forcibly, because in my opinion it would be good for *him*, is still seizure of his earnings, which is plunder.

Besides, if I have the right to force him to help pay for my pet projects, hasn't he equally the right to force me to help pay for his? Perhaps he in turn wants the government to subsidize rock-and-roll, or his new car, or a house in the country? If I have the right to milk him, why hasn't he the right to milk me? If I can be a moral cannibal, why can't he too?

We should beware of the inventors of utopias. They would remake the world according to their vision—with the lives and fruits of the labor of *other* human beings. Is it someone's utopian vision that others should build pyramids to beautify the landscape? Very well, then other men should provide the labor; and if he is in a position of political power, and he can't get men to do it voluntarily, then he must *compel* them to "cooperate"—i.e., he must enslave them.

A hundred men might gain great pleasure from beating up or killing just one insignificant human being; but other men's lives are not theirs to dispose of. "In order to achieve the worthy goals of the next five-year-plan, we must forcibly collectivize the peasants . . ."; but other men's lives are not theirs to dispose of. Do you want to occupy, rent-free, the mansion that another man has worked for twenty years to buy? But other men's lives are not yours to dispose of. Do you want operas so badly that everyone is forced to work harder to pay for their subsidization through taxes? But other men's lives are not yours to dispose of. Do you want to have free medical care at the expense of other people, whether they wish to provide it or not? But this would require them to work longer for you whether they want to or not, and other men's lives are not yours to dispose of.

> The freedom to engage in any type of enterprise, to produce, to own and control property, to buy and sell on the free market, is derived from the rights to life, liberty, and property . . . which are stated in the Declaration of Independence . . . [but] when a government guarantees a "right" to an education or parity on farm products or a guaranteed annual income, it is staking a claim on the property of one group of citizens for the sake of another group. In short, it is violating one of the fundamental rights it was instituted to protect.*

3. *No human being should be a nonvoluntary mortgage on the life of another.* I cannot claim your life, your work, or the products of your efforts as mine. The fruit of one man's labor should not be fair game for every freeloader who comes along and demands it as his own. The orchard that has been carefully grown, nurtured, and harvested by its owner should not be ripe for the plucking for any bypasser who has a yen for the ripe fruit. The wealth that some men have produced should not be fair game for looting by government, to be used for whatever purposes its representatives determine, no matter what their motives in so doing may be. The theft of your money by a robber is not justified by the fact that he used it to help his injured mother.

It will already be evident that libertarian doctrine is embedded in a view of the rights of man. Each human being has the right to live his life as he chooses, compatibly with the equal right of all other human beings to live their lives as they choose.

All man's rights are implicit in the above statement. Each man has the right to life: any attempt by others to take it away from him, or even to injure him, violates this right, through the use of coercion against him. Each man has the right to liberty: to conduct his life in accordance with the alternatives open to him without coercive action by others. And every man has the right to property: to work to sustain his life (and the lives of whichever others he chooses to sustain, such as his family) and to retain the fruits of his labor.

People often defend the rights of life and liberty but denigrate property rights, and yet the right to property is as basic as the other two; indeed, without property rights no other rights are possible. Depriving you of property is depriving you of the means by which you live.

> . . . All that which an individual possesses by right (including his life and property) are morally his to use, dispose of and even destroy, as he sees fit. If I own my life, then it follows that I am free to associate with whom I please and not to associate with whom I please. If I own my knowledge and services, it follows that I may ask any compensation I wish for providing them for another, or I may abstain from providing them at all, if I so choose. If I own my house, it follows that I may decorate it as I please and live in it with whom I please. If I control my own business, it follows that I may charge what I please for my products or services, hire whom I please and not hire whom I please. All that which I own in fact, I may dispose of as I choose to in reality. For anyone to attempt to limit my freedom to do so is to violate my rights.

*William W. Bayes, "What Is Property?" *The Freeman,* July 1970, p. 348.

> Where do my rights end? Where yours begin. I may do anything I wish with my own life, liberty and property without your consent; but I may do nothing with your life, liberty and property without your consent. If we recognize the principle of man's rights, it follows that the individual is sovereign of the domain of his own life and property, and is sovereign of no other domain. To attempt to interfere forcibly with another's use, disposal or destruction of his own property is to initiate force against him and to violate his rights.

I have no right to decide how *you* should spend your time or your money. I can make that decision for myself, but not for you, my neighbor. I may deplore your choice of life-style, and I may talk with you about it provided you are willing to listen to me. But I have no right to use force to change it. Nor have I the right to decide how you should spend the money you have earned. I may appeal to you to give it to the Red Cross, and you may prefer to go to prizefights. But that is your decision, and however much I may chafe about it I do not have the right to interfere forcibly with it, for example by robbing you in order to use the money in accordance with *my* choices. (If I have the right to rob you, have you also the right to rob me?)

When I claim a right, I carve out a niche, as it were, in my life, saying in effect, "This activity I must be able to perform without interference from others. For you and everyone else, this is off limits." And so I put up a "no trespassing" sign, which marks off the area of my right. Each individual's right is his "no trespassing" sign in relation to me and others. I may not encroach upon his domain any more than he upon mine, without my consent. Every right entails a duty, true—but the duty is only that of *forbearance*—that is, of *refraining* from violating the other person's right. If you have a right to life, I have no right to take your life; if you have a right to the products of your labor (property), I have no right to take it from you without your consent. The non-violation of these rights will not guarantee you protection against natural catastrophes such as floods and earthquakes, but it will protect you against the aggressive activities *of other men*. And rights, after all, have to do with one's relations to other human beings, not with one's relations to physical nature.

Nor were these rights created by government; governments—some governments, obviously not all—*recognize* and *protect* the rights that individuals already have. Governments regularly forbid homicide and theft; and, at a more advanced stage, protect individuals against such things as libel and breach of contract. . . .

Government is the most dangerous institution known to man. Throughout history it has violated the rights of men more than any individual or group of individuals could do: it has killed people, enslaved them, sent them to forced labor and concentration camps, and regularly robbed and pillaged them of the fruits of their expended labor. Unlike individual criminals, government has the power to arrest and try; unlike individual criminals, it can surround and encompass a person totally, dominating every aspect of one's life, so that one has no recourse from it but to leave the country (and in totalitarian nations even that is prohibited). Government throughout history has a much sorrier record than any individual, even that of a ruthless mass murderer. The signs we see on bumper stickers are chillingly accurate: "Beware: the Government is Armed and Dangerous."

The only proper role of government, according to libertarians, is that of the protector of the citizen against aggression by other individuals. The government, of course, should never initiate aggression; its proper role is as the embodiment of the *retaliatory* use of force against anyone who initiates its use.

If each individual had constantly to defend himself against possible aggressors, he would have to spend a considerable portion of his life in target practice, karate exercises, and other means of self-defenses, and even so he would probably be helpless against groups of individuals who might try to kill, maim, or rob him. He would have little time for cultivating those qualities which are essential to civilized life, nor would improvements in science, medicine, and the arts be likely to occur. The function of government is to take this responsibility off his shoulders: the government undertakes to defend him against aggressors and to punish them if they attack him. When the government is effective in doing this, it enables the citizen to go about his business unmolested and without constant fear for his life. To do this, of course, government must have physical power—the police, to protect the citizen from aggression within its borders, and the armed forces, to protect him from aggressors outside. Beyond that, the government should not intrude upon his life, either to run his business, or adjust his daily activities, or prescribe his personal moral code.

Government, then, undertakes to be the individual's protector; but historically governments have gone far beyond this function. Since they already have the physical power, they have not hesitated to use it for purposes far beyond that which was entrusted to them in the first place. Undertaking initially to protect its citizens against aggression, it has often itself become an aggressor—a far greater aggressor, indeed, than the criminals against whom it was supposed to protect its citizens. Governments have done what no private citizens can do: arrest and imprison individuals without a trial and send them to slave labor camps. Government must have power in order to be effective—and yet the very means by which alone it can be effective make it vulnerable to the abuse of power, leading to managing the lives of individuals and even inflicting terror upon them.

What then should be the function of government? In a word, the *protection of human rights.*

1. *The right to life:* Libertarians support all such legislation as will protect human beings against the use of force by others, for example, laws against killing, attempted killing, maiming, beating, and all kinds of physical violence.
2. *The right to liberty:* There should be no laws compromising in any way freedom of speech, of the press, and of peaceable assembly. There should be no censorship of ideas, books, films, or of anything else by government.
3. *The right to property:* Libertarians support legislation that protects the property rights of individuals against confiscation, nationalization, eminent domain, robbery, trespass, fraud and misrepresentation, patent and copyright, libel and slander.

Someone has violently assaulted you. Should he be legally liable? Of course. He has violated one of your rights. He has knowingly injured you, and since he has initiated aggression against you he should be made to expiate.

Someone has negligently left his bicycle on the sidewalk where you trip over it in the dark and injure yourself. He didn't do it intentionally; he didn't mean you any harm. Should he be legally liable? Of course; he has, however unwittingly, injured you, and since the injury is caused by him and you are the victim, he should pay.

Someone across the street is unemployed. Should you be taxed extra to pay for his expenses? Not at all. You have not injured him, you are not responsible for the fact that he is unemployed (unless you are a senator or bureaucrat who agitated for further curtailing of business, which legislation passed, with the result that your neighbor was laid off by the curtailed business). You may voluntarily wish to help him out, or better still, try to get him a job to put him on his feet again; but since you have initiated no aggressive act against him, and neither purposely nor accidentally injured him in any way, you should not be legally penalized for the fact of his unemployment. (Actually, it is just such penalties that increase unemployment.)

One man, A, works hard for years and finally earns a high salary as a professional man. A second man, B, prefers not to work at all, and to spend wastefully what money he has (through inheritance), so that after a year or two he has nothing left. At the end of this time he has a long siege of illness and lots of medical bills to pay. He demands that the bills be paid by the government—that is, by the taxpayers of the land, including Mr. A.

But of course B has no such right. He chose to lead his life in a certain way—that was his voluntary decision. One consequence of that choice is that he must depend on charity in case of later need. Mr. A chose not to live that way. (And if everyone lived like Mr. B, on whom would he depend in case of later need?) Each has a right to live in the way he pleases, but each must live with the consequences of his own decision (which, as always, fall primarily on himself). He cannot, in time of need, claim A's beneficence as his right. . . .

Laws may be classified into three types: (1) laws protecting individuals against themselves, such as laws against fornication and other sexual behavior, alcohol, and drugs; (2) laws protecting individuals against aggressions by other individuals, such as laws against murder, robbery, and fraud;

(3) laws requiring people to help one another; for example, all laws which rob Peter to pay Paul, such as welfare.

Libertarians reject the first class of laws totally. Behavior which harms no one else is strictly the individual's own affair. Thus, there should be no laws against becoming intoxicated, since whether or not to become intoxicated is the individual's own decision; but there should be laws against driving while intoxicated, since the drunken driver is a threat to every other motorist on the highway (drunken driving falls into type 2). Similarly, there should be no laws against drugs (except the prohibition of sale of drugs to minors) as long as the taking of these drugs poses no threat to anyone else. Drug addiction is a psychological problem to which no present solution exists. Most of the social harm caused by addicts, other than to themselves, is the result of thefts which they perform in order to continue their habit—and then the *legal* crime is the theft, not the addiction. The actual cost of heroin is about ten cents a shot; if it were legalized, the enormous traffic in illegal sale and purchase of it would stop, as well as the accompanying proselytization to get new addicts (to make more money for the pusher) and the thefts performed by addicts who often require eighty dollars a day just to keep up the habit. Addiction would not stop, but the crimes would: it is estimated that 75 percent of the burglaries in New York City today are performed by addicts, and all these crimes could be wiped out at one stroke through the legalization of drugs. (Only when the taking of drugs could be shown to constitute a threat to *others* should it be prohibited by law. It is only laws protecting people against *themselves* that libertarians oppose.)

Laws should be limited to the second class only: aggression by individuals against other individuals. These are laws whose function is to protect human beings against encroachment by others; and this, as we have seen, is (according to libertarianism) the sole function of government.

Libertarians also reject the third class of laws totally: no one should be forced by law to help others, not even to tell them the time of day if requested, and certainly not to give them a portion of one's weekly paycheck. Governments, in the guise of humanitarianism, have given to some by taking from others (charging a "handling fee" in the process, which, because of the government's waste and inefficiency, sometimes is several hundred percent). And in so doing they have decreased incentive, violated the rights of individuals, and lowered the standard of living of almost everyone.

All such laws constitute what libertarians call *moral cannibalism*. A cannibal in the physical sense is a person who lives off the flesh of other human beings. A *moral* cannibal is one who believes he has a right to live off the "spirit" of other human beings—who believes that he has a moral claim on the productive capacity, time, and effort expended by others.

It has become fashionable to claim virtually everything that one needs or desires as one's *right*. Thus, many people claim that they have a right to a job, the right to free medical care, to free food and clothing, to a decent home, and so on. Now if one asks, apart from any specific context, whether it would be desirable if everyone had these things, one might well say yes. But there is a gimmick attached to each of them: *At whose expense?* Jobs, medical care, education, and so on, don't grow on trees. These are goods and services *produced only by men*. Who, then, is to provide them, and under what conditions?

If you have a right to a job, who is to supply it? Must an employer supply it even if he doesn't want to hire you? What if you are unemployable, or incurably lazy? (If you say "the government must supply it," does that mean that a job must be created for you which no employer needs done, and that you must be kept in it regardless of how much or little you work?) If the employer is forced to supply it at his expense even if he doesn't need you, then isn't *he* being enslaved to that extent? What ever happened to *his* right to conduct his life and his affairs in accordance with his choices?

If you have a right to free medical care, then, since medical care doesn't exist in nature as wild apples do, some people will have to supply it to you for free: that is, they will have to spend their time and money and energy taking care of you whether they want to or not. What ever happened to *their* right to conduct their lives as they see fit? Or do you have a right to violate theirs? Can there be a right to violate rights?

All those who demand this or that as a "free service" are consciously or unconsciously evading the fact that there is in reality no such thing as free services. All man-made goods and services are the result of human expenditure of time and effort. There is no such thing as "something for nothing" in this world. If you demand something free, you are demanding that other men give their time and effort to you without compensation. If they voluntarily choose to do this, there is no problem; but if you demand that they be *forced* to do it, you are interfering with their right not to do it if they so choose. "Swimming in this pool ought to be free!" says the indignant passerby. What he means is that others should build a pool, others should provide the materials, and still others should run it and keep it in functioning order, so that *he* can use it without fee. But what right has he to the expenditure of *their* time and effort? To expect something "for free" is to expect it *to be paid for by others* whether they choose to or not.

Many questions, particularly about economic matters, will be generated by the libertarian account of human rights and the role of government. Should government have no role in assisting the needy, in providing social security, in legislating minimum wages, in fixing prices and putting a ceiling on rents, in curbing monopolies, in erecting tariffs, in guaranteeing jobs, in managing the money supply? To these and all similar questions the libertarian answers with an unequivocal no.

"But then you'd let people go hungry!" comes the rejoinder. This, the libertarian insists, is precisely what would not happen; with the restrictions removed, the economy would flourish as never before. With the controls taken off business, existing enterprises would expand and new ones would spring into existence satisfying more and more consumer needs; millions more people would be gainfully employed instead of subsisting on welfare, and all kinds of research and production, released from the stranglehold of government, would proliferate, fulfilling man's needs and desires as never before. It has always been so whenever government has permitted men to be free traders on a free market. . . .

QUESTIONS FOR REFLECTION

1. How does Hospers define libertarianism?
2. What conception of rights emerges from Hospers's analysis?
3. What, according to Hospers, is the proper function of government? How does his view compare to Mill's? To Locke's?
4. How does Hospers respond to the charge that libertarianism fails to respond to real human needs? Do you find his answer convincing?

AMARTYA SEN

Equality of What?

Amartya Sen is Thomas W. Lamont University professor and professor of economics and philosophy at Harvard University. He is also a Senior Fellow at the Harvard Society of Fellows, Distinguished Fellow of All Souls College, Oxford, and a Fellow of Trinity College, Cambridge. He won the Nobel Prize for economic sciences in 1998. (Source: from The Tanner Lecture on Human Values, *vol. I, Cambridge: Cambridge University Press, 1980, pp. 197–220. Notes have been omitted.)*

3. Rawlsian Equality

Rawls's "two principles of justice" characterize the need for equality in terms of—what he has called—"primary social goods." These are "things that every rational man is presumed to want," including "rights, liberties and opportunities, income and wealth, and the social bases of self-respect." Basic liberties are separated out as having priority over other primary goods, and thus priority is given to the principle of liberty which demands that "each person is to have an equal right to the most extensive basic liberty compatible with a similar liberty for others." The second principle supplements this, demanding efficiency and equality, judging advantage in terms of an index of primary goods. Inequalities are condemned unless they work out to everyone's advantage. This incorporates the "Difference Principle" in which priority is given to furthering the interests of the worst-off. And that leads to maximin, or to leximin, defined not on individual utilities but on the index of primary goods. But given the priority of the liberty principle, no trade-offs are permitted between basic liberties and economic and social gain.

Herbert Hart has persuasively disputed Rawls's arguments for the priority of liberty, but with that question I shall not be concerned in this lecture. What is crucial for the problem under discussion is the concentration on bundles of primary social goods. Some of the difficulties with welfarism that I tried to discuss will not apply to the pursuit of Rawlsian equality. Objective criteria of well-being can be directly accommodated within the index of primary goods. So can be Mill's denial of the parity between pleasures from different sources, since the sources can be discriminated on the basis of the nature of the goods. Furthermore, while the Difference Principle is egalitarian in a way similar to leximin, it avoids the much-criticised feature of leximin of giving more income to people who are hard to please and who have to be deluged in champagne and buried in caviar to bring them to a normal level of utility, which you and I get from a sandwich and beer. Since advantage is judged not in terms of utilities at all, but through the index of primary goods, expensive tastes cease to provide a ground for getting more income. Rawls justifies this in terms of a person's responsibility for his own ends.

But what about the cripple with utility disadvantage, whom we discussed earlier? Leximin will give him more income in a pure distribution problem. Utilitarianism, I had complained, will give him *less*. The Difference Principle will give him neither more nor less on grounds of his being a cripple. His utility disadvantage will be irrelevant to the Difference Principle. This may seem hard, and I think it is. Rawls justifies this by pointing out that "hard cases" can "distract our moral perception by leading us to think of people distant from us whose fate arouses pity and anxiety." This can be so, but hard cases do exist, and to take disabilities, or special health needs, or physical or mental defects, as morally irrelevant, or to leave them out for fear of making a mistake, may guarantee that the *opposite* mistake will be made.

And the problem does not end with hard cases. The primary goods approach seems to take little note of the diversity of human beings. In the context of assessing utilitarian equality, it was argued that if people were fundamentally similar in terms of utility functions, then the utilitarian concern with maximizing the sum-total of utilities would push us simultaneously also in the direction of equality of utility levels. Thus utilitarianism could be rendered vastly more attractive if people really were similar. A corresponding remark can be made about the Rawlsian Difference Principle. If people were basically very similar, then an index of primary goods might be quite a good way of judging advantage. But, in fact, people seem to have very different needs varying with health, longevity, climatic conditions, location, work conditions, temperament, and even body size (affecting food and clothing requirements). So what is involved is not merely ignoring a few hard cases, but overlooking very widespread and real differences. Judging advantage purely in terms of primary goods leads to a partially blind morality.

Indeed, it can be argued that there is, in fact, an element of "fetishism" in the Rawlsian framework. Rawls takes primary goods as the embodiment of advantage, rather than taking advantage to be a *relationship* between persons and goods. Utilitarianism, or leximin, or—more generally—welfarism does not have this fetishism, since utilities are reflections of one type of relation between persons and goods. For example, income and wealth are not valued under utilitarianism as physical units, but in terms of their capacity to create human happiness or to satisfy human desires. Even if utility is not thought to be the right focus for the person–good relationship, to have an entirely good-oriented framework provides a peculiar way of judging advantage.

It can also be argued that while utility in the form of happiness or desire-fulfilment may be an *inadequate* guide to urgency, the Rawlsian framework asserts it to be *irrelevant* to urgency, which is, of course, a much stronger claim. The distinction was discussed earlier in the context of assessing welfarism, and it was pointed out that a rejection of welfarism need not take us to the point in which utility is given no role whatsoever. That a person's interest should have nothing directly to do with his happiness or desire-fulfilment seems difficult to justify. Even in terms of the prior-principle of prudential acceptability in the "original position," it is not at all clear why people in that primordial state should be taken to be so indifferent to the joys and sufferings in occupying particular positions, or if they are not, why their concern about these joys and sufferings should be taken to be morally irrelevant.

4. Basic Capability Equality

This leads to the further question: Can we not construct an adequate theory of equality on the *combined* grounds of Rawlsian equality and equality under the two welfarist conceptions, with some trade-offs among them. I would now like to argue briefly why I believe this too may prove to be informationally short. This can, of course, easily be asserted *if* claims arising from considerations other than well-being were acknowledged to be legitimate. Non-exploitation, or non-discrimination, requires the use of information not fully captured either by utility or by primary goods. Other conceptions of entitlements can also be brought in going beyond concern with personal well-being only. But in what follows I shall not introduce these concepts. My contention is that *even* the concept of *needs* does not get adequate coverage through the information on primary goods and utility.

I shall use a case-implication argument. Take the cripple again with marginal utility disadvantage. We saw that utilitarianism would do nothing for him; in fact it will give him *less* income than to the physically fit. Nor would the Difference Principle help him; it will leave his physical disadvantage severely alone. He did, however, get preferential treatment under leximin, and more generally, under criteria fostering total equality. His low level of total utility was the basis of his claim. But now suppose that he is no worse off than others in utility terms despite his physical handicap because of certain other utility features. This could be because he has a jolly disposition. Or because he has a low aspiration level and his heart leaps up whenever he sees a rainbow in the sky. Or because he is religious and feels that he will be rewarded in after-life, or cheerfully accepts what he takes to be just penalty for misdeeds in a past incarnation. The important point is that despite his marginal utility disadvantage, he has no longer a total utility deprivation. Now not even leximin—or any other notion of equality focussing on total utility—will do much for him. If we still think that he has needs as a cripple that should be catered to, then the basis of that claim clearly rests neither in high marginal utility, nor in low total utility, nor—of course—in deprivation in terms of primary goods.

It is arguable that what is missing in all this framework is some notion of "basic capabilities": a person being able to do certain basic things. The ability to move about is the relevant one here, but one can consider others, e.g., the ability to meet one's nutritional requirements, the wherewithal to be clothed and sheltered, the power to participate in the social life of the community. The notion of urgency related to this is not fully captured by either utility or primary goods, or any combination of the two. Primary goods suffers from fetishist handicap in being concerned with goods, and even though the list of goods is specified in a broad and inclusive way, encompassing rights, liberties, opportunities, income, wealth, and the social basis of self-respect, it still is concerned with good things rather than with what these good things *do* to human beings. Utility, on the other hand, *is* concerned with what these things do to human beings, but uses a metric that focusses not on the person's capabilities but on his mental reaction. There is something still missing in the combined list of primary goods and utilities. If it is argued that resources should be devoted to remove or substantially reduce the handicap of the cripple despite there being no marginal utility argument (because it is expensive), despite there being no total utility argument (because he is so contented), and despite there being no primary goods deprivation (because he has the goods that others have), the case must rest on something else. I believe what is at issue is the interpretation of needs in the form of basic capabilities. This interpretation of needs and interests is often implicit in the demand for equality. This type of equality I shall call "basic capability equality."

The focus on basic capabilities can be seen as a natural extension of Rawls's concern with primary goods, shifting attention from goods to what goods do to human beings. Rawls himself motivates judging advantage in terms of primary goods by referring to capabilities, even though his criteria end up focussing on goods as such: on income rather than on what income does, on the "social bases of self-respect" rather than on self-respect itself, and so on. If human beings were very like each other, this would not have mattered a great deal, but there is evidence that the conversion of goods to capabilities varies from person to person substantially, and the equality of the former may still be far from the equality of the latter.

There are, of course, many difficulties with the notion of "basic capability equality." In particular, the problem of indexing the basic capability bundles is a serious one. It is, in many ways, a problem comparable with the indexing of primary good bundles in the context of Rawlsian equality. This is not the occasion to go into the technical issues involved in such an indexing, but it is clear that whatever partial ordering can be done on the basis of broad uniformity of personal preferences must be supplemented by certain established conventions of relative importance.

The ideas of relative importance are, of course, conditional on the nature of the society. The notion of the equality of basic capabilities is a very general one, but any application of it must be rather culture-dependent, especially in the weighting of different capabilities. While Rawlsian equality has the characteristic of being both culture-dependent and fetishist, basic capability equality avoids fetishism, but remains culture-dependent. Indeed, basic capability equality can be seen as essentially an extension of the Rawlsian approach in a non-fetishist direction.

5. Concluding Remarks

I end with three final remarks. First, it is not my contention that basic capability equality can be the sole guide to the moral good. For one thing morality is not concerned only with equality. For another, while it is my contention that basic capability equality has certain clear advantages over other types of equality, I did not argue that the others were morally irrelevant. Basic capability equality is a partial guide to the part of moral goodness that is associated with the idea of equality. I have tried to argue that as a partial guide it has virtues that the other characterisations of equality do not possess.

Second, the index of basic capabilities, like utility, can be used in many different ways. Basic capability equality corresponds to total utility equality, and it can be extended in different directions, e.g., to leximin of basic capabilities. On the other hand, the index can be used also in a way similar to utilitarianism, judging the strength of a claim in terms of incremental contribution to *enhancing* the index value. The main departure is in focussing on a *magnitude* different from utility as well as the primary goods index. The new dimension can be utilised in different ways, of which basic capability equality is only one.

Last, the bulk of this lecture has been concerned with rejecting the claims of utilitarian equality, total utility equality, and Rawlsian equality to provide a sufficient basis for the equality-aspect of morality—indeed, even for that part of it which is concerned with needs rather than deserts. I have argued that none of these three is sufficient, nor is any combination of the three.

This is my main thesis. I have also made the constructive claim that this gap can be narrowed by the idea of basic capability equality, and more generally by the use of basic capability as a morally relevant dimension taking us beyond utility and primary goods. I should end by pointing out that the validity of the main thesis is not conditional on the acceptance of this constructive claim.

QUESTIONS FOR REFLECTION

1. How might Mill's idea that some goods are of higher quality than others be accommodated within Rawls's theory of justice?
2. Why does Sen reject Rawls's Difference Principle in its application to people with disabilities?
3. What problem does the diversity of people's desires and needs pose for Rawls's theory of justice?
4. What are basic capabilities? Why do other theories fail to take account of them?
5. Suppose that some people have few capabilities, through no fault of their own, and that attempting to equalize their capabilities with those of others would require either impoverishing or handicapping everyone else. What does Sen's theory imply in such a case?
6. Describe a case in which equality of capabilities conflicts with Rawls's difference principle. Is there any principle that determines which consideration should take precedence?
7. Might a concern for equality of capabilities require significant restrictions of liberty—of what Rawls calls basic liberties?

CHARLES MURRAY

from *Losing Ground: American Social Policy, 1950–1980*

Charles Murray is W. H. Brady Scholar at the American Enterprise Institute.
(Source: From Losing Ground: American Social Policy, 1950–1980 *by Charles Murray.*

CHAPTER 16 / THE CONSTRAINTS ON HELPING

Laws of Social Programs

. . . Let me suggest some characteristics . . . that occur so widely and for such embedded reasons that they suggest laws. That is, no matter how ingenious the design of a social transfer program may be, we cannot—in a free society—design programs that escape their influence. . . .

> #1. The Law of Imperfect Selection. Any objective rule that defines eligibility for a social transfer program will irrationally exclude some persons.

It can always be demonstrated that some persons who are excluded from the Food Stamps program are in greater need than some persons who receive Food Stamps. It can always be demonstrated that someone who is technically ineligible for Medicaid really "ought" to be receiving it, given the intent of the legislation.

These inequities, which are observed everywhere, are not the fault of inept writers of eligibility rules, but an inescapable outcome of the task of rule-writing. Eligibility rules must convert the concept of "true need" into objectified elements. The rules constructed from these bits and pieces are necessarily subject to what Herbert Costner has called "epistemic error"—the inevitable gap between quantified measures and the concept they are intended to capture. We have no way of defining "truly needy" precisely—not those who truly need to stop smoking, nor those truly in need of college scholarships or subsidized loans or disability insurance. Any criterion we specify will inevitably include a range of people, some of whom are unequivocally the people we intended to help, others of whom are less so, and still others of whom meet the letter of the eligibility requirement but are much less needy than some persons who do not.

Social welfare policy in earlier times tended to deal with this problem by erring in the direction of exclusion—better to deny help to some truly needy persons than to let a few slackers slip through. Such attitudes depended, however, on the assumption that the greater good was being served. Moral precepts had to be upheld. Whenever a person was inappropriately given help, it was bad for the recipient (undermining his character) and a bad example to the community at large.

When that assumption is weakened or dispensed with altogether, it follows naturally that the Law of Imperfect Selection leads to programs with constantly broadening target populations. If persons are not to blame for their plight, no real harm is done by giving them help they do not fully "need." No moral cost is incurred by permitting some undeserving into the program. A moral cost *is* incurred by excluding a deserving person. No one has a scalpel sharp enough to excise only the undeserving. Therefore it is not just a matter of political expedience to add a new layer to the eligible population rather than to subtract one (though that is often a factor in the actual decision-making process). It is also the morally correct thing to do, given the premises of the argument.

> #2. The Law of Unintended Rewards. Any social transfer increases the net value of being in the condition that prompted the transfer.

A deficiency is observed—too little money, too little food, too little academic achievement—and a social transfer program tries to fill the gap—with a welfare payment, Food Stamps, a compensatory education program. An unwanted behavior is observed—drug addiction, crime, unemployability—and the program tries to change that behavior to some other, better behavior—through a drug rehabilitation program, psychotherapy, vocational training. In each case, the program, however unintentionally, *must* be constructed in such a way that it increases the net value of being in the condition that it seeks to change—either by increasing the rewards or by reducing the penalties.

For some people in some circumstances, it is absurd to think in terms of "net value," because they so clearly have no choice at all about the fix they are in or because the net value is still less desirable than virtually any alternative. Paraplegics receiving Medicaid cannot easily be seen as "rewarded" for becoming paraplegics by the existence of free medical care. Poor children in Head Start cannot be seen as rewarded for being poor. Persons who are in the unwanted condition *completely involuntarily* are not affected by the existence of the reward.

But the number of such pure examples is very small. Let us return to the case of the middle-aged worker who loses his job, wants desperately to work, but can find nothing. He receives Unemployment Insurance, hating every penny of it. He would seem to be "completely involuntarily" in his situation and his search for a job unaffected by the existence of Unemployment Insurance. In fact, however, his behavior (unless he is peculiarly irrational) *is* affected by the existence of the Unemployment Insurance. For example, the cushion provided by Unemployment Insurance may lead him to refuse to take a job that requires him to move to another town, whereas he would take the job and uproot his home if he were more desperate. Most people (including me) are glad that his behavior is so affected, that he does not have to leave the home and friends of a lifetime, that he can wait for a job opening nearby. But he is not "completely involuntarily" unemployed in such a case, and the reason he is not is that the Unemployment Insurance has made the condition of unemployment more tolerable.

Our paraplegic anchors one end of the continuum labeled "Degree of Voluntarism in the Conditions that Social Policy Seeks to Change or Make Less Painful," and our unemployed worker is only slightly to one side of him—but he is to one side, not in the same place. The apparent unattractiveness of most of the conditions that social policy seeks to change must not obscure the continuum involved. No one chooses to be a paraplegic, and perhaps no one chooses to be a heroin addict. But the distinction remains: very few heroin addicts developed their addiction by being tied down and forcibly injected with heroin. They may not have chosen to become addicts, but they *did* choose initially to take heroin.

Let us consider the implications in terms of the archetypical social program for helping the chronic unemployed escape their condition, the job-training program.

Imagine that a program is begun that has the most basic and benign inducement of all, the chance to learn a marketable skill. It is open to everybody. By opening it to all, we have circumvented (for the time being) the Law of Unintended Rewards. All may obtain the training, no matter what their job history, so no unintended reward is being given for the condition of chronic unemployment.

On assessing the results, we observe that the ones who enter the program, stick with it, and learn a skill include very few of the hardcore unemployed whom we most wanted to help. The typical "success" stories from our training program are persons with a history of steady employment who wanted to upgrade their earning power. This is admirable. But what about the hardcore unemployed? A considerable number entered the program, but almost all of them dropped out or failed to get jobs once they left. Only a small proportion used the training opportunity as we had hoped. The problem of the hardcore unemployed remains essentially unchanged.

We may continue to circumvent the Law of Unintended Rewards. All we need do is continue the job-training program unchanged. It will still be there, still available to all who want to enroll, but we will do nothing to entice participation. Our theory (should we adopt this stance) is that, as time goes on, we will continue to help at least a few of the hardcore unemployed who are in effect skimmed from the top of the pool. We may even hope that the number skimmed from the top will be larger than the number who enter the pool, so that, given enough time, the population of hardcore unemployed will diminish. But this strategy is a gradualist one and relies on the assumption that other conditions in society are not creating more hardcore unemployed than the program is skimming off.

The alternative is to do something to get more of the hardcore unemployed into the program, and to improve the content so that more of them profit from the training. And once this alternative is taken, the program planner is caught in the trap of unintended rewards. Because we cannot "draft" people into the program or otherwise coerce their participation, our only alternative is to make it more attractive by changing the rules a bit.

Suppose, for example, we find that the reason many did not profit from the earlier program was that they got fired from (or quit) their new jobs within a few days of getting them, and that the reason they did so had to do with the job-readiness problem. The ex-trainee was late getting to work, the boss complained, the ex-trainee reacted angrily and was fired. We observe this to be a common pattern. We know the problem is not that the ex-trainee is lazy or unmotivated, but that he has never been socialized into the discipline of the workplace. He needs more time, more help, more patience than other workers until he develops the needed work habits. Suppose that we try to compensate—for example, by placing our trainees with employers who are being subsidized to hire such persons. The employer accepts lower productivity and other problems in return for a payment to do so (such plans have been tried frequently, with mixed results). Given identical work at identical pay, the ex-trainee is being rewarded for his "credential" of hardcore unemployment. He can get away with behavior that an ordinary worker cannot get away with.

May we still assume that the program is making progress in preparing its trainees for the real world marketplace? Will the hardcore unemployed modify their unreliable behavior? What will be the effect on morale and self-esteem among those trainees who were succeeding in the program before the change of rules? It is tempting to conclude that the program has already ceased to function effectively for anyone anymore, that the change in rules has done more harm than good. But my proposition is for the moment a more restricted one: The reward for unproductive behavior (both past and present) now exists.

What of the case of a drug addict who is chronically unemployed because (let us assume) of the addiction? It might seem that the unintended reward in such a case is innocuous; it consists of measures to relieve the addict of his addiction, measures for which the nonaddict will have no need or use. If we were dealing with an involuntary disability—our paraplegic again—the argument would be valid. But in the case of drug addiction (or any other behavior that has its rewards), a painless cure generally increases the attractiveness of the behavior. Imagine, for example, a pill that instantly and painlessly relieved dependence on heroin, and the subsequent effects on heroin use.

Thus we are faced with the problem we observed in the thought experiment. The program that seeks to change behavior must offer an inducement that unavoidably either adds to the attraction of, or reduces the penalties of engaging in, the behavior in question. The best-known example in real life is the thirty-and-a-third rule for AFDC recipients. It becomes more advantageous financially to hold a job than not to hold a job (the intended inducement for AFDC recipients to work), but it also becomes more advantageous to be on AFDC (the unintended reward to nonrecipients).

We are now ready to tackle the question of when a social program can reasonably be expected to accomplish net good and when it can reasonably be expected to produce net harm. Again let us think in terms of a continuum. All social programs, I have argued, provide an unintended reward for being in the condition that the program is trying to change or make more tolerable. But some of these unintended rewards are so small that they are of little practical importance. Why then can we not simply bring a bit of care to the design of such programs, making sure that the unintended reward is *always* small? The reason we are not free to do so lies in the third law of social programs:

> #3. The Law of Net Harm. The less likely it is that the unwanted behavior will change voluntarily, the more likely it is that a program to induce change will cause net harm.

A social program that seeks to change behavior must do two things. It must induce participation by the persons who are to benefit, as described under the Law of Unintended Rewards. Then it must actually produce the desired change in behavior. It must succeed, and success depends crucially on one factor above all others: The price that the participant is willing to pay.

The more that the individual is willing to accept whatever needs to be done in order to achieve the desired state of affairs, the broader the discretion of the program designers. Thus, expensive health resorts can withhold food from their guests, hospitals can demand that their interns work inhuman schedules, and elite volunteer units in the armed forces can ask their trainees to take risks in training exercises that seem (to the rest of us) suicidal. Such programs need offer no inducement at all except the "thing in itself" that is the *raison d'être* of the program—a shapelier body, a career as a physician, membership in the elite military unit. Similarly, the drug addict who is prepared to sign over to a program a great of deal of control over his own behavior may very well be successful—witness the sometimes impressive success rates of private treatment clinics.

The smaller the price that the participant is willing to pay, the greater the constraints on program design. It makes no difference to an official running a training program for the hardcore unemployed that (for example) the Marine Corps can instill exemplary work habits in recruits who come to the Corps no more "job-ready" than the recruits to the job-training program. If the training program tried for one day to use the techniques that the Marine Corps uses, it would lose its participants. Boot camp was not part of the bargain the job trainees struck with the government when they signed on. Instead, the training program must not only induce persons to join the program (which may be fairly easy). It must also induce them to stay in the program, induce them to cooperate with its curriculum, and induce them, finally, to adopt major changes in outlook, habits, and assumptions. The program content must be almost entirely carrot.

There is nothing morally reprehensible in approaches that are constrained to use only positive inducements. The objections are practical.

First, it is guaranteed that success rates will be very low. The technology of changing human behavior depends heavily on the use of negative reinforcement in conjunction with positive reinforcement. The more deeply engrained the behavior to be changed and the more attractions it holds for the person whose behavior is involved, the more important it is that the program have both a full tool kit available to it *and* the participant's willingness to go along with whatever is required. The Marine Corps has both these assets. Social programs to deal with the hardcore unemployed, teenaged mothers, delinquents, and addicts seldom do.

Second, as inducements become large—as they must, if the program is dealing with the most intractable problems—the more attractive they become to people who were not in need of help in the first place. We do not yet know how large they must finally become. We do know from experience, however, that quite generous experimental programs have provided extensive counseling, training, guaranteed jobs, and other supports—and failed. We can only guess at what would be enough—perhaps a matter of years of full-time residential training, followed by guaranteed jobs at double or triple the minimum wage; we do not know. Whatever they are, however, consider their effects on the people not in the program. At this point, it appears that any program that would succeed in helping large numbers of the hardcore unemployed will make hardcore unemployment a highly desirable state to be in.

The conditions that combine to produce net harm are somewhat different in the theoretical and the practical cases, but they come to the same thing.

Theoretically, any program that mounts an intervention with sufficient rewards to sustain participation and an effective result will generate so much of the unwanted behavior (in order to become eligible for the program's rewards) that the net effect will be to increase the incidence of the unwanted behavior. In practice, the programs that deal with the most intractable behavior problems have included a package of rewards large enough to induce participation, but not large enough to produce the desired result.

My conclusion is that social programs in a democratic society tend to produce net harm in dealing with the most difficult problems. They will inherently tend to have enough of an inducement to produce bad behavior and not enough of a solution to stimulate good behavior; and the more difficult the problem, the more likely it is that this relationship will prevail. The lesson is not that we can do no good at all, but that we must pick our shots.

CHAPTER 17 / CHOOSING A FUTURE

A Proposal for Public Welfare

I begin with the proposition that it is within our resources to do enormous good for some people quickly. We have available to us a program that would convert a large proportion of the younger generation of hardcore unemployed into steady workers making a living wage. The same program would drastically reduce births to single teenage girls. It would reverse the trendline in the breakup of poor families. It would measurably increase the upward socioeconomic mobility of poor families. These improvements would affect some millions of persons.

All these are results that have eluded the efforts of the social programs installed since 1965, yet, from everything we know, there is no real question about whether they would occur under the program I propose. A wide variety of persuasive evidence from our own culture and around the world, from experimental data and longitudinal studies, from theory and practice, suggests that the program would achieve such results.

The proposed program, our final and most ambitious thought experiment, consists of scrapping the entire federal welfare and income-support structure for working-aged persons, including AFDC, Medicaid, Food Stamps, Unemployment Insurance, Worker's Compensation, subsidized housing, disability insurance, and the rest. It would leave the working-aged person with no recourse whatsoever except the job market, family members, friends, and public or private locally funded services. It is the Alexandrian solution: cut the knot, for there is no way to untie it.

It is difficult to examine such a proposal dispassionately. Those who dislike paying for welfare are for it without thinking. Others reflexively imagine bread lines and people starving in the streets. But as a means of gaining fresh perspective on the problem of effective reform, let us consider what this hypothetical society might look like.

A large majority of the population is unaffected. A surprising number of the huge American middle and working classes go from birth to grave without using any social welfare benefits until they receive their first Social Security check. Another portion of the population is technically affected, but the change in income is so small or so sporadic that it makes no difference in quality of life. A third group comprises persons who have to make new arrangements and behave in different ways. Sons and daughters who fail to find work continue to live with their parents or relatives or friends. Teenaged mothers have to rely on support from their parents or the father of the child and perhaps work as well. People laid off from work have to use their own savings or borrow from others to make do until the next job is found. All these changes involve great disruption in expectations and accustomed roles.

Along with the disruptions go other changes in behavior. Some parents do not want their young adult children continuing to live off their income, and become quite insistent about their children learning skills and getting jobs. This attitude is most prevalent among single mothers who have to depend most critically on the earning power of their offspring.

Parents tend to become upset at the prospect of a daughter's bringing home a baby that must be entirely supported on an already inadequate income. Some become so upset that they spend considerable parental energy avoiding such an eventuality. Potential fathers of such babies find themselves under more pressure not to cause such a problem, or to help with its solution if it occurs.

Adolescents who were not job-ready find they are job-ready after all. It turns out that they can work for low wages and accept the discipline of the workplace if the alternative is grim enough. After a few years, many—not all, but many—find that they have acquired salable skills, or that they are at the right place at the right time, or otherwise find that the original entry-level job has gradually been transformed into a secure job paying a decent wage. A few—not a lot, but a few—find that the process leads to affluence.

Perhaps the most rightful, deserved benefit goes to the much larger population of low-income families who have been doing things right all along and have been punished for it: the young man who has taken responsibility for his wife and child even though his friends with the same choice have called him a fool; the single mother who has worked full time and forfeited her right to welfare for very little extra money; the parents who have set an example for their children even as the rules of the game have taught their children that the example is outmoded. For these millions of people, the instantaneous result is that no one makes fun of them any longer. The longer-term result will be that they regain the status that is properly theirs. They will not only be the bedrock upon which the community is founded (which they always have been), they will be recognized as such. The process whereby they regain their position is not magical, but a matter of logic. When it becomes highly dysfunctional for a person to be dependent, status will accrue to being independent, and in fairly short order. Noneconomic rewards will once again reinforce the economic rewards of being a good parent and provider.

The prospective advantages are real and extremely plausible. In fact, if a government program of the traditional sort (one that would "do" something rather than simply get out of the way) could *as plausibly* promise these advantages, its passage would be a foregone conclusion. Congress, yearning for programs that are not retreads of failures, would be prepared to spend billions. Negative side-effects (as long as they were the traditionally acceptable negative side-effects) would be brushed aside as trivial in return for the benefits. For let me be quite clear: I am not suggesting that we dismantle income support for the working-aged to balance the budget or punish welfare cheats. I am hypothesizing, with the advantage of powerful collateral evidence, that the lives of large numbers of poor people would be radically changed for the better.

There is, however, a fourth segment of the population yet to be considered, those who are pauperized by the withdrawal of government supports and unable to make alternate arrangements: the teenaged mother who has no one to turn to; the incapacitated or the inept who are thrown out of the house; those to whom economic conditions have brought long periods in which there is no work to be had; those with illnesses not covered by insurance. What of these situations?

The first resort is the network of local services. Poor communities in our hypothetical society are still dotted with storefront health clinics, emergency relief agencies, employment services, legal services. They depend for support on local taxes or local philanthropy, and the local taxpayers and philanthropists tend to scrutinize them rather closely. But, by the same token, they also receive considerably more resources than they formerly did. The dismantling of the federal services has poured tens of billions of dollars back into the private economy. Some of that money no doubt has been spent on Mercedes and summer homes on the Cape. But some has been spent on capital investments that generate new jobs. And some has been spent on increased local services to the poor, voluntarily or as decreed by the municipality. In many cities, the coverage provided by this network of agencies is more generous, more humane, more wisely distributed, and more effective in its results than the services formerly subsidized by the federal government.

But we must expect that a large number of people will fall between the cracks. How might we go about trying to retain the advantages of a zero-level welfare system and still address the residual needs?

As we think about the nature of the population still in need, it becomes apparent that their basic problem in the vast majority of the cases is the lack of a job, and this problem is temporary. What they need is something to tide them over while finding a new place in the economy. So our first step is to reinstall the Unemployment Insurance program in more or less its previous form. Properly administered, unemployment insurance makes sense. Even if it is restored with all the defects of current practice, the negative effects of Unemployment Insurance *alone* are relatively minor. Our objective is not to wipe out chicanery or to construct a theoretically unblemished system, but to meet legitimate human needs without doing more harm than good. Unemployment Insurance is one of the least harmful ways of contributing to such ends. Thus the system has been amended to take care of the victims of short-term swings in the economy.

Who is left? We are now down to the hardest of the hard core of the welfare-dependent. They have no jobs. They have been unable to find jobs (or have not tried to find jobs) for a longer period of time than the unemployment benefits cover. They have no families who will help. They have no friends who will help. For some reason, they cannot get help from local services or private charities except for the soup kitchen and a bed in the Salvation Army hall.

What will be the size of this population? We have never tried a zero-level federal welfare system under conditions of late-twentieth-century national wealth, so we cannot do more than speculate. But we may speculate. Let us ask of whom the population might consist and how they might fare.

For any category of "needy" we may name, we find ourselves driven to one of two lines of thought. Either the person is in a category that is going to be at the top of the list of services that localities vote for themselves, and at the top of the list of private services, or the person is in a category where help really is not all that essential or desirable. The burden of the conclusion is not that every single person will be taken care of, but that the extent of resources to deal with needs is likely to be very great—not based on wishful thinking, but on extrapolations from reality.

To illustrate, let us consider the plight of the stereotypical welfare mother—never married, no skills, small children, no steady help from a man. It is safe to say that, now as in the 1950s, there is no one who has less sympathy from the white middle class, which is to be the source of most of the money for the private and local services we envision. Yet this same white middle class is a soft touch for people trying to make it on their own, and a soft touch for "deserving" needy mothers—AFDC was one of the most widely popular of the New Deal welfare measures, intended as it was for widows with small children. Thus we may envision two quite different scenarios.

In one scenario, the woman is presenting the local or private service with this proposition: "Help me find a job and day-care for my children, and I will take care of the rest." In effect, she puts herself into the same category as the widow and the deserted wife—identifies herself as one of the most obviously deserving of the deserving poor. Welfare mothers who want to get into the labor force are likely to find a wide range of help. In the other scenario, she asks for an outright and indefinite cash grant—in effect, a private or local version of AFDC—so that she can stay with the children and not hold a job. In the latter case, it is very easy to imagine situations in which she will not be able to find a local service or a private philanthropy to provide the help she seeks. The question we must now ask is: What's so bad about that? If children were always better off being with their mother all day and if, by the act of giving birth, a mother acquired the inalienable right to be with the child, then her situation would be unjust to her and injurious to her children. Neither assertion can be defended, however—especially not in the 1980s, when more mothers of all classes work away from the home than ever before, and even more especially not in view of the empirical record for the children growing up under the current welfare system. Why should the mother be exempted by the system from the pressures that must affect everyone else's decision to work?

As we survey these prospects, important questions remain unresolved. The first of these is why, if federal social transfers are treacherous, should locally mandated transfers be less so? Why should a municipality be permitted to legislate its own AFDC or Food Stamp program if their results are so inherently bad?

Part of the answer lies in conceptions of freedom. I have deliberately avoided raising them—the discussion is about how to help the disadvantaged, not about how to help the advantaged cut their taxes, to which arguments for personal freedom somehow always get diverted. Nonetheless, the point is valid: Local or even state systems leave much more room than a federal system for everyone, donors and recipients alike, to exercise freedom of choice about the kind of system they live under. Laws are more easily made and changed, and people who find them unacceptable have much more latitude in going somewhere more to their liking.

But the freedom of choice argument, while legitimate, is not necessary. We may put the advantages of local systems in terms of the Law of Imperfect Selection. A federal system must inherently employ very crude, inaccurate rules for deciding who gets what kind of help, and the results are as I outlined them in Chapter 16. At the opposite extreme—a neighbor helping a neighbor, a family member helping another family member—the law loses its validity nearly altogether. Very fine-grained judgments based on personal knowledge are being made about specific people and changing situations. In neighborhoods and small cities, the procedures can still bring much individualized information to bear on decisions. Even systems in large cities and states can do much better than a national system; a decaying industrial city in the Northeast and a booming sunbelt city of the same size can and probably should adopt much different rules about who gets what and how much.

A final and equally powerful argument for not impeding local systems is diversity. We know much more in the 1980s than we knew in the 1960s about what does not work. We have a lot to learn about what *does* work. Localities have been a rich source of experiments. Marva Collins in Chicago gives us an example of how a school can bring inner-city students up to national norms. Sister Falaka Fattah in Philadelphia shows us how homeless youths can be rescued from the streets. There are numberless such lessons waiting to be learned from the diversity of local efforts. By all means, let a hundred flowers bloom, and if the federal government can play a useful role in lending a hand and spreading the word of successes, so much the better.

The ultimate unresolved question about our proposal to abolish income maintenance for the working-aged is how many people will fall through the cracks. In whatever detail we try to foresee the consequences, the objection may always be raised: We cannot be *sure* that everyone will be taken care of in the degree to which we would wish. But this observation by no means settles the question. If one may point in objection to the child now fed by Food Stamps who would go hungry, one may also point with satisfaction to the child who would have an entirely different and better future. Hungry children should be fed; there is no argument about that. It is no less urgent that children be allowed to grow up in a system free of the forces that encourage them to remain poor and dependent. If a strategy reasonably promises to remove those forces, after so many attempts to "help the poor" have failed, it is worth thinking about.

But that rationale is too vague. Let me step outside the persona I have employed and put the issue in terms of one last intensely personal hypothetical example. Let us suppose that you, a parent, could know that tomorrow your own child would be made an orphan. You have a choice. You may put your child with an extremely poor family, so poor that your child will be badly clothed and will indeed sometimes be hungry. But you also know that the parents have worked hard all their lives, will make sure your child goes to school and studies, and will teach your child that independence is a primary value. Or you may put your child with a family with parents who have never worked, who will be incapable of overseeing your child's education—but who have plenty of food and good clothes, provided by others. If the choice about where one would put one's own child is as clear to you as it is to me, on what grounds does one justify support of a system that, indirectly but without doubt, makes the other choice for other children? The answer that "What we really want is a world where that choice is not forced upon us" is no answer. We have tried to have it that way. We failed. Everything we know about why we failed tells us that more of the same will not make the dilemma go away.

The Ideal of Opportunity

Billions for equal opportunity, not one cent for equal outcome—such is the slogan to inscribe on the banner of whatever cause my proposals constitute. Their common theme is to make it possible to get as far as one can go on one's merit, hardly a new ideal in American thought.

The ideal itself has never lapsed. What did lapse was the recognition that practical merit exists. Some people are better than others. They deserve more of society's rewards, of which money is only one small part. A principal function of social policy is to make sure they have the opportunity to reap those rewards. Government cannot identify the worthy, but it can protect a society in which the worthy can identify themselves.

I am proposing triage of a sort, triage by self-selection. In triage on the battlefield, the doctor makes the decision—this one gets treatment, that one waits, the other one is made comfortable while waiting to die. In our social triage, the decision is left up to the patient. The patient always has the right to say "I can do X" and get a chance to prove it. Society always has the right to hold him to that pledge. The patient always has the right to fail. Society always has the right to let him.

There is in this stance no lack of compassion but a presumption of respect. People—all people, black or white, rich or poor—may be unequally responsible for what has happened to them in the past, but all are equally responsible for what they do next. Just as in our idealized educational system a student can come back a third, fourth, or fifth time to a course, in our idealized society a person can fail repeatedly and always be qualified for another chance—to try again, to try something easier, to try something different. The options are always open. Opportunity is endless. There is no punishment for failure, only a total absence of rewards. Society—or our idealized society—should be preoccupied with making sure that achievement is rewarded.

There is no shortage of people to be rewarded. Go into any inner-city school and you will find students of extraordinary talent, kept from knowing how good they are by rules we imposed in the name of fairness. Go into any poor community, and you will find people of extraordinary imagination and perseverance, energy and pride, making tortured accommodations to the strange world we created in the name of generosity. The success stories of past generations of poor in this country are waiting to be repeated.

There is no shortage of institutions to provide the rewards. Our schools know how to educate students who want to be educated. Our industries know how to find productive people and reward them. Our police know how to protect people who are ready to cooperate in their own protection. Our system of justice knows how to protect the rights of individuals who know what their rights are. Our philanthropic institutions know how to multiply the effectiveness of people who are already trying to help themselves. In short, American society is very good at reinforcing the investment of an individual in himself. For the affluent and for the middle-class, these mechanisms continue to work about as well as they ever have, and we enjoy their benefits. Not so for the poor. American government, in its recent social policy, has been ineffectual in trying to stage-manage the decision to invest, and it has been unintentionally punitive toward those who would make the decision on their own. It is time to get out of the way. . . .

QUESTIONS FOR REFLECTION

1. Explain Murray's three laws.
2. Are you convinced that Murray's laws are true? Why or why not?
3. What benefits would accrue, according to Murray, if welfare programs were eliminated altogether?
4. Who might be harmed by eliminating welfare programs, in Murray's view? In your view?
5. Is Murray committed to any particular theory of justice?
6. Reynolds's Law: "Subsidizing the markers of status [homeownership, college degrees, etc.] doesn't produce the character traits that result in that status; it undermines them." How does that relate to Murray's laws? Do programs intended to subsidize home ownership and education undermine desirable character traits? Why, or why not?

ELIZABETH S. ANDERSON

What Is the Point of Equality?

Elizabeth S. Anderson is Arthur F. Thurnau Professor and John Rawls Collegiate Professor of Philosophy and Women's Studies at the University of Michigan. (Source: from Ethics 109 (1999): 287–337. Notes are omitted.)

If much recent academic work defending equality had been secretly penned by conservatives, could the results be any more embarrassing for egalitarians? Consider how much of this work leaves itself open to classic and devastating conservative criticisms. Ronald Dworkin defines equality as an "envy-free" distribution of resources. This feeds the suspicion that the motive behind egalitarian policies is mere envy. Philippe Van Parijs argues that equality in conjunction with liberal neutrality among conceptions of the good requires the state to support lazy, able-bodied surfers who are unwilling to work. This invites the charge that egalitarians support irresponsibility and encourage the slothful to be parasitic on the productive. Richard Arneson claims that equality requires that, under certain conditions, the state subsidize extremely costly religious ceremonies that its citizens feel bound to perform. G. A. Cohen tells us that equality requires that we compensate people for being temperamentally gloomy, or for being so incurably bored by inexpensive hobbies that they can only get fulfilling recreation from expensive diversions. These proposals bolster the objection that egalitarians are oblivious to the proper limits of state power and permit coercion of others for merely private ends. Van Parijs suggests that to fairly implement the equal right to get married, when male partners are scarce, every woman should be given an equal tradable share in the pool of eligible bachelors and have to bid for whole partnership rights, thus implementing a transfer of wealth from successful brides to compensate the losers in love. This supports the objection that egalitarianism, in its determination to correct perceived unfairness everywhere, invades our privacy and burdens the personal ties of love and affection that lie at the core of family life.

Those on the left have no less reason than conservatives and libertarians to be disturbed by recent trends in academic egalitarian thought. First, consider those whom recent academic egalitarians have singled out for special attention: beach bums, the lazy and irresponsible, people who can't manage to entertain themselves with simple pleasures, religious fanatics. Thomas Nagel and Gerald Cohen give us somewhat more sympathetic but also pitiable characters in taking stupid, talentless, and bitter people to be exemplary beneficiaries of egalitarian concern. What has happened to the concerns of the politically oppressed? What about inequalities of race, gender, class, and caste? Where are the victims of nationalist genocide, slavery, and ethnic subordination?

Second, the agendas defined by much recent egalitarian theorizing are too narrowly focused on the distribution of divisible, privately appropriated goods, such as income and resources, or privately enjoyed goods, such as welfare. This neglects the much broader agendas of actual egalitarian political movements. For example, gay and lesbian people seek the freedom to appear in public as who they are, without shame or fear of violence, the right to get married and enjoy benefits of marriage, to adopt and retain custody of children. The disabled have drawn attention to the ways the configuration of public spaces has excluded and marginalized them, and campaigned against demeaning stereotypes that cast them as stupid, incompetent, and pathetic. Thus, with respect to both the targets of egalitarian concern and their agendas, recent egalitarian writing seems strangely detached from existing egalitarian political movements.

What has gone wrong here? I shall argue that these problems stem from a flawed understanding of the point of equality. Recent egalitarian writing has come to be dominated by the view that the fundamental aim of equality is to compensate people for undeserved bad luck—being born with poor native endowments, bad parents, and disagreeable personalities, suffering from accidents and illness, and so forth. I shall argue that in focusing on correcting a supposed cosmic injustice, recent egalitarian writing has lost sight of the distinctively political aims of egalitarianism. The proper negative aim of egalitarian justice is not to eliminate the impact of brute luck from human affairs, but to end oppression, which by definition is socially imposed. Its proper positive aim is not to ensure that everyone gets what they morally deserve, but to create a community in which people stand in relations of equality to others.

In this article, I will compare the implications of these two conceptions of the point of equality. The first conception, which takes the fundamental injustice to be the natural inequality in the distribution of luck, can be called "luck egalitarianism" or "equality of fortune." I shall argue that equality of fortune fails the most fundamental test any egalitarian theory must meet: that its principles express equal respect and concern for all citizens. It fails this test in three ways. First, it excludes some citizens from enjoying the social conditions of freedom on the spurious ground that it's their fault for losing them. It escapes this problem only at the cost of paternalism. Second, equality of fortune makes the basis for citizens' claims on one another the fact that some are inferior to others in the worth of their lives, talents, and personal qualities. Thus, its principles express contemptuous pity for those the state stamps as sadly inferior and uphold envy as a basis for distributing goods from the lucky to the unfortunate. Such principles stigmatize the unfortunate and disrespect the fortunate by failing to show how envy can obligate them. Third, equality of fortune, in attempting to ensure that people take responsibility for their choices, makes demeaning and intrusive judgments of people's capacities to exercise responsibility and effectively dictates to them the appropriate uses of their freedom.

The theory I shall defend can be called "democratic equality." In seeking the construction of a community of equals, democratic equality integrates principles of distribution with the expressive demands of equal respect. Democratic equality guarantees all law-abiding citizens effective access to the social conditions of their freedom at all times. It justifies the distributions required to secure this guarantee by appealing to the obligations of citizens in a democratic state. In such a state, citizens make claims on one another in virtue of their equality, not their inferiority, to others. Because the fundamental aim of citizens in constructing a state is to secure everyone's freedom, democratic equality's principles of distribution neither presume to tell people how to use their opportunities nor attempt to judge how responsible people are for choices that lead to unfortunate outcomes. Instead, it avoids bankruptcy at the hands of the imprudent by limiting the range of goods provided collectively and expecting individuals to take personal responsibility for the other goods in their possession.

Justice as Equality of Fortune

The following passage by Richard Arneson aptly describes the conception of justice I aim to criticize: "The concern of distributive justice is to compensate individuals for misfortune. Some people are blessed with good luck, some are cursed with bad luck, and it is the responsibility of society—all of us regarded collectively—to alter the distribution of goods and evils that arises from the jumble of lotteries that constitutes human life as we know it. . . . Distributive justice stipulates that the lucky should transfer some or all of their gains due to luck to the unlucky." This conception of justice can be traced to the work of John Rawls, and has been (I believe mistakenly) attributed to him. Equality of fortune is now one of the dominant theoretical positions among egalitarians, as evidenced by the roster of theorists who endorse it, including Richard Arneson, Gerald Cohen, Ronald Dworkin, Thomas Nagel, Eric Rakowski, and John Roemer. Philippe Van Parijs also incorporates this principle into his theory of equality of resources or assets. Luck egalitarianism relies on two moral premises: that people should be compensated for undeserved misfortunes and that the compensation should come only from that part of others' good fortune that is undeserved.

Part of the appeal of equality of fortune comes from its apparently humanitarian impulse. When decent people see others suffer for no good reason—say, children dying from starvation—they tend to regard it as a matter of obligation that the more fortunate come to their aid. Part of its appeal comes from the force of the obviously correct claim that no one deserves their genetic endowments or other accidents of birth, such as who their parents are or where they were born. This seems to weaken claims of those blessed by their genes or social circumstances to retain all of the advantages that typically flow from such good fortune. Besides these intrinsic sources of appeal, proponents of equality of fortune have tried to build support for egalitarianism by responding to many of the formidable objections that conservatives and libertarians have made against egalitarians of the past.

Consider the following litany of objections to equality. Some critics argue that the pursuit of equality is futile. For no two people are really equal: the diversity of individuals in their talents, aims, social identities, and circumstances ensures that in achieving equality in some domain, one will inevitably create inequalities in others. Give people the same amount of money and the prudent will get more happiness from it than the imprudent. Recent egalitarians have effectively responded to these charges by paying close attention to the problem of defining the proper space in which equality is desirable. Equality is a viable goal once the space of egalitarian concern is defined and the resulting inequalities in other domains are shown to be acceptable. Other critics charge that the quest for equality is wasteful because it would rather throw away goods that can't be evenly divided than let some have more than others. What's worse, it may call for leveling down people's talents when all cannot be lifted to the same high standards. Recent egalitarians adopt a leximin criterion of equality, permitting inequalities as long as they benefit, or, more permissively, don't harm the worst off. So they don't care much about income disparities among the very prosperous. Many proponents of equality of fortune also accept a strong principle of self-ownership, and so deplore interference with people's choices to develop their talents or forced appropriation of those talents.

Luck egalitarians have been most responsive to criticisms of equality based on ideals of desert, responsibility, and markets. Critics of equality object that egalitarians take goods away from the deserving. Proponents of equality of fortune reply that they take from the fortunate only that portion of their advantages that everyone acknowledges is undeserved. On the receiving side, the critics protest that egalitarianism undermines personal responsibility by guaranteeing outcomes independent of people's personal choices. In response, luck egalitarians have moved from an equality of outcome to an equality of opportunity conception of justice: they ask only that people start off with equal opportunities to achieve welfare or access to advantage, or that they start off with an equal share of resources. But they accept the justice of whatever inequalities result from adults' voluntary choices. All place great stress on the distinction between the outcomes for which an individual is responsible—that is, those that result from her voluntary choices—and the outcomes for which she is not responsible—good or bad outcomes that occur independent of her choice or of what she could have reasonably foreseen. Luck egalitarians dub this the distinction between "option luck" and "brute luck."

The Ills of Luck Egalitarianism: a Diagnosis

We have seen that equality of fortune underwrites a hybrid institutional scheme: free markets, to govern the distribution of goods attributable to factors for which individuals are responsible, and the welfare state, to govern the distribution of goods attributable to factors beyond the individual's control. Equality of fortune can thus be seen as an attempt to combine the best of capitalism and socialism. Its free market aspects promote efficiency, freedom of choice, "consumers' sovereignty," and individual responsibility. Its socialist aspects give everyone a fair start in life and protect the innocent against bad brute luck. Equality of fortune could be seen as a doctrine to which socialists might naturally gravitate, after learning the lessons of the follies of comprehensive centralized state economic planning and the considerable virtues of market allocations. By incorporating a very large role for market decisions within their institutional arrangements, luck egalitarians might appear to have disarmed the traditional conservative and libertarian critiques of egalitarianism.

But the counterintuitive judgments that luck egalitarians pass on the cases discussed above suggest a more dismal judgment: equality of fortune appears to give us some of the worst aspects of capitalism and socialism. Egalitarianism ought to reflect a generous, humane, cosmopolitan vision of a society that recognizes individuals as equals in all their diversity. It should promote institutional arrangements that enable the diversity of people's talents, aspirations, roles, and cultures to benefit everyone and to be recognized as mutually beneficial. Instead, the hybrid of capitalism and socialism envisioned by luck egalitarians reflects the mean-spirited, contemptuous, parochial vision of a society that represents human diversity hierarchically, moralistically contrasting the responsible and irresponsible, the innately superior and the innately inferior, the independent and the dependent. It offers no aid to those it labels irresponsible, and humiliating aid to those it labels innately inferior. It gives us the cramped vision of the Poor Laws, where unfortunates breathe words of supplication and submit to the humiliating moral judgments of the state.

How could luck egalitarians go so wrong? Consider first the ways equality of fortune invites problems in the ways it relies on market decisions. It offers a very inadequate safety net for the victims of bad option luck. This reflects the fact that equality of fortune is essentially a "starting-gate theory": as long as people enjoy fair shares at the start of life, it does not much concern itself with the suffering and subjection generated by people's voluntary agreements in free markets. The fact that these evils are the product of voluntary choices hardly justifies them: free choice within a set of options does not justify the set of options itself. In focusing on correcting the supposed injustices of nature, luck egalitarians have forgotten that the primary subject of justice is the institutional arrangements that generate people's opportunities over time.

Some luck egalitarians, most notably Dworkin, also use market decisions to provide guidance on appropriate state allocations at the start of life. The guiding idea here is that individual autonomy is protected by "consumers' sovereignty." Thus, Dworkin suggests that the market prices people actually pay for insurance against bodily injury might be used as a guide for the state's awards of compensation for people who are blamelessly injured in the same ways. But actual market prices for insurance reflect two factors irrelevant to determining the compensation the state might owe to the involuntarily injured: the need to keep compensation extremely low to reduce the moral hazard for nonfatal injuries (high compensation might tempt people to risk greater injuries), and the fact that people insure only against the costs of injury that the state does not already indemnify them against (e.g., workplace disability, public accommodations for the disabled).

Dworkin's resort to the hypothetical insurance purchases of people who don't know their abilities suffers from a larger problem: he never explains why such hypothetical market choices have any relevance at all to determining what citizens owe one another. Since these choices were not, in fact, made, the failure to reflect them in state allocations violates no one's actual autonomous choices. Individuals' market choices vary according to their tastes. But what one is obligated to do for others is not, in general, determined either by one's own or even by the beneficiaries' tastes. We have seen that such taste relativity licenses discrimination against citizens with rare disabilities and against risk-loving citizens. But even if certain people are willing to take risks with themselves, it doesn't follow that they give up their claim on fellow citizens to provide them with the same social insurance benefits against *involuntarily* caused disabilities to which their risk-averse fellows are entitled. Moreover, even if everyone would rationally purchase some insurance for themselves—say, for plastic surgery to correct minor defects in appearance—this fact is hardly sufficient to generate an *obligation* for society to pay for it. If everyone wants it, they could of course vote to include plastic surgery in a national health-care plan. But if they voted not to include it and leave everyone to purchase such insurance from their private resources, it is hard to see how any citizen could have a complaint of justice against the decision of the voters. It is one thing for everyone to decide that something is worth purchasing for their private consumption, quite another to decide that citizens acting collectively are obligated to socialize the costs of providing it to everyone. I conclude that *people's real or hypothetical market choices offer no guidance whatsoever to what citizens are obligated to provide to one another on a collective basis.* This suggests another desideratum for egalitarian theory: it must supply principles for collective willing— that is, for what citizens should will together, not just for what each can will individually.

Now consider the ways luck egalitarianism invites problems in the ways it relies on socialist principles. Equality of fortune tells us that no one should suffer from undeserved misfortune. To implement its principles, the state must make judgments of moral desert or responsibility in assigning outcomes to brute or option luck. To determine whether a smoker who picked up the habit while a soldier shall get state-funded medical treatment for lung cancer, other people must judge whether he should have shown stronger resolve against smoking, given the social pressures he faced from peers and advertisers while serving in the army, the anxiety-reducing benefits of smoking in the highly stressful situation of combat, the opportunities he was offered to overcome his habit after the war, and so forth.

F. A. Hayek has identified the central problem with such merit-based systems of reward: in order to lay a claim to some important benefit, people are forced to obey other people's judgments of what uses they should have made of their opportunities, rather than following their own judgments. Such a system requires the state to make grossly intrusive, moralizing judgments of individual's choices. Equality of fortune thus *interferes with citizens privacy and liberty.* Furthermore, as Arneson and Roemer make clear, such judgments require the state to determine how much responsibility each citizen was capable of exercising in each case. But it is disrespectful for the state to pass judgment on how much people are responsible for their expensive tastes or their imprudent choices.

Furthermore, equality of fortune would not really promote personal responsibility in the way that it claims. To be sure, it denies compensatory rewards to people who are judged responsible for their bad fortune. But this gives individuals an *incentive to deny personal responsibility for their problems,* and to represent their situation as one in which they were helpless before uncontrollable forces. Better social conditions for fostering the spread of a passive, whining victim's mentality could hardly be constructed. They allow citizens to lay claim to such goods as basic medical benefits only at the cost of making an undignified spectacle of themselves. Moreover, it is easier to construct a sob story recounting one's undeserved misfortunes than it is to engage in productive work that is valued by others. In giving people an incentive to channel their self-seeking energies in the former rather than the latter direction, equality of fortune generates a huge *deadweight loss* to society.

In promoting such an unhappy combination of capitalist and socialist institutions, equality of fortune succeeds not in establishing a society of equals, but only in reproducing the stigmatizing regime of the Poor Laws, in which citizens lay claim to aid from the state only on condition that they accept inferior status. Poor Law thinking pervades the reasoning of luck egalitarians. This is most evident in their distinction between the deserving and the undeserving disadvantaged—between those who are not responsible for their misfortune and those who are. Like the Poor Law regime, it abandons those disadvantaged through their own choices to their miserable fates, and defines the deserving disadvantaged in terms of their innate inferiority of talent, intelligence, ability, or social appeal.

Moreover, in classifying those who devote the bulk of their energies to caring for dependents with those who have a voluntarily expensive taste for charity, equality of fortune *assumes atomistic egoism and self-sufficiency as the norm for human beings.* It promises equality only to those who tend only to their own self-interest, who avoid entering into relationships with others that might generate obligations to engage in dependent caretaking, and who therefore can manage to take care of themselves through their own wage earning, without having to depend on market-generated income provided by anyone else. But such a norm for human beings cannot be universalized. Long periods of dependency on others' caretaking are a normal and inevitable part of everyone's life cycle. It is therefore an indispensable condition of the continuation of human society that many adults devote a great deal of their time to such caretaking, however poorly such work may be remunerated in the market. And this, in turn, entails some dependency of caretakers on income generated by others. Equality of fortune, in representing the dependency of caretakers as voluntary deviance from a falsely universalized androcentric norm, ends up justifying the subordination of women to male wage earners and the stigmatization of dependent caretaking relative to self-sufficient wage earning. A more perfect reproduction of Poor Law thinking, including its sexism and its conflation of responsible work with market wage-earning, could hardly be imagined.

What is the Point of Equality?

There must be a better way to conceive of the point of equality. To do so, it is helpful to recall how egalitarian political movements have historically conceived of their aims. What have been the inegalitarian systems that they have opposed? Inegalitarianism asserted the justice or necessity of basing social order on a hierarchy of human beings, ranked according to intrinsic worth. Inequality referred not so much to distributions of goods as to relations between superior and inferior persons. Those of superior rank were thought entitled to inflict violence on inferiors, to exclude or segregate them from social life, to treat them with contempt, to force them to obey, work without reciprocation, and abandon their own cultures. These are what Iris Young has identified as the faces of oppression: marginalization, status hierarchy, domination, exploitation, and cultural imperialism. Such unequal social relations generate, and were thought to justify, inequalities in the distribution of freedoms, resources, and welfare. This is the core of inegalitarian ideologies of racism, sexism, nationalism, caste, class, and eugenics.

Egalitarian political movements oppose such hierarchies. They assert the equal moral worth of persons. This assertion does not mean that all have equal virtue or talent. Negatively, the claim repudiates distinctions of moral worth based on birth or social identity—on family membership, inherited social status, race, ethnicity, gender, or genes. There are no natural slaves, plebeians, or aristocrats. Positively, the claim asserts that all competent adults are equally moral agents: everyone equally has the power to develop and exercise moral responsibility, to cooperate with others according to principles of justice, to shape and fulfill a conception of their good.

Egalitarians base claims to social and political equality on the fact of universal moral equality. These claims also have a negative and a positive aspect. Negatively, egalitarians seek to abolish oppression—that is, forms of social relationship by which some people dominate, exploit, marginalize, demean, and inflict violence upon others. Diversities in socially ascribed identities, distinct roles in the division of labor, or differences in personal traits, whether these be neutral biological and psychological differences, valuable talents and virtues, or unfortunate disabilities and infirmities, never justify the unequal social relations listed above. Nothing can justify treating people in these ways, except just punishment for crimes and defense against violence. Positively, egalitarians seek a social order in which persons stand in relations of equality. They seek to live together in a democratic community, as opposed to a hierarchical one. Democracy is here understood as collective self-determination by means of open discussion among equals, in accordance with rules acceptable to all. To stand as an equal before others in discussion means that one is entitled to participate, that others recognize an obligation to listen respectfully and respond to one's arguments, that no one need bow and scrape before others or represent themselves as inferior to others as a condition ofhaving their claim heard.

Contrast this democratic conception of equality with equality of fortune. First, democratic equality aims to abolish socially created oppression. Equality of fortune aims to correct what it takes to be injustices generated by the natural order. Second, democratic equality is what I shall call a relational theory of equality: it views equality as a social relationship. Equality of fortune is a distributive theory of equality:

it conceives of equality as a pattern of distribution. Thus, equality of fortune regards two people as equal so long as they enjoy equal amounts of some distributable good—income, resources, opportunities for welfare, and so forth. Social relationships are largely seen as instrumental to generating such patterns of distribution. By contrast, democratic equality regards two people as equal when each accepts the obligation to justify their actions by principles acceptable to the other, and in which they take mutual consultation, reciprocation, and recognition for granted. Certain patterns in the distribution of goods may be instrumental to securing such relationships, follow from them, or even be constitutive of them. But democratic egalitarians are fundamentally concerned with the relationships within which goods are distributed, not only with the distribution of goods themselves. This implies, third, that democratic equality is sensitive to the need to integrate the demands of equal recognition with those of equal distribution. Goods must be distributed according to principles and processes that express respect for all. People must not be required to grovel or demean themselves before others as a condition of laying claim to their share of goods. The basis for people's claims to distributed goods is that they are equals, not inferiors, to others.

This gives us a rough conception of equality. How do we derive principles of justice from it? Our investigation of equality of fortune has not been completely fruitless: from its failures, we have gleaned some desiderata for egalitarian principles. First, such principles must identify certain goods to which all citizens must have effective access over the course of their whole lives. Some goods are more important from an egalitarian point of view than others, within whatever space of equality is identified as of particular concern for egalitarians. And starting-gate theories, or any other principles that allow law-abiding citizens to lose access to adequate levels of these goods, are unacceptable. Second, egalitarians should be able to justify such guarantees of lifetime accessibility without resorting to paternalism. Third, egalitarian principles should offer remedies that match the type of injustice being corrected. Private satisfactions cannot make up for public oppression. Fourth, egalitarian principles should uphold the responsibility of individuals for their own lives without passing demeaning and intrusive judgments on their capacities for exercising responsibility or on how well they have used their freedoms. Finally, such principles should be possible objects of collective willing. They should be capable of supplying sufficient reasons for citizens acting together to collectively guarantee the particular goods of concern to egalitarians.

Let us take up the last desideratum first. The determination of what can or must be collectively willed has been the traditional task of social contract theory. In liberal democratic versions of social contract theory, the fundamental aim of the state is to secure the liberty of its members. Since the democratic state is nothing more than citizens acting collectively, it follows that the fundamental obligation of citizens to one another is to secure the social conditions of everyone's freedom. Because libertarians also embrace this formula, it might be thought to lead to inegalitarian implications. Instead of repudiating this formula, democratic equality interprets it. It claims that the social condition of living a free life is that one stand in relations ofequality with others.

This claim might seem paradoxical, given the prevailing view that represents equality and freedom as conflicting ideals. We can see how it is true by considering the oppressive relationships that social equality negates. Equals are not subject to arbitrary violence or physical coercion by others. Choice unconstrained by arbitrary physical coercion is one of the fundamental conditions of freedom. Equals are not marginalized by others. They are therefore free to participate in politics and the major institutions of civil society. Equals are not dominated by others; they do not live at the mercy of others' wills. This means that they govern their lives by their own wills, which is freedom. Equals are not exploited by others. This means they are free to secure the fair value of their labor. Equals are not subject to cultural imperialism: they are free to practice their own culture, subject to the constraint of respecting everyone else. To live in an egalitarian community, then, is to be free from oppression to participate in and enjoy the goods of society, and to participate in democratic self-government.

Egalitarians thus differ from libertarians in advocating a more expansive understanding of the social conditions of freedom. Importantly, they view private relations of domination, even those entered into by consent or contract, as violations of individual freedom. Libertarians tend to identify freedom with formal, negative freedom: enjoying the legal right to do what one wants without having to ask anyone else's permission and without interference from others. This definition of freedom neglects the importance of having the means to do what one wants. In addition, the definition implicitly assumes that, given the material means and internal capacity to do what one wants, the absence of interference from others is all one needs to do what one wants. This ignores the fact that most of the things people want to do require participation in social activities, and hence communication and interaction with others. One cannot do these things if others make one an outcast. A libertarian might argue that freedom of association entails the right of people to refuse to associate with others on any grounds. Yet, a society embodying such an unconditional right hardly needs physical coercion to force others to obey the wishes of those with the power to exclude others from participation in social life. The same point applies to a society in which property is so unequally distributed that some adults live in abject dependence on others, and so live at the mercy of others. Societies that permit the creation of outcasts and subordinate classes can be as repressive as any despotic regime.

Equality in the Space of Freedom: A Capabilities Approach

Amartya Sen has proposed a better way to understand freedom. Consider the states of being and doing that constitute a person's well-being: a person can be healthy, well-nourished, physically fit, literate, an active participant in community life, mobile, happy, respected, confident, and so forth. A person may also care about other states of being and doing that reflect her autonomous ends: she may want to be outgoing, to raise children, practice medicine, play soccer, make love, and so forth. Call such states *functionings*. A person's *capabilities* consist of the sets of functionings she can achieve, given the personal, material, and social resources available to her. Capabilities measure not actually achieved functionings, but a person's freedom to achieve valued functionings. A person enjoys more freedom the greater the range of effectively accessible, significantly different opportunities she has for functioning or leading her life in ways she values most. We can understand the egalitarian aim to secure for everyone the social conditions of their freedom in terms of capabilities. Following Sen, I say that egalitarians should seek equality for all in the space of capabilities.

Sen's capability egalitarianism leaves open a large question, however. *Which* capabilities does society have an obligation to equalize? Some people care about playing cards well, others about enjoying luxury vacations in Tahiti. Must egalitarians, in the name of equal freedom, offer free card-playing lessons and state subsidized vacations in exotic lands? Surely there are limits to which capabilities citizens are obligated to provide one another. We should heed our first desideratum, to identify particular goods within the space of equality that are of special egalitarian concern.

Reflection on the negative and positive aims of egalitarianism helps us meet this requirement. Negatively, people are entitled to whatever capabilities are necessary to enable them to avoid or escape entanglement in oppressive social relationships. Positively, they are entitled to the capabilities necessary for functioning as an equal citizen in a democratic state. While the negative and positive aims of egalitarianism overlap to a large extent, they are not identical. If functioning as an equal citizen were all that egalitarians cared about, they could not object to forced clitoridectomy, by which men control women's sexuality in private relations. But egalitarians also aim at abolishing private relations of domination, and therefore support the functionings needed for individual sexual autonomy. If having the capabilities needed to avoid oppression were all that mattered, then egalitarians would not oppose discrimination among the relatively privileged—for example, the glass ceiling for female executives. But egalitarians also aim at enabling all citizens to stand as equals to one another in civil society, and this requires that careers be open to talents.

Democratic equality thus aims for equality across a wide range of capabilities. But it does not support comprehensive equality in the space of capabilities. Being a poor card player does not make one oppressed. More precisely, the social order can and should be arranged so that one's skill at cards does not determine one's status in civil society. Nor is being a good card player necessary for functioning as a citizen. Society therefore has no obligation to provide free card lessons to citizens. Democratic equality satisfies the first desideratum of egalitarian theory.

Consider further the capabilities that democratic equality does guarantee to citizens. Let us focus on the capabilities necessary for functioning as an equal citizen. Citizenship involves functioning not only as a political agent—voting, engaging in political speech, petitioning government, and so forth—but participating as an equal in civil society. Civil society is the sphere of social life that is open to the general public and is not part of the state bureaucracy, in charge of the administration of laws. Its institutions include public streets and parks, public accommodations such as restaurants, shops, theaters, buses and airlines, communications systems such as broadcasting, telephones, and the Internet, public libraries, hospitals, schools, and so forth. Enterprises engaged in production for the market are also part of civil society, because they sell their products to any customer and draw their employees from the general public. One of the important achievements of the civil rights movement was to vindicate an understanding of citizenship that includes the right to participate as an equal in civil society as well as in government affairs. A group that is excluded from or segregated within the institutions of civil society, or subject to discrimination on the basis of ascribed social identities by institutions in civil society, has been relegated to second-class citizenship, even if its members enjoy all of their political rights.

So, to be capable of functioning as an equal citizen involves not just the ability to effectively exercise specifically political rights, but also to participate in the various activities of civil society more broadly, including participation in the economy. And functioning in these ways presupposes functioning as a human being. Consider, then, three aspects of individual functioning: as a human being, as a participant in a system of cooperative production, and as a citizen of a democratic state. To be capable of functioning as a human being requires effective access to the means of sustaining one's biological existence—food, shelter, clothing, medical care—and access to the basic conditions of human agency—knowledge of one's circumstances and options, the ability to deliberate about means and ends, the psychological conditions of autonomy, including the self-confidence to think and judge for oneself, freedom of thought and movement. To be capable of functioning as an equal participant in a system of cooperative production requires effective access to the means of production, access to the education needed to develop one's talents, freedom of occupational choice, the right to make contracts and enter into cooperative agreements with others, the right to receive fair value for one's labor, and recognition by others of one's productive contributions. To be capable of functioning as a citizen requires rights to political participation, such as freedom of speech and the franchise, and also effective access to the goods and relationships of civil society. This entails freedom of association, access to public spaces such as roads, parks, and public accommodations including public transportation, the postal service, and telecommunications. This also entails the social conditions of being accepted by others, such as the ability to appear in public without shame, and not being ascribed outcast status. The freedom to form relationships in civil society also requires effective access to private spaces, since many such relationships can only function when protected from the scrutiny and intrusions of others. Homelessness—that is, having only public dwelling—is a condition of profound unfreedom.

Three points should be made about the structure of egalitarian guarantees in the space of freedom or capabilities. First, democratic equality guarantees not actual levels of functioning, but effective access to those levels. Individuals are free to choose to function at a lower level than they are guaranteed. For example, they might choose to join a religious group that discourages political participation. Moreover, democratic equality can make access to certain functionings—those requiring an income—conditional upon working for them, provided that citizens have effective access to those conditions—they are physically capable of performing the work, doing so is consistent with their other duties, they can find a job, and so forth. Effective access to a level of functioning means that people can achieve that functioning by deploying means already at their disposal, not that the functioning is unconditionally guaranteed without any effort on their own part. Thus, democratic equality is consistent with constructing the incentive systems needed for a modern economy to support the production needed to support egalitarian guarantees in the first place.

Second, democratic equality guarantees not effective access to equal levels of functioning but effective access to levels of functioning sufficient to stand as an equal in society. For some functionings, equal citizenship requires equal levels. For example, each citizen is entitled to the same number of votes in an election as everyone else. But for other functionings, standing as an equal does not require equal levels of functioning. To be capable of standing as an equal in civil society requires literacy. But in the U.S. context, it does not require literacy in any language other than English, nor the ability to interpret obscure works of literary theory. Democratic equality does not object if not everyone knows a foreign language, and only a few have a Ph.D.-level training in literature. In other countries, multilingual literacy might be required for equal standing.

Third, democratic equality guarantees effective access to a package of capabilities sufficient for standing as an equal over the course of an entire life. It is not a starting-gate theory, in which people could lose their access to equal standing through bad option luck. Access to the egalitarian capabilities is also market-inalienable: contracts whereby individuals irrevocably transfer their fundamental freedoms to others are null and void. The rationale for establishing such inalienable rights might seem difficult to grasp from the point of view of the rights holder. Why shouldn't she be free to trade some of her egalitarian-guaranteed freedoms for other goods that she prefers? Isn't it paternalistic to deny her the freedom to trade?

We can avoid this thought by considering the point of view of the obligation holder. The counterpart to an individual's inalienable right to the social conditions of her freedom is the unconditional obligation of others to respect her dignity or moral equality. Kant would put the point as follows: every individual has a worth or dignity that is not conditional upon anyone's desires or preferences, not even the individual's own desires. This implies that there are some things one may never do to other people, such as to enslave them, even if one has their permission or consent. Contracts into slavery or servitude are therefore invalid. In basing inalienable rights on what others are obligated to do rather than on the rights bearer's own subjective interests, democratic equality satisfies the second desideratum of egalitarian theory: to justify lifetime guarantees without resorting to paternalism.

One advantage of the capabilities approach to equality is that it allows us to analyze injustices in regard to other matters besides the distribution of resources and other divisible goods. One's capabilities are a function not just of one's fixed personal traits and divisible resources, but of one's mutable traits, social relations and norms, and the structure of opportunities, public goods, and public spaces. Egalitarian political movements have never lost sight of the whole range of targets of egalitarian assessment. For example, feminists work to overcome the internal obstacles to choice—self-abnegation, lack of confidence, and low self-esteem—that women often face from internalizing norms of femininity. Gays and lesbians seek the ability to publicly reveal their identities without shame or fear, which requires significant changes in social relations of contempt and hostility, and changes in norms of gender and sexuality. The disabled aim to reconfigure public spaces to make them accessible and adapt work situations to their needs, so that they can participate in productive activity. No mere redistribution of divisible resources can secure the freedoms these groups seek.

Of course, democratic equality is also concerned with the distribution of divisible resources. It requires that everyone have effective access to enough resources to avoid being oppressed by others and to function as an equal in civil society. What counts as "enough" varies with cultural norms, the natural environment, and individual circumstance. For example, cultural norms and climate influence what kind of clothing one needs to be able to appear in public without shame and with adequate protection from the elements. Individual circumstances, such as disabilities, influence how much resources one needs to function as an equal. People without use of their legs may need more resources—wheelchairs, specially adapted vans—to achieve mobility comparable to that of ambulatory persons. Equality in the space of capabilities may therefore demand an unequal division of resources to accommodate the disabled. What citizens ultimately owe one another is the social conditions of the freedoms people need to function as equal citizens. Because of differences in their internal capacities and social situations, people are not equally able to convert resources into capabilities for functioning. They are therefore entitled to different amounts of resources so they can enjoy freedom as equals.

Suppose we abstract from the fact that people have different internal physical and mental capabilities. Would democratic equality demand that external resources be divided equally from the start, as equality of fortune holds? There is no reason to think so. The capabilities relevant to functioning as a human being, as a participant in the system of social cooperation, and as an equal citizen do not include all functionings or all levels of functioning. To function as a human being, one needs adequate nutrition. To eat without being relegated to a subhuman status, one needs access to sources of nutrition besides pet food or the dumpster. But to be able to function as a dignified human being, one does not need the quantity or quality of food intake of a gourmet. Democratic equality therefore requires that everyone have effective access to adequate nutrition, as well as sources of nutrition that one's society considers dignified—fit for consumption in social gatherings. It does not require that everyone have the resources needed for an equal opportunity to function as a gourmet. It therefore does not require criteria for equality of resources that depend on the morally dubious idea that the distribution of resources should be sensitive to considerations of envy.

QUESTIONS FOR REFLECTION

1. Anderson complains that other egalitarians write about cases that are bad public relations. But her complaint goes deeper. What do those other approaches have in common?
2. What is luck egalitarianism? How does Anderson argue against it?
3. Explain Dworkin's idea of hypothetical insurance purchases. How does Anderson argue against it? How might Dworkin respond?
4. What is Hayek's objection to social insurance schemes?
5. Why, according to Anderson, do certain kinds of egalitarianism undermine personal responsibility? What must an egalitarianism be like to avoid that result?
6. What is democratic equality?
7. How does Anderson derive principles of justice from her conception of democratic equality?
8. How does Anderson object to Sen's capabilities view? How does she use democratic equality to solve the problem she sees with his view?

ROBERT RECTOR AND RACHEL SHEFFIELD

Air Conditioning, Cable TV, and an Xbox: What Is Poverty in the United States Today?

Robert Rector is senior research fellow on welfare and family issues at the Heritage Foundation. Rachel Sheffield focuses on policy issues related to welfare, marriage and family, and education as research assistant in the DeVos Center for Religion & Civil Society at the Heritage Foundation. (Source: Report No. 2575 (2011), published by the Heritage Foundation. Reprinted by permission. Notes are omitted.)

Each year for the past two decades, the U.S. Census Bureau has reported that over 30 million Americans were living in "poverty." In recent years, the Census has reported that one in seven Americans are poor. But what does it mean to be "poor" in America? How poor are America's poor?

For most Americans, the word "poverty" suggests destitution: an inability to provide a family with nutritious food, clothing, and reasonable shelter. For example, the Poverty Pulse poll taken by the Catholic Campaign for Human Development asked the general public: "How would you describe being poor in the U.S.?" The overwhelming majority of responses focused on homelessness, hunger or not being able to eat properly, and not being able to meet basic needs. That perception is bolstered by news stories about poverty that routinely feature homelessness and hunger.

Yet if poverty means lacking nutritious food, adequate warm housing, and clothing for a family, relatively few of the more than 30 million people identified as being "in poverty" by the Census Bureau could be characterized as poor. While material hardship definitely exists in the United States, it is restricted in scope and severity. The average poor person, as defined by the government, has a living standard far higher than the public imagines.

As scholar James Q. Wilson has stated, "The poorest Americans today live a better life than all but the richest persons a hundred years ago." In 2005, the typical household defined as poor by the government had a car and air conditioning. For entertainment, the household had two color televisions, cable or satellite TV, a DVD player, and a VCR.

If there were children, especially boys, in the home, the family had a game system, such as an Xbox or a PlayStation. In the kitchen, the household had a refrigerator, an oven and stove, and a microwave. Other household conveniences included a clothes washer, clothes dryer, ceiling fans, a cordless phone, and a coffee maker.

The home of the typical poor family was not overcrowded and was in good repair. In fact, the typical poor American had more living space than the average European. The typical poor American family was also able to obtain medical care when needed. By its own report, the typical family was not hungry and had sufficient funds during the past year to meet all essential needs.

Poor families certainly struggle to make ends meet, but in most cases, they are struggling to pay for air conditioning and the cable TV bill as well as to put food on the table. Their living standards are far different from the images of dire deprivation promoted by activists and the mainstream media.

Regrettably, annual Census reports not only exaggerate current poverty, but also suggest that the number of poor persons and their living conditions have remained virtually unchanged for four decades or more. In reality, the living conditions of poor Americans have shown significant improvement over time.

Consumer items that were luxuries or significant purchases for the middle class a few decades ago have become commonplace in poor households. In part, this is caused by a normal downward trend in price following the introduction of a new product. Initially, new products tend to be expensive and available only to the affluent. Over time, prices fall sharply, and the product saturates the entire population, including poor households.

As a rule of thumb, poor households tend to obtain modern conveniences about a dozen years after the middle class. Today, most poor families have conveniences that were unaffordable to the middle class not too long ago.

Poverty: A Range of Living Conditions

However, there is a range of living conditions within the poverty population. The average poor family does not represent every poor family. Although most poor families are well housed, a small minority are homeless.

Fortunately, the number of homeless Americans has not increased during the current recession. Although most poor families are well fed and have a fairly stable food supply, a sizeable minority experiences temporary restraints in food supply at various times during the year. The number of families experiencing such temporary food shortages has increased somewhat during the current economic downturn.

Of course, to the families experiencing these problems, their comparative infrequency is irrelevant. To a family that has lost its home and is living in a homeless shelter, the fact that only 0.5 percent of families shared this experience in 2009 is no comfort. The distress and fear for the future that the family experiences are real and devastating. Public policy must deal with that distress. However, accurate information about the extent and severity of social problems is imperative for the development of effective public policy.

In discussions about poverty, however, misunderstanding and exaggeration are commonplace. Over the long term, exaggeration has the potential to promote a substantial misallocation of limited resources for a government that is facing massive future deficits. In addition, exaggeration and misinformation obscure the nature, extent, and causes of real material deprivation, thereby hampering the development of well-targeted, effective programs to reduce the problem. Poverty is an issue of serious social concern, and accurate information about that problem is always essential in crafting public policy.

Living Conditions of the Poor

Each year, the U.S. Census Bureau releases its annual report on income and poverty. This report, though widely publicized by the press, provides only a bare count of the number of Americans who are allegedly poor. It provides no data on or description of their actual living conditions.

This does not mean that such information is not available. The federal government conducts several other surveys that provide detailed information on the living conditions of the poor. These surveys provide a very different sense of American poverty. They reveal that the actual standard of living among America's poor is far higher than the public imagines and that, in fact, most of the persons whom the government defines as "in poverty" are not poor in any ordinary sense of the term. Regrettably, these detailed surveys are almost never reported in the mainstream press.

One of the most interesting surveys that measures actual living conditions is the Residential Energy

Consumption Survey (RECS), which the Department of Energy has conducted regularly since 1980. The RECS survey measures energy consumption and ownership of various conveniences by U.S. households. It also provides information on households at different income levels, including poor households.

The first half of this paper uses RECS data to analyze and describe one aspect of the living standards of the poor: ownership and availability of household amenities. The second half provides a broader description of the living standards of America's poor.

Availability of Amenities in Poor Households

This section uses RECS data from 2005, the most recent year for which data are available, to analyze the amenities typically found in poor households. The 2005 RECS data represent the living conditions of the poor before the current recession. Conditions are likely quite similar today.

Because the current recession has increased the number of poor persons in the U.S. since 2005, it

CHART 1

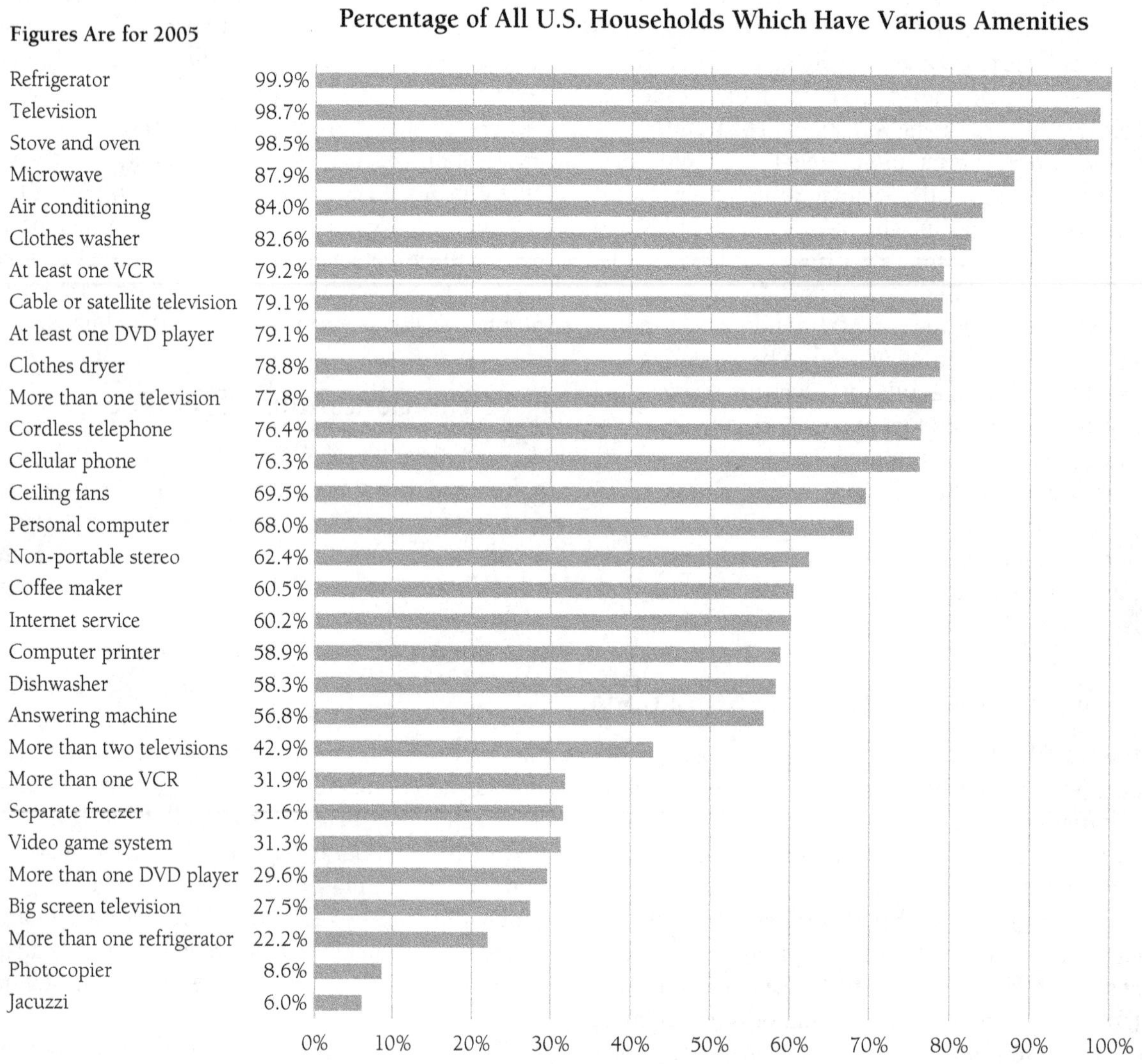

Source: U.S. Department of Energy, Residential Energy Consumption Survey, 2005.

might seem likely that poor households would have fewer amenities and conveniences today than in 2005. However, the increase in poverty during the recession is, to a considerable degree, the result of working-class families losing employment. One would not expect these families to dispose of their normal household conveniences in those circumstances. Thus, paradoxically, the increase in the number of working- and middle-class families who have become temporarily poor is likely to increase slightly the share of poor households that own various items. When the present recession ends, the living conditions of the poor are likely to continue to improve as they have in the past.

Chart 1 shows the percentage of all U.S. households that owned or had available various household amenities and conveniences in 2005. For example, it shows that 84 percent of all U.S. households had air conditioning, 79 percent had cable or satellite television, and 68 percent had a personal computer.

Chart 2 shows the same information for 2005 for poor U.S. households (those with cash incomes below the official poverty thresholds). While poor

CHART 2

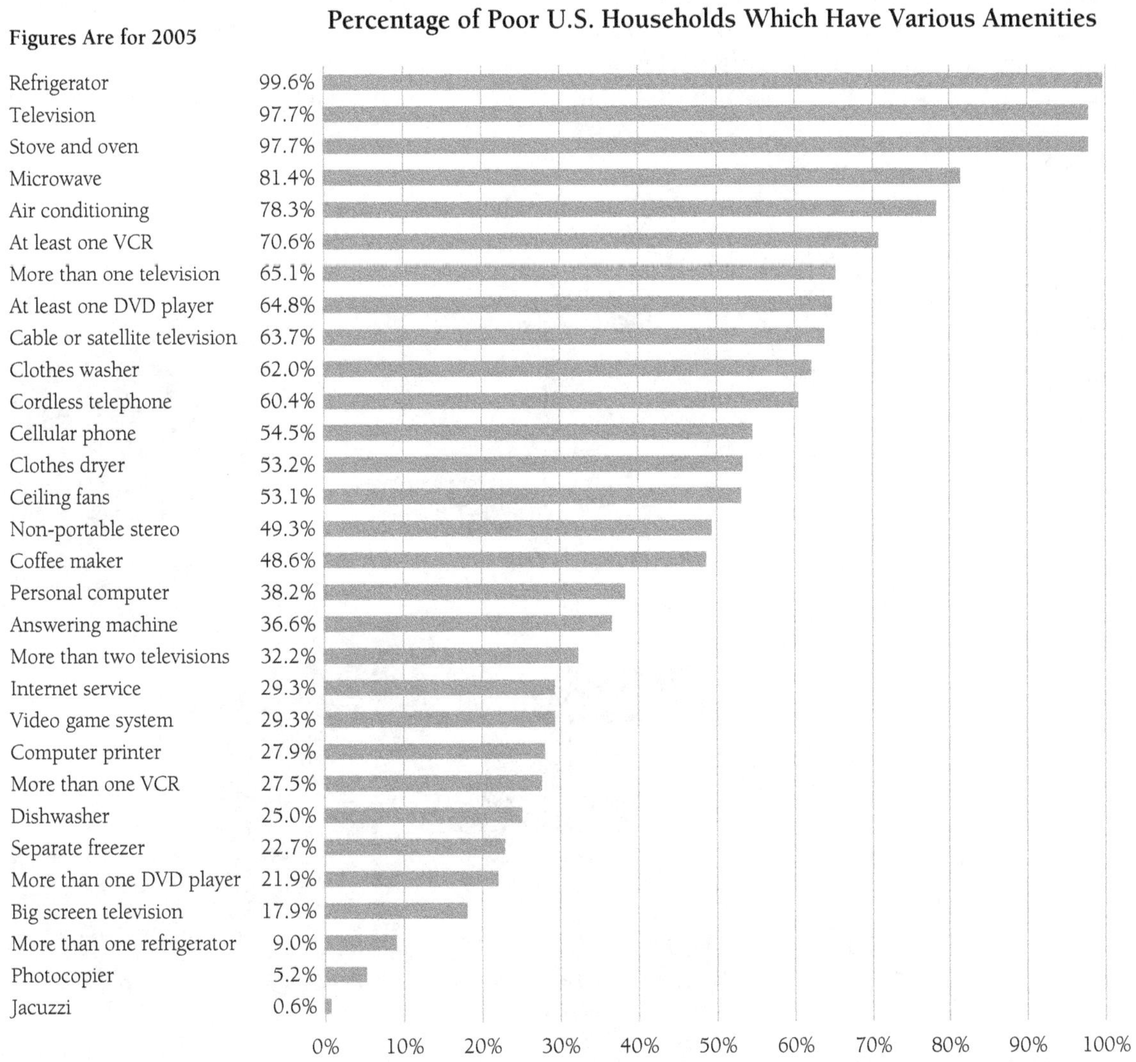

Source: U.S. Department of Energy, Residential Energy Consumption Survey, 2005.

households were slightly less likely to have conveniences than the general population, most poor households had a wide range of amenities. As Chart 2 shows, 78 percent of poor households had air conditioning, 64 percent had cable or satellite TV, and 38 percent had a personal computer.

The Household Amenity Scale

Living conditions can be analyzed by creating a household amenity scale based on the 30 items listed in Chart 1. The RECS database reports which households have each specific amenity. For each affirmative response that a household has a particular amenity, we gave the household one point. All the affirmative responses of the household were then summed to produce an overall amenity score for the household.

Thus, a household's amenity score can range from 0 to 30. A household that responded negatively to all 30 items would have an amenity score of zero, a household that responded affirmatively to half the items would have an amenity score of 15, and a household that answered affirmatively to all 30 items would have a score of 30. The amenity score of a household is roughly equal to the number of amenities present in the household.

Chart 3 provides the cumulative distribution of amenity scores for all U.S. households in 2005, showing the percentage of all households with an amenity score at or below each specified level. The median amenity score for all households is 19. This means that half of all households had a score at or below 19 and half of households had a score at or above 19.

Having determined the median amenity score, we then examined every household with that score

CHART 3

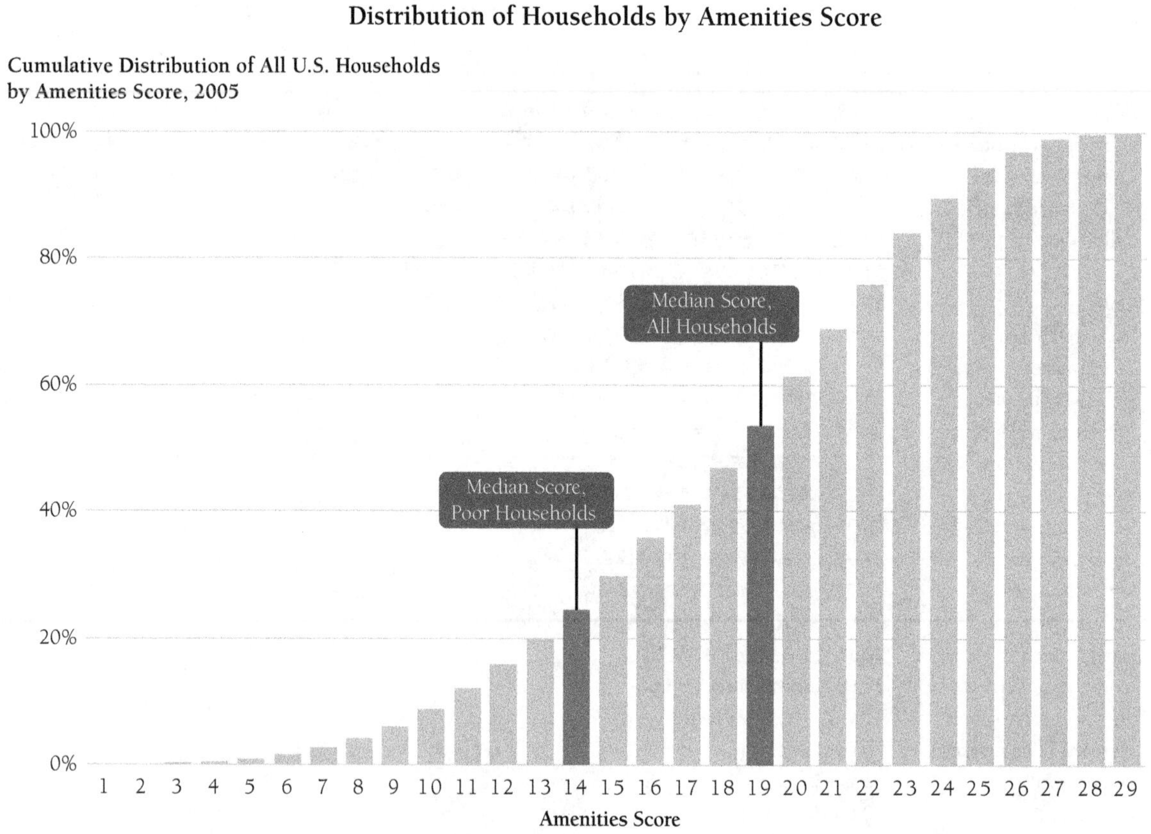

Note: No household owned a total of 30 items.
Source: U.S. Department of Energy, Residential Energy Consumption Survey, 2005.

to determine which amenities appeared most frequently within the median group. (See Table 1.)

- The analysis showed that households with the median amenity score most frequently had the following 19 items: air conditioning, a personal computer, Internet access, a computer printer, a ceiling fan, a cell phone or phones, a cordless phone, and a coffee maker.
- For entertainment, these households had two color televisions, cable or satellite TV, a DVD player, and a VCR.
- In the kitchen, the households had a refrigerator, an oven and stove, an automatic dishwasher, and a microwave.
- In the laundry, they had a washing machine and dryer.

These amenities may then be considered representative of the living standards of the median or typical U.S. household in 2005.

Amenities in the Median Poor Household

We then examined poor households, meaning households with a reported income below the official government poverty income thresholds in 2005. Analysis revealed that poor households had a median household amenity score of 14. This means that half of all poor households had a score at or below 14 and half of households had scores at or above 14.

Having determined that the amenity score of the median poor household was 14, we then examined all poor households with that score to determine which amenities appeared most frequently within the median poor group.

- The analysis showed that median poor households most frequently had the following 14 items: air conditioning, a clothes washer, a clothes dryer, ceiling fans, and a cordless phone.
  - For entertainment, these households had two color televisions, cable or satellite TV, a DVD player, and a VCR.
  - In the kitchen, these poor households had a refrigerator, an oven and stove, a microwave, and a coffee maker.

These items may then be considered representative of the living standards of the median or typical poor U.S. household in 2005.

The median poor household had five fewer amenities than the median household in the general population. Specifically, the typical poor household lacked the following items that were in the typical middle-income household: a personal computer, Internet access, a computer printer, a dishwasher, and a cell phone.

Amenities in Poor Families with Children

Poor families with children have more conveniences and amenities than other poor families. In 2005, the median amenity score for poor families with children was 16. We examined all poor families with children with an amenity score of 16 to

Table 1 AMENITIES IN TYPICAL HOUSEHOLDS

Household	Most Common Amenities
Median U.S. Household, Whole Population (Amenity Score = 19)	Air conditioning, personal computer, Internet access, computer printer, two color televisions, cable or satellite TV, DVD player, VCR, refrigerator, oven and stove, dishwasher, microwave, washing machine, dryer, ceiling fans, cell phone, cordless phone, and coffee maker
Median Poor Household (Amenity Score = 14)	Air conditioning, two color televisions, cable or satellite TV, DVD player, VCR, refrigerator, oven and stove, microwave, coffee maker, clothes washer, dryer, ceiling fans, and cordless phone
Median Poor Family with Children (Amenity Score = 16)	Air conditioning, personal computer, cable or satellite TV, three color televisions, DVD player, VCR, video game system, refrigerator, stove and oven, microwave, coffee maker, cell phone, cordless phone, and clothes washer

Source: U.S. Department of Energy, Residential Energy Consumption Survey, 2005.

determine which items appeared most frequently in these homes.

- These homes typically had both air conditioning and a personal computer.
- For entertainment, they typically had cable or satellite TV, three color televisions, a DVD player, a VCR, and a video game system, such as an Xbox or Play Station.
- In the kitchen, they had a refrigerator, a stove and oven, a microwave, and an automatic coffee maker.
- Other amenities included a cell phone, a cordless phone, and a clothes washer.

These conveniences may be considered representative of the living standards of the median or typical poor family with children in 2005.

Improvement in Poor Households over Time

Because the RECS has reported on the living conditions of the poor for several decades, it is a useful tool for charting the improvement in living conditions among the poor over time. For example, Chart 4 shows the percentage of all households and the percentage of poor households that had any type of air conditioning between 1970 and 2005. Although poor households were less likely to have air conditioning in any given year, the share of households with air conditioning increased steadily for both groups over the 25-year period. By 2005, the two rates converged as air conditioning became nearly universal in U.S. society.

Chart 5 shows the percentage of all households and the percentage of poor households that had central air conditioning between 1970 and 2005. Because central air conditioning is more expensive than window units, it is less common in U.S. society. Nonetheless, the share of the general population and the share of poor households with central air conditioning have increased at a similar pace for the past 25 years.

Finally, Chart 6 shows the share of all households and the share of poor households that had a personal computer from 1990 to 2005. Personal computers were rare in 1990 but spread widely through society over the next 15 years. Computer ownership among the poor increased substantially during the period.

CHART 4

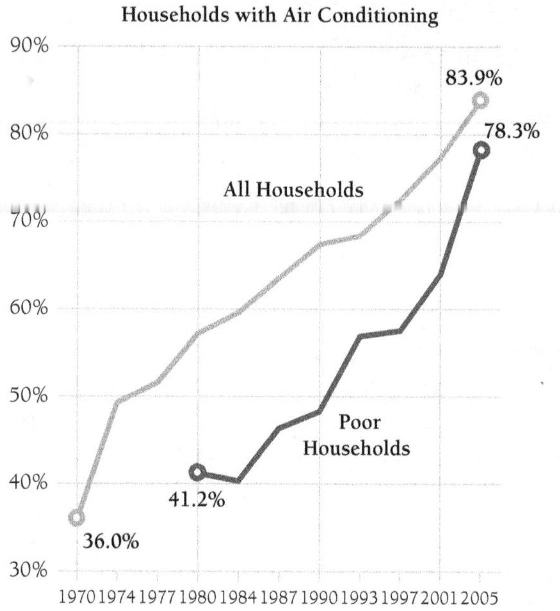

Sources: U.S. Department of Housing and Urban Development, American Housing Survey, and U.S. Department of Energy, Residential Energy Consumption Survey, 2005.

CHART 5

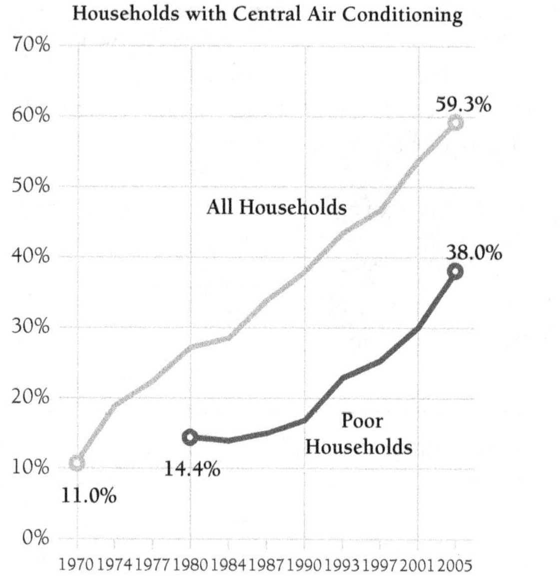

Sources: U.S. Department of Housing and Urban Development, American Housing Survey, and U.S. Department of Energy, Residential Energy Consumption Survey, 2005.

CHART 6

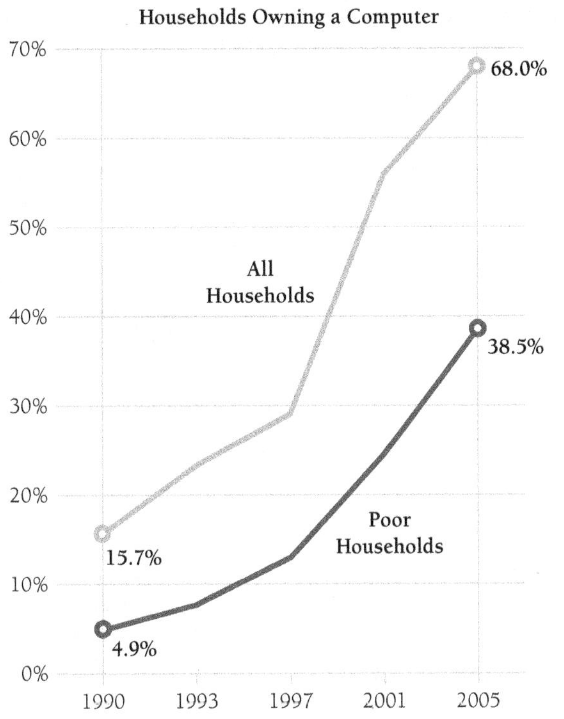

Sources: U.S. Department of Energy, Residential Energy Consumption Survey, 2005.

In 1990, only 5 percent of poor households had a computer. By 2005, the number had risen to almost 40 percent.

Charts 4, 5, and 6 show a common pattern. The share of poor households that have a given amenity tends to equal the share of all U.S. households that had the same amenity 10 to 15 years earlier. There seems to be a general lag effect in which poor households acquire a given amenity roughly a dozen years after the general population acquires it.

Housing and Poverty

Of course, the typical poor family could have a host of modern conveniences and still live in dilapidated, overcrowded housing. However, data from other government surveys show that this is not the case. Poor Americans are well housed and rarely overcrowded. In fact, the houses and apartments of America's poor are quite spacious by international standards. The typical poor American has considerably more living space than does the average European.

Forty-three percent of all poor households own their own homes. The average home owned by persons classified as poor by the Census Bureau is a three-bedroom house with one-and-a-half baths, a garage, and a porch or patio.

Nearly all of the houses and apartments of the poor are in good condition. According to the government's data, only one in 10 has moderate physical problems. Only 2 percent of poor domiciles have "severe" physical problems, the most common of which is sharing a bathroom with another household living in the building.

Food Shortages, Nutrition, and Poverty

It is possible that most poor households could be well housed and have many modern conveniences but still face chronic food shortages and under-nutrition. Poor families might have microwaves but a limited and sporadic supply of food to put in the microwave. Government surveys show that this is not the case for the overwhelming majority of poor families.

On average, the poor are well nourished. The average consumption of protein, vitamins, and minerals is virtually the same for poor and middle-class children. In most cases, it is well above recommended norms. Poor children actually consume more meat than higher-income children consume, and their protein intake averages 100 percent above recommended levels. In fact, most poor children are super-nourished and grow up to be, on average, one inch taller and 10 pounds heavier than the GIs who stormed the beaches of Normandy in World War II.

However, even though the poor, in general, have an ample food supply, some do suffer from temporary food shortages. For example, a poor household with an adequate long-term food supply might need temporarily to cut back meals, eat cheap food, or go without if cash and food stamps run out at the end of the month.

Still, government data show that most poor households do not suffer even from temporary food shortages. As Chart 7 shows, 92.5 percent of poor households assert that they always had "enough food

CHART 7

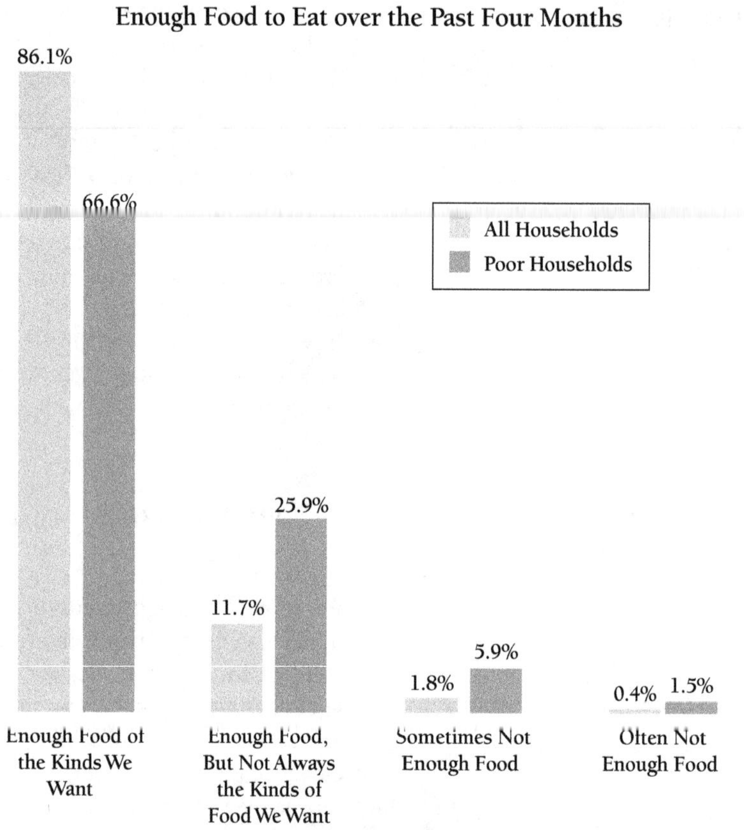

Sources: U.S. Census Bureau, Survey of Income and Program Participation, 2001 Panel, Wave 8 Topical Module, 2003.

to eat" during the previous four months, although 26 percent of these did not always have the foods that they would have preferred. Some 6 percent of poor households state that they "sometimes" did not have enough food, and 1.5 percent say they "often" did not have enough food.

The bottom line is that, although a small portion of poor households report temporary food shortages, the overwhelming majority of poor households report that they consistently have enough food to eat.

Temporary food shortages have increased during the current recession but still remain atypical among poor households. During 2009, less than one poor household in five experienced even a single instance of "reduced food intake and disrupted eating patterns" due to a lack of financial resources. Strikingly, only 4 percent of poor children experienced even a single instance of "reduced food intake and disrupted eating patterns" due to a lack of financial resources.

Food Banks and Soup Kitchens

TV news stories that inform audiences that one in seven Americans are poor routinely depict "the poor" collecting free groceries at a food pantry or eating meals at a free food kitchen. The audience is led to conclude that gathering free food from a charity pantry or eating free meals at a soup kitchen is the norm for those in poverty.

In fact, while the use of food pantries and emergency kitchens has increased during the current recession, poor families generally did not use charity food pantries or soup kitchens. The U.S. Department of Agriculture (USDA) reports that only one poor

Table 2 ODDS OF BEING HOMELESS ON A SINGLE NIGHT IN 2009

	Number of Persons	Odds of Being Homeless on a Single Night within Whole U.S. Population	Odds of Being Homeless on a Single Night within U.S. Poverty Population
Persons in shelters and transitional housing	403,308	1 in 753	1 in 108
Persons on the street/ without shelter	239,759	1 in 1,266	1 in 182
All homeless persons	643,067	1 in 472	1 in 68

Source: U.S. Department of Housing and Urban Development, *2009 Annual Homeless Assessment Report*, p. 8.

family in five took food from a food pantry even once during all of 2009. Far fewer ate at a food kitchen.

In the whole U.S. population, 5.6 million households (4.8 percent of all households) used a food pantry at any point during 2009. Far fewer ate meals at a soup kitchen. Only 625,000 of all U.S. households (0.5 percent) had a member who ate a meal in a free food kitchen at any time in 2009.

Poverty and Homelessness

The mainstream press and activist groups also frequently conflate poverty with homelessness. News stories about poverty often feature homeless families living "on the street." This depiction is seriously misleading because only a small portion of persons "living in poverty" will become homeless over the course of a year. The overwhelming majority of the poor reside throughout the year in non-crowded housing that is in good repair.

The 2009 *Annual Homeless Assessment Report* published by the U.S. Department of Housing and Urban Development (HUD) states that on a given night in 2009, some 643,000 persons in the U.S. were homeless (without permanent domicile). This means that at any given time, one out of 470 persons in the general population or one out of 70 persons with incomes below the poverty level was homeless.

Moreover, two-thirds of these 643,000 homeless persons were residing in emergency shelters or transitional housing. Only 240,000 were without shelter. These "unsheltered" individuals were "on the street," meaning that they were living in cars, abandoned buildings, alleyways, or parks. At any point in 2009, roughly one person out of 1,250 in the general population or one out of 180 poor persons was homeless in the literal sense of being on the street and without shelter. (See Table 2.)

Homelessness is usually a transitional condition. Individuals typically lose housing, reside in an emergency shelter for a few weeks or months, and then reenter permanent housing. The transitional nature of homelessness means that many more people become temporarily homeless over the course of a year than are homeless at any single point in time.

Thus, HUD reports that 1.56 million persons resided in an emergency shelter or transitional housing at least one night during 2009. The year-round total of individuals who ever stayed in a shelter or transitional housing was nearly four times larger than the 403,000 who resided in such facilities on an average night.

Based on the year-round data on shelter use, roughly one person in 195 in the general population resided in emergency shelter or transitional housing for at least one night during a full 12-month period. Roughly one in 25 poor persons (4 percent of all poor persons) resided in an emergency shelter or transitional housing for at least one night during the full year. (See Table 3.)

Despite news stories that assert that the current recession has caused a great increase in homelessness, homeless shelter use, in general, has not increased during the current economic downturn. In addition, shelters are not overcrowded. On a typical night, shelters are not overcrowded. On a

Table 3 ODDS OF RESIDING IN A HOMELESS SHELTER OR TRANSITIONAL HOUSING FOR AT LEAST ONE NIGHT DURING FULL YEAR: 2009

	Number of Persons	Odds of Using a Homeless Shelter in 2009 within Whole U.S. Population	Odds of Using a Homeless Shelter in 2009 within U.S. Poverty Population
Children	330,000	1 in 214	1 in 38
Adults	1,216,000	1 in 190	1 in 21
All persons	1.56 million	1 in 195	1 in 25

Source: U.S. Department of Housing and Urban Development, *2009 Annual Homeless Assessment Report*, p. 8.

typical night, shelters have an average vacancy rate of 10 percent.

While the overall number of homeless has not increased during the current recession, there has been a small increase in the number of families with children who use homeless shelters. Some 168,000 families with children resided in a homeless shelter for at least one night during all of 2010. This figure was up from 130,000 in 2007. The increase of 38,000 families represents only one family out every 1,000 families with children. While the misfortune is real for the families involved, these numbers scarcely show a tidal wave of increased homelessness.

Although news stories often suggest that poverty and homelessness are similar, this is inaccurate. In reality, the gap between the living conditions of a homeless person and the typical poor household is proportionately as great as the gap between the poor household and a middle-class family in the suburbs.

Essential Needs

Although the public equates poverty with physical deprivation, the overwhelming majority of poor households do not experience any form of physical deprivation. Some 70 percent of poor households report that during the course of the past year, they were able to meet "all essential expenses," including mortgage, rent, utility bills, and important medical care.

It is widely supposed that the poor are unable to obtain medical care, but in reality, only 13 percent of poor households report that a family member needed to go to a doctor or hospital at some point in the prior year but was unable because the family could not afford the cost.

Public Understanding of Poverty

In 2005, the typical poor household, as defined by the government, had air conditioning and a car. For entertainment, the household had two color televisions, cable or satellite TV, a DVD player, and a VCR. In the kitchen, it had a refrigerator, an oven and stove, and a microwave. Other household conveniences included a clothes washer, clothes dryer, ceiling fans, a cordless phone, and a coffee maker. The family was able to obtain medical care when needed. Their home was not overcrowded and was in good repair. By its own report, the family was not hungry and had sufficient funds during the past year to meet all essential needs.

The overwhelming majority of the public do not regard a family living in these conditions as poor. For example, a poll conducted in June 2009 asked a nationally representative sample of the public whether they agreed or disagreed with the following statement: "A family in the U.S. that has a decent, uncrowded house or apartment to live in, ample food to eat, access to medical care, a car, cable television, air conditioning and a microwave at home should not be considered poor."

A full 80 percent of Republicans and 77 percent of Democrats agreed that a family living in those living conditions should not be considered poor.

Census Poverty Reports Are Misleading and Inaccurate

Nonetheless, each year, the U.S. Census Bureau issues a report claiming that over 35 million Americans live in poverty. The annual Census poverty report is flawed in two respects.

First, the report provides no information on the actual living conditions of the persons identified as poor. It simply states that a specified number of persons are poor without giving any information on what poverty means in the real world. A detailed description of the living conditions of the poor would greatly enhance public understanding. In fact, without a detailed description of living conditions, public discussions of poverty are meaningless.

Second, the Census report massively undercounts the economic resources provided to poor people. The Census asserts that a household is poor if its "money income" falls below a specified threshold. In 2009, the poverty income threshold for a family of four was $21,756. However, in counting the money income of households, the Census ignores virtually the entire welfare state. For example, there are over 70 means-tested welfare programs that provide cash, food, housing, medical care, and social services to poor and low-income persons. Major means-tested welfare programs include Temporary Assistance for Needy Families; Supplemental Security Income; the Earned Income Tax Credit; food stamps; the Women, Infants, and Children food program; public housing; and Medicaid. (Social Security and Medicare are not means-tested welfare programs.)

In 2008, federal and state governments spent $714 billion on means-tested welfare programs, but the Census counted only about 4 percent of this as "money income" for purposes of determining whether a household was poor. The bottom line is that the economic resources available to poor persons are vastly greater than the Census claims.

In fact, the U.S. Department of Labor finds that the lowest-income one-fifth of households appear to spend $1.87 for every $1.00 of income that the Census says these households have. If the free medical care and public housing subsidies given to these households were counted, then the gap between expenditure and income would be even greater.

Misrepresenting Poverty in America

As noted, for the average American, the word "poverty" implies significant material hardship and deprivation. Politicians, activists, and the mainstream media reinforce this image, asserting that each year, over 35 million Americans live in chronic material deprivation, unable to obtain "the basic material necessities of life."

For example, former Senator and Vice Presidential candidate John Edwards made poverty the centerpiece of his repeated campaigns for the presidency. Edwards proclaimed that 37 million Americans "struggle with incredible poverty." He explicitly equated poverty as defined by the Census Bureau with dramatic unfulfilled material need. According to Edwards, America's poor, who number "one in eight of us . . . do not have enough money for the food, shelter, and clothing they need." The poor, he said, were forced to live in "terrible" circumstances.

In Edwards's stump speeches, the "plague of poverty" in America was typified by a 10-year-old girl who lacked food and clothing. Edwards proclaimed, "Tonight, a 10-year-old little girl will go to bed hungry, hoping and praying that tomorrow will not be as cold as today because she doesn't have the coat to keep her warm." Confronted by skeptics, Edwards's staff ultimately admitted that the girl was "metaphorical," but Edwards continued to feature her in speech after speech.

Liberal advocacy groups routinely echo Edwards's claims. For example, the Children's Defense Fund equates government-defined poverty with daily hardship and suffering. CDF President Marian Wright Edelman states, "It is a moral outrage that in the wealthiest nation on earth there are still 12.8 million children living in poverty" and "inexcusable that 12.8 million children are forced to suffer through hardship every day."

In a campaign to promote higher welfare spending, Catholic Charities USA tells the public that the government-defined poor lack the basic material necessities of life:

> We speak of [the United States] being the land of plenty: a country with living standards so high that others wish to emulate our success. But for nearly 37 million Americans there is another story. What is life like in this other America? How can it be that millions of us lack the basic material necessities of life?

Advocacy groups often equate official poverty with hunger, malnutrition, and homelessness. When asked what it means for children to live in official U.S. poverty, Marion Wright Edelman informed TV audiences that official child poverty means "hopelessness for too many, it means homelessness; it means being hungry." The activist Web site Spotlight on Poverty asserts, "An increasing number of Americans face poverty and, as a result, hunger. . . . In all, 15 percent of American households . . . did not have the resources to obtain adequate nutrition and lead a healthy lifestyle."

Confusing Poverty and Deprivation

Protestations by anti-poverty activists almost always involve two incompatible ideas: that poverty in America is widespread, affecting as many as one in seven Americans, and that being poor in this country means serious material deprivation. The fusion of these two notions leads to a profound misrepresentation of the actual living conditions in the nation.

For example, confusion of this sort can be found in *Just Generosity: A New Vision for Overcoming Poverty in America* by evangelical Ronald J. Sider. Sider begins his book with a chapter entitled "What Does Poverty Look Like?" in which he informs his readers, "In 2005, in the United States, 37 million people lived in poverty in the richest society in human history." He asks, "Who are the poor? Where do they live?" and proceeds to answer these questions with a lengthy description of the home of Mrs. Onita Skyles, a 68-year-old widow:

> The foundation was collapsing. Sections of the floor had rotted. The walls and ceiling were cracked. The tub and toilet had sunk below the floor level and were unusable, and there was no running water. Mrs. Styles cooked with a hot plate and carried water in gallon jugs from a neighbor's house.

He then describes the shack where the Perez family lives: "The walls are old doors, tar paper, chicken wire, and rotting boards. The ground provides a dirt floor. There is no bathroom, no running water, no electricity, no heat. Their toilet is a reeking outhouse across the street."

The descriptions of these two individual households are indeed appalling, but Sider is seriously misleading when he implies that such living conditions are representative of 37 million poor people. In fact, the situations he presents are not at all representative of the poor in America. The described conditions are very unusual and probably found in no more than one in 500 households.

Confronted with this fact, activists usually respond that the exact numbers are irrelevant because no American should live in such deplorable conditions. This may be true, but when formulating effective public policy, it matters a great deal whether one in seven households or one in 500 households live in such conditions.

However, if the goal is greater income redistribution—rather than policies that precisely and effectively target those truly in need—then big numbers matter a lot. Liberal activists continue to insist that very large numbers of Americans live in severe deprivation.

This is no accident. The interlocking assertions that poverty is widespread, affecting one in seven Americans, and that the poor live in desperate conditions are both ideologically necessary for the Left. Together, they provide justification for policies to greatly expand the welfare state and further "spread the wealth." But if one or both assertions proves to be untrue, the impetus for expanding the welfare state is greatly undermined.

QUESTIONS FOR REFLECTION

1. Marxists sometimes contend that justice requires that people's needs be met. Are the needs of a typical poor family in the United States being met? How many people, roughly, have unmet needs in the United States today?
2. The gap between poor and middle-class families suggests that additional income transfers to the poor would largely fund the purchase of personal computers, Internet access, and cell phones. How does that affect the moral status of such transfers?
3. A typical poor person in the United States has more living space than the average European. What are the moral implications of that fact?
4. Is poverty best understood as absolute or relative? Is there an obligation to help people if they fall below a certain level (of being able to meet needs, for instance), or an obligation to help people below the average income level, no matter how well off they are in absolute terms?
5. Rector and Sheffield argue that misunderstanding poverty makes it harder to address homelessness, hunger, and other problems of real deprivation by directing most transfers and programs to people who are not deprived. How so? Do you agree?
6. Critique Rector and Sheffield from the perspective of Rawls or Sen.

AFFIRMATIVE ACTION

The United States, like many other countries, has a history of racial and sexual discrimination. Unlike many other countries, it also has a history of slavery. Discrimination and slavery have long been recognized as evils. Discrimination, for example, might be defined as making a judgment or decision on the basis of irrelevant factors. Race and sex are almost always irrelevant to decisions about whom to hire, whom to fire, whom to admit to a college or university, and other similar decisions. Kant's categorical imperative requires that we judge similar cases similarly—that we judge a case as if our judgment were universal law. To discriminate is to judge similar cases differently, depending on some irrelevant factor such as race or sex. Discrimination thus directly violates Kant's imperative.

The obligation to eliminate discrimination, therefore, is not controversial. What its elimination requires is. In a landmark case, *Brown v. Board of Education,* the Supreme Court held that segregation is a form of discrimination and so must be eliminated. It took a long series of subsequent cases, however, to spell out exactly what that requires. It is wrong to separate students of different race as a matter of law. But is it acceptable to assign students to the nearest school without regard to race, even if, due to housing patterns, some schools fill up with students of a single race? What other changes must occur in society if discrimination is to be ended?

Agreement about the goal of racial equality leaves room for disagreement about the means to that goal. Racial or sexual discrimination, as a violation of Kant's principle, is by its very nature unfair. So, we might think that justice requires making decisions about hiring, firing, admissions, and other matters of economic and political significance in a "color-blind" way, without regard for race, sex, or other irrelevant factors. From another perspective, however, this apparent even-handedness is only apparent, for some of the players in the economic and political game have been harmed by prior discrimination. Setting things right requires, from this point of view, giving those players an advantage to balance the disadvantages they suffer as a result of past injustices. On this conception, then, race, sex, and perhaps other characteristics are no longer irrelevant. The history of discrimination has turned them into relevant factors.

From this perspective have sprung "affirmative-action" programs: programs that give preferences to some people because of their race, sex, ethnic background, or other characteristic. Generally, these programs try to "level the playing field" by granting preference to those who have suffered from prior discrimination or are otherwise disadvantaged. Sometimes, the preference is general, of the form "all other things being equal, we prefer people with the following characteristics"; in other cases, there are explicit quotas for people of different groups. Affirmative-action programs have been a source of controversy. In the United States, they have provoked arguments and lawsuits. In other countries, they have provoked riots and bloodshed.

The University of California operated a quota system at its medical school at Davis. It reserved sixteen of the one hundred places in each class at the medical school for members of minority groups. Alan Bakke, a white male, applied and was rejected. He learned, however, that his grades and test scores were higher than those of many students admitted under the minority quota. Bakke sued, claiming that he had been discriminated against on account of his race. In 1978, the Supreme Court decided in Bakke's favor. The Court stopped short of declaring that taking race and similar qualities into account is unacceptable. The Court did, however, decide that quota systems like that operating at the University of California were unconstitutional, amounting themselves to a form of discrimination. Dissenters on the Court decried the decision, maintaining that there is a great moral difference between using a racial classification against a disadvantaged group and using it to benefit that group. In short, the dissenters insisted that race, sex, and other factors are not irrelevant in themselves, though there is a strong presumption of their irrelevance. Prior discrimination and economic disadvantage may, they claimed, make these factors relevant and even require that they be taken into account in decision making.

Following *Bakke* was a series of decisions on affirmative action in various contexts: education, industry, unions, state government, and others. These decisions are extremely complex. They agree, however, that affirmative-action programs, to be constitutional, must pass strict scrutiny; that is, they must be necessary to achieve a compelling state interest. Racial equality is a compelling state interest, so the crucial question has been, Is this program necessary to achieve it? In the Court's jargon, Is it *narrowly tailored?* The Court has upheld several voluntary race-conscious affirmative-action plans, and even some court-imposed quota systems in cases where there appeared to be ongoing discrimination.

Antonin Scalia argues that the *Bakke* decision makes no sense. The decision, he argues, is constructed to make sure that the University of California and other institutions may continue to discriminate in favor of some groups and against others, so long as they hide what they are doing behind a facade of diversity. The effect of such programs, he contends, is to place a burden on less advantaged whites while harming the very groups they are designed to help.

Bernard Boxill argues in favor of affirmative action on two grounds. First, past injustice requires compensation. African Americans have been subjected to slavery and then to decades of legal and extralegal discrimination. Affirmative action is needed, Boxill argues, to rectify inequalities resulting from that injustice. Second, affirmative action programs have advantages for the future, producing greater equality and enabling people whose talents would otherwise be overlooked to exercise their abilities to everyone's benefit.

Thomas Sowell, an economist, argues that affirmative action brings about far more harm than good. He traces the history of affirmative action in many societies around the world, contending that it uniformly increases racial tensions. Advocates argue that affirmative-action plans are temporary repairs of harm brought about by prior discrimination. Sowell argues that there is no way to determine how much of the economic position of an individual or a group is due to prior discrimination. Consequently, there is no way to tell when the effects of prior discrimination have been eliminated. Once instituted, therefore, preferences never go away; indeed, they expand to more groups, few of whose claims can be founded on prior discrimination.

Finally, the Supreme Court, in a pair of cases concerning admission to the University of Michigan, approved affirmative-action programs, but only "holistic" ones that take race into account in examining an applicant's overall profile.

CHIEF JUSTICE EARL WARREN

Majority Opinion in Brown v. Board of Education (1954)

(*Source:* Brown *v.* Board of Education *347 U.S. 483 [1954].*)

Mr. Chief Justice Warren delivered the opinion of the Court.

These cases come to us from the States of Kansas, South Carolina, Virginia, and Delaware. They are premised on different facts and different local conditions, but a common legal question justifies their consideration together in this consolidated opinion.

In each of the cases, minors of the Negro race, through their legal representatives, seek the aid of the courts in obtaining admission to the public schools of their community on a nonsegregated basis. In each instance, they had been denied admission to schools attended by white children under laws requiring or permitting segregation according to race. This segregation was alleged to deprive the plaintiffs of the equal protection of the laws under the Fourteenth Amendment. In each of the cases other than the Delaware case, a three-judge federal district court denied relief to the plaintiffs on the so-called "separate but equal" doctrine announced by this Court in *Plessy* v. *Ferguson*. Under that doctrine, equality of treatment is accorded when the races are provided substantially equal facilities, even though these facilities be separate. In the Delaware case, the Supreme Court of Delaware adhered to that doctrine, but ordered that the plaintiffs be admitted to the white schools because of their superiority to the Negro schools.

The plaintiffs contend that segregated public schools are not "equal" and cannot be made "equal," and that hence they are deprived of the equal protection of the laws. . . .

In the first cases in this Court construing the Fourteenth Amendment, decided shortly after its adoption, the Court interpreted it as proscribing all state-imposed discriminations against the Negro race. The doctrine of "separate but equal" did not make its appearance in this Court until 1896 in the case of *Plessy* v. *Ferguson,* involving not education but transportation. American courts have since labored with the doctrine for over half a century. In this Court, there have been six cases involving the "separate but equal" doctrine in the field of public education. In *Cumming* v. *County Board of Education* and *Gong Lum* v. *Rice,* the validity of the doctrine itself was not challenged. In more recent cases, all on the graduate school level, inequality was found in that specific benefits enjoyed by white students were denied to Negro students of the same educational qualifications. In none of these cases was it necessary to re-examine the doctrine to grant relief to the Negro plaintiff. And in *Sweatt* v. *Painter,* the Court expressly reserved decision on the question whether *Plessy* v. *Ferguson* should be held inapplicable to public education.

In the instant cases, that question is directly presented. Here, unlike *Sweatt* v. *Painter,* there are findings below that the Negro and white schools involved have been equalized, or are being equalized, with respect to buildings, curricula, qualifications and salaries of teachers, and other "tangible" factors. Our decision, therefore, cannot turn on merely a comparison of these tangible factors in the Negro and white schools involved in each of the cases. We must look instead to the effect of segregation itself on public education.

In approaching this problem, we cannot turn the clock back to 1868 when the Amendment was adopted, or even to 1896 when *Plessy* v. *Ferguson* was written. We must consider public education in the light of its full development and its present place in American life throughout the nation. Only in this way can it be determined if segregation in public schools deprives these plaintiffs of the equal protection of the laws.

Today, education is perhaps the most important function of state and local governments. Compulsory school attendance laws and the great expenditures for education both demonstrate our recognition of the importance of education to our democratic society. It is required in the performance of our most basic public responsibilities, even service in the armed forces. It is the very foundation of good citizenship. Today it is a principal instrument in awakening the child to cultural values, in preparing him for later professional training, and in helping him to adjust normally to his environment. In these days, it is doubtful that any child may reasonably be expected to succeed in life if he is denied the opportunity of an education. Such an opportunity, where the state has undertaken to provide it, is a right which must be made available to all on equal terms.

We come then to the question presented: Does segregation of children in public schools solely on the basis of race, even though the physical facilities and other "tangible" factors may be equal, deprive the children of the minority group of equal educational opportunities? We believe that it does.

In *Sweatt* v. *Painter,* in finding that a segregated law school for Negroes could not provide them equal educational opportunities, this Court relied in large part on "those qualities which are incapable of objective measurement but which make for greatness in a law school." In *McLaurin* v. *Oklahoma State Regents,* the Court, in requiring that a Negro admitted to a white graduate school be treated like all other students, again resorted to intangible considerations: ". . . his ability to study, to engage in discussions and exchange views with other students, and, in general, to learn his profession." Such considerations apply with added force to children in grade and high schools. To separate them from others of similar age and qualifications solely because of their race generates a feeling of inferiority as to their status in the community that may affect their hearts and minds in a way unlikely ever to be undone. The effect of this separation on their educational opportunities was well stated by a finding in the Kansas case by a court which nevertheless felt compelled to rule against the Negro plaintiffs:

"Segregation of white and colored children in public schools has a detrimental effect upon the colored children. The impact is greater when it has the sanction of the law; for the policy of separating the races is usually interpreted as denoting the inferiority of the Negro group. A sense of inferiority affects the motivation of a child to learn. Segregation with the sanction of law, therefore, has a tendency to [retard] the educational and mental development of Negro children and to deprive them of some of the benefits they would receive in a racial[ly] integrated school system."

Whatever may have been the extent of psychological knowledge at the time of *Plessy* v. *Ferguson,* this finding is amply supported by modern authority. Any language in *Plessy* v. *Ferguson* contrary to this finding is rejected.

We conclude that in the field of public education the doctrine of "separate but equal" has no place. Separate educational facilities are inherently unequal. Therefore, we hold that the plaintiffs and others similarly situated for whom the actions have been brought are, by reason of the segregation complained of, deprived of the equal protection of the laws guaranteed by the Fourteenth Amendment. This disposition makes unnecessary any discussion whether such segregation also violates the Due Process Clause of the Fourteenth Amendment.

Because these are class actions, because of the wide applicability of this decision, and because of the great variety of local conditions, the formulation of decrees in these cases presents problems of considerable complexity. On reargument, the consideration of appropriate relief was necessarily subordinated to the primary question—the constitutionality of segregation in public education. We have now announced that such segregation is a denial of the equal protection of the laws.

QUESTIONS FOR REFLECTION

1. What is the "separate but equal" doctrine?
2. Why does the Court find it unconstitutional?
3. How does the Court justify a right to education? What does this right entail?
4. What role do psychological considerations play in the Court's argument?
5. Robert Bork, among others, has argued that psychological considerations are irrelevant and that the Court should have found segregation unconstitutional even if schools for children of different races really were equal in quality and segregation produced no feelings of inferiority. Do you agree? If so, how might such an argument go?

JUSTICE LEWIS POWELL

Majority Opinion in Regents of the University of California *v.* Bakke (1978)

(Source: Regents of the University of California *v.* Bakke *438 U.S. 265 [1978]. Most legal references have been omitted.)*

. . . Mr. Justice Powell announced the judgment of the Court. . . .

I

The Medical School of the University of California at Davis opened in 1968 with an entering class of 50 students. In 1971, the size of the entering class was increased to 100 students, a level at which it remains. No admissions program for disadvantaged or minority students existed when the school opened, and the first class contained three Asians but no blacks, no Mexican-Americans, and no American Indians. Over the next two years, the faculty devised a special admissions program to increase the representation of "disadvantaged" students in each Medical School class. The special program consisted of a separate admissions system operating in coordination with the regular admissions process. . . .

The special admissions program operated with a separate committee, a majority of whom were members of minority groups. On the 1973 application form, candidates were asked to indicate whether they wished to be considered as "economically and/or educationally disadvantaged" applicants; on the 1974 form the question was whether they wished to be considered as members of a "minority group," which the Medical School apparently viewed as "Blacks," "Chicanos," "Asians," and "American Indians." If these questions were answered affirmatively, the application was forwarded to the special admissions committee. No formal definition of "disadvantaged" was ever produced, but the chairman of the special committee screened each application to see whether it reflected economic or educational deprivation. Having passed this initial hurdle, the applications then were rated by the special committee in a fashion similar to that used by the general admissions committee, except that special candidates did not have to meet the 2.5 grade point average cutoff applied to regular applicants. About one-fifth of the total number of special applicants were invited for interviews in 1973 and 1974. Following each interview, the special committee assigned each special applicant a benchmark score. The special committee then presented its top choices to the general admissions committee. The latter did not rate or compare the special candidates against the general applicants, but could reject recommended special candidates for failure to meet course requirements or other specific deficiencies. The special committee continued to recommend special applicants until a number prescribed by faculty vote were admitted. While the overall class size was still 50, the prescribed number was 8; in 1973 and 1974, when the class size had doubled to 100, the prescribed number of special admissions also doubled, to 16.

From the year of the increase in class size—1971—through 1974, the special program resulted in the admission of 21 black students, 30 Mexican-Americans, and 12 Asians, for a total of 63 minority students. Over the same period, the regular admissions program produced 1 black, 6 Mexican-Americans, and 37 Asians, for a total of 44 minority students. Although disadvantaged whites applied to the special program in large numbers, none received an offer of admission through that process. Indeed, in 1974, at least, the special committee explicitly considered only "disadvantaged" special applicants who were members of one of the designated minority groups.

Allan Bakke is a white male who applied to the Davis Medical School in both 1973 and 1974. In both years Bakke's application was considered under the general admissions program, and he received an interview. His 1973 interview was with Dr. Theodore C. West, who considered Bakke "a very desirable applicant to [the] medical school." Despite a strong benchmark score of 468 out of 500, Bakke was rejected. His application had come late in the year, and no applicants in the general admissions process with scores below 470 were accepted after Bakke's application was completed. There were four special admissions slots unfilled at that time, however, for which Bakke was not considered. After his 1973 rejection, Bakke wrote to Dr. George H. Lowrey, Associate Dean and Chairman of the Admissions Committee, protesting that the special admissions program operated as a racial and ethnic quota.

Bakke's 1974 application was completed early in the year. His student interviewer gave him an overall rating of 94, finding him "friendly, well tempered, conscientious and delightful to speak with." His faculty interviewer was, by coincidence, the same Dr. Lowrey to whom he had written in protest of the special admissions program. Dr. Lowrey found Bakke "rather limited in his approach" to the problems of the medical profession and found disturbing Bakke's "very definite opinions which were based more on his personal viewpoints than upon a study of the total problem." Dr. Lowrey gave Bakke the lowest of his six ratings, an 86; his total was 549 out of 600. Again, Bakke's application was rejected. In neither year did the chairman of the admissions committee, Dr. Lowrey, exercise his discretion to place Bakke on the waiting list. In both years, applicants were admitted under the special program with grade point averages, MCAT scores, and benchmark scores significantly lower than Bakke's. The table . . . compares Bakke's science grade point average, overall grade point average, and MCAT scores with the average scores of regular admittees and of special admittees in both 1973 and 1974.

After the second rejection, Bakke filed the instant suit in the Superior Court of California. He sought mandatory, injunctive, and declaratory relief compelling his admission to the Medical School. He alleged that the Medical School's special admissions program operated to exclude him from the school on the basis of his race, in violation of his rights under the Equal Protection Clause of the Fourteenth Amendment, Art. I, 1/8 21, of the California Constitution, and 1/8 601 of Title VI of the Civil Rights Act of 1964. The University cross-complained for a declaration that its special admissions program was lawful. . . .

III

A

. . . The guarantees of the Fourteenth Amendment extend to all persons. Its language is explicit: "No State shall . . . deny to any person within its jurisdiction the equal protection of the laws." It is settled beyond question that the "rights created by the first section of the Fourteenth Amendment are, by its terms, guaranteed to the individual. The rights established are personal rights." The guarantee of equal protection cannot mean one thing when applied to one individual and something else when applied to a person of another color. If both are not accorded the same protection, then it is not equal.

Nevertheless, petitioner argues that the court below erred in applying strict scrutiny to the special admissions program because white males, such as respondent, are not a "discrete and insular minority" requiring extraordinary protection from the majoritarian political process. This rationale, however, has never been invoked in our decisions as a prerequisite to subjecting racial or ethnic distinctions to strict

CLASS ENTERING IN 1973

	SGPA	OGPA	MCAT Percentiles Verbal	Quantitative	Science	General Information
Bakke	3.44	3.46	96	94	97	72
Average of regular admittees	3.51	3.49	81	76	83	69
Average of special admittees	2.62	2.88	46	24	35	33

CLASS ENTERING IN 1974

	SGPA	OGPA	MCAT Percentiles Verbal	Quantitative	Science	General Information
Bakke	3.44	3.46	96	94	97	72
Average of regular admittees	3.36	3.29	69	67	82	72
Average of special admittees	2.42	2.62	34	30	37	18

Applicants admitted under the special program also had benchmark scores significantly lower than many students, including Bakke, rejected under the general admissions program, even though the special rating system apparently gave credit for overcoming "disadvantage."

scrutiny. Nor has this Court held that discreteness and insularity constitute necessary preconditions to a holding that a particular classification is invidious. These characteristics may be relevant in deciding whether or not to add new types of classifications to the list of "suspect" categories or whether a particular classification survives close examination. Racial and ethnic classifications, however, are subject to stringent examination without regard to these additional characteristics. We declared as much in the first cases explicitly to recognize racial distinctions as suspect:

> Distinctions between citizens solely because of their ancestry are by their very nature odious to a free people whose institutions are founded upon the doctrine of equality.
>
> [A]ll legal restrictions which curtail the civil rights of a single racial group are immediately suspect. That is not to say that all such restrictions are unconstitutional. It is to say that courts must subject them to the most rigid scrutiny.

The Court has never questioned the validity of those pronouncements. Racial and ethnic distinctions of any sort are inherently suspect and thus call for the most exacting judicial examination.

B

This perception of racial and ethnic distinctions is rooted in our Nation's constitutional and demographic history. The Court's initial view of the Fourteenth Amendment was that its "one pervading purpose" was "the freedom of the slave race, the security and firm establishment of that freedom, and the protection of the newly-made freeman and citizen from the oppressions of those who had formerly exercised dominion over him." *Slaughter-House Cases* (1873). The Equal Protection Clause, however, was "[v]irtually strangled in infancy by post-Civil-War judicial reactionism." It was relegated to decades of relative desuetude while the Due Process Clause of the Fourteenth Amendment, after a short germinal period, flourished as a cornerstone in the Court's defense of property and liberty of contract. In that cause, the Fourteenth Amendment's "one pervading purpose" was displaced. It was only as the era of substantive due process came to a close that the Equal Protection Clause began to attain a genuine measure of vitality.

By that time it was no longer possible to peg the guarantees of the Fourteenth Amendment to the struggle for equality of one racial minority.

During the dormancy of the Equal Protection Clause, the United States had become a Nation of minorities. Each had to struggle—and to some extent struggles still—to overcome the prejudices not of a monolithic majority, but of a "majority" composed of various minority groups of whom it was said—perhaps unfairly in many cases—that a shared characteristic was a willingness to disadvantage other groups. As the Nation filled with the stock of many lands, the reach of the Clause was gradually extended to all ethnic groups seeking protection from official discrimination. The guarantees of equal protection, said the Court in *Yick Wo,* "are universal in their application, to all persons within the territorial jurisdiction, without regard to any differences of race, of color, or of nationality; and the equal protection of the laws is a pledge of the protection of equal laws."

Although many of the Framers of the Fourteenth Amendment conceived of its primary function as bridging the vast distance between members of the Negro race and the white "majority," the Amendment itself was framed in universal terms, without reference to color, ethnic origin, or condition of prior servitude. As this Court recently remarked in interpreting the 1866 Civil Rights Act to extend to claims of racial discrimination against white persons, "the 39th Congress was intent upon establishing in the federal law a broader principle than would have been necessary simply to meet the particular and immediate plight of the newly freed Negro slaves." And that legislation was specifically broadened in 1870 to ensure that "all persons," not merely "citizens," would enjoy equal rights under the law. Indeed, it is not unlikely that among the Framers were many who would have applauded a reading of the Equal Protection Clause that states a principle of universal application and is responsive to the racial, ethnic, and cultural diversity of the Nation.

Over the past 30 years, this Court has embarked upon the crucial mission of interpreting the Equal Protection Clause with the view of assuring to all persons "the protection of equal laws," in a Nation confronting a legacy of slavery and racial discrimination. Because the landmark decisions in this area arose in response to the continued exclusion of Negroes from the mainstream of American society, they could be characterized as involving discrimination by the "majority" white race against the Negro minority. But they need not be read as depending upon that characterization for their results. It suffices to say that "[o]ver the years, this Court has consistently repudiated '[d]istinctions between citizens solely because of their ancestry' as being 'odious to a free people whose institutions are founded upon the doctrine of equality.'"

Petitioner urges us to adopt for the first time a more restrictive view of the Equal Protection Clause and hold that discrimination against members of the white "majority" cannot be suspect if its purpose can be characterized as "benign."* The clock of our liberties, however, cannot be turned back to 1868. It is far too late to argue that the guarantee of equal protection to *all* persons permits the recognition of special wards entitled to a degree of protection greater than that accorded others.† "The Fourteenth Amendment is not directed solely against discrimination due to a 'two-class theory'—that is, based upon differences between 'white' and Negro."

---

*In the view of Mr. Justice Brennan, Mr. Justice White, Mr. Justice Marshall, and Mr. Justice Blackmun, the pliable notion of "stigma" is the crucial element in analyzing racial classifications. The Equal Protection Clause is not framed in terms of "stigma." Certainly the word has no clearly defined constitutional meaning. It reflects a subjective judgment that is standardless. All state-imposed classifications that rearrange burdens and benefits on the basis of race are likely to be viewed with deep resentment by the individuals burdened. The denial to innocent persons of equal rights and opportunities may outrage those so deprived and therefore may be perceived as invidious. These individuals are likely to find little comfort in the notion that the deprivation they are asked to endure is merely the price of membership in the dominant majority and that its imposition is inspired by the supposedly benign purpose of aiding others. One should not lightly dismiss the inherent unfairness of, and the perception of mistreatment that accompanies, a system of allocating benefits and privileges on the basis of skin color and ethnic origin. Moreover, Mr. Justice Brennan, Mr. Justice White, Mr. Justice Marshall, and Mr. Justice Blackmun offer no principle for deciding whether preferential classifications reflect a benign remedial purpose or a malevolent stigmatic classification, since they are willing in this case to accept mere post hoc declarations by an isolated state entity—a medical school faculty—unadorned by particularized findings of past discrimination, to establish such a remedial purpose.

†Professor Bickel noted the self-contradiction of that view:

"The lesson of the great decisions of the Supreme Court and the lesson of contemporary history have been the same for at least a generation: discrimination on the basis of race is illegal, immoral, unconstitutional, inherently wrong, and destructive of democratic society. Now this is to be unlearned and we are told that this is not a matter of fundamental principle but only a matter of whose ox is gored. Those for whom racial equality was demanded are to be more equal than others. Having found support in the Constitution for equality, they now claim support for inequality under the same Constitution." A. Bickel, The Morality of Consent 133 (1975).

Once the artificial line of a "two-class theory" of the Fourteenth Amendment is put aside, the difficulties entailed in varying the level of judicial review according to a perceived "preferred" status of a particular racial or ethnic minority are intractable. The concepts of "majority" and "minority" necessarily reflect temporary arrangements and political judgments. As observed above, the white "majority" itself is composed of various minority groups, most of which can lay claim to a history of prior discrimination at the hands of the State and private individuals. Not all of these groups can receive preferential treatment and corresponding judicial tolerance of distinctions drawn in terms of race and nationality, for then the only "majority" left would be a new minority of white Anglo-Saxon Protestants. There is no principled basis for deciding which groups would merit "heightened judicial solicitude" and which would not. Courts would be asked to evaluate the extent of the prejudice and consequent harm suffered by various minority groups. Those whose societal injury is thought to exceed some arbitrary level of tolerability then would be entitled to preferential classifications at the expense of individuals belonging to other groups. Those classifications would be free from exacting judicial scrutiny. As these preferences began to have their desired effect, and the consequences of past discrimination were undone, new judicial rankings would be necessary. The kind of variable sociological and political analysis necessary to produce such rankings simply does not lie within the judicial competence—even if they otherwise were politically feasible and socially desirable.

Moreover, there are serious problems of justice connected with the idea of preference itself. First, it may not always be clear that a so-called preference is in fact benign. Courts may be asked to validate burdens imposed upon individual members of a particular group in order to advance the group's general interest. Nothing in the Constitution supports the notion that individuals may be asked to suffer otherwise impermissible burdens in order to enhance the societal standing of their ethnic groups. Second, preferential programs may only reinforce common stereotypes holding that certain groups are unable to achieve success without special protection based on a factor having no relationship to individual worth. Third, there is a measure of inequity in forcing innocent persons in respondent's position to bear the burdens of redressing grievances not of their making.

By hitching the meaning of the Equal Protection Clause to these transitory considerations, we would be holding, as a constitutional principle, that judicial scrutiny of classifications touching on racial and ethnic background may vary with the ebb and flow of political forces. Disparate constitutional tolerance of such classifications well may serve to exacerbate racial and ethnic antagonisms rather than alleviate them. Also, the mutability of a constitutional principle, based upon shifting political and social judgments, undermines the chances for consistent application of the Constitution from one generation to the next, a critical feature of its coherent interpretation. In expounding the Constitution, the Court's role is to discern "principles sufficiently absolute to give them roots throughout the community and continuity over significant periods of time, and to lift them above the level of the pragmatic political judgments of a particular time and place."

If it is the individual who is entitled to judicial protection against classifications based upon his racial or ethnic background because such distinctions impinge upon personal rights, rather than the individual only because of his membership in a particular group, then constitutional standards may be applied consistently. Political judgments regarding the necessity for the particular classification may be weighed in the constitutional balance, but the standard of justification will remain constant. This is as it should be, since those political judgments are the product of rough compromise struck by contending groups within the democratic process. When they touch upon an individual's race or ethnic background, he is entitled to a judicial determination that the burden he is asked to bear on that basis is precisely tailored to serve a compelling governmental interest. The Constitution guarantees that right to every person regardless of his background. . . .

IV

We have held that in "order to justify the use of a suspect classification, a State must show that its purpose or interest is both constitutionally permissible and substantial, and that its use of the classification is 'necessary . . . to the accomplishment' of its purpose or the safeguarding of its interest." The special admissions program purports to serve the purposes of: (i) "reducing the historic deficit of traditionally disfavored minorities in medical schools and in the medical profession," (ii) countering the effects of societal discrimination; (iii) increasing the number of physicians who will practice in communities currently underserved; and (iv) obtaining the educational benefits that flow from an ethnically diverse student body. It is necessary to decide which, if any, of these purposes is substantial enough to support the use of a suspect classification.

A

If petitioner's purpose is to assure within its student body some specified percentage of a particular group merely because of its race or ethnic origin, such a preferential purpose must be rejected not as insubstantial but as facially invalid. Preferring members of any one group for no reason other than race or ethnic origin is discrimination for its own sake. This the Constitution forbids.

B

The State certainly has a legitimate and substantial interest in ameliorating, or eliminating where feasible, the disabling effects of identified discrimination. The line of school desegregation cases, commencing with *Brown*, attests to the importance of this state goal and the commitment of the judiciary to affirm all lawful means toward its attainment. In the school cases, the States were required by court order to redress the wrongs worked by specific instances of racial discrimination. That goal was far more focused than the remedying of the effects of "societal discrimination," an amorphous concept of injury that may be ageless in its reach into the past.

We have never approved a classification that aids persons perceived as members of relatively victimized groups at the expense of other innocent individuals in the absence of judicial, legislative, or administrative findings of constitutional or statutory violations. After such findings have been made, the governmental interest, in preferring members of the injured groups at the expense of others is substantial, since the legal rights of the victims must be vindicated. In such a case, the extent of the injury and the consequent remedy will have been judicially, legislatively, or administratively defined. Also, the remedial action usually remains subject to continuing oversight to assure that it will work the least harm possible to other innocent persons competing for the benefit. Without such findings of constitutional or statutory violations, it cannot be said that the government has any greater interest in helping one individual than in refraining from harming another. Thus, the government has no compelling justification for inflicting such harm. . . .

Hence, the purpose of helping certain groups whom the faculty of the Davis Medical School perceived as victims of "societal discrimination" does not justify a classification that imposes disadvantages upon persons like respondent, who bear no responsibility for whatever harm the beneficiaries of the special admissions program are thought to have suffered. To hold otherwise would be to convert a remedy heretofore reserved for violations of legal rights into a privilege that all institutions throughout the Nation could grant at their pleasure to whatever groups are perceived as victims of societal discrimination. That is a step we have never approved.

C

Petitioner identifies, as another purpose of its program, improving the delivery of health-care services to communities currently underserved. It may be assumed that in some situations a State's interest in facilitating the health care of its citizens is sufficiently compelling to support the use of a suspect classification. But there is virtually no evidence in the record indicating that petitioner's special admissions program is either needed or geared to promote that goal. The court below addressed this failure of proof:

> The University concedes it cannot assure that minority doctors who entered under the program, all of whom expressed an "interest" in practicing in a disadvantaged community, will actually do so. It may be correct to assume that some of them will carry out this intention, and that it is more likely they will practice in minority communities than the average white doctor. Nevertheless, there are more precise and reliable ways to identify applicants who are genuinely interested in the medical problems of minorities than by race. An applicant of whatever race who has demonstrated his concern for disadvantaged minorities in the past and who declares

> that practice in such a community is his primary professional goal would be more likely to contribute to alleviation of the medical shortage than one who is chosen entirely on the basis of race and disadvantage. In short, there is no empirical data to demonstrate that any one race is more selflessly socially oriented or by contrast that another is more selfishly acquisitive.

Petitioner simply has not carried its burden of demonstrating that it must prefer members of particular ethnic groups over all other individuals in order to promote better health-care delivery to deprived citizens. Indeed, petitioner has not shown that its preferential classification is likely to have any significant effect on the problem.

D

The fourth goal asserted by petitioner is the attainment of a diverse student body. This clearly is a constitutionally permissible goal for an institution of higher education. Academic freedom, though not a specifically enumerated constitutional right, long has been viewed as a special concern of the First Amendment. The freedom of a university to make its own judgments as to education includes the selection of its student body. Mr. Justice Frankfurter summarized the "four essential freedoms" that constitute academic freedom:

> It is the business of a university to provide that atmosphere which is most conducive to speculation, experiment and creation. It is an atmosphere in which there prevail "the four essential freedoms" of a university—to determine for itself on academic grounds who may teach, what may be taught, how it shall be taught, and who may be admitted to study.

Our national commitment to the safeguarding of these freedoms within university communities was emphasized in *Keyishian* v. *Board of Regents* (1967):

> Our Nation is deeply committed to safeguarding academic freedom which is of transcendent value to all of us and not merely to the teachers concerned. That freedom is therefore a special concern of the First Amendment. . . . The Nation's future depends upon leaders trained through wide exposure to that robust exchange of ideas which discovers truth "out of a multitude of tongues, [rather] than through any kind of authoritative selection."

The atmosphere of "speculation, experiment and creation"—so essential to the quality of higher education—is widely believed to be promoted by a diverse student body. As the Court noted in *Keyishian,* it is not too much to say that the "nation's future depends upon leaders trained through wide exposure" to the ideas and mores of students as diverse as this Nation of many peoples.

Thus, in arguing that its universities must be accorded the right to select those students who will contribute the most to the "robust exchange of ideas," petitioner invokes a countervailing constitutional interest, that of the First Amendment. In this light, petitioner must be viewed as seeking to achieve a goal that is of paramount importance in the fulfillment of its mission.

It may be argued that there is greater force to these views at the undergraduate level than in a medical school where the training is centered primarily on professional competency. But even at the graduate level, our tradition and experience lend support to the view that the contribution of diversity is substantial. In *Sweatt* v. *Painter,* the Court made a similar point with specific reference to legal education:

> The law school, the proving ground for legal learning and practice, cannot be effective in isolation from the individuals and institutions with which the law interacts. Few students and no one who has practiced law would choose to study in an academic vacuum, removed from the interplay of ideas and the exchange of views with which the law is concerned.

Physicians serve a heterogeneous population. An otherwise qualified medical student with a particular background—whether it be ethnic, geographic, culturally advantaged or disadvantaged—may bring to a professional school of medicine experiences, outlooks, and ideas that enrich the training of its student body and better equip its graduates to render with understanding their vital service to humanity.

Ethnic diversity, however, is only one element in a range of factors a university properly may consider in attaining the goal of a heterogeneous student body. Although a university must have wide discretion in making the sensitive judgments as to who should be admitted, constitutional limitations protecting individual rights may not be disregarded. Respondent urges—and the courts below have held—that petitioner's dual admissions program is a racial classification that impermissibly infringes his rights under the Fourteenth Amendment. As the interest of diversity is compelling in the context of a university's admissions program, the question remains whether the program's racial classification is necessary to promote this interest.

V

A

It may be assumed that the reservation of a specified number of seats in each class for individuals from the preferred ethnic groups would contribute to the attainment of considerable ethnic diversity in the student body. But petitioner's argument that this is the only effective means of serving the interest of diversity is seriously flawed. In a most fundamental sense the argument misconceives the nature of the state interest that would justify consideration of race or ethnic background. It is not an interest in simple ethnic diversity, in which a specified percentage of the student body is in effect guaranteed to be members of selected ethnic groups, with the remaining percentage an undifferentiated aggregation of students. The diversity that furthers a compelling state interest encompasses a far broader array of qualifications and characteristics of which racial or ethnic origin is but a single though important element. Petitioner's special admissions program, focused *solely* on ethnic diversity, would hinder rather than further attainment of genuine diversity. . . .

B

In summary, it is evident that the Davis special admissions program involves the use of an explicit racial classification never before countenanced by this Court. It tells applicants who are not Negro, Asian, or Chicano that they are totally excluded from a specific percentage of the seats in an entering class. No matter how strong their qualifications, quantitative and extracurricular, including their own potential for contribution to educational diversity, they are never afforded the chance to compete with applicants from the preferred groups for the special admissions seats. At the same time, the preferred applicants have the opportunity to compete for every seat in the class.

The fatal flaw in petitioner's preferential program is its disregard of individual rights as guaranteed by the Fourteenth Amendment. Such rights are not absolute. But when a State's distribution of benefits or imposition of burdens hinges on ancestry or the color of a person's skin, that individual is entitled to a demonstration that the challenged classification is necessary to promote a substantial state interest. Petitioner has failed to carry this burden. For this reason, that portion of the California court's judgment holding petitioner's special admissions program invalid under the Fourteenth Amendment must be affirmed. . . .

QUESTIONS FOR REFLECTION

1. Justice Powell argues that the University of California's racial classification should not simply be viewed as "benign." Why?
2. How did the University of California try to justify its affirmative-action program? Why does Justice Powell reject those arguments?
3. What sort of affirmative-action program does Justice Powell find acceptable? How does it differ from the University of California program?

ANTONIN SCALIA

The Disease as a Cure

Antonin Scalia is a justice of the United States Supreme Court. This paper was published before his appointment. (Source: From the Washington University Law Quarterly, *1979, no. 1. Copyright © 1979. Reprinted by permission.)*

I have grave doubts about the wisdom of where we are going in affirmative action, and in equal protection generally. I find this area an embarrassment to teach. Here, as in some other fields of constitutional law, it is increasingly difficult to pretend to one's students that the decisions of the Supreme Court are tied together by threads of logic and analysis—as opposed to what seems to be the fact that the decisions of each of the justices on the court are tied together by threads of social preference and predisposition. Frankly, I do not have it in me to play the game of distinguishing and reconciling the cases in this utterly confused field.

The chaos in which we find ourselves is exemplified well enough by *Bakke* itself. Four of the justices tell us that both the Constitution and Title VI permit racial preference; four of the justices tell us that whatever the Constitution may permit, Title VI forbids it. And the law of the land, pronounced by the one remaining justice, apparently is that Title VI is no different from the Constitution; governmental racial distinctions of any sort are "odious to a free people" and their validity "inherently suspect"; they must pass "the most exacting judicial examination," and can only be justified by a "compelling" state interest. We later learn that the "compelling" interest at issue in *Bakke* is the enormously important goal of assuring that in medical school—where we are dealing with students in an age range of twenty-two to twenty-eight, or in Bakke's case, thirty-three to thirty-nine—we will expose these impressionable youngsters to a great diversity of people. We want them to work and play with pianists, maybe flute players. We want people from the country, from the city. We want bespectacled chess champions and football players. And, oh yes, we may want some racial minorities, too. If that is all it takes to overcome the presumptions against discrimination by race, we have witnessed an historic trivialization of the Constitution. Justice Powell's opinion, which we must work with as the law of the land, strikes me as an excellent compromise between two committees of the American Bar Association on some insignificant legislative proposal. But it is thoroughly unconvincing as an honest, hard-minded, reasoned analysis of an important provision of the Constitution.

There is, of course, a lot of pretense or self-delusion (you can take your choice) in all that pertains to affirmative action. Does anyone really think, for example, that the situation has changed at Davis? So instead of reserving class places for minority students, the school will open all slots to all applicants, but in choosing among them, will take into account the need for diversity—piano players, football players, people from the country, minority students, etc. When it comes to choosing among these manifold diversities in God's creation, will being a piano player, do you suppose, be regarded as more important than having yellow skin?

Or will coming from Oshkosh, Wisconsin, be regarded as more important than having a Spanish surname? It will be very difficult to tell.

Only two results of the *Bakke* decision are certain. First, the judgments that the Davis medical school makes in filling these 100 slots will be effectively unappealable to the courts. (There is no way to establish, for example, that the diversity value of New York City oboists has not been accorded its proper weight.) Second, when all is said and done, it is a safe bet that though there may not be a piano player in the class, there are going to be close to sixteen minority students. And I suspect that Justice Powell's delightful compromise was drafted precisely to achieve these results—just as, it has been charged, the Harvard College "diversity admissions" program, which Mr. Justice Powell's opinion so generously praises, was designed to reduce as inconspicuously as possible the disproportionate number of New York Jewish students that a merit admissions system had produced.

Examples abound to support my suggestion that this area is full of pretense or self-delusion. Affirmative action requirements under Title VI and VII are said repeatedly "not to require the hiring of any unqualified individuals." That gives one a great feeling of equal justice until it is analyzed. Unfortunately, the world of employment applicants does not divide itself merely into "qualified" and "unqualified" individuals. There is a whole range of ability—from unqualified, through minimally qualified, qualified, well qualified, to outstanding. If I cannot get Leontyne Price to sing a concert I have scheduled, I may have to settle for Erma Glatt. La Glatt has a pretty good voice, but not as good as Price. Is she unqualified? Not really—she has sung other concerts with modest success. But she is just not as good as Price. Any system that coerces me to hire her in preference to Price, because of her race, degrades the quality of my product and discriminates on racial grounds against Price. And it is no answer to either of these charges that Glatt is "qualified." To seek to assuage either the employer's demand for quality or the disfavored applicant's demand for equal treatment by saying there is no need to hire any unqualified individuals is a sort of intellectual shell game, which diverts attention from the major issue by firmly responding to a minor one.

But, of course, even the disclaimer of compulsion to hire unqualified individuals loses something when it is translated into practice by the advocates of affirmative action. Consider, for example, the following statement by Professor Edwards: "This is not to say that blacks or women must be thrust into positions for which they are not qualified; however, when the choice is between white males and other qualified or qualifiable individuals, we should open the available positions to those who formerly could not occupy them." Note that what begins with the ritualistic denial of any intent to foster hiring of the unqualified imperceptibly shifts to a call for hiring of the "qualifiable," which surely must be a subcategory of the unqualified. It is typical of the confused level of debate that characterizes this field.

Another example of pretense or self-delusion is the Department of Labor's regulations concerning goals for hiring to overcome "underutilization": "The purpose of a contractor's establishment and use of goals is to insure that he meets his affirmative action obligation. It is not intended and should not be used to discriminate against any applicant or employee because of race, color, religion, sex, or national origin." This is, quite literally, incredible. Once there is established a numerical figure, the failure to meet it will have material, adverse consequences; namely, the substantial risk of cutoff of government contracts and the substantial certainty of disruptive and expensive government investigations. All that we know about human nature and human motivations indicates quite clearly that discrimination often will be produced in an effort to meet or exceed the magic number. I am a businessman who has, let us say, six more jobs to fill, and I am three short of my minority "goal." Reaching the goal will render my government contracts secure and will save thousands of dollars in the expenses necessary to comply with the demands of an equal employment investigation. If I consult my self-interest, which people tend to do, I will hire three minority applicants, even if they are somewhat less qualified than others. When the results that are inevitable are compared with the results that are said to be "intended," one must conclude that the drafter of the regulation is either fooling us or fooling himself. I appreciate, of course, that any antidiscrimination law with teeth in it will generate *some* pressures to favor minority groups. But that is worlds away from the "we-need-three-more-nonwhites" attitude that is the utterly predictable result of so-called "goals."

Judge Wisdom, dissenting in the *Weber* case, makes the following statement: "The Union's duty to bargain in good faith for all its members [an obligation imposed by law] does not prevent it from fairly advancing the national policy against discrimination, even if that requires assisting some of its members more than others." One has to be reminded of the line from *Animal Farm,* to the effect that all animals are created equal but some are more equal than others. And one cannot help but think that a paraphrase of Judge Wisdom's statement would fit very nicely in the mouth of a good old-fashioned racist employer: "We favor all applicants, but we favor white applicants more than others." It is very difficult to take Judge Wisdom's argument as a serious attempt to identify and grapple with the real issue rather than as an elaborate intellectual word game.

Another pretense or self-delusion—perhaps the grandest of all—is the notion that what was involved in the *Weber* case is voluntary private discrimination against whites. As Judge Wisdom put it: "While the government might not be able to require that restorative justice be done, neither should it prevent it." Fancy that! To think that the real issue in *Weber,* and presumably all those "reverse discrimination" cases, is damnable federal regulation: whether the federal government should be able to *prevent* the discrimination against better-qualified employees, which Kaiser and thousands of other businesses throughout the country are champing at the bit to engage in! That is, of course, chimerical. Nobody really believes that Kaiser would have established the challenged program, or the union permitted it, without the "incentive" of federal administrative regulations, which in effect makes the application of what Judge Wisdom calls "restorative justice" a condition for the award of government contracts and for the avoidance of expensive litigation in and out of the courts. To discuss the issue in the fictitious context of voluntarism not only makes any intelligently reasoned decision impossible in the particular case, but poisons the well of legal discourse.

The Restorative Justice Handicapping System

That last quotation concerning "restorative justice" may explain why I feel a bit differently about these issues than, for example, Judge Wisdom or Justice Powell or Justice White. When John Minor Wisdom speaks of "restorative justice," I am reminded of the story about the Lone Ranger and his "faithful Indian companion" Tonto. If you recall the famous radio serial, you know that Tonto never said much, but what he did say was (disguised beneath a Hollywood-Indian dialect) wisdom of an absolutely Solomonic caliber. On one occasion, it seems that the Lone Ranger was galloping along with Tonto, heading eastward, when they saw coming towards them a large band of Mohawk Indians in full war dress. The Lone Ranger reigns in his horse, turns to Tonto, and asks, "Tonto, what should we do?" Tonto says, "Ugh, ride-um west." So they wheel around and gallop off to the west until suddenly they encounter a large band of Sioux heading straight toward them. The Lone Ranger asks, "Tonto, what should we do?" Tonto says, "Ugh, ride-um north." So, they turn around and ride north, and, sure enough, there's a whole tribe of Iroquois headed straight towards them. The Ranger asks, "Tonto, what should we do?" And Tonto says, "Ugh, ride-um south," which they do until they see a war party of Apaches coming right for them. The Lone Ranger says, "Tonto, what should we do?" And Tonto says, "Ugh, what you mean, 'we,' white man?"

I have somewhat the same feeling when John Minor Wisdom talks of the evils that "we" whites have done to blacks and that "we" must now make restoration for. My father came to this country when he was a teenager. Not only had he never profited from the sweat of any black man's brow, I don't think he had ever seen a black man. There are, of course, many white ethnic groups that came to this country in great numbers relatively late in its history—Italians, Jews, Irish, Poles—who not only took no part in, and derived no profit from, the major historic suppression of the currently acknowledged minority groups, but were, in fact, themselves the object of discrimination by the dominant Anglo-Saxon majority. If I can recall in my lifetime the obnoxious "White Trade Only" signs in shops in Washington, D.C., others can recall "Irish Need Not Apply" signs in Boston, three or four decades earlier. To be sure, in relatively recent years some or all of these groups have been the beneficiaries of discrimination against blacks, or have themselves practiced discrimination. But to compare their racial debt—I must use that term, since the concept of "restorative justice" implies it; there is no creditor without a debtor—with that of those who plied the slave trade, and who maintained a formal caste system for many years thereafter, is to confuse a mountain with a molehill. Yet curiously enough, we find that in the system of restorative justice established by the Wisdoms and the Powells and the Whites, it is precisely *these* groups that do most of the restoring. It is they who, to a disproportionate degree, are the competitors with the urban blacks and Hispanics for jobs, housing, education—all those things that enable one to scramble to the top of the social heap where one can speak eloquently (and quite safely) of restorative justice.

To remedy this inequity, I have developed a modest proposal, which I call RJHS—the Restorative Justice Handicapping System. I only have applied it thus far to restorative justice for the Negro, since obviously he has been the victim of the most widespread and systematic exploitation in this country; but a similar system could be devised for other creditor-races, creditor-sexes, or minority groups. Under my system each individual in society would be assigned at birth Restorative Justice Handicapping Points, determined on the basis of his or her ancestry. Obviously, the highest number of points must go to what we may loosely call the Aryans—the Powells, the Whites, the Stewarts, the Burgers, and, in fact (curiously enough), the entire composition of the present Supreme Court, with the exception of Justice Marshall. This grouping of north European races obviously played the greatest role in the suppression of the American black. But unfortunately, what was good enough for Nazi Germany is not good enough for our purposes. We must further divide the Aryans into subgroups. As I have suggested, the Irish (having arrived later) probably owe less of a racial debt than the Germans, who in turn surely owe less of a racial debt than the English. It will, to be sure, be difficult to draw precise lines and establish the correct number of handicapping points, but having reviewed the Supreme Court's jurisprudence on abortion, I am convinced that our justices would not shrink from the task.

Of course, the mere identification of the various degrees of debtor-races is only part of the job. One must in addition account for the dilution of bloodlines by establishing, for example, a half-Italian, half-Irish handicapping score. There are those who will scoff at this as a refinement impossible of achievement, but I am confident it can be done, and can even be extended to take account of dilution of blood in creditor-races as well. Indeed, I am informed (though I have not had the stomach to check) that a system to achieve the latter objective is already in place in federal agencies—specifying, for example, how much dilution of blood deprives one of his racial-creditor status as a "Hispanic" under affirmative action programs. Moreover, it should not be forgotten that we have a rich body of statutory and case law from the Old South to which we can turn for guidance in this exacting task.

But I think it unnecessary to describe the Restorative Justice Handicapping System any further. I trust you find it thoroughly offensive, as I do. It, and the racist concept of restorative justice of which it is merely the concrete expression, is fundamentally contrary to the principles that govern, and should govern, our society. I owe no man anything, nor he me, because of the blood that flows in our veins. To go down that road (or I should say to return down that road), even behind a banner as gleaming as restorative justice, is to make a frightening mistake. This is not to say that I have no obligation to my fellow citizens who are black. I assuredly do—not because of their race or because of any special debt that my bloodline owes to theirs, but because they have (many of them) special needs, and they are (all of them) my countrymen and (as I believe) my brothers. This means that I am entirely in favor of according the poor inner-city child, who happens to be black, advantages and preferences not given to my own children because they do not need them. But I am not willing to prefer the son of a prosperous and well-educated black doctor or lawyer—solely because of his race—to the son of a recent refugee from Eastern Europe who is working as a manual laborer to get his family ahead. The affirmative action system now in place will produce the latter result because it is based upon concepts of racial indebtedness and racial entitlement rather than individual worth and individual need; that is to say, because it is racist.

Evil Fruits of a Bad Seed

But I not only question the principle upon which racial affirmative action is based; I even question its effectiveness in achieving the desired goal of advancing a particular race. Professor Edwards, for example, states in one of his pieces that: "The continued existence of long-standing myths about the inherent inability of blacks to perform certain work has also contributed to their exclusion from significant jobs in the employment market." That strikes me as true, but one may well wonder whether the prescribed solution of affirmative action based on race will eliminate the myths rather than assure their perpetuation. When one reads the *Bakke* case, the most striking factual data is the enormous divergence in the average college grades and average test scores of the regular admittees and the special (minority) admittees of the Davis medical school for the years Bakke was rejected. In 1973 they looked like this:

	Grade Point Average		Medical College Admission Test			
	Science	Overall	Verbal	Quantitative	Science	Gen'l Info.
Regular	3.51	3.49	81	76	83	69
Minority	2.62	2.88	46	24	35	33

Do you suppose the "image" of minority groups has been improved by this? I suggest that, to the contrary, the very ability of minority group members to distinguish themselves and their race has been dreadfully impaired. To put the issue to you in its starkest form: If you must select your brain surgeon from among recent graduates of Davis medical school and have nothing to go on but their names and pictures, would you not be well advised—playing the odds—to eliminate all minority group members? It is well known to the public that the outstanding institutions of higher education graduate the best and the brightest principally through the simple device of admitting only the best and the brightest. And it is obvious to the public that (to the extent these schools flunk *anyone* out) the same factor that produced special admissions will also tend to produce special retention and, ultimately, special graduation. Thus, insofar as "public image" is concerned, the immediate and predictable effect of affirmative action is to establish a second-class, "minority" degree, which is a less certain certificate of quality. In other words, we have established within our institutions of higher education (and wherever else racial affirmative action is applied) a regime reminiscent of major league baseball in the years before Jackie Robinson: a separate "league" for minority students, which makes it difficult for the true excellence of the minority star to receive his or her deserved acknowledgment. To be sure, the students' teachers, and those of us who have the opportunity of examining the students' transcripts, can tell who is or is not outstanding. But those members of the public about whom Professor Edwards is concerned—those who judge by generalities, or by "image," if you will—are they likely to think better or worse of minority graduates? The person who was so ignorant as to say "a Negro simply cannot become a truly outstanding doctor" can now plausibly add "—and the fact that he obtained a degree from one of the best medical schools in the country doesn't prove a thing."

In response to this, the advocates of racial affirmative action might say the following: "Even if, as you say, our system cannot give an increased number of minority students a first-class Davis degree—and indeed, even if it may, as you say, make it impossible for *any* minority student to obtain a first-class Davis degree—at least it gives more minority students the concrete benefits of a first-class Davis education." But that is questionable pedagogy. In grammar school, at least, where the politics of race do not yet seem to have permeated pupil assignment within schools, we do not "help" a disadvantaged student by admitting him into a faster group. Why should college and graduate school be different? During the guns-on-campus disturbances at Cornell, one-half of that school's black students were on academic probation. Why? They were neither stupid nor lazy. As a whole their test scores were in the *upper* 25 per cent of all students admitted to college. But the Cornell student body as a whole was in the upper one per cent. Was it really "helping" these young men and women, either from the standpoint of their personal intellectual development or from the standpoint of their "image" as minority graduates in later life, to place them in an environment where it was quite probable (as probable as such things can ever be) that they did not belong? It solved the political problems of the school administrators, no doubt. And it may have given the administrators, faculty, and alumni the warm feeling that they were doing their part (at no expense, by and large, to their own children) for "restorative justice." But did it really help these young men and women? With few exceptions, I suspect not.

I could mention other harmful, practical effects of racial affirmative action. It has been suggested, for example, that one consequence is to encourage the location of industries in areas where affirmative action problems are likely to be reduced; that is, away from the inner cities where the game of racial percentages produces significantly higher quotas (or, if you prefer, goals). In any case, it is a fact that statistics show an increase in the economic status of blacks in the years immediately preceding affirmative action and a decline thereafter. Whatever else the program may be, it is not demonstrably effective.

Conclusion

I am, in short, opposed to racial affirmative action for reasons of both principle and practicality. Sex-based affirmative action presents somewhat different constitutional issues, but it seems to me an equally poor idea, for many of the reasons suggested above. I do not, on the other hand, oppose—indeed, I strongly favor—what might be called (but for the coloration that the term has acquired in the context of its past use) "affirmative action programs" of many types of help for the poor and disadvantaged. It may well be that many, or even most, of these benefited by such programs would be members of minority races that the existing programs exclusively favor. I would not care if *all* of them were. The unacceptable vice is simply selecting or rejecting them *on the basis of their race.*

A person espousing the views I have expressed of course, exposes himself to charges of, at best, insensitivity or, at worst, bigotry. That is one reason these views are not expressed more often, particularly in academia. Beyond an anticipatory denial, I must content myself with the observation that it must be a queer sort of bigotry indeed, since it is shared by many intelligent members of the alleged target group. Some of the most vocal opposition to racial affirmative action comes from minority group members who have seen the value of their accomplishments debased by the suspicion—no, to be frank, the reality—of a lower standard for their group in the universities and the professions. This new racial presumption, imposed upon those who have lifted themselves above the effects of old racial presumptions, is the most evil fruit of a fundamentally bad seed. From racist principles flow racist results.

QUESTIONS FOR REFLECTION

1. Scalia rejects the justification for affirmative action from rectification or compensation. Why? Do you find his arguments compelling?
2. What harms does affirmative action produce, according to Scalia?
3. Why are discussions of affirmative action filled with "pretense or self-delusion," in Scalia's view?
4. Is diversity a compelling state interest? Why, or why not? What kind of evidence would one have to have to justify either conclusion?
5. If affirmative action programs give preference to members of certain groups, they must thereby place members of some other groups at a relative disadvantage. What are those other groups? Are they being treated unjustly?

BERNARD R. BOXILL

from *Blacks and Social Justice*

Professor Bernard R. Boxill is a professor of philosophy at the University of North Carolina at Chapel Hill. (Source: From Bernard R. Boxill, Blacks and Social Justice, *rev. ed., pp. 147–72. Footnotes have been omitted. Copyright 1984, 1992 by Rowman and Littlefield Publishers. Reprinted by permission.)*

Liberals into Former Liberals

As Michael Kinsley has observed in *Harper's*, "No single development of the past fifteen years has turned more liberals into former liberals than affirmative action." This metamorphosis, if it is not merely an unmasking, is ostensibly due to the belief that affirmative action perverts the just goal of civil rights. That goal, protest the disillusioned liberals, is to guarantee that persons be treated as individuals and judged on their merits; but affirmative action, they complain, guarantees that individuals are treated as mere members of racial groups, and their merits disparaged and ignored.

These liberals are not appeased by Allan Bakke's victory in the Supreme Court in 1978. For although the court ruled that Bakke was wrongly denied admission to the medical school at the University of California at Davis, it allowed that race could be used as a factor in considering applicants. As *Time* announced on its cover: "What Bakke Means. Race: Yes. Quotas: No."

As with busing, the arguments for preferential treatment fell into two classes, backward-looking and forward-looking. Backward-looking arguments justify preferential treatment considered as compensation for past and present wrongs done to blacks and their effects. Forward-looking arguments justify preferential treatment considered as a means to present or future goods, particularly equality. Both the assumptions and the aims of these two kinds of argument must be carefully distinguished.

Backward-looking arguments assume that blacks have been, or are being, wronged. Forward-looking arguments assume that blacks are generally inferior to whites in status, education, and income. Backward-looking arguments aim at compensating blacks. Forward-looking arguments aim at improving the status, education, and income of blacks.

The Backward-Looking Argument

The fundamental backward-looking argument is simply stated: Black people have been and are being harmed by racist attitudes and practices. Those wronged deserve compensation. Therefore, black people deserve compensation. Preferential treatment is an appropriate form of compensation for black people. Therefore black people deserve preferential treatment.

Criticism of this argument falls into two main classes: on the one hand, critics charge that the claims to compensation of the black beneficiaries of preferential treatment are unfounded or vacuously satisfied; on the other hand, they charge that these claims are outweighed by other considerations.

The most common version of the first type always uttered by the critic with an air of having played a trump, is that, since those members of groups that have been discriminated against who benefit from preferential hiring must be minimally qualified, they are not the members of the group who deserve compensation. The philosopher Alan Goldman, for example, argues this way: "Since hiring within the preferred group still depends upon relative qualifications and hence upon past opportunities for acquiring qualifications, there is in fact a reverse ratio established between past discriminations and present benefits, so that those who most benefit from the program, those who actually get jobs, are those who least deserve to." But surely a conclusion that preferential hiring is unjustified based on the argument above is a non sequitur. Let us grant that qualified blacks are less deserving of compensation than unqualified blacks, that those who most deserve compensation should be compensated first, and finally that preferential hiring is a form of compensation. How does it follow that preferential hiring of qualified blacks is unjustified? Surely the assumption that unqualified blacks are more deserving of compensation than qualified blacks does not require us to conclude that qualified blacks deserve no compensation. Because I have lost only one leg, I may be less deserving of compensation than another who has lost two legs, but it does not follow that I deserve no compensation at all.

Even Thomas Nagel, one of the country's leading philosophers and a strong defender of preferential treatment on the basis of the forward-looking argument, resorts to this criticism of the backward-looking argument. Thus he labels a "bad" argument, one that maintains that the "beneficiaries of affirmative action deserve it as compensation for past discrimination," because, he says, "no effort is made to give preference to those who have suffered most from discrimination." Indeed, Nagel makes exactly the same point as Goldman: Because the blacks who benefit from preferential treatment are qualified, "they are not necessarily, or even probably the ones who especially deserve it. Women or blacks who don't have the qualifications even to be considered are likely to have been handicapped more by the effects of discrimination than those who receive preference." But for the reasons given, this criticism is bogus. Furthermore, since Nagel defends preferential treatment on forward-looking, egalitarian grounds, this puts him into deeper trouble than it does those who reject preferential treatment altogether.

For, if preferential treatment makes no effort to give preference to those who have suffered most, neither does it make an effort to give preference to those who are most unequal to whites. In other words, if the qualified have suffered least, they are also least unequal, and it seems a bad strategy, if one is aiming for equality, to prefer them. Nagel could object that preferring the qualified is a good egalitarian strategy because it will lead indirectly to equality. But a variant of the idea is open to the advocate of the backward-looking argument. He could argue that preferential treatment of the qualified also helps to compensate the unqualified insofar as it shows them that if one is qualified, being black is no longer a bar to promotion. . . .

To sum up to this point: The criticism of the backward-looking argument for preferential treatment under consideration is unsound in one of its forms, and irrelevant in the other. Insofar as it assumes that many blacks have escaped wrongful harm as a result of discrimination it is unsound. Even if some blacks have escaped harm this would not be sufficient to make preferential treatment unjustified, because the overwhelming majority it benefited would deserve compensation. Insofar as the criticism assumes the black preferred are less wronged or harmed than other blacks it is irrelevant. The backward-looking argument does not exclude compensating unqualified blacks, or deny that compensating unqualified blacks, or deny that they are more deserving of compensation. Neither does it say that qualified blacks must be compensated first. It asserts only that blacks deserve compensation for the wrongful harms of discrimination. Thus, it is unaffected by the claim that qualified blacks may be the least wronged and harmed of blacks. The fact that qualified blacks are wrongfully harmed at all, and that preferential treatment is appropriate compensation, is sufficient justification for it.

Now, I have admitted that it is a weak argument which tries to justify preferential treatment of qualified blacks applying for desirable places and positions on the grounds that, had there been no discrimination, these blacks would probably have qualified for such places and positions without preferential treatment. The key assumption in this argument is simply not plausible. But if we assume that compensation is owed to blacks as a group, then a stronger version of that argument can be advanced, which goes as follows: Blacks as a group have been wronged, and are disadvantaged, by slavery and discrimination. Consequently, blacks as a group deserve compensation. Furthermore, had it not been for slavery and discrimination, blacks as a group would be more nearly equal in income, education, and well-being to other groups who did not suffer from slavery or the extent and kind of discrimination from which blacks have suffered. Consequently, assuming that compensating a group for wrongful disadvantages requires bringing it to the condition it would have been in had it not been wrongfully disadvantaged, compensating blacks as a group requires making them, as a group, more nearly equal to those other groups. But if blacks as a group were more nearly equal in income, education, and well-being to such groups, some blacks would then fill desirable positions. Accordingly, compensating blacks as a group requires putting some blacks in desirable positions. However, only the blacks who are now most qualified can, fittingly, be placed in desirable positions. Hence, even if those blacks are *not* the very ones who would have filled such places and positions had there been no slavery and discrimination, compensating blacks as a group may specifically require preferential treatment of qualified blacks. . . .

. . . We can form some estimate of the assets blacks as a group had before slavery and discrimination. Consequently, we can apply the ideal conception of compensation, and reasonably propose to place blacks as a group in the position they would have occupied had there been no slavery and discrimination. . . .

. . . [I]t has seemed to many critics that preferential treatment, insofar as it involves preferential admissions and hiring, is unfair to young white males. For example, according to Robert K. Fullinwider, a research associate at the Center for Philosophy and Public Policy at the University of Maryland, the compensation argument for preferential treatment confuses the sound compensation principle—"he who wrongs another shall pay for the wrong"—with the "suspect" principle—"he who benefits from a wrong shall pay for the wrong." To clinch the point, Fullinwider asks us to consider the following ingenious example: A neighbor pays a construction company to pave his driveway, but someone maliciously directs the workmen to pave Fullinwider's driveway instead. Fullinwider admits that his neighbor has been "wronged and damaged" and that he himself has "benefited from the wrong." However, since he is not responsible for the wrong, he denies that he is "morally required to compensate" his neighbor by "paying" him for it.

This example makes us see that not all cases where compensation may be due are straightforward, though one kind of case clearly is. If John steals Jeff's bicycle and "gives" it to me, however innocent I may be, I have no right to it and must return it to Jeff as soon as I discover the theft. Given that this example is unproblematic, in what way does it differ from Fullinwider's, which is problematic?

One difference is that, whereas I can simply hand over Jeff's bicycle to him, Fullinwider cannot simply hand over the pavement in his driveway. It will be objected that the proposal was not that Fullinwider should hand over the pavement, but that he should pay his neighbor for it. But this is a different case. I did not say that I had a duty to pay Jeff for his bicycle. I said that I had a duty to return the bicycle to Jeff. If Jeff told me to keep the bicycle but pay him for it, I do not admit that I would have a duty to do so. I could object fairly that when I accepted the bicycle I did not believe that I would have to pay for it, and if I had thought that I would have to, I might have not accepted it. Paying for the bicycle now would impose on me, because I might have preferred to spend my money in a different way and, being innocent of any wrongdoing, I see no reason why I should be penalized. The point is that though the beneficiary of an injustice has no right to his advantage, if he is innocent of the injustice, he does not deserve to be penalized. Thus, where compensation is concerned, the obligations of the innocent beneficiary of injustice and of the person responsible for the injustice are quite different. Though the former has no right to his benefits, the process of compensation cannot impose any losses on him over and above the loss of his unfair benefits. If compensation is impossible without such loss, it is unjustified. On the other hand, in the case of the person responsible for injustice, even if compensation requires him to give up more than he has unfairly gained, it is still justified.

But, though Fullinwider's example is cogent as far as it goes, it is irrelevant as an argument against preferential hiring. It is cogent as far as it goes because, as the above analysis shows, requiring young white males to pay women and minorities for all the unfair advantages they have enjoyed would indeed be unfair. The advantages cannot, as in my example of the bicycle, simply be transferred from their hands into those of the preferred group. Compensation of this kind would impose on young white males time and effort over and above the cost of the unfair advantages they are required to return. They could justly protest that they are being penalized, because they might not have accepted the advantages had they known what they would cost them—now they are "out" both the advantages and their time and effort. But preferential hiring does not require young white males to pay, at an additional cost to themselves, the price of their advantages. It proposes instead to compensate the injured with goods no one has yet established a right to and therefore in a way that imposes no unfair losses on anyone. And these goods are, of course, jobs.

It may be objected that, although a white male applicant may not have established a right to this or that job, he has a right to fair competition for it, and preferential hiring violates that right. But, on the contrary, by refusing to allow him to get the job because of an unfair advantage, preferential hiring makes the competition fairer. The white male applicant can still complain, of course, that, had he known that preferential hiring would be instituted, he would not have accepted his advantages in the first place. Since, if he knew that preferential hiring would be instituted, he would necessarily also have known that his advantages were unfair, his complaint would amount to his saying that, had he known his advantages were unfair, he would not have accepted them. But then, if he is concerned with fairness, and if preferential hiring makes the competition fairer, he should have no objections to it. Or to state the proposition somewhat less contentiously, preferential hiring imposes no unfair losses on him.

Thus, a fairer application of Fullinwider's example about the driveway to the case of preferential hiring would be as follows: Suppose an "improve-your-neighborhood group" offered a valuable prize for the best driveway on the block. Would Fullinwider be justified in insisting that he deserves to get the prize over his neighbor who has, at further cost to himself, built another, somewhat inferior driveway?

To sum up my discussion of forms of the backward-looking argument for preferential treatment, while I have insisted that all, or nearly all, blacks are victims of racial injustice, I have conceded that it has handicapped some blacks more than others, and that other kinds of injustice have handicapped some whites more than racial injustice has handicapped blacks. Consequently, although the backward-looking argument is the bedrock of the case for preferential treatment, to complete that case we must look forward.

The Forward-Looking Argument

Whereas the backward-looking argument tried to justify preferential treatment as compensation for past wrongful harms, the forward-looking argument tries to justify preferential treatment on the grounds that it may secure greater equality or increase total social utility. Moreover, the fact that blacks were slaves and the victims of discrimination is irrelevant to the forward-looking argument, which, its proponents imply, would not lose force even if blacks had never been slaves and never were discriminated against. All that is relevant to the argument is that blacks are often poor, generally less than equal to whites in education, influence, and income, and preferentially treating them will alleviate their poverty, reduce their inequality, and generally increase total utility.

The forward-looking argument has one very clear advantage over the backward-looking argument. As we have seen, a persistent criticism of the backward-looking argument is that, although some blacks deserve no compensation for discrimination because they have not been harmed by discrimination, they are precisely the ones benefiting from preferential treatment. I have tried to rebut this criticism, but this is unnecessary if the forward-looking argument is adopted. For that argument does not require the assumption that the beneficiaries of preferential treatment have been harmed by discrimination, or even that they have been harmed at all. Indeed, it does not require that they be less than equal to whites, and is consistent with their being relatively privileged. For it endorses a strategy of increasing the incomes and education even of blacks superior in those respects to most whites if, however indirectly, this will, in the long run, effectively increase blacks' equality and increase total social utility.

Now whether or not preferential treatment has such consequences is in the end an empirical question, but some critics, as I will show, insist on concocting specious *a priori* arguments to show that preferential treatment necessarily causes a loss in social utility.

Thus it has been argued that since, by definition, preferential treatment awards positions to the less qualified over the more qualified, and since the more qualified perform more efficiently than the less qualified, therefore preferential treatment causes a loss of utility. But suppose that less qualified blacks are admitted to medical school in preference to more qualified whites, and suppose the resulting black doctors practice in poor black neighborhoods treating serious illnesses, while if the whites they were preferred to had been admitted they would have practiced in affluent white neighborhoods, treating minor illnesses. In that sort of case, it is not at all necessarily true that preferential treatment causes a loss in utility. Some authors try to avoid the force of this argument by switching the basis of their criticism from the fact that preferential treatment may reward the less qualified to the false assertion that preferential treatment may reward the "unqualified." Thus, Goldman reminds us that "all will suffer when unqualified persons occupy many positions." This is criticism of a straw man.

It has also been claimed that the forward-looking argument that preferential treatment increases utility is open to a serious philosophical objection. Thus philosopher George Sher writes that the utilitarian, or forward-looking, defense of preferential treatment is "vulnerable" to the "simple but serious" objection that "if it is acceptable to discriminate in favor of minorities and women when doing so maximizes utility, then it is hard to see why it should not also be acceptable to discriminate against minorities and women when that policy maximizes welfare." And against Thomas Nagel who argues that racial discrimination, unlike reverse discrimination, "has no social advantages . . . and attaches a sense of reduced worth to a feature with which people are born," Sher makes a similar objection. He says that Nagel gives us no reason to believe that "there could never be alternative circumstances in which racial, ethnic, or sexual discrimination had social advantages which did outweigh the sense of reduced worth it produced," and maintains that Nagel still has not shown us that such discrimination is illegitimate under "any circumstances at all."

The serious utilitarian is likely to dismiss Sher's criticisms with the same impatience with which he dismisses the stock criticism that utilitarianism allows slavery. As R. M. Hare notes, it is the "strength" of the utilitarian doctrine that "the utilitarian cannot reason *a priori* that whatever the facts about the world and human nature, slavery is wrong. He has to show it is wrong by showing, through a study of history and other factual observation, that slavery does have the effects (namely the production of misery) that make it wrong." In particular, he is not undone by the arguments of the intuitionist who thinks up "fantastic" examples which show slavery to be right according to the principles of utilitarianism, because these show only that the intuitionist has "lost contact with the actual world." Much the same thing can be said about Sher's notion that there are circumstances in which racial discrimination would be legitimate according to utilitarian principles. . . .

. . . I have used more space in rebutting criticisms than in arguing positively for conclusions. This is because the main arguments for affirmative action are straightforward, and yet philosophers persist in concocting ever more desperately ingenious objections to it. Not that I believe that any one of the various backward- and forward-looking arguments is by itself sufficient to justify affirmative action. Affirmative action is justified by the combined force of these arguments and by the way they complement and support each other. The weaknesses in some are made up by the strengths of others. For example, the weakness in the case for compensation on an individual basis is made up for by the case for compensation on a group basis, and the weaknesses of both these cases are strengthened by considerations stemming from the forward-looking argument. A society which tries to be just tries to compensate the victims of its injustice, and when these victims are easily identified, either as individuals or as a group less than equal to others, the case for treating them preferentially is overwhelming.

QUESTIONS FOR REFLECTION

1. How does Boxill criticize the argument that affirmative action helps those who least need it?
2. How does Boxill justify compensating blacks as a group? Do you find his argument compelling? Why or why not?
3. Do you agree with Boxill that all blacks have been harmed by discrimination and deserve compensation—even Bill Cosby and Oprah Winfrey, for example?
4. How might Boxill respond to the argument that the social and economic position of blacks is due more to culture than to discrimination?
5. What is Boxill's forward-looking argument for affirmative action?

THOMAS SOWELL

"Affirmative Action": A Worldwide Disaster

Thomas Sowell is a senior research fellow at the Hoover Institution at Stanford University. (Source: Reprinted from Commentary *[December 1989], by permission; all rights reserved.)*

Arguments for and against "affirmative action" have raged for about twenty years in the United States. Similar arguments have provoked controversy—and even bloodshed—for a longer or a shorter period, in the most disparate societies, scattered around the world. India, Nigeria, Australia, Guyana, Malaysia, Sri Lanka, Pakistan, and Indonesia are just some of the countries where some groups receive official, government-sanctioned preferences over others. While the American phrase "affirmative action" is used in Australia and Canada, other countries have used a variety of other phrases, such as "positive discrimination" (India), "sons of the soil" preferences (Indonesia, Malaysia), "standardization" (Sri Lanka), or "reflecting the federal character" of the country (Nigeria). The same general principle of government apportionment of coveted positions, to supersede the competition of the marketplace or of academia, was of course also embodied in the *numerus clausus* laws used to restrict the opportunities of Jews in prewar Central and Eastern Europe.

The countries with preferential policies have varied enormously in cultural, political, economic, and other ways. The groups receiving preferences have likewise varied greatly, from locally or nationally dominant groups in some countries to the poorest and most abject groups, such as the untouchables of India. Such vast disparities in settings and people make it all the more striking that there are common patterns among these countries—patterns with serious implications for "affirmative-action" policies in the United States. Among these patterns are the following:

1. Preferential programs, even when explicitly and repeatedly defined as "temporary," have tended not only to persist but also to expand in scope, either embracing more groups or spreading to wider realms for the same groups, or both. Even preferential programs established with legally mandated cut-off dates, as in India and Pakistan, have continued far past those dates by subsequent extensions.
2. Within the groups designated by government as recipients of preferential treatment, the benefits have usually gone disproportionately to those members already more fortunate.
3. Group polarization has tended to increase in the wake of preferential programs, with nonpreferred groups reacting adversely, in ways ranging from political backlash to mob violence and civil war.
4. Fraudulent claims of belonging to the designated beneficiary groups have been widespread and have taken many forms in various countries.

In the United States, as in other countries around the world, the empirical consequences of preferential policies have received much less attention than the rationales and goals of such policies. Too often these rationales and goals have been sufficient unto themselves, both in the political arena and in courts of law. Without even an attempt at empirical assessment of costs versus benefits, with no attempt to pinpoint either losers or gainers, discussions of preferential policies are often exercises in assertion, counter-assertion, and accusation. Illusions flourish in such an atmosphere. So do the disappointments and bitterness to which illusions lead.

Foremost among these illusions is the belief that group "disparities" in "representation" are suspect anomalies that can be corrected by having the government temporarily apportion places on the basis of group membership. Every aspect of this belief fails the test of evidence, in country after country. The prime moral illusion is that preferential policies compensate for wrongs suffered. This belief has been supported only by a thin veneer of emotional rhetoric, seldom examined but often reiterated.

1. The Assumptions of "Affirmative Action"

"Temporary" Policies

When U.S. Supreme Court Justice William J. Brennan described the "affirmative-action" plan in the *Weber* case as "a temporary measure," he was echoing a view widely held, not only in the United States but also around the world. Britain's Lord Scarman likewise said:

> We can and for the present must accept the loading of the law in favor of one group at the expense of others, defending it as a temporary expedient in the balancing process which has to be undertaken when and where there is social and economic inequality.

The rhetoric of transience and the reality of persistence and proliferation are both international features of preferential policies. "Affirmative-action" plans initially justified in the United States by the unique historic sufferings of blacks have been successively extended, over the years, to groups that now add up to several times as many people as the black population—and more than half of the total American population. These include not only American Indians, Hispanics, and Asians, but also women. A very similar pattern emerged in India, where official preferences were established more than forty years ago for untouchables, for some tribal groups, and for unspecified "other backward classes." Since then, so many groups have managed to get themselves included under "other backward classes" that they now outnumber the untouchables and the tribal peoples put together.

Even where no new groups are added to those legally entitled to official preferences, new occupations, institutions, and sectors of the society can fall under the coverage of preferential policies. Malays were granted preferential employment in government back in colonial Malaya under the British. After Malaya became independent Malaysia, and especially after the "New Economic Policy" announced in 1969, preferences spread to university admissions, government loans, occupational licenses, and employment in private businesses, both local and foreign-owned. The island nation of Sri Lanka has followed a pattern much like that of Malaysia. Preferences for the Sinhalese have not spread to other groups but have simply become more pronounced and more widespread over time.

Perhaps the classic example of preferences that spread far beyond their initial group and their original rationale have been the preferences in Pakistan. The desperately poor Bengalis of East Pakistan were "underrepresented" in the civil service, the military, business, and the professions. Even the administration of East Pakistan was filled with West Pakistanis. Preferential policies to correct this were advocated in 1949 as "temporary" expedients to be phased out in five to ten years. In reality, however, these policies have lasted decades beyond this time and in 1984 were extended to 1994 by the late President Zia. Not only did preferential quotas spread well beyond people from the East Pakistan region; they persisted long after East Pakistan broke away in 1971 to form the independent nation of Bangladesh. In other words, those who provided the initial rationale for preferential policies have now disappeared by secession but the policies themselves have acquired a political life of their own.

Despite such patterns in these and other countries, the word "temporary" continues to be used in discussions of preferential policies—judicial and scholarly, as well as popular and political. No argument seems to be considered necessary to show that this transience can be enforced, so that the word "temporary" will be something more than political decoration. Indeed, few seem to feel a need to specify whether the dimensions of "temporary" are to be measured in actual units of time or by the attainment of some preconceived social results. If the latter, then the distinction between "temporary" and "eternal" can be wholly illusory in practice. In short, the nebulousness of the concept of "temporary" preference has matched its futility.

Statistical Disparities

Equally nebulous are the assumptions about the statistical "disparities" and "imbalances" that preferential policies are supposed to correct.

The idea that large statistical disparities between groups are unusual—and therefore suspicious—is commonplace, but only among those who have not bothered to study the history of racial, ethnic, and other groups in countries around the world. Among leading scholars who have in fact devoted years of research to such matters, a radically different picture emerges. Donald L. Horowitz of Duke University, at the end of a massive and masterful international study of ethnic groups—a study highly praised in scholarly journals—examined the idea of a society where groups are "proportionately represented" at different levels and in different sectors. He concluded that "few, if any, societies have ever approximated this description."

A worldwide study of military forces and police forces by Cynthia Enloe of Clark University likewise concluded that "militaries fall far short of mirroring, even roughly, the multi-ethnic societies" from which they come. Moreover, just "as one is unlikely to find a police force or a military that mirrors its plural society, so one is unlikely to find a representative bureaucracy." One reason is that "it is common for different groups to rely on different mobility ladders." Some choose the military, some the bureaucracy, and some various parts of the private sector. Even within the military, different branches tend to have very different racial or ethnic compositions—the Afrikaners, for example, being slightly underrepresented in the South African navy and greatly overrepresented in the South African army, though their utter dominance in the government ensures that they cannot be discriminated against in either branch. Powerless minorities have likewise been greatly overrepresented or even dominant in particular branches of the military or the police—the Chinese in Malaysia's air force and among detectives in the police force, for example.

In the private sector as well, it is commonplace for minorities to be overrepresented, or even dominant, in competitive industries where they have no power to prevent others from establishing rival businesses. Jewish prominence in the clothing industry, not only in the United States, but in Argentina and Chile as well, did not reflect any ability to prevent other Americans, Argentines, or Chileans from manufacturing garments, but simply the advantages of the Jews' having brought needle-trade skills and experience with them from Eastern Europe. The fact that Jews owned more than half the clothing stores in mid-19th-century Melbourne likewise reflected that same advantage, rather than any ability to forbid other Australians from selling clothes. In a similar way, German minorities have been dominant as pioneers in piano manufacturing in colonial America, czarist Russia, Australia, France, and England. Italian fishermen, Japanese farmers, and Irish politicians have been among many other minority groups with special success in special fields in various countries, without any ability to keep out others.

Another distinguished scholar who has studied multi-ethnic societies around the world, Myron Weiner of MIT, refers to "the universality of ethnic inequality." He points out that those inequalities are multidimensional:

> All multi-ethnic societies exhibit a tendency for ethnic groups to engage in different occupations, have different levels (and, often, types) of education, receive different incomes, and occupy a different place in the social hierarchy.

Yet the pattern Professor Weiner has seen, after years of research, as a "universality" is routinely assumed to be an *anomaly,* not only by preferential-policy advocates, but also by the intelligentsia, the media, legislators, and judges—all of whom tend to assume, as a *norm,* what Professor Horowitz has found to exist (or even to be approximated) in "few, if any, societies." That what exists widely across the planet is regarded as an anomaly, while what exists virtually nowhere is regarded as a norm, is a tribute to the effectiveness of sheer reiteration in establishing a vision—and of the difficulties of dispelling a prevailing vision by facts.

Some might try to salvage the statistical argument for discrimination by describing discrimination as also being universal. But, to repeat, groups who are in no position to discriminate against anybody have often been overrepresented in coveted positions—the Chinese in Malaysian universities, the Tamils in Sri Lankan universities, the southerners in Nigerian universities, all during the 1960's, and Asians in American universities today being just some of the minorities of whom this has been true. All sorts of other powerless minorities have dominated particular industries or sectors of the economy, the intellectual community, or government employment. Among businessmen, India's Gujaratis in East Africa, the Lebanese in West Africa, the Chinese in Southeast Asia, the Jews in Eastern Europe, and Koreans and Vietnamese in black ghettos across the United States are just some examples. Among high government officials, the Germans were greatly overrepresented in czarist Russia, as were Christians in the Ottoman empire. Among intellectuals, the Scots were as dominant in 18th- and 19th-century Britain as the Jews have been in other parts of Europe. In short, large statistical disparities have been commonplace, both in the presence of discrimination and in its absence. Indeed, large disparities have been commonplace in the utilization of preferential programs designed to reduce disparities.

The intellectual and political *coup* of those who promote the randomness assumption is to put the burden of proof entirely on others. It is not merely the individual employer, for example, who must disprove this assumption in his own particular case in order to escape a charge of discrimination. All who oppose the randomness assumption find themselves confronted with the task of disproving an elusive plausibility, for which no evidence is offered. As for counter-evidence, no enumeration of the myriad ways in which groups are grossly disparate—in age of marriage, alcohol consumption, immigration patterns, performance in sports, performance on tests—can ever be conclusive, even when extended past the point where the patience of the audience is exhausted.

Those viscerally convinced of the pervasiveness of discrimination and its potency as an explanation of social disparities—and convinced also of the effectiveness of preferential policies as a remedy—are little troubled by the logical shakiness of the statistical evidence. That is all the more reason for others to be doubly troubled—not simply because an incorrect policy may be followed but also, and more importantly, because actions ostensibly based on the rule of law are in substance based on visceral convictions, the essence of lynch law. . . .

Assumptions as Law

Flaws in logic or evidence are unfortunate in intellectual speculation but they are far more serious in courts of law, where major penalties may be inflicted on those whose employees or students, for example, do not have a racial or ethnic composition that meets the preconceptions of other people. Some U.S. Supreme Court Justices have repeatedly treated statistical disparities as tantamount to discrimination and assumed the task of restoring groups to where they would have been otherwise. Even where group disparities in "representation" reflect demonstrable performance disparities, these performance disparities themselves have been taken as proof of societal discrimination. Thus, in the *Weber* case, Justice Harry Blackmun declared that there could be "little doubt that any lack of skill" on the part of minority workers competing with Brian Weber "has its roots in purposeful discrimination of the past." In the *Bakke* case, four Justices declared that the failure of minority medical-school applicants to perform as well as Allan Bakke "was due principally to the effects of past discrimination." The Court's task, therefore, was one of "putting minority applicants in the position they would have been in if not for the evil of racial discrimination."

All this presupposes a range of knowledge that no one has ever possessed. Ironically, this sweeping assumption of knowledge has been combined with an apparent ignorance of vast disparities in performance, disparities favoring groups with no power to discriminate against anybody. From such judicial speculation it is only a short step to the idea of restoring groups to where they would have been—and *what* they would have been—but for the offending discrimination.

What would the average Englishman be like today "but for" the Norman conquest? What would the average Japanese be like "but for" the enforced isolation of Japan for two-and-a-half centuries under the Tokugawa shoguns? What would the Middle East be like "but for" the emergence of Islam? In any other context besides preferential-policy issues, the presumption of knowing the answers to such questions would be regarded as ridiculous, even as intellectual speculation, much less as a basis for serious legal action.

To know how one group's employment, education, or other pattern differs statistically from another's is usually easy. What is difficult to know are the many variables determining the interest, skill, and performance of those individuals from various groups who are being considered for particular jobs, roles, or institutions. What is virtually impossible to know are the patterns that would exist in a non-discriminatory world—the deviations from which would indicate the existence and magnitude of discrimination.

Age distribution and geographic distribution are only two very simple factors which can play havoc with the assumption that groups would be evenly or randomly distributed in occupations and institutions, in the absence of discrimination. When one group's median age is a decade younger than another's—not at all uncommon—that alone may be enough to cause the younger group to be statistically "overrepresented" in sports, crime, and entry-level jobs, as well as in those kinds of diseases and accidents that are more prevalent among the young, while the older group is overrepresented in homes for the elderly, in the kinds of jobs requiring long years of experience, and in the kinds of diseases and accidents especially prevalent among older people.

Another very simple factor operating against an even "representation" of groups is that many ethnic groups are distributed geographically in patterns differing from one another. It would be unlikely that American ethnic groups concentrated in cold states like Minnesota and Wisconsin would be as well represented among citrus growers and tennis players as they are on hockey teams and among skiers. It is also unlikely that groups concentrated in land-locked states would be equally represented in maritime activities, or that groups from regions lacking mineral deposits would be as well-represented among miners or in other occupations associated with extractive industries as groups located in Pennsylvania or West Virginia.

Differences in geographic concentrations among racial and ethnic groups are by no means confined to the U.S. In Brazil, people of German and Japanese ancestry are concentrated in the south. In Switzerland, whole regions are predominantly French, German, or Italian. In countries around the world, an overwhelming majority of the Chinese or the Jewish population is heavily concentrated in a few major cities—often in just one city in a given country. Group differences in geographical distribution can reach right down to the neighborhood level or even to particular streets. In Buenos Aires, people of Italian ancestry have concentrated in particular neighborhoods or on particular streets, according to the places of their own or their ancestral origins in Italy. In Bombay, people from different parts of India are likewise concentrated in particular neighborhoods or on particular streets.

Lest the point be misunderstood, while these two simple and obvious factors—age and location—are capable of disrupting the even "representation" that many assume to exist in the absence of discrimination, there are also innumerable other factors, of varying degrees of complexity and influence, that can do the same. Moreover, differences in age and location may play a significant role in explaining *some* socioeconomic differences between *some* groups but not other socioeconomic differences between those groups, or among other groups. The purpose here is not to pinpoint the reasons for intergroup differences—or even to assume that they can all be pinpointed—but rather to show how arbitrary and unfounded is the assumption that groups would be evenly "represented," in the absence of discrimination. Precisely because the known differences among groups are large and multidimensional, the presumption of weighing these differences so comprehensively and accurately as to know where some group would be "but for" discrimination approaches hubris.

Even the more modest goal of knowing the *general direction* of the deviation of a group's position from where it would have been without discrimination is by no means necessarily achievable. What are the "effects" of centuries of injustice, punctuated by recurring outbursts of lethal mass violence, against the overseas Chinese in Southeast Asia or against the Jews in Europe? Both groups are generally more prosperous than their persecutors. Would they have been still more prosperous in the absence of such adversity? Perhaps—but many peoples with a long history of peace, and with prosperity supplied by nature itself, have quietly stagnated. This is not to say that the Jews and the Chinese would have done so. It is only to say that *we do not know and cannot know.* No amount of good intentions will make us omniscient. No fervent invocation of "social justice" will supply the missing knowledge.

Incentives and Results

"Affirmative-action" policies assume not only a level of knowledge that no one has ever possessed but also a degree of control that no one has ever exercised. Proponents of preferential policies have tended to reason in terms of the rationales and goals of such policies—not in terms of the *incentives* these policies create. Yet these incentives acquire a life of their own, independent of—and often counter to—the avowed goals of preferential policies. Nor are these simply isolated "mistakes" that can be "corrected." They are the fruition of fundamental misconceptions of the degree of control that can be maintained over a whole galaxy of complex social interactions.

At the individual level, the potential beneficiary and the potential loser are not mere blocks of wood passively placed where the policy dictates. Nor are they automatons who continue acting as before, except for modifications specified for them by others. Rather, they respond *in their own ways* to preferential policies. One of these ways was exemplified by a question raised by a group activist seeking preferential hiring in India's city of Hyderabad: "Are we not entitled to jobs just because we are not as qualified?" A Nigerian wrote of "the tyranny of skills." The sense of entitlement—independent of skills or performance—has long been an accompaniment of preferential policies, for the most disparate groups in the most disparate societies.

The late South African economist W. H. Hutt pointed out long ago that the most "virulent" white supporters of early racial-preferential policies in the mines were "those who had not troubled to qualify themselves for promotion," and who therefore relied on being white instead. Today, in the Virgin Islands, even schoolchildren excuse their own substandard academic and behavioral performance by pointing out that government jobs will be waiting for them as U.S. citizens—jobs for which their better-behaved and better-performing West Indian classmates are ineligible. In Malaysia, likewise, "Malay students, who sense that their future is assured, feel less pressure to perform," according to a study there. A study of black colleges in the United States similarly noted that even students planning postgraduate study often showed no sense of urgency about needing to be prepared "because they believed that certain rules would simply be set aside for them." In India, even a fervent advocate of the untouchables, and of preferential policies for them, has urged untouchable students in medical and engineering schools to abandon their "indifference."

The disincentives created by group preferences apply to both preferred and non-preferred groups. As W. H. Hutt wrote of the South African "color bar," these racial preferences "have vitiated the efficiency of the non-whites by destroying incentives" and have also "weakened incentives to efficiency on the part of the whites who have been featherbedded." A very similar principle is found in the very different setting of Jamaica, after it became independent and black-run. There it was the whites who faced the disincentives of the non-preferred. Many withdrew from the competition for public office because they "felt that the day of the black man had come and questioned why they had to make the effort if the coveted job or the national honor would go to the blacks, despite their qualifications." The upshot is that preferential policies represent not simply a transfer of benefits from one group to another, but can also represent a net loss, as both groups perform less well as a result.

Those who initiate preferential policies cannot sufficiently control the reactions of either preferred or non-preferred groups to ensure that such policies will have the desired effect, or even move in the desired direction: Counterproductive reactions that reduce national prosperity or social tranquility adversely affect even members of the preferred group, who are also members of the general society. Whether their gains in one role exceed their losses in the other role is an empirical question whose answer depends on the specifics of each situation. One of the clearly undesired and uncontrolled consequences of preferential policies has been a backlash by non-preferred groups. This backlash has ranged from campus racial incidents in the United States to a bloody civil war in Sri Lanka.

Honors

Nowhere is control more illusory than in the awarding of honors, whose very meaning and effect depend upon other people's opinions. Preferential honors for members of particular groups can easily render suspect not only those particular honors but also honors fully merited and awarded after free and open competition. If one-fifth of the honors received by preferred groups are awarded under double standards, the other four-fifths are almost certain to fall under a cloud of suspicion as well, if only because some of those who lost out in the competition would prefer to believe that they were not bested fairly. It is by no means clear that more real honors—which are ultimately other people's opinions—will come to a group preferentially given awards. Preferential honors can in practice mean a moratorium on recognition of the group's achievements, which can be confounded with patronage or pay-offs. This need not inevitably be so. The point is that the matter is out of the control of those who decide award policy, and in the hands of others observing the outcomes and deciding what to make of them.

Honor is more than a sop to personal vanity. It is a powerful incentive which accomplishes many social tasks, including tasks that are too arduous and dangerous to be compensated by money—even inducing individuals in crisis situations to sacrifice their lives for the greater good of others. In more mundane matters, honor and respect from one's colleagues and subordinates are important and sometimes indispensable aids, without which even the most talented and conscientious individuals sometimes cannot fulfill their promise. To jeopardize the respect and recognition of individuals from preferred groups by rewarding "honors" tainted with double standards is not only to downgrade their own achievements but also to downgrade their chances of accomplishing those achievements in the first place. For example, minority faculty members have often complained about a lack of intellectual and research interaction with their colleagues, and of being thought of as "affirmative-action" professors. After the media revealed that black students were admitted to the Harvard Medical School with lower qualifications, white patients began to refuse to be examined by such students. The negative effects of tainted honors are by no means limited to academia.

Partial Preferences

The illusion of control includes the belief that preferential policies can be extended *partway* into a process while maintaining equal treatment in the remainder of the process. For example, in the early days of "affirmative action" in the United States, it was sometimes asserted that special efforts to recruit minority employees or minority students would be followed by equal treatment at the actual selection stage and afterward. Special concern for particular groups might also mean only special scrutiny to see that they were treated equally. President John F. Kennedy's Executive Order No. 10,925 required that employers who were government contractors "take affirmative action to ensure that the applicants are employed, and that employees are treated during employment without regard to race, creed, color, or national origin." That is virtually the antithesis of what "affirmative action" has come to mean today, either in the United States or in other countries where the term refers to statistical results viewed precisely *with regard* to race, color, creed, or national origin.

The concept of preferential concern stopping partway into a process is not confined to employment or to the United States. In India, a government minister has urged a small lowering of university admissions standards for students from scheduled castes (untouchables) and scheduled tribes, with the proviso that "he was recommending relaxation for admission and not for passing or grading." Similar views were once expressed in the United States, where special recruitment programs for minority students quickly led to lower admission standards for them—and this in turn sometimes led to "affirmative grading," to prevent excessive failures by minority students. Double standards in grading may originate with the individual professor or be a result of administrative pressures. Halfway around the world—in Soviet Central Asia—professors are also pressured to give preferential grading to Central Asian students. In Malaysia, preferential grading is virtually institutionalized. As Gordon P. Means puts it:

> Although grading is supposed to be without reference to ethnicity, all grades must be submitted to an evaluation review committee having heavy Malay representation. Individual faculty members report various instances when grades were unilaterally raised, apparently for purposes of "ethnic balance."

Sometimes preferential grading takes the less direct form of creating special or easier subjects for particular groups, such as Maori Studies in New Zealand, Malay Studies in Singapore, or a variety of ethnic studies in the United States.

Whether in employment, education, or other areas, carefully limited or fine-tuned preferences have repeatedly proved to be illusory. Neither time limitations nor other limitations have in fact stopped their persistence and spread.

A wide variety of moral arguments has been used to justify preferential policies. Some of these arguments have little in common, except for being largely unexamined in the excitement of crusading zeal—and being successful politically. Among the reasons given for preferences are that (1) the group is indigenous; (2) the group has been historically wronged; and (3) the group happens to be less well represented in desirable institutions or occupations, for whatever reason, so that this "imbalance" must be "corrected."

Whatever the arguments for preferential policies, these preferences (as we have seen) can long outlive the validity of those arguments, whether the degree of validity be zero or 100 percent, or anywhere in between. A genuinely disadvantaged group can cling to preferences, or seek more, long after their disadvantages have been redressed. The moral question, therefore, is not simply whether particular groups deserve particular benefits for particular periods of time, or until particular social conditions are achieved. The real quesion is whether the *actual consequences of the particular processes* being initiated are likely to be justified, morally or otherwise. . . .

Historical Compensation

The wrongs of history have been invoked by many groups in many countries as a moral claim for contemporary compensation. Much emotional fervor goes into such claims but the question here is about their logic or morality. Assuming for the sake of argument that the historical claims are factually correct, which may not be the case in all countries, to transfer benefits between two groups of living contemporaries because of what happened between two sets of dead people is to raise the question whether any sufferer is in fact being compensated. Only where both wrongs and compensation are viewed as collectivized and inheritable does redressing the wrongs of history have a moral, or even a logical, basis.

The biological continuity of the generations lends plausibility to the notion of group compensation—but only if guilt can be inherited. Otherwise there are simply windfall gains and windfall losses among contemporaries, according to the accident of their antecedents. Moreover, few people would accept this as a general principle to be applied consistently, however much they may advocate it out of compassion (or guilt) over the fate of particular unfortunates. No one would advocate that today's Jews are morally entitled to put today's Germans in concentration camps, in compensation for the Nazi Holocaust. Most people would not only be horrified at any such suggestion but would also regard it as a second act of gross immorality, in no way compensating the first, but simply adding to the sum total of human sins.

Sometimes a more sociological, rather than moral, claim is made that living contemporaries are suffering from the *effects* of past wrongs and that it is these effects which must be offset by compensatory preferences. Tempting as it is to imagine that the contemporary troubles of historically wronged groups are due to those wrongs, this is confusing causation with morality. The contemporary socioeconomic position of groups in a given society often bears no relationship to the historic wrongs they have suffered. Both in Canada and in the United States, the Japanese have significantly higher incomes than the whites, who have a documented history of severe anti-Japanese discrimination in both countries. The same story could be told of the Chinese in Malaysia, Indonesia, and many other countries around the world, of the Jews in countries with virulent anti-Semitism, and a wide variety of other groups in a wide variety of other countries. Among poorer groups as well, the level of poverty often has little correlation with the degree of oppression. No one would claim that the historic wrongs suffered by Puerto Ricans in the United States exceed those suffered by blacks, but the average Puerto Rican income is lower than the average income of blacks.

None of this proves that historic wrongs have no contemporary effects. Rather, it is a statement about the limitations of our knowledge, which is grossly inadequate to the task undertaken and likely to remain so. To pretend to disentangle the innumerable sources of intergroup differences is an exercise in hubris rather than morality.

As one contemporary example of how easy it is to go astray in such efforts, it was repeated for years that the high rate of single-parent, teenage pregnancy among blacks was "a legacy of slavery." Evidence was neither asked nor given. But when serious scholarly research was finally done on this subject, the evidence devastated this widely held belief. The vast majority of black children grew up in two-parent homes, even under slavery itself, and for generations thereafter. The current levels of single-parent, teenage pregnancy are a phenomenon of the last half of the 20th century and are a disaster that has also struck groups with wholly different histories from that of blacks. Passionate commitment to "social justice" can never be a substitute for knowing what you are talking about.

Those who attribute any part of the socioeconomic fate of any group to factors internal to that group are often accused of "blaming the victim." This may sometimes be part of an attempt to salvage the historical-compensation principle but it deserves separate treatment.

"Blame" and "Victims"

The illusion of morality is often confused with the reality of causation. If group A originates in a country where certain scientific and technological skills are widespread and group B originates in a country where they are not, then when they immigrate to the same third country, they are likely to be statistically "represented" to very different degrees in occupations and institutions requiring such skills. There is nothing mysterious about this, in causal terms. But those who wish to attribute this disparity to institutional discrimination are quick to respond to any mention of group B's lesser scientific-technological background as a case of "blaming the victim." By making the issue *who* is to blame, such arguments evade or preempt the more fundamental question—whether this is a matter of blame in the first place.

Clearly today's living generation—in any group—cannot be *blamed* for the centuries of cultural evolution that went on before they were born, often in lands that they have never seen. Nor can they be blamed for the fact that the accident of birth caused them to inherit one culture rather than another. In causal terms, it would be a staggering coincidence if cultures evolving in radically different historical circumstances were equally effective for all purposes when transplanted to a new society. Blame has nothing to do with it. . . .

"Underrepresentation" and "Life Chances"

Quite aside from claims of historic wrongs, the argument has often been made—on grounds of morality as well as political or social expediency—that the "underrepresentation" of particular groups in desirable roles is an "imbalance" to be "corrected." Majorities have pressed such claims as readily as minorities, in circumstances where their only disadvantages were their own lack of skills or interest, as well as where a plausible case could be made that imposed disabilities have handicapped them.

Among the many unexamined assumptions behind preferential policies is the belief that intergroup friction is a function of the magnitude of income gaps, so that more social harmony can be achieved by reducing these gaps. As with so much that has been said in this area, evidence has been neither asked nor given, while counter-evidence is plentiful, varied, and ignored.

In Bombay, the hosility of the Maharashtrians has been directed primarily at the South Indians, who are somewhat ahead of them economically, rather than against the Gujaratis, who are far ahead of them. Throughout sub-Saharan Africa, there has historically been far more hostility directed by Africans against Asians than against Europeans, who are economically far ahead of both. A similar pattern is found *within* African groups. In Nigeria, for example, the Yoruba were far ahead of the Ibo economically in 1940, while there was a much smaller gap at that time between the Hausa and the Ibo. Yet the hostility and violence between Hausa and Ibo in that era greatly exceeded any friction between either of these groups and the Yoruba. Later, as the Ibos rose, narrowing the gap between themselves and the Yoruba, it was precisely then that Ibo-Yoruba outbreaks of violence occurred.

Advocates of preferential policies often express a related belief, similarly unsupported by evidence, that an even distribution of groups across sectors of the economy tends to reduce social frictions and hostility. Much history suggests the opposite, that (in the words of Professor Horowitz) "the ethnic division of labor is more a shield than a sword."

The utter dominance of particular sectors by particular minority groups has been quietly accepted for generations in many countries—until a specific, organized campaign has been whipped up against the minority, often by members of the majority who are seeking to enter the minority-dominated sector and are finding their competition very formidable. Often majority-group customers or suppliers actually prefer dealing with the minority-run entrepreneurs. Even in the midst of ethnic riots against other groups certain middleman minorities have been spared—the Greeks in the Sudan, Hindus in Burma, Marwaris in Assam. Organized boycotts of minority businessmen have been spearheaded by majority-group business rivals, from Uganda and Kenya to the Philippines and the United States. Contrary to what is widely (and lightly) assumed, neither an even representation of groups nor mass resentment at unevenness is "natural."

Repeatedly, in countries scattered around the world, it has been precisely the rise of newly emerging ethnic competitors—whether in business, government, or the professions—which has produced not only friction with groups already dominant in the sectors concerned but also, and much more importantly, has led the newcomers to whip up their whole group emotionally against the already established group. A Sri Lankan legislator noted this pattern early in that country's interethnic troubles:

> University graduates and people like that are the cause of all the trouble—not the vast mass of the Sinhalese people. It is those men, these middle-class unemployed seeking employment, who are jealous of the fact that a few Tamils occupy seats of office in government—these are the people who have gone round the countryside, rousing the masses and creating this problem.

Halfway around the world a similar charge was made, that "the educated Nigerian is the worst peddler of tribalism." In the very different setting of Hungary in the 1880's, the promotion of anti-Semitism was largely the work of students, intellectuals, and sections of the middle classes, while the Hungarian peasant masses remained relatively unresponsive.

Advocates of preferential policies often see these policies as not only promoting social harmony by reducing gaps in income and "representation," but also as part of a more general attempt to "equalize life chances." Much effort is expended establishing the moral desirability of this goal and the extent to which we currently fall short of it, while little or no effort goes into establishing our *capability* to accomplish such a staggering task. One clue to the magnitude and difficulty of what is being attempted are the various ways in which first-born children excel their siblings. A completely disproportionate number of the famous individuals in history were either first-born or the only child. In more mundane achievements as well, the first-born tend to excel. A study of National Merit Scholarship finalists showed that, even in five-child families, the first-born became finalists more often than all the other siblings combined. The same was true in two-, three-, and four-child families. Such disparities, among people born of the same parents and raised under the same roof, mock presumptions of being able to equalize life chances across broader and deeper differences among people in a large, complex, and, especially, multi-ethnic society.

The abstract moral desirability of a goal cannot preempt the prior question of our capacity to achieve it. This is not even a question of falling short of all that might be hoped for. It is a question of risking counterproductive, disastrous, and even bloody results.

Beneficiaries and Losers

Part of the moral aura surrounding preferential policies is due to the belief that such policies benefit the less fortunate. The losers in this presumed redistribution are seldom specified, though the underlying assumption seems to be that they are the more fortunate.

Empirical evidence for such assumptions is largely lacking and the *a priori* case for believing them is unconvincing. For example, the effects of preferential policies depend on the costs of complementary factors required to use the preferences. These costs can obviously be borne more readily by those who are already more fortunate. Benefits set aside for businessmen of the preferred group are of no use to members of that group who do not happen to own a business, or possess the capital to start one. Preferential admission to medical school is a benefit only to those who have already gone to college. Because preferential benefits tend to be concentrated on more lucrative or prestigious things, they are often within striking distance only for the fortunate few who have already advanced well beyond most other members of the preferred group. In Third World countries, where the great demand is for clerical jobs in the government, the poorer groups in these countries often have difficulty reaching even the modest level of education required for such employment.

Preferential scholarships for Malays in Malaysia are a classic example. Students from families in the lower-income brackets—63 percent of the population—received 14 percent of the university scholarships, while students whose families were in the top 17 percent of the income distribution received more than half of the scholarships. In India, preferential programs for both untouchables and "other backward classes" show the same pattern. In the state of Haryana, 37 different untouchable castes were entitled to preferential scholarships but only 18 actually received any—and just one of these received 65 percent of the scholarships at the graduate levels and 80 percent at the undergraduate level. Similar patterns are found in other parts of the country. In the state of Tamil Nadu, the highest of the so-called "backward classes" (11 percent of the total) received nearly half of all jobs and all university admissions set aside for such classes. The bottom 12 percent received no more than 2 percent of the jobs and university admissions.

In some cases—including the United States—the less fortunate members of a preferred group may actually retrogress while the more fortunate advance under preferential policies. After "affirmative-action" policies took hold in the early 1970's, blacks with little education and little job experience fell further behind the general population—and indeed further behind whites with little education and little job experience. Meanwhile, blacks with college education or substantial job experience advanced economically, both absolutely and relative to whites with the same advantages. Yet another example of the benefits of "affirmative action" to those already more fortunate are the business "set-asides" that give minority entrepreneurs preferential access to government contracts under Section 8(a) of the Small Business Act. Minority businessmen who participate in this program have an average net worth of $160,000. This is not only far higher than the average net worth of the groups they come from, but also higher than the average net worth of Americans in general.

This pattern of simultaneous advance at the top and retrogression at the bottom is not confined to the United States. In India, the era of preferential policies has seen the proportion of untouchables increase significantly among high-level government officials, while the proportion of untouchables who work as landless agricultural laborers has also increased. In Malaysia, the representation of Malays on corporate boards of directors has increased significantly, while the proportion of Malays among the population living below the official poverty level has also increased.

Just as the advocates of preferential policies arbitrarily assume that such policies will benefit the "disadvantaged," so they arbitrarily assume that this will be at the expense of the "privileged." They neither offer evidence of this in advance nor are so impolitic as to collect data on this point after preferential programs have been inaugurated. Such evidence as exists points in the opposite direction. In Bombay, preferential policies to put Maharashtrians into the ranks of business executives had only minor effects on the Gujaratis who were dominant in that occupation, reducing the proportion of Gujarati executives from 52 percent to 44 percent. Among the South Indians, however, their 25-percent representation among Bombay executives was cut in half, to 12 percent. A similar pattern appeared in the very different setting of prewar Hungary, where policies favoring Gentiles had relatively little effect on the Jewish financial and industrial elite but imposed real hardships on the Jewish middle class and lower middle class. In the United States, despite voluminous official statistics on all sorts of racial and ethnic matters, no one seems to have collected data on the actual losers under "affirmative action." It may be significant, however, that those who have protested their losses all the way up to the U.S. Supreme Court have not been named Adams, Cabot, or Rockefeller, but DeFunis, Bakke, and Weber.

II. The Illusion of Compensation

What makes compensation an illusion is not only that sufferers are not in fact compensated, or the effects of historic wrongs redressed—or even accurately identified and separated from innumerable other social factors at work simultaneously. Both the principle of compensation and the particular form of compensation via preferential policies require careful examination.

The Principle of Compensation

Given the mortality of human beings, often the only compensation for historic wrongs that is within the scope of our knowledge and control is purely symbolic compensation—taking from individuals who inflicted no harm and giving to individuals who suffered none. In addition to the moral shakiness and social dangers of such a policy, it also promotes a kind of social irredentism, a set of *a priori* grievances against living people, whether or not they have ever inflicted harm on those who feel aggrieved. In view of the futile but bitter and bloody struggles engendered by territorial irredentism, there is little good to hope for by applying this same principle in a new field.

The factual reality that actual benefits from compensatory preferences tend to be concentrated in the already more fortunate elites among the preferred groups makes the moral case for such policies weaker and the social dangers greater. The more educated, articulate, and more politically sophisticated elites have every incentive to whip up group emotions in favor of more and better preferences, despite the increasing group polarization this may produce, and to be intransigent against any suggestion that any such preferences should ever be reduced or ended. This has been a common pattern in the most disparate countries.

In principle, compensation can take many forms, beginning with a simple transfer of money from one group to another. In practice, however, preferential policies are the form taken in many countries around the world. The implications of that particular form, and of its alternatives, raise still more troubling questions.

The Form of Compensation

If, notwithstanding all philosophic objections to the principle of group compensation, such a policy is in fact chosen, then the particular form of the compensation can make a major difference in the costs and the consequences of compensatory policies. When resources, or the benefits they create, are transferred from group A to group B, this is not necessarily—or even likely—a zero-sum process, in which the value of what is lost by one is the same as the value of what is gained by the other. What is transferred may be subjectively valued differently by the losers and the recipients. There may also be objectively discernible differences in the use of the same resources by the two groups.

Compensatory policies may, in theory, take place through transfers of money, transfers of in-kind benefits, or through differential applications of rules and standards. In Australia, for example, various money and in-kind transfers to the aborigines add up to more than $2,000 annually for every aboriginal man, woman, and child. Such transfers arouse relatively little political opposition or social backlash. Similarly, in the United States, monetary compensation for Japanese Americans interned during World War II aroused relatively little controversy—and even that little controversy quickly subsided, once the decision was made.

Such monetary transfers are less costly to individual members of the majority population the more the majority outnumbers the minority receiving the transfer. Obviously, if group A is 100 times as large as group B, each member of group B can receive $100 at a cost of only one dollar to each member of group A. However, even where the losses sustained by one group are significant, monetary transfers may still be efficient, in the narrowly economic sense that what is lost by one group as a whole is gained by another group, with no direct net loss to society as a whole.

Whatever the merits or demerits of the particular transfer on other grounds, it is not inefficient. Politically and socially, the opposition to such transfers is therefore unlikely to be as great as opposition to the same net transfers in forms that cost more to the losers than is gained by the gainers. Preferential policies often cost the losers more than is gained by the gainers. Preferential policies, by definition, involve a differential application of rules and standards to individuals originating in different groups. Even where the preferences are not stated in terms of differential rules or standards, but rather in terms of numerical quotas, "goals," or "targets," differences in the qualifications of the respective pools of applicants can readily make numerical similarities amount to differences in standards. This is a very common result in countries around the world. In Nigeria, programs to have college-student populations reflect "the federal character" of the country—i.e., tribal quotas under regional names—led to a situation where cutoff scores for admission to the same college varied substantially between students from different tribes or regions. In Sri Lanka, demographic "standardization" policies led to similar disparities in qualification requirements for individuals from different regions of the country. In India, attempts to meet quotas for untouchable students led to drastic reductions in the qualifications they needed for admission to various institutions. Where applicant pools in different groups are different in qualifications, numerical quotas are equivalent to different standards. Therefore preferential policies in general, however phrased, are essentially an application of different rules or standards to individuals from different groups. The question then is: what are the effects of transfers between groups in this particular form?

There are many ways in which intergroup transfers through differential standards can become negative-sum processes, in which what is lost by one group exceeds what is gained by another, thus representing a direct loss to society as a whole—as well as causing indirect losses, due to a larger resistance or backlash than if the recipient group had obtained the same value or benefit in some other form. An obvious example is when a particular group, in which 90 percent of the students admitted to college succeed in graduating, loses places to another group in which only 30 percent of the students graduate. Group A must lose 900 graduates, in order for group B to gain 300 graduates. It might be objected that this overstates the net loss, since there may be some marginal benefit simply from having attended college, even without graduating. Offsetting this, however, is the fact that groups with lower qualifications tend to specialize in easier and less remunerative fields, whether in India, Malaysia, the Soviet Union, or the United States. Therefore group A may lose 900 graduates largely concentrated in mathematics, science, and engineering, while group B gains 300 graduates largely concentrated in sociology, education, and ethnic studies.

The *apparent* losses to one group under preferential policies may also far exceed the real losses, thereby further raising the indirect social costs of backlash and turmoil. For example, an observer of India's preferential policies for untouchables (known officially as "scheduled castes") has commented:

> . . . we hear innumerable tales of persons being deprived of appointments in favor of people who ranked lower than they did in the relevant examinations. No doubt this does happen, but if all these people were, in fact, paying the price for appointments to Scheduled Castes, there would be many more SC persons appointed than there actually are. To illustrate: supposing that 300 people qualify for ten posts available. The top nine are appointed on merit but the tenth is reserved, so the authorities go down the list to find an SC applicant. They find one at 140 and he is appointed. Whereupon all 131 between him and the merit list feel aggrieved. He has not taken 131 posts; he has taken one, yet 131 people believe they have paid the price for it. Moreover, the remaining 159 often also resent the situation, believing that their chances were, somehow, lessened by the existence of SC reservations.

Where certain opportunities are rigidly "set aside" for particular groups, in the sense that members of other groups cannot have them, even if these opportunities remain unused, then there is the potential for a maximum of grievance for a minimum of benefit transfer. Admission to medical school in India's state of Gujarat operates on this principle—and has led repeatedly to bloody riots in which many people have died. Reservations or "set-asides" in general tend to provoke strong objections. The first major setback for "affirmative action" in the U.S. Supreme Court was based on objections to reserved-admissions places for minority applicants in the 1978 *Bakke* case. A later major setback occurred in *City of Richmond* v. *Croson* (1989), where minority business set-asides were struck down by the Supreme Court. Similarly, in India, an exhaustive, scholarly legal study of preferential policies found: "Virtually all of the litigation about compensatory discrimination has involved reservations, even though preferences in the form of provisions of facilities, resources, and protections directly affect a much larger number of recipients." This litigation has been initiated mostly by non-preferred individuals who complain of being adversely affected. In some ultimate sense, non-preferred individuals are just as much adversely affected by preferences in other forms that direct resources away from them and toward preferred groups. But it is preference in the specific form of "reservation" or "set-aside" that seems most to provoke both violence and litigation.

By contrast, resource transfers designed to enable disadvantaged groups to meet standards are accepted while attempts to bring the standards down to them are overwhelmingly rejected. In the United States, preferential policies have repeatedly been rejected in public-opinion polls. However, the same American public has strongly supported "special educational or vocational courses, free of charge, to enable members of minority groups to do better on tests." More than three-fifths of all whites even support "requiring large companies to set up special training programs for members of minority groups." The issue is not simply whether one is for or against the advancement of particular groups or is willing to see transfers of resources for their betterment. The method by which their betterment is attempted matters greatly in terms of whether such efforts have the support or the opposition of others.

III. Replacing Illusions

With all the empirical weaknesses, logical flaws, and social dangers of preferential policies, why have they become so popular and spread so rapidly around the world? One reason is that their *political* attractions are considerable. They offer an immediate response—a quick fix—at relatively little government expense, to the demands of vocal, aroused, and often organized elites, speaking in the name of restive masses. This restiveness of the masses is by no means incidental. Violence has frequently preceded preferences, from the American ghetto riots of the 1960's to the Malay and Indonesian riots against the Chinese at about the same time, to terrorism in India, and massive mob violence against the Tamils in Sri Lanka. This violence by the masses is typically used politically to promote elite purposes via preferential policies. An international study of ethnic conflicts concluded:

> Preferences tend to respond to middle-class aspirations almost entirely. They do little or nothing about the resentments of those who do not aspire to attend secondary school or university, to enter the modern private sector or the bureaucracy, or to become businessmen. Although lower-class resentments are often profound—it is not, after all, the middle class that typically participates in ethnic violence—the resentments may have nothing to do with occupational mobility and preferences do not address them.

Preferential policies, then, are politically attractive as a response, however socially ineffective or counterproductive such policies may later prove to be in practice. At a sufficiently superficial level, the moral attractions of preferential policies are considerable as well. Even in South Africa, moral appeals were made on behalf of a "civilized labor policy"—protecting European workers' customary standard of living from being undercut by Africans and Indians accustomed to living on less—and clergy, intellectuals, and others not personally benefiting joined in support of these policies on that basis. Preferential policies allow intellectuals as well as politicians to be on the side of the angels (as locally defined at the time) at low cost—or rather, at a low down payment, for the real costs come later, and have sometimes been paid in blood.

The last refuge of a failed policy is "the long run," in which it will supposedly be a success. In other words, those who predicted the short run wrongly ask to be trusted with the much harder task of predicting the long run rightly. This argument, used to defend the counterproductive effects of preferential policies, is far less defensible in an international perspective where older preferential policies (as in India or Sri Lanka) have progressed from intergroup political hostility to bloodshed in the streets and deaths by the thousands, while newer programs (as in the United States) are still in the process of increasing group polarization, and the even more recent preferential policies taking shape in Australia and New Zealand are still at the stage of optimistic predictions.

Even the most damning indictment of a policy is almost certain to be met with the response: "But what would you replace it with?" However effective as a political tactic, such a question confuses rather than clarifies. It is like an arbitrary prohibition against saying that the emperor has no clothes, until a complete wardrobe has been designed. The question misconceives policy, and human actions in general, in yet another way: no one who extinguishes a forest fire or removes a cancer has to "replace" it with anything. We are well rid of evils.

This is not to say that none of the aspects of social issues raised during "affirmative-action" controversies should ever be addressed by public policy. The case for public policy in general, or for a particular public policy, must be made on the individual merits of the particular issues raised—but not as a general "replacement" for some discredited policy.

What must be replaced are the social illusions and misconceptions underlying preferential policies, for any alternative policy based on the same illusions and misconceptions will have the same fatal weaknesses in its structure. In some countries and for some purposes social policy may wish to ameliorate the lot of the less fortunate or make it possible for individuals or groups to acquire the knowledge and skills necessary for their own advancement. It is infinitely more important that such efforts be based on facts and logic than that there be one particular scheme selected from innumerable possibilities as the uniquely designated "replacement" for existing policy.

We may or may not be able to agree on what the ideal, or even a viable, policy must be. What we can agree on is far more fundamental: We can agree to *talk* sense. That will mean abandoning a whole vocabulary of political rhetoric which preempts factual questions by arbitrarily calling statistical disparities "discrimination," "exclusion," "segregation," and the like. It will mean confronting issues instead of impugning motives. It will mean specifying goals and defending those specifics, rather than speaking in terms of seeking some nebulously unctuous "change" or "social justice." Perhaps more than anything else, talking sense will mean examining policies in terms of the incentives they create, and the results to which these incentives lead, rather than the hopes they embody. It will mean that evidence takes precedence over assertion and reiteration. . . .

VI. Politics versus Progress

. . . Could some judicious blend of preferential programs and programs designed to improve the performances of less educated groups work? Here the problem is that the two kinds of programs create incentives that work at cross-purposes, even if their goals are the same. Forcing students to meet higher standards—a painful process for them and their teachers alike—will be made all the more difficult if the students know that these standards are unnecessary for them to reach whatever educational or employment goals they have, or even to be promoted to the next grade. If group-representation statistics are the standard by which institutions will be judged, other standards will be sacrificed for the sake of body count. This is true not only of educational institutions but of other institutions as well.

Political feasibility is the greatest obstacle to new policies with an overriding goal of advancing the less fortunate because time is the key ingredient in such advancement on a large scale. Even in the extreme case of South Africa, where massive transfers of the nation's resources were focused on a small minority of its people, in *addition* to preferential policies pursued in utter disregard of the losses and even tragedies suffered by others as a result, it was decades before the Afrikaner "poor whites" became middle-class. Only in terms of political appearances are preferential policies a "quick fix." The dangers of an actual retrogression among the masses of the beneficiary group cannot be dismissed, either from an analytical or an empirical perspective. Even greater dangers have materialized in countries that have experienced bloodshed in the wake of group polarization brought on by preferential policies.

While current political feasibility may be the touchstone of the professional politician, it cannot be the last word for others. In many countries, what is most politically feasible are policies that further a continued drift in the direction of group polarization and the dangers and disasters this entails. Specific alternative policies will differ for different groups and different countries. What is crucial is that these alternatives be examined in terms of the incentives they create and the results to which such incentives can be expected to lead—regardless of the rationales, aspirations, or symbolism of these policies. Determining in this way what *should* be done is not an exercise in utopianism, for once there is a consensus on what needs to be done, that in itself changes what is politically feasible.

The starting point for rethinking and reform must be a recognition that "affirmative action" has been a failure in the United States and a disaster in other countries that have had such policies longer. Indeed, a growing polarization and increasing numbers of ugly racial incidents (especially on campuses that are strongholds of "affirmative action") may be early warnings that we too may be moving from the stage of mere failure to the stage of social disaster.

QUESTIONS FOR REFLECTION

1. What patterns does Sowell find in affirmative-action programs around the world?
2. What are Sowell's responses to arguments from compensation? Do you find them convincing?
3. To what incentives do affirmative-action policies give rise, according to Sowell? How are these incentives harmful, in his view?
4. Some advocates of affirmative action believe that race is a good proxy for disadvantage in general. Sowell disagrees. Why? What evidence does he present?

CHIEF JUSTICE WILLIAM REHNQUIST

Majority Opinion in Gratz et al. *v.* Bollinger et al. (2003)

(*Source:* Jennifer Gratz and Patrick Hamacher, Petitioners, *v.* Lee Bollinger et al., *539 U.S. 244 (2003). Most legal references have been omitted.)*

Chief Justice Rehnquist delivered the opinion of the Court.

We granted certiorari in this case to decide whether "the University of Michigan's use of racial preferences in undergraduate admissions violate[s] the Equal Protection Clause of the Fourteenth Amendment, Title VI of the Civil Rights Act of 1964, or 42 U. S. C. §1981." Because we find that the manner in which the University considers the race of applicants in its undergraduate admissions guidelines violates these constitutional and statutory provisions, we reverse that portion of the District Court's decision upholding the guidelines.

I

A

Petitioners Jennifer Gratz and Patrick Hamacher both applied for admission to the University of Michigan's (University) College of Literature, Science, and the Arts (LSA) as residents of the State of Michigan. Both petitioners are Caucasian. Gratz, who applied for admission for the fall of 1995, was notified in January of that year that a final decision regarding her admission had been delayed until April. This delay was based upon the University's determination that, although Gratz was "'well qualified,'" she was "'less competitive than the students who ha[d] been admitted on first review.'" Gratz was notified in April that the LSA was unable to offer her admission. She enrolled in the University of Michigan at Dearborn, from which she graduated in the spring of 1999.

Hamacher applied for admission to the LSA for the fall of 1997. A final decision as to his application was also postponed because, though his "'academic credentials [were] in the qualified range, they [were] not at the level needed for first review admission.'" Hamacher's application was subsequently denied in April 1997, and he enrolled at Michigan State University. . . .

B

The University has changed its admissions guidelines a number of times during the period relevant to this litigation, and we summarize the most significant of these changes briefly. The University's Office of Undergraduate Admissions (OUA) oversees the LSA admissions process. In order to promote consistency in the review of the large number of applications received, the OUA uses written guidelines for each academic year. Admissions counselors make admissions decisions in accordance with these guidelines.

OUA considers a number of factors in making admissions decisions, including high school grades, standardized test scores, high school quality, curriculum strength, geography, alumni relationships, and leadership. OUA also considers race. During all periods relevant to this litigation, the University has considered African-Americans, Hispanics, and Native Americans to be "underrepresented minorities," and it is undisputed that the University admits "virtually every qualified . . . applicant" from these groups.

During 1995 and 1996, OUA counselors evaluated applications according to grade point average combined with what were referred to as the "SCUGA" factors. These factors included the quality of an applicant's high school (S), the strength of an applicant's high school curriculum (C), an applicant's unusual circumstances (U), an applicant's geographical residence (G), and an applicant's alumni relationships (A). After these scores were combined to produce an applicant's "GPA 2" score, the reviewing admissions counselors referenced a set of "Guidelines" tables, which listed GPA 2 ranges on the vertical axis, and American College Test/Scholastic Aptitude Test (ACT/SAT) scores on the horizontal axis. Each table was divided into cells that included one or more courses of action to be taken, including admit, reject, delay for additional information, or postpone for reconsideration.

In both years, applicants with the same GPA 2 score and ACT/SAT score were subject to different admissions outcomes based upon their racial or ethnic status. For example, as a Caucasian in-state applicant, Gratz's GPA 2 score and ACT score placed her within a cell calling for a postponed decision on her application. An in-state or out-of-state minority applicant with Gratz's scores would have fallen within a cell calling for admission.

In 1997, the University modified its admissions procedure. Specifically, the formula for calculating an applicant's GPA 2 score was restructured to include additional point values under the "U" category in the SCUGA factors. Under this new system, applicants could receive points for underrepresented minority status, socioeconomic disadvantage, or attendance at a high school with a predominantly underrepresented minority population, or underrepresentation in the unit to which the student was applying (for example, men who sought to pursue a career in nursing). Under the 1997 procedures, Hamacher's GPA 2 score and ACT score placed him in a cell on the in-state applicant table calling for postponement of a final admissions decision. An underrepresented minority applicant placed in the same cell would generally have been admitted.

Beginning with the 1998 academic year, the OUA dispensed with the Guidelines tables and the SCUGA point system in favor of a "selection index," on which an applicant could score a maximum of 150 points. This index was divided linearly into ranges generally calling for admissions dispositions as follows: 100–150 (admit); 95–99 (admit or postpone); 90–94 (postpone or admit); 75–89 (delay or postpone); 74 and below (delay or reject).

Each application received points based on high school grade point average, standardized test scores, academic quality of an applicant's high school, strength or weakness of high school curriculum, in-state residency, alumni relationship, personal essay, and personal achievement or leadership. Of particular significance here, under a "miscellaneous" category, an applicant was entitled to 20 points based upon his or her membership in an underrepresented racial or ethnic minority group. The University explained that the "'development of the selection index for admissions in 1998 changed only the mechanics, not the substance of how race and ethnicity were considered in admissions.'"

In all application years from 1995 to 1998, the guidelines provided that qualified applicants from underrepresented minority groups be admitted as soon as possible in light of the University's belief that such applicants were more likely to enroll if promptly notified of their admission. Also from 1995 through 1998, the University carefully managed its rolling admissions system to permit consideration of certain applications submitted later in the academic year through the use of "protected seats." Specific groups—including athletes, foreign students, ROTC candidates, and underrepresented minorities—were "protected categories" eligible for these seats. A committee called the Enrollment Working Group (EWG) projected how many applicants from each of these protected categories the University was likely to receive after a given date and then paced admissions decisions to permit full consideration of expected applications from these groups. If this space was not filled by qualified candidates from the designated groups toward the end of the admissions season, it was then used to admit qualified candidates remaining in the applicant pool, including those on the waiting list.

During 1999 and 2000, the OUA used the selection index, under which every applicant from an underrepresented racial or ethnic minority group was awarded 20 points. Starting in 1999, however, the University established an Admissions Review Committee (ARC), to provide an additional level of consideration for some applications. Under the new system, counselors may, in their discretion, "flag" an application for the ARC to review after determining that the applicant (1) is academically prepared to succeed at the University, (2) has achieved a minimum selection index score, and (3) possesses a quality or characteristic important to the University's composition of its freshman class, such as high class rank, unique life experiences, challenges, circumstances, interests or talents, socioeconomic disadvantage, and underrepresented race, ethnicity, or geography. After reviewing "flagged" applications, the ARC determines whether to admit, defer, or deny each applicant. . . .

II

B

Petitioners argue, first and foremost, that the University's use of race in undergraduate admissions violates the Fourteenth Amendment. Specifically, they contend that this Court has only sanctioned the use of racial classifications to remedy identified discrimination, a justification on which respondents have never relied. Petitioners further argue that "diversity as a basis for employing racial preferences is simply too open-ended, ill-defined, and indefinite to constitute a compelling interest capable of supporting narrowly-tailored means." But for the reasons set forth today in *Grutter* v. *Bollinger,* the Court has rejected these arguments of petitioners.

Petitioners alternatively argue that even if the University's interest in diversity can constitute a compelling state interest, the District Court erroneously concluded that the University's use of race in its current freshman admissions policy is narrowly tailored to achieve such an interest. Petitioners argue that the guidelines the University began using in 1999 do not "remotely resemble the kind of consideration of race and ethnicity that Justice Powell endorsed in *Bakke*." Respondents reply that the University's current admissions program *is* narrowly tailored and avoids the problems of the Medical School of the University of California at Davis program (U. C. Davis) rejected by Justice Powell. They claim that their program "hews closely" to both the admissions program described by Justice Powell as well as the Harvard College admissions program that he endorsed. Specifically, respondents contend that the LSA's policy provides the individualized consideration that "Justice Powell considered a hallmark of a constitutionally appropriate admissions program." For the reasons set out below, we do not agree.

It is by now well established that "all racial classifications reviewable under the Equal Protection Clause must be strictly scrutinized." *Adarand Constructors, Inc.*v. *Peña* (1995). This "'standard of review . . . is not dependent on the race of those burdened or benefited by a particular classification.'" Thus, "any person, of whatever race, has the right to demand that any governmental actor subject to the Constitution justify any racial classification subjecting that person to unequal treatment under the strictest of judicial scrutiny." *Adarand.*

To withstand our strict scrutiny analysis, respondents must demonstrate that the University's use of race in its current admission program employs "narrowly tailored measures that further compelling governmental interests." Because "[r]acial classifications are simply too pernicious to permit any but the most exact connection between justification and classification," *Fullilove* v. *Klutznick* (1980) (Stevens, J., dissenting), our review of whether such requirements have been met must entail "'a most searching examination.'" *Adarand* (quoting *Wygant* v. *Jackson Bd. of Ed.* (1986) (plurality opinion of Powell, J.)). We find that the University's policy, which automatically distributes 20 points, or one-fifth of the points needed to guarantee admission, to every single "underrepresented minority" applicant solely because of race, is not narrowly tailored to achieve the interest in educational diversity that respondents claim justifies their program.

In *Bakke*, Justice Powell reiterated that "[p]referring members of any one group for no reason other than race or ethnic origin is discrimination for its own sake." He then explained, however, that in his view it would be permissible for a university to employ an admissions program in which "race or ethnic background may be deemed a 'plus' in a particular applicant's file." He explained that such a program might allow for "[t]he file of a particular black applicant [to] be examined for his potential contribution to diversity without the factor of race being decisive when compared, for example, with that of an applicant identified as an Italian-American if the latter is thought to exhibit qualities more likely to promote beneficial educational pluralism." Such a system, in Justice Powell's view, would be "flexible enough to consider all pertinent elements of diversity in light of the particular qualifications of each applicant."

Justice Powell's opinion in *Bakke* emphasized the importance of considering each particular applicant as an individual, assessing all of the qualities that individual possesses, and in turn, evaluating that individual's ability to contribute to the unique setting of higher education. The admissions program Justice Powell described, however, did not contemplate that any single characteristic automatically ensured a specific and identifiable contribution to a university's diversity. Instead, under the approach Justice Powell described, each characteristic of a particular applicant was to be considered in assessing the applicant's entire application.

The current LSA policy does not provide such individualized consideration. The LSA's policy automatically distributes 20 points to every single applicant from an "underrepresented minority" group, as defined by the University. The only consideration that accompanies this distribution of points is a factual review of an application to determine whether an individual is a member of one of these minority groups. Moreover, unlike Justice Powell's example, where the race of a "particular black applicant" could be considered without being decisive, the LSA's automatic distribution of 20 points has the effect of making "the factor of race . . . decisive" for virtually every minimally qualified underrepresented minority applicant.

Also instructive in our consideration of the LSA's system is the example provided in the description of the Harvard College Admissions Program, which Justice Powell both discussed in, and attached to, his opinion in *Bakke*. The example was included to "illustrate the kind of significance attached to race" under the Harvard College program. It provided as follows:

"The Admissions Committee, with only a few places left to fill, might find itself forced to choose between A, the child of a successful black physician in an academic community with promise of superior academic performance, and B, a black who grew up in an inner city ghetto of semi-literate parents whose academic achievement was lower but who had demonstrated energy and leadership as well as an apparently abiding interest in black power. If a good number of black students much like A but few like B had already been admitted, the Committee might prefer B; and vice versa. If C, a white student with extraordinary artistic talent, were also seeking one of the remaining places, his unique quality might give him an edge over both A and B. Thus, the critical criteria are often individual qualities or experience *not dependent upon race but sometimes associated with it*." (emphasis added).

This example further demonstrates the problematic nature of the LSA's admissions system. Even if student C's "extraordinary artistic talent" rivaled that of Monet or Picasso, the applicant would receive, at most, five points under the LSA's system. At the same time, every single underrepresented minority applicant, including students A and B, would automatically receive 20 points for submitting an application. Clearly, the LSA's system does not offer applicants the individualized selection process described in Harvard's example. Instead of considering how the differing backgrounds, experiences, and characteristics of students A, B, and C might benefit the University, admissions counselors reviewing LSA applications would simply award both A and B 20 points because their applications indicate that they are African-American, and student C would receive up to 5 points for his "extraordinary talent."

Respondents emphasize the fact that the LSA has created the possibility of an applicant's file being flagged for individualized consideration by the ARC. We think that the flagging program only emphasizes the flaws of the University's system as a whole when compared to that described by Justice Powell. Again, students A, B, and C illustrate the point. First, student A would never be flagged. This is because, as the University has conceded, the effect of automatically awarding 20 points is that virtually every qualified underrepresented minority applicant is admitted. Student A, an applicant "with promise of superior academic performance," would certainly fit this description. Thus, the result of the automatic distribution of 20 points is that the University would never consider student A's individual background, experiences, and characteristics to assess his individual "potential contribution to diversity." Instead, every applicant like student A would simply be admitted.

It is possible that students B and C would be flagged and considered as individuals. This assumes that student B was not already admitted because of the automatic 20-point distribution, and that student C could muster at least 70 additional points. But the fact that the "review committee can look at the applications individually and ignore the points," once an application is flagged, is of little comfort under our strict scrutiny analysis. The record does not reveal precisely how many applications are flagged for this individualized consideration, but it is undisputed that such consideration is the exception and not the rule in the operation of the LSA's admissions program. Additionally, this individualized review is only provided *after* admissions counselors automatically distribute the University's version of a "plus" that makes race a decisive factor for virtually every minimally qualified underrepresented minority applicant.

Respondents contend that "[t]he volume of applications and the presentation of applicant information make it impractical for [LSA] to use the . . . admissions system" upheld by the Court today in *Grutter*. But the fact that the implementation of a program capable of providing individualized consideration might present administrative challenges does not render constitutional an otherwise problematic system. Nothing in Justice Powell's opinion in *Bakke* signaled that a university may employ whatever means it desires to achieve the stated goal of diversity without regard to the limits imposed by our strict scrutiny analysis.

We conclude, therefore, that because the University's use of race in its current freshman admissions policy is not narrowly tailored to achieve respondents' asserted compelling interest in diversity, the admissions policy violates the Equal Protection Clause of the Fourteenth Amendment. We further find that the admissions policy also violates Title VI and 42 U. S. C. § 1981. Accordingly, we reverse that portion of the District Court's decision granting respondents summary judgment with respect to liability and remand the case for proceedings consistent with this opinion.

It is so ordered.

QUESTIONS FOR REFLECTION

1. How does the Michigan admissions process described here differ from that described in *Bakke?*
2. What does it mean for a consideration of race to be "narrowly tailored"?
3. Why does the Court reject the Michigan system as not narrowly tailored?
4. Could a large university such as Michigan design a system taking race into account that would be narrowly tailored and capable, in practice, of handling tens of thousands of applications?

JUSTICE SANDRA DAY O'CONNOR

Majority Opinion in Grutter v. Bollinger et al. (2003)

(*Source:* Barbara Grutter, Petitioner, *v.* Lee Bollinger et al., *539 U.S. 306 [2003]. Most legal references have been omitted.)*

Justice O'Connor delivered the opinion of the Court.

This case requires us to decide whether the use of race as a factor in student admissions by the University of Michigan Law School (Law School) is unlawful.

I

A

The Law School ranks among the Nation's top law schools. It receives more than 3,500 applications each year for a class of around 350 students. Seeking to "admit a group of students who individually and collectively are among the most capable," the Law School looks for individuals with "substantial promise for success in law school" and "a strong likelihood of succeeding in the practice of law and contributing in diverse ways to the well-being of others." More broadly, the Law School seeks "a mix of students with varying backgrounds and experiences who will respect and learn from each other." In 1992, the dean of the Law School charged a faculty committee with crafting a written admissions policy to implement these goals. In particular, the Law School sought to ensure that its efforts to achieve student body diversity complied with this Court's most recent ruling on the use of race in university admissions. See *Regents of Univ. of Cal.* v. *Bakke* (1978). Upon the unanimous adoption of the committee's report by the Law School faculty, it became the Law School's official admissions policy.

The hallmark of that policy is its focus on academic ability coupled with a flexible assessment of applicants' talents, experiences, and potential "to contribute to the learning of those around them." The policy requires admissions officials to evaluate each applicant based on all the information available in the file, including a personal statement, letters of recommendation, and an essay describing the ways in which the applicant will contribute to the life and diversity of the Law School. In reviewing an applicant's file, admissions officials must consider the applicant's undergraduate grade point average (GPA) and Law School Admissions Test (LSAT) score because they are important (if imperfect) predictors of academic success in law school. The policy stresses that "no applicant should be admitted unless we expect that applicant to do well enough to graduate with no serious academic problems."

The policy makes clear, however, that even the highest possible score does not guarantee admission to the Law School. Nor does a low score automatically disqualify an applicant. Rather, the policy requires admissions officials to look beyond grades and test scores to other criteria that are important to the Law School's educational objectives. So-called "'soft' variables" such as "the enthusiasm of recommenders, the quality of the undergraduate institution, the quality of the applicant's essay, and the areas and difficulty of undergraduate course selection" are all brought to bear in assessing an "applicant's likely contributions to the intellectual and social life of the institution."

The policy aspires to "achieve that diversity which has the potential to enrich everyone's education and thus make a law school class stronger than the sum of its parts." The policy does not restrict the types of diversity contributions eligible for "substantial weight" in the admissions process, but instead recognizes "many possible bases for diversity admissions." The policy does, however, reaffirm the Law School's longstanding commitment to "one particular type of diversity," that is, "racial and ethnic diversity with special reference to the inclusion of students from groups which have been historically discriminated against, like African-Americans, Hispanics and Native Americans, who without this commitment might not be represented in our student body in meaningful numbers." By enrolling a "'critical mass' of [under-represented] minority students," the Law School seeks to "ensur[e] their ability to make unique contributions to the character of the Law School."

The policy does not define diversity "solely in terms of racial and ethnic status." Nor is the policy "insensitive to the competition among all students for admission to the [L]aw [S]chool." Rather, the policy seeks to guide admissions officers in "producing classes both diverse and academically outstanding, classes made up of students who promise to continue the tradition of outstanding contribution by Michigan Graduates to the legal profession."

B

Petitioner Barbara Grutter is a white Michigan resident who applied to the Law School in 1996 with a 3.8 grade point average and 161 LSAT score. The Law School initially placed petitioner on a waiting list, but subsequently rejected her application. In December 1997, petitioner filed suit in the United States District Court for the Eastern District of Michigan against the Law School, the Regents of the University of Michigan, Lee Bollinger (Dean of the Law School from 1987 to 1994, and President of the University of Michigan from 1996 to 2002), Jeffrey Lehman (Dean of the Law School), and Dennis Shields (Director of Admissions at the Law School from 1991 until 1998). Petitioner alleged that respondents discriminated against her on the basis of race in violation of the Fourteenth Amendment; Title VI of the Civil Rights Act of 1964; and Rev. Stat. § 1977, as amended, 42 U. S. C. § 1981.

Petitioner further alleged that her application was rejected because the Law School uses race as a "predominant" factor, giving applicants who belong to certain minority groups "a significantly greater chance of admission than students with similar credentials from disfavored racial groups." Petitioner also alleged that respondents "had no compelling interest to justify their use of race in the admissions process." Petitioner requested compensatory and punitive damages, an order requiring the Law School to offer her admission, and an injunction prohibiting the Law School from continuing to discriminate on the basis of race. Petitioner clearly has standing to bring this lawsuit.

II

A

We last addressed the use of race in public higher education over 25 years ago. In the landmark *Bakke* case, we reviewed a racial set-aside program that reserved 16 out of 100 seats in a medical school class for members of certain minority groups. The decision produced six separate opinions, none of which commanded a majority of the Court. Four Justices would have upheld the program against all attack on the ground that the government can use race to "remedy disadvantages cast on minorities by past racial prejudice." Four other Justices avoided the constitutional question altogether and struck down the program on statutory grounds. Justice Powell provided a fifth vote not only for invalidating the set-aside program, but also for reversing the state court's injunction against any use of race whatsoever. The only holding for the Court in *Bakke* was that a "State has a substantial interest that legitimately may be served by a properly devised admissions program involving the competitive consideration of race and ethnic origin." Thus, we reversed that part of the lower court's judgment that enjoined the university "from any consideration of the race of any applicant."

Since this Court's splintered decision in *Bakke,* Justice Powell's opinion announcing the judgment of the Court has served as the touchstone for constitutional analysis of race-conscious admissions policies. Public and private universities across the Nation have modeled their own admissions programs on Justice Powell's views on permissible race-conscious policies.

B

The Equal Protection Clause provides that no State shall "deny to any person within its jurisdiction the equal protection of the laws." Because the Fourteenth Amendment "protect[s] *persons*, not *groups*," all "governmental action based on race—a *group* classification long recognized as in most circumstances irrelevant and therefore prohibited—should be subjected to detailed judicial inquiry to ensure that the *personal* right to equal protection of the laws has not been infringed." *Adarand Constructors, Inc.* v. *Peña* (1995) (emphasis in original; internal quotation marks and citation omitted). We are a "free people whose institutions are founded upon the doctrine of equality." *Loving* v. *Virginia* (1967) (internal quotation marks and citation omitted). It follows from that principle that "government may treat people differently because of their race only for the most compelling reasons." *Adarand Constructors, Inc.* v. *Peña.*

We have held that all racial classifications imposed by government "must be analyzed by a reviewing court under strict scrutiny." This means that such classifications are constitutional only if they are narrowly tailored to further compelling governmental interests. "Absent searching judicial inquiry into the justification for such race-based measures," we have no way to determine what "classifications are 'benign' or 'remedial' and what classifications are in fact motivated by illegitimate notions of racial inferiority or simple racial politics." *Richmond* v. *J. A. Croson Co.* (1989) (plurality opinion). We apply strict scrutiny to all racial classifications to "'smoke out' illegitimate uses of race by assuring that [government] is pursuing a goal important enough to warrant use of a highly suspect tool."

Strict scrutiny is not "strict in theory, but fatal in fact." *Adarand Constructors, Inc.* v. *Peña* (internal quotation marks and citation omitted). Although all governmental uses of race are subject to strict scrutiny, not all are invalidated by it. As we have explained, "whenever the government treats any person unequally because of his or her race, that person has suffered an injury that falls squarely within the language and spirit of the Constitution's guarantee of equal protection." But that observation "says nothing about the ultimate validity of any particular law; that determination is the job of the court applying strict scrutiny." When race-based action is necessary to further a compelling governmental interest, such action does not violate the constitutional guarantee of equal protection so long as the narrow-tailoring requirement is also satisfied.

Context matters when reviewing race-based governmental action under the Equal Protection Clause. See *Gomillion* v. *Lightfoot* (1960) (admonishing that, "in dealing with claims under broad provisions of the Constitution, which derive content by an interpretive process of inclusion and exclusion, it is imperative that generalizations, based on and qualified by the concrete situations that gave rise to them, must not be applied out of context in disregard of variant controlling facts"). In *Adarand Constructors, Inc.*v. *Peña,* we made clear that strict scrutiny must take "'relevant differences' into account." Indeed, as we explained, that is its "fundamental purpose." Not every decision influenced by race is equally objectionable and strict scrutiny is designed to provide a framework for carefully examining the importance and the sincerity of the reasons advanced by the governmental decisionmaker for the use of race in that particular context.

III

A

With these principles in mind, we turn to the question whether the Law School's use of race is justified by a compelling state interest. Before this Court, as they have throughout this litigation, respondents assert only one justification for their use of race in the admissions process: obtaining "the educational benefits that flow from a diverse student body." In other words, the Law School asks us to recognize, in the context of higher education, a compelling state interest in student body diversity.

We first wish to dispel the notion that the Law School's argument has been foreclosed, either expressly or implicitly, by our affirmative-action cases decided since *Bakke*. It is true that some language in those opinions might be read to suggest that remedying past discrimination is the only permissible justification for race-based governmental action. See, *e.g., Richmond* v. *J. A. Croson Co.* (plurality opinion) (stating that unless classifications based on race are "strictly reserved for remedial settings, they may in fact promote notions of racial inferiority and lead to a politics of racial hostility"). But we have never held that the only governmental use of race that can survive strict scrutiny is remedying past discrimination. Nor, since *Bakke,* have we directly addressed the use of race in the context of public higher education. Today, we hold that the Law School has a compelling interest in attaining a diverse student body.

The Law School's educational judgment that such diversity is essential to its educational mission is one to which we defer. The Law School's assessment that diversity will, in fact, yield educational benefits is substantiated by respondents and their *amici*. Our scrutiny of the interest asserted by the Law School is no less strict for taking into account complex educational judgments in an area that lies primarily within the expertise of the university. Our holding today is in keeping with our tradition of giving a degree of deference to a university's academic decisions, within constitutionally prescribed limits.

We have long recognized that, given the important purpose of public education and the expansive freedoms of speech and thought associated with the university environment, universities occupy a special niche in our constitutional tradition. In announcing the principle of student body diversity as a compelling state interest, Justice Powell invoked our cases recognizing a constitutional dimension, grounded in the First Amendment, of educational autonomy: "The freedom of a university to make its own judgments as to education includes the selection of its student body." From this premise, Justice Powell reasoned that by claiming "the right to select those students who will contribute the most to the 'robust exchange of ideas,'" a university "seek[s] to achieve a goal that is of paramount importance in the fulfillment of its mission." Our conclusion that the Law School has a compelling interest in a diverse student body is informed by our view that attaining a diverse student body is at the heart of the Law School's proper institutional mission, and that "good faith" on the part of a university is "presumed" absent "a showing to the contrary."

As part of its goal of "assembling a class that is both exceptionally academically qualified and broadly diverse," the Law School seeks to "enroll a 'critical mass' of minority students." The Law School's interest is not simply "to assure within its student body some specified percentage of a particular group merely because of its race or ethnic origin." That would amount to outright racial balancing, which is patently unconstitutional. Rather, the Law School's concept of critical mass is defined by reference to the educational benefits that diversity is designed to produce.

These benefits are substantial. As the District Court emphasized, the Law School's admissions policy promotes "cross-racial understanding," helps to break down racial stereotypes, and "enables [students] to better understand persons of different races." These benefits are "important and laudable," because "classroom discussion is livelier, more spirited, and simply more enlightening and interesting" when the students have "the greatest possible variety of backgrounds."

The Law School's claim of a compelling interest is further bolstered by its *amici,* who point to the educational benefits that flow from student body diversity. In addition to the expert studies and reports entered into evidence at trial, numerous studies show that student body diversity promotes learning outcomes, and "better prepares students for an increasingly diverse workforce and society, and better prepares them as professionals."

These benefits are not theoretical but real, as major American businesses have made clear that the skills needed in today's increasingly global marketplace can only be developed through exposure to widely diverse people, cultures, ideas, and viewpoints. What is more, high-ranking retired officers and civilian leaders of the United States military assert that, "[b]ased on [their] decades of experience," a "highly qualified, racially diverse officer corps . . . is essential to the military's ability to fulfill its [principal] mission to provide national security." The primary sources for the Nation's officer corps are the service academies and the Reserve Officers Training Corps (ROTC), the latter comprising students already admitted to participating colleges and universities. At present, "the military cannot achieve an officer corps that is *both* highly qualified *and* racially diverse unless the service academies and the ROTC used limited race-conscious recruiting and admissions policies." (emphasis in original). To fulfill its mission, the military "must be selective in admissions for training and education for the officer corps, *and* it must train and educate a highly qualified, racially diverse officer corps in a racially diverse setting." (emphasis in original). We agree that "[i]t requires only a small step from this analysis to conclude that our country's other most selective institutions must remain both diverse and selective."

We have repeatedly acknowledged the overriding importance of preparing students for work and citizenship, describing education as pivotal to "sustaining our political and cultural heritage" with a fundamental role in maintaining the fabric of society. *Plyler* v. *Doe* (1982). This Court has long recognized that "education . . . is the very foundation of good citizenship." *Brown* v. *Board of Education* (1954). For this reason, the diffusion of knowledge and opportunity through public institutions of higher education must be accessible to all individuals regardless of race or ethnicity. The United States, as *amicus curiae*, affirms that "[e]nsuring that public institutions are open and available to all segments of American society, including people of all races and ethnicities, represents a paramount government objective." And, "[n]owhere is the importance of such openness more acute than in the context of higher education." Effective participation by members of all racial and ethnic groups in the civic life of our Nation is essential if the dream of one Nation, indivisible, is to be realized.

Moreover, universities, and in particular, law schools, represent the training ground for a large number of our Nation's leaders. *Sweatt* v. *Painter* (1950) (describing law school as a "proving ground for legal learning and practice"). Individuals with law degrees occupy roughly half the state governorships, more than half the seats in the United States Senate, and more than a third of the seats in the United States House of Representatives. The pattern is even more striking when it comes to highly selective law schools. A handful of these schools accounts for 25 of the 100 United States Senators, 74 United States Courts of Appeals judges, and nearly 200 of the more than 600 United States District Court judges.

In order to cultivate a set of leaders with legitimacy in the eyes of the citizenry, it is necessary that the path to leadership be visibly open to talented and qualified individuals of every race and ethnicity. All members of our heterogeneous society must have confidence in the openness and integrity of the educational institutions that provide this training. As we have recognized, law schools "cannot be effective in isolation from the individuals and institutions with which the law interacts." See *Sweatt* v. *Painter*. Access to legal education (and thus the legal profession) must be inclusive of talented and qualified individuals of every race and ethnicity, so that all members of our heterogeneous society may participate in the educational institutions that provide the training and education necessary to succeed in America.

The Law School does not premise its need for critical mass on "any belief that minority students always (or even consistently) express some characteristic minority viewpoint on any issue." To the contrary, diminishing the force of such stereotypes is both a crucial part of the Law School's mission, and one that it cannot accomplish with only token numbers of minority students. Just as growing up in a particular region or having particular professional experiences is likely to affect an individual's views, so too is one's own, unique experience of being a racial minority in a society, like our own, in which race unfortunately still matters. The Law School has determined, based on its experience and expertise, that a "critical mass" of underrepresented minorities is necessary to further its compelling interest in securing the educational benefits of a diverse student body.

B

Even in the limited circumstance when drawing racial distinctions is permissible to further a compelling state interest, government is still "constrained in how it may pursue that end: [T]he means chosen to accomplish the [government's] asserted purpose must be specifically and narrowly framed to accomplish that purpose." *Shaw* v. *Hunt* (1996) (internal quotation marks and citation omitted). The purpose of the narrow tailoring requirement is to ensure that "the means chosen 'fit' . . . th[e] compelling goal so closely that there is little or no possibility that the motive for the classification was illegitimate racial prejudice or stereotype." *Richmond* v. *J. A. Croson Co.* (plurality opinion).

Since *Bakke,* we have had no occasion to define the contours of the narrow-tailoring inquiry with respect to race-conscious university admissions programs. That inquiry must be calibrated to fit the distinct issues raised by the use of race to achieve student body diversity in public higher education. Contrary to Justice Kennedy's assertions, we do not "abandon[] strict scrutiny." Rather, as we have already explained, we adhere to *Adarand's* teaching that the very purpose of strict scrutiny is to take such "relevant differences into account."

To be narrowly tailored, a race-conscious admissions program cannot use a quota system—it cannot "insulat[e] each category of applicants with certain desired qualifications from competition with all other applicants." *Bakke* (opinion of Powell, J.). Instead, a university may consider race or ethnicity only as a "'plus' in a particular applicant's file," without "insulat[ing] the individual from comparison with all other candidates for the available seats." In other words, an admissions program must be "flexible enough to consider all pertinent elements of diversity in light of the particular qualifications of each applicant, and to place them on the same footing for consideration, although not necessarily according them the same weight."

We find that the Law School's admissions program bears the hallmarks of a narrowly tailored plan. As Justice Powell made clear in *Bakke,* truly individualized consideration demands that race be used in a flexible, nonmechanical way. It follows from this mandate that universities cannot establish quotas for members of certain racial groups or put members of those groups on separate admissions tracks. Nor can universities insulate applicants who belong to certain racial or ethnic groups from the competition for admission. Universities can, however, consider race or ethnicity more flexibly as a "plus" factor in the context of individualized consideration of each and every applicant.

We are satisfied that the Law School's admissions program, like the Harvard plan described by Justice Powell, does not operate as a quota. Properly understood, a "quota" is a program in which a certain fixed number or proportion of opportunities are "reserved exclusively for certain minority groups." *Richmond* v. *J. A. Croson Co.* (plurality opinion). Quotas "'impose a fixed number or percentage which must be attained, or which cannot be exceeded,'" *Sheet Metal Workers* v. *EEOC* (1986) (O'Connor, J., concurring in part and dissenting in part), and "insulate the individual from comparison with all other candidates for the available seats." *Bakke,* (opinion of Powell, J.). In contrast, "a permissible goal . . . require[s] only a good-faith effort . . . to come within a range demarcated by the goal itself," *Sheet Metal Workers* v. *EEOC,* and permits consideration of race as a "plus" factor in any given case while still ensuring that each candidate "compete[s] with all other qualified applicants," *Johnson* v. *Transportation Agency, Santa Clara Cty.* (1987).

Justice Powell's distinction between the medical school's rigid 16-seat quota and Harvard's flexible use of race as a "plus" factor is instructive. Harvard certainly had minimum *goals* for minority enrollment, even if it had no specific number firmly in mind. ("10 or 20 black students could not begin to bring to their classmates and to each other the variety of points of view, backgrounds and experiences of blacks in the United States"). What is more, Justice Powell flatly rejected the argument that Harvard's program was "the functional equivalent of a quota" merely because it had some "'plus'" for race, or gave greater "weight" to race than to some other factors, in order to achieve student body diversity.

The Law School's goal of attaining a critical mass of underrepresented minority students does not transform its program into a quota. As the Harvard plan described by Justice Powell recognized, there is of course "some relationship between numbers and achieving the benefits to be derived from a diverse student body, and between numbers and providing a reasonable environment for those students admitted." "[S]ome attention to numbers," without more, does not transform a flexible admissions system into a rigid quota. Nor, as Justice Kennedy posits, does the Law School's consultation of the "daily reports," which keep track of the racial and ethnic composition of the class (as well as of residency and gender), "suggest[] there was no further attempt at individual review save for race itself" during the final stages of the admissions process. To the contrary, the Law School's admissions officers testified without contradiction that they never gave race any more or less weight based on the information contained in these reports. Moreover, as Justice Kennedy concedes, between 1993 and 2000, the number of African-American, Latino, and Native-American students in each class at the Law School varied from 13.5 to 20.1 percent, a range inconsistent with a quota.

The Chief Justice believes that the Law School's policy conceals an attempt to achieve racial balancing, and cites admissions data to contend that the Law School discriminates among different groups within the critical mass. But, as The Chief Justice concedes, the number of underrepresented minority students who ultimately enroll in the Law School differs substantially from their representation in the applicant pool and varies considerably for each group from year to year.

That a race-conscious admissions program does not operate as a quota does not, by itself, satisfy the requirement of individualized consideration. When using race as a "plus" factor in university admissions, a university's admissions program must remain flexible enough to ensure that each applicant is evaluated as an individual and not in a way that makes an applicant's race or ethnicity the defining feature of his or her application. The importance of this individualized consideration in the context of a race-conscious admissions program is paramount.

Here, the Law School engages in a highly individualized, holistic review of each applicant's file, giving serious consideration to all the ways an applicant might contribute to a diverse educational environment. The Law School affords this individualized consideration to applicants of all races. There is no policy, either *de jure* or *de facto,* of automatic acceptance or rejection based on any single "soft" variable. Unlike the program at issue in *Gratz* v. *Bollinger*, the Law School awards no mechanical, predetermined diversity "bonuses" based on race or ethnicity. Like the Harvard plan, the Law School's admissions policy "is flexible enough to consider all pertinent elements of diversity in light of the particular qualifications of each applicant, and to place them on the same footing for consideration, although not necessarily according them the same weight."

We also find that, like the Harvard plan Justice Powell referenced in *Bakke,* the Law School's race-conscious admissions program adequately ensures that all factors that may contribute to student body diversity are meaningfully considered alongside race in admissions decisions. With respect to the use of race itself, all underrepresented minority students admitted by the Law School have been deemed qualified. By virtue of our Nation's struggle with racial inequality, such students are both likely to have experiences of particular importance to the Law School's mission, and less likely to be admitted in meaningful numbers on criteria that ignore those experiences.

The Law School does not, however, limit in any way the broad range of qualities and experiences that may be considered valuable contributions to student body diversity. To the contrary, the 1992 policy makes clear "[t]here are many possible bases for diversity admissions," and provides examples of admittees who have lived or traveled widely abroad, are fluent in several languages, have overcome personal adversity and family hardship, have exceptional records of extensive community service, and have had successful careers in other fields. The Law School seriously considers each "applicant's promise of making a notable contribution to the class by way of a particular strength, attainment, or characteristic—*e.g.*, an unusual intellectual achievement, employment experience, nonacademic performance, or personal background." All applicants have the opportunity to highlight their own potential diversity contributions through the submission of a personal statement, letters of recommendation, and an essay describing the ways in which the applicant will contribute to the life and diversity of the Law School.

What is more, the Law School actually gives substantial weight to diversity factors besides race. The Law School frequently accepts nonminority applicants with grades and test scores lower than underrepresented minority applicants (and other nonminority applicants) who are rejected. . . . This shows that the Law School seriously weighs many other diversity factors besides race that can make a real and dispositive difference for nonminority applicants as well. By this flexible approach, the Law School sufficiently takes into account, in practice as well as in theory, a wide variety of characteristics besides race and ethnicity that contribute to a diverse student body. Justice Kennedy speculates that "race is likely outcome determinative for many members of minority groups" who do not fall within the upper range of LSAT scores and grades. But the same could be said of the Harvard plan discussed approvingly by Justice Powell in *Bakke,* and indeed of any plan that uses race as one of many factors. . . .

Petitioner and the United States argue that the Law School's plan is not narrowly tailored because race-neutral means exist to obtain the educational benefits of student body diversity that the Law School seeks. We disagree. Narrow tailoring does not require exhaustion of every conceivable race-neutral alternative. Nor does it require a university to choose between maintaining a reputation for excellence or fulfilling a commitment to provide educational opportunities to members of all racial groups. . . . Narrow tailoring does, however, require serious, good faith consideration of workable race-neutral alternatives that will achieve the diversity the university seeks. . . .

We agree with the Court of Appeals that the Law School sufficiently considered workable race-neutral alternatives. The District Court took the Law School to task for failing to consider race-neutral alternatives such as "using a lottery system" or "decreasing the emphasis for all applicants on undergraduate GPA and LSAT scores." But these alternatives would require a dramatic sacrifice of diversity, the academic quality of all admitted students, or both.

The Law School's current admissions program considers race as one factor among many, in an effort to assemble a student body that is diverse in ways broader than race. Because a lottery would make that kind of nuanced judgment impossible, it would effectively sacrifice all other educational values, not to mention every other kind of diversity. So too with the suggestion that the Law School simply lower admissions standards for all students, a drastic remedy that would require the Law School to become a much different institution and sacrifice a vital component of its educational mission. The United States advocates "percentage plans," recently adopted by public undergraduate institutions in Texas, Florida, and California to guarantee admission to all students above a certain class-rank threshold in every high school in the State. The United States does not, however, explain how such plans could work for graduate and professional schools. Moreover, even assuming such plans are race-neutral, they may preclude the university from conducting the individualized assessments necessary to assemble a student body that is not just racially diverse, but diverse along all the qualities valued by the university. We are satisfied that the Law School adequately considered race-neutral alternatives currently capable of producing a critical mass without forcing the Law School to abandon the academic selectivity that is the cornerstone of its educational mission.

We acknowledge that "there are serious problems of justice connected with the idea of preference itself." *Bakke* (opinion of Powell, J.). Narrow tailoring, therefore, requires that a race-conscious admissions program not unduly harm members of any racial group. Even remedial race-based governmental action generally "remains subject to continuing oversight to assure that it will work the least harm possible to other innocent persons competing for the benefit." To be narrowly tailored, a race-conscious admissions program must not "unduly burden individuals who are not members of the favored racial and ethnic groups." *Metro Broadcasting, Inc.* v. *FCC* (1990) (O'Connor, J., dissenting).

We are satisfied that the Law School's admissions program does not. Because the Law School considers "all pertinent elements of diversity," it can (and does) select nonminority applicants who have greater potential to enhance student body diversity over underrep-resented minority applicants. As Justice Powell recognized in *Bakke,* so long as a race-conscious admissions program uses race as a "plus" factor in the context of individualized consideration, a rejected applicant "will not have been foreclosed from all consideration for that seat simply because he was not the right color or had the wrong surname. . . . His qualifications would have been weighed fairly and competitively, and he would have no basis to complain of unequal treatment under the Fourteenth Amendment."

We agree that, in the context of its individualized inquiry into the possible diversity contributions of all applicants, the Law School's race-conscious admissions program does not unduly harm nonminority applicants.

We are mindful, however, that "[a] core purpose of the Fourteenth Amendment was to do away with all governmentally imposed discrimination based on race." *Palmore* v. *Sidoti* (1984). Accordingly, race-conscious admissions policies must be limited in time. This requirement reflects that racial classifications, however compelling their goals, are potentially so dangerous that they may be employed no more broadly than the interest demands. Enshrining a permanent justification for racial preferences would offend this fundamental equal protection principle. We see no reason to exempt race-conscious admissions programs from the requirement that all governmental use of race must have a logical end point. The Law School, too, concedes that all "race-conscious programs must have reasonable durational limits."

In the context of higher education, the durational requirement can be met by sunset provisions in race-conscious admissions policies and periodic reviews to determine whether racial preferences are still necessary to achieve student body diversity. Universities in California, Florida, and Washington State, where racial preferences in admissions are prohibited by state law, are currently engaged in experimenting with a wide variety of alternative approaches. Universities in other States can and should draw on the most promising aspects of these race-neutral alternatives as they develop. . . .

The requirement that all race-conscious admissions programs have a termination point "assure[s] all citizens that the deviation from the norm of equal treatment of all racial and ethnic groups is a temporary matter, a measure taken in the service of the goal of equality itself." *Richmond* v. *J. A. Croson Co.* . . .

We take the Law School at its word that it would "like nothing better than to find a race-neutral admissions formula" and will terminate its race-conscious admissions program as soon as practicable. . . . It has been 25 years since Justice Powell first approved the use of race to further an interest in student body diversity in the context of public higher education. Since that time, the number of minority applicants with high grades and test scores has indeed increased. We expect that 25 years from now, the use of racial preferences will no longer be necessary to further the interest approved today.

IV

In summary, the Equal Protection Clause does not prohibit the Law School's narrowly tailored use of race in admissions decisions to further a compelling interest in obtaining the educational benefits that flow from a diverse student body. Consequently, petitioner's statutory claims based on Title VI and 42 U. S. C. § 1981 also fail. . . . The judgment of the Court of Appeals for the Sixth Circuit, accordingly, is affirmed

It is so ordered.

QUESTIONS FOR REFLECTION

1. Explore the diversity rationale at issue in this case.
2. How does the Law School's admissions process differ from the undergraduate process rejected in *Gratz?*
3. What benefits might diversity bring to an educational institution? Do they constitute a compelling state interest?
4. What is a "critical mass" of minority students? Why does Justice O'Connor consider it important?
5. Justice O'Connor argues that the Law School's admissions process is narrowly tailored. Analyze and evaluate her argument.

IMMIGRATION

We are in the midst of a great period of migration. The seventeenth and eighteenth centuries saw massive movements of people from Europe to the Americas. Another great migration to the United States occurred in the late nineteenth and early twentieth centuries. Those who feared being overwhelmed by tides of immigrants then restricted immigration to much lower levels. In the past few decades, however, immigration, both legal and illegal, has increased dramatically. The direction of immigration has also changed. Immigrants to the United States now hail mostly from Latin America rather than from Europe. Immigrants to Europe hail mostly from North Africa, South Asia, and the Middle East.

From a moral point of view, immigration raises several profound questions. Do people have a right to emigrate? To immigrate? To work where they choose? If immigration controls are morally acceptable, what kinds of controls should they be? Who should decide? May residents of a nation seek to preserve their own economic welfare, culture, and identity? What obligations do people have to others outside their own community or nation?

Immanuel Kant raises some of these questions, holding that the central obligation we have to those outside our nation is hospitality. By that he means three things:

1. We have no obligation to receive others into our country.
2. We must treat those whom we choose to receive without hostility.
3. We have no obligation to grant anyone permanent occupancy.

A nation, when considering whether to allow immigration, is essentially in the position of those who own property. They are under no obligation to allow anyone onto their property. If they do allow it, however, they must treat the visitor with respect. Nevertheless, they have no obligation to allow anyone else permanent use of that property. Indeed, that is more than anyone has a right to ask.

Some have objected to Kant's position, holding that the division of humankind into nations is an unfortunate artifact of a particular historical era. Ideally, they say, we would all be citizens of one world community. Kant rejects this idea outright. A world government, Kant argues, "would end in one universal monarchy." The larger the territory the government oversees, the further removed it is from the interests, values, concerns, and consent of any local community. Therefore, Kant insists, "laws always lose in vigor what government gains in extent; hence a condition of soulless despotism falls into anarchy after stifling seeds of good."

John Rawls presents a modern version of Kant's position, defending "familiar and traditional principles of justice among free and independent peoples," many of which Kant himself articulated:

1. *Liberty*. Peoples must respect the freedom and independence of all other peoples.
2. *Contracts*. Peoples must observe treaties.
3. *Equality*. Peoples are equal parties to agreements.
4. *Nonintervention*. Peoples must not intervene in the affairs of other peoples.
5. *Jus ad bellum*. Peoples may fight wars only in self-defense.
6. *Rights*. Peoples must respect human rights.
7. *Jus in bello*. Peoples must conduct war according to moral principles.
8. *Assistance*. Peoples must help other peoples who suffer under unjust or indecent governments.

Rawls explicitly declines to put certain principles on this list. Peoples do not, for example, have a right to self-determination or secession. They have no right to subjugate or discriminate against other peoples or minorities within their own borders. And they have no right to immigrate into another people's territory without their consent. A people may restrict immigration, among other reasons, to protect their own culture and governing principles.

Garrett Hardin argues against immigration on consequentialist grounds. He compares a nation to a lifeboat that can support only a certain number of people. Allowing more people into the lifeboat can easily lead to a "tragedy of the commons," making everyone worse off. The problem is exacerbated by differences in rates of reproduction. Demographic trends between native populations and immigrant populations often differ markedly. In much of Europe, for example, the average native woman has fewer than two children—less than replacement level. The average immigrant woman, in contrast, has between three and four children. Under such circumstances, Hardin argues, liberal immigration policies are suicidal. We have an obligation to future generations to bequeath them a nation that is "a decent place to live."

Robert Putnam considers the effects of immigration and diversity on "social capital," the social networks and norms of trust and cooperation that enable people to work together effectively. The diversity that arises from immigration has a variety of beneficial effects. But it also has costs. There is an increased potential for conflicts between groups. More surprisingly, there is a loss of social capital even within groups. People in diverse communities trust everyone less, even members of their own group. They have lower confidence in government and participate in it less. They give less to charity, volunteer less, expect less of others, and are less happy. "Diversity," Putnam concludes, "seems to bring out the turtle in all of us."

Finally, Michael Huemer argues for a prima facie right to immigrate. Someone who, by the use of physical force, prevented another person from getting to a marketplace to buy food or get a job does something wrong and violates that person's rights. If people in the United States want to hire immigrants, rent apartments to them, sell them houses and land, and so on, it is wrong to keep them out of the country. The wrong is not merely theoretical; millions of people suffer, and hundreds die, from current immigration policies.

IMMANUEL KANT

from *Perpetual Peace*

(Source: Immanuel Kant, Perpetual Peace *[London: Vernor and Hood, 1796].)*

THIRD DEFINITIVE ARTICLE FOR A PERPETUAL PEACE

"The Law of World Citizenship Shall Be Limited to Conditions of Universal Hospitality"

The cosmopolitical right shall be limited to conditions of universal hospitality.

In this article, as well as in the preceding ones, it is a question of right, not of philanthropy. Hospitality there signifies solely the right every stranger has of not being treated as an enemy in the country in which he arrives. One may refuse to receive him, if it can be done without endangering his existence; but dares not act hostilely towards him, so long as he does not offend any one. The question is not about the right of being received and admitted into the house of an individual: this benevolent custom demanding particular conventions. *One speaks here only of the right all men have, of demanding of others to be admitted into their society;* a right founded upon that of the common possession of the surface of the earth, whose spherical form obliges them to suffer others to subsist contiguous to them, because they cannot disperse themselves to an indefinite distance, and because originally one has not a greater right to a country than another. The sea and uninhabitable deserts divide the surface of the globe; but the ship and the camel, that vessel of the desert, re-establish the communication and facilitate the right which the human species all possess, of profiting in common by its surface. The inhospitality of the inhabitants of the coasts (for instance of the coast of Barbary) their custom of taking the vessels in the neighbouring seas, or that of reducing to slavery the unhappy wretches shipwrecked on their shores; the barbarous practice which in their sandy deserts the Bedouin Arabs exercise of pillaging all those who approach their wandering tribes; all these customs then are contrary to the right of nature, which, nevertheless, in ordaining hospitality, was contented with fixing the conditions on which one may endeavour to form connections with the inhabitants of a country. In this manner distant regions may contract amicable relations with each other, sanctioned in the end by public laws, and thus insensibly mankind may approach towards a cosmopolitical constitution.

At how great a distance from this perfection are the civilized nations, and especially the commercial nations of Europe? At what an excess of injustice do we not behold them arrive, when they discover strange countries and nations? (which with them is the same thing as to conquer). America, the countries inhabited by the negroes, the Spice Islands, the Cape, &c. were to them countries without proprietors, for the inhabitants they counted as nothing. Under pretext of establishing factories in Hindostan, they carried thither foreign troops, and by their means oppressed the natives, exited wars among the different states of that vast country; spread famine, rebellion, perfidy, and the whole deluge of evils that afflict mankind, among them.

The Chinese and Japanese, whom experience has taught to know the Europeans, wisely refuse their entry into the country, though the former permit their approach, which the latter grant to one European nation only, the Dutch; still, however, excluding them like captives from every communication with the inhabitants. The worst, or to speak with the moralist, the best of the matter is, that all these outrages are to no purpose; that all the commercial companies, guilty of them, touch upon the instant of their ruin; that the sugar islands, that den of slavery the most refined and cruel, produce no real revenue, and are profitable only indirectly, serving views not very laudable, namely, to form sailors for the navies, consequently to carry on war in Europe; which service the render to powers who boast the most of piety, and who, whilst they drink iniquity like water, pretend to equal the elect in point of orthodoxy.

The connections, more or less near, which have taken place among the nations of the earth, having been carried to that point, that a violation of rights, committed in one place, is felt throughout the whole, the idea of a cosmopolitical right can no longer pass for a fantastic exaggeration of right; but is the last step of perfection necessary to the tacit code of civil and public right; these systems at length conducting towards a public right of men in general, and towards a perpetual peace, but to which one cannot hope continually to advance, except by means of the conditions here indicated.

SUPPLEMENT

Supplement the first.— Of the guarantee for a perpetual peace

The guarantee of this treaty is nothing less than the great and ingenious artist, nature (*natura dædala rerum*). Her mechanical march evidently announces the grand aim of producing among men, against their intention, harmony from the very bosom of their discords. Hence it is that we call it *destiny,* viewing it as a cause absolute in its effects, but unknown as to the laws of its operations. But the regular order which we observe in the course of the events of this world, makes us call it *Providence,* inasmuch as we discern in her the profound wisdom of a superior cause, which predetermines the course of fate, and makes it tend to the final purpose of human existence. It is true, we do not discover this providence the methodical arrangements of nature, nor can we by reasonings deduce it therefrom; we can only suppose it, which we do, as often as we refer the modes of things to some end. We stand even in need of this supposition to form to ourselves an idea of the possibility of an order of nature, analagous to the operations of human art. The idea of a relation of this mechanism to the moral end which reason immediately prescribes, though rash in theory, is a well founded truth in practice; for instance, by making this physical order of nature serve towards the realization of the duty of a perpetual peace. Since reason cannot apply the relations of causes and effects, to any other objects, than such as experience has made known to us, it is more modest and conformable to the limits of the human understanding, to employ the word *nature,* when theory and not religion is the question, preferably to that of *Providence,* which intimates a pretended knowledge of its mysteries, and a flight as temerarious as that of Icarus, towards the sanctuary of its impenetrable designs.

Before we determine the manner in which nature guarantees a perpetual peace, it will be necessary to examine the situation in which she places the beings that figure upon this vast stage, and the measures she has taken to render this peace necessary to them.

These are her preparatory arrangements.

I. She has in every climate provided for the existence of man.
II. She has by means of war dispersed them, in order to populate the most inhospitable regions.
III. She has, by the same means, compelled them to contract relations more or less legal.

That in the vast plains which border the icy sea, the moss however grows, which the rein deer digs from beneath the snow, in order to make itself subservient to the nourishment or to the conveyance of the Ostic or the Samoied; that the saline sandy deserts should contain the camel, which appears created for the very purpose of traversing them, is already wonderful. Still more clearly marked does this end appear in the care nature has taken to place on the shores of the icy sea, besides the animals covered with furs, seals and whales, whose flesh serves as food and whose fat as firing to the inhabitants. But the maternal providence of nature is most wonderfully manifested by the singular manner in which she furnishes (in a manner not well known) those countries destitute of vegetation with wood, without which the inhabitants could have neither canoes, weapons, or huts; being, besides, too much occupied with defending themselves against the wild beasts, to live in peace with each other. But probably it was war alone which carried them into these climates. The first instrument of war was without doubt the horse, being tamed and trained up for combat when the earth began to be peopled with inhabitants. The elephant served in later times to the luxury of states already formed. As also the culture of divers sorts of corn, originally herbs now unknown; and the increase and improvement of fruit trees, by transplanting and ingrafting them, since primæval Europe produced only wild apple and pear trees; these operations then could only take place after an established constitution secured to every proprietor the enjoyment of his possessions. But before this could take place, it was necessary that men who at first subsisted in a state of anarchic liberty, either by the chace or the fishery, should have passed from the pastoral life to a life of agriculture; that salt and iron should be discovered (probably the two first objects of commerce between different nations) to produce among them pacific relations, and to contract, even with the most distant, some relations of convention and society.

Now as nature has provided an existence for men in every part of the earth, she insists upon their living in every part; and so despotic is this her will, that they obey it even against their inclination, and without being forced to it by any moral law. War is the only means she employs to obtain this end. By this means she has separated people, whose identity of language proclaims that of their origin. We find the Samoiedes on the coasts of the icy sea speak the mongul language of the inhabitants of the Altaish mountains, situated two hundred miles from them; between these two we find a mongul nation of horsemen, and of course warlike; is it not probable that the latter should have driven the former into these inhospitable icy lands, into which they would certainly not have penetrated from inclination? It is the same with the Finlanders, who, in the northern extremity of Europe, are called Laplanders. They have been separated by the Goths and Salmatians from the Hungarians, whose language is the same with theirs. What can have carried into the north of America the Esquimaux, that race of men so entirely different from all other nations of the new world, descended perhaps from some European adventurers; and into the south the Pesheras as far as to the fire island, if it was not war, of which nature makes use to people all the earth?

As to war itself, it requires no particular motive; it appears ingrafted on human nature; it passes even for an act of greatness, to which the love of glory alone, without any other motive, impels. Thus, among the savages of America, as among the Europeans in the times of chivalry, military valour obtained great honours, not only during war, which would be just, but also when in order to signalize itself it undertakes war; so that a kind of dignity is attached to war itself, and that philosophers are found who commend it as a noble prerogative of humanity, forgetting this sentence of a Greek: "War is an evil, inasmuch as it produces more wicked men than it takes off."

Enough has been said of the measures nature takes to lead mankind, considering them as they compose a class of animals, to the end she has proposed to herself.

We have now to examine what is most essential relatively to a perpetual peace, that is to say, what nature has done with regard to it; how she favours the moral views of man, and guarantees the execution of the laws reason prescribes to him; so that whatever man should do freely, according to the civil, public, and cosmopolitical right, if he neglects it, he shall be forced to do it, by a constraint of nature, without prejudice to his liberty.

When I say nature wills that this or that arrive, this does not mean that she makes it a duty to us; it is practical reason alone that can prescribe laws to free beings without constraining them; but it means, that nature does it herself, whether we will or no.

"Fata volentem ducunt, nolentem trahunt."

I. If even intestine discords were not to force a people to submit to the constraint of laws, they would be compelled thereto by the external means of war; nature having placed, as has already been seen, by the side of each people, another neighbouring people, which presses upon it, and obliges it to form itself into a state, in order to form a power capable of opposing the enterprises of the other. Now as a republican constitution is the only one that is entirely conformable to the rights of man, it is also the most difficult to establish and to maintain; so much so, that it has been said it required angels, and not men under the dominion of interested inclinations, to realize a form of government so sublime. But nature employs these interested inclinations themselves, to give to the general will, with the respect due to reason, upon which it is founded, the efficacious practice it stands in need of. The question is, only so to organize a state (and this is certainly, not beyond the power of mortals) that the action and re-action of these various inclinations either annihilates or moderates their injurious effect, and by rendering it null to reason, force man to be, if not a good moral being, at least a good citizen.

The problem of a constitution is solvable even to a nation of devils (I shall be forgiven what is offensive in the expression) if this people is but endowed with understanding. "A multitude of reasonable beings de-sire for their preservation universal laws, though every one among them has a secret inclination to exempt himself from the observance of them. A constitution must therefore be given them, that so confines their individual passions, one by means of the other, that, in their public conduct, their effect becomes as inconsiderable as if they had not these hostile 'dispositions.'" A problem like this must be solvable. It does not require that one should obtain the desired effect of a moral reform in man. It only demands that one should derive advantage from the mechanism of nature, in order so to direct the opposition of personal interests, that all the individuals who compose a nation should constrain one another to range themselves beneath the coercive power of a legislation, and thus introduce a pacific state of legislation.

However imperfect the organization of the existing states may be, they nevertheless give us a proof of what has been advanced. They approach in some degree to what the idea of right exacts in their external conduct, though the intrinsic principles of morality do certainly not contribute towards it, nor can they contribute towards it, as it is not for morality to lead to a good constitution, but for this latter to produce the moral reform in man. The example here cited sufficiently shews that the mechanism of nature, according to which the interested propensities ought to defeat each other even in their effects, may serve reason as the means of procuring to the principle of right the sovereignty to which it tends, and to the state the establishment and sure maintenance of an external and even internal peace.

Here nature in an absolute manner *wills* that right should at length obtain the victory. What one neglects to do, she does herself, though by very unpleasant means.

Vous pliez d'un roseau le fragile soutien;
Courbez trop, il rompra. Qui veut trop, ne
veut rien.

[Bend the tender stem of a reed;
Bend it too much and it breaks.
He who attempts too much attempts nothing.]

BOUTERWECK.

II. The idea of the law of nations supposes the reciprocal independence of several neighbouring and separate states; and although this situation is in itself a state of war, if a federative union prevents not hostilities, reason yet prefers this co-existence of states to their union under one superior power to the rest, which would at length end in an universal monarchy. For the laws always lose in energy what the government gains in extent; and a despotism, which, destroying the minds, stifles the germs of every good, and sooner or later degenerates into anarchy.

However there is no state, the chief of which does not desire to secure to himself a constant state of peace by the conquest of the whole universe, if it were possible. But nature opposes this: she employs two means in order to prevent nations from mixing one with another, a diversity of language and religion.*

It is true, this variety contains the germ of reciprocal hatred, and furnishes even frequently a pretext for war: but in proportion as men come nearer in their principles, in consequence of progress in their civilization, the difference of language and of religions leads to and secures a well-founded peace, not like that of despotism, upon the grave of liberty and by means of the extinction of all power, but by the equilibrium they maintain with each other in spite of the contest resulting from their diversity.

*Diversity of religion: a very singular expression! It is precisely as if one spake of a diversity of morals. There may be different kinds of historical faith attached to relative events, not to religion, but to its establishment, and which appertain to the jurisdiction of the learned; there may likewise be different books of religion (the Zendavesta, the Veda, the Koran, &c.) but there is only one religion, true for all men and all times. These can therefore be only accidental means, which serve as a vehicle to religion, and change according to times and places.

If nature wisely separates nations, which every state would seek to combine, by artifice or force, and even according to the principles of the law of nations; who, on the other hand, through the interested spirit of all nations, produces an union between them, which the idea of the cosmopolitical right alone would not have sufficiently secured from war and violence. It is the spirit of commerce that sooner or later takes hold of every nation, and is incompatible with war: the power of money being that which of all others gives the greatest spring to states, they find themselves obliged to labour at the noble work of peace, though without any moral view; and instantly seek to stifle, by mediations, war, in whatever part it may break out, as if for this purpose they had contracted a perpetual alliance; great associations in a war are naturally rare, and less frequently still successful. It is in this manner that nature, by means of the human propensities, guarantees a perpetual peace; and though the assurance which she gives us thereof is not sufficient to predict theoretically, yet it prevents us from regarding it as a chimerical aim, and makes it thereby a duty in us to contribute towards it.

QUESTIONS FOR REFLECTION

1. What obligations does a nation have to those who would like to enter it, in Kant's view?
2. What is Kant's attitude toward colonialism?
3. Many people consider European colonization of the Americas and the consequent displacement of its native inhabitants to have been a gross injustice and yet oppose contemporary controls on immigration. Are these positions compatible?
4. How is it possible for good government to emerge from a group of self-interested people, according to Kant?
5. Why does Kant reject the idea of world government?

GARRETT HARDIN

Living on a Lifeboat

Garrett Hardin (1915–2003) was professor of human ecology at the University of California at Santa Barbara. (Source: Bioscience *24 [1974].)*

Susanne Langer has shown that it is probably impossible to approach an unsolved problem save through the door of metaphor. Later, attempting to meet the demands of rigor, we may achieve some success in cleansing theory of metaphor, though our success is limited if we are unable to avoid using common language, which is shot through and through with fossil metaphors. (I count no *fewer* than five in the preceding two sentences.)

Since metaphorical thinking is inescapable it is pointless merely to weep about our human limitations. We must learn to live with them, to understand them, and to control them. "All of us," said George Eliot in *Middlemarch,* "get our thoughts entangled in metaphors, and act fatally on the strength of them." To avoid unconscious suicide we are well advised to pit one metaphor against another. From the interplay of competitive metaphors, thoroughly developed, we may come closer to metaphor-free solutions to our problems.

No generation has viewed the problem of the survival of the human species as seriously as we have. Inevitably, we have entered this world of concern through the door of metaphor. Environmentalists have emphasized the image of the earth as a spaceship—Spaceship Earth. Kenneth Boulding is the principal architect of this metaphor. It is time, he says, that we replace the wasteful "cowboy economy" of the past with the frugal "spaceship economy" required for continued survival in the limited world we now see ours to be. The metaphor is notably useful in justifying pollution control measures.

Unfortunately, the image of a spaceship is also used to promote measures that are suicidal. One of these is a generous immigration policy, which is only a particular instance of a class of policies that are in error because they lead to the Tragedy of the Commons. These suicidal policies are attractive because they mesh with what we unthinkingly take to be the ideals of "the best people." What is missing in the idealistic view is an insistence that rights and responsibilities must go together. The "generous" attitude of all too many people results in asserting inalienable rights while ignoring or denying matching responsibilities.

For the metaphor of a spaceship to be correct the aggregate of people on board would have to be under unitary sovereign control. A true ship always has a captain. It is conceivable that a ship could be run by a committee. But it could not possibly survive if its course were determined by bickering tribes that claimed rights without responsibilities.

What about Spaceship Earth? It certainly has no captain, and no executive committee. The United Nations is a toothless tiger, because the signatories of its charter wanted it that way. The spaceship metaphor is used only to justify spaceship demands on common resources without acknowledging corresponding spaceship responsibilities.

An understandable fear of decisive action leads people to embrace "incrementalism"—moving toward reform by tiny stages. As we shall see, this strategy is counterproductive in the area discussed here if it means accepting rights before responsibilities. Where human survival is at stake, the acceptance of responsibilities is a precondition to the acceptance of rights, if the two cannot be introduced simultaneously.

Lifeboat Ethics

Before taking up certain substantive issues let us look at an alternative metaphor, that of a lifeboat. In developing some relevant examples the following numerical values are assumed. Approximately two-thirds of the world is desperately poor, and only one-third is comparatively rich. The people in poor countries have an average per capita GNP (Gross National Product) of about $200 per year, the rich, of about $3,000. (For the United States it is nearly $5,000 per year.) Metaphorically each rich nation amounts to a lifeboat full of comparatively rich people. The poor of the world are in other, much more crowded lifeboats. Continuously, so to speak, the poor fall out of their lifeboats and swim for a while in the water outside, hoping to be admitted to a rich lifeboat, or in some other way to benefit from the "goodies" on board. What should the passengers on a rich lifeboat do? This is the central problem of "the ethics of a lifeboat."

First we must acknowledge that each lifeboat is effectively limited in capacity. The land of every nation has a limited carrying capacity. The exact limit is a matter for argument, but the energy crunch is convincing more people every day that we have already exceeded the carrying capacity of the land. We have been living on "capital"—stored petroleum and coal—and soon we must live on income alone.

Let us look at only one lifeboat—ours. The ethical problem is the same for all, and is as follows. Here we sit, say 50 people in a lifeboat. To be generous, let us assume our boat has a capacity of 10 more, making 60. (This, however, is to violate the engineering principle of the "safety factor." A new plant disease or a bad change in the weather may decimate our population if we don't preserve some excess capacity as a safety factor.)

The 50 of us in the lifeboat see 100 others swimming in the water outside, asking for admission to the boat, or for handouts. How shall we respond to their calls? There are several possibilities.

One. We may be tempted to try to live by the Christian ideal of being "our brother's keeper," or by the Marxian ideal of "from each according to his abilities, to each according to his needs." Since the needs of all are the same, we take all the needy into our boat, making a total of 150 in a boat with a capacity of 60. The boat is swamped, and everyone drowns. Complete justice, complete catastrophe.

Two. Since the boat has an unused excess capacity of 10, we admit just 10 more to it. This has the disadvantage of getting rid of the safety factor, for which action we will sooner or later pay dearly. Moreover, *which* 10 do we let in? "First come, first served?" The best 10? The neediest 10? How do we *discriminate? And what* do we say to the 90 who are excluded?

Three. Admit no more to the boat and preserve the small safety factor. Survival of the people in the lifeboat is then possible (though we shall have to be on our guard against boarding parties).

The last solution is abhorrent to many people. It is unjust, they say. Let us grant that it is.

"I feel guilty about my good luck," say some. The reply to this is simple: *Get out and yield your place to others.* Such a selfless action might satisfy the conscience of those who are addicted to guilt, but it would not change the ethics of the lifeboat. The needy person to whom a guilt-addict yields his place will not himself feel guilty about his sudden good luck. (If he did he would not climb aboard.) The net result of conscience-stricken people relinquishing their unjustly held positions is the elimination of their kind of conscience from the lifeboat. The lifeboat, as it were, purifies itself of guilt. The ethics of the lifeboat persist, unchanged by such momentary aberrations.

This then is the basic metaphor within which we must work out our solutions. Let us enrich the image step by step with substantive additions from the real world.

Reproduction

The harsh characteristics of lifeboat ethics are heightened by reproduction, particularly by reproductive differences. The people inside the lifeboats of the wealthy nations are doubling in numbers every 87 years, those outside are doubling every 35 years, on the average. And the relative difference in prosperity is becoming greater.

Let us, for a while, think primarily of the U.S. lifeboat. As of 1973 the United States had a population of 210 million people, who were increasing by 0.8% per year, that is doubling in number every 87 years.

Although the citizens of rich nations are outnumbered two to one by the poor, let us imagine an equal number of poor people outside our lifeboat—a mere 210 million poor people reproducing at a quite different rate. If we imagine these to be the combined population of Colombia, Venezuela, Ecuador, Morocco, Thailand, Pakistan, and the Philippines, the average rate of increase of the people "outside" is 3.3% per year. The doubling time of this population is 21 years.

Suppose that all these countries, and the United States, agreed to live by the Marxian ideal, "to each according to his needs," the ideal of most Christians as well. Needs, of course, are determined by population size, which is affected by reproduction. Every nation regards its rate of reproduction as a sovereign right. If our lifeboat were big enough in the beginning it might be possible to live *for a while* by the Christian-Marxian ideals. *Might*.

Initially, in the model given, the ratio of non-Americans to Americans would be one to one. But consider what the ratio would be 87 years later. By this time Americans would have doubled to a population of 420 million. The other group (doubling every 21 years) would now have swollen to 3,540 million. Each American would have more than eight people to share with. How could the lifeboat possibly keep afloat?

All this involves extrapolation of current trends into the future and is consequently suspect. Trends may change. Granted: but the change will not necessarily be favorable. If—as seems likely—the rate of population increase falls faster in the ethnic group presently inside the lifeboat than it does among those now outside, the future will turn out to be even worse than mathematics predicts, and sharing will be even more suicidal.

Ruin in the Commons

The fundamental error of the sharing ethics is that they lead to the tragedy of the commons. Under a system of private property the people who own property recognize their responsibility to care for it, for if they don't they will eventually suffer. A farmer, for instance, if he is intelligent, will allow no more cattle in a pasture than its carrying capacity justifies. If he overloads the pasture weeds take over, erosion sets in, and the owner loses in the long run.

But if a pasture is run as a commons open to all, the right of each to use it is not matched by an operational responsibility to take care of it. It is no use asking independent herdsmen in a commons to act responsibly, for they dare not. The considerate herdsman who refrains from overloading the commons suffers more than a selfish one who says his needs are greater. (As Leo Durocher says, "Nice guys finish last.") Christian-Marxian idealism is counterproductive. That it *sounds* nice is no excuse. With distribution systems, as with individual morality, good intentions are no substitute for good performance.

A social system is stable only if it is insensitive to errors. To the Christian-Marxian idealist a selfish person is a sort of "error." Prosperity in the system of the commons cannot survive errors. If *everyone* would only restrain himself, all would be well; but it takes *only one less than everyone* to ruin a system of voluntary restraint. In a crowded world of less than perfect human beings—and we will never know any other—mutual ruin is inevitable in the commons. This is the core of the tragedy of the commons.

One of the major tasks of education today is to create such an awareness of the dangers of the commons that people will be able to recognize its many varieties, however disguised. There is pollution of the air and water because these media are treated as commons. Further growth of population and growth in the per capita conversion of natural resources into pollutants require that the system of the commons be modified or abandoned in the disposal of "externalities."

The fish populations of the oceans are exploited as commons, and ruin lies ahead. No technological invention can prevent this fate; in fact, all improvements in the art of fishing merely hasten the day of complete ruin. Only the replacement of the system of the commons with a responsible system can save oceanic fisheries.

The management of western rangelands, though nominally rational, is in fact (under the steady pressure of cattle ranchers) often merely a government-sanctioned system of the commons, drifting toward ultimate ruin for both the rangelands and the residual enterprisers. . . .

Immigration Creates a Commons

From this point on, *it will be assumed that immigrants and native-born citizens are of exactly equal quality*, however quality may be defined. The focus is only on quantity. The conclusions reached depend on nothing else, so all charges of ethnocentrism are irrelevant.

World food banks move food to the people, thus facilitating the exhaustion of the environment of the poor. By contrast, unrestricted immigration moves people to the food, thus speeding up the destruction of the environment in rich countries. Why poor people should want to make this transfer is no mystery; but why should rich hosts encourage it? This transfer, like the reverse one, is supported by both selfish interests and humanitarian impulses.

The principal selfish interest in unimpeded immigration is easy to identify; it is the interest of the employers of cheap labor, particularly that needed for degrading jobs. We have been deceived about the forces of history by the lines of Emma Lazarus inscribed on a plaque within the Statue of Liberty:

Give me your tired, your poor,
Your huddled masses yearning to breathe free,
The wretched refuse of your teeming shore,
Send these, the homeless, tempest-tossed, to me;
I lift my lamp beside the golden door.

The image is one of an infinitely generous earth-mother, passively opening her arms to hordes of immigrants who come here on their own initiative. Such an image may have been adequate for the early days of colonization, but by the time these lines were written (1886) the force for immigration was largely manufactured inside our own borders by factory and mine owners who sought cheap labor not to be found among laborers already here. One group of foreigners after another was thus enticed into the United States to work at wretched jobs for wretched wages.

At present, it is largely the Mexicans who are being so exploited. It is particularly to the advantage of certain employers that there be many illegal immigrants. Illegal immigrant workers dare not complain about their working conditions for fear of being repatriated. Their presence reduces the bargaining power of the Mexican-American laborers. Cesar Chavez repeatedly pleaded with congressional committees to close the doors to more Mexicans so that those here can negotiate effectively for higher wages and decent working conditions. Chavez understood the ethics of a lifeboat.

The interests of the employers of cheap labor are well served by the silence of the intelligentsia of the country. WASPs—White Anglo-Saxon Protestants—are particularly reluctant to call for a closing of the doors to immigration for fear of being called ethnocentric bigots. It was, therefore, an occasion of pure delight for this particular WASP to be present at a meeting when the points he would like to have made were made better by a non-WASP speaking to other non-WASPs. It was in Hawaii, and most of the people in the room were second-level Hawaiian officials of Japanese ancestry. All Hawaiians are keenly aware of the limits of their environment, and the speaker had asked how it might be practically and constitutionally possible to close the doors to more immigrants to the islands. (To Hawaiians, immigrants from the other 49 states are as much of a threat as those from other nations. There is only so much room in the island, and the islanders know it. Sophistical arguments that imply otherwise do not impress them.)

Yet the Japanese-Americans of Hawaii have active ties with the land of their origin. This point was raised by a Japanese-American member of the audience who asked the Japanese-American speaker: "But how can we shut the doors now? We have many friends and relations in Japan that we'd like to bring to Hawaii some day so that they can enjoy this beautiful land."

The speaker smiled sympathetically and responded slowly: "Yes, but we have children now and someday we'll have grandchildren. We can bring more people here from Japan only by giving away some of the land that we hope to pass on to our grandchildren some day. What right do we have to do that?"

To be generous with one's own possessions is one thing; to be generous with posterity's is quite another. This, I think, is the point that must be gotten across to those who would, from a commendable love of distributive justice, institute a ruinous system of the commons, either in the form of a world food bank or that of unrestricted immigration. Since every speaker is a member of some ethnic group it is always possible to charge him with ethnocentrism. But even after purging an argument of ethnocentrism the rejection of the commons is still valid and necessary if we are to save at least some parts of the world from environmental ruin. Is it not desirable that at least some of the grandchildren of people now living should have a decent place in which to live?

QUESTIONS FOR REFLECTION

1. What is a tragedy of the commons?
2. Why, according to Hardin, does immigration lead to a tragedy of the commons?
3. Is a country analogous to a lifeboat, in your view? Why or why not?
4. What is the Marxist-Christian attitude toward immigration? How does Hardin criticize it?
5. What role does our obligation to future generations play in Hardin's argument?

ROBERT D. PUTNAM

E Pluribus Unum: *Diversity and Community in the Twenty-First Century The 2006 Johan Skytte Prize Lecture*

Robert D. Putnam is Peter and Isabel Malkin Professor of Public Policy at Harvard University and director of the Manchester Graduate Summer Programme in Social Change at the University of Manchester.
(Source: Robert D. Putnam, "E Pluribus Unum: Diversity and Community in the Twenty-First Century," *Scandinavian Political Studies,* vol. 30, no. 2, 2007.

One of the most important challenges facing modern societies, and at the same time one of our most significant opportunities, is the increase in ethnic and social heterogeneity in virtually all advanced countries. The most certain prediction that we can make about almost any modern society is that it will be more diverse a generation from now than it is today. This is true from Sweden to the United States and from New Zealand to Ireland. In this article, I want to begin to explore the implications of that transition to a more diverse, multicultural society for "social capital"—the concept for which I have been honored by the Skytte Prize committee.

I begin with a word or two about this concept, which has been the subject of an exponentially expanding and controversial literature over the last fifteen years. I prefer a "lean and mean" definition: social networks and the associated norms of reciprocity and trustworthiness. The core insight of this approach is extremely simple: like tools (physical capital) and training (human capital), social networks have value. Networks have value, first, to people who are in the networks. For example, economic sociologists have shown repeatedly that labor markets are thoroughly permeated by networks so that most of us are as likely to get our jobs through whom we know as through what we know. Indeed, it has been shown that our lifetime income is powerfully affected by the quality of our networks. Similarly, much evidence is accumulating about the health benefits of social ties.

What makes social networks even more interesting, however, is that they also have implications for bystanders. For example, criminologists have taught us the power of neighbourhood networks to deter crime. My wife and I have the good fortune to live in a neighbourhood of Cambridge, Massachusetts, that has a good deal of social capital: barbecues and cocktail parties and so on. I am able to be in Uppsala, Sweden, confident that my home is being protected by all that social capital, even though—and this is the moment for confession—I actually never go to the barbecues and cocktail parties. In other words, I benefit from those social networks even though I am not actually in them myself. In the language of economics, social networks often have powerful externalities.

Social capital comes in many forms, not all fungible. Not all networks have exactly the same effects: friends may improve health, whereas civic groups strengthen democracy. Moreover, although networks can powerfully affect our ability to get things done, nothing guarantees that what gets done through networks will be socially beneficial. Al Qaeda, for instance, is an excellent example of social capital, enabling its participants to accomplish goals they could not accomplish without that network. Nevertheless, much evidence suggests that where levels of social capital are higher, children grow up healthier, safer and better educated, people live longer, happier lives, and democracy and the economy work better. So it seems worthwhile to explore the implications of immigration and ethnic diversity for social capital. In this article, I wish to make three broad points:

- Ethnic diversity will increase substantially in virtually all modern societies over the next several decades in part because of immigration. Increased immigration and diversity are not only inevitable, but over the long run they are also desirable. Ethnic diversity is, on balance, an important social asset, as the history of my own country demonstrates.
- In the short to medium run, however, immigration and ethnic diversity challenge social solidarity and inhibit social capital. In support of this provocative claim I wish to adduce some new evidence, drawn primarily from the United States. . . .
- In the medium to long run, on the other hand, successful immigrant societies create new forms of social solidarity and dampen the negative effects of diversity by constructing new, more encompassing identities. Thus, the central challenge for modern, diversifying societies is to create a new, broader sense of "we."

The Prospects and Benefits of Immigration and Ethnic Diversity

Figure 1 provides illustrative evidence that immigration has grown remarkably across the advanced nations of the world over the last half century. This chart shows the trends in six different countries, selected more or less at random, with quite different historical trajectories: the United States, Ireland, Sweden, Germany, Britain and France. Although these countries began at somewhat different starting points in the 1960s (France relatively higher, Ireland relatively lower), the general

FIGURE 1. **Growth of Immigration in Selected OECD Countries, 1960–2005.**

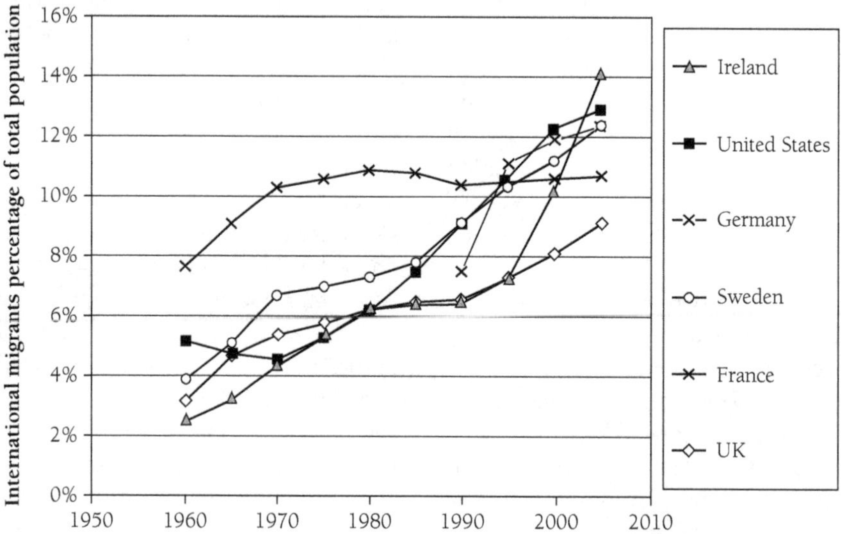

Source: Population Division of the Department of Economic and Social Affairs of the United Nations Secretariat, "Trends in Total Migrant Stock: The 2005 Revision," http://esa.un.org/migration, 27 September 2006.

pattern is a clear convergence toward a much higher number of immigrants as a fraction of the total population.

Of course, not all immigrants are ethnically different from the native population: Danish immigrants do not significantly alter the ethnic mix in Sweden, nor do Canadian immigrants in the United States. Conversely, much of the ethnic diversity in the United States, especially black-white diversity, is entirely unrelated to immigration since the ancestors of most African-Americans have been in the United States longer than the ancestors of most white Americans. So diversity and immigration are not identical, and in our subsequent, more detail analyses we will need to make that distinction more explicit and rigorous. Nonetheless, as a general rule, the mounting wave of immigration depicted in Figure 1 has increased ethnic diversity in the receiving countries. Moreover, because immigrant groups typically have higher fertility rates than native-born groups, ethnic diversity in virtually all of these countries would still increase in the years ahead, even if all new immigration were somehow halted.

So our societies will inevitably be more ethnically diverse tomorrow than they are today. And that diversity will be a valuable national asset. It is not merely that national cuisine is enhanced by immigration, or even that culture of all sorts is enhanced by diversity, though culture and cuisine in my own country provide powerful evidence of those benefits.

- Creativity in general seems to be enhanced by immigration and diversity. Throughout history, for example, immigrants have accounted for three to four times as many of America's Nobel Laureates, National Academy of Science members, Academy Award film directors and winners of Kennedy Center awards in the performing arts as native-born Americans. If we were to include second-generation immigrants (i.e., the children of immigrants), the contribution of immigrants would be even greater. Many (though not all) of the scores of studies of collective creativity in work groups (in business, education and so on) find that diversity fosters creativity. Scott Page has powerfully summarized evidence that diversity (especially intellectual diversity) produces much better, faster problem-solving.
- Immigration is generally associated with more rapid economic growth. The economics profession has debated the short-run economic consequences of immigration for native workers. While there are important distributional effects to be considered, especially the impact of immigration on low-wage native workers in the US, the weight of the evidence suggests that the net effect of immigration is to increase national income. One recent study, for example, suggests that the income of native-born Americans rises more rapidly, *ceteris paribus*, if they are living in places with more immigrants than if they are living in places with fewer immigrants.
- In advanced countries with aging populations, immigration is important to help offset the impending fiscal effects of the retirement of the baby-boom generation. In my country, for example, young immigrant workers (documented and undocumented) contribute financially to our Social Security system, but will not draw benefits for several decades, if at all, thus mitigating the otherwise unsustainable imbalance in the medium term between outflow and inflow into our national coffers. This effect is even more important in the more rapidly aging nations of Europe and East Asia.
- New research from the World Bank has highlighted yet another benefit from immigration, one of special relevance to the Nordic countries that have long played a disproportionate role on issues of global development. This new research suggests that immigration from the global South to the richer North greatly enhances development in the South, partly because of remittances from immigrants to their families back home and partly because of the transfer of technology and new ideas through immigrant networks. So powerful is this effect that despite "brain drain" costs, increasing annual northward immigration by only three percentage points might produce net benefits greater than meeting all our national targets for development assistance *plus* canceling all Third World debt plus abolishing all barriers to Third World trade.

In short, immigration and multicultural diversity have powerful advantages for both sending and receiving countries. Yet what about the effects on social capital?

Immigration and Diversity Foster Social Isolation

In the theoretical toolkit of social science we find two diametrically opposed perspectives on the effects of diversity on social connections. The first, usually labelled the "contact hypothesis," argues that diversity fosters interethnic tolerance and social solidarity. As we have more contact with people who are unlike us, we overcome our initial hesitation and ignorance and come to trust them more. Some of the most striking evidence in support of the contact hypothesis came originally from a famous study of the American soldier during the Second World War. White soldiers were asked how they would feel about having black soldiers serving in the same platoon with them. . . . [A]mong white soldiers who in fact had no contact with black soldiers, most opposed the idea. On the other hand, white soldiers who had been assigned to units with black soldiers were much more relaxed about the idea of racial integration.

Evidence of this sort suggested to social psychologists, beginning with Gordon Allport in the 1950s, the optimistic hypothesis that if we have more contact with people of other ethnic and racial backgrounds (or at least more contact in the right circumstances), we will all begin to trust one another more. More formally, according to this theory, diversity reduces ethnocentric attitudes and fosters out-group trust and solidarity. If black and white children attend the same schools, for example, race relations will improve. This logic was an important part of the legal case that led the United States Supreme Court to require racial desegregation in the famous *Brown v. Board of Education* case in 1954. For progressives, the contact theory is alluring, but I think it is fair to say that most (though not all) empirical studies have tended instead to support the so-called "conflict theory," which suggests that, for various reasons—but above all, contention over limited resources—diversity fosters out-group distrust and in-group solidarity. On this theory, the more we are brought into physical proximity with people of another race or ethnic background, the more we stick to "our own" and the less we trust the "other."

The evidence that diversity and solidarity are negatively correlated (controlling for many potentially confounding variables) comes from many different settings:

- Across workgroups in the United States, as well as in Europe, internal heterogeneity (in terms of age, professional background, ethnicity, tenure and other factors) is generally associated with lower group cohesion, lower satisfaction and higher turnover.
- Across countries, greater ethnic heterogeneity seems to be associated with lower social trust.
- Across local areas in the United States, Australia, Sweden, Canada and Britain, greater ethnic diversity is associated with lower social trust and, at least in some cases, lower investment in public goods.
- Among Peruvian micro-credit cooperatives, ethnic heterogeneity is associated with higher default rates; across Kenyan school districts, ethnolinguistic diversity is associated with less voluntary fundraising; and in Himalayan Pakistan, clan, religious, and political diversity are linked with failure of collective infrastructure maintenance.
- Across American census tracts, greater ethnic heterogeneity is associated with lower rates of car-pooling, a social practice that embodies trust and reciprocity.
- Within experimental settings such as prisoner's dilemma or ultimatum games, players who are more different from one another (regardless of whether or not they actually know one another) are more likely to defect (or "cheat"). Such results have been reported in many countries, from Uganda to the United States.
- Within the Union (northern) Army in the American Civil War, the casualty rate was very high and the risks of punishment for desertion were very low, so the only powerful force inhibiting the rational response of desertion was loyalty to one's fellow soldiers, virtually all of whom were other white males. Across companies in the Union Army, the greater the internal heterogeneity (in terms of age, hometown, occupation, etc.), the higher the desertion rate.

Advocates of the conflict and contact theories clearly disagree about the balance of the empirical evidence, but in their shared focus on ethnocentric attitudes, they share one fundamental assumption–namely that in-group trust and out-group trust are negatively correlated. I believe this assumption is unwarranted and may have obscured some of the most interesting and unexpected consequences of diversity for social capital. In order to explain why, I need to remind you of an important distinction now commonly made in the field of social capital—that is, the distinction between "bonding" social capital (ties to people who are *like* you in some important way) and "bridging" social capital (ties to people who are *unlike* you in some important way). So, my bonding social capital consists of my ties to other white, male, elderly professors, and my bridging social capital reflects my ties to people of a different generation or a different race or a different gender.

Too often, without really thinking about it, we assume that bridging social capital and bonding social capital are inversely correlated in a kind of zero-sum relationship: if I have lots of bonding ties, I must have few bridging ties, and vice versa. As an empirical matter, I believe that assumption is often false. In other words, high bonding might well be compatible with high bridging, and low bonding with low bridging. In the United States, for example, whites who have more non-white friends *also* have more white friends. This article is not the place for an extended discussion of that empirical issue, but the theoretical point helps to clarify the relationship between diversity and social capital.

Contact theory suggests that diversity erodes the in-group/out-group distinction and enhances out-group solidarity or bridging social capital, thus lowering ethnocentrism. Conflict theory suggests that diversity enhances the in-group/out-group distinction and strengthens in-group solidarity or bonding social capital, thus increasing ethnocentrism. However, virtually none of the hundreds of empirical studies of this broad topic has ever actually measured in-group attitudes. Instead, researchers have typically measured out-group attitudes (positive or negative) and have simply *assumed* that in-group attitudes must vary inversely. Thus, they have presumed (without evidence) that their measures of out-group attitudes were straightforward measures of ethnocentrism. However, once we recognize that in-group and out-group attitudes need not be reciprocally related, but can vary independently, then we need to allow, logically at least, for the possibility that diversity might actually reduce *both* in-group *and* out-group solidarity—that is, both bonding *and* bridging social capital. We might label this possibility "constrict theory" (a term suggested by my colleague, Abby Williamson).

I now present some initial evidence from the United States on the issue of how diversity (and by implication, immigration) affects social capital. The evidence comes from a large nationwide survey, the Social Capital Community Benchmark Survey, carried out in 2000, with a total sample size of roughly 30,000. Embedded within the nationwide sample is a representative national sample of 3,000, as well as smaller samples representative of 41 very different communities across the United States, ranging from large metropolitan areas like Los Angeles, Chicago, Houston and Boston to small towns and rural areas like Yakima, Washington, rural South Dakota and the Kanawha Valley in the mountains of West Virginia. While these 41 sites vary with respect to geographic scope from two inner city neighbourhoods to several largely rural states, for the most part they represent metropolitan areas. These community sites differ in many ways (size, economic profile, region, educational levels, etc.), but for our purposes it is important that they differ greatly in their ethnic diversity. For example, Los Angeles and San Francisco (roughly 30–40 percent white) are among the most ethnically diverse human habitations in history, whereas in our rural South Dakota county (95 percent white) celebrating "diversity" means inviting a few Norwegians to the annual Swedish picnic.

Another important methodological feature of this survey is that it was conducted simultaneously with the national census of 2000, and virtually every interview in our survey was "geo-coded" (i.e., for the vast majority of our respondents, we know exactly where they live, and thus we know the demographic characteristics of the census tract within which they live). Thus, we know not only the race, education, income, marital status and so on of our respondents, but also the race, education, income, marital status and so on of their neighbours. The variability of the thousands of census tracts within which our respondents live is even greater than the variability across the 41 sample communities. Some respondents live in neighbourhoods that are almost completely homogeneous, while others live in neighbourhoods that are extremely diverse in every respect. For our detailed and most sophisticated analyses presented below, we use the individual as the unit of analysis, linking his or her attitudes and behavior to the characteristics of his or her neighbourhood. For expository purposes, however, I begin by using the community as the unit of analysis, showing how the diversity of a community is linked to the average level of social capital in that community.

One last methodological preliminary: For present purposes, we adopt the basic fourfold categorization of race and ethnicity that was used in the concurrent census: Hispanic, non-Hispanic white, non-Hispanic black and Asian. This classification scheme, like all such schemes, is "socially constructed"—that is, it is not God-given, or biological, or timeless and unchanging, or uniquely defensible. Indeed, the social construction of ethnicity will be an important part of my concluding remarks. However, this typology has two advantages for present purposes. First, it is widely used in public and private discourse in contemporary America, and second, it allows us to treat respondents (from our survey) and their neighbours (from the census) in parallel ways.

I begin with probably the least surprising, but in some respects most misleading, finding from our survey. Figure 2 arrays our 41 communities according to their ethnic diversity and the average level of *inter-racial trust* expressed by our respondents in those communities. We asked every respondent how much he or she trusted whites, blacks, Asian-Americans

FIGURE 2. Racial Homogeneity and Inter-racial Trust.

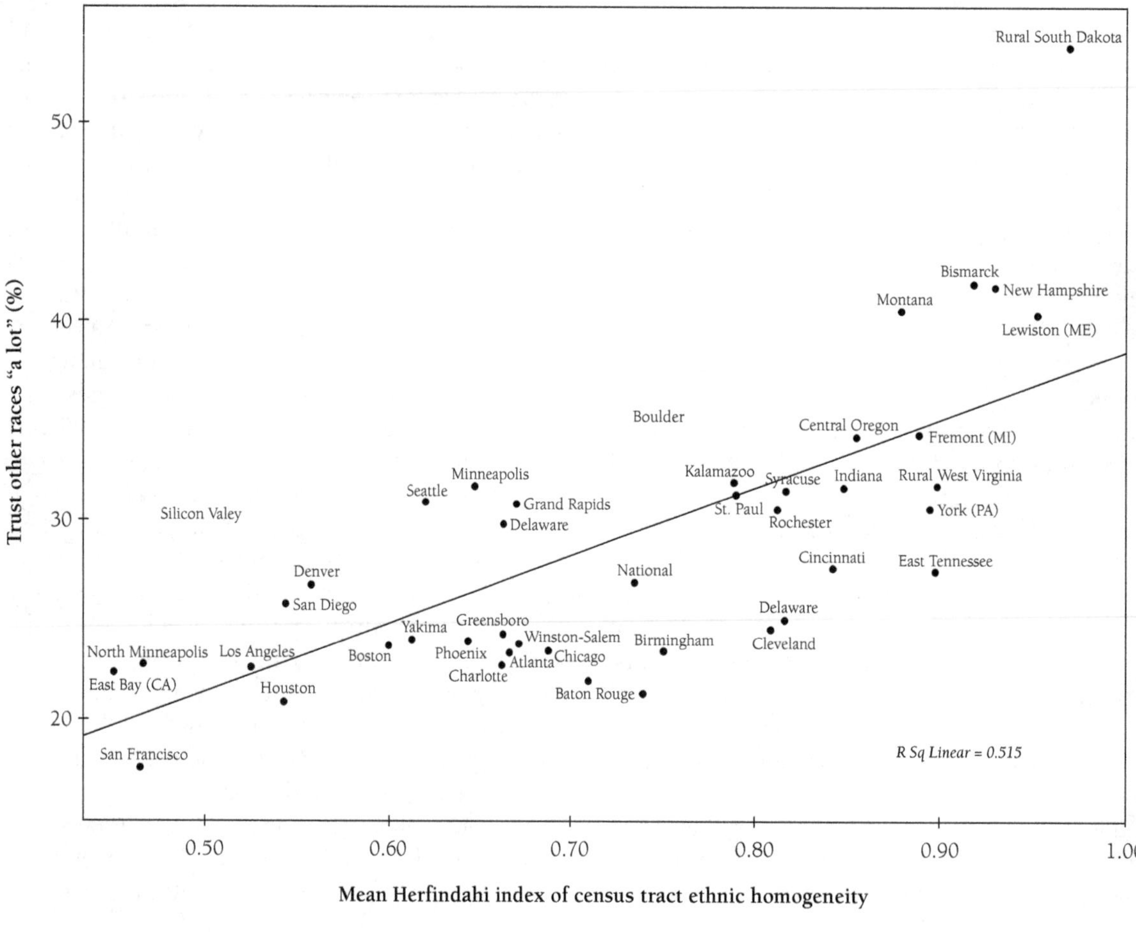

and Hispanics (or Latinos), and we know the respondent's own ethnicity, so this measure is simply the average trust expressed toward the other three ethnic categories. Obviously, Figure 2 shows a strong positive relationship between inter-racial trust and ethnic homogeneity. Inter-racial trust is relatively high in homogeneous South Dakota and relatively low in heterogeneous San Francisco or Los Angeles. The more ethnically diverse the people we live around, the less we trust them. This pattern may be distressing normatively, but it seems to be consistent with conflict theory. Had we stopped our inquiry at this point (as previous studies of conflict and contact theory have done), we would have rejected contact theory, at least in its simplest form, and accepted conflict theory. However, as we shall see momentarily, the story is actually more complicated.

Figure 3 is directly comparable to Figure 2, except that here our measure of social capital is trust in "people who live in your neighbourhood." Because of *de facto* residential segregation, most Americans' neighbours are of the same race as their own. And yet Figure 3 shows virtually the same pattern. The differences across our 41 sites are very substantial in absolute terms. In highly diverse Los Angeles or San Francisco, for example, roughly 30 percent of the inhabitants say that they trust their neighbours "a lot," whereas in the ethnically homogeneous communities of North and South Dakota, 70–80 percent of the inhabitants say the same. In more diverse communities, people trust their neighbours less.

Figure 4 repeats the story, but with one important difference. Now we ask about trust in people of the respondent's *own* race: how much do whites trust other whites, blacks other blacks, Hispanics other Hispanics, and Asians other Asians? This figure charts an entirely unexpected correlation for it shows that in-group trust, too, is lower in more diverse

FIGURE 3. Racial Homogeneity and Trust of Neighbours.

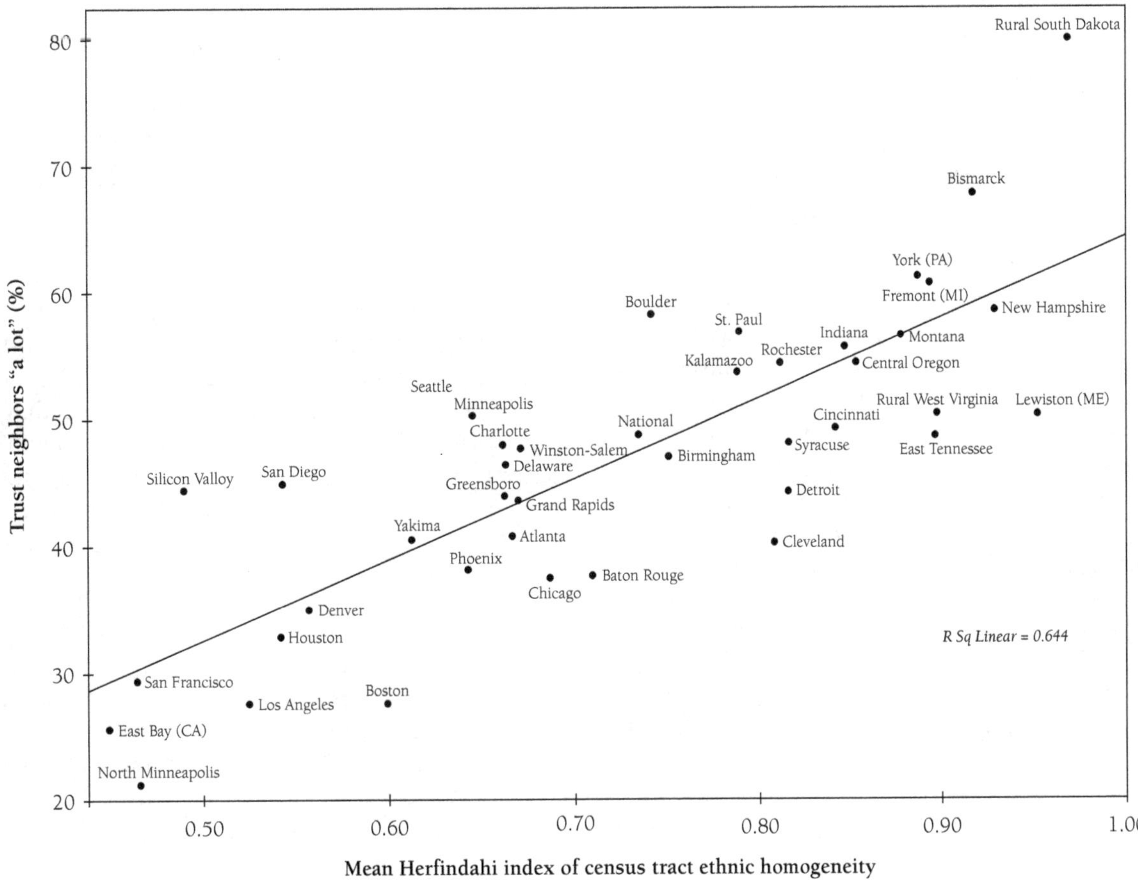

FIGURE 4. Racial Homogeneity and Intra-racial Trust.

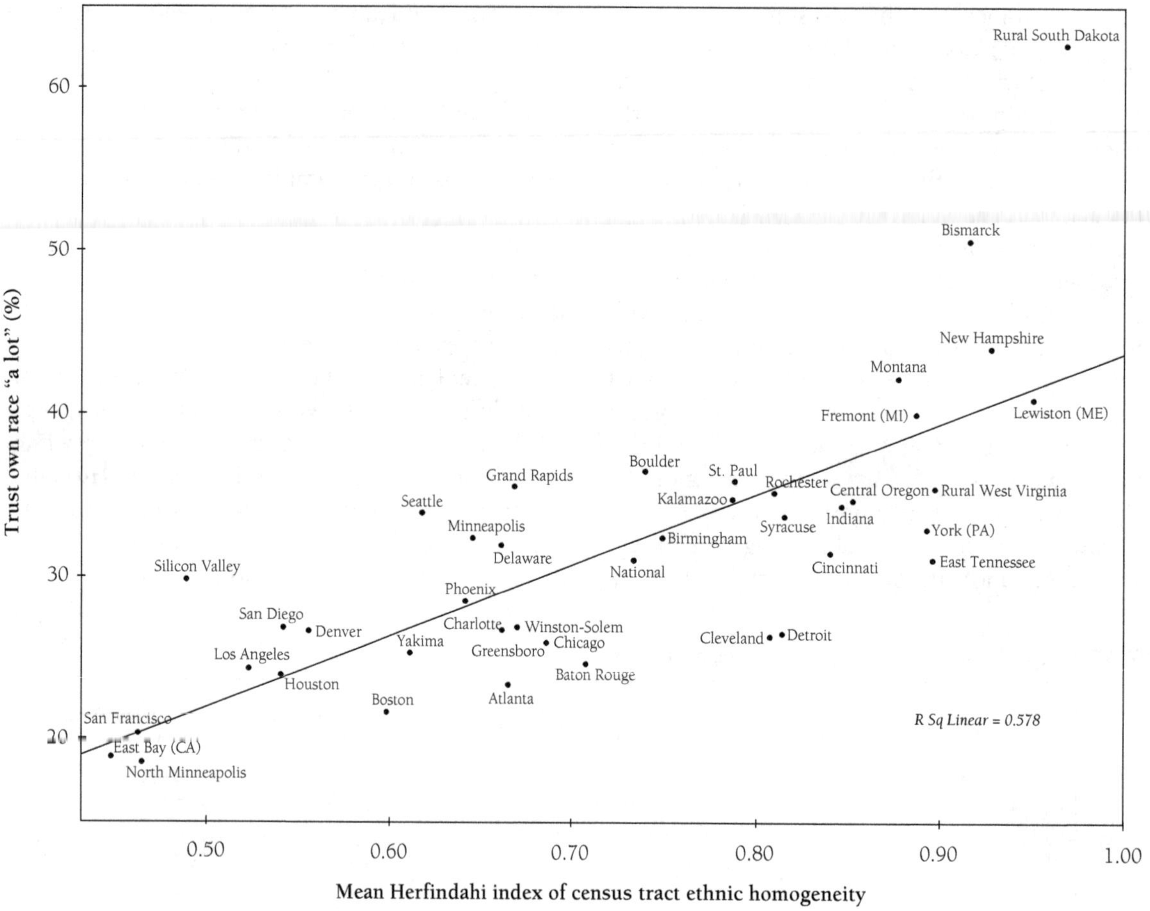

settings. Whereas Figures 2 and 3 are inconsistent with contact theory, Figure 4 is inconsistent with conflict theory. In other words, in more diverse settings, Americans distrust not merely people who do not look like them, but even people who *do*.

Finally, Figure 5 completes the story by arraying community diversity and "ethnocentric trust"—that is, trust in one's own race *minus* trust in other races. This figure clearly shows that ethnocentric trust is completely uncorrelated with ethnic diversity. Thus, it suggests that *neither* conflict theory *nor* contact theory corresponds to social reality in contemporary America. Diversity seems to trigger *not* in-group/out-group division, but anomie or social isolation. In colloquial language, people living in ethnically diverse settings appear to "hunker down"—that is, to pull in like a turtle. Figures 2 to 5, taken together, suggest support for what I earlier tentatively labelled "constrict theory."

So far I have limited my presentation to evidence regarding social trust, and it is true that the most impressive and substantial patterns we have so far discovered involve trust of various sorts, including even trust of shop clerks. However, a wide array of other measures of social capital and civic engagement are also negatively correlated with ethnic diversity. In areas of greater diversity, our respondents demonstrate:

- Lower confidence in local government, local leaders and the local news media.
- Lower political efficacy—that is, confidence in their own influence.
- Lower frequency of registering to vote, but more interest and knowledge about politics and more participation in protest marches and social reform groups.

FIGURE 5. Racial Homogeneity and Ethnocentric Trust.

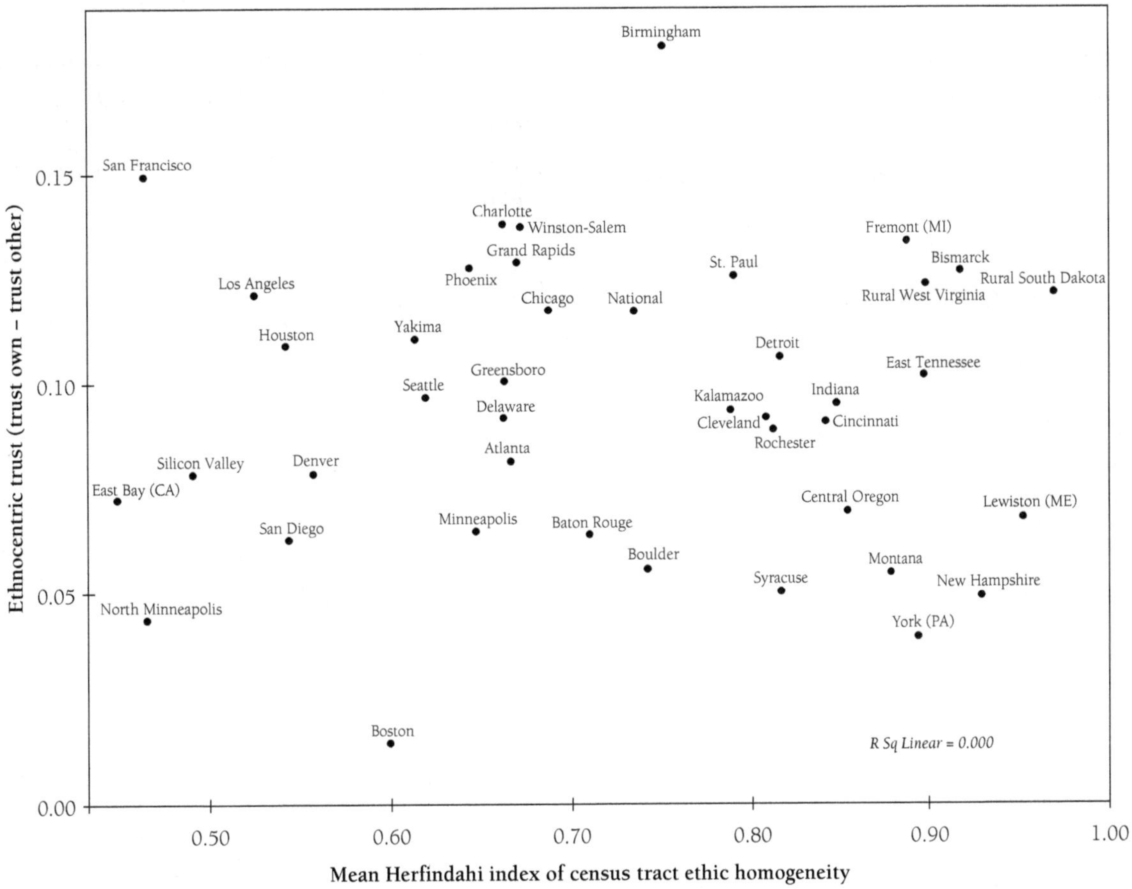

- Less expectation that others will cooperate to solve dilemmas of collective action (e.g., voluntary conservation to ease a water or energy shortage).
- Less likelihood of working on a community project.
- Lower likelihood of giving to charity or volunteering.
- Fewer close friends and confidants.
- Less happiness and lower perceived quality of life.
- More time spent watching television and more agreement that "television is my most important form of entertainment."

To be sure, some dimensions of social capital and civic engagement seem relatively unaffected by ethnic diversity in American communities. For example, organizational activity of various sorts, including religious activity, is essentially uncorrelated with diversity, once we control for confounding variables, and as I have already noted, several measures of political engagement are positively correlated with diversity. Nevertheless, a reasonably coherent, consistent image emerges from this analysis.

Diversity does *not* produce "bad race relations" for ethnically defined group hostility, our findings suggest. Rather, inhabitants of diverse communities tend to withdraw from collective life, to distrust their neighbours, regardless of the colour of their skin, to withdraw even from close friends, to expect the worst from their community and its leaders, to volunteer less, give less to charity and work on community projects less often, to register to vote less, to agitate for social reform *more,* but have less faith that they can actually make a difference, and to huddle unhappily in front of the television. Note that this pattern encompasses attitudes and behavior, bridging and bonding social capital, public and private connections. Diversity, at least in the short run, seems to bring out the turtle in all of us.

QUESTIONS FOR REFLECTION

1. What is social capital?
2. What are some benefits of immigration and diversity?
3. How, according to Putnam, does diversity encourage social isolation?
4. What is the contact theory? The conflict theory?
5. What is "constrict theory"? Give an example of something that might reduce both in-group and out-group solidarity.
6. What are some of the short-term negative effects of diversity?

MICHAEL HUEMER

Is There a Right to Immigrate?

Michael Huemer is associate professor of philosophy at the University of Colorado at Boulder. *(Source: from* Social Theory and Practice *36 [2010]: 429–461. Reprinted by permission of the publishers. Notes are omitted.)*

1. The Immigration Question

Every year, close to one million individuals from foreign nations migrate to the United States legally. But many more are turned away. Individuals seeking to enter without the permission of the U.S. government are regularly barred at the border, and those discovered in the territory without authorization are forcibly removed. The government expels over one million people from the country each year. Hundreds of thousands continue to try to smuggle themselves in, occasionally dying in the attempt. On the face of it, this raises ethical questions. Is it right to forcibly prevent would-be immigrants from living in the United States? Those excluded seem, on the face of it, to suffer a serious harm. Why are we justified in imposing this harm?

Some reason that, just as a private club may exercise its discretion as to whom to admit or exclude, so a nation-state has the right to choose whom to admit or exclude. Some believe that we must exclude most would-be immigrants in order to maintain the integrity of our national culture. Others argue that immigrants cause economic hardship for existing citizens—that they take jobs from American workers, depress wages, and place an undue burden on social services provided by the state. Some go so far as to warn that unchecked immigration would bring on environmental, economic, and social catastrophes that would reduce the United States to the status of a Third World country.

Few would question the state's right to exclude at least some potential migrants. For example, the state may deny entry to international terrorists or fugitives from the law. The interesting question concerns the vast majority of other potential immigrants—ordinary people who are simply seeking a new home and a better life. Does the state have the right to exclude these ordinary people?

In the following, I argue that the answer to this question is no. I shall assume that we are considering ordinary, noncriminal migrants who wish to leave their country of origin for morally innocent reasons, whether to escape persecution or economic hardship, or simply to join a society they would prefer to live in. Though I shall conduct the discussion in terms of the situation of the United States, most of my arguments apply equally well to other countries.

My strategy is to argue, first, that immigration restriction is at least a prima facie violation of the rights of potential immigrants. This imposes a burden on advocates of restriction to cite some special conditions that either neutralize or outweigh the relevant prima facie right. I then examine the most popular justifications offered for restricting immigration, finding that none of them offers a credible rationale for claiming either that such restriction does not violate rights or that the rights violation is justified. This leaves immigration restrictions ultimately unjustified.

A word about theoretical assumptions. In my view, most general theories or theoretical approaches in political philosophy—liberal egalitarianism, contractarianism, utilitarianism, and so on—are too controversial to form a secure basis for reasoning. It is not known which, if any, of those theories are correct. I have therefore sought to minimize the reliance on such theories. This does not mean that I assume that all such broad theories are false; I merely refrain from resting my arguments on them. Thus, I do not assume utilitarianism, contractarianism, libertarian rights theory, liberal egalitarianism, nor any general account of harm or rights. Nor do I assume the negation of any of those theories. Instead, I aim to rest conclusions on widely shared ethical intuitions about relatively specific cases. The method is to describe a case in which nearly everyone will share a particular, clear intuitive evaluation of some action, and then to draw a parallel from the case described to some controversial case of interest. This methodology follows a well-established tradition in applied ethics; I propose that the approach be applied to the issue of immigration. The approach can, of course, be subjected to criticism, particularly for the weight placed on common ethical intuitions, but this is not the place for a general discussion of the value of ethical intuition. In any event, the intuitive premises I shall rely on are, I hope, much less controversial than the broad philosophical theories of the sort mentioned above, and much less initially controversial than the immigration issue itself.

2. Immigration Restriction as a Prima Facie Rights Violation

In this section, I aim to show that immigration restriction is a prima facie rights violation. A prima facie rights violation is an action of a sort that *normally*—that is, barring any special circumstances—violates someone's rights. For example, killing a human being is a prima facie rights violation: in normal circumstances, to kill someone is to violate his rights. But there are special circumstances that may alter this verdict: euthanasia and self-defense killings do not violate rights, for instance. Furthermore, even when an action violates rights, it may sometimes be justified nevertheless, because the victim's rights may be *outweighed* by competing moral considerations. Thus, killing one innocent person may be justified, though a violation of the victim's right to life, if it is necessary to prevent the deaths of one million others. Or so it seems to me.

The claim that an action is a prima facie rights violation, then, is not a very strong claim. It does not entail that the action is wrong all things considered, for there may be special circumstances that prevent the action from being an actual rights violation, or that render it justified despite its violation of rights. But nor is the claim entirely without force: to accept that an action is a prima facie rights violation has the effect of shifting a normative presumption. It becomes the burden of those who advocate the act in question to identify the special exculpatory or justificatory circumstances that make what tends to be a wrongful rights violation either not a rights violation in this case, or a justified rights violation. Those who oppose the act in question need only rebut such efforts.

Now before we turn to the case of immigration, consider the following scenario. Marvin is in desperate need of food. Perhaps someone has stolen his food, or perhaps a natural disaster destroyed his crops; whatever the reason, Marvin is in danger of starvation. Fortunately, he has a plan to remedy the problem: he will walk to the local marketplace, where he will buy bread. Assume that in the absence of outside interference, this plan would succeed: the marketplace is open, and there are people there who are willing to trade food to Marvin in exchange for something he has. Another individual, Sam, is aware of all this and is watching Marvin. For some reason, Sam decides to detain Marvin on his way to the marketplace, forcibly preventing him from reaching it. As a result, Marvin returns home empty-handed, where he dies of starvation.

What is the proper assessment of Sam's action? Did Sam harm Marvin? Did he violate Marvin's rights? Was Sam's action wrong?

It seems to me that there are clear answers to these questions. Sam's behavior in this scenario was both extremely harmful to Marvin and a severe violation of Marvin's rights. Indeed, if Marvin's death was reasonably foreseeable, then Sam's act was an act of murder. Unless there obtained some unusual circumstances not mentioned in the preceding description, Sam's behavior was extremely wrong.

Intuitively, Sam's behavior would still be wrong if the harm suffered by Marvin were less severe. Suppose that, rather than dying soon after returning home, Marvin foreseeably suffers from serious malnutrition. Again, assume that this misfortune would have been avoided had Marvin been able to trade in the marketplace, but Sam forcibly prevented him from doing so. In this case, again, it seems that Sam violates Marvin's rights and wrongfully harms Marvin.

What do these examples show? I think they show, to begin with, that individuals have a prima facie, negative right not to be subjected to seriously harmful coercion. Sam's behavior in the scenario was, by stipulation, coercive—it involved a use or threat of physical force against Marvin, significantly restricting his freedom of action. It was also extremely harmful, resulting in Marvin's starvation. These facts seem to explain why Sam's action was a violation of Marvin's rights, and why it was wrong.

How do we know that Sam harmed Marvin? A "harm" is commonly understood as a setback to someone's interests. Marvin's death by starvation certainly sets back his interests. Moreover, in my view, no philosophical *theory* of harm is required in this case. Perhaps there are borderline cases in which one would need to appeal to a theory to determine whether an event counted as a harm or not. But the story of starving Marvin presents no such difficult case. Marvin's death is a paradigm case of a harm.

Still, there are some who draw a distinction between *harming* someone (making oneself the agent of harm) and merely *allowing a harm* to befall someone. And some believe that allowing harm is much less wrong than harming, perhaps not even wrong at all. This view is controversial. Fortunately, we need not resolve that controversy here, because the case of Sam and Marvin is not a case of a mere allowing of harm. If Sam had merely stood by and refused to give Marvin food, then it could be said that Sam *allowed* Marvin to die. But that is not the story. The story is that Marvin is going to get some food, and Sam *actively and forcibly intervenes* to stop Marvin from getting it. This is a harming and, since the harm involved is death, it is a killing. I take all this to be the judgment of common sense.

I am not claiming here that all acts of coercion are harmful. Paternalistic coercion, for instance, need not be harmful. Nor are all harmful actions coercive. One might harm a person, for instance, by spreading false rumors about her, without any exercise of physical force. I am only claiming that *this* action, Sam's forcible interference with Marvin's effort to reach the marketplace, was both harmful and coercive. Similarly, I am not claiming that all coercion violates rights, nor that all harmful acts violate rights. I claim only that, when an action is seriously harmful *and* coercive, it tends for that reason to be a rights violation, other things being equal—that is, it is a prima facie rights violation. Sam's behavior in the scenario described violates Marvin's rights, because it is an act of extremely harmful coercion, and there are no relevant extenuating circumstances. Sam's behavior could be justified if, for example, it was necessary to prevent the deaths of a million innocent persons; or, perhaps, if Marvin had for some reason contracted Sam to forcibly prevent Marvin from going to the marketplace. But assume that nothing like that is the case. The case is just as originally described, with no special circumstances. Few would doubt, then, that Sam's behavior is unacceptable.

How does all this relate to U.S. immigration policy? The role of Marvin is played by those potential immigrants who seek escape from oppression or economic hardship. The marketplace is the United States: were they allowed in, most immigrants would succeed in meeting their needs (to a greater extent, at least, than they will if they are not allowed in). The role of Sam is played by the government of the United States, which has adopted severe restrictions on entry. These restrictions are imposed by coercion: armed guards are hired to patrol the borders, physically barring unauthorized entry, and armed officers of the state forcibly detain and expel immigrants who are found residing in the country illegally. As in the case of Sam's detention of Marvin, the U.S. government's exclusion of undocumented immigrants is also very harmful to most of those excluded: many suffer from oppression or poverty that could and would be remedied if only they were able to enter the country of their choice. In view of this, the actions of the U.S. government, prima facie, constitute serious violations of the rights of potential immigrants—specifically, the government violates their prima facie right not to be harmfully coerced.

How might advocates of restriction object to this reasoning? Some might argue that the United States, in refusing entry to potential immigrants, merely fails to confer a benefit, or that it merely allows a harm to occur, rather than actually *harming* the potential immigrants. On some views, individuals have a right not to be harmed in certain ways, but no right to positive assistance. There are at least two reasons why one might think that immigration restrictions merely allow harm. First, it might be thought that the United States is not the *cause* of the harms that potential immigrants suffer. Perhaps the harms are caused by natural disasters, or corrupt foreign governments. This claim is controversial; nevertheless, I shall grant it for the sake of argument. Second, it might be thought that the U.S. does not harm potential immigrants by refusing them entry, because the good they are denied is only a good that would be provided by the United States itself, and it might be thought that a withholding of benefits that would be conferred by oneself—even if that withholding requires active agency—is a mere failure to benefit, rather than a harming.

In response to the first point, we must recognize that it is possible to harm a person even when one is not the originating cause of the harm that person suffers: one can harm a person by preventing that person from averting or remedying a harm originated by someone or something else. That is the lesson of the Sam-Marvin case: Sam did not cause Marvin to be out of food to begin with. We may suppose that Marvin was initially in danger of starvation because a natural disaster destroyed his crops, or because thieves (entirely unconnected to Sam) stole his food. This initial situation would be no fault of Sam's. Nevertheless, when Sam actively and coercively interferes with Marvin's efforts to remedy the problem, Sam then becomes responsible for Marvin's misfortune.

In response to the second point, note that the agent to whom I am ascribing a wrong is not the United States (the society as a whole) but rather the U.S. government. In denying entry to potential immigrants, the U.S. government refuses to provide certain benefits to them, including all the social services that they would receive were they granted U.S. residence. But that is not the harm that I am claiming the government imposes on potential immigrants. (Perhaps that is a harm imposed by the state, perhaps not—but it is not what my argument rests upon.) The U.S. government also fails to provide assistance in the form of foreign aid to most of these would-be immigrants. But again, that is not the harm that I charge the U.S. government with imposing. The way the government harms potential immigrants is by excluding them from a certain physical area, and thereby effectively excluding them from interacting in important and valuable ways with people (other than the government itself) who are in that region. Many Americans would happily trade with or employ these would-be immigrants, in a manner that would enable the immigrants to satisfy their needs. The government does not merely refuse to give goods to the potential immigrants, nor does it merely refuse, itself, to trade with them. It expends great effort and resources on actively stopping Americans from trading with or employing them in the relevant ways.

The point can be seen perhaps more clearly by returning to the case of Marvin. If Sam refuses to sell Marvin food, then Sam thereby fails to confer a benefit on Marvin. But when Sam actively stops Marvin from trading with anyone in the marketplace, when there are merchants present who would be glad to trade with Marvin, Sam thereby harms Marvin. He does not merely fail to benefit Marvin.

Sam's action might be justified if there were special circumstances not previously specified, circumstances that either cancelled the right that Marvin normally has not to be harmfully coerced, or that morally outweighed Marvin's rights. Likewise, what we have said so far does not establish that the U.S. government's restrictions on immigration are wrong *tout court,* but only that those defending the policy incur a burden of providing a justification for these restrictions. In light of the seriousness of the harms involved in this case, the justification for immigration restrictions must be correspondingly clear and powerful.

3. Reasons for Restriction

Harmful coercion is sometimes justified. It may be justified when necessary to defend an innocent party against harmful coercion. It may be justified when necessary to prevent much worse consequences. It may be justified because of a prior agreement made by the coercee. And there may be other circumstances that justify harmful coercion as well. Some believe, for instance, that harmful coercion may be justified because of a need to rectify severe economic inequality. The latter claim is controversial, as would be many other alleged justifications for harmful coercion. This illustrates one reason why a general theory of the conditions for justified harmful coercion would be difficult to devise and still more difficult to defend.

Fortunately, it may turn out that we do not need any such general theory. Some sorts of reasons, including some mentioned in the preceding paragraph, are generally accepted as legitimate justifications for harmful coercion. Equally, there are some sorts of reasons that we can see intuitively, even without a general theory, *not* to be legitimate justifications for harmful coercion. For instance, one is not justified in harmfully coercing a person simply because one wants the victim's shoes, or because one hates the race to which the victim belongs, or because one disagrees with the victim's philosophical beliefs. Whatever is the correct theory of justifications for harmful coercion, *those* reasons surely will not qualify. The task at hand is to determine whether there are any circumstances that justify the harmful coercion involved in immigration restrictions. Given that immigration restriction is a prima facie rights violation, the burden of proof falls on advocates of restriction. Thus, we may proceed by considering the reasons they have offered for restricting immigration. If it turns out that all of these reasons fall into the category of things that clearly do not count as valid justifications for harmful coercion, then it is fair to draw the conclusion that immigration restrictions are unjustified.

3.1. Immigration and Employment

In popular discourse, the most common sort of argument for limiting or eliminating immigration is economic. It is said that immigrants take jobs away from American workers, and that they cause a lowering of wage rates due to their willingness to work for lower wages than American workers. At the same time, economists are nearly unanimous in agreeing that the overall economic effects of immigration on existing Americans are positive. These claims are mutually consistent: there are certain industries in which immigrants are disproportionately likely to work. Preexisting workers in those industries are made worse off due to competition with immigrant workers. According to one estimate, immigration during the 1980s may have reduced the wages of native-born workers in the most strongly affected industries by about 1–2% (5% for high school dropouts). At the same time, employers in those industries and customers of their businesses are made better off due to lower production costs, and the economic gains to these latter groups outweigh the economic losses to the workers. Some economists have accused immigration opponents of overlooking the economic benefits of immigration due to a bias against foreigners or members of other races.

Let us leave aside the question of the overall effects of immigration on the economy, and focus instead on the following question. Granted that immigration makes some American workers economically worse off, does this show that immigration restriction does not violate the rights of would-be immigrants, or that if it does, the rights violation is nevertheless justified? More generally, does the following constitute a valid justification for harmful coercion: that the coercive action is necessary to prevent someone else from suffering slight to moderate economic disadvantage through marketplace competition?

It seems to me that it does not. Consider two related examples. In the first example, I am being considered for a particular job, for which I know that Bob is the only other candidate. I also know that Bob is willing to work for a lower salary than the salary that I could obtain if I were the only candidate. On the day Bob is scheduled to have his job interview, I accost him and physically restrain him from going to the interview. When confronted about my seemingly unacceptable conduct, I explain that my action was necessary to protect myself against Bob's taking the job that I would otherwise have, or my being forced to accept a lower salary in order to get the job. Does this provide an adequate justification for my behavior? Does it show that, contrary to initial appearances, my harmful coercion does not really violate Bob's rights? Alternatively, does it show that my action, though a rights violation, was an ethically justified rights violation?

Certainly not. The mere fact that Bob is competing with me for a job that I desire, or that Bob is willing to accept a lower salary than I could obtain if I did not have to compete with him, does not invalidate or suspend Bob's right not to be subjected to harmful coercion. Nor does my interest in having less economic competition *outweigh* Bob's right not to be coercively harmed. If my need for the job in question were very much greater than Bob's need, then some might argue that I would be justified in overriding Bob's rights. We need not decide exactly when a right may be overridden, nor whether a greater economic need could constitute an adequate basis for overriding a competitor's right to be free from harmful coercion; we need not decide these things here, because we can simply stipulate that Bob has at least as much need for the job for which we are competing as I do. In such a case, no one would say that Bob's right to be free from coercive harms is suspended or outweighed.

My second example is a modified version of the story of Sam and Marvin. As before, Marvin plans to walk to the local marketplace to obtain life-sustaining food. Due to his economic circumstances, Marvin will have to buy the cheapest bread available at the market. Sam's daughter, however, also plans to go to the market, slightly later in the day, to buy some of this same bread. This bread is often in short supply, so that the vendor may run out after Marvin's purchase. Sam's daughter could buy more expensive bread, but she would prefer not to. Knowing all this, Sam fears that if Marvin is allowed to go to the market, his daughter will be forced to pay a slightly higher price for bread than she would like. To prevent this from happening, he accosts Marvin on the road and physically restrains him from traveling to the market. Is Sam's action permissible?

Suppose Sam claims that his harmful coercion does not violate Marvin's rights, because it is necessary to protect his daughter from economic disadvantage. Certainly this defense falls flat. A person's right to be free from harmful coercion is not so easily swept aside. Likewise for the suggestion that Sam's action, though a rights violation, is justified because his daughter's interest in saving money outweighs Marvin's rights. No one would accept such feeble justifications.

Yet this seems analogous to the common economic argument for immigration restriction. The claim seems to be that we are justified in forcibly preventing individuals—many of whom are seeking escape from dire economic distress—from entering the American labor market, because American workers would suffer economic disadvantage through price competition. No one claims that American workers would be disadvantaged to anything like the degree that potential immigrants are disadvantaged by being forcibly excluded from the market. Nevertheless, the prospect of a modest lowering of American wages and narrowing of employment opportunities is taken to either suspend or outweigh the rights of needy foreigners. The ethical principle would have to be that a person's right to be free from extremely harmful coercion is sometimes held in abeyance simply by virtue of the fact that such coercion is necessary to protect third parties from modest economic disadvantage resulting from marketplace competition. The implausibility of this principle is shown by the examples of Bob and Marvin above.

3.2. The State's Duty to Its Citizens

Perhaps immigration restriction can be justified by reflection on the special obligations governments owe to their own citizens, as distinct from foreign nationals. Few doubt that there are such duties. States must provide their citizens protection from criminals and hostile foreign governments. A state does not have the same obligation to protect foreign citizens from criminals or other governments. Those who endorse a social contract theory of political authority may explain this by appeal to the idea that noncitizens of a given state are not party to the social contract with that state; the state therefore lacks the contractual obligations to noncitizens that it bears to citizens.

Perhaps this leads to a rationale for immigration restriction. Perhaps the state has a general duty to serve the interests of its own citizens, including their economic interests, and no such duty, or no duty nearly as strong, to further the interests of foreign nationals. As a result, when the interests of American citizens come into conflict with those of foreigners, the American government must side with its own citizens, even when this results in a lowering of global social utility. Limitations on migration into the United States run contrary to the interests of would-be immigrants, but since those would-be immigrants are not presently U.S. citizens, the U.S. government has either no duty or a much weaker duty to consider their interests, as compared to the interests of its own citizens. Perhaps this gives some traction to the argument that American workers are disadvantaged because of competition with immigrants. Alternatively, one might argue that immigrants impose a financial burden on government providers of social services, such as health care, education, and law enforcement. Since these social programs are financed through revenues collected from existing U.S. citizens, the government's consideration for the interests of its current citizens dictates that it limit the amount of immigration into the country.

Begin with the observation that immigration disadvantages American workers through labor market competition. There are two obstacles to regarding this as a justification for immigration restriction, even if we accept that the state has a much stronger obligation to protect the interests of its own citizens than it has to protect the interests of others. First, only some current citizens would be disadvantaged by increased immigration—those citizens who work in industries that immigrants are disproportionately likely to join. This is a relatively small portion of the population. All other current citizens would either fail to be significantly affected or actually be benefited by increased immigration. As mentioned earlier, most economists believe that the overall economic impact of immigration on current citizens is positive. Thus, if we consider only the interests of current citizens, it is at best unclear that immigration restrictions are beneficial. If we also give *some* weight to the interests of the immigrants themselves, it seems that the case for free immigration is clear.

Second, there are some obligations that any moral agent owes to other persons, merely in virtue of their status as persons. The special obligations that governments owe to their citizens, whatever these obligations may consist in, do not eliminate the obligation to respect the human rights of noncitizens. In particular, the government's duty to give special consideration to its own citizens' interests cannot be taken to imply that the government is entitled to coercively impose grave harms on non-citizens for the sake of securing small economic benefits for citizens.

Consider again the case of starving Marvin. In the last version of the story, Sam coercively prevented Marvin from reaching the local marketplace, on the grounds that doing so was necessary to prevent his daughter from having to pay a higher than normal price for her bread. This action seems unjustified. Would Sam succeed in defending his behavior if he pointed out that, as a father, he has special obligations to his daughter, and that these imply that he must give greater weight to her interests than to the interests of non-family members? Certainly the premise is true—if anything, parents have even stronger and clearer duties to protect the interests of their offspring than a government has to protect its citizens' interests. But this does not negate the rights of non-family members not to be subjected to harmful coercion. One's special duties to one's offspring imply that if one must choose between giving food to one's own child and giving food to a non-family member, one should generally give the food to one's own child. But they do not imply that one may use force to stop non-family members from obtaining food, in order to procure modest economic advantages for one's own children.

Next, consider the charge that immigrants create a fiscal burden due to their consumption of social services. On the whole, immigrants pay slightly less in taxes than the cost of the social services they consume. This is mainly because immigrants tend to have lower-than-average incomes, and thus pay relatively low taxes. Some economists believe, however, that in the long run (over a period of decades), increased immigration would have a net positive fiscal impact.

Assume that immigrants impose a net fiscal burden on government. Would this fact justify forcibly preventing a large number of potential immigrants from entering the country? To answer this, first we must ask whether the state presently has an obligation to provide social services to potential immigrants, even at a net cost to the state. On some theories of distributive justice, it could be argued that the state has such an obligation, even though these potential immigrants are not presently citizens. If so, then the state obviously may not exclude potential immigrants for the purpose of shirking this duty.

Suppose, on the other hand, that the state has no such obligation to provide social services to potential immigrants, at least not without collecting from them sufficient revenues to cover the expenditure. If this is true, the state would perhaps be justified in denying social services to immigrants, raising taxes on immigrants, or charging special fees to immigrants for the use of social services. But it remains implausible that the state would be justified in excluding potential immigrants from the territory entirely. It is not typically a satisfactory defense for a harmful act of coercion to say that because of a policy one has voluntarily adopted, if one did not coerce one's victim in this way, one would instead confer a benefit on the person that one does not wish to confer.

Suppose, for example, that Sam runs a charity organization. He has made a policy of offering free food to all poor people who enter the local marketplace. Unfortunately, the organization is running short on cash, so Sam is looking for ways to cut costs. When he learns that Marvin is heading to the market to buy some food, he decides to save money by forcibly preventing Marvin from reaching the market. Marvin would be better off being allowed into the marketplace, even without free food, since he could still buy some inexpensive food with his limited funds. But Sam has already made a policy of offering free food to all poor people in the marketplace, so he would in fact offer free food to Marvin, were Marvin to make it there. Is it permissible for Sam to coercively inflict a serious harm on Marvin, in order to avoid having to either break his policy or give free food to Marvin?

Surely not. Perhaps Sam would be justified in altering his policy and refusing to give free food to Marvin when he arrives at the marketplace—this would be permissible, provided that Sam has no humanitarian obligation to assist Marvin. But whether or not Sam has any such humanitarian duties, he surely has no right to actively prevent Marvin from getting his own food. If Marvin had been coming to the market to *steal* Sam's food, perhaps then again Sam would be justified in excluding him. Even this claim would be controversial; if Marvin's condition of need were sufficiently urgent, some would say that Sam must let him take the food. But whatever one thinks about that question, surely Sam cannot justify barring Marvin from the opportunity to *buy* food from others, merely on the grounds that if Sam permits him to do so, then Sam will also voluntarily give him some food.

I have considered the possibilities both that the state owes potential immigrants a duty to help them satisfy their needs, and that the state owes them no such duty. But perhaps the situation is more complex. Perhaps the state presently owes no duty to aid potential immigrants, but if and when they become residents in its territory, the state will *then* owe them a duty to provide the same level of services as it provides to native-born citizens. If so, the state could not, ethically, protect its financial interests by opening the borders and simply providing lower levels of social services to the mass of incoming immigrants.

In assessing this view, we must take account of the distinction between residents and citizens. It is much more plausible that states are obligated to help citizens satisfy their needs, than that states are obligated to help all *residents* do so. So it is not clear that the suggestion of the preceding paragraph could justify preventing foreigners from residing in the United States, as opposed to justifying a refusal to grant citizenship. Nevertheless, let us assume that the state has a duty to offer equal levels of social services to all residents, once they are here. Even if mere residency somehow entitles one to equal levels of social services with native-born citizens, it is not plausible that this entitlement is *inalienable,* that is, that it cannot be voluntarily waived. The state therefore has at least one available strategy, apart from immigration restriction, for protecting its financial interests. This is to make a grant of legal residency or citizenship to potential immigrants contingent on the immigrants' agreement to waive their right to receive certain social services. Alternatively, the state could require new immigrants to agree to pay a higher tax rate, sufficient to cover the government's expected costs. The availability of these alternatives undercuts any justification the state could plausibly be claimed to have, in virtue of its fiscal interests, for excluding most potential immigrants from the country.

It could be questioned whether the policy suggested in the preceding paragraph is permissible. If foreigners have a *right* to immigrate, one could argue, then the state must allow them to exercise that right, whether or not they agree to waive other rights (including rights that they may come to have in the future). This may be correct. But whether or not it is correct, my argument of the preceding paragraph stands. For my claim was not that the state in fact ought to require potential immigrants to waive their (future) right to receive social services. I claim only that the state ought *not* to prohibit potential immigrants from entering the country, given that there is an alternative method of achieving the same goal, and that this alternative is less coercive and less harmful. It may of course be that *neither* alternative is permissible. But in any event, the unnecessarily coercive alternative is not permissible. In general, whether one may coercively harm innocent others to protect one's economic interests is open to debate. Perhaps there are circumstances in which one may do so. But even if one may do so, surely one may not employ *more* harmful coercion than is necessary to achieve one's goal.

QUESTIONS FOR REFLECTION

1. What is a prima facie right?
2. Explain the case of starving Marvin. What are its implications for the immigration debate?
3. In what sense are immigration restrictions coercive?
4. Discuss the strengths and weaknesses of Huemer's analogy between starving Marvin and immigration controls.
5. Huemer doubts that immigrants harm the employment prospects of Americans, but, even if they do, he contends that immigration restrictions on this basis would violate potential immigrants' rights. Evaluate his argument.
6. Suppose the United States were to opt for an open borders policy, allowing anyone into the country who wanted to come. What would result? Does that provide an argument for or against Huemer's position?
7. Suppose that the German Army had "immigrated" to Denmark, Norway, France, and other countries in 1940. Are there circumstances in which immigration would amount to invasion? Could a nation permissibly take steps to prevent it?
8. Could rapid immigration by people from the same area cause permanent harm to the unity of a nation? Under what circumstances? Would a country have a right to try to prevent that harm by restricting immigration?

Credits

CPSIA information can be obtained
at www.ICGtesting.com
Printed in the USA
LVHW011240190521
687817LV00002B/2

MHL000040482